To Gail and Steven Spector

Preface

Industrial/organizational or I/O psychology is an exciting field that has been enjoying continual growth throughout the industrialized world during its almost 100-year history. What began as a tiny subspecialty of psychology, known only to a few practitioners and professors, has grown to be one of the major specialties in psychology worldwide. This attention is due to two factors. First, I/O is concerned with the workplace, so its findings and principles are relevant to everyone who holds a job. Second, I/O has developed proven methods that organizations find of value. I/O psychologists are often called on to help organizations develop a more efficient and healthier workforce.

The field of I/O psychology has a dual nature. First, it is the science of people at work. This aspect ties it to other areas of psychology, such as cognitive and social psychology. Second, I/O psychology is the application of psychological principles of organizational and work settings. There is no other area of psychology in which a closer correspondence between application and science exists, making I/O a good example of how society can benefit from the study of psychology.

The field of I/O is a large and diverse one. Many topics are covered, ranging from methods of hiring employees to theories of how organizations work. It is concerned with helping organizations get the most from their employees or human resources, as well as helping organizations take care of employee health, safety, and well-being. For this reason, a single text can provide only an overview of the major findings and methods that I/O psychologists use. The goal of this book is to provide such an overview, as well as a comprehensive understanding of the field. Each of the major areas that comprise I/O psychology is covered.

Part One of this book provides an overview of the I/O field. Chapter 1 covers the nature of the field and its history. I/O psychology is discussed as both a practice and a science. The chapter describes what a career in I/O psychology involves and what it takes to become an I/O psychologist. Chapter 2 is an overview of the basic principles of I/O research methods.

The remainder of the book is divided into four parts. Part Two focuses on assessment. Chapter 3 discusses the assessment of jobs, called job analysis; Chapter 4 focuses on the assessment of employee job performance; and Chapter 5 explores the way in which employee characteristics are measured. Part Three contains two chapters. Chapter 6 deals with the methods that organizations use to hire new employees. Chapter 7 follows those new employees, as well as experienced ones, through their training programs.

The four chapters in Part Four discuss the relationship between the individual and the organization. Chapter 8 covers theories of motivation. Chapter 9 focuses on how people feel about their jobs—their attitudes about the job and the emotions they experience at work. The topic of Chapter 10 is productive and counterproductive work behavior. Chapter 11 deals with occupational health psychology, a rapidly emerging field that is concerned with worker health, safety, and well-being.

The final part of the book, Part Five, is concerned with the social context of work. Chapter 12 explores small work groups and work teams and their effect on the individual.

Chapter 13 discusses leadership and supervision in the workplace. Chapter 14, the last chapter, takes an organization perspective. It covers organizational development and organizational theory.

▶ SPECIAL FEATURES

In each chapter of the book, there are "Learning by Doing" exercises that actively engage the student with the material in the chapter. All of the exercises ask the student to address an I/O issue or answer a particular question. Some involve interviewing working individuals about an aspect of their work experience. Others require observations of a public work setting, such as a retail store or restaurant. Still others are accomplished through the web. These experiences are designed to enhance the student's knowledge of how information can be used to address a problem.

In all but the first two chapters, there are two special features. First, there are detailed summaries of research studies from one of the major I/O journals. Each "International Research" was chosen to give added insight through a study that is relevant to topics covered in the chapter. The implications of each study for the practice of I/O psychology are also discussed. Second, a case study describes how a practicing I/O psychologist was able to help an organization with a problem. These "I/O Psychology in Practice" cases were chosen to represent the wide variety of settings and applied work that involve I/O psychologists.

At the end of each "I/O Psychology in Practice" case are discussion questions. The purpose of these questions is to encourage students to think about the principles discussed in the book. They require students to apply the chapter principles to a real situation. The questions can be used in a variety of ways. They can be assigned to groups of students or to individuals. They can be used for in-class debates, discussions, oral presentations, or written assignments. The cases themselves are provided to help show students the connections between practice and research in the I/O field. Students often have a difficult time seeing the relevance to their lives of much of what they study in college. I/O psychology is a field that is relevant to almost everyone.

▶ CHANGES TO THE SIXTH EDITION

My goal with all six editions is to provide a text that is as current as possible, covering both the traditional core material of the field and the exciting new emerging areas and findings. The first major task I had with the revision was to update the material and add important new developments. The science of I/O psychology is rapidly developing, with new findings and insights emerging almost daily. I added more than 170 new references. with almost all of them from 2007 or later. The overall organization of the book retains the original 14 chapters.

Although early development of I/O psychology took place primarily in the United States and the United Kingdom, in the 21st century I/O psychology is international in scope. Across all the editions of this book, there has been material concerning the international nature of the I/O field, and the book attempts a broader focus than just the United States. In this edition, I have added material on the development of I/O psychology (or occupational psychology) in the United Kingdom, which occurred at the same time as in the United States.

A characteristic of American I/O psychology during most of the 20th century was its major concern with employee performance and productivity—and how these contribute to organizational functioning. Much of this was driven by the applied job market and the sorts of services that organizations were willing to purchase from consultants or hire psychologists to provide. In the United Kingdom and other European countries, the emphasis was more on employee health and well-being. In recent years, there has been a cross-fertilization, with many American I/O psychologists becoming interested in health and well-being, while American perspectives on productivity techniques have been adopted elsewhere. One offshoot of the movement toward concern with employees can be seen in the emerging field of occupational health psychology (OHP), which is developing in large part out of I/O psychology. OHP is a multidisciplinary field that is concerned with the health, safety, and well-being of employees. It developed first in the United Kingdom and other European countries and has been making rapid advances in the United States over just the past few years. OHP topics have been included in this book since the first edition, but the sixth edition provides more balance between issues of employee performance and well-being.

Content Changes in the Sixth Edition

Although all of the topics covered in the first five editions are still here, some have been expanded or modified, and new ones have been added. Of particular note are the following new or substantially updated topics:

Alcohol and stress
Bullying/mobbing
Emotional labor
History of I/O psychology in the United Kingdom
Humanitarian work psychology
Incivility
Musculoskeletal disorders
Respites
Violence prevention climate

ACKNOWLEDGMENTS

In writing all six editions of this book, I was lucky to have had advice and assistance from many people. I express my sincere thanks to the many colleagues and students who provided such help, as well as the Wiley people who did a superb job.

First are the members of the University of South Florida I/O psychology group:

Tammy Allen
Walter Borman
Michael Brannick
Michael Coovert
Russell Johnson, now at Michigan State University
Edward Levine
Carnot Nelson
Steve Stark

There are colleagues and friends from around the world who provided feedback and information:

Seymour Adler, Assessment Solutions, Inc.
Julian Barling, Queens University, Canada
John Bernardin, Florida Atlantic University
Stephen Bluen, Gordon Institute of Business Science, South Africa
Peter Chen, Colorado State University
Yochi Cohen-Charash, Baruch University
Steven Cronshaw, University of Guelph, Canada
Donald Davis, Old Dominion University
Dov Eden, Tel Aviv University, Israel
Barbara Ellis, Charleston, South Carolina
Michael Frese, University of Giessen, Germany
Yitzhak Fried, Wayne State University
Barbara Fritzsche, University of Central Florida
Joan Hall, Naval Air Warfare Center Training Systems Division
Paul Jackson, University of Sheffield, England
Richard Jeanneret, PAQ Services, Inc.
Steve Jex, Bowling Green State University
Boris Kabanoff, University of New South Wales, Australia
Filip Lievens, University of Ghent, Belgium
John C. Munene, Makere University, Uganda
Lakshmi Narayanan, Florida Gulf Coast University
Brian O'Connell, ICF International
Richard Perlow, University of Lethbridge
Mark Peterson, Florida Atlantic University
Ivan Robertson, University of Manchester Institute of Science and Technology, England
Juan Sanchez, Florida International University
Arie Shirom, Tel Aviv University, Israel
Oi-Ling Siu, Lingnan University
Dirk Steiner, Universite de Nice-Sophia, France
Paul Taylor, University of Waiko, New Zealand

In addition, 12 I/O psychologists provided the "Psychology in Practice" cases:

Jonathan Canger, Marriott
Janis Cannon-Bowers, University of Central Florida
Jeanne Carsten, JP Morgan Chase
Stephen Cohen, Strategic Leadership Collaborative
Anna Erickson, Questar
Chuck Evans, Jackson Leadership Systems
Amanda Gartshore, Chromis Consulting Ltd.
Kate Keenan, Formulas4Life
Christopher McGivern, Employee Feedback
Gemma Phillips-Pike, GP Psychology Consultancy
Lynn Summers, North Carolina State Personnel
Tom White, Changelink, Australia

The reviewers of the various drafts of the book did a superb job, and the comments of every one of them were a tremendous help.

Robert B. Bechtel, University of Arizona
John Binning, Illinois State University
Valentina Bruk Lee, Florida International University
David V. Day, Pennsylvania State University
Janet Barnes Farrell, University of Connecticut
M. Jocelyne Gessner, University of Houston
Sigrid Gustafson, American Institutes for Research
Jane Halpert, De Paul University
Leslie Hammer, Portland State University
Joseph Horn, University of Texas at Austin
David Kravitz, George Mason University
Marjorie Krebs, Gannon University
Karl Kuhnert, University of Georgia
Dan Landis, University of Mississippi
Terese Macan, University of Missouri–St. Louis
Karen Maher, California State University at Long Beach
Patrick McCarthy, Middle Tennessee State University
John Meyer, University of Western Ontario
Susan Mohammad, Pennsylvania State University
George Neuman, Northern Illinois University
Kimberly O'Brien, Central Michigan University
Diana Odom-Gunn, University of California
Stephanie Payne, Texas A&M University
Gerald L. Quatman, Xavier University
Ann Marie Ryan, Michigan State University
Steven Scher, Eastern Illinois University
Susan Shapiro, Indiana University East
Kenneth Shultz, California State University at San Bernardino
Steven Stern, University of Pittsburgh at Johnstown
Ladd Wheeler, University of Rochester
H. A. Witkin, Queens College

I also would like to thank the people at John Wiley who made the book possible. First is my editor, Eileen McKeever, who ran interference on lots of details and made the process run smoothly. Then there is the production staff who did an outstanding job of turning my manuscript into a book. They are my production editor, Elaine Chew, and photo editor, Sheena Goldstein. Thanks for the production of additional material for this international student version also go to Gemma Phillips-Pike.

Finally, I would like to thank my wife, Gail Spector, for helping in many ways, including helping me make the hundreds of little decisions involved in writing a book.

Brief Contents

Contents

PART I
INTRODUCTION

PART II

ASSESSMENT OF JOBS, PERFORMANCE, AND PEOPLE

CHAPTER 4

Performance Appraisal 74

CHAPTER 5

Assessment Methods for Selection and Placement 101

▶ CHAPTER 10

Productive and Counterproductive Employee Behavior 238

▶ CHAPTER 11

Occupational Health Psychology 263

PART V

THE SOCIAL CONTEXT OF WORK

PART I

INTRODUCTION

(*PhotoDisc, Inc./Getty Images, Inc.*)

CHAPTER 1

Introduction

CHAPTER 1 OUTLINE

Most people in the industrialized world come into direct or indirect contact with organizations every day. If you go to a supermarket to buy groceries, that store is part of an organization. On a given day, you might encounter a few employees, such as the produce manager who helps you find some fresh grapes, the checker who rings up your order, and the bagger who puts all your items in bags. The organization, however, might employ thousands and even tens of thousands of individuals who are collectively responsible for seeing to it that the products you wish to purchase are continually available at each of its stores. This requires the coordinated action of many individuals, likely cutting across many countries. Needless to say, managing such a complex enterprise is extremely difficult. The managers responsible hire a great many specialists to assist them. They often turn to industrial/organizational (I/O) psychologists for help with many of their employee-related problems. For example, I/O psychologists have helped:

AT&T develop assessment centers to choose the best managers.

General Electric (GE) develop systems to provide job performance feedback to employees.

The U.S. Army use psychological tests to place recruits in the appropriate jobs.

The U.S. Postal Service develop procedures to reduce assaults by employees.

If you go to work for a large organization, there is a good chance that your work life will be affected by I/O psychology. An I/O psychologist may have designed the application form that you will fill out to get the job, the salary and benefit package that you will be offered, the training that you will receive, and the structure of the tasks that will comprise your job. I/O psychologists are involved in issues related to employee health, job performance, motivation, safety, selection (hiring), and training. They can also deal with the design of equipment and job tasks. This book discusses all of these areas, and more.

There are two equally important aspects of the I/O psychology field. First, I/O psychology involves the scientific study of the human side of organizations. Many I/O psychologists, particularly those who are professors at universities, conduct research about people at work. Second, I/O psychology includes the application of the principles and findings of I/O research. Most I/O psychologists are involved in practice, either as consultants or as employees of organizations. What distinguishes the practice of I/O psychology from that of many other fields is that I/O psychology is an evidence-based field, meaning that the things practitioners do are based on scientific methods and principles. This book reviews the major findings from I/O science and explores how practicing I/O psychologists apply those findings in organizational settings.

I/O psychology is an eclectic field that has borrowed concepts, ideas, techniques, and theories from many other disciplines. Experimental psychology provided the historical basis of the I/O field. Its principles and techniques, such as psychological testing, were applied by several early experimental psychologists to problems of organizations. As we will discuss later in this chapter, one of the earliest examples occurred when psychologist Robert Yerkes convinced the army to use psychological tests during World War I. Other influences on the I/O field have come from industrial engineering, management, social psychology, and sociology. Although I/O psychology had its beginnings largely in the United States, it has become an international activity, especially in industrialized countries.

This chapter contains an overview of the I/O field. It covers the major activities and employment settings for I/O psychologists and presents a brief history of the field. The chapter discusses what training is needed to become an I/O psychologist and where that training is offered, not only in the United States but also throughout the world. The research process will be discussed, and the major publication outlets for I/O research will be listed. I/O psychologists are very concerned with the ethical treatment of people, which is another topic that we will cover.

Chapter 2 contains a discussion of the research methods used in I/O psychology. Chapters 3 to 14 cover the major topics of the field, beginning with a focus on the assessment of jobs and people in Chapters 3 to 5. Covered in Chapters 6 and 7 are two major areas that are relevant to developing productive employees—selecting good people and training them to do their jobs well. Chapters 8 to 11 are concerned with the individual in the context of the organization and cover motivation, how people feel about their jobs, employee behavior, and employee health and safety (i.e., occupational health psychology). Chapters 12 to 14 deal with the individual employee in the social context of the organization. Major topics discussed include groups and teams, leadership, techniques to change organizations, and theories of organizations.

Objectives: The student who studies this chapter should be able to:

- Define I/O psychology.
- Describe the major activities of I/O psychologists.
- Summarize the history of the I/O field.
- Explain the importance of research and how it relates to practice.

WHAT IS I/O PSYCHOLOGY?

Psychology is the science of human (and nonhuman) behavior, cognition, emotion, and motivation. It can be subdivided into many different specializations, some of which are concerned primarily with psychological science (experimental psychology) and others of which are concerned with both psychological science and the application of that science to real-world problems outside of the research setting. I/O psychology (along with clinical psychology) falls into the latter category of being concerned with both psychological science and its application.

As its two-part name implies, the field of I/O psychology contains two major divisions: the industrial (or personnel) and the organizational. Although the contents of the two major divisions overlap and cannot be easily separated, each grew out of different traditions in the history of the field. Industrial psychology, which was the original name for the field, is the older branch and tends to take a management perspective of organizational efficiency through the appropriate use of human resources or people. It is concerned with issues of efficient job design, employee selection, employee training, and performance appraisal. Organizational psychology developed from the human relations movement in organizations. It is concerned with understanding behavior and enhancing the well-being of employees in the workplace. Organizational topics include employee attitudes, employee behavior, job stress, and supervisory practices. The major topics of the field, however, cannot easily be characterized as strictly industrial (I) or organizational (O). Motivation, for example, is relevant to the I concerns of employee efficiency and performance, but it is also relevant to the O concern with the happiness and well-being of employees, as well as understanding human behavior in organizational settings. Even though the I and O areas cannot always be clearly distinguished, together they suggest the broad nature of the field.

The largest subarea of psychology concerned with application of scientific findings is clinical psychology. Clinical psychologists deal with the study and treatment of psychological disorders and problems. **Industrial/organizational psychology** is a smaller, but more rapidly growing psychology subfield that is concerned with the development and application of scientific principles to the workplace. I/O psychologists do not deal directly with employees' emotional or personal problems. This activity falls in the domain of clinical psychology. An I/O psychologist, however, might recommend hiring a clinical psychologist to help with such problems as employee alcoholism or post-traumatic stress disorder (PTSD). It is important to note that there are a variety of terms associated with I/O psychology. In the UK, the field tends to be called Occupational Psychology. Whereas in Europe, Work and Organizational Psychology is the most commonly used. Broadly speaking, I/O Psychologists will focus on the same issues in the same way as Occupational Psychologists and Work and Organizational Psychologists. However, for brevity, the term of I/O Psychology will be used throughout this book.

▶ ACTIVITIES AND SETTINGS OF I/O PSYCHOLOGISTS

I/O psychologists do many different jobs in a wide variety of settings. We often divide I/O settings into those that are concerned with practice and those that are concerned with scientific research. The practice activities involve the use of psychological principles to solve real-world problems, such as excessive job stress or poor job performance. Research provides principles that can be applied in practice. Both practice and research are equally important within the I/O field. One major objective of I/O psychology is to help organizations function more effectively. In order to do so, the field must have research findings on which to base practice. Not all research is done with practice in mind, however. Some psychologists study work behavior just to learn why people do the things they do at work. As with all forms of basic research, often the findings of such activities can be applied to important human problems.

Although settings can be classified as either practice or research, there is considerable overlap in activities across the two. Many I/O psychologists in research settings get involved in practice, and psychologists in practice settings do research. Furthermore, some practice activities require research to determine the best approach to solve the problem at hand. Existing principles might not be available in all cases. In fact, I/O psychologists often don't have ready-made answers, but rather they have the means of finding answers.

Most research settings are the colleges and universities at which I/O psychologists are professors. Practice settings include consulting firms, government, the military, and private corporations. Consulting firms provide I/O services to organizations that hire them. Large consulting firms might have hundreds of employees providing services to organizations throughout the world. I/O psychologists often work for governments (city, county, state, or national), the military (usually as civilian specialists), and private corporations. I/O psychologists in each of these practice settings might be doing the same sorts of activities. Figure 1.1 shows the percentage of I/O psychologists found in each of the major settings.

Many I/O psychologists are college or university professors. Most are in psychology departments, but frequently they can be found in colleges of business administration or other places on campus as well. Although they spend much of their time doing research and teaching students, they do far more than that. Many are involved in practice as consultants to organizations, and some have started their own consulting firms to pursue this interest. The following list describes the major activities of professors:

Teach courses

Do research

Write research papers and present them at meetings

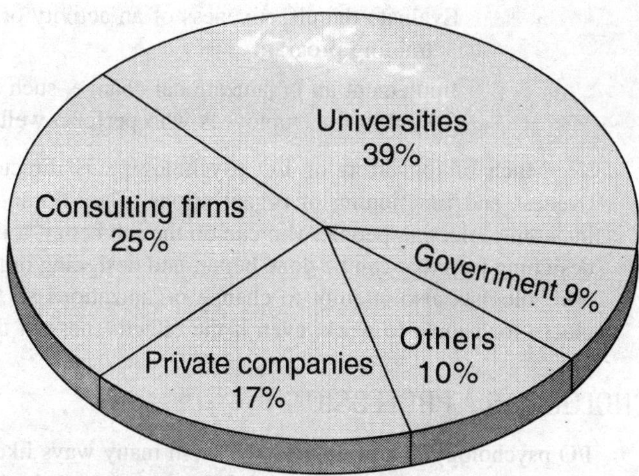

Figure 1.1 Percentage of I/O psychologists who work in various settings. From *Society for Industrial and Organizational Psychology 2006 member survey: Overall report.* Available at http://www.siop.org/reportsandminutes/survey_results06.aspx.

Publish articles in scientific journals

Provide consulting services to organizations

Write textbooks

Mentor graduate and undergraduate students

Provide information to the public

Develop courses

Keep up with their field

Help administer the teaching function of their university

The basic functions of a professor are to create and disseminate knowledge. Each activity in this list is concerned with one or both of these functions.

Practicing I/O psychologists do many of the same things as their academic colleagues, including conducting research and teaching college courses. The major focus of a practice job, however, is the application of the findings and principles of the field. The following list of activities shows what practicing I/O psychologists do:

Analyze the nature of a job (job analysis)

Conduct an analysis to determine the solution to an organizational problem

Conduct a survey of employee feelings and opinions

Design an employee performance appraisal system

Design an employee selection system

Design a training program

Develop psychological tests

Evaluate the effectiveness of an activity or practice, such as a training program

Implement an organizational change, such as a new reward system for employees who perform well

Much of the effort of I/O psychologists is directed toward enhancing the effectiveness and functioning of organizations. They do so by focusing on several aspects, including selecting people who can do the job better, training people to do the job better, designing jobs that can be done better, and designing organizations to function better. I/O psychologists also attempt to change organizations so that they are healthier and safer places for people to work, even if the effectiveness of the organization is not improved.

I/O PSYCHOLOGY AS A PROFESSION

I/O psychology is a profession that is in many ways like the profession of accounting or law. Some countries require that I/O psychologists be licensed to practice, for example parts of the US and UK. Many I/O psychologists work for consulting firms that provide services for a fee to client organizations. These services are provided in much the same way that an accounting firm or law firm provides them.

I/O psychologists belong to several professional/scientific societies. In the United States, there are several national and regional societies. The Society for Industrial and Organizational Psychology (SIOP), which is a division of the American Psychological Association (APA), is the largest organization in the United States that is comprised entirely of I/O psychologists. It has more than 8,200 members, with about 48% of them being student affiliates. Although SIOP is an American association, it is rapidly becoming international, with about 12% of its members from other countries, which represents a doubling in the international membership in the past four years. The Academy of Management is a larger organization than SIOP, but the majority of its members are not psychologists. It is comprised of people who have interests in the broad field of management, mostly professors from colleges of business administration. Many I/O psychologists, primarily those who are college professors, are active members of this organization.

There are also professional associations of I/O psychologists in many other countries throughout the world. Australia has the College of Organisational Psychologists, Canada has its own Society for Industrial and Organizational Psychology, the British Psychological Society has its Division of Occupational Psychology, and many similar associations exist throughout Europe. Over a dozen of them have formed the European Association of Work and Organizational Psychology (EAWOP). Also very relevant to I/O psychologists is the International Association of Applied Psychology, Division of Organizational Psychology, which is the largest division. I/O psychologists from around the world, and especially those with interests in cross-cultural and international issues, are members.

I/O PSYCHOLOGY AS A SCIENCE

Research is one of the major activities of I/O psychologists. Research can develop new methods and procedures for such activities as selecting and training employees. Often such research is conducted for a specific organization to solve a particular problem—for example, for a company that has a high employee turnover (quitting) rate. Other research focuses on understanding some organizational phenomenon, such as the cause of employee theft or the effect of job attitudes. Results of these sorts of research studies are presented at professional meetings and published in scientific journals.

The national and international associations noted earlier all have conferences, usually annually, where results of research are presented. The annual meeting of SIOP, for example, attracts close to 4,000 practitioners and researchers who share and discuss their research findings and ideas. Practitioners often find such meetings to be a good place to learn about new solutions to their organizational problems. Researchers can find out about the latest findings before they are published in the scientific journals.

Scientific journals of the field represent the major outlet for research results. Some major journals are produced by professional associations, whereas others are published privately. For example, the *Journal of Applied Psychology* is published by the APA, and the *Journal of Occupational and Organizational Psychology* is published by the British Psychological Society. Table 1.1 lists the major journals that publish research on I/O topics. Most are like magazines that are published in four to six issues per year. One, the *International Review of Industrial and Organizational Psychology*, is published once a year and summarizes the state of knowledge on various topics.

I/O researchers, most of whom are college professors, submit articles for possible publication to these journals. Their work is then sent to experts in the field for a critique. Articles are revised based on the critiques, and often several rounds of revision and resubmission will be necessary before an article is accepted for publication. Only the 10% to 20% of submitted articles that survive a rigorous peer review process will be published in the best journals. Peer review helps maintain high standards for published work so that the best research makes it into print.

Publication of research papers is a competitive and difficult endeavor. College professors, particularly those without tenure, are under tremendous pressure to be successful at publication. I/O programs at most universities have a "publish or perish" system that requires professors to be active researchers who contribute to the knowledge base of the field. This is true of all scientific disciplines in most universities. A publication record in the best journals is a major determiner of career success for a professor, as reflected

TABLE 1.1 Journals That Publish I/O Research and Theory

Academy of Management Journal	*Journal of Applied Psychology*
Academy of Management Review	*Journal of Business and Psychology*
Administrative Science Quarterly	*Journal of Management*
Applied Psychology: An International Review	*Journal of Occupational and Organizational Psychology*
Group and Organization Studies	*Journal of Occupational Health Psychology*
Human Factors	*Journal of Organizational Behavior*
Human Relations	*Journal of Vocational Behavior*
Human Resources Management Review	*Organizational Behavior and Human Decision Processes*
International Journal of Selection and Assessment	*Organizational Research Methods*
International Review of Industrial and Organizational Psychology	*Personnel Psychology*
	Work & Stress

in the ability to find a job, earn tenure, get promoted, and receive raises. Keep in mind, however, that one of the major functions of a university is to create and disseminate new knowledge for the benefit of society, so there is a good reason to emphasize research.

▶ HISTORY OF THE FIELD OF I/O PSYCHOLOGY[1]

I/O psychology is a twentieth century invention, with roots in the late 1800s and early 1900s. It has existed almost from the beginning of the psychology field. The first psychologists to do I/O work were experimental psychologists who were interested in applying the new principles of psychology to problems in organizations. Early work in the United States focused on issues of job performance and organizational efficiency, and in the United Kingdom, it was on employee fatigue and health (Kreis, 1995). As the field matured during the first half of the century, it expanded into the areas that it covers today.

Two psychologists are credited with being the main founders of the American I/O field. Hugo Münsterberg and Walter Dill Scott were both experimental psychologists and university professors who became involved in applying psychology to problems of organizations. Münsterberg, who came to the United States from his native Germany, was particularly interested in the selection of employees and the use of the new psychological tests. Landy (1992) posits that Münsterberg's inability to gain the respect of colleagues at Harvard University was the motivation for his shift to the emerging field of industrial psychology. Scott was interested in many of the same things as Münsterberg, as well as the psychology of advertising. Scott wrote a pioneering textbook, *The Theory of Advertising* (1903), and Münsterberg wrote the first American I/O textbook, *Psychology and Industrial Efficiency* (1913).

A major influence on the I/O field was the work of Frederick Winslow Taylor, an engineer who studied employee productivity throughout his career during the late nineteenth and early twentieth centuries. Taylor developed what he called *Scientific Management* as an approach to handling production workers in factories. Scientific Management includes several principles to guide organizational practices. In his writings, Taylor (1911) suggested the following:

1. Each job should be carefully analyzed so that the optimal way of doing tasks can be specified.
2. Employees should be selected (hired) according to characteristics that are related to job performance. Managers should study existing employees to find out what personal characteristics are important.
3. Employees should be carefully trained to do their job tasks.
4. Employees should be rewarded for their productivity to encourage high levels of performance.

Though refined over the years, these same ideas are still considered valuable today.

Another influence from the field of engineering can be seen in the work of Frank and Lillian Gilbreth, a husband-and-wife team who studied efficient ways of performing tasks. They combined the fields of engineering and psychology (Frank was an engineer

[1]Note that this section is based on Katzell and Austin's (1992) history of the I/O field unless otherwise noted.

and Lillian a psychologist) in studying how people perform tasks. Their best-known contribution was the *time and motion study*, which involved measuring and timing people's motions in doing tasks with the goal of developing more efficient ways of working. Although the basic ideas were Taylor's, the Gilbreths refined and used their new technique to help many organizations (Van De Water, 1997). Some historians claim that Lillian was the first to receive an American I/O Ph.D. (Koppes, 1997) in 1915, although most historians give this distinction to Bruce V. Moore in 1921. The Gilbreths' work served as the foundation of what would later become the field of human factors, which is the study of how best to design technology for people. In later years, Lillian turned her attention to designing consumer products and invented the foot-pedal trash can and refrigerator door shelves, among other things (Koppes, 1997). However, the Gilbreths themselves are best known as the subjects of the popular movie *Cheaper by the Dozen*, which chronicled their lives as working parents of 12 children.

World War I saw the beginning of the use of I/O psychology to assist in the war effort in both the United Kingdom and the United States. The beginning of I/O psychology in the United Kingdom is marked by the establishment of the Health of Munitions Committee (HMC) in 1915 in order to deal with issues of employee health, safety, and efficiency that were exacerbated by productivity demands due to the war (Kries, 1995). In the United States, on the other hand, entry into the war in 1917 encouraged a number of psychologists, led by Robert Yerkes, to offer their services to the army. The best-known accomplishment of the group was the development of the Army Alpha and Army Beta group tests for mental ability. One of the biggest problems for the army was placing new recruits in jobs for which they were best suited. The newly invented psychological tests seemed to the psychologists to be an efficient way to solve that problem. This was the first large-scale application of psychological testing to place individuals in jobs. It provided a foundation for mass testing that has been used ever since in educational settings (e.g., the Scholastic Aptitude Test, now the SAT) and employment settings.

During the decades between the two world wars, I/O psychology expanded into most of the areas that we see today. As organizations grew in size, they began hiring I/O psychologists to address many of their increasing employee problems, particularly those that were relevant to productivity in the United States. At the same time, research on I/O topics began to accumulate. In 1921 in the United Kingdom, psychologist Charles

Charles Myers (*Library of the London School of Economics & Political Science, NIIP Collection*)

Hugo Münsterberg (*Archives of the History of American Psychology*)

Walter Dill Scott (*Archives of the History of American Psychology*)

Frederick Winslow Taylor (*Jacques Boyer/Roger-Viollet/The Image Works*)

Robert Yerkes (*Archives of the History of American Psychology*)

Myers co-founded the National Institute of Industrial Psychology (NIIP), an organization devoted to improving efficiency and working conditions of British employees. Its focus on employee well-being follows the work of the earlier HMC and characterizes not only British but also European I/O psychology during the early development of the field (Kwiatkowski, Duncan, & Shimmin, 2006). At the same time, in 1921 Penn State University awarded what many consider the first American Ph.D. in what was then called industrial psychology to Bruce V. Moore. I/O psychologists began organizing into consulting firms that would provide services to organizations for a fee. The most well-known of these was the American company Psychological Corporation, founded in 1921 by James McKeen Cattell, which today is called Harcourt Assessment. One of the most important events of this period was the Hawthorne studies, which continued for more than 10 years at the Western Electric Company in the United States.

Before the Hawthorne studies, American I/O psychologists focused almost exclusively on issues of employee productivity and organizational efficiency, including the assessment of employee abilities and the efficient design of jobs. Although the Hawthorne researchers set out to study these topics, they quickly discovered what their British colleagues had previously found (Kwiatkowski et al., 2006): It is difficult to separate employee productivity from social aspects of organizational life. Their study of supervision and work groups helped draw attention to the O or organizational side of the field.

The best known of the Hawthorne studies was the investigation of lighting-level effects (Roethlisberger & Dickson, 1939). The objective of this study was to determine the lighting level that would produce optimal performance on a factory task. The researchers conducted an experiment in which a group of employees was taken to a special room where lighting levels were changed. Lights were made brighter and dimmer from day to day to see the effects on productivity. The researchers were surprised to find that over the course of the experiment, productivity increased and seemed to have little to do with lighting levels. Many explanations of these results have been advanced and debated. The most frequently discussed is that knowledge of being in an experiment, or what has come to be called the **Hawthorne Effect**, caused increases in performance. Whatever the reason, it seems clear that social factors can be more important than physical factors in people's job performance.

World War II had a tremendous stimulating effect on the development of the I/O field for countries on both sides of the conflict, most notably the United States and United Kingdom (Warr, 2007). Psychologists dealt with problems that spanned the entire scope of both I and O work, including the selection of recruits, placement of recruits in different jobs, training, morale, performance appraisal, team development, and equipment design. Prior to World War II, the APA limited its interests to experimental psychology and rejected attempts by I/O psychologists to make practice, which was considered nonscientific, part of its mission. As a result of the war, however, the APA opened its doors to applied psychology, and Division 14 of Industrial and Business Psychology was formed in 1944 (Benjamin, 1997). After the war, the two areas of industrial and organizational psychology continued to expand. For example, Arthur Kornhauser conducted research on how work conditions can have effects on both the mental health and the personal life of employees, thus producing some of the early American work on what is now called occupational health psychology (Zickar, 2003). In 1970, Division 14 of the APA changed its name to the Division of Industrial and Organizational Psychology and is today called the **Society for Industrial and Organizational Psychology (SIOP)**. The society's website (http://www.siop.org) is an important resource for information about the field, including information about graduate school, job postings, and society business.

Another event in the United States that helped shape the field of I/O psychology was the passage of the Civil Rights Act of 1964. This act set into motion forces that have had a tremendous impact on how organizations hire and treat employees, and not only in the United States. When discrimination against minorities and women became illegal, organizations had to change many of their employment practices. I/O psychologists were called upon to help develop procedures that would eliminate discrimination in the workplace. The passage of the Americans With Disabilities Act (ADA) in 1990 extended protection against discrimination to persons with disabilities. Here again I/O psychologists have been called upon to find ways to eliminate unlawful discrimination.

The history of the field is full of examples of how I/O psychologists have helped improve organizations and work conditions for employees. The field has grown tremendously from an initial focus on efficiency and productivity, especially in the United States, to the many diverse areas we find today. I/O psychology has much to contribute to the operation of organizations and the well-being of employees. Its future looks bright, as organizations continue to need help with employee issues, as discussed throughout this book.

▶ I/O PSYCHOLOGY BEYOND THE UNITED STATES AND UNITED KINGDOM

Our discussion of the history of I/O has focused largely on the United States and to a lesser extent on the United Kingdom, where the field had its beginnings and most (but not all) of its early development. However, I/O psychology exists throughout the world, and many of its findings and principles have come from other countries. One indication of both the rapid spread of the field and its globalization can be seen in the nationalities of authors who publish in what are considered the leading journals in the field, the US-based *Journal of Applied Psychology* and *Personnel Psychology*. Cascio and Aguinis (2008) showed that the percentage of non-American authors of papers published in these two journals increased fivefold, from 5% in the mid-1960s to 25% in the mid-2000s. We are seeing increasing numbers of journal articles coming from Australia, Canada, Greater China, Germany, Israel, Korea, the Netherlands, New Zealand, Scandinavia, and Singapore, just to mention a few places. Another indication of the spread of I/O psychology beyond the United States and United Kingdom is the increasing number of I/O master's and Ph.D. programs outside of these two countries. Throughout the six editions of this textbook, the list has continued to grow as new programs are established throughout the world. Another trend is for researchers to partner across countries to conduct cross-cultural research. This work is important because not all principles used in the West will necessarily work in other countries or cultures. We will discuss some of these studies throughout the book.

An interesting aspect of the I/O field internationally is that cultural, historical, and political conditions helped shape the nature of the field and the sorts of things that are studied, giving each country its own I/O flavor (Warr, 2007). Zickar and Gibby (2007) noted that American I/O psychology has historically focused on employee productivity and the assessment of individual differences that can be used for employee selection (see Chapters 5 and 6). Warr (2007) contrasted the American perspective with that of the United Kingdom, noting that the latter had a much greater focus on employee health and well-being. In recent decades, the rapid globalization of the world economy and widespread electronic communication have meant cross-fertilization of the field across countries and a greater convergence of ideas and methods. One factor is that some of the large American I/O consulting firms, such as Development Dimensions International and Personnel Decisions International, established offices around the world, which both introduced American I/O methods overseas and introduced the methods from overseas to the United States.

▶ WHAT IT TAKES TO BECOME AN I/O PSYCHOLOGIST

The most common route to becoming an I/O psychologist is to earn a graduate degree (master's or Ph.D.) in I/O psychology from one of the many I/O psychology graduate programs that exist throughout the world. Many people who do I/O work have other backgrounds, such as in other areas of psychology or in business administration. Some of these people consider themselves to be I/O psychologists and may hold jobs with that title. In the United States, most I/O psychologists hold a Ph.D. degree. Although it is possible to be an I/O psychologist with a master's degree in the I/O field, such people are often referred to as master's level I/O psychologists to reflect their lower degree status. One can have a successful career as an I/O psychologist with a master's degree, but opportunities and salaries are better with the Ph.D.

In some countries, such as Canada, the situation is similar to that in the United States. However, in other places, as in much of Europe, the Ph.D. is not as common as the master's degree. Rather, the master's degree is considered a practice degree, whereas the Ph.D. is a research credential. An individual who wishes to be a practitioner will likely have a master's degree and then may be required to apply for a subsequent license to practice after obtaining experience in the field i.e. Chartered Psychologist in the UK. If one continues on to earn a Ph.D., he or she is most likely to be interested in research and will be found in a research institute or a university. It is possible for a practitioner to have a Ph.D., but it is not considered as important as in the United States and Canada.

Admission to graduate programs is quite competitive, especially for the well-established Ph.D. programs in the US. Most base admission largely, but not exclusively, on undergraduate grades. Prior applied and research experience can be helpful, especially for top Ph.D. programs. Letters of recommendation from faculty members are usually required. I/O graduate programs are challenging and require skills in both communication (verbal and written) and mathematics. Thus to do well, a student should properly prepare as an undergraduate. A solid background in basic mathematics (i.e., algebra) and statistics is a good start. Good basic communication skills, especially writing, are also valuable. It is always wise to take a course in I/O psychology before making the choice to pursue this career. Interestingly, many students enter graduate school without having taken this course. Finally, a good background in basic psychology will make things easier. Students who have other undergraduate majors and don't have this background find they have a lot of catching up to do, especially in the first year.

The training of I/O psychologists includes both the practice and the research sides of the field. An I/O psychologist is trained to be a scientist-practitioner, or someone who is able to conduct scientific research and apply principles to problems of organizations. Students are exposed to procedures for applying principles of the field, as well as to research methodology. The specific content and emphasis can differ among graduate programs, especially when comparing these programs across countries. There are many excellent programs offering terminal master's degrees to people who do not wish to spend the extra years it would take to earn the Ph.D. These programs offer training that is usually oriented more toward practice than science, in part because they do not have sufficient time to cover each side of the field in depth and in part because they are intended to train practitioners. The Ph.D. programs can offer a better balance between practice and science because they take over twice as long to complete. These programs train people to be both practitioners and researchers.

A master's degree can be completed in about two years, while a Ph.D. can be completed in about four to six years by a person who has a bachelor's degree. Programs vary, but a master's program will include coursework on research methodology and the various areas of the I/O field, which will be discussed in this book. A Ph.D. program covers the same areas, as well as general psychology and more extensive research methodologies. For this degree, societies dedicated to I/O Psychology, i.e. the British Psychological Society, will suggest of a list of areas that should be covered that includes each of the chapters in this book. In addition, there is practicum experience working in an organizational setting with a practicing I/O psychologist and research experience (e.g., a master's thesis or doctoral dissertation) done under the supervision of a committee of I/O faculty members.

The job market for I/O psychologists in the United States has been excellent, although it does fluctuate with general economic conditions. Surveys of I/O psychologists done by the APA over the years have generally found less than 1% unemployment among those who wish to work. Khanna and Medsker (2010) reported the results of a salary survey of SIOP members' incomes in 2009. The median salary was $74,500 per year for individuals with a master's degree and $105,000 per year for those with a Ph.D. Salary varied by region of the country, type of employment, and industry. For example, individuals with their own consulting firms had the highest median income ($184,000). College professors working in psychology departments earned less than those working for business schools, and college professors in departments that had doctoral programs earned more than professors in departments that did not. The median starting salary for a new Ph.D. was $75,000 per year and for a new M.A. $55,000. Women earned 16.4% less than men on average, but this difference was accounted for by factors other than gender itself. For example, female I/O psychologists on average have less job experience than males because until relatively recently I/O psychology was a predominantly male profession. Finally, it should be kept in mind that these are median salaries, meaning that half the people make more and half less than these numbers.

The gender distribution of I/O psychology has been becoming increasingly balanced in the numbers of men and women. In the 1960s, only about 8% of Ph.D.s in I/O psychology were awarded to women. Interestingly, prior to 1930, women comprised a much higher proportion of practicing I/O psychologists than they did in 1960. Although accurate estimates of numbers are impossible to make (Koppes, 1997), women may have comprised as much as 25% of the I/O psychologists in the 1920s. In the past few decades, women have entered the field in increasing numbers, and today they earn about half or more of the Ph.D.s awarded in the United States. The membership of SIOP in 2006 was 36.7% female, which represents a sizeable increase over the 1960s. This trend can also be found elsewhere in the world.

▶ INTERNET RESOURCES FOR I/O PSYCHOLOGISTS AND STUDENTS

There are a number of internet resources that are helpful to I/O psychologists and students. Most societies have websites devoted to their field. Perhaps the most useful for I/O psychology is the SIOP website (http://www.siop.org), which contains a great deal of information about the I/O field. Of perhaps most interest to students is SIOP's detailed information on almost all of the I/O graduate programs in Canada and the United States, as well as a sample from overseas. For each program, admission requirements, size of the program, and other vital information are provided. In addition, there are links to each program's website. SIOP's quarterly newsletter, *The Industrial/Organizational Psychologist* or *TIP*, is here as well. This book's author has also developed a website that contains information about I/O psychology as a career, advice about getting into graduate school (also contained in the book's Appendix), useful links concerning I/O psychology, and information about his research interests. Table 1.2 contains a number of useful websites relevant to I/O psychology.

▶ ETHICS OF THE I/O FIELD

Psychology has had a long tradition of concern with ethical behavior and the welfare of people. I/O psychologists in the United States follow an ethical code that has been developed over the years by the APA. The code includes both ethical principles and statements of appropriate professional conduct. Although the association has little enforcement power other than to terminate a psychologist's membership, most I/O psychologists are guided by these principles in their professional work.

The basic philosophy of the ethical code is that psychologists should do their best to avoid harming other people through their professional work. This means that a psychologist should avoid committing any illegal or immoral act that might harm someone either physically or psychologically. On the other hand, psychologists have a social responsibility to use their talents to help other people. In other words, the goal of the profession is to improve the human condition through the application of psychology. For the I/O psychologist, this means helping to improve organizations so that they function better and helping to improve the well-being of employees.

The APA ethical code contains six principles, each of which is listed in Table 1.3. As you can see from the table, these principles are concerned with basic ethical standards of honesty, integrity, respect for others, and responsibility. The code also contains a detailed list of appropriate and inappropriate behaviors; too long to reprint here, they can be found on the APA website at http://www.apa.org/ethics.

Many psychologists follow the code of ethics of the Academy of Management. Although it is somewhat different from the APA code, the two codes are compatible. The Academy of Management code deals with standards of behavior for its members in

TABLE 1.2 I/O Psychology Internet Resources

Web address	Description
http://shell.cas.usf.edu/~spector	Paul Spector's website: Contains information about several research topics and about the I/O field.
http://www.aomonline.org/	Academy of Management (AOM): Contains information about this I/O-related association and the field itself.
http://www.apa.org	American Psychological Association (APA): Contains information about the association, lots of psychology links, and abstracts of articles in APA journals.
http://www.bps.org.uk/	British Psychological Society (BPS): Contains information about the major British psychology society and its I/O psychology division.
http://www.eawop.org/web/	European Association of Work and Organizational Psychology (EAWOP). Provides information about this Europe-wide I/O psychology society.
http://www.hfes.org	Human Factors and Ergonomics Society (HFES): Contains information about the association and its publications.
http://www.iaapsy.org/	International Association of Applied Psychology (IAAP): Their Division of Work and Organizational Psychology website has information about I/O outside of the United States.
http://www.siop.org	Society for Industrial and Organizational Psychology (SIOP): Contents of *TIP* and lots of information about the field and about graduate programs.
http://www.sohp-online.org/	Society for Occupational Health Psychology (SOHP): Contains information about the society and about the field of occupational health psychology.
http://www.hr-software.net/ EmploymentStatistics	Employment Statistics: Mostly selection-oriented information and links.
http://online.onetcenter.org	Occupational Information Network, O*NET: The U.S. Department of Labor job information site.

TABLE 1.3 Six Ethical Principles from the American Psychological Association Code

Competence: A psychologist only does work that he or she is competent to perform.

Integrity: Psychologists are fair and honest in their professional dealings with others.

Professional and Scientific Responsibility: Psychologists maintain high standards of professional behavior.

Respect for People's Rights and Dignity: Psychologists respect the rights of confidentiality and privacy of others.

Concern for Other's Welfare: Psychologists attempt to help others through their professional work.

Social Responsibility: Psychologists have a responsibility to use their skills to benefit society.

Source: From "Ethical Principles of Psychologists and Code of Conduct," by the American Psychological Association, 1992, *American Psychologist, 47,* pp. 1597–1611.

three domains of organizational work—practice, research, and teaching. It, too, is based on the principles that one does not harm others and that one has the responsibility to use his or her talents to benefit society. Similar to this is the ethical standards listed by the British Psychological Society, www.bps.org.uk.

HUMANITARIAN WORK PSYCHOLOGY

For the most part, I/O psychology is a field that developed in the Western developed world, where organizations have the resources to hire I/O psychologists as consultants. In much of the world, however, people live in poverty, work in unhealthy conditions, and have received no benefit from the accumulated knowledge from the I/O field or the expertise of practicing I/O psychologists. The humanitarian work psychology movement is an attempt to remedy this problem by mobilizing I/O psychologists to use their skills to help reduce poverty and promote health and well-being in the workplace in countries where large numbers of people lack access to economic and workplace well-being. The Global Task Force for Humanitarian Work Psychology is a group of psychologists who are finding ways to link I/O psychology with development agencies like the United Nations and governments of developing countries so that their expertise can be brought to bear on these problems (Berry, Reichman, Klobas, MacLachlan, Hui, & Carr, 2011). Berry et al. (2011) explain that I/O psychologists have a great deal to offer the humanitarian effort with their expertise in assessing people's needs for specific programs and interventions, evaluating how well programs work, developing strategies for implementing programs, and determining how best to handle a variety of issues concerning people at work. Much of this work can involve helping humanitarian agencies to work more effectively. For example, I/O selection procedures (see Chapters 5 and 6) can be very useful in choosing which volunteers can be psychologically resilient enough to handle field assignments as aid workers under adverse circumstances such as following a disaster (Berry et al., 2011).

CHAPTER SUMMARY

The field of industrial/organizational (I/O) psychology is one of the major areas of psychology. It is a diverse field concerned with the human side of organizations. The I/O field can be divided into two major areas. The industrial side is concerned with organizational efficiency through the appraisal, selection, and training of people and the design of jobs. The organizational side is concerned with understanding the behavior of people on the job and protecting their health, safety, and well-being.

I/O psychology is both a practice and a science. Most I/O psychologists can be found working for organizations to address issues and problems involving people. They are practitioners who work either as consultants to many organizations or as employees of a single organization. A little over a third of I/O psychologists are college professors (see Figure 1.1), most of whom conduct research to develop better methods and procedures to deal with employee problems at work or to understand employee behavior.

An I/O psychologist needs to earn a graduate degree from an I/O psychology program in a university. Many such programs may be found throughout the United States and the rest of the industrialized world—for example, Australia, Canada, China, Europe,

Israel, New Zealand, and South Africa—with new programs being added in other places. Although the field began largely in the United States and United Kingdom, it has rapidly expanded throughout most of the world. Many of the findings discussed in this book have come from studies done with organizations and people throughout the world.

There are many associations of I/O psychologists (and others with similar interests) that allow for the dissemination of ideas and research findings of the field. This is done by holding conventions and by publishing scientific journals. These associations also have developed codes of ethical conduct for their members. For example, both the Academy of Management and the American Psychological Association have published ethical standards. The basic philosophy in these ethical codes is that I/O psychologists should take care not to harm anyone and that I/O psychologists have a social responsibility to use their skills to benefit others.

LEARNING BY DOING

Graduate Study in I/O Psychology

Go to the SIOP website, http://www.siop.org or the British Psychological website www.bps.org.uk. Go to "Graduate Training Program University Listing" and choose the program of your choice (they are listed by university). Click on the university name and review the information provided here, as well as on the program's own site. Answer the following questions.

1. What is the focus of the program (i.e., what does the description say the program is about)?
2. How many faculty are in the program?
3. How many students are there?
4. How many of the faculty are cited in this textbook (check the Author Index)?

Advantages of Association Membership

Go to the SIOP website, http://www.siop.org or the British Psychological Society website www.bps.org.uk. From the material there, list the advantages to psychologists and students of being a member of the association.

CHAPTER **2**

Research Methods in I/O Psychology

CHAPTER 2 OUTLINE

Imagine that you are a practicing I/O psychologist working for a company. You are assigned the task of determining if a new training program is effective in producing better performance in employees. Perhaps employees are being trained in the use of a new web-based system that is supposed to increase employee productivity. How would you go about finding out if the training works? Would you review the program and see if it looks as if it should be effective, or would you conduct a research study to determine its effects?

The problem with the first approach is that a training program that looks as if it should be effective does not always produce the desired results. The only way to be certain that training accomplishes its purpose is to conduct a research study. To conduct a study to determine training effectiveness requires knowledge of research methodology, a topic in which I/O psychologists today are extensively trained. Whether an I/O psychologist is in a job that involves primarily practice or research, he or she needs to know the methods that are used for conducting studies.

Research is the foundation of both the practice and the science of I/O. In many practice jobs, I/O psychologists are hired to provide research skills so that questions concerning whether or not programs work can be determined scientifically. This is important for evaluating the success of organizational practices (such as training programs). Research is also important for the development of new practices, such as procedures for hiring people.

I/O psychology is a science because the methods used to expand knowledge of organizational phenomena are scientific methods. This means that the I/O psychologist gathers data or information in a systematic way to address research questions of interest, such as these:

"Does the training program work?"

"Will the new absence policy result in better employee attendance?"

Each scientific study begins with a research question, which defines the purpose of the study. An investigation is planned using a particular design or structure in which data are collected. For example, in a simple experiment to test a training program, you might divide a sample of employees into two groups, only one of which receives the training. After the training has been completed, the two groups would be compared on their job performance. The basic experiment defines one of the simplest designs for an investigation. Data would be collected on performance and analyzed using a statistical test, which in this case would probably be a t-test. (See the discussion of inferential statistics later in this chapter.) Conclusions would be drawn concerning the effects of the training by considering statistical results in the context of the investigation's design. With the training program, it is hoped that the trained group will perform better than the nontrained group after the training has been completed. If this were the finding, one feasible conclusion would be that the training worked. In any given study, however, there can be many competing explanations for results that must be addressed with further research. In the training study, perhaps the trained people performed better because they felt management was paying attention to them and not because the training itself was effective, similar to what happened in the Hawthorne studies we discussed in

Chapter 1. With organizational studies (as well as those in any science), one cannot always be certain why results occurred, but with proper research design, competing explanations can be eliminated.

This chapter covers the four major components of a research study. First, it discusses the nature of research questions and how they are refined into testable research hypotheses. Second, it reviews several types of research designs and how they are used as the basis of organizational research studies. Third, it addresses the basic principles of measurement, which define how observations of the phenomena of interest are collected. Fourth, it shows how statistics are used to draw conclusions from the data of an investigation. In addition, this chapter reviews the major principles of research ethics.

Objectives: The student who studies this chapter should be able to:

- Explain the major concepts of research design.
- Describe the major types of research designs and list their advantages and limitations.
- Discuss the types of reliability and validity.
- Explain how inferential statistics can be used to draw conclusions about data.
- State the major principles of research ethics.

▶ RESEARCH QUESTIONS

Every study begins with a research question. This is true for studies done by practicing I/O psychologists, whose questions address an immediate issue for an organization, such as the effectiveness of a procedure or program. It is just as true for I/O scientists, whose research is addressing questions that they believe are scientifically important, even if they are not of immediate concern to any particular organization.

Research questions can be general or specific. A general question would be:

"What causes people to like or dislike their jobs?"

The problem with this sort of question is that it is not sufficiently specific to provide the basis of a study. Too many different factors could be studied as possible influences on liking the job. To be useful, the question should specify exactly what is being studied. A better question that is more specific is:

"Does level of pay affect how much people like their jobs?"

This question specifies the particular influence on liking the job. It tells the researcher exactly what to study as a possible cause of liking the job. To address this question, the researcher needs to assess people's pay levels and their feelings about their jobs.

As we will see in Chapter 9, pay itself is not as important as the fairness of pay policies. People tend to be satisfied when they believe that they have been treated fairly when it comes to pay. They will be dissatisfied if they believe they have been unfairly treated, even if their pay is very high. Thus, the amount of pay is not necessarily the most important factor.

Many investigations go beyond raising questions by stating specific theoretical hunches or hypotheses about the outcomes of a study. A **hypothesis** is the researcher's best guess about what the results of a study will be. Rather than merely raising the question, the hypothesis is a theoretical answer. Thus, one might hypothesize that:

"People who are well paid will like their jobs better than people who are not."

or

"People who are fairly paid will like their jobs more than people who are not."

The hypothesis is a statement of the results that the researcher expects to find. Research studies are conducted to confirm hypotheses. In other words, do the results come out the way they were predicted?

Most hypotheses and research questions come from prior research and theory. Although occasionally a researcher will have a sudden inspirational research idea, most studies and theories come from hard work in studying the research literature of an area. This is the way that all sciences advance and evolve as individual studies become the foundations for later work. The best advice one can give a new researcher is to look to other people's research for new hypotheses and research questions.

The hypothesis and research question is the basis of the study and in some ways its most critical aspect. Without a specific and well-formulated question, it is difficult to design a study that will adequately address it. The question defines the goal or objective of the study, as well as the phenomena of interest. When both are known, the researcher can design the study and choose the measurement techniques much more easily than when the researcher has only an imprecise idea of what he or she is trying to accomplish.

▶ IMPORTANT RESEARCH DESIGN CONCEPTS

The design of an investigation specifies the structure of the study. A large number of common designs are used in organizational research. Each has its own particular strengths and weaknesses, so that no design is necessarily superior to the others. Before discussing the various types of designs, we will define several concepts that must be understood first.

Variables

Variables are the basic building blocks of a design. A **variable** is an attribute or characteristic of people or things that can vary (take on different values). People's abilities (e.g., intelligence), attitudes (e.g., job satisfaction), behavior (e.g., absence from work), and job performance (e.g., weekly sales) are all common variables in organizational research. Every subject's standing on each variable, is quantified (converted to numbers) so that statistical methods can be applied.

Variables can be classified into one of two types. In experiments, **independent variables** are those that are manipulated by the researcher, while **dependent variables** are those that are assessed in response to the independent variables. In other words, the independent variables are assumed to be the cause of the dependent variables. In the training program example, employees are assigned to either a group that is trained or a group that is not trained. Group assignment (trained or not trained) is the independent variable. It is manipulated because the researcher creates the training and decides who does and does not get trained. Subsequent job performance is the dependent variable because it is not manipulated by the researcher but is merely assessed after training.

Research Setting

The research setting can be classified as either field or laboratory. A **field setting** is one in which the phenomenon of interest naturally occurs. Organizations are field settings in which to study employee behavior. **Laboratory settings** are artificial environments in which phenomena of interest do not normally occur. They occur only because the researcher created them in that setting. The same physical location can be the setting for either a field or a laboratory study, depending on what is studied. A university classroom is a field setting in which to study student learning but a laboratory setting in which to study reactions to job conditions.

Most I/O research occurs in organizational field settings, but some of it takes place in the laboratory as well. Dipboye (1990) reported that 29% of I/O studies published in major I/O journals are laboratory studies. Laboratory studies can involve any aspect of work. For example, many researchers create simulated job conditions to test people's reactions. Taken together, the results of both field and laboratory studies help enhance our understanding of organizational phenomena (Dipboye, 1990).

Generalizability

Generalizability of results means that the conclusions of a study can be extended to other groups of people, organizations, settings, or situations. Generalizability is often a concern with laboratory studies because we cannot be certain that the results will hold for organizational settings. The more dissimilar the study is to the organizational setting in terms of both conditions and subjects, the less confidence there can be in the generalizability of the results. The only sure way to be certain about generalizability is to replicate the study in the field setting. If the results in the laboratory are also found in the field, we can have confidence in the generalizability of the laboratory findings.

Generalizability can also be a concern in field studies, for studies done in one organization or with one group of subjects might not have the same results in other places or with other groups of subjects. For example, a study done with nurses in a hospital might have different results from the same study done with physicians. Furthermore, results found in a hospital might be different from results found in a university. Of even greater concern is generalizability across countries and cultures. We cannot be certain that the findings from all of our American and Western research will generalize to countries with different cultures, such as China or India. Finally, even if we wish to generalize only within a single occupation in a single organization, conditions of the study might hold only for the setting in which the study is conducted. A training program that is conducted as part of a study might differ somewhat from the program that is implemented throughout the organization. Trainees and trainers can be affected by knowing they are participants in a research study, just as in the Hawthorne studies we discussed in Chapter 1. This knowledge can motivate the trainers to perform their training tasks in a more effective way than they would if the training was for other purposes. Thus, a training program might work well in the research phase but not in the implementation phase of a training development project.

Control

Every study offers several possible explanations for why the results occurred. **Control** refers to procedures that allow researchers to rule out certain explanations for results other than the hypotheses they wish to test. For example, suppose we wish to find out if salary affects how much people like their jobs. We could conduct a survey of employees in various organizations, asking them how much they are paid and how much they like their jobs. We might find that the higher the salary, the greater the liking. However, with this sort of design, there are many uncontrolled variables that might be the real cause of liking. For example, perhaps the higher-paid people are in different types of jobs than the lower-paid people. If the higher-paid people are all professional athletes and the lower-paid people are all sales clerks, it will be difficult to conclude that level of pay caused liking differences. This is because the type of job was uncontrolled, and it is a possible alternative explanation for the results.

Control can be achieved by a number of procedures. For the most part, they involve either holding constant or systematically varying the level of one or more variables. With the pay survey example, one might hold constant the type of job by limiting the survey to people of only one occupation. If the subjects of the study all had the same job, job type could not have accounted for the results because it was controlled. One could also control for job type by systematically varying it. Subjects could be chosen so that there would be equal numbers of higher- and lower-paid people in each of several job types. For example, the study might be limited to groups of actors and athletes that had about the same mix of higher- and lower-paid people.

Control can be achieved in experiments by the use of the **control group**. A control group is a collection of people who receive a condition or manipulation different from the one of interest. In determining the effectiveness of a training program, the group that did not get trained and is compared to the group that did get trained is called the *control group*. A control group can sometimes be exposed to some manipulation that is used to control specific variables of concern. For example, with a training study it is possible that training has a nonspecific or Hawthorne Effect. A person who knows he or she has been trained might perform better because of increased effort rather than increased skills. This is important to know because there is no need to send someone through expensive and time-consuming training if it does not have the intended effect. The control group can be given bogus or placebo training to control for the Hawthorne Effect. If individuals who are told they are being trained but receive little actual training perform as well as the trained group, the researcher will know that the training did not achieve its intended results.

Laboratory experiments are often conducted in I/O psychology because they provide the strongest control over many variables that might affect results. Even though a laboratory study may lack the generalizability of a field study, a researcher might choose this more controlled approach. It is common for research on new topics to begin in the laboratory so that a researcher can see if, under highly controlled conditions, a hypothesis might hold. If it does, field studies can follow to be sure the results generalize to the settings of ultimate interest—organizations.

Random Assignment and Random Selection

Random refers to a process that eliminates systematic influences on how subjects are treated in a study. The term *random* is used in two ways—random assignment and random selection.

Random assignment occurs when we assign people to various treatment conditions or levels of an independent variable in a nonsystematic way. This means that every subject of our study has an equal chance of being assigned to every condition. In a training study, each employee who participates would have an equal chance of being assigned to the trained group or to the control group. The random assignment process is a means of controlling for subject variables that are not of interest in the study. We expect that on average subjects in both groups will be more or less equivalent in their characteristics. For example, they should be of approximately the same ability, age, motivation, and tenure.

Random selection means that we choose the subjects of our investigation by a nonsystematic method. This means that every possible subject of our study has an equal chance of being chosen to participate. Random selection is important if we wish to draw accurate conclusions about the entire group of interest. If we wish to find out how the employees of a given organization feel about their jobs, unless we are going to study all of them, we want to be sure that the group we choose is a random sample. Otherwise, we run the risk of choosing employees who do not feel the same way about their jobs as the majority of employees. It would not be a good idea to conduct a survey of a large organization and only get the views of top management. Their feelings are not likely to reflect those of employees at the lower levels of the organization.

Random assignment is used as a means of control by which groups of subjects can be made more or less equivalent to one another on variables not being studied. This is a powerful means of control used in experimental studies such as our training study example. Random selection enhances generalizability by choosing subjects who represent the people of interest. This might mean choosing a sample from all employees of a given organization or from all working people in an entire country.

Confounding

Confounding occurs when two or more variables are intertwined in such a way that conclusions cannot be drawn about either one. For example, age is confounded with job tenure (how long people have been on their jobs). This is because one cannot be on the job a long time unless one is relatively old. A 25-year-old cannot have been on the job for 20 years. If you were to find that age was associated with job performance, you could not be certain that it was not job tenure that was the important variable. Age might relate to performance only because the older employees had longer job tenure on average.

With commission sales jobs, pay is determined by job performance. Employees who sell the most product have the highest pay. This confounds pay and performance. If you wished to relate either variable to another variable of interest, you could not easily know which was the more important factor. For example, if job satisfaction related to performance, you could not be certain if pay or performance was the reason for satisfaction.

Often control procedures can be used to unconfound variables. For example, one might study the age-performance connection in only a sample of newly hired employees. Control could be achieved over tenure by limiting the study to those people with approximately the same low level of job tenure. You might study the performance-satisfaction connection by limiting the study to employees who were not on commission or other pay-for-performance systems.

Statistical procedures can also be used to control for confounding. Although it is beyond our scope here, there are many complex statistics that allow for statistical control of unwanted confounding variables. Much of the research in the literature of I/O psychology is concerned with testing for the confounding effects of variables. Often this helps us to understand why two variables, such as performance and satisfaction, are related.

▶ RESEARCH DESIGNS

A **research design** is the basic structure of a scientific study. Research designs can be classified along a continuum from those that involve active manipulation of conditions (experimental) to those that involve relatively passive observation of people. The various designs have their strengths and weaknesses, and rarely will a particular design allow us to draw definitive conclusions about a research question. To do so requires the use of a variety of designs that produce similar results.

Experiments

An **experiment** is a design in which there are one or more independent variables and one or more dependent variables, as well as random assignment of subjects. An independent variable contains two or more levels or conditions of interest. The following have been independent variables in organizational experiments:

Length of daily work shift (in hours)

Pay categories (in dollars)

Availability or nonavailability of training

Setting or nonsetting of job goals

The dependent variable is measured but not manipulated by the researcher and is presumed to be caused by the independent variable. Examples of some frequently studied dependent variables in organizational research are:

Frequency of absences from work

Satisfaction with the job

Job performance

Turnover (quitting the job)

The experiment can be distinguished from other designs by two particular features. First, in an experiment, subjects are assigned at random to two or more conditions that represent the levels of the independent variable or variables. Even though other research designs may have levels of independent variables, to be a true experiment there must be random assignment. Second, the experiment usually involves the creation of the independent variable levels by the researcher. For example, a researcher might design experimental training programs. Sometimes, however, the independent variable levels may occur naturally, and the researcher merely assigns subjects to those levels. In an organization, for example, there might be ongoing training programs that the researcher assigns people to at random.

Most experiments in the I/O literature have taken place in the laboratory (Schaubroeck & Kuehn, 1992). However, experiments can be conducted in more naturalistic settings. The **field experiment** is conducted within an organization rather than the laboratory. The many field experiments that have been conducted are often only approximations of true experiments and are called *quasi-experiments* (Shadish, 2002). In a **quasi-experiment design**, one or more of the features of a true experiment have been compromised. Very often there is not random assignment to the levels of the independent variable. In a training study, members of one work group might be given the training, while members of another serve as the control group. Observed differences between the trained and untrained employees might result from the work group itself rather than the training because of the lack of random assignment.

The major advantage of the experiment is the ability to draw causal conclusions. If the experiment is done properly, one can be reasonably certain that the independent variable is the cause of the dependent variable. If the experiment is conducted in the laboratory, however, one cannot be certain that the results will generalize to the field. With field experiments, generalizability is more likely.

Even with the experiment, however, there can be alternative explanations for results. Often the independent variable will be confounded with another variable. For example, suppose you are interested in determining whether the number of training sessions employees receive affects their job performance. One group might get 5 sessions and the other 10 sessions. However, the total training time is confounded because the second group gets twice the time of training as the first. You could control total time by making the sessions for the 5-session group twice as long as those for the 10-session group. Unfortunately, now the length of session is confounded with the number of sessions. Disentangling the effects of session length, session number, and total training time can be difficult. It can require several experiments to reach a definitive conclusion.

Survey Designs

The survey design is one of the simplest and easiest to conduct of all the major designs. A **survey design** uses a series of questions chosen to study one or more variables of interest. These questions are then asked of a sample of respondents at a single point in time, or they can be asked repeatedly at two or more points in time. Surveys can be presented in a variety of formats, with the most efficient being either the paper-and-pencil **questionnaires** that respondents complete and return to the researcher or the web-based equivalents that are completed online. In recent years, online companies, including Surveymonkey and Zoomerang, have begun offering web-based survey services to researchers for a fee. Surveys can also be conducted through interview methods, either by telephone or face to face.

The most common version of the survey involves collecting all data directly from the respondents, but some studies use other data sources as well. For example, one can survey employees about their jobs and get additional information from coworkers or supervisors. Studies of job performance often get performance data from supervisors rather than the employees who are being studied. It is also common to ask customers or peers to provide assessments of job performance. For example, some restaurants ask customers to fill out a card indicating how good the service was. This can be used as a measure of performance if the waiter or waitress is identified.

Most surveys use a **cross-sectional design**, meaning that all data were collected at a single point in time. A **longitudinal design** is one in which data are collected at more than one point in time. For example, one might collect data on people's feelings about the job when they are first hired and on their performance a year later. This design allows one to see if initial feelings predict later job performance. Many studies of employee turnover are longitudinal, with turnover assessed a year or more after an initial survey to assess variables believed to be related to turnover. This sort of study involves both a survey and one other type of data, turnover assessed from organizational records.

Using a survey design to study organizational phenomena has two advantages. First, the survey is a quick and relatively inexpensive way to find out how people feel about the job. Second, the survey is usually conducted on employees who are asked about their own jobs. This means that generalizability is not as big a problem as it is with laboratory experiments.

Surveys have two major disadvantages. First, employees are not always good sources of information about the variables of interest. For example, self-appraisals of job performance are usually biased in favor of the employee (Harris & Schaubroeck, 1988). In other words, people overrate their own performance. Second, the cross-sectional nature of most surveys makes it difficult to draw conclusions about which variables were likely to be the cause of which other variables. For example, a survey of teachers might find that their reports of their job stress relate to their reports of their job performance. From this alone, it cannot be determined that stress caused performance, performance caused stress, or a third variable (e.g., job tenure) caused both. The use of longitudinal designs can be more helpful in drawing causal conclusions. Studies in which employee feelings about their jobs predict their later turnover, for example, have provided convincing evidence that job attitudes are a causal factor in turnover (Gerhart, 1990).

Perhaps the biggest problem in conducting a survey is assuring a sufficiently high response rate. **Response rate** is the percentage of those surveyed who agree to participate. If the response rate is low because only a small percentage of people are willing to provide data, the generalizability of results could be questioned, especially if you wish to determine the average level of a variable, such as mean level of motivation. The responses of these few people might not be the same as those of the people who did not participate. Procedures have been developed to increase response rates, such as avoiding threatening questions and sending reminder letters (Fowler, 1988; Kalton, 1983).

Observational Designs

In an **observational design**, the researcher observes employees in their organizational settings. Observations can be done either with the employees' knowledge (obtrusive method) or without it (unobtrusive method). With **obtrusive methods**, the researcher might watch individual employees conducting their jobs for a period of time. Employees would know that the observer was conducting research about a particular aspect of their jobs. With **unobtrusive methods**, the subjects of study might be aware that the researcher was present, but they would not know that they were being studied.

In some obtrusive studies, observers assess specific behaviors or events of interest. For example, observers might record the number of times workers take breaks. In other obtrusive studies, the observer might rate the workers' job conditions or reactions to their jobs. For example, Glick, Jenkins, and Gupta (1986) asked observers to estimate how much employees liked their jobs after watching them for about 2 hours.

The unobtrusive observational study can be conducted in many ways. A well-designed study can be quite simple but requires creativity and ingenuity to think of a reasonable way to assess the variables of interest. Often such studies are done by having a person pretend to be doing something other than recording people's behavior. The guard at the entrance of an office building can keep track of the arrival times of employees in a study of tardiness. Such data might also be gathered from a videotape of the entrance that has the time recorded on the picture.

One disadvantage of the obtrusive study is that the researcher can affect the phenomenon being studied. Remember how in the Hawthorne studies job performance kept going up no matter what lighting levels were chosen (see Chapter 1)? Employee motivation was affected by the research process, making it seem that lighting had no effect on performance. This is why unobtrusive methods can be valuable, although it is not always possible to use them because of ethical and legal requirements to respect people's privacy.

Qualitative Studies

Thus far we have been discussing quantitative methods in which researchers define variables, take quantitative measurements of those variables, and use statistical analysis to draw inferences. An alternative approach to research relies on nonquantitative methods to study organizational phenomena. There are many types of **qualitative methods** (Strauss & Corbin, 1990), including case studies, participant observations (the researcher spends time in an organization observing employees), and interviews. In pure form, the qualitative approach involves observing behavior in an organization and then recording those observations in a narrative form. Conclusions and generalizations can be drawn from repeated observations of the same phenomenon without quantifying the results. The qualitative approach can be a good means of generating hypotheses and theories from observations of what happens in organizational settings.

Other forms of qualitative methods involve content analysis of interviews, responses to open-ended questions, and written materials. In this sort of qualitative study, trained judges are asked to sort materials into categories that are given descriptive names. The frequency of each category is then calculated. An example of this approach is a cross-national comparative study of job stress by C. Liu, Spector, and Shi (2007). Both American and Chinese employees were asked to describe a stressful incident at work. Judges read the incidents and placed them into categories. The frequencies with which types of stressful incidents were mentioned were compared across countries, showing that Americans are more likely than Chinese to mention lack of control and less likely to mention making mistakes as being stressful.

▶ MEASUREMENT

Measurement is the process of assigning numbers to characteristics of people or things. Variables in every study must be measured or quantified so that data analysis can be conducted to draw conclusions. One of the most critical steps in planning a research study is deciding how each variable will be measured. The nature of measurement determines in part the type of data analysis that can be done.

Measurement can be classified as either categorical or continuous. With **categorical measurement**, the values of the variable represent discrete categories and not the amount of the characteristic of interest. Numbers are assigned arbitrarily to people or things so that low values do not represent less of the characteristic than high values. Player numbers on a sports team and job titles are categorical because (in most cases) they are arbitrary substitutes for the name of the person in the former case or the title of the job in the latter.

Continuous measurement is used when the numbers represent the amount of the characteristic in question. Higher numbers represent more of the characteristic than lower numbers, so that inferences can be made based on the value of a variable. Dependent variables are usually continuous in large part because continuous measurement allows for a variety of sophisticated data analysis methods. Much of the work of both the I/O practitioner and the I/O researcher involves the assessment or measurement of jobs and people. Number of training sessions and total sales per month are continuous measures.

In experiments, the levels of the independent variables are often categorically measured by numbering them arbitrarily when the levels do not represent an underlying characteristic that can be measured continuously. For example, the independent variable of the method of information presentation in a training program would not represent a continuously quantified dimension. There might be four levels of presentation—for example, below are four discrete items that are numbered arbitrarily.

1 = Book	3 = Lecture
2 = Computer	4 = Videotape

Classical Measurement Theory

According to **classical measurement theory**, every observation of a variable can be divided into two components: true score and error. The true score is assumed to represent the variable of interest. The error is comprised of random influences on the observed score that are independent of the true score. Because errors are random, they are as likely to deflate as inflate the observed values of the variable. Thus, if multiple observations of a variable are taken on the same person or thing, the errors will average out to approximately zero and disappear. Suppose you wish to weigh yourself on a bathroom scale with a needle that tends to stick, randomly indicating a too high or too low weight on successive attempts. If you weigh yourself several times and average the observations, the resulting mean is likely to be close to your true weight. For example, suppose you weigh 120 pounds and the observed scores are:

116, 118, 122, 124

Each of these observed weights is inaccurate because of an error component. The magnitudes of the error components are:

−4, −2, 2, 4, respectively.

The average of the four error components is zero. This means that if you average the four observations of weight, the errors will disappear and the resulting mean will be the correct weight of 120 pounds.

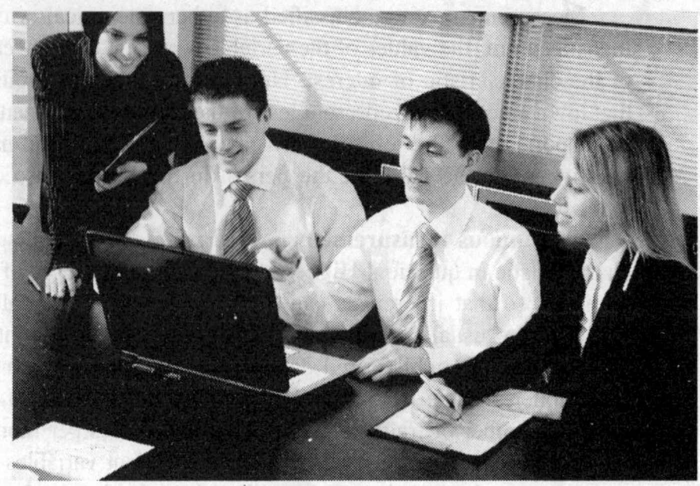

Most I/O research is conducted in the workplace. (© *Konstantin Chagin, sourced from Shutterstock images*)

Psychological tests use multiple items to increase accuracy of measurement by averaging out error. Each item of the test contains both a true score and an error component. By combining the items with random errors, those errors should cancel each other out. This leaves a more accurate measurement of the true score.

Even the elimination of error with multiple measures, however, does not guarantee that what was assessed reflects what was intended to be assessed. Depending on the measurement process, many factors may affect the observed score beyond the intended variable and error. For example, rating scales that ask people to indicate the characteristics of their jobs can be affected by the responder's cognitive processes, feelings about the job, mood, and personality (Spector, 1992). The multitude of influences on an observed score is one factor that makes it difficult to interpret the meaning of results from a single study.

Reliability

Reliability is the consistency of measurement across repeated observations of a variable for the same subject. In classical measurement theory terms, it reflects the relative sizes of the error and true score components. When the error component is small, there will be little variation from observed score to observed score on the same subject, and so the measurement process is reliable. As the error component increases, observations will differ each time the subject is assessed, and so the measurement process is unreliable.

There are several types of reliability that can be classified as either internal consistency or test-retest. We often take multiple measurements of each subject on the variable of interest to increase the accuracy of measurement by averaging out the error components, as we discussed in the previous section. **Internal consistency reliability** refers to how well the multiple measures for the same subject agree. If each measure is presumed to assess the same true score, then differences in scores on each measure reflect error or unreliability.

The instrument that uses multiple measures most often is a psychological test that combines multiple items into a total score for the variable of interest. The items must be interrelated for the test to have internal consistency reliability. Usually the more items there are in a test, the better will be its internal consistency. Multiple-item measures are used to assess many of the variables discussed throughout this book, including abilities, job attitudes, perceptions of the job environment, and personality.

Multiple measures are also used when we ask people to rate variables of interest. For example, employee job performance can be assessed by asking supervisors to rate the performance of subordinates. Supervisors are asked to indicate how well subordinates perform by using a rating scale, such as the following:

How would you rate the performance of your staff assistant?

_______ Excellent
_______ Good
_______ Fair
_______ Poor

Performance ratings are very much like grades given to students by teachers. For research purposes, two or more people might be asked to rate each employee's performance. The ratings can be combined in the same way that multiple items on a test are combined. **Inter-rater reliability** is the extent to which ratings by two or more raters are related to one another.

Test-retest reliability refers to the consistency of measurement when it is repeated over time. If you were to assess a person's job satisfaction several times in a row, a reliable scale would give you the same score each time. This assumes, of course, that the satisfaction remained constant. Similarly, a psychological test or other measuring device should give you the same value for a subject each time unless the underlying score changes. The time span over which test-retest reliability is assessed is dependent on how stable the variable is assumed to be. With tests of some human attributes such as intelligence, high levels of reliability have been found over time spans of decades.

Both internal consistency reliability and test-retest reliability are necessary properties for a useful measuring device. If a measure contains too much error, it will not give sufficiently accurate measurement to be useful. The first required property of a measure is reliability. Reliability is not enough, however. Just because a measuring device is consistent does not mean that it assesses the variable of interest. The interpretation of scores from any measuring device represents its validity, which we discuss next.

Validity

Validity has to do with the inferences that are made about what an observed score measures or represents. In classical measurement theory, it refers to our interpretation of the true score component. Thus, validity refers to the inferences made about a measuring device rather than the device itself. For example, an intelligence test is considered valid if people who score high do better than people who score low on tasks that in theory require intelligence, such as doing well in college courses and solving logic problems. **Construct validity** means that we are able to give an interpretation to scores on a measure (see Table 2.1). To say that a measure has construct validity is to say that we have confidence in our interpretation of what that measure represents. We attribute construct validity to

TABLE 2.1 Four Types of Validity for a Measure and What Each One Means

Type	Meaning
Face	Measure looks like what it assesses
Content	Measure assesses entire variable
Criterion-related	Measure relates to what is expected
Construct	Interpretation of a measure's meaning

standard intelligence tests because we have decades of research showing that scores on these tests predict expected performance in school and on the job.

There are several different ways to assess construct validity, all of which involve inferences that can be made about measures (also described in Table 2.1). **Face validity** means that a measure appears to assess what it was designed to assess. An item from a scale to assess how people feel about their jobs such as:

"Do you like your job?"

might be considered to have face validity because it appears to assess what was intended. An issue of concern with face validity is the perspective of those judging it. Sometimes experts in a domain are asked to judge the face validity of a measure. I/O psychologists can be used as experts for measures of organizational variables.

Face validity does not provide particularly strong evidence to support construct validity. Often a measuring device might appear to have face validity, but it does not assess what was intended. The question "Have you stolen from your employer?" might appear to be a face-valid measure of honesty, but if dishonest employees lie in their answers, the question will not be a valid measure of honesty. Although we sometimes rely on face validity to interpret our measures, it is far from sufficient for establishing construct validity.

Content validity means that a multiple-item measure of a variable does an adequate job of covering the entire domain of the variable. This is best seen in determining whether or not the questions on a course examination do a good or poor job of adequately covering the entire body of material students were assigned. A single question would generally be inadequate to cover all the material in a single chapter of a textbook. The question:

"What is content validity?"

would not represent an adequate and content-valid examination on this chapter. A content-valid exam would ask many questions that cover a good sampling of the topics in the chapter. As with face validity, experts are used to judge the content validity of a measure.

Criterion-related validity means that scores on a measure of interest relate to other measures that they should relate to in theory. As noted earlier, scores on an intelligence test that is considered valid should relate to performance on tasks that in theory require intelligence, such as taking examinations in college courses. Intelligence tests have been shown to relate to many variables, including job and school performance, lending confidence to the interpretation of what they represent. The ability of intelligence tests to predict performance makes them valuable tools for the practitioner who wishes to select employees for jobs (see Chapter 5). Although criterion-related validity is important for building a case for construct validity, it is not sufficient. Sometimes we can find support for our predictions for reasons other than what we expect.

The four types of validity are summarized in Table 2.1. The first three—face, content, and criterion-related—represent ways to assess validity. Combined they provide evidence for the fourth, construct validity of a measure. Construct validity is inferred based on research evidence. It is our best guess about what a measure represents.

STATISTICS

Most studies carried out by I/O psychologists require statistical methods for the data analysis. Two types of statistics are used. Descriptive statistics summarize the results of a study, and inferential statistics help interpret the results using a variety of statistical tests. In this section, we review descriptive statistics and the purpose of several inferential statistics tests.

Descriptive Statistics

The designs discussed in this chapter result in the collection of data on samples of several individuals or jobs. When such data are collected in a study, it is all but impossible to make sense of them without some sort of summary analysis. **Descriptive statistics** provide ways of reducing large amounts of data to summary statistics, such as means or variances. These statistics can be interpreted much more easily than the original data.

Measures of Central Tendency and Dispersion

Several different statistics measure the center of a group of scores. The **arithmetic mean** is the sum of the observations divided by the number of observations. For example, suppose we have the following numbers of absences in a year for five employees:

2, 3, 4, 5, 6

The mean of these five numbers is four absences per year. It is computed by taking the sum of the five numbers (20) and dividing it by the number of employees (5). The **median** is the middle number when the observations are rank ordered from lowest to highest. In this case, 4 is also the median because there are two observations below and two above this value.

The measure of central tendency might indicate the middle score, but it does not give any indication about how much the observations differ from one another in value. For example, the observations of

48, 49, 50, 51, 52

have the same mean of 50 as

0, 1, 50, 99, 100

even though there is a larger difference among observations in the second case. Measures of dispersion indicate the degree to which the observations differ from one another.

The **variance** is a dispersion measure that is the arithmetic mean of the squared differences between each observation and the arithmetic mean of the same observations. For example, the arithmetic mean of the absence frequencies

2, 3, 4, 5, 6

is 4. The differences between each observation and the mean of 4 are

−2, −1, 0, 1, 2

Squaring each of these differences results in

4, 1, 0, 1, 4

The arithmetic mean of these numbers is 2 (10 divided by 5), which is the variance. The **standard deviation** is the square root of the variance, which is 1.4 in this example. It is frequently reported in research papers as the measure of dispersion.

Correlation

Measures of central tendency and dispersion are useful for summarizing groups of observations from a single variable. **Correlation** is a statistic used to indicate the degree to which two continuous variables are related (magnitude) and the direction of the relation. This is important because many research questions concern the relations among variables. For example, a question such as:

"Does level of pay relate to job performance?"

is likely to be answered by computing a correlation statistic between a measure of pay and a measure of job performance.

The descriptive statistic most commonly used to assess correlation is the **Pearson product-moment correlation coefficient**. This statistic can be computed when there are two observations, each representing a different variable, on every subject in a given

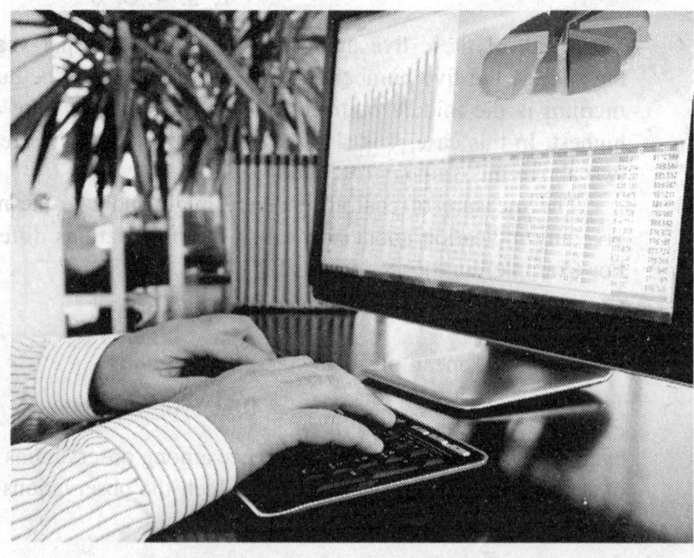

I/O researchers analyze their data by computer. (© *NAN728, sourced from Shutterstock images*)

TABLE 2.2 Hypothetical Data Showing Three Possible Associations Between Pay and Job Performance

Positive Association		Negative Association		No Association	
Job Performance	Pay	Job Performance	Pay	Job Performance	Pay
1	1	1	12	1	1
2	2	2	11	2	12
3	3	3	10	3	3
4	4	4	9	4	10
5	5	5	8	5	5
6	6	6	7	6	8
7	7	7	6	7	7
8	8	8	5	8	6
9	9	9	4	9	9
10	10	10	3	10	4
11	11	11	2	11	11
12	12	12	1	12	2

sample. Table 2.2 contains hypothetical observations of pay and job performance for 12 employees of an organization. Each employee has an observation for each variable. The table contains three possible associations reflected in how the observations of the two variables are paired. Each of the three cases is plotted in Figure 2.1.

In the first case, a positive association or correlation exists between pay and job performance. Employees who have low pay also have low job performance, and employees who have high pay also have high job performance. In Figure 2.1a, the two variables are plotted with performance on the vertical axis and pay on the horizontal axis. The observations form a straight line from the lower left to the upper right of the graph. This means that pay and performance are positively correlated, with a value of 1.0.

Figure 2.1b illustrates negative association or correlation. Employees who have low pay have high job performance, and employees who have high pay have low job performance. The observations form a straight line from the upper left to the lower right of the graph. This indicates negative correlation between pay and job performance. This time the value for the correlation coefficient is −1.0.

Figure 2.1c illustrates little association between pay and performance. Some employees with low pay have low job performance, and some have high job performance. Some employees with high pay have low performance, and some have high performance. The observations do not form a straight line but are scattered widely throughout the graph, meaning that the value for the correlation coefficient is approximately zero (0).

Figures 2.1a and 2.1b illustrate perfect correlation because the observations form a straight line. In almost all studies, there is likely to be a much smaller association between variables, reflected in correlation coefficients that are closer to 0 than the upper limit of 1 in absolute value. In I/O research, correlation coefficients rarely exceed .50. In many domains, correlations can be considerably smaller. Figure 2.2 is a plot of 50

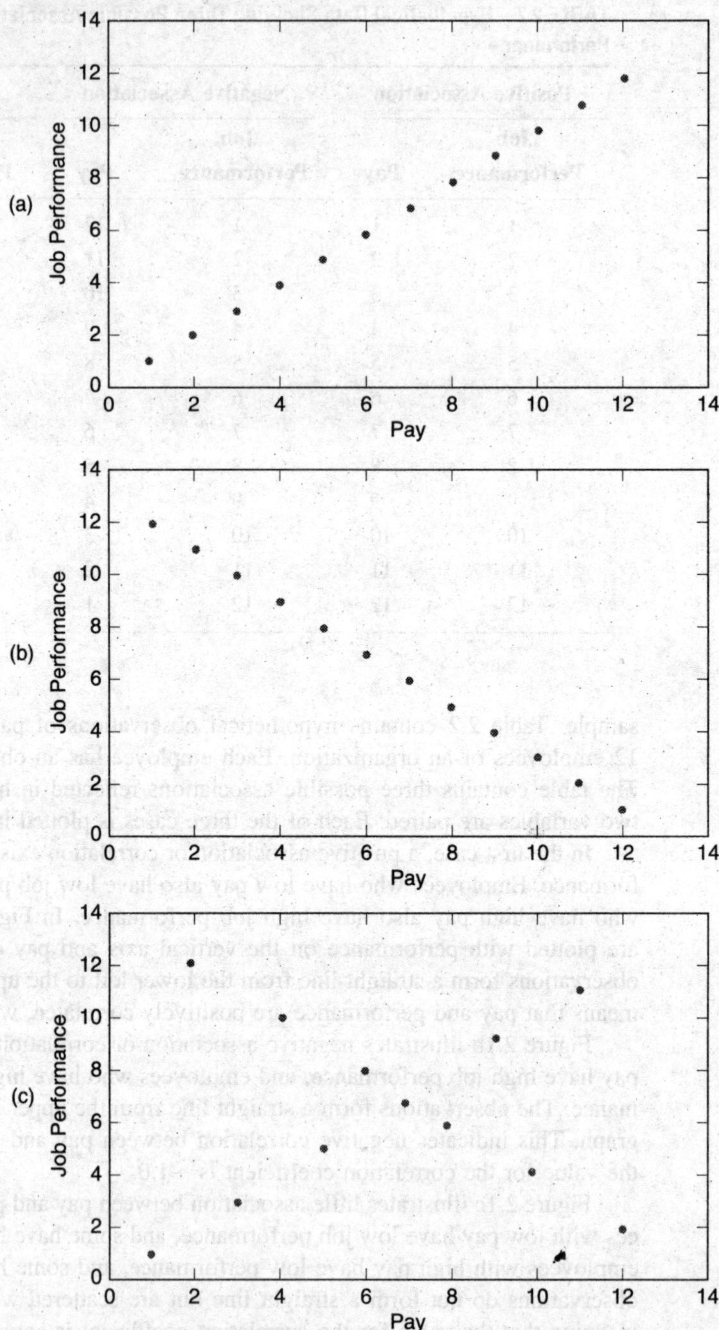

Figure 2.1 Three possible associations between income and job performance: (a) positive association; (b) negative association; (c) no association.

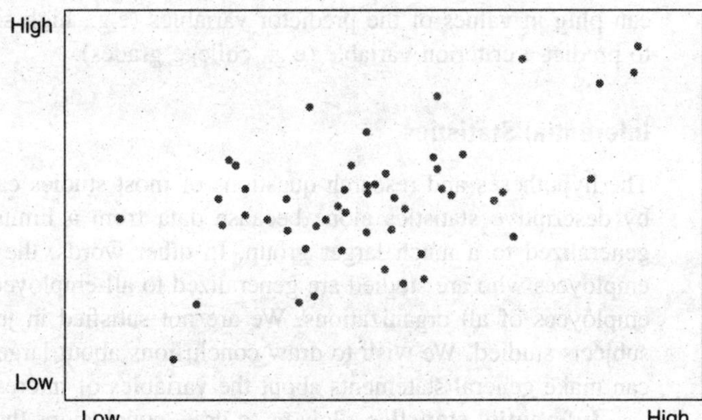

Figure 2.2 Plot showing 50 observations of two variables that are correlated at approximately .50.

observations on two variables that have a correlation between them of approximately .50. The points form an elliptical shape from the lower left to the upper right. The direction of the plot indicates a positive association. If the observations had lined up from the upper left to the lower right, the magnitude of the correlation would have been the same, but it would have been negative in sign (−.50).

Regression

An important by-product of correlated variables is that you can use one to predict the other. With the case illustrated in Figure 2.1a, we can predict that employees with low pay will have low performance and employees with high pay will have high performance. Precise predictions can be made when the numerical value for performance is predicted from the numerical value for pay. This calculation is done using a regression equation that is computed from a set of data.

The **regression equation** provides a mathematical formula that allows for the prediction of one variable from another. If you enter the value of one variable (called the **predictor**) into the equation, it will give you the value for the other variable (called the **criterion**). In almost all cases, the two variables will not be perfectly correlated, so prediction of the criterion from the predictor will not be completely accurate. However, even relatively imprecise predictions can be helpful in many situations in which predictions are made. For example, psychological tests (e.g., the Scholastic Aptitude Test or SAT) are used to select students for admission to colleges and universities because they have been shown to predict grade point average. Even though predictions are imperfect, use of the test can result in better average performance by the students, who are admitted based on test scores.

It is also possible to combine data from two or more predictor variables in order to predict a criterion variable. **Multiple regression** is a technique that enables the researcher to combine the predictive power of several variables to improve prediction of a criterion variable. For example, both high school grades and scores on the SAT can be combined to predict college grades. An equation can be developed from a sample of subjects that can plug in values of the predictor variables (e.g., high school grades and SAT scores) to predict a criterion variable (e.g., college grades).

Inferential Statistics

The hypotheses and research questions of most studies cannot be adequately addressed by descriptive statistics alone because data from a limited sample of people must be generalized to a much larger group. In other words, the data from a small sample of employees who are studied are generalized to all employees of the organization or to all employees of all organizations. We are not satisfied in just noting the results with the subjects studied. We wish to draw conclusions about larger groups of people so that we can make general statements about the variables of interest.

Inferential statistics allow us to draw conclusions that generalize from the subjects we have studied to all the people of interest by allowing us to make inferences based on probabilities. The findings from a research study involving a small group of subjects are extended to other subjects by using statistical tests that are based on probability.

For example, suppose we conduct a training experiment and wish to extend the results to a larger population of employees. Twenty employees of an organization are randomly assigned to one of two groups of 10 each. One group receives the training, and the other is a control group that does not. The dependent variable is performance on the job. Table 2.3 contains hypothetical data from the study. The performance scores of subjects within each group varied from one another, even though every subject in each of the two groups had the same treatment assigned to that group. This variability among subjects who receive the same treatment in an experiment is called **error variance**, which makes it difficult to draw conclusions just by looking at descriptive statistics. This is because the variability among subjects treated the same will produce differences in means between groups. If we were to place subjects into groups randomly, it is unlikely that those groups would have the same mean on the variable of interest. If many different groups of subjects were taken at random from the same organization, it is unlikely that

TABLE 2.3 Hypothetical Data for an Experiment Comparing a Trained Group to a Control Group

Control-Group Performance	Trained-Group Performance
1	2
1	4
2	5
2	5
3	6
3	6
4	7
4	8
5	8
10	9
Mean 3.6	Mean 6.0

the mean performance of many of them would be the same. There will be variability from sample to sample. Interpreting the results of a study means deciding if observed differences between means are due to error variance or the treatment in question.

If the performance scores in each group were equivalent and produced the same mean, it would be obvious that the training was ineffective. On the other hand, if the performance scores of the trained subjects were all higher than the performance scores of the control group subjects, it would be obvious that the training worked as expected. Neither case is likely to occur in an actual study, making the interpretation of results difficult based on inspection of means alone. The data illustrated in Table 2.3 are typical of the results usually found. Even though the trained-group mean is higher than the control-group mean, there is overlap in the scores of subjects across the two groups. Some control-group subjects performed better than some trained-group subjects, and the best performer was in the control group. To interpret these results, you must decide if there is enough difference between the groups to conclude that the training worked or if the differences were due to error variance.

Inferential statistics or *statistical tests* are procedures that help you decide if the results can be attributed to error variance or the experimental treatment. The tests allow you to calculate the probability that the observed results, the differences between means in this case, were not due to error variance. If the probability of finding the mean difference by chance is less than 1 in 20 (.05), the conclusion is reached that the difference was likely due to the training rather than error variance. This is called **statistical significance**, meaning that the probability of finding the observed results by chance alone is less than .05.

There are dozens of different statistical tests, each used for a different situation. Some are used for various experimental designs, whereas others are used for nonexperimental designs, and many can be used for both. Some are limited to two variables, such as the one independent variable and the one dependent variable in the present example. Others can be used with an unlimited number of variables. Table 2.4 lists several of the most commonly used statistical tests in I/O research. Although they may have different purposes, all are based on the same underlying principle of determining if the probability of the test statistic is statistically significant.

An independent group *t*-test is used in the present example to see if the two groups differ significantly on a dependent variable. If there are two or more groups, the **analysis**

TABLE 2.4 Five Commonly Used Inferential Statistics Tests and Their Usage

Independent Group *t*-test: Used to determine if two groups of subjects differ significantly on a dependent variable.

Analysis of Variance (ANOVA): Used to determine if two or more groups of subjects differ significantly on a dependent variable.

Factorial ANOVA: Used to determine the significance of effects of two or more independent variables on a dependent variable.

***t*-test for Correlation:** Used to determine if the correlation between two variables is significantly greater than zero.

Multiple Regression: Used to determine if two or more predictor variables can significantly predict a criterion variable.

of variance (ANOVA) would be used. This would allow you to compare two different training methods to a control group. In most experiments, however, there are two or more independent variables. For example, suppose you wish to compare the trained group to the control group separately for men and women. You could randomly assign 10 men to the control group and 10 men to the trained group. Similarly, you could randomly assign 10 women to the control group and 10 women to the trained group. This would produce a factorial design consisting of the training variable and the gender variable, each of which had two levels. A **factorial design** has two or more independent variables. **Factorial ANOVA** is a statistical test that is used to analyze the data from a factorial design. It tells us if the subjects in the various groups differ significantly on the dependent variable.

The correlation coefficient can be tested to see if it is significantly different from zero. This is done with a variation of the t-test. A significant correlation means that there is significant association between two variables and that you can predict one variable from the other better than by chance. When more than two variables are related to a third, multiple regression is used. There are significance tests that show whether two or more predictor variables in the regression analysis are related significantly to the criterion variable. Again, significance means that the criterion can be predicted by the predictors better than by chance.

Meta-Analysis

A single study is never considered to offer a definitive answer to a research question. To achieve confidence in a conclusion about a phenomenon of interest, we need to conduct several studies. It is not unusual, however, for different studies to yield somewhat different results. The same sampling error that produces differences among means taken from the same population will produce differences in the results of inferential statistical tests. To make sense of conflicting results across studies requires the use of a special type of analysis called meta-analysis.

A **meta-analysis** is a quantitative way of combining results of studies, much like our statistics summarize the results across individual subjects (Hunter & Schmidt, 1990; Rosenthal, 1991). A meta-analysis can summarize statistically the results of different studies in the domains of interest to I/O psychologists. Such analyses can be simple descriptive summaries of results or very complex mathematical and statistical procedures.

Perhaps the simplest form of meta-analysis summarizes the results of multiple studies with means of descriptive statistics. A meta-analysis might report that the mean correlation between two variables has been found to be a particular value, such as .40. For example, suppose you found five studies that reported the following correlations between job satisfaction and pay level:

.20, .22, .24, .26, .28

A simple meta-analysis of these five studies would conclude that the mean correlation between these two variables was .24. More-complex analyses could also be conducted to explore other aspects of these studies. If some studies were conducted on managers and others on nonmanagers, one could test to see if the correlations were different for the two types of employees.

In this book, the results of studies are often summarized by referring to meta-analyses. These analyses have become popular in the I/O research literature. It can be difficult to read several studies and make sense of the findings without the use of some sort of method such as meta-analysis. In most areas that have been frequently studied, meta-analyses can be found to help interpret and summarize what those individual studies have found.

Mediator and Moderator Variables

Regardless of the design, experimental or nonexperimental, research studies help us to determine the extent to which two or more variables are related to one another. Some studies, however, are intended to explore more complex relationships among variables. A mediator is a variable that is part of the intervening process between two other variables. In other words, it explains why two variables relate to one another. For example, we know that ability relates to performance, so if you score well on the quantitative portion of the SAT, you will likely do well in statistics classes. This fact alone does not really tell us why these variables are related. One possibility is that ability enhances motivation, and motivation results in greater effort and thereby better performance. Thus students who score well on the SAT have more confidence in their abilities and are motivated to work hard in quantitative courses. They work harder in their statistics classes, and that effort leads to better performance. In this example, motivation is a mediator.

A moderator is a variable that affects the relationship between two other variables. Participants at one level of the moderator variable will have a different relationship between two other variables than participants at another level. Gender serves as a moderator if the relationship between two variables is different for men and women. For example, suppose the correlation between SAT scores and statistics grades is .50 for women but only .10 for men. Gender would be said to moderate the relationship between SAT scores and grades. Continuous variables can also be moderators. For example, it might be that the relationship between SAT scores and grades is stronger for older than younger students. In this case, age has moderated that relationship.

Mediation and moderation are frequently confused, even in journal articles. Remember that a mediator is an intervening variable that explains the relationship between two other variables. It is concerned with the causal chain of events in which one variable causes the mediator, which in turn causes another variable. A moderator is a variable that changes the relationship between two other variables. That is, the relationship is different at one level of the moderator than another.

▶ ETHICS OF RESEARCH

The ethical principles of I/O psychologists hold for research as well as for practice. The overriding ethical consideration is that the researcher must protect the well-being of subjects. This means that manipulations, such as an experimental training procedure, should not be used if they are known to cause harm. Even with nonexperimental studies, such as surveys, the researcher must take care to protect identities when appropriate. If respondents to a survey provide negative feedback about their supervisors, supervisors should not be able to find out who provided the feedback. This way there can be no retaliation against a subordinate for saying something that the supervisor did not like.

At times, however, conflicting demands can make it difficult to decide what is correct ethically. It would be considered unethical to violate confidentiality and disclose the identities of surveyed employees. On the other hand, a psychologist who works for an organization has an ethical responsibility to that organization much as he or she would have to an individual. That responsibility might extend to identifying disgruntled employees who might cause trouble or need help. A psychologist might have to weigh the well-being of individuals against the well-being of the organization. This responsibility to two parties creates an ethical dilemma because two conflicting demands are placed on the psychologist. It is difficult to know the right thing to do in all such situations. An I/O psychologist must carefully weigh the costs to all people involved in taking different actions. An ethical psychologist will discuss the issue with other psychologists and with superiors in the hope of reaching an ethical and satisfactory decision. In some cases, the psychologist might be forced to take the organization's side or risk being fired.

It is a good idea to try to foresee these situations and avoid them. If you suspect that supervisors might demand to know employee identities, conduct surveys anonymously. If you do not know the identities, you cannot disclose them. Even so, ethical dilemmas can arise in both practice and research. They can be difficult to resolve because someone might be harmed no matter what action is taken. For example, a psychologist might become aware of company policy violations committed by an employee. If nothing is said, the company might suffer damage, but if the person is turned in, he or she might get fired.

Another ethical principle is that subjects of studies should be informed about the nature and purpose of a study before they participate. If there is even a slight possibility that participation has some drawbacks, the subjects should be asked to sign an **informed consent form**. These forms explain the nature of a study and what is expected of the subjects, and they inform the subjects that they can withdraw from the experiment at any time. Although using these forms can be awkward in field settings, informed consent means that the subjects understand possible risks. This protects the researcher from legal action as a result of harm, either real or imagined, that someone claims occurred from participation. Keep in mind that I/O practitioners also are concerned about ethics, but informed consent is not typically used when employees are asked to do things that are part of their jobs or are required as part of their employment rather than for research itself.

▶ CHAPTER SUMMARY

I/O psychology is a science because the methods used in research are scientific methods. This means that I/O psychologists collect and analyze data to address organizational issues and questions. An I/O research study begins with a research question, which defines the purpose of the study. The question leads to a research hypothesis, which is the researcher's best guess about how a study will turn out. A specific hypothesis will serve as the basis for the design of a study.

An I/O study can take place in either a field or a laboratory setting. In a field setting, the phenomenon in question occurs naturally; in a laboratory, it is created. Generalizability means that the results of a given study can be extended to other settings and situations. Control is an important component of research studies in that it allows one to rule out alternative explanations for results. There are many different approaches to achieving control in studies. Random assignment refers to choosing subjects in a nonsystematic way, so that every individual has an equal chance of being assigned to different treatment conditions. Random selection means that every possible subject has an equal chance of being chosen to participate in the study. Confounding occurs when two or more variables are intertwined and related in a way that makes it difficult to draw conclusions about either one.

Research designs can be divided into experimental and nonexperimental forms. In experimental designs, the researcher randomly assigns subjects to conditions that are constructed for the study. Nonexperimental designs involve observation without assignment of subjects or construction of conditions.

Measurement is the process by which characteristics of people or things are quantified. Reliability refers to the consistency of measurement, whereas validity means that inferences can be drawn about the meaning of a measure. The data generated by a study are analyzed with statistical methods. Descriptive statistics summarize the data from a study, and inferential statistics allow for the interpretation of findings.

Ethical principles of research apply to the studies that I/O psychologists conduct. In general, researchers should ensure that their studies do not harm anyone. This is accomplished by taking care that procedures are not dangerous or harmful. Subjects should be informed about the nature of a study by having them read and sign an informed consent form. They should be allowed the opportunity to decline participation. Care should be taken to protect the identities of subjects when information they provide could be used against them in a detrimental way.

LEARNING BY DOING

Methods Used In I/O Research

Find an article that describes a research study from one of the I/O journals listed in Table 1.1. Answer the following questions about that article.

1. What is the research question being addressed?
2. What is one hypothesis from the paper?
3. What kind of research design was used?
4. What do the authors tell us about the reliability of their measures?
5. What is one inferential statistic the authors report in their study?
6. What is the most important conclusion from the study?

PART II

ASSESSMENT OF JOBS, PERFORMANCE, AND PEOPLE

(© Yuri Arcurs, sourced from Shutterstock images)

CHAPTER 3

Job Analysis

CHAPTER 3 OUTLINE

How would you describe the job of a police officer? What are the different tasks that police officers do, and how much time do they spend doing each one? How difficult is it to learn the various tasks, and how long does it take? What personal characteristics does it take to do each task, as well as the entire job? These questions are addressed by a variety of techniques that I/O psychologists refer to as job analysis.

Even for the most familiar jobs, a job analysis is necessary to provide an accurate picture of all the details of the job and all the characteristics required of the people who will do it. For example, everyone is somewhat familiar with the job of a police officer. However, the public perception of the job is based to a large extent upon depictions in movies and television programs, such as *Law and Order* and *CSI*. Television programs focus on the more dramatic aspects of the job, which may be rarely performed. Most police officers spend more time carrying out routine patrol duties and completing paperwork than on apprehending criminals (Bernardin, 1988). The firing of a weapon is a common occurrence on television, but it is rarely done by most police officers on the job. A thorough job analysis would provide an accurate picture of what police officers do all day on the job. The police officer's job has been thoroughly studied with many different job analysis methods and procedures. We look at some of them throughout this chapter.

There are two different categories of job analyses—job oriented and person (or employee) oriented. The job-oriented job analysis focuses on the tasks that are done on the job, whereas the person-oriented job analysis is concerned with the personal characteristics needed for a job. In other words, the job-oriented procedures describe jobs, and the person-oriented procedures describe the characteristics people need to perform jobs. Both are important tools for describing jobs and their requirements.

In this chapter, we discuss the job-oriented and person-oriented approaches, as well as the particular methods that are used for each. In addition, we discuss the uses and purposes of job analysis information, the sources of information that goes into a job analysis, and the reliability and validity of job analysis methods. Finally, we discuss job evaluation, which is a job analysis technique used to set salary levels.

Objectives: The student who studies this chapter should be able to:

- List the uses of job analysis information.
- Describe the sources and ways of collecting job analysis information.
- Discuss the different job analysis methods.
- Describe the evidence for reliability and validity of job analysis methods.
- Explain how job evaluation is used to set salary levels for jobs.

WHAT IS JOB ANALYSIS?

Job analysis is a method for describing jobs and/or the human attributes necessary to perform them. According to Brannick, Levine, and Morgeson (2007, p. 8), there are three elements that comprise a formal job analysis:

1. The procedure must be systematic. This means the analyst specifies a procedure in advance and follows it.

2. A job is broken into smaller units. We describe components of jobs rather than the overall job.
3. The analysis results in some written product, either electronic or on paper.

There is no one way to do a job analysis. Many methods provide different types of information about jobs and human attributes needed for jobs. As noted earlier, job analysis techniques can be used to collect information that is job oriented or person oriented, depending on the purpose of the job analysis.

The Job-Oriented Approach

The **job-oriented job analysis** provides information about the nature of tasks done on the job. Some methods describe the tasks themselves. Other methods provide information about characteristics of tasks. For example, a task for a police officer would be:

Completes report after arresting a suspect

The statement above describes something a police office does. A characteristic of an officer's job would be:

Uses pencils and pens

The characteristic isn't a specific task but describes common features that cut across tasks. A police officer performs many tasks involving writing, such as completing reports of many types and giving citations to motorists. The purposes of the job analysis determine which type of approach would be more useful. The task descriptions provide a picture of what people do on a job, whereas the characteristics of tasks can be used to compare the nature of tasks across different kinds of jobs. Police officers and teachers share the characteristic of using pencils and pens to do tasks, so there can be some similarities in types of tasks, even though the specific tasks themselves may vary.

Tasks can be divided into a hierarchy in which higher-level descriptions are broken down into smaller and smaller pieces of the job. For example, one of the major tasks

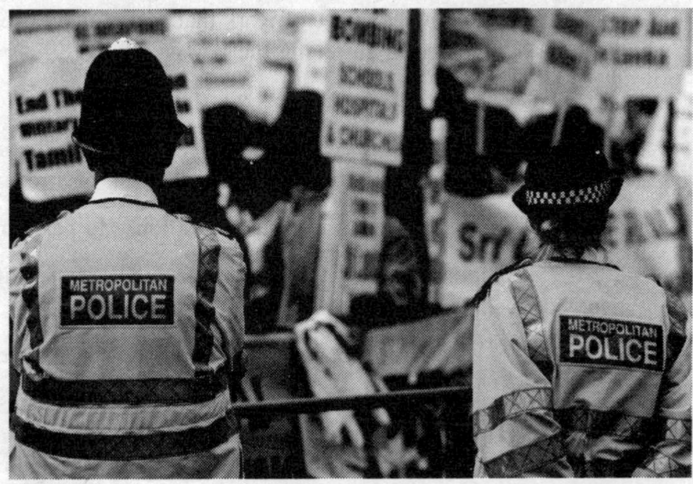

A job analysis is needed to describe what a police officer does at work. (© *Nila Newsom, sourced from Shutterstock images*)

performed by police officers is apprehending suspects. This police function can be further broken down into the specific actions that are involved, such as:

Go to suspect's house to make arrest

Knock on door and identify self

Handcuff suspect

Inform suspect of legal rights

Put suspect in car

Drive suspect to police station

Brannick et al. (2007) discussed a hierarchy that contains five levels of specificity:

1. Position
2. Duty
3. Task
4. Activity
5. Element

A *position* is a collection of duties that can be performed by a single individual. Typically each employee has a single position, although it is possible that one individual holds more than one position. Furthermore, a number of similar positions might be given the same title; for example, several police officers within a department might have the title of "patrol officer," although each has a separate position and collection of tasks. One position might be assigned to patrol an area of the city by car, another to patrol on foot, and a third to work at a desk in the station.

A *duty* is a major component of a job. For a police officer, a duty would be:

Enforce the law

Each duty is accomplished by performing one or more associated tasks.

A *task* is a complete piece of work that accomplishes some particular objective. One of the tasks involved in enforcing the law is:

Arrest suspects who violate the law

Each task can be divided into *activities*, which are the individual parts that make up the task. In this case, activities that make the task of arresting suspects would include:

Driving to a suspect's house to perform an arrest

To accomplish this activity, a number of very specific actions or *elements* are involved, such as:

Turn the ignition key to start the automobile engine

For most jobs, there are several duties; each duty is associated with several tasks; each task is associated with several activities; and each activity can be broken down into several elements. This means that a job analysis can contain a great deal of very specific information about what happens on a particular job. A job analysis that goes to the level of job elements results in a long and detailed report.

TABLE 3.1 Examples of KSAOs and Associated Tasks

KSAO	Task
Knowledge of legal arrest procedures	Arrest suspects
Skill in using a firearm	Practice shooting firearm on firing range
Ability to communicate with others	Mediate a dispute between two people to prevent violent incident
Courage (as other personal characteristic)	Enter dark alley to apprehend suspect

The Person-Oriented Approach

A **person-oriented job analysis** provides a description of the characteristics or KSAOs necessary for a person to successfully perform a particular job. **KSAOs** are the employee's knowledge, skills, abilities, and other characteristics necessary for a job. The first three characteristics focus mainly on job performance itself; the "other" characteristics relate to job adjustment and satisfaction, as well as performance.

Knowledge is what a person needs to know to do a particular job. For example, a carpenter should have knowledge of local building codes and power tool safety.

Skill is what a person is able to do on the job. A carpenter should have skill in reading blueprints and in using power tools.

Ability is a person's aptitude or capability to do job tasks or learn to do job tasks. It is a person's potential to develop skills. Most skills require one or more abilities. The skill of using power tools requires several abilities, including hand-eye coordination. In order to build the roof on a house, a carpenter should have good balance and an ability to work quickly.

Finally, **other personal characteristics** include anything relevant to the job that is not covered by the other three characteristics. A carpenter should have a willingness to do manual tasks and to work outdoors.

Although they might seem to overlap, KSAOs and tasks are very distinct. A task is something a person does. A KSAO is an attribute or characteristic of the person required to do a particular task or tasks. Tasks define what is done on a job, whereas KSAOs describe the sort of person needed. Table 3.1 provides some examples of tasks and associated KSAOs.

Many job analysis methods have been developed to do both job- and person-oriented analyses. Some are specific to one of the two major types of analyses, whereas others can be used for either one or both. The appropriateness of a particular method is determined by its purpose, the next topic we discuss.

► PURPOSES OF JOB ANALYSIS

Job analysis information has many purposes. It can serve as the foundation on which many other activities and functions are built. Ash and Levine (1980) outlined 11 common uses of job analysis information, 5 of which we discuss in this section of the chapter, along with 2 not on their list. A sixth use of job analysis information for setting salary levels will be discussed later under the heading "Job Evaluation." The 11 uses are listed in Table 3.2.

TABLE 3.2 Eleven Uses of Job Analysis Information

Use	Description
Career development	Define KSAOs necessary for advancement
Legal issues	Show job relevance of KSAOs
Performance appraisal	Set criteria to evaluate performance
Recruitment and selection of employees	Delineate applicant characteristics to be used as the basis for hiring
Training	Suggest areas for training
Setting salaries	Determine salary levels for jobs
Efficiency/safety	Design jobs for efficiency and safety
Job classification	Place similar jobs into groupings
Job description	Write brief descriptions of jobs
Job design	Design content of jobs
Planning	Forecast future need for employees with specific KSAOs

Source: Based on "A Framework for Evaluating Job Analysis Methods," by R. A. Ash and E. L. Levine, 1980, *Personnel Psychology, 57*, 53–59.

Career Development

Many organizations have systems that allow employees to move up through the ranks to higher and higher positions. This is referred to as a **career ladder**: A progression of positions is established for individuals who acquire the necessary skills and maintain good job performance. Perhaps the best-known career ladder system is in the military. Personnel move up through the ranks from lieutenant to captain to major to colonel to general. Not everyone can climb to the top of the ladder because of limited opportunities for promotion and inability to achieve the necessary KSAOs.

In recent years, **competency systems** have become popular in organizations to reward employees for acquiring the knowledge and skills needed to both improve performance and be promoted (Levenson, Van der Stede, & Cohen, 2006). Such systems require the identification of critical competencies, the availability of the means of learning and developing competencies, and a procedure for evaluating progress.

Job analysis contributes to career development by providing a picture of the KSAO requirements for jobs at each level of the career ladder and by identifying the key competencies. Knowledge of KSAO requirements can be incorporated into employee development and training programs that can focus on skills necessary for career advancement. This benefits employees because they are told exactly what they need to be eligible for promotion. It benefits organizations because they develop a readily available supply of candidates for upper-level positions.

Legal Issues

Most industrialized countries have laws prohibiting discriminatory employment practices, especially in the hiring of employees. In Canada and the United States, for example, it is illegal to discriminate on the basis of age, color, disability, gender, race, or religion. Although the specific groups that are protected against discrimination vary from country to country, the basic idea that decisions affecting people should be fair is almost universal. Fairness in employment means that decisions should be based on job performance or job potential rather than irrelevant personal characteristics. Job analysis provides a list of relevant KSAOs as the basis for hiring rather than irrelevant personal characteristics.

An important legal concept in U.S. employment is that of **essential functions**, which are actions that must be done on a job. A receptionist must answer the telephone, for example. A nonessential function might be done occasionally but is not important for a person in that position to do. A custodian might receive an occasional phone call, but answering the phone is not an important part of the job.

The concept of essential function is important in deciding whether or not to hire a person with a disability. In the United States, an organization might be able to legally deny employment to a person with a disability who cannot perform essential functions under certain conditions (see Chapter 6). It is illegal to refuse to hire individuals with disabilities because they cannot perform nonessential functions because these functions can easily be done by someone else or do not need to be done at all. With nonessential functions, and at times with essential functions, an organization is required to make reasonable accommodations so that the person is able to do the job (Cleveland, Barnes-Ferrell, & Ratz, 1997), as we will discuss at greater length in Chapter 5.

Job analysis is used to identify essential functions and KSAOs (Mitchell, Alliger, & Morfopoulos, 1997). This can help ensure that decisions about actions that affect people are based on personal factors that are job relevant. For example, a legally defensible system to hire people should be based on KSAOs that have been shown to be relevant to the job in question. Promotion decisions should be based at least in part on the KSAOs of the possible candidates for the position. Only those individuals who possess the established characteristics that are necessary for the job should be considered. When KSAOs are derived from a properly conducted job analysis, employee actions based on those KSAOs are likely to be legal. Furthermore, employees and job applicants will probably believe that they were fairly treated and will be unlikely to file a lawsuit claiming discrimination.

Performance Appraisal

A well-designed performance appraisal system will be based on a job analysis. Criterion development, determining the major components of job performance to be evaluated, is one of the major uses of job analysis information. A job-oriented analysis provides a list of the major components of a job, which can be used as dimensions for performance evaluation.

The behavior-focused performance appraisal methods to be discussed in Chapter 4 are based on a job analysis. The specific behaviors contained in such instruments are collected with **critical incidents** from a job analysis (Flanagan, 1954). These critical incidents are instances of behavior that represent different levels of job performance from outstanding to poor, and they become an important part of the assessment of performance. A poor incident would describe how a person actually did something that was ineffective, such as a police officer getting into an argument with a citizen that resulted in violence. A good incident would describe how a person did something that worked well, such as a police officer defusing a potentially violent encounter by allowing a person to explain his or her side of the story.

Selection

The first step in deciding who to hire for a job is determining the human attributes or KSAOs necessary for success on that job. This means that a person-oriented job analysis should be the first step in the design of an employee selection system. Once the KSAOs for a job are identified, procedures can be chosen to determine how well job applicants fit the requirements for the job. This is done by using methods such as interviews and psychological tests to assess individual characteristics (see Chapter 5).

A person-oriented job analysis produces a list of the KSAOs for a particular job. These KSAOs include both the characteristics that a job applicant is usually expected to have at the time of hiring and the characteristics that will be developed on the job through experience and training. Most accountant positions in large organizations, for example, require a college degree in accounting. This ensures that most applicants will have a reasonable level of knowledge about accounting principles and procedures. Specific knowledge about the organization's own policies and practices is gained on the job. This leads us to the next use of job analysis information—training.

Training

The KSAOs for a job suggest the areas in which training efforts should be directed. The KSAOs that applicants do not have when they apply for a position are areas for training after they are hired. An effective training program in an organization should be based on a thorough analysis of the KSAO requirements for a job. The KSAO requirements can be compared to the KSAOs of applicants or employees. Deficiencies on the part of applicants or employees are the areas toward which training efforts might be directed if the characteristics can be acquired. For example, one cannot train a person to be taller if there is a height requirement for a job.

Vocational Counseling

A major function of schooling, including at the university level, is to assist students in making vocational choices about their future careers. A number of vocational counseling tools exist to help individuals match their KSAOs to the KSAO requirements of jobs. Some of these tools attempt to match individual preferences and personalities to occupations that they would enjoy. Other approaches match individual capabilities to job requirements. Job analysis is particularly useful for matching KSAOs of people with those of occupations.

Converse, Oswald, Gillespie, Field, Bizot, and Smither (2004) provided an example of how job analysis can be used for vocational counseling. They used job analysis to determine KSAO requirements for specific occupations. A battery of ability tests was administered to a sample of individuals, and their ability profiles were matched to the requirements for each of the available jobs. Scores indicating how well the individual KSAOs matched job requirements were computed in order to demonstrate the best- and worst-fitting occupations for each person. For example, one person's abilities were a good match for occupations involving driving, such as a truck driver or subway operator but were a poor match for health-related occupations such as a physician's assistant or physician. Another person was a good match for factory machine operator but was a poor match for biologist.

INTERNATIONAL RESEARCH

Psychologists have long recognized that there are vast individual differences in what people find to be stressful—what one person finds unpleasant another finds enjoyable. The authors of this study were interested in exploring a personality variable's role in occupational stress and in seeing if the job context plays a role as well.

This study was conducted in Finland with a sample of 734 local government employees from six health care facilities. A questionnaire was used to assess the personality characteristic of need for structure and emotional strain at work. Job complexity was assessed with data from the *Dictionary of Occupational Titles* database. The personality variable was related to strain in the entire sample—individuals who were high in need for structure tended to be high in strain at work. However, when the authors added job complexity to the analysis, they found that this was true only for individuals in highly complex jobs. For individuals with simple jobs, there was no relation between personality and strain.

The authors concluded that job context is an important element in job stress. Individual differences alone do not account for strain but it is the combination of individual differences plus circumstances that result in strain. In this case, when jobs are simple, there is presumably high structure, and so there is little reason for those high in need for structure to experience the job any differently than those who are low in that need. However, when jobs are complex and structure is low, the effects of this personality variable emerge.

As noted in Chapter 1, Scandinavian research is almost all concerned with employee well-being, and this study is no exception. Job analysis studies are often concerned with employee selection or performance appraisal, whereas in Finland such a technique is used to study occupational stress.

Source: From "Personal Need for Structure and Occupational Strain: An Investigation of Structural Models and Interaction with Job Complexity," by M. Elovainio and M. Kivimäki, 1999, *Personality and Individual Differences, 26,* 209–222.

Research

An additional use of job analysis information is in research. Many researchers are interested in determining the role of job requirements or task characteristics in many organizational phenomena that we will discuss in this book, ranging from employee motivation and performance to health and safety. For example, Elovainio and Kivimäki (1999) used job analysis data in their study of individual differences in job stress (see the International Research box). In this Finnish study, it was shown that people who have an aversion to change and uncertainty are likely to experience high levels of emotional strain (anxiety and tension) at work—but only if their jobs are complex, as determined by job analysis. If their jobs are simple, these individuals are no more likely to experience strain than are people who enjoy change and uncertainty.

HOW JOB ANALYSIS INFORMATION IS COLLECTED

Job analysis information is collected in several ways. All of them use people who are trained in quantifying job characteristics and the KSAOs necessary to accomplish the different aspects of jobs. These people either survey the employees who do the job in question or experience the job firsthand by doing it themselves or observing it being done.

Who Provides the Information?

Most job analysis information comes from one of four different sources:

Job analysts	Job incumbents
Supervisors	Trained observers

Job analysts and trained observers actually do the job or spend time observing employees doing the job and translate those experiences into a job analysis. Incumbents and supervisors are considered to be **subject matter experts** or SMEs, people with detailed knowledge about the content and requirements of their own jobs or the jobs they supervise. They are asked to provide information about jobs either in interviews or by completing job analysis questionnaires.

Approaches to Collecting Job Analysis Information

People can provide job analysis information in many ways. The four most commonly used are:

Perform the job

Observe employees on the job

Interview SMEs

Administer questionnaires to SMEs

Perform Job

One way to collect job analysis information is for the job analyst to actually do some of the job tasks or the whole job. The job can be performed as an employee would, or the tasks can be performed under simulated conditions. By doing the job, the analyst gains insight into the nature of the job tasks and how the job tasks interrelate. It also provides an appreciation for the context in which employees do their jobs. Both an insurance salesperson and a police officer, for example, operate an automobile, but the conditions under which they do so can be very different.

Although this method can provide good information, it is not often used. Experiencing the job by doing it can be costly and time consuming. The analyst can require extensive training before he or she can do the job. Some jobs are dangerous, particularly for an inexperienced person. Finally, this approach does not clearly indicate that tasks can differ among employees with the same job title.

Observe Employees Working

Another way to collect information about a job is to observe people doing it. Observers can be job analysts or people trained to observe others. Observers are often given forms to complete about the jobs they observe. The form could contain a list of activities, and the observer would indicate how often the observed employee does each one. As with the prior technique, observing employees can give insights into the context in which job tasks are performed. It can also be expensive and time consuming. Furthermore, employees might not behave in the same manner when they know they are being observed.

Interview Employees

One of the most popular ways to collect information about jobs is by interviewing SMEs who are familiar with them. The experts are usually job incumbents and their supervisors. Interviews are carried out by job analysts or trained interviewers. Interviews are often used to generate lists of all tasks and activities done by everyone who has the same job title. Some tasks might be performed by few employees. Other tasks might be performed by every employee but only on rare occasions.

Administer a Questionnaire

The questionnaire is the most efficient means of collecting job analysis information. It can contain hundreds of questions about the job and can be administered easily to thousands of employees. No other technique can provide as much information about jobs with as little effort on the part of the job analyst. The same questionnaire can be given to every employee with the same job title. Comparisons can be made among groups that have the same job title but may differ on some characteristics, such as location.

Multiple Approaches

Each of the four ways of collecting job analysis information has its own set of advantages and limitations in providing a picture of what a job is like. Table 3.3 lists the advantages and limitations of each method. In practice, multiple ways are often used so that the limitations of one are offset by the strengths of another. For example, a job analyst might do the job to get a feel for the context of the job and then administer questionnaires to get detailed information from a wide cross section of employees with the same job title.

METHODS OF JOB ANALYSIS

Many methods have been developed to conduct job analysis. These methods use the different sources of information and the different ways of collecting information. Some of the methods focus on either the job or the person, whereas others focus on both. The methods vary in their use of the four sources of job analysis information and the four ways of collecting information. Many of these methods use more than one source and more than one way of collecting information. One reason that so many methods exist is that they are not all suited to the same purposes. Levine, Ash, Hall, and Sistrunk (1983) found that job analysts rated different methods as being best suited to different purposes.

In this section, we discuss four of the many job analysis methods: The Job Components Inventory, Functional Job Analysis, and Position Analysis Questionnaire are general methods that can be used to compare different jobs; the task inventory is used to provide a description of the specific components and tasks of an individual job. Each method has its own particular strengths and was developed to address a particular purpose.

Job Components Inventory

The **Job Components Inventory (JCI)** was developed in Great Britain to address the need to match job requirements to worker characteristics (Banks, Jackson, Stafford, & Warr, 1983). This method allows for the simultaneous assessment of the job requirements and a person's KSAOs. In other words, the KSAOs for a job and for an individual are

TABLE 3.3 Advantages and Limitations of Four Techniques Used by the Job Analyst to Collect Job Analysis Information

Perform the Job		
	Advantages:	Provides the context in which the job is done
		Provides extensive detail about the job
	Limitations:	Fails to show differences among jobs with the same title
		Is expensive and time consuming
		Can take extensive training of analyst
		Can be dangerous to analyst
Interview Employees Who Perform the Job		
	Advantages:	Provides multiple perspectives on a job
		Can show differences among incumbents with the same job
	Limitations:	Is time consuming compared to questionnaires
		Fails to show context in which the tasks are done
Observe Employees Performing the Job		
	Advantages:	Provides relatively objective view of the job
		Provides the context in which the job is done
	Limitations:	Is time consuming
		Might cause employees to change their behavior because they know they are being observed
Administer Questionnaires to Employees Who Perform the Job		
	Advantages:	Is efficient and inexpensive
		Shows differences among incumbents in the same job
		Is easy to quantify and analyze statistically
		Is easy to compare different jobs on common job dimensions
	Limitations:	Ignores the context in which the job is done
		Limits respondents to the questions asked
		Requires knowledge of the job to design the questionnaire
		Allows job incumbents to easily distort answers to make their jobs seem more important than they are

listed. The degree of correspondence of the lists is used to determine if an individual is suited to a particular job or if the person needs additional training in order to perform a particular job adequately. The JCI has been used in school settings for both curriculum development and vocational guidance.

The JCI covers over 400 features of jobs that can be translated into skill requirements. Five components of job features are represented in the JCI:

1. Use of tools and equipment
2. Perceptual and physical requirements
3. Mathematics
4. Communication
5. Decision making and responsibility

TABLE 3.4 Examples of Frequently Needed Skills for British Clerical Occupations Grouped by the Five Components of the Job Components Inventory

Component	Skill
Use of tools and equipment	Use of pens
	Use of telephone
Perceptual and physical requirements	Selective attention
	Wrist/finger/hand speed
Mathematics	Use of decimals
	Use of whole numbers
Communication	Provision of advice or help to people
	Receipt of written information
Decision making and responsibility	Ability to decide on sequencing of work
	Ability to decide on standards of work

Source: From "Skills Training for Clerical Work: Action Research Within the Youth Opportunities Programme," by M. H. Banks and E. M. Stafford, 1982, *BACIE Journal, 37,* 57–66.

Examples of the skill requirements for each of the five components for clerical jobs in Great Britain can be found in Table 3.4. Just about any job can be analyzed with the JCI so that its skill requirements can be matched to those of potential employees. An existing database of job requirements for many jobs can be used with people who wish to know how well their own skills match those of a chosen career.

Functional Job Analysis

Functional Job Analysis (FJA) (Fine & Wiley, 1971) uses observation and interviews with SMEs to provide both a description of a job and scores on several dimensions concerning the job and potential workers. The dimensions are applicable to all jobs, so that the procedure can be used to make comparisons among jobs. FJA was the job analysis method used by the U.S. Department of Labor to produce the ***Dictionary of Occupational Titles*** **(DOT)** (U.S. Department of Labor, 1977, 1991). This rather large document contains job analysis information for more than 20,000 jobs. The index from the 1977 edition lists jobs from abalone diver to zyglo inspector, both of which are described in Table 3.5. The DOT description for a police officer job is shown in Table 3.6. The printed DOT has been replaced with an expanded, electronic resource, the Occupational Information Network.

TABLE 3.5 The First and Last Entries in the *Dictionary of Occupational Titles,* Fourth Edition, 1977 Index*

ABALONE DIVER: Gathers or harvests marine life, such as sponges, abalone, pearl oysters, and geoducks from sea bottom wearing wet suit and scuba gear, or diving suit with air line extending to surface.

ZYGLO INSPECTOR: Applies iron oxide and zyglo solutions to ferrous metal parts and examines parts under fluorescent and black lighting to detect defects, such as fissures, weld breaks, or fractures.

*Condensed from the original.

TABLE 3.6 Description of a Police Officer Job From the *Dictionary of Occupational Titles*, Fourth Edition, 1977*

Patrols assigned beat to control traffic, prevent crime and arrest violators. Notes suspicious persons and establishments and reports to superior officer. Disperses unruly crowds at public gatherings. Issues tickets to traffic violators. May notify public works department of location of abandoned vehicles to tow away. May accompany parking meter personnel to protect money collected.

*Condensed from the original.

Occupational Information Network

Enlisting the help of many I/O psychologists from both research firms and universities, the U.S. Department of Labor launched the **Occupational Information Network (O*NET)** in the 1990s, and its development and refinement are an ongoing process. This information system is a computer-based resource for job-related information on approximately 1,100 groups of jobs sharing common characteristics (Peterson, Mumford, Borman, Jeanneret, Fleishman, Levin, et al., 2001). It is available in a number of forms, including CD-ROM for the personal computer and via the world wide web (http://online.onetcenter.org). The idea is to make this database widely available to individuals and organizations.

O*NET began with much of the raw material that went into the DOT, but the contents of the O*NET are far more extensive than anything previously attempted. It provides a tremendous amount of information about the content of jobs and the KSAOs needed by individuals in those jobs. The *O*NET98 Data Dictionary* (U.S. Department of Labor, 1998) lists over 450 separate dimensions along which jobs are described and rated. Table 3.7 (column 1) shows the six domains of the O*NET content model. Half of the domains (Experience Requirements, Worker Requirements, and Worker Characteristics) list KSAOs. Occupation Requirements and Occupation Specific Information are concerned with characteristics of job tasks. Occupation Characteristics deals with other kinds of information concerning the labor market and wages for a job.

With O*NET, it is possible to look up a particular job and get a description and detailed information about the six domains. Although the underlying data are the same, the version for personal computers and the online version provide information in a somewhat different format. Table 3.7 shows a sample of the information provided for a police officer, organized by the six domains. The officer information overlaps with that provided by the Positional Analysis Questionnaire (compare the third column of Table 3.7 with Table 3.9), which isn't surprising, as Jeanneret and Strong (2003) showed that corresponding O*NET and Position Analysis Questionnaire dimension scores are strongly related.

Position Analysis Questionnaire

The **Position Analysis Questionnaire (PAQ)** (McCormick, Jeanneret, & Mecham, 1972) is an instrument that can be used to analyze any job. The questionnaire itself contains 189 items dealing with the task requirements or elements of jobs. A KSAO profile for a job can be developed from the elements. The elements of the PAQ are general and allow comparisons of different jobs on a common set of dimensions or KSAOs.

The elements of the PAQ are organized into six major categories, each of which is further divided into several minor categories (Table 3.8). The elements cover a wide

TABLE 3.7 Sample of Information Provided by O*NET for a Police Patrol Officer Job

Domain	Contents of Domain	Examples of Patrol Officer Information
Experience Requirements	Training, learning, licensing	Training in vocational schools, related on-the-job experience, or an associate's degree. May require a bachelor's degree.
Worker Requirements	Basic skills, cross-functional skills, general knowledge, education	Skill in problem identification and speaking. Knowledge of public safety and law.
Worker Characteristics	Abilities, interests, work styles	Quick reaction time and far vision. Interested in work activities that assist others. Achievement oriented.
Occupation Requirements	Generalized work activities, work context, organizational context	Working with the public, operating vehicles or equipment.
Occupation Specific information	Occupational knowledge, occupation skills, tasks, machines, tools and equipment	Patrols specific area, maintains order, arrests perpetrators, monitors traffic.
Occupation Characteristics	Labor market information, occupation outlook, wages	Employment projections suggest an increase of 17.8% from 1996 to 2006. National median wages are $34,632.

Source: O*NET98 Database files accessed with O*NET98 Viewer Version 1.0, U.S. Department of Labor.

TABLE 3.8 Major Categories of the PAQ

Category	Example
Information input	Collecting or observing information
Mediation processes	Decision making and information processing
Work output	Manipulating objects
Interpersonal activities	Communicating with other people
Work situation and job context	Physical and psychological working conditions
Miscellaneous aspects	Work schedule

Source: From "A Study of Job Characteristics and Job Dimensions as Based on the Position Analysis Questionnaire (PAQ)," by E. J. McCormick, P. R. Jeanneret, and R. C. Mecham, 1972, *Journal of Applied Psychology, 56*, 347–368.

variety of task requirements, including the inputting and processing of information, the use of equipment and tools, general body movements, interpersonal interaction, and work context. The elements can be translated into KSAOs for any job. A job that involves using mathematics, for example, requires skill in this area. Because the PAQ generates a standard list of KSAOs, jobs can be compared on their KSAO requirements.

The PAQ produces a profile of the task elements and KSAOs for a job. The profile compares a given job to the hundreds of jobs in the PAQ database. It indicates the percentile score for each element and KSAO in comparison to all jobs. A low score means that the element or KSAO is a less important part of the target job than it is for

TABLE 3.9 PAQ KSAOs and Task Elements for a Police Officer

KSAOs	Task Elements
Far visual acuity	Interpreting what is sensed
Simple reaction time	Being aware of environmental conditions
Movement detection	Controlling machines and/or processes
Rate control	Engaging in general personal contact
Auditory acuity	Wearing specified versus optional apparel

Source: Job Profile, PAQ Number 003 127, used by permission of PAQ Services.

jobs in general. A high score means that the element or KSAO is a more important part of the target job than it is for jobs in general. A percentile of 50 means that the job is average on the element or dimension in question.

Table 3.9 contains a sample of the most important elements and KSAOs for a police officer job. As the table shows, a police officer job involves engaging in general personal contact and wearing specified versus optional apparel. Table 3.9 also contains several sample KSAOs for a police officer job. The two most important are far visual acuity and simple reaction time. Note that both of these were identified by O*NET as well.

Task Inventory

A **task inventory** is a questionnaire that contains a list of specific tasks that might be done on a job that is being analyzed. The inventory also contains one or more rating scales for each task. Ratings might be made on dimensions such as:

Amount of time spent doing the task

Criticality of the task for doing a good job

Difficulty of learning the task

Importance of the task

Job incumbents usually are asked to complete the inventory for their own job. Results are compiled across incumbents to give a picture of the average importance or time spent for each task in a particular job.

When several people complete a task inventory, they are certain to give somewhat different ratings on the same dimensions for each task. This can reflect differences in how individuals make judgments about their jobs. In other words, if two people spend the same amount of time on a task, one might give it a higher time-spent rating than the other. An alternative possibility is that differences in ratings across people reflect real differences in tasks (Harvey & Wilson, 2000; Sanchez & Levine, 2000). There can be large differences in the content of jobs with the same title in the same organization. For example, Lindell, Clause, Brandt, and Landis (1998) found that (among emergency preparedness departments) the number of employees in the work unit affected ratings made concerning amount of time spent in various tasks. It seems likely that the smaller the work group, the larger the number of tasks each person must perform.

Most task inventories are used for purposes in which differences among people with the same job are of no particular interest, but there are two notable exceptions. Conte,

INTERNATIONAL RESEARCH

Lack of agreement among raters of a task inventory is usually interpreted as lack of reliability. In this study, the authors viewed disagreement from a different perspective. They believed that people in the same job would differ in the amount of time they spent in various tasks. Furthermore, the researchers believed that the time-spent differences might relate to sales performance of stockbrokers. In other words, people who are high performers might spend their time differently on the job than people who are low performers.

To test this idea, the authors conducted a job analysis with 580 stockbrokers as subject matter experts. Each one completed a task inventory with 160 tasks. Ratings of amount of time spent were made for each task. In addition, data were collected for each stockbroker's sales performance (dollars sold) for the prior year.

The amount of time spent in some of the tasks correlated significantly with sales performance. For example, the following tasks were associated with high sales:

Dealing with corporate clients and clients in non-business settings, and

Advising and helping other stockbrokers.

The authors noted that it might be tempting to conclude that their results suggest effective strategies for stockbrokers to adopt for good sales performance. They believed, however, that the strategies might be the effect rather than the cause of good performance. A stockbroker with many clients is likely to have many opportunities to spend time with them away from the office setting. He or she is also likely to have high sales volume because of the number of clients. A stockbroker with few clients has fewer opportunities for client contact outside the office setting or for sales. Thus the activity of spending time with clients away from the office may not be the cause of high sales volume but just the by-product of having many clients. The major contribution of this study is that it shows that there can be important differences among people in the same job. It might prove useful if job analysts provided information to organizations about employee differences in time spent doing tasks.

Source: From "Time-Spent Responses as Time Allocation Strategies: Relations With Sales Performance in a Stockbroker Sample," by W. C. Borman, D. Dorsey, and L. Ackerman, 1992, *Personnel Psychology, 45,* 763–777.

Dean, Ringenbach, Moran, and Landy (2005) showed that feelings about the job related to job analysis ratings. Individuals who were satisfied with their jobs reported spending more time on various tasks than people who were dissatisfied. Similarly, in a study of stockbrokers, ratings of time spent in several tasks predicted the individual's sales performance (Borman, Dorsey, & Ackerman, 1992). For example, stockbrokers who spent more time with clients away from the office sold more than their counterparts who spent less time (see the International Research box). Whether the time spent is the cause or the result of good performance and satisfaction with the job is not totally clear in these studies. Further study is needed to determine why task inventory ratings vary among people.

A task inventory for even a fairly simple job can contain hundreds of tasks. To make interpretation easier, tasks are often placed into dimensions that represent the major components of a job. The dimensions for a police officer job that came from a task inventory are shown in Table 3.10. Each of these dimensions was associated with several specific tasks, and each task was rated by SMEs on a variety of different scales. A better understanding of this job can be gained by considering the individual tasks in the context of the major dimensions.

A task inventory often is a major component of an extensive job analysis project that collects several different types of information about jobs and people. Edward

TABLE 3.10 Major Dimensions of a Police Officer Job From a Task Analysis

Driving a car or other police vehicle	Investigating accidents and related problems
Making arrests	Issuing tickets and citations, such as those for traffic violations
Interviewing witnesses and other people	Responding to disturbances, such as family quarrels
Maintaining vigilance during routine patrol	Providing service to citizens

Source: From *Selection of Police Officers, Report Supplement No. 1: Job Analysis*, by R. M. Guion and K. M. Alvares, 1980, Bowling Green, OH: Bowling Green State University.

Levine's *Combination Job Analysis Method* (C-JAM) (Brannick et al., 2007) is one such approach. C-JAM uses both interviews and questionnaires to collect information about KSAOs and tasks. It produces a detailed picture of the KSAOs for a job and the tasks performed. Table 3.11 contains an example of several KSAOs for a police officer job analyzed with C-JAM.

Choosing a Job Analysis Method

We have discussed only a few of the many available job analysis methods. With such a wide variety of methods, how can one choose? Each method has its own advantages and limitations, and not every method is appropriate for every application. Levine et al. (1983) asked job analysis experts to rate the effectiveness of seven job analysis methods for 11 purposes. Each method was better suited for some purposes than others. FJA was seen as being relatively effective for almost all purposes; however, it was also seen as one of the most time-consuming to complete. Choice of method requires consideration of several factors, including cost and purpose.

Job Analysis Methods for Work Teams

So far we have discussed job analysis methods that are designed for jobs that are done individually. However, more and more work in organizations is being done by teams rather than individuals, requiring the use of special job analysis methods. As pointed out by Brannick et al. (2007), team job analysis is similar to the other methods we have already discussed in that the same sources and data collection approaches can be adapted. However, there are specific KSAOs and tasks necessary for communication and coordination among team members. For example, Stevens and Campion (1999) noted

TABLE 3.11 Examples of KSAOs for a Police Officer Job Analyzed With C-JAM

Knowledge of laws, statutes, ordinances (including types of crimes)	Skill in handling/maintaining handgun/shotgun
Knowledge of where/when to conduct interview/interrogation	Ability to enforce laws, statutes, ordinances
Skill in operating special equipment (helicopter, boat, MDT, voice radio, etc.)	Ability to take charge of a situation
	Integrity (moral/ethical/honesty)
	Courage

Source: From *Job Analysis of Deputy Sheriff in the Pinellas County Sheriff's Office*, by E. L. Levine and D. P. Baker, 1987, unpublished paper, University of South Florida, Tampa.

that teamwork requires special KSAOs related to communication, conflict resolution, goal setting, problem solving, and task coordination among team members.

RELIABILITY AND VALIDITY OF JOB ANALYSIS INFORMATION

Job analysis information depends on the judgment of people who either do or observe others do a job. People's judgments are imperfect, so it is important to determine how reliable and valid each job analysis method is. Studies have addressed this issue for some of the methods. In general, results suggest that different people's ratings of jobs are often reasonably reliable. In other words, there will be a relatively high correlation among different people's ratings of the same job for at least some job analysis methods. Validity is a more difficult question, and some researchers have begun to study the question of what job analysis ratings actually represent. In other words, are they accurate representations of task characteristics and KSAO requirements, or do they reflect something else?

Reliability

Dierdorff and Wilson (2003) used meta-analysis (see Chapter 2), which allowed them to summarize the results of 46 studies that reported reliabilities for various job analysis methods. They found a mean test-retest reliability of .83, suggesting that people are quite consistent over time in making their job analysis ratings. Inter-rater agreement (whether or not different job analysts agree in their ratings) was somewhat lower, depending on the types of raters (e.g., analysts vs. SMEs) and the dimensions being rated. Correlations among ratings by different rater types ranged from .48 to .81.

Several studies have examined the reliability of task inventory ratings. Wilson, Harvey, and Macy (1990) found that test-retest reliabilities varied considerably for different rating scales, such as amount of time spent doing the task or importance of the task. Although some reliabilities were very high, others were unacceptably low. Sanchez and Fraser (1992) also found that inter-rater reliabilities among job incumbents varied across different rating scales and across different jobs as well.

Taken together, the studies suggest that job analysis ratings can be reasonably reliable. As noted here, there are exceptions with task inventory ratings. Care should be taken in deciding which scales to use for rating tasks when job incumbents are the SMEs. The next question is whether or not job analysis ratings are valid.

Validity

The best evidence for the validity of job analysis ratings comes from studies that compared different methods or sources of information, such as incumbents versus supervisors. Spector, Brannick, and Coovert (1989) summarized the results of nine studies that reported correlations among methods or sources that ranged from .47 to .94. These results are suggestive of validity for job analysis ratings, but an intriguing study raises some doubts about the interpretation of source agreement. J. E. Smith and Hakel (1979) compared the PAQ ratings of trained job analysts with the ratings of college students who were given only job titles. The students' ratings correlated very well with the ratings of the analysts. This seemed strange because the analysts conducted in-depth interviews with incumbents, whereas the students were given limited information about the job. Smith and Hakel wondered if the analyst ratings reflected preconceived notions about the job rather than the information gathered with the job analysis procedures. If this is the case, then job analysis ratings might be less valid than I/O psychologists usually assume.

Other researchers who have studied the correspondence in ratings of students and trained job analysts have reached different conclusions. Cornelius, DeNisi, and Blencoe (1984) believed that students have accurate knowledge about many jobs; therefore, both job analysts and students can provide valid indicators of job information. Although students have accurate knowledge, more extensive information can be gathered in a thorough job analysis conducted by trained analysts (Cornelius et al., 1984).

Green and Stutzman (1986) conducted a job analysis in which they had job incumbents complete a task inventory. The task inventory included tasks that no one did on the job the researchers were analyzing. Over half of the incumbents indicated that they did at least one fake task. This finding suggests that many people are either careless or not completely honest when they complete task inventories. Whether or not this reduces the accuracy of the task inventory was not determined by this study. Hacker (1996), however, followed up on this research by conducting a similar study and comparing incumbents who endorsed fake tasks with those who did not. He found that both groups of people did not differ in their ratings of all other tasks or in the reliability of their ratings of all other tasks. His results suggest that this phenomenon does not affect job analysis results.

The research on the validity of job analysis ratings suggests that they can provide useful information, but they are not perfect and are potentially subject to some biases because they are based on human judgment (Morgeson & Campion, 1997; Morgeson, Delaney-Klinger, Mayfield, Ferrara, & Campion, 2004). Green and Stutzman's (1986) results emphasize that incumbents are not necessarily accurate in making their ratings. However, that accuracy is not constant across different kinds of job analysis ratings. Dierdorff and Morgeson (2009) showed that people are more accurate when rating specific tasks (e.g., recording medical information on patients) than when rating traits people need to do the job (e.g., dependability). They argued that the more specific the task or trait is and the easier it is to observe, the more reliable and accurate ratings will be. Sanchez and Levine (1994) attempted to improve job analysis results by training incumbents in how to rate their jobs. Although their results were only partially successful, such training might prove useful in the future. Even though there is a need to improve job analysis procedures, the various methods are important tools used by I/O psychologists.

▶ JOB EVALUATION

Job evaluation refers to a family of quantitative techniques that are used to scientifically determine the salary levels of jobs (Morgeson, Campion, & Maertz, 2001). These techniques are very much like the job analysis methods we have already discussed. In fact, the job analysis methods sometimes are used to conduct job evaluation. For example, Robinson, Wahlstrom, and Mecham (1974) used the PAQ to conduct a job evaluation. The major difference between job analysis and job evaluation is that job evaluation has the specific purpose of determining the relative salaries for different jobs by mathematically combining job information.

Perhaps the most popular job evaluation method is the point method (Treiman, 1979). There are four steps involved in conducting a point method job evaluation. First, a panel, often managers or other organization members, determines the compensable factors for the job. **Compensable factors** are characteristics that will serve as the basis for the evaluation. They include:

Consequences of error on the job	Education required
Responsibility	Skill required

Second, a panel (comprised of new people or the same people) judges the degree to which each job has each compensable factor. This is done on a quantitative scale so that each job gets points for each factor. A particular job, for example, might get 2 points out of a possible 20 for consequences of errors made and 20 points out of a possible 20 for education. This would mean that the job would be low on consequences for error and high on education level required.

Third, the points for the factors are summed for each job to provide a total score. In this example, the job would get a total of 22 points (2 + 20) for the two factors. These numbers are not in dollar units, and so they do not indicate the actual salary level. Rather, the numbers are relative, so that the higher the number, the higher the salary the job should have.

The fourth and final step is to plot the actual salaries for each job in an organization against the point totals for each job. If the salary system is fair according to the compensable factors, the plot should be a straight line. This means that the more points a job has, the higher the salary for that job. If the point for a particular job is not on the straight line, the job is either overpaid (point is above the line) or underpaid (point is below the line). Steps can then be taken to bring the job into line with the other jobs with similar totals. Jobs that are paid too much according to the system can have salaries frozen. Jobs that are paid too little can be given salary increases.

Although the job evaluation can indicate the relative value of a job, other factors enter into salary levels. One of the biggest influences is the market wage for a job. A hospital might find, for example, that physicians are overpaid in relation to nurses. However, it would not be feasible for a hospital to set salaries completely according to compensable factors. The cost of paying nurses much higher salaries would be prohibitive. Paying physicians much lower wages would result in not being able to hire or retain them. Thus, the wages paid throughout the area or country must be considered. A salary survey can be conducted to find out what other organizations pay each position. To conduct such a survey, all hospitals in the area could be contacted to determine their salary levels for nurses and physicians.

The point system is just one of many different job evaluation methods. There are also several varieties of point systems. They are all used to determine the pay levels of jobs by estimating their comparative worth. Research on the various methods suggests that they may be interchangeable. Studies have shown that the results of different methods are often quite similar (e.g., Gomez-Mejia, Page, & Tornow, 1982).

Comparable Worth

It is well known that in the United States and other countries women's salaries are lower on average than men's. Some of the differences are attributable to the fact that jobs held primarily by women, such as secretaries, are paid less than jobs held primarily by men, such as electricians (Allen & Sanders, 2002). Although the Equal Pay Act of 1963 made it illegal in the United States to pay women less than men for the same job, there is no law preventing an organization from paying women less than men in a different job.

The concept of **comparable worth** means that different but comparable jobs should be paid the same. If jobs that are held predominantly by women contribute as much to the organization as jobs held primarily by men, the jobs should be paid the same. The difficulty is finding a common measure by which to gauge the comparable worth of jobs. Job evaluation provides a means of doing so.

To do a comparable worth study with job evaluation, one would first apply one of the job evaluation methods to the jobs of an organization. Those jobs that are held primarily by men would be compared to those held primarily by women. It is likely that at least some of the jobs held mainly by women would be underpaid according to the compensable factors. Using mathematical procedures, it would be possible to calculate how much adjustment each of the underpaid jobs should receive. If made, those adjustments could accomplish comparable worth between the predominantly female and predominantly male jobs.

The use of job evaluation to establish comparable worth has not been without critics (e.g., Eyde, 1983). Part of the difficulty is that the judgments used in a job evaluation can be biased in ways that perpetuate the lower salaries of women. For example, Schwab and Grams (1985) found that people who assign points to jobs in organizations are influenced by knowledge of current salaries. As a result, lower-paid jobs are given fewer points than they deserve, and higher-paid jobs are given more points than they deserve. Job evaluations might undervalue the lower-paid predominantly female jobs and overvalue the higher-paid predominantly male jobs.

Perhaps the biggest impediment to achieving comparable worth is not bias in job evaluation but the cost involved in substantially raising salaries in predominantly female occupations, such as clerks and elementary school teachers. The adjustments of these salaries would be extremely expensive unless they were accompanied by reductions in the salaries of other jobs. In addition, there is the issue of market wages, which is a major influence on the salary levels set by organizations. Although some progress has been made in the United States, it seems unlikely that comparable worth will be achieved in the near future.

▶ CHAPTER SUMMARY

Job analysis is a method for describing jobs and the personal attributes necessary to do a job. The job-oriented approach provides information about the nature of and the tasks involved in a job. The person-oriented approach describes the KSAOs (knowledge, skills, abilities, and other personal characteristics) a person must have for a job. There are dozens of job analysis methods that provide information about the job, the person, or both.

Job analysis information has many purposes. It can be used for:

- Career development of employees
- Legal issues, such as ensuring fairness in employee actions
- Performance appraisal
- Selection
- Training
- Vocational counseling
- Research

Most job analysis information comes from one of four different sources:

Job analysts	Job incumbents
Supervisors	Trained observers

They provide their information through one of the following ways:

- Performing the job themselves
- Interviewing people who do the job
- Observing people doing the job
- Giving questionnaires to people who do the job

Many different methods can be used to conduct a job analysis; no one method stands out as being superior to the others. Each has its particular advantages and limitations. The job analyst's purpose should determine which method is chosen. Four popular methods are:

- Job Components Inventory
- Functional Job Analysis
- Position Analysis Questionnaire
- Task inventory

Most job analysis methods have been found to be reasonably reliable. Inadequate research attention has been given to exploring their validity. Existing research has shown promise, but there is evidence that people are not always accurate in their job analysis ratings. More attention should be directed to studying ways to increase the accuracy of job analysis information.

Job evaluation is one of a family of techniques that are used to set salary levels. Job evaluation procedures are much like job analysis, and often job analysis methods are used to conduct job evaluation. Research suggests that many of the different job evaluation techniques give similar results when applied to the same jobs. Job evaluation has been used in an attempt to reduce the salary inequities between men and women. The concept of comparable worth means that jobs that make equivalent contributions to an organization should be paid the same.

I/O PSYCHOLOGY IN PRACTICE

(*Courtesy of Gemma Phillips-Pike*)

This case deals with a job analysis conducted by Gemma Phillips-Pike as part of a recruitment campaign for prison officers. Gemma Phillips-Pike, a Chartered Psychologist, received her MSc in Occupational Psychology from Cardiff University, Wales in 2006. She is currently Director of GP Psychology Consultancy which specializes in the selection and assessment of employees as well as employee development and helping organizations improve their overall employee engagement. Phillips-Pike is also a visiting lecturer at the University of West of England, Bristol.

A FTSE 100 company operating privately-owned prisons required support with their recruitment of prison officers. One prison required 60 prison officers to be recruited. It was decided that assessment centers would be the best way to assess candidates for the role. Before assessment centers could be designed, a current job description was required. Phillips-Pike was required to develop an up-to-date job description for the prison officer role.

Various job analysis data was collected for the development of the updated job description. Phillips-Pike initially obtained data from *written material* held such as training manuals and performance contracts. Then *job holder reports* were obtained by interviewing those prison officers who had achieved good performance appraisal scores in order to assess what knowledge, skills and abilities they possessed which helped them in their role. In addition, *colleague reports* were collected from those who worked with prison officers first hand to provide an external perspective as to what the role required. Finally, through *directly observing* existing prison officers in their role a full profile could be generated as to what the role required. When conducting a job analysis it is important to collect as much data on the role as possible, therefore, it is often the case that external consultants are used for this purpose as it can be a time-consuming and in-depth process requiring specific skills.

Once all the data had been collated it was analysed and an updated job description was created which mapped onto the existing organizational competency framework. It was reviewed by Senior Management within the organization and by a team set up to oversee the recruitment process, which included a number of prison officer representatives.

Once the job description had been generated, the assessment center design could commence. In total, 140 candidates went through the initial assessment center process. In total 60 were offered the role of prison officer. As part of a longer-term process, subsequent objective performance data were collected on those employees and criterion related validity was assessed and the process was reevaluated on the basis of these findings. The job description is still being used today as the basis of prison officer selection within this organization.

Discussion Questions

1. Why was it important to conduct a job analysis before developing the assessment center?
2. Why is it important to collect a number of different forms of job analysis data?
3. How would this job analysis help a company if they were sued for discriminating against a handicapped person?
4. What are the benefits of using an external consultant to conduct a job analysis?

LEARNING BY DOING

Conducting a Job Analysis Interview

One way to conduct a job analysis is to interview employees who hold the job in question. Choose a person you know (acquaintance, family member, or friend) who is currently employed in a job you have never held yourself. Interview that person about the job, taking careful notes of what he or she tells you. You should ask about the following:

1. Job title
2. Brief description of the job
3. The most important tasks involved in the job
4. The most important KSAOs needed for the job

Write a brief report that provides an overview of what you learned about the job.

CHAPTER 4

Performance Appraisal

CHAPTER 4 OUTLINE

Imagine that you are a manager for a large organization and you are given the task of determining how well your subordinates are doing their jobs. How would you go about appraising their job performance to see who is and who is not doing a good job? Would you watch each person perform his or her job? If you did watch people, how would you know what to look for? Some people might appear to work very hard but in fact accomplish little that contributes to the organization's objectives. For many jobs, it might not be readily apparent how well a person is doing just by observing him or her unless you have a good idea of what constitutes good job performance. Performance is best appraised by measuring a person's work against a criterion or standard of comparison.

In this chapter, we are concerned with issues involved in the appraisal of employee job performance. First, there is the issue of the criterion or standard of comparison by which performance is judged and measured. Before we can appraise performance, we must have a clear idea of what good performance is. Once we know that, we can address the second issue of developing a procedure to assess it. Performance appraisal is a two-step process of first defining what is meant by good performance (criterion development) followed by the implementation of a procedure to appraise employees by determining how well they meet the criteria. Before we discuss criteria and procedures for appraising performance, we look at the major reasons for engaging in this potentially time-consuming activity.

Objectives: The student who studies this chapter should be able to:

- List the uses of job performance information.
- Discuss the importance of criteria for performance appraisal.
- Describe the various methods of performance appraisal, as well as their advantages and limitations.
- Discuss how to conduct a legally defensible performance appraisal.

WHY DO WE APPRAISE EMPLOYEES?

The first question that we address is the rationale for organizations to appraise the performance of their employees. Performance appraisal can be a time-consuming chore that most managers and their subordinates dislike. Why then do most large organizations appraise employee job performance at least once per year? The reason is that job performance data can benefit both employees and organizations. Performance data can be used for administrative decisions, employee development and feedback, and research to determine the effectiveness of organizational practices and procedures.

Administrative Decisions

Many administrative decisions that affect employees are based, at least in part, on their job performance. Most large organizations use job performance as the basis for many negative and positive actions. Negative actions toward an employee include both demotion and termination (firing), and some organizations have policies that require the firing of unsatisfactorily performing employees. Positive actions include promotion and pay raises, and many organizations have merit pay systems that tie raises to the level of job performance.

The basis for using job performance data for administrative decisions can be found in both contract and law. A union contract will often specify that job performance is the basis for particular administrative decisions, such as pay raises. A contract can also state that performance appraisals will not be done. Civil service (government) employees in the United States can be fired only for unsatisfactory job performance or violation of work rules. Rule violations include assaulting a coworker, being convicted of a felony, falling asleep on the job, and not showing up for work when scheduled. Even so, many fired U.S. government employees have been reinstated because of long records of satisfactory performance on the job. The United States is not the only country that has laws requiring administrative decisions to be based on job performance. In Canada, for example, the legal requirement that employee firing must be based on job performance has been extended to private companies, as well as the government.

Employee Development and Feedback

In order for employees to improve and maintain their job performance and job skills, they need job performance feedback from their supervisors. One of the major roles of supervisors is to provide information to their subordinates about what is expected on the job and how well they are meeting those expectations. Employees need to know when they are performing well so that they will continue to do so, as well as when they are not so that they can change what they are doing. Even employees who are performing well on the job can benefit from feedback about how to perform even better. Feedback can also be helpful in telling employees how to enhance their skills to move up to higher positions. A new trend is for companies to go beyond the once per year evaluation in designing a comprehensive performance management system. In addition to the annual appraisal, such systems can include goal setting and periodic coaching and feedback sessions between the employee and supervisor. Whereas the annual review might be used for administrative purposes, the interim reviews would be used only for feedback, thus reducing some of the anxiety and defensiveness employees experience when being evaluated for raises and promotions. The performance management system at Wachovia Bank is described in the I/O Psychology in Practice case in this chapter.

Research

Many of the activities of practicing I/O psychologists concern the improvement of employee job performance. The efforts of I/O psychologists can be directed toward designing better equipment, hiring better people, motivating employees, and training employees. Job performance data can serve as the criterion against which such activities are evaluated. To do so, one can conduct a research study. A common design for such a study involves comparing employee performance before and after the implementation of a new program designed to enhance it. A better design would be an experiment in which one group of employees receives a new procedure, while a control group of employees does not. The two groups could be compared to see if the group that received the new procedure had better job performance than the control group that did not. Better job performance by the trained group would serve as good evidence for the effectiveness of the training program.

▶ PERFORMANCE CRITERIA

A criterion is a standard against which you can judge the performance of anything, including a person. It allows you to distinguish good from bad performance. Trying to assess performance without criteria is like helping a friend find a lost object when the friend will not tell you what it is. You cannot be of much help until you know what it is you are looking for. In a similar way, you cannot adequately evaluate someone's job performance until you know what the performance should be.

Characteristics of Criteria

Actual Versus Theoretical Criterion

Criteria can be classified as either actual or theoretical. The theoretical criterion is the definition of what good performance is rather than how it is measured. In research terminology, the **theoretical criterion** is a theoretical construct. It is the idea of what good performance is. The **actual criterion** is the way in which the theoretical criterion is assessed or operationalized. It is the performance appraisal technique that is used, such as counting a salesperson's sales.

Table 4.1 contains theoretical and corresponding actual criteria for five different jobs. As can be seen, both criteria can be quite different for some jobs. For others, the correspondence between the theoretical and actual criteria is quite close. For example, for an insurance salesperson, the theoretical criterion is to sell, and the actual criterion is a count of the sales the person made. For an artist, the correspondence is not as close. The theoretical criterion of producing great works of art is matched to the actual criterion of asking art experts for an opinion about the person's work. In this case, there is room for subjectivity about who is deemed an art expert and about the expert judgments of what is and is not good art. As these cases illustrate, the criteria for different jobs may require quite different assessment approaches.

Contamination, Deficiency, and Relevance

Our actual criteria are intended to assess the underlying theoretical criteria of interest. In practice, however, our actual criteria are imperfect indicators of their intended theoretical performance criteria. Even though an actual criterion might assess a piece of the intended theoretical criterion, there is likely some part of the theoretical criterion that is left out. On the other hand, the actual criterion can be biased and can assess something other than the theoretical criterion. Thus the actual criterion often provides only a rough estimate of the theoretical criterion it is supposed to assess.

Three concepts help explain this situation: criterion contamination, criterion deficiency, and criterion relevance. **Criterion contamination** refers to that part of the actual criterion that reflects something other than what it was designed to measure. Contamination can arise from biases in the criterion and from unreliability. Biases are common when people's judgments and opinions are used as the actual criterion. For example, using the judgments of art experts as the actual criterion for the quality of someone's artwork can reveal as much about the biases of the judges as it does about

TABLE 4.1 Examples of Theoretical and Actual Criteria for Five Jobs

Job	Theoretical Criterion	Actual Criterion
Artist	Create great works of art	Judgments of art experts
Insurance salesperson	Sell insurance	Monthly sales
Store clerk	Provide good service to customers	Survey of customer satisfaction with service
Teacher	Impart knowledge to students	Student achievement test scores
Weather forecaster	Accurately predict the weather	Compare predictions to actual weather

the work itself. Because there are no objective standards for the quality of art, experts will likely disagree with one another when their judgments are the actual criterion for performance.

Unreliability in the actual criterion refers to errors in measurement that occur any time we try to assess something. As discussed in Chapter 2, measurement error is part of the measurement process and is comprised of random errors that make our measurement inaccurate. It is reflected in the inconsistency in measurement over time. If we were to assess the job performance of someone repeatedly over time, the measure of performance would vary from testing to testing even if the performance (theoretical criterion) remained constant. This means that our actual performance criterion measures will have less than perfect reliabilities.

Criterion deficiency means that the actual criterion does not adequately cover the entire theoretical criterion. In other words, the actual criterion is an incomplete representation of what we are trying to assess. This concept was referred to in Chapter 2 as content validity. For example, student achievement test scores in mathematics could be used as an actual performance criterion for elementary school teachers. It would be a deficient criterion, however, because elementary school teachers teach more than just mathematics. A less deficient criterion would be student scores on a comprehensive achievement test battery, including mathematics, reading, science, and writing.

Criterion relevance is the extent to which the actual criterion assesses the theoretical criterion it is designed to measure, or its construct validity (see Chapter 2). The closer the correspondence between the actual and theoretical criteria, the greater the relevance of the actual criterion. All of the actual criteria in Table 4.1 would seem to have some degree of relevance for assessing their intended theoretical criteria. Theoretical criteria can be quite abstract, such as producing great works of art; therefore, it can be difficult to determine the relevance of a criterion. As with the validity of any assessment device, relevance concerns the inferences and interpretations made about the meaning of our measurements of performance.

Criterion contamination, deficiency, and relevance are illustrated in Figure 4.1. The actual criterion is represented in the figure by the lower circle, and the theoretical criterion is represented by the upper circle. The overlap between the two circles (shaded area) represents the extent to which the actual criterion is assessing the theoretical, which

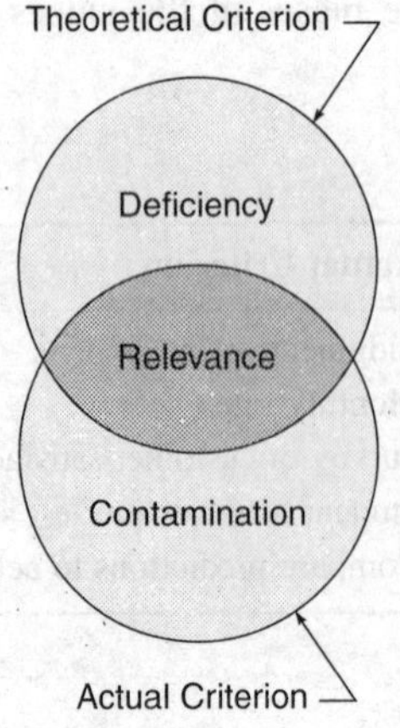

Figure 4.1 Criterion contamination, relevance, and deficiency. The lower circle represents the actual criterion, and the upper circle represents the theoretical criterion. Contamination is the part of the actual criterion (nonshaded area) that does not overlap the theoretical criterion. Deficiency is the part of the theoretical criterion that is not overlapped by the actual criterion (nonshaded area). Relevance is represented by the overlap between the actual and theoretical criteria (darker shaded area).

is criterion relevance. The part of the lower circle that does not overlap the theoretical criterion (unshaded area) is contamination because the actual criterion is assessing something else, which is measurement error. The part of the upper circle that does not overlap the lower (unshaded area) is criterion deficiency because part of the theoretical criterion is not assessed.

Level of Specificity

Most jobs are complex and involve many different functions and tasks. Job performance criteria can be developed for individual tasks or for entire jobs. For some purposes, it may be better to assess performance on an individual task, such as making arrests for a police officer or selling products for a salesperson, whereas for other purposes the entire person's job performance is of interest. For developing an employee's skills, it is better to focus at the individual task level so that feedback can be specific. The person might be told that he or she types too slowly or makes too many errors. This sort of specific feedback can be helpful for an employee who wishes to improve performance. For administrative purposes, overall job performance might be of more concern. The person who gets promoted might be the one whose overall performance has been the best. The particular methods used to assess performance should be based on the purposes of the assessment information.

Criterion Complexity

Because most jobs involve multiple tasks and most tasks can be evaluated from several perspectives, criteria can become quite complex. Job performance even on a single task can usually be assessed along a quality dimension (how well the person does the task) and a quantity dimension (how much or how quickly the person does the task). The complexity of job performance means that multiple criterion measures are necessary to assess performance adequately. These might involve only quality, only quantity, or both. It can be at the level of specificity of a single task or at the level of the person's entire job. The nature of the job and the purposes of the assessment information determine the nature of the criteria that are used, as well as the level of specificity.

It takes close observation to see how well an employee is doing the job. (© *rgerhardt, sourced from Shutterstock images*)

The nature of some jobs requires that quality be the major focus, whereas for others quantity may take priority. In athletics, sometimes one or the other serves as the criterion for winning a competition. In gymnastics, quality is the criterion used. Judges score each gymnast's performance along a quality dimension, and the person with the highest score wins. In track and field events, the criterion is concerned with quantity—jumping farthest, jumping highest, running fastest, or throwing farthest. The quality of jumping form or running style is not relevant, and so there are no judges to rate performance in these events. With jobs, there can be an emphasis on quality or quantity, often depending on the nature of the tasks involved. For a sales job, the emphasis is usually on the quantity of sales, whereas for a teacher it is on the quality of instruction.

There are many other possible criteria beyond work quality and quantity. Table 4.2 contains a performance appraisal form that has eight rather general criteria that are relevant to many jobs. For example, maintaining a professional appearance on the job is relevant when public image is important. Many organizations expect employees who meet the public to display a certain image. This might involve a dress code that specifies the sort of clothing that is appropriate for work, such as a business suit. Factories can have dress codes that are concerned not with public image but with safety. Ties are often forbidden because they could get caught in machinery, resulting in a serious accident and injury.

There are two ways to deal with the complex nature of criteria. The *composite criterion approach* involves combining individual criteria into a single score. If employees receive a number to represent performance on each of four dimensions, a composite would be the average of the four dimension scores for each employee. If a person received the following performance scores on a 1-to-5 scale:

Attendance = 5	Work quality = 4
Professional appearance = 4	Work quantity = 5

his or her composite performance score would be the average of the dimension scores, or 4.5, computed as $(5 + 4 + 4 + 5)/4$. A grade point average would be a composite score for school performance. The *multidimensional approach* does not combine the individual criterion measures. In the previous example, there would be four scores per employee.

TABLE 4.2 Example of a Performance Appraisal Form With Eight Criterion Dimensions

	Rating Categories				
Dimension	**Poor**	**Fair**	**Adequate**	**Good**	**Outstanding**
Attendance	_____	_____	_____	_____	_____
Communicating with others	_____	_____	_____	_____	_____
Following directions	_____	_____	_____	_____	_____
Instructing others	_____	_____	_____	_____	_____
Motivating others	_____	_____	_____	_____	_____
Professional appearance	_____	_____	_____	_____	_____
Work quality	_____	_____	_____	_____	_____
Work quantity	_____	_____	_____	_____	_____

The composite approach is preferred for comparing the performance of individual employees. It is easier to compare employees when each has a single performance score. The multidimensional approach is preferred when feedback is given to employees. It gives specific information about the various dimensions of performance rather than general feedback about overall performance.

Dynamic Criteria

Criteria are usually considered as constant or static standards by which employee performance can be judged. Some I/O psychologists believe, however, that job performance itself is variable over time. This means that the best performer on the job at one point in time will not be best at another point in time. Performance variability makes assessment difficult because performance will not be the same throughout the time period for which it is measured. If someone performs well for part of the year and not well for the other part, how should his or her performance be assessed?

Variability of performance over time is referred to as the **dynamic criterion**, although it is the performance and not the standard that changes. The dynamic criterion idea has generated some controversy among I/O psychologists, with some believing performance is stable and others suggesting it is not (Schmitt & Chan, 1998). On the one hand, Deadrick and Madigan (1990) provided data for sewing machine operators in a clothing factory that indicated performance was stable over short periods of time (weeks) but was not very consistent over long periods of time (months). On the other hand, Vinchur, Schippmann, Smalley, and Rothe (1991) found that the job performance of manufacturing employees was reasonably stable over a 5-year time span. Deadrick, Bennett, and Russell (1997) pointed out that employee performance tends to improve over time, at least early in an employee's tenure, and that factors that determine the performance of new employees are not necessarily the same as those that determine later performance improvement. Thus looking at people's performance over time will show that it is variable and that the best performers don't necessarily remain the best performers in the long run.

Contextual Performance

Criteria for most jobs concern tasks that are specifically required and are certainly listed in a job analysis of that job. However, it has been recognized that employees do a great deal more for organizations than what is required, and these extra behaviors are essential for organizations to function smoothly. **Contextual performance** consists of extra voluntary things employees do to benefit their coworkers and organizations, such as volunteering to carry out extra tasks or helping coworkers (Borman, Buck, Hanson, Motowidlo, Stark, & Drasgow, 2001). Although not specifically required, contextual performance is noticed and appreciated by managers, and their ratings of subordinate performance will be affected by it (Johnson, 2001). This all suggests that contextual performance should be considered in developing criteria for jobs. We will return to the issue of contextual performance in Chapter 10 when we discuss organizational citizenship behavior.

▶ METHODS FOR ASSESSING JOB PERFORMANCE

The job performance of individuals can be assessed in many ways. The most common procedures can be divided into two categories—objective performance measures and

INTERNATIONAL RESEARCH

An important issue in performance appraisal concerns the accuracy of supervisor ratings. In this study, the researchers had available not only supervisor ratings but also data on objective performance with which to compare them.

This study was conducted in Finland in a state-owned company that provided banking and transportation services. Participants were 208 supervisors who together rated the performance of 268 female salespersons. For each salesperson, data were collected on the actual sales productivity during the prior year. In addition, each salesperson was rated by her supervisor on a five-point rating scale ranging from poor (1) to very good (5). Because the nature of each measure was different, each was standardized to a mean of zero and a standard deviation of 1. Thus a salesperson with average productivity should have a score of zero, and her supervisor rating would also be expected to be zero. By comparing the scores for each salesperson, the researchers were able to determine if the supervisor underrated, overrated, or accurately rated the salesperson.

The results found that roughly a third of the ratings fell into each of the accuracy categories, although there were somewhat more overratings than underratings. This should not be surprising because rating leniency is quite common. Supervisors had a tendency to overrate those employees they knew best, perhaps suggesting there was some favoritism expressed toward those subordinates who had developed good working relationships with their supervisors. Furthermore, they found that female supervisors gave more accurate ratings than male supervisors.

These findings show that most ratings of performance are not accurate when compared to objective performance and that the relationship a supervisor has with a subordinate affects ratings. However, it should be kept in mind that this was a case in which performance had an objective and quantifiable outcome—sales. In cases in which there is no such standard, we might expect accuracy to suffer even more. Furthermore, the ratings here were done solely for the purposes of the research and are likely to be more accurate than ratings done for administrative purposes, where subordinates might suffer consequences of less than outstanding evaluations.

Source: From "Performance Rating Accuracy: Convergence Between Supervisor Assessment and Sales Productivity," by L. Sundvik and M. Lindeman, (1998), *International Journal of Selection and Assessment, 6,* 9–15.

subjective judgments. *Objective measures* are counts of various behaviors (e.g., number of days absent from work) or of the results of job behaviors (e.g., total monthly sales). *Subjective measures* are ratings by people who should be knowledgeable about the person's job performance. Usually supervisors provide job performance ratings of their subordinates. Both types of measures can be useful, but studies have shown that when both are used for the same employees, they don't always agree on the level of performance (Sundvik & Lindeman, 1998, see International Research), suggesting they likely reflect different aspects of job performance. Both objective and subjective measures will be presented in the following discussion.

Objective Measures of Job Performance

Organizations keep track of many employee behaviors and results of behaviors. Human resource departments record the number of absences, accidents, incidents, and latenesses for each employee. Some organizations keep track of the productivity of each employee, as well. Productivity data must be collected if an organization has an incentive system that pays employees for what they produce, such as a commission or piece rate.

TABLE 4.3 Examples of Objective Measures of Job Performance

Performance	Measure
Absences	Days absent per year
Accidents	Number of accidents per year
Incidents at work (e.g., assaults)	Number of incidents per year
Latenesses	Days late per year
Productivity (e.g., sales)	Dollar amount of sales

Five common objective measures of job performance are listed in Table 4.3. Each is an objective count of the number of behaviors or amount of work produced. Such data are usually found in organization records, but they can be collected specifically to assess performance. Two of the measures are concerned with attendance—number of times absent and number of times late for work. Accidents include both automotive and nonautomotive, such as being injured by a machine in a factory. Incidents are the number of times the individual is involved in a work incident that is considered important for the particular job. For example, in a psychiatric inpatient facility incident reports record the number of times a staff person is assaulted by a patient. For a police officer, shooting incident reports become part of the employee's record. Productivity is the amount of work produced by an individual.

The attendance measures are applicable to the majority of jobs because most have scheduled work hours. For jobs that are unstructured in terms of work schedule (e.g., college professor), attendance is not a criterion for job performance. The other three objective measures are specific to a particular job. For example, the type of incidents recorded is a function of the nature of the job and job environment. Records of incidents of assaults by students might be kept for urban public school teachers, but they are not likely to be kept for college professors. Teachers are assaulted relatively frequently in large American cities, but college professors are rarely the target for violence. The productivity measure chosen must match the nature of the work done. Specific productivity measures for some common jobs are listed in Table 4.4. As you can see, the nature of productivity can be very different from job to job. This makes it difficult to compare the performances of people who hold different jobs.

Using objective measures to assess job performance has several advantages. First, it can be easy to interpret the meaning of objective measures in relation to job performance criteria. For example, it is obvious that no absences in the past year is a good indicator of

TABLE 4.4 Examples of Objective Productivity Measures for Several Jobs

Job	Measure
Assembly-line worker	Number of units produced
College professor	Number of publications
Lawyer	Number of cases won
Salesperson	Amount of sales
Surgeon	Number of operations performed

satisfactory attendance and that four work-related traffic accidents in the prior 6 months are an indicator of unsatisfactory driving performance. Second, the quantitative nature of objective measures makes it easy to compare the job performance of different individuals in the same job. For attendance measures, comparisons can be made of individuals across different jobs as long as they all require that the person work on a particular schedule. Third, objective measures can be tied directly to organizational objectives, such as making a product or providing a service. Finally, objective measures can often be found in organizational records, so that special performance appraisal systems do not have to be initiated. These data often are collected and stored, frequently in computers, for reasons other than employee performance appraisal, making performance appraisal a relatively easy task to accomplish.

Unfortunately, objective performance measures also have several limitations. Many of the objective measures are not appropriate for all jobs. When jobs do not involve countable output, productivity is not a feasible measure of performance. Also, it is not always obvious what number is considered satisfactory performance. For example, how many absences per year should be considered good performance? Data taken from records can be contaminated and inaccurate. Sometimes behaviors and productivity are attributed to the wrong person or are never recorded. People can also distort records by omitting bad incidents for individuals who are being favored, and employees might fail to report accidents and injuries.

Objective measures are often deficient as indicators of job performance criteria. They tend to focus on specific behaviors, which may be only part of the criterion, and they may ignore equally important parts (Borman, Bryant, & Dorio, 2010). Measures of productivity focus on work quantity rather than quality. Although quantity might be more important in some jobs, it is difficult to imagine a job in which quality is not also somewhat important. Finally, what is reflected in an objective measure is not necessarily under the control of the individual being assessed (Borman et al., 2010). Differences in the productivity of factory workers can be caused by differences in the machinery they use, and differences in the sales performance of salespeople can be caused by differences in sales territories. A person who is assaulted at work may have done nothing wrong and may have been unable to avoid the incident. A police officer who uses his or her weapon might have been forced into it by circumstances rather than poor job performance. In using objective measures to assess individuals, these other factors should be taken into account.

Subjective Measures of Job Performance

Subjective measures are the most frequently used means of assessing the job performance of employees. Most organizations require that supervisors complete performance appraisal rating forms on each of their subordinates annually. There are many types of rating forms that different organizations use to assess the performance of their employees. In this section, we discuss several different types.

Graphic Rating Forms

The most popular type of subjective measure is the **graphic rating form**, which is used to assess individuals on several dimensions of performance. The graphic rating form focuses on characteristics or traits of the person or the person's performance. For example, most forms ask for ratings of work quality and quantity. Many include personal traits such as appearance, attitude, dependability, and motivation.

A graphic rating form, illustrated in Table 4.2, consists of a multipoint scale and several dimensions. The scale represents a continuum of performance from low to high and usually contains from four to seven values. The scale in the table contains five scale points, ranging from "poor" to "outstanding," with "adequate" in the middle. The form also contains several dimensions of job performance along which the employee is to be rated. This form includes attendance and work quality. To use the form, a supervisor checks off his or her rating for each of the dimensions.

Behavior-Focused Rating Forms

The graphic rating forms just discussed focus on dimensions that are trait oriented, such as dependability, or on general aspects of performance, such as attendance. The behavior-focused forms concentrate on behaviors that the person has done or could be expected to do. Behaviors are chosen to represent different levels of performance. For attendance, an example of a good behavior would be "can be counted on to be at work every day on time," whereas a poor behavior would be "comes to work late several times per week." The rater's job is to indicate which behaviors are characteristic of the person being rated. The way in which the form is scored is dependent on the particular type of form.

There are several different types of behavior-focused rating forms. We will discuss three of them:

Behaviorally Anchored Rating Scale (Smith & Kendall, 1963)
Mixed Standard Scale (Blanz & Ghiselli, 1972)
Behavior Observation Scale (Latham & Wexley, 1977)

All three of these scales provide descriptions of behavior or performance rather than traits, but they differ in the way they present the descriptions and/or the responses.

The **Behaviorally Anchored Rating Scale (BARS)** is a rating scale in which the response choices are defined in behavioral terms. An example for the job of college professor is shown in Figure 4.2. This scale is designed to assess performance on the dimension of Organizational Skills in the Classroom. The rater chooses the behavior that comes closest to describing the performance of the person in question. The behaviors are ordered from bottom to top on the scale along the continuum of performance effectiveness.

A BARS performance evaluation form contains several individual scales, each designed to assess an important dimension of job performance. A BARS can be used to assess the same dimensions as a graphic rating form. The major difference is that the BARS uses response choices that represent behaviors, while the graphic rating form asks for a rating of how well the person performs along the dimension in question. Thus both types of rating forms can be used to assess the same dimensions of performance for the same jobs.

The **Mixed Standard Scale (MSS)** provides the rater with a list of behaviors that vary in their effectiveness. For each statement, the rater is asked to indicate if:

1. The ratee is better than the statement
2. The statement fits the ratee
3. The ratee is worse than the statement

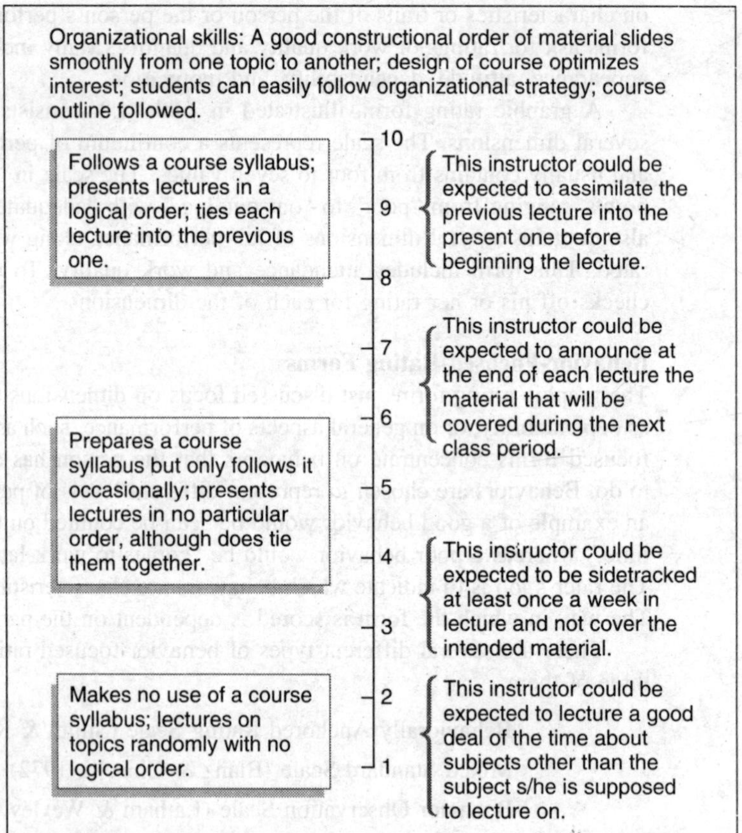

Figure 4.2 An example of a BARS for a college professor. From *Performance Appraisal: Assessing Human Behavior at Work*, by H. J. Bernardin and R. W. Beatty, 1984, Boston, MA: Kent. Reprinted with permission.

There are several dimensions of performance in an MSS, and each dimension has several behaviors associated with it. An example of three statements that reflect performance for the dimension of Relations with Other People is shown in Table 4.5. The three statements represent good, satisfactory, and poor job performance along the dimension.

In an MSS, the statements for the various dimensions are presented in a random order. The rater is not told the specific dimensions associated with each behavior, although the nature of the behaviors is certainly clear. The original idea of Blanz and Ghiselli (1972) was that the mixed order of presentation of the statements would make it more difficult for the raters to bias their ratings than is true of the other types of rating forms. When Dickinson and Glebocki (1990) compared responses to both the mixed and the sorted (by dimension) orders, they found that subjects responded similarly in their ratings with both orders. Thus it does not seem to matter if the dimensions are identified or if the statements are mixed up.

The **Behavior Observation Scale (BOS)** contains items that are based on critical incidents, making it somewhat like an MSS. A **critical incident** (Flanagan, 1954) is

TABLE 4.5 Three Items for an MSS to Assess the Dimension of Relations With Other People

Good Performance

Is on good terms with everyone. Can get along with people even when he or she doesn't agree with them.

Satisfactory Performance

Gets along with most people. Only very occasionally does he or she have conflicts with others on the job, and these are likely to be minor.

Poor Performance

Has the tendency to get into unnecessary conflicts with other people.

Note: Each item is rated on the following scale: For each item on the scale, indicate if the employee is:

Better than the item

As good as the item

Worse than the item

Source: From "The Mixed Standard Scale: A New Rating System," by F. Blanz and E. E. Ghiselli (1972), *Personnel Psychology*, 25, 185–199.

an event reflecting either effective or ineffective behavior by an employee. An example of a poor incident for a teacher would be "slapping a child who made a disrespectful comment." With the BOS, raters are asked to indicate for each item the amount of time the employee engaged in that behavior. The developers of the scale recommend having raters indicate the percentage of time the employee does each behavior by using the following percentage options:

0% to 64%

65% to 74%

75% to 84%

85% to 94%

95% to 100%

This scale is different from the MSS in that the raters indicate frequency rather than comparing employee behavior with the item. In theory, it should indicate how often employees engage in performance-relevant behavior.

Use of the frequency ratings has been criticized by Kane and Bernardin (1982). They point out that frequency of a behavior is not a good indicator of performance because a given frequency might reflect good performance for one behavior and poor performance for another. They give as examples two behaviors for police officers. An 85% to 94% frequency of occurrence would be outstanding for obtaining arrest warrants but abysmal for being vindicated in the use of lethal force. Thus considerable judgment can be required in interpreting the meaning of frequency ratings with the BOS. Of course, judgment is required in interpreting many measures of job performance.

Development of Behavior-Focused Forms

Development of behavior-focused forms takes considerable effort from several people in an organization. Because such a form focuses on specific behaviors, it must be developed

TABLE 4.6 Four Steps in Developing a Behavior-Focused Rating Form to Assess Job Performance

Step 1: Perform job analysis to define job dimensions
Step 2: Develop descriptions of effective and ineffective job performance from critical incidents
Step 3: Have knowledgeable judges place descriptions into job dimensions
Step 4: Have knowledgeable judges rate the effectiveness of the descriptions

for a specific job or family of jobs. The process involves four steps and can take a long time to complete. Each of the four steps is listed in Table 4.6.

Step 1 is a job analysis that identifies the specific dimensions of performance, such as making arrests and writing reports for a police officer. Step 2 involves writing the descriptions of behaviors that vary in their effectiveness or ineffectiveness on the job. This can be done by collecting critical incidents from people who are knowledgeable about the job in question, such as employees who do the job or their supervisors. Critical incidents can provide examples that vary from extremely effective to extremely ineffective performance.

Step 3 involves having judges (knowledgeable people) sort the descriptions of behavior into dimensions to verify that the descriptions reflect the intended dimensions. The final step is to have judges rate the descriptions of behavior along a continuum of effectiveness. With a BARS, these ratings allow for the placement of the descriptions along the scale for each dimension, as in Figure 4.2. With an MSS, the ratings are used to place statements into the three categories of good, satisfactory, and poor.

Cognitive Processes Underlying Ratings

The development of sound performance appraisal methods requires that we understand the cognitive processes that affect rating behavior. I/O psychologists have studied these processes and have devised several models to explain ratings. Some of these models focus on how people utilize information to make judgments. Others are concerned with how people's views of job performance influence their evaluation of an employee.

Models of the Rating Process

There have been several competing models of the cognitive processes that influence ratings of performance (e.g., DeNisi, Cafferty, & Meglino, 1984; Feldman, 1981). These models suggest that the rating process involves several steps (see Ilgen, Barnes-Farrell, & McKellin, 1993), including:

Observing performance

Storing information about performance

Retrieving information about performance from memory

Translating retrieved information into ratings

The process begins with observation of the employee by the supervisor. Next, observations of performance are stored in the supervisor's memory. When asked to rate performance, the supervisor must retrieve information about the employee from his or her memory. The information is then used in some manner to decide what performance rating to give for each dimension of job performance.

The various models describe how humans process information at each step. One idea is that people use **schemata** (categories or frames of reference) to help interpret and organize their experiences (Borman, 1987). Perhaps the best-known schema is the *stereotype*—a belief about characteristics of the members of a group. The characteristics can be favorable or unfavorable. For example, one stereotype might be that private-sector managers are hardworking.

Another type of schema is a *prototype*, which is a model of some characteristic or type of person. One might think of a particular fictional or real person as the prototype of a good manager. Some people might consider Bill Gates, the founder of Microsoft, to be a prototype of a good corporate manager. A person who has the salient characteristics of the prototype might be thought of as a good manager. If the salient characteristics of the prototype are blond hair (or looking like Gates), managers who are blond (or look like Gates) might be seen as better in performance than their counterparts who have brown hair (or do not resemble Gates). The prototype is the standard used to assign people to the good manager category.

Schemata might influence all four steps in the evaluation process. They might affect what behaviors a supervisor chooses to observe, how the behaviors are organized and stored in memory, how they are retrieved, and how they are used to decide on ratings. The use of schemata, however, does not necessarily imply that they lead to inaccurate ratings. In many ways, the use of schemata can simplify experience so that it can be more easily interpreted. It is possible that this leads to accurate judgments about employee performance (Lord & Maher, 1989).

In theory, it should be possible to make use of these cognitive models to help raters do a more accurate job of evaluating job performance. Jelley and Goffin (2001) attempted this with an experiment in which college students were asked to rate the performance of a videotaped college instructor using a BOS. Although results were somewhat inconsistent, the authors were able to find some accuracy increases after priming the raters' memory. This was done by having them do some preliminary global ratings designed to stimulate recall of the performance observed. This approach shows some promise in helping improve ratings, but more research will be needed to determine whether these models will ultimately prove useful.

Content of Subordinate Effectiveness

If schemata affect job performance ratings, it is important that we understand the schemata of people who appraise performance. In other words, appraisal techniques might be improved if they were designed to effectively utilize the schemata of supervisors. If the dimensions on an appraisal form match the dimensions in supervisors' schemata about performance, it will be easier for supervisors to do their ratings. There has been some research that is relevant to this issue.

Borman (1987) studied the content of U.S. Army officers' schemata of subordinate job performance. When asked to describe the differences in characteristics between effective and ineffective soldiers, these officers generated 189 descriptive items. Borman then used complex statistical analysis to reduce the 189 items to six meaningful dimensions. Effective soldiers were seen as having the following characteristics:

Working hard

Being responsible

Being organized
Knowing the technical parts of the job
Being in control of subordinates
Displaying concern for subordinates

Borman concluded that these dimensions represent the characteristics that officers use to judge soldiers' performance. He also noted that in his sample of experienced officers, there was good agreement about what constituted good job performance. These results suggest that experienced supervisors might have schemata that accurately represent effective performance. These six dimensions could be used as the basis for any of the rating forms we discussed earlier.

Werner (1994) conducted a study in which he asked experienced supervisors to rate the performance of secretaries as described in a series of incidents. One of the variables of interest in this study was the sort of information that the supervisors used in making their ratings. Werner found that the following dimensions were seen as most important:

Attendance	Work accuracy
Job knowledge	Work quantity

Werner suggested that these four dimensions might represent the characteristics that define the schemata of his supervisors. He also suggested that supervisors should let subordinates know the content of their schemata. Subordinates are likely to attempt to perform well in those areas that the supervisor believes are important for good performance.

Rater Bias and Error

It is the nature of human judgment to be imperfect. When supervisors or other people make performance ratings, they are likely to exhibit rating biases and rating errors. These biases and errors can be seen in the pattern of ratings, both within the rating forms for individuals and across rating forms for different people. These within-form and across-form patterns are called halo and distributional errors, respectively.

Halo Errors

Halo error occurs when a rater gives an individual the same rating across all rating dimensions, despite differences in performance across dimensions. In other words, if the person is rated as being outstanding in one area, he or she is rated outstanding in all areas, even though he or she may be only average or even poor in some areas. For example, a police officer might be outstanding in completing many arrests (high quantity) but might do a poor job in paperwork. A supervisor might rate this officer high on all dimensions, even though it is not uniformly deserved. Similarly, if a person is rated as poor in one area, the ratings are poor for all areas, even though he or she may be satisfactory on some performance dimensions. This rating error occurs within the rating forms of individuals as opposed to occurring across the forms of different individuals.

Table 4.7 shows a pattern of responses that reflects a halo error. The table shows the ratings of four individuals across five dimensions of performance. Ratings ranged from 1 (poorest performance) to 5 (best performance). This is a halo pattern because the ratings for each individual employee are the same across the different dimensions, even though

TABLE 4.7 Job Performance Ratings for Four Employees on Five Dimensions Illustrating a Halo Error Pattern

Dimension	Employee 1	Employee 2	Employee 3	Employee 4
Attendance	5	3	1	4
Communication	5	3	1	4
Following directions	5	3	1	4
Work quality	5	3	1	4
Work quantity	5	3	1	4

each person received different ratings. Such a patterns suggests that raters are unable to distinguish among dimensions. The person is seen as uniform in performance across dimensions.

Although a pattern of similar ratings might indicate a rating error, it is possible that employee performance is consistent across dimensions. This means that halo patterns might accurately indicate that dimensions of actual performance are related. This possibility has led to considerable discussion in the I/O literature about the meaning of halo (e.g., Balzer & Sulsky, 1992; Murphy, Jako, & Anhalt, 1993; Solomonson & Lance, 1997; Viswesvaran, Schmidt, & Ones, 2005). Part of this discussion concerns how to separate the error from "true" halo. *True halo* means that an employee performs at the same level on all dimensions.

Another concern with halo has been explaining cognitive processes that would lead a rater to exhibit halo error. Several researchers have theorized that raters rely on a general impression of the employee when making dimension ratings (Lance, LaPointe, & Fisicaro, 1994; Nathan & Lord, 1983). According to this view, salient pieces of information are used to form a general impression of an employee. The impression forms the basis of performance ratings. This suggests that raters may be better able to provide information about global performance than dimensions of performance.

Distributional Errors

Distributional errors occur when a rater tends to rate everyone the same. **Leniency errors** occur when the rater rates everyone at the favorable end of the performance scale. **Severity errors** occur when the rater rates everyone at the unfavorable end of the performance scale. **Central tendency** errors occur when a rater rates everyone in the middle of the performance scale. The leniency pattern can be seen across ratings of different people. Table 4.8 shows a leniency pattern in that all four people were given ratings at the favorable end of the performance scale. Each person received ratings of 4 and 5 on a five-point scale. It is possible, however, that a distributional error pattern does not reflect errors. All ratees might have performed the same, leading to similar ratings.

Control of Rater Bias and Error

Two approaches have been developed to control and eliminate rater bias and error. One approach is to design better performance appraisal forms that will be resistant to these problems. The other is to train raters to avoid rating errors. Although both approaches have shown promise, research studies have yielded conflicting results about their ability to reduce errors (Bernardin & Beatty, 1984).

TABLE 4.8 Job Performance Ratings for Four Employees on Five Dimensions Illustrating a Leniency Error Pattern

Dimension	Employee 1	Employee 2	Employee 3	Employee 4
Attendance	4	5	5	5
Communication	4	5	5	5
Following directions	5	4	4	4
Work quality	4	5	4	5
Work quantity	5	4	5	5

Error-Resistant Forms to Assess Performance

The behavior-focused rating scales, such as the BARS and the MSS, were originally developed in part to eliminate rating errors. The idea is that raters will be able to make more accurate ratings if they focus on specific behaviors rather than traits. These behaviors are more concrete and require less idiosyncratic judgment about what they represent. For example, it should be easier to rate accurately how often a person is absent from work than the somewhat abstract trait of dependability.

Many studies have compared the various behavior-focused rating forms with graphic rating forms, as well as with one another. These comparisons have found that sometimes the behavior-focused forms yield fewer errors (such as halo and leniency) than the graphic rating scales and sometimes they do not (Bernardin & Beatty, 1984; Latham, Skarlicki, Irvine, & Siegel, 1993). Furthermore, scales that merely ask raters to check whether or not individuals have engaged in specific behaviors may result in less leniency than graphic rating scales (Yun, Donahue, Dudley, & McFarland, 2005). After reviewing the literature on rating forms, Borman et al. (2010) concluded that there is little advantage to using behavior-based scales over graphic rating scales. It seems that efforts to improve rater accuracy should focus on things other than the design of the rating instruments.

Rater Training to Reduce Errors

Rater training has also been attempted in many studies, with mixed results (Hedge & Kavanagh, 1988; Latham, 1986). At least some of the discrepancy in research findings may be the result of differences in the types of training that have been studied. Perhaps the most popular training is **rater error training** or **RET**. The objective of RET is to familiarize raters with rater errors and to teach them to avoid these rating patterns. Although most studies have found that this sort of training reduces rating errors, it is often at the cost of rating accuracy (e.g., Bernardin & Pence, 1980; Hedge & Kavanagh, 1988). In other words, the raters might reduce the number of halo and leniency patterns in their ratings by forcing ratings to vary, whether or not they accurately reflect how well the person has done, but those ratings are less accurate in reflecting the true level of performance.

How could it be possible that the reduction of errors also results in a reduction in accuracy? One possible explanation lies in the nature of the rating errors. As noted earlier in this discussion, rater errors are inferred from the pattern of ratings. It is possible that the performance of individuals is similar across different performance dimensions (true halo) or that all individuals in a supervisor's department perform their jobs equally well.

Training raters to avoid the same ratings across either dimensions or people will result in their concentrating on avoiding certain patterns rather than on accurately assessing job performance. Bernardin and Pence (1980) suggested that RET might be substituting one series of rating errors for another.

Nathan and Tippins (1990) offered a different explanation of why halo errors are associated with greater accuracy in job performance ratings. They speculated that raters who exhibited less halo in their ratings might have given too much weight to inconsequential negative events. For example, a supervisor might have given an otherwise reliable employee a low rating in attendance because he or she was sick for one week in the prior year. Raters who exhibited a halo pattern in their ratings paid less attention to such rare instances and tended to consider the person's usual performance. This may have resulted in ratings that were more accurate because they were influenced more by general performance than by rare instances of good or poor performance in one or more dimensions.

Results have been more promising with types of training other than RET. Those training procedures teach raters how to observe performance-relevant behavior and how to make judgments based on those observations. Hedge and Kavanagh (1988), for example, found that this observation training increased rating accuracy but did not reduce rating errors (see the International Research box). Perhaps the most promising is **frame of reference training** (Day & Sulsky, 1995), which attempts to provide a common understanding of the rating task. Raters are given specific examples of behavior that would represent various levels of performance for each dimension to be rated. Results with this kind of training have thus far proven to be promising in increasing rating accuracy and providing the rater with a more accurate understanding of the criteria for good performance (Gorman & Rentsch, 2009). One limitation to this line of research is that it has mostly been conducted in laboratory settings with college students, so it is not clear how well the results would generalize to managers rating their employees in the field.

INTERNATIONAL RESEARCH

Several studies have found that training raters to avoid rating errors can reduce their accuracy in evaluating job performance. Hedge and Kavanagh (1988) wanted to see if other types of training would be more effective in increasing the accuracy of performance ratings.

Fifty-two supervisors were randomly assigned to one of four treatment groups. The first group received rater error training designed to familiarize the rater with rating errors and ways to avoid them. The second group received training in ways to observe behavior relevant to a job performance. The third group received training in ways to make proper judgments about performance based on observed behavior. The last group was a control group that received no training.

Both before and after training, all groups watched a videotape of a person performing a job. They then rated the person's performance on several performance dimensions. The videotaped performance was assessed by a panel of experts who provided a standard for comparison of the appraisals by members of each group in the study. Accuracy of performance rating was assessed as the discrepancy between the raters' appraisal of the videotape and the expert panel's judgment of the videotape.

The results showed that those who received rater error training had decreased rating errors and accuracy. This finding was consistent with prior research on this sort of training. The other two types of training were successful in increasing accuracy but at the cost of increased rating errors. The authors concluded that these two types of training showed promise for increasing rating accuracy. They also concluded that the rating patterns often thought to reflect rating errors may not represent mistakes. Rather, these patterns may accurately indicate the level of performance of individuals on the job. For example, individuals might perform at the same level for different dimensions. The implications of this study are that different types of rater training might help organizations get more accurate performance appraisals.

Source: From "Improving the Accuracy of Performance Evaluations: Comparisons of Three Methods of Performance Appraiser Training," by J. W. Hedge and M. Kavanagh, (1988) *Journal of Applied Psychology, 73,* 68–73.

Other Factors That Influence Job Performance Ratings

So far we have discussed how the ratings of supervisors can be affected by their cognitive processes and by the design of the rating form (and training in how to use it). Other factors can also affect the ratings given by supervisors, including supervisor feelings about the subordinate, supervisor mood, supervisor perceptions about subordinate motives for performance, cultural factors, and the race of both the rater and the ratee.

The idea that supervisors give better ratings to subordinates they like is supported by research (e.g., Ferris, Judge, Rowland, & Fitzgibbons, 1994). This has concerned some people that ratings might be biased and reflect favoritism. However, there is some evidence that liking can be the result of good job performance, as supervisors like those who work well for them (Robbins & DeNisi, 1994). It is particularly important for a new employee to be seen as a good performer because that perception will likely lead to being liked by supervisors, which can result in receiving extra support that leads to even better performance in the future (Lefkowitz, 2000).

The continuation of good performance ratings can be influenced by supervisor expectations about performance independent of liking. Murphy, Gannett, Herr, and Chen (1986) found that judgments of performance were influenced by the rater's expectations about the ratee's performance. People are likely to forget instances of behavior that do not fit their view of the person they are evaluating. Thus a person who is liked and performs well will continue to be seen as a good performer, even if performance has recently slipped. This can produce biased ratings when performance changes over time.

The mood of the rater at the time of appraisal can affect ratings. In a laboratory study, Sinclair (1988) assigned participants to a condition in which their mood was experimentally manipulated to be more depressed or elated. They were then asked to read a description of a professor's behavior and rate that professor's performance. Results showed that participants in a depressed mood rated the professor's performance lower than subjects in the elated mood condition. The depressed participants were also more accurate and exhibited less halo. Sinclair explained the results as reflecting the better information-processing ability of people when they are in depressed moods.

Managers' views of subordinate motivation can be a factor in their ratings of job performance, but interestingly such views can be subject to cultural factors. DeVoe and Iyengar (2004) assessed manager perceptions of their employees as being intrinsically motivated (wanting to do a good job for its own sake) and extrinsically motivated (working hard for rewards) and then linked those perceptions to ratings of job performance. American and Latin managers considered intrinsic motivation to be more important for performance than extrinsic motivation, whereas Asian managers considered both types of motivation to be equally important.

It has been well established that Black employees on average receive lower performance appraisal ratings than White employees (McKay & McDaniel, 2006). Interestingly the race of the rater seems to have no effect on ratings for Whites, but it does on ratings for Blacks. As shown by Stauffer and Buckley (2005), Black and White raters give similar ratings to Whites and rated Blacks lower on average than Whites. However, that difference between the ratings is much larger for White than for Black raters. If it is presumed that Black raters would have less bias than White raters against Black employees, these findings suggest the possibility that White raters are biased against Black employees. Of course, alterative explanations are that Black raters are biased in favor of Blacks and overrate them and that both Black and White raters are biased in favor of Whites and overrate them relative to Blacks. At this time, we don't know the extent to which bias is operating in these ratings either for or against Black and White employees.

360-Degree Feedback

In most organizations, the direct supervisor of each employee is responsible for assessing job performance. However, it can be helpful to get multiple perspectives on job performance (Furnham & Stringfield, 1994), and the use of multiple perspectives is becoming standard practice in the evaluation of managers and others (Rowson, 1998). Ratings by peers, self, and subordinates (for supervisors) can be a useful complement to supervisor ratings and can be helpful in providing feedback for employee development (Maurer, Mitchell, & Barbeite, 2002). In particular, discrepancies between the ratings by self (the employee's own ratings of performance) and others can show those areas in which other people see the employee differently from how the employee views himself or herself.

The use of multiple perspectives for manager feedback has been called **360-degree feedback** (Baldwin & Padgett, 1993). A manager is evaluated by peers, subordinates, and supervisors on several dimensions of performance. In addition, the manager completes a rating of his or her own performance. Research has shown that people in these different positions show only modest agreement in their ratings (Brett & Atwater, 2001; Carless, Mann, & Wearing, 1998; Fletcher & Baldry, 2000), suggesting that they provide different perspectives on a person's performance. Another advantage of using multiple raters is that the effects of the biases of individuals can be reduced. For example, it has been shown that people give higher ratings in 360-degree evaluations to those they like (Antonioni & Park, 2001). For example, the effects of favoritism on the part of the immediate supervisor are diminished when additional information from other raters is added to the appraisal. This can lead to increased trust of and better attitudes about the appraisal system on the part of those being evaluated (Mayer & Davis, 1999).

The purpose of 360-degree systems is to enhance performance, especially for those individuals who are the most in need of performance improvement. These systems have been shown to have positive effects for some individuals but not all. Contrary to these systems' intended purpose, it is the best and not the worst performers who seem to benefit most from 360-degree feedback (Bailey & Austin, 2006). Furthermore, Atwater and Brett (2005) found that those individuals who received low ratings from others and rated themselves low as well had the worst reactions to feedback, suggesting that if one knows his or her performance is poor, having those beliefs corroborated by others was not helpful.

THE IMPACT OF TECHNOLOGY ON PERFORMANCE APPRAISAL

Advances in technology, particularly the web, have greatly expanded what is practical in performance appraisal. For large companies, the amount of data that is involved in monitoring performance can be staggering. For example, one of the difficulties with 360-degree feedback is the logistics of organizing this large rating task. Each target manager must nominate several subordinates and several peers to provide ratings, do a self-rating, and get his or her supervisor's rating. In some organizations, this might represent 8 or more ratings completed per manager, and if there are 10,000 managers, there are 80,000 ratings to track and process. This is an expensive and difficult task for a company to do manually.

There are two places in which we see technology having an impact on performance appraisal—monitoring of objective productivity and implementation of performance management systems. Many employees today work on computer systems, such as reservation specialists for airlines and telephone operators. The systems that allow them to complete their job tasks are also capable of tracking productivity, and such data are routinely collected in many organizations. The use of computers allows for the easy analysis of performance across millions of employee-customer transactions, and it can be a built-in feature of the task software employees use to do their jobs each day.

Computerized, web-based employee performance management systems help managers clarify goals and expectations, provide coaching and feedback, and evaluate performance (see the I/O Psychology in Practice case study in this chapter). Such systems automate the entire process, making 360-degree feedback systems economically feasible for large companies. Each target manager can log onto the system and nominate the peers, subordinates, and others who will provide ratings. The system notifies individuals to do those ratings and then pulls together all of the rating information into a report. Consulting firms can be found that specialize in providing the computer services to conduct a 360-degree feedback project.

LEGAL ISSUES IN PERFORMANCE APPRAISAL

Many countries have laws that prohibit discrimination against minorities and women (as well as other groups) in the workplace. These laws cover organizational actions that affect the employment status of people, such as promotions and terminations. Such employee actions are often based at least in part on the person's performance; therefore, the performance appraisal system of an organization can become the target for legal action. In many countries, it is illegal to discriminate in performance appraisal on the basis of certain non-performance-related factors, such as age, gender, mental or physical disability, or race.

In the United States, there have been an increasing number of court challenges to performance-based employee actions, such as promotions and terminations (Latham et al., 1993). Organizations that have lost such cases have been unable to demonstrate to the court's satisfaction that their performance appraisal systems did not discriminate

TABLE 4.9 Six Points of a Legally Defensible Performance Appraisal System

1. Perform job analysis to define dimensions of performance
2. Develop rating form to assess dimensions from step 1
3. Train raters in how to assess performance
4. Have higher management review ratings, and allow employees to appeal their evaluations
5. Document performance, and maintain detailed records
6. Provide assistance and counseling to poor-performing employees prior to actions against them

Source: Adapted from "Performance Appraisal and Terminations: A Review of Court Decisions Since Brito v. Zia With Implications for Personnel Practices," by G. V. Barrett and M. G. Kernan, 1987, *Personnel Psychology*, 40, 489–503.

against certain groups. Subjective methods are especially likely to evoke legal challenges because they allow room for supervisors to express prejudices against certain groups of people. It can be difficult for a supervisor to prove in court that his or her ratings were fair and unbiased when, for example, Blacks get lower performance ratings than Whites (McKay & McDaniel, 2006), as noted earlier.

Barrett and Kernan (1987) suggested six components that should be part of a legally defensible performance appraisal system. As shown in Table 4.9, the system should begin with a job analysis to derive the dimensions of performance for the particular job. The job analysis will ensure that the dimensions chosen are job relevant. Raters should receive training in how the rating form is to be used to assess performance. To help minimize personal bias, upper management should review performance appraisals. Performance and the reasons for the employee action should be documented and recorded. It is easier to take action against an employee when the performance, good or poor, has been documented for a long period of time. This eliminates the appearance that the latest appraisal was given to justify a particular action affecting an employee. Finally, it is a good idea to provide assistance and counseling to employees whose performance is unsatisfactory. This shows that the organization has done everything possible for an unsatisfactory employee before taking action against him or her.

Werner and Bolino (1997) analyzed the outcomes of 295 U.S. court cases in which performance appraisals were challenged as being discriminatory. Performance appraisal systems that were based on a job analysis, gave written instructions to raters, offered employees the opportunity to have input, and used multiple raters were far less likely to result in an organization losing the case. For example, while overall organizations lost 41% of cases, those that used multiple raters lost only 11% of cases. The use of these four practices combined should result in a relatively safe performance appraisal system from a legal perspective.

Allowing employees to have input into performance appraisals also has benefits beyond legal issues. Research has shown that giving employees the opportunity to sit down with supervisors and discuss appraisals openly can lead to better attitudes (Korsgaard & Roberson, 1995). In one study, this occurred even though employees who were allowed input actually had lower ratings than those who were not (Taylor, Tracy, Renard, Harrison, & et al., 1995). Perceptions of fairness in this study even reduced employee intentions of quitting the job. To be effective and perceived as fair, performance appraisal systems should include Barrett and Kernan's (1987) six steps, as well as input by employees.

▶ CHAPTER SUMMARY

Job performance data have many organizational uses, including administrative decision making, employee development, employee feedback, and research. The first step in evaluating job performance is to develop performance criteria that define good and poor performance. Once criteria are set, specific methods to measure them can be chosen.

Job performance measures can be classified as either objective or subjective. Objective measures are counts of the output of a job, such as the number of sales for a salesperson or the number of units produced for a factory worker. Subjective measures are ratings by supervisors (or other individuals who are familiar with the person's job performance). Subjective measures are the more commonly used of the two methods, but they suffer from biases and errors attributable to human judgment. Two different approaches have been taken to reduce rating errors in subjective measures: design of the rating form and rater training.

Several different types of rating forms have been devised to increase the accuracy of performance ratings. The Behaviorally Anchored Rating Scale (BARS) asks raters to indicate which of several behaviors comes closest to representing the job performance of the individual. The Mixed Standard Scale (MSS) asks raters to indicate if the individual's performance is worse than, as good as, or better than each of several items of performance behavior. The Behavior Observation Scale (BOS) asks raters to indicate how often ratees perform each of the listed behaviors. Research comparing the behavior-focused rating forms with other types of measures has failed to find consistent evidence for greater accuracy.

Rater training is another approach that has been attempted to reduce errors. Research has suggested that rater error training can reduce rating accuracy, even if it is successful in reducing rating errors. Observation training that focuses on observing performance-related behavior and making judgments of performance has shown promise in increasing accuracy. At the present time, however, it would be premature to conclude that either approach will prove useful in helping supervisors provide accurate performance ratings.

Several factors have been shown to relate to job performance ratings, although it is not entirely clear whether they result in rater bias or not. Whether the rater likes the subordinate, rater mood, perceived motives of the employee for performance, cultural factors, and both rater and ratee race all affect ratings.

Feedback from multiple sources can be helpful for employees wishing to improve their performance. Managers receive 360-degree feedback from a comparison of their self-ratings with those of peers, subordinates, and supervisors.

In the United States and many other countries, performance appraisal is a legal process as well as a technical one. Organizations are required by U.S. law to avoid discrimination in their performance appraisal procedures. Failure to comply with such legal requirements can make an organization subject to lawsuits. A number of specific practices, such as basing the system on a job analysis and providing rater training, reduce the chances that an organization will lose in court if challenged.

I/O PSYCHOLOGY IN PRACTICE

(*Courtesy of Amanda Gartshore*)

This case deals with the development of a comprehensive performance appraisal and management system that Amanda Gartshore worked on for a large company from the banking sector. Gartshore, a Chartered Occupational Psychologist, received her MSc in Occupational Psychology in 1998 from the University of Surrey. She is currently the Director of Chromis Consulting Ltd, an occupational psychology company, which specializes in senior and graduate selection along with development, including the design of development centres and coaching at all management levels. At the time of this case, she was part of the HR function at a UK subsidiary of a major US bank, where there were approximately 1,000 employees. As part of her role, Gartshore was involved primarily in performance management.

One of Gartshore's initial projects was to assist with the implementation of an internal performance appraisal system. The system was in its infancy and performance criteria needed to be generated for each individual job role. Managers were given this responsibility, whereby they were expected to develop performance criteria for the staff they managed based on job descriptions. Gartshore provided training to help managers define observable and measurable performance criteria. The main focus was on ensuring fairness of the criteria and consistency across departments, thus ensuring levels of reliability and validity. The performance appraisal outcomes were rated on a scale of 1 to 4, which were linked to performance-related pay, so it was of crucial importance that a fair and accurate system be developed.

This performance appraisal system tied together annual performance reviews with goal setting and employee development. The system ran on an annual cycle beginning in January when each manager would meet with each of their subordinates to discuss his or her performance and to agree performance standards and goals for the upcoming year. These specified not only what was to be accomplished but also how it was to be done, thus providing a balanced emphasis on both work quality and quantity. Following this initial review at the start of the year, managers and their subordinates would meet for quarterly reviews to monitor progress and discuss development needs. At the end of each calendar year they would have a final review meeting where the performance standards and goals would be reviewed, taking into account performance throughout the year. Each manager would then provide a rating on the scale of 1 to 4 for each subordinate—1 being 'well exceeded expectations', 2 being 'exceeded expectations', 3 being 'achieved expectations'. A rating of 4 either meant that the employee did not meet expectations or that they were in a new role and still in training. Based on these ratings set pay increases would be approved for the following year. A '1' rating also guaranteed a percentage bonus.

Gartshore reviewed the quality of the ratings and statistically analysed the data in order to ensure the process was reliable and valid. It was expected that the reviews of all 1,000 employees would fit the normal distribution curve which they did overall, but the distribution was more skewed in smaller departments. Gartshore would therefore focus on teams and where clusters of similar ratings appeared she would meet with the managers to challenge the decisions made and see whether the clustering was justifiable. As you can see, this performance appraisal system goes far beyond just completing the usual "report card" on every employee each year.

Discussion Questions

1. Do you think you'd like working in a company with this sort of performance system? Why or why not?
2. Why would a company from the banking sector invest so much effort into performance evaluation?
3. Why are managers required to provide quarterly reviews? Isn't a once-a-year system enough?
4. Do you think goal setting will increase employee motivation and performance (see Chapter 8's section on goal setting)?
5. What are the inherent issues in a 'pay for performance' system?

LEARNING BY DOING

Determining Criteria for a Job

Criteria for a job can be determined by interviewing employees who hold it. Choose a person you know (acquaintance, family member, or friend) who is currently employed in a job you have never held yourself. Interview him or her about the criteria for performance, taking careful notes. You should ask about the following.

1. What are the major functions of this job?
2. For each function, what is it the employee is supposed to accomplish?
3. For each function, what constitutes acceptable performance and outstanding performance?
4. What would best reflect good performance on this job?

Critical Incidents of Performance

Critical incidents can be quite useful in developing job performance measures. Collect 10 critical incidents, half reflecting effective and half reflecting ineffective performance. Ask people you know to provide examples that they have observed. The same person could give you both an effective and an ineffective incident. It is best to get incidents from several people. Use the incidents to define one or more dimensions of job performance that might be included on a performance rating scale.

CHAPTER 5

Assessment Methods for Selection and Placement

CHAPTER 5 OUTLINE

- JOB-RELATED CHARACTERISTICS
- PSYCHOLOGICAL TESTS
  - Characteristics of Tests
  - Ability Tests
  - Knowledge and Skill Tests
  - Personality Tests
  - Emotional Intelligence Tests
  - Integrity Tests
  - Vocational Interest Tests
  - Drug Testing
- BIOGRAPHICAL INFORMATION
- INTERVIEWS
- WORK SAMPLES
- ASSESSMENT CENTERS
- ELECTRONIC ASSESSMENT
  - Electronic Administration of Psychological Tests
  - Computer Adaptive Testing
- CHAPTER SUMMARY
- I/O PSYCHOLOGY IN PRACTICE
- LEARNING BY DOING

Suppose you find yourself responsible for deciding whom to hire for a particular job. It might be hiring a computer programmer, or a plumber, or a secretary, or a teacher. There are several job applicants, and your task is to decide which one to hire. How would you go about making your choice? Would you interview each one and pick the person who seemed to be best suited for the job? How would you know what characteristics or qualities to look for in a potential employee? Furthermore, how would you go about finding out if applicants have the necessary characteristics? Procedures for the assessment of characteristics for selection (hiring) and placement (assigning current employees to jobs) are the topic of this chapter.

One of the earliest applications of psychology to the human problems of organizations had to do with the assessment of people for selection and placement. During World War I, the U.S. Army became one of the first organizations to use large-scale testing of people to determine their job assignments (placement). After the war, large organizations saw the potential value of assessing job applicants for selection and other employment decisions, and the use of testing and other techniques became commonplace. This is true not only in the United States but also in most of the industrialized world, including Canada, Western Europe, and Israel (McCulloch, 1993).

This chapter discusses five techniques for the assessment of characteristics that are frequently used for selection and placement. A *psychological test* consists of a standard set of items or tasks that a person completes under controlled conditions. Most involve paper-and-pencil tasks, such as answering questions or solving problems, although some involve manipulation of physical objects to assess such characteristics as manual dexterity and eye-hand coordination. Psychological tests can be used to assess ability, interests, knowledge, personality, and skill. *Biographical information forms* ask about relevant prior experiences, such as level of education and work experience. Some forms can be quite detailed, asking not only about objective facts but about opinions and subjective reactions as well. The *interview* is a meeting between the job applicant and someone at the employing organization who will have input into the hiring decision. This can be done face to face or via technology such as a telephone or webcam. A *work sample* is a test that asks a person to perform a simulated job. The person is given the necessary materials and tools and must perform a particular task, such as assembling a motor, under controlled conditions. An *assessment center* is a series of exercises, including simulated job tasks, that measure how well a person can perform a job. It is commonly used to assess potential for a management or other white-collar job.

Each of the five assessment techniques can be used to determine a person's suitability for a particular job. Often more than one technique is used at the same time to get a more complete picture of how well an individual's characteristics match those necessary for a job. These assessment techniques can have uses other than selection and placement, however. They can be useful for employee development by showing a person's strengths and weaknesses, which can then be addressed by training. Many of these techniques are used to assess human characteristics in research studies concerned with almost all the topics discussed throughout this book. In the next chapter, we will see how the five techniques are used to help choose people for jobs.

Objectives: The student who studies this chapter should be able to:

- Define KSAOs.
- Describe the five assessment methods in the chapter.
- Discuss the advantages and limitations of each assessment method in the chapter.
- Explain how computers and technology are used to facilitate assessment.

TABLE 5.1 KSAOs for a Computer Sales Associate

Knowledge	Knowledge of computer systems Knowledge of computer software	Abilities	Ability to understand complex technology Ability to communicate with other people
Skills	Skill in using a cash register Skill in completing monetary transactions	Other	Neat appearance Outgoing, friendly personality

JOB-RELATED CHARACTERISTICS

Many different characteristics of people, or KSAOs (knowledge, skill, ability, and other personal characteristics), are needed for a job. (See Chapter 3 for a more extensive discussion of KSAOs in the context of job analysis.) *Knowledge* refers to what the person knows about a job, such as legal knowledge for an attorney. A *skill* is something that a person is able to do, such as program a computer or type. *Ability* is the capability to learn something, such as the ability to learn to play a musical instrument or to speak a foreign language. *Other personal characteristics* are every other human attribute not covered by the first three. Included are interests, personality, physical characteristics (such as height or eye color), and prior experience relevant for the job.

Table 5.1 contains examples of KSAOs for a sales associate in a computer store. Such a person should have knowledge of the product that he or she will sell, as well as the ability to understand complex computer systems. It is important that the person can work a cash register and handle monetary transactions. Finally, the person must have a neat appearance and a friendly, outgoing personality. When we hire a computer sales associate, these are some of the KSAOs for which we will select people.

The KSAOs for each job can be determined by a detailed and thorough study, which is called a *job analysis*. (See Chapter 3 for a discussion of job analysis.) This involves a number of techniques that result in a list of the necessary KSAOs for the job in question. Once KSAOs are determined, procedures can be chosen or developed to assess them in job applicants or current employees. The idea is to select or place people who have the necessary KSAOs for the jobs available. Although this process does not guarantee that all the people chosen will be successful on the job, it increases the chances of making good choices over using other selection and placement approaches.

All five of the assessment techniques that we discuss attempt to measure KSAOs that are relevant for job performance and other organizationally relevant variables. As with all assessment techniques, the properties of reliability and validity are critical (see Chapter 2 for a discussion of these properties). That is, all measures must be consistent (reliable) and must pass stringent tests for validity. In other words, evidence must exist that they can accomplish the tasks for which they are used in organizations. If a test is to be used to select police officers, for example, it must be shown to predict how well a police officer will do on the job.

PSYCHOLOGICAL TESTS

A **psychological test** is a standardized series of problems or questions that assess a particular individual characteristic. Psychological tests are commonly used to assess many KSAOs, including knowledge, skills, abilities, attitudes, interests, and personality. They are comprised of multiple items, which are indicators of the characteristic of interest.

Each item can be completed relatively quickly, making it feasible to include many items to assess each characteristic and to assess several characteristics at one time.

Multiple items provide increased reliability and validity over a single indicator of the characteristic. Single-item measures tend to have low reliability because a person can easily make a mistake on any one item. For example, an item can be misinterpreted or misread. Consider the following item that might be encountered on a test:

> I'm not usually the first one to volunteer for a new work assignment.

If a person misreads the item and does not notice that the second word is *not*, the meaning of the item will be reversed. His or her response to the item will be the opposite of what it should be, and the item will not be an accurate indicator of the characteristic of interest. If it is likely that only a few people will make this error, the item may retain some reliability and validity. The reliability and validity are better for a multiple-item test than that for a single-item test because the impact of occasional errors on each person's score is reduced. The contribution of each item to the total score when there are many items is quite small.

Characteristics of Tests

Many different types of tests are available that can assess hundreds of individual characteristics. The nature of the characteristic of interest helps determine which test is used. For example, a test to assess mathematical ability will most certainly be composed of math problems. A test of physical strength, on the other hand, will likely involve the lifting of heavy objects. A discussion of the four distinguishing characteristics of tests follows.

Group Versus Individually Administered Tests

A **group test** can be administered to several people at once. The test itself can be in a printed form (e.g., a booklet), or it can be displayed on a computer screen. In the former case, a group of people can be administered the test in a room at the same time, as is typically done with a course exam. In the latter case, several individuals can take the test simultaneously, either in the same location (e.g., a computer lab) or in different locations. In employment settings, there is often concern about testing conditions and test security, so a test administrator will control access to the test (e.g., hand out tests or log people onto a computer), time the test, and make sure that the individual taking the test is the candidate. An individual test is one that a test administrator gives to a single test taker at a time rather than to a group of individuals. This is necessary because either the administrator has to score the items as the test proceeds or an apparatus is involved that only one person can use at a time. The test administrator sets the pace of the individual items. This approach is often used in administering cognitive ability tests to children. Because of its greater efficiency, the group test is preferred when it is feasible.

Closed-Ended Versus Open-Ended Tests

With a **closed-ended test**, the test taker must choose one from several possible responses, as in a multiple-choice test. An **open-ended test** is like an essay exam. The test taker must generate a response rather than choosing a correct response. Whereas the closed-ended test is preferred because of its greater ease in scoring, the open-ended test is more appropriate for some characteristics. For example, writing ability is best assessed by asking a person to write an essay. Experts can read and score the essay for a number of characteristics, such as clarity of expression and grammatical accuracy. These characteristics would be more difficult, if not impossible, to assess with a closed-ended test.

Paper-and-Pencil Versus Performance Tests

With a **paper-and-pencil test**, the test is on a piece of paper or other printed (or electronic) medium, and the responses are made in written form, often with a pencil. A multiple-choice course examination is a paper-and-pencil test that presents the exam questions on paper, and the responses are made in pencil on the exam itself or on a separate answer sheet. Although we continue to use the name, quite often employment tests today are administered electronically, with responses made via keyboard or mouse. Open-ended tests can also be paper-and-pencil tests if they ask people to record their responses in some form, either by writing on paper or by typing on a computer. A **performance test** involves the manipulation of apparatuses, equipment, materials, or tools. Perhaps the most widely used performance test is a typing test. With this sort of performance test, the test taker demonstrates his or her typing ability on an actual keyboard under standardized conditions. This tests the typing ability itself rather than typing knowledge, which could be assessed with a paper-and-pencil test of knowledge about typing.

Power Versus Speed Tests

A **power test** gives the test taker almost unlimited time to complete the test. A **speed test** has a strict time limit. It is designed so that almost no one can finish all items in the allotted time. There are two ways in which the speed test is used. First, a speed test can contain challenging items that must be completed under time pressure. Some instructors use speed tests for classroom examinations under the presumption that the better-prepared students will be able to answer the questions more quickly than those that are less well prepared. The drawback to this use of speed tests is that the test taker is at a disadvantage if he or she is a slow reader or writer. The second use is with a test that is designed to assess a person's speed in doing a particular task. A typing test is timed because its purpose is to assess a person's typing speed, as well as accuracy.

Ability Tests

An ability or aptitude is a person's capacity to do or learn to do a particular task. Cognitive abilities, such as intelligence, are relevant to tasks that involve information processing and learning. Psychomotor abilities, such as manual dexterity, involve body movements and manipulation of objects. The importance of each ability is dependent on the nature of the tasks of interest. Some job tasks require mostly cognitive abilities (e.g., programming a computer), whereas others rely mainly on psychomotor abilities (e.g., sweeping a floor). Many tasks require both types of abilities (e.g., repairing a computer or complex piece of eouipment).

Cognitive Ability Tests

An intelligence or IQ test of general cognitive ability is the best-known **cognitive ability test**. There are also tests of individual cognitive abilities, such as mathematical or verbal ability. The items on such tests represent individual problems to solve. Such tests can be administered to large groups of individuals simultaneously and provide an inexpensive and efficient means of assessing job applicants.

Numerical

For answers which should have a decimal point, the decimal point is printed on the answer line for you to use.

EXAMPLE

There are 8 gallons of water in a tank which can hold 16.5 gallons. How many gallons can be added to this tank .... 8.5 .... gallons	16.5 − 8 8.5

Verbal

EXAMPLE A

Which does not belong?

(A) red, (B) green, (C) purple, (D) sweet A B C D

Red, green, and *purple* are colors but *sweet* (choice D) is not a color and does not belong with the words. Therefore, the D had been marked as shown on the right of the question.

Figure 5.1 Two sample items from the Personnel Tests for Industry (PTI). Reproduced by permission. *(Copyright 1969 by the Psychological Corporation, All rights reserved.)*

Figure 5.1 contains two sample items from the Personnel Tests for Industry (PTI), a test designed to assess mathematical and verbal ability. The items are problems involving mathematical and verbal reasoning. The test was designed for group administration and can be completed in about 25 minutes. The PTI was produced by the Psychological Corporation (now Harcourt Assessment), which is one of the oldest and best-known publishers of employment tests.

All test takers are not proficient in the local language; therefore, some tests have been developed that do not rely on reading ability. Figure 5.2 contains two items from the Beta II, which is a nonverbal intelligence test. The items involve problem solving without words. The first item asks the test taker to find his or her way through the maze. The second item asks the test taker to solve a coding problem using numbers and shapes. The test administrator reads instructions to test takers for each type of item. Instructions can be given in any language.

Research has consistently shown that cognitive ability tests are valid predictors of job performance across a large number of different kinds of jobs (Ones, Dilchert, Viswesvaran, & Salgado, 2010). People who score well on cognitive ability tests tend to perform better on the job. Cognitive ability tests have a long history of use by large organizations for employee selection because of their efficiency and validity. In a survey of 703 SIOP members, Murphy, Cronin, and Tam (2003) found consensus among I/O psychologists that such tests are fair and useful for selection.

Psychomotor Ability Tests

Psychomotor ability tests assess such things as ability to manipulate objects and use tools. They involve both the coordination between senses and movement (e.g., eye-hand

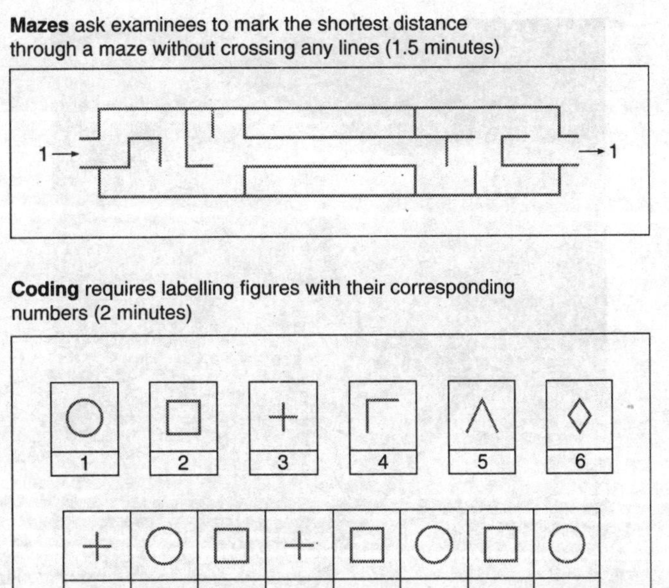

Mazes ask examinees to mark the shortest distance through a maze without crossing any lines (1.5 minutes)
1
1
Coding requires labelling figures with their corresponding numbers (2 minutes)
1
2
3
4
5
6

Figure 5.2 Two sample items from the Beta II Examination (2nd edition), a nonverbal intelligence test. Reproduced by permission. (*Copyright 1978 by the Psychological Corporation. All rights reserved.*)

coordination) and the accuracy of movements. Many psychomotor tests are performance tests rather than paper-and-pencil tests because the abilities of interest involve manipulation of objects rather than cognitive elements. People are scored on their ability to perform motor tasks, such as putting pegs in holes or using simple tools to manipulate objects.

Figures 5.3 and 5.4 show two psychomotor tests. Figure 5.3 depicts a therapeutic tool which assesses the ability to use simple tools to manipulate small objects. This test involves removing and reassembling several fasteners using wrenches and a screwdriver. The score is based on the time it takes to complete the task. Figure 5.4 shows the Purdue Pegboard Dexterity Test, which assesses hands, fingers, and arm movement accuracy and speed. The test involves sequential insertion of pegs and assembly of pegs, collars, and washers, and scores are based on the speed and accuracy with which the person can accomplish the task.

Knowledge and Skill Tests

An ability test is intended to assess a person's capability or potential to learn. A **knowledge and skill test**, often called an **achievement test**, is designed to assess a person's present level of proficiency. A knowledge test assesses what the person knows, and a skill test assesses what a person is able to do.

In practice, it is difficult to totally separate ability from knowledge and skill, for ability tests rely to some extent on knowledge and skill, and knowledge and skill tests rely to some extent on ability. The major difference between the two types of tests is the

Figure 5.3 Using therapeutic tool for improving fine motor and sensory function. Reproduced by permission. (*PhotoAlto/Michele Constantini/Getty Images Inc.*)

Figure 5.4 Doctor testing patient with Purdue Pegboard Dexterity Test. (© *Radius Images/Alamy*)

emphasis placed on prior knowledge and skill in performing specific tasks. For example, a psychomotor ability test might assess how quickly a person could put pegs in holes as an indicator of eye-hand coordination, whereas a psychomotor skill test might assess how well a person can type. Typing skill is the product of several different abilities.

Many different knowledge and skill areas can be assessed with a test. Some tests focus on general skills, such as math and reading. Others are useful for assessing skills at particular job tasks, such as typing. With a typing test, the test taker is given the task of typing some materials under standardized conditions. The person is scored on the number of words per minute typed and the number of typing errors. As with ability tests, some knowledge and skill tests are paper-and-pencil tests and some are performance tests.

Figure 5.5 contains three items from the Bennett Mechanical Comprehension Test. This test assesses a combination of mechanical ability and knowledge about tools. This sort of test is useful for determining if a person has a good understanding of how mechanical things work and how tools can be used. Note that this is a knowledge test and assesses a person's knowledge about tools rather than his or her skill in using tools. Actual tool use is a skill that involves both cognitive and psychomotor elements.

Personality Tests

A **personality trait** is the predisposition or tendency to behave in a particular way across different situations. A person who prefers to do things with other people is said to be high on the trait of sociability. A person who frequently influences others is said to be high on the trait of dominance. Personality traits can be important because certain classes of behavior can be relevant for job performance and other behaviors in organizations. Sociability can be an important trait for a salesperson who must interact with other people, whereas dominance can be an important trait for a supervisor who must direct the activities of others.

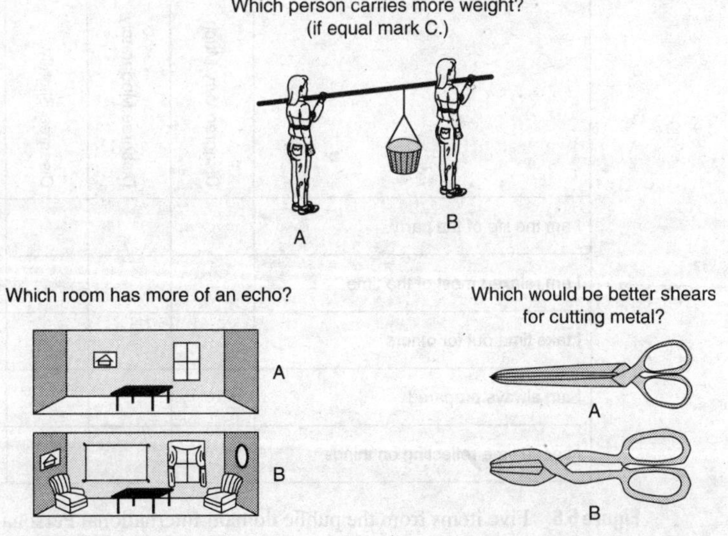

Figure 5.5 Three sample items from the Bennett Mechanical Comprehension Test (BMCT). Reproduced by permission. (*Copyright 1980 by the Psychological Corporation, All rights reserved.*)

Paper-and-pencil **personality tests** can be useful tools for assessing personality traits. Some personality tests are designed to assess a single personality trait; personality inventories assess multiple dimensions and are sometimes used to provide profiles of individuals across several personality traits. They can also characterize people into types, which are combinations of different traits. For example, the extraverted type of person tends to be high on the traits of activity, optimism, sociability, and talkativeness, whereas the introverted type tends to be high on carefulness, quietness, passivity, and unsociability (Pervin, 1993).

Figure 5.6 contains five sample items from the public domain International Personality Item Pool (Goldberg, Johnson, Eber, Hogan, Ashton, Cloninger et al., 2006). This web-based resource (http://ipip.ori.org) provides more than 2,000 personality items that can be used to assess a wide variety of traits. The sample items in the figure are used to assess the Big Five personality theory dimensions of extraversion, emotional stability, agreeableness, conscientiousness, and openness to experience. The Big Five will be discussed in Chapter 10. As with ability tests, many standard tests can be purchased from commercial testing companies, such as Harcourt Assessment and Psychological Assessment Resources.

Researchers frequently use personality tests to study many different aspects of people's behavior in organizations, but there are two major concerns with the use of personality tests for employee selection. First, there is the possibility that job applicants will fake responses to the test by answering the items in the manner they believe will put them in the most favorable light (Birkeland, Manson, Kisamore, Brannick, & Smith, 2006). It is feared that faking will undermine the validity of the test (Heggestad, Morrison, Reeve, & McCloy, 2006). Research has revealed, however, that attempts at distortion will not necessarily invalidate a personality test used for employee selection (J. Hogan,

	Disagree Very Much	Disagree Moderately	Disagree Slightly	Agree Slightly	Agree Moderately	Agree Very Much
I am the life of the party						
I am relaxed most of the time						
I take time out for others						
I am always prepared						
I spend time reflecting on things						

Figure 5.6 Five items from the public domain International Personality Item Pool (IPIP) (Goldberg et al., 2006) that assess the Big Five personality dimensions. In order from top to bottom, the items are from the subscales of extraversion, emotional stability, agreeableness, conscientiousness, and openness to experience. The IPIP website is http://ipip.ori.org.

Barrett, & Hogan, 2007). This might be because an individual who knows how he or she should appear on a personality test will also know how he or she should behave at work to be effective. Thus the test might be assessing a person's self-presentation skills (Marcus, 2009). Second, personality tests do not always appear to be as job relevant as other assessment devices. *Job relevance* means that what an assessment tool measures is linked to the KSAO requirements of the job. A typing test, for example, is obviously relevant for a secretary who must type as part of the job requirements. It is harder to show that a personality trait such as dominance is important for job performance. This has led some to question whether or not it is appropriate to use these tests.

Despite concerns over the use of personality tests for employee selection, such tests have been growing in popularity among practitioners and researchers in organizations (Ones & Anderson, 2002). Several researchers have conducted meta-analyses to investigate the relation between personality and job performance. This technique of data analysis allows for the statistical combination of results across multiple studies of the same phenomenon (see Chapter 2). Such analyses have shown that personality can predict performance, although the magnitude of these correlations is modest (Dudley, Orvis, Lebiecki, & Cortina, 2006; Salgado, 2003). One difficulty with drawing conclusions about the validity of personality tests from the existing meta-analyses is that those analyses group together tests that assessed many different traits for the prediction of performance on many different types of jobs. Some of those traits may have represented job-relevant characteristics; others may have been unimportant for success. Existing evidence suggests that specific personality traits chosen to be relevant to job performance on particular jobs will do an even better job of predicting performance (Paunonen, Rothstein, & Jackson, 1999; Tett, Steele, & Beauregard, 2003).

Emotional Intelligence Tests

A characteristic that falls between a personality trait and a cognitive ability is **emotional intelligence (EI)**. It is defined as the ability people have to control and recognize emotions in themselves and in others. In theory, this ability makes people more socially skilled, enabling them to be aware of and to control their impact on others. In a work setting, this means being able to work smoothly with colleagues, and in supervisory positions, it means the ability to exert leadership. Salovey and Mayer (1989) are credited with kicking off interest among psychologists in the idea that emotional intelligence is an important ability. Unfortunately various researchers who study it have adopted somewhat different definitions and conceptions, and exaggerated claims both inside the field and in the popular media have caused confusion and controversy.

There are two types of EI assessments (Joseph & Newman, 2010). The trait type measures EI as a personality characteristic that is accessible to the person's awareness. These trait assessments look like a personality test in that people respond to each item concerning how well it describes them. The ability type has a multiple-choice format with one right answer per question. It is based on the assumption that people cannot directly report their EI because it is not accessible to awareness. Rather, a person reveals his or her EI by choosing the correct answers on the test, just as he or she would indicate cognitive ability with a general intelligence test.

Research with various EI tests has shown that they can predict job performance. For example, a meta-analysis by Joseph and Newman (2010) found that on average

EI trait tests correlate .32 and EI ability tests correlate .16 with job performance. EI has also been shown to relate to students' college grade point averages (GPAs) (Rode, Mooney, Arthaud-Day, Near, Baldwin, Rubin, et al., 2007) and for managers to the job satisfaction of their subordinates (Sy, Tram, & O'Hara, 2006), although correlations are often quite small. However, research does not support the claims that EI is one of the most important characteristics for job success. Joseph and Newman (2010) found that EI ability measures related to performance only in jobs that require employees to manage their own emotions—that is, to engage in emotional labor (see Chapter 9). An important issue with EI research, however, is that some have questioned the construct validity of the EI measures used in these studies, suggesting that EI ability measures overlap with measures of cognitive ability and personality (Christiansen, Janovics, & Siers, 2010), which are the real underlying factors relating to performance (Landy, 2005). At the current time, we know that EI measures relate to a number of important variables, but the construct validity of these measures is in dispute among researchers.

Integrity Tests

An **integrity test** is designed to predict whether or not an employee will engage in counterproductive or dishonest behavior on the job. The behaviors these tests are designed to predict include cheating, sabotage, theft, and unethical behavior. They also are sometimes used to predict absence and turnover. Wanek, Sackett, and Ones (2003) noted that there are two different types of integrity tests—overt and personality.

The *overt integrity test* assesses a person's attitudes and prior behavior. It asks the person to indicate agreement or disagreement with statements concerning honesty and moral behavior. An example of such an item would be the following:

It is alright to lie if you know you won't get caught.

The test taker is also asked how often he or she has done a number of counterproductive behaviors. A possible item might be the following:

How often have you stolen something from your employer?

The *personality integrity test* assesses personality characteristics that have been found to predict counterproductive behavior. Whereas the overt integrity tests are obvious assessments of honesty and integrity, the personality tests are hidden in their purpose. In fact, standard personality inventories often are used as integrity tests. We discussed personality tests earlier in this chapter.

Research on integrity tests has shown that they can predict counterproductive behavior at work, including absence, theft, and other behaviors potentially damaging to organizations (Ashton, 1998; Ones & Viswesvaran, 1998). This is true for both overt and personality integrity tests, which are also related to one another (Marcus, Lee, & Ashton, 2007). Interestingly, research has shown that integrity tests may do a better job of predicting absence, general counterproductive behavior, and job performance than they do theft itself (Wanek, 1999). Part of the problem with conducting validation studies is that accurate data on employee theft are difficult to obtain because many employees who steal are never caught. Thus it is difficult to determine how well the test can predict stealing when you don't know for certain which employees were dishonest. However, as Wanek pointed out, these tests have been shown to predict useful behaviors at work besides theft, so there can be benefits beyond control of theft from using integrity tests for selection. For example, Van Iddekinge, Taylor, and Eidson (2005) showed that a commercially available integrity test was able to predict job performance.

Vocational Interest Tests

A **vocational interest test** matches either the interests or the personality of the test taker to those of people in a variety of different occupations and occupational categories. Interests are assessed by asking the test taker to indicate his or her preferences for engaging in various activities, such as between attending a sporting event and visiting a museum. Personality is relevant, as specific traits might drive people's interests; for example, people who are outgoing and extraverted might prefer activities that involve contact with other people (Larson, Rottinghaus, & Borgen, 2002). Data from vocational interest tests are available about the answers of people in many different occupations. The test taker's answers are matched to those of people in different occupations to see how well he or she fits each occupation.

Interest and personality profiles vary considerably from occupation to occupation. Therefore, any individual test taker will match some occupations and not others. Because occupations tend to group together into categories, a person can be matched to an occupational category. One such occupational category is artistic, which involves creative processes, such as interior design and photography.

One of the most popular vocational interest tests is the Self-Directed Search (Holland, 1994). This test provides scores on six personality types (Figure 5.7). Each type is associated with a particular family of occupations. As shown in the figure, the Investigative type

The **Realistic** type likes jobs such as automobile mechanic, aircraft controller, surveyor, farmer, or electrician.

The **Investigative** type likes investigative jobs such as biologist, chemist, physicist, anthropologist, geologist, or medical technologist.

The **Artistic** type likes artistic jobs such as composer, musician, stage director, writer, interior decorator, or actor/actress.

The **Social** type likes social jobs such as teacher, religious worker, counselor, clinical psychologist, psychiatric case worker, or speech therapist.

The **Enterprising** type likes enterprising jobs such as salesperson, manager, business executive, television producer, sports promoter, or buyer.

The **Conventional** type likes conventional jobs such as bookkeeper, stenographer, financial analyst, banker, cost estimator, or tax expert.

Figure 5.7 The six personality types and associated occupations as assessed by the Self-Directed Search. Adapted and reproduced by special permission of the Publisher, Psychological Assessment Resources, Inc., 16204 North Florida Avenue, Lutz, FL 33549, from *You and Your Career* by John L. Holland, Ph. D. (*Copyright 1985 by PAR, Inc. Further reproduction is prohibited without permission from PAR, Inc.*)

likes investigative-type jobs that include scientific fields such as biology and geology. The profile of scores on the six types can guide a person in choosing a career.

The match between a person's vocational interests and the nature of his or her job is related to how satisfied the person is with that job (Rottinghaus, Hees, & Conrath, 2009). A person who takes a job that is a poor match will likely be unhappy with it, whereas a person who takes a job that is a good match will probably like it. The idea behind the tests is to encourage people to select careers that match their interests. Vocational interest tests are frequently used for vocational guidance in helping people decide what careers to pursue.

Drug Testing

Organizations in the United States and elsewhere have turned to drug testing with both applicants and employees as a means of controlling drug use at work, and estimates are that as many as 30 million Americans undergo such tests each year (Mastrangelo & Popovich, 2000). Such testing is of particular importance in jobs that are safety-sensitive, meaning that impaired performance could lead to accidents or injury, such as air traffic controllers and bus drivers. However, such tests have been controversial, with many people considering them an unfair invasion of privacy. Paronto, Truxillo, Bauer, and Leo (2002) surveyed 1,484 individuals about their attitudes toward drug testing. They found that respondents considered drug testing more acceptable for jobs that were safety-sensitive than for jobs that were not.

▶ BIOGRAPHICAL INFORMATION

One of the easiest ways to find out about people is to ask them what you wish to know. In an employment setting, basic information about people is obtained from an application form. Although they can differ from organization to organization, standard application forms contain questions about education, job skills, personal characteristics, and work history. Some forms can be quite detailed, asking about specific experiences, such as extracurricular school activities (e.g., participation in sports). Most ask about biographical information concerning education and relevant work experience that might be necessary for a particular job.

The **biographical inventory** asks much more detailed background questions than a typical application form. Whereas application forms ask about prior level of education and work experience, the biographical inventory asks about specific experiences at school and work, or even in other areas of life. Some of the questions ask about objective, verifiable facts, such as

"What was your grade point average in college?"

Others ask about opinions or subjective experiences, such as

"Did you enjoy college?"

If a biographical inventory contains enough of the second type of question, it begins to approximate a psychological test that assesses interests and personality instead of prior life experiences (Schmitt & Chan, 1998). Most inventories use a multiple-choice response

TABLE 5.2 Sample Items From a Biographical Inventory

When you were in grade school and people were being picked for teams, when were you usually picked?	Did you attend your high school prom?
During high school, what grades did you get in chemistry class?	In your first full-time job, how often did you initiate conversation with your immediate supervisor?

format that can be easily scored. Possible answers to the question about enjoying college might be

"Enjoyed very much"
"Enjoyed somewhat"
"Enjoyed a little"
"Didn't enjoy at all"

Table 5.2 contains some examples of inventory items.

Stokes and Searcy (1999) distinguished empirical from rational biographical inventories. The **empirical biographical inventory** is developed by administering a large number of potential items to a group of employees in a particular job. Those items that are related to job performance are retained for the scale. The **rational biographical inventory** is developed by beginning with an analysis of KSAO requirements and then devising items that reflect those KSAOs.

Biographical inventories been shown to predict job performance (Breaugh, 2009; Stokes, Toth, Searcy, Stroupe, & Carter, 1999). In a direct comparison, Stokes and Searcy (1999) found similar predictive power for both the empirical and the rational types of inventories. Furthermore, biographical inventories have been found to add predictability over and above personality tests, suggesting they don't just assess the same thing (McManus & Kelly, 1999—see the International Research box; Mount, Witt, & Barrick, 2000). Furthermore, biographical inventories tend to be resistant to applicant faking in order to look good on the test because many items are factual in nature and give the appearance of verifiability (J. West & Karas, 1999).

INTERNATIONAL RESEARCH

One of the criticisms of biographical inventories is that they just assess personality and offer limited advantages over a personality inventory. McManus and Kelly (1999) wanted to see how well a biographical inventory could stand up against a personality inventory in predicting job performance.

The study was conducted in five insurance companies in the United States. Participants in the study were 116 newly hired insurance sales representatives. During the application process, each one completed a widely used off-the-shelf biographical inventory designed for the insurance industry called the Initial Career Profile (ICP). A 124-item personality battery was included to measure what many consider the Big Five underlying dimensions of personality: extraversion, agreeableness, conscientiousness, emotional stability, and openness to experience (see Chapter 10). The ICP was used for selecting applicants, but the personality battery was not. Six months after an applicant was hired, his or her job performance was assessed with a five-item rating scale completed by the immediate supervisor. This produced two scores—one for the main tasks involved in sales and the other for more-general displays of effort and motivation. Both job performance scores were strongly correlated at .69.

Results showed that both the ICP and the personality battery were related to job performance. The biographical inventory correlated .25 and .26 with sales and effort, respectively. Of the personality variables, extraversion correlated with performance the most strongly, with correlations of .29 and .22, respectively. Conscientiousness correlated lowest, with nonsignificant correlations of almost zero. This surprised the authors because prior studies have suggested conscientiousness should relate to performance. When they analyzed the personality battery and the ICP together, they found that combined they did a better job of predicting performance than alone, suggesting that the biographical inventory was not just assessing the same thing as the personality battery.

Source: From "Personality Measures and Biodata: Evidence Regarding Their Incremental Predictive Value in the Life Insurance Industry," by M. A. McManus and M. L. Kelly, 1999, *Personnel Psychology, 52,* 137–148.

The biggest criticism of biographical inventories has been limited to the empirical variety and concerns the fact that items are chosen based entirely on their ability to predict performance rather than on an apparent link to job requirements. Sometimes an item can predict performance even though it cannot be linked to a KSAO necessary for job performance. These items are combined into scores that predict performance but do not reflect job-related KSAOs. Many questions in such inventories can appear completely unrelated to the job or job performance. Applicants may consider some questions to be an invasion of privacy, such as questions about high school dating behavior. Finally, such inventories can often have limited generalizability (Mumford, 1999) and might be useful only for the job and location for which they were developed. On the other hand, rational inventories can often be used for many jobs and locations.

▶ INTERVIEWS

An interview is a face-to-face meeting between one or more interviewers who are collecting information or making hiring decisions and an interviewee. Almost all organizations use the interview in hiring for almost all positions. Perhaps one reason for the universal use of this technique is that it is widely accepted. Studies across Europe and the United States have shown that people rate interviews as among the most fair selection procedures that organizations use (Bertolino & Steiner, 2007; Ispas, Ilie, Iliescu, Johnson, & Harris, 2010).

There are two types of interviews conducted in organizational settings. During an *unstructured interview*, the interviewer asks whatever questions come to mind. It can be much like a conversation between the interviewer and interviewee in which the nature of the interaction between the two people determines in large part what is discussed. By contrast, during a **structured interview**, the interviewer has a preplanned series of questions that are asked of every person who is interviewed. This makes the interview relatively standard, although the interaction between the two people can still affect what gets discussed. Nevertheless, the use of a standard set of questions allows the interviewer to collect the same information about each interviewee.

Campion, Palmer, and Campion (1997) discussed 15 ways in which structure can be introduced into an interview. There is no one way in which such interviews are conducted.

Some interviews are moderately structured in that the questions to be asked or just the topics to be covered are specified and standardized. Others have strict requirements that questions be asked in a set order, that the same phrasing be used, that interviewees not be asked to elaborate on any answer even if it is unclear, and that interviewees not be allowed to ask questions themselves until the end. In the extreme, the interview is much like an open-ended test with an oral rather than a written response. Campion et al. suggested that the more highly structured approaches are probably the most valid, and therefore as much structure as possible should be introduced into the interview.

The interview can be used in two ways. One is as an alternative to an application form or a written questionnaire to collect information. Questions can ask about attitudes ("Did you like your last job?"); job experiences ("Have you ever supervised anyone?"); personal background ("What was your major in college?"); and preferences ("Would you mind working weekends?"). The other way the interview can be used is to make inferences about a person's suitability for a job based on both the person's answers to the questions and his or her behavior in the interview situation. The interview can be considered as a sample of interpersonal behavior, showing how well a person communicates and relates to the interviewer.

Interviewers can be asked to make ratings on job-related dimensions, such as communication skills and relevant experience. They sometimes make overall ratings of applicant suitability for the job. These ratings can be subject to the same problems as performance appraisal ratings, which we discussed in Chapter 4. Interviewer biases and cognitive processes can reduce the accuracy of judgments and ratings (Dipboye & Gaugler, 1993).

The structured interview can be a good way to collect information that builds on that provided in the application form. Specific questions can ask for more detail about the provided information. For example, an application form will typically ask the person to list all prior jobs. In the interview, the interviewee might be asked to describe each job and to explain how his or her prior work experiences might be relevant to the job at hand.

An interview has two advantages over an application form. First, the interview allows for longer and more detailed answers to questions that do not have short or simple answers. Most people find it easier to talk than write. Second, the interview allows both the interviewer and the interviewee to ask one another for clarification. The interviewer can ask the interviewee to explain an unclear answer or to provide additional details. The interviewee can ask the interviewer to rephrase an unclear question or to indicate if the appropriate level of detail has been given.

The disadvantage of the interview is that the interviewer can affect the answers of the interviewee. Even with the most carefully constructed structured interview and thoroughly trained interviewer, the interaction between interviewer and interviewee will differ from interview to interview. Differences among interviewers in their ability to conduct an interview and in their personalities could affect the interview process and the interviewee's responses (Dipboye & Gaugler, 1993). This is not a concern with application forms because there is relatively little interaction between the person administering it and the person completing it.

Research evidence supports the use of structured interviews, but not necessarily unstructured ones, in making employment decisions. Ratings of interviewee employment suitability from a structured interview have been shown to predict future job performance across many different studies (Judge, Higgins, & Cable, 2000; Wiesner & Cronshaw, 1988). Wiesner and Cronshaw (1988) conducted a meta-analysis of over 100 interview

The interview is used for almost all hiring. (© *Adam Gregor, sourced from Shutterstock images*)

studies in which they compared structured and unstructured interviews. The average correlation between interview outcome and job performance was larger for the structured interview studies ($r = .34$) than for the unstructured interview studies ($r = .17$). Schmidt and Zimmerman (2004) argued that much of the difference in interview validity can be attributed to the lower reliability of unstructured interviews compared to that of structured interviews. With unstructured interviews, multiple interviewers will not agree very well on the applicant's suitability to be hired, and this lack of agreement hurts the ability of the interview to predict future job success. Another problem with the unstructured interview is that it leaves too much room for biases. An interviewer might decide on the basis of appearance, for example, that an applicant is unsuited. Cable and Judge (1997) found that interviewers' hiring decisions were related to how attractive they found the applicant and how much they liked him or her. Interviewers might not be as thorough in questioning a disliked or unattractive applicant and might fail to discover important job-related qualifications that might lead to hiring. Stewart, Dustin, Barrick, and Darnold (2008) conducted simulated interviews that showed how eye contact and firmness of handshake affect interviewers' ratings of interview performance. Given the existence of biases, it should not be surprising that interviewers fail to agree about applicants.

Several factors contribute to the validity of the structured interview. Huffcutt, Roth, and McDaniel (1996) conducted a meta-analysis showing that cognitive ability is related to interview outcomes and is a factor in their validity. Dipboye and Gaugler (1993) discussed six factors that are listed in Table 5.3. These factors involve the design of the questions asked, the information available and not available to the interviewer, the ratings made by the interviewer, and the training given to the interviewer. P. E. Roth and Campion (1992) found good validity for a structured interview that contained most of the factors noted as important by Dipboye and Gaugler.

With all the research focus on the validity of interviews, issues about what interviews actually assess have been overlooked. Huffcutt, Conway, Roth, and Stone (2001) did an extensive analysis of the specific personal characteristics assessed in interviews that provides insight into why they are able to predict future performance. The authors conducted a literature review and identified 47 interview studies that provided information about the KSAOs covered. The most commonly assessed were personality traits

TABLE 5.3 Factors That Can Enhance the Reliability and Validity of a Structured Interview

The interviewer should ask standardized questions.
The interviewer should have detailed information about the job in question.
The interviewer should not have prior information about the interviewee, such as psychological test scores.
The interviewer should not evaluate the interviewee until the interview is completed.
The interviewer should make ratings of individual dimensions of the interviewee, such as educational background and relevance of prior work history, rather than a global rating of suitability for the job.
Interviewers should receive training in how to conduct a valid structured interview.

Source: Adapted from "Cognitive and Behavioral Processes in the Selection Interview," by R. L. Dipboye and B. B. Gaugler, 1993, in N. Schmitt and W. C. Borman (Eds.), *Personnel Selection in Organizations*, San Francisco, CA: Jossey-Bass.

and interpersonal skills. Furthermore, structured and unstructured interviews tended to focus on different things. Structured interviews targeted job knowledge and skills, person-organization fit, and interpersonal skills, whereas unstructured interviews targeted general intelligence, education, and prior experience.

Technology has also made it possible to conduct interviews remotely. Telephone and webcam interviews have become increasingly popular when applicants are located at great distances. Research has shown that this can result in higher ratings for interviewees in telephone interviews (Straus, Miles, & Levesque, 2001) and videophone interviews (Chapman & Rowe, 2001). This was particularly true for individuals who were physically unattractive (Straus et al., 2001), suggesting a possible bias in interviews where the interviewer can see the interviewee. Schmidt and Rader (1999) conducted a meta-analysis of structured telephone interview studies and found that the average correlation with performance was about the same as for face-to-face interviews. One of the limitations of the telephone is not allowing for observation of nonverbal information—such as appearance, facial expression, and gestures—and these elements can be important to assess for some jobs such as sales. Furthermore, as Chapman, Uggerslev, and Webster (2003) found, applicants may have better attitudes toward face-to-face interviews than telephone or videophone interviews. Thus it seems unlikely that face-to-face interviews will disappear anytime soon.

WORK SAMPLES

A **work sample** is an assessment device that requires a person to demonstrate how well he or she can perform the tasks involved in a job under standardized conditions. It is a type of simulation in which a person does a job or part of a job under testing conditions rather than actual job conditions.

A work sample is like a psychological test except that it is designed to measure a higher-level skill. A test measures a basic skill, such as eye-hand coordination or manual dexterity. A work sample assesses the skill in doing a particular task, such as driving a bulldozer, which is composed of several basic skills performed in the context of a particular set of conditions. For some applications, the higher-level skill may be more important to assess than the basic skills because a work sample indicates how well a person can actually do a particular task. The psychological test indicates if a person has the requisite basic skills that should in theory predict how well he or she could do the task—but not how well he or she can actually do it.

The typical work sample gives the applicant the materials and tools necessary to accomplish the task. The person is instructed to complete the task quickly but accurately. A score is computed based on the accuracy with which the task is completed and the amount of time it took. For example, a person might be asked to disassemble and reassemble an electric motor or a small gasoline engine. A trained observer would score the person on accuracy and speed. Perhaps the most familiar work sample is the driving test that is required of applicants for a driver's license. The applicant is asked to complete a series of maneuvers with the automobile, while the test administrator records the scores for each one. To get the license, the applicant must achieve a total score that meets a prearranged criterion. A work sample in an organizational setting might be used the same way to determine if a person is suitable for a particular job.

Work samples have been found to be good predictors of future job performance (Robertson & Kandola, 1982). The close correspondence between the assessment situation and the job itself certainly has much to do with the success of the work sample in predicting performance. As with most simulation techniques, the work sample has a high degree of job relevance. This increases the likelihood that people will accept its use as a predictor of important skills in employee selection. There are several limitations to keep in mind, however. For many work samples, the applicant must already have experience with the task, work samples can be costly to develop, and the work sample is specific to a particular type of job (Callinan & Robertson, 2000).

▶ ASSESSMENT CENTERS

An **assessment center** measures how well a person is able to perform some of the tasks of a specific job. It consists of several exercises that are designed to simulate various job tasks. Most assessment centers are designed to assess management skills, but they are used for nonmanagement jobs as well. The exercises can take several days to complete and are often administered to several individuals at a time. This technique is widely used by many types of employers. For example, in a survey of British employers, Keenan (1995) found that 44% used assessment centers to hire college graduates. In the United States, the assessment center is used primarily for hiring and promotion decisions, although it can also be used to help employees enhance job skills (Bell & Arthur, 2008; Spychalski, Quiñones, Gaugler, & Pohley, 1997).

Assessment center exercises have a high level of realism because they simulate many of the actual tasks included in the job. For example, the person being assessed, or *assessee*, may be asked to role-play being a manager in a given situation. This might involve dealing with a subordinate or handling the paperwork for the job. The assessee's performance on each exercise is scored by a panel of trained *assessors*. The assessors are asked to evaluate the person's performance on each of several dimensions relevant to the job in question. For a manager's job, these can involve communicating, dealing with other people, making decisions, and planning. Table 5.4 contains the dimensions from a typical assessment center for managers described by Harris, Becker, and Smith (1993).

An assessment center can contain many different activities and exercises. The assessee might participate in an interview and take a battery of psychological tests, in

TABLE 5.4 Dimensions Scored in an Assessment Center

Oral communication
Oral comprehension
Problem solving
Interpersonal relations
Coaching
Planning
Written communication

Source: From "Does the Assessment Center Scoring Method Affect the Cross-Situational Consistency of Ratings?" by M. M. Harris, A. S. Becker, and D. E. Smith, 1993, *Journal of Applied Psychology, 78,* 675–678.

addition to completing several simulation exercises. The exercises might include an in-basket exercise, a leaderless group exercise, a problem-solving simulation, and role plays. Each exercise yields scores on several dimensions, and usually each dimension is assessed by several exercises. In addition, there is an overall assessment of the person's potential for the job in question.

An **in-basket exercise** asks the assessee to pretend that it is the first day of a new job and he or she has found a series of items in his or her in-basket. Items include e-mails, letters, memos, and phone messages. The assessee's task is to deal with each item in an appropriate manner, deciding what action, if any, to take by making notes on each item. An example of a memo that could be part of an in-basket exercise is shown in Table 5.5. To score well, the person must handle the memo in an appropriate and constructive manner. Ignoring the memo or writing a nasty reply to the sender would not be a constructive action. Leaving a note for the secretary to complete the report or doing so himself or herself would be better.

In a **leaderless group exercise**, several assessees are given a problem to solve together. The problem might be a competitive one, such as dividing up a scarce resource such as deciding which department gets a new piece of equipment. Each member of the group might be asked to role-play a particular management position. The problem can also be a cooperative one, in which all group members must generate a solution to an organizational problem, such as deciding whether or not to market a new product.

TABLE 5.5 Example of a Memorandum for an In-Basket Exercise

Memorandum

TO: Robert Jones, Manager of Marketing
FROM: Deborah Smith, Director of Human Resources
SUBJECT: New Position

On October 15 of this year, you requested an additional secretarial position for your department. I have been instructed by the company president to provide you the position. Before I can do so, however, you need to provide me with a complete justification for why you need this position. Please complete a Position Justification Report and return it to me. I need it by the end of the week, or the position will be delayed until the first of the year.

In a *problem-solving simulation*, the assessee is given a problem and is asked to come up with a solution, perhaps by producing a report. The problem provides sufficient background information from which to write the report. For example, the assessee could be given information about the costs for and projected income from opening a new assembly plant. His or her task would be to produce a feasibility report for opening the plant.

A *role-play exercise* requires that the assessee pretend to be a particular person in a specific organizational role, such as the manager of human resources. The task is to handle a problem or situation, such as counseling a troubled employee or dealing with an irate customer.

Assessors rate each assessee on each dimension by both observing behavior and reviewing materials produced during the exercises. Each person is scored on the various dimensions and may get an overall score. The dimension scores can be used to give the person feedback about his or her strengths and weaknesses. The overall score is useful if assessment center performance is to be used to make hiring or promotion decisions.

Research on the assessment center has found it to be a valid device for the selection of employees (Arthur, Day, McNelly, & Edens, 2003). This means that scores on the assessment center are correlated with job performance. For example, Shechtman (1992) found that scores in an assessment center given to university students upon admission predicted their job performance as teachers from 2 to 5 years after graduation, with a correlation of .27. Dayan, Kasten, and Fox (2002) found that assessment center ratings predicted job performance both 2 and 4 years later for police officers, with correlations of .30 and .21, respectively.

Although the overall scores in an assessment center have been shown to be valid, questions have been raised about the construct validity of the individual dimension scores (Bowler & Woehr, 2009; Lance, Lambert, Gewin, Lievens, & Conway, 2004). In other words, we are not certain that the intended dimensions of the assessment center are actually what is being measured. Different exercises are designed to assess a common set of dimensions. Because the same dimensions are assessed across exercises, scores on corresponding dimensions from different exercises should correlate well. For example, the score for leadership in the in-basket exercise should relate to the score for leadership in the leaderless group exercise. On the other hand, the different dimension scores within the same exercise should not be highly correlated because the dimensions are supposed to be measures of different, distinct characteristics. High correlations among dimension ratings are similar to halo errors in performance appraisal (see Chapter 4).

The problem with assessment centers is that the various dimension scores given to assessees within an exercise, such as an in-basket exercise, are too highly correlated. Furthermore, the scores given to assessees on the same dimensions across different exercises are not correlated enough. The high correlations across dimensions within exercises suggest that assessors are assessing only a single dimension rather than multiple dimensions. One possibility is that assessors are able to judge only overall exercise performance rather than the individual dimensions. The low correlations between dimensions across exercises suggest that each exercise might assess a different characteristic.

On balance, research on assessment centers raises the possibility that each exercise measures a single trait rather than multiple dimensions and that the different exercises may assess different things (Lance, Foster, Gentry, & Thoresen, 2004). Lievens, Chasteen, Day, and Christiansen (2006) suggested that each exercise provides a different set of opportunities for the assessee to display behavior relevant to performance in a unique way. One might reflect leadership and another might tap problem solving. Thus it should be no surprise that dimension scores are not very high across exercises. At the present time, we are not certain exactly what the different KSAOs assessed might be. Thus use of the assessment center to give specific feedback about individual KSAOs (e.g., decision making or leadership) is questionable. Russell and Domm (1995) provided evidence that ratings reflect how well the individual performs the role for the job being simulated rather than how well he or she does each dimension. Regardless of why it works, the assessment center does a good job of predicting future job performance. For that reason, it is a popular assessment device for selection and placement (see the International Research box).

INTERNATIONAL RESEARCH

Assessment centers use several different types of exercises to measure the various abilities thought to be essential for job success. The idea is to combine scores for each ability across several exercises, which should improve reliability and validity. Research has shown, however, that people's scores on individual ability dimensions from exercise to exercise are not highly correlated. In other words, a person might do well on a dimension (e.g., decision making) on one exercise and poorly on the same dimension on another exercise. This suggests that the assessment center may not measure the intended dimensions. If it did measure individual dimensions of ability, scores should be similar across different exercises.

Chan (1996) conducted a study that illustrates this problem of poor correlations among dimension scores across exercises in an assessment center that still has validity. The study involved the Singapore Police Force, which asked the author to design an assessment center for it. Assessees were 46 officers who were possible candidates for promotion. Six exercises were written, including an in-basket and a leaderless group exercise. Fourteen dimensions were assessed, although not every dimension was measured in each exercise. The center was validated against two job performance criteria—current job performance rating and subsequent promotion 2 years after the assessment.

Correlations were computed among all ratings in the assessment center, both among all measures of the same dimension across exercises and among all ratings within exercises. If the dimension scores were valid, the former should have been larger than the latter. The results were the opposite, in that the mean correlation among measures of the same dimension was larger than that among measures of different dimensions within exercises (.07 versus .71, respectively). The lack of significant relation among measures of the same dimensions suggests they measure different things, while the very high correlations among all ratings within exercises reflect a single thing for each exercise.

The assessment center resulted in two overall ratings—overall performance and promotability in the future. Overall performance correlated quite well with actual promotion assessed 2 years later but not at all with the most recent performance appraisal by the supervisor. The assessment center rating of promotability also correlated strongly with future promotion strongly and only modestly with the supervisor rating of performance. These results demonstrate the validity of the center, even though the exercises did not do an adequate job of assessing what they were initially designed to measure.

The results of this study are quite consistent with many others in showing the doubtful validity of dimension scores. On the other hand, the strong prediction of future promotions was very encouraging. Whereas many assessment center studies are contaminated, in that results are used to help determine future promotions, such was not the case here. The assessment center is an effective technique, even though we are not certain what it actually measures.

Source: From "Criterion and Construct Validation of an Assessment Centre," by D. Chan, 1996, *Journal of Occupational and Organizational Psychology*, 69, 167–181.

Research efforts have been made to improve the validity of dimension ratings in assessment centers. Reilly, Henry, and Smither (1990) reasoned that perhaps assessors are unable to adequately assess individual dimensions because they have too much information to process. Each exercise provides a great deal of information, and often that information must be organized in some way for judgments to be made. To help assessors organize information, the researchers provided a checklist of 273 behaviors to use to rate performance in the exercises. The assessors used the checklist to note the specific behaviors performed by each assessee before making their ratings. The results of the study showed that correlations between dimensions within exercises got smaller and correlations between corresponding dimensions across exercises got larger than those typically found in assessment centers. Thus the validities of the dimension scores improved. These results suggest that one problem with assessment centers as they are currently conducted is that they overload the assessor's ability to accurately assess dimensions. Providing checklists of behaviors imposed structure on the judgment task and improved the validity of the exercise ratings.

Means to improve assessment center ratings were also found by Arthur, Woehr, and Maldegen (2000). They were able to produce good correlations within dimensions across exercises by carefully constructing their assessment center. Most of their assessors were I/O psychologists, and all received careful training about how to translate specific behaviors into ratings. Finally, Lievens (2001) was able to increase the accuracy of assessment center ratings through the use of frame-of-reference training (see Chapter 4). Raters were given examples of effective and ineffective behaviors so they could build a common understanding of performance during training. A combination of all these approaches—using checklists, offering frame-of-reference training, and more carefully choosing assessors and conducting the centers—will likely produce the best results.

▶ ELECTRONIC ASSESSMENT

One of the fastest-growing trends in organizational assessment is the use of electronic media rather than paper and pencil. What began as a move to computerize test administration and scoring on personal computers has exploded with new kinds of assessments and approaches being developed. Lievens and Sackett (2006), for example, discussed the use of video-based assessment, where each item is presented as a video clip illustrating an event that might occur at work. Such assessments can provide a realistic situation that is difficult to describe fully with text. One of the major catalysts for electronic assessment has been the web, which makes it possible to link an applicant with an assessment almost anywhere in the world. Applicant recruitment services, such as Monster.com, have incorporated assessments into what previously was the initial application process. Electronic technology is expanding the use of assessment, as it has made that assessment cheaper and more convenient.

Electronic Administration of Psychological Tests

Paper-and-pencil psychological tests can be adapted for administration electronically. The test taker can read each item on a computer screen or display and respond with the keyboard, mouse, or other interface device. There are two major advantages to this approach. First, the test can be scored automatically as soon as the last item is answered, which can speed up the selection process. Second, a test can be put on a website, allowing access from almost anywhere in the world. An applicant doesn't have to come to a particular testing site to take the test. Of course, steps must be taken to monitor test taking so that cheating doesn't occur. There are two major disadvantages (McBride, 1998). First, developing a computer testing system can be expensive and time consuming, although the increasing availability of off-the-shelf electronic assessments can reduce that cost. Hardware and software costs can be considerable, especially compared to the small cost of printed test booklets and pencils. The use of computer-scannable answer sheets, however, allows for cheap computer scoring of large numbers of tests, thus eliminating one advantage of computer administration. Second, computerized tests are not necessarily equivalent to printed tests, especially for speed tests, which time how many correct items a person can do in a given interval. One such test is a clerical speed and accuracy test in which the test taker must compare two strings of letters and indicate if they are the same or not—for example:

abdiel *versus* abdifl
ghicbe *versus* ghicbe

Response time per item can be different when using computer versus paper and pencil for the same items, making scores nonequivalent.

Potosky and Bobko (2004) contrasted web-based with paper-and-pencil tests. They noted that for speed tests, where the test taker has a limited amount of time, adjustments must be made for the load times of web pages. Furthermore, test-taking strategies are likely to vary between the two formats. It is easy with paper-and-pencil tests to skip around, so that the test taker might choose to complete certain types of items first and other types last. Since web-based tests allow fewer items per screen than paper does per page, it can discourage skipping around, and thus items are more likely to be completed in order. Care must be taken in comparing scores of tests taken with the two formats.

It might seem that computer administration has the potential for increasing the accuracy of personality tests in which people often distort or fake their responses—people are sometimes better able to reveal themselves honestly to a machine, such as a computer, than to another person. A computer might seem more impersonal than a paper-and-pencil test to a test taker. Richman, Kiesler, Weisband, and Drasgow (1999) conducted a meta-analysis to see if the tendency to respond in a favorable direction was the same for computer as for paper-and-pencil administration of personality tests. Overall, the results suggested no differences. However, in looking more closely at the results, Richman et al. noticed that there was somewhat less distortion when the person was alone. When an experimenter was in the room, any feeling of anonymity was apparently lost, and there were no differences between the computer and paper-and-pencil administrations.

A still more complex type of computer assessment that measures complex problem solving has become popular in Germany (Funke, 1998; Kleinmann & Strauss, 1998). These assessments provide the applicant with a simulation of a complex work situation, such as running an airport or factory, that is somewhat like a computer game. The person is given a fixed amount of time to run the simulation, and various indicators of performance are calculated by the computer. Research with these assessments has provided impressive initial evidence that they can predict future job performance for jobs in which problem-solving skill is important (Kleinmann & Strauss, 1998).

Computers are not the only technology that is being used to increase the efficiency of assessment. Van Iddekinge, Eidson, Kudisch, and Goldblatt (2003) developed a telephone-based system for administering a biographical inventory. Applicants were able to dial a toll-free number and answer yes/no questions about their backgrounds using the keys on their telephones. Van Iddekinge et al. showed that this type of assessment was able to predict job performance for those subsequently hired. However, it required designing an inventory in a yes/no format, which is more limiting than other media, such as pencil and paper.

Computer Adaptive Testing

Computer adaptive testing (CAT) is a flexible computerized approach to item administration where items given to a test taker are chosen based on prior correct or incorrect responses. For an ability test where some items are more difficult than others, the session begins by giving the test taker a moderately difficult item. If the person gets the item correct, a more difficult item is presented. If the person gets it incorrect, an easier item is chosen. As the test proceeds, the computer chooses items that are at the appropriate level of difficulty for the particular test taker. Thus each test taker gets a somewhat different set of items, depending on his or her pattern of correct and incorrect answers. By doing this, CAT is more efficient than standard testing because it can achieve the same level of reliability with fewer items (Penfield, 2006). There is also less concern about security than with nonadaptive testing, since each test taker gets a different set of items, thus making it more difficult to cheat (Reynolds & Dickter, 2010). For these reasons, this approach has been used for mass testing, such as the computerized version of the Graduate Record Examination (GRE). CAT is not without disadvantages, however. Perhaps the biggest is that the tests take considerable time and resources to develop. A well-designed test will likely have hundreds of items, and data on each item must be collected from a thousand or more test takers in order to determine difficulty levels (Reynolds & Dickter, 2010). Thus it takes a lot more time and money to develop a computer adaptive test than a nonadaptive test.

▶ CHAPTER SUMMARY

One of the major tasks I/O psychologists do for organizations is the assessment of people's characteristics for selection and placement. These characteristics can be classified as the knowledge, skill, ability, and other personal characteristics, or KSAOs, necessary for successful performance on the job.

The five major methods used to assess KSAOs are:

Psychological test

Biographical inventory

Interview

Work sample

Assessment center

A psychological test is a standardized series of problems or questions given to a person to assess a particular individual characteristic. Tests are commonly used to assess many KSAOs, including knowledge, skill, ability, attitudes, interests, and personality.

The biographical inventory asks for detailed information about the person's past experience, both on and off the job. It asks for far more extensive information than the typical job application form.

An interview is a face-to-face meeting between an interviewee and one or more interviewers who are collecting information or making hiring decisions. During an unstructured interview, the interviewer asks whatever questions come to mind. By contrast, during a structured interview the interviewer has a preplanned series of questions that are asked of every person who is interviewed. In both types, the interviewer often makes overall judgments about the interviewee's suitability for the job.

A work sample is an assessment device that requires a person to demonstrate how well he or she can perform job tasks under standardized conditions. It is a type of simulation in which a person does a job or part of a job under testing conditions rather than actual job conditions.

The assessment center consists of several different types of exercises that take place over one or more days. Although most assessment centers are used to identify future management potential, they can be used to assess the potential of people for many different types of jobs.

Electronic assessment has become commonplace, especially for the administration of psychological tests. The most common use of electronic media is the administration of a paper-and-pencil test by computer. Often the test is almost identical to the printed version, with items displayed on the screen and a response made with a keyboard or mouse. Computer adaptive testing (CAT) is a more sophisticated approach in which the items administered to an individual are customized, depending on correct and incorrect answers to prior questions. Such tests can yield better reliabilities with fewer items, but they are costly to develop and are therefore best left to mass-testing situations.

I/O PSYCHOLOGY IN PRACTICE

(Courtesy of Jon Canger)

Many of the I/O functions of organizations are moving to the web. Dr. Jonathan Canger has been finding new and innovative ways to use this technology in employee recruitment and selection. Dr. Canger received his Ph.D. in I/O psychology from the University of South Florida in 1990. He has worked for a variety of large organizations, including Coca-Cola, Motorola, and Verizon Wireless, where he is currently Associate Director for Talent Acquisition and Assessment. He was at the time of this case Vice President for Organizational Development at TMP Worldwide, a 10,000-employee national firm that provides a variety of employee recruitment and consulting services. His current responsibilities involve helping the company function more effectively through effective management of employees. He is involved in designing systems to help employees develop their work skills, planning future needs for top managers, and overseeing organizational changes to make the organization function more smoothly. One of the projects he began prior to moving into his current position involved the development of personality tests that could be used to better match people to jobs and organizations.

The best-known service provided by TMP is the Monster career search website. Monster was the 454th dotcom website to be established, and it is one of the few that are currently profitable. It is also one of the most popular: 10% of all web visits in the world are to the Monster site. The site is a career portal, where potential job applicants can for no cost browse lists of available jobs and leave résumés on file (there are currently 14 million) for prospective employers. It is the employer who must pay a fee for listing its jobs or browsing the résumé database.

Dr. Canger came up with the idea of adding personality assessments to the Monster site to assist both applicants and employers in finding better matches. The idea was to put a personality scale online where prospective applicants could easily complete it and have it electronically scored. This information could then be used to help determine which jobs to apply for (applicant side) and who to hire (employer side). Because the number of individuals who would ultimately complete these assessments would be enormous (potentially tens of millions), it wasn't feasible to purchase an existing assessment from one of the psychological testing companies. Dr. Canger and his team decided to develop their own assessment from scratch.

The first step was to compile a pool of potential personality items. The team decided to use the Big Five theory to provide the underlying dimensions that would be measured. In addition, they added items concerning work values taken from the O*NET (see Chapter 3). These included achievement, recognition, and working conditions. All the items were administered to about 2,000 employees of various organizations in Australia, New Zealand, the United Kingdom, and the United States. This allowed Dr. Canger's team to refine the assessment.

Phase 1 of this project was to put the assessment on the Monster website, available as part of a career development service that has a nominal fee. People could get feedback about their own personalities and how they could match to potential employers and jobs. Phase 2 added a component to provide employers with information about potential applicants so employers could better match people to jobs. Phase 3, scheduled to be operational by the time you read this, will add specific hiring recommendations to employers about individuals, not unlike an I/O consultant who provides selection services.

This is an innovative system for two reasons. First, it is entirely web-based, with both applicants and employers working at different ends of the same integrated computer system. Second, generally information about personality is used only by the employer as opposed to potential applicants. Providing this information to both sides should allow for better matching, as both the applicants and the employers will be working toward achieving good matches between the person and the organization.

Discussion Questions

1. What are the advantages and disadvantages of web-based assessments?
2. Why would it be important to the organization to match the person's personality to the job or organization?
3. Why did Dr. Canger and his team collect initial data in more than one country?
4. What is the advantage of using the Big Five personality dimensions and the O*NET values?
5. What are the advantages to applicants and employers of using the Monster website for recruitment?

LEARNING BY DOING

Choosing Selection Tools for a Job

Go to the O*NET website, http://online.onetcenter.org, and go to the "Find Occupation" section. From the top, enter an occupation and review the summary for it. Choose at least 10 KSAOs from the O*NET overview. For each, explain the assessment method you would use to assess it.

Student Selection

List five KSAOs for the job of college student. For each, explain the assessment method you would use to assess it.

PART III

SELECTING AND TRAINING EMPLOYEES

(© *Dean Mitchell/iStockphoto*)

CHAPTER 6

Selecting Employees

CHAPTER 6 OUTLINE

Did you ever apply for a job with an organization that required you to complete some sort of an assessment? Most employers will have you complete an application form, but many will also include assessments like the ones we discussed in Chapter 5. The most common are psychological tests, although biographical inventories, simulations, and work samples might also be used. Did you wonder, as you were completing the test, what they were trying to learn about you and why they couldn't just ask? Some tests are fairly obvious, such as a test of mathematical skill, but personality tests often contain questions that seemingly have little to do with the job. Did you feel that the assessments you completed were reasonable, or did they include questions that you felt were none of the organization's business or were not relevant to the job? If the selection system was scientifically developed, the assessments you encountered should have been relevant and would help to predict whether or not you would be successful. Chances are that if you encountered these sorts of assessments, I/O psychologists had something to do with developing them.

Two of the most important functions of any organization are the recruitment and selection of employees. The health and well-being of an organization depend in large part on a steady flow of new people. Employees must be hired to fill newly created positions and to replace people who have left. Acquiring new employees can be a costly and difficult undertaking. It involves the following four steps (Figure 6.1):

Planning the need for new employees

Getting appropriate people to apply for positions (recruitment)

Deciding whom to hire (selection)

Getting the selected people to take the jobs

Employee recruitment and selection involve legal issues in many countries, particularly those in North America and Europe. As we have already discussed, there are strictly enforced laws in many countries prohibiting discrimination in actions that affect employees. The most frequent target of equal employment opportunity efforts has been the hiring process. An I/O psychologist who gets involved in employee selection must be an expert in the legal issues concerning selection.

In this chapter, we discuss how organizations recruit and select new employees, using the four steps listed earlier and shown in Figure 6.1. Most of the efforts of I/O psychologists involve selection, so we spend more time on that topic than the others. This is not to say, however, that the selection step is the most important. Rather, it is selection that has been the major focus of I/O practice and research since the beginning of the field. In addition to the four steps, we discuss the value or utility of the scientific approach to selection. We also cover the legal issues involved in employee recruitment and selection from the perspective of civil rights legislation.

Objectives: The student who studies this chapter should be able to:

- Explain how organizations conduct human resource planning.
- Discuss methods of recruitment.
- Explain the steps involved in conducting a validation study.
- Describe how scientific approaches to selection can have utility for organizations.
- Relate the principles of legal selection.

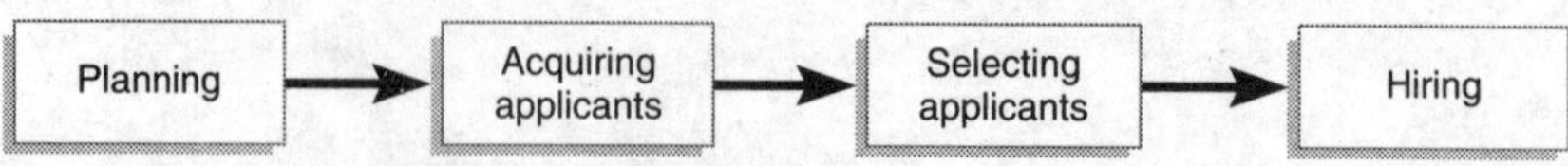

Figure 6.1 Four steps for acquiring new employees.

▶ THE PLANNING OF HUMAN RESOURCE NEEDS

In order for an organization to stay healthy, it must have a steady supply of human resources or people. These human resources are necessary to fill vacancies created by people who leave the organization. They are also needed to fill new positions that are created by organizational changes or expansion. To do a good job in recruiting the people needed by an organization, careful planning is necessary. Human resource plans must include both a consideration of the organization's needs for people and the supply of possible people to hire (Cascio, 1998).

Forecasts of human resource demands usually list the number of people needed in each job category, such as the number of clerks or teachers. Table 6.1 is an example of a projection that might be made by a manufacturing organization that is facing a gradual automation of its factories. The number of assembly-line workers needed declines steadily, while the number of technicians registers a corresponding increase. This is a common trend in industry, and it is important that organizations plan for reduction in one type of employee and increase in another. The organization can take a variety of actions to deal with the shifting nature of jobs and job requirements. The selection approach would replace assemblers with technicians. The training approach would turn assemblers into technicians. The first approach can be less expensive because it would cost more to provide training to employees who continue to get paid while they are learning a new job. The second approach has the advantage of doing the least harm to current employees. It provides considerable benefits to individuals who are given a new and more marketable skill. A training approach is necessary, however, when there is an inadequate supply of people with the necessary skills in the labor market, which is a situation that is becoming increasingly common in the United States and many other countries. This has necessitated somewhat of a shift from a pure selection approach to a training and staff development approach in which existing employees are offered retraining when old skills become obsolete. Training will be the topic for Chapter 7.

The supply of people to hire in the labor market can be estimated in a variety of ways. Organizations can keep track of the number of people who apply for various positions. In addition, government agencies provide information about the number of available workers in different job categories. In the United States, several agencies provide this sort of information (Table 6.2), including the Bureau of Labor Statistics of the U.S. Department of Labor (http://www.bls.gov). A comparison of the demand and supply of people for various jobs is an important component in choosing between a selection or a training approach to meeting future human resource needs.

Both the globalization of the world economy and technological advances have produced tremendous shifts in the demand for people with various job-related skills. The demand for semiskilled and unskilled assemblers in factories has been declining in

TABLE 6.1 Projections of Employees Needed for an Organization Undergoing Automation of Its Manufacturing Processes

Job Classification	Now	Year 1	Year 2	Year 3	Year 4
Assemblers	20,000	16,000	10,000	5,000	4,000
Technicians	20	200	400	600	1,000

TABLE 6.2 Sources of Labor Market Information for the United States

Bureau of Labor Statistics of the U.S. Department of Labor
Engineering Manpower Commission
National Science Foundation
Office of Education
Public Health Service of the U.S. Department of Health and Human Services
U.S. Employment Service

Source: From *Applied Psychology in Personnel Management*, 5th ed. (p. 163), by W. F. Cascio, 1998, Englewood Cliffs, NJ: Prentice Hall.

industrialized countries such as Canada and the United States. The demand for people to fill many highly skilled jobs has been increasing—and should continue to increase for at least the next decade. Demand is expected to decline for jobs in manufacturing and mining, and during the 2000s we have seen a loss in such jobs in the United States. Demand should increase for jobs in health-related fields and technology. Figure 6.2 shows the 20 occupations requiring a college degree that have the most job openings in the United States, projected from 2004 to 2014, according to the U.S. Department of Labor's Bureau of Labor Statistics. I/O psychology is among the 25 fastest-growing U.S. occupations (U.S. Department of Labor, 2010).

▶ RECRUITING APPLICANTS

A challenge for many organizations is getting people to apply for available positions. To be able to hire good people, an organization must have a large pool of job applicants from which to choose. For some jobs, it may be relatively easy to recruit applicants because there are many available people who are easily attracted. For jobs in which there is an undersupply of people, an organization must expend considerable effort to attract the right people to fill its job vacancies. Several methods can be used to recruit applicants for a vacant position. Some require little effort, such as putting a position vacancy notice on the organization's own website or posting the position on a job search website like Yahoo! HotJobs or Monster. Other actions may require the full-time efforts of one or more people—for example, as recruiters to interview potential applicants at colleges and universities across the country.

Six possible sources of applicants that are commonly used by organizations are:

Advertising	School recruiters
Employee referral	Walk-ins
Employment agencies	The web

The choice of sources depends on the ease with which organizations can recruit applicants. Some organizations find that they get enough walk-in applicants to cover the jobs that they have, so more time-consuming methods are unnecessary. (A walk-in applicant is someone who applies for a job on his or her own without action on the part of the organization.) For low-level positions, many organizations rely on their own company websites (Chapman & Webster, 2003). In a competitive job market, however, many organizations

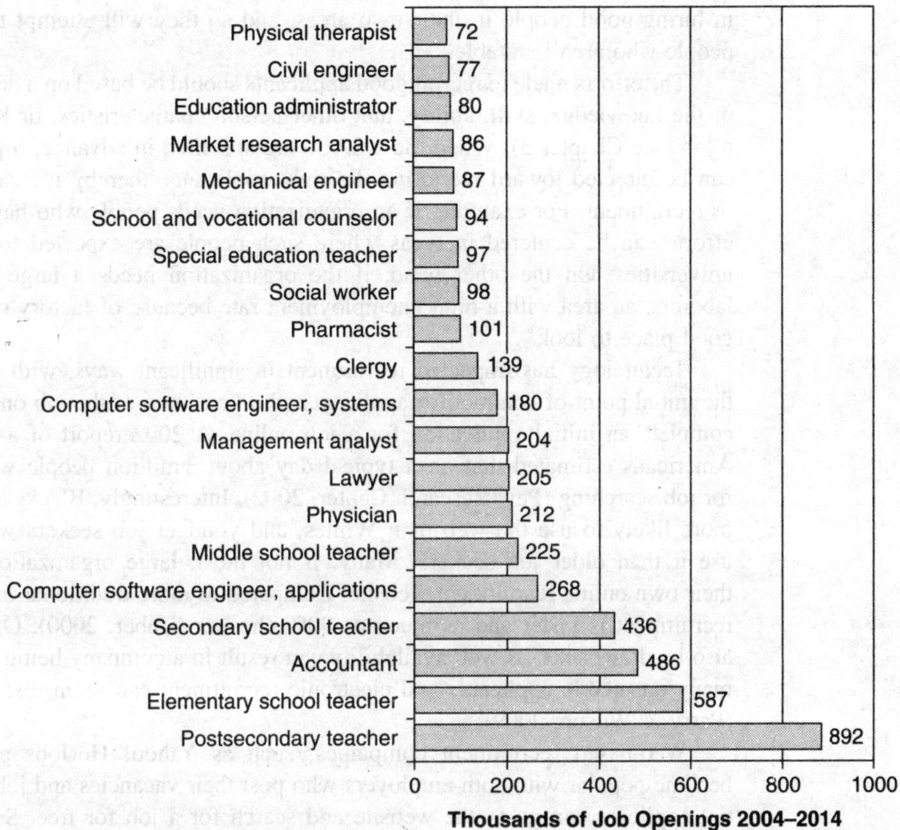

Figure 6.2 Fastest-growing occupations requiring a college degree in the United States, 2004–2014. From "The 2004–14 Job Outlook for College Graduates," by O. Crosby and R. Moncarz, 2006, *Occupational Outlook Quarterly* (Fall), 42–57.

might be attempting to attract the same individuals. Here time-consuming methods might be necessary to attract the people who are needed.

The different sources of job applicants do not necessarily attract the same quality of applicant. Zottoli and Wanous (2000) reviewed 50 years of research on applicant source and found consistent evidence that inside sources (employee referrals of acquaintances/friends, rehires of those who once worked there, and transfers from inside the organization) provide employees who perform better and remain on the job longer on average than outside sources (advertising or employment agencies). Furthermore, employees hired through inside sources tend to be more satisfied with their jobs, likely because they have more realistic expectations about what the job will entail (Moser, 2005). McManus and Ferguson (2003) also found that inside sources provided the best applicants; in addition, they found that applicants who learned of the job through the internet were of better quality than those who found it through newspapers and other outside sources. Zottoli and Wanous suggested two reasons for the superiority of inside sources. First, such applicants receive more accurate information about the job and so they prescreen themselves out of jobs for which they aren't suited. Second, recommenders will assess fit before suggesting someone for a job. Employees can have a personal stake in hiring good people in their own areas, and so they will attempt to screen out those people who aren't suitable.

The efforts made to recruit good applicants should be based on a detailed specification of the knowledge, skill, ability, and other person characteristics, or KSAOs, needed for a job (see Chapter 3). When the KSAOs are specified in advance, organizational efforts can be directed toward recruiting the right applicants, thereby increasing the efficiency of recruitment. For example, if an organization needs people who have computer skills, efforts can be centered in areas where such people are expected to be, such as large universities. On the other hand, if the organization needs a large supply of manual laborers, an area with a high unemployment rate because of factory closings might be a good place to look.

Technology has impacted recruitment in significant ways, with the web becoming the initial point of contract for applicants who first learn of the job online and who often complete an initial application for a job online. A 2002 report of a national survey of Americans estimated that on a typical day about 3 million people were using the web for job searching (Pew Research Center, 2002). Interestingly, Blacks and Hispanics were more likely to use the web than Whites, and younger job seekers were more likely to use it than older job seekers. Many, if not most, large organizations today maintain their own online recruitment website. Compared to more traditional methods, web-based recruitment is faster and as much as 90% cheaper (Cober, 2000). Of course, there can also be drawbacks, as web availability can result in a company being swamped with too many unsuitable applicants and electronic recruitment can seem distant and impersonal (Parry & Wilson, 2009).

Web-based recruitment companies, such as Yahoo! HotJobs and Monster, have become popular with both employers who post their vacancies and job seekers. A potential applicant can go to the website and search for a job for free. Sophisticated search features allow for searches by geographic region, job title, and even salary level. Applications can be completed for many jobs online. Employers must pay to post positions or to browse résumés of prospective employees who did not specifically apply. These web services can do far more than just post jobs, however. They provide prescreening, online assessments, and systems to help manage recruitment.

Breaugh and Starke (2000) pointed out that recruitment is not just a matter of collecting applications and conducting assessments. Part of recruitment is marketing the organization and making it attractive to applicants. Turban and Cable (2003) conducted a study in the placement office of a university, finding that companies with better reputations as good employers attracted more and better (higher GPA) applicants. Given that prospective applicants' initial contact with the organization is through the web, it is important that the organization's website be attractive, informative, and user friendly (Allen, Mahto, & Otondo, 2007; Sylva & Mol, 2009).

▶ SELECTING EMPLOYEES

If an organization is lucky, it will have many more good applicants than the number of vacant jobs. As we will see in this section, the more selective an organization can be, the better the chances that the person hired will be a good employee. This is because many of the employee selection procedures developed by I/O psychologists work best when there are several applicants from which to choose. These procedures are based on statistical methodologies used to develop selection systems. We first discuss the criterion-related validity approach to employee selection taken by I/O psychologists. This approach is based on scientific principles and statistics. We then briefly discuss alternative procedures that are often used because of practical considerations. Next, we cover the utility of our selection techniques. Utility is concerned with the benefits that organizations achieve from using scientific selection.

How Do Organizations Select Employees?

The purpose of employee selection is to hire people who are likely to be successful on the job, as organizational performance is dependent on having employees who perform their jobs well. Perhaps the approach used most often by organizations is to have a manager interview the applicants and decide subjectively which one to hire. Such purely subjective hiring procedures, however, have been shown to be biased and inaccurate. A better approach is to use scientific methods that have been shown to work in almost a century of research on employee selection.

Two important elements in employee selection must be considered. First is the *criterion*, which is the definition of good employee performance. Although it may seem obvious that we hire the person who is expected to be the best performer, it is not easy to define what we mean by good performance. Job performance involves many different aspects. Some employees may work very accurately, whereas others work very fast. It is not always easy to decide if we should hire based on one aspect of the criterion (e.g., attendance) or another (e.g., work quantity). These issues were discussed at length in Chapter 4. To use scientific selection methods, we first must know what the criterion is for the job in question.

The second element is the *predictor*, which is anything assessed in job applicants that relates to the criterion. In Chapter 5, we discussed several methods for assessing characteristics that are relevant to job requirements. These techniques can be used to assess KSAOs that are necessary for job success. Measures of KSAOs can be used as predictors of a criterion of job performance. Knowledge of the subject matter, for example, should be a good predictor for the job performance of a classroom teacher. It is not the only predictor, for knowledge alone does not make someone a good teacher.

Determining if a given predictor relates to a criterion requires a **validation study**, which is a research study that attempts to show that the predictor relates to the criterion. To conduct this sort of study, both the criterion and the predictor are quantified. Data are collected for a group of employees on both the criterion and the predictor variables. Because they are both quantified, a statistical test can be conducted to see if they are significantly related. The correlation coefficient indicates how well the two variables relate to each other. If the two variables are significantly related statistically, you can conclude that the predictor is valid in terms of the criterion. The implication is that you could use information about the predictor to forecast the applicant's likely performance on the job.

Conducting a good validation study is a complex and difficult undertaking. First, you must carefully analyze the job and job requirements using job analysis. The results of the job analysis can be used to develop criteria for the job and to pick predictors. Data are collected to verify that the chosen predictors are valid. Such valid predictors will become part of the organization's employee selection system. We discuss this process in greater detail in the next section of the chapter.

Conducting a Validation Study

Conducting a validation study involves five steps:

1. Conduct a job analysis.
2. Specify job performance criteria.
3. Choose predictors.
4. Validate the predictors.
5. Cross-validate.

Conducting a job analysis provides the information needed to proceed with the next two steps of specifying criteria and choosing predictors. Once these steps are completed, data can be collected on a sample of employees to determine if the criteria are related to the predictors. If they are, the results must be replicated on a second sample to verify the results. The five steps are illustrated in Figure 6.3.

Step 1: Conduct a Job Analysis

As we discussed in Chapter 3, a job analysis provides information about the tasks involved in a job. It also provides information about the characteristics (KSAOs) an employee needs to be successful on a job. These two types of information are not independent, for the specification of KSAOs often is derived from an analysis of the tasks required for the job.

As we discuss later in the section on legal issues, an important concept in employee selection is job relevance—the correspondence between the KSAOs needed for job success and the KSAOs of the job applicant. For successful and legal selection, these two types of KSAO requirements should correspond. Hiring people with characteristics that are not related to the job requirements or without characteristics that are related would be foolish at best and illegal at worst if it results in discrimination. Thus it would make sense to hire on the basis of physical strength if the job requires heavy lifting, such as a dock worker. It makes little sense to have a strength requirement for school teachers.

A job analysis can be used in many ways as the basis for a validation study. The job analysis can identify the major components of the job. Next, an analysis can be done

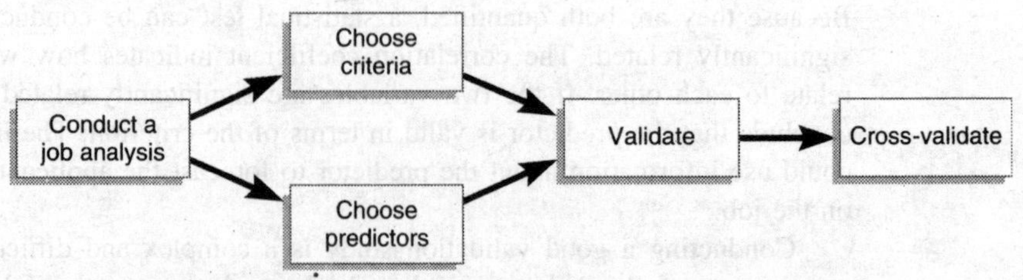

Figure 6.3 The five steps for conducting a validation study.

to specify the KSAOs necessary to accomplish each component. From this information, a list of performance criteria and potential predictors can be made.

For example, a major component for a manager's job might be managing a budget. Managers often have to develop budgets and manage their resources so that they do not exceed them. One KSAO that would be important for managing a budget is knowledge of basic mathematics, such as addition and subtraction. People hired to be managers should have this basic knowledge.

Step 2: Specify Job Performance Criteria

Once you have a good idea about what a job entails, you can begin to develop criteria for good job performance. For example, if a manager is required to manage a budget, a reasonable criterion might be how well the manager stayed within the budget. There can be many reasons for not staying within the budget, so this criterion alone is not sufficient for evaluating how well a person performs the job. However, for a validation study we are interested in using criteria that might be predicted by one or more of our predictors. For example, if a test of mathematical ability is found to predict how well a manager can stay within a budget, then we can expect to hire managers who do better on the criterion if that test is used to help select them.

Step 3: Choose Predictors

As we develop our criteria for a job, we also choose potential predictors of performance on those criteria. Potential predictors might be chosen to assess KSAOs directly, as with a psychological test of mathematical ability. Other predictors might be less direct as measures of a KSAO. We often assume that college graduates have certain knowledge and ability, such as being able to do basic mathematics and to write in their native language. Using education level as a predictor can eliminate the need to assess many KSAO requirements for a job. This is why many organizations prefer to hire college graduates. Care must be taken, however, that requiring a college degree is reasonable for the job in question. A degree would be overkill if the job required only basic arithmetic and a fourth-grade reading level.

In Chapter 5, we discussed five methods that can be used to assess KSAOs. All these methods are frequently used as predictors in validation studies and have been shown to be valid predictors of job performance:

- Assessment centers
- Psychological tests
- Biographical inventories
- Work samples
- Interviews

These tools might predict other nonperformance criteria as well, such as job satisfaction. Although few organizations select employees based on the likelihood that they will enjoy the job, it is possible to conduct such a validation study to find appropriate and valid predictors. Criteria chosen for validity studies usually are concerned with an aspect of job performance or other behavior that is directly related to accomplishment of organizational objectives.

Step 4: Validate the Predictors

After the criteria and predictors are chosen, the data collection phase of the validation study can proceed. In this step, measures of the criterion and the predictors are taken on a sample of people to see if the predictor relates to the criterion. A good field test of the predictor is done in the organizational setting in which it is expected to be used in the future. Most validation studies are done in actual organizational settings as opposed to laboratory settings. In the laboratory, you might determine that a human attribute relates to task performance, but you cannot be certain that it will generalize to the organization. By conducting field studies in the settings in which selection tools will ultimately be used, the likelihood of generalization is maximized.

There are two types of study designs for conducting a validation study. In a **concurrent validation study**, both the criterion and the predictor scores are collected from a sample of participants at more or less the same point in time. Usually the participants are current employees who are assessed on both criteria and predictors. A sample of employees might be asked to provide predictor data by taking an assessment test. Test scores would then be correlated with employees' most recent performance evaluation. If the two are related, we assume that scores on the predictor at the time of application for a job will predict later performance on the job.

In a **predictive validity study**, the predictors are measured before the criterion. A sample of job applicants is assessed on the predictor, but scores on that predictor are not used in deciding who to hire. In other words, we hire applicants who are both high and low on the predictor. Some time (from a few months to a few years) after this group of new hires has been on the job, we assess the criterion or criteria. We conduct statistical analyses to see if the predictor relates significantly to the criterion or criteria. If the predictor can predict future performance, we can have reasonable confidence in the predictor as a valid selection device.

It might seem that the predictive design would be superior to the concurrent in validating predictors because the predictive design tests the predictor on applicants rather than employees who already have been selected and trained. Because the predictor is used on applicants, generalizability should be maximized. Research has shown, however, that the two designs are equally effective in validating predictors. Validity coefficients, the correlations between scores on the criterion and predictor, have been found to be about the same in studies using the two different types of designs (Schmitt, Gooding, Noe, & Kirsch, 1984). This is good news for organizations because predictive designs take a long time to conduct. You might have to wait a year after collecting predictor scores to collect criterion scores. Furthermore, for some organizations it could take months or years before a sufficient number of people are hired to conduct the analysis. A concurrent study can be conducted in as little as a few days if the predictor can be administered quickly and the criterion scores are readily available.

Step 5: Cross-Validate

The final step in a validation study is to **cross-validate** or replicate the results of one sample with those of another sample. This is done to be certain that our results are due to a real correlation between the criterion and predictor and not a statistical error. In any study involving statistics, significance can occur by chance as opposed to occurring due to real relations among the variables of interest. Such statistical errors are called

Alpha or Type 1 errors. To protect ourselves from making an error in our conclusions about whether or not a predictor can forecast a criterion, we cross-validate or repeat our analyses on another sample of participants. It is extremely unlikely that we will find the same results twice if there is no relation among the variables of interest. In other words, two successive Alpha errors are unlikely.

To conduct a cross-validation, we need two samples. The first sample is used to determine if the criterion and predictor are significantly correlated. A second sample is used to see if the significant relationship found in the first sample can be repeated on the second. The predictor is validated on the first sample and then double-checked or cross-validated on the second. Cross-validation adds to our confidence that the predictor can forecast the criterion or criteria of interest. In most field settings, cross-validation is done by taking the original sample and dividing it randomly in half. The first half is used for the validation, and the second is used for the cross-validation.

Validity Generalization

At times, it is not necessary to collect data to validate a selection test or other assessment device. Selection tests that are valid in one setting are often valid in many other settings. **Validity generalization** means that validities of selection devices are generalizable or transportable from job to job and organization to organization (Schmidt & Hunter, 1977). If a test predicts performance for an administrative assistant in one organization, for example, it will predict for an administrative assistant in another organization.

The idea of validity generalization has been widely accepted among I/O psychologists (Murphy, 2000), at least as long as the jobs and tests in question are comparable. If you validate a test for the selection of people in a particular job, the test should be valid for the same job in a different organization. It should also be valid for a job that has the same KSAO requirements. If the second job is different from the job for which the test was valid, the test in the second case may or may not be valid. The only way to be certain would be to conduct another validation study on the second job to determine if the test predicts the criterion.

How Predictor Information Is Used for Selection

Once it is determined that a predictor or predictors are valid forecasters of future performance criteria, it must be decided how best to use the predictor information. Two popular uses of predictor information are as hurdles and as predictors in a regression equation. With either approach, multiple predictors can be used in combination. Often prediction is better with several rather than single predictors because multiple KSAOs are necessary for job success.

Multiple Hurdles

The **multiple hurdles** approach sets a passing score for each predictor. If an applicant achieves that score, then the hurdle is passed. For example, a computer salesperson should have several KSAOs in order to be successful on the job. One obvious KSAO is knowledge of computer principles. Completion of a college degree in computers could serve as an indicator of the KSAO, and the applicant would pass this hurdle if he or she had such a degree. Another important KSAO might be communication skills so that the person can relate well to customers. This might be assessed with a communication skills exercise. Applicants would have to have a passing score on the communication exercise to pass this hurdle.

It is efficient to use multiple hurdles in a specified order and eliminate applicants as the assessment process goes from hurdle to hurdle. It would make financial sense to order the predictors in terms of cost from least to most expensive. For example, only those computer sales applicants with college degrees would be given the communication skills exercise, since the earning of a degree can be seen in an initial application, whereas the exercise will have some additional cost to administer. Many organizations use relatively inexpensive preliminary screening methods as hurdles so that expensive assessments are not used with people who easily could have been screened out earlier in the process.

Regression Approach

The *regression approach* uses the score from each predictor in an equation to provide a numerical estimate or forecast of the criterion. With the computer sales job, an equation could predict the actual dollar amount of sales per month. Predictors for that job might be GPA in college and scores on the communication exercise. Both quantitative variables (GPA and exercise score) can be combined mathematically to provide forecasted criterion scores (e.g., monthly sales). Individuals who are forecasted to have the best criterion scores would be those who are hired.

With a single-predictor variable, a linear regression equation is calculated from a sample of data. To compute an equation, you must have data on both the criterion and the predictor so that you can compare how well the forecasted criterion scores match the real criterion scores. The general form of a linear regression equation is

$$Y = b \times X + a$$

where X is the predictor, Y is the criterion, b is the slope, and a is the intercept. When the equation is used, a and b are known quantities. A forecasted value for the criterion (Y) can be computed by replacing X with values of the predictor.

The regression equation is developed from the data of a validation study. In addition to the correlation coefficient, a regression equation can be computed for a sample of data on a criterion and predictor. As noted earlier, this equation provides a means of forecasting the criterion from the predictor. For example, monthly sales for a salesperson might be forecasted from scores on the communication exercise. The most accurate forecast might be achieved from a regression equation such as the following:

$$\text{Sales} = \$400 \times \text{Exercise Score} + \$2{,}000$$

In this equation, a is \$2,000 and b is \$400. If a person had an exercise score of 10, his or her sales would be predicted to be \$6,000:

$$\text{Sales} = \$400 \times 10 + \$2{,}000$$
$$\text{Sales} = \$6{,}000$$

If another person had a test score of 5, his or her sales would be predicted to be \$4,000:

$$\text{Sales} = \$400 \times 5 + \$2{,}000$$
$$\text{Sales} = \$4{,}000$$

Obviously, the first person would be preferred because his or her forecasted performance is higher.

A similar procedure is applied when there are two or more predictors. This case involves the use of multiple correlation and multiple regression. Multiple correlation is the correlation between a criterion and two or more predictors simultaneously. The multiple correlation coefficient is indicated by an R. Multiple regression is a statistical technique that provides an equation relating two or more predictors simultaneously to a criterion. The equation can be used to forecast the criterion from scores on the predictors. In many cases, several predictors combined can provide a more accurate forecast of the criterion than any of them alone.

The general form of a multiple regression equation is

$$Y = (b_1 \times X_1) + (b_2 \times X_2) + a$$

for the two-predictor case. In this equation, the Xs are predictors, Y is the criterion, a is the intercept, and the bs are regression coefficients. The coefficients and intercept are computed from sample data. The equation is solved by substituting values of the predictors for the Xs. A forecasted value for the criterion is then computed.

For example, we can combine the scores on the communication exercise with GPA in college. Assume that both of these predictors relate to sales performance. Combined they might provide more-accurate forecasts than either one alone. If each predictor had a correlation of .40 with sales, combined they would likely have a multiple correlation that is greater than .40. The magnitude of the multiple correlation is a function of how strongly each predictor variable correlates with the criterion variable and how strongly the predictor variables correlate with one another. The multiple correlation will have the largest value when the predictor variables are uncorrelated with one another. This would show that combined the predictors are more accurate than either one alone in forecasting the criterion.

A multiple regression analysis would provide an equation that would forecast sales from both the exercise score and the college GPA. The equation could be used to forecast the sales from scores on the two predictors. Suppose that the predictor equation was the following:

$$\text{Sales} = (\$2{,}000 \times \text{GPA}) + (\$1{,}000 \times \text{Exercise}) + \$2{,}000$$

In this equation, a is \$2,000, and the bs are \$2,000 and \$1,000. To use the equation, multiply GPA by \$2,000, and add it to the exercise score multiplied by \$1,000. To this total add \$2,000. The resulting number is an estimate of the person's future monthly sales. If a person had a college GPA of 2.0 and an exercise score of 4, his or her forecasted sales would be \$10,000. A person with a 4.0 college GPA and an exercise score of 10 would be forecasted to have sales of \$20,000.

The magnitude of the relation between the predictors and the criterion determines how accurate the prediction is likely to be. If the predictors correlate strongly with the criterion, the forecasted values for sales are likely to be fairly accurate. If the predictors do not correlate very well with the criterion, the forecasts will not be very accurate. Even when predictors relate to criteria modestly, however, using the scientific approach we have discussed can still result in hiring better-performing employees than using nonscientific approaches.

Every regression equation must be cross-validated to be sure that it continues to make reasonably accurate forecasts. An equation that is generated from a sample of data will make the most accurate predictions possible for that sample. For statistical reasons that are beyond the scope of this book, it is not likely that the same equation will be as accurate when used on a second sample. To perform a cross-validation, the equation generated from one sample of data is applied to a second sample of data. Usually the accuracy of forecasting will be reduced when using the first sample equation on the second sample. If the regression equation yields nonsignificant results when used on a second sample, it should not be used.

An implication of using the regression approach is that a low score on one predictor can be compensated for by a high score on another. The multiple hurdles approach avoids this problem because an applicant must reach the passing score for each predictor. This can be important because a person often must have a reasonable level on every KSAO even if some KSAOs are very high. For example, in selecting a surgeon there are two equally important KSAOs. He or she must have the knowledge of how to operate and the manual skill to do so. A high level of one KSAO cannot overcome a deficiency in the other. Skill with a scalpel is insufficient if the surgeon does not know where to cut. The limitation of the regression approach can be overcome by combining it with the hurdles approach. First, applicants would be screened using the hurdles. A regression equation would then be applied only to those who made it past the hurdles.

Even when validation studies have been conducted, it is far more common for companies to use subjective approaches to combine results of different predictors than to use formal multiple hurdles or regression results, the latter of which is rare in practice. Ganzach, Kluger, and Klayman (2000) conducted a study that compared the subjective approach with multiple regression for the recruitment of Israeli soldiers. They found that regression was superior in forecasting a measure of performance, suggesting there can be advantages to this approach but that a combination of regression and subjective judgment worked best (see the International Research box).

INTERNATIONAL RESEARCH

Although it has been known for a long time that subjective judgment can be less accurate than objective procedures for combining information to make decisions, most organizations use the subjective approach for making hiring decisions. Ganzach, Kluger, and Klayman (2000), in this study of selection in the Israeli Army, wanted to compare these two approaches.

This study was conducted in a field setting in Israel, where military service is compulsory. Participants were 26,197 males who were interviewed prior to being drafted into the army. Each interview took approximately 20 minutes and was conducted by one of 116 highly trained professional interviewers who underwent a 3-month training program. At the end of the interview, the interviewer made ratings on six traits: activity, pride in the service, sociability, responsibility, independence, and promptness. A global rating of expected success in the army of the interviewee was also made. The criterion was the number of disciplinary actions taken against the interviewee during his subsequent 3-year service. Because most participants (83%) had no disciplinary actions taken and few had more than one or two, the criterion was collapsed to two levels: had actions and didn't have actions.

A multiple regression analysis was conducted between the six trait ratings and the criterion, and a correlation was computed between the global rating and the criterion. Results showed that the six trait ratings, combined with a regression equation to maximize prediction, was more accurate than the global ratings, with correlations of .28 versus .23, respectively. In other words, the statistical combination of the individual trait ratings did a better job predicting the subsequent criterion than the human's global judgment. However, the six trait ratings combined with the multiple regression equation did even better when used with the global judgment, with a correlation of .30. This suggested that there can be advantages to combining both approaches to achieve maximum prediction.

Source: From "Making Decisions From an Interview: Expert Measurement and Mechanical Combination," by Y. Ganzach, A. N. Kluger, and N. Klayman, 2000, *Personnel Psychology, 53,* 1–20.

Alternatives to Conducting Validation Studies

Most organizations select employees without going through costly and time-consuming validation studies. Organizations do not always hire enough people to conduct such studies, which can require more than 100 participants to do properly. Other times organizations do not wish to invest the money or time to conduct these studies. For an organization with hundreds of different jobs, it could cost millions of dollars to conduct validation studies for every position.

An alternative approach is to rely on the established validity of selection tools that can be linked to KSAO requirements. With this approach, one conducts a job analysis to determine KSAOs. Established methods to assess each KSAO are then chosen. If the job analysis results indicate that cognitive ability is needed, an existing cognitive ability test can be chosen. This approach relies heavily on existing research findings concerning the validities of existing methods. It does not involve data collection to test for validity of predictors. An organization can often rely on validity generalization results to help guide its choice of selection methods.

It is possible to purchase existing selection devices that have been developed elsewhere. Psychological testing companies have validated tests for sale to organizations. As we discussed in Chapter 5, many tests exist to assess hundreds of different characteristics. It is even possible to hire members of consulting firms to administer all sorts of assessments, including assessment centers, interviews, simulation exercises, and tests. Sometimes it is less expensive for an organization to buy assessment services than to do its own. This is likely to be true with a small company that has few people to assess or a large company that is hiring few people into a particular type of position.

No matter how selection decisions are made, once it is decided whom to hire, procedures must be initiated to get that person to take the job. An organization has many ways to entice a person to join it, including offering fringe benefits and restructuring the job to suit the individual. One procedure that is often used is the realistic job preview, which we discuss next.

► GETTING APPLICANTS TO ACCEPT AND KEEP JOBS OFFERED

The recruitment job is not over when it is decided who will be offered a job. The next step is being sure that the applicants that an organization wishes to hire are interested in accepting the job offer. Installing the most accurate selection system possible is of little value if the applicants who are identified as potentially good employees will not take the job that is offered. Of equal importance is ensuring that individuals who take a job do not quit in a short period of time because they find that they do not like the job.

Convincing an applicant to accept a job involves several strategies. First, it is important for the recruitment process to be a positive one and for the prospective employee to feel he or she has been treated fairly (Hausknecht, Day, & Thomas, 2004). Second, salary and compensation offers should be comparable to those of other organizations for similar jobs in the same area (Chapman, Uggerslev, Carroll, Piasentin, & Jones, 2005). One way to make sure that offers are competitive is to conduct a salary survey to find out what other organizations are paying. This is done by contacting organizations and asking them what they pay for particular positions. Another way to handle compensation is to negotiate salary and other rewards with the potential employee. Many organizations are flexible in their benefits and salaries and may be able to tailor them to the demands of applicants. One such approach is the **cafeteria benefits** program, in which employees are allowed to choose their benefits from a long list of possibilities, such as different types of insurance policies. Organizations can also offer flexibility in the content of jobs so that a potential employee can modify the job to his or her liking.

Third, the behavior of recruiters is an important influence on applicants accepting job offers. Chapman et al. (2005) showed that it is important for recruiters to be personable and provide honest information about the job. Providing a falsely positive view of an organization can result in high turnover as new employees find that conditions are not as favorable as they were presented to be. A person may find that the job is intolerable because of some situation that he or she did not know about at the time the job was accepted. For example, a person may not have been told that the job involved extensive travel during the summer. A person who finds that job conditions are unacceptable will be likely to quit. Recruitment will have to begin again to find a replacement.

The **realistic job preview (RJP)** is used to give job applicants accurate information about the job and the organization. It is most typically accomplished with a brochure or videotaped presentation (Wanous, 1989). A good RJP provides an accurate view of both the favorable and the unfavorable aspects of a job so that a person who accepts a job will do so with accurate and realistic expectations. A person who knows what he or she is going to encounter will be more likely to remain on a job if unfavorable, but anticipated, conditions arise. If conditions exist that a person cannot tolerate, he or she will refuse the job offer. Another person who is willing to accept the situation will be hired and will be more likely to stay on the job.

Research with the RJP has shown benefits but surprisingly not for turnover. Premack and Wanous (1985) conducted a meta-analysis of 21 RJP experiments conducted in organizations. This analysis of the results of these studies indicated that RJPs reduce initial expectations about the job and organization. They also reduce the number of employees who accept job offers by the organization. In addition, RJPs increase job performance and job satisfaction, probably because people who would have been unhappy on a job are screened out before they accept the job. Those who accept the job are likely to have less favorable, but probably more realistic, perceptions of the organization because of the RJP. However, other research has shown that RJPs have little effect on turnover (Meglino, Ravlin, & DeNisi, 2000), suggesting that this might not be the best way to reduce turnover itself, despite other positive results.

INTERNATIONAL RESEARCH

Field experiments are difficult to conduct in organizational settings. This study by Meglino, DeNisi, and Ravlin (1993) is an example of a field experiment that was conducted over a relatively long period of time. Its purpose was to investigate the effects of a realistic job preview (RJP) on the turnover of employees who varied in experience on the job in question. Although many studies have shown the effects of RJPs on turnover, these researchers thought that the effects would differ between experienced and inexperienced employees.

Subjects were applicants for the job of correctional officer who were randomly assigned either to receive or not to receive the RJP. The subjects were further divided into two groups depending on their prior experience in a similar job. Data were collected concerning whether or not each applicant took the job and how long each applicant stayed on the job. Thus, there were two dependent variables—job acceptance and job survival.

The results showed that the impact of the RJP was different for the experienced and inexperienced applicant groups. The experienced applicants were less likely to take the job if they were exposed to the RJP. They were more likely to quit the job during a 3- to 9-month probationary period, and they were less likely to quit after the probationary period if they were given the RJP. The inexperienced applicants were more likely to accept the job after seeing the RJP. The RJP had no significant effect on their turnover rate. These results show that the effects of the RJP might not be the same on everyone. Perhaps the RJP was more meaningful to experienced applicants who had a context in which to interpret the information. They knew that a particular feature of the job would be unpleasant, even though it might not initially seem to be so. Results also show that the effects can differ over time. Positive effects on turnover might not occur immediately.

Overall, it has been found that RJPs can be an effective and relatively inexpensive way of decreasing unwanted employee turnover. This study shows that organizations should consider carefully the characteristics of applicants when deciding to implement a preview because they might not reduce turnover for experienced employees.

Source: From "Effects of Previous Job Exposure and Subsequent Job Status on the Functioning of a Realistic Job Preview," by B. M. Meglino, A. S. DeNisi, and E. C. Ravlin, 1993, *Personnel Psychology, 46*, 803–822.

The surprising lack of effects of an RJP on turnover might be explained by the complicating effect of job experience. Meglino, DeNisi, and Ravlin (1993) conducted a field experiment in which applicants for a correctional officer position were assigned to either an RJP or a control condition without an RJP. Applicants in each group were classified according to prior experience as a correctional officer. The results showed that the impact of the RJP on turnover was different for the experienced and inexperienced applicant groups (see the International Research box). These results show that the effects of the RJP might not be the same on everyone, although in general RJPs have been shown to have positive effects.

▶ THE UTILITY OF SCIENTIFIC SELECTION

Perhaps the most important question to ask about the scientific approach to employee selection concerns its utility or value. What is the payoff to an organization for using this difficult and time-consuming approach to selection? The answer is not easy to determine. Research has shown that scientific selection can result in the hiring of better employees, but its effects on overall organizational functioning are not as easy to determine. This is because individual units of an organization do not always use selection systems as they were designed (Van Iddekinge, Ferris, Perrewe, Perryman, Blass, & Heetderks, 2009). The study of these effects is called **utility analysis**. I/O psychologists have developed mathematical procedures for conducting utility analyses of selection procedures. In this section, we first discuss in general how selection devices can result in the hiring of better employees. We then consider how utility analysis has been used to show how these selection procedures can have important effects on organizational functioning.

How Valid Selection Devices Work

An understanding of utility analysis must begin with an understanding of how selection devices work. Three basic concepts form the foundation of this discussion:

Baserate

Selection ratio

Validity

These three factors determine the extent to which scientific selection will result in hiring better-performing employees. If it does so, then we must consider the cost of using the selection device in determining its utility.

Baserate

The **baserate** is the percentage of applicants who would be successful on the job if all of them were hired. For some jobs, most applicants would be capable of performing well, making the baserate close to 100%. For other jobs, relatively few applicants would be successful, making the baserate close to 0%. A baserate of 50% results in the maximum utility because it offers the most room for improvement in accuracy of forecasting. Suppose you know the baserate from prior experience with employees on a job. If 50% have been successful in the past, the best accuracy rate you could expect by guessing which applicants would be successful is 50%. If you guessed that every applicant would be successful or unsuccessful, you would expect to be correct half the time. Using a predictor, you could improve your accuracy up to 100%. This would represent a difference of 50% in accuracy between the baserate and your predictor.

If you know that the baserate is less or more than 50%, you can achieve better than 50% accuracy of forecasting by guessing that every applicant will be successful (if the baserate is greater than 50%) or not successful (if the baserate is less than 50%). For example, a 60% baserate would give about 60% accuracy if you guess that everyone will be successful. A baserate of 40% would give about 60% accuracy if you guess that everyone will be unsuccessful (40% of people successful means that 60% are not successful). In both cases, the biggest possible gain in forecasting accuracy is from 60% to 100%.

The more the baserate differs from 50% in either direction (the majority of employees are successful or not successful), the smaller is the room for improvement if we had perfect forecasting. Thus all baserates that are greater or less than 50% give less room for gain than 50%.

Selection Ratio

The **selection ratio** is the proportion of job applicants that an organization must hire. It is calculated as the number of positions to fill divided by the number of applicants.

Some organizations find that they have many applicants for each vacant position. Their selection ratio will be low. Other organizations find that they have few applicants for each vacant position. Their selection ratio will be high. For example, if there are 100 job applicants for each job, the selection ratio will be $^1/_{100}$. If there are two applicants for each position, the selection ratio will be $^1/_2$. Low selection ratios produce the greatest utility because they allow an organization to be more selective in whom it hires for each position. In the long run, an organization can hire better people when there are many applicants from which to choose.

Validity

The validity of a selection device is the magnitude of correlation between it and the criterion. The larger the correlation is, the more accurately the criterion can be forecasted by the selection device. The more accurate the forecast of the criterion is, the greater is the utility because utility is based in part on increasing the success rate over the baserate.

How Valid Predictors Increase Success Rates

Figure 6.4 illustrates how baserate, selection ratio, and validity combine to increase the success rate of those hired. The figure graphs the criterion and predictor scores for a fictitious sample of 20 job applicants. The horizontal axis represents scores on the predictor variable, and the vertical axis represents scores on the criterion variable of job performance. The individual job applicants are represented by the points on the graph. Each point shows the criterion and predictor score for an applicant.

The baserate is represented by the horizontal line across the middle of the graph. Cases above the line are in the successful range on the criterion, and cases below the line are in the unsuccessful range. The cutoff score on the predictor is represented by the vertical line running down the center of the graph. With a multiple hurdle approach, a cutoff score is chosen to determine who is eligible to be hired and who is not. In this case, applicants who score higher than the cutoff on the predictor (right side of vertical

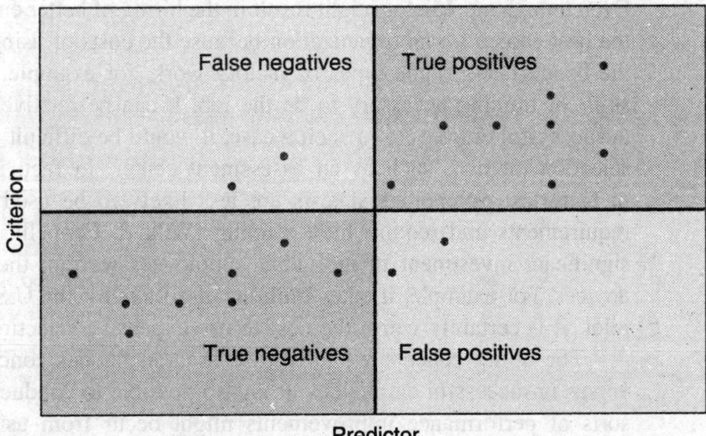

Figure 6.4 How a valid selection device increases the accuracy of selection.

line) are hired, and applicants who score lower than the cutoff on the predictor (left side of vertical line) are not hired. In the figure, half of the applicants had predictor scores that were higher than the cutoff.

The graph is divided into four quadrants. The upper right quadrant contains applicants who would be hired if the predictor is used and who would be successful on the job. They are referred to as *true positives*. The lower right quadrant contains people who would be hired if the predictor is used but who would be unsuccessful on the job. They are the *false positives*. The lower left quadrant contains people who would not be hired if the predictor is used and who would not be successful on the job. They are the *true negatives*. Finally, the upper left quadrant contains applicants who would not be hired if the predictor is used but who would be successful on the job. They are the *false negatives*. There are eight true negatives and eight true positives, and there are two false negatives and two false positives.

If a predictor is valid, the points on the graph will be in the shape of an ellipse. This will produce a more accurate prediction over the baserate if a cutoff score on a predictor is used to choose employees. The baserate in Figure 6.4 is 50%, meaning that half of the cases will be successful on the job if all are hired. If the predictor scores are used with the cutoff shown in the graph, eight people will be successful and two will not be. This improves the accuracy of prediction from the 50% baserate to 80%. This gain is a reflection of the potential utility of selection and can be substantial when conditions are favorable. As noted earlier in this discussion, the best situation occurs when the baserate is 50% and the selection ratio is low. The greater the validity is, the greater the potential utility of scientific selection will be.

So far we have seen how valid predictors can help identify those individuals who will be successful on the job. This is an important part of utility, but it is not the only part. The other important issue concerns the cost of using the selection device and the cost of poor selection. It is the gain in using the selection system versus the cost that determines utility, as we will see next.

Computing the Utility of Scientific Selection

Even though a predictor might result in the hiring of better employees, it is not necessarily the best choice for an organization because the costs of using the predictor might exceed the benefits. For some types of factory work, for example, there is little in the way of skills or training necessary to do the job. It can be relatively inexpensive to replace an unsuccessful employee. In such a case, it would be difficult to justify using an expensive selection method, such as an assessment center. In fact, it has been found that even in factories, psychological tests are less likely to be used in jobs that have few skill requirements and require little training (Wilk & Cappelli, 2003). Jobs that result in a significant investment in individual employees warrant the use of expensive selection devices. For example, it takes millions of dollars for the U.S. Air Force to train a fighter pilot. It is certainly worth the cost to use expensive selection procedures in this case.

The utility concept we have discussed so far has concerned identifying successful versus unsuccessful employees. It is also possible to conduct utility analyses to see what sorts of performance improvements might occur from using a valid selection device to choose employees. If a selection device is valid, we would expect that on average individuals chosen with it will have better job performance. Several studies have shown that the highest performers can be up to 16 times more productive than the lowest performers on jobs with countable output, such as factory work (Campbell, Gasser, & Oswald, 1996). If we can compute the monetary value of that performance gain, we can compute the utility of using a selection device.

Several approaches have been suggested to conduct this sort of utility analysis (e.g., Raju, Burke, & Normand, 1990). Each is based on mathematical equations that provide estimates of monetary gain from using a selection device. The various approaches make their own assumptions and have their own variation on the equations. Each requires finding the relation between performance and monetary gain. For some jobs, this can be straightforward. For example, the performance of a salesperson can be translated into the monetary value of sales made. For other jobs, the translation is not so easy. How would you estimate the monetary value for a teacher's performance? It is possible to do so, usually by asking SMEs to make subjective judgments.

There has been much debate in the I/O field about the best approach to utility analysis. Some of the discussion has concerned how people make judgments about the monetary value of job performance (Becker & Huselid, 1992). These authors have expressed concern that people are not necessarily accurate in their judgments, making utility estimates inaccurate. Other authors have noted that utility analyses have failed to consider all the major factors involved in utility (Russell, Colella, & Bobko, 1993), resulting in somewhat inflated estimates of gains. As but one example, Boudreau (1983) discussed how increased profits from a more productive workforce should be adjusted for taxes to yield the real bottom-line utility estimate.

Although it can be challenging to compute the monetary gain that scientific selection can provide to organizations, research has shown that it can be considerable. Van Iddekinge et al. (2009) studied the effects of using a scientific selection system on the financial performance of individual restaurants in a fast-food organization. Their results showed that units that used the company's selection system had more satisfied customers and were more profitable than units that did not.

The idea of computing utility is not limited to employee selection. Landy, Farr, and Jacobs (1982) suggested that the approach could be used to estimate the monetary gain of other organizational practices, such as giving employees job performance feedback. If you can estimate the gain in performance from such a procedure, you can compute the utility in terms of monetary gain. Such analyses would share the same limitations as the utility analyses used for employee selection.

One further issue should be noted concerning the use of utility analysis. Such mathematical procedures provide a theoretical estimate of how much gain in performance would occur if more capable people were hired. Although in theory more capable people should perform better, in practice, the expected gains may never occur. Organizations are complex social systems that affect people's behavior in a variety of ways. Job performance can be both enhanced and inhibited by factors both internal and external to organizations. As we will see throughout the remainder of this book, being able to perform does not mean that the organizational conditions and constraints will allow it. A capable person might not perform well because the equipment or support to do so is not available. Even a highly talented machinist will be unproductive if his or her machine is defective and keeps breaking. Nevertheless, utility analysis is valuable because it shows that selection procedures can be of benefit to organizations.

▶ INTERNATIONAL DIFFERENCES IN SELECTION PRACTICES

Selection practices vary greatly among organizations or even branches of the same organization in different countries. Ryan, McFarland, Baron, and Page (1999) surveyed managers from 959 organizations in 20 countries concerning their selection practices and in particular the selection devices they used. The interview, former employer reference check, and application form were most popular and were used universally. This was not true when it came to psychological tests. Although the most popular around the world were personality and cognitive ability tests, there was considerable difference in how much they were used from country to country. Biographical inventories and interviews were most popular in Greece, whereas tests were most popular in Belgium and Spain. Zibarras and Woods (2010) surveyed 579 U.K. organizations about their selection practices and contrasted them to U.S. organizations. American companies were more likely to use background checks, biographical inventories, unstructured interviews, and work samples and less likely to use ability tests.

Newell and Tansley (2001) noted that there were differences in selection practices across countries, even where job requirements and situations were similar, and furthermore that often less-valid procedures were preferred over more-valid ones. They suggested several societal factors that account for this. First, before selection procedures can be used, managers have to know about them. Until fairly recently, communication among managers across national borders was limited, and so information about a better selection approach discovered in one place wouldn't always be known in another. Although the internet has reduced the limitations of physical distance and national boundary, there are still language barriers in many places. Eleftheriou and Robertson (1999), in their survey of selection practices among Greek companies, found that cost and lack of familiarity were reasons psychological tests were not used more frequently. Second, laws and regulations influence selection procedures. In the United States, antidiscrimination laws have shaped how selection must be done (see the following section on legal issues). In many European countries, such as Germany and Sweden, unions are quite powerful, and they influence selection procedures much more than in the United States. Third, economic factors put limits on which approaches are done. In less wealthy countries, expensive assessments are not an option. Finally, there are culture differences in values and what is considered important. For example, in some countries achievement is more important than symbols of status. In the former, the college GPA would be considered more important than the status of the institution attended, but the opposite might be true in the latter.

▶ LEGAL ISSUES

Throughout the industrialized world, it is becoming an accepted value that organizations should not be discriminatory in their practices that affect employees, such as hiring and promotion. These countries have laws that protect the rights of people from discriminatory actions by organizations. The particular groups of people who are protected by these laws vary from country to country. Most offer protection to women, and many offer protection to Blacks. A group is likely to be protected by law if it represents a reasonably large minority of a country and if members of that groups have been victims of discrimination. Thus in countries with large Black minorities, Blacks are likely to be offered protection. In countries with few Blacks, this protection might not be found in the law.

In this section, we discuss the legal issues involved in employee selection both inside and outside the United States. Although the United States was a leader in the development of legal protection from discrimination, many countries have not been far behind in this area, and some have pulled ahead in some ways. This discussion offers a contrast between the handling of the problem of discrimination in the United States and in other countries.

Legal Selection in the United States

Prior to 1964 in the United States, discrimination against ethnic minorities and women was widespread for many jobs, particularly the most desirable and highest-paying ones. In 1964, the Civil Rights Act changed the way organizations selected employees because it expanded legal protections from discrimination and provided a mechanism to enforce it. Legislation in the following years has broadened the legal protection to groups that were not covered by the Civil Rights Act of 1964. Discrimination in hiring and other areas of employment has not been eliminated completely in the United States, with over 146,000 federal and state discrimination complaints being filed in 2005 alone (Goldman, Gutek, Stein, & Lewis, 2006). Nevertheless, tremendous progress has been made over the past few decades.

The Civil Rights Act of 1964 made it illegal to discriminate against minorities and other groups in employment and other areas of life in U.S. society. Subsequent legislation and Supreme Court cases have produced a complex and confusing array of legal requirements for employee selection. The Civil Rights Act of 1991 was an attempt to rectify some of the confusion produced by years of sometimes conflicting Supreme Court decisions. Table 6.3 lists six of the most significant Supreme Court cases and the major outcome of each. Although the underlying principles of nondiscrimination are simple, implementing a selection system that meets legal requirements is complicated.

TABLE 6.3 Six Significant U.S. Supreme Court Discrimination Cases and Their Outcomes

Case	Outcome
Griggs v. Duke Power (1971)	Selection methods that have adverse impact must be valid.
Rowe v. General Motors (1972)	Legal protection against discrimination holds for performance appraisals.
Albemarle Paper Company v. Moody (1975)	Organizations must use rigorous validation procedures.
Baake v. Regents of the University of California (1978)	Discrimination laws protect everyone, and quotas for admission to graduate school are illegal.
Wards Cove Packing Company v. Atonio (1987)	This case made it more difficult for individuals to win discrimination cases. It was an impetus for the Civil Rights Act of 1991.
Price Waterhouse v. Hopkins (1988)	Promotions cannot be based on gender stereotyping (e.g., requiring a female employee to act or look more feminine).

TABLE 6.4 Civil Rights Legislation in the United States Protecting Various Groups

Legislation	Covers
Civil Rights Act of 1964	Gender, national origin, race, religion
Age Discrimination Act of 1967 (Amended 1968)	Age
Pregnancy Discrimination Act of 1978	Pregnancy
Americans With Disabilities Act of 1990	Mental and physical disabilities

This is due in part to the changing requirements of the Congress and Supreme Court and in part to the technical complexities in employee selection systems.

The first issue that we address is the concept of *protected classes*. Although the law states that discrimination against anyone is illegal, certain groups of people have been the target of protection under the law. These groups are called **protected classes** and are comprised of people who have been the target of discrimination in the past. African Americans, Hispanics, Native Americans, and women all represent protected classes. Table 6.4 lists the major federal discrimination laws and the specific groups each covers. At the present time, it is illegal to discriminate on the basis of:

Age	Color
Disability	Gender
National origin	Race
Religion	

It is conceivable that other groups will become protected classes in the future, and individual states are free to offer protection to additional groups not covered by U.S. law. For example, sexual orientation is included in some states, and some organizations have extended this protection even though it is not mandated by the law.

Uniform Guidelines on Employee Selection

In 1978, the U.S. government produced a set of guidelines for legal selection called the **Uniform Guidelines on Employee Selection Procedures** (1978, August 25). Although originally intended to apply to government agencies, the guidelines were eventually adopted as acceptable legal practices for all organizations. The guidelines define several important concepts for selection and provide a procedure by which organizations can conduct legal selection. They provide more than just a statement of legal requirements. They outline the proper way to develop a valid employee selection system, which provides an additional advantage to an organization that follows them.

One of the most important concepts embodied in the Uniform Guidelines is **adverse impact**, which refers to the impact of a given selection practice on a protected class. It is usually defined in terms of selection ratios of the protected class and a comparison group (e.g., White males). Adverse impact occurs when the **four-fifths rule** is violated, meaning that the selection ratio for the protected class is less than 80%, or four-fifths, of that of the comparison group (Roth, Bobko, & Switzer, 2006). For example, suppose that 60% of male applicants were offered a job. Female applicants would experience adverse impact if fewer than 48% of them (four-fifths of 60%) were offered a job (Table 6.5). This four-fifths rule recognizes that an equal number of applicants from

TABLE 6.5 Applying the Four-Fifths Rule for Adverse Impact Against Women

Case 1: No Adverse Impact Against Women

Gender	Number of Applicants	Number Hired	Percent Hired	4/5ths Threshold
Men	100	60	60%	
Women	80	40	50%	48%

There is no adverse impact because 50% is above the 48% threshold.

Case 2: Adverse Impact Against Women

Gender	Number of Applicants	Number Hired	Percent Hired	4/5ths Threshold
Men	100	60	60%	
Women	80	20	25%	48%

There is adverse impact against women because 25% is below the 48% threshold.

Note: In the first case, 60% of male applicants and 50% of female applicants were hired. Because 50% is more than 4/5ths of 60%, there is no adverse impact against women. In the second case, 60% of male applicants but only 25% of female applicants were hired. Because 25% is less than 4/5ths of 60%, there is adverse impact against women.

every possible group is unlikely. Of importance here is the percentage of applicants who are hired, not the actual numbers.

Adverse impact is a threshold for possible discrimination in selection. It is not necessarily illegal to use a selection device that has adverse impact on a protected class.

Civil rights legislation says that each of these people should have an equal opportunity to be hired for a job. (© *Neustockimages/iStockphoto*)

If a selection device or procedure has adverse impact, there are further tests to decide its legality. To be legal, a selection device must be job relevant. This means that it assesses a KSAO that is necessary for job success. One way to establish job relevance is by showing that a selection device is a valid predictor of job performance.

If selection practices produce adverse impact, an organization must be ready to defend itself from legal challenges. Tests of cognitive ability and physical strength are both likely to have adverse impact on some groups. Their use can be justified only if a job analysis shows that these attributes are necessary KSAOs for the job and if the tests are shown to be valid. An organization that fails to do both a job analysis and to use valid selection methods risks using procedures that are unfair to the adversely affected groups. Although it is legal to require that those who are hired have the required KSAOs to do a job, it is illegal to require KSAOs that are not necessary for success on the job.

Essential Functions and Reasonable Accommodation

The 1990 Americans With Disabilities Act (ADA) extended legal protection from discrimination to people with disabilities. Two concepts came from this legislation. **Essential functions**, as we discussed in Chapter 3, refer to KSAOs that are an important part of the job. For example, typing is an essential function for a secretary, but lifting heavy objects is not. It can be illegal to deny a job to a person with a disability based on a KSAO that relates only to nonessential functions. The idea is that rarely done tasks, such as lifting a heavy object, that require a KSAO that an otherwise competent employee does not have can be done by someone else.

The second concept is **reasonable accommodation** for an employee with a disability. An organization must make allowances that are feasible to enable a person with a disability to perform the job. For example, an organization should not fail to hire someone in a wheelchair just because he or she has to climb two steps to get into the building for work. A minor and reasonable accommodation would be to provide a ramp so the person can access the building without much difficulty and having to climb the stairs. Providing help in doing nonessential functions for a job can be another reasonable accommodation. It is not yet clear what other actions are reasonable and what actions to help a worker with a disability are too difficult or expensive for an organization. Undoubtedly, future court cases will determine how far organizations must go to make reasonable accommodations for employees with disabilities.

Affirmative Action

Affirmative action consists of a variety of practices that organizations use to increase the number of protected class members in targeted jobs. Its purpose is to address the lingering effects of past discrimination in hiring by allowing certain groups to catch up in acquiring jobs that were at one time unavailable to them. Kravitz (2008) distinguished between programs designed to increase the number of minority applicants and those that give preferential treatment to minorities in job offers. The former type of opportunity enhancement program increases the number of minority applicants by engaging in extra recruitment efforts (e.g., advertising in media that target minorities) or by offering training so more minorities have the KSAOs required for a job. Affirmative action is not a quota system and does not require the hiring of anyone without the necessary KSAOs. The U.S. Supreme Court has consistently ruled against entities using such practices except in extraordinary circumstances (Kravitz, Harrison, Turner, Levine, Chaves, Brannick, Denning, Russell, & Conard, 1997), for example, an organization refused to comply with legal selection practices and blatantly discriminates in their hiring. Nevertheless, the Court also let stand the California law that prohibited most forms of preferential treatment. This does not mean, however, that other forms of affirmative action have been eliminated.

Organizations that have more than 50 employees and government contracts exceeding $50,000 are required by executive order to have an affirmative action program. This requirement affects most colleges and universities whose faculties have government research grants. For most other organizations, this activity is voluntary, although some employers that have been caught using discriminatory practices have been ordered or strongly encouraged by a court to adopt an affirmative action program to end their illegal practices. Most large organizations in the United States practice some form of affirmative action, although some do so more rigorously than others. The widespread practice can be seen in the prominently displayed notice that an employer is an "Affirmative Action" employer, common on the stationery of many organizations and most universities.

The intent of an affirmative action program is to remedy the widespread problem of discrimination. Such programs should be introduced carefully because they can have unintended detrimental effects on the groups they are designed to help. Heilman and her colleagues have found that women who are given preferential treatment in hiring can have a negative view of themselves and other women (Heilman, Kaplow, Amato, & Stathatos, 1993), and such negative views can affect self-confidence (Heilman & Alcott, 2001). This effect has been found with minority candidates as well (Evans, 2003). Furthermore, a person who is hired under affirmative action is likely to be seen as incompetent, and that stigma of affirmative action is difficult to overcome in the minds of coworkers (Heilman, Battle, Keller, & Lee, 1998). Research has also shown adverse effects on nonbeneficiaries when preferential treatment has been perceived as unfair (e.g., as reverse discrimination) (Heilman, McCullough, & Gilbert, 1996).

Kravitz (2008) argued that the problems with and debates over affirmative action have all concerned preferential treatment. Programs concerned with other aspects of affirmative action have shown promise and do not share the same drawbacks. He suggested that affirmative action programs should focus on both increasing the number of minority applicants and retaining minority employees. Attracting applicants can be accomplished by doing a better job marketing the organization to minority applicants and by increasing the pool of minorities with the necessary KSAOs through educational programs. Retention can be accomplished with programs that improve the working environment and experiences for minorities—for example, by offering mentoring and training and by reducing negative experiences, such as ethnic bullying. Kravitz notes that to be effective, these programs should be available to everyone, and not just minorities. For example, a program to decrease incivility should focus on incivility toward everyone, and not just minorities. The advantage of being inclusive with such programs is that they improve working experiences for everyone, and not just minorities.

Legal Selection Outside the United States

Many countries throughout the industrialized world have discrimination laws similar to those in the United States. Some countries are as vigorous as the United States in enforcing antidiscrimination laws (e.g., Canada and South Africa), whereas others are more lax (e.g., Australia and England). Although the United States may have taken the lead, other countries give employees even more protection and extend protection to additional groups not specifically mentioned in U.S. law. How different countries approach their discrimination problems depends on the nature of those problems and their societies. In 1995, the United Kingdom instituted the Disability Discrimination Act, which is much like the ADA in the United States. As in the United States, there is resistance by employers, especially those who have negative attitudes about persons with disabilities and who have little knowledge of what the law actually requires (Jackson, Furnham, & Willen, 2000).

Canada is much like the United States in terms of laws and vigor of enforcement, although Canada also disallows discrimination based on sexual preference, which the United States does not. To avoid legal problems, organizations in Canada need to follow practices to those they would follow in the United States. Ireland is a more homogeneous society than Canada or the United States, having fewer minority groups of sufficient size to push for legal protection. In Ireland, discrimination on the basis of gender or marital status is illegal, but the law is silent about Blacks or other minority groups (Federation of Irish Employers, 1991).

The countries mentioned here, as well as the remainder of at least the industrialized world, have endorsed the idea that employee selection should be based on the job-relevant attributes of people. With this approach, the person hired is the person who can best do the job. This will eliminate unfairness in selection that results from discriminatory practices. It should also help organizations enhance their effectiveness by hiring the best-qualified people, regardless of age, color, disability, gender, national origin, race, religion, sexual preference, or other personal characteristic that is irrelevant for job success.

▶ CHAPTER SUMMARY

One of the most important functions of an organization is the recruitment and selection of new employees. To remain effective, an organization must have a supply of skilled people with the necessary attributes or KSAOs to do the job. Acquiring such people involves a four-step procedure:

Planning the need for new employees

Getting appropriate people to apply for positions (recruitment)

Deciding who to hire (selection)

Getting the selected people to take the jobs

Planning the need for new employees requires the use of forecasting methods. This involves comparing the need for people with particular KSAOs with the number of such people who might be available in the area. Future planning for organizational changes and expansions must consider the availability of people to fill the necessary positions. Failure to consider these issues can result in the inability to find the people necessary to carry out an important organizational function.

Getting people to apply for jobs can be a difficult task if there is a shortage of qualified people. The problem is more often one of getting the right people to apply, because there can be a surplus of people with certain skills and a shortage of people with others. There are a number of ways that organizations acquire applicants, including advertising, using recruiters, and using web-based services.

Scientific selection involves the use of selection devices that have been shown to predict job performance. To develop a system of effective or valid selection devices involves a five-step procedure: The KSAOs are identified with a job analysis, the criteria are chosen, the potential predictors are chosen, the predictors are validated with a research study, and finally, the predictors are cross-validated with a second sample or study.

Once an organization has decided whom to hire, it must convince the person to take the job. To do so, an organization must be sure that it offers rewards that are equivalent to those offered by other organizations. One procedure that has been used to ensure a better match between a person and a job is the realistic job preview (RJP), which provides accurate information about the job that allows an applicant to make an informed decision about accepting a job offer.

Utility analysis is used to determine the benefits of using a predictor to hire people. These analyses are based on mathematical formulas that require an estimate of the monetary value of good job performance. There have been disagreements among researchers about the best way to conduct utility analysis. Nevertheless, the results of utility analyses have shown that scientific selection can have substantial benefits for organizations.

Employee selection is not only a scientific process; it is also a legal process. Most industrialized countries have laws against discriminatory selection practices. In the United States, it is illegal to discriminate on the basis of age, color, disability, gender, national origin, race, or religion. To avoid legal problems, an organization must base selection decisions on job-relevant factors.

I/O PSYCHOLOGY IN PRACTICE

(*Courtesy of Anna Erickson*)

This case concerns the development of an unusual assessment device to measure the artistic ability of employees. It was carried out by Dr. Anna Erickson, who was an I/O psychologist for SBC Communications Inc., which owns several telephone companies, including Pacific Bell and Southwestern Bell Inc. Dr. Erickson received her Ph.D. in I/O psychology in 1995 from Iowa State University. At the time of this project, her role in the company was to do selection research, although she also has done projects in the areas of job analysis, performance appraisal, planning for future employee needs, and surveys of employee opinions. At the present time, she is Director of Marketing Research and is responsible for conducting studies of customer preferences for and reactions to telephone company products and services, such as call waiting and caller ID. This is not an unusual job for an I/O psychologist, for the methods and techniques are much the same as those for more traditional I/O work discussed in this book.

One type of employee hired by the telephone company is a yellow page artist who sketches ads for company customers. The company decided to expand the advertising services, which requires a higher level of artistic talent than is necessary for ad sketches. Supervisors of the ad artists were asked to recommend individuals for the more artistic jobs, but this procedure led to widespread controversy and a union grievance over favoritism. Clearly a new procedure had to be found that would be seen as fair to the employees, while providing a valid means of choosing good artists.

Dr. Erickson was asked to solve this problem, but unfortunately no existing assessments for artists could be found. She would have to invent a new assessment device, while at the same time gaining the support of the employees. To accomplish this objective, she put together a task force of employees and managers. At the same time, she studied the research literature on creativity and discovered that, despite the seemingly subjective nature of art, experts show a high degree of interrater agreement when evaluating it. This gave her the idea of developing an assessment center in which raters would be faculty members from a well-known university art department.

The first step in developing the center was to conduct a job analysis to identify KSAOs for the job. Results showed that there were two important components to assess. First, the artist had to deal with customers, and second, he or she had to do the creative work. The customer service part was assessed with a structured interview. The creative part was assessed by having experts rate the quality of a portfolio the person submitted and the performance of the person in a simulation. All ratings were done blind, with the rater not knowing whose work was being assessed.

The task force was unanimous in approving this assessment procedure. It accomplished the goal of settling the union grievance. Dr. Erickson conducted a validation study of the assessment center and found it predicted very well professor ratings of their art students' employability. Those students who were rated most capable and employable did best in the assessment center. It is now being used for placement and selection in the company. This case illustrates how often employees perceive effective selection as fair selection.

Discussion Questions

1. Why was it important to have employee acceptance of the new assessment center?
2. Do you think supervisor nomination was an unfair way to decide who got the jobs?
3. How else could this assessment center be validated other than with the procedure used?
4. Can you think of other ways to measure artistic creativity?

LEARNING BY DOING

Job Market for an Occupation

Go to the O*NET website, http://online.onetcenter.org, and then go to "Find Occupation." From the top, enter an occupation and you will get a summary for it. Go to the bottom where it shows "Wages & Employment Trends." Choose a state and hit the GO button. Write a brief report that compares your state with the United States in terms of wages and growth in the number of people needed.

How Companies Approach Minority Hiring

Choose a large company (e.g., a Fortune 500 company like General Motors or Verizon) and go to its website. Search for evidence and write a report listing ways in which it encourages minorities to apply and values diversity in its workforce.

CHAPTER 7

Training

CHAPTER 7 OUTLINE

If you accept a job with a large organization, it is almost certain that you will go through some sort of formal training program. Even people with college degrees need additional instruction in order to do most jobs. Even simple jobs require training. For example, every employee at a McDonald's restaurant gets trained. The person who makes French fries is taught the proper way to do the job. A restaurant manager receives hundreds of hours of training, much of it in a classroom setting. There is much to learn to be able to do most jobs well. Future trends suggest that the need for training will increase in most jobs as they become more and more technically oriented.

Training is one of the major human resource activities of both large and small organizations in both the private and the public (government) sectors throughout the world. It is a necessary activity for both new and experienced employees. New employees must learn how to do their jobs, whereas experienced employees must learn to keep up with job changes and how to improve their performance. In many organizations, a person will not be considered for a promotion until certain training has been completed and certain skills mastered. Learning in many jobs is a lifelong process that does not stop with a certain level of education.

Five steps are required for effective organizational training programs, as shown in Figure 7.1. The first step of a training program is to conduct a *needs assessment* study in order to determine who needs training and what kind of training is needed. The second step is to set objectives so that it will be clear what the training should accomplish. The third step is to design the training program. The fourth step is to deliver the training to those employees designated by the needs assessment. The final step is to evaluate the training to be certain that it reached its objectives. If the training was ineffective, the process should continue until an effective program is achieved. Each step should be based on the one that precedes it.

In this chapter, we discuss all five steps in the training process. All but the delivery step fall within the domain of I/O psychology. Most training is conducted by professional trainers who specialize in its delivery. I/O psychologists are often behind the scenes, helping to design the training that others will actually deliver. Most of the training conducted in organizations, however, does not involve I/O psychologists.

Objectives: The student who studies this chapter should be able to:

- List the steps involved in developing and implementing a training program in an organization.
- Describe how needs assessment is conducted.
- Explain the various factors that affect learning and transfer of training.
- Discuss the various training methods, including their advantages.
- Discuss how training is evaluated.

NEEDS ASSESSMENT

A needs assessment is conducted to determine which employees need training and what the content of their training should be (Arthur, Bennett, Edens, & Bell, 2003). It is too often the case that training resources are wasted by training the wrong people or teaching the wrong content. A needs assessment can ensure that training resources are wisely spent on areas in which there is a demonstrated training need.

Figure 7.1 Five steps to developing an effective training program.

According to Goldstein (1993), needs assessment should focus on three levels: organization, job, and person. The *organization level* is concerned with the objectives of the organization and how they are addressed by the performance of employees. An analysis of the organization's objectives can offer hints about the training that is needed. For example, if an organization has the goal of minimizing injuries, it would seem reasonable to train employees in principles of workplace safety. If the goal is to maximize productivity, training would involve principles of production efficiency.

The *job level* is concerned with the nature of tasks involved in each job. A job analysis can be used to identify the major tasks and then the necessary KSAOs for each task. From the list of KSAOs, a series of training needs can be specified. A police officer, for example, must have knowledge of legal arrest procedures. This would be a rather obvious area in which training would be provided.

The *person level* is concerned with how well job applicants or present employees are able to do job tasks. In other words, it assesses the KSAO levels of people rather than jobs. A comparison of the KSAOs of jobs and individual employees suggests the areas of greatest potential training need. An employee development plan can be created for each employee both to remedy areas of deficiency in knowledge and skill and to enhance knowledge and skill that would allow the employee to take on additional responsibilities or be promoted.

So far we have discussed needs assessment from the perspective of what should be included in an organization's training program. This approach, however, says nothing about the content of a training program that might already be in use. Ford and Wroten (1984) developed a procedure for determining the extent to which a training program meets training needs. It is somewhat like a job analysis, except that the training is analyzed rather than the job. To conduct such an analysis, SMEs review the content of the training program and compile a list of the KSAOs that are addressed. A separate group of SMEs reviews the KSAO list and rates the importance of each one to the job in question. This procedure can identify how well the program components match the training needs for the job. Programs can be adopted or modified on the basis of this procedure.

Despite the importance of needs assessment, organizations do not often use it. A survey of 1,000 large private companies in the United States found that only 27% use some sort of needs assessment before conducting training of their management-level people (Saari, Johnson, McLaughlin, & Zimmerle, 1988). Too often training resources are wasted because the needs assessment that might have redirected that effort was never performed. A well-conducted needs assessment can help organizations make the most of their training resources.

▶ OBJECTIVES

One of the most important steps in developing a training program is setting objectives. Unless you are clear about the purpose of training, it is difficult to design a training program to achieve it. Part of this step is to define the criteria for training success. The objectives of training are based on criteria and should include a statement of what a trainee should be able to do or know after training. The training criterion is a statement of how achievement of the training objective can be assessed. The training objective of acquiring knowledge, for example, can be assessed by seeing if trainees can meet a criterion of achieving a cutoff score on a knowledge test.

Criteria serve as the basis for the design of organizational training. Once we know what the training criterion is, we can design appropriate training to achieve it. Criteria also serve as the standards against which training programs can be evaluated, which we discuss in the section on training evaluation. Training objectives should be based on the results of the needs assessment.

▶ TRAINING DESIGN

Most organizational training is conducted with the expectation that employees will apply what they have learned on the job. This is called **transfer of training**. Transfer is affected by a number of factors in both the job environment and the training itself, and there is no guarantee that training will always transfer (Taylor, Russ-Eft, & Taylor, 2009). Individual differences in characteristics among trainees also are an important consideration in whether or not training will transfer. Figure 7.2 is a model of transfer developed by Baldwin and Ford (1988). Their model describes how features of the training design can affect how well trainees learn and in turn how well the training transfers to the job. They also noted that individual differences among trainees and characteristics of the work environment are important influences.

In this section, we discuss the training design factors that affect both learning and transfer. In addition, we cover eight popular techniques used to deliver training. Training can be done in a variety of ways, from the relatively passive lecture to the very involving simulation. In the former case, the trainee listens to a presentation, whereas in the latter case he or she gets to try out the new skill. Each of the eight methods is useful in some training situations.

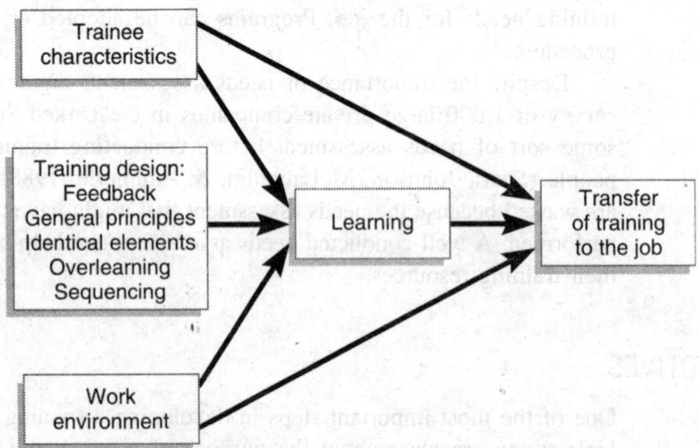

Figure 7.2 This model of transfer of training shows how characteristics of the trainee, training program, and work environment affect learning and transfer of training. Adapted from "Transfer of Training: A Review and Directions for Future Research," by T. T. Baldwin and J. K. Ford, 1988, *Personnel Psychology, 41,* 63–105.

Trainee Characteristics

Individual differences among people in both ability and motivation are important factors in learning (Herold, Davis, Fedor, & Parsons, 2002). Not everyone is equally able to learn specific tasks, and where one person is better able to learn cognitive tasks, another has more ability at motor tasks. Thus some people are skilled academicians and others are world-class athletes. These differences are important when it comes to the design of training. Not everyone has the same ability to learn a given task, and training needs to recognize these differences.

Bunker and Cohen (1977) studied the effectiveness of a training program designed to instruct telephone company employees in basic electronics theory. The mathematical ability of each trainee was assessed before training, and a measure of electronics knowledge was taken both before and after training. Results showed that those trainees with the highest level of mathematical ability gained the most from training. In order to get each trainee up to a given level of knowledge, more training would be necessary for the low-ability trainees. A good strategy for training is to give each individual trainee the amount of training necessary for him or her to reach the training criterion. This can mean that some people get more training than others.

Ability is not the only individual trainee characteristic that affects training outcomes. Attitudes and motivation can affect outcomes both in training and on the job (Noe & Schmitt, 1986). People who do not wish to learn are not likely to get much benefit from a training program. One of the most important factors that must be considered is how to motivate employees to do their best in a training situation. This can be done by giving external rewards for successful completion (e.g., promotion) or by making the training interesting to the trainees. Colquitt, Le Pine, and Noe (2000) conducted a meta-analysis of training motivation studies. They found that, not unexpectedly, motivation consistently relates to transfer of training, as well as to good employee attitudes.

People also differ in the best way to learn new material. Some people are good at learning from a presentation, whereas others do well with written materials. People's capacities and preferences for different types of training are important considerations and should be taken into account if possible. People who do not read well should be trained with verbal approaches. Others who like to study and think about material might do better with a written manual.

Design Factors That Affect Transfer of Training

The transfer of training model in Figure 7.2 specifies five design factors that affect transfer. Each factor should be considered in the design of a training program. Appropriate use of the factors will maximize the likelihood of transfer. Ignoring them might result in a training program that is ineffective in impacting behavior on the job.

Feedback

Feedback is an important component of learning. Without some sort of feedback, it is doubtful that learning can occur at all. Feedback should be built into the training as appropriate so that the trainee can tell if he or she is learning the correct material.

Training that is intended to impart information or knowledge can build in feedback in two ways. First, trainees can be tested on the information with an examination. Second, trainees can ask questions of the trainer. Both of these procedures are a regular part of most college or university courses. Training that is intended to teach a skill should allow the trainees to practice and get feedback as they learn. For example, training in driving an automobile should allow the person to drive with an instructor who will give feedback. Feedback is also built into the task itself. Trainees can tell if they are staying on the road and if they are driving straight.

General Principles

General principles mean that training should teach why something is done as well as how it should be done. Many training programs include a section on principles behind the material being taught. With computer training, there might be an introduction to the principles of computer and software design. This would be brief and rather general, but it would give the trainees a general idea of what the computer is and how it works. The purpose of teaching the general principles is that it provides a framework for learning. It has been found that including general principles where appropriate enhances learning (Baldwin & Ford, 1988).

Identical Elements

A training program that has good transfer of training capability should include **identical elements**, which means that the responses in the training situation are identical to those in the job situation. It also means that the stimuli the person perceives will be identical in both settings. The closer the match is in both responses and stimuli, the easier it will be for trainees to apply what has been learned in training to the job setting.

A flight simulator is a training device that takes advantage of the identical elements idea. A flight simulator allows the trainee to fly an airplane without leaving the ground. There are two types—high fidelity and low fidelity. The high-fidelity simulator is extremely realistic and might be a cockpit from a real aircraft mounted on a moving platform that simulates the motion of the airplane. The motions of the simulator match the movements of the controls. If the trainee pulls back on the stick, for example, the front of the cockpit tilts upward. A low-fidelity simulator is best illustrated by a computer game that simulates flying. Even though these low-fidelity simulator games do not contain all the elements of a real airplane, many of the elements are authentic. For this reason, the U.S. Navy uses such games to help train their pilots on some aspects of flying. To complete training, however, they must use the high-fidelity simulators. The simulator provides training that transfers well to actual flying because there are many identical elements (Figure 7.3).

Overlearning

Overlearning refers to giving the trainee practice beyond that necessary to reach a criterion for success in training. The idea is that a person first learns the material and then continues to overlearn it. Through overlearning, the person consolidates the new knowledge or skill so that he or she can use what has been learned with little thought. He or she has achieved **automaticity**, meaning that a task (e.g., driving a car or riding a bicycle) can be done smoothly without the person having to mentally monitor or pay attention to how he or she is performing. This results in much more effective performance and should be the goal for much organizational training (Ford & Kraiger, 1995).

Figure 7.3 Pilots learn many of the skills of flying an airplane in a flight simulator such as the one shown in this picture. (© *Rasch, sourced from Shutterstock images*)

Athletes practice their skills until they have become so overlearned that automaticity is achieved. In athletics, the actions that are performed are often so complex and done in such short periods of time that it is not possible to think about all the elements. Overlearned elements are performed automatically and quickly. On the job, the same principle can apply, as overlearned skills can be used when there is not enough time to think about how to perform a task. For example, in a hospital emergency room, there is little time to think about every task that needs to be done to save a person's life. Equipment must be used quickly and automatically when a person is in critical condition.

Overlearning can be built into training through practice and repetition. Information and knowledge training can include repetition of important concepts to ensure that the person rehearses the information. Examinations can also allow the person to rehearse, thus helping to consolidate what has been learned. With manual skills, sufficient practice should be allowed so that the skill becomes overlearned. It is not sufficient to allow the person to try the skill until he or she can do it correctly one time. Repeated practice is necessary to provide overlearning. The more the person gets to practice, the more likely it is that he or she can apply what has been learned on the job.

Driskell, Willis, and Copper (1992) conducted a meta-analysis of overlearning studies. They analyzed the amount of performance gain as a function of the amount of overlearning. Overlearning was defined as practice in the training session that continued after the trainees first achieved the criterion level for having learned the task. Overlearning in these studies ranged from 0% (no overlearning) to 200% (twice the amount of training after the training criterion was reached as before it was reached). If it took 2 hours of training for the trainee to reach the criterion, 200% overlearning would be an extra 4 hours of training. Figure 7.4 summarizes the results. The greater the overlearning (horizontal axis), the greater the amount of learning (vertical axis). It should be kept in mind, however, that most of the studies included in this meta-analysis investigated short-term learning where the time between the training and the assessment of learning was no more than a week. Furthermore, the overlearning occurred in a single training session. Rohrer, Taylor, Pashler, Wixted, and Cepeda (2005) compared short-term (1-week) and

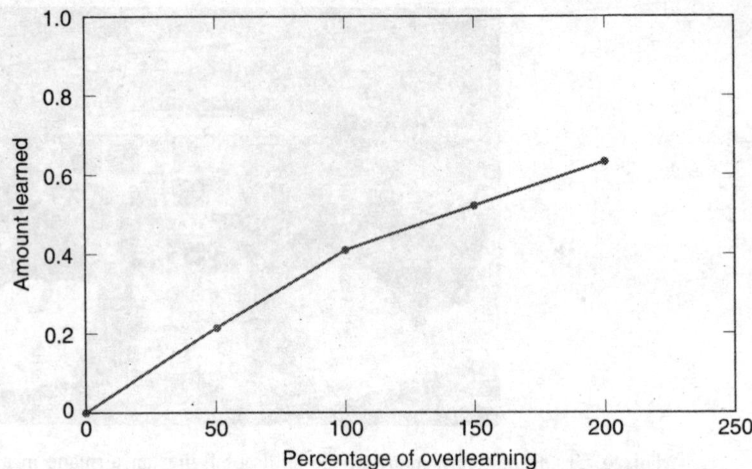

Figure 7.4 Learning is enhanced by the amount of overlearning training. Increasing the amount of training after the initial criterion is reached will increase the amount of learning. From "Effect of Overlearning on Retention," by J. E. Driskell, R. P. Willis, and C. Copper, 1992, *Journal of Applied Psychology, 77*, 615–622.

long-term (9-week) retention of learned material. They found that although the overlearners retained more material throughout the study, almost all of the initial gain disappeared by the ninth week. They suggested that the problem with retention length can be solved by incorporating spaced training in which extra practice occurs over extended periods of time and not all in a single long training session. Spaced training will be discussed next.

Sequencing of Training Sessions

There are two aspects of sequencing training sessions: *part* versus *whole* and *massed* versus *spaced*. **Part training** refers to breaking a task into components, which are learned one at a time. After the components are learned, the entire task is taught as a whole. **Whole training** occurs when the entire task is taught at one time rather than breaking it into individual components.

Part training is preferred over whole training when tasks are too complex to be learned all at once. It would be difficult to learn to play golf or tennis using the whole approach. It would be better in this case to learn one aspect of the game at a time, such as swinging the golf club or serving the tennis ball. To concentrate on all aspects of the game would be very difficult. Learning to ride a bicycle, on the other hand, is taught whole. One does not usually learn the components separately, such as pedaling and steering.

Massed training means that the training sessions are long in duration and take place over a relatively short period of time. **Spaced training** means that training sessions are relatively short and are spread out over time. Massed and spaced are relative terms that can be used to refer to some training programs as being more massed or spaced than other programs. A training program that holds sessions 1 hour per day for 10 days is more spaced than a program that meets once for 10 hours.

Massed training can be very efficient. For that reason, it is often used for organizational training when it is easier to allow a person to leave work for training for a day than for 1 hour a day for 8 days. With many jobs, a replacement will have to be found while the person is in training, and it can be difficult to find a replacement for an hour at a time. The person might have to be paid for an entire day to fill in for 1 hour. Furthermore, considerable travel time may be needed to get to the training site, which might be in another city. For these practical reasons, massed training is often used.

On the other hand, spaced training can be more effective than massed training in the long term and produces better learning (Cepeda, Pashler, Vul, Wixted, & Rohrer, 2006). Furthermore, the optimal spacing interval is dependent on how long people need to retain the information. In a series of experiments, Cepeda and colleagues manipulated the length of spaced training trials and then assessed retention of the learned material for up to a year later. They found that the ideal spacing was determined by how long the material had to be retained, such that longer intervals were better for long-term retention. They suggested that spacing training sessions over weeks and even months might be needed for optimal training design (Cepeda, Coburn, Rohrer, Wixted, Mozer, & Pashler, 2009; Cepeda, Vul, Rohrer, Wixted, & Pashler, 2008). These results are most relevant for knowledge and skill that an employee needs but does not use regularly—for example, first aid or CPR (cardiopulmonary resuscitation). In such cases, follow-up refresher training should be given periodically. For knowledge and skill that are regularly used on the job, spaced refresher sessions might not be necessary.

At least part of the problem with massed training is that it can produce boredom, which interferes with learning, and there are limits to how long a person can learn before fatigue comes into play. Imagine learning to play tennis in 10-hour sessions. The fatigue would make it impossible to get the full benefit of the training. Even with mental tasks, a person is not efficient when he or she is tired. Any student who has crammed for an exam has learned that massed training is not always the best procedure.

Work Environment

Training in organizations takes place in the context of a complex work environment. Whether or not the skills learned in training are used on the job is dependent in large part on the environment of the job. Just because management provides training does not mean that employees or their direct supervisors will support its transfer to the job. It is not uncommon for direct supervisors of lower-level employees to tell their subordinates that the new procedures or skills learned in training are not to be used in their departments. Supportive environments where supervisors and other people encourage the application of learned principles produce employee motivation to learn and increased transfer of training (Machin & Fogarty, 2003). Unless there is support by employees and their supervisors, the best training will not have its intended effects. Getting that support is a complex problem that goes beyond the proper design of training.

Another issue concerns whether or not the opportunity arises to use the new training. For example, employees might be trained in using a new computer system. The system might not be available to them on the job, meaning that the training could have no effect. This issue goes back to the idea of needs assessment. People should not receive training in an area that they will not encounter on the job.

Training Methods

Many different methods for training are available. Because each has its advantages and limitations, there is no one best way to train, and all of them can be effective in the right situation (Callahan, Kiker, & Cross, 2003). As noted earlier, different individuals may do well with different approaches. The best training programs are flexible and can adapt to the demands of what and who are being trained.

In this section, we discuss eight different training methods that are frequently used in organizational training. These methods can be used in combination because a good training program may need to take advantage of the strengths of different methods for different aspects of training. For example, the training of pilots may involve many, if not all, of these methods. The learning of complex tasks can require the use of a variety of approaches. Table 7.1 lists all eight methods and summarizes the major advantages of each.

Audiovisual Instruction

Audiovisual instruction involves the electronic presentation of materials using an audiotape, videotape, DVD, or computer. Although audio recordings and films have long been used for training, technology has been expanding the ease and flexibility with which such media can be used. It is commonplace for lecturers in business and higher education to use computer-based tools such as PowerPoint to add audiovisual elements to

TABLE 7.1 Advantages of Eight Training Methods

Method	Advantages
Audiovisual instruction	Presents material that could not otherwise be heard or seen Can train many people at once
Autoinstruction	Gives immediate feedback to trainees Provides individualized pacing
Conference	Allows for feedback to trainees Provides a high level of trainee involvement
Lecture	Is economical Is a good information-giving method
Modeling	Provides a high level of feedback Provides practice of new skills
On-the-job training	Gives exposure to the actual job Ensures a high level of transfer
Role playing	Provides a high level of feedback Provides practice of new skills
Simulation	Ensures a high level of transfer Provides practice of new skills

Source: Adapted from "Selection, Training, and Development of Personnel," by W. C. Borman, N. G. Peterson, and T. L. Russell, 1992, in G. Salvendy (Ed.), *Handbook of Industrial Engineering* (2nd ed.), New York, NY: John Wiley & Sons.

presentations. These methods can also be used by individuals in autoinstruction, which is the next method we will discuss.

Autoinstruction

Autoinstruction refers to any training method that is self-paced and does not use an instructor. The most well-known technique is **programmed instruction**, which divides the material to be covered into a series of individual chunks or frames. Each frame contains a piece of information, a question to be answered, and the answer to the question from the prior frame. The person works at his or her own pace. There is repetition built in, as the same material is presented more than once. There is also feedback, as the person must answer questions and is then given the correct answers almost immediately. Although the medium for programmed instruction was originally a book or manual, the computer is able to provide a much more flexible approach to autoinstruction training.

Conference

A **conference** is a meeting of trainees and a trainer to discuss the material in question. The distinguishing feature of the conference is that participants can discuss the material and ask questions. It also allows for a free flow of ideas so that the discussion can go beyond the prepackaged materials. Thus the conference can be used to create an active learning environment that engages the trainees. It is especially effective when used with trainees who have already acquired expertise with the material. It is the major teaching method used at the Ph.D. level in the training of I/O psychology students.

Lecture

A **lecture** is a presentation by a trainer to a group of trainees. Its major advantage is its efficiency. One trainer can present material to a large number of trainees. At some universities, lectures are given to thousands of students at one time. The greatest strength of the lecture is also its greatest weakness. The mass presentation to many people limits the amount of feedback that can be given. If there were even 40 people in a lecture and each person asked one question, the lecturer would have little time to present. For situations in which feedback is not needed, the lecture can be a very effective means of training.

Modeling

Modeling involves having trainees watch someone perform a task and then model what they have seen. The model can be live or recorded. Models can show both effective and ineffective examples of behavior. This approach is often used for the training of supervisory skills, such as giving negative feedback to an employee who is performing poorly. The examples of supervisory behavior are shown, and then the trainees attempt to imitate what they have seen. The trainer's role is to encourage the trainees to try the approaches and to give them feedback about how well they imitated what they saw.

Research on the modeling approach has provided support for its ability to train people in interpersonal skills, such as communicating with others. Taylor, Russ-Eft, and Chan's (2005) meta-analysis showed that modeling was effective in enhancing learning performance as assessed by both paper-and-pencil tests and simulations. Simon and Werner (1996) reported better learning with modeling than with autoinstruction or lecture in training U.S. naval personnel to use a new data processing system on a personal computer.

On-the-Job Training

On-the-job training is not a particular method but is any method used to show employees how to do the job while they are doing it. The greatest amount of job training often occurs while the person is doing the various job tasks. On-the-job training can be an informal system whereby a new employee watches an experienced employee to see how the job should be done. It can also involve a formal training program such as an **apprenticeship**, which is commonly used for jobs for which it may take years to fully train the employee. For this sort of job, the other methods might not be feasible because the organization will not want to pay a person for years of training without productivity. If the person quits before training is completed, the training effort has been wasted. An apprentice is an employee who can serve as an assistant to the trainer. The trainer is an employee who is doing the job and training the apprentice at the same time. This approach is often used to train people in trade occupations, such as electricians and plumbers.

Role-Playing

A **role play** is a type of simulation in which the trainee pretends to be doing a task. It usually involves an interpersonal situation, such as giving a person advice or feedback, and is used frequently for supervisory training. The role play is part of the modeling procedure we discussed earlier. The role play itself does not involve first observing another person perform the behavior. It can be an effective training technique, but it is costly in that only a few trainees can be trained at one time.

Simulations

As discussed earlier, a **simulation** is a technique in which specialized equipment or materials are used to portray a task situation. Trainees are to pretend that the situation is real and carry out their tasks as they would in the actual situation. Simulations can be used for training people in the use of equipment, such as automobiles or airplanes. They can also be used to simulate other situations, such as a business decision simulation that asks the trainee to pretend to be an organization member who has been given a problem to solve or task to accomplish. For example, a simulation might involve running an airport or a factory (Funke, 1998). These simulations can be made very realistic, for they can be based on real examples from the same organization. The simulation shares the limitation of the role play in that only a few trainees can participate at one time, although with the use of computer-based approaches, this may not be a serious limitation because computers are widely available in many organizations.

Electronic Training

Electronic training or **E-learning** is the latest trend in both organizational training and university education. It involves the use of electronic tools to provide training, and several of the training methods discussed here can be done electronically. Some forms of E-learning merely make use of a computer or technology to deliver training originally developed for another medium, such as web-broadcasting a lecture so people can watch it remotely on their computers or televisions. Other, more sophisticated approaches allow for complex, individualized training methods that incorporate sophisticated assessments to both provide feedback and make training more efficient by matching it to the level of the trainee. Practice can continue until a criterion level of proficiency is achieved, and already learned material can be skipped. One rapidly growing practice is the use of the web for training delivery. Training materials can be put online so they are available to employees at all times. This makes training available whenever and wherever the employee comes across a situation in which the training is needed rather than having to wait until a training session is available.

DeRouin, Fritzsche, and Salas (2005) noted several potential advantages of E-learning that make it attractive to organizations. First, it can give the learner a great deal of control over the training experience by being able to determine where and when the training is delivered and, with some methods, the order of the material. Second, technology allows for rapid development and modification of training materials as they are needed. A training module written in PowerPoint can be put together and e-mailed to employees or posted on a website in a very short time. Third, E-learning can be combined with other, more traditional methods, producing **blended learning**. For example, a classroom lecture can be coupled with some E-learning exercises. Finally, E-learning can be easily customized to meet individual employee needs. For example, a training program might include assessments that determine when the learner has mastered the material and is ready to move to the next topic. Newton and Doonga (2007) surveyed training managers of organizations who noted that the major advantages for them were the flexibility in where training could be done, the efficiency of delivery, and not having employees absent to attend training sessions. Rather, employees can complete training in small sessions during the workday (e.g., during breaks).

On the other hand, there are drawbacks to E-learning. As noted earlier, motivation is an important element in training, and it can be a particular concern with E-learning (Brown, 2005). Since it is self-paced, there is no trainer or other trainees to help motivate a trainee who has little intrinsic interest in the material. Another problem with this approach is that typically employees are asked to complete training at their own pace when they can find time. Oiry (2009) noted that employees complain that their supervisors are reluctant to provide breaks for training, given the demands of heavy workloads. This problem is reduced when an employee is given a day off to attend training.

E-learning is certainly popular for delivery of organizational training, and it seems to have become a common part of organizational life. Studies have shown that it can produce learning that is equivalent to or in some situations even better than learning from classroom instruction (Sitzmann, Kraiger, Stewart, & Wisher, 2006). Of course, as with all training methods, it is suitable for some but not all training situations.

Mentoring

Many organizations have found that new and inexperienced employees can benefit from being mentored by more senior and usually higher-level employees. **Mentoring** is a special kind of work relationship between two employees where the more experienced offers advice/coaching, counseling, and friendship and serves as a role model (Baranik, Roling, & Eby, 2010). Furthermore, although most mentor situations involve employees of different organizational levels and often a mentor is the protégé's supervisor, mentors can also be peers who are at the same level but are just more experienced (Allen, McManus, & Russell, 1999). Mentoring can be thought of as a kind of training that not only helps a new employee get oriented to the job but also helps that employee develop his or her career with the company over a considerable period of time (Young & Perrewe, 2004). Research has shown that those mentored or protégés derive a number of benefits from mentoring, including better job performance, quicker promotion, better job attitudes, and less turnover (Allen, Eby, Poteet, Lentz, & Lima, 2004; Blickle, Witzki, & Schneider, 2009). There are also benefits to the mentors, including improved personal satisfaction, enhanced job performance, recognition by others, and future loyalty of the protégés, which can be helpful (Eby, Durley, Evans, & Ragins, 2006).

O'Brien, Biga, Kessler, and Allen (2010) wondered if there are gender differences in receiving and providing mentoring in general and career assistance or emotional support in particular. They conducted a meta-analysis of 41 mentoring studies that looked at experiences of men and women. Their results showed that on the protégé side, men and women were equally likely to receive mentoring, but that women were more likely than men to receive emotional support from a mentor. On the mentor side, men were more likely to provide career assistance, whereas women were more likely to provide emotional support. Given the small size of the effects, one should not stereotype individual men and women, as both genders engage in both forms of mentoring.

Mentoring occurs quite naturally as relationships develop between people at work, but many organizations have formal mentoring programs in which mentors and protégés are assigned to one another (Raabe & Beehr, 2003). Formal programs can be useful

INTERNATIONAL RESEARCH

Not every employee is able to find a mentor or have a good mentoring relationship. Aryee, Lo, and Kang (1999) were interested in determining the characteristics of protégés that led to receiving mentoring from older, more experienced employees.

Participants in this study were 184 Chinese employees of various local and multinational companies in Hong Kong. The researchers mailed each a copy of a questionnaire that contained questions about their mentoring experiences, some personality tests, and questions about their age and gender. The mentoring experiences were measured with two scales. One concerned the extent to which the participant had received mentoring from an experienced manager. The other asked about the efforts the participant had made to seek out a mentor.

Results showed that both mentoring scales were correlated—employees who sought mentors were more likely to find them than employees who waited for mentors to find them. Both mentoring scales were related to the participant's achievement striving and extraversion (outgoingness). Older employees were more likely to find mentors than were younger employees (but keep in mind that most participants were between the ages of 25 and 30). Finally, both men and women were equally likely to seek and find mentors.

The magnitude of correlation between the two mentoring scales (.40) was rather low, suggesting that although seeking a mentor raised employees' chances of finding one, they were often not successful in doing so. Those employees who were successful were likely to be ambitious, hardworking, and outgoing, based on their personality test scores. They were also likely to be older—in this sample in their 30s rather than early 20s. Finally, gender didn't make a difference in mentoring—men and women were equally likely to be protégés.

Source: From "Antecedents of Early Career Stage Mentoring Among Chinese Employees," by S. Aryee, S. Lo, and I. L. Kang, 1999, *Journal of Organizational Behavior, 20*, 563–576.

because not all employees are likely to find mentors on their own. Individuals who are achievement oriented and sociable are most likely to find mentors naturally (Aryee, Lo, & Kang, 1999) (see the International Research box). Assigned mentorships don't always work as well as those that develop naturally (Allen & Eby, 2003), as assigned mentor-protégé relationships are not always good. Allen, Eby, and Lentz (2006) studied the experiences of mentors and protégés, asking about several features of their mentor program and whether or not they derived benefits. Their responses showed that allowing both mentor and protégé to have input into their pairing and providing training were important factors in achieving a successful mentoring experience. In the extreme, mentoring can become dysfunctional when the relationship between mentor and protégé becomes destructive, with the mentor being overly critical and even undermining the protégé. Such negative experiences can be worse than no mentor at all and can create significant problems for protégés (Eby, Durley, Evans, & Ragins, 2008).

Executive Coaching

High-level executives and managers, especially in private companies, are sometimes paired with a consultant who can serve as an executive coach to help him or her improve job performance. **Executive coaching** was originally designed to assist high-level managers with performance problems, but it has evolved to become a means of helping even well-performing managers enhance their management skills (Bono, Purvanova, Towler, & Peterson, 2009). There are many ways in which a coach can operate. One way is to solicit feedback from employees who interact with the executive, perhaps using 360-degree feedback (see Chapter 4). The coach then meets with the executive to help interpret the feedback and devise an action plan to improve in areas that are deficient. For example, if subordinates and peers note problems with communication, a plan to enhance such skills can be devised. The coach might work with the executive for an extended period of time, providing continual advice and feedback.

One concern with executive coaching is that there is no particular background or credentials one needs to be a coach, and there is no consensus concerning the KSAOs required (Bono et al., 2009). Coaches can be found with a variety of backgrounds, including I/O psychology (see this chapter's I/O Psychology in Practice). The scant research concerning effectiveness suggests that executive coaching can have positive effects (Grant, Curtayne, & Burton, 2009). For example, Baron and Morin (2010) found that managers who were coached increased their self-efficacy, which means they felt more confident about their management abilities. As we will see in Chapter 8, self-efficacy is an important prerequisite to good job performance.

► DELIVERY OF A TRAINING PROGRAM

Even the most well-designed training program will be ineffective unless it is properly delivered. In most organizations, specialists who are skilled in training deliver the program. They may or may not be experts in the content of the training or in training design. Content is the responsibility of SMEs who know the particular topics that the training will cover. I/O psychologists and people from several other fields are experts at program design. Because program delivery is not a frequent activity of an I/O psychologist, we continue with the next topic: training evaluation.

▶ EVALUATION OF A TRAINING PROGRAM

As far as an I/O psychologist is concerned, a training program is not completed until its effectiveness has been evaluated. An evaluation is a piece of research to see whether or not the program had its intended effects. This is important because many training programs are ineffective. For example, Morrow, Jarrett, and Rupinski (1997) evaluated the utility of 18 training programs in an organization and found that 5 cost more than they returned in improved performance on the job. The principles of research design, as discussed in Chapter 2, are very much involved in the design of evaluation. There is little difference between conducting an evaluation study for a training program and conducting a research study to determine the effects of any intervention that is tried in an organization. Thus the principles and techniques of research methodology that we discussed in Chapter 2 apply to the evaluation of a training program.

Carrying out a training evaluation requires five steps (Figure 7.5). The first step is to define the criteria for evaluation. As we have discussed several times in this book, you must have criteria before you can evaluate something. Criteria are the standards used for comparison that allow you to determine if training has been effective. Once criteria have been selected, a design for the study and the measures used to assess the criteria can be selected (steps 2 and 3). Step 4 is collecting the data for the study. Step 5 is analyzing the data and reaching conclusions about the effectiveness of the training program. We discuss each of these steps in greater detail now.

Set Criteria

Training criteria serve as the standard by which training can be evaluated. If you know what the training is supposed to achieve, you can design an evaluation study to determine if the goals were met. Suppose a manufacturing company is selling too many defective products. It might set as a training objective teaching employees to reduce errors in their manufacturing tasks. The criterion could be a specified reduction in the number of defective products. When the criterion is specific, such as a reduction of 10%, it is relatively easy to evaluate the effectiveness of the training program.

Training criteria are classified into two levels—training level and performance level—both of which are important in evaluating training. **Training-level criteria** are concerned with what people are able to do at the end of training in the training environment itself rather than on the job. **Performance-level criteria** are concerned with the person's performance on the job rather than in the training setting. In other words, performance criteria are concerned with transfer of training. Thus training level

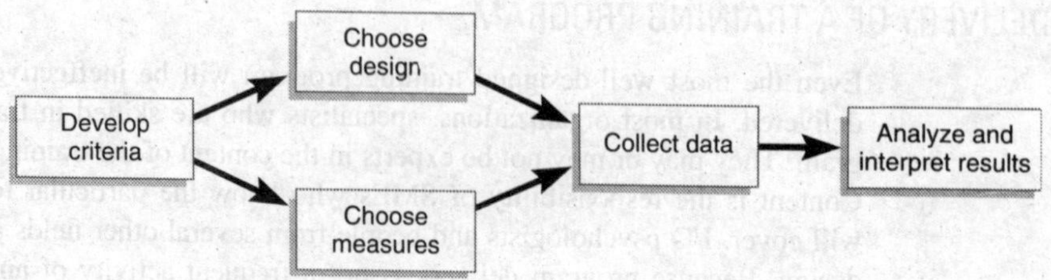

Figure 7.5 Five steps to evaluating a training program.

is concerned with what the person learned, whereas performance level is concerned with the effects of the training on the job itself.

Performance-level and training-level criteria work hand in hand in evaluating the effectiveness of training. The performance level is important because it shows whether or not the training has had the intended effects on the job. Because most training is intended to affect job performance, a training program without effects at the performance level is ineffective. On the other hand, it is important to know what the employees learned in the training. The best criterion for this is at the training level. Someone might learn a great deal and for some reason not apply it to the job. Failure to have an effect on the job might be due to other factors. For example, a person might know what to do and how to do it, but the opportunity to apply the knowledge might never occur. Employees might be given a first aid course to help them better handle work accidents. If no accidents occur, the employees will not show any effects at the performance level.

Another useful way of classifying criteria is to divide them into four types, two of which can be placed in the performance level and two in the training level (Kirkpatrick, 1977):

Reactions	Behavior
Learning	Results

Reactions criteria refer to how much each trainee liked the training and how much the trainee believed he or she got out of it. It is assessed with a questionnaire given to each trainee at the end of the training session. **Learning criteria** refer to what the person learned in training—what the trainee is able to demonstrate behaviorally in terms of knowledge and skills acquired in training. It might be assessed with an examination given at the end of training. Both of these criterion types relate to the training level. They are frequently used in colleges and universities. Student evaluations are reactions criteria, and exam scores are learning criteria.

Behavior criteria concern the trainee's behaviors on the job that might have been due to training. This type of criterion looks at whether or not the person is doing the things he or she was taught. **Results criteria** deal with whether the training had its intended effect. Did the training reduce costs or increase productivity? This final type of criterion serves as the bottom line for the effectiveness of a training program. Both behavior and results criteria relate to the performance level because they focus on what happens on the job rather than in the training setting.

All of these criterion types are important because each is a partial indicator of training success. A meta-analysis of 34 training studies showed that most criteria assessed within the same study are only slightly correlated with one another (Alliger et al., 1997). Furthermore, in any given training program, only some of the criteria may show the desired results. Campion and Campion (1987) conducted a study in which they evaluated a training program against four different criteria. Their results showed that the training of interview skills was effective at the training level but not at the performance level. On the other hand, Maurer, Solamon, Andrews, and Troxtel (2001) were able to show that training in how to interview was effective in enhancing performance in interviews away from the training situation. Thus we can see that interview training can show transfer but does not always show transfer. These studies demonstrate that one must be careful not to assume training will have the intended effects and that one should include criteria at both levels to thoroughly evaluate effectiveness (see the International Research box).

INTERNATIONAL RESEARCH

Sometimes events occur in organizations that produce the equivalent of an experiment. Such was the case when the availability of training for only some employees allowed Campion and Campion (1987) to conduct a naturally occurring experiment to evaluate the effects of training. Employees were assigned to be either trained or untrained merely because the organization had insufficient resources and time for everyone to be trained. After the training was completed, the researchers assessed everyone using four criteria to compare the trained and untrained employees.

This study took place in an electronics company that needed to move a large number of employees from manufacturing jobs to marketing jobs. Many of the employees lacked interview skills. The managers of the organization were concerned that their employees would be unable to perform well enough in an interview to transfer to another job. To remedy the deficiency, an interview skills training program was developed and implemented.

Roughly half of the eligible employees were given training and half were not. The training was evaluated with each of the four types of criteria: reactions, learning, behavior, and results. The reactions criterion was assessed with a questionnaire at the end of the training. The majority of participants believed the training was worthwhile. Learning was assessed with a test given to the trained employees at the beginning and end of training. This knowledge test showed that the participants learned about proper interview behavior during the training.

The behavior criterion was assessed by having the interviewers who later interviewed all employees rate how well they performed. According to this criterion, the trained group performed the same as the untrained group. Finally, the results criterion was assessed by noting the number of job offers each employee received. Here again there were no differences between the trained and untrained individuals.

These results suggested that the training was effective in teaching the employees interview skills but ineffective in helping them perform better in an actual job interview. From the organization's point of view, the training did not meet its objectives. The reasons for this failure are not clear. Perhaps the training was unnecessary because most employees already had good interview skills. Perhaps the training included the wrong material. In either case, this study demonstrates why it is important for organizations to assess different types of criteria when evaluating a training program.

Source: From "Evaluation of an Interviewee Skills Training Program in a Natural Field Experiment," by M. A. Campion and J. E. Campion, 1987, *Personnel Psychology, 40,* 675–691.

Choose Design

A *design* is the structure of a study that specifies how data are collected, whether it is a study of training or some other phenomenon. With a training evaluation, the type of criterion sets limits on the designs that can be used. For reactions criteria, the only feasible design is one that assesses participants once at the end of training. It makes no sense to assess nonparticipants as a control group or to assess participants before they go through training. People who are not going to be trained cannot have a reaction to what they have not experienced. People who have not yet been trained cannot have a reaction to what they are about to experience.

Other criteria can be assessed with many different types of designs. The two most popular are pretest-posttest and control group. The *pretest-posttest design* assesses trainees before and after training. The *control group design* compares trainees with a group of employees who have not received the training. Each design has its advantages and limitations in evaluating a training program.

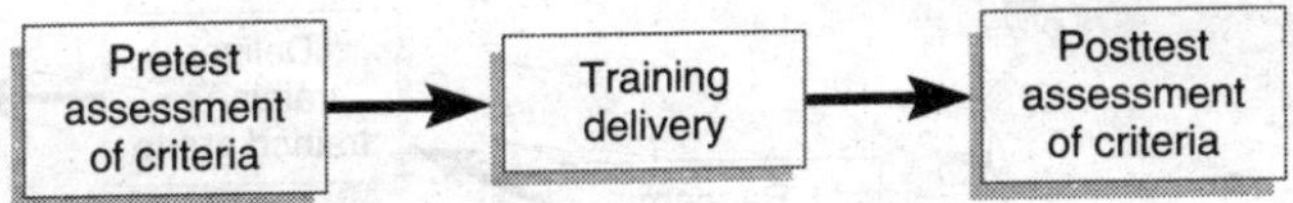

Figure 7.6 Structure of a pretest-posttest training evaluation design.

Pretest-Posttest

The **pretest-posttest design** is intended to provide information about how much the trainees gained from the training. It can be used to assess the amount learned in the training itself or the amount of change in behavior back on the job. To conduct a study with this design, the measures of interest are assessed before the training begins (pretest) and again after it has been completed (posttest). Figure 7.6 illustrates the structure of this design. Both pretest and posttest measures are part of the training program. It is not unusual for a training program to begin with a test to see what trainees know and conclude with a test to see what they have learned. Assessments can also occur on the job well before and well after training. For example, if a training program is intended to improve productivity, measures of productivity could be taken for the 6 months prior to and the 6 months after training. Some training may not show effects on the job for a long period of time. Thorough evaluation would not be possible immediately after training.

The pretest-posttest design is popular because it is a practical design to use in organizations. It is usually easy to build in an assessment at the beginning and end of a training program. The assessment can also be used as a means of providing feedback. The major drawback of this design is that it is difficult to attribute changes to the training itself rather than other events in the organization. This is particularly true for performance criteria. If a training program is designed to improve job performance, gains in performance from before to after training might have occurred for many reasons. Just making supervisors aware that performance is a problem could motivate them to put pressure on subordinates to perform. This increased attention to performance would coincide with the training and might be the cause of the performance gains. To find out if the training itself was the cause of the improvement would require a research design with a control group.

Control Group

A control group design compares employees who have received training to equivalent employees who have not been trained. Figure 7.7 illustrates the structure of this design. To conduct a control group study, a group of employees is selected for the study. Half are assigned at random to the trained group, and the other half are the controls who receive no training. At the end of the training program, all employees in the study are assessed on the measures of interest. The comparison between the two subgroups of employees indicates the effects of the training.

This design is more difficult to use in an organization because it is not always possible to assign employees at random to the two groups. In addition, there can be contamination as the trained employees tell the untrained control group employees what they have learned. However, this design is an improvement over the pretest-posttest when you wish to determine the effects of training. It helps control for the possibility that it was something other than training that caused the changes that you observed in employees.

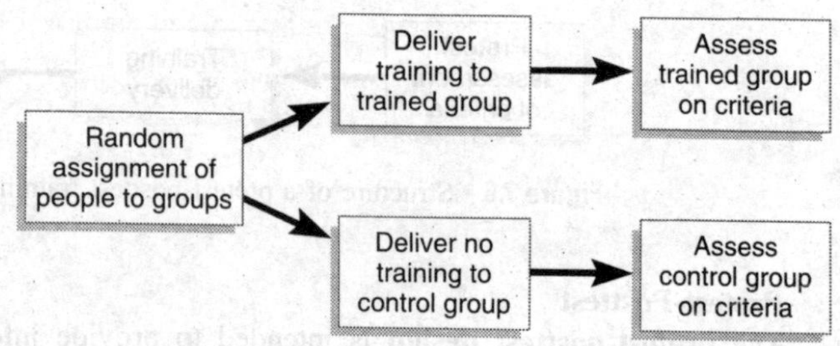

Figure 7.7 Structure of a control group training evaluation design.

Choose Measures of the Criteria

Once criteria have been chosen, the actual measures of those criteria need to be selected. The criterion of interest determines to a great extent what sorts of measures can be used to assess it. Reactions criteria require the use of a questionnaire that trainees can complete to give their reactions. The specific design of the questionnaire must be decided. There are many ways to ask people their reactions to training. For example, questions can ask how much the trainee learned or if the training was enjoyable.

Learning criteria usually involve some sort of test given at the end of training. Training intended to increase knowledge about a topic can be evaluated with a knowledge test, much like an examination given in school. Training to enhance other types of skills requires a different approach, such as a role play or simulation test. Assessment of performance criteria requires measuring trainee behavior or results in the job setting rather than in training.

Collect Data

Although the underlying logic of an evaluation study is simple and straightforward, carrying out the study can be a difficult undertaking because collecting the data poses many practical problems. People are not always cooperative, and many things can and do go wrong. It is difficult to perform pure random assignment in an organization, so that compromises have to be made. Often this means that the trained group comes from one department and the control group from another. Differences between the trained and untrained employees might then be caused by department differences on the criteria of interest.

The best possible design should always be planned. Every researcher knows that the plan might not be carried out without problems. This means that modifications might have to be made during the study. A good researcher is able to deal effectively with problems that occur during the data collection step of the study. If this step is conducted properly, it will be possible to draw conclusions about the effectiveness of the training program.

Analyze and Interpret Data

The data from evaluation studies are analyzed with inferential statistics. With a pretest-posttest design, the statistics indicate how much the trainees changed from the pretest to the posttest. With a control group study, the statistics show how much difference, if any, exists between the trained and untrained employees. In both cases, the statistic used could be as simple as a t-test.

If all four prior steps of the training evaluation have been well done, it will be possible to reach a confident conclusion about the effectiveness of the training program. It is always a good idea to evaluate training, and it should be evaluated at both the performance and the training levels. Training will often be effective at only one of the two levels, so assessment of both will give useful information about the effects the training might have had.

If training works at both levels, it can be considered effective and should continue. Training that does not work at either level should be considered ineffective and eliminated or modified. Training that is effective at the training level but not the performance level is probably the wrong approach or an incomplete solution to the problem. A productivity problem might be due to inadequate knowledge or skill, but it can be caused by other factors as well. In a manufacturing plant, poor productivity can be caused by poor equipment maintenance or poor supervision. Training of equipment operators is unlikely to affect their productivity if it is being reduced by one of these two factors. An evaluation of training would likely show that the operators learned but that productivity stayed the same.

The development of a new training program should always include an evaluation component. Training that is found to be ineffective should not continue but should be modified if that would increase its effectiveness. A good strategy for developing training is to pilot test it before implementation. A small group of employees could be put through the training, and then the training would be evaluated at several levels. It would not be implemented throughout the organization until it had been found to be effective during pilot testing. This approach also allows for the modification of training so that it can be improved before full implementation throughout the organization. This strategy for developing training programs should result in making the most of training resources.

CHAPTER SUMMARY

Training is one of the most important activities of organizations. The design of effective training programs is a five-step process:

Determine training needs through needs assessment
Set objectives for training
Design training
Deliver training
Evaluate training

The first step of a training program is to determine the need for training. This includes not only what should be trained but also who should be trained. Once the training need is established by a needs assessment, the objectives for the training should be decided. From the objectives, a series of training criteria should be developed by which to judge the effectiveness of the training.

The design of effective training should consider characteristics of trainees. Different individuals might have different training needs. It should also incorporate the principles of good training and the methods that will be used. Many principles determine whether or not a particular training program will be effective:

Feedback	Overlearning
General principles	Sequencing of training sessions
Identical elements	

Many training methods can be used. Each has its strengths and limitations, and no one method is necessarily better than the others. Choice of method depends on what and who are trained. E-learning, the use of technology to deliver training, has become commonplace in organizations. Web-based training can be effective and efficient if used properly. Mentoring is a special relationship between an experienced and an inexperienced employee in which the former helps the latter develop his or her job skills.

Training evaluation is done by conducting a research study to determine if the training was effective. The evaluation process includes five steps:

Select criteria

Choose a research design

Choose measures

Collect data

Analyze data and interpret results

A well-conducted evaluation study can provide valuable information about whether or not a training program is having its intended effects on individuals and organizations. A training program that is ineffective should be eliminated or modified so that it is effective. In the long run, a policy of evaluating training will lead to better use of training resources and a more effective workforce.

I/O PSYCHOLOGY IN PRACTICE

(*Courtesy of Charles Evans*)

This case concerns executive coaching—the development of management skills in high-level corporate executives—which was one of the major responsibilities of Dr. Charles Evans, an I/O psychologist working for RHR International, an international consulting firm in Toronto, Canada. Dr. Evans received his Ph.D. in I/O psychology from the University of Guelph in Canada in 1994. His RHR responsibilities were to work on projects for client organizations, which are some of the largest corporations in the world. Most of his work was in the areas of employee assessment and performance appraisal, as well as executive coaching.

As an executive coach, Dr. Evans's major function was to provide assistance and feedback to executives who need to enhance their managerial skills. Often people who are promoted to high levels in organizations find that success on the job requires new approaches to dealing with people rather than the approaches they had used effectively at lower levels.

A common problem is that executives are too autocratic and focused on results. Although subordinates at lower levels might have responded constructively to direct orders, middle- and higher-level managers do not. Instead, executives need to use skills in communication and persuasion. One must gain support for taking actions that require cooperation from many people for success. Individuals who lack these skills must develop them, or they will remain ineffective.

Dr. Evans addressed these and other problems by collecting information about the individual and then giving feedback based on that information. He conducted a structured interview to assess the individual's background and interpersonal skills. A 360-degree feedback (see Chapter 4) was conducted, and the results were discussed with the person to let him or her know how he cr she comes across to peers, subordinates, and supervisors. Dr. Evans assisted the person in coming up with a development plan to address deficiencies and improve management skills. He served as a coach to the person in helping figure out ways to do a better job.

Dr. Evans did this work mainly in North America, but his firm works with executives throughout the world. Companies pay executives very high salaries, and they are willing to spend a lot on their development, including hiring a private coach to help enhance their management skills. Such efforts can help organizations function better because their executives are more effective in dealing with people.

Discussion Questions

1. Why would a high-level executive want to enhance management skills?
2. How do you tell a person who has risen to the top of an organization that he or she needs to handle people more effectively?
3. Which of the training methods would be most effective here?
4. How would you go about evaluating what Dr. Evans does?

LEARNING BY DOING

Training Needs Assessment

One of the major methods of needs assessment is to survey employees about their training needs. Choose a person you know (acquaintance, family member, or friend) who is currently employed in a job you have never held yourself. Interview him or her about the training needs for the job. Ask about the three or four most important areas in which training is needed. You should ask about the following:

1. Job title
2. Areas in which training is needed
3. KSAOs that would be enhanced by the training
4. Tasks that would be facilitated by the training

Write a brief report that provides an overview of what you learned about the job.

E-Learning at Your University

Find a course at your university that uses some form of E-learning. Review whatever materials you can find about the course (e.g., catalog description or syllabus). Explain the specific E-learning methods used in the course and whether or not blended learning is being used. Discuss how the specific topics of the course fit or fail to fit the E-learning method being used.

PART IV

THE INDIVIDUAL AND THE ORGANIZATION

(*Corbis Stock Market*)

CHAPTER 8

Theories of Employee Motivation

CHAPTER 8 OUTLINE

- WHAT IS MOTIVATION?
- WORK MOTIVATION THEORIES
- NEED THEORIES
  - Need Hierarchy Theory
  - Two-Factor Theory
- REINFORCEMENT THEORY
- EXPECTANCY THEORY
- SELF-EFFICACY THEORY
- JUSTICE THEORIES
- GOAL-SETTING THEORY
- CONTROL THEORY
- ACTION THEORY
- CHAPTER SUMMARY
- I/O PSYCHOLOGY IN PRACTICE
- LEARNING BY DOING

Bill Gates, the founder and former head of Microsoft Corporation, is known for his arduous work schedule. When running the company, he typically spent 12 hours a day at the office and worked several hours more at home. He did not own a television set because he said it was too distracting. By the time he was in his mid-30s, Gates had amassed a fortune of several billion dollars, and he became one of the richest people in the world. Yet he still continued to work harder than almost anyone, even though he did not need more money. What drove Gates to work so hard? He said that he was motivated by challenges and the desire to learn new things.

Few people work as hard as Bill Gates did. Furthermore, not everyone works for the challenge as he did. A variety of factors motivate people to work hard. The necessity to make money is certainly one of them, but there are others, which can be tangible, such as an insurance benefit, or intangible, such as a sense of accomplishment. Theories of motivation explain why people work hard. They also explain other types of work behavior that do not involve job performance. Most of the theories, however, have focused on job performance because job performance has been a central variable for the I/O field.

This chapter discusses job performance in terms of several popular theories, with a focus on motivation rather than ability. (In Chapter 10, we will explore other things that affect performance.) It also covers explanations for other forms of work behavior, such as turnover. The chapter begins by defining motivation in the context of the work environment. It then introduces work motivation theories and provides a brief overview of the nine theories to be covered. Each theory is next discussed in greater detail, along with the research evidence for its validity.

Objectives: The student who studies this chapter should be able to:

- Define motivation.
- List the major work motivation theories that are discussed in this chapter.
- Describe how each of the major work motivation theories explains work behavior.
- Compare and contrast the major work motivation theories.

WHAT IS MOTIVATION?

Motivation is generally defined as an internal state that induces a person to engage in particular behaviors. From one perspective, it has to do with the direction, intensity, and persistence of behavior over time. *Direction* refers to the choice of specific behaviors from a large number of possible behaviors. For example, an employee might decide to volunteer for an extra work project that will require him or her to work overtime instead of going home on time and watching television. *Intensity* refers to the amount of effort a person expends at doing a task. If an employee is asked to sweep a floor, the person can exert a lot of effort by sweeping hard and fast or exert a little effort by sweeping softly and slowly. *Persistence* refers to the continuing engagement in a behavior over time. An employee might try to accomplish something over an extended period of time, such as studying to pass the CPA exam to become a certified public accountant, even though it might take several attempts.

From another perspective, motivation is concerned with the desire to acquire or achieve some goal. That is, motivation derives from a person's wants, needs, or desires. Some people, for example, are highly motivated to acquire money. It is presumed that a high level of motivation to have money affects the behavior relevant to acquiring it.

WORK MOTIVATION THEORIES

Work motivation theories are most typically concerned with the reasons, other than ability, that some people perform their jobs better than others. Depending on the situation, these theories can predict people's choice of task behavior, their effort, or their persistence. Presuming that people have the necessary ability and that constraints on performance are relatively low, high levels of motivation should lead to good job performance. (See the discussion of job performance in Chapter 10.)

The theories covered in this chapter view employee motivation from very different perspectives. According to need theories, people are motivated to acquire certain categories of things, such as food or recognition. Need hierarchy theory classifies all human needs into a small number of categories, and it presumes that people's behavior is directed toward fulfilling their needs. Two-factor theory says that various aspects of work address one of two categories of need. One category concerns the nature of the job itself, and the other concerns rewards such as pay.

Reinforcement theory views behavior as the result of rewards or reinforcements. As opposed to need theories, reinforcement theory describes motivation as the result of environmental influences rather than internally generated motives. Expectancy theory, like reinforcement theory, attempts to relate environmental rewards to behavior. Unlike reinforcement theory, it is concerned with human cognitive processes that explain why rewards can lead to behavior.

Self-efficacy theory is concerned with how people's beliefs about their own capabilities can affect their behavior. According to this theory, motivation to attempt a task is related to whether or not the person believes he or she is capable of successfully accomplishing the task.

Justice theories are quite different from the other theories in that they are concerned with people's values rather than needs, beliefs, or reinforcements. These theories presume that people universally value fairness in their social relations at work. Situations in which unfairness or inequity exists are presumed to motivate employees to remedy the unfairness.

Goal-setting theory explains how people's goals and intentions can result in behavior. Like need theories, it notes that motivation begins inside the person, but it also shows how environmental influences can shape motivation and behavior. Cognitive control theory is also concerned with goals but focuses attention on feedback toward goal attainment and how discrepancies between goals and the current situation motivate behavior. Action theory was developed in Germany to explain volitional (self-motivated and voluntary) behavior at work. It is another cognitive theory that explains how goals are translated into behaviors that persist until the person reaches his or her objective.

Even though these various theories view motivation from different perspectives, they do not necessarily lead to different predictions about behavior. Portions of some of these theories can be complementary, and efforts have been made to integrate features of some of them. For example, Locke and Latham (1990) combined aspects of expectancy and self-efficacy theories with their goal-setting theory. In the remainder of this chapter, the various motivation theories will be discussed in detail.

These theories can be described along a continuum from distal to proximal (Kanfer, 1992). **Distal motivation theories** deal with processes that are far removed from the behavior. **Proximal motivation theories** deal with processes that are close to the behavior. Need theories are distal because they deal with general needs that can be translated into behavior in many ways. Goal-setting theory is more proximal because it deals with goals that lead to specific behaviors, such as a goal by a salesperson to sell a particular amount of product.

NEED THEORIES

The two need theories discussed here view motivation as deriving from people's desires for certain things. It is implied that needs can differ both within the same person over time and across different people. Need theories were quite popular in the psychological literature at one time. In recent years, I/O researchers have turned their attention to more cognitively oriented theories, such as the control, goal-setting, and self-efficacy theories. Perhaps the major reason for the declining interest in need theories is that research on needs has failed to find strong relations with job performance, possibly because needs are distal constructs that are far removed from job performance. That is, the rather general needs in these theories can be satisfied in many ways and with many different behaviors. Thus, a particular need is not likely to be strongly associated with any particular behavior. A person who has a high need to accomplish challenging tasks, for example, can fulfill that need either on or off the job. Nevertheless, need theories have contributed to our understanding of work motivation by showing how people can vary in the rewards they want out of work.

Need Hierarchy Theory

Maslow's **need hierarchy theory** (Maslow, 1943) states that fulfillment of human needs is necessary for both physical and psychological health. Human needs are arranged in a hierarchy that includes physical, social, and psychological needs. Figure 8.1 illustrates the need hierarchy from the lowest level, physical needs, to the highest level, psychological needs. The lowest level, physiological needs, includes the physical necessities for survival, such as air, food, and water. The second level consists of safety needs, those things that protect us from danger. This level includes the need for security and shelter. The third level is the love needs, which include the need for love, affection, and affiliation with others. The fourth level is esteem needs, which involve self-respect and the respect of others. Finally, there is self-actualization, which Maslow did not define precisely. It refers to fulfilling personal life goals and reaching one's potential, or as Maslow stated, "the desire to become . . . everything that one is capable of becoming" (Maslow, 1943, p. 382).

According to Maslow, a need must be unmet to be motivating, and people are motivated by the lowest-level need that is unmet at the moment. That is, if two levels of needs are unmet, the lower-level need will dominate. Thus a hungry person would not be concerned with danger and might risk stealing food even though the punishment for theft is severe. A person with unmet safety needs would not be concerned with going to a party and having a good time with friends. Maslow recognized, however, that there can be exceptions to the hierarchy and that some individuals can find certain higher-order needs to be more important than lower-level ones. Furthermore, many individuals in

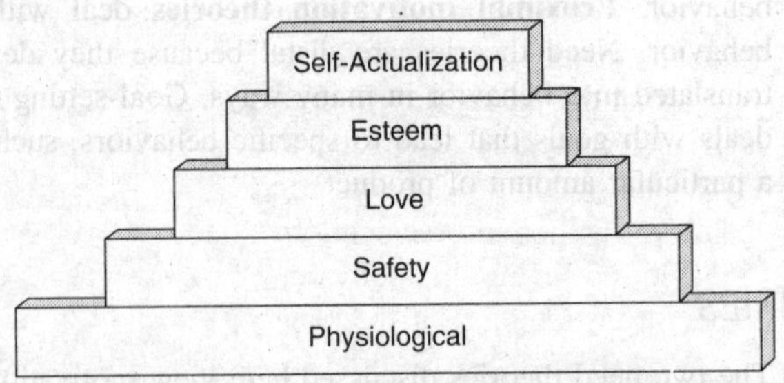

Figure 8.1 Maslow's needs hierarchy.

Western society have the first four needs met and may never have experienced deprivations of one or more of them, especially food. Therefore, the basic needs are not motivating.

Research on need hierarchy theory has not been very supportive. Locke and Henne (1986) noted that at least part of the difficulty is that Maslow's statement of the theory is rather vague, making it difficult to design good tests of it. Despite its lack of empirical support, need hierarchy theory has had a positive impact on organizations. It continues to be taught to both current and future managers. This helps focus attention on the importance of meeting employees' needs at work.

Two-Factor Theory

Herzberg's (1968) **two-factor theory** states that motivation comes from the nature of the job itself, not from external rewards or job conditions. The human needs that work addresses are divided into two categories—those deriving from the animal nature of human beings, such as the physiological needs, and those relating to the higher-level, uniquely human ability for psychological growth. Job aspects relevant to the animal needs are called **hygiene factors** and include pay, supervision, coworkers, and organizational policies. Job aspects relevant to growth needs are called **motivator factors** and include achievement, recognition, responsibility, and the nature of the work itself. According to Herzberg, the way to motivate employees and make them satisfied with their jobs is to provide appropriate levels of motivator factors. Hygiene factors, no matter how favorable, cannot lead to motivation or satisfaction with work.

Most researchers consider Herzberg's theory to be invalid (Locke & Henne, 1986). The major problem with the theory is that the two-factor structure has not been supported by research. Despite shortcomings in the theory, Herzberg has been influential. His work helped focus the field on the important issue of providing meaningful work to people. It led to the application of job enrichment in many organizations. It also was the basis for Hackman and Oldham's (1976) job characteristics theory, which is discussed in Chapters 9 and 10.

► REINFORCEMENT THEORY

Reinforcement theory describes how rewards or reinforcements can affect behavior. The theory does not deal with internal states such as motivation, so in a sense it is a nonmotivational theory. It explains behavior as a function of prior reward experiences or "reinforcement history." Behavior is seen as a response to the environment.

The major tenet of reinforcement theory is the **law of effect** (Thorndike, 1913). This states that the probability of a particular behavior increases if it is followed by a reward or reinforcement. Conversely, the probability of a behavior decreases if it is followed by a punishment. Behaviors become established through the pairing or associating of behavior with reinforcement. In other words, rewards are *contingent* on a particular behavior occurring. In a job context, this means that performance-relevant behaviors will increase in frequency if they are rewarded.

Rewards can be tangible (money) or intangible (praise). They can be given by the organization or be a by-product of tasks themselves. Thus the organization can provide a bonus for good performance, or good performance can provide a sense of accomplishment by itself. Both can be equally reinforcing and lead to continued good performance.

This rather simple idea that behavior increases if it is rewarded is the basis of incentive systems, such as piece rates for factory workers and commissions for salespeople. With **incentive systems**, rewards are contingent on individual units of productivity, such as attaching the door of a refrigerator or selling an automobile. For jobs with countable output, it can be relatively easy to institute incentive systems. For other jobs, there can be specific, measurable performance-relevant behaviors that can be quantified. For example, telephone operators can be rewarded for answering the phone within a specified number of rings. With many jobs, however, it is not feasible to develop incentive systems as discussed here. For example, it would be quite difficult to design a piece-rate system for public school teachers. Good performance for a teacher is not easy to divide into individual units of productivity or individual behaviors that can be rewarded.

Research has shown that rewards can be effective in enhancing job performance. Stajkovic and Luthans (2003) conducted a meta-analysis of 72 studies of the effects of rewards, both monetary and nonmonetary, on job performance. They found that on average reward systems result in a 16% increase in performance, but monetary rewards have a bigger impact on performance (23%) than nonmonetary rewards. Although rewards can enhance job performance under some conditions, such conditions do not always exist in organizations (Coch & French, 1948). Additional influences by other

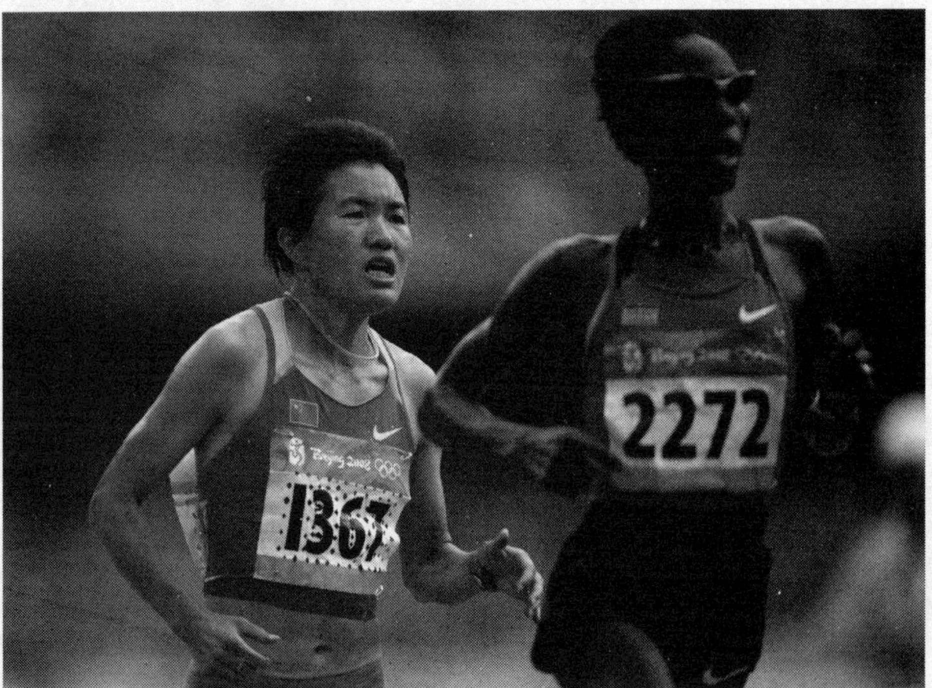

It requires a tremendous amount of motivation to win a marathon. Most jobs require far less effort than running a marathon. (© *OLIVIER MORIN/AFP/Getty Images, Inc.*)

employees, constraints in the environment (e.g., inadequate equipment), and the indifference of individuals to particular rewards can result in the failure of incentive systems.

Many organizations have applied reinforcement theory principles to influence the behavior of employees. These efforts have involved not only job performance but other behaviors as well. The control of employee absence, for example, has been the focus of reinforcement programs. Some organizations allow employees a certain number of sick leave days in a year. To encourage attendance, employees are paid for the sick leave days they do not use. Other organizations reward each employee who meets a criterion of attendance for a given period of time (e.g., no absences in a month). A rather unusual absence control program was a lottery system studied by Pedalino and Gamboa (1974). With this system, all employees present at work each day were allowed to draw a card from a standard deck of playing cards. At the end of a week, each employee with perfect attendance had a five-card poker hand. The eight employees with the best poker hands won a prize of $20. This system was found to reduce absence frequency by about 18%.

Although the principles of reinforcement theory can be useful, the theory itself has fallen out of favor among most I/O psychologists, as well as psychologists in general. The major reason is probably that reinforcement theory gives little insight into motivational processes (Locke, 1980). It merely describes relations between reinforcement and behavior. In addition, some people object to the idea of using rewards to regulate behavior. They believe that these programs represent an unethical form of manipulation. Many of those who hold this position are assuming that the techniques of reinforcement have more power over people than they actually do. Under the proper circumstances, people will voluntarily work harder for rewards that they want. Reinforcement theory says nothing about whether or not a person will want a reward. This issue is addressed by expectancy theory, which we discuss next.

► EXPECTANCY THEORY

Expectancy theory attempts to explain how rewards lead to behavior by focusing on internal cognitive states that lead to motivation. Reinforcement theory states that reinforcement will lead to behavior; expectancy theory explains when and why this will occur. The basic idea is that people will be motivated when they believe that their behavior will lead to rewards or outcomes that they want. If they do not believe that rewards will be contingent on their behavior, they will not be motivated to perform that behavior. If they do not want the contingent rewards, they will not be motivated to perform a behavior.

Several somewhat different versions of expectancy theory have been adapted to the I/O domain. The oldest and most well known is Vroom's (1964) theory that motivation or force is a mathematical function of three types of cognitions. The equation relating force to cognitions is

$$\text{Force} = \text{Expectancy} \times \Sigma(\text{Valences} \times \text{Instrumentalities})$$

In this equation, **force** represents the amount of motivation a person has to engage in a particular behavior or sequence of behaviors that is relevant to job performance. It could be thought of as the motivation to perform. **Expectancy** is the subjective probability that a person has about his or her ability to perform a behavior. It is similar to self-esteem or self-confidence in that a person believes he or she can perform the job at a particular level. *Subjective probability* means that people can vary in the certainty of their beliefs. A subjective probability of zero means that the person is certain that he or she is incapable of performing successfully. A subjective probability of 1.0 means that the person is absolutely convinced, without the slightest doubt, that he or she can perform successfully. A subjective probability of .50 means that the person believes there is a 50/50 chance of success.

Valence is the value of an outcome or reward to a person. It is the extent to which a person wants or desires something. In the job setting, money is a frequent reward that can have different valence levels for different people. **Instrumentality** is the subjective probability that a given behavior will result in a particular reward. For any given situation, there can be more than one reward or outcome for a behavior. For each possible outcome, a valence and instrumentality are multiplied. Then each valence-instrumentality product is summed into a total, and the total is multiplied by expectancy to produce a force score. If the force score is high, the person will be motivated to achieve the outcomes of the job. If the force score is low, the person will not be motivated to achieve the outcomes.

Table 8.1 shows how possible combinations of values for expectancy, valence, and instrumentality are combined into a force score. This case presumes that there is a single outcome. As the table shows, only when all three components are high will force be high. If any one of the three components is low, force will be low. If any one of the three components equals zero, there will be no motivation.

In most situations, more than one outcome is possible, so that the situation is more complex because the valence-instrumentality for each outcome is combined. The way this works is best illustrated with an example. Suppose you are at work on a Friday afternoon and your boss asks for a volunteer to work overtime for extra pay. You find your job rather boring and view the prospect of working extra hours as somewhat aversive. In this case, there are two outcomes—receiving extra money and enduring several hours of boredom. If you believe that you are capable of working overtime, your expectancy will be high. Assuming that you believe both that you will get the overtime pay and that you will be bored, both instrumentalities will be high. The final factor that determines your motivation to work overtime will be the relative valences of the two outcomes. If the positive valence or desire for money is greater than the negative valence or desire to avoid the boredom,

TABLE 8.1 The Relation of Expectancy, Valence, and Instrumentality to Force

Expectancy Score	Valence Score	Instrumentality Score	Force Score
High	High	High	High
High	High	Low	Low
High	Low	High	Low
High	Low	Low	Very low
Low	High	High	Low
Low	High	Low	Very low
Low	Low	High	Very low
Low	Low	Low	Extremely low

then you will be motivated to volunteer. If the positive valence for money is less than the negative valence for boredom, then you will be motivated to avoid volunteering.

Expectancy theory can also predict a person's choice of behavior from two or more options. Suppose that you have a dinner date, and you must choose between working overtime and going on the date. For each possible course of action, there will be an expectancy, valences, and instrumentalities. Thus there will be a force to work overtime and a force to go on the date. The course of action with the greater force is the one in theory that you will take.

There has been research support for the predictions of expectancy theory. Studies have shown that performance is related to the individual components of expectancy theory, as well as to the multiplicative combination (Van Eerde & Thierry, 1996). In the typical study, a sample of employees is surveyed and asked to indicate their expectancies that they can perform the job, as well as their valences and instrumentalities for each of a number of possible outcomes. In addition, supervisors are asked to provide job performance ratings for each employee. The total force score is then correlated with performance.

Van Eerde and Thierry (1996) conducted a meta-analysis of expectancy theory studies that looked not only at predictions of job performance but at effort and preferences as well. Although the study showed that the force score related to measures of job performance as expected, it related more strongly to measures of effort. Similarly, the force score related more strongly to an individual's preference for something other than their actual choice—for example, wanting to quit a job versus actually quitting. These findings demonstrate that motivation is only one element in the processes that lead to behavior at work. A person might be motivated to work harder, but this doesn't necessarily produce better job performance. Having a preference for something is not the same as making an actual choice, for other factors can be important, such as not being able to find another job when you want to quit your present one.

SELF-EFFICACY THEORY

Self-efficacy theory states that motivation and performance are determined in part by how effective people believe they can be (Bandura, 1982). In other words, people with high **self-efficacy** believe they are capable of accomplishing tasks and will be motivated to put forth effort. People with low self-efficacy do not believe they are capable of accomplishing tasks and will not be motivated to put forth effort. In a way, this is like a self-fulfilling prophecy in which a person behaves in a manner that fulfills his or her initial belief. Of course, people with high self-efficacy can be effective only if they have the necessary ability and constraints on performance at work are not insurmountable.

The self-efficacy concept itself is concerned with specific tasks or courses of action, and people vary in their self-efficacy across different tasks. Thus, a student might have high self-efficacy for taking essay tests and low self-efficacy for taking multiple-choice tests. This can explain why many students complain that they are good at one type of test and not the other. The theory would predict that students exert greater effort when taking the type of test for which their self-efficacy is higher.

Self-efficacy is much like the concept of expectancy. The major difference is that expectancy is concerned with a specific activity at a particular point in time, whereas self-efficacy is concerned with the general feeling that a person is or is not capable in some domain of life, such as playing tennis. For example, a person might have a high level of expectancy that if he or she makes the effort, he or she can win a tennis game. A high level of self-efficacy is the belief that one is a good player. Obviously, these two concepts are closely related, for the person with high self-efficacy should have a high expectancy, but they are not the same. The person who believes he or she is good at tennis might not be confident about winning if he or she is playing one of the best professional players in the world. Self-efficacy theory and expectancy theory are compatible in predicting that people will do well at tasks when they believe they can succeed. Expectancy theory also considers the influence of rewards on motivation, a subject that is not addressed by self-efficacy theory.

The theory of self-efficacy has been well tested, and research has been quite supportive inside and outside of the workplace (Bandura & Locke, 2003). Studies in the training domain have shown that self-efficacy for particular tasks relates to performance in training on those tasks. For example, McIntire and Levine (1991) conducted a longitudinal study of self-efficacy and performance among students taking college-level typing courses. They assessed self-efficacy before the course began and at the end of the course. They also assessed the number of words per minute typed and the grade at the end of the course. Finally, each student was asked to set a goal for the number of words per minute he or she would be able to type by the end of the course. The results were that self-efficacy before the class predicted the number of words per minute typed at the end of the course but not the grade in the course. Self-efficacy was also related to the goal set, with greater self-efficacy associated with setting a higher goal. These results suggest that self-efficacy can be a factor in future performance. The results with goals suggest that self-efficacy might operate through the setting of goals, so that students with high self-efficacy set harder goals, which results in better performance. Goal setting is discussed in detail later in this chapter.

Similar results with self-efficacy have been found in other training studies. Mathieu, Martineau, and Tannenbaum (1993) found that self-efficacy assessed before a bowling class was related to students' subsequent performance at the end of class. Locke and Latham (1990) conducted a meta-analysis of 13 studies relating self-efficacy to performance in both laboratory and field settings. They found a mean correlation of .39, with correlations as high as .74.

Whereas at least some of the observed relation between people's self-efficacy and their performance can be attributed to motivational effects of self-efficacy, some of the relation might also be due to the effects of successful performance on self-efficacy. W. D. Davis, Fedor, Parsons, and Herold (2000) studied self-efficacy in aircraft pilot training. Those students who performed well in simulation training developed high self-efficacy for actual subsequent flying. In the McIntire and Levine (1991) study, course grade related to self-efficacy at the end of the class but not the beginning, suggesting that students who achieved better grades enhanced their self-efficacy. Karl, O'Leary-Kelly, and Martocchio (1993) found that positive feedback on a speed reading task raised the self-efficacy of people who were initially low in self-efficacy.

Eden and his associates conducted a series of studies in the workplace in which they manipulated self-efficacy to see its effects on job performance. These experimental studies controlled for ability and initial motivation by randomly assigning subjects to have their self-efficacy raised or not by providing information or training. Eden refers to this as the **Galatea effect**, in which people's beliefs about their own capabilities lead them to perform better, as in a self-fulfilling prophecy. Eden and Aviram (1993) successfully applied this approach to increase the job search success of unemployed people. Similarly, Eden and Zuk (1995) used this technique to convince naval cadets in the Israel Defense Forces that they were unlikely to get seasick. This illness creates significant problems for all navies because it can interfere with job performance at sea. Eden and Zuk conducted an experiment in which cadets were randomly assigned to one of two groups—a group that attended a briefing where they were assured that seasickness was unlikely and would not interfere with their performance or a control group that was given no such briefing. While at sea, the briefed cadets had less seasickness and performed better than the control group. This very simple technique to enhance self-efficacy was quite effective.

In another military study, this time in the United States, Jex, Bliese, Buzzell, and Primeau (2001) linked self-efficacy to soldier stress and well-being. They found that individuals with high levels of self-efficacy reported feeling low levels of work overload and psychological distress. Taken together, all this research suggests that high self-efficacy contributes to both effective performance and employee well-being.

Self-efficacy theory is a useful theory with implications for the work setting. It suggests that motivation and performance, and perhaps well-being, can be enhanced by raising the self-efficacy of employees. Bandura (1982) discussed how self-efficacy can develop through a series of successes with increasingly difficult tasks. An organization can apply this principle by structuring the assignments of employees in such a way that they succeed at increasingly challenging tasks. This strategy can be particularly important with new employees, who may take some period of time to become adept at all aspects of the job. Relatively simple assignments can be given to new employees, with more difficult tasks introduced slowly to allow the person to experience few, if any, failures. As the person experiences success on more and more difficult tasks, his or her self-efficacy should increase. Karl et al. (1993) suggested using this approach in training programs. Morin and Latham (2000) showed that training can successfully raise self-efficacy (see the International Research box).

INTERNATIONAL RESEARCH

It has been well established in the research literature that self-efficacy is related to performance. An important question concerns how self-efficacy can be raised.

Morin and Latham (2000) conducted a study in Ontario, Canada, to explore the role of self-efficacy and skill enhancement in performance. Participants were 41 supervisors and engineers in a paper mill. Each participant sat through a 1-day interpersonal communication skills training session that included listening to a lecture, watching videotaped performances, and completing role-play exercises. Evaluation at the completion of the training showed that communication skills had increased. However, the researchers felt that just raising skills was not enough; rather, a second intervention was needed to raise self-efficacy.

Following the 1-day training, participants were randomly assigned to one of four follow-up conditions: mental practice training, goal-setting training, both, or a control condition of neither. Mental practice taught participants how to mentally rehearse their communication skills. It was hypothesized that this would raise self-efficacy by increasing confidence in the newly learned skills. The goal setting was not expected to impact self-efficacy because it dealt not with enhancing the skills but with the setting of improvement goals. Approximately 1 month after completion of the follow-up training, two peers of each participant rated their communication behavior on the job.

Results showed that the two conditions involving mental practice raised self-efficacy and communication performance on the job. The other two conditions had no effect on self-esteem or on performance. This led the authors to conclude that skill enhancement acquired from training is insufficient for enhancing performance in communication. Rather, it is necessary to raise self-efficacy as well as skills to achieve performance gain.

Source: From "The Effect of Mental Practice and Goal Setting as a Transfer of Training Intervention on Supervisors' Self-Efficacy and Communication Skills: An Exploratory Study," by L. Morin and G. P. Latham, (2000) *Applied Psychology: An International Review, 49,* 566–578.

▶ JUSTICE THEORIES

A different approach to motivation is provided by justice theories, which focus on norms for fair treatment of employees by their organizations. The underlying assumption of these theories is that people value fairness and that they are motivated to maintain fairness in relationships between themselves and organizations.

Equity theory (Adams, 1965) states that people are motivated to achieve a condition of fairness or equity in their dealings with other people and with organizations. According to Adams (1965), employees who find themselves in inequitable situations will experience dissatisfaction and emotional tension, which they will be motivated to reduce. The theory specifies conditions under which inequity will occur and what employees are likely to do to reduce it.

Inequity is a psychological state that arises from employees' comparisons of themselves with others. What is specifically compared are ratios of outcomes to inputs. **Outcomes** are the rewards or everything of personal value that an employee gets from working for an organization, including pay, fringe benefits, good treatment, enjoyment, and status. **Inputs** are the contributions made by the employee to the organization. They include not only the work that the employee accomplishes but the experience and talents that he or she brings to the job as well. Thus an employee with many years of job experience would have greater inputs than an employee just starting out in a career.

The theory posits that employees make psychological comparisons of their own outcome/input ratios to those of other employees. That is, employees psychologically evaluate how much they receive from the job (outcomes) in relation to their contributions (inputs), which is represented as the ratio

Outcomes/Inputs

Each employee compares his or her ratio to the ratios of people chosen for comparison. These comparison people or *others* might be employees doing the same job inside or outside the organization. They might also be people who have different types of jobs. The comparison involves the entire ratio and not the individual outcomes or inputs. Thus a person may believe a situation is equitable even though his or her outcomes are less than inputs. It is only when the employee believes that his or her ratio is different from other people's that inequity exists. This difference can be in either direction. That is, an employee can experience *underpayment* inequity if he or

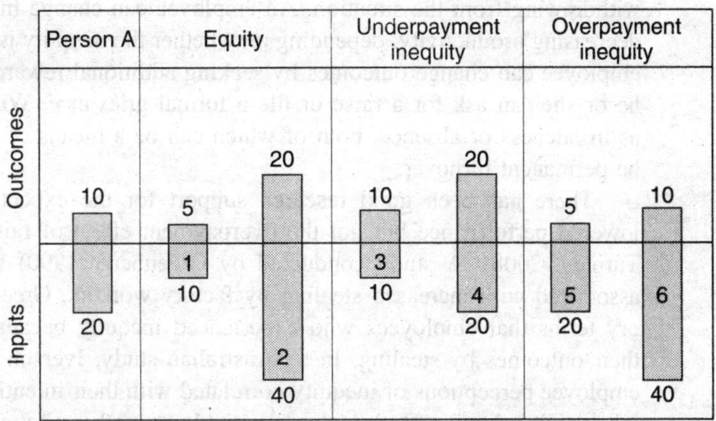

Figure 8.2 An illustration of equity and inequity. Person A has twice as many inputs as outcomes (see bars in first column). The other six bars represent comparison others' inputs and outcomes. Person A will experience equity or inequity depending on whom he or she chooses as a comparison. Cases 1 and 2 illustrate equity, where both inputs are double outcomes. Case 3 represents underpayment because the outcomes are the same as Person A's, but inputs are only half. Case 4 is underpayment because inputs are the same as Person A's, but outcomes are double. Case 5 is overpayment because inputs are the same as Person A's, but outcomes are half. Case 6 is overpayment because outcomes are the same as Person A's, but inputs are double.

she believes that other people get more outcomes for their inputs. *Overpayment* inequity exists when an employee believes he or she is getting more outcomes for his or her inputs than other people are getting.

Figure 8.2 illustrates several possible comparison situations. In each case, it is presumed that the target employee (Person A) has a ratio of 10/20. That is, Person A receives one unit of outcome for each two units of input. Note that the outcome and input scores do not have to be equal. It is the comparison of ratios that is important, not the comparison of outcomes to inputs. In the first two cases, the comparison other also has a ratio that reduces to one outcome per two inputs, so equity is achieved. In the first case, the outcomes are half of Person A's (5), but the inputs are half as well (10). In the second case, both the outcomes and the inputs are double (20 and 40, respectively). The next two cases illustrate underpayment inequity. That is, Person A's ratio is lower than the comparison other's, resulting in a feeling of underpayment. In the third case, the comparison other is getting the same outcomes but is giving only half the inputs (10/10), and in the fourth case, the comparison other is getting double the outcomes for the same inputs. The last two cases involve overpayment inequity. That is, Person A is receiving more outcomes per unit of input than the comparison other. In case 5, the comparison other receives half the outcomes for the same inputs, and in case 6 the comparison other receives the same outcomes for double the inputs.

According to Adams (1965), underpayment inequity induces anger and overpayment inequity induces guilt. In either case, the employee will be motivated to reduce the inequity through several possible mechanisms. Three of these mechanisms are particularly relevant to the organizational setting—changing inputs, changing outcomes, and withdrawing from the situation. An employee can change inputs by either increasing or decreasing productivity, depending on whether the inequity is over- or underpayment. An employee can change outcomes by seeking additional rewards from work. For example, he or she can ask for a raise or file a formal grievance. Withdrawal can be temporary, as in lateness or absence, both of which can be a means of reducing inputs. It can also be permanent turnover.

There has been good research support for the expected underpayment effect of lowered performance but not the overpayment effect of raised performance (Bolino & Turnley, 2008). A study conducted by Greenberg (1990) showed that a pay cut was associated with increased stealing by factory workers. Greenberg argued in equity theory terms that employees who experienced inequity because of the pay cut increased their outcomes by stealing. In an Australian study, Iverson and Roy (1994) found that employee perceptions of inequity correlated with their intentions to quit the job and with job search behavior. Both of these variables have been found to predict turnover (Blau, 2007), as we will discuss in Chapter 10.

Recent research on fairness in the workplace has replaced equity theory with the somewhat different perspective of **fairness theory** (Cropanzano, Byrne, Bobocel, & Rupp, 2001). Rather than focusing on the fair allocation or distribution of rewards, fairness theory distinguishes between the distribution of rewards and the procedures by which rewards are allocated. **Distributive justice** is similar to equity and concerns the fairness with which rewards are found among people. **Procedural justice** is concerned with the fairness of the reward distribution process as opposed to the results of that distribution. Although in many cases it might be expected that procedural justice would lead to distributive justice, this is not always the case. For example, past reward policies may have created a situation in which some people are paid more than others for similar inputs, a case that represents distributive injustice. A new procedure that gives the underpaid a small salary adjustment each year to make up for it might be seen as procedural justice, even though it might take years to make up the difference.

Another distinction from equity theory is that fairness theory doesn't assume that perceptions of injustice necessarily come from a social comparison with others. Rather, it suggests that people perceive injustice when something negative happens and they perceive it to have been done purposefully by another person in an unfair way. For example, suppose a company fails to give employees an annual raise. This would be a negative event which employees will see as unfair if they perceive that management has withheld the raise purposefully and that the basis for doing so is unreasonable. If the company has announced financial problems, employees might see this as beyond management's control and might not perceive the situation as unfair. However, if management fails to provide a convincing explanation, employees will likely feel the situation is unfair.

There have been many studies relating both distributive and procedural justice perceptions by employees to many organizationally relevant outcomes. Cohen-Charash and Spector (2001) conducted a meta-analysis of these studies and found, as might be expected from equity theory, that both forms of justice are related to job performance, job satisfaction, and intention of quitting the job. Injustice has been shown to be related to both positive behaviors, such as volunteering to do extra work (Fassina, Jones, & Uggerslev, 2008), and negative behaviors that harm organizations, such as excessive absence (Jones, 2009). Interestingly Sweeney and McFarlin (1997) found that procedural justice is more important for women, but distributive justice is more important for men. Apparently for women the procedure by which rewards are allocated is more important, but for men the results are what matter most.

▶ GOAL-SETTING THEORY

The theory of motivation that has been the most useful for I/O psychologists is **goal-setting theory** (Locke & Latham, 1990). Principles of goal setting have been widely used in organizations, although this is not necessarily based on the theory. For example, Yearta, Maitlis, and Briner (1995) noted that 79% of British organizations use some form of goal setting. Various goal-setting programs have been widely used throughout the industrialized world.

The basic idea of this theory is that people's behavior is motivated by their internal *intentions*, *objectives*, or *goals*—the terms are used here interchangeably. Goals are quite "proximal" constructs, for they can be tied quite closely to specific behaviors. For example, a salesperson might have the goal of selling a certain amount of product in a given month. Because goals can be tied closely to particular behaviors relevant for performance, goal-setting theory has been strongly tied to behavior.

According to the theory, a goal is what a person consciously wants to attain or achieve. Goals can be specific, such as "receive an 'A' on the next exam," or general, such as "do well in school." General goals such as doing well in school are often associated with a number of more specific goals such as receiving an "A" in a particular course. People can vary in their **goal orientation**—that is, in whether they focus their efforts on learning (**learning orientation**) or on achieving certain levels of job performance (**performance orientation**). A person with a learning orientation is primarily concerned with enhancing knowledge and skill, whereas a person with a performance orientation focuses efforts on enhancing performance on specific job tasks (DeShon & Gillespie, 2005; Payne, Youngcourt, & Beaubien, 2007). However, goal strategies that might be effective for one orientation will not necessarily be optimal for the other. Kozlowski and Bell (2006) noted that there can be an incompatibility between the two orientations in that focusing on performance directs attention away from learning. Most of the research on goal setting has focused on performance and does not necessarily apply to learning goals.

Locke and Henne (1986) noted four ways in which goals affect behavior. First, goals direct attention and action to behaviors that the person believes will achieve the goal. A student who has the goal of making an "A" on an exam will engage in studying behavior, such as reading the assigned material and reviewing class notes. Second, goals mobilize effort in that the person tries harder. The student with the goal of an "A" will concentrate harder to learn the material. Third, goals increase persistence, resulting in more time spent on the behaviors necessary for goal attainment. The student who wants an "A" will spend more time studying. Finally, goals can motivate the search for effective strategies to attain them. The conscientious student will attempt to learn effective ways of studying and good test-taking strategies.

Goal-setting theory predicts that people will exert effort toward accomplishing their goals and that job performance is a function of the goals set. From an organizational standpoint, goal setting can be an effective means of maintaining or increasing job performance, and many organizations have used goal setting to do so. According to Locke

(2000), several factors are necessary for goal setting to be effective in improving job performance (Table 8.2). First, employees must have *goal commitment*, which means that they accept the goal. An organizational goal is not necessarily an individual employee goal, and only goals of the individual person will motivate behavior. Second, *feedback* is necessary because it allows people to know whether or not their behavior is moving them toward or away from their goals. It is difficult for goals to direct behavior unless the person receives feedback. Third, the more difficult the goal, the better the performance is likely to be. A goal of a 4.0 GPA is likely to result in better performance than a goal of 3.5, which is likely to result in better performance than a goal of 3.0. Although people will not always reach their goals, the harder the goal, the better the performance, at least until the point at which the person is working at the limit of his or her capacity. Fourth, specific hard goals are more effective than vague "do your best" goals. Vague goals can be effective, but specific goals that allow the person to know when they are met are best. Finally, self-set goals are usually better than organizationally assigned goals. It is generally best to either allow employees to set their own goals or at least allow them input into setting goals rather than having supervisors assign goals without employee involvement. This leads to better goal acceptance, which is necessary for goals to be effective.

Goal-setting theory has been shown to be effective at increasing job performance (e.g., Ludwig & Goomas, 2009). Not only have its propositions been the subject of considerable research, but goal setting is a popular means of increasing job performance as well. For example, H. J. Klein, Wesson, Hollenbeck, and Alge (1999) described a meta-analysis of 83 studies, showing that greater goal commitment is associated with better performance. The theory and research surrounding goal-setting theory have underscored important factors (shown in Table 8.2) that should be incorporated into a goal-setting program.

Although research has shown that goal setting can be effective, some researchers discussed its limitations. Yearta et al. (1995) noted that most goal-setting studies involved single goals, such as increased production in a factory. They showed that with more complex jobs and multiple goals, performance was lower when goals were difficult. Doerr, Mitchell, Klastorin, and Brown (1996) showed that group goals were better than individual goals for increasing speed of production in a fish-processing plant (see the International Research box). Ambrose and Kulik (1999) listed several drawbacks of goal setting. The most important are that employees sometimes focus so much on the goals that they ignore other equally important aspects of the job and that goals can conflict, so that working on one prevents achieving another. Finally, Drach-Zahavy and Erez (2002) discussed how difficult goals can actually lead to worse performance when stress

TABLE 8.2 Important Factors for Goal Setting to Improve Job Performance

1. Goal acceptance by the employee.
2. Feedback on progress toward goals.
3. Difficult and challenging goals.
4. Specific goals.

Source: "Work Motivation Theories," by E. A. Locke and D. Henne, (1986) in C. L. Cooper and I. T. Robertson (Eds.), *International Review of Industrial and Organizational Psychology 1986*. Chichester, England: John Wiley.

INTERNATIONAL RESEARCH

There has been a trend in large organizations toward the use of work groups and teams rather than individuals to accomplish work. Thus, it is important that we understand how groups and individuals differ in their behavior and reactions. One area of concern is how to motivate people who work in groups. Goal setting can be an effective motivational technique for individuals, but will it be equally effective with groups?

This study was conducted in a fish-processing plant in the northwestern United States with a workforce consisting entirely of non-Americans. These employees worked 2 to 3 hours per day cleaning and dressing salmon that arrived by boat. During the course of the study, 39 employees participated in an experiment with goal setting. Three conditions were created—group goal, individual goal, and no goal. An initial baseline measure of production speed was taken to serve as the standard against which to set goals. The goals represented working at a consistent pace that was faster than typically maintained. Employees were given feedback as well as an incentive of state lottery tickets for goal achievement.

To meet the group goal, the output of everyone combined had to achieve the predetermined amount. For the individual condition, each person had his or her own goal. Results showed that productivity was significantly higher for both conditions than for the no goal control condition, although productivity for the group goal condition was even higher than for the individual goal condition. Mean time to process 50 fish was 538 versus 570 seconds for the group and individual goal conditions, respectively. The no goal condition mean was 702 seconds.

These results demonstrate that in production situations, goal setting can be quite effective. Furthermore, groups might respond even more favorably than individuals. As discussed in Chapter 12, groups can have powerful effects on members, and conditions that motivate groups can have enhanced effects on individuals in those groups. However, it should be recognized that this study involved single goals with very simple tasks. These effects might not occur in situations where things are more complex. Nevertheless, goal setting can be a powerful motivational tool if applied appropriately in the proper setting.

Source: From "Impact of Material Flow Policies and Goals on Job Outcomes," by K. H. Doerr, T. R. Mitchell, T. D. Klastorin, and K. A. Brown, 1996, *Journal of Applied Psychology*, *81*, 142–152.

is high. Putting all this together suggests that difficult goals work best when situations are relatively simple (single goals and simple jobs) and there are low levels of stress.

▶ CONTROL THEORY

Control theory (Klein, 1989) builds upon goal-setting theory by focusing on how feedback affects motivation to maintain effort toward goals. As shown in Figure 8.3, the process explained by the theory begins with a goal that the person is intending to accomplish. The goal might be assigned by a supervisor or chosen by the individual, but the theory says that the person must believe the goal is attainable and accept it. Over time, as the person works toward the goal, feedback about performance will be given. The person will evaluate the feedback by comparing current goal progress to some internal standard or expected progress. If progress is insufficient, the person will be motivated to take action, which might include goal reevaluation and modification or adoption of different strategies to improve performance. This might be simply exerting more effort (working harder) or adopting new approaches that might be more effective (working smarter).

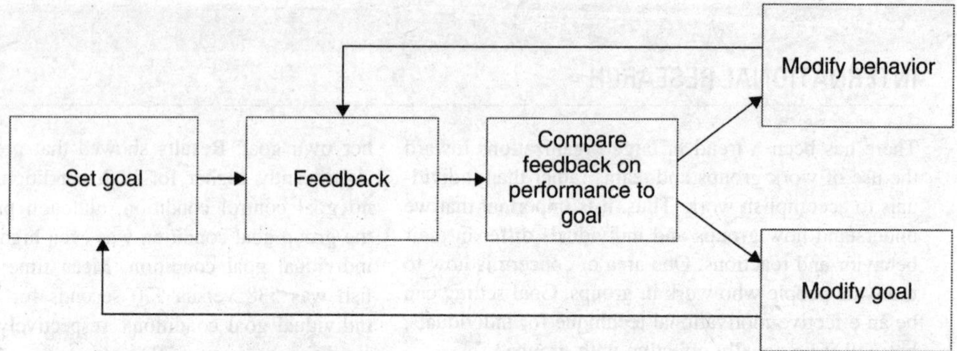

Figure 8.3 Control theory suggests that people set goals and then evaluate feedback about how well their performance is achieving their goals. Discrepancies can motivate people to modify their behaviors or their goals.

Evidence has been provided in support of control theory predictions. For example, Donovan and Williams (2003) studied the goals and performance of university track and field athletes during an 8-week season. Before the season, each athlete set goals for the first meet and the entire season. Each week the athletes completed progress reports that included their weekly performance and goals for the following week. They tended to revise their future goals based on discrepancy between their performance and prior goals, and the amount of goal adjustment was greater for the proximal next week goals than the distal season goals. This showed that feedback did result in adjustment to goals rather than just increased effort toward meeting the goals originally set,

▶ ACTION THEORY

Action theory is a comprehensive German theory of work behavior that describes a process linking goals and intentions to behaviors (Frese & Zapf, 1994). This theory proposes that work motivation theories should focus mainly on goal-oriented or volitional (voluntary) behaviors called actions. Such actions are the product of a conscious intent to accomplish something, which can be as small as finishing one piece on an assembly line or as large as achieving a promotion at work. The major focus of this theory is on the actions themselves and on the processes leading to actions.

Action theory describes the **action process** linking a hierarchy of cognitions to both actions and feedback from the environment. Figure 8.4 illustrates this sequence. It begins with an initial desire to accomplish or have something, and that desire leads to specific goals and objectives to achieve or acquire it. These goals in the workplace are often tied to tasks (similar to tasks in a job analysis) that define the nature of what the individual employee is supposed to accomplish at work. The theory points out that there is an important distinction between external tasks and internal tasks. An external task is assigned by the organization to the employee, whereas an internal task is chosen by the employee himself or herself. An important element is the redefinition process whereby the employee translates an external task into an internal one. In other words, the employee changes the assigned task to suit himself or herself.

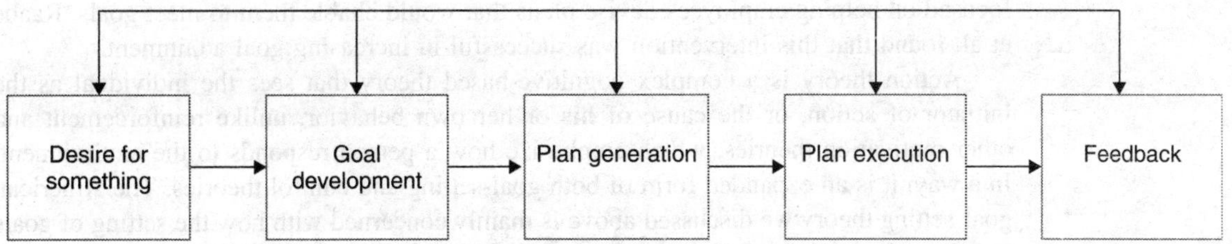

Figure 8.4 The action process from German action theory.

The next step after goals are set is to translate those goals into plans. Plans are specific steps chosen to accomplish the goals and are specifications of actions and sequences of actions. Next, the plan is executed, and execution involves actions. Finally the person receives feedback either from the environment itself or from other people. This feedback informs the employee about whether progress is being made toward the goal. Positive feedback can help maintain actions that are part of plans, and negative feedback can lead to modification of goals, plans, or actions.

An example of the process would be the following. You want to make a lot of money, so you set the goal of landing a well-paying job when you graduate college. Your plan might be to major in a field in which such jobs are plentiful and to have a high GPA. Your actions will address these aspects of the plan, such as investigating job opportunities of various majors and studying for classes. Feedback is provided by grades, and if you find your GPA is not high enough, you might change your goal and decide to settle for a lower-paying job, change your plan and choose a different major, or change your actions and study harder.

Action theory also contains personality variables. One of the most important is **action versus state orientation**. A person who is action oriented is one who tends to follow the action process. He or she sets goals, formulates plans, and then sticks with them until the goals are achieved. State-oriented people are the opposite. They have difficulty committing to a course of action, are easily distracted, and give up when faced with setbacks (Kuhl & Beckmann, 1994). Research has shown that action-oriented people tend to perform better on the job (Diefendorff, Hall, Lord, & Strean, 2000; Jaramillo, Locander, Spector, & Harris, 2007), perhaps in part due to the fact that state-oriented people have a tendency to procrastinate (Van Eerde, 2000).

Research has also tended to support some of the predictions made from action theory. For example, Sonnentag (1998) studied the cognitive processes underlying the task behavior of high- and average-performing computer software programmers, making some predictions based on action theory. As expected, high performers were able to understand the problem more quickly so they could move on to the planning stage (step 3 of the action sequence) and to make better use of feedback (step 5). The study of high-performing individuals within an action theory framework can be potentially useful in suggesting ways to train employees to be more effective.

Action theory has also proven useful in the design of an organizational intervention intended to enhance employee motivation. Raabe, Frese, and Beehr (2007) designed an intervention that was used in a German company to increase the extent to which employees enhanced their job skills and managed their own careers. Whereas a goal theory-based intervention would have focused only on goals, this action theory approach focused on helping employees devise plans that would enable them to meet goals. Raabe et al. found that this intervention was successful in increasing goal attainment.

Action theory is a complex cognitive-based theory that sees the individual as the initiator of action, or the cause of his or her own behavior, unlike reinforcement and other motivation theories, which emphasize how a person responds to the environment. In a way, it is an expanded form of both goal-setting and control theories. The American goal-setting theory we discussed above is mainly concerned with how the setting of goals translates into job performance (Farr, Hofmann, & Ringenbach, 1993). Control theory focuses on how feedback concerning goal progress affects behavior. Action theory goes further than each of these theories in examining the cognitive processes that intervene between goals and performance.

▶ CHAPTER SUMMARY

This chapter discussed nine theories that consider motivation from very different perspectives. The two need theories—need hierarchy and two-factor—view motivation as arising from internal needs. Need hierarchy theory classifies human needs into five categories. Needs are rather broad, and the theory's predictions are imprecise, as it cannot identify very well what specific behaviors are likely to arise. A person with a high level of achievement need, for example, might work hard on the job to achieve success. On the other hand, he or she might direct most of his or her efforts to achievement outside of work. Two-factor theory states that motivation comes from two categories of needs that are addressed by work.

Reinforcement theory takes a situational view and states that behavior is a function of a person's reinforcement history. According to this theory, job-relevant behaviors that are rewarded are likely to be repeated in the future. Expectancy theory attempts to explain how rewards lead to behavior. It states that people will perform well if they believe that their efforts will lead to successful performance, that successful performance will lead to rewards and if they want the rewards.

Self-efficacy theory states that people's beliefs about their own capabilities are an important component of motivation. A person who believes that he or she is incapable of performing on the job is not likely even to try. A high level of self-efficacy or belief in one's own capability is a necessary component in work motivation and subsequent job performance.

Justice theories state that people value fair and equitable treatment by their organizations. Equity theory states that people compare themselves to others on the ratio of outcomes to inputs at work, and discrepancies in ratios can motivate people to take action. This might include changing the level of contribution to the organization, changing the rewards obtained from work, or quitting. More-modern justice theories focus on both the distribution of rewards (distributive justice) and the fairness of procedures by which rewards are allocated among people (procedural justice).

Goal-setting theory posits that people's behaviors are directed by conscious goals and objectives. The theory underscores several factors that are important determinants of how well goal setting can improve job performance. Four are particularly important: goal commitment by employees, feedback about progress toward goals, goal difficulty, and specificity of goals.

Control theory extends goal-setting theory by focusing attention on feedback toward goal attainment. It suggests that people set goals and then seek information about how well they are progressing toward goal achievement. Discrepancies between expected and actual goal progress will motivate individuals to either reassess and modify their goals or change their behaviors to make better progress.

German action theory describes the action process linking goals to behavior. The process begins with the desire to achieve something, and that desire is translated into a goal. Plans are generated to achieve the goal, and plan execution involves actions. Feedback occurs in response to actions and can result in modification of the prior steps.

Although these various theories view motivation from different perspectives, they are not necessarily incompatible, and in fact elements of various theories have been integrated. Locke and Latham (1990) discussed consistencies between features of expectancy theory, self-efficacy theory, and goal-setting theory. In particular, they saw self-efficacy as an important ingredient in goal commitment. A person with low self-efficacy concerning the achievement of a goal is not likely to become committed to that goal.

I/O PSYCHOLOGY IN PRACTICE

(Courtesy of Lynn Summers)

This case concerns a goal-based theft-control program that Dr. Lynn Summers helped design. Dr. Summers received his Ph.D. in I/O psychology in 1977 from the University of South Florida. He has worked for a variety of organizations and is currently a human resources specialist with the North Carolina Office of State Personnel. Prior to that, he was Vice President of Performaworks Corporation, a company that provides I/O services via the internet. One of its specialties is 360-degree feedback (see Chapter 4) done online. The peers, subordinates, and supervisors of an employee can complete an assessment about him or her on a web page. After viewing the feedback from these various perspectives, the employee prepares an improvement plan by interacting with an online program. Performaworks also does other types of assessments and opinion surveys using the internet. It is one example of how I/O psychologists can use the internet for business. Before helping to found the company, Dr. Summers had his own consulting practice. One of his projects was helping an organization deal with employee theft.

Dr. Summers was asked by a national fast-food chain to devise a program to control theft in its restaurants. In the restaurant industry, internal theft is a much larger problem than theft due to robbery. This chain wanted to do something about employees who were either stealing food for themselves or giving food to friends for free. Dr. Summers investigated the situation and helped a team of employees representing different restaurants come up with six different interventions. Of interest here is a goal-setting procedure, which turned out to be the most effective.

The goal-setting procedure was quite simple. In each restaurant, the manager assigned a small group of employees responsibility for control of the theft of a particular item, such as chicken breasts. The group was shown how to figure out the number of chicken breasts that were "missing" each day. It was also assigned a specific goal for reducing the number.

The company found that the goal-setting program was quite effective in that thefts were reduced. What no one is certain about is why it worked. The employees were not instructed in how they should go about reducing the theft—they were given only a goal. It is possible that members of the group had been stealing, and they merely stopped. It is also possible that the group members knew which people were stealing and put pressure on them to stop. At the very least, the program directed employee attention to the problem, and as we discussed previously, this is one of the ways goal setting enhances performance. No matter why it worked, this case illustrates that goal setting can be an effective means of changing behavior. Often managers need only set a goal and then allow their subordinates the latitude to figure out how to achieve it.

Discussion Questions

1. What factors cause employees to steal?
2. Why did the goal-setting program reduce stealing?
3. What other interventions might have reduced stealing?
4. How widespread do you think employee theft is in large organizations?

LEARNING BY DOING

Motivation Case at Work

Find an example of motivation that relates to one of the theories discussed in the chapter. It could be an item from a newspaper or one of the online news services. Give the background for your case, explaining who the person is and what he or she did. Then explain how it relates to one of the theories in the chapter.

How Companies Motivate Their Employees

Find an example of how companies motivate their employees. This can be from your own work experience, the experience of someone you know, or something you found on the internet. Explain the approach and how it relates to one or more of the theories in this chapter.

CHAPTER **9**

Feelings About Work: Job Attitudes and Emotions

CHAPTER 9 OUTLINE

- THE NATURE OF JOB SATISFACTION
- HOW PEOPLE FEEL ABOUT THEIR JOBS
- THE ASSESSMENT OF JOB SATISFACTION
  - Job Descriptive Index (JDI)
  - Minnesota Satisfaction Questionnaire (MSQ)
  - Job in General Scale (JIG)
  - Is Global Satisfaction the Sum of Facets?
- ANTECEDENTS OF JOB SATISFACTION
  - Environmental Antecedents of Job Satisfaction
  - Personal Antecedents of Job Satisfaction
  - Person-Job Fit
- POTENTIAL EFFECTS OF JOB SATISFACTION
  - Job Satisfaction and Job Performance
  - Job Satisfaction and Turnover
  - Job Satisfaction and Absence
  - Health and Well-Being
  - Job and Life Satisfaction
- ORGANIZATIONAL COMMITMENT
  - Assessment of Organizational Commitment
  - Organizational Commitment and Other Variables
- EMOTIONS AT WORK
  - Causes and Consequences of Emotions at Work
  - Emotional Labor
- CHAPTER SUMMARY
- I/O PSYCHOLOGY IN PRACTICE
- LEARNING BY DOING

National polls of American workers have typically found that the majority are satisfied with their jobs. For example, the Society for Human Resource Management (2009) conducted a 2009 survey that found 86% of employees were satisfied with their jobs. A 2002 poll suggests that Canadians are even more satisfied than Americans, with 92% of respondents saying they like their jobs (Shields, 2006).

One of the major tasks I/O psychologists perform is assessing employee attitudes about their jobs, especially their job satisfaction, and determining ways to improve it. I/O researchers have extensively studied the causes and consequences of job satisfaction since the beginning of the I/O field itself. It is one of the two most studied variables in I/O psychology (the other one is job performance). Much of this popularity, as we will see, derives from the relative ease with which it can be assessed. Another reason for the popularity of the study of job satisfaction is that it is a central variable in many theories that deal with organizational phenomena, such as the nature of work, supervision, and the job environment. Job satisfaction has been posited as a cause of important employee and organizational outcomes ranging from job performance to health and longevity.

Job satisfaction, however, is not the only variable that reflects how people feel about work. Organizational commitment is another attitude that concerns people's feelings of attachment to their jobs and organizations. Feelings also include both positive and negative emotions that are experienced at work, such as anger over unfair treatment and joy over receiving a promotion.

In this chapter, we begin with a discussion of job satisfaction, including how it is measured, its potential causes, and its possible consequences. Job satisfaction is often included in studies of all sorts of organizational phenomena. You will see it frequently mentioned throughout most of the remaining chapters of this book. We will also include a discussion of organizational commitment, which relates to many of the same variables as job satisfaction. Finally, we will discuss emotions in the workplace, both their causes and their consequences.

Objectives: The student who studies this chapter should be able to:

- Define job satisfaction and organizational commitment.
- Characterize the differences between job satisfaction and organizational commitment.
- Explain how job satisfaction and organizational commitment are measured.
- Summarize the findings on possible causes and effects of job satisfaction and organizational commitment.
- Discuss how emotions are experienced by employees at work and how they impact organizations.

THE NATURE OF JOB SATISFACTION

Job satisfaction is an attitudinal variable that reflects how people feel about their jobs overall, as well as various aspects of the jobs. In simple terms, job satisfaction is the extent to which people like their jobs; job dissatisfaction is the extent to which they dislike them.

There have been two approaches to the study of job satisfaction—the global approach and the facet approach. The *global approach* treats job satisfaction as a single, overall

TABLE 9.1 Common Job Satisfaction Facets

Pay	Job conditions
Promotion opportunities	Nature of the work itself
Fringe benefits	Communication
Supervision	Security
Coworkers	

feeling toward the job. Many studies assess people's overall satisfaction, and many of the findings discussed in this chapter reflect that variable.

The alternative approach is to focus on job **facets** or different aspects of the job, such as rewards (pay or fringe benefits), other people on the job (supervisors or coworkers), job conditions, and the nature of the work itself. A list of the most often studied facets appears in Table 9.1. The facet approach permits a more complete picture of job satisfaction. An individual typically has different levels of satisfaction with the various facets. He or she might be very dissatisfied with pay and fringe benefits but at the same time be very satisfied with the nature of the work and supervisors. This is a typical pattern for Americans, as we will see in the next section.

HOW PEOPLE FEEL ABOUT THEIR JOBS

As noted earlier, surveys show that the majority of Americans like their jobs (Society for Human Resource Management, 2009), but this doesn't mean they like all aspects of their jobs equally. The typical American pattern of facet satisfaction is shown in Figure 9.1, with data from the norms (Spector, 2008) of the Job Satisfaction Survey (JSS) (Spector, 1985). The JSS is a scale that assesses eight popular facets of job satisfaction. The norms are based on the job satisfaction scores of 36,380 employees from more than 100 organizations throughout the United States. The figure shows that Americans are typically

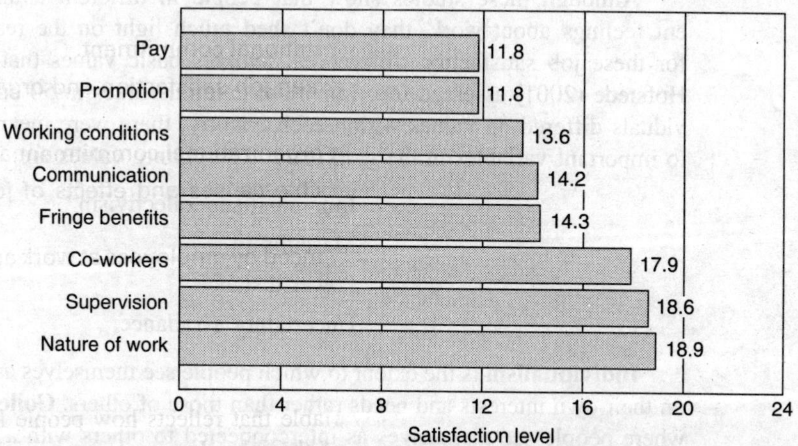

Figure 9.1 The mean satisfaction levels for various facets of the Job Satisfaction Survey. Satisfaction level is indicated on the horizontal axis. The numbers next to the bars are the means for each facet. They range from a low of 11.8 for pay and promotion to a high of 18.9 for nature of work. From "Measurement of Human Service Staff Satisfaction: Development of the Job Satisfaction Survey," by P. E. Spector, 1985, *American Journal of Community Psychology, 13,* 693–713.

TABLE 9.2 Job Satisfaction of Managers in 24 Countries, Listed From Most to Least Satisfied

1. Canada	9. New Zealand	17. France
2. Sweden	10. Ukraine	18. Bulgaria
3. Israel	11. Slovenia	19. Romania
4. Estonia	12. Poiand	20. South Africa
5. India	13. Spain	21. People's Republic of China
6. United States	14. Taiwan	22. Hong Kong
7. Belgium	15. Brazil	23. Japan
8. Germany	16. Australia	24. England

Source: "Do National Levels of Individualism and Internal Locus of Control Relate to Well-Being: An Ecological Level International Study," by P. E. Spector, C. L. Cooper, J. I. Sanchez, M. O'Driscoll, K. Sparks, P. Bernin, A. Büssing, P. Dewe, P. Hart, L. Lu, K. Miller, L. Renault de Moraes, G. M. Ostognay, M. Pagon, H. Pitariu, S. Poelmans, P. Radhakrishnan, V. Russinova, V. Salamatov, J. Salgado, S. Shima, O. L. Siu, J. B. Stora, M. Teichmann, T. Theorell, P. Vlerick, M. Westman, M. Widerszal-Bazyl, P. Wong, & S. Yu, 2001, *Journal of Organizational Behavior, 22*, 815–832.

very satisfied with their supervisors, coworkers, and nature of the work they do. They are less satisfied with rewards, such as pay, promotion opportunities, and fringe benefits.

Multinational surveys have found that job satisfaction levels are not the same across countries. Pichler and Wallace (2009) compared mean job satisfaction among samples from 27 European countries. They found that satisfaction was highest in Scandinavia (Denmark, Finland, and Sweden), Germany, and Austria and was lowest in Eastern Europe (Bulgaria, Slovakia, Poland, and Latvia). Spector, Cooper, Sanchez, O'Driscoll, Sparks et al. (2001) compared job satisfaction levels among managers in 24 countries across the globe and found significant differences. Table 9.2 lists the countries in order from highest to lowest satisfaction, and shows that Americans came in sixth (although there were no significant differences among the top nine). Managers from Asian countries (China and Japan) tended to be lower.

Although these studies show that people in different countries may have different feelings about work, they don't shed much light on the reasons. One explanation for these job satisfaction differences involves basic values that vary across countries. Hofstede (2001) assessed four important cultural values in 50 countries. Although individuals differed on values within each country, there were mean differences that relate to important variables in the workplace. The culture values are:

Individualism/collectivism

Masculinity

Power distance

Uncertainty avoidance

Individualism is the extent to which people see themselves as autonomous and focus on their own interests and needs rather than those of others. **Collectivism** is the opposite, where people see themselves as interconnected to others with a focus on the groups to which they belong. Western nations such as Australia, Canada, the United Kingdom, and the United States are high on individualism, while Asian countries (China and Korea) and Latin countries (Ecuador and Guatemala) tend to be high on collectivism. **Masculinity** reflects the extent to which organizations focus on achievement and job performance as opposed to the health and well-being of employees. Scandinavian countries are low on this value, which is reflected in their strong emphasis on health and well-being at work, while high countries include Japan and Austria. The United States is in the upper third.

Power distance is the tolerance people have for power and status differences among levels of an organization and society. Countries with high power distance tend to produce managers who demand obedience from subordinates. Latin countries, such as Guatemala and Panama, tend to be high, while Austria and Israel are lowest. The United States is in the lower half of the scale. **Uncertainty avoidance** reflects the level of comfort in situations that are unpredictable. In organizations, people can maintain predictability by adhering to formal procedures and rules; thus in countries high on this dimension, organizations tend to be very rule oriented. Countries highest on this dimension are Greece and Portugal, while the lowest are Singapore and Jamaica. The United States is in the lower third on uncertainty avoidance.

These dimensions have been found to relate to many organizational variables. In the job satisfaction area, Hui, Yee, and Eastman (1995) showed that individualism/collectivism scores for a country significantly related to satisfaction with social aspects of work. People from collectivist countries were more satisfied with coworkers than were people from individualist countries. Similarly Huang and Van de Vliert (2003) found that power distance relates to job satisfaction; people who are tolerant of large power distances are less satisfied with their jobs.

THE ASSESSMENT OF JOB SATISFACTION

Job satisfaction is almost always assessed by asking people how they feel about their jobs, either by questionnaire or by interview. Most of the time questionnaires are used because they are very easy to administer and require relatively little time and effort on the part of the researcher. They can also be done anonymously, which allows employees to be more candid in expressing their attitudes. Sometimes, more often in practice than in research, employees are interviewed about their satisfaction. A few cases can be found in which job satisfaction was assessed by asking supervisors (Spector, Dwyer, & Jex, 1988) or observers (Glick, Jenkins, & Gupta, 1986) to estimate another person's satisfaction, but such estimates are not likely to be completely accurate, since only the individual employees really know their own attitudes.

Job Descriptive Index (JDI)

Of all the job satisfaction scales available, the **Job Descriptive Index (JDI)** (P. C. Smith, Kendall, & Hulin, 1969) has been the most popular with researchers. It is also the most thoroughly and carefully validated. This scale assesses five facets:

Work
Pay
Promotion opportunities
Supervision
Coworkers

Many users of the scale have summed the facet results into an overall job satisfaction score. However, this practice is not recommended by one of the scale's developers, Patricia Cain Smith (Ironson, Smith, Brannick, Gibson, & Paul, 1989), as we will discuss after we cover satisfaction scales.

Table 9.3 contains a sample of the scale's 72 items and their respective subscales. Each item is an adjective or short phrase that is descriptive of the job. Possible responses

TABLE 9.3 Sample Items From the Job Descriptive Index (JDI)

Think of the opportunities for promotion that you have now. How well does each of the following words or phrases describe these? In the blank beside each word below, write

Y for "Yes" if it describes your opportunities for promotion

N for "No" if it does NOT describe them

? if you cannot decide

OPPORTUNITIES FOR PROMOTION

Dead-end job

Unfair promotion policy

Regular promotions

Think of the work you do at present. How well does each of the following words or phrases describe your work? In the blank beside each word below, write

Y for "Yes" if it describes your work

N for "No" if it does NOT describe it

? if you cannot decide

WORK ON PRESENT JOB

Routine

Satisfying

Good

Think of the pay you get now. How well does each of the following words or phrases describe your present pay? In the blank beside each word below, write

Y for "Yes" if it describes your pay

N for "No" if it does NOT describe it

? if you cannot decide

PRESENT PAY

Income adequate for normal expenses

Insecure

Less than I deserve

Think of the kind of supervision that you get on your job. How well does each of the following words or phrases describe this? In the blank beside each word below, write

Y for "Yes" if it describes the supervision you get on your job

N for "No" if it does NOT describe it

? if you cannot decide

SUPERVISION

Impolite

Praises good work

Doesn't supervise enough

Think of the majority of the people that you work with now or the people you meet in connection with your work. How well does each of the following words or phrases describe these people? In the blank beside each word below, write

Y for "Yes" if it describes the people you work with

N for "No" if it does NOT describe them

? if you cannot decide

CO WORKERS (PEOPLE)

Boring

Responsible

Intelligent

Source: From the Job Descriptive Index, which is copyrighted by Bowling Green State University. The complete forms, scoring key, instructions, and norms can be obtained from Department of Psychology, Bowling Green State University, Bowling Green, OH 43403.

are "yes," "uncertain," and "no." For each subscale, a brief explanation of the facet is provided, followed by the items concerning that subscale.

The JDI has been used frequently by organizational researchers. The extensive body of research using the scale provides extensive evidence for its validity. The biggest limitation of the scale is that it has only five subscales and might not cover all facets of the job that one might wish to study.

Minnesota Satisfaction Questionnaire (MSQ)

Another popular job satisfaction scale is the **Minnesota Satisfaction Questionnaire (MSQ)** (Weiss, Dawis, Lofquist, & England, 1966). This scale comes in two forms, a 100-item long version and a 20-item short version. Both versions have items that ask about 20 facets of job satisfaction, but facet scores are computed only for the long form. The short form is used to assess either global satisfaction or intrinsic and extrinsic satisfaction. *Intrinsic satisfaction* refers to the nature of the job tasks themselves and how people feel about the work they do. *Extrinsic satisfaction* concerns other aspects of the work situation, such as fringe benefits and pay. Both types of satisfaction are the combination of several facets.

The 20 facets of the MSQ are shown in Table 9.4. Each of the MSQ items is a statement that describes a facet. The employee is asked to indicate how satisfied he or she is with each one. For example, an item for the Activity facet is "Being able to keep busy all the time." The overall scale has been shown to have good reliability and evidence for validity. Several researchers, however, have questioned how the items have been classified into the intrinsic and extrinsic groups (C. A. Schriesheim, Powers, Scandura, Gardiner, et al., 1993).

Job in General Scale (JIG)

Ironson et al. (1989) developed a scale of global job satisfaction that contains items that do not reflect the various facets of the job. The **Job in General Scale (JIG)** was patterned on the JDI. It contains 18 items that are adjectives or short phrases about the

TABLE 9.4 Dimensions From the Minnesota Satisfaction Questionnaire (MSQ)

Activity	Ability utilization
Independence	Company policies and practices
Variety	Compensation
Social status	Advancement
Supervision (human relations)	Responsibility
Supervision (technical)	Creativity
Moral values	Working conditions
Security	Coworkers
Social service	Recognition
Authority	Achievement

Source: From *Instrumentation for the Theory of Work Adjustment*, by D. J. Weiss, R. Dawis, L. H. Lofquist, and G. W. England, 1966, Minnesota Studies in Vocational Rehabilitation, xxi, Minneapolis: University of Minnesota.

TABLE 9.5 Three Items From the Job in General Scale (JIG)

Think of your job in general. All in all, what is it like most of the time? In the blank beside each word or phrase below, write

Y for "Yes" if it describes your job

N for "No" if it does NOT describe it

? if you cannot decide

JOB IN GENERAL

Undesirable

Better than most

Rotten

Source: From the Job in General Scale, which is copyrighted by Bowling Green State University. The complete forms, scoring key, instructions, and norms can be obtained from Department of Psychology, Bowling Green State University, Bowling Green, OH 43403.

job in general. Three of the items are shown in Table 9.5. The scale has good reliability and correlates well with other scales of overall job satisfaction.

Is Global Satisfaction the Sum of Facets?

Researchers have debated whether global job satisfaction is the sum of facets or something different. Patricia Cain Smith, the developer of the JDI and JIG, has argued that they are separate (Ironson et al., 1989). Many researchers, however, have treated the sum of facet scores as an indicator of overall job satisfaction. Each MSQ item reflects a specific facet, so that the total score is a sum of facets. This is justified by the fact that facets often correlate well with overall job satisfaction. For example, Ironson et al. (1989) found a .78 correlation of the JIG with the JDI Work scale. On the other hand, the summing of subscale scores presumes that all facets have been assessed and that each makes an equal contribution to global satisfaction. It seems unlikely that each facet has the same importance to every individual. Thus the sum of facets is an approximation of overall job satisfaction, but it may not exactly match the global satisfaction of individuals.

▶ ANTECEDENTS OF JOB SATISFACTION

What makes people like or dislike their jobs? This question has been addressed in hundreds of research studies. Most of them have taken an environmental perspective. They have investigated features of jobs and organizations that lead employees to be satisfied or dissatisfied. Several studies have shown, however, that people with the same jobs and highly similar job conditions can vary considerably in their satisfaction. Findings such as these have led some researchers to take a personality perspective. Their purpose has been to show that certain types of people are inclined to like or dislike their jobs. Still other researchers have taken the interactionist perspective of person-job fit, which combines the environmental and personality approaches. Person-job fit recognizes that different people prefer different features of a job. It attempts to learn which sorts of people are satisfied with which sorts of job conditions. Job satisfaction, according to

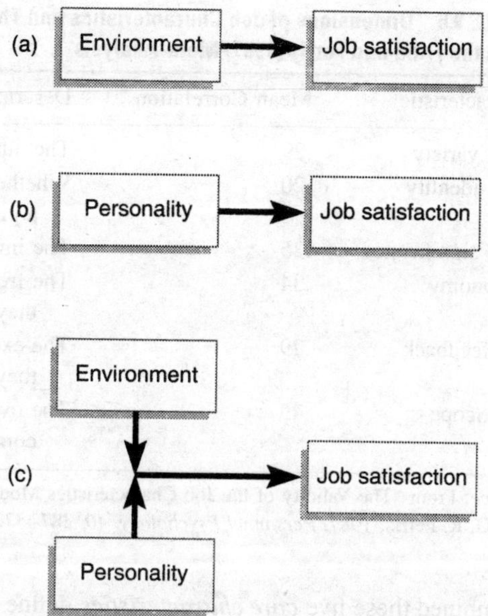

Figure 9.2 Three models illustrating (a) the impact of the job environment on job satisfaction, (b) the impact of personality on job satisfaction, and (c) the joint influence of the environment and personality on job satisfaction

this view, is the product of appropriately matching the individual to the job. All three perspectives—environment, personality, and interactionist—are illustrated in Figure 9.2.

Environmental Antecedents of Job Satisfaction

As we will discuss, there is research evidence showing that aspects of the job and job environment relate to job satisfaction. In other words, some situations will produce satisfaction and others will produce dissatisfaction. In this section, we will look at characteristics of job tasks, pay, justice in the workplace, and the impact of stressful job conditions.

Job Characteristics

Job characteristics refer to the content and nature of job tasks themselves. There are only a few characteristics studied as contributors to job satisfaction. Five are part of Hackman and Oldham's (1976) influential job characteristics theory (see Chapter 10 for additional details of the theory):

Skill variety: The number of different skills necessary to do a job;

Task identity: Whether or not an employee does an entire job or a piece of a job;

Task significance: The impact a job has on other people;

Autonomy: The freedom employees have to do their jobs as they see fit; and

Task feedback: The extent to which it is obvious to employees that they are doing their jobs correctly.

TABLE 9.6 Dimensions of Job Characteristics and Their Mean Correlations with Job Satisfaction From the Fried and Ferris (1987) Meta-Analysis

Characteristic	Mean Correlation	Description of Characteristic
Skill variety	.29	The number of different skills necessary to do a job
Task identity	.20	Whether or not an employee does an entire job or a piece of a job
Task significance	.26	The impact a job has on other people
Autonomy	.34	The freedom employees have to do their jobs as they see fit
Job feedback	.29	The extent to which it is obvious to employees that they are doing their jobs correctly
Job Scope	.45	The overall complexity of a job, computed as a combination of all five individual characteristics

Source: From "The Validity of the Job Characteristics Model: A Review and Meta-Analysis," by Y. Fried and G. R. Ferris, 1987, *Personnel Psychology, 40,* 287–322.

Combined these five *core characteristics* define the **scope** or complexity and challenge of a job. It is assumed by job characteristics theory that high scope leads to job satisfaction and low scope leads to boredom and dissatisfaction.

Dozens of studies across many different types of jobs have shown that each of the five characteristics relates to job satisfaction. Fried and Ferris (1987) conducted a meta-analysis of studies relating the Hackman and Oldham characteristics to global satisfaction. As discussed in Chapter 2, meta-analysis is a quantitative procedure for combining results of different studies. Table 9.6 contains Fried and Ferris's mean correlations across various studies of the relations between job characteristics and global job satisfaction. You can see that correlations ranged from .20 for task identity to .45 for job scope. Scope was assessed by combining scores on all five core characteristics.

One limitation of most studies that have addressed the influence of job characteristics on job satisfaction is that the job characteristics were assessed with questionnaires given to the employees themselves. As discussed in Chapter 2, merely demonstrating that variables are correlated does not mean that one necessarily causes the other. For example, people who like their jobs are likely to describe them in more favorable terms than people who dislike them, thereby reporting higher levels of job scope. Thus, job satisfaction might be the cause rather than the consequence of job characteristics as reported by employees on questionnaires. Although the Fried and Ferris (1987) results are consistent with the view that certain job characteristics can lead to job satisfaction, more evidence is needed to give confidence to this conclusion.

Unfortunately studies that have used different methodologies have not always been supportive of the idea that these five job characteristics lead to job satisfaction. For example, Spector and Jex (1991) used both questionnaires and job analysis techniques to assess job characteristics in a sample of employees who represented a wide range of jobs. Whereas the questionnaire measure of job characteristics correlated with job satisfaction, the job analysis data did not.

On the other hand, quasi-experimental field studies in which job characteristics were modified provide some support for at least a short-term effect of job characteristics on job satisfaction. Holman, Axtell, Sprigg, Totterdell, and Wall (2010) found that job satisfaction improved for individuals whose jobs had core characteristics increased over a period of 9 months. Griffin (1991) conducted a similar quasi-experiment that also showed that increasing levels of core characteristics resulted in increased job satisfaction. However, job satisfaction returned to the level found before the change in jobs by the time of a 2-year follow-up. His results suggest that changes in job satisfaction may be short-lived and that once people get used to job changes, job satisfaction returns to a baseline level; in other words, the job satisfaction change is due to the novelty of the situation.

Although the relation between employees' reports of their job characteristics and job satisfaction is consistent across samples in the United States and other Western countries, it might not be universal. Pearson and Chong (1997) were unable to find the same results in Malaysia (see the International Research box). The five core characteristics were unrelated to job satisfaction in a sample of nurses. The researchers argued that in this collectivistic Asian culture, it might be more important to focus on relationships among coworkers and supervisors as a means of achieving high job satisfaction than on the nature

INTERNATIONAL RESEARCH

Many studies conducted in the United States and Europe have shown that job characteristics are related to job satisfaction. A question of concern to researchers is whether such results will hold in countries that are very different culturally. Pearson and Chong (1997) conducted a study of job characteristics in the collectivist southeast Asian country of Malaysia. They hypothesized that because of the Chinese values of Malaysians, the core job characteristics involving the nature of tasks have little effect on job satisfaction. However, because of their values, Malaysians are more sensitive to interpersonal aspects of work, and those should relate more strongly to job satisfaction.

Participants in this study were 286 nurses of a large hospital. Questionnaires were distributed anonymously in English containing measures of job characteristics, job satisfaction, and Chinese values with the Chinese Value Survey. This survey measures four dimensions, including Confucian work dynamism, which reflects the teaching of Confucius, and moral discipline, which concerns self-control and moral behavior. Included were the five core characteristics of autonomy, feedback, skill variety, task identity, and task significance, plus the interpersonal dimension of feedback from others. This last dimension concerned the extent to which supervisors and other people provided feedback about how well the person was doing the job.

As expected, there were no significant correlations of any of the five core job characteristics with job satisfaction. Malaysians did not find jobs high on these dimensions to be more satisfying. However, there was a correlation of feedback from others with job satisfaction ($r = .40$). The authors explained these results as reflecting the greater collectivism of the Malaysians, who put great value on receiving feedback from others. To further test the idea that values were responsible for the results, participants were divided into those who strongly endorsed Chinese values and those who didn't. Correlations of the core job characteristics with job satisfaction were higher for those low on Chinese values than those high on Chinese values. For example, autonomy correlated .24 with job satisfaction for those low on Chinese values but only .07 for those high. This study clearly shows that results from one country cannot always be generalized to another.

Source: From "Contributions of Job Content and Social Information on Organizational Commitment and Job Satisfaction: An Exploration in a Malaysian Nursing Context," by C. A. L. Pearson and J. Chong, 1997, *Journal of Occupational and Organizational Psychology, 70*, 357–374.

of job tasks. However, a study conducted in more developed and Westernized Hong Kong found relations between job characteristics and job satisfaction quite similar to those found in the United States (Wong, Hui, & Law, 1998). Clearly we need to be careful about generalizing results from one country to another and not assume that what works here will work everywhere.

Pay

Although pay itself is associated to some extent with global satisfaction, as might be expected it relates even more strongly with the facet of pay satisfaction. Brasher and Chen (1999) surveyed recent college graduates and found that their level of starting pay relates more strongly to pay satisfaction (correlation = .36) than to global satisfaction (correlation = .17). Furthermore, it is the fairness with which pay is distributed, or equity (see Chapter 8 for a discussion of justice theories), that is a more important determinant of pay satisfaction than the actual level of pay itself (Williams, McDaniel, & Nguyen, 2006). You can find people making minimum wage who are satisfied with pay, whereas professional athletes and entertainers might be dissatisfied with six- and even seven-figure salaries.

All this leads to the hypothesis that if we compare the pay and pay satisfaction of people across different jobs, we will find little or no correlation. People who make more money are not necessarily more satisfied when they have different jobs. On the other hand, if we have a sample of people who all do the same job, those who make more money should be more satisfied. Research support for this hypothesis comes from two studies. Spector (1985) found a mean correlation of only .17 between salary level and pay satisfaction in three heterogeneous samples in which employees held different jobs. Rice, Phillips, and McFarlin (1990) found a much larger .50 correlation between pay and job satisfaction in a sample of mental health professionals holding the same jobs. Pay satisfaction is affected by how an individual's salary compares to those of others in the same job rather than to those of people in general. More direct support for the link with fairness comes from the research on justice and pay satisfaction. In their meta-analysis, Cohen-Charash and Spector (2001) found that distributive and procedural justice (see Chapter 8) are strongly correlated with pay satisfaction, with correlations of .58 and .45, respectively (see Table 9.7).

Justice

As noted in the Chapter 8 discussion of justice theories, perceptions of fairness are important determinants of people's behavior and reactions to work. Distributive justice

TABLE 9.7 Correlations of Distributive Justice and Procedural Justice With Job Satisfaction

Job Satisfaction Type	Distributive Justice	Procedural Justice
Global job satisfaction	.39	.40
Pay satisfaction	.58	.45
Supervisor satisfaction	.36	.47
Nature of work satisfaction	.32	.31

Source: From "The Role of Justice in Organizations: A Meta-Analysis," by Y. Cohen-Charash and P. E. Spector, 2001, *Organizational Behavior and Human Decision Processes, 86*, 538–551.

is the extent to which people perceive the allotment of rewards at work to be fair, whereas procedural justice is the extent to which people perceive the process by which rewards at work are allocated to be fair. These two forms of justice have been linked to both global and facet job satisfaction in the Cohen-Charash and Spector (2001) meta-analysis. Overall job satisfaction and facet satisfactions of pay, supervision, and nature of work correlate significantly with both forms of justice (see Table 9.7). Note that for pay satisfaction, distributive justice has a larger correlation than procedural justice. This suggests that the distribution of pay is more important for satisfaction than the procedures for distribution, although both are certainly important. For supervision satisfaction, procedural justice is more important than distributive justice, perhaps because it is the supervisor who decides on the procedures by which assignments and rewards are allocated.

Personal Antecedents of Job Satisfaction

The majority of studies of the causes of job satisfaction have taken an environmental perspective. Some researchers, however, feel that personal characteristics are also important in determining job satisfaction (e.g., Staw & Cohen-Charash, 2005). Personal characteristics include demographics (e.g., age, gender, and race), as well as personality. In this section, we will discuss factors that may play a role in people's reactions to jobs and their job satisfaction.

Personality

The idea that job satisfaction may be caused in part by personality can be traced back to the Hawthorne studies. The Hawthorne researchers noticed that certain individuals, whom they called the *chronic kickers*, were continually complaining about the job (Roethlisberger, 1941). No matter what the researchers did for them, the chronic kickers always had new complaints. More recently Bowling, Beehr, and Lepisto (2006) explored the stability of satisfaction by studying people who changed employers. They found that the job satisfaction of these individuals was correlated across a 5-year span of time. In other words, the job satisfaction of people on one job correlated with their satisfaction on another. Bowling et al. concluded that job satisfaction is caused in part by underlying personality. Some people are predisposed to like their jobs, whereas others are predisposed not to like them. T. Newton and Keenan (1991) did a similar study, but found evidence that job environment, as well as personality, is important. They studied a group of British engineers during their first 4 years on the job after college. They also found consistency in job satisfaction over time, but in addition they found that engineers who changed jobs increased their satisfaction. Dormann and Zapf (2001) conducted a meta-analysis of such studies showing that job satisfaction is far more stable over time when people remain on the same job (mean correlation = .42) than when they change jobs (mean correlation = .18). Thus, although personality may contribute to satisfaction, job conditions are also important.

Even stronger evidence for personality than consistency across time was provided by Staw, Bell, and Clausen (1986) who studied people's job satisfaction over the span of decades (see the International Research box). They found that personality assessed in adolescents predicted job satisfaction up to 50 years later.

These studies showing consistency in job satisfaction over time support the idea that personality is important, but they don't shed much light on the nature of relevant

INTERNATIONAL RESEARCH

One of the limitations of many I/O studies is that data are collected at a single point in time. The study by Staw, Bell, and Clausen (1986) stands out as a rare example of a long-term longitudinal study of job satisfaction. The study spanned 50 years, comparing the personality of adolescents with their later job satisfaction.

The study made use of data from the Intergenerational Studies begun at the University of California, Berkeley, during the 1920s. Three groups of subjects were assessed using interviews and questionnaires several times during their lives. Staw et al. (1986) had several judges, who were either clinical psychologists or psychiatric social workers, read the extensive material in each subject's file and rate them on several personality characteristics. Scores on 17 characteristics were combined into affective disposition scores. Examples of the characteristics include thin-skinned, punitive, condescending, hostile, distrustful, irritable, and moody.

Results showed that affective disposition assessed as young as early adolescence correlated significantly with job satisfaction assessed up to 50 years later. For the 46 subjects who had data at adolescence and decades later on the job, the correlation between disposition and satisfaction was .37. This is larger than many of the correlations found between job conditions and job satisfaction.

There are several explanations for these results, as noted by Staw et al. First, it may be that affective disposition, as assessed here, relates to a person's view of the world. People with a negative disposition might perceive all aspects of their lives, including their jobs, as worse than people with a more positive disposition. Alternatively, disposition might lead to job choice, with negative people seeking out worse jobs than positive people. Although this study cannot answer these questions, it demonstrates that through some as-yet-to-be-determined mechanism, personality is a likely precursor to job satisfaction. These results suggest that organizations should carefully consider characteristics of individuals when implementing job changes intended to enhance job satisfaction.

Source: From "The Dispositional Approach to Job Attitudes: A Lifetime Longitudinal Test," by B. M. Staw, N. E. Bell, and J. A. Clausen, 1986, *Administrative Science Quarterly, 31*, 56–77.

personality traits. Quite a few specific traits have been studied, with particular attention being paid to two of them—negative affectivity and locus of control.

Negative affectivity (NA) is the tendency for an individual to experience negative emotions, such as anxiety or depression, across a wide variety of situations. Watson, Pennebaker, and Folger (1986) extended the NA idea to the workplace, hypothesizing that high NA individuals would likely be dissatisfied because they tend to view all aspects of their world in a negative way. This is consistent with the idea of the chronic kicker, mentioned earlier, in that some people just dwell on negative aspects of life. This theoretical idea is supported by Connolly and Viswesvaran (2000), who conducted a meta-analysis of 27 studies that found a mean correlation between NA and job satisfaction of −.27, showing that individuals who are high on NA tend to score low on job satisfaction.

Locus of control refers to whether or not people believe they are in control of reinforcements in life. People who believe that they control reinforcements are termed *internals*. People who believe that fate, luck, or powerful others control reinforcements are termed *externals*. Internals have been found to be more satisfied with their jobs than externals (Ng, Sorensen, & Eby, 2006; Q. Wang, Bowling, & Eschleman, 2010).

Although the research on these personality traits has shown a connection with job satisfaction, the reasons are not well delineated. Watson et al. (1986) suggested that NA relates to job satisfaction because the high NA person perceives and experiences the job negatively, regardless of the actual conditions. It is possible that externals experience their jobs in a similar way. There are other mechanisms that are equally plausible. For example, Spector (1982) hypothesized that one reason for the higher satisfaction of internals is their higher job performance. Individuals who perform better might be better rewarded and thus like their jobs better. Personality might also be related to job choice. Perhaps people with certain personality traits choose better jobs and therefore have higher satisfaction. Clearly research is needed to determine why personality relates to job satisfaction.

Gender

Most studies that have compared men and women in their global job satisfaction have found few differences. Meta-analytic studies involving multiple samples and thousands of employees have failed to find gender differences (Witt & Nye, 1992). Greenhaus, Parasuraman, and Wormley (1990) found no significant gender differences in their study, even though the distribution of jobs was not the same in their sample for both genders—males were more likely to have managerial/professional jobs, and females were more likely to have clerical jobs. This suggests that women may be happier with lower pay and less responsibility than men, perhaps because their expectations are lower about what they will receive or because they compare themselves to other women who are in similar circumstances.

Age

The workforces in many countries have been getting older because of both the changing demographic makeup of the population (there are more elderly people) and legislation that has made age discrimination illegal. A question that has been of interest to I/O psychologists concerns possible changes in job satisfaction over a person's life span. Many studies (e.g., Siu, Lu, & Cooper, 1999) have shown that older workers are more satisfied with their jobs than younger workers. Two large sample surveys, one conducted in England (Clark, Oswald, & Warr, 1996) and the other in nine countries including the

Most Americans say that they like their jobs. (© *Peter Bernik, sourced from Shutterstock images*)

United States (Birdi, Warr, & Oswald, 1995), found a curvilinear relation between age and job satisfaction. In these studies, job satisfaction at first declines with age, reaching the lowest level at around age 26 to 31, and then increases through the rest of the working career. Although some of this pattern might be due to age, it is also likely that other factors are important as well. One factor is tenure on the job. It has been shown that job satisfaction is high at the time of hiring and then declines after an initial honeymoon period (Boswell, Shipp, Payne, & Culbertson, 2009). Age is confounded with tenure on the job (only older workers can have long years of service), and so part of the relationship with age might be due to tenure. Very young workers will be new to a job, and thus their job satisfaction is high. As employees get older, their average tenure increases, and so many of them will be past the honeymoon period and experience lowered job satisfaction. Over time, however, job satisfaction will increase, perhaps as employees adjust to working life.

Cultural and Ethnic Differences

Another trend in the composition of the workforce in the United States and other countries is that it is becoming increasingly multicultural. In addition, large organizations frequently have facilities in multiple countries and employ people from those countries. For example, American automobile manufacturers have plants outside the United States, and Japanese automobile manufacturers such as Toyota have plants in the United States. If organizations are to deal appropriately with a diverse workforce, then they must understand how people of various ethnic, racial, and cultural backgrounds view and feel about their jobs.

Several studies have compared the job satisfaction of Black and White employees in the United States. Some of these studies have found that Blacks have slightly lower satisfaction (Greenhaus et al., 1990). Studies that have found differences in satisfaction have also noted differences in other variables, suggesting that job experiences might differ in at least some organizations. For example, Blacks had lower mean performance ratings than Whites in the Greenhaus et al. (1990) study. Perhaps the factors leading to lower ratings resulted in lowered job satisfaction. Somers and Birnbaum (2001) studied Black and White employees of a hospital and found that there were no differences between them after demographic variables (e.g., age and education) and type of work were controlled.

Person-Job Fit

Most researchers have tended to treat environmental and personal factors as independent influences on job satisfaction. In other words, they have studied characteristics of jobs or of individuals that may lead to satisfaction. Another approach, however, is to look at the interaction of both factors. The person-job fit approach states that job satisfaction will occur when there is a good match between the person and the job. There are many ways that people and jobs fit, however, including the correspondence between task demands and personal abilities (Greguras & Diefendorff, 2009).

Much of the research on person-job fit has looked at the correspondence between what people say they want on a job and what they say they have (e.g., L.-Q. Yang, Che, & Spector, 2008). For example, employees could be asked how much autonomy they have and how much they want. The difference between having and wanting represents the amount of fit of person to job. Studies have been quite consistent in showing that the smaller the discrepancy between having and wanting, the greater the job satisfaction. For example, Verquer, Beehr, and Wagner (2003) conducted a meta-analysis of 21 person-job fit studies and found that various measures of fit were correlated with job satisfaction.

Another approach to studying the interplay of the job and person is to look at the interaction of specific person and job variables in predicting job satisfaction. That is, person variables are used as moderators of the relation between job variables and job satisfaction. A **moderator variable** affects the relation between two other variables. One might find that a particular job variable relates to job satisfaction for people at one level of a person variable and not for people at another level. For example, men might react differently than women to a job condition. Thus there might be a positive correlation between the job condition and job satisfaction for men and no correlation for women. We would say that gender has moderated the relation between the job condition and job satisfaction. It determines whether or not the two variables are correlated.

In the job characteristics area, many studies have attempted to find the sorts of people who would react most positively to high-scope jobs (i.e., those high on the five core job characteristics of Hackman and Oldham, 1976). One personality characteristic that comes from Hackman and Oldham's (1976) theory is **growth need strength (GNS)**. This characteristic refers to a person's desire for the satisfaction of higher-order needs, such as autonomy and achievement. Meta-analyses of studies that have addressed the effects of GNS have shown that it moderates the relation between job characteristics and job satisfaction (Loher, Noe, Moeller, & Fitzgerald, 1985). Correlations between these two variables are greater for individuals who are high in GNS than for individuals who are low.

This relation is illustrated in Figure 9.3. The horizontal axis of the graph represents the scope of the job; the vertical axis represents job satisfaction. One line is for high GNS people, and the other line is for low GNS people. As the graph shows, people who are high in GNS will be satisfied with high-scope jobs and not with low-scope jobs.

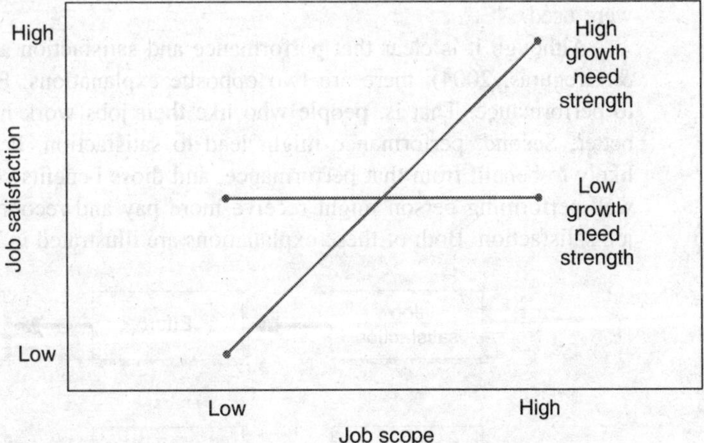

Figure 9.3 The moderating effect of growth need strength on the job scope–job satisfaction relation. Scope is represented by the horizontal axis of the graph. Job satisfaction is on the vertical axis. For people high in growth need strength, satisfaction is high when scope is high and low when scope is low. For people who are low in growth need strength, satisfaction is unaffected by level of job scope.

The scope of the job is not important for people low in GNS. Their satisfaction stays constant, regardless of job scope.

▶ POTENTIAL EFFECTS OF JOB SATISFACTION

A number of organizationally relevant variables are thought to be the result of job satisfaction or dissatisfaction. Some are behaviors that have an important impact on the well-being of organizations. Three of these are job performance, turnover, and employee absence. Job satisfaction is also linked to variables that are of direct relevance to the health and well-being of employees.

Job Satisfaction and Job Performance

The idea that job satisfaction and job performance are related seems intuitively obvious. After all, shouldn't satisfied employees be productive employees? Judge, Thoresen, Bono, and Patton (2001) conducted a thorough meta-analysis of 312 studies and found that there is a modest relationship—the average correlation is .20 between job performance and global satisfaction. Two other investigators, Iaffaldano and Muchinsky (1985), found that the correlation with individual facets, however, is variable, ranging from .05 for pay satisfaction to .20 for satisfaction with intrinsic aspects of the job.

At least part of the reason for the relatively small mean correlations found in these meta-analyses may have to do with the measures of job performance available in many studies. Most studies rely on supervisor ratings of performance, which suffer from several limitations, as discussed in Chapter 4. Supervisors frequently exhibit rating errors, especially when ratings are for organizational purposes. This can produce inaccuracy in performance ratings, which introduces extra error into the statistics. Relations of satisfaction with performance would likely be stronger if more accurate measures of performance were used.

Although it is clear that performance and satisfaction are related (Schleicher, Watt, & Greguras, 2004), there are two opposite explanations. First, satisfaction might lead to performance. That is, people who like their jobs work harder and therefore perform better. Second, performance might lead to satisfaction. People who perform well are likely to benefit from that performance, and those benefits could enhance satisfaction. A well-performing person might receive more pay and recognition, which might increase job satisfaction. Both of these explanations are illustrated in Figure 9.4. In the top part of

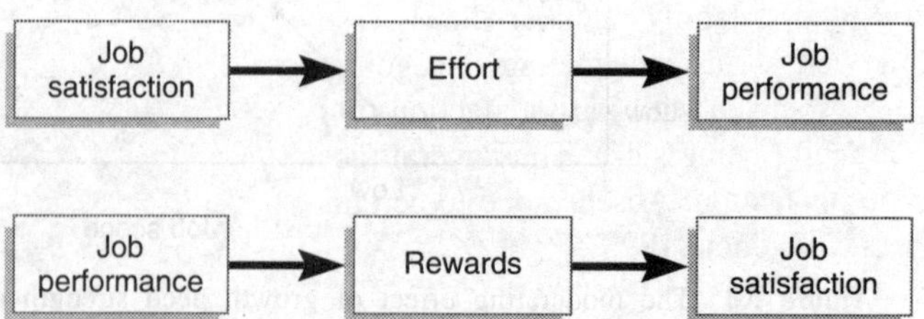

Figure 9.4 Two possible models illustrating why job performance relates to job satisfaction. In the first model, job satisfaction leads to increased effort on the job, which leads to job performance. In the second, job performance leads to rewards, which lead to job satisfaction. As noted in the text, evidence exists to support the second model.

the figure, satisfaction leads to effort, which in turn leads to performance. In the bottom part, performance leads to rewards and rewards lead to satisfaction.

Jacobs and Solomon (1977) conducted a study that supports the second explanation. They hypothesized that satisfaction and performance are related more strongly when performance leads to rewards. The rationale is that employees who perform well will be more satisfied because they have received rewards. Jacobs and Solomon found support for their hypothesis that a performance-reward linkage leads to stronger satisfaction-performance relations.

Job Satisfaction and Turnover

Quitting the job, or *turnover*, has been tied to job satisfaction. Many studies have shown that dissatisfied employees are more likely than satisfied employees to quit their jobs (Blau, 2007).

Correlations between job satisfaction and turnover have been interpreted as indicating the effects of satisfaction on behavior. One reason that it has been possible to demonstrate such a linkage between job satisfaction and turnover has to do with the designs of turnover studies and the nature of turnover. Most turnover studies are predictive, assessing job satisfaction in a sample of employees on one occasion and then waiting some period of months or years to see who quits. The predictive nature of these studies allows the conclusion that dissatisfaction is a factor that leads employees to quit their jobs.

Job Satisfaction and Absence

Conventional wisdom suggests that absence from work is the by-product of employee job dissatisfaction. People who dislike their jobs will be more likely to avoid work than people who like their jobs. Several meta-analyses have looked at this question, and they show that the connection between job satisfaction and absence is inconsistent and usually quite small. For example, Bowling and Hammond (2008) found a mean correlation of −.12 between absence and global job satisfaction. Tharenou (1993), on the other hand, found correlations as high as −.34 between absence and job satisfaction in a sample of Australian blue-collar workers. Why some studies find stronger absence–job satisfaction correlations than others is not entirely clear, but it seems that they can be related under some circumstances.

One possible reason for the small relation between satisfaction and absence is that a person can be absent for many reasons (Kohler & Mathieu, 1993), including employee illness, family member illness (especially children), personal business, and fatigue, as well as just not feeling like going to work. Whereas some of these reasons might be associated with job satisfaction (not feeling like going to work), others probably are not (child being sick). Thus overall absence is not likely to have a strong relation with job satisfaction. Absence due to certain reasons will likely be more strongly related (Kohler & Mathieu, 1993).

Health and Well-Being

I/O psychologists have been concerned that job dissatisfaction might be an important factor in employee health and well-being. Correlational studies show that job satisfaction relates to a variety of health-related variables. For example, dissatisfied employees report more physical symptoms, such as sleep problems and upset stomach, than their satisfied counterparts (Bowling & Hammond, 2008). Dissatisfaction has also been found to correlate with negative emotions at work, such as anxiety and depression (Bowling & Hammond, 2008; Jex & Gudanowski, 1992). These negative emotional states could be considered indicators of psychological health or well-being at work. Evidence relating job satisfaction to more-serious health problems, such as heart disease, has been harder to produce (Heslop, Smith, Metcalfe, Macleod, & Hart, 2002).

Job and Life Satisfaction

Another important issue concerns the contribution of job satisfaction to overall **life satisfaction**—how satisfied a person is with his or her life circumstances. Life satisfaction is considered to be an indicator of overall happiness or emotional well-being. Studies of life satisfaction have found that it correlates with job satisfaction (Bowling & Hammond, 2008).

Three hypotheses have been proposed about how job and life satisfaction might affect one another (Rain, Lane, & Steiner, 1991). The *spillover hypothesis* suggests that satisfaction (or dissatisfaction) in one area of life affects or spills over to another. Thus problems and dissatisfaction at home can affect satisfaction with work, whereas problems and dissatisfaction at work can affect satisfaction with home. The *compensation hypothesis* says that dissatisfaction in one area of life will be compensated for in another. A person with a dissatisfying job will seek satisfaction in other aspects of life. A person with a dissatisfying home life might seek satisfaction in work. The *segmentation hypothesis* states that people compartmentalize their lives and that satisfaction in one area of life has no relation to satisfaction in another.

The three hypotheses lead to contradictory predictions about the correlation between job and life satisfaction. Spillover predicts a positive correlation in that satisfaction at work will affect satisfaction in other areas of life. Compensation predicts a negative correlation because dissatisfaction in one area of life will be compensated for by satisfaction in another. Segmentation predicts no correlation because people keep satisfaction with different areas of life separated. Rain et al. (1991) pointed out that research has consistently found a positive correlation between job and life satisfaction. Thus the spillover hypothesis is the only one supported by research.

▶ ORGANIZATIONAL COMMITMENT

Organizational commitment is another popular attitudinal variable in the work domain. It is strongly related to job satisfaction, but it is distinctly different in focusing on the attachment of the individual to the organization rather than on whether an individual likes or dislikes the job. The study of organizational commitment has taken two perspectives—the global and the component. The original global perspective is based on the work of Mowday, Steers, and Porter (1979), which considers organizational commitment to be a global feeling that involves three things:

1. An acceptance of the organization's goals
2. A willingness to work hard for the organization
3. The desire to stay with the organization

Subsequently a three-component commitment perspective was developed (Meyer, Allen, & Smith, 1993). The three components of commitment are:

Affective
Continuance
Normative

Affective commitment occurs when the employee wishes to remain with the organization because of an emotional attachment. **Continuance commitment** exists when a person must remain with the organization because he or she needs the benefits and salary or cannot find another acceptable job. **Normative commitment** comes from the values of the employee. The person believes that he or she owes it to the organization to remain out of a sense that this is the right thing to do.

Meyer et al. (1993) discussed the nature and origins of the three components of commitment. Figure 9.5 shows the major influences on each. As you can see, there are different factors involved in each component. Affective commitment arises from job conditions and met expectations. That is, did the job provide the rewards that the employee expected? Continuance commitment is produced by the benefits accrued from working for the organization and by the lack of available alternative jobs. Normative commitment comes from the employee's personal values and from the obligations that the person

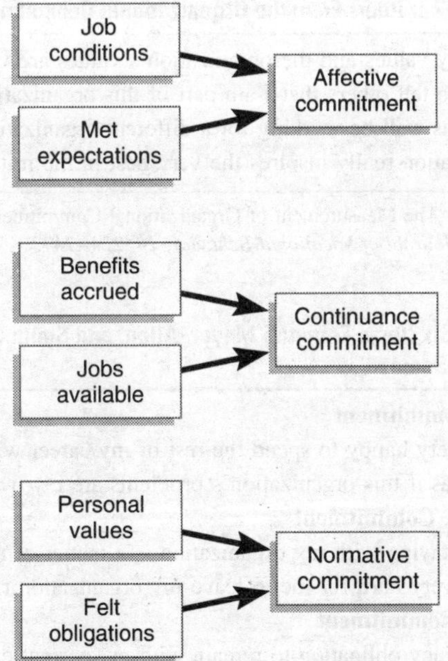

Figure 9.5 Antecedents of the three components of organizational commitment. Each type of commitment has different antecedents. Affective commitment arises from favorable experiences on the job. Continuance is produced by the investments in the job and the difficulty in finding another job. Normative commitment derives from a sense of obligation either because of the person's values or from favors done for the person by the organization.

feels toward the employer. These obligations come from favors that the organization has done, such as paying the person's school expenses.

Assessment of Organizational Commitment

Organizational commitment is measured with self-report scales not unlike those used to assess job satisfaction. Four items from the most popular scale, developed by Mowday et al. (1979), are shown in Table 9.8. The items tap the three aspects of commitment—acceptance of goals, willingness to work hard, and intention to stay with the organization. All three components relate strongly to one another, and combined they indicate global commitment.

The three components in the Meyer et al. (1993) conception of commitment can be assessed with a scale they developed. Table 9.9 contains two of the items for each component. As opposed to the Mowday et al. (1979) scale, the components in the Meyer et al. (1993) scale produce separate scores. Research with the scale has found support for the idea that the three types of commitment are separate variables (Dunham, Grube, & Castaneda, 1994). Hackett, Bycio, and Hausdorf (1994) noted that the Mowday et al. (1979) scale assesses mainly affective commitment. It correlates strongly with the affective commitment subscale but not with the continuance and normative subscales of the Meyer et al. (1993) scale.

TABLE 9.8 Four items From the Organizational Commitment Questionnaire

I find that my values and the organization's values are very similar.
I am proud to tell others that I am part of this organization.
I could just as well be working for a different organization as long as the type of work was similar.
This organization really inspires the very best in me in the way of job performance.

Source: From "The Measurement of Organizational Commitment," by R. T. Mowday, R. M. Steers, and L. W. Porter, 1979, *Journal of Vocational Behavior, 14,* 224–247.

TABLE 9.9 Six Items From the Meyer, Allen, and Smith (1993) Three-Component Organizational Commitment Scale

Affective Commitment
I would be very happy to spend the rest of my career with this organization
I really feel as if this organization's problems are my own
Continuance Commitment
Right now, staying with my organization is a matter of necessity as much as desire
It would be very hard for me to leave my organization right now, even if I wanted to
Normative Commitment
I do not feel any obligation to remain with my current employer
Even if it were to my advantage, I do not feel it would be right to leave my organization now

Source: From "Commitment to Organizations and Occupations: Extension and Test of a Three-Component Conceptualization," by J. P. Meyer, N. J. Allen, and C. A. Smith, 1993, *Journal of Applied Psychology, 78,* 538–551.

TABLE 9.10 Mean Correlations of Organizational Commitment Types With Four Work Variables

Variable	Affective Commitment	Continuance Commitment	Normative Commitment
Job satisfaction	.50	.09	.29
Job performance	.22	−.09	.06
Turnover intention	−.48	−.15	−.29
Turnover	−.17	−.20	−.13

Source: From "The Construct of Work Commitment: Testing an Integrative Framework," by A. Cooper-Hakim and C. Viswesvaran, 2005, *Psychological Bulletin, 131,* 241–259.

Organizational Commitment and Other Variables

Organizational commitment has been included in studies involving many organizational variables. Cooper-Hakim and Viswesvaran (2005) conducted a meta-analysis of nearly 1,000 studies, relating commitment to several hypothesized variables proposed as consequences. Table 9.10 summarizes their results, relating the three components of commitment to four important variables. Job satisfaction relates most strongly to affective commitment, which isn't surprising considering that both variables are attitudes about the job. Job performance also relates most strongly and positively to affective commitment, at about the same level as does job satisfaction, as was discussed earlier. Continuance commitment relates negatively to job performance, although the relationship is rather small. These results suggest that people who are working because of an emotional attachment will tend to perform better, but those who are working because they feel they have to will actually perform worse.

Turnover in particular has been a focus of much commitment research (Somers, 2009). Because commitment refers to the attachment of people to jobs, we would expect it to be related to turnover. Those with low commitment should be more likely to quit their job than those with high commitment. Cooper-Hakim and Viswesvaran (2005) found that turnover (last row of the table) correlates negatively with all three components, with continuance commitment relating most strongly. The pattern with turnover intentions is different in that continuance commitment has the weakest correlation of the three components. These results suggest that affective commitment relates most strongly to the desire to quit, as reflected in intentions, but it is the actual investments in the job, reflected in continuance commitment, that are most important in translating intentions to turnover itself.

Commitment has been studied in relation to potential antecedent variables as well. Meyer, Stanley, Herscovitch, and Topolnytsky (2002) conducted a meta-analysis of 155 studies showing that commitment is associated with job stress (people who perceive their jobs to be stressful have low commitment) and organizational justice (people who feel they have been unfairly treated have low commitment). However, relationships with these variables are stronger for affective commitment than either continuance or normative commitment. Continuance commitment is most strongly related to how well skills can transfer from the current job to another job, which makes sense, since lack of transferability would make it difficult for someone to switch jobs, thus producing a higher level of continuance commitment.

As with job satisfaction, there have been few gender or racial differences found with organizational commitment. For example, Ng, Butts, Vandenberg, DeJoy, and Wilson (2006) found that men and women, and Whites and non-Whites, have the same level of organizational commitment.

One must be cautious in generalizing these organizational commitment findings to other countries. Robert, Probst, Martocchio, Drasgow, and Lawler (2000) surveyed employees of a multinational company in four countries: India, Mexico, Poland, and the United States. Organizational commitment correlated strongly with intent to quit in the United States (as expected) and Poland. However, the correlation was somewhat smaller in Mexico, and it was nonsignificant in India. Apparently Indians and Mexicans who have low commitment are less inclined to quit their jobs than Americans and Poles who have low commitment.

Perhaps one reason for these cross-national differences has to do with culture values. As discussed earlier in the chapter, individualism-collectivism concerns whether people focus is on themselves (individualism) or on others (collectivism). Being members of collectivist societies, Indians and Mexicans might display more loyalty to their employers and resist translating low commitment into turnover. Indeed, Cohen (2006) showed that collectivists in Israel have greater organizational commitment and are more likely to engage in behaviors to help their employers than are individualists.

The idea of commitment has been extended from the organization to other work-related domains. Vandenberghe, Bentein, and Stinglhamber (2004) developed scales to assess commitment to one's supervisor and to one's work group or peers. They showed that commitment to the group is a better predictor of turnover than commitment to the organization or supervisor. Group commitment has also been shown to relate to work group performance (Neininger, Lehmann-Willenbrock, Kauffeld, & Henschel, 2010). These findings illustrate how it can be relationships with one's work peers that matter most in deciding whether or not to remain with an employer, and it can affect how well coworkers work together.

Meyer et al. (1993) developed the idea of **occupational commitment**, which concerns the occupation or profession rather than a particular organization. People might be very committed to their occupation, such as accounting or law, and uncommitted to their current employer. The focus of a person's commitment is important in determining his or her responses. For example, Keller (1997) found that occupational commitment among engineers and scientists relates to an objective measure of performance (number of articles published), but organizational commitment does not. Success in publication may be relevant to how individuals view their occupations but not their organizations. On the other hand, Cropanzano, Howes, Grandey, and Toth (1997) found that occupational commitment is less strongly related than organizational commitment to intention of quitting the job. In their meta-analysis of occupational commitment studies, K. Lee, Carswell, and Allen (2000) found that the mean correlation with job satisfaction ($r = .37$) is smaller than is typically found for organizational commitment. We might expect that occupational commitment will relate most strongly to behaviors relevant to success in that occupation. Organizational commitment will relate most strongly to behaviors and variables relevant to the present job.

Finally, in unionized occupations and workplaces, people can vary in the extent to which they are committed to their unions. Such commitment has been shown to relate to the time and effort one puts into union activities. For example, Fullagar, Gallagher, Clark, and Carroll (2004) showed that union commitment predicted participation in union activities over a span of 10 years. This suggests, as with job satisfaction, that some forms of commitment can be quite stable over a long period of time.

EMOTIONS AT WORK

For most people, the job is an important component of life, providing not only resources (pay and fringe benefits) to acquire the necessities of life but a sense of purpose and social contact as well. It is inevitable that people will react emotionally to workplace events and situations. Accomplishment of a major work project will likely result in positive feelings, such as pride and joy, whereas a heated argument with a supervisor will certainly induce feelings of anger and annoyance. Furthermore, the expression of emotion at work can sometimes be an important part of the job. Salespeople are expected to smile and be friendly, whereas police officers often are expected to act stern in dealing with someone committing a crime.

It is important to distinguish emotion states and moods. An emotional state is the immediate experience of a particular emotion, such as anger or fear, that is generally in response to a situation, such as being yelled at by your supervisor. A mood is a longer-term state that is less specific, with a positive or a negative direction (a good mood or a bad mood) rather than specific feelings such as joy or sadness (Fisher, 2000). Both emotion states and moods are important to study in the workplace.

Causes and Consequences of Emotions at Work

Brief and Weiss (2002) discussed how things that are stressful and aversive at work (including punishments) can produce negative emotion states and moods. This might include the need to juggle conflicting demands (e.g., having a child become ill the day of an important meeting at work), too much time pressure, and unfair treatment. They also discussed things that can induce positive emotions, which can be stimulated by the positive moods of coworkers and supervisors. In particular, rewards at work can induce positive emotion—for example, a bonus or raise, as well as less tangible rewards such as recognition by supervisors.

Emotions are associated with employee behavior and other variables that have implications for organizations. Ashkanasy, Hartel, and Daus (2002) compared the effects of positive and negative moods. They noted that positive mood is associated with greater creativity, higher job satisfaction, less turnover, more contextual performance (e.g., volunteering to do extra work that isn't required; see Chapter 4), and better job performance. Negative moods, on the other hand, are associated with low job satisfaction and more absence and turnover. As we will see in Chapter 10, emotions have also been linked to counterproductive work behavior (e.g., directing verbal aggression toward coworkers and purposely withholding effort), with positive emotion leading to low levels of these harmful behaviors and negative emotion to high levels (Fox, Spector, & Miles, 2001).

Evidence linking mood to job satisfaction comes from a study by Fuller, Stanton, Fisher, Spitzmüller, Russell, and Smith (2003). They asked 14 employees to complete measures on more than 1,000 occasions of stressful events, their mood, and their job satisfaction. Results showed, as expected, that stressful events lead to more negative mood and that positive moods are associated with greater job satisfaction.

Emotional Labor

It has long been recognized by private-sector companies that the emotional expressions by employees who deal with clients and customers is an important part of customer service (Grandey, Fisk, Mattila, Jansen, & Sideman, 2005). Such encounters can be difficult for employees who encounter a public that can be rude and even abusive at times (Grandey & Diamond, 2009). Many companies have emotion display rules requiring the expression of positive emotions such as smiling at customers and appearing to be enjoying work (Diefendorff, Richard, & Croyle, 2006), even if customers are not being particularly nice. The required expression of certain emotions at work is called **emotional labor**, recognizing that it can take effort for employees to maintain the appearance of positive feelings (Glomb & Tews, 2004).

Emotional labor has been shown to have both positive and negative effects on employees, depending on a number of factors. Perhaps the most important is how emotional labor is performed. Deep acting is a form of emotional labor in which the individual experiences the emotion he or she is trying to display. Surface acting, on the other hand, is a form of emotional labor in which the person fakes feeling good, while hiding his or her real feelings. Surface acting, or pretending to be happy when experiencing the opposite emotion, leads to **emotional dissonance**, which is stressful and has been associated with negative effects (Zapf, 2002). On the other hand, deep acting, or making yourself feel positive emotions that are displayed to others, can have positive effects on well-being. For example, Judge, Woolf, and Hurst (2009) showed that job satisfaction is oppositely related to deep and surface acting. People who deep act tend to like their jobs, and people who surface act tend to dislike them. Similarly, H. A. M. Johnson and Spector (2007) found that deep acting and surface acting are related oppositely to the emotional exhaustion component of burnout (see Chapter 11 for a discussion of burnout). Individuals who surface act experience more exhaustion than individuals who do not. Individuals who deep act experience less exhaustion than individuals who do not. Finally Yanchus, Eby, Lance, and Drollinger (2010) found that surface acting is associated with low levels of life satisfaction.

There are both individual and organizational factors that affect emotional labor and its possible impact on employees. First, it has been found that women (H. A. M. Johnson & Spector, 2007) and older workers (Dahling & Perez, 2010) are more likely to engage in deep acting than men and younger workers. Furthermore, the relationship between acting and well-being differs by gender and personality. The negative effects of surface acting are greater for women than men (H. A. M. Johnson & Spector, 2007) and for introverts than extraverts (Judge et al., 2009). Furthermore, the negative effects of emotional labor are reduced when the employee has high levels of autonomy and control (Grandey, Fisk, & Steiner, 2005; H. A. M. Johnson & Spector, 2007). Having control over the situation, such as being given latitude in how to deal with a rude customer, will tend to reduce negative effects, presumably because the employee does not have to fake being happy while being treated rudely by a customer.

The form of emotional labor performed can affect not only the employee but also customers who observe it. Groth, Thurau, and Walsh (2009) studied the reactions that customers have to the emotional labor of customer service employees. Subjects were students who were asked to complete a survey during a customer service encounter and to request that the customer service employee who waited on them complete a parallel survey asking about their emotional labor. Results showed that customers can detect whether the employee is engaging in deep or surface acting. More important is the finding that deep acting results in more positive perceptions of the service encounter. Thus it would seem that only deep acting can really accomplish the organizational purpose of emotional labor by enhancing the quality of the service encounter for the customer.

▶ CHAPTER SUMMARY

Job satisfaction is the extent to which people like or dislike their jobs (global satisfaction) or aspects of their jobs (facet satisfaction). It is usually measured with questionnaires administered to employees. Several popular job satisfaction scales are available:

Job Descriptive Index (JDI)
Minnesota Satisfaction Questionnaire (MSQ)
Job in General Scale (JIG)

Research has linked job satisfaction to a number of job environment variables. It has been shown to correlate with job characteristics, pay, and justice. Job satisfaction has also been found to correlate with personal characteristics, including age, and with various personality variables, such as negative affectivity and locus of control.

Research has also linked job satisfaction to several employee behaviors. Lack of satisfaction seems to be a cause of employee turnover. It is related modestly to job performance and slightly to absence, although it is not clear that satisfaction is the cause of either. There is evidence that performance may be the cause of satisfaction. Job satisfaction has been linked to employee health-related variables, but we will need future research to tell us specifically how job attitudes might affect disease.

Organizational commitment is another attitudinal variable that has been popular among I/O researchers. Commitment concerns the employee's attachment to the organization. It correlates strongly with job satisfaction, but it is conceptually different. Three components of commitment have been identified as affective, continuance, and normative. Organizational commitment has many of the same correlates as job satisfaction, including job satisfaction, job performance, turnover, stress, and justice.

The experience of positive emotions by employees on the job can have positive effects on employees and organizations, whereas the experience of negative emotions can have the opposite effects. The requirement to engage in emotional labor can have positive effects on customers of customer service employees but negative effects on employees, particularly if they fake the emotions (surface acting) and have low control over the service encounter.

I/O PSYCHOLOGY IN PRACTICE

(*Courtesy of Christopher McGivern*)

This case is a job satisfaction project carried out by Christopher McGivern. McGivern received a Master's degree in Occupational Psychology from Birkbeck, University of London in 1976. He has over 25 years' experience of employee surveys and organization development in several companies. McGivern founded his first employee survey business in 1980. It grew into one of the leading specialists in the field, merging with another consultancy in 2006. Currently, McGivern is the Director of Employee Feedback, a specialist employee survey provider.

One consulting project was a job satisfaction survey done for an incident management and roadside assistance provider. They employ around 400 people, mainly based in a call center environment. At the commencement of the project, a considerable amount of change had taken place and a new HR Director had been appointed. As a way of understanding the state of the business, an employee survey was conducted. The top team were hopeful that the survey would provide an impetus for change, providing guidance as to where best to focus their efforts for maximum impact.

McGivern began this project by interviewing several groups of employees. From the interviews he was able to develop a satisfaction questionnaire appropriate to the issues of the organization. He surveyed all the employees using the questionnaire and found that satisfaction was quite low. In particular, there was dissatisfaction with both pay and communication. The results of the study were compiled into a report that was given to the top team for review. They used the report to target action and subsequently improved wages and communication. One year later McGivern repeated the survey and found that job satisfaction had significantly increased. Furthermore, the largest increases were in the facets of pay and communication satisfaction. Every year for the last six years an employee survey has been run and action plans developed. Year-on-year increases in employee engagement and satisfaction have been seen, with response rates now consistently high. In addition, this company is now listed in the '100 Best Companies to Work for' guide. This case illustrates that job satisfaction surveys can be used to improve the work conditions for employees.

Discussion Questions

1. What sorts of things would you expect to raise the job satisfaction of employees?
2. Do you think the results of this project would have been different if McGivern had not received the backing of the entire top team?
3. What effects would you expect if the top team had ignored the results of this study?
4. Can you think of another way McGivern could have assessed job satisfaction?

LEARNING BY DOING

Job Satisfaction Facets

Take the list of common job satisfaction facets in Table 9.1. Ask at least five working people you know to indicate for each one whether they are satisfied or not on their current job. Then for each facet, compute the percentage of people who said they are satisfied. How does the pattern of satisfaction match with Figure 9.1? Note that security is not shown in the figure. If this is done in class, you could combine data with other students.

Observing Emotional Labor

Go to a store or restaurant and observe the interaction between sales clerks or servers and customers. Watch five different employees as they interact with a customer during the initial encounter. Record whether or not the employee expressed any form of emotion. Did the employee smile (or even laugh)? Did the customer return the smile? Did the employee make physical contact (e.g., shake hands or pat the customer's back)? As an alternative, try this in two or more organizations and see whether there are differences in the behavior of employees toward customers.

CHAPTER 10

Productive and Counterproductive Employee Behavior

CHAPTER 10 OUTLINE

On November 14, 1991, Thomas McIlvane, a former U.S. Postal Service employee, brought a rifle to the Royal Oak, Michigan, office and opened fire on his coworkers. Four people were killed and four were wounded before he shot and killed himself as well. His reason was apparently anger over being fired for insubordination, and a subsequent investigation suggested that he had been treated poorly by supervisors. In reaction to this and similar incidents, the Postal Service has implemented an employee assistance program to offer counseling services to troubled employees. This program is designed to deal with emotional problems and involves clinical rather than I/O psychologists.

Although it has received the most media attention, the Postal Service is not the only organization in which such incidents of violence have occurred. For example, on June 25, 2008, Wesley Higdon, an employee of Atlantis Plastics in Henderson, Kentucky, killed five of his coworkers following an argument with his supervisor. Nevertheless, extreme violence at work is rather rare. Most aggressive acts in the workplace have far less violent results, and so the news media pay little attention. Fights among employees that do not result in homicide or serious injury are not unusual events, and most go unreported to police. Even more common is verbal aggression among employees. Aggression and other forms of counterproductive work behavior (CWB) such as sabotage, theft, and withdrawal (absence, tardiness, and turnover) are a tremendous problem for organizations.

Rotundo and Sackett (2002) distinguish three classes of performance-related behavior engaged in by employees. CWB consists of acts that are harmful to organizations and people in organizations, as we have already discussed. Task performance concerns the core dimensions of performance that are described in a job analysis and are likely the focus of the performance appraisal system. For example, a customer service employee waits on customers, and a teacher conducts classes. Organizational citizenship behavior (OCB) is similar to the contextual performance that we discussed in Chapter 4. It consists of activities that go beyond the core dimensions of a job but that support the performance of the organization. This might include volunteering to do extra work or helping a coworker with a task. The latter two areas of performance are beneficial to the organization. In this chapter, we will discuss all three of these performance-related areas.

Objectives: The student who studies this chapter should be able to:

- **Discuss how environmental and personal characteristics impact job performance.**
- **Explain how the principles of human factors can be used to enhance job performance.**
- **Summarize the research on organizational citizenship behavior.**
- **Summarize the research on the causes of employee withdrawal.**
- **Discuss how counterproductive work behavior can result from environmental and personal factors.**

PRODUCTIVE BEHAVIOR: TASK PERFORMANCE

For an organization to achieve its purposes, individual employees must perform their jobs at some reasonable level of proficiency. This is as true for government organizations, in which poor performance means a failure to provide mandated public services, as it is for private companies, in which poor performance can mean bankruptcy. From a societal standpoint, it is in everyone's best interest for organizations to have employees who perform their jobs well. Good performance enhances organizational productivity, which directly enhances the goods and services provided to the public, as well as the national and global economies.

People can perform their jobs well only if they have both the necessary ability and the necessary motivation. Organizational practices and job conditions can enhance these personal characteristics or serve as constraints that interfere with job performance. These three factors—ability, motivation, and organizational constraints—are illustrated

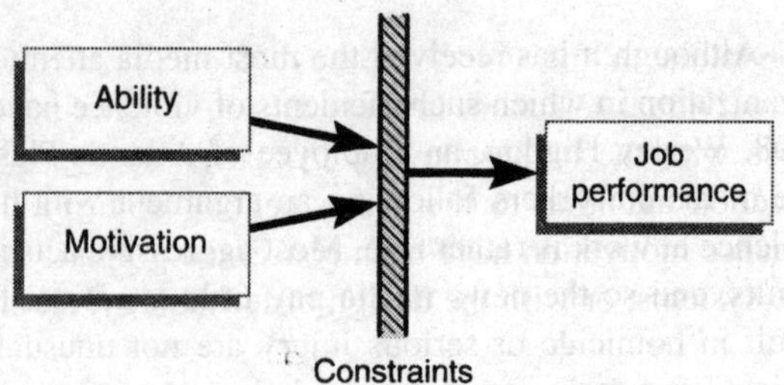

Figure 10.1 Good job performance requires both ability and motivation. Organizational constraints, such as inadequate training, can interfere with good performance.

in Figure 10.1. The figure shows how ability and motivation lead to performance but can be blocked by constraints.

Ability and Task Performance

Most selection efforts by I/O psychologists focus on identifying the necessary abilities and skills for specific jobs and finding people who have them. First, worker-oriented job analysis methods (as discussed in Chapter 3) are used to determine the necessary KSAOs (knowledge, skill, ability, and other personal characteristics) for a job. Once the KSAOs are identified, selection procedures are implemented to find individuals who have the appropriate characteristics. Although KSAOs deal with a variety of attributes, most selection devices (see Chapter 5) are designed to assess ability and skill. Finally, in addition to what employees bring with them, additional knowledge and skills can be developed through training. If an organization is to have a workforce with the necessary attributes for good job performance, all three steps—job analysis, selection, and training—must be followed.

It has been well established that various measures of ability relate to job performance (see Chapters 5 and 6). As might be expected, the nature of the job determines the mix of specific abilities necessary. For example, Gutenberg, Arvey, Osburn, and Jeanneret (1983) showed that cognitive ability predicts performance for most jobs. The more mentally demanding the job, however, the stronger was the relation between cognitive ability and job performance. In other words, cognitive ability is more important for mentally demanding jobs (e.g., engineer) than for simple jobs (e.g., file clerk). Caldwell and O'Reilly (1990) demonstrated that matching people's abilities to the KSAO requirements from a job analysis can be a useful strategy for enhancing job performance. They also found that employees whose abilities matched their jobs are more satisfied. These results are consistent with the notion that job performance might lead to satisfaction (see Chapter 9). Employees who have the characteristics necessary for good performance will be more successful on the job and will be more satisfied.

Motivation and Task Performance

Motivation is an individual characteristic, but it can arise from both within the worker (e.g., personality) and environmental conditions. Organizational attempts to enhance motivation in the workforce have focused more on environmental interventions than on individual selection. In theory, one might assess motivation in job applicants and hire those with the highest levels. I/O psychologists, however, have directed most of their selection attention to the assessment of ability rather than of motivation. Attempts to enhance motivation have been concerned primarily with the structure of jobs, with incentive systems, or with the design of technology, all of which are discussed in this chapter.

Personal Characteristics and Task Performance

Several employee characteristics are relevant to job performance and may affect ability to do the job. Others affect employee motivation to work hard (Tett & Burnett, 2003). In most cases, it is difficult to disentangle the effects of ability from the effects of motivation on job performance. For example, people with high levels of ability can also have high levels of motivation. As their ability leads to good performance and associated rewards, their motivation to perform may be enhanced. High-ability people might perform better because they are more skilled or because they put forth more effort—or both.

Cognitive ability (mathematical and verbal reasoning) has been found to predict job performance over a wide variety of jobs (Schmitt, Gooding, Noe, & Kirsch, 1984). In Chapters 3 and 5, we discussed how specific measures of ability are related to job performance, so ability will not be discussed again here. This chapter is concerned with the "Big Five" personality characteristics, which many researchers believe represent the basic dimensions of human personality. We also discuss how locus of control and age relate to performance.

The "Big Five" and Task Performance

Many psychologists today believe that human personality can be described by five dimensions, called the **Big Five:** extraversion, emotional stability, agreeableness, conscientiousness, and openness to experience (Barrick & Mount, 1991). Table 10.1 presents a brief description of each dimension.

Several meta-analyses have summarized relations between each of the five dimensions and task performance (Hurtz & Donovan, 2000; Salgado, 2003). Both meta-analysis studies concluded that personality is associated with job performance, with conscientiousness being the best predictor. Furthermore, Hurtz and Donovan (2000) discovered that certain personality dimensions are correlated more strongly with

TABLE 10.1 Description of the "Big Five" Dimensions of Personality

Dimension	Description
Extraversion	Sociable, gregarious, assertive, talkative
Emotional stability	Low levels of anxious, depressed, angry, worried, insecure
Agreeableness	Courteous, flexible, good-natured, cooperative
Conscientiousness	Dependable, responsible, hardworking, achievement oriented
Openness to experience	Imaginative, curious, broadminded, intelligent

Source: From "The Big Five Personality Dimensions and Job Performance: A Meta-Analysis," by M. R. Barrick and M. K. Mount, 1991, *Personnel Psychology, 44,* 1–26.

performance for some jobs than others. Although mean correlations are not large, these studies provide evidence that personality is an important factor for job performance across different kinds of jobs. However, even stronger correlations can be found by closely matching the particular personality traits to the particular job and task (Hogan & Holland, 2003; Tett, Steele, & Beauregard, 2003). For example, one might expect that emotional stability would predict performance in a job that requires the ability to handle stress, such as a police officer. Extraversion would be relevant to salespeople who must deal one-on-one with potential customers.

Locus of Control and Performance

Locus of control concerns people's beliefs about their ability to control reinforcements in their environment (see Chapter 9). Research has shown that *internals*, those who believe they can control reinforcements, have higher levels of job motivation than *externals*, those who do not believe they can control reinforcements (Ng, Sorensen, & Eby, 2006; Wang, Bowling, & Eschleman, 2010). Although the greater motivation of internals might be expected to result in better job performance, the effects relationship of locus of control to performance is quite small (Ng et al., 2006), suggesting that the locus of control–task performance relation can be complex. Blau (1993) studied how locus of control related to two different task performance dimensions of bank tellers (see the International Research box). Blau noted that internals have been shown to have higher levels of work motivation, which should lead them to display more initiative on the job. Externals, on the other hand, have been shown to be more conforming and would be expected to respond better to highly structured tasks that allow for little personal initiative. This is exactly what he found. Internals performed better in developing important job skills, whereas externals performed better on the routine clerical tasks that were highly structured. Blau's study suggests that relations between personality and job performance can depend on the particular dimension of performance.

INTERNATIONAL RESEARCH

Most of the research on job performance has failed to consider that different aspects of performance might be influenced by different factors. Blau's (1993) study is an exception in that it looked at the relation of locus of control with three different measures of performance. Blau hypothesized that internals would do better in some areas of performance, but externals would do better in others. Specifically, internals would perform better at tasks requiring independence and initiative, and externals would perform better at tasks requiring compliance with rules and supervisory directives.

Subjects for this study were 146 bank tellers (also known as cashiers). Locus of control in the work domain and three performance measures (productivity, money shortages, and self-development) were assessed. Productivity was an objective measure of the volume of work processed by each teller, and it represents a highly structured part of the job. Money shortage was an objective measure of accuracy in accounting, which is also a highly structured part of the job. Self-development, assessed by supervisors, was the extent to which employees enhanced their skills through their own initiative and independent action.

As Blau predicted, the correlations with locus of control differed across the different performance measures. The correlations were .27, .05, and −.30 for productivity, money shortages, and self-development, respectively. Externals performed significantly better than internals in productivity, but internals performed significantly better in self-development. The correlation between locus of control and money shortages was not significant. The correlation between productivity and self-development was negative, suggesting that the employees who had the highest levels of productivity had the lowest levels of self-development.

These results suggest that different people can do well at different aspects of the same job. The tellers who were the most productive were the poorest at self-development. Perhaps this shows that individuals differed in how much time and effort they put into different aspects of the job. Externals may have focused on the day-to-day requirements for productivity. Internals, on the other hand, may have put effort into learning new tasks, perhaps with the personal objective of receiving future promotions. This study emphasizes that job performance can be quite complex. Organizations should recognize that there can be more than one way to be a productive employee.

Source: From "Testing the Relationship of Locus of Control to Different Performance Dimensions," by G. Blau, 1993, *Journal of Occupational and Organizational Psychology, 66,* 125–138.

Age and Performance

Many people assume that job performance declines with age. The stereotype of the nonproductive older worker probably has roots in the fact that many physical abilities decline with age. For example, professional athletes almost always retire before they reach 40 years of age. Research has shown that the stereotype is incorrect, however. Older workers in many jobs are as productive as their younger coworkers.

Ng and Feldman (2008) conducted a meta-analysis of 280 studies relating age to task performance, as well as other performance-related variables. Rather than finding that job task performance declines with age, their study found little to no relationship. If anything, older workers perform tasks slightly better than younger workers, engage in more OCB, have fewer accidents, and are less likely to be absent from or late to work. Although some abilities might decline with age, other skills and a level of job wisdom that may lead to greater efficiency may increase with experience (Warr, 2001). What older workers lack in physical ability they may more than compensate for by better task strategies, better management of time, and more efficient approaches. The physical demands of the majority of jobs are well within the ability range of most older workers unless they are in poor health. Of course, poor health can adversely affect the job performance of even the youngest workers.

Environmental Conditions and Task Performance

The job environment can affect task performance in many ways. The environment can have a positive or negative influence on employee motivation, leading to an increase or decrease in employee efforts. Similarly, the environment can be structured to facilitate performance by making it easier for individuals to accomplish their jobs, or it can contain constraints that interfere with performance. One study showed that something as simple as allowing employees to listen to music over stereo headsets improves task performance, apparently by reducing tension (Oldham, Cummings, Mischel, Schmidtke, & Zhou, 1995). In this chapter, we will look at somewhat more complex factors of job characteristics, incentive systems, technology design, and organizational constraints.

Job Characteristics and Task Performance

One of the most influential theories that relate the nature of jobs to performance is Hackman and Oldham's (1976, 1980) job characteristics theory. This theory is based on the presumption that people are motivated by the intrinsic nature of job tasks. When work is interesting and enjoyable, people will like their jobs (as discussed in Chapter 9), be highly motivated, and perform well.

Job characteristics theory is illustrated in Figure 10.2. This theory states that features of jobs induce psychological states that lead to satisfaction, motivation, and task performance. The job features, or core characteristics (described in Table 9.6), lead to three psychological states. Skill variety, task identity, and task significance lead to experienced meaningfulness of work; autonomy leads to feelings of responsibility; and feedback leads to knowledge of results. These three states are critical to the satisfaction and motivation of employees. When jobs induce them, individuals will be motivated and satisfied and will perform better.

The levels of the core characteristics determine how motivating a job is likely to be. Hackman and Oldham (1976) noted that the **Motivation Potential Score (MPS)** of a job can be calculated by combining scores on the core characteristics. Specifically, the following formula is used:

MPS = (Skill Variety + Task Significance + Task Identity)/3 × Autonomy × Feedback

Note that the three characteristics leading to experienced meaningfulness are averaged. The average is multiplied by autonomy and feedback, which lead to experienced responsibility and knowledge of results, respectively. The multiplicative nature of the formula implies that a job cannot be motivating if it leads to low levels of even one of

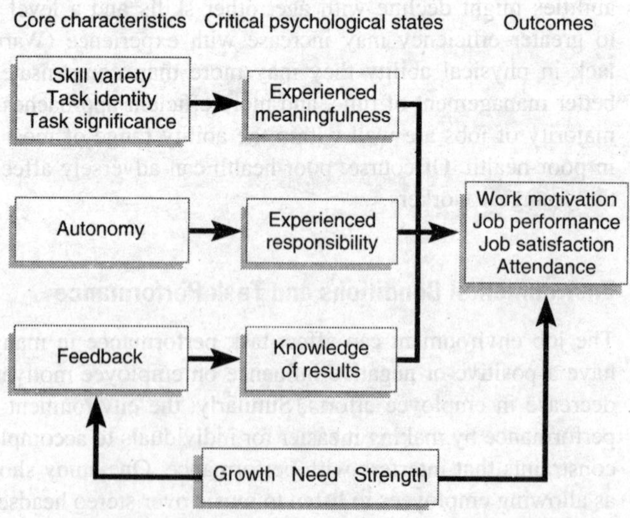

Figure 10.2 Hackman and Oldham's (1976) job characteristics model. *Source:* From "Motivation Through the Design of Work: Test of a Theory," by J. R. Hackman and G. R. Oldham, 1976, *Organizational Behavior and Human Performance, 16,* 250–279.

the three psychological states. If one of the three multiplied terms equals zero, the MPS will be zero.

There is one last piece of the theory: the moderator effect of growth need strength (GNS). As noted in Chapter 9, GNS is a personality variable that concerns the need for fulfillment of higher-order needs, such as personal growth, autonomy, and achievement. According to Hackman and Oldham (1976), the connection from job characteristics to psychological states to outcomes holds mainly for individuals who are high on GNS. This means that this is a person-job fit theory, in which only certain types of people will respond well to high MPS jobs. Hackman and Oldham had little to say about low GNS people and what might motivate them.

Studies that used employee self-reports as measures of the core characteristics have supported their relation with motivation and performance (Fried & Ferris, 1987), as well as the moderating effect of GNS (Loher, Noe, Moeller, & Fitzgerald, 1985). Research using other methods has been more equivocal. Although studies can be found demonstrating that changing or redesigning jobs to be higher in MPS results in better job performance, other studies show no effect from job redesign. An interesting longitudinal study by Griffin (1991) showed that the effects of job redesign are a temporary increase in job satisfaction and a delayed increase in task performance. These results suggest that the connection among job conditions, satisfaction, and performance is more complex than the job characteristics theory would lead us to expect.

Incentive Systems and Performance

A possible way of increasing task performance, at least performance quantity, is incentive systems that reward employees for each unit of work performed (see Chapter 8's discussion of reinforcement theory). Such systems are common with salespeople who receive commissions and with factory workers who are on **piece-rate systems** that pay them for each unit of production. Incentive systems work through motivation by rewarding employees for behavior beneficial to the organization. Most such systems reward task performance, although examples can be found that reward employees for other behaviors such as attendance.

Although incentive systems can increase productivity, they have not been universally successful. Yukl and Latham (1975), for example, found that a piece-rate system increased the productivity of only two of three groups with which it was implemented. In their classic study of factory workers, Coch and French (1948) documented how peer pressure within work groups could undermine the effects of a piece-rate system. They gave as an example how the productivity of one factory worker was cut in half by pressure from coworkers.

In order for an incentive system to be effective, three elements must be in place. First, the employees must have the ability to increase productivity. If they are working at the limit of their capability, introducing an incentive system will not improve performance. Second, employees must want the incentives. Not everyone is willing to work harder for money or other rewards. For an incentive system to work, the incentive must be something that people want. Finally, an incentive system will not work if there are physical or psychological constraints on performance. A salesperson in a store cannot sell if there are no customers. Figure 10.3 shows how the three elements combine to determine the effectiveness of an incentive system.

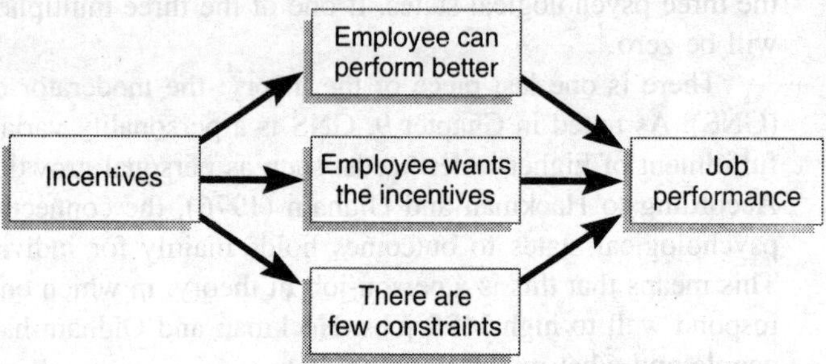

Figure 10.3 Incentives can lead to improved performance if employees are able to perform better, if they want the incentives, and if there are few constraints.

Design of Technology

The Hawthorne studies showed that social factors can be more important than the physical environment in job performance. There is no doubt, however, that the physical features of job settings can affect performance. The field of **human factors** (also called **ergonomics** or **engineering psychology**) is concerned with the interface between people and the physical environment, including tools, equipment, and technology. Human factors psychologists are involved in the design of the physical environment to make jobs safer and easier to accomplish. Through their work over the past few decades, human factors psychologists have developed sound design principles and procedures. The influence of the field can be found in the design of everything from automobiles and consumer appliances to military aircraft and nuclear power plants.

Displays and Controls

The major focus of human factors is on the interaction between people and tools, machines, or technology. Two major areas of concern are the presentation of information to the person and the manipulation of tools or machines by the person.

In an automobile, the driver must be given information about speed. He or she also must control the speed and direction of the vehicle. Human factors principles tell engineers how best to present information and design controls that maximize precision and reduce human error.

A machine can provide information to a person in many ways. The nature and use of the information determine how it should best be presented. Most machine information is provided through either the visual or the auditory channel, or sometimes both. For danger or warning signals, such as at a railway crossing, it is best to use both, such as a bell and flashing lights.

With machines, information can be provided in a visual display. Two different types of visual displays for quantitative information (airplane altitude) are shown in Figure 10.4. The upper display in the figure is a two-point style, which is like a traditional clock with the shorter and heavier hand representing altitude in thousands of feet and the longer and thinner hand representing hundreds of feet. The lower display is a digital display, which indicates the altitude by showing the numerals. Obviously, in an airplane there is a need to be able to determine altitude both quickly and accurately because errors can

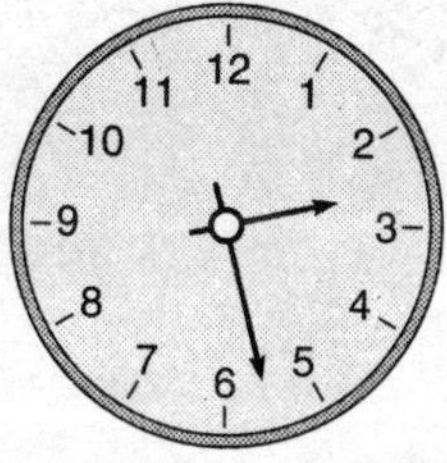

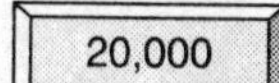

Figure 10.4 Types of altitude displays for an aircraft. *Source:* From "Control and Tools" (p. 214), by J. R. Buck, 1983, in B. H. Kantowitz and R. D. Sorkin (Eds.), *Human Factors: Understanding People-System Relationships*, New York, NY: John Wiley.

lead to disaster. The digital display is superior to the two-point because it is easy to mix up the two hands (Buck, 1983). For example, 2,100 feet can be misread as 1,200 feet, which could present a problem for anyone attempting to fly over a 2,000-foot-high mountain.

The manipulation of the machine by the person, often in response to information provided by a display, is accomplished through controls. The design of the best control is also determined by the particular purpose and situation. Most controls are worked with either the hand or the foot, although other possibilities can be found (e.g., the knee or elbow). Hand controls are best when fine or precise motions are necessary, such as for steering an automobile. Foot controls are best when force is more important than precision, such as with a brake pedal for an automobile.

There are a number of important design considerations pertaining to controls. First, they should be located in a logical place, with controls for the same function together. A well-designed automobile console, for example, will place the lighting controls together, the windshield wiper and washer controls together, the heater and air conditioner controls together, and so on. A control to work a front window should be in front of a control to work a back window, and a control to work a feature on the right side of the car should be to the right of a control to work the same feature on the left side.

Second, vital controls that can produce important consequences should be recognizable by touch. This is not important for the volume control on a car radio, but it is vital for the landing gear on an airplane. Figure 10.5 illustrates several different knobs for stick-type levers, such as the shift lever of an automobile. Each of these can be discriminated by touch alone. Knobs such as these are used in airplanes.

Third, controls should provide appropriate feedback so that the person knows that the function has been accomplished (Wickens, Lee, Liu, & Becker, 2004). With an on/off switch, the person might hear a click and feel a tactile sensation indicating that the switch has been activated or deactivated. Some switches use springs so that the person can feel the lever lock into place. Finally, the directions in which controls are moved should logically match the directions in which the machine will move. For example, an increase in some factor should involve moving a switch either clockwise, up, or to the right as opposed to counterclockwise, down, or to the left. This is the general rule followed with most equipment with volume controls, such as radios and televisions. Levers to move a device to the right should move clockwise or to the right, as in most vehicles.

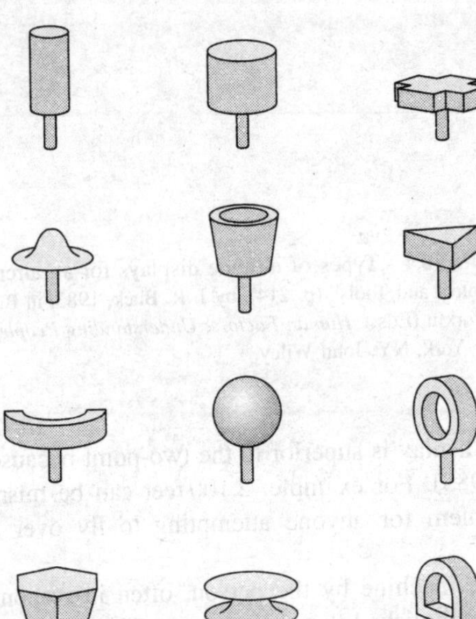

Figure 10.5 Examples of shift knobs that can be discriminated by touch alone. Source: From *Human Factors: Understanding People-System Relationships* (p. 311), edited by B. H. Kantowitz and R. D. Sorkin, 1983, New York, NY: John Wiley.

Computer-Human Interaction

These principles of displays and controls have been available for many years, so there is not much need to conduct research on them today. Instead, human factors psychologists have turned their attention to computer-human interaction. *Computer-human interaction* is the interplay of people with computers and associated technologies that have led to tremendous changes in the workplace for both blue- and white-collar work. Automation and computerization have changed the nature of many jobs, so that individuals must use computer-based systems to accomplish a growing number of tasks. Web-based systems are rapidly replacing physical paper-and-pencil systems for many tasks, such as paying bills.

A major issue for computer-human interaction is communication between human and machine. That is, how best should computers provide information to people, and how best can people tell computers what they wish done? In order for people to communicate effectively with computers, they must develop a conceptual understanding or **mental model** of how the computer operates (Wickens et al., 2004). A person who knows how to drive an automobile, for example, has a mental model of how the operation of the controls results in the appropriate movement of the vehicle.

Frese (1987) noted that efficient use of computers by people can arise by focusing on two essential elements: training people and appropriate system design. Training is necessary because in many jobs people are hired without all the necessary skills for the computer system they must use. Even when people do have the necessary skills, computer systems and software are constantly changing, requiring a continued training effort to maintain proficiency. Research on computer training has suggested ways in which it can enhance performance. Augustine and Coovert (1991), for example, have shown that the use of animated models can be quite effective in enhancing performance of computer tasks. Animated models show the computer system in action rather than giving a written description or instructions. This approach is similar to the demonstration portion of a video game (e.g., Nintendo Wii or Microsoft X-Box) that shows the game in action.

Attention to system design is essential because many existing systems are poorly designed and inefficient. Research on computer-human interaction has provided many insights about how best to design systems that people can learn and use efficiently. Coovert (1990) argued that the best systems represent problems in a way that matches how people who use them represent problems. Systems that require people to adopt new ways of looking at familiar problems are difficult to learn.

Although this was not always the case, today's electronic devices such as smart phones are designed with the user in mind. Information is displayed on a touch screen that makes it easy to interact with the device. Icons (small pictures on the screen) are used that represent the functions you wish to use. For example, on a Droid phone if you touch the icon that looks like a telephone handset, it brings up the dial screen. Touch the icon of a person, and it takes you to your personal phone book. Icons at the top of the screen provide important information, such as a picture of a battery that shows how much battery power is left, and a picture of vertical bars of increasing length to indicate signal strength. The use of icons that are easy to learn and intuitively obvious makes it possible to use a complex smart phone that is in actuality a handheld computer, without extensive computer training.

So far we have discussed the interaction of individual people with technology, but technology can also be used to facilitate collaboration among employees working together. **Computer-supported cooperative work** or CSCW is the study of how technology can be used to help people work together on tasks (Coovert & Thompson, 2001). Computer-based technologies allow people in remote locations to send almost instantaneous messages (e-mail or texting) or to see and hear one another (videoconferencing). People can work in virtual teams that "meet" only electronically. Research on the effects and effectiveness of such technologies compared to live communication is new, but already we know there are differences. For example, people working together via e-mail, compared to live interaction, are less inhibited (are more likely to make hostile comments and insult one another), are less likely to conform to one another's opinions, have more trouble reaching decisions, and have more trouble coordinating their efforts (Coovert & Thompson, 2001). Research needs to be done in this area to figure out how to overcome these problems, either by better design of the technology or by better training of people to be more effective users of CSCW.

The principles of human factors can be used to design tools and equipment so that people can perform their tasks more easily and efficiently. Whether or not this translates into better overall task performance depends on many other factors. If employees are not motivated to perform well, making their job tasks easier through better equipment design might mean that they do the same work with less effort. Furthermore, constraints in the work environment, which we discuss next, may prevent better performance, even though certain tasks might be accomplished more efficiently.

From a human factors perspective, the goal is to design technology that will be helpful to people. However, technology can come with a price, and not all effects are positive. The introduction of computers in manufacturing has changed jobs but not always for the better. Although new factory systems might be more efficient, they can increase employee boredom and stress (Wall & Davids, 1992). Often the person who used to be an active participant on the assembly line is relegated to passively watching a machine operate. The loss of control over tasks to the machine can be associated with job dissatisfaction and poor emotional well-being (Mullarkey, Jackson, Wall, Wilson, & Grey-Taylor, 1997).

Organizational Constraints

Organizational constraints are aspects of the work environment that interfere with or prevent good task performance. They can arise from any aspect of the job, including the physical environment; supervisory practices; and the lack of needed training, tools, equipment, or time. Peters and O'Connor (1980) outlined eight different areas of constraints, which they derived from critical incidents. They asked 62 employed people to describe an incident in which something at work interfered with their job performance. From an analysis of the incidents, they came up with the constraint areas. Each is shown in Table 10.2, along with a brief description.

According to Hochwarter, Witt, Treadway, and Ferris (2006), organizational constraints have a detrimental effect on job performance, preventing employees from adequately using their skills to perform job tasks. H. J. Klein and Kim (1998) found that salespeople's reports of constraints were correlated with their objective sales performance. Individuals who scored highest on constraints sold the least amount. Tesluk and Mathieu (1999) reported similar findings for the performance of road maintenance and construction crews. Higher levels of constraints led to lower levels of performance for crews as rated by managers. O'Connor, Peters, Rudolf, and Pooyan (1982) further demonstrated that constraints can be potentially detrimental to employee well-being, as well as performance. They found that high levels of situational constraints, as reported by employees, were associated with job dissatisfaction and frustration. Jex and Gudanowski (1992) found similar results, as well as a tendency for employees reporting high levels of constraints to be more likely to intend to quit their jobs. Thus it seems that organizational constraints can have detrimental effects not only on task performance but on employee satisfaction, frustration, and possibly turnover as well. This conclusion must be tempered by the fact that most constraint studies have relied entirely

TABLE 10.2 Eight Organizational Constraint Areas

Job-related information: For example, data and information needed for the job.

Tools and equipment: Tools, equipment, instruments, and machinery necessary for the job, such as computers or trucks.

Materials and supplies: Materials and supplies necessary for the job, such as lumber or paper.

Budgetary support: Money necessary to acquire resources to do the job.

Required services and help from others: Help available from other people.

Task preparation: Whether or not the employee has the KSAOs necessary for the job.

Time availability: The amount of time available for doing job tasks.

Work environment: The physical features of the job environment, such as buildings or weather.

Source: From "Situational Constraints and Work Outcomes: The Influences of a Frequently Overlooked Construct," by L. H. Peters and E. J. O'Connor, 1980, *Academy of Management Review, 5,* 391–397.

on employee self-reports for all the data. Studies using other methods will be necessary to determine the importance of the job environment itself rather than just people's perceptions.

ORGANIZATIONAL CITIZENSHIP BEHAVIOR (OCB)

Organizational citizenship behavior (OCB) is behavior that goes beyond the core task requirements of the job (tasks listed in a job description) and is typically beneficial to the organization. OCB is usually assessed by having supervisors rate their subordinates on OCB behaviors. Sample items from C. Smith, Organ, and Near's (1983) popular OCB scale are shown in Table 10.3. Note that although some of these items fit the definition of going beyond requirements (e.g., making suggestions), others do not (e.g., being punctual).

Organ and Konovsky (1989) divided OCB into two categories of behaviors: those that are specifically required and those that are not. *Altruism* is helping another employee or supervisor with a problem, even though it is not required. It might involve helping a coworker who has been absent or making suggestions to improve conditions. *Compliance* is doing what needs to be done and following rules, such as coming to work on time and not wasting time.

OCB can be an important aspect of an employee's behavior that contributes to overall organizational effectiveness. Individuals who are high on OCB are not necessarily the best performers in other areas, however. MacKenzie, Podsakoff, and Fetter (1991) assessed OCB and objective sales performance of salespeople. They found little relation between the two types of behavior. Employees who had the best sales records were no different in terms of their OCB from those who had the poorest records. In some cases, salespeople who performed poorly in sales may have made significant contributions to the organization through their OCB. P. M. Podsakoff, Ahearne, and MacKenzie (1997) studied 40 work crews in a paper mill, assessing the OCBs of individual members in relation to the crew's overall performance rather than individual employee performance. Results showed that higher levels of OCB among crew members are associated with higher total crew productivity and fewer defects. Likewise, N. P. Podsakoff, Whiting, Podsakoff, and Blume's (2009) meta-analysis showed that high levels of OCB among people in work groups is associated with organization profitability and customer satisfaction.

Several factors have been suggested as antecedents of OCB. A meta-analysis of OCB studies by Hoffman, Blair, Meriac, and Woehr (2007) suggested that OCB is most likely when employees are satisfied with their jobs, have high levels of affective commitment,

TABLE 10.3 Four Items From the Organizational Citizenship Behavior Scale

Assists supervisor with his or her work
Makes innovative suggestions to improve department
Is punctual
Gives advance notice if unable to come to work

Source: From "Cognitive Versus Affective Determinants of Organizational Citizenship Behavior," by D. W. Organ and M. Konovsky, 1989, *Journal of Applied Psychology, 74,* 157–164.

feel they are treated fairly, and have good relations with their supervisors. There are also personality characteristics that relate to OCB. Kaplan, Bradley, Luchman, and Haynes (2009) in their meta-analysis found that high levels of OCB were associated with high levels of negative affectivity (the tendency to experience negative emotions) and high levels of positive affectivity (the tendency to experience positive emotions). In addition, OCB may be contagious—people who work in groups where people tend to perform OCB are likely to perform it themselves (Bommer, Miles, & Grover, 2003). Some of these results have been shown to hold in other countries as well. Farh, Podsakoff, and Organ (1990) found that OCB correlated with job satisfaction and employee perceptions of supervisor supportive behavior in Taiwan. Munene (1995) found OCB related to job satisfaction and organizational commitment in Nigeria.

McNeely and Meglino (1994) divided OCB into acts that help other employees (OCBI) and acts that benefit the organization (OCBO). They found that different types of OCB are related to different variables; for example, OCBI correlates with the individual's concern for others, whereas OCBO correlates with employees' perceived equity, and both correlate with job satisfaction. Similarly, organizational commitment has been linked to both types of OCB, with it being more strongly related to OCBO than OCBI in the United States (Lavelle et al., 2009) and Turkey (Wasti, 2005). However, OCB is related to affective and not continuance commitment (Johnson & Chang, 2006). Furthermore, Lee and Allen (2002) reported that both OCBI and OCBO relate to positive mood at work, but only OCBO relates to procedural justice. The results of all these studies suggest that the two types of OCB have different combinations of causes, with some causes shared and some unique.

Although OCB is often thought of as altruistic acts that individuals do for selfless reasons, recent research suggests that in at least some instances, OCB can be a strategy for getting ahead at work. Hui, Lam, and Law (2000), in a study conducted in a multinational bank among tellers, assessed levels of OCB in employees before and after receiving a promotion. In addition, before promotion employees were asked if they believed engaging in OCB would improve chances of promotion. For those who thought it would, OCB levels were high before promotion and declined after promotion, suggesting these employees increased their OCB as a tactic for obtaining a desired promotion but then reduced their OCB once their goal had been achieved.

▶ COUNTERPRODUCTIVE WORK BEHAVIOR: WITHDRAWAL

On any given day in almost any large organization, some people will come to work late, some people will miss the entire workday, and some people will quit the job permanently. All of these *withdrawal* behaviors involve employees not being at work when scheduled or needed, either temporarily (absence and lateness) or permanently (turnover). Most of the research on withdrawal behaviors has considered them to be related phenomena. As noted by Mitra, Jenkins, and Gupta (1992), some researchers have considered absence and turnover to be alternative reactions to job dissatisfaction. Both may reflect attempts by employees to escape, either temporarily or permanently, from situations they find unpleasant.

In their meta-analysis, Mitra et al. (1992) found that absence and turnover are moderately correlated with one another. In other words, employees who quit their jobs are likely to have had relatively high levels of absence before they quit. In a similar meta-analysis, Koslowsky, Sagie, Krausz, and Singer (1997) found that lateness (not getting to work on time) correlates with both absence and turnover. Late people are often absent people and are likely to quit. Although correlations among withdrawal measures might mean that they have similar causes, other explanations are possible. For example, individuals who plan to quit their jobs might use up their sick leave rather than forfeit it upon leaving, and they might be absent and late to engage in job hunting.

Absence

Absence, employees not showing up for work when scheduled, can be a major problem for organizations. Many jobs require someone's presence even when the scheduled person is not there. In such cases, absence requires that organizations either overstaff so that enough people will be available each day or have substitutes on call. Whereas the idea of substitutes for teachers is undoubtedly familiar to everyone, many organizations, especially factories, have substitutes available for other types of work, as well. Often the on-call substitutes are regular employees who may be asked to work an extra shift to fill in, frequently at higher overtime salary rates.

The major approach to understanding why absence occurs has focused on withdrawal as a response to dissatisfying jobs and job conditions. Absence and job satisfaction are related, but research has found quite small correlations between them. As noted in Chapter 9, Bowling and Hammond's (2008) meta-analysis found a −.10 correlation between absence and job satisfaction. Farrell and Stamm (1988) conducted a meta-analysis of 72 absence studies and noted that the two best predictors are prior absence history and the organization's absence policy rather than job satisfaction. People who have frequently been absent in the past are likely to be absent in the future. Organizations that have policies designed to control absence by either rewarding attendance or punishing absence have less absence.

Although it seems obvious that absence might arise from an employee being ill or being unmotivated to go to work, family responsibilities can be another major factor. Goff, Mount, and Jamison (1990) found that having primary responsibility for child care predicted absence with a correlation considerably higher than that typically found with job satisfaction. Erickson, Nichols, and Ritter (2000) found that absence was associated with the number of children under six years old. In a study conducted in Finland, absence rates were highest for young women who were presumably of childbearing age (Elovainio, Kivimäki, Vahtera, Virtanen, & Keltikangas-Jarvinen, 2003). Taken together, these studies support the idea that absence can be caused by having to take care of children, a form of work-family conflict (see Chapter 11), whether or not the employee likes his or her job.

Dalton and Mesch (1991) asked subjects to classify their absence into one of two categories: due to illness or due to other circumstances. They found that the two types of absence had different correlates. Absence due to illness, but not due to other circumstances, was related to job satisfaction and gender. The dissatisfied and women were ill more frequently. Absence due to other circumstances was related to job tenure and absence policy. Organizations with longer-tenured employees and less restrictive policies had more absence. These results suggest that the different types of absences have different causes that might be reduced with different procedures.

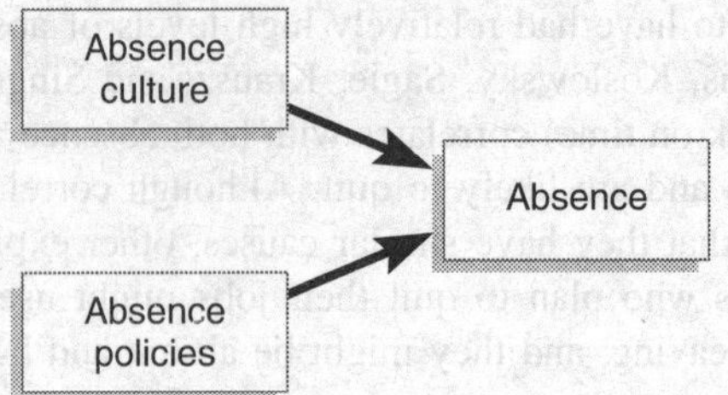

Figure 10.6 Both the absence culture of the work group and organizational absence policies contribute to employee absence.

Nicholson and Johns (1985) have taken a different approach to the explanation of absence. They noted that absence can be caused by the absence culture of a work group or organization. That is, in any work group or organization there will be accepted social rules governing the appropriate amount of and reasons for absence. One organization might have a culture that encourages absence whenever an employee does not feel like coming to work. Another might encourage employees to come to work unless it is absolutely impossible for them to do so. In support of this idea, Mathieu and Kohler (1990) showed that absence runs in groups—that is, individuals are more likely to be absent if their coworkers are absent.

Figure 10.6 illustrates that absence culture and absence policies are the two biggest factors in absence. Although job satisfaction has been the focus of most absence research, it seems that its potential effects are overshadowed by culture and policies. A dissatisfied individual who might want to escape work by calling in sick is not likely to do so if absence is punished or is viewed by coworkers as unacceptable. Organizations can reduce absence by changing policies to encourage attendance and discourage absence. A simple procedure found in one study was merely to mail each employee a letter indicating the number of days he or she had been absent (Gaudine & Saks, 2001). Just knowing that management was concerned about absence was enough to convince employees to reduce it.

Lateness

For many jobs, employees are on fixed work schedules, but often employees will fail to get to work on time. Some employees might be able to make up the time by skipping breaks, taking a short lunch, or staying late. However, often employees fail to make up the time, or the time cannot be made up; for example, if a professor is late for class, the time won't usually be rescheduled. Lateness produces costs for organizations that call in substitutes and can put an unfair burden on coworkers who might have to take up the slack.

Lateness, like absence, can have many causes. Koslowsky (2000) noted that although attitudes, such as job dissatisfaction, have been linked to lateness, other important causes are commuting distance and ease and work-family conflict. People who have long commutes can get stuck in traffic. Individuals with children, for example, might be late because a child is sick and must be taken to the doctor. Another important factor is national culture. Promptness is considered more important in some countries than in others; for example, Americans value it more than Brazilians do. Organizations also have their own lateness cultures, just as they have absence cultures (Elicker, Foust, O'Malley, & Levy, 2008).

Foust, Elicker, and Levy (2006) argued that attitudes about lateness itself are more important determinants of lateness behavior than other, more general job attitudes. They developed a lateness attitude scale that asked about both one's own behavior (feeling guilty for being late) and coworkers' behavior (being let down when coworkers are late). They administered their new scale as part of a survey of employees. It was a better predictor of lateness than was either job satisfaction or organizational commitment. Finally, Iverson and Deery (2001) investigated both lateness and leaving early from work, which they found were related. Coming late and leaving early were associated with perceptions of injustice (see Chapter 8) and job dissatisfaction.

Turnover

In every organization, employees will quit their jobs from time to time. The quitting of employees is called **turnover**. The percentage of the workforce that quits in a given period of time is called the *turnover rate*. When the rate becomes excessive, the organization's workforce can become too inexperienced and untrained, resulting in inefficiency and difficulties in achieving the organization's objectives. Turnover is a problem if good performers quit but not if the quitters are people who perform poorly. Trevor, Gerhart, and Boudreau (1997) studied the relation between task performance and turnover. They found a curvilinear relation in that the best and worst employees were most likely to quit. Turnover can have beneficial results if better replacements can be found for poor performers. However, good performers might also quit because often the best people are those who are the most attractive to other organizations. For the best performers, good salary raises reduced turnover.

Poor performers will quit for several reasons. When pay and other rewards are contingent on performance, they may quit because rewards are low (Williams, 1999). Furthermore, if they know they are not doing well on the job, they may attempt to find jobs for which they are better suited. Alternatively, it is not uncommon for supervisors to "encourage" turnover by targeting individuals for harassment. Poor performers might be denied rewards, given distasteful work assignments, and treated unkindly in order to get them to quit.

Serious difficulties can arise from this approach to creating turnover and can produce more problems than it solves. It can affect employees who are not the intended target. The harassment of one employee can create a hostile and uncomfortable work environment for everyone. Legal ramifications are also possible, for harassed employees might file lawsuits. If the supervisor and target of harassment are of a different gender or from different ethnic backgrounds, a discrimination case might be filed. Finally, harassment is an unethical behavior, and even poorly performing employees should be dealt with in a fair and honest manner.

The second issue that determines the costs of turnover to organizations concerns the expense involved in replacing people who have quit. For some jobs, recruiting and hiring can be costly and time consuming. Hiring high-level executives can take months of searching for applicants, conducting extensive and expensive out-of-town interviews, and offering expensive bonuses and benefits. For other jobs, a long period of training might

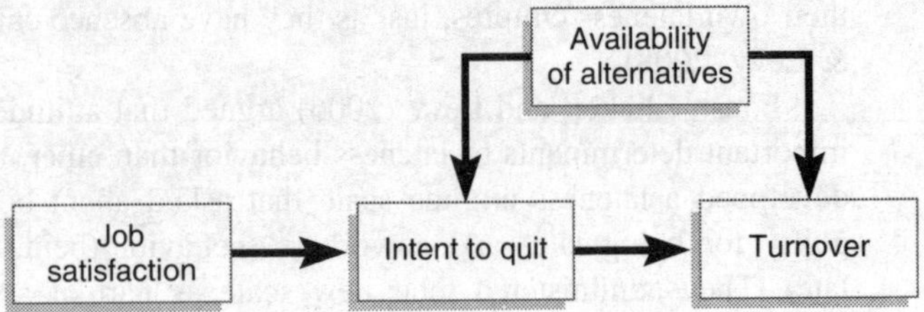

Figure 10.7 Employee turnover as a function of job satisfaction and unemployment rate.

be required before an employee is able to be fully productive. In the armed services, it can take more than a year to fully train a fighter pilot. If there is a high level of pilot turnover, the cost to the government will be great.

Job satisfaction has been a central variable in the research on turnover (Griffeth, Hom, & Gaertner, 2000). Figure 10.7 illustrates how the turnover process is thought to work. It shows that job satisfaction leads to intention to quit, which leads to turnover. Furthermore, the relation between intention to quit and turnover is moderated by the unemployment rate. People who are dissatisfied with their jobs are likely to intend to quit them. Intentions are often precursors to behavior that leads to quitting. It is unlikely, however, that people will quit their jobs unless they have another job available. As shown in the model, the unemployment rate, which reflects the availability of alternative employment, affects whether or not dissatisfaction and intentions are translated into turnover.

There is good support for the propositions in this model. First, job satisfaction and intention of quitting correlate with one another (Bowling & Hammond, 2008), which is consistent with the idea that satisfaction leads to intention. Second, Blau (2007) found that both job satisfaction and intention of quitting correlate with job search behaviors, such as applying for another job and going on a job interview. Third, Griffeth et al. (2000) found in their meta-analysis that both job satisfaction and intention to quit predict future turnover, with satisfaction having a smaller magnitude of correlation ($r = -.17$) than intention ($r = .35$). The predictive nature of these studies supports the idea that job satisfaction and intention are precursors of turnover. Finally, studies have shown that the unemployment rate moderates the relations between job satisfaction and turnover and between intention and turnover (e.g., Trevor, 2001). These studies show that when the unemployment rate is low and alternative job opportunities are plentiful, there is a strong relation of satisfaction and intention with turnover. When the unemployment rate is high and alternative job opportunities are scarce, however, there is little predictability of turnover by intention and job satisfaction. In other words, dissatisfied people may wish to quit their jobs, but they can do so only when alternative employment is available.

Dickter, Roznowski, and Harrison (1996) tracked the quitting of individuals who either liked or disliked their jobs over several years. For both groups, likelihood of turnover increased from the time of hiring until about 2 years on the job, after which it declined. Dissatisfied individuals were more likely to quit than their satisfied counterparts until about 4 years on the job. After 4 years, differences disappeared. Apparently, the effects of job satisfaction on turnover are time limited, as perhaps those who dislike their jobs and wish to quit eventually give up and make the best of the situation.

Although many employees quit their jobs because they are unhappy with them, there are other reasons for turnover (Maertz & Griffeth, 2004). First, a person might quit for health reasons. Heart attack survivors will often make drastic changes in their lifestyles, which can include quitting their jobs. Second, a person might become disabled on a job due to an accident that prevents him or her from continuing to perform essential tasks on the job. As noted in Chapter 11, motor vehicle accidents are a common source of serious injury on the job. Third, people will sometimes quit jobs they like to pursue other life interests. These might include continuing their education or training for athletic pursuits such as the Olympics. Fourth, people might quit because of family reasons, such as pregnancy (Lee, Wilbur, Kim, & Miller, 2008). Finally, people might quit because their spouse has been offered a better job in another location.

Some of these reasons go beyond the workplace, but organizations can do a great deal to address some of these causes of turnover. An organization can create a safer work environment to reduce injuries and can encourage healthy behavior to reduce illness. Many organizations have instituted employee wellness programs, which can include exercise programs, smoking and weight control classes, and stress management workshops. Organizational policies and practices can help employees pursue other interests while continuing to work. For example, on-site child care and flexible work schedules can make it easier for employees with young children to continue their jobs. With on-site child-care programs, child care is provided at the place of employment so that employees can take their children to work and spend breaks and lunch periods with them. Having their children nearby can provide peace of mind that makes it easier for employees to focus attention on work. Flexible work schedules that allow employees to work at times that do not interfere with other interests can keep some employees from quitting their jobs.

▶ COUNTERPRODUCTIVE WORK BEHAVIOR: AGGRESSION, SABOTAGE, AND THEFT

Instances of irate employees shooting their coworkers and often themselves have brought national attention to the issue of employee aggression. Although these relatively rare (Neuman & Baron, 1997), but extreme, examples fall more within the domain of clinical psychology or criminology, the issue of less extreme employee behavior that is damaging to organizations is an important one for the I/O field. **Counterproductive work behavior** or CWB (often called desk rage in the popular media) refers to behaviors that harm the organization and other people at work, such as coworkers, supervisors, and customers. CWB can consist of engaging in physical and verbal aggression, directing hostile and nasty behavior at a coworker, destroying organizational property, purposely doing work incorrectly, stealing, and withholding task performance.

Sabotage and theft have been recognized as major problems for organizations. Sabotage, the destruction of property or intentional withholding of performance, results in both direct costs from the damage to property and indirect costs from the loss of productivity while property needed for work is being repaired. Although many acts of sabotage are blatant, such as burning down a building, most are surreptitious and difficult to prove. It is often impossible to determine if an equipment-damaging accident was really accidental. For example, an employee might purposely ignore warning signals on a piece of equipment, such as the indicator light that a truck is low on oil or water. In some cases, employees might remove the oil or water, knowing that it will damage the equipment. If the employee is careful, it will be difficult to prove that he or she purposely sabotaged the equipment.

Employee theft has been estimated to cost U.S. businesses billions of dollars per year (Greenberg, 2002). In a national survey of retailers, employees were found to be responsible for more theft than shoplifters (Hollinger, Dabney, Lee, Hayes, Hunter, & Cummings, 1996). Organizations spend considerable money and resources to control theft. Many organizations have tried to weed out potential thieves with the use of paper-and-pencil integrity tests to assess honesty (see Chapter 5). Others have resorted to lie detector tests, either for job applicants or for current employees.

Bennett and Robinson (2000) conducted an anonymous mail survey of Toledo, Ohio, residents chosen at random from the telephone book. They asked about a long list of CWBs that went well beyond just sabotage and theft and found that many were quite common. For example, a quarter of people admitted to falsifying a receipt to get reimbursed for money they didn't spend, a third of people said they played a mean prank on someone at work, 52% of people said they took property from work without permission, 61% neglected to follow instructions, and 78% made fun of someone at work.

Figure 10.8 is a model of the causes of CWB. It begins with stressful job conditions, such as organizational constraints (as discussed earlier in this chapter), or injustice. For example, on the day he assaulted his coworkers, Thomas McIlvane had lost the final appeal of his dismissal from the post office. Stressful conditions and injustice induce negative emotions, such as anger or fear. These feelings in turn lead to behaviors that can be constructive, such as developing more effective strategies to overcome the conditions or injustice, or destructive, such as CWB.

Beliefs about control determine in part whether individuals choose constructive or destructive responses. An employee who believes that constructive efforts can be effective is likely to attempt them. An employee who believes that he or she cannot control the situation might resort to CWB as a means of coping with the negative emotion.

The illegal nature of many counterproductive behaviors has made research difficult to conduct with other than anonymous surveys. Support for the model presented earlier comes mainly from questionnaire studies that ask employees to report about their jobs and reactions. These studies have shown that employee reports of stressful job conditions (Spector, Fox, Penney, Bruursema, Goh, & Kessler, 2006) and injustice (Hershcovis, Turner, Barling, Arnold, Dupre, Inness, et al., 2007) relate to negative emotions and CWB. In addition to workplace factors, CWB has been shown to relate to personality. Perhaps the best personality predictor of CWB is trait anger, which is the tendency to

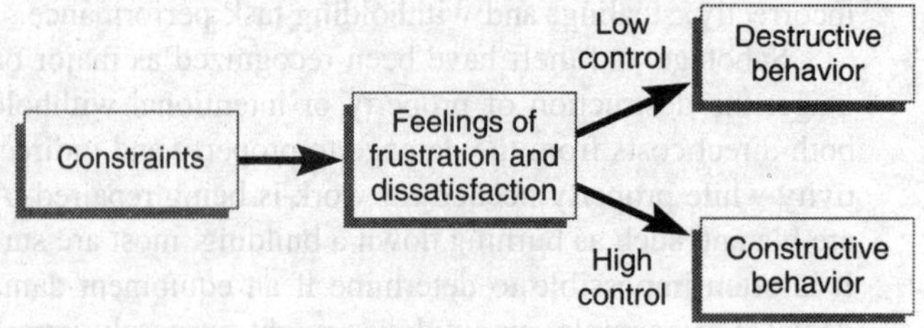

Figure 10.8 A model of the causes of counterproductive work behavior, or CWB.

experience anger even from minor provocations (Spielberger, 1996). Not surprisingly, individuals who are high on trait anger are more likely to engage in CWB (Hershcovis et al., 2007). However, it isn't just the tendency to experience anger that relates to CWB but the tendency to experience other negative emotions as well. Individuals who are high on the trait of negative affectivity (see Chapter 9) are more likely to engage in CWB (Penney & Spector, 2005). Finally, CWB has been studied in relation to the Big Five dimensions of personality discussed earlier in this chapter. Individuals who are low on agreeableness, conscientiousness, and emotional stability are more likely to engage in CWB (Berry, Ones, & Sackett, 2007). The correct (or perhaps it is best to say incorrect) combination of individual personality and workplace factors will maximize the likelihood than an employee will engage in CWB.

Unfortunately, almost all studies of CWB have been conducted in North America, so little is known about CWB in countries that are culturally dissimilar to Canada and the United States. One exception is a study of CWB conducted in Turkey (Bayram, Gursakal, & Bilgel, 2009) that showed similar relationships of stressful job conditions and job satisfaction with CWB (see the International Research box).

INTERNATIONAL RESEARCH

Counterproductive work behavior (CWB) consists of a variety of acts that are harmful to organizations. Almost all research on CWB has been conducted in North America, with a notably rare exception from Turkey.

Bayram, Gursakal, and Bilgel (2009) conducted a study to see the sorts of CWB that Turkish employees engage in and if variables from North American studies that relate to CWB show similar relationships in Turkey. In addition, they compared the frequency of individual CWB across several industries to see if they differ, which is something that has not been investigated in the past.

The study was conducted in the Turkish city of Bursa, one of the leading financial centers of Turkey. A sample of 766 white-collar employees completed anonymous surveys. These employees came from several industries, including the automotive, food, machinery, and textile industries. Employees were asked to indicate how often they engaged in 45 different types of CWB, how satisfied they were with their jobs, the extent to which they experienced organizational constraints, and how often they got into conflicts with others at work. The scales used in the study were Turkish translations of those used in a similar American study (Spector et al., 2006), making it possible to contrast findings from the two countries.

The results showed industry differences in the overall amount of CWB, with the most occurring in the food industry and the least in the machinery industry. This suggests that it will be important to consider industry and perhaps occupation in future studies. The results also showed considerable differences in how often employees said they engaged in various acts, with the most frequent being calling in sick when the employee was not and taking overly long breaks. A comparison of the results of this study with those of the comparable American study (Spector et al., 2006) showed that Turks engage in some behaviors more frequently and others less frequently than Americans. For example, Turks reported less withdrawal from work (e.g., 54% of Americans versus 28% of Turks said they called in sick when they were not), and less verbally aggressive behaviors (e.g., 26% of Americans versus 14% of Turks said they insulted someone at work). On the other hand, Turks reported more theft at work (26% versus 13%) and more physical aggression, such as hitting or pushing someone (15% versus 3%).

Similar to the American study, CWB is associated with job satisfaction, organizational constraints, and conflicts with others. The magnitude of correlations is similar between CWB and both job satisfaction and conflicts with others between the two countries. Correlations between CWB and organizational constraints, however, were quite different. Although the correlations were significant in both countries, they were twice as large in Turkey as in the United States. This suggests that Turks might be more sensitive to organizational constraints than Americans.

The findings of this study suggest that there are many similarities between Americans and Turks in their responses to the workplace and in their CWB, but there are also differences. On the one hand, Turks, like Americans, will likely respond to stressful and dissatisfying job conditions with CWB. However, the nature of the behavior chosen is likely very much influenced by national culture.

Source: From "Counterproductive Work Behavior Among White-Collar Employees: A Study From Turkey," by N. Bayram, N. Gursakal, and N. Bilgel, 2009, *International Journal of Selection and Assessment, 17*, 180–188.

Labor Unrest and Strikes

Another area in which counterproductive behavior occurs as a response to anger or unfair treatment is in labor-management disputes. The history of organized labor contains many acts of violence on both sides. A tactic often used by unions is to "attack" the organization by withholding output. In addition, sabotage and even violence can be common during union actions, such as strikes. These actions are counterproductive from the organization's viewpoint, although not necessarily from the employees'.

Labor unrest and strikes can occur for many reasons. Often these actions are accompanied by frustration on the part of employees who believe that they are not treated fairly. These beliefs can lead to a variety of counterproductive behaviors such as work slowdowns or sabotage. Anger and perceptions of unfair treatment have been associated with strikes (Giacalone & Knouse, 1990).

CHAPTER SUMMARY

The productive and counterproductive behavior of employees at work is a vital area of concern to the I/O field. Three areas of performance are task performance, organizational citizenship behavior (OCB), and counterproductive work behavior (CWB).

Task performance is a central variable for the I/O field. Much of the research and practice of I/O psychologists is concerned with understanding, assessing, or enhancing task performance. Performance results from the interplay of ability and motivation. Both environmental and personal factors are important influences. Personality characteristics, such as the Big Five and locus of control, have been shown to relate to performance. Job characteristics, incentive systems, and technology are important environmental influences.

One of the major objectives of the human factors field is to enhance task performance through the design of tools and equipment. Although the Hawthorne studies suggested that the social environment could be more important than the physical, the physical environment can still influence task performance. Physical aspects, such as lighting and sound levels, as well as the design of equipment and the ways in which information is presented, all have important influences on performance.

Organizational constraints are features of the work environment that interfere with good task performance. Such conditions can lead to lower job satisfaction and employee turnover.

Organizational citizenship behavior (OCB) is behavior that goes beyond the core task requirements of the job and is beneficial to the organization. It involves both altruistic behavior (helping others) and compliance behavior (following rules). OCB is important because it can contribute to organizational well-being. Both job satisfaction and supportive supervisory behavior are correlated with how much employees engage in OCB.

Withdrawal behavior—absence, lateness, and turnover—are forms of CWB that can create problems for organizations. Most of the research on these variables has considered them to be reactions to job dissatisfaction. This seems to be more true for turnover, at least during times of plentiful jobs, than for absence and lateness, which correlate only slightly with job satisfaction. Furthermore, withdrawal can arise from many causes, with only some related to job attitudes.

More serious forms of CWB (e.g., aggression at work, hostility toward others, sabotage, and theft) can produce tremendous costs to organizations. The research conducted on these behaviors suggests that they are reactions to stressful job conditions and injustice that produce negative emotions. Furthermore, employees who believe they have little control at work are more likely to engage in destructive behavior. Personality characteristics of trait anger, trait anxiety, agreeableness, conscientiousness, and emotional stability have been linked to CWB.

I/O PSYCHOLOGY IN PRACTICE

(*Courtesy of Jeanne Carsten*)

This case concerns a turnover project carried out by Dr. Jeanne M. Carsten. Dr. Carsten received her Ph.D. in I/O psychology in 1987 from the University of South Florida. Since then, she has been employed by JP Morgan Chase in New York City, one of the largest financial institutions in the world. Her current job title is Manager of Strategic Planning and Implementation. In her work for the company, she has covered many areas of I/O, including attitude surveys, employee development, selection, and training. One of her major functions is to carry out projects designed to address specific organizational problems.

The first major project she was assigned when she was newly hired was to find a solution to an excessive turnover rate among bank tellers (also known as cashiers). Although high turnover is normal and expected with these employees, the management of the bank believed that its rate had become excessive. Dr. Carsten was charged with finding out why and suggesting solutions.

The first phase of this project was to collect information. Interviews were conducted with tellers and their supervisors to find out why they were quitting. Tellers were asked about problems they encountered on the job. In addition, a salary survey was conducted to see if other banks were paying their tellers more, which they were.

The second phase was to prepare and present an action plan to the management of the bank. There were 12 recommendations, including raising salaries, training teller supervisors to provide better assistance to their subordinates, clarifying job performance standards, and offering additional teller training.

During the final phase of the project, almost all of the recommendations were implemented. Afterward, the turnover rate declined by almost 50%. Without a control group, one cannot be certain what caused improvement in the turnover rate. During the course of the project, the national unemployment rate increased, which would have reduced turnover. Dr. Carsten points out that the turnover rate became lower than that at other banks, however, lending support to the idea that the changes were effective. Furthermore, many of the changes, such as improving supervisory practices and clarifying performance standards, may have been of benefit for reasons other than turnover reduction. This case illustrates how an I/O psychologist who works for an organization can help improve working conditions for employees.

Discussion Questions

1. Why do you think the bank tellers quit their jobs?
2. What factors would encourage you to stay on a job that you did not like?
3. Do you think that Dr. Carsten's interventions did anything else besides reduce turnover?
4. Do you think that employees at this bank might have engaged in other forms of withdrawal behavior?

LEARNING BY DOING

Human Factors Design of Automobiles

Inspect an automobile for examples of human factors that have been incorporated into the design. Make a list of features involving displays (e.g., instrument panel) and controls. How many examples of the principles discussed in the chapter can you find?

Organizational Citizenship Behavior

Ask at least five employed friends or family members to provide examples of OCB they have seen at work. First, give each person a definition of OCB (behavior that helps the organization but goes beyond the core tasks required for the job). Then record the examples that they give you. How many of these examples benefit the organization, how many benefit other people, and how many benefit both?

CHAPTER 11

Occupational Health Psychology

CHAPTER 11 OUTLINE

- OCCUPATIONAL HEALTH AND SAFETY
  - Accidents and Safety
  - Infectious Disease Exposure
  - Loud Noise
  - Musculoskeletal Disorders (MSDs)
  - Harmful Substance Exposure
  - Workplace Violence
- WORK SCHEDULES
  - Night Shifts
  - Long Shifts
  - Flexible Work Schedules
- OCCUPATIONAL STRESS
  - The Occupational Stress Process
  - Job Stressors
  - Alcohol as a Coping Mechanism
- WORK-FAMILY CONFLICT
- BURNOUT
- CHAPTER SUMMARY
- I/O PSYCHOLOGY IN PRACTICE
- LEARNING BY DOING

Movies and television programs like *World Trade Center* and *Rescue Me* have underscored the dramatic and often dangerous aspects of a firefighter's job. Having to go into burning buildings, like the World Trade Center, that might collapse at any moment and to deal with the injured and dying is clearly stressful. Does performing such jobs have an adverse impact on firefighters' health and well-being? Del Ben, Scotti, Chen, and Fortson (2006) surveyed firefighters from one U.S. state and found that about 5% showed all the signs of a posttraumatic stress disorder (PTSD), whereas 22% showed some symptoms.

TABLE 11.1 Frequent Sources of Illness and Injury for Workers in Some Common Occupations

Source	Occupation
Infectious disease	Dentist, nurse
Loud noise	Airline baggage handler, musician
Physical assault (fatal)	Police officer, taxi driver
Physical assault (nonfatal)	Nursing home aide, psychiatric nurse
Repetitive actions and lifting	Data entry clerk, nurse
Toxic substances	Exterminator, farmer

Their study did not include firefighters who might have quit their jobs due to PTSD or other health-related problems, so likely the percentage of cases is even higher. As this study illustrates, characteristics of jobs and job-related experiences have an important impact on health and well-being. In this case, the firefighters noted that having to deal with someone's death and being injured or nearly killed were the most traumatic events they encountered. This is not the only occupation that deals with these issues. People in health professions, such as nurses and physicians, deal with injury and death, whereas police officers and individuals in dangerous occupations deal with the possibility of being injured or even killed on the job.

Table 11.1 lists some frequent sources of illness and injury on the job, along with some common occupations for which each is particularly problematic. These sources represent concrete physical conditions at work, such as equipment or toxic substances, likely to affect physical health. The effects of these sources tend to be direct, although for some people exposure over a long period of time must occur for illness or injury to develop. For example, it can take years to become injured or develop a disability from repetitive motions, such as typing. Certain occupations are more likely than others to exhibit each of these sources, although employees on most jobs might encounter any of them. Those who work outdoors, such as park rangers and roofers, are most likely to encounter either extremely hot or extremely cold conditions, but even office workers might encounter extremes of temperature if their buildings do not have adequate heating or air conditioning. Whereas police officers and taxi drivers are among the most likely to be victims of assault, virtually anyone might be assaulted at work, although for most jobs the chances are remote.

In addition to the physical conditions listed in Table 11.1, certain nonphysical conditions might affect physical health and emotional well-being. Nonstandard work schedules, such as night-shift work, have been implicated as causes of both physical and psychological problems. Several nonphysical work conditions are frequently discussed in the literature under the general topic of occupational stress. Such conditions as workload, lack of control, role ambiguity, role conflict, and organizational constraints have all been associated with physical health or emotional well-being.

In this chapter, we are concerned with both physical and psychological aspects of employee health, safety, and well-being at work that comprise **occupational health psychology**, or OHP. This emerging subfield of psychology (and other disciplines such as medicine and public health) is concerned with psychological factors that contribute to occupational health and well-being. It deals with psychological reactions to physical and nonphysical work conditions, as well as behavior that has implications for health. Included in this chapter will be discussion of physical conditions that affect health, occupational stress, occupational accidents, the interplay between work and family, and burnout.

Objectives: The student who studies this chapter should be able to:

- Describe the causes of accidents and the steps that can be taken to prevent them.
- List the major physical work conditions that affect employee health.
- Explain how work schedules can affect employee health and well-being.
- Discuss the nature of occupational stress, including its causes and effects.
- Define burnout and state how it relates to employee health and well-being.

OCCUPATIONAL HEALTH AND SAFETY

Physical work conditions tend to have direct physical effects on people. Sometimes the effects are immediate, as when an employee is injured in an automobile accident. Other times illness or injury may develop after exposure to a harmful condition (e.g., loud noise) or toxic substance at work for many years. There are steps that can be taken to avoid or minimize accidents and exposures to harmful conditions through the adoption of safe workplace design and safe procedures for doing the job. In addition to physical effects, illness and injury can have psychological consequences that are detrimental to emotional well-being. Serious illness and injury are almost certainly associated with some level of psychological distress and trauma, particularly when they result in disability.

In this section, we first discuss accidents and safety related behavior. Accidents are events that occur at work that cause immediate injury, such as getting a hand caught in a machine or cutting a finger with a knife. As we will see, accidents are a major problem in the workplace that have tremendous costs for both employees and organizations. Next, we will cover five common exposures that can produce injury and illness at work:

Infectious disease

Loud noise

Repetitive actions or lifting

Toxic substances

Workplace violence

Often exposure is the result of unsafe behavior or poor workplace design that places an employee in a position to be harmed but could have been avoided.

Accidents and Safety

Accidents are the fifth leading cause of death among Americans after heart disease, cancer, stroke, and respiratory disease (National Safety Council, 2005–2006). One of the major accomplishments of the 20th century in the United States was reducing the workplace accident rate by 90% to the point where today most workers are safer at work than anywhere else, with only 10% of accidental death occurring on the job for workers. However, in 2008 there were still 5,214 workplace fatalities (Bureau of Labor Statistics, 2010). Furthermore, the number of nonfatal accidents far exceeds the number of workplace fatalities. For example, Glasscock, Rasmussen, Carstensen, and Hansen (2006) found in a Danish study that 36% of farm workers reported being injured in the prior year, and about a third of them required medical attention. Accident rates can be even higher for young farmworkers who are inexperienced and more prone to take risks than older workers (Cigularov, Chen, & Stallones, 2009).

Figure 11.1 shows the major types of fatal workplace accidents in the United States in 2008 (Bureau of Labor Statistics, 2010). As you can see, motor vehicles were the leading cause, accounting for 3%. Figure 11.2 shows the accident rates for nine categories of jobs. Agriculture/fishing/forestry/hunting and mining are the most dangerous, whereas

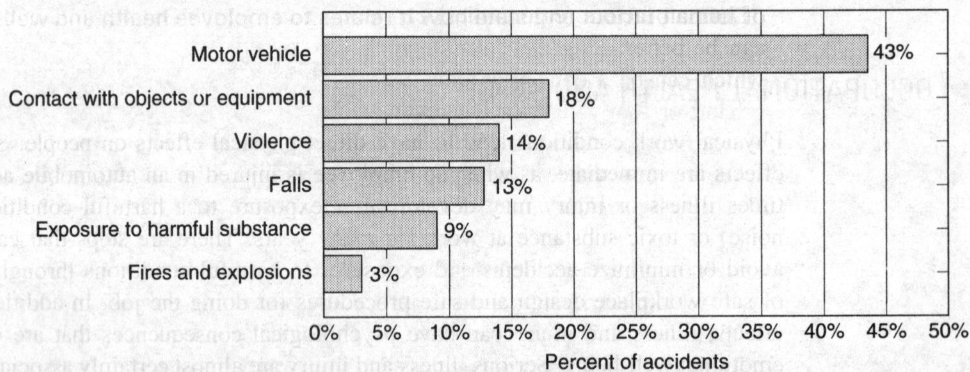

Figure 11.1 Major types of fatal work accidents for 2008 in the United States. From Census of Fatal Occupational Injuries Charts, 1992–2008 (Revised Data). U.S. Department of Labor, 2010, Author.

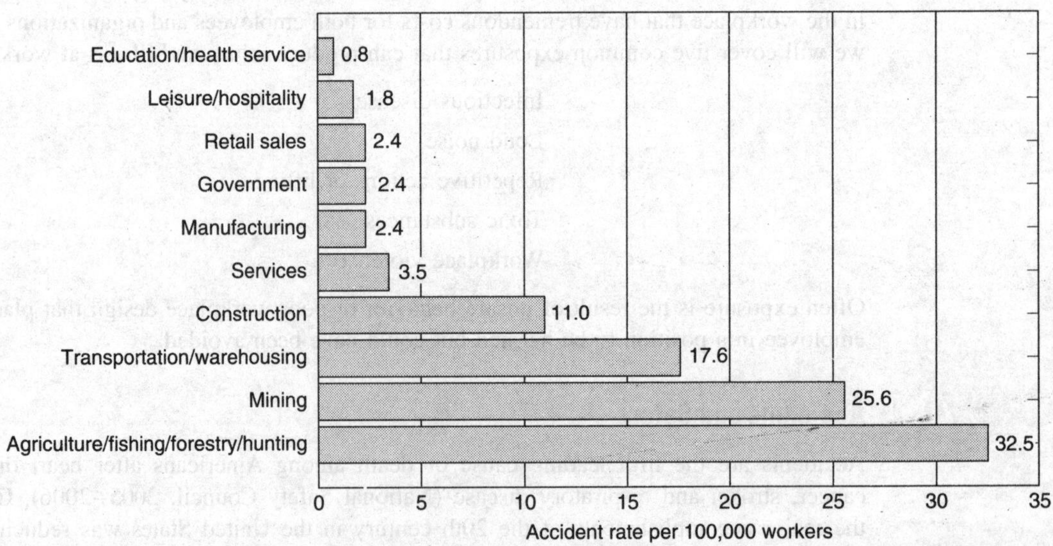

Figure 11.2 Fatal accident rates for several categories of jobs for 2008 in the United States. From Census of Fatal Occupational Injuries Charts, 1992–2008 (Revised Data). U.S. Department of Labor, 2010, Author.

education/health service and sales are the safest. Another factor related to fatalities is gender. Men comprise 57% of the workforce in the United States (based on hours worked), but they account for 93% of fatalities (Bureau of Labor Statistics, 2010). Much of this is due to men being disproportionally found in the most dangerous occupations.

Preventing accidents has been a major concern because of both employee and organization costs. Taken together, both fatal and nonfatal accidents are expensive, costing an estimated $140 billion annually in the United States alone (National Safety Council, 2005–2006), much of which is paid by employers and their insurance companies. Many different approaches have been tried to prevent accidents. Some involve design of equipment, whereas others focus on people. The best strategy depends on the particular situation and an analysis of accident causes. Often solutions can be fairly simple, such as having employees wear protective goggles to prevent eye injuries. The application of human factors (ergonomics) can be effective when equipment is poorly designed (or can be better designed) from a safety standpoint. An example is the push lawnmower, which can be a dangerous device. At one time, the design allowed an operator to get a hand or foot caught in the revolving blade. All new lawnmowers sold in the United States must be designed with a handle release switch that turns off the engine (or blade) when the operator lets go of the handle. Such a system makes it difficult for a person to accidentally stick a hand or foot into a moving blade. Better design can be quite effective in reducing accidents and injuries, and as an additional benefit, it can reduce strains for the employee as well (Kompier, Aust, van den Berg, & Siegrist, 2000).

A major difficulty in preventing workplace accidents is getting the cooperation of employees in using the appropriate safety equipment and engaging in safe behaviors. People can often find safety devices inconvenient and safety equipment uncomfortable. Some people tape down the handle release switch on a lawnmower because they find it annoying and fail to use safety goggles because they are uncomfortable. Accepted workplace practices among employees might preclude the use of particular practices because they are thought to waste time, take too much effort, or even reflect a person's lack of courage in facing dangerous situations. Factors relating to accidents are listed in Table 11.2.

Safety climate is the shared perception by employees of an organization that safe procedures, practices, and behaviors are encouraged and rewarded by managers (Zohar, 2010). Climate is reflected in both the policies of the organization and the practices relevant to safety, such as the use of safety equipment. Studies have clearly shown a link between safety climate and accidents (Clarke, 2010), between safe behavior and injuries on the job (Beus, Payne, Bergman, & Arthur, 2010). Those organizations that are high on safety climate have employees who behave more safely and have fewer accidents than employees in organizations that are low on safety climate. These studies have used a cross-sectional design with both climate and other variables measured at the same time. This leaves open the possibility that safety climate is the result of accidents rather than the cause. A more conclusive study was conducted by Neal and Griffin (2006). They

TABLE 11.2 Factors Associated With Work Accidents and Safety

Management commitment to safety	Safety climate
Nonwork stressors	Safety training
Personality characteristics	Work stressors
Production versus safety emphasis	

found that safety climate predicted accidents up to 3 years later, making it unlikely that accidents could have caused climate.

Accidents can also be affected by the balance in emphasis between productivity and safety (Humphrey, Moon, Conlon, & Hofmann, 2004). For example, Kaminski (2001) studied accidents in 86 small manufacturing plants in the United States. She found that pay incentive systems were associated with injuries on the job. Jobs were safer if assembly-line workers were paid per hour rather than based on productivity, since the latter encouraged working fast to the detriment of safety.

Stress both on and off the job can be another important factor. For example, Savery and Wooden (1994) surveyed Australian workers from 61 different organizations. They found that frequency of stressful events (e.g., divorce) is related to work accidents. How people feel about their jobs and their attitudes about safety also affect accidents and injuries. Individuals who are satisfied with their jobs (Barling, Kelloway, & Iverson, 2003) and those who have positive attitudes about safety (Newnam, Griffin, & Mason, 2008) are less likely to have accidents at work.

Finally, individual differences are also a factor in accidents and injuries. Christian, Bradley, Wallace, and Burke (2009) conducted a meta-analysis that summarized studies relating personality to workplace accidents. They found that the Big Five dimensions of conscientiousness and emotional stability both related negatively to accidents: Individuals who are high on both traits are less likely to have accidents than individuals who score low. Conscientious people tend to carefully follow rules, so one would expect that conscientious employees would follow safety rules and therefore avoid accidents. The reason that individuals high in emotional stability are able to avoid accidents is less clear, but perhaps it is because they are less prone to experience stress, and as noted earlier, such experiences are linked to accidents.

Ludwig and Geller (1997) successfully used goal setting (see Chapter 8) to encourage safer driving behavior in a sample of pizza deliverers. They asked drivers to set goals concerning the percentage of times they will come to a complete and safe stop before pulling into traffic. The goal setting improved not only the targeted behavior but also other safety behaviors for which goals had not been set, such as seatbelt use. Goals can be an effective means of improving not only job performance, as we discussed in Chapter 8, but safety as well.

Infectious Disease Exposure

Employees who must deal with the public (e.g., hairstylist, police officer, sales clerk, and teacher) may be exposed to infectious disease, although most such cases result in relatively minor illnesses, such as a cold or flu. Exposure to serious infectious diseases is of particular concern to people in the health care professions who must deal with seriously ill and dying patients. Of particular concern is exposure to HIV and hepatitis B (HBV), both of which can be fatal. A protocol has been adopted globally that all health care workers comply with: The **Universal Precautions** is a set of safety procedures designed to help health care professionals avoid contact with patient bodily fluids. They include actions such as:

Disposing of sharp objects (e.g., needles) in a special *sharps* container

Wearing disposable gloves when handling blood or body fluids

Immediately cleaning all bodily fluid spills with disinfectant

Wearing aprons and masks

Unfortunately large numbers of health care workers fail to follow Universal Precautions even though research shows that these procedures are highly effective. Gammon, Morgan-Samuel, and Gould (2008) summarized results of 37 studies of Universal Precautions conducted throughout the world. They found that compliance was rather disappointing. Although compliance is quite high for some acts, such as disposing of sharp objects properly (91%), it is low for others, such as wearing masks (30%). The proper handling of sharp objects is of particular concern for nurses, for whom accidental needle sticks and other sharps injuries are common. Talas (2009) noted that 4% of hospital nurses receive a sharps injury each year, whereas injury rates for nursing students, who are inexperienced, are almost 10 times as high. Clearly there is a great deal of work to be done to reduce infectious disease exposure in health care workers, especially students. Likely the same factors that are important with accidents in general would hold for infectious disease exposure as well, such as a safety climate that encourages following the Universal Precautions.

Loud Noise

Loud noise occurs at many jobs, particularly those involving heavy equipment or machinery. Airports, construction sites, factories, and mines can all be noisy places, exposing employees to conditions that can affect both their health and their job performance.

The intensity of noise is measured in **decibel (dB)** units. The decibel scale is a logarithmic scale, meaning that the relation between decibel level and sound intensity is not linear. Increasing the sound level by 10 dB is an increase of 10 times in sound intensity, and increasing it by 20 dB is an increase of 100 times in sound intensity. The decibel levels of several common sounds found in the workplace are shown in Figure 11.3.

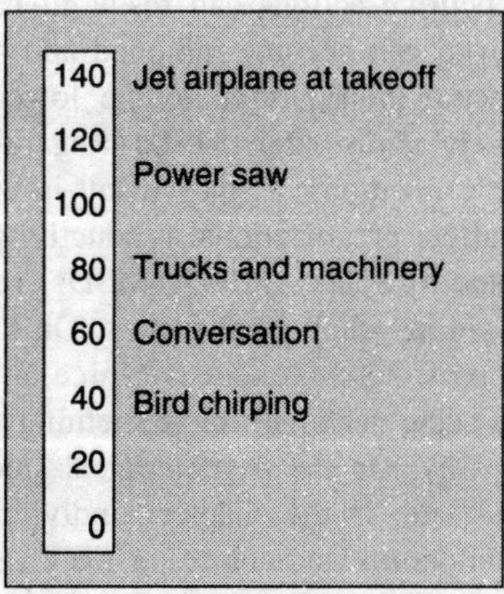

Figure 11.3 Sound intensity levels in decibels for some common sounds. From *Sound Sense,* by National Safety Council, 1992, Itasca, IL: Author.

Exposure to extremely loud noises, such as explosions, can severely damage a person's sense of hearing, sometimes permanently. Noise of this magnitude is painful, and most people avoid places where such noises occur. Of even more concern at work is continuous exposure to moderately loud noise that exceeds 85 dB (National Safety Council, 1992). If continued over a period of months or years, moderately loud noise can lead to permanent hearing loss, particularly in the higher frequencies. Because noise of this intensity is not typically painful, however, many employees will do nothing to avoid it. It is quite common for employees in noisy work environments to suffer from hearing loss. Hearing damage can also be caused by exposure to loud music. Using ear buds to listen to music at high volume levels can be particularly dangerous because the dB level in the ear can be quite high.

Because of the potential for hearing damage, many countries have laws governing the legal levels of noise to which an employee can be exposed. Employees who work in noisy environments are given hearing protection to prevent hearing loss. It is common, for example, to see airline employees wear such protection when they are around jets that have their engines running. As with universal precautions, employees often fail to use hearing protection, thus increasing exposure to health-damaging conditions.

Besides hearing damage, there is evidence suggestive of a link between noise exposure at work and cardiovascular disease. Melamed, Fried, and Froom (2001) showed that exposure to noise relates to level of blood pressure for individuals in complex, but not simple, jobs. Presumably noise interferes with the greater concentration that complex jobs require, thus serving as a job stressor (see the discussion of stressors later in this chapter).

Musculoskeletal Disorders (MSDs)

Many jobs require physical actions of various body parts that can become injured. Some injuries might occur through repeated motions, such as on a traditional assembly-line where an employee performs the same operation over and over. Other jobs require the lifting of heavy objects or people, such as warehouse workers who have to load trucks. Repetitive actions can result in **repetitive strain injuries**, in which the body parts involved can become inflamed and sometimes permanently damaged. Lifting can result in acute injury, often to the lower back. Both kinds of injuries are forms of **musculoskeletal disorder (MSD)**. Regardless of the type, such injuries are an important issue for organizations, as they result in employee absence and inefficiency, which can adversely affect organizational productivity (Escorpizo, 2008).

As noted by Faucett (2005), MSDs are related to both the biomechanics of job tasks and employee psychological factors. On the biomechanical side, injuries can occur due to repetition of motion, excessive force on the body, and improper posture. Thus a back injury can occur when lifting something that is too heavy while bending the back in the wrong way. On the psychological side, MSDs are related to job stress (which we will discuss later in the chapter). Individuals are more likely to have an MSD if they have low autonomy and control at work (Larsman & Hanse, 2009), are dissatisfied with work (Sobeih, Salem, Daraiseh, Genaidy, & Shell, 2006), and feel anxious or depressed (Sprigg, Stride, Wall, Holman, & Smith, 2007).

Jobs vary in both their incidence of MSD and where in the body incumbents tend to experience injury (Nordander, Ohlsson, Akesson, Arvidsson, Balogh, Hansson et al., 2009). For example, urban transit workers who drive buses or trains are most at risk for back or neck pain (Greiner & Krause, 2006). Nurses are subject to back injury from lifting patients (Rickett, Orbell, & Sheeran, 2006). Dentists also tend to have neck and back injuries, but they experience shoulder and wrist/hand problems, as well (Palliser, Firth, Feyer, & Paulin, 2005). Salespeople who are on their feet all day are at risk for leg and lower-back pain (Pensri, Janwantanakul, & Chaikumarn, 2009). Workers who do a lot of keyboard work or typing are at risk for **carpal tunnel syndrome**, which is a wrist injury that causes pain, numbness, and weakness in the fingers and hands. It is brought on by repeated use of the fingers and wrist.

MSDs can be reduced with relatively inexpensive strategies. First, the proper design of tools and equipment can go a long way to reduce the strain on the body that can result in these injuries. Figure 11.4 shows a wrist rest that can help prevent carpal tunnel syndrome in people who use computer keyboards. It is a bar that helps keep the typist's wrists straight so that the strain on the wrist is reduced. Split keyboards in which the keys are placed at an angle so the wrists can remain straight are becoming increasingly popular. Acute lifting injuries can be reduced by the use of mechanical devices that take the heavy load (Rickett et al., 2006).

A second strategy is to allow employees to take frequent rest breaks. In Sweden, there are laws governing the maximum amount of time an employee can be asked to use a computer keyboard without a break and the maximum amount of time he or she can

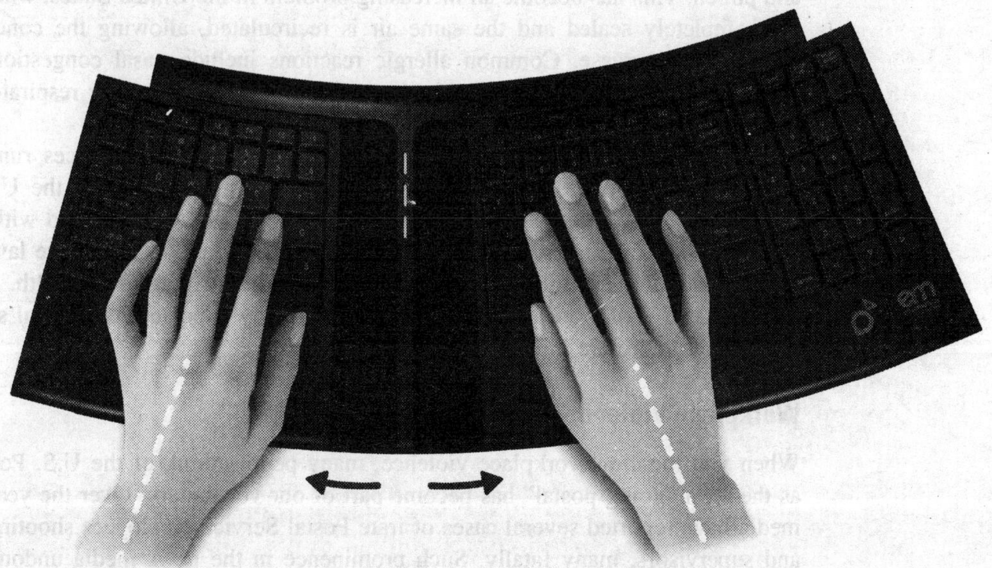

Figure 11.4 A split keyboard that helps reduce strain on a person's wrist when using a computer. (*Photo courtesy of Handout/MCT/NewsCom.*)

type in a day. In the United States, similar legislation has been debated but not enacted. A combination of both equipment design and rest breaks can be successful in reducing the likelihood that employees will contract debilitating MSDs.

Harmful Substance Exposure

The exposure of employees to harmful and toxic substances has been given more and more attention as research has shown how such substances can affect health. The problem with exposure to many substances is that adverse health effects such as cancer can take years or decades to develop. Furthermore, not every person exposed will develop symptoms. This makes it difficult to determine the effects of exposure because many things might contribute to a particular person contracting an illness.

Employees in many jobs can be exposed to harmful substances, often in unexpected places. Employees in chemical plants and exterminators and farmworkers who use insecticides can expect to be exposed. Office workers in enclosed buildings do not, but they can be exposed to various chemicals, such as toners from copying machines and solvents that might be used to clean ink. Furthermore, people vary in sensitivity to a variety of substances. Reactions to exposure can range from fairly minor symptoms such as headaches or nausea to serious conditions that can permanently damage vital organs such as the kidneys or liver. At times, only a few sensitive individuals will exhibit symptoms, but it is not unusual for most of the individuals in an office to become ill, leading to what has been termed the *sick building* phenomenon, which can arise from harmful substances or microorganisms.

Another issue concerns allergy to various substances, most commonly dust, mold, and pollen. This has become an increasing problem in the United States, where buildings are completely sealed and the same air is recirculated, allowing the concentration of allergens to increase. Common allergic reactions include nasal congestion, coughing, watery eyes, and skin rash, but employees with asthma and other respiratory illnesses can experience serious and even fatal medical conditions.

Organizations that expose their employees to harmful substances run the risk of lawsuits by employees who become ill or develop a disability. In the United States, the Occupational Safety and Health Administration (OSHA) is charged with seeing that workplace safeguards are used to protect workers. Many countries have laws to protect employees from harmful substances and other conditions that affect health. As shown in Table 11.1, 8% of workplace fatalities are caused by exposure to harmful substances at work. Even more are injured or made sick.

Workplace Violence

When you mention workplace violence, many people think of the U.S. Postal Service, as the term "going postal" has become part of our vocabulary. Over the years, the news media have reported several cases of irate Postal Service employees shooting coworkers and supervisors, many fatally. Such prominence in the news media undoubtedly gives an erroneous impression that the workplace is particularly dangerous and that coworkers are a significant threat. Although homicide does occur in the workplace, it is not the setting in which most homicides occur. The Bureau of Labor Statistics (2010) reported that there were 526 workplace homicides in the United States in 2008, which is about 3%

TABLE 11.3 Occupations Associated With Four Types of Workplace Violence

Violence Type	Definition	Occupation Likely to Experience It
Type 1	Strangers committing a crime	Convenience store clerk Taxi driver
Type 2	Client/customer/patient	Nurse Social worker
Type 3	Other employees	Any job with coworker contact
Type 4	Relationship	Any job

of the U.S. homicide total of 16,272 that year (Federal Bureau of Investigation, 2010a). Furthermore, coworker homicide is quite unusual, with approximately 15% of workplace homicide being due to coworkers (Sygnatur & Toscano, 2000). Even more rare is for a homicide victim to be a woman. Although women are 43% of the U.S. workforce (according to hours worked), they comprise only 19% of homicide victims (Bureau of Labor Statistics, 2010).

There are four types of workplace violence depending on the relationship between the perpetrator and the workplace (Merchant & Lundell, 2001). Type 1 is violence by individuals with no business relationship with the organization, such as someone committing a robbery. Type 2 is violence by clients, customers, or patients of the organization. Type 3 is performed by other employees. Type 4 is relationship (e.g., intimate partner) violence that spills over to the workplace. The nature of the job determines in large part whether or not these different types are possible. Table 11.3 lists occupations most at risk for the various types.

For most occupations, fatal assaults are extremely rare, with employees being safer at work than almost anywhere else they can be. However, there are a few occupations for which homicide is a more significant risk. Whereas the national average workplace homicide rate is .70 cases per 100,000 employees, the risk is far greater for taxi drivers (41.4), liquor store clerks (7.5), police officers (7.0), and gas station attendants (4.8) (National Institute for Occupational Safety and Health, 1996). In the United States, there were 41 law enforcement officers who were homicide victims in 2008 (Federal Bureau of Investigation, 2010b).

Of course, nonfatal assault is a far more common occupational hazard, especially for those who work with the public. A survey of employers found that 4.3% of more than 7 million U.S. workplaces experienced at least one case of workplace violence in the prior year (Bureau of Labor Statistics, 2006). People who work in health care settings such as nursing homes, police, prison staff, and teachers are at particular risk of Type 2 violence (National Institute for Occupational Safety and Health, 2004); in most cases, there is little or no serious physical injury, although employees can still be subject to psychological trauma (Walsh & Clarke, 2003).

There are a number of job and organizational factors that can contribute to being a target of physical violence. Some have to do with the nature of the work itself and how employees are exposed to potentially violent situations. LeBlanc and Kelloway (2002) analyzed the nature of jobs that were particularly prone to violence exposure. Jobs in which employees had physical control over others (e.g., prison staff), handle weapons (police officer), have contact with individuals taking medication (nurses), and exercise security functions (law enforcement officer) are particularly at risk. At the organization level, workplaces differ in the extent to which they reward and support employee actions that help avoid violence. Just as with safety climate, violence prevention climate can be encouraged by supervisors in order to minimize employee risk of being assaulted (Kessler, Spector, Chang, & Parr, 2008).

▶ WORK SCHEDULES

Whereas most employed people work standard schedules of approximately 8 daylight hours per day during weekdays, the use of nonstandard schedules involving longer work shifts, nights, and weekends has become commonplace. Of particular interest to I/O psychologists have been three types of schedules: night shifts, long work shifts, and flextime.

Night Shifts

Many organizations, such as hospitals and police departments, run 24 hours per day, requiring the use of two or three shifts of workers to cover the entire day. A typical three-shift sequence is:

8 A.M. to 4 P.M.

4 P.M. to 12 A.M.

12 A.M. to 8 A.M.

referred to as the day, evening, and night or graveyard shifts, respectively. Some organizations hire people to work a fixed shift; that is, they work the same shift all the time. Other organizations use rotating shifts: Employees work one shift for a limited length of time—say, a month—and then switch or rotate to another shift.

The major health problem with working night shifts is that the typical sleep/waking cycle is disturbed. Associated with this cycle are the **circadian rhythms** of physiological changes that occur throughout the day. These include body temperature changes and changes in hormone levels in the bloodstream. It has been suggested that night shifts can cause health problems by disrupting these natural rhythms.

The most obvious health problem in working night shifts is sleep disturbance—either being unable to fall asleep or having a poor quality of sleep (Daus, Sanders, & Campbell, 1998). Although this can happen, there are ways to minimize these negative effects. Many organizations use rotating shifts, where employees alternate among shifts over time. Thus they might work days one week, evenings the next, and then nights. Karlson, Eek, Orbaek, and Osterberg (2009) showed that the negative effects of rotating shifts can be minimized by rotating backward (day to night to evening) and keeping people on each shift for several weeks. Barton and Folkard (1991) found that employees on temporary night shifts have greater sleep problems than employees who work permanent night shifts but that permanent night-shift workers are no more likely to have sleep problems than day-shift workers. These results suggest that permanent shifts might cause fewer problems than rotating shifts. Another aspect of the Barton and Folkard study is that their nurses volunteered for the shifts they were in. Given that people vary in their ability to

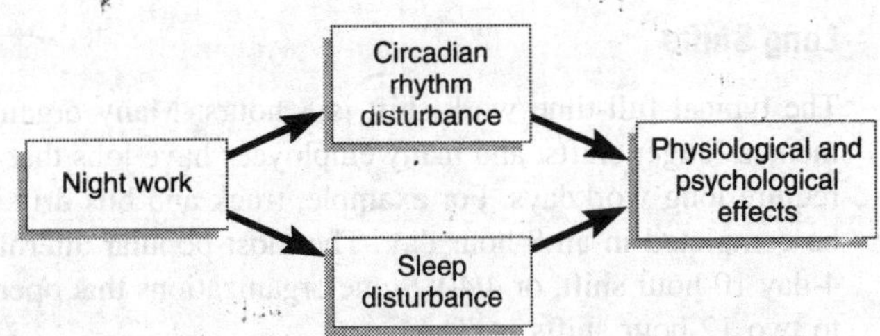

Figure 11.5 Night work leads to both circadian rhythm disturbance and sleep problems. These in turn lead to physical problems such as stomach upset and psychological problems such as anxiety.

adapt to night work (Willis, O'Connor, & Smith, 2008), it is likely that volunteers would consist of people who are able to tolerate working at night.

Sleep disturbance is not the only health problem that has been associated with night-shift work. Digestive system problems have been shown to be more frequent in night-shift workers (Koller, Kundi, & Cervinka, 1978). Akerstedt and Theorell (1976) studied physiological changes in workers before, during, and after a period of night-shift work. In this study, the blood levels of the hormone gastrin, which is related to stomach acid secretion, was assessed twice a day over a period of 5 weeks. Results showed a decrease in gastrin during the time the workers were on the night shift. Although this study shows that night-shift work can have physiological effects, it is not clear why they occur. Was it the disruption of the circadian rhythms that upset the secretion of gastrin, or was it lack of sleep (Figure 11.5)? Whatever it was, at least one solution to night-shift effects is to allow several consecutive days of rest per week (Totterdell, Spelten, Smith, Barton, & Folkard, 1995).

In addition to health problems, shift work can cause social problems. Having to work nights and sleep days can isolate a person from family and friends. Bohle and Tilley (1998) surveyed hospital nurses concerning their feelings about shiftwork. The best predictor of dissatisfaction was conflict between work and nonwork activities. Individuals who reported high levels of conflict tended to report the greatest dissatisfaction with shiftwork.

Long-distance drivers sometimes work long shifts that can interrupt sleep patterns. (© *Andrey Pavlov, sourced from Shutterstock images*)

Long Shifts

The typical full-time work shift is 8 hours. Many organizations, however, have implemented longer shifts, and many employees have jobs that do not have fixed shifts but can require long workdays. For example, truck and bus drivers may have routes that cannot be completed in an 8-hour day. The most popular alternative long work schedule is the 4-day 10-hour shift, or 4/40. Some organizations that operate 24 hours per day have gone to two 12-hour shifts per day.

One important difficulty with the long workday is fatigue (Bendak, 2003). A 10- to 12-hour day can be quite tiring if the work is mentally or physically demanding. On the other hand, many employees like the longer days because it gives them more time to recover from work and more usable free time per week (Bendak, 2003), and long shifts can result in both better job performance and job satisfaction (Baltes, Briggs, Huff, Wright, & Neuman, 1999). On the other hand, Raggatt (1991) conducted a study of Australian bus drivers that showed how long shifts might have serious health effects (see the International Research box). The length of work shift was associated with sleep problems, alcohol consumption, and use of stimulants. These outcomes were also associated with job dissatisfaction and poor health. Thus long work shifts can have detrimental effects for some jobs. For other jobs, long shifts might be beneficial.

It is not only long shifts, however, that can have detrimental effects on people. The number of hours worked per week can expose employees to higher work demands and other stressful things at work (Ng & Feldman, 2008). Long workweeks have been linked to hypertension (high blood pressure) in working people (H. Yang, Schnall, Jauregui, Su, & Baker, 2006). This detrimental effect seems to occur only in people who work long hours nonvoluntarily, which is often the case in organizations that have downsized or reduced their number of employees (Sparks, Cooper, Fried, & Shirom, 1997). Survivors usually wind up working more hours to cover tasks of colleagues who have been laid off. The European Council adopted rules in the mid-1990s restricting work hours in member countries, including maximum hours worked per day and week (13 and 48, respectively). Such restrictions have not been implemented in the United States and other non-European industrialized countries.

INTERNATIONAL RESEARCH

Job stressors take many forms and can be detrimental to the well-being of employees. Role clarity and its antithesis, role ambiguity, have been studied by many researchers. In this study, Lang, Thomas, Bliese and Adler (2007) studied the effect of role clarity on job demands and psychological and physical strain to see whether there was a link.

The study conducted at the National Advanced Leadership Camp (NALC) in Washington focused on Army cadets during their 5-week intensive training course. In total 1,418 cadets took part in this research. All cadets were surveyed after 26 consecutive days of training and evaluation. By this time the cadets had been exposed to many demands, having their day-to-day performance constantly observed during military tasks. Cadets were asked to rate on a number of self-reported scales the impact of the job demands they experienced during the course, their own perception of role clarity during their time at NALC, and their perceived psychological and physical strain. The Cadet Evaluation Score, a quantifiable measure of leadership performance, was used to measure individual cadet performance on day 35. The individual's survey data from day 26 was eventually paired with their performance score on the final day of the course.

Results showed that the cadets who experienced high demands but perceived their role clarity to be high reported lower levels of both psychological and physical strain; the opposite was found where cadets experienced high demands but perceived their role clarity as low. Therefore, it was concluded that role clarity could be considered to be a significant moderator of the relationship between job demands and job strain.

This study provided evidence that individuals who clearly understand what is expected of them in their job role may feel less impact from the job demands than those who experience ambiguity in their role. Role clarity therefore indicates that employees can withstand greater levels of job demands. This is especially important to note in jobs which are hierarchically structured and where increased decision latitude is not possible. It may mean that despite not being able to allow employees to decide when they work or how they work, providing role clarity improves their resilience to job demands. It is therefore important for organizations to encourage the development of clear role functions and responsibilities, in order to support employees more fully, especially under conditions of increased job demands.

Source: Lang, J. Thomas, J. Bliese, P. & Adler, A. (2007). Job Demands and Job Performance: The Mediating Effect of Psychological and Physical Strain and the Moderating Effect of Role Clarity. *Journal of Occupational Health Psychology,* 12(2), 116–124.

Flexible Work Schedules

Fixed daily work schedules are still the norm, but many employees have flexible schedules, known as **flextime**, that allow them to determine, at least in part, the hours of the day that they work. In 2004, about 30% of U.S. workers did not work a fixed schedule. There are many varieties, from systems requiring only that employees work their allotted hours per day to systems that allow employees the option of starting their shift an hour early or an hour late. As we note in the discussion of work-family issues later in the chapter, flextime can be part of a family-friendly policy that allows working parents more flexibility to fulfill child-care responsibilities.

From the organization's perspective, an advantage of a flexible work schedule is that it allows employees to take care of personal business on their own time rather than on work time. Thus an employee could have a doctor's visit in the morning and begin the shift late. In their meta-analysis, Baltes et al. (1999) confirmed that there is less absence, and Ralston (1989) found less tardiness with flextime than with fixed work schedules, as might be expected. Relations with job performance and satisfaction have been less consistent. Baltes et al. (1999) found that objective measures of productivity are higher with flextime but that supervisor ratings of performance are not. Job satisfaction is slightly higher with flextime, but the magnitude of effect is small.

▶ OCCUPATIONAL STRESS

Everyone has experienced **stress** at one time or another. Taking an exam is a situation that is stressful for most students, particularly for those who want good grades. On most jobs, there are situations that employees find stressful. Being reprimanded by a supervisor, having too little time to complete an important assignment, and being told that you might be fired are all situations that almost anyone would find stressful. In this section, we review what is known about the effects of occupational stress.

The Occupational Stress Process

To understand occupational stress, you must first understand several concepts that are involved in the stress process. A **job stressor** is a condition or situation at work that requires an adaptive response on the part of the employee (Jex & Beehr, 1991). Being reprimanded, having too little time, and being told about the possibility of being fired are all examples of job stressors. A **job strain** is a negative reaction by an employee to a stressor, such as anger, anxiety, or a physical symptom such as a headache. Jex and Beehr (1991) categorize strains into:

Psychological reactions

Physical reactions

Behavioral reactions

(See Table 11.4) Psychological reactions involve emotional responses such as anxiety and frustration. Physical reactions include symptoms such as headaches and stomach distress and illnesses such as cancer. Behavioral reactions are responses to job stressors and include substance use (e.g., alcohol), smoking, accidents, and counterproductive work behavior (CWB).

TABLE 11.4 Examples of Job Strains From Each of the Three Categories of Job Strains

Job Strain	Examples of Specific Outcomes
Psychological reactions	Anger
	Anxiety
	Frustration
	Job dissatisfaction
Physical reactions	Physical symptoms
	Dizziness
	Headache
	Heart pounding
	Stomach distress
	Illness
	Cancer
	Heart disease
Behavioral reactions	Accidents
	Smoking
	Substance use
	Turnover

Source: From "Emerging Theoretical and Methodological Issues in the Study of Work-Related Stress," by S. M. Jex and T. A. Beehr, 1991, *Research in Personnel and Human Resources Management, 9*, 311–365.

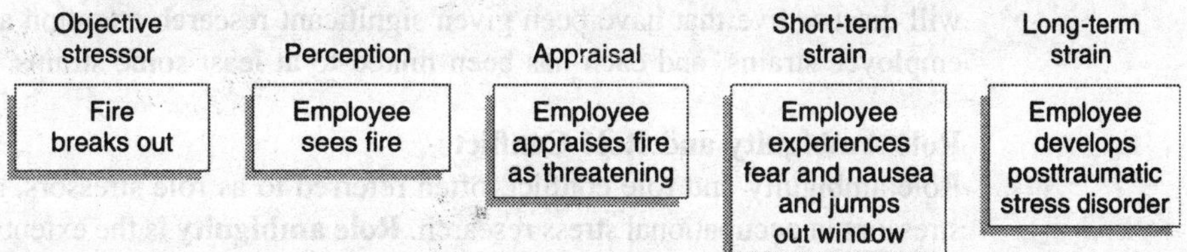

Figure 11.6 A five-step model of the job stress process. An objective stressor (step 1) leads to its perception (step 2), and it is appraised by the individual (step 3). If it is appraised to be a challenge or threat, it can lead to short-term strains (step 4) and eventually to long-term strains (step 5). From "Methodological Issues in the Study of Work Stress: Objective vs Subjective Measurement of Work Stress and the Questions of Longitudinal Studies" (pp. 375–411), by M. Frese and D. Zapf, 1988, in C. L. Cooper and R. Payne (Eds.), *Causes, Coping and Consequences of Stress at Work*, Oxford, England: John Wiley.

Models of the occupational stress process presume that job stressors lead to job strains. It is generally recognized, however, that the process is not automatic and that the employee's perception and appraisal of the stressor are essential parts of the process. Appraisal is the extent to which a person interprets an event or situation to be personally threatening. Not everyone will see the same situation as a job stressor. One person who is given an extra work assignment sees it as an opportunity to make a good impression on the supervisor, while another sees it as an unfair imposition on his or her free time.

Figure 11.6 (based on Frese & Zapf, 1988) illustrates how job stressors lead to job strains. In this model, job stressors (step 1) are objective conditions or situations in the work environment. For example, there might be a fire at work. In order for the fire to become a stressor, the employee must be aware of its existence. This leads to step 2, which is perception of the stressor. Perception alone, however, is not sufficient to lead to strain. The employee must appraise the stressor as aversive or threatening (step 3). If a building is on fire, virtually anyone would appraise the situation as threatening. If it is only an ashtray that is on fire, it is doubtful that many would find it a threat. If the location is filled with flammable materials, however, even a lit match would be dangerous. It is the interpretation or appraisal of the situation that determines if it will lead to the next steps, which involve strain. Strains in this model are divided into short term (step 4) and long term (step 5). Short-term strains occur immediately. Upon seeing a fire, an employee might experience fear (psychological reaction), become nauseated (physical reaction), and jump out a window (behavioral reaction). If the person experienced a severe enough trauma from the experience, he or she might develop PTSD, which would be a long-term strain.

Job Stressors

There are many things in the work environment that can be stressful. Some are conditions that can occur across most jobs, such as conflicts with coworkers or heavy workloads. Others can be specific to particular occupations. For example, Parasuraman and Purohit (2000) found that a major stressor for orchestra musicians is being asked to do something that violates their sense of artistic integrity. This situation could not likely exist for a nurse who must instead deal with the stress of dying patients. Although many different conditions at work might serve as job stressors, relatively few have been studied. We will discuss five that have been given significant research attention as possible causes of employee strains, and each has been linked to at least some strains.

Role Ambiguity and Role Conflict

Role ambiguity and role conflict, often referred to as role stressors, are the most studied stressors in occupational stress research. **Role ambiguity** is the extent to which employees are uncertain about what their job functions and responsibilities are. Many supervisors fail to provide clear guidelines and directions for their subordinates, leading to ambiguity about what the employee is supposed to do.

Role conflict arises when people experience incompatible demands either at work (intrarole) or between work and nonwork (extrarole). *Intrarole conflict* arises from multiple demands on the job. For example, two supervisors might ask the person to do incompatible tasks. One might ask the person to take more care in doing the work, and the other might ask the person to work faster. These demands are incompatible in that the employee would have to work more slowly to be more careful. The incompatibility would be reflected in role conflict.

Extrarole conflict occurs between demands from work and nonwork domains. Such conflict commonly occurs when employees have children and the needs of children conflict with the demands of the job. When a child is sick, a parent may have to stay home from work, thus experiencing role conflict. This particular type of role conflict is discussed in the next section on work-family conflict.

The research on role ambiguity and role conflict has focused primarily on psychological strains. The results of S. E. Jackson and Schuler's (1985) meta-analysis showed that high levels of both role stressors are associated with low levels of job satisfaction and high levels of anxiety/tension and intention to quit the job. Glazer and Beehr (2005) showed that role variables relate to psychological strains not only in the United States but in Hungary, Italy, and the United Kingdom as well. Correlations with behavioral strains, such as absence and job performance (Tubre & Collins, 2000), are quite small in most studies. It should be kept in mind that most studies of job performance use supervisor ratings, which (as discussed in Chapter 4) can be quite inaccurate. Fried, Ben-David, Tiegs, Avital, and Yeverechyahu (1998) improved on the typical job performance measure by seeking specific information about performance (e.g., "the employee is assigned the most difficult tasks in the department" and "the employee is capable of reading technical drawings") rather than the more typical ratings of work quality and quantity. Relations of role ambiguity and role conflict with this measure of job performance were considerably higher than typically found, suggesting that researchers need to pay more attention to the quality of performance measures in future studies. Of course, we must be careful in awaiting replication before drawing firm conclusions.

Most of the research on role stressors has used self-report scales completed by employees. This means that in the five-step model, role stressors were assessed at the level of appraisal (step 3). It is unclear whether objective job conditions were responsible for these appraisals or whether those conditions resulted in psychological strains. Jex and Beehr (1991) wondered if role ambiguity and role conflict are perhaps not very important stressors. Their lack of importance is underscored by studies in which employees are asked to relate the most stressful thing that has happened to them in the recent past. Incidents that reflect role ambiguity or role conflict are seldom mentioned (C. Liu, Spector, & Shi, 2007).

Workload

Workload concerns the work demands that the job places on an employee, and it can be of two types: quantitative and qualitative. *Quantitative workload* is the amount of work that a person has. A heavy quantitative workload means that a person has too much to do. *Qualitative workload* is the difficulty of work relative to a person's capabilities. A heavy qualitative workload means that the employee cannot easily do job tasks because they are difficult for him or her. It is possible for a person to experience only one type of workload in a job. He or she might have a lot of work to do that is not necessarily difficult, or difficult work to do that is not necessarily plentiful.

Research has found that workload relates to all three types of strains—psychological, physical, and behavioral (Jex & Beehr, 1991). This research has involved a variety of methodologies that allow us to draw more definitive conclusions about the possible outcomes of this stressor.

Questionnaire studies have shown that employee reports of their workloads correlate with a variety of strains. Spector, Dwyer, and Jex (1988) found significant correlations of workload with the psychological strains of anxiety, frustration, job dissatisfaction, and intention of quitting and the physical strains of health symptoms. Jamal (1990) found significant correlations of workload with the strains of job dissatisfaction, intention of quitting, and health symptoms. Karasek, Gardell, and Lindell (1987) found that workload is associated with the strains of depression, exhaustion, job dissatisfaction, health symptoms, and heart disease. These three studies were quite geographically diverse, having been conducted in the United States, Canada, and Sweden, respectively.

Social Stressors

When asked to relate the most stressful incidents that happened recently at work, employees frequently mention those that involve relationships with people (C. Liu et al., 2007). Being able to get along well with people is an important element in well-being, and failing to get along can be a serious source of strain. Because employed individuals spend so much of their time at work, social relationships with coworkers, supervisors, and others can be some of the most important in their lives. Stressful incidents concerning other people are considered **social stressors**. They include having interpersonal conflicts, as well as being mistreated by others, including organization members (e.g., coworkers, supervisors, or subordinates), and nonmembers (clients, customers, patients, or members of the public).

Interpersonal conflicts occur when people get into arguments and disputes with others. Conflicts can range from mild disagreements to heated and nasty exchanges that can become physical. Bowling and Beehr (2006) conducted a meta-analysis of 28 studies relating interpersonal conflict at work to job strains. They found that conflict relates to physical strains of health symptoms (e.g., headache and stomach distress) and psychological strains of anxiety, depression, and job dissatisfaction at work. Dormann and Zapf (1999) conducted a longitudinal study in East Germany from 1990 to 1991, assessing a sample of workers before and after reunification of the country (see the International Research box). They surveyed a sample of employees including scales of social stressors (conflict and poor relationships with coworkers and supervisors) and depressive symptoms (feeling sad and a sense of worthlessness). They found that social stressors were associated with depressive symptoms over time, suggesting that poor relations lead to psychological strain.

INTERNATIONAL RESEARCH

Social aspects of work can be very important for the well-being of employees. Conflict and poor relationships among employees, as well as lack of social support, can be important contributors to job strain. In this German study, Dormann and Zapf (1999) studied social aspects of work in relation to depressive symptoms to see if they were linked.

This study was conducted in Dresden, in what was formerly East Germany, to explore the impact of social stressors on psychological strain during the period of reunification of Germany from 1990 to 1991. This was a time of considerable upheaval, which makes it a good period in which to study occupational stress. A door-to-door survey method was used, with streets being chosen randomly and then every fourth apartment visited. Residents were asked to participate if they were between 16 and 65 years old and working full-time. Scales to assess social stressors (animosity and conflict with others at work), social support (extent to which others at work provide assistance and emotional support), and depressive symptoms (feeling sad and a sense of worthlessness) were administered by interviewers. Because this was a longitudinal study, interviewers returned to those houses where residents completed the initial survey after 3 months and then a year. By using a longitudinal design, it is possible to draw more confident conclusions about the possible effect of stressors on strains. As is characteristic of longitudinal studies, there was attrition (loss) of participants across the three time periods, and sample sizes ranged from 230 to 529 for the various analyses.

Results showed that social stressors were correlated with depressive symptoms even across the year time period of the study. This supported the idea that social stressors led to depressive symptoms. Furthermore, it was found that social support was a moderator of the relation between social stressors and depressive symptoms. For those employees who reported low social support at work (but not those who reported high), there was a positive relation between social stressors and depressive symptoms. That is, the higher the symptoms the higher the stressors the higher the symptoms.

This study provided evidence that social aspects of work can be an important element in psychological strain. A combination of high social stressors and low social support is associated with high levels of depressive symptoms. It is important for organizations to encourage the development of good employee relationships, and immediate supervisors can be the means for accomplishing this if they are trained to be sensitive to employee conflicts and to provide social support.

Source: From "Social Support, Social Stressors at Work, and Depressive Symptoms: Testing for Main and Moderating Effects With Structural Equations in a Three-Wave Longitudinal Study," by C. Dormann and D. Zapf, 1999, *Journal of Applied Psychology, 84,* 874–884.

Whereas interpersonal conflict assumes a two-way interaction among two or more people, some social stressors are mainly unidirectional, with one or more individual targets being mistreated in some way by one or more actors. Such stressors can range from rather mild forms of *incivility* to more intense forms of verbal abuse and aggression. Sometimes such incidents can escalate into physical confrontations and even violence. As with violence, nonphysical acts can be perpetrated by individuals inside and outside of the organization. Regardless of whether the actor is an organization member, such as a coworker or supervisor (Hershcovis, 2010), or a nonmenber, such as a customer (Milam, Spitzmueller, & Penney, 2009), being a target of mistreatment can be stressful. Such experiences have been linked to a number of both psychological and physical strains, such as anxiety, depression, physical symptoms like headaches, and job dissatisfaction (Bowling & Beehr, 2006).

As explained by S. Lim, Cortina, and Magley (2008), **incivility** consists of low-intensity verbal acts of rudeness and insensitivity that are not always clearly intended to harm someone else. This might consist of making disparaging comments or sarcastic remarks, giving hostile looks, or ignoring someone. The common element is that the target feels that he or she was treated disrespectfully, even though the actor might not feel any offense was intended. Thus incivility is very much a personal issue in that the same experience will not be interpreted as uncivil by all targets. Nevertheless, it has been shown that individuals who feel they were targets of incivility will report symptoms of strain, such as emotional distress and job dissatisfaction (Lim et al., 2008).

More-extreme forms of mistreatment can involve clear cases of employee abuse that in the extreme can be considered forms of bullying (Rayner & Keashly, 2005). **Bullying** is a repeated pattern of abusive behavior directed toward someone over time. It can consist of both verbal and physical acts, with some bullies resorting to physical aggression and threats of violence. Although it is often thought that bullying involves a single actor who might single out one or more individuals as targets, bullying in the workplace can involve multiple actors targeting a single person, sometimes termed **mobbing** (Zapf & Einarsen, 2005), which is more prevalent in Europe than North America. Zapf and Einarsen (2005) referred to bullying and mobbing as extreme forms of social stressors than can have serious effects on targets. In addition to emotional and physical strains, individuals exposed to this stressor can require medical treatment and can show signs of severe strain not unlike PTSD.

Organizational Politics

Organizational politics is the perception by employees that coworkers and supervisors engage in self-serving behavior in which they put their own interests above those of the organization and other people. Furthermore, rewards are perceived to be based on favoritism rather than merit (Kacmar & Carlson, 1997). Organizational politics can be considered a stressor in that it leads to strains. For example, Hochwarter, Kacmar, Perrewé, and Johnson (2003) surveyed 311 employees from a variety of organizations. They found that perceptions of organizational politics are associated with both psychological and physical strains. Similarly, Vigoda (2002) in a series of three Israeli studies found that politics is associated with psychological and physical strains, as well as low organizational commitment and low job satisfaction.

Control

Control is the extent to which employees are able to make decisions about their work. Such decisions involve all aspects of work, including when to work, where to work, how to work, and what tasks to do. Employees with a high level of control are able to set their own work schedules, choose their own tasks, and decide how to complete those tasks. In a low-control job, the work schedule is set, tasks are assigned, and often even the procedures for accomplishing tasks are specified. College professors have a high level of control because they decide what courses they teach, how they will teach them, and often even when and where their classes will be held. Factory workers usually have little control because they work a fixed schedule, are given a specific task to do, and may be told exactly how to do that task. In many factories, the work is paced by machine. In

TABLE 11.5 Mean Correlations of Perceived Control With Job Strains From Spector's (1986) Meta-Analysis

Stressor	Mean Correlation
Job satisfaction	.30
Organizational commitment	.26
Job involvement	.41
Emotional distress	−.25
Intent to quit	−.17
Health symptoms	−.25
Absence	−.19
Job performance	.20
Turnover likelihood	−.22

Source: From "Perceived Control by Employees: A Meta-Analysis of Studies Concerning Autonomy and Participation at Work," by P. E. Spector, 1986, *Human Relations, 11,* 1005–1016.

other words, the work comes down a conveyor belt at a fixed rate, and the worker must keep up with the machine, thus having very little control over work pacing.

Control is an extremely important component of the occupational stress process. It is also a component of job characteristics theory (see Chapters 9 and 10). Studies have found that employee perceptions of control are associated with all three categories of strain, although results are most consistent with psychological strain. Table 11.5 shows the mean correlations of perceived employee control with several strains reported in Spector's (1986) meta-analysis. As you can see from the table, high levels of control are associated with high levels of job satisfaction, organizational commitment, job involvement, and performance. Low levels of control are associated with high levels of emotional distress, intent to quit the job, health symptoms, absence, and turnover.

The control studies summarized in Spector's (1986) meta-analysis concern employee perceptions about how much control they have at work. In most of these studies, control and strains were assessed with questionnaires given to employees. This sort of study makes it difficult to know if job strains are the result of perceived control or if perceived control is the result of strains. Perhaps employees who dislike their jobs or employees who have low commitment or employees who are in poor health perceive their jobs to be low in control, even though the job may not be. As noted previously, there is evidence that how people feel about work affects their perception of the job, including the amount of control they have (Spector, 1992). In other words, the supposed strain might cause the supposed stressor rather than the reverse. To make things even more complicated, it has been found that employees who perform well on the job are given more control (Dansereau, Graen, & Haga, 1975), suggesting that performance affects the amount of control the employee has. Perhaps the extra control given to good performers raises their job satisfaction. Rather than the strain being caused by the stressor, the stressor is caused by the strain. However, there have been some studies of objective control that allow us to draw more firm conclusions about its role in occupational stress.

Studies of objective or actual control help solve the problem of inferring the effects of control on strains because they do not rely on employee reports about control. That is, they allow us to draw conclusions about the effects of low control assessed independently of the employee's perception or appraisal, or at step 1 of the occupational stress model in Figure 11.5. Results with objective measures are not always the same as results with reports of control. For example, C. Liu, Spector, and Jex (2005) showed that O*NET (see Chapter 3) scores for control are associated with absence and illness but not with psychological strains. Employee perceptions of control, on the other hand, are associated with illness and psychological strains but not absence.

Machine Pacing

One area in which objective control has been studied is *machine-paced work*, which means that a machine controls when the worker must make a response. Factory work is the best example when the conveyor belt controls the speed at which the employee works. Computer technology has introduced machine pacing into nonfactory work as well. Millions of people worldwide sit at computer terminals all day doing what is not much different from simple factory work. They respond to information that comes on the screen at a pace that is set by the machine.

The effects of machine pacing and other work conditions were studied for years by a research group at the University of Stockholm in Sweden. A major focus of this research is to understand how human physiology is affected by job stressors, such as machine pacing. Two types of stress-related hormones have been studied—catecholamines (adrenaline and noradrenaline) and cortisol. These substances help prepare the body for action when danger or challenge occurs. Adrenaline is often said to help energize the performance of athletes during competition. Its actions can be felt as "butterflies" in the stomach. Cortisol helps control swelling during injury (Sarafino, 1990).

The University of Stockholm research has shown that both control and workload affect physiological responses. In a series of studies, these researchers assessed the level of employees' hormones by analyzing urine samples at home and at work. They found that as workload increases, the amounts of adrenaline and noradrenaline increased (Frankenhaeuser & Johansson, 1986). When people work hard, their bodies may use these two hormones to help energize performance. Control also has an effect on these two catecholamines. Employees who were machine paced had higher levels of adrenaline and noradrenaline than employees who were self paced (Johansson, 1981). The effects of control on cortisol are somewhat different. With machine pacing (low control), the cortisol level increases from home to work. With self-pacing (high control), however, the cortisol level decreases from home to work (Frankenhaeuser & Johansson, 1986). The researchers hypothesized that distress is the important component in these results. Lack of control is presumed to increase the level of cortisol because the lack of control distresses the employees, and distress is associated with the secretion of cortisol.

In addition to physiological reactions, machine pacing has been associated with psychological strains and health symptoms. Compared to self-paced work, machine-paced work has been found to be associated with anxiety (Broadbent & Gath, 1981), dissatisfaction, and health symptoms (M. J. Smith, Hurrell, & Murphy, 1981). All of these studies combined have provided reasonably convincing evidence that job stressors can have both physiological and psychological effects. They have not demonstrated, however, that these effects lead directly to serious illness. Johansson (1989) pointed out that frequent high levels of catecholamines and cortisol have been associated with heart disease. Thus we might speculate that working under conditions that cause distress would be a risk factor in the development of later illness.

The Demand/Control Model

The **demand/control model** (Karasek, 1979) states that the effects of job stressors are a complex interplay of demands and employee control. Demands are stressors such as workload that require adaptation. Put another way, a demand taxes an employee's ability to cope with the environment. According to the theory, demands lead to strain only when there is insufficient control. Stated another way, having control reduces the negative effects of demands; that is, it serves as a *stress buffer*. Figure 11.7 illustrates how control affects the relation between demands and strain. It shows that when control is high, demands (stressors) do not lead to strain. When control is low, however, strains increase as stressors increase. The model implies that giving people control at work can be a successful strategy for reducing or buffering the negative effects of job stressors.

Research support for the demand/control model has been mixed, with only some studies finding the hypothesized effect (Häusser, Mojzisch, Niesel, & Schulz-Hardt, 2010). At least some of the reason for the inconsistent results may concern the measures of demands and control, which have differed across studies. Wall, Jackson, Mullarkey, and Parker (1996) showed that the nature of control matters in their test of the model. They found support for the model with a measure that focuses on control over employees' immediate tasks but not with a measure of more general control. Another possible factor is that most studies measure the general or typical levels of demands, control and strain. When G. D. Bishop and colleagues (2003) assessed control, demands, and blood pressure

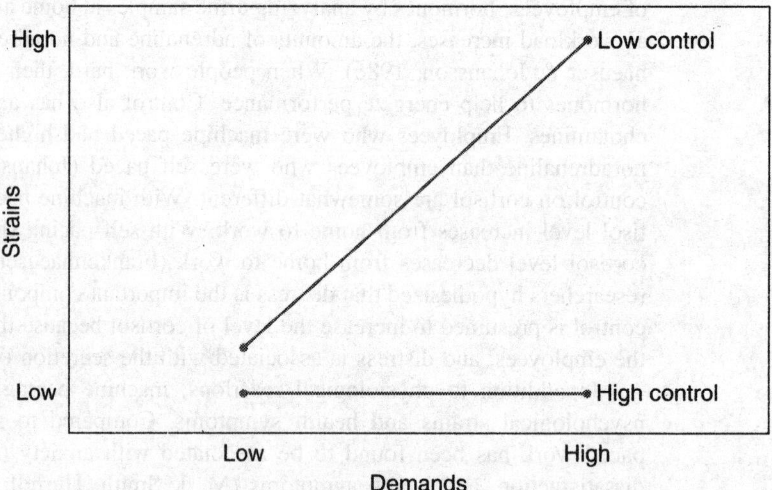

Figure 11.7 The demand/control model. When control is high, there is no relation between demands and strain. When control is low, strain increases as demands increase.

repeatedly over the day, they found that high demand–low control events are associated with elevated pressure, just as the theory predicts.

Alcohol as a Coping Mechanism

Employees can engage in a variety of behaviors to cope with workplace stressors. Some of those behaviors can be directed toward elimination or reduction of stressors, such as figuring out more efficient ways to cope with heavy workloads. Others can involve finding ways to cope with the strains produced by stressors. The consumption of alcohol can be a means of coping with stressful job conditions. For example, Frone (2008) conducted a national survey of Americans, finding that alcohol consumption is related to the stressors of job insecurity and workload. Similarly Bacharach, Bamberger, and Doveh (2008) found in their study of New York City firefighters that alcohol is used as a means of coping with distress on the job, such as having to deal with suicide attempts or incidents with fatalities.

The use of alcohol to cope with stressors can be affected by both individual and organizational factors. For example, M. Wang and colleagues studied alcohol use among employees in China. They found that individuals who are high in negative affectivity (the tendency to experience negative emotions; see Chapter 9) are more likely than those who are low to use alcohol to cope with stressful job conditions (S. Liu, Wang, Zhan, & Shi, 2009). Furthermore, peer norms are an influence on drinking behavior, as people are more likely to drink if their coworkers see drinking as being acceptable (M. Wang, Liu, Zhan, & Shi, 2010).

Although the moderate use of alcohol likely has little or no effect on organizations, heavy drinking can be a significant problem. Drinking at work can create obvious problems, as workplace intoxication can reduce job performance and increase the risk of accidents and injuries on the job. However, drinking off the job can create problems for the organization as well. Heavy drinking at home, for example, has been related to absence (Bacharach, Bamberger, & Biron, 2010), perhaps due to hangover-related illness.

▶ WORK-FAMILY CONFLICT

Work-family conflict is a form of extrarole conflict (see the role conflict discussion earlier in the chapter) in which the demands of work interfere with those of the family—for example, having to spend time at work leaves insufficient time for home (Baltes & Heydens-Gahir, 2003)—or the demands of the family interfere with those of work—for example, having to take a sick child to the doctor might require a person to be absent from work. The problem can be particularly acute for two-career couples with children and for single parents. With both parents working or with single parents, conflicts are certain to arise over issues such as staying home with sick children and participating in school functions.

There are several factors that contribute to the experience of work-family conflict. On the organization side, having to work many hours (M. T. Ford, Heinen, & Langkamer, 2007) and lack of schedule flexibility (Major, Klein, & Ehrhart, 2002) can lead to conflict. Work-family conflict has also been shown to relate to role conflict and role ambiguity (M. T. Ford et al., 2007). On the employee side, personality can be a factor; for example, research has shown that individuals who are high on negative affectivity (the tendency to experience negative emotions) report more work-family conflict (Bruck & Allen, 2003; Wayne, Musisca, & Fleeson, 2004). Of course, such individuals have a tendency to experience high levels of various stressors and strains.

Work-family conflict can have a number of negative effects on both men and women. In their meta-analysis of work-family conflict studies, T. D. Allen, Herst, Bruck, and Sutton (2000) found a mean correlation of −.23 with job satisfaction. Individuals who report high levels of work-family conflict tend to report low job satisfaction. Work-family conflict has also been linked to work stress, with high levels of work-family conflict being associated with strains of anxiety (M. T. Ford et al., 2007), depression and physical health symptoms (Major et al., 2002), absence and lateness (Hammer, Bauer, & Grandey, 2003), and dissatisfaction with life in general (Michel, Mitchelson, Kotrba, LeBreton, & Baltes, 2009).

Although having both parent and work roles can have detrimental effects, particularly for women who usually assume the major responsibility for children, dual roles can have positive effects as well (Langan-Fox, 1998). Work can provide enhanced self-esteem and social support from others, which for some people counteracts the more negative effects of dual roles. Likewise, there can be a positive impact of work on the family and family on work. Hanson, Hammer, and Colton (2006) pointed out that coworkers can help with family issues, and family members can help with work issues.

Organizations that are concerned with work-family conflict have taken steps to help their employees. Two of the most frequently used approaches are flexible work schedules and on-site child care in the workplace. Both make it easier for employees with children to manage family and work responsibilities. Flexible schedules allow an individual to take time off to deal with nonwork demands, such as taking a sick child to the doctor. On-site child care makes it easier for parents by enabling them to take their children with them to work. Parents can visit their children during breaks, and they are nearby in case of illness. Scandura and Lankau (1997) surveyed male and female managers about flexible hours and their job attitudes. Flexible hours were associated with greater job satisfaction for both men and women who had children living with them but not for men and women without children. Chiu and Ng (1999) looked at what they termed women-friendly practices (e.g., child-care facilities, maternity benefits, flexible work hours, and family counseling) in Hong Kong companies and found they have a positive effect on women's but not men's attitudes. Despite the potential benefits of flexible work arrangements and other policies designed to reduce work-family conflict, they are not always fully utilized due to a lack of support by supervisors (Shockley & Allen, 2010).

▶ BURNOUT

Burnout is a distressed psychological state that an employee might experience after being on the job for a period of time. A person suffering from burnout is emotionally exhausted and has low work motivation, having little energy and enthusiasm for the job. Originally, the concept was developed to explain the reactions of employees in the helping professions, such as psychotherapists and social workers. The early burnout researchers believed that burnout is the result of working intensely with other people, and there is research to support that idea. For example, Bakker, Schaufeli, Sixma, Bosveld, and Van Dierendonck (2000) found that patient demands are associated with burnout in physicians. More recently, however, the idea has been extended to workers in all sorts of jobs, even those who have little contact with others.

Burnout is assessed with scales administered to employees. The most popular scale, the Maslach Burnout Inventory (MBI) (Maslach, 1998), measures three components of burnout:

Emotional exhaustion,
Depersonalization, and
Reduced personal accomplishment.

Emotional exhaustion is the feeling of tiredness and fatigue at work. *Depersonalization* is the development of a cynical and callous feeling toward others. *Reduced personal accomplishment* is the feeling that the employee is not accomplishing anything worthwhile at work. Table 11.6 lists some of the by-products of each burnout component. For example, emotional exhaustion should lead to absence and fatigue.

Feelings of burnout have been found to correlate with many job stressor and job strain variables and might be considered a type of strain. Burnout has been associated with stressors such as role ambiguity, role conflict (Beehr, Bowling, & Bennett, 2010), and lack of control (Fernet, Guay, & Senecal, 2004). It has also been associated with absence, turnover, poor performance (Swider & Zimmerman, 2010), and physical symptoms (Beehr et al., 2010). It has even been linked to increased risk for cardiovascular disease (Melamed, Shirom, Toker, Berliner, & Shapira, 2006). Figure 11.8 shows some

TABLE 11.6 The Three Burnout Components and Expected Results of Each

Component	Results
Emotional exhaustion	Absence
	Fatigue
Depersonalization	Callous and uncaring treatment of clients and other people
	Hostility toward other people
Reduced personal accomplishment	Low motivation
	Poor performance

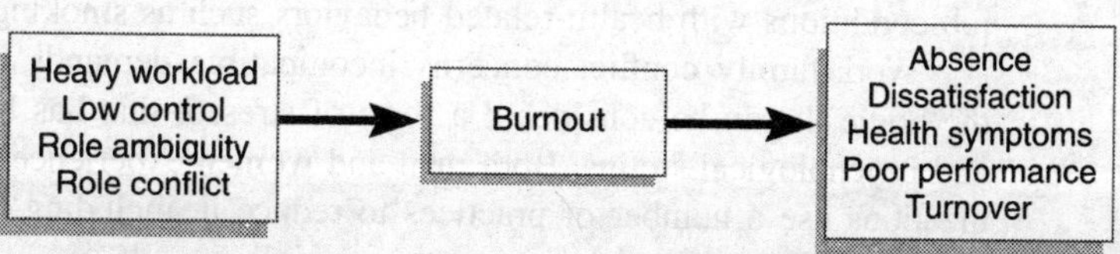

Figure 11.8 Job stressors and job strains that have been associated with burnout. From "A Review and an Integration of Research on Job Burnout," by C. L. Cordes and T. W. Dougherty, 1993, *Academy of Management Review, 18,* 621–656.

of the job stressors and strains that correlate with burnout. These stressors are possible causes of burnout.

As we have seen in many other areas of I/O psychology, research in the burnout domain has been dominated by self-report survey methods. From these studies, we know many of the variables that are correlated with burnout. We are not yet certain about the causes of burnout and how organizations can prevent it. Research does suggest two ways to reduce burnout. First, burnout can be reduced by getting a break or **respite** from work, either by psychologically detaching from or forgetting about work during nonwork hours (Fritz, Yankelevich, Zarubin, & Barger, 2010) or by taking a vacation (Fritz & Sonnentag, 2006). Unfortunately vacation effects are likely to be short-lived, with burnout levels returning after a few weeks back on the job. Second, it has been suggested that organizations encourage managers to provide emotional support to employees by providing positive feedback and engaging in discussions of positive aspects of work as a means of reducing burnout (Kahn, Schneider, Jenkins-Henkelman, & Moyle, 2006).

▶ CHAPTER SUMMARY

Work can be a dangerous place, not only for blue-collar workers who must use hazardous equipment and substances but for white-collar workers as well. Many hazards have immediate consequences, such as an injury from an accident. Often, however, the effects of work conditions do not show up for many years, such as a cancer that is produced from years of exposure to a carcinogenic chemical.

Accidents are a major cause of death for people of working age. The causes of accidents involve both employee and organizational factors. Programs directed toward both eliminating physical hazards in the workplace and encouraging safe behavior through development of a safety climate seem most effective in reducing accidents.

Physical work conditions tend to have effects that are primarily physical. Exposure to infectious disease can cause illness, exposure to loud noise can cause hearing loss, repetitive actions and lifting can cause musculoskeletal disorders (MSDs), and exposure to toxic substances can cause injury. Nonphysical conditions can have effects that are both physical and psychological. Work schedules, for example, have been associated with job satisfaction and physical symptoms.

Research has shown that occupational stress can be a factor in psychological strain. Although much of the evidence is circumstantial, support is accumulating for the idea that work demands and control have important physical health implications. Some of the effects of job stressors, however, may be indirect. For example, research has associated job conditions with health-related behaviors such as smoking and alcohol use.

Work-family conflict concerns incompatible demands between the workplace and the home. It can be considered a form of stressor that has been linked to both physical and psychological strains. Both men and women experience work-family conflict. Organizations use a number of practices to reduce it, including flexible work schedules and on-site child care.

Burnout is a psychological state involving fatigue and lack of motivation for work. Research on burnout has found that burnout is associated with many job stressors and strains and may itself be considered a psychological strain.

I/O PSYCHOLOGY IN PRACTICE

(*Courtesy of Kate Keenan*)

This case discusses how Kate Keenan works with organizations to improve their well-being by reducing stress levels for employees. Keenan, a Chartered Psychologist, received her M.Phil in occupational psychology from Birkbeck in 1978 and a MSc. in Mental Health Studies from Kings College London in 2002. She is the Director of a coaching and mentoring business, Formulas 4 Life, a member of the British Psychology Society South West of England Committee and has been a Non-Executive Director of a National Health Service Trust. She is the author of the 'Management Guide' series of books, one of which offers specific guidance on handling stress. Her role is to help organizations apply principles of psychology to issues involving management of stress in the workplace. Keenan helps companies by training their employees on the issues surrounding stress—introducing the concept of stress, the triggers, and ways in which it can be managed. She deals with all areas of OHP, including accidents, burnout, stress, and the development of bespoke stress policies.

One of her projects was a stress education programme based in a large energy supplier in the UK. This is a safety-critical industry very much concerned with assessing and reducing occupational risk and thus highly motivated to reduce stress levels, as research suggests that heightened stress may act as a precursor to an increase in accidents. As many of the day-to-day work activities the employees engage in have the potential for injury, it was a key focus to manage stress in the workplace.

The goal of this project was to educate middle management upwards on the definition of stress, its causes and some of the techniques by which it can be managed. Kate Keenan worked in collaboration with the HR Team to develop an approach to informing all staff about the organization's stress policy. Initially, a briefing pack for stress in the organization was designed, which included information on stress along with contact numbers for free confidential counseling services. All middle managers upwards were invited to attend a training day where they were educated on stress and its effects. They were then given the briefing packs and a scripted statement to disseminate to their teams in a subsequent timetabled meeting. This process ensured that managers were well informed as to the causes of stress, recognizing those suffering from stress and techniques which would enable them to help. It also provided managers with information to share with their team.

The results of this stress education program showed an uptake in the confidential counseling service, of which previously employees had little knowledge. In addition, as employee awareness of stress increased it was found that absenteeism and turnover of staff decreased. Overall, employees felt supported and empowered by management as the organization had clearly taken ownership of the stress issue and encouraged all teams to work together to reduce the incidence of stress at work.

Kate Keenan's approach has been widely used throughout the industry to inform organizations about the steps they should take to reduce levels of stress in the workplace. This project illustrates how positive change in organizations can be accomplished by providing specific information and knowledge about the types of effective actions that can be taken to resolve an important problem.

Discussion Questions

1. Why would an energy supplier be concerned about the stress levels of their employees?
2. What else might an organization do to reduce stress levels other than provide training?
3. How might an organization reduce stressors in an organisation?
4. Some managers would argue that employee well-being is not their concern and that employees should be responsible for managing their own stress. Counter this argument and explain why stress reduction is the concern of management.

LEARNING BY DOING

Safety in the Workplace

Choose a workplace that you have access to as a customer, employee, or visitor. It could be your own university. Look for instances in which safety procedures are used. This could include the posting of safety messages (e.g., to use safety equipment), the wearing of safety gear, the availability or use of safety equipment, or other signs of safety practices. Make a record of what you found that can be discussed in class or compared with the findings of other students.

Workplace Stress

Do a mini-replication of the Keenan and Newton (1985) study. Ask five people you know (acquaintances, family members, or friends) to relate a stressful event that occurred to them in the past 30 days. Ask them to describe what led up to it, what happened, and how they responded. When you have all five, look them over and see what the nature of the events was. In particular, see how many occurred at work compared to outside of work. See if any involved work-family conflict. Of the workplace events, see if they fit any of the stressors we have discussed, such as role ambiguity, role conflict, workload, lack of control, or social stressors. What was the typical response to a stressful event?

PART V

THE SOCIAL CONTEXT OF WORK

(*Getty Images*)

CHAPTER 12

Work Groups and Work Teams

CHAPTER 12 OUTLINE

On July 3, 1988, the U.S. Navy guided missile cruiser *Vincennes* shot down an Iranian airliner, killing all 290 persons onboard. Responsibility for firing the fatal missile was shared by several members of the Anti-Air Warfare Team. This team is supposed to be able to identify hostile aircraft correctly and to shoot only when threatened. Obviously something went wrong, and much of the blame can be placed on poor teamwork. Someone mistakenly identified the airliner as hostile, and over the next few stressful minutes no one corrected the mistake. The Navy spent considerable time and effort since the tragedy trying to determine how best to prevent similar mistakes in the future, and in more than 2 decades since the *Vincennes* incident, the error has not been repeated. I/O psychologists were very much involved in this effort to improve teamwork through research (see this chapter's I/O Psychology in Practice).

The U.S. Navy is not the only organization in which people work in teams. Teams can be found in factories, hospitals, schools, and stores. Any job that requires the coordinated actions of more than one person can involve teams. Not all groups of people in organizations work in teams, however. In many work settings, we find groups of people who work relatively independently but still come in contact with one another. College professors, salesclerks, security guards, and teachers often do most of their work without the help of coworkers, although they come into contact with many other people in their organizations doing similar work. Even the most independent employees are affected by the behavior of others with whom they interact at work.

In this chapter, we turn our attention from the individual employee to groups of employees. We will see how the behavior of individuals is very much affected by the behavior of other people in the work environment. One cannot fully understand the behavior of individuals without considering the influence of others because people rarely work totally alone and unaffected by others.

We begin this discussion by distinguishing work groups from work teams. Four important group and two important team concepts will be discussed:

Roles

Norms

Group cohesiveness

Process loss

Team commitment

Team mental model

Next, the chapter covers the effects of groups on job performance. Techniques for enhancing group and team performance are included.

Objectives: The student who studies this chapter should be able to:

- Define work groups and work teams and note the distinction between them.
- Explain the four important group and two important team concepts.
- Summarize the findings on group performance.
- Talk about the advantages and disadvantages of group diversity.
- Discuss the procedures that can be used to enhance work group and team performance.

WORK GROUPS VERSUS WORK TEAMS

A **work group** is a collection of two or more people who interact with one another and share some interrelated task goals. These two characteristics—interaction and interrelatedness—distinguish a group from just a collection of people. A university department faculty is a work group. The members of the faculty interact with one another from time to time, and they have interrelated goals involving the education of students. Each faculty member teaches courses that, taken together, constitute the requirements for the major course of study. On the other hand, all of the students of the university are not a group because they do not all interact with one another, although subsets of them do, and they do not all share interrelated goals. Rather, each student has an individual goal that is unrelated to the goals of other students.

A **work team** is a type of work group, but a team has three specific properties (M. A. West, Borrill, & Unsworth, 1998):

1. The actions of individuals must be interdependent and coordinated.
2. Each member must have a particular, specified role.
3. There must be common task goals and objectives.

For example, each person on a surgical team has a specific role. A surgeon does the cutting and sewing, a surgical nurse assists and hands instruments to the surgeon, and an anesthesiologist keeps the patient unconscious and monitors vital signs. The actions of these people are coordinated. The cutting cannot begin until the patient is asleep. The surgeon cannot sew unless the nurse hands him or her the tools. There is a common goal of successfully completing the surgery without losing the patient.

The distinction between a group and a team is an important one. All teams are groups, but not all groups are teams. A group consists of people who work together but can do their jobs without one another. A team is a group of people who cannot do their jobs, at least not effectively, without the other members of their team. For the remainder of this chapter, all group principles will apply to teams, but team concepts don't necessarily apply to groups.

Virtual Teams

As we discussed in Chapter 10, technology (computer-supported cooperative work) has made it possible for people to work in teams without face-to-face contact. These **virtual teams** communicate via e-mail, instant messaging, telephone, web cameras, and other technologies. Virtuality, however, is not an all-or-none phenomenon. Teams vary in their use of virtual tools such as e-mail and telephone (Kirkman & Mathieu, 2005), with some teams having members who are geographically separated, thus precluding face-to-face interaction, whereas others are located in the same place but choose to communicate virtually at least some of the time.

Comparisons of face-to-face with virtual groups suggest that the former often function more effectively. A meta-analysis of 52 studies that compared face-to-face with virtual groups shows that the virtual groups have worse task performance, take more time to complete tasks, and have lower group-member satisfaction (Baltes, Dickson, Sherman, Bauer, & LaGanke, 2002). Some of these findings might be due to the use of mainly text-based virtual tools in these studies. The use of richer media—for example, using video plus voice—results in better performance than just text alone (Martins, Gilson, & Maynard, 2004). Furthermore, the type of group task might also affect performance. As we will see later in the chapter, virtual brainstorming can be superior to the face-to-face version.

▶ IMPORTANT GROUP AND TEAM CONCEPTS

There are four important group and two important team concepts that underlie much group and team behavior. The first three (roles, norms, and group cohesiveness) describe important aspects of groups and teams that help us understand how they operate. The fourth (process loss) is concerned with what sorts of things happen in work groups and teams that prevent people from putting all of their efforts into job performance. Team commitment and team mental model are characteristics important to teams but not groups.

Roles

The concept of **role** implies that not everyone in a group or team has the same function or purpose. Instead, different individuals have different jobs and responsibilities in the group or team. In a surgical team, one person has the role of surgeon, another of nurse, and another of anesthesiologist. In a well-running work team, each role is clearly defined, and all team members know exactly what their roles are.

Formal roles are specified by the organization and are part of the formal job description. In a surgical team, each person's job title—surgeon, nurse, or anesthesiologist—defines the role in a formal way. There may be organizational documents, such as written job descriptions and job analyses, that define roles. **Informal roles** arise from group interaction rather than from the formal rules and specifications of organizations. Groups can invent roles that do not exist formally, or a group's informal roles can supersede the formal ones.

An example of an informal role in a work group is that of greeting card sender. It is common in a work group for employees to send cards to one another during special occasions, such as birthdays or weddings. A group member might take on the role of buying and sending cards at the appropriate times. An example of the informal superseding the formal occurs when one person has the formal title of supervisor, but another person is the actual and informal leader. This can occur in combat teams when the members view the lower-ranking experienced sergeant rather than the higher ranking but inexperienced lieutenant as the leader.

Groups vary considerably in the extent to which roles are specialized among members. In a surgical team, for example, the training and credentials are such that little overlap in roles can occur among the surgeon, nurse, and anesthesiologist. With other groups or teams, members can change roles or rotate responsibilities over time. In an academic department of a university, it is common for faculty to take turns being the chairperson.

Norms

Norms are unwritten rules of behavior accepted by members of a work group. These rules can cover everything from style of dress and manner of speech to how hard everyone

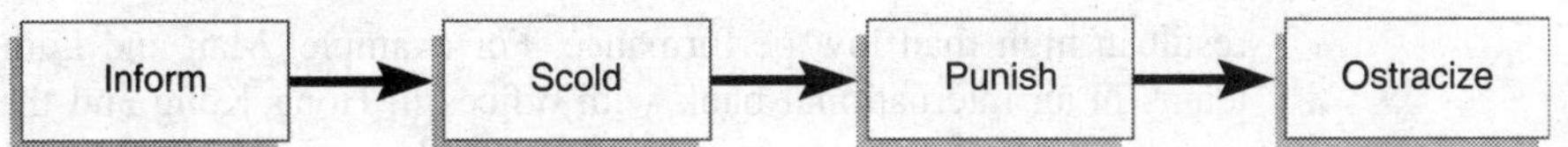

Figure 12.1 Norm violators are informed, scolded, punished, and then ostracized from the group.

works. Norms can exert powerful influences on individual behavior because many groups will strenuously enforce them. As illustrated in Figure 12.1, violation of norms will bring increasingly stronger pressure to bear on the violator, beginning by informing the member of the norm, then scolding the member for violation, and then punishing the member either verbally or physically (violence); when these steps are ineffective, the member will be ostracized (C. L. Jackson & LePine, 2003). A good illustration of norms can be found in Coch and French's (1948) classic study of a pajama factory with a piece-rate system. In this factory, employees assembled pajamas and could work at their own pace. Groups, however, would adopt production norms that specified how much members should produce. Coch and French documented the output of a worker who began to exceed the 50-unit per hour production norm of her work group. When group members pressured her, she restricted her output to about 45 units per hour. A short time later the group was disbanded, and within a matter of days the worker's output more than doubled.

Work group norms can have a bigger impact on member behavior than supervisors or organizational practices. In the Coch and French (1948) study, production was restricted, even though a piece-rate system was in place. Employees would sacrifice the opportunity to make extra money to keep from violating group norms. Clearly norms could prove quite useful as a means of enhancing productivity if they could be appropriately directed. The changing of group norms can be difficult for the management of an organization, which must structure the changes so that it is in the best interest of the group to adopt them. For example, group incentive systems can be an effective means of getting groups to adopt high production norms. With such a system, all members of the group are given rewards, such as a monetary bonus, if the group achieves some specified level of performance. As demonstrated by Coch and French, however, incentive systems will not always motivate groups to perform well.

Group Cohesiveness

Group cohesiveness is the sum of forces attracting group members and keeping the group together. For a group to be highly cohesive, most, if not all, members must have strong motives to remain in the group. A high level of group cohesiveness has important implications for group behavior. Norms tend to be strongly enforced in groups that are highly cohesive. The violation of a norm, particularly an important one, can be threatening to a group's existence. If group continuation is vitally important to group members, the conformity to norms will be a critical issue. In the workplace, people are often dependent on their jobs for economic survival, and the work group can be as important as the family. Threats to the well-being of the group are taken seriously.

Cohesive groups strongly enforce their norms, and work groups might adopt norms for high or low productivity. For this reason, correlations between cohesiveness and job performance have been somewhat inconsistent across studies. However, a meta-analysis (Beal, Cohen, Burke, & McLendon, 2003) suggests that cohesiveness is more likely to result in high than low performance. For example, Man and Lam (2003) studied work teams in an international bank with offices in Hong Kong and the United States. Team members completed questionnaires asking about cohesiveness, and supervisors provided ratings of team performance. Results showed that cohesive teams are rated higher in team performance.

Team Conflict

When people work in teams, they must coordinate their actions in order to accomplish task goals. There are decisions to be made about what procedures to follow, how to allocate resources, and how to distribute tasks to team members. It is unlikely that everyone will always agree, which can lead to conflicts about issues that are important to team members. How teams deal with such conflicts can determine how effective they can be. Conflicts can be distinguished as cooperative versus competitive (Hempel, Zhang, & Tjosvold, 2009). A **cooperative conflict** is one in which individuals openly share diverging views, respect one another's opinions, and focus on finding a solution that is acceptable to team members. A **competitive conflict**, on the other hand, is one in which team members promote their own points of view, have little regard for others' opinions, and try to get their own position adopted. Cooperative conflict in teams has been shown to relate positively to team performance and competitive conflict has been shown to relate negatively (Hempel et al., 2009; Somech, Desivilya, & Lidogoster, 2009). Thus it is important for members of teams to adopt a cooperative style in order for teams to function well.

Process Loss

Much of the time and effort of work group members is devoted to accomplishing organizational objectives through the performance of individuals. Much effort, however, goes into other group functions that have little to do directly with job performance, including time spent in group maintenance functions such as norm enforcement and conflict resolution among members. It can also involve social activities, such as meals or conversation, that enhance group cohesiveness, which can be important for efficient group functioning. All the time and effort expended on activities not directly related to production or task accomplishment are referred to as **process loss**.

Groups vary tremendously in the amount of time they devote to maintenance activities. Some groups have problems with norm violators and interpersonal conflicts that can consume a great deal of time and energy. Other groups run smoothly with little friction and few internal distractions. In the following section on group performance, we will see that groups do not always perform as well as we might expect. Process loss can have a lot to do with the inefficiency that sometimes occurs in groups. Nevertheless, a certain amount of process loss is necessary and may lead to better future performance by the group.

Team Commitment

The organizational commitment concept has been extended to a number of different entities, including the team. **Team commitment** is the strength of an individual's involvement in a team and consists of the acceptance of team goals, willingness to work hard for the team, and desire to remain in the team (J. W. Bishop & Scott, 2000). Therefore, we might expect that high team commitment would be associated with high team performance, low turnover, and team satisfaction. Research has found support for at least two of these expectations. J. W. Bishop, Scott, and Burroughs (2000) found in an automobile parts manufacturing company that work team performance is positively related to team commitment. J. W. Bishop and Scott (2000) studied sewing machine operators and found that their team commitment was related to coworker and supervisor satisfaction, as well as organizational commitment. Van Der Vegt, Emans, and Van De Vliert (2000), in a study conducted in the Netherlands, reported significant positive correlations of team commitment with general job satisfaction and team satisfaction (see the International Research box).

INTERNATIONAL RESEARCH

Task interdependence, the extent to which people's tasks require them to share resources or work together, is an important element in distinguishing groups from teams. Groups consist of people who may or may not be very interdependent but merely work in proximity to one another, whereas teams are interdependent. In this study conducted in the Netherlands, Van Der Vegt, Emans, and Van De Vliert (2000) investigated the extent to which interdependence relates to team commitment and team member job satisfaction. They argued that task interdependence can enhance job satisfaction, team satisfaction, and team commitment. This is because the demands for working closely together lead to camaraderie and good interpersonal relationships that most people find enjoyable.

Participants were 148 employees of a technical consulting firm who were organized into 22 work teams. Questionnaires were mailed to employees by higher-management members who asked them to participate. Scales were included to measure task interdependence, job satisfaction, team satisfaction, and team commitment. Teams varied in the tasks they were assigned, with some requiring more interdependence than others.

Results showed that task interdependence was significantly and positively correlated with job satisfaction (.18), team satisfaction (.29), and team commitment (.45). Thus, the greater the interdependence, the more satisfied and committed the team members were. Furthermore, team commitment was strongly correlated with job satisfaction (.59) and team satisfaction (.69).

These results support Van Der Vegt et al.'s arguments that interdependence leads to job satisfaction, task satisfaction, and team commitment. Of course, since this was a cross-sectional questionnaire study, we can't be certain that interdependence was the cause, but we can say that interdependence appears to play an important role in how people feel about their jobs and teams.

Source: From "Team Members' Affective Responses to Patterns of Intragroup Interdependence and Job Complexity," by G. S. Van Der Vegt, B. Emans, and E. Van De Vliert, 2000, *Journal of Management, 26,* 633–655.

Team commitment seems much like group cohesiveness, but it is a broader construct. Whereas cohesiveness is only the attraction of the individuals to the group, commitment also involves acceptance of team goals and willingness to work hard for the team. Of course, all of these elements are highly related, so in practice cohesive teams will be committed teams.

Team Mental Model

When people work in teams, they must have some common conception of what they are to do together. A **team mental model** refers to the shared understanding among team members of the task, team, equipment, and situation (Mohammed & Dumville, 2001). Smith-Jentsch, Mathieu, and Kraiger (2005) explained that mental models are complex and can be divided into two types, one concerned with taskwork and the other teamwork. The taskwork model concerns the nature of the job that needs to be done. In a surgical team, all members have to share an understanding of the surgery they jointly perform and their particular roles. This does not mean that the mental models have to be identical but just compatible (Cannon-Bowers & Salas, 2001). The nurse may not have the same understanding of the patient's illness that the surgeon does, but both share an understanding of what they need to accomplish and what each person does. When the surgeon asks for an instrument, the nurse knows what to do because they share that understanding. The teamwork model is the shared conception of the team and how its members are to work together. A shared mental model of teamwork facilitates team performance because members know how to coordinate efforts with one another.

In order for a team to perform effectively, there must be a sufficiently shared team mental model. Teams in which the mental model is inadequate will fail to coordinate, will be inefficient, and will be likely to make errors. Conflicts can also arise out of misunderstandings or because team members get frustrated with one another because each person expects the other to do tasks that are not getting done. Research has shown that quality of team mental model relates to team performance, with both accuracy and similarity of mental models among team members leading to better performance (DeChurch & Mesmer-Magnus, 2010; Edwards, Day, Arthur, & Bell, 2006).

▶ GROUP AND TEAM PERFORMANCE

There is a widespread belief that group performance is superior to individual performance for many tasks. This belief is based on the notion that something emerges in the interaction among people that enables a group to be better than the sum of its members. In other words, people inspire one another to be better than they would have been alone. It is true that for some tasks the coordinated efforts of two or more people are necessary because a single individual could not accomplish them alone. For example, several people are needed to build a house. Some tasks may require more than two hands, and others may require the lifting of objects that one person cannot do alone. For many tasks, however, groups are not necessarily better than individuals. Part of the reason is process loss—group members distract and keep one another from concentrating solely on the task at hand. There are additional reasons that we discuss as we compare the performance of individuals with that of groups.

Performance in the Presence of Others

One of the earliest known research findings concerning groups in psychology is that task performance is affected by the presence of others. In the late 1800s, Norman Triplett

Performing in front of an audience raises arousal, as this person will certainly experience. (© *Yuri Arcurs, sourced from Shutterstock images*)

noted that the performance of bicycle riders was faster when they were racing against other people than when they were racing alone (Triplett, 1897). Subsequent research with laboratory tasks, however, did not always find that people performed better in the presence of others. Performance was better in the presence of others in some studies but worse in other studies.

The most widely accepted explanation for these results was put forth by Zajonc (1965), who noticed that the type of task determined if performance is enhanced or inhibited by the presence of others. He suggested that the presence of others increases physiological arousal, which has effects on task performance. Performance is improved (the **social facilitation** effect) by other-induced arousal when the task is simple or well learned, such as bicycle riding. On the other hand, performance is decreased (the **social inhibition** effect) by other-induced arousal when the task is complex or new to the individual, such as solving a complex mathematics problem. These results suggest that for complex tasks, people should be given private space that allows them to keep their arousal levels relatively low. For simple tasks, the arousal produced by the presence of others can enhance performance, but other people can also be a distraction in the workplace, leading to poorer performance. There are no guarantees.

Group Versus Individual Performance on Additive Tasks

When researchers compare individuals to groups on task performance, they are usually concerned with an **additive task**. The output of the task is countable, and the total output is the sum of the individual group-member outputs. The total output for a group of cashiers in a supermarket would be additive because the total sales are the sum of all the individual cashiers' sales. The effects of group process on additive task performance can be seen by comparing the output of an interacting group of people with an equal number of individuals who do not interact. The noninteracting individuals are referred to

TABLE 12.1 Strength of Object Pulling and Pushing as a Function of Group Size

Size of Group	Expected Pull (KGS)	Actual Pull (KGS)	Percentage of Actual to Expected Performance
1	1	1	100
2	2	1.86	93
4	4	3.08	77
8	8	3.92	49

Source: From "Ringelmann Rediscovered: The Original Article," by D. A. Kravitz and B. Martin, 1986, *Journal of Personality and Social Psychology, 50,* 936–941.

as a **nominal group**. Their output reflects the output of a given number of individuals. The output of the interacting group, by comparison, reflects how well the same number of people will perform in a group.

Research dating back to the 19th century has consistently shown that nominal groups do as well as and usually better than interacting groups (J. H. Davis, 1969). This finding is well illustrated by research done over 100 years ago by an agricultural engineer in France named Maximilien Ringelmann. Kravitz and Martin (1986) described Ringelmann's research in which he compared the task performance of groups and individuals. Ringelmann noted that the sum of individual efforts often surpassed the effort of an equal number of people working in a group. Table 12.1 summarizes how group and individual efforts compare. It shows the results across several different types of tasks involving the pulling and pushing of objects. The first column shows the number of people in the group. The second column shows the expected output of a group, which was calculated as the number of people in the group times the average individual performance. In other words, a group of two people should produce double the output of a single person, and a group of four people should produce four times the output of a single person. The third column shows the actual performance of the group. As the table illustrates, the actual interacting group output is considerably less than the expected group output. The percentage that the interacting group output is of the expected group output declines as the group size increases (see column 4). Clearly something is happening with the interacting group that is inhibiting performance.

There are at least two explanations for the group effect on additive task performance. The first explanation is the possibility of process loss. Group members might interfere with one another's task performance, or they might spend time and effort on group maintenance activities rather than on the task at hand. This might explain inhibited performance in some studies, but with the rope-pulling task this does not seem likely. The nature of the task required that all group members concentrate their efforts on pulling the rope at the same time when a signal was given. Group members could not have been doing something else at the time.

A second and more likely explanation is a phenomenon called **social loafing**—people do not put forth as much effort in a group as they would if they were working alone, and the larger the group, the less effort each person exerts. Latané, Williams, and Harkins (1979) found this phenomenon to be widespread in both laboratory and field settings. The social loafing effect can be diminished when group members believe that their individual output is being assessed. In a field study, social loafing was lower when employees felt their individual productivity was visible to others (Liden, Wayne, Jaworski, & Bennett, 2004). The phenomenon may also be limited to individualistic cultures, such as Australia, Canada, England, and the United States (see the discussion of culture values in Chapter 9), where emphasis is placed on the self rather than on society. Earley (1989) found that Chinese management trainees who came from a collectivist country, where emphasis is placed on the group and society, did not demonstrate social loafing.

Brainstorming

Groups are often said to be superior to individuals in generating ideas or solutions to problems (Osborn, 1957). The theory is that group members inspire one another to generate ideas that they would not have thought of alone. **Brainstorming** is a group technique that is supposed to result in improved performance with this type of task. A group is given instructions to generate ideas without being critical or judgmental in any way. Ideas will be evaluated and modified later.

Unfortunately, research has failed to find that the performance of interacting groups that brainstorm is superior to that of nominal groups (McGlynn, McGurk, Effland, Johll, & Harding, 2004). Rather than inspiring one another, group members often inhibit one another. Part of the difficulty is undoubtedly attributable to process loss. The group may not spend as much time as individuals generating ideas. Perhaps even more important, individuals can be reluctant to share ideas in the group because of shyness or social anxiety. Alone a person might be more confident and secure in generating ideas. Finally, when working in a live group, members are spending most of their time listening to others rather than generating options.

Electronic brainstorming has been shown to enhance performance in an idea-generation task with the use of computers (Dennis & Valacich, 1993). Individuals are asked to enter ideas into a computer rather than writing them down. This technique has been found to produce performance equal to or better than that of nominal groups (the combined output of individuals who worked alone) and better than that of groups of individuals who shared their ideas. In Gallupe, Bastianutti, and Cooper's (1991) computer brainstorming study, subjects were aware that several people were working on the same task at the same time and that as ideas were entered onto the computer, they would be seen by everyone. Individuals were not known to one another, which may have reduced the social anxiety that could have inhibited performance in an interacting group. In a similar study, however, Valacich, Dennis, and Nunamaker (1992) found that anonymity made no difference in the performance of brainstorming individuals linked by computer. This study suggests that social anxiety is not the reason for the poorer performance of interacting groups.

Gallupe, Cooper, Grisé, and Bastianutti (1994) conducted a study that showed how electronic brainstorming produces better performance in part because people do not have to wait their turn for others to speak. They can type their responses as they think of them. When electronic brainstormers had to wait their turn to enter their responses onto the computer, performance was about the same as that for the interacting groups. This suggests that process loss is responsible for the poorer performance of interacting groups compared to computer or nominal brainstorming groups.

Paulus (2000) argued that the basic idea that group members inspire one another may be correct but that group process gets in the way. He has shown that exposure to the ideas of others can help people generate more ideas. He suggested a procedure whereby people first get together in a group to discuss ideas and then work alone to generate options. Research has shown that the initial group session helps facilitate the subsequent solitary session and results in increased performance (Paulus, 2000).

Group Problem Solving

So far we've shown that for additive tasks and brainstorming, nominal groups do better than interacting groups. This is not to say that individuals always outperform groups, however, as there are tasks that can be better done when people interact. Problem-solving tasks involve finding the solution to a given situation, such as solving a puzzle. For some problems, there can be a correct answer, but for others there might be a variety of solutions that could be reasonable. Performance is assessed as the time to find the right answer in the former case or the time to find a suitable answer (or the quality of the answer) in the latter. Studies of group problem solving often compare groups to their individual members, contrasting the group time to solve the problem with the time of the single best performer. Studies of problem solving have often found that groups perform as well or better than their best member, suggesting that for this sort of task a group can be a good choice (Bonner, Baumann, & Dalal, 2002).

Group Decision Making

Groups within organizations frequently make decisions ranging from those that are relatively unimportant (e.g., the color of the new stationery) to those that significantly affect the lives and well-being of thousands (e.g., closing a plant and laying off all the workers). Organizations differ tremendously in the extent to which important decisions are made by individual managers (the autocratic approach) or by groups (the democratic approach). Even in the most autocratic organizations, however, it is common for individuals to make decisions only after consultation with a group or committee. The president of the United States consults the cabinet for important decisions, and the presidents of corporations usually have their "inner circles" of associates who serve the same purpose.

Evaluating the quality of a decision is not always an easy or straightforward undertaking. Often the evaluation depends on the values of the person doing the determination and the criterion chosen for comparison. If a government decides to go to war, the decision might be considered good by one person because the war was won and bad by another because many people were killed. For example, many Americans supported President George W. Bush's decision to use military force against Iraq in 2003 to overthrow the Saddam Hussein government, whereas others believed it was a bad decision that would cost too many lives. Similarly, if a company president decides to downsize and lay off thousands of employees, it might be considered a good decision by stockholders whose shares might go up in value and a poor decision by employees who might lose their jobs. A solution to this dilemma is to evaluate a decision against the objective that it was meant to obtain. The Iraq War might be considered a good decision because it accomplished the objective of overthrowing Hussein. If the criterion considers the cost in human life and money, the decision might be considered to have been a poor one.

A layoff might be a good decision if it results in a financially healthier company, but a bad decision if it does not.

We review two areas of group decisions in this section. First is the issue of whether groups take more risks or are more conservative in their decisions than individuals. As we will see in our discussion of group polarization, this question has no simple answer. The second issue concerns how groups sometimes make inappropriate decisions, even though most of the group members know the decision is a poor one. This is the phenomenon of groupthink.

Group Polarization

If a group of people decides on one of several possible courses of action, will the choice involve greater or lesser risk than the choice made by an individual? In other words, are groups riskier or more conservative than individuals in their decisions? This question has been addressed by hundreds of studies comparing group decisions to the decisions of individuals. The answer is that group decisions often differ from the decisions of individuals, but whether they are riskier or more conservative depends on the nature of the decision.

The typical risky-decision study asks individuals and groups to choose one option from a series of options that vary in risk. For example, a decision task might involve deciding the acceptable odds of survival for undergoing elective surgery. Table 12.2 is one of the choice-dilemmas (Kogan & Wallach, 1964) that have been used in many risk studies. In these studies, subjects are first asked to make an individual decision. The subjects are then placed into groups and are asked to come to a group decision. In most studies, the group decisions are more extreme than the mean of the individual decisions. For example, suppose that five subjects choose the following acceptable odds for the surgery problem: 20, 20, 20, 60, and 80 chances out of 100 of dying in surgery. The mean of their choices is 40. When placed in a group, however, the same five people are likely to reach a group decision that is closer to the majority position of 20 than the mean of the individuals alone.

In groups, the majority position typically holds more weight than the minority position, and the shift of the group is toward the majority view. If the majority of the group members make a risky choice, the group decision is likely to be riskier than the mean of its individuals. If the majority make a conservative choice, the group is likely to shift its decision in a conservative direction. This deviation from the group mean is called **group polarization** (Lamm & Myers, 1978), meaning that the group is more extreme (closer to one pole or the other) than the mean of its individuals.

TABLE 12.2 A Risk-Related Choice Task Used in Group Decision Research

Mr. B, a 45-year-old accountant, has recently been informed by his physician that he has developed a severe heart ailment. The disease would be sufficiently serious to force Mr. B to change many of his strongest life habits—reducing his workload, drastically changing his diet, giving up favorite leisure-time pursuits. The physician suggests that a delicate medical operation could be attempted which, if successful, would completely relieve the heart condition. But its success could not be assured, and in fact, the operation might prove fatal.

Source: From *Risk Taking: A Study in Cognition and Personality*, by N. Kogan and M. A. Wallach, 1964, New York, NY: Holt, Rinehart and Winston.

A number of explanations have been offered for the group polarization phenomenon. One likely explanation is that the members who hold the minority view will likely conform to the majority, especially if one member's choice is far from the choices of the other group members. The individuals who find that others made the same choice that they did are likely to be convinced that theirs was the best choice. Most of the group discussion will be directed to convincing the minority that they should adopt the "correct" majority viewpoint. Although most of the research on group decision shifts has concerned risk-related decisions, this phenomenon probably holds for any type of choice situation. For example, decision shift would be expected in deciding how much money to spend on an item.

Groupthink

High-level decision-making groups in corporations and governments typically are comprised of experts who should be able to make good decisions. Unfortunately, something can happen to decision-making processes when groups of people get together, leading

The decision that led to the *Challenger* disaster was likely caused by groupthink, according to Moorhead, Ference, and Neck (1991). (*NASA/ScienceSource/Photo Researchers*)

them to make decisions that any reasonably bright, informed individual would probably never make. Janis (1972) conducted in-depth analyses of decision fiascoes and developed a theory of what can go wrong when groups make decisions. **Groupthink** is a phenomenon that can occur when groups make decisions that individual members know are poor ones (Janis, 1972). Janis noted as examples the Ford Motor Company's decision to produce the Edsel, an automobile that lost $300 million; the Kennedy administration's decision to invade Cuba at the Bay of Pigs, an invasion that was a total failure; and the Johnson administration's decision to escalate the Vietnam War, which the United States never won. Moorhead, Ference, and Neck (1991) analyzed the decision to launch the space shuttle *Challenger* in 1986. Despite warnings that cold weather could cause serious mechanical failures, NASA officials decided to launch the shuttle in freezing temperatures, resulting in a tragic accident that killed the entire crew.

According to Janis (1972), groupthink is likely to occur in highly cohesive groups with strong leaders when the social pressures to maintain conformity and harmony in the group take precedence over sound decision making. The likelihood of groupthink is increased when decision-making groups isolate themselves from outside ideas and influences. Note the following sequence of events: Suppose that the leader of the group presents a bad idea at a meeting. Each member might initially suspect that the idea is a poor one but is reluctant to be the one to say so. Much like the story "The Emperor's New Clothes," no one wants to stick his or her neck out and question the leader's decision. As each individual looks around the room and notices that everyone is silent, he or she may begin to doubt his or her initial judgment. After all, if everyone else seems to be going along, perhaps the idea is not so bad. As the group process gets rolling, even the most minor reservation is quickly rationalized away, and pressure is put on individual members to conform to the group point of view. Some of the factors leading to groupthink are illustrated in Figure 12.2.

Janis (1972) offered several suggestions for avoiding groupthink. Two major themes appear throughout these suggestions. First, group leaders should serve as impartial moderators in group meetings rather than attempting to control the decision alternatives that are recommended. Second, group members at every stage of the decision-making process should critically evaluate decision alternatives and continually seek information that might support or refute the wisdom of a decision. Janis discussed specific actions that groups should take to maintain a critical and objective frame of mind. For example, groups should periodically break into smaller subgroups to discuss critical issues, and

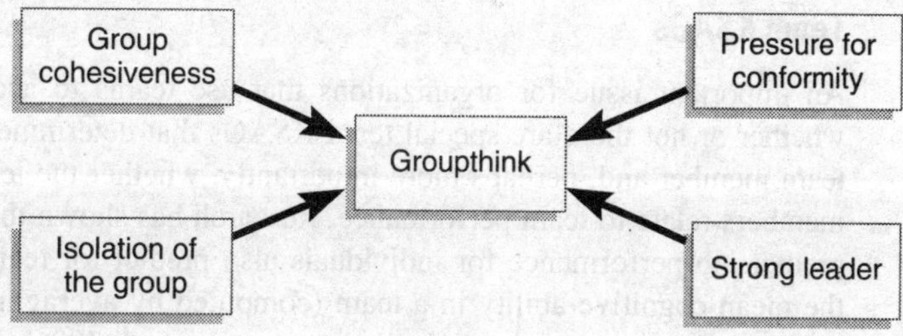

Figure 12.2 Several factors can lead to groupthink. Of the four shown here, group cohesiveness seems unnecessary, according to Aldag and Fuller (1993).

members of the decision-making groups should discuss issues with subordinates. These actions can help groups avoid getting caught in a cycle of groupthink that can result in making the wrong decision.

Aldag and Fuller (1993) reviewed the research on groupthink. They noted that few good tests of its propositions exist and that those that do exist support only part of the theory. For example, group cohesiveness does not seem to be necessary for groupthink to occur. Janis (1972), however, offered sound advice about how to avoid bad group decisions by soliciting a variety of views. This is a potential advantage of having diversity in the backgrounds of group members. A diverse group is likely to have different perspectives on a problem and its solution. We will discuss group diversity later in the chapter.

Team Innovation

Organizations today find themselves in a rapidly changing and competitive world that requires them to adapt and change. Much of that change occurs at the level of work teams that implement new innovations in the workplace. Innovation is the introduction of new ideas, procedures, or products into a team (De Dreu, 2006). Innovation is not the same as creativity in that team members don't necessarily invent the innovations that they adopt. Innovation is the process of introducing changes regardless of whether they were invented or borrowed.

Teams innovate out of necessity, from both internal factors (organizational constraints and workload) and external factors (turbulent environment) (Anderson, De Dreu, and Nijstad, 2004). A turbulent and challenging environment is the case for high-tech companies that produce products in rapidly advancing fields. Extreme competition requires constant innovation for organizations to maintain their market share and survive. Teams also innovate because of organizational constraints that require innovations to overcome obstacles and heavy workloads that require new ways to get work done more efficiently.

Teams vary in their orientation to innovation. Those teams that take time to critically discuss how they do things and how they can do them better are the best innovators (Somech, 2006). Such discussions involve sharing differences of opinion that can produce conflicts about tasks among members. A moderate level of such conflict is optimal in facilitating innovation in teams (De Dreu, 2006), especially when that conflict is cooperative (see the discussion on team conflict earlier in this chapter).

Team KSAOs

An important issue for organizations that use teams to accomplish important work is whether or not there are special team KSAOs that determine whether a person is a good team member and, perhaps more importantly, whether the levels of team KSAOs among members relate to team performance. Research has shown that at least some KSAOs that predict job performance for individuals also predict for teams. For example, the higher the mean cognitive ability in a team (computed by averaging team member scores), the higher the team performance is likely to be (Stewart, 2006). Determining additional team KSAOs that also relate to team performance would inform both selection and training of members.

As might be expected, several team KSAOs have been identified that relate to team performance. Three are particularly important:

1. To be a good team member requires knowledge of teamwork (Hirschfeld, Jordan, Feild, Giles, & Armenakis, 2006). Such knowledge is concerned with how individuals can effectively work together in teams and develop good working relationships with others.
2. An effective team member has good social skills (Morgeson, Reider, & Campion, 2005). Beyond knowing how to work in teams, a person must have skills in communicating with and influencing others.
3. Certain personality characteristics make a person particularly suited to teamwork. Jackson, Colquitt, Wesson, and Zapata-Phelan (2006) showed that individuals who are collectivistic as opposed to individualistic (see Chapter 9) in their values perform better in teams.

Taken together, these studies suggest that the most effective team members have knowledge of how to work in teams and skill in doing so, as well as a personality that is suited to working closely with others.

▶ GROUP DIVERSITY

Demographic shifts have resulted in increasing numbers of minorities and women in the workplace, not only in North America but in much of the rest of the industrialized world (Triandis, 2003). Coupled with the greater reliance on teamwork, group diversity has become an important issue for organizations (Mohammed & Angell, 2004). Diversity or differences among people can be divided into two types: cognitive and demographic (Van der Vegt & Janssen, 2003). Cognitive diversity concerns people's knowledge, skills, and values. Demographic diversity consists of more visible attributes of people, such as age, gender, and race-ethnicity. An important issue concerns the impact of diversity within work groups on member performance and reactions.

Jackson, Joshi, and Erhardt (2003) reviewed 63 studies that addressed the impact of diversity within groups—that is, the effect on groups of having members that are different from one another. They noted that diversity can have both positive and negative effects but that results across studies are inconsistent. Some of the reasons are that different types of diversity have been investigated in different studies and that diversity can have different effects depending on the task. Mannix and Neale (2005), for example, concluded that cognitive diversity is likely to be helpful for team innovation, but demographic diversity is not. However, demographic diversity is helpful when there is a need to get the perspectives of a diverse population of potential clients or customers in marketing situations (Jackson & Joshi, 2004).

Organizational context is also important for diversity. Van der Vegt and Janssen (2003) found no relation of either cognitive or demographic diversity with performance in teams from a Dutch company. However, the diverse groups were the best performers when the job required coordinating with teammates and the worst performers when the job could be done independently. In another Dutch study, a similar pattern was found for job satisfaction when the joint influences of diversity and group goals were investigated (Schippers, Den Hartog, Koopman, & Wienk, 2003). There is no overall correlation between diversity and job satisfaction. However, members of teams with group goals are more satisfied if they are diverse; members of teams with individual goals are more satisfied if they are not diverse. Taken together, these studies suggest that diversity can have negative effects when people have no stake in getting along with one another because their jobs are independent or their goals are not linked. However, when there is a necessity to work well with others, not only does the negative aspect of diversity disappear, but also there can be significant advantages in both performance and satisfaction.

▶ INTERVENTIONS WITH WORK GROUPS IN ORGANIZATIONS

Most organizations consist of a network of interrelated work groups. In order for the organization to function effectively, individuals must coordinate their efforts within their own groups, and groups must coordinate their efforts with one another. In this section, we discuss three techniques that can be used to improve group functioning. The autonomous work team is an alternative to the traditional organization of a factory. Items are assembled by small teams of employees rather than by all production employees. The autonomous work team idea has been adapted for nonmanufacturing organizations as well. Quality circles are groups of employees who meet to provide suggestions to management about how to improve productivity. Team building is a family of procedures used to improve the functioning of teams.

Autonomous Work Teams

In the traditional factory, the assembly of a product is broken down into many small operations. For large, complex products, like an automobile, there can be hundreds or thousands of operations, each done by a separate employee. Because assembling a product

Autonomous work groups at Butler Corporation assemble entire grain dryers, which is the cylinder surrounded by steam. (© *Stan Zack/Alamy*)

requires the coordinated effort of a large number of people, many resources must be devoted to supervision. The autonomous work team is an alternative system whereby an entire product is assembled by a small team of employees. A factory will be comprised of many work teams, each assembling an entire product. Because assembly of a product involves only the coordination of team members, relatively few resources are necessary for supervision. Teams are relied on to manage themselves, requiring far fewer supervisors.

The details of how autonomous work teams operate vary from organization to organization. One such system, described by Hackman and Oldham (1980), was implemented by the Butler Corporation when it opened a new grain dryer plant. A grain dryer is a large piece of farm equipment that contains over 3,000 parts (see photograph). At Butler, each dryer is assembled by an autonomous work team. Each team is responsible for managing itself and for product assembly. Ten distinguishing characteristics of the teams at Butler are listed in Table 12.3. As you can see, each member of the team learns each operation, so that after about 18 months on the job every employee can assemble an entire dryer. The team is responsible for the quality of the finished product, which it must test before sending it out of the plant. If a dryer is defective after it is placed into use on a farm, a team member might have to make a service call to fix it. The role of supervisors is different at Butler. There are few of them, and their major function is to offer advice and training to team members. The approach is participative with frequent staff meetings and an advisory committee comprised of members from different teams.

Research has shown that autonomous work teams can benefit employees and organizations. Job satisfaction is sometimes higher with autonomous work teams than more traditional approaches (Cordery, Mueller, & Smith, 1991). Job performance has been found to be the same in manufacturing organizations (Wall, Kemp, Jackson, & Clegg, 1986) or better (Banker, Field, Schroeder, & Sinha, 1996). However, the decreased need for supervisory personnel can result in an overall greater efficiency for these autonomous work teams, even when productivity is the same (see the International Research box). Although there can be advantages to autonomous work teams, they aren't suitable for all

TABLE 12.3 Distinguishing Features of Autonomous Work Groups at Butler Corporation

1. Employees frequently rotated jobs.
2. After about 18 months, most employees knew the entire production process.
3. Groups designed and purchased their own tools.
4. Group members went on service calls to do warranty repairs.
5. Quality control inspection was done by group members.
6. There were few supervisors.
7. Group members participated in hiring and firing.
8. Supervisors served as coaches providing counseling and training.
9. There were weekly group meetings and monthly plant meetings.
10. There were employee advisory groups to management.

Source: From *Work Redesign*, by J. R. Hackman and G. R. Oldham, 1980, Reading, MA: Addison-Wesley.

situations. Langfred (2005) found that to be in an autonomous team means surrendering some individual autonomy. Thus such teams are best suited to tasks that require a high level of interdependent effort among members to complete tasks.

INTERNATIONAL RESEARCH

It is rare in field settings to be able to do a true experiment in which two or more experimental conditions are created and subjects are randomly assigned to them. Wall, Kemp, Jackson, and Clegg (1986) conducted a *quasi-experiment*, meaning that the design of the study was an approximation to an experiment. Two factories that represented the two experimental conditions of interest were compared, but employees were not randomly assigned to work at each factory. It is therefore possible that the observed effects were due to differences in the two factories rather than the autonomous work group treatment.

The study was conducted at a candy manufacturing company in England. Officials of the company decided to experiment with autonomous work groups by trying them at one factory. The researchers were enlisted to evaluate the effects of the new system. The productivity, job satisfaction, and mental health of employees at the autonomous work group factory were compared to those factors for employees at a matched factory that used the traditional assembly-line approach. Data were collected 6 months, 18 months, and 30 months after the new factory began operation.

The results showed that employees in the autonomous work group factory were more satisfied with their jobs than employees in the traditional factory. Their productivity, however, was not better. In fact, during the first 6 months of operation, the productivity of the autonomous work groups was quite disappointing. Much of the difficulty was attributed to problems with new equipment and the time needed for training employees in the new production procedures. By the 30-month time period, performance in both factories was equivalent. Because the autonomous work group factory had fewer supervisors, however, it was found to be more cost efficient.

One finding illustrates the difficulties in drawing conclusions from quasi-experimental studies. The turnover rate was found to be higher in the autonomous work group factory than the traditional factory. This finding was surprising because employees of the former factory were more satisfied with their jobs than employees of the latter factory. The authors noted that the unemployment rate in the area of England where the autonomous work group factory was located was lower than it was where the traditional factory was located. They speculated that the unemployment rate may have been the cause of the turnover rate differences rather than the type of factory. Because of the design of the study, we cannot be certain why the difference occurred. This study does provide evidence to support the idea that autonomous work groups can be more cost efficient than traditional factory structures. Organizations should be aware, however, that extra effort and time may be needed for successful implementation of the system.

Source: From "Outcomes of Autonomous Workgroups: A Long-Term Field Experiment," by T. D. Wall, N. J. Kemp, P. R. Jackson, and C. W. Clegg, 1986, *Academy of Management Journal, 29,* 280–304.

Quality Circles

A quality circle is a group intervention that gives employees the opportunity to have greater input into issues at work. **Quality circles** are groups of employees who meet periodically to discuss problems and propose solutions relevant to their jobs. Typically the groups are comprised of people who have similar jobs in manufacturing organizations, and discussions revolve around issues of product quality and production efficiency. As with autonomous work teams, the use of quality circles has been attempted in all types of organizations.

In theory, quality circles have benefits for both employees and organizations. They allow individual employees to enjoy greater participation, which many find stimulating and enjoyable. It can be a welcome break from routine work to spend time discussing work problems with colleagues. For the organization, it should mean better production procedures because the people who do the work are often the most knowledgeable about what the problems are and how they can be solved.

Too little research has been done on quality circles to draw any firm conclusions about their effects on employees or organizations (Van Fleet & Griffin, 1989). The few studies that have investigated quality circle benefits have yielded somewhat mixed results (Bettenhausen, 1991). Marks, Mirvis, Hackett, and Grady (1986) conducted one of the few studies that compared participants with nonparticipants in the same organization. They found that employees who participate in the quality circle program are more productive and have fewer absences than employees who do not. These results are quite promising, but they need to be replicated in other organizations before we can conclude that quality circles will increase productivity and reduce absence.

The quality circle idea has been adapted to focus on employee health rather than job performance. The German **health circle** or Gesundheitszirkel is an intervention in which groups of employees discuss ways to improve health and well-being. Aust and Ducki (2004) identified 11 studies with results that showed mostly positive effects of health circles. Not only did studies show that many suggestions were implemented, but some found increases in both health and well-being as well.

Team Building

Team building refers to any of a number of activities designed to enhance the functioning of work groups or teams. Some team-building efforts are task oriented—they attempt to help team members improve how they accomplish their team tasks. Other efforts are interpersonally oriented—they are concerned with how well team members communicate and interact. This approach presumes that teams will perform better when their members can communicate and interact with one another effectively (Buller, 1986).

There is no one particular way in which team building is done, but three factors characterize team-building efforts (Buller, 1986). First, team building is a planned activity—that is, it consists of one or more exercises or experiences that are designed to accomplish a particular objective. Second, team building is typically conducted or *facilitated* by a consultant or trainer who is an expert in the particular form of team building that is being done. It would be difficult for a team to run itself through team building, for the trainer is an integral part of the experience. Third, team building usually involves an existing work team. Individuals are trained in team building to enhance their individual team skills within their work teams.

Team building often involves team members discussing problems and coming up with solutions. The role of the team trainer is to facilitate the discussion by getting team members talking to one another. This might involve directing questions such as these at individuals:

> "Tom, what sorts of problems have you been having with product quality?"
>
> "Ellen, why don't you seem to get the information that you need?"

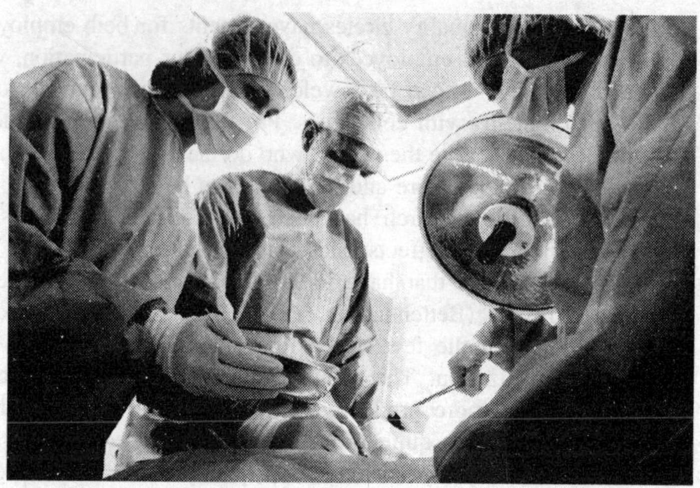

Team building can be valuable for all sorts of teams. (© *stefanolunardi, sourced from Shutterstock images*)

or summarizing and reflecting back to the group the points that have been made:

> "It sounds like everyone is concerned that there are too many defective parts."
>
> "I guess everyone feels uninformed about decisions."

The trainer's job is to get people to raise issues, identify problems, and discuss possible solutions. The trainer might also have to mediate conflicts if the discussion leads to arguments among team members.

Studies have shown that team building can have positive effects on teams and team members. C. Klein and colleagues (C. Klein, DiazGranados, Salas, Le, Burke, Lyons, et al., 2009) conducted a comprehensive meta-analysis to summarize the results of 20 team-building studies. Their analyses showed that team building resulted in better team performance, more efficient team coordination, enhanced team skills by members, and better attitudes about the team. As might be expected, team building had larger effects on team members (skills and attitudes) than team performance because the focus of these interventions is individual members. Furthermore, interventions that were task oriented had larger effects than those that were interpersonally oriented, although both types of intervention were effective.

▶ CHAPTER SUMMARY

Much of the work done today in organizations is performed by work groups or work teams. Work groups are collections of individuals who interact at work and share interrelated task goals. Work teams are a type of work group, but the tasks of individual members are coordinated and interrelated; the team members have different roles; and the team has a common objective or task goal.

Four concepts relate to work groups. *Roles* distinguish the specific positions and functions of individuals in a group or team. *Norms* are group rules of behavior that in many groups are rigidly enforced. *Group cohesiveness* is the sum of forces holding the group together. Highly cohesive groups rigidly enforce their norms. *Team conflict* arises from disagreements and disputes among team members. *Competitive conflict* has detrimental effects, whereas *cooperative conflict* has positive effects on teams. *Process loss* is the time and effort that group members spend keeping the group operating rather than working on tasks. Two additional concepts are important for teams: *Team commitment* is the involvement members have in their team. *Team mental model* is the shared understanding team members have about the task and situation.

The presence of other people affects task performance. Simple or well-learned tasks are facilitated by the presence of others; complex or new tasks are inhibited by the presence of others. Group performance is often inferior to the combined performance of an equal number of individuals working alone. For additive tasks (the total performance is the sum of each individual's performance), the phenomenon of social loafing is that the larger the group, the less effort each individual expends.

Group polarization explains that, depending on the situation, group decisions can be riskier or more conservative than individual decisions. Groupthink occurs when highly talented decision makers are placed in decision groups and make bad decisions. Rapidly changing environments necessitate that teams innovate by adopting new ways of working. Finally, team KSAOs are characteristics of individuals that make them well suited to working effectively in teams.

Three interventions have the potential for improving group functioning and performance. Autonomous work teams are given the responsibility for entire jobs, such as assembling whole products like appliances and automobiles. Quality circles are groups of employees who meet periodically to come up with solutions to work problems. Team building is one of a number of interventions designed to improve the functioning of work teams.

I/O PSYCHOLOGY IN PRACTICE

(*Courtesy of Janis Cannon-Bowers*)

This case concerns a U.S. Navy team development training program created and carried out by Dr. Janis Cannon-Bowers. Dr. Cannon-Bowers received her Ph.D. in I/O psychology in 1988 from the University of South Florida. From her graduation until 2003, when she accepted a faculty position at the University of Central Florida, she worked at the Naval Air Warfare Center Training Systems Division in Orlando, Florida, where she held the title of Research Psychologist. Her major responsibility was to conduct research on team performance and training to develop new and more effective approaches. As a result of her research, she became involved in training naval officers in team development.

There were two naval tragedies in the late 1980s that led to a great deal of research into team performance. In 1987, the U.S.S. *Stark* was hit by an Iraqi missile, and in 1988 the U.S.S. *Vincennes* shot down an Iranian airliner. An investigation into the causes of both incidents revealed that poor teamwork was a major factor. This led to the U.S. Navy's effort to find ways to improve the performance of teams. Dr. Cannon-Bowers was part of this research effort, but her work also involved interventions aimed at improving team performance on navy ships.

Many different teams on combat ships carry out complex and dangerous functions, often under the severe stress of combat. Under such conditions, there is no time for group deliberation because all functions must be carried out quickly and efficiently, with life-and-death decisions being made in a matter of seconds. It is vitally important that teams are developed into well-functioning units that do their jobs efficiently. On a combat ship, it is the commanding officer (C.O.) who must see to it that the various teams develop into effective units. To do so, the C.O. must have skills in team development.

Dr. Cannon-Bowers and her colleagues designed a team development training program for C.O.s that she conducted at the U.S. Navy's Surface Warfare School. The program was intended to give the C.O.s insights into team functioning and sound training principles. It covers the ways to:

1. Give feedback
2. Accept criticism by subordinates
3. Create a climate for learning
4. Develop a "shared mental model" or common understanding of the team's functions
5. Avoid groupthink

The response to the training by the C.O.s was positive. They found the training program to be informative and useful. From the perspective of participant reaction criteria, it was successful. Whether this translates directly into better team performance on ships still needs to be determined, but initial results suggest that it does.

Discussion Questions

1. Do you think Dr. Cannon-Bowers's program will prove to be effective?
2. What steps could the U.S. Navy take to improve the team performance of ship personnel?
3. Is awareness of the causes of groupthink enough for team members to avoid it?
4. How would you go about giving feedback to subordinates if you were a ship's C.O.?

LEARNING BY DOING

Team Innovation

Find an individual (friend, acquaintance, or family member) who is a member of a work team. Ask him or her to relate a case in which his or her team adopted some new way of working (e.g., a new type of equipment or a new procedure). Ask the following questions.

1. What was the nature of the innovation?
2. What motivated the team to adopt the innovation?
3. Who suggested the innovation (i.e., team member, manager, or someone else)?
4. Were alternative innovations considered?
5. Was the original innovation idea modified to suit this particular team?

CHAPTER

13

Leadership and Power in Organizations

CHAPTER 13 OUTLINE

- WHAT IS LEADERSHIP?
- SOURCES OF INFLUENCE AND POWER
  - French and Raven's (1959) Bases of Power
  - Yukl's (1989) Sources of Political Power
  - Political Skill
- ABUSE OF SUPERVISORY POWER: SEXUAL AND ETHNIC HARASSMENT
- APPROACHES TO THE UNDERSTANDING OF LEADERSHIP
  - The Trait Approach
  - The Leader Behavior Approach
  - Fiedler's Contingency Theory
  - Path-Goal Theory
  - Leader-Member Exchange (LMX) Theory
  - Transformational Leadership Theory
  - Vroom-Yetton Model
- WOMEN IN LEADERSHIP POSITIONS
  - Gender and Leadership Style
- CROSS-CULTURAL ISSUES IN LEADERSHIP
- CHAPTER SUMMARY
- I/O PSYCHOLOGY IN PRACTICE
- LEARNING BY DOING

What makes a person a good leader? Was President Bill Clinton a good leader? During both of his terms, the media reported constant rumors and scandals. He was impeached, was sued for sexual harassment, and was the target of an ongoing criminal investigation through his entire presidency. His opponents attacked his character constantly, arguing that he was morally unfit for the job. Yet in the midst of serious charges of immoral behavior and perjury and an impeachment trial in the U.S. Senate, poll after poll found that the overwhelming majority (two-thirds) of Americans approved of his performance in office. The U.S. economy was the strongest in decades with the stock market breaking records, the federal budget was balanced, serious crime was on the decline, and welfare reform seemed to be successful. Were these signs of his effectiveness or merely coincidences? How would you go about determining how effective he was? Is good leadership a matter of character or a matter of being able to get important things done? Will the same person be a good leader in all situations? These are important questions to both government and nongovernment organizations. The answers tell us whom to choose as our leaders, and they tell leaders how they must act to be effective.

In this chapter, we deal with the important domain of leadership in organizations. We discuss the nature of leadership and how leaders influence followers. We summarize what is presently known about the personal characteristics that relate to good leadership performance and the effects of leader behavior on subordinates. We see how good leadership is the result of leader behavior, leader characteristics, and the leadership situation. Finally, we discuss women in leadership positions, and cross-cultural differences in leadership.

Objectives: The student who studies this chapter should be able to:

- Define leadership.
- Explain the five sources of power and three sources of political power.
- Summarize the major approaches and theories of leadership.
- Compare and contrast the major approaches and theories of leadership.
- Discuss how men and women compare on leadership.

WHAT IS LEADERSHIP?

You probably have an intuitive idea of what leadership is. A *leader* is the one in charge or the boss of other people. Just because you are in charge, however, does not mean that people will listen to you or do what you say. What at first seems simple is quite complex, as we discuss in this chapter. Leadership scholars have come up with many different definitions of leadership, and no one definition has been universally accepted (Yukl, 1989). A common idea that runs through various definitions is that leadership involves influencing the attitudes, beliefs, behaviors, and feelings of other people. Even nonleaders influence others, but leaders exert a disproportionate influence—that is, a leader is more influential than a nonleader.

Within an organization, leaders are often associated with supervisory positions; however, being a supervisor does not guarantee that you will be able to influence others. Furthermore, many leaders in organizations have no formal organizational title. Informal leaders often arise in work groups and may be more influential over the behavior of group members than the actual supervisors. Formal and informal leadership is an aspect of the formal and informal roles that we discussed in Chapter 12. An organization assigns the role of leader (e.g., manager or supervisor) to a person. An individual develops the informal leader role through interaction with colleagues. A person who is particularly skilled might find that others look to him or her for guidance, perhaps more so than to their own supervisors. The amount of influence a person has over others is determined by several personal and organizational factors, which we discuss next.

▶ SOURCES OF INFLUENCE AND POWER

French and Raven's (1959) Bases of Power

French and Raven (1959) described five bases of power one person has over another, such as a supervisor over a subordinate. **Power** is the extent to which one person can influence another to do something. The power bases listed in Table 13.1 involve both individual characteristics and organizational conditions, and they concern the relationship between leader and follower, or between supervisor and subordinate. Although bases of power are discussed as characteristics of the supervisor, power arises from the interaction between subordinate and supervisor. The supervisor makes an influence attempt, but it is the behavior of the subordinate that determines whether or not it is effective. Table 13.1 indicates how supervisors can use each power base.

Expert power is based on the knowledge and expertise that the supervisor has. A subordinate is likely to follow the directives of a person who he or she believes has special knowledge or expertise about the issue at hand. Note that it is the expertise the subordinate believes the supervisor has that is important rather than the actual expertise. Although actual expertise affects perceived expertise, some people are better than others at appearing to be experts. Titles (doctor), college degrees (Ph.D.), certifications (certified public accountant), and distinctions (Nobel Prize winner) can enhance the perceived expert power of an individual. Expert power can be particularly effective because the subordinate is likely to be convinced that the supervisor's directive is correct and should be followed.

Referent power is the extent to which the subordinate likes and identifies with the supervisor. A person is likely to be influenced by another whom he or she admires or likes. This source of power can be developed through personal relationships with other people. It can also be enhanced by raising the status of the supervisor. A person with celebrity status is likely to have a high level of referent power. Some corporate leaders have become national celebrities with referent power, such as Donald Trump.

Legitimate power is the power inherent in a supervisor's job title. It is derived from the subordinate's belief that the supervisor has the legitimate right or authority to be in charge. Much of the strength of this power derives from the subordinate's values

TABLE 13.1 The Five French and Raven Bases of Interpersonal Influence and Power and How They Can Be Used

Base	Use
Expert	Give information
Referent	Get subordinates to like you
Legitimate	Get a high-level position or rank
Reward	Give rewards for compliance
Coercive	Give punishments for noncompliance

Source: From "The Bases of Social Power" (pp. 150–167), by J. R. P. French, Jr., and B. Raven, 1959, in D. Cartwright (Ed.), *Studies in Social Power*, Ann Arbor, MI: Institute for Social Research.

about the rights of supervisors. If the subordinate refuses to recognize the authority of the supervisor, there will be no power in the supervisor's title.

Reward power is the ability of the supervisor to reward subordinates with bonuses, desirable job assignments, promotions, or raises. **Coercive power** is the ability of the supervisor to punish subordinates with disciplinary actions, fines, firing, or salary reductions. Organizations differ in the extent to which supervisors can give out punishments and rewards. In private companies, it is not unusual for a supervisor to be able to give raises and promotions to subordinates. In government organizations, an individual supervisor might not be able to do so because these rewards are determined by legislative action.

All five types of power can be effective if used properly. The major limitation of reward power is that subordinates might become accustomed to it and perform only when the reward is available. For example, salespeople on commission might be reluctant to do anything other than selling. Coercive power can have detrimental effects because subordinates might become angry and strike back, either directly or indirectly; for example, they might engage in counterproductive work behavior (see Chapter 10). Aguinis, Nesler, Quigley, Suk-Jae-Lee, and Tedeschi showed that the expert, referent, and reward bases of power are associated with good relationships between college professors and their students. On the other hand, coercive power is associated with poor relationships.

Yukl's (1989) Sources of Political Power

French and Raven's bases of power are concerned with the influences people have on one another in any setting. Yukl's (1989) sources of political power are concerned specifically with power in organizations. According to Yukl, *political action* is the process by which people gain and protect their power within the organization. He outlined three means by which political power is achieved and maintained in organizations (Figure 13.1).

Controlling decision processes involves controlling and influencing important decisions in the organization, such as the allocation of resources. This sort of power can be achieved by serving on appropriate committees (e.g., finance) or taking on the right tasks (preparation of the budget). Influence in the U.S. Congress is largely based on being on the most powerful House or Senate committees.

Forming coalitions means entering into agreements with others to support your position in return for your support of the others' position. Again, this is often seen in legislative bodies when different factions agree to support each other in favored positions.

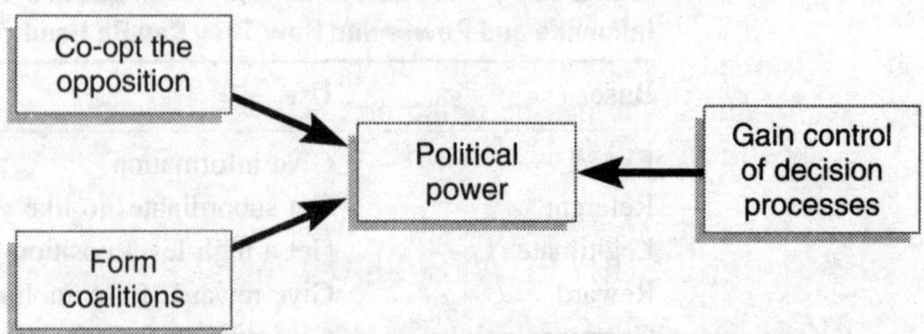

Figure 13.1 Yukl (1989) discussed how political power tactics can be a means of achieving political power in an organization. From *Leadership in Organizations*, by G. A. Yukl, 1989, Englewood Cliffs, NJ: Prentice Hall.

Senators who support an important issue such as expanding equal employment opportunity to other groups might agree to help those who support the issue of gun control in return for support of their issue.

Co-opting involves trying to diffuse another faction's opposition by allowing its members to participate in the decision. The hope is that this will make it difficult for them to remain in opposition. For example, a local government that wishes to take action to reduce the pollution produced by local industry is sure to run into opposition. A political approach to reducing or co-opting that opposition is to assign the task to a committee that includes industry representation—but not enough representation to determine the committee's actions.

This type of political action concerns how power is acquired and is different from the self-serving organizational politics discussed in Chapter 11. The sort of political actions discussed here can be used for good purposes and are quite common in both government and nongovernment organizations. Gaining influence in large organizations can be more a matter of achieving political rather than individual power. Even the president of the United States does not have the personal power to get laws enacted that might solve the nation's worst problems. Since Jimmy Carter, every U.S. president had campaigned on a promise to get Congress to pass a balanced federal budget. It wasn't until three administrations later that President Clinton was able to fulfill this promise.

Political Skill

If leadership is about influencing other people, then political skill is an important component. **Political skill** is the extent to which a person is able to influence others to engage in behavior that is beneficial to that person or to the organization (Zellars, Perrewe, Rossi, Tepper, & Ferris, 2008). Such skill can be used in a self-serving way, as we discussed in the Chapter 11 section on politics, but it also can be used to benefit others and the organization. Ferris and his colleagues (Ferris, Treadway, Kolodinsky, Hochwarter, Kacmar, Douglas, et al., 2005) have divided political skill into four dimensions. Social astuteness is the ability to understand people and social situations. This is not unlike emotional intelligence (see Chapter 5), but social astuteness does not involve just understanding emotions. Interpersonal influence is the skill of convincing other people to engage in the behavior desired or to accept a particular position. Networking ability involves developing relationships with a wide range of individuals and managing those relationships to accomplish objectives. Finally, apparent sincerity is the skill of appearing to be or really being honest, open, and trustworthy. Taken together, this suggests that the politically skilled understand social interactions, are able to influence others, can build networks of allies who can be relied on, and exude an aura of integrity. Research has shown that political skill in leaders does result in leader effectiveness (Ferris et al., 2005).

ABUSE OF SUPERVISORY POWER: SEXUAL AND ETHNIC HARASSMENT

When used appropriately, the various forms of power can provide tools to enhance the functioning of organizations. They can also be used to help individuals have positive feelings about work and perform their jobs well, but there is a potentially negative side to power. Some supervisors will use their power to mistreat subordinates. In some cases, the supervisor believes that punitive measures are necessary to get people to perform well; in other cases, the supervisor simply enjoys wielding power over others.

Supervisors who enjoy abusing others might do so in any number of ways. Employee harassment occurs when supervisors are free to demand that their subordinates do exactly what they are told, regardless of the appropriateness of their demands. Thus an individual might be required to do personal favors or be punished. Some supervisors use a harsh and punitive style and may belittle subordinates for even minor mistakes. This produces an intimidating and uncomfortable work environment for subordinates. Some supervisors might engage in sexual harassment by mistreating subordinates of a different gender or sexual orientation. Others might engage in ethnic harassment—the mistreatment of employees based on their ethnic or racial background (Bergman, Palmieri, Drasgow, & Ormerod, 2007; Schneider, Hitlan, & Radhakrishnan, 2000). Fox and Stallworth (2005) found that the most common forms of ethnic harassment include derogatory comments, ethnic jokes, and exclusion of the target person from employee interactions.

Perhaps the best-known form of power abuse is **sexual harassment**, which is behavior of a sexual nature that

Is unwanted

Can adversely affect a person's employment

Interferes with a person's job performance

Creates a hostile and intimidating work environment

The sorts of behaviors that comprise sexual harassment include

Unwelcome sexual advances and requests

Unwanted physical contact or touching

Use of offensive language

Repeated requests for a date

Threats of punishment for noncompliance with requests

Sexual harassment is illegal in the United States and many other countries. In the United States, it is covered by civil rights legislation and is considered a form of discrimination. Many cases have resulted in lawsuits, with companies having to pay damages to employees in excess of $100,000. Although sexual harassment is the act of an individual, organizations have been held accountable for the behaviors of their employees. Thus organizations are expected to prevent their supervisors and others from engaging in sexual harassment.

It is difficult to know exactly how widespread sexual harassment might be. Surveys in the United States (e.g., Schneider, Swan, & Fitzgerald, 1997) and elsewhere (Cho & Wilke, 2010) have asked men and women if they have encountered one or more instances of behavior that can be considered sexual harassment, such as crude comments or jokes or unwanted requests for a date. Ilies, Hauserman, Schwochau, and Stibal (2003) conducted a meta-analysis of 55 such studies and concluded that 58% of women reported experiencing these sorts of behaviors at work. One must be cautious in interpreting this to mean that a majority of women have been victims of sexual harassment (Fitzgerald, Drasgow,

Hulin, Gelfand, & Magley, 1997). Many of these behaviors become harassment only when they are unwanted and are repeated often enough to create a hostile or intimidating work environment. An isolated comment or simple request for a date is not harassment, so one should not interpret such surveys as indicating that a majority of women have been victims. In fact, Ilies et al. (2003) noted that fewer than half of those women who reported experiencing these behaviors felt they were actually harassed. It should be noted that although sexual harassment is often considered a woman's problem, recent studies have shown that men can also be targets (Berdahl & Moore, 2006).

Another issue is that people vary in the extent to which they perceive actions by supervisors and others to be harassment (Timmerman & Bajema, 2000). In other words, harassment is in the eye of the beholder—and in the attribution an employee makes about the intent and motives of the other person (Luthar & Pastille, 2000). For example, Wayne (2000) asked college students to read a real sexual harassment case, but she manipulated the gender and organizational level of the perpetrator and victim. The person was more likely to be judged to have harassed when the victim was of a higher level (e.g., supervisor) than a lower level (subordinate). Wayne argued that the perception of the situation is determined in part by whether or not the person's behavior is contrary to expectations. A certain degree of coerciveness is seen as expected in supervisors but not subordinates, and so for supervisors there may be a higher threshold for perceiving their behavior as sexual harassment.

Sexual and other forms of employee harassment are serious matters that organizations should attempt to control. They often reflect a general climate of abusiveness in which racial, sexual, and general harassment occurs together (Berdahl & Moore, 2006). When supervisors and other employees engage in certain forms of harassment, they can get their organizations into legal difficulties. The costs of legal problems, however, are probably quite small in comparison to the hidden costs to organizations. Sexual and ethnic harassment can be stressful, leading to job dissatisfaction, psychological strain, and physical strain (Lance, Dawson, Birkelbach, & Hoffman, 2010; Willness, Steel, & Lee, 2007). It should be kept in mind that actual cases of sexual harassment were not identified and that one cannot be certain from such cross-sectional surveys (see Chapter 2) that harassment is the cause of strain. It is possible that employees who are under strain are more likely to perceive situations as harassing. However, there is enough evidence from the study of various forms of employee mistreatment (see the discussion of social stressors in Chapter 11) to suggest that sexual harassment and other forms of abuse can have serious detrimental effects on people. Organization management would be wise to make efforts to safeguard its employees from victimization by supervisors as well as others who abuse their power.

▶ APPROACHES TO THE UNDERSTANDING OF LEADERSHIP

Many approaches to the study and understanding of leadership have been taken. The trait approach is concerned with determining the personal characteristics of good leaders. It asks the question

"Who will make a good leader?"

The behavior approach is concerned with finding out which leader behaviors are effective. It asks the question

"What do good leaders do?"

The contingency approach (Fiedler's and path-goal) assumes that good leadership is a function of the interplay of the person, his or her behavior, and the situation. It asks the question

"Under a given condition, who will be a good leader and what behavior is likely to be effective?"

The leader-member exchange theory and the charismatic/transformational approaches focus on the relationships between subordinates and supervisors. They ask the question

"How does the interaction between subordinate and supervisor affect the subordinate's behavior?"

All of these approaches have contributed to our understanding of leadership, and we discuss them in this section. We also cover the Vroom-Yetton model for deciding how to approach decision-making tasks in work groups.

The Trait Approach

The oldest approach to the study of leadership is the *trait approach*. It is based on the presumptions that some people make better leaders than others and that it is possible to determine the traits of good leaders. Some proponents of this approach would argue that good leadership is a function of the person and that a person who is a good leader in one situation would be a good leader in any situation. It would follow that various leaders, such as Alexander the Great, Winston Churchill, Martin Luther King Jr., and George Washington, could have been great leaders in other times and situations. This does not seem likely, however, since each man had different attributes and adopted a different approach to leadership that was appropriate to his circumstances.

Most of the research studies that have attempted to uncover the traits of good leaders have used one of two approaches. One approach used a methodology similar to employee selection studies, which were discussed in Chapter 6. A sample of leaders, often supervisors in an organization, is identified for study, and a criterion for leadership performance, typically job performance, is chosen. The supervisors are assessed on the criterion and on the personal traits of interest. These might include measures of various abilities, job experiences, motivation, and personality. Relationships between the personal characteristics and performance are interpreted as the effects of traits on leader performance.

Various studies have used many different measures of personal characteristics, as well as different measures of performance. Randle (1956), for example, assessed about 100 different traits of managers. Although many studies have used well-validated measures, many have used untested instruments developed for the particular study. Some of these measures were not of good quality, especially in early studies conducted before we fully understood some of the biases that affect psychological measurement. This has contributed to the inconsistency of results across studies in predicting leader performance. Nevertheless, research on manager performance has shown that personal traits such as cognitive ability can predict managerial performance (Hogan, Curphy, & Hogan, 1994).

The second approach is concerned with *leader emergence*—that is, who in a group will become the leader. These studies had groups of people work on a laboratory task, and the criterion was who became the leader of the group. The performance of the leader would not usually be assessed. It is possible that the personal characteristics that resulted in an individual's becoming the leader (for example, physical attractiveness) would not necessarily result in that person being a good leader.

It should come as no surprise that results across many of these studies are inconsistent. Some studies found that certain characteristics are associated with leader emergence and performance, whereas others did not. To make sense out of an inconsistent literature, Judge, Bono, Ilies, and Gerhardt (2002) conducted a meta-analysis to combine results across studies statistically. They found that effective and emergent leaders were high on the Big Five traits of emotional stability, extraversion, openness to experience, and conscientiousness.

The Leader Behavior Approach

The *leader behavior approach* is concerned with what leaders do rather than what their personal characteristics might be. Although leader behavior studies have dealt with specific behaviors, most have concentrated on leadership styles. A *leadership style* is a cluster of related behaviors that represent an approach to dealing with subordinates. For example, some supervisors prefer to allow subordinates to have input into decisions that affect them. Such a style of asking advice and having discussions about issues is called *participative.* Other supervisors do not involve subordinates in decisions. Rather, they make the decision and announce it to the group. This style in which subordinates are given little input is called *autocratic.*

The most influential research program to study leader behaviors is the Ohio State Leadership Studies, which were begun in 1945 (Stogdill, 1963). This series of studies was designed to uncover the effects of specific supervisory behaviors on subordinates. The Ohio State researchers began by collecting about 1,800 critical incidents that represented either very good or very bad instances of supervisory behavior. They used these incidents as the basis for developing a 150-item questionnaire on leader behavior. The questionnaire was administered to several samples of employees, who answered each item about their supervisors. A complex statistical procedure called *factor analysis* was used to see if the 150 items could be reduced to a smaller number of underlying dimensions of leadership. The dimensions, which were based on the intercorrelations among the 150 items, showed that two aspects of leadership were represented, which they called consideration and initiating structure.

Consideration is the amount of concern that supervisors show for the happiness and welfare of their subordinates. It includes friendly and supportive behavior that makes the workplace pleasant for subordinates. **Initiating structure** is the extent to which the supervisor defines his or her own role and makes clear what is expected of subordinates. It includes assigning tasks to subordinates and scheduling the work. One of the major contributions of the Ohio State Leadership Studies was the development of scales to assess these dimensions. The most widely used is the Leader Behavior Description Questionnaire

TABLE 13.2 Eight Items From the Consideration and Initiating Structure Scales of the Leader Behavior Description Questionnaire (LBDQ), Form XII

Consideration Items
He or she is friendly and approachable.
He or she does little things to make it pleasant to be a member of the group.
He or she puts suggestions made by the group into operation.
He or she treats all members of the group as his or her equals.
Initiating Structure Items
He or she lets group members know what is expected of them.
He or she encourages the use of uniform procedures.
He or she tries out his or her ideas in the group.
He or she makes his or her attitudes clear to the group.

Note: Items were modified to eliminate the generic "he."
Source: From *Manual for the Leader Behavior Description Questionnaire–Form XII*, by R. M. Stogdill, 1963, Columbus, OH: Ohio State University.

(LBDQ), which is completed by subordinates about their supervisor. Table 13.2 contains four items that assess consideration and four items that assess initiating structure.

Many studies have used the LBDQ in an attempt to discover the effects of leader behavior on subordinates. A good example is Fleishman and Harris's (1962) study of production workers in a truck manufacturing plant. Data were collected from subordinates of 57 supervisors with the LBDQ. The grievance and turnover rates were also collected for each supervisor's work group. Grievances can be considered behavioral measures of dissatisfaction with conditions of work. In unionized and government organizations, grievances require hearings that can consume considerable employee time. An excessive grievance rate can destroy the efficiency of a work group because people are spending time in unproductive ways.

Fleishman and Harris (1962) found that the mean LBDQ scores for the supervisors are related to the grievance and turnover rates in their departments. Supervisors with low scores on consideration and high scores on initiating structure had higher turnover rates and more grievances among subordinates than supervisors who were high on consideration and low on initiating structure. The supervisors scoring lowest on consideration had a turnover rate that was about four times higher than the supervisors scoring highest (Figures 13.2 and 13.3).

Although it is tempting to interpret these results as a demonstration of the effects of leader behavior on important subordinate behaviors, there are two major difficulties in doing so. First, the LBDQ might not be a good indicator of supervisory behavior and might be telling us as much about subordinates as their supervisors. Several studies have attempted to find out what subordinate reports about their supervisors really mean. It has been found that the reports are affected by the biases and stereotypes of the subordinates. In a series of studies, college students were asked to view a videotape of a supervisor interacting with subordinates. At random, all subjects who watched the same tape were told that the supervisor was rated either high or low in performance. Subjects who were

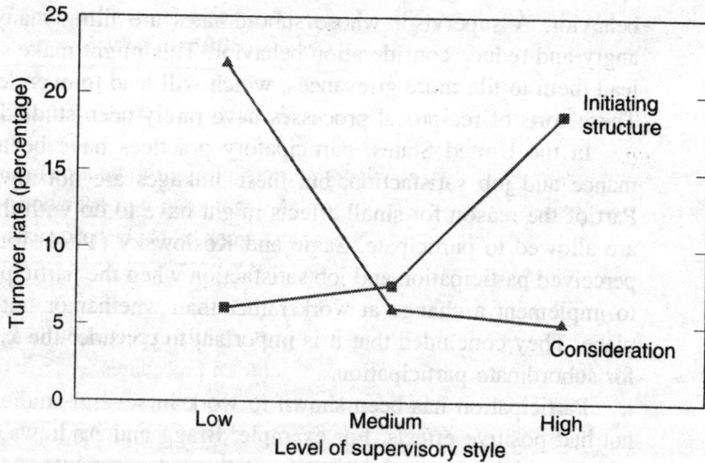

Figure 13.2 Turnover rate as a result of both the consideration and the initiating structure of supervisors. From "Patterns of Leadership Behavior Related to Employee Grievances and Turnover," by E. A. Fleishman and E. F. Harris, 1962, *Personnel Psychology, 15,* 43–56.

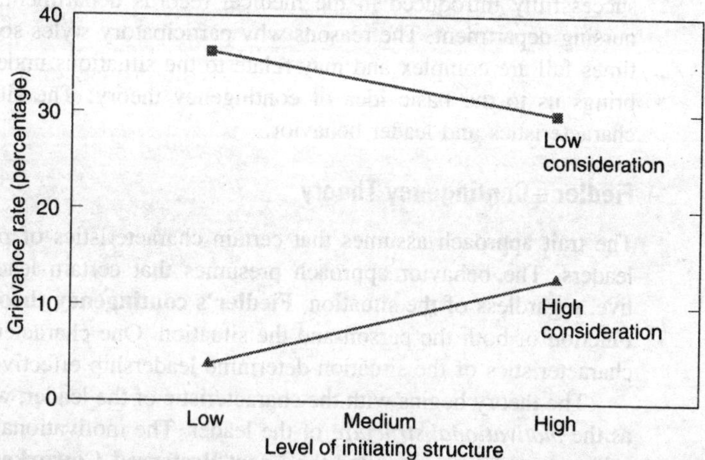

Figure 13.3 Grievance rate as a result of both the consideration and the initiating structure of supervisors. From "Patterns of Leadership Behavior Related to Employee Grievances and Turnover," by E. A. Fleishman and E. F. Harris, 1962, *Personnel Psychology, 15,* 43–56.

told that the supervisor was a good performer rated him differently on the LBDQ than subjects who were told he was a poor performer (Lord, Binning, Rush, & Thomas, 1978).

The second problem concerns drawing causal conclusions from data collected at one time in a cross-sectional research design (see Chapter 2). We cannot be certain from a study such as Fleishman and Harris's (1962) if the grievance and turnover rates are caused by supervisor behavior or if supervisor behavior is caused by the grievance and turnover rate. Studies have shown that supervisor behavior can be affected by subordinate behavior (Lowin & Craig, 1968), particularly job performance. Yukl (1989) concluded that a reciprocal relationship probably exists between supervisor style and subordinate behavior. A supervisor whose subordinates are filing many grievances might become angry and reduce consideration behavior. This might make subordinates more angry and lead them to file more grievances, which will lead to even less consideration, and so on. These sorts of reciprocal processes have rarely been studied in I/O psychology.

In the United States, participatory practices have been linked to both job performance and job satisfaction, but these linkages are not always strong (Wagner, 1994). Part of the reason for small effects might have to do with the areas in which employees are allowed to participate. Sagie and Koslowsky (1994) found larger relations between perceived participation and job satisfaction when the participation involved deciding how to implement a change at work rather than whether or not to implement it in the first place. They concluded that it is important to consider the kinds of decisions appropriate for subordinate participation.

Participation has been shown to work in several studies. In others, however, it has not had positive effects. For example, Bragg and Andrews (1973) conducted a study in which participants worked in two of three departments. At the beginning of the study, the supervisor of the hospital laundry department changed from an autocratic to a participative style. Over the next 18 months, there were positive effects on attendance, job performance (a 42% increase), and job satisfaction. This supervisory approach was then successfully introduced in the medical records department, but it could not be in the nursing department. The reasons why participatory styles sometimes succeed and sometimes fail are complex and may relate to the situations under which they are tried. This brings us to the basic idea of contingency theory: The situation interacts with leader characteristics and leader behavior.

Fiedler's Contingency Theory

The trait approach assumes that certain characteristics of people will make them good leaders. The behavior approach presumes that certain leader behaviors will be effective, regardless of the situation. **Fiedler's contingency theory** states that leadership is a function of both the person and the situation. One characteristic of the leader and three characteristics of the situation determine leadership effectiveness.

The theory begins with the characteristic of the leader, which Fiedler (1978) refers to as the *motivational structure* of the leader. The motivational structure is assessed with a self-report instrument called the **Least Preferred Coworker (LPC) scale**. Although the name implies that it assesses the coworker, the scale actually measures a characteristic of the leader, not the subordinate. The LPC asks the leader to think about the person with whom he or she has had the most trouble working—that is, the coworker with whom he or she would least like to work. The leader then describes his or her least preferred coworker using a semantic differential scale (Osgood, Teannenbaum, & Suci, 1957). The LPC consists of 18 bipolar adjective items, and for each item the leader indicates which of the two words with opposite meanings best describes someone, such as pleasant versus unpleasant or friendly versus unfriendly. (Examples from the LPC scale appear in Table 13.3.)

Fiedler's (1978) theory is also concerned with the situational variable of leader situational control. *Situational control* concerns the amount of power and influence the leader has over subordinates. It is the extent to which the supervisor's actions will predictably lead to subordinate behavior. There are three characteristics of the leadership

TABLE 13.3 Four Items From Fiedler's Least Preferred Coworker Scale (LPC)

Pleasant	___	___	___	___	___	___	___	___	Unpleasant
Friendly	___	___	___	___	___	___	___	___	Unfriendly
Rejecting	___	___	___	___	___	___	___	___	Accepting
Tense	___	___	___	___	___	___	___	___	Relaxed

Source: From "The Contingency Model and the Dynamics of the Leadership Process" (pp. 59–112), by F. E. Fiedler, 1978, in L. Berkowitz (Ed.), *Advances in Experimental Social Psychology* (Vol. 11), New York, NY: Academic Press.

situation that comprise situational control: *Leader-member relations* is the extent to which subordinates get along with and support their supervisors. *Task structure* is the extent to which subordinate job tasks are clearly and specifically defined. *Position power* refers to the amount of power and influence that the supervisor has, including the ability to give out rewards and punishments. A supervisor with good leader-member relations, highly structured tasks for subordinates, and high position power will be in a situation of high control. A supervisor with poor leader-member relations, low task structure for subordinates, and low position power will be in a situation of low control.

According to Fiedler's (1978) theory, the LPC of the supervisor determines the situations in which he or she will perform well. Individuals who are low on LPC do well under both very high and very low situational control. Individuals who are high on LPC will do best under conditions of moderate situational control. Take, for example, the situation in which the leader doesn't get along well with subordinates, the subordinates have unstructured tasks, and the leader has little power. This is an unfavorable situation, and the low LPC leader would be expected to be more effective than the high LPC leader. However, if the situation is moderately favorable, where relations are poor, but task structure is high and the leader has moderate power, the high LPC person should be more effective than the low LPC person. Figure 13.4 illustrates how supervisor performance is a function of situational control for individuals high and low in LPC.

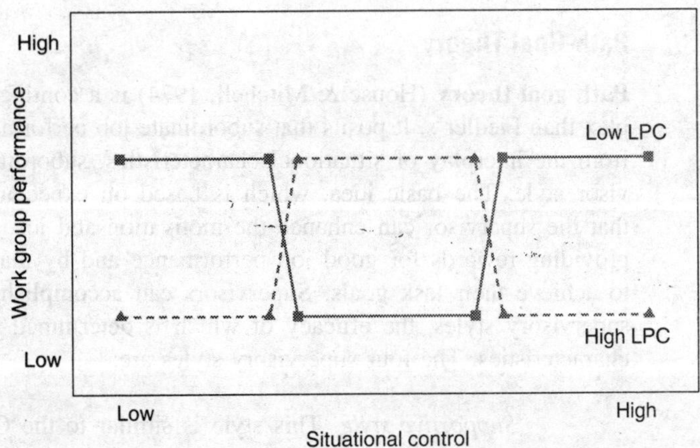

Figure 13.4 Group performance as a result of both the situational control and the LPC of the leader. Adapted from "The Contingency Model and the Dynamics of the Leadership Process," by F. E. Fiedler, 1978, in L. Berkowitz (Ed.), *Advances in Experimental Social Psychology* (Vol. 11), New York, NY: Academic Press.

Research on contingency theory has provided mixed support for its validity, and Fiedler certainly has his critics. Two meta-analyses combined the results of many tests of the theory (Peters, Hartke, & Pohlmann, 1985; Strube & Garcia, 1981). Both found that leader performance was a joint function of LPC and situational control, although the predictions of the theory were not completely upheld. What is not clear at the present time is exactly why LPC and situational control interact. The major difficulty is that no one, not even Fiedler, is quite sure what LPC represents. LPC was intended to measure something about leader motivation, but it is not clear that motivation is assessed. Fiedler (1978) states that low LPC leaders are more concerned with getting tasks done than with having good relationships with subordinates, whereas high LPC leaders have the opposite motivations, being more concerned with having good relationships with subordinates than with getting the job done. At this time, all we can say for sure is that the LPC assesses some unknown but important characteristic of leaders.

Although the theory states that the situation determines the best leader characteristics, Fiedler (1978) does not believe that a supervisor should attempt to adapt his or her style to the particular situation. He believes that supervisors should modify the situation to be appropriate to their own leadership style. To this end, he has developed a training program called **Leader Match**. Fiedler summarized the results of several field experiments comparing Leader Match–trained supervisors with untrained controls. The results showed better group performance for the trained supervisors. Some question has been raised, however, about whether Leader Match training results in leaders changing the situation according to theory or whether the results of the Leader Match research are due to other factors (Jago & Ragan, 1986).

Despite the criticisms of the theory, Fiedler has been one of the most influential people in the study of leadership. His major contribution has been to show us that leadership involves the complex interaction of leader characteristics with the leadership situation. His work has been extended by theorists who have developed more complex contingency theories. One of these is path-goal theory, which we discuss next.

Path-Goal Theory

Path-goal theory (House & Mitchell, 1974) is a contingency theory that is more complex than Fiedler's. It posits that subordinate job performance and job satisfaction result from the interplay of situational characteristics, subordinate characteristics, and supervisor style. The basic idea, which is based on expectancy theory (see Chapter 8), is that the supervisor can enhance the motivation and job satisfaction of subordinates by providing rewards for good job performance and by making it easier for subordinates to achieve their task goals. Supervisors can accomplish this by adopting one of four supervisory styles, the efficacy of which is determined by situational and subordinate characteristics. The four supervisory styles are:

Supportive style. This style is similar to the Ohio State Leadership Studies' style of consideration. It involves showing concern for the needs and welfare of subordinates.

Directive style. This style is similar to the Ohio State Leadership Studies' style of initiating structure. It involves structuring job tasks for subordinates and letting them know what is expected.

Participative style. This style involves seeking input from subordinates and allowing them to participate in decision making.

Achievement style. This style involves emphasizing achievement and good performance. It includes setting challenging task goals and emphasizing high performance standards.

Subordinate characteristics include personality variables, such as locus of control and self-perceived ability. Locus of control is the extent to which subordinates believe that they can control rewards in their lives. A person with an internal locus of control believes that he or she is able to control rewards. A person with an external locus of control believes that rewards are controlled by others or by outside forces. Self-perceived ability is the extent to which the subordinate believes he or she is capable of doing the task well. It is similar to self-efficacy, which was discussed in Chapter 8, but it is specific to the particular task at hand. Situational characteristics include aspects of tasks, such as dangerousness, repetitiveness, and structure.

House and Mitchell (1974) derived a series of hypotheses based on the basic ideas of the theory. These hypotheses describe how certain supervisory styles affect subordinates under certain conditions. For example:

1. When tasks are boring, dangerous, stressful, or tedious, a supportive style will be the most appropriate. Subordinates who must deal with these situations will have their anxiety lowered and their self-esteem raised by a supportive supervisor.
2. When tasks are unstructured and subordinates are inexperienced, a directive style will be most appropriate because subordinates will be uncertain about what to do. A directive supervisor will increase subordinates' effort and job satisfaction by telling them what is expected and what they should do.

Unfortunately researchers have focused attention on only a few of the hypotheses of path-goal theory, particularly the second hypothesis given here. Although some of this research has supported the theory (Podsakoff, MacKenzie, Ahearne, & Bommer, 1995), many of the findings are inconsistent (Wofford & Liska, 1993). In part, the inconsistency may be due to methodological weaknesses in some of the studies. Another possibility is that some of the propositions are not quite correct.

Keller (1989) noted that not all individuals are bothered by lack of structure on a job and that in fact some people might prefer it. People who prefer unstructured tasks should be more satisfied with a low-structure job and would respond negatively to a directive supervisory style. Samples of employees from four organizations were assessed on subordinate need for structure, job performance, job satisfaction, and directive supervisory style (Keller, 1989). The results are consistent with predictions that subordinates who have a high need for structure respond favorably to directive supervision (see the International Research box). Keller's study suggests that one of the propositions should be modified to take subordinate personality into account.

INTERNATIONAL RESEARCH

One of the hypotheses of path-goal theory is that when task structure is low, initiating structure by the supervisor will result in subordinate satisfaction. In other words, when subordinates are unsure about what is expected, clarification by the supervisor will be appreciated. Keller (1989) noted that research support for this hypothesis has been inconsistent across studies. He reasoned that a mistake of path-goal theory is assuming that all employees find lack of structure unpleasant. His hypothesis is that the subordinate's need for clarity determines his or her reaction to initiating structure in a job with low structure.

In this study, a survey was conducted among professionals in research and development (R&D) organizations. Because this work involves discovering new knowledge and technologies, an R&D job can have little structure. Respondents to the survey completed scales to assess the extent to which they need and prefer clarity on the job, the initiating structure of their supervisor, and their job satisfaction.

Data analyses showed that Keller's hypothesis is correct. Those individuals with a high need for clarity are more satisfied with high-initiating structure than low-initiating structure. Individuals with a low need for clarity are more satisfied with low-initiating structure than high-initiating structure. This study suggests that supervisors should consider the personality of each subordinate in deciding the most appropriate supervision method.

Source: From "A Test of the Path-Goal Theory of Leadership With Need for Clarity as a Moderator in Research and Development Organizations," by R. T. Keller, 1989, *Journal of Applied Psychology, 74,* 208–212.

Future research will be needed to show which of the original House and Mitchell (1974) hypotheses can be supported. It seems likely, in light of Keller's (1989) findings, that new hypotheses involving the interplay of situations, subordinates, and supervisors will be developed. One implication of Keller's findings is that different supervisory approaches might be necessary with different subordinates. This brings us to the leader-member exchange theory of leadership, which is concerned with the interactions of each subordinate-supervisor dyad or pair.

Leader-Member Exchange (LMX) Theory

The **leader-member exchange (LMX) theory** (Dansereau, Graen, & Haga, 1975) focuses on the subordinate-supervisor dyad rather than on the supervisor and work group. Dansereau et al. argued that one of the major limitations of most leadership research is its implicit assumptions that each supervisor's group of subordinates is sufficiently homogeneous to justify studying it as a unit and that each supervisor adopts the same style across all subordinates. On the contrary, they propose that supervisors treat individual subordinates differently.

Dansereau et al. (1975) discussed two types of relationships that develop between supervisors and subordinates. The **cadre** or **in-group** consists of subordinates who are trusted and influential members of the work group. The supervisor treats them with consideration and adopts a participative style with them. The **hired hands** or **out-group**, by contrast, is subordinates who are supervised with a directive style and are given little input into decisions. These relationships evolve over time, with characteristics of subordinates affecting the category in which they find themselves. To become part of the cadre, a subordinate must be perceived as dependable and hardworking. In return for cadre status, a subordinate must be prepared to exert effort on the job beyond the minimum expected.

In their research, Dansereau et al. (1975) found that within work groups supervisors had two distinct groups in terms of how much participation was allowed. Members of the cadre were more satisfied with their jobs, believed they had better relationships with supervisors, and were less likely to quit than the hired hands. Care must be taken, however, in concluding that the satisfaction and turnover differences were the result of supervisor treatment. It is likely that supervisor behavior toward each subordinate was as much a function of the subordinate's job performance as it was a cause of that performance (Bauer & Green, 1996).

One contribution of the leader-member exchange approach is that it focuses attention on the importance of individual relationships within each supervisor-subordinate dyad. The idea was the basis of an intervention study in which supervisors were trained to enhance their relationships with each subordinate. Graen, Novak, and Sommerkamp (1982) conducted a field experiment in which one group of supervisors was trained in leader-member exchange. The training was intended to help supervisors improve their relationships with subordinates. Each trained supervisor had meetings with individual subordinates to discuss work issues and the working relationship between them. The subordinates of the trained supervisors subsequently had better job performance and higher job satisfaction than a control group in which supervisors were not trained.

Research has shown that the quality of LMX relationships, as perceived by subordinates, is associated with several important work variables. For example, subordinates who report good LMX relationships with their supervisors are rated higher in job performance and organizational citizenship behavior by those supervisors than are subordinates who report poor LMX relationships (Petruzzello, Gapin, Snook, & Smith, 2009; Radloff, 1977; Vidyarthi, Liden, Anand, Erdogan, & Ghosh, 2010). In their meta-analysis of 79 studies, Gerstner and Day (1997) showed that individuals who have good relationships with their supervisors tend to have higher job satisfaction, are more committed to their employers, and perceive the job as less stressful than individuals with poor relationships with supervisors. Taken together, these studies suggest that good relationships between supervisor and subordinate are important because they benefit employees and organizations.

There have been criticisms and limitations noted about the LMX theory of leadership. First, differential treatment of subordinates within a work group can be destructive (Yukl, 1989). Equity theory, as discussed in Chapter 8, describes how employees can react negatively to unequal treatment. The higher turnover rate and lower job satisfaction of the hired hands in the Dansereau et al. (1975) study might well be interpreted as a response to inequity. Schriesheim (1980) pointed out that supervisors often direct influence attempts at entire work groups at one time rather than treating each individual differently. She believed that a focus on both work groups and individual dyads makes the most sense for understanding leadership. LMX theory has helped focus attention on the relationship between subordinate and supervisor. It also has led to an understanding that supervisors do not act the same way with all subordinates.

Transformational Leadership Theory

Transformational leadership theory deals with leaders who have considerable and unusual influence over their followers; in other words, they are **charismatic leaders**. It is in some ways a return to the trait approach because it focuses on characteristics of leaders in relation to effectiveness. However, it differs from prior approaches in going beyond linking traits to performance and in attempting to determine how leaders affect their followers. A **transformational leader** is one who leads by inspiring others to adopt high goals and strive to achieve them. He or she articulates a vision for followers and encourages them to pursue it. Gardner and Avolio (1998) explained that certain leaders are able to convince followers of their competence and the importance of a vision. They engage in behaviors that make them appear to be creative, innovative, powerful, and trustworthy. Much of the leader's influence derives from beliefs by followers that only by following the leader will they be able to achieve the vision, such as making the company profitable. Leaders like Abraham Lincoln, Winston Churchill, John F. Kennedy, and Martin Luther King, Jr., are examples of transformational leaders. King's vision of a free society reflected in his "I have a dream" speech on August 28, 1963, in Washington, D.C., is an example of a vision statement that inspires.

Bass and Riggio (2006) argued that transformational leadership has four components. Idealized influence is the extent to which leaders encourage followers with their statements and model high standards of behavior. Inspirational motivation is providing a vision, such as King's dream. Intellectual stimulation is encouraging followers to question the status quo and think of better ways to do things. Individualized consideration is paying attention to the development and well-being of followers. Taken together, this suggests that transformational leaders inspire by articulating a vision for the group, encouraging and supporting followers, and setting an example to follow.

Research on transformational leadership shows that it relates to several subordinate variables that are important for organizational functioning. For example, individuals who perceive their supervisors to be transformational tend to be high on job performance (Keller, 2006; Yang, Spector, Chang, Gallant-Roman, & Powell, 2010), job satisfaction (Judge & Piccolo, 2004), organizational citizenship behavior, organizational commitment,

Dr. Martin Luther King, Jr. (left) and President John F. Kennedy (right) were charismatic leaders who championed civil rights in the United States. (© *Bettmann/CORBIS*)

and perceptions of justice (Pillai, Schriesheim, & Williams, 1999). Furthermore, although it might seem that transformational leadership is innate, researchers have been successful at training people to exhibit the behaviors. For example, Towler (2003) conducted a laboratory experiment in which business students were randomly assigned to receive transformational training versus control training. They subsequently delivered a role-play speech to a supposed group of employees. Those who received the transformational training were rated by trained observers to be higher on transformational leadership than the controls. Barling, Weber, and Kelloway (1996) were able to successfully train bank managers to be more transformational and showed that this training had an impact on the financial performance of their branches.

Existing studies are quite suggestive that transformational leadership has considerable potential for application. If transformational leaders have more productive and satisfied subordinates and if such leadership can be taught, organizations would benefit by encouraging supervisors to adopt this approach. More studies like Barling et al. (1996) are needed to confirm their promising results.

Vroom-Yetton Model

The **Vroom-Yetton model** (Vroom & Yetton, 1973) is a different kind of leadership theory from the theories we have discussed so far. Rather than describing how the leadership process works, Vroom-Yetton is a prescriptive model that indicates the supervisory approach that is expected to be most effective in a particular situation when making decisions. Note that Vroom-Yetton is designed only for decision making and not for other aspects of supervisor behavior, such as generating solutions to problems and directing the activities of subordinates. The model is based on psychological principles that can help inform the best decision-making practices based on characteristics of a particular situation. A manager can use the model to help choose the way to handle each situation in which a decision must be made.

The model specifies the following five approaches to making a decision, which range from the autocratic to democratic:

1. Supervisor makes the decision alone.
2. Supervisor gets information from subordinates and makes the decision alone.
3. Supervisor discusses the problem with some subordinates and then makes the decision.
4. Supervisor discusses the problem with all subordinates in a meeting and makes the decision.
5. Supervisor presents the problem to all subordinates in a meeting and lets them decide.

As you can see, the supervisor can act independently (approach 1), turn over the problem to the group (approach 5), or adopt various stages of sharing the decision from merely soliciting information (approach 2) to actually discussing the problem and considering others' viewpoints (approach 3 or 4).

The decision-making situation is defined by seven characteristics that address the problem itself and the subordinates:

1. Quality requirement for the result (is it important to make the right decision?).
2. Sufficiency of information the supervisor has.
3. Problem structure (is it clear what has to be done or is the situation ambiguous?).
4. Necessity for subordinate acceptance of the decision.
5. Likelihood of subordinate acceptance of the decision if made by the supervisor alone.
6. Subordinate commitment to solving the problem.
7. Subordinate conflict over solutions.

Each of the characteristics is translated into a yes/no question (e.g., "Is the problem structured?"). The pattern of answers determines the best practice. For example, if quality isn't important (characteristic 1), acceptance by subordinates is important (characteristic 4), and subordinates are unlikely to accept a decision made unilaterally by the supervisor (characteristic 5), the best approach is to allow the subordinates to make the decision. On the other hand, if quality is not an issue and if acceptance isn't important, any of the five approaches should be equally effective. In most cases, the more democratic approaches are appropriate, and it is only in limited situations that being autocratic can be effective.

Vroom and Yetton (1973) provided decision tools based on their model that can be used by managers to help choose a decision-making approach. The specific approach recommended depends on whether you wish to minimize the time necessary for a decision or maximize the likelihood of group acceptance of the decision. Not surprisingly, making a decision yourself can often be the quickest approach, but it isn't necessarily the most effective. There are paper-and-pencil materials (tables and decision trees) that one can use to follow the answers to all seven questions to the recommended decision-making approaches. They also have developed computer software that displays the questions, allows you to enter answers, and then provides advice about how to approach the situation.

A limited number of studies have tested the Vroom-Yetton model. For the most part, the findings support the recommendations of the theory. Vroom and Jago (1988) compiled results across six studies that compared the effectiveness of decisions that conformed with the theory's advice with those that failed to conform. The success rate for decisions made in accordance with the theory was higher than for decisions made in violation of it—62% versus 37%, respectively. On the other hand, Field and House (1990) provided only mixed support for the theory. They had a sample of supervisors and their subordinates report on the process and effectiveness of a decision. Although the supervisor data supported the Vroom-Yetton model, the subordinate data did not. Field and House were hesitant to conclude that the theory was invalid and called for additional research to test it.

The Vroom-Yetton model has the potential to be the most useful of the leadership theories from the perspective of the practicing manager who wishes to use the latest findings to guide his or her supervisory approach. This theory offers very specific advice about how to supervise, whereas the other theories provide principles that one would have to figure out how to apply. After working with the Vroom-Yetton model for awhile, a manager will likely learn the underlying principles, making it unnecessary to consult a table or software each time a new decision situation in encountered. At the present time, the research findings have been promising, but too few studies have been conducted in field settings to test whether or not following the theory leads to better decision outcomes, in terms of either decision quality or decision speed.

WOMEN IN LEADERSHIP POSITIONS

Women have made considerable strides in achieving management and supervisory positions in organizations throughout most of the world. It was estimated that by 1999 about 46% of all management jobs in the United States were held by women. Despite their success at the lower levels of management, American women are still underrepresented at the higher levels of organizations. Their numbers, however, have been increasing, with more than 15% of top corporate management positions being held by women by 2002 (Northhouse, 2004). One study of MBA graduates' career progression found that men had higher starting salaries and that their salaries went up more quickly with age than did women's (Goldberg, Finkelstein, Perry, & Konrad, 2004). However, it is unclear how typical these results might be, as another study of high-level executives in a financial services corporation found little difference between men's and women's compensation (Lyness & Thompson, 1997). Perhaps some industries have made progress in equating men's and women's salary progressions, whereas others are lagging behind.

What do these two women have in common? They were both leaders of their countries. Although the United States has never had a woman as president, other countries have had female leaders. Both Golda Meir of Israel (left) and Margaret Thatcher of the United Kingdom (right) were prime ministers of their countries. (© *Bettmann/CORBIS*)

Although women have more difficulty than men achieving high-level positions in most organizations, this problem is not found in all organizations. Powell and Butterfield (1994) found that females who applied for promotion were more (not less) likely than men to be promoted to top management in the U.S. civil service. In part, the gender difference was attributed to better job performance by the female applicants. The lack of bias against women may have been due to fairer promotion practices and commitment to equal employment opportunity in U.S. government agencies.

Many explanations have been advanced for the **glass ceiling** phenomenon that symbolizes women's difficulty in getting beyond the lower levels of management. Some of these explanations have focused on differences between men and women in their career preparation and their attitudes, whereas others are concerned with bias against women as high-level managers. For example, in a Dutch study van Vianen and Fischer (2002) found that women were less ambitious, cared less about salary and status, and were more concerned with work-family conflict than men. These factors may explain why fewer women might seek promotions to higher management, but it doesn't explain why those who wish to achieve higher levels have a more difficult time doing so.

The bias explanation has to do with the attitudes and stereotypes of those at the top levels of organizations who make decisions about hiring. Research by Schein and colleagues (Schein, Mueller, Lituchy, & Liu, 1996) demonstrated how subtle stereotypes about characteristics of men and women put women at a disadvantage for management selection. They asked people to describe the characteristics of managers, men, and women and found that the descriptions of managers overlapped with descriptions of men but not with descriptions of women. It was concluded that the reason a woman might have difficulty getting promoted is that she is not seen as having the characteristics necessary for the position. It is not that the decision maker is consciously discriminating against women. Rather, the male candidates seem to fit the requirements for the job better than the female candidates. According to this view, equal access to high-level management jobs will require attitude change on the part of those who do the hiring. Furthermore, this phenomenon seems to be universal, for they found similar results in China, Germany, Japan, the United Kingdom, and the United States.

On the other hand, bias on the part of decision makers is unlikely to be a complete explanation either. Lyness and Thompson (2000) surveyed matched samples of middle- to upper-level male and female managers about their career progression. They found that women are more likely than men to report feeling they don't fit in with colleagues. Whether this reflects that women have a harder time adapting to management ranks, are finding colleagues and supervisors less accepting of them, or merely perceive less fit is unclear. However, even if it is just perception, feeling out of place would be likely to affect confidence and behavior in a way that might adversely affect career progression.

Powell and Butterfield (1994) suggested that the U.S. federal government may be a model of how to eliminate the glass ceiling. Important factors include a strong management commitment to equal employment opportunity and uniform selection procedures that reduce subjectivity in decisions.

Gender and Leadership Style

Do men and women in leadership positions differ in their supervisory styles? Our stereotypes of men and women suggest that women would be more concerned with the feelings and emotional well-being of subordinates (consideration) and men would be more concerned with getting the job done (initiating structure). Research on gender differences in leadership suggests that the answer is complex.

Eagly and Johnson (1990) conducted a meta-analysis of studies that compared the leadership styles of men and women. They combined the results of over 160 leadership studies and arrived at several conclusions. One is that the stereotypic styles of men being high in structure and women being high in consideration have been found in laboratory research with students but not in field studies with actual leaders. They had two explanations for this finding. First, in an organizational setting, there are environmental constraints and requirements that may force male and female supervisors to adopt similar styles. Second, organizations may select women who have leadership styles similar to men's. In laboratory studies, subjects are selected more randomly, and there are fewer constraints on the leader behaviors that the participants adopt. Thus whereas females may be inclined to supervise differently than men do, organizational settings do not allow them to express that inclination.

On the other hand, when men and women are compared on their autocratic or democratic tendencies, gender differences are found in both the laboratory and the field. Men have been found to be more autocratic and women more democratic in their styles. Eagly and Johnson (1990) pointed out that each style will probably be more effective under different organizational circumstances. They noted that research is needed to determine whether there are gender differences in actual supervisory performance.

Men and women have also been compared in the extent to which their subordinates see them as transformational. Bass, Avolio, and Atwater (1996) found, based on three samples, that women were either the same as or higher than men on transformational leadership. Unfortunately their study does not permit conclusions about effectiveness. Nevertheless, it suggests that there are gender differences in leadership style.

▶ CROSS-CULTURAL ISSUES IN LEADERSHIP

It would be a mistake to assume that all of the findings and theories discussed in this chapter apply universally to all countries and cultures. How leaders are viewed and what might be effective are not necessarily the same across all countries. For example, the attributes associated with good leadership can be culturally determined. The most comprehensive study of this issue is the 62-country Global Leadership and Organizational Effectiveness (Project GLOBE) Research Program (House, Hanges, Ruiz-Quintanilla, Dorfman, Javidan, Dickson, et al., 1999). One of the findings of GLOBE is that there are many specific attributes of managers that are universal but there are others that vary across countries. For example, being intelligent and being trustworthy are universally seen as positive characteristics. However, being individualistic (focusing on self rather than others) and being willing to take risks are seen as more positive in some countries than in others.

Similarly, Ensari and Murphy (2003) asked students from a collectivist country (Turkey) and an individualist country (United States) to read descriptions of managers that vary in their behavior and in their performance and then to rate how transformational the leader is. The Turkish students' ratings were influenced most by the performance of the managers, whereas the American students focused mainly on behaviors. To the extent that perceptions of transformational leadership affect employee attitudes and behavior, this suggests that the specific behaviors of managers are more important in the United States than Turkey, where results are paramount. Of course, this needs to be replicated in an organizational setting with practicing managers.

Another important issue concerns cultural differences in the effectiveness of different leader behaviors. Scandura, Von Glinow, and Lowe (1999) investigated this issue by comparing employees from the United States with those in the Middle Eastern countries of Jordan and Saudi Arabia (see the International Research box). They found that consideration is more strongly related to leadership effectiveness than initiating structure in the United States but that the opposite was true in the Middle East. This suggests that using American approaches in another country that is culturally dissimilar may not be effective.

INTERNATIONAL RESEARCH

It has generally been well established that certain supervisory styles are more effective than others. It is unclear, however, whether the same styles will be universally effective in countries with different cultural practices. Scandura, Von Glinow and Lowe (1999) conducted a study comparing leadership styles in the United States with those in the Middle East. The authors felt that the cultural differences between these two areas would result in different styles as being effective.

Surveys were administered to 144 employees from the United States, 47 from Jordan, and 60 from Saudi Arabia. Data from both Middle Eastern countries were combined. Scales included the Leader Behavior Description Questionnaire (LBDQ), which assessed consideration and initiating structure, global job satisfaction, and perceived effectiveness of the supervisor. The Middle East survey was translated into Arabic.

In the U.S. sample, consideration correlates more strongly than initiating structure with job satisfaction (.61 vs. .20, respectively) and perceived effectiveness (.65 vs. .30, respectively). The Middle East sample shows the opposite pattern: Consideration correlates less strongly than initiating structure with job satisfaction (.22 vs. .38, respectively) and perceived effectiveness (.25 vs. .34, respectively). Furthermore, neither of these styles correlates as strongly with job satisfaction or effectiveness in the Middle East as consideration did in the United States.

These findings suggest that consideration is more important to Americans than to Middle Easterners. As Scandura et al. pointed out, the Arabic view of leadership tends to be far more militaristic than the American view. Thus the Arabic view of a leader is someone more autocratic and task oriented. Middle Easterners have less expectation of consideration, and so this style is less important. It should be kept in mind, however, that for the American sample there was a correlation between initiating structure and both job satisfaction and effectiveness, and for the Middle Eastern sample there was a correlation between consideration and both of these outcomes. Thus it is the relative importance that differs.

Source: From "When East Meets West: Leadership 'Best Practices' in the United States and the Middle East" (pp. 171–233), by T. A. Scandura, M. A. Von Glinow, and K. B. Lowe, 1999, in W. H. Mobley, M. J. Gessner, and V. Arnold (Eds.), *Advances in Global Leadership* (Vol. 1), Stamford, CT: JAI.

Preferences for directive versus participative management might also vary across countries. Narayanan, Menon, and Spector (1999) asked clerical employees in India and the United States to describe the most stressful incident that had happened to them at work in the prior month. Trained judges analyzed the content of the incidents, placing them into categories. In the United States, lack of control was the second most often mentioned stressful incident, mentioned by almost a fourth of participants. In India, the most often mentioned stressful incident was insufficient structure provided by supervisors, mentioned by a little over a fourth of the participants. Not one American mentioned insufficient structure, and not one Indian mentioned lack of control. In another study, Euwema, Wendt, and van Emmerik (1997) surveyed employees in 33 countries (including India and the United States) concerning the leadership styles of their supervisors and found, finding that directive approaches have more negative effects on people from individualistic than collectivistic countries. The results of both studies suggest that leadership style preferences and effectiveness may differ across countries.

Despite such differences in leadership preferences and effectiveness, there are some aspects of leadership that transcend culture. Transformational leadership has been shown to relate to job performance in Singapore, much as it does in more Western countries (Lim & Ployhart, 2004). Furthermore, transformational leadership is related to positive job attitudes in China and India (Walumbwa, Wang, Lawler, & Shi, 2004). Taken together, these results show that there might be some universal characteristics of leaders that are effective across countries. Of course, this doesn't mean that transformational leaders behave in exactly the same way in different countries, as what it takes to be transformational is likely determined to a large extent by culture.

▶ CHAPTER SUMMARY

Leadership is an important function in organizations in which the efforts of many individuals must be coordinated and directed. Leadership refers to the disproportionate influence that one person has over others, and in organizations it is typically associated with management and supervisory positions. Leaders' influence over their followers is based on a number of factors. French and Raven (1959) provided five bases of power and influence:

Expert
Referent
Legitimate
Reward
Coercive

Yukl (1989) added the political influence tactics of:

Controlling decisions
Forming coalitions
Co-opting

There have been many approaches to the study of leadership. The trait approach attempts to find characteristics that make people good leaders. The leader behavior approach, represented by the Ohio State Leadership Studies, views leadership from the perspective of behaviors that are and are not effective. Contingency theories, such as Fiedler's and path-goal, state that leadership is a complex interaction of leader characteristics and the leadership situation. The leader-member exchange theory points out that leadership can be fully understood only by focusing attention on the often unique interactions of a supervisor with each subordinate. Transformational leadership theories look at the way some leaders are able to have a profound influence on the attitudes, beliefs, behaviors, and values of subordinates. Finally, the Vroom-Yetton model is a prescriptive theory that tells a supervisor how best to approach a decision situation.

Although women have made great strides in the workplace, they still face a glass ceiling, making it more difficult for them to obtain high-level management positions than for men. One explanation for this phenomenon has to do with the stereotypes of women's behavior. It is interesting that research has found few differences in the consideration and initiating structure styles of men and women managers, but women seem to be more democratic than men.

The theories discussed in this chapter were developed and tested primarily in Western developed countries. It is unclear to what extent they all hold in culturally dissimilar countries. Research suggests that there likely are some aspects of leadership that are and are not universal. Directive leadership styles, for example, are perceived differently across countries.

I/O PSYCHOLOGY IN PRACTICE

(*Courtesy of Dr. Stephen L. Cohen*)

This case concerns development of a training program to teach transformational leadership skills to corporate managers. Dr. Steve Cohen headed the team of consultants that implemented the program. Dr. Cohen received his Ph.D. in I/O psychology from the University of Tennessee in 1971. He began his career as a college professor but decided shortly after earning tenure that he preferred the world of consulting. Over the next 25 years, he has alternated between working for a consulting firm and running his own. Today he is Managing Director, Learning Solutions Group, for Dove Consulting in Minneapolis. Dove is a 110-employee international strategy and organizational effectiveness firm. The Learning Solutions Group specializes in developing training programs and employee performance improvement systems.

One of the most interesting projects on which he has worked involved the challenging task of training competent managers to become transformational and visionary leaders. A major global food and beverage company, headquartered in the United States with facilities in 170 countries, contracted with Dove to train their 7,500 managers to change their management approach. This company had been successful for decades, and top management felt employees at all levels had become relatively complacent. Managers did a good job of running the day-to-day business, but they had adopted a short-term focus, tended to avoid risk, and lacked a vision for the future. As described in this chapter, a transformational leader is just the opposite, in that he or she inspires followers to aspire to do better through the promotion of a vision for the future.

The project began with the development of a leadership competency model that described the ideal manager of the future for their business. Turning existing managers into the ideal served as the ultimate objective of the project. Next came the development of the curriculum. This started with a needs assessment to determine the existing skill levels and deficiencies of managers. Dr. Cohen's team then designed and developed training materials to address the skills identified in the needs assessment. They pilot tested the materials and then trained the trainers (not psychologists) who would ultimately deliver the training to the 7,500 managers throughout the world. Finally, the project was evaluated through the use of 360-degree feedback. Subordinates, peers, and supervisors completed rating scales that contained items reflecting transformational leadership behaviors.

The methods used for training were quite eclectic. Some were traditional paper-and-pencil materials provided to both trainers and trainees, and some of the training occurred in a classroom setting. However, Dr. Cohen has been a leader in the use of electronic technologies for training, and much of the material was provided online. Managers could log onto the company website and find self-paced materials, as well as resources for them to manage their own development. This approach not only provided an efficient means of conducting training with minimal use of trainers but also allowed for an individualized approach that helps trainees create a plan and track progress toward completion.

Discussion Questions

1. Why did Dr. Cohen train trainers instead of conducting training himself?
2. What are the advantages and disadvantages of the web-based approach?
3. Why was it necessary to first conduct a needs assessment?
4. What is one advantage and one disadvantage of having all leaders in a company adopt a transformational approach?

LEARNING BY DOING

Transformational Leadership

Choose a public leader such as a head of state who you believe is transformational. Find evidence from one or more of the leader's speeches that confirms that he or she is transformational. Which of the four components of transformational leadership does it reflect? Find an example of a vision statement the leader has used.

Abuse of Power

Who is Helen Green, for what company did she work, and what does she have to do with abuse of power? Explain how her experience adversely affected her and the company for which she worked.

CHAPTER 14

Organizational Development and Theory

CHAPTER 14 OUTLINE

- ORGANIZATIONAL DEVELOPMENT
  - Employee Acceptance of Change
  - Management by Objectives
  - Survey Feedback
  - Team Building
  - T-Group
  - Effectiveness of OD Programs
- ORGANIZATIONAL THEORIES
  - Bureaucracy Theory
  - Theory X/Theory Y
  - Open System Theory
  - Sociotechnical Systems Theory
  - Comparison of the Theories
- CHAPTER SUMMARY
- I/O PSYCHOLOGY IN PRACTICE
- LEARNING BY DOING

So far our focus in this book has been on the individual employee or small groups of employees in the context of the organization. In this last chapter, we change our perspective from the individual to the organization itself. We deal with two important topics—organizational development and organizational theory.

Organizations in the modern industrialized world find themselves in a rapidly evolving environment that requires appropriate changes in both their structure and their function. The field of *organizational development* helps organizations make changes that are rationally planned and implemented. Organizational change is often forced by circumstances and crises that are beyond the control of those in charge, resulting in hurried changes in response to an emergency. Companies such as AIG in the financial crisis in 2008 and British Petroleum with the Gulf of Mexico oil spill in the summer of 2010 likely institute organizational change with insufficient time to plan the best way to implement that change. Such precipitous changes can have unintended consequences that can be damaging to the organization in the long term.

For example, many organizations today are experiencing *downsizing*—reduction in the number of employees. Although downsizing is often necessary, it is too often carried out from a purely financial perspective without consideration of the effects on employees and on the organization itself. The projected savings from layoffs may never materialize because productivity is compromised by the social disruption of people's jobs. Surviving employees might be demotivated and unproductive, and many of the best employees might have left, thus leaving behind a less skilled workforce. Organizational development can help by considering the human side of organizational change and the best way to carry it out so that the organization remains effective. In this chapter, we explore how organizational development can help and some of the specific techniques involved.

Organizational theories describe how organizations work. Some focus on the structure of organizations, including the various components and how they interrelate. Others are concerned with the interpersonal aspects of organizations, including communication and how people relate to one another. Finally, some focus on the interaction of the interpersonal and technical sides of organizations: In other words, how do people affect the technology of the organization, and how does the technology affect people? All of these approaches are discussed in this chapter as we cover four important organizational theories.

Objectives: The student who studies this chapter should be able to:

- Explain what organizational development is and how it is applied.
- Describe the organizational development techniques discussed and indicate the effectiveness of each.
- Discuss each of the organizational theories presented in the chapter.
- Show the linkages among the four organizational theories discussed.

ORGANIZATIONAL DEVELOPMENT

Organizational development (OD) is a family of techniques designed to help organizations change for the better. They involve the use of behavioral science principles and procedures that help employees improve performance and interact with coworkers more effectively. An OD effort involves an entire organization or a large component of it, and it is intended to result in substantial changes in how the organization operates. Such changes can involve a reorganization in which new departments are created and old ones eliminated, with functions moved from area to area and person to person. An OD effort, however, is typically much more than a reorganization, and often reorganization isn't even involved. It usually involves changing how people do their work, how they communicate with one another, and how they coordinate their efforts.

An OD effort or program involves employees at all levels of the organization. It is implemented by a person or persons referred to as change agents. The **change agent** is the catalyst for change within the organization. He or she is an expert in working with organizations to improve their functioning. The change agent might be an employee of the organization, as in the case at the end of the chapter. In most instances, however, the change agent is an outside consultant who is hired to implement the OD program. Many consulting firms throughout the world specialize in organizational development.

The change agent's job is to act as a guide and trainer for the organizational development process. He or she might conduct classes in which employees are trained in new ways to communicate or operate within their organizations. He or she might conduct group sessions during which organization members plan changes that will improve the organization. The role of the change agent in these sessions is to serve as the group facilitator or moderator, keeping everyone focused on the task at hand and helping to mediate disputes among people. In short, the change agent assists the organization members in their OD effort. The change agent usually does not come into the organization with a specific plan for change, only the process by which employees can redesign their organization.

Organizational development and other changes are not easy to implement. Armenakis and Bedeian (1999) discussed how it is a multistage process that an organization must go through to successfully implement a change. It begins with employees first learning that a change needs to occur, which in many cases will induce anxiety and disbelief. Next, the specific form of the change has to be determined, often with the participation of the employees affected. Once a plan is produced, the change can be implemented. Typically there will be some degree of resistance to the change that must be overcome. Finally, the new ways of operating must be consolidated and become part of the accepted way people operate.

Employee Acceptance of Change

Management's desire to introduce change does not guarantee that it will be successful. Employees who have to change their behavior or use new equipment and techniques effectively must be willing to accept the change rather than resisting and must commit to making it successful. Change can be stressful, leading to negative emotions and feelings of uncertainty that can affect acceptance (Fugate, Kinicki, & Prussia, 2008; Rafferty & Griffin, 2006). Both individual employee and organizational factors combine to determine people's willingness to accept change. On the individual side, people who are flexible and like to try new things are likely to accept change (Choi & Price, 2005). Furthermore, people who have had positive experience with change in the past will be more likely to accept it in the future (Cunningham, Woodward, Shannon, MacIntosh, Lendrum, Rosenbloom, et al., 2002).

On the organizational side, leadership is an important element in employee acceptance of change (Furst & Cable, 2008). Transformational leaders can effectively encourage followers to accept change (Bommer, Rich, & Rubin, 2005; Groves, 2005). Of particular importance is the leader's articulation of a vision that is consistent with the change. In other words, an effective transformational leader will explain to followers how the change will enable them to reach important goals more easily and will convince them that change is welcome. Wanberg and Banas (2000) noted how sufficient information about change and participation by employees in the process were associated with employee acceptance of change within U.S. government agencies over a 14-month period (see the International Research box). K. J. Klein, Conn, and Sorra (2001) studied change in 39 U.S. manufacturing plants and found that sufficient financial resources and support from management are associated with successful change efforts.

INTERNATIONAL RESEARCH

Even the most well-designed organizational change will induce some level of resistance among employees. An issue of concern is determining what factors might mitigate that resistance. Wanberg and Banas (2000) studied organizational change in U.S. public housing organizations funded by the U. S. Department of Housing and Urban Development (HUD). In the midst of a radical restructuring of HUD and its operations, surveys were conducted to determine those factors that might lead to favorable employee reactions to organizational change.

Participants in this study were members of the National Association of Housing and Redevelopment Officials (NAHRO) from two states in the U.S. Surveys were administered to 173 employees who were attending state NAHRO conferences. A number of scales assessed characteristics of the individual employees and their perceptions of organizational conditions. Included was a measure of resilience, which was comprised of high self-esteem, an optimistic outlook on life, and feelings of control. Organizational scales assessed information sharing (the extent to which employees were informed about changes) and participation in changes. Two months later participants were mailed a questionnaire that assessed their openness to organizational change, job satisfaction, and turnover intentions. One year later organizations were contacted to determine whether or not each participant had quit his or her job.

Results showed that the two most important factors in openness to change were the extent to which employees felt informed and participation. Personality was also a factor, with resilience associated with openness. Furthermore, openness was associated with job satisfaction and intention to quit, and both job satisfaction and intention to quit were associated with turnover. This suggests that forced change can lead to dissatisfaction and intention of quitting, which can lead to subsequent turnover.

This study shows that people vary in their openness to organizational change and that resilient people are more likely to endorse rather than resist it. Furthermore, these results suggest that providing sufficient information about impending changes and allowing employees to participate in change planning and implementation can go a long way to increasing openness and reducing resistance, thus facilitating effective organizational change.

Source: From "Predictors and Outcomes of Openness to Changes in a Reorganizing Workplace," by C. R. Wanberg and J. T. Banas, 2000, *Journal of Applied Psychology, 85,* 132–142.

Management by Objectives

Management by objectives (MBO) is an organizational change technique that is based on goal setting (see Chapter 8). Each employee's own goals are coordinated with the goals of both supervisors and subordinates. In a typical MBO program, goal setting begins by having those at the top of the organization set broad objectives for the entire organization. The process of setting goals or objectives then filters down level by level, with all employees' goals being related to the goals of their superiors. The goals serve as motivational tools to direct effort, as criteria against which employee performance is appraised, and as the means of coordinating everyone's efforts toward a common set of organizational objectives.

Implementation of an MBO program typically begins with the change agent meeting with the top officials of the organization to set organizationwide goals and objectives. These goals must be as concrete and measurable as possible because everyone else's goals must be linked to them. A goal such as:

Improve the functioning of the organization

is a worthy goal, but it is too vague to be of much value in directing effort. A better goal would be:

Increase sales by 20%

This goal is specific and measurable, allowing everyone to know precisely what needs to be done and when it has been achieved.

In the next step, the change agent meets with managers and trains them in the goal-setting process. The program will work only when managers understand how to state measurable goals and how to set goals with subordinates and superiors. The third step is a series of meetings involving every subordinate-supervisor pair in the organization, usually beginning at the top and working down the organization level by level. The technique involves active participation by subordinates, who negotiate their goals with their supervisor, with the requirement that subordinates' goals must be consistent with those of the higher levels. Once all goals have been set, employees try to achieve them. After a 6- to 12-month period, each employee's job performance is evaluated against progress toward his or her goals. The entire process is illustrated in Figure 14.1.

Research on MBO has supported its use as an effective means of increasing organizational performance. Rodgers and Hunter (1991) conducted a meta-analysis of the effectiveness of MBO. They found positive effects on employee productivity in 68 of the 70 studies they reviewed. The combined results of 23 of the studies indicated an average increase in productivity of 39% as a result of the program. Rodgers and Hunter did an additional analysis in which they separated the 23 studies into three groups based on the extent to which top management was committed to the MBO program. As shown in Table 14.1, organizations with the highest levels of management commitment had far better results than those with the lowest levels (57% vs. 6% increase in productivity).

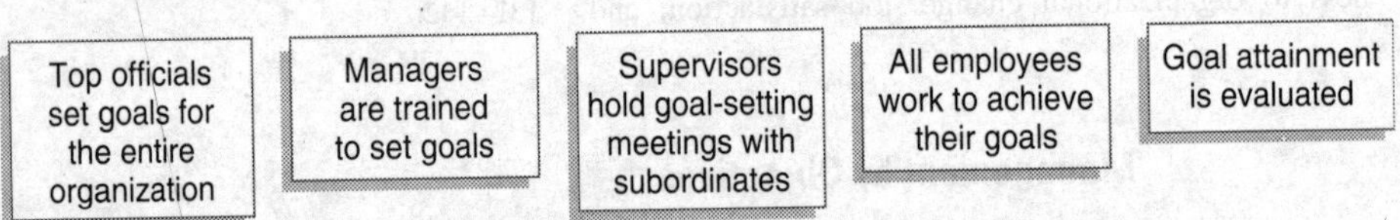

Figure 14.1 The five steps of implementing a management by objectives (MBO) program.

TABLE 14.1 Effect of Management Commitment on Performance Gain After Implementation of Management by Objectives

Level of Commitment	Percentage Gain in Productivity
High	56.5
Medium	32.9
Low	6.1

Source: Adapted from "Impact of Management by Objectives on Organizational Productivity," by R. Rodgers and J. E. Hunter, 1991, *Journal of Applied Psychology, 76,* 322–336.

The high success rate found by Rodgers and Hunter (1991) is probably an overestimate of how well MBO has worked across the many organizations in which it has been tried. These studies likely represent some of the better efforts at implementing MBO. Many organizations have made attempts to implement MBO without full management commitment or necessary resources. Such half-hearted attempts are likely to have little effect on the organization, with employees setting easy goals and exerting little effort toward achieving them.

Survey Feedback

Survey feedback is an OD technique that involves conducting a survey of employee attitudes and opinions and then feeding back the results to the entire organization. The idea is that employees can express their opinions in a nonthreatening way through anonymous or confidential questionnaires. The survey data can then be used as the starting point for discussions about needed changes in the organization.

A survey feedback program consists of two major stages. First, the change agent designs and administers questionnaires to the employees of the organization. Employees are asked about job satisfaction, perceptions of job conditions, and problems at work. Standardized scales can be used to assess some of these variables; for example, the Job Descriptive Index (Smith, Kendall, & Hulin, 1969) can be used to measure job satisfaction (see Chapter 9). Other items and custom-made scales might be developed specifically for each organization by the change agent after interviews with a sample of employees. The advantage of using standardized scales is that results from the organization can be compared to results from other organizations. That way one knows if employee job satisfaction is unusually high or low compared to similar organizations. The advantage of custom-made scales is that they can be much more targeted and deal with issues of concern to employees only in the specific organization. Thus one can find out with a standardized scale how employees feel about their pay in general, but it would take a custom-made scale to find out how they feel about a particular pay policy.

The second stage of a survey feedback program is providing feedback about the survey to employees. Data from the survey are compiled into a report, and the report is presented to employees, usually at a series of group meetings. The change agent might run the meetings, during which employees discuss the results and potential solutions to the problems uncovered by the survey. A successful program will result in the implementation of solutions to organizational problems.

Studies on the effectiveness of survey feedback have tended to find positive results from its use. Bowers (1973) reported the results of a large-scale longitudinal study involving more than 14,000 employees from 23 organizations. Positive changes in employee reports of job satisfaction and job conditions were found after survey feedback programs were introduced. In a meta-analysis of OD studies, survey feedback was found to have a modest positive impact on the job satisfaction of employees who participated (Neuman, Edwards, & Raju, 1989). It gives employees an opportunity to air their grievances in a constructive atmosphere. It also can provide for increased participation by employees in policy decisions that affect the entire organization. If done properly, survey feedback can help solve problems and give employees a greater sense of involvement in the organization.

Team Building

Team building refers to many techniques that are designed to enhance the functioning of work teams. As discussed in Chapter 12, team building can focus on tasks, such as smooth coordination of effort, or interpersonal issues, such as communication. With the task-oriented approach, the change agent helps work teams improve their task performance by learning how to work together more effectively. With the interpersonal approach, the change agent helps work teams improve their communication and interaction. Part of this effort can be directed toward reducing interpersonal conflict within work teams.

Team building can be an essential part of an OD effort because many of the tasks of organizations are conducted by work teams rather than individuals. An organization in which work teams do not work well will have a hard time being effective. Improving team functioning can go a long way toward improving an organization. In Chapter 12, we saw how the U.S. Navy is committed to finding ways to improve team functioning through training. Also noted in Chapter 12 was a comprehensive meta-analysis that shows that team building tends to have positive effects on team functioning and team performance (Klein, DiazGranados, Salas, Le, Burke, Lyons, et al., 2009). In their meta-analysis, Neuman et al. (1989) found that team building has a positive effect on job satisfaction.

T-Group

The **T-group** or training group is an intervention designed to enhance the communication and interpersonal skills of individual employees through the use of specific group exercises. There are many variations of the T-group. Most are conducted at a site away from work, take place over a 3-day to 2-week period, and involve several people who do not know one another. The idea is for the group of strangers to experience a series of interpersonal skills exercises with a trainer or facilitator to guide them.

A T-group experience encourages participants to experiment with their interpersonal behavior in a situation in which they receive nonjudgmental feedback. This allows group members to gain insights into their effects on others and how they are perceived by others. The purpose is for organizational members, most often managers, to increase their interpersonal skills in the hope that they will be more effective on the job.

At one time, the T-group was a popular intervention, with many large organizations sending their management staffs to an off-site location for training. It is not as popular at the present time for at least two reasons. First, research on the T-group has found that although individuals can be positively affected by the experience, there is typically either no effect or negative effects on the workplace. For example, Bowers (1973) found detrimental changes in reports of job conditions and job satisfaction among employees who participated in T-groups. Second, the T-group experience can be very much like group psychotherapy, with individuals exploring sensitive and potentially threatening aspects of themselves. There have been reports of individuals being hurt and upset by the T-group. Some have raised the issue that it is unethical for an organization to require T-group attendance.

Although T-groups have lost much of their popularity, organizations are still very much concerned with communication skills. To enhance such skills, organizations can use a variety of other methods. For example (as discussed in Chapter 7), behavior modeling has been found to be effective in teaching interpersonal skills. This method involves having employees watch people enact appropriate ways to communicate with others on the job. Trainees then practice what they have seen, under the direction of a trainer. This approach can be effective in enhancing interpersonal skills without the potentially harmful effects of the T-group. Thus organizations have alternatives that they can use to enhance the communication skills of their employees.

Effectiveness of OD Programs

The many different approaches to OD make it difficult to define precisely what a legitimate OD program is. Many involve more than one technique, including some combination of the four discussed in this section. An OD program might begin with survey feedback to identify issues. MBO or team building might be implemented next if the survey feedback process suggests that they are appropriate interventions. The wide variety of approaches and the complexity of the programs make it difficult to determine the effectiveness of particular OD techniques.

Another problem is that research on an entire organization is difficult to accomplish. If one implements an OD effort and wishes to assess the results, what will serve as the control group? The ideal OD study would randomly assign a sample of organizations (as opposed to individual participants) to one of two groups—intervention or control. This sort of design would require the cooperation of many organizations and is not generally feasible. Most OD studies are conducted in a single organization, with comparisons made before and after the OD program. For example, one can compare the performance of employees before and after OD implementation, but one cannot be certain what has caused any differences that are found. A variety of things might have occurred that have nothing to do with the OD program, and some of those might have been the real cause of differences.

Perhaps the most reasonable conclusion is that OD programs, if properly applied and supported by top management, can be effective. Meta-analyses have found that many OD techniques are effective (Guzzo, Jette, & Katzell, 1985; Neuman et al., 1989). Except for T-groups, there have been few reports of detrimental effects on organizations. The majority of large U.S. corporations seem to believe in the value of OD. In a survey of Fortune 500 companies, McMahan and Woodman (1992) found that most had internal OD professionals who were actively working to improve their organizations: 38% of the companies had OD staffs of 6 or more people, and 14% had staffs of 21 or more people. These results are probably an overestimate of the amount of OD activity in large U.S. companies, for the participation rate in the study was only about one-fifth of the eligible companies, and those actively engaged in OD were probably more likely to participate in the study. Nevertheless, they suggest that OD is an important activity in many large organizations.

ORGANIZATIONAL THEORIES

Organizational theories describe the structure and functioning of organizations and deal with issues such as:

1. The distinguishing characteristics of organization
2. The structure of organizations
3. The interrelationships among people in organizations
4. The interactions among people and technology in organizations

Descriptive theories explain how existing organizations work. A good descriptive theory will provide an accurate picture of how organizations are structured and how they operate. **Prescriptive theories** indicate how organizations should operate. Proper application of a good prescriptive theory will lead to an effective and efficient organization.

In practice, the distinction between descriptive and prescriptive theories may not be totally clear. Elements of both may appear in a given theory. Prescriptive theories that tell us what to do may in fact be descriptive of certain types of organizations. The first theory we discuss, bureaucracy, describes a particular type of organization, but its developer intended it to be prescriptive.

In this section, we discuss four different theoretical approaches to understanding organizations. *Bureaucracy* is the oldest theory and dates back to the 19th century. It is concerned with the structure of a particular type of organization that has been quite popular over the past century. *Theory X/Theory Y* is concerned with the interpersonal aspects of an organization. It is not an overall theory but describes how the attitudes of managers toward subordinates determine the organizational practices that are adopted. *Open system theory* describes the 10 components common to all general systems, including organizations. *Sociotechnical systems theory* is concerned with the interaction between the people and the technology of an organization.

Bureaucracy Theory

Bureaucracy theory, initially developed by Max Weber in the late 1800s, is a classical theory of the structure of an organization (Weber, 1947). In the early days of large organizations, little was known about effective techniques to structure and manage them. Weber's idea was to create a rational structure and several principles that would allow for the orderly and efficient functioning of an organization. Although we tend to think of a bureaucracy today as an inefficient and unresponsive organization, it represented an improvement over many of the organizational structures that existed at the time it was invented. Early organizations were often disorganized and inefficient. Bureaucracy theory provides characteristics and principles that were presumed to be important for an effective organization. We will discuss four of them:

Division of labor

Delegation of authority

Span of control

Line versus staff

These principles can be useful for describing how most organizations operate, even those that are not bureaucratic in nature.

Division of Labor

Division of labor refers to the organization's specialized job positions, each of which is responsible for different tasks. For a complex process, such as manufacturing an automobile, the total job is divided into many individual parts. For an entire manufacturing organization, the design, production, sale, and delivery of products are handled by different people in different departments.

The advantage of a division of labor is that each job requires relatively few skills. Therefore, it will not be difficult to find people who have the necessary KSAOs to do the job, it will take little time to train them, and individuals can become quite proficient because they have few tasks to master. The major disadvantage is that it requires resources to coordinate the activities of many specialized people. In a factory, for example, many managers and supervisors are needed to make sure that all employees do their jobs properly and that the efforts of employees are coordinated. This leads us to the next characteristic, delegation of authority.

Delegation of Authority

Most organizations are hierarchically structured with one person at the top who has ultimate authority and control. Reporting to the top person will be one or more people who have authority and control over others who are below them in the hierarchy. At each level of the hierarchy, except the first, people report to others who are their superior. At the last or bottom level are people who report to someone above them, but no one reports to them. An example of the organizational chart for a hierarchically structured organization is shown in Figure 14.2.

Division of labor means that no one in the organization does the entire work of the organization. Thus, the person at the top is dependent on all those below to produce the organization's goods or services. In order to accomplish this, each person must allow **delegation of authority** to those below to accomplish a particular job. Thus the top person might delegate authority for the design of a product to the research and development manager, for the running of a factory to a plant manager, for the selling of the product to a sales manager, and for the distribution of the product to a distribution manager. The people who report to each of these managers will be given authority to do whatever their jobs require. The efforts of different individuals are coordinated through a network of hierarchical supervision or **chain of command**: Each person is responsible for those tasks and functions over which he or she has authority.

Span of Control

Span of control refers to the number of subordinates who report to each supervisor. In a given bureaucracy, there will be an optimal span of control. Because everyone except

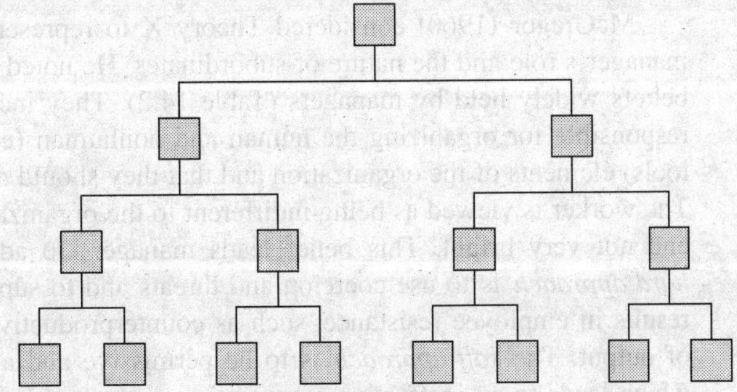

Figure 14.2 An organizational chart for a hierarchically structured organization. In such organizations—for example, a bureaucracy—each person reports to a single supervisor.

the person at the top has a supervisor, too small a span of control results in needing too many managers. Too large a span of control is chaotic because one person cannot adequately supervise the work of many people. The number of people someone can adequately supervise depends on two factors. First, the more skilled the subordinates, the less supervisory time they take. A person who is unskilled will need constant help and direction. A person who knows the job well will need only occasional attention. Second, the person's supervisory style helps determine the optimal span of control. A directive style requires considerable time for each subordinate. Each time a decision or problem arises, the supervisor must take time to deal with it. A participative style allows for a larger span of control because subordinates are allowed to deal with many of their own problems and make their own decisions, thereby freeing the time of their supervisors.

Line Versus Staff

Each position in an organization can be classified as either line or staff. A *line position* is involved directly with the organization's major purpose. In the military, it would be combat soldiers; in education, it would be teachers; in manufacturing, it would be assemblers; and in retailing, it would be salespeople. Line positions also include all the levels of supervision above these positions. A *staff position* supports the activities of a line position. The administration of salary and fringe benefits, employee selection, and training are all considered to be staff functions performed by people in staff positions.

Theory X/Theory Y

McGregor's (1960) **Theory X/Theory Y** is a human relations theory concerned with the interaction between supervisors and subordinates. The basic idea is that the attitudes and beliefs of supervisors about their subordinates determine the organization's management approach, which in turn affects how subordinates behave. This is a self-fulfilling prophecy in that managers treat subordinates according to how they are expected to behave, and this treatment causes subordinates to behave as expected. For example, a manager who believes that subordinates will not do their jobs properly without close supervision is likely to supervise closely. The closely supervised subordinates will undoubtedly believe that they are not trusted and will probably not work well when the supervisor is absent. Although the manager might believe that the close supervision is the result of subordinate behavior, the opposite is the case.

McGregor (1960) considered Theory X to represent the conventional view of the manager's role and the nature of subordinates. He noted eight propositions that represent beliefs widely held by managers (Table 14.2). They include the idea that managers are responsible for organizing the human and nonhuman (equipment, money, supplies, and tools) elements of the organization and that they should direct and motivate subordinates. The worker is viewed as being indifferent to the organization's needs, lazy, unmotivated, and not very bright. This belief leads managers to adopt one of two strategies. The *hard approach* is to use coercion and threats and to supervise closely, an approach that results in employee resistance, such as counterproductive work behavior and restriction of output. The *soft approach* is to be permissive and avoid conflict with subordinates, which leads to an ineffective organization.

Theory Y is McGregor's preferred management view, which he believes will lead to more satisfied employees and more effective organizations. It has four propositions

TABLE 14.2 McGregor's Theory X/Theory Y Propositions

Theory X

Managers are responsible for organizing elements of the organization.

Managers should direct the activities of subordinates.

Employees are resistant to organizational needs.

The average employee is lazy.

The average employee lacks ambition and dislikes responsibility.

The average employee is concerned for himself or herself and not the organization.

The average employee is resistant to change.

The average employee is gullible and not very bright.

Theory Y

Managers are responsible for organizing elements of the organization.

Employees are not by nature resistant to organization needs. They have become that way because of prior organization experiences.

Managers should make it possible for subordinates to recognize and develop their organizational capabilities.

Managers should create organizational conditions so that subordinates can achieve their own goals through achieving organizational goals.

Source: From *The Human Side of Enterprise*, by D. M. McGregor, 1960, New York, NY: McGraw-Hill.

(see Table 14.2), which cover both the role of managers and the nature of subordinates. According to Theory Y, managers are responsible for organizing rather than directing the various human and nonhuman elements of the organization. Subordinates are capable and not inherently unmotivated or unresponsive to organizational needs. It is the responsibility of managers to arrange conditions so that employees can fulfill their own goals by directing efforts toward organizational goals. This last point is very much like the path-goal leadership theory idea (see Chapter 13), that leaders should provide the means by which subordinates can achieve personal rewards through good job performance. The supervisory approach adopted by the Theory Y manager is likely to be quite different from his or her Theory X counterpart. Rather than relying on directive approaches, the Theory Y manager stresses employee autonomy and development. Emphasis is placed on the setting of goals and objectives for employees, with their supervisors helping by removing constraints and providing guidance.

McGregor believed that movement toward Theory Y would be a slow process because the experiences of most people have been in Theory X situations. Today we can see many examples of the Theory Y approach. For example, the autonomous work team is based on the philosophy that subordinates are capable of managing themselves. As organizations continue to experience pressure to reduce costs by downsizing, it will become necessary to give more responsibility to lower-level employees. Doing so will require adoption of a Theory Y approach.

Theory X and Theory Y are not the only possible approaches for managing people. Ouchi (1981) proposed an approach to management that is based on Japanese practices. **Theory Z** assumes that long-term employment is the basis of effective organizations. People who can count on spending their entire career in the same organization will have high levels of commitment. They will be willing to put more effort into helping their organizations to be successful because they have a personal stake in the long-term success of their employers.

Open System Theory

According to Katz and Kahn's (1978) **open system theory**, an organization can be viewed as a type of open system. The idea comes from the natural sciences, which view biological organisms such as plants, animals, bacteria, and viruses as open systems. Although organizations are different from biological organisms, they do share many characteristics (see Figure 14.3).

Katz and Kahn (1978) noted 10 characteristics of open systems, which are listed in Table 14.3. Open systems such as organizations import energy, transform the energy into

Figure 14.3 Organizations can be thought of as open systems that share many of the characteristics of biological organisms. (© *Ronnie Howard, sourced from Shutterstock images*)

TABLE 14.3 The 10 Organizational Characteristics From Katz and Kahn's Open System Theory and an Organizational Example of Each

Characteristic	Example
1. Import energy	Hire people
2. Transform energy	Make products
3. Output products	Sell products
4. Cycles of events	Work shifts
5. Escape entropy	Stay profitable
6. Input information	Do a market survey
7. Homeostasis	Balance the annual budget
8. Specialization	Create specialized job titles
9. Coordination and integration	Supervise employees
10. Equifinality	There are many effective ways to run an organization

From *The Social Psychology of Organizations* (2nd ed.), by D. Katz & R. L. Kahn, 1978, New York: John Wiley.

something else, and output some product or service. All organizations import people and materials, produce goods and services, and deliver those goods and services to customers. Even government organizations provide services to citizens, including education, health care, protection, and transportation.

Open systems undergo cycles of events, and organizations are no different. Most organize their finances by fiscal years; employees have weekly work schedules; and for many organizations, the day is broken into two or more work shifts. Universities organize instruction by semesters and semesters are organized into academic years. Many employees are hired according to time-limited contracts, especially in professional sports organizations such as baseball, basketball, football, and soccer teams.

Open systems must somehow escape entropy—the decay and destruction of the system. With a biological organism, entropy results in death. For an organization, entropy also can result in death, although often "dying" organizations are absorbed by other organizations. With private-sector organizations, entropy can be indicated by the economic health of the company. Organizations that are efficient in transforming their inputs into goods and services that can be sold at a reasonable profit will survive. Those that cannot produce goods and services at a profit will have their finances erode until they can no longer pay employees or input energy. When this situation occurs, they will cease to function unless additional energy is available. This might occur if an external entity provides the funds to continue. It is what happened to Chrysler Corporation and General Motors in 2008 when the U.S. government loaned them money to keep them in business.

In addition to energy, open systems input information about their environments. Organizations have many people who are information specialists of various types. Organizations have accountants to deal with financial matters and lawyers to deal with legal issues, helping the organization maintain its homeostasis. Just as the thermostat in a house keeps the temperature constant, systems in organizations maintain certain conditions. An organization must maintain an appropriate number of employees, have the proper equipment in working order, have the necessary materials, and balance a budget. All these maintain the organization's homeostasis.

As open systems grow and become more complex, they develop specialized functions. As organizations become larger, they tend to divide work into more and more specialized functions. A small organization might have a single individual perform all accounting, human resources, and legal functions. A large corporation will have entire departments and often divisions for each of these functions. As functions become more specialized, open systems develop structures for coordination and integration. In organizations, this function is accomplished through supervision and the chain of command.

The final characteristic of an open system is equifinality—a system can reach a particular state from many different starting points using many different methods. From an open system perspective, there is no one correct way to structure and operate an organization. Successful organizations can function in a variety of ways. For example, a product can be produced with an autonomous work team or with a traditional assembly line.

Open system theory is descriptive in providing a framework to understand the characteristics of organizations. It does not provide prescriptive insights into how an organization should be run, as does McGregor's Theory X/Theory Y.

Sociotechnical Systems Theory

Sociotechnical systems theory views an organization in terms of the interrelations between people and technology in the context of the organizational environment. *People* include the employees of the organization and their relationships with one another. *Technology* consists of the equipment, materials, tools, and other nonhuman objects in the organization. The *environment* is the physical and social conditions in which the organization must function. The theory deals with how people affect technology and how technology affects people. Sociotechnical systems theory is prescriptive in that it uses research findings to provide principles of good organizational design.

The origins of sociotechnical systems theory can be found in a paper by Trist and Bamforth (1951) in which they describe the effects of technological change in the British coal industry (see Figure 14.4). Prior to the change, coal mining was done by small groups of men who controlled their own work pace. Members of each group worked together in close proximity inside the dangerous environment of the mine. The introduction of machinery resulted in changes in the work group relationships among the men and the loss of worker control over work pace. Individuals now operated large pieces of machinery alone, without the close support of colleagues. This led to increases in absence and health complaints among the miners. Trist and Bamforth's paper made the linkages between the human and technological aspects of organizations very clear.

Since Trist and Bamforth's (1951) paper, sociotechnical systems theory has undergone development and frequent application (Winterton, 1994). Cooper and Foster (1971) noted several principles of the theory. **Joint optimization** is the idea that the social and

Figure 14.4 Technological changes in coal mining have sometimes disrupted the social system of miners, resulting in employee problems. (© *Jeff Morgan 08/Alamy*)

technological systems should be designed to fit one another as well as possible. Machines and equipment should be easy for people to use, and people should be organized into tasks and jobs so that machines and equipment can function well. This means not only that human factors should be part of equipment design but also that available technology should be considered in designing the human side of organizations. The introduction of word processing on personal computers in offices during the 1980s is an example of this approach. Because employees using this technology were not experts in computers, both hardware and software had to be designed to be as easy to use as possible. To get the full advantage out of word processing, however, the computers could not be designed just to mimic the typewriters they were replacing. The use of additional functions required that they had to operate somewhat differently. This necessitated extensive training for clerical employees with limited computer experience. Many managers of organizations, however, violated sociotechnical systems principles by thinking that all they needed to do was order computers and have them put on employees' desks.

Unit control of variances concerns who handles work problems when they arise. In many organizations, each employee is responsible for handling only routine assigned tasks. When there is a variance from normal routine—for example, a machine breaks or a customer has a problem—specialists or supervisors are called to handle it. The idea of unit control is that variances should be handled by the employee or employees who encounter them. Thus the operator of the machine should be allowed to fix it, and the salesclerk should be allowed to help a customer with a problem. In an office, employees who use word processors should be able to solve all but the most difficult problems they encounter. This approach enhances the motivation, self-efficacy, and skills of the employee, and it saves the time of the specialist and supervisor.

Implementation of the sociotechnical systems approach results in self-regulation by the individual employees or groups of employees. Thus the autonomous work team approach is a major way in which these ideas have been introduced into organizations (Majchrzak & Borys, 1998). The existence of self-regulating or self-managed units implies a different function for management. Rather than directing the actions of employees, managers spend time counseling and supporting the activities of work units and facilitating their interactions.

The ideas of sociotechnical systems theory have been widely applied in organizations and will probably continue to spread for at least two reasons. First, as noted earlier in this chapter, there has been a worldwide trend toward downsizing organizations by trimming the size of management staffs (Kozlowski, Chao, Smith, & Hedlund, 1993). With fewer managers, individual employees will have to work more independently. Second, organizations today find themselves in a rapidly changing environment that requires the flexibility to adapt to changing demands. The principles of sociotechnical systems theory describe how organizations can function well under such conditions (Liu, Shah, & Schroeder, 2006).

Research on sociotechnical systems theory applications has been supportive. Two studies conducted in the United Kingdom, for example, found that the unit control principle has positive effects on productivity. Wall, Corbett, Martin, Clegg, and Jackson (1990) hypothesized, based on sociotechnical systems theory, that allowing factory workers to deal with machine problems themselves reduces the amount of time that machines are "down" for adjustment or repair. They found that not only does this form of unit control

INTERNATIONAL RESEARCH

There is perhaps no better setting in which to apply the principles of sociotechnical systems theory than an automated factory that mixes people with industrial robots. Such was the case in this study of productivity in a British factory by Wall, Jackson, and Davids (1992). This factory produced drill bits on a robotics assembly line where four humans interacted with six robots. The robots did most of the assembly work, which involved forming metal into drill bits. The workers fed the material to the first robot, unloaded the finished bits from the last robot, and made minor adjustments to the machines.

Relying on principles of sociotechnical systems theory, the researchers recommended to management that the workers' jobs be redesigned to allow them to deal with machine problems, which are common with industrial robots. Management refused the idea because of objections by the engineers, who believed that the machine operators could not handle this responsibility. Management had also instituted an incentive system for the operators, however, but because the assembly-line speed was controlled by the robots, the only way to increase productivity was to reduce downtime. The operators took it upon themselves to handle the machine problems, and once they proved they could do so, the engineers withdrew their objections. Thus the experiment occurred accidentally.

Data on downtime were collected for 6 months before and 8 months after the operators expanded their jobs. Downtime was reduced significantly from the period of time before to that after the intervention. It is interesting that the number of short stoppages (less than 15 minutes) increased, but the number of long stoppages (15 minutes to an hour) decreased. Overall, the number of stoppages was the same, but the time lost for stoppages decreased. This suggests that when the operators dealt with the problems themselves, they could do so more quickly and reduce the lost time. The researchers estimated that productivity increases resulted in as much as $2,400 in profit per week.

This study shows that the sociotechnical approach, even when implemented in an unplanned way, can have beneficial effects on productivity. A similar study by some of the same researchers (see Chapter 12) showed that it can have positive effects on people as well (Wall, Corbett, Martin, Clegg, & Jackson, 1990). Organizations could benefit by carefully applying the principles of sociotechnical systems theory. Note that in this study employees were offered an incentive for improving productivity. The combination of increased motivation (the incentive) and accidental job redesign resulted in reduced downtime. Imposing this sort of job change without considering employee motivation and preferences might not have the same effects and can even result in counterproductive behavior if employees resist the change.

Source: From "Operator Work Design and Robotics System Performance: A Serendipitous Field Study," by T. D. Wall, P. R. Jackson, & K. Davids, 1992, *Journal of Applied Psychology, 77,* 353–362.

enhancement decrease downtime, it also decreases employee feelings of job pressure and increases their job satisfaction. In a similar study in another British factory, Wall, Jackson, and Davids (1992) found that when factory workers assume responsibility for fixing machine problems, productivity increases because of a reduction of machine downtime (see the International Research box).

Meta-analyses of interventions based on sociotechnical systems theory have indicated a high degree of success. Pasmore, Francis, Haldeman, and Shani (1982) analyzed the results of 134 studies and found that the majority have positive effects on criteria of productivity, costs, employee withdrawal, employee attitudes, safety, grievances, and

TABLE 14.4 Percentage of Studies Reporting Various Positive Effects of Sociotechnical Systems Theory Interventions

Effect	Percentage Successful
Productivity	87
Cost	89
Absence	81
Turnover	65
Attitudes	94
Safety	88
Grievances	89
Quality	97

Source: Adapted from "Sociotechnical Systems: A North American Reflection on Empirical Studies of the Seventies,'" by W. Pasmore, C. Francis, J. Haldeman, and A. Shani, 1982, *Human Relations, 12,* 1179–1204.

work quality (Table 14.4). Guzzo et al. (1985) found positive effects of sociotechnical systems interventions on productivity and turnover.

Comparison of the Theories

Each of the four theories we have discussed is distinct, and each tends to focus on different aspects of organizations. There are some common ideas and connections among them, however. The rigid structure of the bureaucracy lends itself to a Theory X approach. In a bureaucracy, each person's job is clearly defined, with the individual having relatively little autonomy or discretion. This tends to be associated with the leadership style defined as Theory X, which includes close supervision and nonparticipative approaches.

Sociotechnical systems theory applications have tended to be consistent with Theory Y ideas. One of the main sociotechnical systems approaches has been the autonomous work team (see Chapter 12). The idea is to give employees autonomy and discretion in how they do their jobs. This assumes that management adopts a trusting view of employees. One cannot allow someone discretion without being confident that he or she will do the job properly. Thus the application of sociotechnical systems theory requires a Theory Y philosophy that employees can be trusted to do the job.

Open system theory is quite different. It describes the functioning of an organization in terms of 10 rather general principles and does not recommend specific practices. One can use the principles to describe the processes of an organization that might be based on the other theories. For example, the ways in which employees are supervised is covered by the principles of coordination and integration; however, there is little in the theory to tell us how we should coordinate and integrate. Of course, the principle of equifinality tells us that there can be many effective ways to run an organization, which is consistent with the principles of sociotechnical systems theory (Walker, Stanton, Salmon, & Jenkins, 2008).

These theories provide a broad perspective on organizations and how they function. Some have led to specific applications such as the autonomous work group based on sociotechnical systems theory. Others have affected the philosophies of those who manage organizations rather than describing particular techniques. Theory X/Theory Y, for example, is well known to managers and has had some influence on their practices.

▸ CHAPTER SUMMARY

We took an organizational perspective in this chapter, briefly reviewing two areas—organizational development and organizational theory. Organizational development is the application of behavioral science principles to improve the functioning of organizations. We discussed four specific techniques that can be used separately or in combination. Management by objectives (MBO) sets interlinked goals throughout an organization. Survey feedback uses the results of an employee survey as the basis for group discussion and organization improvement. Team building is a family of techniques that can be used with work teams to improve their functioning. T-groups are training groups that engage in a series of group exercises designed to enhance the communication and interpersonal skills of individuals.

Existing evidence suggests that MBO, survey feedback, and team building can be effective interventions, with positive effects on both employees and organizations. On the other hand, T-groups have not been found to be effective and have been associated with detrimental effects.

Organizational theories describe how organizations can and should work. Bureaucracy theory is a classical theory that focuses on the structural components of organizations. Theory X/Theory Y is a human relations theory that focuses on how management philosophy affects the behavior of employees. Open system theory describes organizations in terms of 10 characteristics of open systems. Sociotechnical systems theory is concerned with the interrelations between the human and technical sides of organizations. This theory has led to many interventions, and most of those reported in the research literature have been successful.

I/O PSYCHOLOGY IN PRACTICE

(*Courtesy of Tom White*)

This case is an effort to help employees cope with organizational change brought about by a corporate downsizing. Dr. Tom White served as the architect and primary change agent for this organizational development project. Dr. White received his Ph.D. in I/O psychology in 1985 from the University of South Florida. Immediately after graduation, he moved to Australia, where he has worked as an I/O psychologist ever since. At the time of this case, he was Organization Development Manager for Compaq Computer Corporation in Australia before it merged with Hewlett-Packard.

Among Dr. White's responsibilities was facilitating organizational change and development. He was also involved with conflict resolution among employees, leadership development, planning for the future, and team building. His role was mainly that of an internal consultant and facilitator. This means he functioned as change agent to help the organization manage the frequent change necessitated by rapid technological development in the computer industry.

An important project Dr. White undertook was to help employees cope with a corporate downsizing that was necessary to keep the company profitable in the extremely competitive computer industry. Despite the company's reputation of caring for employees, heavy losses in recent years required drastic action to cut costs, including having to let go as many as 30% of employees in some areas. This downsizing was a traumatic experience for survivors of the layoffs, many of whom lost close friends at work. The entire company was disrupted, as people found it difficult to work effectively. Dr. White's job was to find a way to help survivors deal with the situation.

The approach chosen was based on techniques to help people cope with the death of a family member. A series of 2-day sessions was conducted with 100 employees or more in each session. During the sessions, which were conducted by managers, employees engaged in a series of small-group activities to help them grieve for their losses while focusing on plans for the future. Two themes were letting go of the past and committing to the future. Dr. White's role was to organize the companywide activity and instruct managers in how to conduct sessions. This is a typical role for a change agent, in that managers have to actually implement change. A psychologist will be a facilitator and resource for those who do the change.

Once the full program was completed, which took a month, an evaluation was conducted to determine its effectiveness. Results showed that employees became more accepting of change and more trusting of management. Employee job performance increased, as did overall productivity of the workforce. Overall, this organizational change effort was beneficial to both the employees and the organization.

Discussion Questions

1. Why didn't Dr. White take a more active role in running the sessions?
2. How can a change agent facilitate change if managers have all the power in the organization?
3. What KSAOs are needed for a person to do organizational development?
4. Why is it important to evaluate programs such as Dr. White's?

LEARNING BY DOING

Organizational Development

Go to the website of a company that does organizational development and answer the following questions.

1. What are the backgrounds of the individuals in the company?
2. What services does the company provide?
3. Can you find out whether the company uses any of the four techniques discussed in the chapter?
4. Does it specialize in a particular industry?

Open Systems Theory

Take an organization (it could be your college or university) with which you are familiar. For each of the 10 open systems theory characteristics, note one example from the organization.

Evaluations of the program were conducted [illegible] [illegible] a month [illegible] [illegible] [illegible] compared [illegible] [illegible] [illegible] afterwards. Results showed that employees became more accepting of changes and more positive about the program. Employees [illegible] performance [illegible] [illegible] [illegible] [illegible] [illegible] [illegible]. Overall, the organizational change efforts [illegible] [illegible] to both the employees and the organization.

2. How can a [illegible] [illegible] [illegible] [illegible] [illegible] [illegible] [illegible] [illegible] [illegible] [illegible]?

References

Adams, J. S. (1965). Inequity in social exchange. In L. Berkowitz (Ed.), *Advances in experimental social psychology* (pp. 276–299). New York, NY: Academic Press.

Aguinis, H., Nesler, M. S., Quigley, B. M., Suk-Jae-Lee, & Tedeschi, J. T. (1996). Power bases of faculty supervisors and educational outcomes for graduate students. *Journal of Higher Education*, *67*, 267–297.

Akerstedt, T., & Theorell, T. (1976). Exposure to night work: Serum gastrin reactions, psychosomatic complaints and personality variables. *Journal of Psychosomatic Research*, *20*, 479–484.

Aldag, R. J., & Fuller, S. R. (1993). Beyond fiasco: A reappraisal of the groupthink phenomenon and a new model of group decision processes. *Psychological Bulletin*, *113*, 533–552.

Allen, D. G., Mahto, R. V., & Otondo, R. F. (2007). Web-based recruitment: Effects of information, organizational brand, and attitudes toward a web site on applicant attraction. *Journal of Applied Psychology*, *92*, 1696–1708.

Allen, J., & Sanders, K. (2002). Gender gap in earnings at the industry level. *European Journal of Women's Studies*, *9*, 163–180.

Allen, T. D., & Eby, L. T. (2003). Relationship effectiveness for mentors: Factors associated with learning and quality. *Journal of Management*, *29*, 469–486.

Allen, T. D., Eby, L. T., & Lentz, E. (2006). The relationship between formal mentoring program characteristics and perceived program effectiveness. *Personnel Psychology*, *59*, 125–153.

Allen, T. D., Eby, L. T., Poteet, M. L., Lentz, E., & Lima, L. (2004). Career benefits associated with mentoring for proteges: A meta-analysis. *Journal of Applied Psychology*, *89*, 127–136.

Allen, T. D., Herst, D. E., Bruck, C. S., & Sutton, M. (2000). Consequences associated with work-to-family conflict: A review and agenda for future research. *Journal of Occupational Health Psychology*, *5*, 278–308.

Allen, T. D., McManus, S. E., & Russell, J. E. (1999). Newcomer socialization and stress: Formal peer relationships as a source of support. *Journal of Vocational Behavior*, *54*, 453–470.

Alliger, G. M., Tannenbaum, S. I., Bennett, W., Jr., Traver, H., & Shotland, A. (1997). A meta-analysis of the relations among training criteria. *Personnel Psychology*, *50*, 341–358.

Ambrose, M. L., & Kulik, C. T. (1999). Old friends, new faces: Motivation research in the 1990s. *Journal of Management*, *25*, 231–292.

American Psychological Association. (1992). Ethical principles of psychologists and code of conduct. *American Psychologist*, *47*, 1597–1611.

Anderson, N., De Dreu, C. K., & Nijstad, B. A. (2004). The routinization of innovation research: A constructively critical review of the state-of-the-science. *Journal of Organizational Behavior*, *25*, 147–173.

Antonioni, D., & Park, H. (2001). The relationship between rater affect and three sources of 360-degree feedback ratings. *Journal of Management*, *27*, 479–495.

Armenakis, A. A., & Bedeian, A. G. (1999). Organizational change: A review of theory and research in the 1990s. *Journal of Management*, *25*, 293–315.

Arthur, W., Jr., Bennett, W., Jr., Edens, P. S., & Bell, S. T. (2003). Effectiveness of training in organizations: A meta-analysis of design and evaluation features. *Journal of Applied Psychology*, *88*, 234–245.

Arthur, W., Jr., Day, E. A., McNelly, T. L., & Edens, P. S. (2003). A meta-analysis of the criterion-related validity of assessment center dimensions. *Personnel Psychology*, *56*, 125–154.

Arthur, W., Jr., Woehr, D. J., & Maldegen, R. (2000). Convergent and discriminant validity of assessment center dimensions: A conceptual and empirical reexamination of the assessment center construct-related validity paradox. *Journal of Management*, *26*, 813–835.

Aryee, S., Lo, S., & Kang, I. L. (1999). Antecedents of early career stage mentoring among Chinese employees. *Journal of Organizational Behavior*, *20*, 563–576.

Ash, R. A., & Levine, E. L. (1980). A framework for evaluating job analysis methods. *Personnel Psychology*, *57*, 53–59.

Ashkanasy, N. M., Hartel, C. E. J., & Daus, C. S. (2002). Diversity and emotion: The new frontiers in organizational behavior research. *Journal of Management*, *28*, 307–338.

Ashton, M. C. (1998). Personality and job performance: The importance of narrow traits. *Journal of Organizational Behavior*, *19*, 289–303.

Atwater, L. E., & Brett, J. F. (2005). Antecedents and consequences of reactions to developmental 360 degrees feedback. *Journal of Vocational Behavior*, *66*, 532–548.

Augustine, M. A., & Coovert, M. D. (1991). Simulations and information order as influences in the development of mental models. *SIGCHI Bulletin*, *23*, 33–35.

Aust, B., & Ducki, A. (2004). Comprehensive health promotion interventions at the workplace: Experiences with health circles in Germany. *Journal of Occupational Health Psychology*, *9*, 258–270.

Bacharach, S. B., Bamberger, P., & Biron, M. (2010). Alcohol consumption and workplace absenteeism: The moderating effect of social support. *Journal of Applied Psychology*, *95*, 334–348.

Bacharach, S. B., Bamberger, P. A., & Doveh, E. (2008). Firefighters, critical incidents, and drinking to cope: The adequacy of unit-level performance resources as a source of vulnerability and protection. *Journal of Applied Psychology*, *93*, 155–169.

Bailey, C., & Austin, M. (2006). 360 degree feedback and developmental outcomes: The role of feedback characteristics, self-efficacy and importance of feedback dimensions to focal managers' current role. *International Journal of Selection and Assessment*, *14*, 51–66.

Bakker, A. B., Schaufeli, W. B., Sixma, H. J., Bosveld, W., & Van Dierendonck, D. (2000). Patient demands, lack of reciprocity, and burnout: A five-year longitudinal study among general practitioners. *Journal of Organizational Behavior*, *21*, 425–441.

Baldwin, T. T., & Ford, J. K. (1988). Transfer of training: A review and directions for future research. *Personnel Psychology*, *41*, 63–105.

Baldwin, T. T., & Padgett, M. T. (1993). Management development: A review and commentary. In C. L. Cooper & I. T. Robertson (Eds.), *International review of industrial and organizational psychology: 1993* (pp. 35–85). Chichester, England: John Wiley.

Baltes, B. B., Briggs, T. E., Huff, J. W., Wright, J. A., & Neuman, G. A. (1999). Flexible and compressed workweek schedules: A meta-analysis of their effects on work-related criteria. *Journal of Applied Psychology*, *84*, 496–513.

Baltes, B. B., Dickson, M. W., Sherman, M. P., Bauer, C. C., & LaGanke, J. (2002). Computer-mediated communication and group decision making: A meta-analysis. *Organizational Behavior and Human Decision Processes*, *87*, 156–179.

Baltes, B. B., & Heydens-Gahir, H. A. (2003). Reduction of work-family conflict through the use of selection, optimization, and compensation behaviors. *Journal of Applied Psychology*, *88*, 1005–1018.

Balzer, W. K., & Sulsky, L. M. (1992). Halo and performance appraisal research: A critical examination. *Journal of Applied Psychology*, *77*, 975–985.

Bandura, A. (1982). Self-efficacy mechanism in human agency. *American Psychologist*, *37*, 122–147.

Bandura, A., & Locke, E. A. (2003). Negative self-efficacy and goal effects revisited. *Journal of Applied Psychology*, *88*, 87–99.

Banker, R. D., Field, J. M., Schroeder, R. G., & Sinha, K. K. (1996). Impact of work teams on manufacturing performance: A longitudinal study. *Academy of Management Journal*, *39*, 867–890.

Banks, M. H., Jackson, P. R., Stafford, E. M., & Warr, P. B. (1983). The Job Components Inventory and the analysis of jobs requiring limited skill. *Personnel Psychology*, *36*, 57–66.

Baranik, L. E., Roling, E. A., & Eby, L. T. (2010). Why does mentoring work? The role of perceived organizational support. *Journal of Vocational Behavior*, *76*, 366–373.

Barling, J., Kelloway, E., & Iverson, R. D. (2003). Accidental outcomes: Attitudinal consequences of workplace injuries. *Journal of Occupational Health Psychology*, *8*, 74–85.

Barling, J., Weber, T., & Kelloway, E. (1996). Effects of transformational leadership training on attitudinal and financial outcomes: A field experiment. *Journal of Applied Psychology*, *81*, 827–832.

Baron, L., & Morin, L. (2010). The impact of executive coaching on self-efficacy related to management soft-skills. *Leadership and Organization Development Journal*, *31*, 18–38.

Barrett, G. V., & Kernan, M. C. (1987). Performance appraisal and terminations: A review of court decisions since Brito v. Zia with implications for personnel practices. *Personnel Psychology*, *40*, 489–503.

Barrick, M. R., & Mount, M. K. (1991). The Big Five personality dimensions and job performance: A meta-analysis. *Personnel Psychology*, *44*, 1–26.

Barton, J., & Folkard, S. (1991). The response of day and night nurses to their work schedules. *Journal of Occupational Psychology*, *64*, 207–218.

Bass, B. M., Avolio, B. J., & Atwater, L. E. (1996). The transformational and transactional leadership of men and women. *Applied Psychology: An International Review*, *45*, 5–34.

Bass, B. M., & Riggio, R. E. (2006). *Transformational leadership* (2nd ed.). Mahwah, NJ: Lawrence Erlbaum.

Bauer, T. N., & Green, S. G. (1996). Development of leader-member exchange: A longitudinal test. *Academy of Management Journal*, *39*, 1538–1567.

Bayram, N., Gursakal, N., & Bilgel, N. (2009). Counterproductive work behavior among white-collar employees: A study from Turkey. *International Journal of Selection and Assessment*, *17*, 180–188.

Beal, D. J., Cohen, R. R., Burke, M. J., & McLendon, C. L. (2003). Cohesion and performance in groups: A meta-analytic clarification of construct relations. *Journal of Applied Psychology*, *88*, 989–1004.

Becker, B. E., & Huselid, M. A. (1992). Direct estimates of SDy and the implications for utility analysis. *Journal of Applied Psychology*, *77*, 227–233.

Beehr, T. A., Bowling, N. A., & Bennett, M. M. (2010). Occupational stress and failures of social support: When helping hurts. *Journal of Occupational Health Psychology*, *15*, 45–59.

Bell, S. T., & Arthur, W., Jr. (2008). Feedback acceptance in developmental assessment centers: The role of feedback message, participant personality, and affective response to the feedback session. *Journal of Organizational Behavior*, *29*, 681–703.

Bendak, S. (2003). 12-h workdays: Current knowledge and future directions. *Work and Stress*, *17*, 321–336.

Benjamin, L. T., Jr. (1997). Organized industrial psychology before Division 14: The ACP and the AAAP (1930–1945). *Journal of Applied Psychology*, *82*, 459–466.

Bennett, R. J., & Robinson, S. L. (2000). Development of a measure of workplace deviance. *Journal of Applied Psychology*, *85*, 349–360.

Berdahl, J. L., & Moore, C. (2006). Workplace harassment: Double jeopardy for minority women. *Journal of Applied Psychology*, *91*, 426–436.

Bergman, M. E., Palmieri, P. A., Drasgow, F., & Ormerod, A. J. (2007). Racial and ethnic harassment and discrimination: In the eye of the beholder? *Journal of Occupational Health Psychology*, *12*, 144–160.

Bernardin, H. J. (1988). Police officer. In S. Gael (Ed.), *Job analysis handbook* (pp. 1242–1254). New York, NY: John Wiley.

Bernardin, H. J., & Beatty, R. W. (1984). *Performance appraisal: Assessing human behavior at work*. Boston, MA: Kent.

Bernardin, H. J., & Pence, E. C. (1980). Effects of rater training: Creating new response sets and decreasing accuracy. *Journal of Applied Psychology, 65*, 60–66.

Berry, C. M., Ones, D. S., & Sackett, P. R. (2007). Interpersonal deviance, organizational deviance, and their common correlates: A review and meta-analysis. *Journal of Applied Psychology, 92*, 410–424.

Berry, M. O. N., Reichman, W., Klobas, J., MacLachlan, M., Hui, H. C., & Carr, S. C. (2011). Humanitarian work psychology: The contributions of organizational psychology to poverty reduction. *Journal of Economic Psychology, 32*, 240–247..

Bertolino, M., & Steiner, D. D. (2007). Fairness reactions to selection methods: An Italian study. *International Journal of Selection and Assessment, 15*, 197–205.

Bettenhausen, K. L. (1991). Five years of groups research: What we have learned and what needs to be addressed. *Journal of Management, 17*, 345–381.

Beus, J. M., Payne, S. C., Bergman, M. E., & Arthur, W., Jr. (2010). Safety climate and injuries: An examination of theoretical and empirical relationships. *Journal of Applied Psychology, 95*, 713–727.

Birdi, K., Warr, P., & Oswald, A. (1995). Age differences in three components of employee well-being. *Applied Psychology: An International Review, 44*, 345–373.

Birkeland, S. A., Manson, T. M., Kisamore, J. L., Brannick, M. T., & Smith, M. A. (2006). A meta-analytic investigation of job applicant faking on personality measures. *International Journal of Selection and Assessment, 14*, 317–335.

Bishop, G. D., Enkelmann, H. C., Tong, E. M., Why, Y. P., Diong, S. M., Ang, J., & Khader, M. (2003). Job demands, decisional control, and cardiovascular responses. *Journal of Occupational Health Psychology, 8*, 146–156.

Bishop, J. W., & Scott, K. D. (2000). An examination of organizational and team commitment in a self-directed team environment. *Journal of Applied Psychology, 85*, 439–450.

Bishop, J. W., Scott, K. D., & Burroughs, S. M. (2000). Support, commitment, and employee outcomes in a team environment. *Journal of Management, 26*, 1113–1132.

Blanz, F., & Ghiselli, E. E. (1972). The mixed standard scale: A new rating system. *Personnel Psychology, 25*, 185–199.

Blau, G. (1993). Testing the relationship of locus of control to different performance dimensions. *Journal of Occupational and Organizational Psychology, 66*, 125–138.

Blau, G. (2007). Does a corresponding set of variables for explaining voluntary organizational turnover transfer to explaining voluntary occupational. *Journal of Vocational Behavior, 70*, 135–148.

Blickle, G., Witzki, A. H., & Schneider, P. B. (2009). Mentoring support and power: A three year predictive field study on protege networking and career success. *Journal of Vocational Behavior, 74*, 181–189.

Bohle, P., & Tilley, A. J. (1998). Early experience of shiftwork: Influences on attitudes. *Journal of Occupational and Organizational Psychology, 71*, 61–79.

Bolino, M. C., & Turnley, W. H. (2008). Old faces, new places: Equity theory in cross-cultural contexts. *Journal of Organizational Behavior, 29*, 29–50.

Bommer, W. H., Miles, E. W., & Grover, S. L. (2003). Does one good turn deserve another? Coworker influences on employee citizenship. *Journal of Organizational Behavior, 24*, 181–196.

Bommer, W. H., Rich, G. A., & Rubin, R. S. (2005). Changing attitudes about change: Longitudinal effects of transformational leader behavior on employee cynicism about organizational change. *Journal of Organizational Behavior, 26*, 733–753.

Bonner, B. L., Baumann, M. R., & Dalal, R. S. (2002). The effects of member expertise on group decision-making and performance. *Organizational*

Behavior and Human Decision Processes, *88*, 719–736.

Bono, J. E., Purvanova, R. K., Towler, A. J., & Peterson, D. B. (2009). A survey of executive coaching practices. *Personnel Psychology*, *62*, 361–404.

Borman, W. C. (1987). Personal constructs, performance schemata, and "folk theories" of subordinate effectiveness: Explorations in an army officer sample. *Organizational Behavior and Human Decision Processes*, *40*, 307–322.

Borman, W. C., Bryant, R. H., & Dorio, J. (2010). The measurement of task performance as criteria in selection research. In J. L. Farr & N. T. Tippins (Eds.), *Handbook of employee selection*. New York, NY: Routledge.

Borman, W. C., Buck, D. E., Hanson, M. A., Motowidlo, S. J., Stark, S., & Drasgow, F. (2001). An examination of the comparative reliability, validity, and accuracy of performance ratings made using computerized adaptive rating scales. *Journal of Applied Psychology*, *86*, 965–973.

Borman, W. C., Dorsey, D., & Ackerman, L. (1992). Time-spent responses as time allocation strategies: Relations with sales performance in a stockbroker sample. *Personnel Psychology*, *45*, 763–777.

Borman, W. C., Peterson, N. G., & Russell, T. L. (1992). Selection, training, and development of personnel. In G. Salvendy (Ed.), *Handbook of industrial engineering* (2nd ed., pp. 882–914). New York, NY: John Wiley.

Boswell, W. R., Shipp, A. J., Payne, S. C., & Culbertson, S. S. (2009). Changes in newcomer job satisfaction over time: Examining the pattern of honeymoons and hangovers. *Journal of Applied Psychology*, *94*, 844–858.

Boudreau, J. W. (1983). Economic considerations in estimating the utility of human resource productivity improvement programs. *Personnel Psychology*, *36*, 551–576.

Bowers, D. G. (1973). OD techniques and their results in 23 organizations: The Michigan ICL study. *Journal of Applied Behavioral Science*, *9*, 21–43.

Bowler, M. C., & Woehr, D. J. (2009). Assessment center construct-related validity: Stepping beyond the MTMM matrix. *Journal of Vocational Behavior*, *75*, 173–182.

Bowling, N. A., & Beehr, T. A. (2006). Workplace harassment from the victim's perspective: A theoretical model and meta-analysis. *Journal of Applied Psychology*, *91*, 998–1012.

Bowling, N. A., Beehr, T. A., & Lepisto, L. R. (2006). Beyond job satisfaction: A five-year prospective analysis of the dispositional approach to work attitudes. *Journal of Vocational Behavior*, *69*, 315–330.

Bowling, N. A., & Hammond, G. D. (2008). A meta-analytic examination of the construct validity of the Michigan Organizational Assessment Questionnaire Job Satisfaction Subscale. *Journal of Vocational Behavior*, *73*, 63–77.

Bragg, J., & Andrews, I. (1973). Participative decision making: An experimental study in a hospital. *Journal of Applied Behavioral Science*, *9*, 727–735.

Brannick, M. T., Levine, E. L., & Morgeson, F. P. (2007). *Job and work analysis*. Thousand Oaks, CA: Sage.

Brasher, E. E., & Chen, P. Y. (1999). Evaluation of success criteria in job search: A process perspective. *Journal of Occupational and Organizational Psychology*, *72*, 57–70.

Breaugh, J. A. (2009). The use of biodata for employee selection: Past research and future directions. *Human Resource Management Review*, *19*, 219–231.

Breaugh, J. A., & Starke, M. (2000). Research on employee recruitment: So many studies, so many remaining questions. *Journal of Management*, *26*, 405–434.

Brett, J. F., & Atwater, L. E. (2001). 360 degrees feedback: Accuracy, reactions, and perceptions of usefulness. *Journal of Applied Psychology*, *86*, 930–942.

Brief, A. P., & Weiss, H. M. (2002). Organizational behavior: Affect in the workplace. *Annual Review of Psychology*, *53*, 279–307.

Broadbent, D. E., & Gath, D. (1981). Symptom levels in assembly-line workers. In G. Salvendy & M.

J. Smith (Eds.), *Machine pacing and occupational stress* (pp. 244–252). London, England: Taylor & Francis.

Brown, K. G. (2005). A field study of employee e-learning activity and outcomes. *Human Resource Development Quarterly*, *16*, 465–480.

Bruck, C. S., & Allen, T. D. (2003). The relationship between Big Five personality traits, negative affectivity, Type A behavior, and work-family conflict. *Journal of Vocational Behavior*, *63*, 457–472.

Buck, J. R. (1983). Controls and tools. In B. H. Kantowitz & R. D. Sorkin (Eds.), *Human factors* (pp. 195–231). New York, NY: John Wiley.

Buller, P. F. (1986). The team building–task performance relation: Some conceptual and methodological refinements. *Group and Organization Studies*, *11*, 147–168.

Bunker, K. A., & Cohen, S. L. (1977). The rigors of training evaluation: A discussion and field demonstration. *Personnel Psychology*, *30*, 525–541.

Bureau of Labor Statistics. (2006). Survey of workplace violence prevention, 2005. Retrieved June 6, 2010, from http://www.bls.gov/iif/oshwc/osnr0026.pdf

Bureau of Labor Statistics. (2010). Census of fatal occupational injuries charts, 1992–2008 (revised data). Retrieved June 5, 2010, from http://www.bls.gov/iif/oshwc/cfoi/cfch0007.pdf

Cable, D. M., & Judge, T. A. (1997). Interviewers' perceptions of person-organization fit and organizational selection decisions. *Journal of Applied Psychology*, *82*, 546–561.

Caldwell, D. F., & O'Reilly, C. A. (1990). Measuring person-job fit with a profile-comparison process. *Journal of Applied Psychology*, *75*, 648–657.

Callahan, J. S., Kiker, D., & Cross, T. (2003). Does method matter? A meta-analysis of the effects of training method on older learner training performance. *Journal of Management*, *29*, 663–680.

Callinan, M., & Robertson, I. T. (2000). Work sample testing. *International Journal of Selection and Assessment*, *8*, 248–260.

Campbell, J. P., Gasser, M. B., & Oswald, F. L. (1996). The substantive nature of job performance variability. In K. R. Murphy (Ed.), *Individual differences and behavior in organizations* (pp. 258–299). San Francisco, CA: Jossey-Bass.

Campion, M. A., & Campion, J. E. (1987). Evaluation of an interviewee skills training program in a natural field experiment. *Personnel Psychology*, *40*, 675–691.

Campion, M. A., Palmer, D. K., & Campion, J. E. (1997). A review of structure in the selection interview. *Personnel Psychology*, *50*, 655–702.

Cannon-Bowers, J. A., & Salas, E. (2001). Reflections on shared cognition. *Journal of Organizational Behavior*, *22*, 195–202.

Carless, S. A., Mann, L., & Wearing, A. J. (1998). Leadership, managerial performance and 360-degree feedback. *Applied Psychology: An International Review*, *47*, 481–496.

Cascio, W. F. (1998). *Applied psychology in personnel management* (5th ed.). Englewood Cliffs, NJ: Prentice Hall.

Cascio, W. F., & Aguinis, H. (2008). Research in industrial and organizational psychology from 1963 to 2007: Changes, choices, and trends. *Journal of Applied Psychology*, *93*, 1062–1081.

Cepeda, N. J., Coburn, N., Rohrer, D., Wixted, J. T., Mozer, M. C., & Pashler, H. (2009). Optimizing distributed practice: Theoretical analysis and practical implications. *Experimental Psychology*, *56*, 236–246.

Cepeda, N. J., Pashler, H., Vul, E., Wixted, J. T., & Rohrer, D. (2006). Distributed practice in verbal recall tasks: A review and quantitative synthesis. *Psychological Bulletin*, *132*, 354–380.

Cepeda, N. J., Vul, E., Rohrer, D., Wixted, J. T., & Pashler, H. (2008). Spacing effects in learning: A temporal ridgeline of optimal retention. *Psychological Science*, *19*, 1095–1102.

Chan, D. (1996). Criterion and construct validation of an assessment centre. *Journal of Occupational and Organizational Psychology*, *69*, 167–181.

Chapman, D. S., & Rowe, P. M. (2001). The impact of videoconference technology, interview structure, and interviewer gender on interviewer evaluations in the employment interview: A field experiment. *Journal of Occupational and Organizational Psychology*, *74*, 279–298.

Chapman, D. S., Uggerslev, K. L., Carroll, S. A., Piasentin, K. A., & Jones, D. A. (2005). Applicant attraction to organizations and job choice: A meta-analytic review of the correlates of recruiting outcomes. *Journal of Applied Psychology*, *90*, 928–944.

Chapman, D. S., Uggerslev, K. L., & Webster, J. (2003). Applicant reactions to face-to-face and technology-mediated interviews: A field investigation. *Journal of Applied Psychology*, *88*, 944–953.

Chapman, D. S., & Webster, J. (2003). The use of technologies in the recruiting, screening, and selection processes for job candidates. *International Journal of Selection and Assessment*, *11*, 113–120.

Chiu, W. C., & Ng, C. W. (1999). Women-friendly HRM and organizational commitment: A study among women and men of organizations in Hong Kong. *Journal of Occupational and Organizational Psychology*, *72*, 485–502.

Choi, J. N., & Price, R. H. (2005). The effects of person-innovation fit on individual responses to innovation. *Journal of Occupational and Organizational Psychology*, *78*, 83–96.

Christian, M. S., Bradley, J. C., Wallace, J., & Burke, M. J. (2009). Workplace safety: A meta-analysis of the roles of person and situation factors. *Journal of Applied Psychology*, *94*, 1103–1127.

Christiansen, N. D., Janovics, J. E., & Siers, B. P. (2010). Emotional intelligence in selection contexts: Measurement method, criterion-related validity, and vulnerability to response distortion. *International Journal of Selection and Assessment*, *18*, 87–101.

Cigularov, K. P., Chen, P. Y., & Stallones, L. (2009). Error communication in young farm workers: Its relationship to safety climate and safety locus of control. *Work and Stress*, *23*, 297–312.

Clark, A., Oswald, A., & Warr, P. (1996). Is job satisfaction U-shaped in age? *Journal of Occupational and Organizational Psychology*, *69*, 57–81.

Clarke, S. (2010). An integrative model of safety climate: Linking psychological climate and work attitudes to individual safety outcomes using meta-analysis. *Journal of Occupational and Organizational Psychology*, *83*, 553–578.

Cleveland, J. N., Barnes-Ferrell, J. L., & Ratz, J. M. (1997). Accommodation in the workplace. *Human Resource Management Review*, *7*, 77–107.

Cober, R. T. (2000). The quest for the qualified job surfer: It's time the public sector catches the wave. *Public Personnel Management*, *29*, 479.

Coch, L., & French, J. R. (1948). Overcoming resistance to change. *Human Relations*, *1*, 512–532.

Cohen, A. (2006). The relationship between multiple commitments and organizational citizenship behavior in Arab and Jewish culture. *Journal of Vocational Behavior*, *69*, 105–118.

Cohen-Charash, Y., & Spector, P. E. (2001). The role of justice in organizations: A meta-analysis. *Organizational Behavior and Human Decision Processes*, *86*, 278–321.

Colquitt, J. A., LePine, J. A., & Noe, R. A. (2000). Toward an integrative theory of training motivation: A meta-analytic path analysis of 20 years of research. *Journal of Applied Psychology*, *85*, 678–707.

Connolly, J. J., & Viswesvaran, C. (2000). The role of affectivity in job satisfaction: A meta-analysis. *Personality and Individual Differences*, *29*, 265–281.

Conte, J. M., Dean, M. A., Ringenbach, K. L., Moran, S. K., & Landy, F. J. (2005). The relationship between work attitudes and job analysis ratings: Do rating scale type and task discretion matter? *Human Performance*, *18*, 1–21.

Converse, P. D., Oswald, F. L., Gillespie, M. A., Field, K. A., Bizot, E. B., & Smither, J. W. (2004). Matching individuals to occupations using abilities and the O*NET: Issues and an application in career guidance. *Personnel Psychology*, *57*, 451–487.

Cooper, R., & Foster, M. (1971). Sociotechical systems. *American Psychologist*, *26*, 467–474.

Cooper-Hakim, A., & Viswesvaran, C. (2005). The construct of work commitment: Testing an integrative framework. *Psychological Bulletin*, *131*, 241–259.

Coovert, M. D. (1990). Development and evaluation of five user models of human-computer interaction. *End-user training* (pp. 105–139). Oxford, England: Walter De Gruyter.

Coovert, M. D., & Thompson, L. F. (2001). *Computer supported cooperative work: Issues and implications for workers, organizations, and human resource management*. Thousand Oaks, CA: Sage.

Cordery, J. L., Mueller, W. S., & Smith, L. M. (1991). Attitudinal and behavioral effects of autonomous group working: A longitudinal field study. *Academy of Management Journal*, *34*, 464–476.

Cornelius, E. T., DeNisi, A. S., & Blencoe, A. G. (1984). Expert and naive raters using the PAQ: Does it matter? [Comment/Reply]. *Personnel Psychology*, *37*, 453–464.

Cropanzano, R., Byrne, Z. S., Bobocel, D., & Rupp, D. E. (2001). Moral virtues, fairness heuristics, social entities, and other denizens of organizational justice. *Journal of Vocational Behavior*, *58*, 164–209.

Cropanzano, R., Howes, J. C., Grandey, A. A., & Toth, P. (1997). The relationship of organizational politics and support to work behaviors, attitudes, and stress. *Journal of Organizational Behavior*, *18*, 159–180.

Cunningham, C. E., Woodward, C. A., Shannon, H. S., MacIntosh, J., Lendrum, B., Rosenbloom, D., & Brown, J. (2002). Readiness for organizational change: A longitudinal study of workplace, psychological and behavioural correlates. *Journal of Occupational and Organizational Psychology*, *75*, 377–392.

Dahling, J. J., & Perez, L. A. (2010). Older worker, different actor? Linking age and emotional labor strategies. *Personality and Individual Differences*, *48*, 574–578.

Dalton, D. R., & Mesch, D. J. (1991). On the extent and reduction of avoidable absenteeism: An assessment of absence policy provisions. *Journal of Applied Psychology*, *76*, 810–817.

Dansereau, F., Graen, G., & Haga, W. J. (1975). A vertical dyad linkage approach to leadership within formal organizations: A longitudinal investigation of the role making process. *Organizational Behavior and Human Performance*, *13*, 46–78.

Daus, C. S., Sanders, D. N., & Campbell, D. P. (1998). Consequences of alternate work schedules. In C. L. Cooper & I. T. Robertson (Eds.), *International review of industrial and organizational psychology: 1998* (pp. 185–223). Chichester, England: John Wiley.

Davis, J. H. (1969). *Group performance*. Reading, MA: Addison-Wesley.

Davis, W. D., Fedor, D. B., Parsons, C. K., & Herold, D. M. (2000). The development of self-efficacy during aviation training. *Journal of Organizational Behavior*, *21*, 857–871.

Day, D. V., & Sulsky, L. M. (1995). Effects of frame-of-reference training and information configuration on memory organization and rating accuracy. *Journal of Applied Psychology*, *80*, 158–167.

Dayan, K., Kasten, R., & Fox, S. (2002). Entry-level police candidate assessment center: An efficient tool or a hammer to kill a fly? *Personnel Psychology*, *55*, 827–849.

De Dreu, C. K. (2006). When too little or too much hurts: Evidence for a curvilinear relationship between task conflict and innovation in teams. *Journal of Management*, *32*, 83–107.

de Haas, S., Timmerman, G., & Hoing, M. (2009). Sexual harassment and health among male and female police officers. *Journal of Occupational Health Psychology*, *14*, 390–401.

Deadrick, D. L., Bennett, N., & Russell, C. J. (1997). Using hierarchical linear modeling to examine dynamic performance criteria over time. *Journal of Management*, *23*, 745–757.

Deadrick, D. L., & Madigan, R. M. (1990). Dynamic criteria revisited: A longitudinal study of performance stability and predictive validity. *Personnel Psychology*, *43*, 717–744.

DeChurch, L. A., & Mesmer-Magnus, J. R. (2010). The cognitive underpinnings of effective teamwork: A meta-analysis. *Journal of Applied Psychology, 95*, 32–53.

Del Ben, K. S., Scotti, J. R., Chen, Y. C., & Fortson, B. L. (2006). Prevalence of posttraumatic stress disorder symptoms in firefighters. *Work and Stress, 20*, 37–48.

DeNisi, A. S., Cafferty, T. P., & Meglino, B. M. (1984). A cognitive view of the performance appraisal process: A model and research propositions. *Organizational Behavior and Human Performance, 33*, 360–396.

Dennis, A. R., & Valacich, J. S. (1993). Computer brainstorms: More heads are better than one. *Journal of Applied Psychology, 78*, 531–537.

Derouin, R. E., Fritzsche, B. A., & Salas, E. (2005). E-learning in organizations. *Journal of Management, 31*, 920–940.

DeShon, R. P., & Gillespie, J. Z. (2005). A motivated action theory account of goal orientation. *Journal of Applied Psychology, 90*, 1096–1127.

DeVoe, S. E., & Iyengar, S. S. (2004). Managers' theories of subordinates: A cross-cultural examination of manager perceptions of motivation and appraisal of performance. *Organizational Behavior and Human Decision Processes, 93*, 47–61.

Dickinson, T. L., & Glebocki, G. G. (1990). Modifications in the format of the mixed standard scale. *Organizational Behavior and Human Decision Processes, 47*, 124–137.

Dickter, D. N., Roznowski, M., & Harrison, D. A. (1996). Temporal tempering: An event history analysis of the process of voluntary turnover. *Journal of Applied Psychology, 81*, 705–716.

Diefendorff, J. M., Hall, R. J., Lord, R. G., & Strean, M. L. (2000). Action-state orientation: Construct validity of a revised measure and its relationship to work-related variables. *Journal of Applied Psychology, 85*, 250–263.

Diefendorff, J. M., Richard, E. M., & Croyle, M. H. (2006). Are emotional display rules formal job requirements? Examination of employee and supervisor perceptions. *Journal of Occupational and Organizational Psychology, 79*, 273–298.

Dierdorff, E. C., & Morgeson, F. P. (2009). Effects of descriptor specificity and observability on incumbent work analysis ratings. *Personnel Psychology, 62*, 601–628.

Dierdorff, E. C., & Wilson, M. A. (2003). A meta-analysis of job analysis reliability. *Journal of Applied Psychology, 88*, 635–646.

Dipboye, R. L. (1990). Laboratory vs. field research in industrial and organizational psychology. In C. L. Cooper & I. T. Robertson (Eds.), *International review of industrial and organizational psychology: 1990* (pp. 1–34). Chichester, England: John Wiley.

Dipboye, R. L., & Gaugler, B. B. (1993). Cognitive and behavioral processes in the selection interview. In N. Schmitt & W. C. Borman (Eds.), *Personnel selection in organizations*. San Francisco, CA: Jossey-Bass.

Doerr, K. H., Mitchell, T. R., Klastorin, T. D., & Brown, K. A. (1996). Impact of material flow policies and goals on job outcomes. *Journal of Applied Psychology, 81*, 142–152.

Donovan, J. J., & Williams, K. J. (2003). Missing the mark: Effects of time and causal attributions on goal revision in response to goal-performance discrepancies. *Journal of Applied Psychology, 88*, 379–390.

Dormann, C., & Zapf, D. (1999). Social support, social stressors at work, and depressive symptoms: Testing for main and moderating effects with structural equations in a three-wave longitudinal study. *Journal of Applied Psychology, 84*, 874–884.

Dormann, C., & Zapf, D. (2001). Job satisfaction: A meta-analysis of stabilities. *Journal of Organizational Behavior, 22*, 483–504.

Drach-Zahavy, A., & Erez, M. (2002). Challenge versus threat effects on the goal-performance relationship. *Organizational Behavior and Human Decision Processes, 88*, 667–682.

Driskell, J. E., Willis, R. P., & Copper, C. (1992). Effect of overlearning on retention. *Journal of Applied Psychology, 77*, 615–622.

Dudley, N. M., Orvis, K. A., Lebiecki, J. E., & Cortina, J. M. (2006). A meta-analytic investigation of conscientiousness in the prediction of job performance: Examining the intercorrelations and the incremental validity of narrow traits. *Journal of Applied Psychology*, *91*, 40–57.

Dunham, R. B., Grube, J. A., & Castaneda, M. B. (1994). Organizational commitment: The utility of an integrative definition. *Journal of Applied Psychology*, *79*, 370–380.

Eagly, A. H., & Johnson, B. T. (1990). Gender and leadership style: A meta-analysis. *Psychological Bulletin*, *108*, 233–256.

Earley, P. (1989). Social loafing and collectivism: A comparison of the United States and the People's Republic of China. *Administrative Science Quarterly*, *34*, 565–581.

Eby, L. T., Durley, J. R., Evans, S. C., & Ragins, B. R. (2006). The relationship between short-term mentoring benefits and long-term mentor outcomes. *Journal of Vocational Behavior*, *69*, 424–444.

Eby, L. T., Durley, J. R., Evans, S. C., & Ragins, B. R. (2008). Mentors' perceptions of negative mentoring experiences: Scale development and nomological validation. *Journal of Applied Psychology*, *93*, 358–373.

Eden, D., & Aviram, A. (1993). Self-efficacy training to speed reemployment: Helping people to help themselves. *Journal of Applied Psychology*, *78*, 352–360.

Eden, D., & Zuk, Y. (1995). Seasickness as a self-fulfilling prophecy: Raising self-efficacy to boost performance at sea. *Journal of Applied Psychology*, *80*, 628–635.

Edwards, B. D., Day, E. A., Arthur, W., Jr., & Bell, S. T. (2006). Relationships among team ability composition, team mental models, and team performance. *Journal of Applied Psychology*, *91*, 727–736.

Eleftheriou, A., & Robertson, I. (1999). A survey of management selection practices in Greece. *International Journal of Selection and Assessment*, *7*, 203–208.

Elicker, J. D., Foust, M. S., O'Malley, A. L., & Levy, P. E. (2008). Employee lateness behavior: The role of lateness climate and individual lateness attitude. *Human Performance*, *21*, 427–441.

Elovainio, M., & Kivimäki, M. (1999). Personal need for structure and occupational strain: An investigation of structural models and interaction with job complexity. *Personality and Individual Differences*, *26*, 209–222.

Elovainio, M., Kivimäki, M., Vahtera, J., Virtanen, M., & Keltikangas-Jarvinen, L. (2003). Personality as a moderator in the relations between perceptions of organizational justice and sickness absence. *Journal of Vocational Behavior*, *63*, 379–395.

Ensari, N., & Murphy, S. E. (2003). Cross-cultural variations in leadership perceptions and attribution of charisma to the leader. *Organizational Behavior and Human Decision Processes*, *92*, 52–66.

Erickson, R. J., Nichols, L., & Ritter, C. (2000). Family influences on absenteeism: Testing an expanded process model. *Journal of Vocational Behavior*, *57*, 246–272.

Escorpizo, R. (2008). Understanding work productivity and its application to work-related musculoskeletal disorders. *International Journal of Industrial Ergonomics*, *38*, 291–297.

Euwema, M. C., Wendt, H., & van Emmerik, H. (2007). Leadership styles and group organizational citizenship behavior across cultures. *Journal of Organizational Behavior*, *28*, 1035–1057.

Evans, D. C. (2003). A comparison of the other-directed stigmatization produced by legal and illegal forms of affirmative action. *Journal of Applied Psychology*, *88*, 121–130.

Eyde, L. D. (1983). Evaluating job evaluation: Emerging research issues for comparable worth analysis. *Public Personnel Management*, *12*, 425–444.

Farh, J. L., Podsakoff, P. M., & Organ, D. W. (1990). Accounting for organizational citizenship behavior: Leader fairness and task scope versus satisfaction. *Journal of Management*, *16*, 705–721.

Farr, J. L., Hofmann, D. A., & Ringenbach, K. L. (1993). Goal orientation and action control theory: Implications for industrial and organizational psychology. In C. L. Cooper & I. T. Robertson (Eds.), *International review of industrial and organizational psychology: 1993* (pp. 193–232). Chichester, England: John Wiley.

Farrell, D., & Stamm, C. L. (1988). Meta-analysis of the correlates of employee absence. *Human Relations*, *41*, 211–227.

Fassina, N. E., Jones, D. A., & Uggerslev, K. L. (2008). Meta-analytic tests of relationships between organizational justice and citizenship behavior: Testing agent-system and shared-variance models. *Journal of Organizational Behavior*, *29*, 805–828.

Faucett, J. (2005). Integrating "psychosocial" factors into a theoretical model for work-related musculoskeletal disorders. *Theoretical Issues in Ergonomics Science*, *6*, 531–550.

Federal Bureau of Investigation. (2010a). 2008 crime in the United States. Retrieved June 6, 2010, from http://www.fbi.gov/ucr/cius2008/data/table_07.html

Federal Bureau of Investigation. (2010b). 2008 law enforcement officers killed & assaulted. Retrieved June 6, 2010, from http://www.fbi.gov/ucr/killed/2008/data/table_01.html

Federation of Irish Employers. (1991). *Personnel policies and procedures guidelines*. Dublin, Ireland: Baggot Bridge House.

Feldman, J. M. (1981). Beyond attribution theory: Cognitive processes in performance appraisal. *Journal of Applied Psychology*, *66*, 127–148.

Fernet, C., Guay, F., & Senecal, C. (2004). Adjusting to job demands: The role of work self-determination and job control in predicting burnout. *Journal of Vocational Behavior*, *65*, 39–56.

Ferris, G. R., Judge, T. A., Rowland, K. M., & Fitzgibbons, D. E. (1994). Subordinate influence and the performance evaluation process: Test of a model. *Organizational Behavior and Human Decision Processes*, *58*, 101–135.

Ferris, G. R., Treadway, D. C., Kolodinsky, R. W., Hochwarter, W. A., Kacmar, C. J., Douglas, C., & Frink, D. D. (2005). Development and validation of the Political Skill Inventory. *Journal of Management*, *31*, 126–152.

Fiedler, F. E. (1978). The contingency model and the dynamics of the leadership process. In L. Berkowitz (Ed.), *Advances in experimental social psychology* (pp. 59–112). New York: Academic Press.

Field, R. H., & House, R. J. (1990). A test of the Vroom-Yetton model using manager and subordinate reports. *Journal of Applied Psychology*, *75*, 362–366.

Fine, S. A., & Wiley, W. W. (1971). *An introduction to functional job analysis methods for manpower analysis* [Monograph No. 4]. W. E. Upjohn Institute.

Fisher, C. D. (2000). Mood and emotions while working: Missing pieces of job satisfaction? *Journal of Organizational Behavior*, *21*, 185–202.

Fitzgerald, L. F., Drasgow, F., Hulin, C. L., Gelfand, M. J., & Magley, V. J. (1997). Antecedents and consequences of sexual harassment in organizations: A test of an integrated model. *Journal of Applied Psychology*, *82*, 578–589.

Flanagan, J. C. (1954). The critical incident technique. *Psychological Bulletin*, *51*, 327–358.

Fleishman, E. A., & Harris, E. F. (1962). Patterns of leadership behavior related to employee grievances and turnover. *Personnel Psychology*, *15*, 43–56.

Fletcher, C., & Baldry, C. (2000). A study of individual differences and self-awareness in the context of multi-source feedback. *Journal of Occupational and Organizational Psychology*, *73*, 303–319.

Ford, J. K., & Kraiger, K. K. (1995). The application of cognitive constructs and principles to the instructional systems model of training: Implications for needs assessment, design, and transfer. In C. L. Cooper & I. T. Robertson (Eds.), *International review of industrial and organizational psychology: 1995* (pp. 1–48). Chichester, England: John Wiley.

Ford, J. K., & Wroten, S. P. (1984). Introducing new methods for conducting training evaluation and for linking training evaluation to program redesign. *Personnel Psychology*, *37*, 651–665.

Ford, M. T., Heinen, B. A., & Langkamer, K. L. (2007). Work and family satisfaction and conflict: A meta-analysis of cross-domain relations. *Journal of Applied Psychology*, *92*, 57–80.

Foust, M. S., Elicker, J. D., & Levy, P. E. (2006). Development and validation of a measure of an individual's lateness attitude. *Journal of Vocational Behavior*, *69*, 119–133.

Fowler, F. J., Jr. (1988). *Survey research methods* (Rev. ed.). Thousand Oaks, CA: Sage.

Fox, S., Spector, P. E., & Miles, D. (2001). Counterproductive work behavior (CWB) in response to job stressors and organizational justice: Some mediator and moderator tests for autonomy and emotions. *Journal of Vocational Behavior*, *59*, 291–309.

Fox, S., & Stallworth, L. E. (2005). Racial/ethnic bullying: Exploring links between bullying and racism in the US workplace. *Journal of Vocational Behavior*, *66*, 438–456.

Frankenhaeuser, M., & Johansson, G. (1986). Stress at work: Psychobiological and psychosocial aspects. *International Review of Applied Psychology*, *35*, 287–299.

French, J. R. P., Jr., & Raven, B. (1959). The bases of social power. In D. Cartwright (Ed.), *Studies in social power* (pp. 150–167). Ann Arbor, MI: Institute for Social Research.

Frese, M. (1987). Human-computer interaction in the office. In C. L. Cooper & I. T. Robertson (Eds.), *International review of industrial and organizational psychology: 1987* (pp. 117–165). Chichester, England: John Wiley.

Frese, M., & Zapf, D. (1988). Methodological issues in the study of work stress: Objective vs subjective measurement of work stress and the question of longitudinal studies. In C. L. Cooper & R. Payne (Eds.), *Causes, coping and consequences of stress at work* (pp. 375–411). Oxford, England: John Wiley.

Frese, M., & Zapf, D. (1994). *Action as the core of work psychology: A German approach*. Palo Alto, CA: Consulting Psychologists Press.

Fried, Y., Ben-David, H. A., Tiegs, R. B., Avital, N., & Yeverechyahu, U. (1998). The interactive effect of role conflict and role ambiguity on job performance. *Journal of Occupational and Organizational Psychology*, *71*, 19–27.

Fried, Y., & Ferris, G. R. (1987). The validity of the Job Characteristics Model: A review and meta-analysis. *Personnel Psychology*, *40*, 287–322.

Fritz, C., & Sonnentag, S. (2006). Recovery, well-being, and performance-related outcomes: The role of workload and vacation experiences. *Journal of Applied Psychology*, *91*, 936–945.

Fritz, C., Yankelevich, M., Zarubin, A., & Barger, P. (2010). Happy, healthy, and productive: The role of detachment from work during nonwork time. *Journal of Applied Psychology*, *95*, 977–983.

Frone, M. R. (2008). Are work stressors related to employee substance use? The importance of temporal context assessments of alcohol and illicit drug use. *Journal of Applied Psychology*, *93*, 199–206.

Fugate, M., Kinicki, A. J., & Prussia, G. E. (2008). Employee coping with organizational change: An examination of alternative theoretical perspectives and models. *Personnel Psychology*, *61*, 1–36.

Fullagar, C. J., Gallagher, D. G., Clark, P. F., & Carroll, A. E. (2004). Union commitment and participation: A 10-year longitudinal study. *Journal of Applied Psychology*, *89*, 730–737.

Fuller, J. A., Stanton, J. M., Fisher, G. G., Spitzmuller, C., Russell, S. S., & Smith, P. C. (2003). A lengthy look at the daily grind: Time series analysis of events, mood, stress, and satisfaction. *Journal of Applied Psychology*, *88*, 1019–1033.

Funke, J. (1998). Computer-based testing and training with scenarios from complex problem-solving research: Advantages and disadvantages. *International Journal of Selection and Assessment*, *6*, 90–96.

Furnham, A., & Stringfield, P. (1994). Congruence of self and subordinate ratings of managerial practices as a correlate of supervisor evaluation. *Journal of Occupational and Organizational Psychology*, *67*, 57–67.

Furst, S. A., & Cable, D. M. (2008). Employee resistance to organizational change: Managerial influence tactics and leader-member exchange. *Journal of Applied Psychology*, *93*, 453–462.

Gallupe, R., Bastianutti, L. M., & Cooper, W. H. (1991). Unblocking brainstorms. *Journal of Applied Psychology*, *76*, 137–142.

Gallupe, R., Cooper, W. H., Grisé, M. L., & Bastianutti, L. M. (1994). Blocking electronic brainstorms. *Journal of Applied Psychology*, *79*, 77–86.

Gammon, J., Morgan-Samuel, H., & Gould, D. (2008). A review of the evidence for suboptimal compliance of healthcare practitioners to standard/universal infection control precautions. *Journal of Clinical Nursing*, *17*, 157–167.

Ganzach, Y., Kluger, A. N., & Klayman, N. (2000). Making decisions from an interview: Expert measurement and mechanical combination. *Personnel Psychology*, *53*, 1–20.

Gardner, W. L., & Avolio, B. J. (1998). The charismatic relationship: A dramaturgical perspective. *Academy of Management Review*, *23*, 32–58.

Gaudine, A. P., & Saks, A. M. (2001). Effects of an absenteeism feedback intervention on employee absence behavior. *Journal of Organizational Behavior*, *22*, 15–29.

Gerhart, B. (1990). Voluntary turnover and alternative job opportunities. *Journal of Applied Psychology*, *75*, 467–476.

Gerstner, C. R., & Day, D. V. (1997). Meta-analytic review of leader-member exchange theory: Correlates and construct issues. *Journal of Applied Psychology*, *82*, 827–844.

Giacalone, R. A., & Knouse, S. B. (1990). Justifying wrongful employee behavior: The role of personality in organizational sabotage. *Journal of Business Ethics*, *9*, 55–61.

Glasscock, D. J., Rasmussen, K., Carstensen, O., & Hansen, O. N. (2006). Psychosocial factors and safety behaviour as predictors of accidental work injuries in farming. *Work and Stress*, *20*, 173–189.

Glazer, S., & Beehr, T. A. (2005). Consistency of implications of three role stressors across four countries. *Journal of Organizational Behavior*, *26*, 467–487.

Glick, W. H., Jenkins, G., & Gupta, N. (1986). Method versus substance: How strong are underlying relationships between job characteristics and attitudinal outcomes? *Academy of Management Journal*, *29*, 441–464.

Glomb, T. M., & Tews, M. J. (2004). Emotional labor: A conceptualization and scale development. *Journal of Vocational Behavior*, *64*, 1–23.

Goff, S. J., Mount, M. K., & Jamison, R. L. (1990). Employer supported child care, work/family conflict, and absenteeism: A field study. *Personnel Psychology*, *43*, 793–809.

Goldberg, C. B., Finkelstein, L. M., Perry, E. L., & Konrad, A. M. (2004). Job and industry fit: The effects of age and gender matches on career progress outcomes. *Journal of Organizational Behavior*, *25*, 807–829.

Goldberg, L. R., Johnson, J. A., Eber, H. W., Hogan, R., Ashton, M. C., Cloninger, C., & Gough, H. G. (2006). The International Personality Item Pool and the future of public-domain personality measures. *Journal of Research in Personality*, *40*, 84–96.

Goldman, B. M., Gutek, B. A., Stein, J. H., & Lewis, K. (2006). Employment discrimination in organizations: Antecedents and consequences. *Journal of Management*, *32*, 786–830.

Goldstein, I. L. (1993). *Training in organizations: Needs assessment, development, and evaluation* (3rd ed.). Monterey, CA: Brooks/Cole.

Gomez-Mejia, L. R., Page, R. C., & Tornow, W. W. (1982). A comparison of the practical utility of traditional, statistical, and hybrid job evaluation approaches. *Academy of Management Journal*, *25*, 790–809.

Gorman, C., & Rentsch, J. R. (2009). Evaluating frame-of-reference rater training effectiveness using performance schema accuracy. *Journal of Applied Psychology*, *94*, 1336–1344.

Graen, G. B., Novak, M. A., & Sommerkamp, P. (1982). The effects of leader-member exchange and job design on productivity and satisfaction: Testing a dual attachment model. *Organizational Behavior and Human Performance*, *30*, 109–131.

Grandey, A. A., & Diamond, J. A. (2009). Interactions with the public: Bridging job design and emotional labor perspectives. *Journal of Organizational Behavior*, *31*, 338–350.

Grandey, A. A., Fisk, G. M., Mattila, A. S., Jansen, K. J., & Sideman, L. A. (2005). Is "service with a smile" enough? Authenticity of positive displays during service encounters. *Organizational Behavior and Human Decision Processes*, *96*, 38–55.

Grandey, A. A., Fisk, G. M., & Steiner, D. D. (2005). Must "service with a smile" be stressful? The moderating role of personal control for American and French employees. *Journal of Applied Psychology*, *90*, 893–904.

Grant, A. M., Curtayne, L., & Burton, G. (2009). Executive coaching enhances goal attainment, resilience and workplace well-being: A randomised controlled study. *Journal of Positive Psychology*, *4*, 396–407.

Green, S. B., & Stutzman, T. M. (1986). An evaluation of methods to select respondents to structured job-analysis questionnaires. *Personnel Psychology*, *39*, 543–564.

Greenberg, J. (1990). Employee theft as a reaction to underpayment inequity: The hidden cost of pay cuts. *Journal of Applied Psychology*, *75*, 561–568.

Greenberg, J. (2002). Who stole the money, and when? Individual and situational determinants of employee theft. *Organizational Behavior and Human Decision Processes*, *89*, 985–1003.

Greenhaus, J. H., Parasuraman, S., & Wormley, W. M. (1990). Effects of race on organizational experiences, job performance evaluations, and career outcomes. *Academy of Management Journal*, *33*, 64–86.

Greguras, G. J., & Diefendorff, J. M. (2009). Different fits satisfy different needs: Linking person-environment fit to employee commitment and performance using self-determination theory. *Journal of Applied Psychology*, *94*, 465–477.

Greiner, B. A., & Krause, N. (2006). Observational stress factors and musculoskeletal disorders in urban transit operators. *Journal of Occupational Health Psychology*, *11*, 38–51.

Griffeth, R. W., Hom, P. W., & Gaertner, S. (2000). A meta-analysis of antecedents and correlates of employee turnover: Update, moderator tests, and research implications for the next millennium. *Journal of Management*, *26*, 463–488.

Griffin, R. W. (1991). Effects of work redesign on employee perceptions, attitudes, and behaviors: A long-term investigation. *Academy of Management Journal*, *34*, 425–435.

Groth, M., Thurau, T. H., & Walsh, G. (2009). Customer reactions to emotional labor: The roles of employee acting strategies and customer detection accuracy. *Academy of Management Journal*, *52*, 958–974.

Groves, K. S. (2005). Linking leader skills, follower attitudes, and contextual variables via an integrated model of charismatic leadership. *Journal of Management*, *31*, 255–277.

Gutenberg, R. L., Arvey, R. D., Osburn, H. G., & Jeanneret, P. (1983). Moderating effects of decision-making/information-processing job dimensions on test validities. *Journal of Applied Psychology*, *68*, 602–608.

Guzzo, R. A., Jette, R. D., & Katzell, R. A. (1985). The effects of psychologically based intervention programs on worker productivity: A meta-analysis. *Personnel Psychology*, *38*, 275–291.

Hacker, G. R. (1996). *A theoretical approach to the selection of job analysis respondents*. Unpublished doctoral dissertation, University of South Florida.

Hackett, R. D., Bycio, P., & Hausdorf, P. A. (1994). Further assessments of Meyer and Allen's (1991) three-component model of organizational commitment. *Journal of Applied Psychology*, *79*, 15–23.

Hackman, J. R., & Oldham, G. R. (1976). Motivation through the design of work: Test of a theory. *Organizational Behavior and Human Performance*, *16*, 250–279.

Hackman, J. R., & Oldham, G. R. (1980). *Work redesign*. Reading, MA: Addison-Wesley.

Hammer, L. B., Bauer, T. N., & Grandey, A. A. (2003). Work-family conflict and work-related withdrawal behaviors. *Journal of Business and Psychology*, *17*, 419–436.

Hanson, G. C., Hammer, L. B., & Colton, C. L. (2006). Development and validation of a multidimensional scale of perceived work-family positive spillover. *Journal of Occupational Health Psychology*, *11*, 249–265.

Harris, M. M., Becker, A. S., & Smith, D. E. (1993). Does the assessment center scoring method affect the cross-situational consistency of ratings? *Journal of Applied Psychology*, *78*, 675–678.

Harris, M. M., & Schaubroeck, J. (1988). A meta-analysis of self-supervisor, self-peer, and peer-supervisor ratings. *Personnel Psychology*, *41*, 43–62.

Harvey, R. J., & Wilson, M. A. (2000). Yes Virginia, there is an objective reality in job analysis. *Journal of Organizational Behavior*, *21*, 829–854.

Hausknecht, J. P., Day, D. V., & Thomas, S. C. (2004). Applicant reactions to selection procedures: An updated model and meta-analysis. *Personnel Psychology*, *57*, 639–683.

Häusser, J. A., Mojzisch, A., Niesel, M., & Schulz-Hardt, S. (2010). Ten years on: A review of recent research on the Job Demand-Control (-Support) model and psychological well-being. *Work and Stress*, *24*, 1–35.

Hedge, J. W., & Kavanagh, M. J. (1988). Improving the accuracy of performance evaluations: Comparison of three methods of performance appraiser training. *Journal of Applied Psychology*, *73*, 68–73.

Heggestad, E. D., Morrison, M., Reeve, C. L., & McCloy, R. A. (2006). Forced-choice assessments of personality for selection: Evaluating issues of normative assessment and faking resistance. *Journal of Applied Psychology*, *91*, 9–24.

Heilman, M. E., & Alcott, V. B. (2001). What I think you think of me: Women's reactions to being viewed as beneficiaries of preferential selection. *Journal of Applied Psychology*, *86*, 574–582.

Heilman, M. E., Battle, W. S., Keller, C. E., & Lee, R. (1998). Type of affirmative action policy: A determinant of reactions to sex-based preferential selection? *Journal of Applied Psychology*, *83*, 190–205.

Heilman, M. E., Kaplow, S. R., Amato, M. A., & Stathatos, P. (1993). When similarity is a liability: Effects of sex-based preferential selection on reactions to like-sex and different-sex others. *Journal of Applied Psychology*, *78*, 917–927.

Heilman, M. E., McCullough, W. F., & Gilbert, D. (1996). The other side of affirmative action: Reactions of nonbeneficiaries to sex-based preferential selection. *Journal of Applied Psychology*, *81*, 346–357.

Hempel, P. S., Zhang, Z. X., & Tjosvold, D. (2009). Conflict management between and within teams for trusting relationships and performance in China. *Journal of Organizational Behavior*, *30*, 41–65.

Herold, D. M., Davis, W., Fedor, D. B., & Parsons, C. K. (2002). Dispositional influences on transfer of learning in multistage training programs. *Personnel Psychology*, *55*, 851–869.

Hershcovis, M. S. (2010). Towards a multi-foci approach to workplace aggression: A meta-analytic review of outcomes from different perpetrators. *Journal of Organizational Behavior*, *31*, 24–44.

Hershcovis, M. S., Turner, N., Barling, J., Arnold, K. A., Dupré, K. E., Inness, M., . . . Sivanathan, N. (2007). Predicting workplace aggression: A meta-analysis. *Journal of Applied Psychology*, *92*, 228–238.

Herzberg, F. (1968, January/February). One more time: How do you motivate employees? *Harvard Business Review*, 52–62.

Heslop, P., Smith, G. D., Metcalfe, C., Macleod, J., & Hart, C. (2002). Change in job satisfaction, and its association with self-reported stress, cardiovascular risk factors and mortality. *Social Science and Medicine*, *54*, 1589–1599.

Hirschfeld, R. R., Jordan, M. H., Feild, H. S., Giles, W. F., & Armenakis, A. A. (2006). Becoming team players: Team members' mastery of teamwork knowledge as a predictor of team task proficiency and observed teamwork effectiveness. *Journal of Applied Psychology*, *91*, 467–474.

Hochwarter, W. A., Kacmar, C., Perrewé, P. L., & Johnson, D. (2003). Perceived organizational support as a mediator of the relationship between politics perceptions and work outcomes. *Journal of Vocational Behavior*, *63*, 438–456.

Hochwarter, W. A., Witt, L., Treadway, D. C., & Ferris, G. R. (2006). The interaction of social skill and organizational support on job performance. *Journal of Applied Psychology*, *91*, 482–489.

Hoffman, B. J., Blair, C. A., Meriac, J. P., & Woehr, D. J. (2007). Expanding the criterion domain? A quantitative review of the OCB literature. *Journal of Applied Psychology*, *92*, 555–566.

Hofstede, G. (2001). *Culture's consequences* (2nd ed.). Thousand Oaks, CA: Sage.

Hogan, J., Barrett, P., & Hogan, R. (2007). Personality measurement, faking, and employment selection. *Journal of Applied Psychology*, *92*, 1270–1285.

Hogan, J., & Holland, B. (2003). Using theory to evaluate personality and job-performance relations: A socioanalytic perspective. *Journal of Applied Psychology*, *88*, 100–112.

Hogan, R., Curphy, G. J., & Hogan, J. (1994). What we know about leadership: Effectiveness and personality. *American Psychologist*, *49*, 493–504.

Holland, J. L. (1994). *Self-Directed Search Form R* (4th ed.). Lutz, FL: Psychological Assessment Resources.

Hollinger, R. C., Dabney, D. A., Lee, G., Hayes, R., Hunter, J., & Cummings, M. (1996). *1996 national retail security survey final report*. Gainesville, FL: University of Florida.

Holman, D. J., Axtell, C. M., Sprigg, C. A., Totterdell, P., & Wall, T. D. (2010). The mediating role of job characteristics in job redesign interventions: A serendipitous quasi-experiment. *Journal of Organizational Behavior*, *31*, 84–105.

House, R. J., Hanges, P. J., Ruiz-Quintanilla, S. A., Dorfman, P. W., Javidan, M., Dickson, M., et al. (1999). Cultural influences on leadership and organizations: Project GLOBE. *Advances in global leadership* (Vol. 1, pp. 171–233). Stamford, CN: JAI Press.

House, R. J., & Mitchell, T. R. (1974). Path-goal theory of leadership. *Contemporary Business*, *3*, 81–98.

Huang, X., & Van de Vliert, E. (2003). Where intrinsic job satisfaction fails to work: National moderators of intrinsic motivation. *Journal of Organizational Behavior*, *24*, 159–179.

Huffcutt, A. I., Conway, J. M., Roth, P. L., & Stone, N. J. (2001). Identification and meta-analytic assessment of psychological constructs measured in employment interviews. *Journal of Applied Psychology*, *86*, 897–913.

Huffcutt, A. I., Roth, P. L., & McDaniel, M. A. (1996). A meta-analytic investigation of cognitive ability in employment interview evaluations: Moderating characteristics and implications for incremental validity. *Journal of Applied Psychology*, *81*, 459–473.

Hui, C., Lam, S. S., & Law, K. K. (2000). Instrumental values of organizational citizenship behavior for promotion: A field quasi-experiment. *Journal of Applied Psychology*, *85*, 822–828.

Hui, C., Yee, C., & Eastman, K. L. (1995). The relationship between individualism-collectivism and job satisfaction. *Applied Psychology: An International Review*, *44*, 276–282.

Humphrey, S. E., Moon, H., Conlon, D. E., & Hofmann, D. A. (2004). Decision–making and behavior fluidity: How focus on completion and emphasis on safety changes over the course of projects. *Organizational Behavior and Human Decision Processes*, *93*, 14–27.

Hunter, J. E., & Schmidt, F. L. (1990). *Methods of meta-analysis: Correcting error and bias in research findings*. Thousand Oaks, CA: Sage.

Hurtz, G. M., & Donovan, J. J. (2000). Personality and job performance: The Big Five revisited. *Journal of Applied Psychology*, *85*, 869–879.

Iaffaldano, M. T., & Muchinsky, P. M. (1985). Job satisfaction and job performance: A meta-analysis. *Psychological Bulletin*, *97*, 251–273.

Ilgen, D. R., Barnes-Farrell, J. L., & McKellin, D. B. (1993). Performance appraisal process research in the 1980s: What has it contributed to appraisals in use? *Organizational Behavior and Human Decision Processes*, *54*, 321–368.

Ilies, R., Hauserman, N., Schwochau, S., & Stibal, J. (2003). Reported incidence rates of work-related sexual harassment in the United States: Using meta-analysis to explain reported rate disparities. *Personnel Psychology*, *56*, 607–631.

Ilies, R., Nahrgang, J. D., & Morgeson, F. P. (2007). Leader-member exchange and citizenship behaviors: A meta-analysis. *Journal of Applied Psychology*, *92*, 269–277.

Ironson, G. H., Smith, P. C., Brannick, M. T., Gibson, W. M., & Paul, K. B. (1989). Constitution of a Job in General Scale: A comparison of global, composite, and specific measures. *Journal of Applied Psychology*, *74*, 193–200.

Ispas, D., Ilie, A., Iliescu, D., Johnson, R. E., & Harris, M. M. (2010). Fairness reactions to selection methods: A Romanian study. *International Journal of Selection and Assessment*, *18*, 102–110.

Iverson, R. D., & Deery, S. J. (2001). Understanding the "personological" basis of employee withdrawal: The influence of affective disposition on employee tardiness, early departure, and absenteeism. *Journal of Applied Psychology*, *86*, 856–866.

Iverson, R. D., & Roy, P. (1994). A causal model of behavioral commitment: Evidence from a study of Australian blue-collar employees. *Journal of Management*, *20*, 15–41.

Jackson, C. J., Furnham, A., & Willen, K. (2000). Employer willingness to comply with the Disability Discrimination Act regarding staff selection in the UK. *Journal of Occupational and Organizational Psychology*, *73*, 119–129.

Jackson, C. L., Colquitt, J. A., Wesson, M. J., & Zapata-Phelan, C. P. (2006). Psychological collectivism: A measurement validation and linkage to group member performance. *Journal of Applied Psychology*, *91*, 884–899.

Jackson, C. L., & LePine, J. A. (2003). Peer responses to a team's weakest link: A test and extension of LePine and Van Dyne's model. *Journal of Applied Psychology*, *88*, 459–475.

Jackson, S. E., & Joshi, A. (2004). Diversity in social context: A multi-attribute, multilevel analysis of team diversity and sales performance. *Journal of Organizational Behavior*, *25*, 675–702.

Jackson, S. E., Joshi, A., & Erhardt, N. L. (2003). Recent research on team and organizational diversity: SWOT analysis and implications. *Journal of Management*, *29*, 801–830.

Jackson, S. E., & Schuler, R. S. (1985). A meta-analysis and conceptual critique of research on role ambiguity and role conflict in work settings. *Organizational Behavior and Human Decision Processes*, *36*, 16–78.

Jacobs, R., & Solomon, T. (1977). Strategies for enhancing the prediction of job performance from job satisfaction. *Journal of Applied Psychology*, *62*, 417–421.

Jago, A. G., & Ragan, J. W. (1986). The trouble with {leader match} is that it doesn't match Fiedler's contingency model. *Journal of Applied Psychology*, *71*, 555–559.

Jamal, M. (1990). Relationship of job stress and Type-A behavior to employees' job satisfaction, organizational commitment, psychosomatic health problems, and turnover motivation. *Human Relations*, *43*, 727–738.

Janis, I. L. (1972). Victims of groupthink: A psychological study of foreign-policy decisions and fiascoes. 277.

Jaramillo, F., Locander, W. B., Spector, P. E., & Harris, E. G. (2007). Getting the job done: The moderating role of initiative on the relationship between intrinsic motivation and adaptive selling. *Journal of Personal Selling and Sales Management*, *27*, 59–74.

Jeanneret, P., & Strong, M. H. (2003). Linking O*Net job analysis information to job requirement predictors: An O*Net application. *Personnel Psychology*, *56*, 465–492.

Jelley, R., & Goffin, R. D. (2001). Can performance-feedback accuracy be improved? Effects of rater priming and rating-scale format on rating accuracy. *Journal of Applied Psychology*, *86*, 134–144.

Jex, S. M., & Beehr, T. A. (1991). Emerging theoretical and methodological issues in the study of work-related stress. *Research in Personnel and Human Resources Management*, *9*, 311–365.

Jex, S. M., Bliese, P. D., Buzzell, S., & Primeau, J. (2001). The impact of self-efficacy on stressor-strain relations: Coping style as an explanatory mechanism. *Journal of Applied Psychology*, *86*, 401–409.

Jex, S. M., & Gudanowski, D. M. (1992). Efficacy beliefs and work stress: An exploratory study. *Journal of Organizational Behavior*, *13*, 509–517.

Johansson, G. (1981). Psychoneuroendocrine correlates of unpaced and paced performance. In G. Salvendy & M. J. Smith (Eds.), *Machine pacing and occupational stress* (pp. 277–286). London, England: Taylor & Francis.

Johansson, G. (1989). Stress, autonomy, and the maintenance of skill in supervisory control of automated systems. *Applied Psychology: An International Review*, *38*, 45–56.

Johnson, H.-A. M., & Spector, P. E. (2007). Service with a smile: Do emotional intelligence, gender, and autonomy moderate the emotional labor process? *Journal of Occupational Health Psychology*, *12*, 319–333.

Johnson, J. W. (2001). The relative importance of task and contextual performance dimensions to supervisor judgments of overall performance. *Journal of Applied Psychology*, *86*, 984–996.

Johnson, R. E., & Chang, C. H. (2006). "I" is to continuance as "We" is to affective: The relevance of the self-concept for organizational commitment. *Journal of Organizational Behavior*, *27*, 549–570.

Jones, D. A. (2009). Getting even with one's supervisor and one's organization: Relationships among types of injustice, desires for revenge, and counterproductive work behaviors. *Journal of Organizational Behavior*, *30*, 525–542.

Joseph, D. L., & Newman, D. A. (2010). Emotional intelligence: An integrative meta-analysis and cascading model. *Journal of Applied Psychology*, *95*, 54–78.

Judge, T. A., Bono, J. E., Ilies, R., & Gerhardt, M. W. (2002). Personality and leadership: A qualitative and quantitative review. *Journal of Applied Psychology*, *87*, 765–780.

Judge, T. A., Higgins, C. A., & Cable, D. M. (2000). The employment interview: A review of recent research and recommendations for future research. *Human Resource Management Review*, *10*, 383–406.

Judge, T. A., & Piccolo, R. F. (2004). Transformational and transactional leadership: A meta-analytic test of their relative validity. *Journal of Applied Psychology*, *89*, 755–768.

Judge, T. A., Thoresen, C. J., Bono, J. E., & Patton, G. K. (2001). The job satisfaction–job performance relationship: A qualitative and quantitative review. *Psychological Bulletin*, *127*, 376–407.

Judge, T. A., Woolf, E. F., & Hurst, C. (2009). Is emotional labor more difficult for some than for others? A multilevel, experience-sampling study. *Personnel Psychology*, *62*, 57–88.

Kacmar, K., & Carlson, D. S. (1997). Further validation of the Perception of Politics Scale (POPs): A multiple sample investigation. *Journal of Management*, *23*, 627–658.

Kahn, J. H., Schneider, K. T., Jenkins-Henkelman, T. M., & Moyle, L. L. (2006). Emotional social support and job burnout among high-school teachers: Is it all due to dispositional affectivity? *Journal of Organizational Behavior*, *27*, 793–807.

Kalton, G. (1983). *Introduction to survey sampling*. Thousand Oaks, CA: Sage.

Kaminski, M. (2001). Unintended consequences: Organizational practices and their impact on workplace safety and productivity. *Journal of Occupational Health Psychology*, *6*, 127–138.

Kane, J. S., & Bernardin, H. (1982). Behavioral observation scales and the evaluation of performance appraisal effectiveness. *Personnel Psychology*, *35*, 635–641.

Kanfer, R. (1992). Work motivation: New directions in theory and research. In C. L. Cooper & I. T. Robertson (Eds.), *International review of industrial and organizational psychology: 1992* (pp. 1–53). Chichester, England: John Wiley.

Kaplan, S., Bradley, J. C., Luchman, J. N., & Haynes, D. (2009). On the role of positive and negative affectivity in job performance: A meta-analytic investigation. *Journal of Applied Psychology*, *94*, 162–176.

Karasek, R. A. (1979). Job demands, job decision latitude, and mental strain-implications for job redesign. *Administrative Science Quarterly*, *24*, 285–308.

Karasek, R. A., Gardell, B., & Lindell, J. (1987). Work and non-work correlates of illness and behaviour in male and female Swedish white collar workers. *Journal of Occupational Behaviour*, *8*, 187–207.

Karl, K. A., O'Leary-Kelly, A. M., & Martocchio, J. J. (1993). The impact of feedback and self-efficacy on performance in training. *Journal of Organizational Behavior*, *14*, 379–394.

Karlson, B., Eek, F., Orbaek, P., & Osterberg, K. (2009). Effects on sleep-related problems and self-reported health after a change of shift schedule. *Journal of Occupational Health Psychology*, *14*, 97–109.

Katz, D., & Kahn, R. L. (1978). *The social psychology of organizations* (2nd ed.). New York, NY: John Wiley.

Katzell, R. A., & Austin, J. T. (1992). From then to now: The development of industrial-organizational psychology in the United States. *Journal of Applied Psychology*, *77*, 803–835.

Keenan, T. (1995). Graduate recruitment in Britain: A survey of selection methods used by organizations. *Journal of Organizational Behavior*, *16*, 303–317.

Keller, R. T. (1989). A test of the path-goal theory of leadership with need for clarity as a moderator in research and development organizations. *Journal of Applied Psychology*, *74*, 208–212.

Keller, R. T. (1997). Job involvement and organizational commitment as longitudinal predictors of job performance: A study of scientists and engineers. *Journal of Applied Psychology*, *82*, 539–545.

Keller, R. T. (2006). Transformational leadership, initiating structure, and substitutes for leadership: A longitudinal study of research and development project team performance. *Journal of Applied Psychology*, *91*, 202–210.

Kessler, S. R., Spector, P. E., Chang, C. H., & Parr, A. D. (2008). Organizational violence and aggression: Development of the three-factor Violence Climate Survey. *Work and Stress*, *22*, 108–124.

Khanna, C., & Medsker, G. J. (2010). 2009 income and employment survey results for the Society for Industrial and Organizational Psychology. *Industrial/Organizational Psychologist*, *48*(1), 23–38.

Kirkman, B. L., & Mathieu, J. E. (2005). The dimensions and antecedents of team virtuality. *Journal of Management*, *31*, 700–718.

Kirkpatrick, D. L. (1977). Evaluating training programs: Evidence versus proof. *Training and Development Journal*, *31*, 9–12.

Klein, C., DiazGranados, D., Salas, E., Le, H., Burke, C. S., Lyons, R., & Goodwin, G. F. (2009). Does team building work? *Small Group Research*, *40*, 181–222.

Klein, H. J. (1989). An integrated control theory model of work motivation. *Academy of Management Review*, *14*, 150–172.

Klein, H. J., & Kim, J. S. (1998). A field study of the influence of situational constraints, leader-member exchange, and goal commitment on performance. *Academy of Management Journal*, *41*, 88–95.

Klein, H. J., Wesson, M. J., Hollenbeck, J. R., & Alge,
B. J. (1999). Goal commitment and the goal-setting process: Conceptual clarification and empirical synthesis. *Journal of Applied Psychology*, *84*, 885–896.

Klein, K. J., Conn, A. B., & Sorra, J. S. (2001). Implementing computerized technology: An organizational analysis. *Journal of Applied Psychology*, *86*, 811–824.

Kleinmann, M., & Strauss, B. (1998). Validity and application of computer-simulated scenarios in personnel assessment. *International Journal of Selection and Assessment*, *6*, 97–106.

Kogan, N., & Wallach, M. A. (1964). *Risk taking: A study in cognition and personality*. New York, NY: Holt, Rinehart & Winston.

Kohler, S. S., & Mathieu, J. E. (1993). Individual characteristics, work perceptions, and affective reactions influences on differentiated absence criteria. *Journal of Organizational Behavior*, *14*, 515–530.

Koller, M., Kundi, M., & Cervinka, R. (1978). Field studies of shift work at an Austrian oil refinery· I Health and psychosocial wellbeing of workers who drop out of shiftwork. *Ergonomics*, *21*, 835–847.

Kompier, M. A., Aust, B., van den Berg, A. M., & Siegrist, J. (2000). Stress prevention in bus drivers: Evaluation of 13 natural experiments. *Journal of Occupational Health Psychology*, *5*, 11–31.

Koppes, L. L. (1997). American female pioneers of industrial and organizational psychology during the early years. *Journal of Applied Psychology*, *82*, 500–515.

Korsgaard, M., & Roberson, L. (1995). Procedural justice in performance evaluation: The role of instrumental and non-instrumental voice in performance appraisal discussions. *Journal of Management*, *21*, 657–669.

Koslowsky, M. (2000). A new perspective on employee lateness. *Applied Psychology: An International Review*, *49*, 390–407.

Koslowsky, M., Sagie, A., Krausz, M., & Singer, A. D. (1997). Correlates of employee lateness: Some theoretical considerations. *Journal of Applied Psychology*, *82*, 79–88.

Kozlowski, S. W., & Bell, B. S. (2006). Disentangling achievement orientation and goal setting: Effects on self-regulatory processes. *Journal of Applied Psychology*, *91*, 900–916.

Kozlowski, S. W. J., Chao, G. T., Smith, E. M., & Hedlund, J. (1993). Organizational downsizing: Strategies, interventions, and research implications. In C. L. Cooper & I. T. Robertson (Eds.), *International review of industrial and organizational psychology: 1993* (pp. 263–332). Chichester, England: John Wiley.

Kravitz, D. A. (2008). The diversity-validity dilemma: Beyond selection—The role of affirmative action. [Comment/Reply]. *Personnel Psychology*, *61*, 173–193.

Kravitz, D. A., Harrison, D. A., Turner, M. E., Levine, E. L., Chaves, W., Brannick, M. T.,. . . Conard, M. A. (1997). *Affirmative action: A review of psychological and behavior research*. Bowling Green, OH: Society for Industrial and Organizational Psychology.

Kravitz, D. A., & Martin, B. (1986). Ringelmann rediscovered: The original article. [Comment/Reply]. *Journal of Personality and Social Psychology*, *50*, 936–941.

Kreis, S. (1995). Early experiments in British scientific management: The Health of Munitions Workers' Committee, 1915–1920. *Journal of Management History*, *1*, 65–78.

Kuhl, J., & Beckmann, J. (1994). *Volition and personality: Action versus state orientation*. Seattle, WA: Hogrefe & Huber.

Kwiatkowski, R., Duncan, D. C., & Shimmin, S. (2006). What have we forgotten—and why? *Journal of Occupational and Organizational Psychology*, *79*, 183–201.

Lamm, H., & Myers, D. G. (1978). Group-induced polarization of attitudes and behavior. In L. Berkowitz (Ed.), *Advances in experimental and social psychology* (pp. 145–195). New York, NY: Academic Press.

Lance, C. E., Foster, M. R., Gentry, W. A., & Thoresen, J. D. (2004). Assessor cognitive processes in an operational assessment center. *Journal of Applied Psychology*, *89*, 22–35.

Lance, C. E., Lambert, T. A., Gewin, A. G., Lievens, F., & Conway, J. M. (2004). Revised estimates of dimension and exercise variance components in assessment center postexercise dimension ratings. *Journal of Applied Psychology*, *89*, 377–385.

Lance, C. E., LaPointe, J. A., & Fisicaro, S. A. (1994). Tests of three causal models of halo rater error. *Organizational Behavior and Human Decision Processes*, *57*, 83–96.

Landy, F. J. (1992). Hugo Munsterberg: Victim or visionary? *Journal of Applied Psychology*, *77*, 787–802.

Landy, F. J. (2005). Some historical and scientific issues related to research on emotional intelligence. *Journal of Organizational Behavior*, *26*, 411–424.

Landy, F. J., Farr, J. L., & Jacobs, R. R. (1982). Utility concepts in performance measurement. *Organizational Behavior and Human Performance*, *30*, 15–40.

Langan-Fox, J. (1998). Women's careers and occupational stress. In C. L. Cooper & I. T. Robertson (Eds.), *International review of industrial and organizational psychology: 1998* (pp. 273–304). Chichester, England: John Wiley.

Langfred, C. W. (2005). Autonomy and performance in teams: The multilevel moderating effect of task interdependence. *Journal of Management*, *31*, 513–529.

Larsman, P., & Hanse, J. J. (2009). The impact of decision latitude, psychological load and social support at work on the development of neck, shoulder and low back symptoms among female human service organization workers. *International Journal of Industrial Ergonomics*, *39*, 442–446.

Larson, L. M., Rottinghaus, P. J., & Borgen, F. H. (2002). Meta-analyses of Big Six interests and Big Five personality factors. *Journal of Vocational Behavior*, *61*, 217–239.

Latané, B., Williams, K., & Harkins, S. (1979). Many hands make light the work: The causes and consequences of social loafing. *Journal of Personality and Social Psychology*, *37*, 822–832.

Latham, G. P. (1986). Job performance and appraisal. In C. L. Cooper & I. T. Robertson (Eds.), *International review of industrial and organizational psychology: 1986* (pp. 117–155). Chichester, England: John Wiley.

Latham, G. P., Skarlicki, D. P., Irvine, D., & Siegel, J. P. (1993). The increasing importance of performance appraisals to employee effectiveness in organizational settings in North America. In C. L. Cooper & I. T. Robertson (Eds.), *International review of industrial and organizational psychology: 1993* (pp. 87–132). Chichester, England: John Wiley.

Latham, G. P., & Wexley, K. N. (1977). Behavioral observation scales for performance appraisal purposes. *Personnel Psychology*, *30*, 255–268.

Lavelle, J. J., Brockner, J., Konovsky, M. A., Price, K. H., Henley, A. B., Taneja, A., & Vinekar, V. (2009). Commitment, procedural fairness, and organizational citizenship behavior: A multifoci analysis. *Journal of Organizational Behavior*, *30*, 337–357.

LeBlanc, M. M., & Kelloway, E. (2002). Predictors and outcomes of workplace violence and aggression. *Journal of Applied Psychology*, *87*, 444–453.

Lee, H., Wilbur, J., Kim, M. J., & Miller, A. M. (2008). Psychosocial risk factors for work-related musculoskeletal disorders of the lower-back among long-haul international female flight attendants. *Journal of Advanced Nursing*, *61*, 492–502.

Lee, K., & Allen, N. J. (2002). Organizational citizenship behavior and workplace deviance: The role of affect and cognitions. *Journal of Applied Psychology*, *87*, 131–142.

Lee, K., Carswell, J. J., & Allen, N. J. (2000). A meta-analytic review of occupational commitment: Relations with person- and work-related variables. *Journal of Applied Psychology*, *85*, 799–811.

Lefkowitz, J. (2000). The role of interpersonal affective regard in supervisory performance ratings: A literature review and proposed causal model. *Journal of Occupational and Organizational Psychology*, *73*, 67–85.

Levenson, A. R., Van der Stede, W. A., & Cohen, S. G. (2006). Measuring the relationship between managerial competencies and performance. *Journal of Management*, *32*, 360–380.

Levine, E. L., Ash, R. A., Hall, H., & Sistrunk, F. (1983). Evaluation of job analysis methods by experienced job analysts. *Academy of Management Journal*, *26*, 339–348.

Liden, R. C., Wayne, S. J., Jaworski, R. A., & Bennett, N. (2004). Social loafing: A field investigation. *Journal of Management*, *30*, 285–304.

Lievens, F. (2001). Assessor training strategies and their effects on accuracy, interrater reliability, and discriminant validity. *Journal of Applied Psychology*, *86*, 255–264.

Lievens, F., Chasteen, C. S., Day, E. A., & Christiansen, N. D. (2006). Large-scale investigation of the role of trait activation theory for understanding assessment center convergent and discriminant validity. *Journal of Applied Psychology*, *91*, 247–258.

Lievens, F., & Sackett, P. R. (2006). Video-based versus written situational judgment tests: A comparison in terms of predictive validity. *Journal of Applied Psychology*, *91*, 1181–1188.

Lim, B. C., & Ployhart, R. E. (2004). Transformational leadership: Relations to the five-factor model and team performance in typical and maximum contexts. *Journal of Applied Psychology*, *89*, 610–621.

Lim, S., Cortina, L. M., & Magley, V. J. (2008). Personal and workgroup incivility: Impact on work and health outcomes. *Journal of Applied Psychology*, *93*, 95–107.

Lindell, M. K., Clause, C. S., Brandt, C. J., & Landis, R. S. (1998). Relationship between organizational context and job analysis task ratings. *Journal of Applied Psychology*, *83*, 769–776.

Liu, C., Spector, P. E., & Jex, S. M. (2005). The relation of job control with job strains: A comparison of multiple data sources. *Journal of Occupational and Organizational Psychology*, *78*, 325–336.

Liu, C., Spector, P. E., & Shi, L. (2007). Cross-national job stress: A quantitative and qualitative study. *Journal of Organizational Behavior*, *28*, 209–239.

Liu, G., Shah, R., & Schroeder, R. G. (2006). Linking work design to mass customization: A sociotechnical systems perspective. *Decision Sciences*, *37*, 519–545.

Liu, S., Wang, M., Zhan, Y., & Shi, J. (2009). Daily work stress and alcohol use: Testing the cross-level moderation effects of neuroticism and job involvement. *Personnel Psychology*, *62*, 575–597.

Locke, E. A. (1980). Latham versus Komaki: A tale of two paradigms. *Journal of Applied Psychology*, *65*, 16–23.

Locke, E. A. (2000). Motivation, cognition, and action: An analysis of studies of task goals and knowledge. *Applied Psychology: An International Review*, *49*, 408–429.

Locke, E. A., & Henne, D. (1986). Work motivation theories. In C. L. Cooper & I. T. Robertson (Eds.), *International review of industrial and organizational psychology: 1986* (pp. 1–35). Chichester, England: John Wiley.

Locke, E. A., & Latham, G. P. (1990). *A theory of goal setting and task performance*. Englewood Cliffs, NJ: Prenuce-Hall.

Loher, B. T., Noe, R. A., Moeller, N. L., & Fitzgerald, M. P. (1985). A meta-analysis of the relation of job characteristics to job satisfaction. *Journal of Applied Psychology*, *70*, 280–289.

Lord, R. G., Binning, J. F., Rush, M. C., & Thomas, J. C. (1978). The effect of performance cues and leader behavior on questionnaire ratings of leadership behavior. *Organizational Behavior and Human Performance*, *21*, 27–39.

Lord, R. G., & Maher, K. J. (1989). Cognitive processes in industrial and organizational psychology. In C. L. Cooper & I. T. Robertson (Eds.), *International review of industrial and organizational psychology: 1989* (pp. 49–91). Chichester, England: John Wiley.

Lowin, A., & Craig, J. R. (1968). The influence of level of performance on managerial style: An experimental object-lesson in the ambiguity of correlational data. *Organizational Behavior and Human Performance*, *3*, 440–458.

Ludwig, T. D., & Geller, E. (1997). Assigned versus participative goal setting and response generalization: Managing injury control among professional pizza deliverers. *Journal of Applied Psychology*, *82*, 253–261.

Ludwig, T. D., & Goomas, D. T. (2009). Real-time performance monitoring, goal-setting, and feedback for forklift drivers in a distribution centre. *Journal of Occupational and Organizational Psychology*, *82*, 391–403.

Luthar, H. K., & Pastille, C. (2000). Modeling subordinate perceptions of sexual harassment: The role of superior-subordinate social-sexual interaction. *Human Resource Management Review*, *10*, 211–244.

Lyness, K. S., & Thompson, D. E. (1997). Above the glass ceiling? A comparison of matched samples of female and male executives. *Journal of Applied Psychology*, *82*, 359–375.

Lyness, K. S., & Thompson, D. E. (2000). Climbing the corporate ladder: Do female and male executives follow the same route? *Journal of Applied Psychology*, *85*, 86–101.

Machin, M., & Fogarty, G. J. (2003). Perceptions of training-related factors and personal variables as predictors of transfer implementation intentions. *Journal of Business and Psychology*, *18*, 51–71.

MacKenzie, S. B., Podsakoff, P. M., & Fetter, R. (1991). Organizational citizenship behavior and objective productivity as determinants of managerial evaluations of salespersons' performance. *Organizational Behavior and Human Decision Processes*, *50*, 123–150.

Maertz, C. P., Jr., & Griffeth, R. W. (2004). Eight motivational forces and voluntary turnover: A theoretical synthesis with implications for research. *Journal of Management*, *30*, 667–683.

Majchrzak, A., & Borys, B. (1998). Computer-aided technology and work: Moving the field forward. In C. L. Cooper & I. T. Robertson (Eds.), *International review of industrial and organizational psychology: 1998* (pp. 305–354). Chichester, England: John Wiley.

Major, V. S., Klein, K. J., & Ehrhart, M. G. (2002). Work time, work interference with family, and psychological distress. *Journal of Applied Psychology*, *87*, 427–436.

Man, D. C., & Lam, S. S. (2003). The effects of job complexity and autonomy on cohesiveness in collectivistic and individualistic work groups: A cross-cultural analysis. *Journal of Organizational Behavior*, *24*, 979–1001.

Mannix, E., & Neale, M. A. (2005). What differences make a difference? The promise and reality of diverse teams in organizations. *Psychological Science in the Public Interest*, *6*, 31–55.

Marcus, B. (2009). "Faking" from the applicant's perspective: A theory of self-presentation in personnel selection settings. *International Journal of Selection and Assessment*, *17*, 417–430.

Marcus, B., Lee, K., & Ashton, M. C. (2007). Personality dimensions explaining relationships between integrity tests and counterproductive behavior: Big Five, or one in addition? *Personnel Psychology*, *60*, 1–34.

Marks, M. L., Mirvis, P. H., Hackett, E. J., & Grady, J. F. (1986). Employee participation in a quality circle program: Impact on quality of work life, productivity, and absenteeism. *Journal of Applied Psychology*, *71*, 61–69.

Martins, L. L., Gilson, L. L., & Maynard, M. (2004). Virtual teams: What do we know and where do we go from here? *Journal of Management*, *30*, 805–835.

Maslach, C. (1998). A multidimensional theory of burnout. In C. L. Cooper (Ed.), *Theories of organizational stress* (pp. 68–85). Oxford, England: Oxford University Press.

Maslow, A. H. (1943). A theory of human motivation. *Psychological Review*, *50*, 370–396.

Mastrangelo, P. M., & Popovich, P. M. (2000). Employees' attitudes toward drug testing, perceptions of organizational climate, and withdrawal from the employer. *Journal of Business and Psychology*, *15*, 3–18.

Mathieu, J. E., & Kohler, S. S. (1990). A cross-level examination of group absence influences on individual absence. *Journal of Applied Psychology*, *75*, 217–220.

Mathieu, J. E., Martineau, J. W., & Tannenbaum, S. I. (1993). Individual and situational influences on the development of self-efficacy: Implications for training effectiveness. *Personnel Psychology*, *46*, 125–147.

Maurer, T. J., Mitchell, D. R., & Barbeite, F. G. (2002). Predictors of attitudes toward a 360-degree feedback system and involvement in post-feedback management development activity. *Journal of Occupational and Organizational Psychology*, *75*, 87–107.

Maurer, T. J., Solamon, J. M., Andrews, K. D., & Troxtel, D. D. (2001). Interviewee coaching, preparation strategies, and response strategies in relation to performance in situational employment interviews: An extension of Maurer, Solamon, and Troxtel (1998). *Journal of Applied Psychology*, *86*, 709–717.

Mayer, R. C., & Davis, J. H. (1999). The effect of the performance appraisal system on trust for management: A field quasi-experiment. *Journal of Applied Psychology*, *84*, 123–136.

McBride, J. R. (1998). Innovations in computer-based ability testing: Promise, problems, and perils. In M. D. Hakel (Ed.), *Beyond multiple choice: Evaluating alternatives to traditional testing for selection* (pp. 23–39). Mahwah, NJ: Lawrence Erlbaum.

McCormick, E. J., Jeanneret, P. R., & Mecham, R. C. (1972). A study of job characteristics and job dimensions as based on the Position Analysis Questionnaire (PAQ). *Journal of Applied Psychology*, *56*, 347–368.

McCulloch, S. (1993). Recent trends in international assessment. *International Journal of Selection and Assessment*, *1*, 59–61.

McGlynn, R. P., McGurk, D., Effland, V. S., Johll, N. L., & Harding, D. J. (2004). Brainstorming and task performance in groups constrained by evidence. *Organizational Behavior and Human Decision Processes*, *93*, 75–87.

McGregor, D. M. (1960). *The human side of enterprise*. New York, NY: McGraw-Hill.

McIntire, S. A., & Levine, E. L. (1991). Combining personality variables and goals to predict performance. *Journal of Vocational Behavior*, *38*, 288–301.

McKay, P. F., & McDaniel, M. A. (2006). A reexamination of black-white mean differences in work performance: More data, more moderators. *Journal of Applied Psychology*, *91*, 538–554.

McMahan, G. C., & Woodman, R. W. (1992). The current practice of organization development within the firm. *Group and Organization Management*, *17*, 117–134.

McManus, M. A., & Ferguson, M. W. (2003). Biodata, personality, and demographic differences of recruits from three sources. *International Journal of Selection and Assessment*, *11*, 175–183.

McManus, M. A., & Kelly, M. L. (1999). Personality measures and biodata: Evidence regarding their incremental predictive value in the life insurance industry. *Personnel Psychology*, *52*, 137–148.

McNeely, B. L., & Meglino, B. M. (1994). The role of dispositional and situational antecedents in prosocial organizational behavior: An examination of the intended beneficiaries of prosocial behavior. *Journal of Applied Psychology*, *79*, 836–844.

Meglino, B. M., DeNisi, A. S., & Ravlin, E. C. (1993). Effects of previous job exposure and subsequent job status on the functioning of a realistic job preview. *Personnel Psychology*, *46*, 803–822.

Meglino, B. M., Ravlin, E. C., & DeNisi, A. S. (2000). A meta-analytic examination of realistic job preview effectiveness: A test of three counterintuitive propositions. *Human Resource Management Review*, *10*, 407–434.

Melamed, S., Fried, Y., & Froom, P. (2001). The interactive effect of chronic exposure to noise and job complexity on changes in blood pressure and job satisfaction: A longitudinal study of industrial employees. *Journal of Occupational Health Psychology*, *6*, 182–195.

Melamed, S., Shirom, A., Toker, S., Berliner, S., & Shapira, I. (2006). Burnout and risk of cardiovascular disease: Evidence, possible causal paths, and promising research directions. *Psychological Bulletin*, *132*, 327–353.

Merchant, J. A., & Lundell, J. A. (2001). *Workplace violence: A report to the nation*. Iowa City, IA: University of Iowa.

Meyer, J. P., Allen, N. J., & Smith, C. A. (1993). Commitment to organizations and occupations: Extension and test of a three-component conceptualization. *Journal of Applied Psychology*, *78*, 538–551.

Meyer, J. P., Stanley, D. J., Herscovitch, L., & Topolnytsky, L. (2002). Affective, continuance, and normative commitment to the organization: A meta-analysis of antecedents, correlates, and consequences. *Journal of Vocational Behavior*, *61*, 20–52.

Michel, J. S., Mitchelson, J. K., Kotrba, L. M., LeBreton, J. M., & Baltes, B. B. (2009). A comparative test of work-family conflict models and critical examination of work-family linkages. *Journal of Vocational Behavior*, *74*, 199–218.

Milam, A. C., Spitzmueller, C., & Penney, L. M. (2009). Investigating individual differences among targets of workplace incivility. *Journal of Occupational Health Psychology*, *14*, 58–69.

Mitchell, K. E., Alliger, G. M., & Morfopoulos, R. (1997). Toward an ADA-appropriate job analysis. *Human Resource Management Review*, *7*, 5–26.

Mitra, A., Jenkins, G., & Gupta, N. (1992). A meta-analytic review of the relationship between absence and turnover. *Journal of Applied Psychology*, *77*, 879–889.

Mohammed, S., & Angell, L. C. (2004). Surface- and deep-level diversity in workgroups: Examining the moderating effects of team orientation and team process on relationship conflict. *Journal of Organizational Behavior*, *25*, 1015–1039.

Mohammed, S., & Dumville, B. C. (2001). Team mental models in a team knowledge framework: Expanding theory and measurement across disciplinary boundaries. *Journal of Organizational Behavior*, *22* 89–106.

Moorhead, G., Ference, R., & Neck, C. P. (1991). Group decision fiascoes continue: Space shuttle *Challenger* and a revised groupthink framework. *Human Relations*, *44*, 539–550.

Morgeson, F. P., & Campion, M. A. (1997). Social and cognitive sources of potential inaccuracy in job analysis. *Journal of Applied Psychology*, *82*, 627–655.

Morgeson, F. P., Campion, M. A., & Maertz, C. P. (2001). Understanding pay satisfaction: The limits of a compensation system implementation. *Journal of Business and Psychology*, *16*, 133–149.

Morgeson, F. P., Delaney-Klinger, K., Mayfield, M. S., Ferrara, P., & Campion, M. A. (2004). Self-presentation processes in job analysis: A field experiment investigating inflation in abilities, tasks, and competencies. *Journal of Applied Psychology*, *89*, 674–686.

Morgeson, F. P., Reider, M. H., & Campion, M. A. (2005). Selecting individuals in team settings: The importance of social skills, personality characteristics, and teamwork knowledge. *Personnel Psychology*, *58*, 583–611.

Morin, L., & Latham, G. P. (2000). The effect of mental practice and goal setting as a transfer of training intervention on supervisors' self-efficacy and communication skills: An exploratory study. *Applied Psychology: An International Review*, *49*, 566–578.

Morrow, C. C., Jarrett, M., & Rupinski, M. T. (1997). An investigation of the effect and economic utility of corporate-wide training. *Personnel Psychology*, *50*, 91–119.

Moser, K. (2005). Recruitment sources and post-hire outcomes: The mediating role of unmet expectations. *International Journal of Selection and Assessment*, *13*, 188–197.

Mount, M. K., Witt, L., & Barrick, M. R. (2000). Incremental validity of empirically keyed biodata scales over GMA and the five factor personality constructs. *Personnel Psychology*, *53*, 299–323.

Mowday, R. T., Steers, R. M., & Porter, L. W. (1979). The measurement of organizational commitment. *Journal of Vocational Behavior*, *14*, 224–247.

Mullarkey, S., Jackson, P. R., Wall, T. D., Wilson, J. R., & Grey-Taylor, S. M. (1997). The impact of technology characteristics and job control on worker mental health. *Journal of Organizational Behavior*, *18*, 471–489.

Mumford, M. D. (1999). Construct validity and background data: Issues, abuses, and future directions. *Human Resource Management Review*, *9*, 117–145.

Munene, J. (1995). "Not-on-seat": An investigation of some correlates of organisational citizenship behaviour in Nigeria. *Applied Psychology: An International Review*, *44*, 111–122.

Murphy, K. R. (2000). Impact of assessments of validity generalization and situational specificity on the science and practice of personnel selection. *International Journal of Selection and Assessment*, *8*, 194–206.

Murphy, K. R., Cronin, B. E., & Tam, A. P. (2003). Controversy and consensus regarding the use of cognitive ability testing in organizations. *Journal of Applied Psychology*, *88*, 660–671.

Murphy, K. R., Gannett, B. A., Herr, B. M., & Chen, J. A. (1986). Effects of subsequent performance on evaluations of previous performance. *Journal of Applied Psychology*, *71*, 427–431.

Murphy, K. R., Jako, R. A., & Anhalt, R. L. (1993). Nature and consequences of halo error: A critical analysis. *Journal of Applied Psychology*, *78*, 218–225.

Narayanan, L., Menon, S., & Spector, P. (1999). A cross-cultural comparison of job stressors and reactions among employees holding comparable jobs in two countries. *International Journal of Stress Management*, *6*, 197–212.

Nathan, B. R., & Lord, R. G. (1983). Cognitive categorization and dimensional schemata: A process approach to the study of halo in performance ratings. *Journal of Applied Psychology*, *68*, 102–114.

Nathan, B. R., & Tippins, N. (1990). The consequences of halo "error" in performance ratings: A field study of the moderating effect of halo on test validation results. *Journal of Applied Psychology*, *75*, 290–296.

National Institute for Occupational Safety and Health. (1996). Violence in the workplace: Risk factors and prevention strategies. Retrieved May 29, 2010, from http://www.cdc.gov/niosh/violcont.html

National Institute for Occupational Safety and Health. (2004). Workplace violence prevention strategies and research needs. Retrieved June 6, 2010, from http://www.cdc.gov/niosh/docs/2006-144/pdfs/2006-144.pdf

National Safety Council. (1992). *Sound sense*. Itasca, IL: Author.

National Safety Council. (2005–2006). *Injury facts* (2005–2006 ed.). Itasca, IL: Author.

Neal, A., & Griffin, M. A. (2006). A study of the lagged relationships among safety climate, safety motivation, safety behavior, and accidents at the individual and group levels. *Journal of Applied Psychology*, *91*, 946–953.

Neininger, A., Lehmann-Willenbrock, N., Kauffeld, S., & Henschel, A. (2010). Effects of team and organizational commitment—A longitudinal study. *Journal of Vocational Behavior*, *76*, 567–579.

Neuman, G. A., Edwards, J. E., & Raju, N. S. (1989). Organizational development interventions: A meta-analysis of their effects on satisfaction and other attitudes. *Personnel Psychology*, *42*, 461–489.

Neuman, J. H., & Baron, R. A. (1997). Aggression in the workplace. In R. A. Giacalone & J. Greenberg (Eds.), *Antisocial behavior in organizations* (pp. 37–67). Thousand Oaks, CA: Sage.

Newell, S., & Tansley, C. (2001). International uses of selection methods. In C. L. Cooper & I. T. Robertson (Eds.), *International review of industrial and organizational psychology* (pp. 195–213). Chichester, England: John Wiley.

Newnam, S., Griffin, M. A., & Mason, C. (2008). Safety in work vehicles: A multilevel study linking safety values and individual predictors to work-related driving crashes. *Journal of Applied Psychology*, *93*, 632–644.

Newton, R., & Doonga, N. (2007). Corporate e-learning: Justification for implementation and evaluation of benefits. A study examining the views of training managers and training providers. *Education for Information*, *25*, 111–130.

Newton, T., & Keenan, T. (1991). Further analyses of the dispositional argument in organizational behavior. *Journal of Applied Psychology*, *76*, 781–787.

Ng, T. W., Butts, M. M., Vandenberg, R. J., DeJoy, D. M., & Wilson, M. G. (2006). Effects of management communication, opportunity for learning, and work schedule flexibility on organizational commitment. *Journal of Vocational Behavior*, *68*, 474–489.

Ng, T. W., & Feldman, D. C. (2008a). Long work hours: A social identity perspective on meta-analysis data. *Journal of Organizational Behavior*, *29*, 853–880.

Ng, T. W., & Feldman, D. C. (2008b). The relationship of age to ten dimensions of job performance. *Journal of Applied Psychology*, *93*, 392–423.

Ng, T. W., Sorensen, K. L., & Eby, L. T. (2006). Locus of control at work: A meta-analysis. *Journal of Organizational Behavior*, *27*, 1057–1087.

Nicholson, N., & Johns, G. (1985). The absence culture and the psychological contract: Who's in control of absence? *Academy of Management Review*, *10*, 397–407.

Noe, R. A., & Schmitt, N. (1986). The influence of trainee attitudes on training effectiveness: Test of a model. *Personnel Psychology*, *39*, 497–523.

Nordander, C., Ohlsson, K., Akesson, I., Arvidsson, I., Balogh, I., Hansson, G. A., ... Skerfving, S. (2009). Risk of musculoskeletal disorders among females and males in repetitive/constrained work. *Ergonomics*, *52*, 1226–1239.

Northhouse, P. G. (2004). *Leadership theory and practice* (3rd ed.). Thousand Oaks, CA: Sage.

O'Brien, K. E., Biga, A., Kessler, S. R., & Allen, T. D. (2010). A meta-analytic investigation of gender differences in mentoring. *Journal of Management*, *36*, 537–554.

O'Connor, E. J., Peters, L. H., Rudolf, C. J., & Pooyan, A. (1982). Situational constraints and employee affective reactions: A partial field replication. *Group and Organization Studies*, *7*, 418–428.

Oiry, E. (2009). Electronic human resource management: Organizational responses to role conflicts created by e-learning. *International Journal of Training and Development*, *13*, 111–123.

Oldham, G. R., Cummings, A., Mischel, L. J., Schmidtke, J. M., & Zhou, J. (1995). Listen while you work? Quasi-experimental relations between personal-stereo headset use and employee work responses. *Journal of Applied Psychology*, *80*, 547–564.

Ones, D. S., & Anderson, N. (2002). Gender and ethnic group differences on personality scales in selection: Some British data. *Journal of Occupational and Organizational Psychology*, *75*, 255–276.

Ones, D. S., Dilchert, S., Viswesvaran, C., & Salgado, J. F. (2010). Cognitive abilities. In J. L. Farr & N. Tippins (Eds.), *Handbook of employee selection* (pp. 255–275). New York, NY: Routledge.

Ones, D. S., & Viswesvaran, C. (1998). Gender, age, and race differences on overt integrity tests: Results across four large-scale job applicant datasets. *Journal of Applied Psychology*, *83*, 35–42.

Organ, D. W., & Konovsky, M. (1989). Cognitive versus affective determinants of organizational citizenship behavior. *Journal of Applied Psychology*, *74*, 157–164.

Osborn, A. F. (1957). *Applied imagination* (Rev. ed.). New York, NY: Scribner.

Osgood, C. E., Teannenbaum, P. H., & Suci, G. J. (1957). *The measurement of meaning*. Urbana, IL: University of Illinois Press.

Ouchi, W. G. (1981). *Theory Z*. New York, NY: Avon.

Palliser, C., Firth, H., Feyer, A., & Paulin, S. (2005). Musculoskeletal discomfort and work-related stress in New Zealand dentists. *Work and Stress*, *19*, 351–359.

Parasuraman, S., & Purohit, Y. S. (2000). Distress and boredom among orchestra musicians: The two faces of stress. *Journal of Occupational Health Psychology*, *5*, 74–83.

Paronto, M. E., Truxillo, D. M., Bauer, T. N., & Leo, M. C. (2002). Drug testing, drug treatment, and marijuana use: A fairness perspective. *Journal of Applied Psychology*, *87*, 1159–1166.

Parry, E., & Wilson, H. (2009). Factors influencing the adoption of online recruitment. *Personnel Review*, *38*, 655–673.

Pasmore, W. A., Francis, C., Haldeman, J., & Shani, A. (1982). Sociotechnical systems: A North American reflection on empirical studies of the seventies. *Human Relations*, *35*, 1179–1204.

Paulus, P. B. (2000). Groups, teams, and creativity: The creative potential of idea-generating groups. *Applied Psychology: An International Review*, *49*, 237–262.

Paunonen, S. V., Rothstein, M. G., & Jackson, D. N. (1999). Narrow reasoning about the use of broad personality measures for personnel selection [Comment/Reply]. *Journal of Organizational Behavior*, *20*, 389–405.

Payne, S. C., Youngcourt, S. S., & Beaubien, J. (2007). A meta-analytic examination of the goal orientation nomological net. *Journal of Applied Psychology*, *92*, 128–150.

Pearson, C. A., & Chong, J. (1997). Contributions of job content and social information on organizational commitment and job satisfaction: An exploration in a Malaysian nursing context. *Journal of Occupational and Organizational Psychology*, *70*, 357–374.

Pedalino, E., & Gamboa, V. U. (1974). Behavior modification and absenteeism: Intervention in one industrial setting. *Journal of Applied Psychology*, *59*, 694–698.

Penfield, R. D. (2006). Applying Bayesian item selection approaches to adaptive tests using polytomous items. *Applied Measurement in Education*, *19*, 1–20.

Penney, L. M., & Spector, P. E. (2005). Job stress, incivility, and counterproductive work behavior (CWB): The moderating role of negative affectivity. *Journal of Organizational Behavior*, *26*, 777–796.

Pensri, P., Janwantanakul, P., & Chaikumarn, M. (2009). Prevalence of self-reported musculoskeletal symptoms in salespersons. *Occupational Medicine*, *59*, 499–501.

Pervin, L. A. (1993). *Personality: Theory and research* (6th ed.). New York, NY: John Wiley.

Peters, L. H., Hartke, D. D., & Pohlmann, J. T. (1985). Fiedler's Contingency Theory of Leadership: An application of the meta-analysis procedures of Schmidt and Hunter. *Psychological Bulletin*, *97*, 274–285.

Peters, L. H., & O'Connor, E. J. (1980). Situational constraints and work outcomes: The influences of a frequently overlooked construct. *Academy of Management Review*, *5*, 391–397.

Peterson, N. G., Mumford, M. D., Borman, W. C., Jeanneret, P., Fleishman, E. A., Levin, K. Y., . . . Dye, D. M. (2001). Understanding work using the occupational information network (O*NET). *Personnel Psychology*, *54*, 451–492.

Pew Research Center. (2002). Online job hunting: A Pew internet project data memo. Retrieved September 29, 2010, from http://www.pewinternet.org/Press-Releases/2002/Online-Job-Hunting-A-Pew-Internet-Project-Data-Memo.aspx

Pichler, F., & Wallace, C. (2009). What are the reasons for differences in job satisfaction across Europe? Individual, compositional, and institutional explanations. *European Sociological Review*, *25*, 535–549.

Pillai, R., Schriesheim, C. A., & Williams, E. S. (1999). Fairness perceptions and trust as mediators for transformational and transactional leadership: A two-sample study. *Journal of Management*, *25*, 897–933.

Podsakoff, N. P., Whiting, S. W., Podsakoff, P. M., & Blume, B. D. (2009). Individual- and organizational-level consequences of organizational citizenship behaviors: A meta-analysis. *Journal of Applied Psychology*, *94*, 122–141.

Podsakoff, P. M., Ahearne, M., & MacKenzie, S. B. (1997). Organizational citizenship behavior and the quantity and quality of work group performance. *Journal of Applied Psychology*, *82*, 262–270.

Podsakoff, P. M., MacKenzie, S. B., Ahearne, M., & Bommer, W. H. (1995). Searching for a needle in a haystack: Trying to identify the illusive moderators of leadership behaviors. *Journal of Management*, *21*, 423–470.

Potosky, D., & Bobko, P. (2004). Selection testing via the internet: Practical considerations and exploratory empirical findings. *Personnel Psychology*, *57*, 1003–1034.

Powell, G. N., & Butterfield, D. (1994). Investigating the "glass ceiling" phenomenon: An empirical study of actual promotions to top management. *Academy of Management Journal*, *37*, 68–86.

Powell, G. N., Butterfield, D., & Parent, J. D. (2002). Gender and managerial stereotypes: Have the times changed? *Journal of Management*, *28*, 177–193.

Premack, S. L., & Wanous, J. P. (1985). A meta-analysis of realistic job preview experiments. *Journal of Applied Psychology*, *70*, 706–719.

Raabe, B., & Beehr, T. A. (2003). Formal mentoring, versus supervisor and coworker relationships: Differences in perceptions and impact. *Journal of Organizational Behavior*, *24*, 271–293.

Raabe, B., Frese, M., & Beehr, T. A. (2007). Action regulation theory and career self-management. *Journal of Vocational Behavior*, *70*, 297–311.

Rafferty, A. E., & Griffin, M. A. (2006). Perceptions of organizational change: A stress and coping perspective. *Journal of Applied Psychology*, *91*, 1154–1162.

Raggatt, P. T. (1991). Work stress among long-distance coach drivers: A survey and correlational study. *Journal of Organizational Behavior*, *12*, 565–579.

Rain, J. S., Lane, I. M., & Steiner, D. D. (1991). A current look at the job satisfaction/life satisfaction relationship: Review and future considerations. *Human Relations*, *44*, 287–307.

Raju, N. S., Burke, M. J., & Normand, J. (1990). A new approach for utility analysis. *Journal of Applied Psychology*, *75*, 3–12.

Ralston, D. A. (1989). The benefits of flextime: Real or imagined? *Journal of Organizational Behavior*, *10*, 369–373.

Randle, C. W. (1956). How to identify promotable executives. *Harvard Business Review*, *34*, 122–134.

Raver, J. L., & Nishii, L. H. (2010). Once, twice, or three times as harmful? Ethnic harassment, gender harassment, and generalized workplace harassment. *Journal of Applied Psychology*, *95*, 236–254.

Rayner, C., & Keashly, L. (2005). Bullying at work: A perspective from Britain and North America. In S. Fox & P. E. Spector (Eds.), *Counterproductive work behavior: Investigations of actors and targets*. (pp. 271–296). Washington, DC: American Psychological Association.

Reilly, R. R., Henry, S., & Smither, J. W. (1990). An examination of the effects of using behavior checklists on the construct validity of assessment center dimensions. *Personnel Psychology*, *43*, 71–84.

Reynolds, D. H., & Dickter, D. N. (2010). Technology and employee selection. In J. L. Farr & N. T. Tippins (Eds.), *Handbook of employee selection* (pp. 171–193). New York, NY: Routledge.

Rice, R. W., Phillips, S. M., & McFarlin, D. B. (1990). Multiple discrepancies and pay satisfaction. *Journal of Applied Psychology*, *75*, 386–393.

Richman, W. L., Kiesler, S., Weisband, S., & Drasgow, F. (1999). A meta-analytic study of social desirability distortion in computer-administered questionnaires, traditional questionnaires, and interviews. *Journal of Applied Psychology*, *84*, 754–775.

Rickett, B., Orbell, S., & Sheeran, P. (2006). Social-cognitive determinants of hoist usage among health care workers. *Journal of Occupational Health Psychology*, *11*, 182–196.

Robbins, T. L., & DeNisi, A. S. (1994). A closer look at interpersonal affect as a distinct influence on cognitive processing in performance evaluations. *Journal of Applied Psychology*, *79*, 341–353.

Robert, C., Probst, T. M., Martocchio, J. J., Drasgow, F., & Lawler, J. J. (2000). Empowerment and continuous improvement in the United States, Mexico, Poland, and India: Predicting fit on the basis of the dimensions of power distance and individualism. *Journal of Applied Psychology*, *85*, 643–658.

Robertson, I. T., & Kandola, R. S. (1982). Work sample tests: Validity, adverse impact and applicant reaction. *Journal of Occupational and Organizational Psychology*, *55*, 171–183.

Robinson, D. D., Wahlstrom, O. W., & Mecham, R. C. (1974). Comparison of job evaluation methods: A "policy-capturing" approach using the Position Analysis Questionnaire. *Journal of Applied Psychology*, *59*, 633–637.

Rode, J. C., Mooney, C. H., Arthaud-Day, M. L., Near, J. P., Baldwin, T. T., Rubin, R. S., & Bommer, W. H. (2007). Emotional intelligence and individual performance: Evidence of direct and moderated effects. *Journal of Organizational Behavior*, *28*, 399–421.

Rodgers, R., & Hunter, J. E. (1991). Impact of management by objectives on organizational productivity. *Journal of Applied Psychology*, *76*, 322–336.

Roethlisberger, F. J. (1941). *Management and morale*. Cambridge, MA: Harvard University Press.

Roethlisberger, F. J., & Dickson, W. J. (1939). *Management and the worker*. Cambridge, MA: Harvard University Press.

Rohrer, D., Taylor, K., Pashler, H., Wixted, J. T., & Cepeda, N. J. (2005). The effect of overlearning on long-term retention. *Applied Cognitive Psychology*, *19*, 361–374.

Rosenthal, R. (1991). *Meta-analytic procedures for social research* (Rev. ed.). Thousand Oaks, CA: Sage.

Roth, P. E., & Campion, J. E. (1992). An analysis of the predictive power of the panel interview and pre-employment tests. *Journal of Occupational and Organizational Psychology*, *65*, 51–60.

Roth, P. L., Bobko, P., & Switzer, F. S., III. (2006). Modeling the behavior of the 4/5ths rule for determining adverse impact: Reasons for caution. *Journal of Applied Psychology*, *91*, 507–522.

Rottinghaus, P. J., Hees, C. K., & Conrath, J. A. (2009). Enhancing job satisfaction perspectives: Combining Holland themes and basic interests. *Journal of Vocational Behavior*, *75*, 139–151.

Rotundo, M., & Sackett, P. R. (2002). The relative importance of task, citizenship, and counterproductive performance to global ratings of job performance: A policy-capturing approach. *Journal of Applied Psychology*, *87*, 66–80.

Rowson, A. M. (1998). Using 360 degree feedback instruments up, down and around the world: Implications for global implementation and use of multi-rater feedback. *International Journal of Selection and Assessment*, *6*, 45–48.

Russell, C. J., Colella, A., & Bobko, P. (1993). Expanding the context of utility: The strategic impact of personnel selection. *Personnel Psychology*, *46*, 781–801.

Russell, C. J., & Domm, D. R. (1995). Two field tests of an explanation of assessment centre validity. *Journal of Occupational and Organizational Psychology*, *68*, 25–47.

Ryan, A. M., McFarland, L., Baron, H., & Page, R. (1999). An international look at selection practices: Nation and culture as explanations for variability in practice. *Personnel Psychology*, *52*, 359–391.

Saari, L. M., Johnson, T. R., McLaughlin, S. D., & Zimmerle, D. M. (1988). A survey of management training and education practices in U.S. companies. *Personnel Psychology*, *41*, 731–743.

Sagie, A., & Koslowsky, M. (1994). Organizational attitudes and behaviors as a function of participation in strategic and tactical change decisions: An application of path-goal theory. *Journal of Organizational Behavior*, *15*, 37–47.

Salgado, J. F. (2003). Predicting job performance using FFM and non-FFM personality measures. *Journal of Occupational and Organizational Psychology*, *76*, 323–346.

Salovey, P., & Mayer, J. D. (1989). Emotional intelligence. *Imagination, Cognition and Personality*, *9*, 185–211.

Sanchez, J. I., & Fraser, S. L. (1992). On the choice of scales for task analysis. *Journal of Applied Psychology*, *77*, 545–553.

Sanchez, J. I., & Levine, E. L. (1994). The impact of raters' cognition on judgment accuracy: An extension to the job analysis domain. *Journal of Business and Psychology*, *9*, 47–57.

Sanchez, J. I., & Levine, E. L. (2000). Accuracy or consequential validity: Which is the better standard for job analysis data? *Journal of Organizational Behavior*, *21*, 809–818.

Sarafino, E. P. (1990). *Health psychology: Biopsychosocial interactions*. New York, NY: John Wiley.

Savery, L. K., & Wooden, M. (1994). The relative influence of life events and hassles on work-related injuries: Some Australian evidence. *Human Relations*, *47*, 283–305.

Scandura, T. A., & Lankau, M. J. (1997). Relationships of gender, family responsibility and flexible work hours to organizational commitment and job satisfaction. *Journal of Organizational Behavior*, *18*, 377–391.

Scandura, T. A., Von Glinow, M. A., & Lowe, K. B. (1999). When East meets West: Leadership "best practices" in the United States and the Middle East. In W. H. Mobley, M. J., Gessner, & V. Arnold (Eds.). *Advances in global leadership* (Vol. 1, pp. 235–248). New York, NY: Elsevier Science/JAI Press.

Schaubroeck, J., & Kuehn, K. (1992). Research design in industrial and organizational psychology. In C. L. Cooper & I. T. Robertson (Eds.), *International review of industrial and organizational psychology: 1992* (pp. 99–121.). Chichester, England: John Wiley.

Schein, V. E., Mueller, R., Lituchy, T., & Liu, J. (1996). Think manager—think male: A global phenomenon? *Journal of Organizational Behavior*, *17*, 33–41.

Schippers, M. C., Den Hartog, D. N., Koopman, P. L., & Wienk, J. A. (2003). Diversity and team outcomes: The moderating effects of outcome interdependence and group longevity and the mediating effect of reflexivity. *Journal of Organizational Behavior*, *24*, 779–802.

Schleicher, D. J., Watt, J. D., & Greguras, G. J. (2004). Reexamining the job satisfaction–performance relationship: The complexity of attitudes. *Journal of Applied Psychology*, *89*, 165–177.

Schmidt, F. L., & Hunter, J. E. (1977). Development of a general solution to the problem of validity generalization. *Journal of Applied Psychology*, *62*, 529–540.

Schmidt, F. L., & Rader, M. (1999). Exploring the boundary condition for interview validity: Meta-analytic validity findings for a new interview type. *Personnel Psychology*, *52*, 445–464.

Schmidt, F. L., & Zimmerman, R. D. (2004). A counterintuitive hypothesis about employment interview validity and some supporting evidence. *Journal of Applied Psychology*, *89*, 553–561.

Schmitt, N., & Chan, D. (1998). *Personnel selection: A theoretical approach*. Thousand Oaks, CA: Sage.

Schmitt, N., Gooding, R. Z., Noe, R. A., & Kirsch, M. (1984). Metaanalyses of validity studies published between 1964 and 1982 and the investigation of study characteristics. *Personnel Psychology*, *37*, 407–422.

Schneider, K. T., Hitlan, R. T., & Radhakrishnan, P. (2000). An examination of the nature and correlates of ethnic harassment experiences in multiple contexts. *Journal of Applied Psychology*, *85*, 3–12.

Schneider, K. T., Swan, S., & Fitzgerald, L. F. (1997). Job-related and psychological effects of sexual harassment in the workplace: Empirical evidence from two organizations. *Journal of Applied Psychology*, *82*, 401–415.

Schriesheim, C. A., Powers, K. J., Scandura, T. A., Gardiner, C. C., & Lankau, M. E. (1993). Improving construct measurement in management research: Comments and a quantitative approach for assessing the theoretical content adequacy of paper-and-pencil survey-type instruments. *Journal of Management*, *19*, 385–417.

Schriesheim, J. F. (1980). The social context of leader-subordinate relations: An investigation of the effects of group cohesiveness. *Journal of Applied Psychology*, *65*, 183–194.

Schwab, D. P., & Grams, R. (1985). Sex-related errors in job evaluation: A "real-world" test. *Journal of Applied Psychology*, *70*, 533–539.

Shadish, W. R., Cook, T. D., & Campbell, D. T. (2002). *Experimental and quasi-experimental designs for generalized causal inference*. Boston, MA: Houghton Mifflin.

Shechtman, Z. (1992). A group assessment procedure as a predictor of on-the-job performance of teachers. *Journal of Applied Psychology*, *77*, 383–387.

Shields, M. (2006). Unhappy on the job. *Health Reports*, *17*, 33–37.

Shockley, K. M., & Allen, T. D. (2010). Investigating the missing link in flexible work arrangement utilization: An individual difference perspective. *Journal of Vocational Behavior*, *76*, 131–142.

Simon, S. J., & Werner, J. M. (1996). Computer training through behavior modeling, self-paced, and instructional approaches: A field experiment. *Journal of Applied Psychology*, *81*, 648–659.

Sinclair, R. C. (1988). Mood, categorization breadth, and performance appraisal: The effects of order of information acquisition and affective state on halo, accuracy, information retrieval, and evaluations. *Organizational Behavior and Human Decision Processes*, *42*, 22–46.

Sitzmann, T., Kraiger, K., Stewart, D., & Wisher, R. (2006). The comparative effectiveness of web-based and classroom instruction: A meta-analysis. *Personnel Psychology*, *59*, 623–664.

Siu, O. L., Lu, L., & Cooper, C. L. (1999). Managerial stress in Hong Kong and Taiwan: A comparative study. *Journal of Managerial Psychology*, *14*, 6–25.

Smith, C., Organ, D. W., & Near, J. P. (1983). Organizational citizenship behavior: Its nature and antecedents. *Journal of Applied Psychology*, *68*, 653–663.

Smith, J. E., & Hakel, M. D. (1979). Convergence among data sources, response bias, and reliability and validity of a structured job analysis questionnaire. *Personnel Psychology*, *32*, 677–692.

Smith, M. J., Hurrell, J. J., Jr., & Murphy, R. K., Jr. (1981). Stress and health effects in paced and unpaced work. In G. Salvendy & M. J. Smith (Eds.), *Machine pacing and occupational stress* (pp. 261–267). London, England: Taylor & Francis.

Smith, P. C., & Kendall, L. (1963). Retranslation of expectations: An approach to the construction of unambiguous anchors for rating scales. *Journal of Applied Psychology*, *47*, 149–155.

Smith, P. C., Kendall, L. M., & Hulin, C. L. (1969). The measurement of satisfaction in work and retirement: A strategy for the study of attitudes. 186.

Smith-Jentsch, K. A., Mathieu, J. E., & Kraiger, K. (2005). Investigating linear and interactive effects of shared mental models on safety and efficiency in a field setting. *Journal of Applied Psychology*, *90*, 523–535.

Sobeih, T. M., Salem, O., Daraiseh, N., Genaidy, A., & Shell, R. (2006). Psychosocial factors and musculoskeletal disorders in the construction industry: A systematic review. *Theoretical Issues in Ergonomics Science*, *7*, 329–344.

Society for Human Resource Management. (2009). 2009 employee job satisfaction: Understanding the factors that make work gratifying. Retrieved June 1, 2010, from http://www.shrm.org/Research/SurveyFindings/Articles/Documents/09-0282_Emp_Job_Sat_Survey_FINAL.pdf

Society for Industrial and Organizational Psychology. (1985). *Guidelines for education and training at the doctoral level in industrial/organizational psychology*. College Park: University of Maryland.

Solomonson, A. L., & Lance, C. E. (1997). Examination of the relationship between true halo and halo error in performance ratings. *Journal of Applied Psychology*, *82*, 665–674.

Somech, A. (2006). The effects of leadership style and team process on performance and innovation in functionally heterogeneous teams. *Journal of Management*, *32*, 132–157.

Somech, A., Desivilya, H. S., & Lidogoster, H. (2009). Team conflict management and team effectiveness: The effects of task interdependence and team identification. *Journal of Organizational Behavior*, *30*, 359–378.

Somers, M. J. (2009). The combined influence of affective, continuance and normative commitment on employee withdrawal. *Journal of Vocational Behavior*, *74*, 75–81.

Somers, M. J., & Birnbaum, D. (2001). Racial differences in work attitudes: What you see depends on what you study. *Journal of Business and Psychology*, *15*, 579–591.

Sonnentag, S. (1998). Expertise in professional software design: A process study. *Journal of Applied Psychology*, *83*, 703–715.

Sparks, K., Cooper, C., Fried, Y., & Shirom, A. (1997). The effects of hours of work on health: A meta-analytic review. *Journal of Occupational and Organizational Psychology*, *70*, 391–408.

Spector, P. E. (1982). Behavior in organizations as a function of employee's locus of control. *Psychological Bulletin*, *91*, 482–497.

Spector, P. E. (1985). Measurement of human service staff satisfaction: Development of the Job Satisfaction Survey. *American Journal of Community Psychology*, *13*, 693–713.

Spector, P. E. (1986). Perceived control by employees: A meta-analysis of studies concerning autonomy and participation at work. *Human Relations*, *39*, 1005–1016.

Spector, P. E. (1992). A consideration of the validity and meaning of self-report measures of job conditions. In C. L. Cooper & I. T. Robertson (Eds.), *International review of industrial and organizational psychology: 1992* (pp. 123–151). West Sussex, England: John Wiley.

Spector, P. E. (2008). Job Satisfaction Survey norms. Retrieved June 1, 2010, from http://shell.cas.usf.edu/~pspector/scales/jssnormstotal.html

Spector, P. E., Brannick, M. T., & Coovert, M. D. (1989). Job analysis. In C. L. Cooper & I. T. Robertson (Eds.), *International review of industrial and organizational psychology: 1989* (pp. 281–328). Oxford, England: John Wiley.

Spector, P. E., Cooper, C. L., Sanchez, J. I., O'Driscoll, M., Sparks, K., Bernin, P., . . . Yu, S. (2001). Do national levels of individualism and internal locus of control relate to well-being: An ecological level international study. *Journal of Organizational Behavior*, *22*, 815–832.

Spector, P. E., Dwyer, D. J., & Jex, S. M. (1988). Relation of job stressors to affective, health, and performance outcomes: A comparison of multiple data sources. *Journal of Applied Psychology*, *73*, 11–19.

Spector, P. E., Fox, S., Penney, L. M., Bruursema, K., Goh, A., & Kessler, S. (2006). The dimensionality of counterproductivity: Are all counterproductive behaviors created equal? *Journal of Vocational Behavior*, *68*, 446–460.

Spector, P. E., & Jex, S. M. (1991). Relations of job characteristics from multiple data sources with employee affect, absence, turnover intentions, and health. *Journal of Applied Psychology*, *76*, 46–53.

Spielberger, C. D. (1996). *State-Trait Anger Expression Inventory, research edition: Professional manual*. Lutz, FL: Psychological Assessment Resources.

Sprigg, C. A., Stride, C. B., Wall, T. D., Holman, D. J., & Smith, P. R. (2007). Work characteristics, musculoskeletal disorders, and the mediating role of psychological strain: A study of call center employees. *Journal of Applied Psychology*, *92*, 1456–1466.

Spychalski, A. C., Quiñones, M. A., Gaugler, B. B., & Pohley, K. (1997). A survey of assessment center practices in organizations in the United States. *Personnel Psychology*, *50*, 71–90.

Stajkovic, A. D., & Luthans, F. (2003). Behavioral management and task performance in organizations: Conceptual background, meta-analysis, and test of alternative models. *Personnel Psychology*, *56*, 155–194.

Stauffer, J. M., & Buckley, M. (2005). The existence and nature of racial bias in supervisory ratings. *Journal of Applied Psychology*, *90*, 586–591.

Staw, B. M., Bell, N. E., & Clausen, J. A. (1986). The dispositional approach to job attitudes: A lifetime longitudinal test. *Administrative Science Quarterly*, *31*, 56–77.

Staw, B. M., & Cohen-Charash, Y. (2005). The dispositional approach to job satisfaction: More than a mirage, but not yet an oasis: Comment [Comment/Reply]. *Journal of Organizational Behavior*, *26*, 59–78.

Stevens, M. J., & Campion, M. A. (1999). Staffing work teams: Development and validation of a selection test for teamwork settings. *Journal of Management*, *25*, 207–228.

Stewart, G. L. (2006). A meta-analytic review of relationships between team design features and team performance. *Journal of Management*, *32*, 29–55.

Stewart, G. L., Dustin, S. L., Barrick, M. R., & Darnold, T. C. (2008). Exploring the handshake in employment interviews. *Journal of Applied Psychology*, *93*, 1139–1146.

Stogdill, R. M. (1963). *Manual for the Leader Behavior Description Questionnaire—Form XII*. Columbus, OH: Ohio State University.

Stokes, G. S., & Searcy, C. A. (1999). Specification of scales in biodata form development: Rational vs. empirical and global vs. specific. *International Journal of Selection and Assessment*, *7*, 72–85.

Stokes, G. S., Toth, C. S., Searcy, C. A., Stroupe, J. P., & Carter, G. W. (1999). Construct/rational biodata dimensions to predict salesperson performance: Report on the U.S. Department of Labor sales study. *Human Resource Management Review*, *9*, 185–218.

Straus, S. G., Miles, J. A., & Levesque, L. L. (2001). The effects of videoconference, telephone, and face-to-face media on interviewer and applicant judgments in employment interviews. *Journal of Management*, *27*, 363–381.

Strauss, A., & Corbin, J. (1990). *Basics of qualitative research*. Thousand Oaks, CA: Sage.

Strube, M. J., & Garcia, J. E. (1981). A meta-analytic investigation of Fiedler's contingency model of leadership effectiveness. *Psychological Bulletin*, *90*, 307–321.

Sundvik, L., & Lindeman, M. (1998). Performance rating accuracy: Convergence between supervisor assessment and sales productivity. *International Journal of Selection and Assessment*, *6*, 9–15.

Sweeney, P. D., & McFarlin, D. B. (1997). Process and outcome: Gender differences in the assessment of justice. *Journal of Organizational Behavior*, *18*, 83–98.

Swider, B. W., & Zimmerman, R. D. (2010). Born to burnout: A meta-analytic path model of personality, job burnout, and work outcomes. *Journal of Vocational Behavior*, *76*, 487–506.

Sy, T., Tram, S., & O'Hara, L. A. (2006). Relation of employee and manager emotional intelligence to job satisfaction and performance. *Journal of Vocational Behavior*, *68*, 461–473.

Sygnatur, E. F., & Toscano, G. A. (2000, Spring). Work-related homicides: The facts. *Compensation and Working Conditions*, 3–8.

Sylva, H., & Mol, S. T. (2009). E-recruitment: A study into applicant perceptions of an online application system. *International Journal of Selection and Assessment*, *17*, 311–323.

Talas, M. S. (2009). Occupational exposure to blood and body fluids among Turkish nursing students during clinical practice training: Frequency of needlestick/sharp injuries and hepatitis B immunisation. *Journal of Clinical Nursing*, *18*, 1394–1403.

Taylor, F. W. (1911). *Scientific management*. New York, NY: Harper & Row.

Taylor, M. S., Tracy, K. B., Renard, M. K., Harrison, J. K., & Carroll, S. J. (1995). Due process in performance appraisal: A quasi-experiment in procedural justice. *Administrative Science Quarterly*, *40*, 495–523.

Taylor, P. J., Russ-Eft, D. F., & Chan, D. W. (2005). A meta-analytic review of behavior modeling training. *Journal of Applied Psychology*, *90*, 692–709.

Taylor, P. J., Russ-Eft, D. F., & Taylor, H. (2009). Transfer of management training from alternative perspectives. *Journal of Applied Psychology*, *94*, 104–121.

Tesluk, P. E., & Mathieu, J. E. (1999). Overcoming roadblocks to effectiveness: Incorporating management of performance barriers into models of work group effectiveness. *Journal of Applied Psychology*, *84*, 200–217.

Tett, R. P., & Burnett, D. D. (2003). A personality trait-based interactionist model of job performance. *Journal of Applied Psychology*, *88*, 500–517.

Tett, R. P., Steele, J. R., & Beauregard, R. S. (2003). Broad and narrow measures on both sides of the personality–job performance relationship. *Journal of Organizational Behavior*, *24*, 335–356.

Tharenou, P. (1993). A test of reciprocal causality for absenteeism. *Journal of Organizational Behavior*, *14*, 269–287.

Thorndike, E. L. (1913). *Educational psychology: The psychology of learning* (Vol. 2). New York, NY: Teachers College Press.

Timmerman, G., & Bajema, C. (2000). The impact of organizational culture on perceptions and experiences of sexual harassment. *Journal of Vocational Behavior*, *57*, 188–205.

Totterdell, P., Spelten, E., Smith, L., Barton, J., & Folkard, S. (1995). Recovery from work shifts: How long does it take? *Journal of Applied Psychology*, *80*, 43–57.

Towler, A. J. (2003). Effects of charismatic influence training on attitudes, behavior, and performance. *Personnel Psychology*, *56*, 363–381.

Treiman, D. J. (1979). *Job evaluation: An analytical review (Interim report to the Equal Employment Opportunity Commission)*. Washington, DC: National Academy of Sciences.

Trevor, C. O. (2001). Interactions among actual ease-of-movement determinants and job satisfaction in the prediction of voluntary turnover. *Academy of Management Journal*, *44*, 621–638.

Trevor, C. O., Gerhart, B., & Boudreau, J. W. (1997). Voluntary turnover and job performance: Curvilinearity and the moderating influences of salary growth and promotions. *Journal of Applied Psychology*, *82*, 44–61.

Triandis, H. C. (2003). The future of workforce diversity in international organisations: A commentary. *Applied Psychology: An International Review*, *52*, 486–495.

Triplett, N. (1897). The dynamogenic factors in pacemaking competition. *American Journal of Psychology*, *8*, 507–533.

Trist, E. L., & Bamforth, K. W. (1951). Some social and psychological consequences of the longwall method of coal-getting. *Human Relations*, *4*, 3–38.

Tubre, T. C., & Collins, J. M. (2000). Jackson and Schuler (1985) revisited: A meta-analysis of the relationships between role ambiguity, role conflict, and job performance. *Journal of Management*, *26*, 155–169.

Turban, D. B., & Cable, D. M. (2003). Firm reputation and applicant pool characteristics. *Journal of Organizational Behavior*, *24*, 733–751.

U.S. Department of Labor. (1977). *Dictionary of occupational titles* (4th ed.). Washington DC: U.S. Government Printing Office.

U.S. Department of Labor. (1991). *Dictionary of occupational titles* (5th ed.). Washington, DC: U.S. Government Printing Office.

U.S. Department of Labor. (1998). *O*NET98 data dictionary release 1.0*. Washington, DC: Department of Labor Employment and Training Administration.

U.S. Department of Labor. (2010). Top 50 fastest-growing occupations. Retrieved September 30, 2010, from http://www.acinet.org/acinet/oview1.asp?Level=BAplus

Uniform Guidelines on Employee Selection Procedures, 43 Fed. Reg. 38295 (1978, August 25).

Valacich, J. S., Dennis, A. R., & Nunamaker, J. (1992). Group size and anonymity effects on computer-mediated idea generation. *Small Group Research*, *23*, 49–73.

Van De Water, T. J. (1997). Psychology's entrepreneurs and the marketing of industrial psychology. *Journal of Applied Psychology*, *82*, 486–499.

Van Der Vegt, G. S., Emans, B., & Van De Vliert, E. (2000). Team members' affective responses to patterns of intragroup interdependence and job complexity. *Journal of Management*, *26*, 633–655.

Van der Vegt, G. S., & Janssen, O. (2003). Joint impact of interdependence and group diversity on innovation. *Journal of Management*, *29*, 729–751.

Van Eerde, W. (2000). Procrastination: Self-regulation in initiating aversive goals. *Applied Psychology: An International Review*, *49*, 372–389.

Van Eerde, W., & Thierry, H. (1996). Vroom's expectancy models and work-related criteria: A meta-analysis. *Journal of Applied Psychology*, *81*, 575–586.

Van Fleet, D. D., & Griffin, R. W. (1989). Quality circles: A review and suggested research directions. *International review of industrial and organizational psychology: 1989* (pp. 213–233). Oxford, England: John Wiley.

Van Iddekinge, C. H., Eidson, C. E., Jr., Kudisch, J. D., & Goldblatt, A. M. (2003). A biodata inventory administered via interactive voice response (IVR) technology: Predictive validity, utility, and subgroup differences. *Journal of Business and Psychology*, *18*, 145–156.

Van Iddekinge, C. H., Ferris, G. R., Perrewé, P. L., Perryman, A. A., Blass, F. R., & Heetderks, T. D. (2009). Effects of selection and training on unit-level performance over time: A latent growth modeling approach. *Journal of Applied Psychology*, *94*, 829–843.

Van Iddekinge, C. H., Taylor, M. A., & Eidson, C. E., Jr. (2005). Broad versus narrow facets of integrity: Predictive validity and subgroup differences. *Human Performance*, *18*, 151–177.

van Vianen, A. E., & Fischer, A. H. (2002). Illuminating the glass ceiling: The role of organizational culture preferences. *Journal of Occupational and Organizational Psychology*, *75*, 315–337.

Vandenberghe, C., Bentein, K., & Stinglhamber, F. (2004). Affective commitment to the organization, supervisor, and work group: Antecedents and outcomes. *Journal of Vocational Behavior*, *64*, 47–71.

Verquer, M. L., Beehr, T. A., & Wagner, S. H. (2003). A meta-analysis of relations between person-organization fit and work attitudes. *Journal of Vocational Behavior*, *63*, 473–489.

Vidyarthi, P. R., Liden, R. C., Anand, S., Erdogan, B., & Ghosh, S. (2010). Where do I stand? Examining the effects of leader-member exchange social comparison on employee work behaviors. *Journal of Applied Psychology*, *95*, 849–861.

Vigoda, E. (2002). Stress-related aftermaths to workplace politics: The relationships among politics, job distress, and aggressive behavior in organizations. *Journal of Organizational Behavior*, *23*, 571–591.

Vinchur, A. J., Schippmann, J. S., Smalley, M., & Rothe, H. F. (1991). Productivity consistency of foundry chippers and grinders: A 6-year field study. *Journal of Applied Psychology*, *76*, 134–136.

Viswesvaran, C., Schmidt, F. L., & Ones, D. S. (2005). Is there a general factor in ratings of job performance? A meta-analytic framework for disentangling substantive and error influences. *Journal of Applied Psychology*, *90*, 108–131.

Vroom, V. H. (1964). *Work and motivation*. New York, NY: John Wiley.

Vroom, V. H., & Jago, A. G. (1988). *The new leadership: Managing participation in organizations*. Englewood Cliffs, NJ: Prentice-Hall.

Vroom, V. H., & Yetton, P. W. (1973). *Leadership and decision-making*. Pittsburgh, PA: University of Pittsburgh Press.

Wagner, J. A. (1994). Participation's effects on performance and satisfaction: A reconsideration of research evidence. *Academy of Management Review*, *19*, 312–330.

Walker, G. H., Stanton, N. A., Salmon, P. M., & Jenkins, D. P. (2008). A review of sociotechnical systems theory: A classic concept for new command and control paradigms. *Theoretical Issues in Ergonomics Science*, *9*, 479–499.

Wall, T. D., Corbett, J., Martin, R., Clegg, C. W., & Jackson, P. R. (1990). Advanced manufacturing technology, work design, and performance: A change study. *Journal of Applied Psychology*, *75*, 691–697.

Wall, T. D., & Davids, K. (1992). Shopfloor work organization and advanced manufacturing technology. In C. L. Cooper & I. T. Robertson (Eds.), *International review of industrial and organizational psychology: 1992* (pp. 363–398). Chichester, England: John Wiley.

Wall, T. D., Jackson, P. R., Mullarkey, S., & Parker, S. K. (1996). The demands-control model of job strain: A more specific test. *Journal of Occupational and Organizational Psychology*, *69*, 153–166.

Wall, T. D., Jackson, P. R., & Davids, K. (1992). Operator work design and robotics system performance: A serendipitous field study. *Journal of Applied Psychology*, *77*, 353–362.

Wall, T. D., Kemp, N. J., Jackson, P. R., & Clegg, C. W. (1986). Outcomes of autonomous workgroups: A long-term field experiment. *Academy of Management Journal*, *29*, 280–304.

Walsh, B. R., & Clarke, E. (2003). Post-trauma symptoms in health workers following physical and verbal aggression. *Work and Stress*, *17*, 170–181.

Walumbwa, F. O., Avolio, B. J., & Zhu, W. (2008). How transformational leadership weaves its influence on individual job performance: The role of identification and efficacy beliefs. *Personnel Psychology*, *61*, 793–825.

Walumbwa, F. O., Cropanzano, R., & Hartnell, C. A. (2009). Organizational justice, voluntary learning behavior, and job performance: A test of the mediating effects of identification and leader-member exchange. *Journal of Organizational Behavior*, *30*, 1103–1126.

Walumbwa, F. O., Wang, P., Lawler, J. J., & Shi, K. (2004). The role of collective efficacy in the relations between transformational leadership and work outcomes. *Journal of Occupational and Organizational Psychology*, *77*, 515–530.

Wanberg, C. R., & Banas, J. T. (2000). Predictors and outcomes of openness to changes in a reorganizing workplace. *Journal of Applied Psychology*, *85*, 132–142.

Wanek, J. E. (1999). Integrity and honesty testing: What do we know? How do we use it? *International Journal of Selection and Assessment*, *7*, 183–195.

Wanek, J. E., Sackett, P. R., & Ones, D. S. (2003). Towards an understanding of integrity test similarities and differences: An item-level analysis of seven tests. *Personnel Psychology*, *56*, 873–894.

Wang, M., Liu, S., Zhan, Y., & Shi, J. (2010). Daily work-family conflict and alcohol use: Testing the cross-level moderation effects of peer drinking norms and social support. *Journal of Applied Psychology*, *95*, 377–386.

Wang, Q., Bowling, N. A., & Eschleman, K. J. (2010). A meta-analytic examination of work and general locus of control. *Journal of Applied Psychology*, *95*, 761–768.

Wanous, J. P. (1989). Installing a realistic job preview: Ten tough choices. *Personnel Psychology*, *42*, 117–134.

Warr, P. (2001). Age and work behaviour: Physical attributes, cognitive abilities, knowledge, personality traits, and motives. In C. L. Cooper & I. T. Robertson (Eds.), *International review of industrial and organizational psychology: 2001* (pp. 1–36). Chichester, England: John Wiley.

Warr, P. B. (2007). Some historical developments in I-O psychology outside the United States. In L. L. Koppes, P. W. Thayer, A. J. Vinchur, & E. Salas (Eds.), *Historical perspectives in industrial and organizational psychology* (pp. 81–107). Mahwah, NJ: Lawrence Erlbaum.

Wasti, S. (2005). Commitment profiles: Combinations of organizational commitment forms and job outcomes. *Journal of Vocational Behavior*, *67*, 290–308.

Watson, D., Pennebaker, J. W., & Folger, R. (1986). Beyond negative affectivity: Measuring stress and satisfaction in the workplace. *Journal of Organizational Behavior Management*, *8*, 141–157.

Wayne, J. H. (2000). Disentangling the power bases of sexual harassment: Comparing gender, age, and position power. *Journal of Vocational Behavior*, *57*, 301–325.

Wayne, J. H., Musisca, N., & Fleeson, W. (2004). Considering the role of personality in the work-family experience: Relationships of the Big Five to work-family conflict and facilitation. *Journal of Vocational Behavior*, *64*, 108–130.

Weber, M. (1947). *The theory of social and economic organization* (A. M. Henderson & T. Parsons, Trans. and Eds.). New York, NY: Oxford University Press.

Weiss, D. J., Dawis, R., Lofquist, L. H., & England, G. W. (1966). *Instrumentation for the theory of work adjustment. (Minnesota Studies in Vocational Rehabilitation, XXI)*. Minneapolis, MN: University of Minnesota.

Werner, J. M. (1994). Dimensions that make a difference: Examining the impact of in-role and extra-role behaviors on supervisory ratings. *Journal of Applied Psychology*, *79*, 98–107.

Werner, J. M., & Bolino, M. C. (1997). Explaining U.S. courts of appeals decisions involving performance appraisal: Accuracy, fairness, and validation. *Personnel Psychology*, *50*, 1–24.

West, J., & Karas, M. (1999). Biodata: Meeting clients' needs for a better way of recruiting entry-level staff. *International Journal of Selection and Assessment*, *7*, 126–131.

West, M. A., Borrill, C. S., & Unsworth, K. L. (1998). Team effectiveness in organizations. In C. L. Cooper & I. T. Robertson (Eds.), *International review of industrial and organizational psychology: 1998* (pp. 1–48). Chichester, England: John Wiley.

Wickens, C. D., Lee, J., Liu, Y., & Becker, S. G. (2004). *An introduction to human factors engineering*. Upper Saddle River, NJ: Parson Prentice Hall.

Wiesner, W. H., & Cronshaw, S. F. (1988). A meta-analytic investigation of the impact of interview format and degree of structure on the validity of the employment interview. *Journal of Occupational Psychology*, *61*, 275–290.

Wilk, S. L., & Cappelli, P. (2003). Understanding the determinants of employer use of selection methods. *Personnel Psychology*, *56*, 103–124.

Williams, C. R. (1999). Reward contingency, unemployment, and functional turnover. *Human Resources Management Review*, *9*, 549–576.

Williams, M. L., McDaniel, M. A., & Nguyen, N. T. (2006). A meta-analysis of the antecedents and consequences of pay level satisfaction. *Journal of Applied Psychology*, *91*, 392–413.

Willis, T. A., O'Connor, D. B., & Smith, L. (2008). Investigating effort-reward imbalance and work-family conflict in relation to morningness-eveningness and shift work. *Work and Stress*, *22*, 125–137.

Willness, C. R., Steel, P., & Lee, K. (2007). A meta-analysis of the antecedents and consequences of workplace sexual harassment. *Personnel Psychology*, *60*, 127–162.

Wilson, M. A., Harvey, R. J., & Macy, B. A. (1990). Repeating items to estimate the test-retest reliability of task inventory ratings. *Journal of Applied Psychology*, *75*, 158–163.

Winterton, J. (1994). Social and technological characteristics of coal-face work: A temporal and spatial analysis. *Human Relations*, *47*, 89–118.

Witt, L., & Nye, L. G. (1992). Gender and the relationship between perceived fairness of pay or promotion and job satisfaction. *Journal of Applied Psychology*, *77*, 910–917.

Wofford, J., & Liska, L. Z. (1993). Path-goal theories of leadership: A meta-analysis. *Journal of Management*, *19*, 857–876.

Wong, C., Hui, C., & Law, K. S. (1998). A longitudinal study of the job perception–job satisfaction relationship: A test of the three alternative specifications. *Journal of Occupational and Organizational Psychology*, *71*, 127–146.

Yanchus, N. J., Eby, L. T., Lance, C. E., & Drollinger, S. (2010). The impact of emotional labor on work-family outcomes. *Journal of Vocational Behavior*, *76*, 105–117.

Yang, H., Schnall, P. L., Jauregui, M., Su, T. C., & Baker, D. (2006). Work hours and self-reported hypertension among working people in California. *Hypertension*, *48*, 744–750.

Yang, L. Q., Che, H., & Spector, P. E. (2008). Job stress and well-being: An examination from the view of person-environment fit. *Journal of Occupational and Organizational Psychology*, *81*, 567–587.

Yearta, S. K., Maitlis, S., & Briner, R. B. (1995). An exploratory study of goal setting in theory and practice: A motivational technique that works? *Journal of Occupational and Organizational Psychology*, *68*, 237–252.

Young, A. M., & Perrewé, P. L. (2004). The role of expectations in the mentoring exchange: An analysis of mentor and prótegé expectations in relation to perceived support. *Journal of Managerial Issues*, *16*, 103–126.

Yukl, G. A. (1989). *Leadership in organizations*. Englewood Cliffs, NJ: Prentice Hall.

Yukl, G. A., & Latham, G. P. (1975). Consequences of reinforcement schedules and incentive magnitudes for employee performance: Problems encountered in an industrial setting. *Journal of Applied Psychology*, *60*, 294–298.

Yun, G. J., Donahue, L. M., Dudley, N. M., & McFarland, L. A. (2005). Rater personality, rating format, and social context: Implications for performance appraisal ratings. *International Journal of Selection and Assessment*, *13*, 97–107.

Zajonc, R. B. (1965). Social facilitation. *Science*, *149*, 269–274.

Zapf, D. (2002). Emotion work and psychological well-being: A review of the literature and some conceptual considerations. *Human Resource Management Review*, *12*, 237–268.

Zapf, D., & Einarsen, S. (2005). Mobbing at work: Escalated conflicts in organizations. In S. Fox & P. E. Spector (Eds.), *Counterproductive work behavior: Investigations of actors and targets* (pp. 237–270). Washington, DC: American Psychological Association.

Zellars, K. L., Perrewé, P. L., Rossi, A. M., Tepper, B. J., & Ferris, G. R. (2008). Moderating effects of political skill, perceived control, and job-related self-efficacy on the relationship between negative affectivity and physiological strain. *Journal of Organizational Behavior*, *29*, 549–571.

Zibarras, L. D., & Woods, S. A. (2010). A survey of UK selection practices across different organization sizes and industry sectors. *Journal of Occupational and Organizational Psychology*, *83*, 499–511.

Zickar, M. J. (2003). Remembering Arthur Kornhauser: Industrial psychology's advocate for worker well-being. *Journal of Applied Psychology*, *88*, 363–369.

Zickar, M. J., & Gibby, R. E. (2007). Four persistent themes throughout the history of I-O psychology in the United States. In L. L. Koppes, P. W. Thayer, A. J. Vinchur, & E. Salas (Eds.), *Historical perspectives in industrial and organizational psychology* (pp. 61–80). Mahwah, NJ: Lawrence Erlbaum.

Zohar, D. (2010). Thirty years of safety climate research: Reflections and future directions. *Accident Analysis and Prevention*, *42*, 1517–1522.

Zottoli, M. A., & Wanous, J. P. (2000). Recruitment source research: Current status and future directions. *Human Resource Management Review*, *10*, 353–382.

Glossary

360-degree feedback: A performance appraisal technique that provides feedback from several perspectives, including peers, subordinates, supervisors, and self.

Ability: The capability of developing a skill or learning a task; a person's aptitude for learning.

Ability test: A test designed to assess a person's abilities or aptitudes.

Achievement test: A psychological test designed to assess a person's level of knowledge or skill; also called a knowledge and skill test.

Action process: From action theory, a series of steps describing the process by which a person translates desire for something into behavior.

Action theory: A motivation theory that links a person's goals to his or her behavior.

Action versus state orientation: A personality variable concerning a person's ability to carry out a sequence of activities to accomplish a goal. An action-oriented individual is able to self-regulate behaviors to achieve goals, whereas a state-oriented person has difficulty doing so.

Actual criterion: The way in which the theoretical criterion is assessed; the operationalization of a construct.

Additive task: A task in which a group's performance is the sum of individual members' performances. For example, total sales for a group of salespeople in a store is the sum of each person's individual sales.

Adverse impact: Potential unfairness in the treatment of minority group or protected class members. In hiring, it occurs if the protected class's selection ratio is less than four-fifths of the nonprotected class's selection ratio.

Affective commitment: A type of organizational commitment in which the person has an emotional attachment to his or her organization.

Affirmative action: A program designed to increase the number of minority or protected class members in an organization.

Analysis of variance (ANOVA): A statistical test used to compare group means.

Application form: A form completed by a job applicant; asks for background information.

Apprenticeship: An on-the-job training method. The trainee learns by assisting an experienced employee; most often used to teach a skilled trade such as carpentry or plumbing.

Arithmetic mean: The sum of scores divided by the number of scores.

Assessment center: A series of assessment exercises, including simulations of work tasks, that are used to assess a person's potential for a job. It is most frequently used to determine an employee's suitability for promotion into a management position.

Audiovisual instruction: A training method that uses pictures and sound to present material.

Autoinstruction: Any self-taught method of training.

Automaticity: A state where a skill or task is so well learned that a person can do it automatically with little conscious monitoring or thought. Professional athletes achieve this level of task performance.

Autonomy: The extent to which an employee is able to decide how to do his or her job.

Baserate: How often something occurs. In selection, it is the proportion of people hired who will be successful on the job.

Behavior criteria: Methods of evaluating training by assessing changes in trainee behavior on the job.

Behavior Observation Scale (BOS): A behavior-based job performance instrument. Raters are given a list of behaviors and indicate how often the ratee performs each one.

Behaviorally Anchored Rating Scale (BARS): A behavior-based job performance instrument. Raters are given several behaviors shown on a scale and are asked to indicate which one is most characteristic of the ratee's performance.

Big Five: The five dimensions considered to represent the major factors of human personality: Agreeableness, Conscientiousness, Emotional Stability, Extraversion, and Openness to Experience.

Biographical inventory: A selection tool in which the job applicant provides extensive background information.

Blended learning: A training course or program that combines an E-learning method with a traditional method of classroom delivery, such as lecture.

Brainstorming: A group method whereby individuals meet to generate solutions to a problem.

Bullying: A pattern of abusive behavior directed toward one or more individuals.

Bureaucracy: A highly structured organizational form having the characteristics outlined in Max Weber's bureaucracy theory.

Bureaucracy Theory: A classical theory initially developed by German sociologist Max Weber that was based on several principles, such as division of labor, delegation of authority, span of control, and line versus staff, to create a rational structure for an orderly and efficiently functioning organization.

Burnout: An aversive emotional state that is thought to be the result of job stress. It is characterized by a lack of enthusiasm for the job and a lost sense of the importance of the job.

Cadre: A term from leader-member exchange (LMX) theory that refers to individuals who are favored by their supervisors.

Cafeteria benefits: An employee benefit program in which individuals are allowed to customize their fringe benefits by choosing several from a long list of benefits, such as different types of insurance plans.

Career ladder: A system in an organization that defines a progression of promotion opportunities, such as ranks in the military.

Carpal tunnel syndrome: A repetitive strain injury of the wrist brought on by continually performing the same motions.

Categorical measurement: A measurement technique in which numbers represent arbitrary categories of a variable rather than positions along an underlying continuum.

Central tendency error: The tendency for a rater to give everyone mid-range ratings across all dimensions of performance.

Chain of command: In bureaucracy theory, the idea that directives flow down the organization from supervisor to subordinate.

Change agent: The person (or persons) who implements the changes in an organizational development plan.

Charismatic leader: A leader who has an unusual amount of influence on followers and can change their attitudes and beliefs.

Circadian rhythms: Physical body changes throughout the day involving hormone levels and temperature.

Classical measurement theory: A theory that states that a measure is composed of a true score component and an error component.

Closed-ended test: A test that requires the test taker to choose from among 2 or more options.

Coercive power: Power based on the use of punishments.

Cognitive ability test: A test that assesses cognitive or mental abilities, such as mathematical or verbal reasoning. The most commonly used cognitive ability tests are intelligence tests.

Cohesiveness: The attraction that group members have toward the group; the importance of the group to group members.

Collectivism: A culture value referring to the focus a person has on others as opposed to the self. It is the opposite of individualism.

Combination Job Analysis Method (C-JAM): A job analysis technique that involves several methods, including interviews and questionnaires.

Comparable worth: The idea that jobs having equivalent value to an organization should be paid the same; refers to differences in pay levels between jobs held predominantly by men and jobs held predominantly by women.

Compensable factors: In job evaluation, the variables that are used as the basis of the analysis.

Competency system: An organizational practice in which critical competencies (KSAOs) for a job are identified and employee progress toward developing those competencies is tracked.

Competitive conflict: A conflict in a team in which team members promote their own points of view, have little regard for others' opinions, and try to get their own position adopted.

Computer adapted testing (CAT): A computer administered test that chooses items to administer based on answers to previous questions.

Computer-supported cooperative work (CSCW): Work involving two or more people that is done through the use of computers and other similar technologies, often from remote locations.

Concurrent validation study: A validation strategy in which the predictor and criterion are assessed at the same time.

Conference: A training method in which trainees meet to discuss the material.

Confounding: A state that occurs when two or more variables are intertwined in such a way that conclusions about either one alone cannot be made.

Consideration: A supervisory style characterized by concern with the well-being of subordinates. One of the dimensions of the Leader Behavior Description Questionnaire that was developed during the Ohio State Leadership Studies.

Construct validity: The ability to confidently interpret the meaning of an instrument and the ability to conclude that we understand what it is that an instrument actually measures.

Content validity: The instrument in question adequately covers the entire domain intended. For a final examination, content validity would mean that all of the curriculum has been included as opposed to only a small part.

Contextual performance: Behavior that is not required of employees but that benefits the organization. Also called organizational citizenship behavior.

Continuance commitment: A type of organizational commitment based on the investments an individual has in his or her organization, such as pensions and seniority.

Continuous measurement: A measurement technique in which numbers represent an underlying continuum of a variable from low to high.

Control: Any of a number of research procedures that eliminate the possibility that unwanted variables caused the results.

Control group: A comparison group in an experiment; often a group that did not receive the treatment of interest.

Control theory: A motivation theory that focuses on how feedback affects the goal setting process.

Cooperative conflict: A conflict in a team in which individuals openly share diverging views, respect one another's opinions, and focus on finding a solution that is acceptable to team members.

Correlation: The association between two variables.

Correlation coefficient: A statistic that indicates the strength of association between two variables.

Counterproductive work behavior (CWB): Employee behavior that hurts the organization or employees of the organization.

Criterion: A standard of comparison. For performance appraisal, it is the definition of good performance. In a regression equation it is the variable on the left-hand side of the equation that is predicted by the predictor variables.

Criterion contamination: The extent to which an actual criterion assesses something other than the theoretical criterion.

Criterion deficiency: The extent to which a theoretical criterion is not assessed by the actual criterion.

Criterion relevance: The extent to which the actual criterion assesses the theoretical criterion.

Criterion-related validity: The instrument in question is related to a criterion to which it is theoretically expected to relate.

Critical incident: An example of either good or poor job performance; often used to conduct job analysis.

Cross-sectional design: A design for a study in which all data are collected at the same time.

Cross-validate: To replicate the results of one sample with those of another sample.

Cutoff score: A score that serves as the threshold for selection. Individuals who reach the cutoff are hired, whereas those who are below the cutoff are not.

CWB: *See* Counterproductive work behavior.

Decibel (dB): A measure of sound intensity.

Delegation of authority: From bureaucracy theory, the principle that each manager should assign the responsibility for portions of work to subordinates.

Demand/control model: A model of job stress that suggests how control can reduce the negative effects of job stressors.

Dependent variable: In an experiment, the variable that changes as a result of manipulating the independent variable.

Descriptive statistics: Statistics that summarize a distribution of scores, such as means and standard deviations.

Descriptive theory: An organizational theory that explains how existing organizations operate.

***Dictionary of Occupational Titles* (DOT):** A book that contains descriptions of more than 20,000 jobs in the United States.

Distal motivation theory: A motivation theory that deals with variables that are remote from the behavior, such as needs.

Distributive justice: The form of justice concerning a fair division of rewards among people.

Division of labor: Principle from bureaucracy theory that suggests how work should be divided into a series of tasks that are assigned to different individuals.

Dynamic criterion: The idea that job performance changes over time.

E-learning: The use of electronic technology such as the internet to deliver training.

Emotional dissonance: A state a person experiences when having to pretend he or she is experiencing one emotion while actually experiencing an incompatible emotion, such as acting happy when sad.

Emotional intelligence (EI): A cluster of abilities involving the control and recognition of emotions in one's self and others.

Emotional labor: A requirement of a job to exhibit a particular emotion, most frequently enthusiasm and happiness. Common with customer service jobs, such as sales. Also called emotion work.

Empirical biographical inventory: A biographical inventory developed by conducting statistical analyses of a large number of items to see which ones predict job performance.

Engineering psychology: The branch of psychology concerned with the interaction of people and technology; also called ergonomics and human factors.

Equity theory: A motivation theory that bases work motivation on the balance between perceived contributions (inputs) and rewards (outcomes).

Ergonomics: The branch of psychology concerned with the interaction of people and technology; also called engineering psychology and human factors.

Error: According to classical test theory, the part of an observed score that does not represent the construct of interest.

Error variance: Variability among subjects in the same experimental condition.

Essential function: A job task that an employee must be able to perform.

Executive coaching: A training technique in which a high-level executive or manager is paired with a consultant who provides one-on-one training to enhance management skills.

Expectancy: The belief that effort will lead to good job performance.

Expectancy theory: A motivation theory that bases work motivation on a person's expectancy that behavior will lead to desired rewards.

Experiment: A research design in which subjects are randomly assigned to conditions or treatments created by the researcher.

Expert power: Influence based on the perceived expertise of the individual.

Face validity: What a measure appears to assess.

Facet: A dimension of job satisfaction, such as pay or supervision.

Factorial analysis of variance (ANOVA): A statistical technique for analyzing data from experiments with more than one independent variable.

Factorial design: An experimental design for a study that has two or more independent variables.

Fairness theory: A theory suggesting that people make judgments about situations being fair or unfair based on negative outcomes that are seen as purposeful and unreasonable.

Feedback: Information given to a person about his or her performance.

Fiedler's contingency theory: A theory that considers leader effectiveness to be a joint outcome of the leader and the leadership situation.

Field experiment: An experiment conducted in the setting in which the behavior in question naturally occurs.

Field setting: A research setting in which behavior naturally occurs.

Flextime: A work schedule that allows employees to choose some of their work hours.

Force: The term in expectancy theory that represents the level of motivation to engage in a behavior.

Formal role: An established role in an organization, such as supervisor.

Four-fifths rule: The threshold for adverse impact. If the percentage of a minority group hired is less than four-fifths that of the majority group, the four-fifths rule has been violated.

Frame of reference training: A form of training for raters who conduct performance appraisal in which they are given a common and consistent frame of reference on which to base judgments.

Functional Job Analysis (FJA): A method of job analysis that produces scores on common dimensions; used to compile the *Dictionary of Occupational Titles*.

Galatea effect: A type of self-fulfilling prophecy in which a belief in being able to do something well results in better performance by an individual. It is similar to self-efficacy.

General principles: A general overview of the area being taught that should be given to trainees.

Generalizability: The extent to which findings in a study can be extended to other settings.

Glass ceiling: The phenomenon that minorities and women can progress only to a certain level in organizations.

Goal orientation: An individual's focus on either enhancing knowledge and skill (learning orientation) or enhancing performance on job tasks (performance orientation).

Goal-setting theory: A motivation theory that considers motivation to be enhanced by the setting of goals.

Graphic rating form: A performance appraisal technique in which employees are rated on dimensions of performance, such as work quality or work quantity.

Group cohesiveness: *See* Cohesiveness.

Group polarization: The tendency of a group to take more extreme positions than the mean of individuals' positions.

Group test: A psychological test administered to groups of individuals at the same time.

Groupthink: Poor decision making that results from certain group processes.

Growth need strength (GNS): A personality variable from job characteristics theory that concerns the level of a person's need for things that can be gotten from complex work, such as recognition and sense of accomplishment.

Halo error: The tendency for a rater to give an individual the same rating across different dimensions of performance.

Hawthorne Effect: Study results that are produced by the subjects' knowledge that they are research participants.

Health circle: An organized group of employees who meet to formulate recommendations to improve employee health and well-being.

Hired hands: In leader-member exchange (LMX) theory, the individuals who are not favored by the supervisor.

Human factors: The branch of psychology concerned with the interaction of people and technology; also called engineering psychology and ergonomics.

Humanitarian work psychology: A movement within I/O psychology to assist in humanitarian efforts—for example, to fight poverty.

Hygiene factors: In two-factor theory, the job factors that fall outside the nature of the work itself, such as pay and other rewards.

Hypothesis: A researcher's best guess about the outcome of a study.

Identical elements: In training, the correspondence between responses made in training and responses necessary on the job.

In-basket exercise: A simulation exercise used in an assessment center; asks the assessee to show what he or she would do with a series of items that might be found in a manager's in-basket.

Incentive system: A compensation system in which employees are paid for their level of productivity.

Incivility: Rude and demeaning behavior when often the intention of the actor is ambiguous; a mild form of mobbing or bullying.

Independent variable: The variable in an experiment that is manipulated by the researcher.

Individual test: A psychological test administered to only one person at a time.

Individualism: A culture value referring to the focus a person has on the self as opposed to others. It is the opposite of collectivism.

Industrial/organizational (I/O) psychology: An applied branch of psychology that is concerned with understanding people in organizations.

Inferential statistics: A branch of statistics that is concerned with generalizing results from the data at hand to all possible cases. It relies on statistical tests that are based on probability.

Informal role: A role that develops in a work group that was not intended by the organization.

Informed consent form: A consent form that explains a study to a potential subject before he or she agrees to participate.

In-group: *See* Cadre.

Initiating structure: A supervisory style characterized by concern with task accomplishment; one of the dimensions of the Leader Behavior Description Questionnaire that was developed during the Ohio State Leadership Studies.

Inputs: In equity theory, the contributions made by an employee.

Instrumentality: In expectancy theory, the belief that performance will lead to rewards.

Integrity test: A test designed to predict employee counterproductive behavior.

Internal consistency reliability: The agreement among multiple items in a test or multiple ratings by different raters.

Inter-rater reliability: The association between the ratings of two (or more) raters who rate the same subject on the same variable.

Interview: A face-to-face meeting between two or more people for the purpose of sharing information; used for data collection and employee selection.

Job analysis: A method for describing jobs and characteristics necessary for jobs.

Job characteristics model: A model that relates employee motivation and satisfaction to job characteristics.

Job Components Inventory (JCI): A method of job analysis that matches job requirements to characteristics of people.

Job Descriptive Index (JDI): A five-facet measure of job satisfaction.

Job evaluation: A mathematical procedure for determining the relative value of a job to an organization.

Job in General (JIG) scale: A measure of overall job satisfaction.

Job satisfaction: A person's attitudes and feelings about his or her job and facets of the job.

Job strain: A physical or psychological reaction to a job stressor.

Job stressor: A stressful job condition.

Job-oriented job analysis: Any job analysis method that focuses on the content of jobs.

Joint optimization: The concept from sociotechnical systems theory that the social system and technical system of an organization must be designed to complement one another.

Knowledge: What it is necessary to know for a job.

Knowledge and skill test: A psychological test designed to assess a person's knowledge or skills; also called an achievement test.

KSAOs: The knowledge, skills, abilities, and other personal characteristics necessary for good job performance.

Laboratory setting: A research setting in which the behavior of interest does not naturally occur.

Law of effect: The psychological principle that says a behavior that is rewarded will be more likely to reoccur and a behavior that is punished will be less likely to reoccur.

Leader Behavior Description Questionnaire (LBDQ): A scale to assess leadership style, including consideration and initiating structure.

Leader Match: A procedure based on Fiedler's contingency theory that trains leaders to modify situations to match their personal characteristics.

Leaderless group exercise: An assessment center exercise in which assessees are placed in a group without a leader to observe their interpersonal behavior.

Leader-member exchange (LMX) theory: A theory that views leadership from the perspective of individual leader-subordinate pairs.

Learning criteria: Methods of evaluating training by assessing how much trainees have learned from the training.

Learning orientation: A goal orientation that focuses attention on enhancing knowledge and skill.

Least Preferred Coworker (LPC) scale: A measure used to assess a personality characteristic of a leader. The LPC is an important component of Fiedler's contingency theory.

Lecture: A training method in which trainees listen to a presentation.

Legitimate power: Influence based on followers' beliefs that a person has the right to ask for compliance, usually based on rank or title.

Leniency error: The tendency for a rater to give everyone high ratings across dimensions of performance.

Life satisfaction: A person's attitudes about his or her overall life.

Locus of control: A personality variable that refers to people's tendencies to attribute rewards to themselves (internals) or to other people or things (externals).

Longitudinal design: A design for a study in which data are collected at different times.

Management by objectives (MBO): An organizational change technique that involves setting interrelated goals throughout an organization.

Masculinity: A culture value reflecting an emphasis on achievement as opposed to the well-being of others.

Massed training: Training in which sessions take place over a relatively short period of time. It is the opposite of spaced training.

Mean: A measure of the center of a distribution; the sum of observations divided by the number of observations.

Measurement: The process of assigning numbers to characteristics of people or things.

Median: A measure of the center of a distribution; the middle score in a rank-ordered group of observations.

Mediator variable: A variable that intervenes in the process by which two variables are related and explains that relationship.

Mental model: A person's conception or cognitive representation of something, such as how a computer works.

Mentoring: The kind of workplace relationship in which experienced employees assist less experienced employees in career development.

Merit pay: Pay based on level of job performance.

Meta-analysis: A mathematical summary of the results of several samples or studies of the same phenomenon.

Minnesota Satisfaction Questionnaire (MSQ): A 20-facet job satisfaction scale.

Mixed Standard Scale (MSS): A behavior-based performance appraisal method.

Mobbing: Occurs when one or more employees harass and mistreat a particular individual at work; similar to bullying.

Modeling: A training method in which the trainee first observes someone executing a behavior and then practices it.

Moderator variable: A variable that affects the relation between two other variables.

Motivation: The underlying force that explains why people engage in a behavior.

Motivation Potential Score (MPS): From job characteristics theory, the overall complexity or scope of a job.

Motivator factors: In two-factor theory, the job factors that are inherent in the job itself.

Motor task: A task that involves body movements, such as placing pegs in holes or walking.

Multiple hurdles: A selection method whereby applicants must achieve a certain score on each predictor to be hired.

Multiple regression: A statistical procedure for combining several predictors to forecast a criterion.

Musculoskeletal disorder (MSD): An injury to the muscles, bones, and connective tissue caused by either an acute episode (e.g., lifting) or repetitive strain.

Need hierarchy theory: A motivation theory that considers motivation to be based on a hierarchy of five basic human needs.

Negative affectivity (NA): A personality variable that refers to a tendency to experience negative emotions across many different situations.

Nominal group: Several noninteracting people who serve as a comparison to an interacting group in group research.

Norm: A standard of behavior in a group of people.

Normative commitment: A type of organizational commitment in which a person feels he or she has to stay at an organization out of a sense of obligation or values.

Objective test: A test that has fixed response choices that the test taker picks from for each item.

Observational design: A research design in which people are observed on the job.

Obtrusive method: A data collection method in which subjects are aware that they are being studied.

OCB: *See* Organizational citizenship behavior.

Occupational commitment: Attachment to one's occupation or profession. regardless of employer or organization.

Occupational health psychology (OHP): An interdisciplinary subfield of psychology concerned with employee health, safety, and well-being.

Occupational Information Network (O*NET): The U.S. Department of Labor's extensive database on jobs and worker requirements for jobs.

OHP: *See* Occupational health psychology.

On-the-job-training: A training method in which the trainee learns the job while doing it.

Open system theory: A theory that describes organizations as having all the features of an open system.

Open-ended test: A test that requires the test taker to write out his or her answer, such as an essay examination.

Organizational citizenship behavior (OCB): Behavior that is not required of employees but that benefits the organization. Also called contextual performance.

Organizational commitment: The attachment that a person has for his or her job. *See also* Affective commitment, Continuance commitment, *and* Normative commitment.

Organizational constraints: Conditions in an organization that prevent employees from performing well.

Organizational development (OD): One of a family of methods used to improve the functioning of organizations.

Other: In equity theory, the person used for comparison of inputs and outcomes.

Other personal characteristics: Characteristics of people relevant to jobs other than knowledge, skill, or ability.

Outcomes: In equity theory, the rewards a person gets from a job.

Out-group: *See* Hired hands.

Overlearning: Training that continues after a trainee first reaches a criterion of learning the skill.

Paper-and-pencil test: A written test that requires either indicating the correct answer from several choices or writing an answer to an open-ended question.

Part training: Training of individual subtasks one at a time. It is the opposite of whole training.

Path-goal theory: A leadership theory that emphasizes how leaders can enhance subordinate motivation by clarifying the paths between behavior and rewards.

Pearson product-moment correlation coefficient: The most frequently used measure of association between two continuous variables.

Performance appraisal: The formal procedures that an organization uses to assess job performance of employees.

Performance orientation: A goal orientation that focuses attention on enhancing performance on specific job tasks.

Performance test: A test that requires the test taker to perform tasks involving manipulation of objects.

Performance-level criteria: Measures that indicate how well training is transferred to the job.

Personality test: A test designed to assess people's patterns of behavior or feelings.

Personality trait: The tendency of a person to engage in certain types of behavior or respond to situations in particular ways.

Person-oriented job analysis: Any job analysis method that focuses on characteristics necessary for a job.

Piece-rate system: A system that pays employees for each unit of production.

Political skill: The skill of being able to influence others to accomplish either personal or organizational objectives.

Position Analysis Questionnaire (PAQ): A job analysis method that describes jobs and necessary job characteristics along common dimensions.

Power: The ability to influence other people.

Power distance: A culture value reflecting tolerance for large power and status differences among levels in an organization.

Power test: A test without a time limit.

Predictive validity study: A study in which predictor information is used to forecast a criterion that is assessed at a later time.

Predictor: A variable that is used to forecast a criterion.

Prescriptive theory: An organizational theory that explains how organizations should function.

Pretest-posttest design: A research design in which the same criterion variable is assessed before and after the treatment occurs.

Procedural justice: The form of justice concerning the fairness of the process by which rewards are allocated.

Process loss: Time spent by group members that is not devoted to task accomplishment.

Programmed instruction: A training method in which trainees work at their own pace.

Protected classes: Groups of people who are given special legal protection because of past discrimination against them.

Proximal motivation theory: A motivation theory that deals with variables that are closely linked to behavior, such as goals or intentions.

Psychological test: A standardized series of problems or questions that measure characteristics of people.

Psychomotor ability test: A psychological test designed to assess physical abilities, such as eye-hand coordination.

Qualitative method: Research that minimizes the use of quantitative and statistical methods.

Quality circle: A group of employees who meet to discuss ways to improve their work.

Quasi-experiment design: A research design that has some but not all the features of an experiment. For example, there might not be random assignment of subjects to conditions.

Questionnaire: A paper-and-pencil or online instrument used to collect information; can be completed by respondents themselves.

Random assignment: Placing subjects into treatment conditions in an experiment so that each subject has an equal chance of being in each condition.

Random selection: Choosing subjects for a study so that every possible subject has an equal chance of participating.

Rater error training (RET): A training program designed to familiarize individuals who rate performance with rating errors and techniques to avoid them.

Rational biographical inventory: A biographical inventory based on theory and research concerning the prior experiences that would be expected to relate to job performance.

Reactions criteria: Methods of evaluating training by assessing trainee reactions to the training.

Realistic job preview (RJP): Information given to job applicants to let them know what the job and organization are like.

Reasonable accommodation: A principle from the Americans With Disabilities Act that requires organizations to provide reasonable assistance or modifications to the job or workplace so that people with disabilities can perform the job.

Referent power: Influence based on the subordinate's liking for the supervisor.

Regression equation: A mathematical equation that allows the prediction of one variable from another.

Reinforcement theory: A motivation theory that considers behavior to be a function of rewards.

Reliability: The consistency of a measure; how well scores for the same subject are replicable across repeated measurements of the same variable.

Repetitive strain injury: An injury brought on by making the same motion continuously, such as typing on a computer keyboard.

Research design: The structure of a research study.

Respite: A break from work such as a vacation.

Response rate: The percentage or proportion of contacted people who participate in a survey.

Results criteria: Methods of evaluating training by assessing the impact of the training on the organization, such as profits.

Reward power: Influence based on giving rewards.

Role: A person's position in a group or team.

Role ambiguity: Employee uncertainty about what is expected of him or her on the job.

Role conflict: Incompatible demands placed on an employee.

Role play: A training technique that involves having the trainee pretend to perform a task.

Salary survey: A survey of employers to determine salary levels for certain jobs.

Sample: The subjects chosen for a study.

Schemata: Cognitive categories or frames of reference.

Scientific management: The application of scientific principles to managing people's job performance; developed by Frederick Winslow Taylor.

Scope: The complexity and challenge of a job.

Selection ratio: The proportion of job applicants who are hired for a job.

Self-efficacy: The belief that a person has in his or her ability to perform a task well.

Self-efficacy theory: A motivation theory based on the idea that people perform well when they believe they are capable of doing the job.

Severity error: In performance appraisal, the assignment of low ratings to all ratees.

Sexual harassment: Behavior of a sexual nature that adversely affects a person's ability to do his or her job.

Simulation: A training method that allows people to practice a skill in an artificial and controlled situation.

SIOP: *See* Society for Industrial and Organizational Psychology.

Skill: How well a person is able to do a task.

Skill variety: A dimension of the job characteristics model that involves the number of skills required to do a job.

Social facilitation: The improvement in performance that sometimes occurs when in the presence of other people. Research has shown that simple or well-learned tasks are facilitated by the presence of others, whereas performance on complex or new tasks is inhibited. *See* Social inhibition.

Social inhibition: The decline in performance that sometimes occurs when in the presence of other people. Research has shown that complex or new tasks are inhibited by the presence of others, whereas performance on simple or well-learned tasks is facilitated. *See* Social facilitation.

Social loafing: A group phenomenon whereby the larger the group, the smaller the effort made by each member on a task.

Social stressor: A stressful job condition that arises from interactions among people, such as bullying or interpersonal conflict.

Society for Industrial and Organizational Psychology (SIOP): The division of the American Psychological Association that is the world's largest association of I/O psychologists.

Sociotechnical systems theory: A theory that states that organizations should consider both the human and the technological demands of tasks in designing work environments.

Spaced training: Training in which sessions are spread out over time. It is the opposite of massed training.

Span of control: A principle of bureaucracy theory that is concerned with the number of people that a supervisor can oversee.

Speed test: A test with a time limit.

Standard deviation: A measure of dispersion for a distribution of scores; the square root of the variance.

Statistical significance: A rule of thumb for evaluating the results of a statistical test.

Statistical test: A quantitative procedure based on probability that allows for the interpretation of study outcomes.

Stress: Physiological and psychological responses to demands that are perceived to be challenging or threatening.

Structured interview: An interview in which the questions are standardized across interviewees.

Subject matter expert: A person who is knowledgeable about a topic.

Survey design: A research design in which subjects are asked to answer questions, usually with an interview or questionnaire.

Survey feedback: An organizational change technique in which employees are surveyed and the survey information is fed back to all levels of the organization.

Tailored testing: A testing procedure that adjusts the level of item difficulty to the test taker's ability.

Task identity: A dimension from the job characteristics model that identifies the extent to which a person does an entire job.

Task inventory: A job analysis technique that produces a detailed list of the tasks for a job.

Task significance: A dimension from the job characteristics model that represents the extent to which a particular job impacts other people.

Team building: A procedure that is used to improve the functioning of work teams.

Team commitment: The attachment a person has to his or her team and teammates.

Team mental model: The cognitive conception a team member has about the various tasks each member of the team has and how the various tasks interrelate.

Telecommute: Work at home while communicating with work-related people via modem and telephone.

Test-retest reliability: The consistency of a measure when it is repeated over time.

T-group: An organizational change technique that has employees attend training sessions over a period of days to learn interpersonal skills.

Theoretical criterion: The conceptual definition of what constitutes good job performance.

Theory X/Theory Y: A theory that proposes that how a manager views subordinate characteristics affects his or her approach to supervision.

Theory Z: The Japanese style of management for large organizations that assumes employees will spend their entire careers with one organization.

Time and motion study: An analysis of task performance involving the observation and timing of subject motions. The purpose is to determine ways to eliminate or modify motions to make performance more efficient.

Training-level criteria: Measures that indicate how well a trainee does in training.

Transfer of training: The application of what was learned in training to the job itself.

Transformational leader: *See* Charismatic leader.

True halo: The extent to which a person's performance across different dimensions is at the same level.

T-test: A statistical test used to compare two means.

Turnover: An employee's quitting his or her job.

Two-factor theory: A motivation theory that considers job satisfaction and dissatisfaction to be separate factors rather than opposite ends of the same continuum.

Type A/B personality: A personality variable; a person can be hard driving and impatient (Type A) or easygoing and relaxed (Type B).

Uncertainty avoidance: A culture value reflecting tolerance for ambiguity and uncertainty, which is reflected in the tendency to be rule oriented.

Uniform Guidelines on Employee Selection Procedures: A document produced by the U.S. government that describes appropriate and legally defensible selection procedures.

Unit control of variances: A principle of sociotechnical systems theory that recommends allowing employees who encounter problems to solve them.

Universal Precautions: Suggested safety procedures for health care workers to reduce chances of accidental exposure to infectious diseases such as AIDS/HIV and hepatitis B.

Unobtrusive method: A method of research in which subjects do not know that they are being studied.

Utility analysis: The analysis of the financial benefits to an organization of taking a course of action, such as implementing a particular selection system.

Valence: In expectancy theory, the value or worth a person gives to an outcome.

Validation study: A study undertaken to determine if a predictor is related to a criterion.

Validity: The interpretation given to the meaning of a measure.

Validity generalization: A principle that states that if a predictor is a valid indicator of a criterion in one setting, it will be valid in another similar setting.

Variable: A characteristic of a person or thing that varies.

Variance: The degree to which scores differ among individuals in a distribution of scores.

Violence prevention climate: A shared perception by a group of employees that their organization has policies and practices to protect them from workplace violence.

Virtual team: Two or more individuals who have interdependent tasks and separate roles and who interact remotely via e-mail, telephone, and other technologies.

Vocational interest test: A test that matches the interests of test takers to those of people in various professions.

Vroom-Yetton model: A model that indicates the best approach to making decisions that involve subordinates.

Whole training: Training that focuses on an entire task at one time rather than on parts of the task. It is the opposite of part training.

Work group: Two or more individuals who interact and share common task goals.

Work sample: A test that includes tasks from a job.

Work team: A work group in which members have interdependent tasks and individual task-related roles.

Work-family conflict: A form of role conflict in which family demands and work demands conflict.

Author Index

D

E

F

Subject Index

Get the ebook FREE!

To get a free PDF copy of this book (sold separately for $29.99) purchase the print book and register it at the Manning website following the instructions inside this insert.

That's it!
Thanks from Manning!

Dependency Injection

DESIGN PATTERNS USING SPRING AND GUICE

DHANJI R. PRASANNA

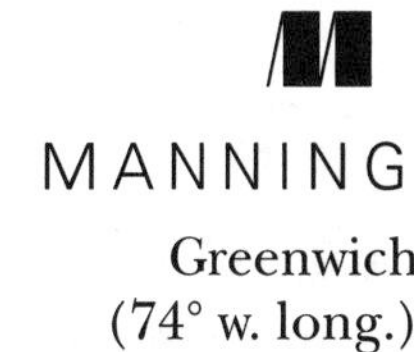

Greenwich
(74° w. long.)

For online information and ordering of this and other Manning books, please visit www.manning.com. The publisher offers discounts on this book when ordered in quantity. For more information, please contact

Special Sales Department
Manning Publications Co.
Sound View Court 3B fax: (609) 877-8256
Greenwich, CT 06830 email: orders@manning.com

Manning Publications Co.
Sound View Court 3B
Greenwich, CT 06830

Development Editor: Tom Cirtin
Copyeditor: Linda Recktenwald
Typesetter: Gordan Salinovic
Cover designer: Leslie Haimes

ISBN 978-1-933988-55-9
Printed in the United States of America
1 2 3 4 5 6 7 8 9 10 – MAL – 14 13 12 11 10 09

To my parents

*"If you want to make an apple pie from scratch,
you must first create the universe."*

—Carl Sagan

brief contents

contents

preface

The reasonable man adapts himself to the world; the unreasonable one persists in trying to adapt the world to himself. Therefore, all progress depends on the unreasonable man.

—George Bernard Shaw

So, novice-expert-aficionado-learner, welcome to our dependency injection theme park! We'll begin this tour of dependency injection at the gate: by first defining the problem it solves.

The tour will then proceed down the streams of specific implementations and popular technologies, examining quick solutions in such frameworks as Guice, Spring, and PicoContainer, among others. A long break will follow for the purpose of theoretical nourishment, where we shall discuss the foundational idioms behind dependency injection, its core *viral* ideology, its types and practices.

Then, we'll peruse the hall of curiosities where we consider such peculiar notions as objects with managed state, lifecycle, and modularity and examine their curious aspectual behaviors.

In turn, we'll descend into the caverns of pitfalls, nuances, and corner cases that ought to titillate and horrify the strongest of constitutions; for when you cross these lines you can expect the demons of class loading, dynamic proxying, and unintended encapsulation to rear their ugly heads, only to be shown up by even greater challenges of concurrency.

We'll make a round about the marvelous gilded architectures of enterprise applications, casting a purposeful eye at their grandeur, which is composed of modular, remote-able service models that separate cleanly between compartments of the enterprise—particularly those nefarious tiers, web and business.

These will leave us with a meditation on the big picture—how we can marry these elegant idioms of dependency injection with their many suitors: applications, third-party libraries, and frameworks.

Finally, dear tourist, you will be presented with a purposed comparison of popular dependency injection frameworks, gauging their performance, features, safety, and rigor (as a functioning example in chapter 11).

The theme park metaphor aside, I have attempted to structure this book as a journey. While the ideas and engineering patterns explored in this book do not refer to a particular language, many of the examples will be in Java. The frameworks we explore will primarily be well-known Java libraries that are widely in use.

A basic understanding of Java (or C#) is preferable; however, for you to get the best out of this book I also recommend familiarity with the principles of object-oriented programming (particularly encapsulation, polymorphism, and inheritance).

acknowledgments

I would not be in the position of having authored this book without the grace and assistance of many people who have been involved in the project, and who have put up with my taxing demeanor during the months of development and writing it took to complete. To all of them, I owe an unrepayable debt.

Foremost, Bob Lee: from the first email I sent him, and every single one since, he has shown me nothing but kindness and encouragement. He not only recommended publishers for my book, but was also instrumental in my joining Google, where I now work on interesting and compelling projects. I am fortunate to count him as a colleague and a friend.

Jesse Wilson, the Guice team lead and the technical reviewer for this book, has been one of my most stalwart defenders, critics, and friends in recent months. Jesse never tires or loses cheer and is infectious. Large parts of my work at Google, in open source, and of this book are owed to him.

Apache Wicket Developer, Manning author, and good friend Eelco Hillenius was responsible for directing me to Manning. He went out on a proverbial limb, championing me and Guice to Manning. Acquisitions editor Mike Stephens was the one who suggested the idea of a software engineering book focusing on design patterns. But most important to this book's development was Tom Cirtin, my editor at Manning. Tom's generosity, sense of humor, and keen eye helped me more than I can express. He pushed me when he had to, and politely steered me from disaster wherever it brewed. I applaud and thank him for his efforts.

Tom Wilson, my team lead at ThoughtWorks, put up with months of my trying behavior while having the courage to listen to every worthwhile idea I brought up and to shoot down every worthless one. Paul Hammant, the PicoContainer author, carefully reviewed many of my early drafts and suggested many corrections. Jon Tirsen, Kevin Bourrillion, Josh Bloch, and Ghassan Mishergi at Google always had time for my rantings and my incessant and often obtuse questioning. Concurrency experts Tim Peierls and Brian Goetz corrected me at different times about pants being up or down. Mike Brock and Michael Neale from Red Hat kept me honest by telling me when I was being silly. Brad Dwyer, Jody Elson, and Dr. George Corliss never refused a request to read or comment on drafts. Thanks also to Robbie Vanbrabant, who contributes to warp-persist, and Mike Bain, my great friend and the best iteration manager ThoughtWorks has ever had.

A special note of thanks to the many reviewers who read my manuscript a number of times during development, contributing feedback and insights along the way that helped make this a much better book. I am grateful to them for their time and efforts: Dan Dobrin, Frank Wang, Paul King, Rick Wagner, Robert Hanson, Shreekanth Joshi, Wahid Sadik, Dave Corun, Sam Newman, Andrew Konkol, David Strong, Patrick Steger, Jon Skeet, Martyn Fletcher, Marcus Baker, Howard Lewis Ship, Mark Seemann, Ramarao Kanneganti, and King Wang.

I would also like to thank the production team at Manning for turning my manuscript into the book you are now reading: copyeditor Linda Recktenwald, proofreader Elizabeth Martin, typesetter Gordan Salinovic, cover designer Leslie Haimes, and project manager Mary Piergies.

I owe a massive debt to Josh McDonald, who created the elegant and subtle theme that is in all the illustrations and who was kind enough to draw many of them. Also for his contributions to my open source project work as well as the many beers he has put back on my account.

Special words of appreciation to Yutgong Au, my close friend and closet artistic genius, who created many of the icons and line drawings in this book, producing them at a moment's notice any time I asked for them.

And to Zac Steacy for being my all around best friend, every day.

about this book

This book is intended for newcomers to dependency injection as well as for seasoned framework users. It is a guide to design patterns and best practices when using dependency injection, an increasingly indispensable tool in any programmer's arsenal.

Who should read this book

The book is for anyone who writes code and is interested in learning best practices for designing large, developer-scale applications. It is also intended for an audience of architects and professionals seeking to identify and correct common anti-patterns in design. All the examples are written in Java using Spring or Guice. But the lessons apply equally to other statically typed languages like C#. Whether you're a developer, architect, team lead, or novice programmer, you will find this book useful.

Roadmap

The book is divided into 11 chapters.

- Chapters 1-4 provide a thorough introduction to testability and the reasons for using dependency injection, its various design patterns, and usage idioms, particularly how to choose these patterns and apply them in various situations.
- Chapters 5-6 focus on scopes, which, are a way of managing state in your application without polluting logic with infrastructure concerns. They also explore deep problems with common idioms such as the *static* singleton anti-pattern and solutions using dependency injection, and examine scopes for web applications and other purposes.

- Chapter 7 talks about how to manage your application's lifecycle via the dependency injector. This involves sending objects notifications of important events in the life of the application and designing custom lifecycle infrastructure for your own uses.
- Chapter 8 deals with aspect oriented programming (or AOP) as it applies to dependency injection, how it helps save on boilerplate code, and reduces the risk of errors. A large part of this chapter is devoted to potential problems and pitfalls in using this powerful technique.
- Chapters 9-11 investigate concurrency and design and look at case studies in performance, design, and design integration with third party frameworks. Chapter 11 is a case study on how to build a complete web application using the concepts presented throughout the book.

Finally, there are two appendixes that discuss alternate approaches to dependency injection frameworks, SmartyPantsIOC for Flex and the Butterfly Container.

Code conventions and downloads

All source code in listings or in the text is in a `fixed-width font like this` to separate it from ordinary text. In listings, **`bold code`** indicates code that has changed from the previous example, or that will change in the next example. Code annotations accompany some of the listings, highlighting important concepts. In some cases, numbered bullets link to explanations that follow in the text.

You can download the source code for this book from the publisher's website at www.manning.com/DependencyInjection.

Software requirements

To use the code in this book, you need the Sun Java SDK (which is free) running on Linux, Windows, or Mac OS X. You'll also find it useful to download libraries for the Spring Framework (http://springframework.org) and Google Guice (http://code.google.com/p/google-guice). Both are open source and free to download from the links provided. Other tools will be referenced where they're relevant. At your discretion you may choose to use a Java IDE such as IntelliJ IDEA, but this is not strictly necessary.

Author Online

Purchase of *Dependency Injection* includes free access to a private web forum run by Manning Publications where you can make comments about the book, ask technical questions, and receive help from the author and from other users. To access the forum and subscribe to it, point your web browser to http://www.manning.com/DependencyInjection. This page provides information on how to get on the forum once you are registered, what kind of help is available, and the rules of conduct on the forum. It also provides links to the source code for the examples in the book, errata, and other downloads.

Manning's commitment to our readers is to provide a venue where a meaningful dialog between individual readers and between readers and the authors can take place. It is not a commitment to any specific amount of participation on the part of the author, whose contribution to the Author Online remains voluntary (and unpaid). We suggest you try asking the author some challenging questions lest his interest stray!

You can also ask the author a question at http://twitter.com/dhanji.

about the cover illustration

The figure on the cover of *Dependency Injection* is captioned "Le Créole de Cayenne," a descendent of colonialists in French Guiana, an overseas region of France located in South America. Cayenne is the capital of French Guiana. The city stands on a former island at the mouth of the Cayenne River on the Atlantic coast. The illustration is taken from a 19th-century edition of Sylvain Maréchal's four-volume compendium of regional and world dress customs published in France. Each illustration is finely drawn and colored by hand.

The rich variety of Maréchal's collection reminds us vividly of how culturally apart the world's towns and regions were just 200 years ago. Isolated from each other, people spoke different dialects and languages. In the streets or in the countryside, it was easy to identify where they lived and what their trade or station in life was just by their dress.

Dress codes have changed since then and the diversity by region and nation, so rich at the time, has faded away. It is now hard to tell apart the inhabitants of different continents, let alone different towns or regions. Perhaps we have traded cultural diversity for a more varied personal life–certainly for a more varied and fast-paced technological life.

At a time when it is hard to tell one computer book from another, Manning celebrates the inventiveness and initiative of the computer business with book covers based on the rich diversity of regional life of two centuries ago, brought back to life by Maréchal's pictures.

1 Dependency injection: what's all the hype?

This chapter covers:

- Seeing an object as a service
- Learning about building and assembling services
- Taking a tour of pre-existing solutions
- Investigating the Hollywood Principle
- Surveying available frameworks

"We all agree that your theory is crazy, but is it crazy enough?"

—Niels Bohr

So you're an expert on dependency injection (DI); you know it and use it every day. It's like your morning commute—you sleepwalk through it, making all the right left turns (and the occasional wrong right turns before quickly correcting) until you're comfortably sitting behind your desk at work. Or you've heard of DI and Inversion of Control (IoC) and read the occasional article, in which case this is your first commute to work on a new job and you're waiting at the station, with a strong suspicion you are about to get on the wrong train and an even stronger suspicion you're on the wrong platform.

Or you're somewhere in between; you're feeling your way through the idea, not yet fully convinced about DI, planning out that morning commute and looking for the best route to work, *MapQuesting* it. Or you have your own home-brew setup that works just fine, thank you very much. You've no need of a DI technology: You bike to work, get a lot of exercise on the way, and are carbon efficient.

Stop! Take a good, long breath. Dependency injection is the art of making work come home to you.

1.1 Every solution needs a problem

Most software today is written to automate some real-world process, whether it be writing a letter, purchasing the new album from your favorite band, or placing an order to sell some stock. In object-oriented programming (OOP), these are *objects* and their interactions are *methods.*

Objects represent their real-world counterparts. An `Airplane` represents a 747 and a `Car` represents a Toyota; a `PurchaseOrder` represents you buying this book; and so on.

Of particular interest is the interaction between objects: An airplane flies, while a car can be driven and a book can be opened and read. This is where the value of the automation is realized and where it is valuable in simplifying our lives.

Take the familiar activity of writing an email; you compose the message using an email application (like Mozilla Thunderbird or Gmail) and you send it across the internet to one or more recipients, as in figure 1.1. This entire activity can be modeled as the interaction of various objects.

Figure 1.1 Email is composed locally, delivered across an internet relay, and received by an inbox.

This highlights an important precept in this book: the idea of an *object acting as a service.* In the example, email acts as a message composition service, internet relays are delivery agents, and my correspondent's inbox is a receiving service.

1.1.1 Seeing objects as services

The process of emailing a correspondent can be reduced to the composing, delivering, and receiving of email by each responsible object, namely the `Emailer`, `InternetRelay`, and `RecipientInbox`. Each object is a *client* of the next.

`Emailer` uses the `InternetRelay` as a service to *send* email, and in turn, the `InternetRelay` uses the `RecipientInbox` as a service to *deliver* sent mail.

The act of composing an email can be reduced to more granular tasks:

- Writing the message
- Checking spelling
- Looking up a recipient's address

And so on. Each is a fairly specialized task and is modeled as a specific service. For example, "writing the message" falls into the domain of editing text, so choosing a `TextEditor` is appropriate. Modeling the `TextEditor` in this fashion has many advantages over extending `Emailer` to write text messages itself: We know exactly where to look if we want to find out what the logic looks like for editing text.

- Our `Emailer` is not cluttered with distracting code meant for text manipulation.
- We can reuse the `TextEditor` component in other scenarios (say, a calendar or note-taking application) without much additional coding.
- If someone else has written a general-purpose text-editing component, we can make use of it rather than writing one from scratch.

Similarly, "checking spelling" is done by a `SpellChecker`. If we wanted to check spelling in a different language, it would not be difficult to swap out the English `SpellChecker` in favor of a French one. `Emailer` itself would not need to worry about checking spelling—French, English, or otherwise.

So now we've seen the value of decomposing our services into objects. This principle is important because it highlights the relationship between one object and others it uses to perform a service: An object depends on its services to perform a function.

In our example, the `Emailer` depends on a `SpellChecker`, a `TextEditor`, and an `AddressBook`. This relationship is called a *dependency*. In other words, `Emailer` is a client of its dependencies.

Composition also applies transitively; an object may depend on other objects that themselves have dependencies, and so on. In our case, `SpellChecker` may depend on a `Parser` to recognize words and a `Dictionary` of valid words. `Parser` and `Dictionary` may themselves depend on other objects.

This composite system of dependencies is commonly called an *object graph*. This object graph, though composed of many dependencies, is functionally a single *unit*.

Let's sum up what we have so far:

- *Service*—An object that performs a *well-defined* function when called upon
- *Client*—Any consumer of a service; an object that calls upon a service to perform a *well-understood* function

The service–client relationship implies a clear *contract* between the objects in the role of performing a specific function that is formally understood by both entities. You will also hear them referred to as:

- *Dependency*—A specific service that is *required* by another object to fulfill its function.
- *Dependent*—A client object that needs a dependency (or dependencies) in order to perform its function.

Not only can you describe an object graph as a system of discrete services and clients, but you also begin to see that a client cannot function *without* its services. In other words, an object cannot function properly without its dependencies.

NOTE DI as a subject is primarily concerned with reliably and efficiently building such object graphs and the strategies, patterns, and best practices therein.

Let's look at ways of building object graphs before we take on DI.

1.2 Pre-DI solutions

Figure 1.2 shows a simple relationship between an object and its dependency.

Were you asked to code such a class without any other restrictions, you might attempt something like this:

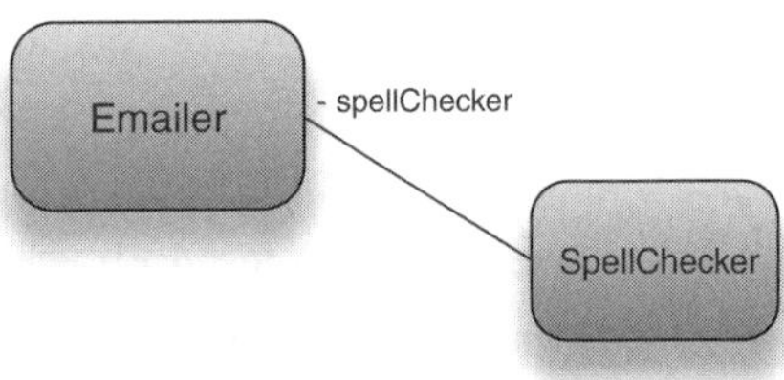

Figure 1.2 Object `Emailer` is composed of another object, `SpellChecker`.

```
public class Emailer {
    private SpellChecker spellChecker;
    public Emailer() {
        this.spellChecker = new SpellChecker();
    }

    public void send(String text) { .. }
}
```

Then constructing a working `Emailer` (one with a `SpellChecker`) is as simple as constructing an `Emailer` itself:

```
Emailer emailer = new Emailer();
```

No doubt you have written code like this at some point. I certainly have. Now, let's say you want to write a unit test for the `send()` method to ensure that it is checking spelling before sending any message. How would you do it? You might create a *mock* `SpellChecker` and give that to the `Emailer`. Something like:

```
public class MockSpellChecker extends SpellChecker {
    private boolean didCheckSpelling = false;
    public boolean checkSpelling(String text) {
        didCheckSpelling = true;
return true;
    }

    public boolean verifyDidCheckSpelling()
        { return didCheckSpelling; }          <-- Called by test to verify behavior
}
```

Of course, we can't use this mock because we are unable to substitute the internal spellchecker that an `Emailer` has. This effectively makes your class *untestable*, which is a showstopper for this approach.

This approach also prevents us from creating objects of the same class with different behaviors. See listing 1.1 and figure 1.3.

Listing 1.1 An email service that checks spelling in English

```
public class Emailer {
    private SpellChecker spellChecker;
```

```
    public Emailer() {
        this.spellChecker = new EnglishSpellChecker();
    }
    ...
}
```

In this example, the `Emailer` has an `EnglishSpellChecker`. Can we create an `Emailer` with a `FrenchSpellChecker`? We cannot! `Emailer` encapsulates the *creation* of its dependencies.

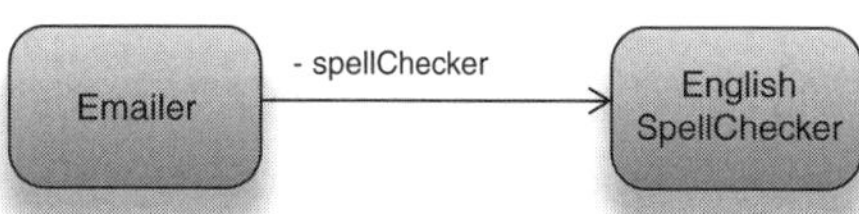

Figure 1.3 An email service that checks spelling in English

What we need is a more flexible solution: *construction by hand* (sometimes called manual dependency injection), where instead of a dependent creating its own dependencies, it has them provided externally.

1.2.1 Construction by hand

Naturally, the solution is not to encapsulate the creation of dependencies, but what does this mean and to whom do we offload this burden? Several techniques can solve this problem. In the earlier section, we used the object's constructor to create its dependencies. With a slight modification, we can keep the structure of the object graph but offload the burden of creating dependencies. Here is such a modification (see figure 1.4):

```
public class Emailer {
    private SpellChecker spellChecker;
    public void setSpellChecker(SpellChecker spellChecker) {
        this.spellChecker = spellChecker;
    }
    ...
}
```

Notice that I've replaced the constructor that created its own `SpellChecker` with a method that *accepts* a `SpellChecker`. Now we can construct an `Emailer` and substitute a mock `SpellChecker`:

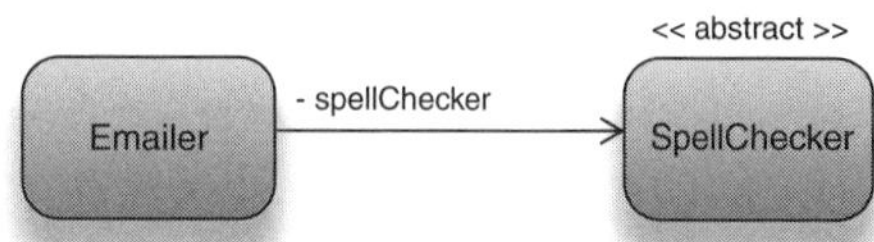

Figure 1.4 An email service that checks spelling using an abstract spelling service

```
    @Test
    public void ensureEmailerChecksSpelling() {
        MockSpellChecker mock = new MockSpellChecker();
        Emailer emailer = new Emailer();
        emailer.setSpellChecker(mock);        <-- Pass in mock dependency for testing
        emailer.send("Hello there!");

        assert mock.verifyDidCheckSpelling();    <-- Verify the dependency was used properly
    }
```

Similarly, it is easy to construct `Emailers` with various behaviors. Here's one for French spelling:

```
Emailer service = new Emailer();
service.setSpellChecker(new FrenchSpellChecker());
```

And one for Japanese:

```
Emailer service = new Emailer();
service.setSpellChecker(new JapaneseSpellChecker());
```

Cool! At the time of creating the Emailer, it's up to you to provide its dependencies. This allows you to choose particular flavors of its services that suit your needs (French, Japanese, and so on) as shown in figure 1.5.

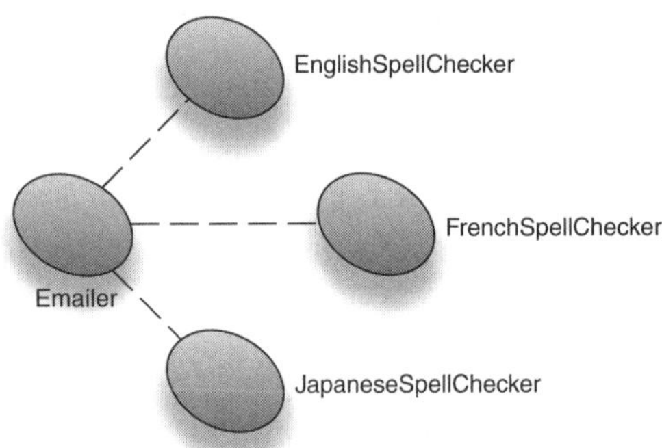

Figure 1.5 The same `Emailer` class can now check spelling in a variety of languages.

Since you end up connecting the pipes yourself at the time of construction, this technique is referred to as construction by hand. In the previous example we used a setter method (a method that accepts a value and sets it as a dependency). You can also pass in the dependency via a constructor, as per the following example:

```
public class Emailer {
    private SpellChecker spellChecker;
    public Emailer(SpellChecker spellChecker) {
        this.spellChecker = spellChecker;
    }
    ...
}
```

Then creating the Emailer is even more concise:

```
Emailer service = new Emailer(new JapaneseSpellChecker());
```

This technique is called *constructor injection* and has the advantage of being explicit about its contract—you can never create an Emailer and forget to set its dependencies, as is possible in the earlier example if you forget to call the `setSpellChecker()` method. This concept is obviously very useful in OOP. We'll study it in greater detail in the coming chapters.

NOTE The idea of connecting the pipes together, or giving a client its dependency, is sometimes also referred to as "injecting" objects into one another and other times as "wiring" the objects together.

While construction by hand definitely helps with testing, it has some problems, the most obvious one being the burden of knowing how to construct object graphs being placed on the client of a service. If I use the same object in many places, I must repeat code for wiring objects in all of those places. Construction by hand, as the name suggests, is really tedious! If you alter the dependency graph or any of its parts, you may be forced to go through and alter all of its clients as well. Fixing even a small bug can mean changing vast amounts of code.

Another grave problem is the fact that users need to know how object graphs are wired internally. This violates the principle of encapsulation and becomes problematic when dealing with code that is used by many clients, who really shouldn't have to care about the internals of their dependencies in order to use them. There are also potent arguments against construction by hand that we will encounter in other forms in the coming chapters. So how can we offload the burden of dependency creation and not shoot ourselves in the foot doing so? One answer is the *Factory pattern.*

1.2.2 The Factory pattern

Another time-honored method of constructing object graphs is the Factory design pattern (also known as the Abstract Factory[1] pattern). The idea behind the Factory pattern is to offload the burden of creating dependencies to a third-party object called a factory (shown in figure 1.6). Just as an automotive factory creates and assembles cars, so too does a Factory pattern create and assemble object graphs.

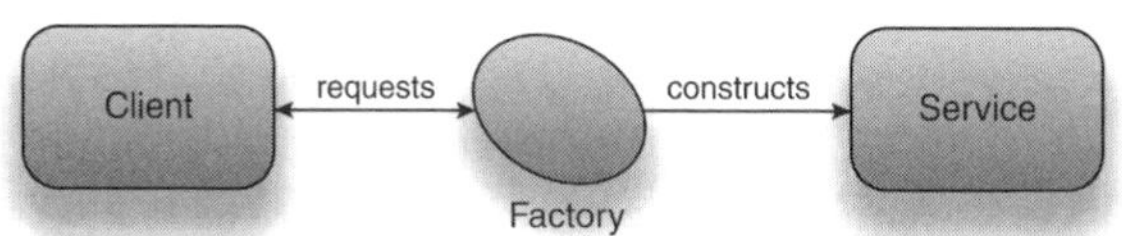

Figure 1.6 A client requests its dependencies from a Factory.

Let's apply the Factory pattern to our `Emailer`. The `Emailer`'s code remains the same (as shown in listing 1.2).

Listing 1.2 An email service whose spellchecker is set via constructor

```
public class Emailer {
    private SpellChecker spellChecker;
    public Emailer(SpellChecker spellChecker) {
        this.spellChecker = spellChecker;
    }
    ...
}
```

Instead of constructing the object graph by hand, we do it inside another class called a factory (listing 1.3).

Listing 1.3 A "French" email service Factory pattern

```
public class EmailerFactory {
    public Emailer newFrenchEmailer() {
        return new Emailer(new FrenchSpellChecker());
    }
}
```

1 Erich Gamma et al., *Design Patterns: Elements of Reusable Object-Oriented Software* (Addison-Wesley Professional Computing Series, 1994). Sometimes called the "Gang of Four" book.

Notice that the Factory pattern is very explicit about what kind of `Emailer` it is going to produce; `newFrenchEmailer()` creates one with a French spellchecker. Any code that uses French email services is now fairly straightforward:

```
Emailer service = new EmailerFactory().newFrenchEmailer();
```

The most important thing to notice here is that the client code has no reference to spellchecking, address books, or any of the other *internals* of `Emailer`. By adding a level of abstraction (the Factory pattern), we have separated the code *using* the `Emailer` from the code that *creates* the `Emailer`. This leaves client code clean and concise.

The value of this becomes more apparent as we deal with richer and more complex object graphs. Listing 1.4 shows a Factory that constructs our `Emailer` with many more dependencies (also see figure 1.4).

Listing 1.4 A Factory that constructs a Japanese emailer

```
public class EmailerFactory {
    public Emailer newJapaneseEmailer() {
        Emailer service = new Emailer();
        service.setSpellChecker(new JapaneseSpellChecker());
        service.setAddressBook(new EmailBook());
        service.setTextEditor(new SimpleJapaneseTextEditor());
        return service;
    }
}
```

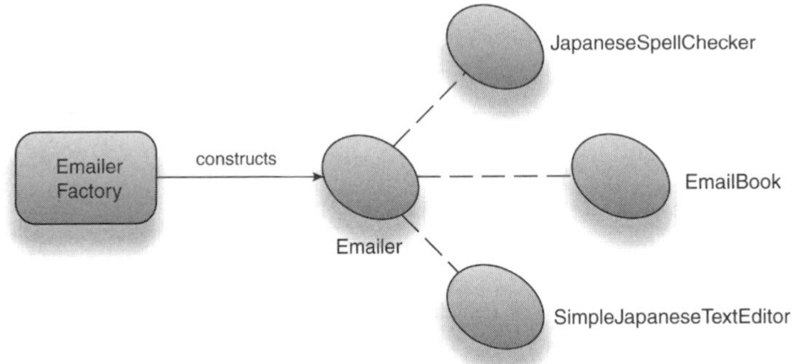

Figure 1.7 `Emailer-Factory` constructs and assembles a Japanese `Emailer` with various dependencies.

Code that uses such an `Emailer` is as simple and readable as we could wish:

```
Emailer emailer = new EmailerFactory().newJapaneseEmailer();
```

The beauty of this approach is that client code only needs to know which Factory to use to obtain a dependency (and none of its internals).

Now how about testing this code? Are we able to mock `Emailer`'s dependencies? Sure; our test can simply ignore the Factory and pass in mocks:

```
@Test
public void testEmailer() {
    MockSpellChecker spellChecker =
```

```
        new MockSpellChecker();          Create mocks for
    ...                                  each dependency

    Emailer emailer = new Emailer();
    emailer.setSpellChecker(spellChecker);     Set mocked
    ...                                        dependencies on emailer

    emailer.send("Hello there!");

    //verify emailer's behavior
    assert ...;                    <-- Ensure everything worked
}
```

So far, so good. Now let's look at a slightly different angle: How can we test *clients* of `Emailer`? Listing 1.5 shows one way.

Listing 1.5 A client uses `Emailer` to send messages typed by a user

```
public class EmailClient {
    private Emailer emailer =
        new EmailerFactory().newEnglishEmailer();     <-- Get ourselves an Emailer from its Factory

    public void run() {
        emailer.send(someMessage());     <-- Send message and confirm to user

        confirm("Sent!");
    }
}
```

This client does not know anything about `Emailer`'s internals; instead, it depends on a Factory. If we want to test that it correctly calls `Emailer.send()`, we need to use a mock. Rather than set the dependency directly, we must pass in the mock via the Factory, as in listing 1.6.

Listing 1.6 Test sets up a mock instance for `EmailClient` using `Emailer`'s Factory

```
    @Test
    public void testEmailClient() {
        MockEmailer mock = new MockEmailer();
        EmailerFactory.set(mock);         <-- Set mock instance on factory using a static method

        new EmailClient().run();

        assert mock.correctlySent();      <-- Verify that the mock was used correctly by EmailClient
    }
```

In this test, we pass in `MockEmailer` using the static method `EmailerFactory.set()`, which stores and uses the provided object rather than creating new ones (listing 1.7).

Listing 1.7 A client uses `Emailer` to send messages typed by a user

```
public class EmailerFactory {
    private static Emailer instance;     <-- Static holder stores mock instance for later use

    public Emailer newEmailer() {
        if (null == instance)            <-- If no mock is present, create a new Emailer with dependencies
            return new Emailer(..);
```

```
        return instance;
    }
                                                Save mock instance
    static void set(Emailer mock) {        <--  to static holder
        instance = mock;
    }
```

In listing 1.7, `EmailerFactory` has been heavily modified to support testing. A test can first set up a mock instance via the static `set()` method, then verify the behavior of any clients (as shown in listing 1.6).

Unfortunately, this is not the complete picture, since forgetting to clean up the mock can interfere with other `Emailer`-related tests that run later. So, we must *reset* the Factory at the end of every test:

```
@Test
public void testEmailClient() {
    MockEmailer mock = new MockEmailer();
    EmailerFactory.set(mock);

    new EmailClient().run();
                                              Reset factory's
    assert mock.correctlySent();              state to null
    EmailerFactory.set(null);           <--
}
```

We're not quite out of the woods yet. If an exception is thrown before the Factory is reset, it can still leave things in an erroneous state. So, a safer cleanup is required:

```
@Test
public void testEmailClient() {
    MockEmailer mock = new MockEmailer();
    EmailerFactory.set(mock);
    try {
        new EmailClient().run();

        assert mock.correctlySent();          Reset factory's state
    } finally {                               inside a finally block
        EmailerFactory.set(null);       <--
    }
}
```

Much better. A lot of work to write a simple assertion, but worth it! Or is it? Even this careful approach is insufficient in broader cases where you may want to run tests in parallel. The static mock instance inside `EmailerFactory` can cause these tests to clobber each other from concurrent threads, rendering them useless.

NOTE This is an essential problem with shared state, often portended by the *Singleton pattern*. Its effects and solutions are examined more closely in chapter 5.

While the Factory pattern solves many of the problems with construction by hand, it obviously still leaves us with significant hurdles to overcome. Apart from the testability problem, the fact that a Factory must accompany every service is troubling. Not only this, a Factory must accompany *every* variation of *every* service. This is a sizable amount of distracting clutter and adds a lot of peripheral code to be tested and maintained. Look at the example in listing 1.8, and you'll see what I mean.

Listing 1.8 Factories that create either French or Japanese email services

```
public class EmailerFactory {
    public Emailer newJapaneseEmailer() {
        Emailer service = new Emailer();
        service.setSpellChecker(new JapaneseSpellChecker());
        service.setAddressBook(new EmailBook());
        service.setTextEditor(new SimpleJapaneseTextEditor());
        return service;
    }
    public Emailer newFrenchEmailer() {
        Emailer service = new Emailer();
        service.setSpellChecker(new FrenchSpellChecker());
        service.setAddressBook(new EmailBook());
        service.setTextEditor(new SimpleFrenchTextEditor());
        return service;
    }
}
```

Specific dependencies of a Japanese email service

Specific dependencies of a French email service

If you wanted an English version of the `Emailer`, you would have to add yet another method to the Factory. And consider what happens when we replace `EmailBook` with a `PhoneAndEmailBook`. You are forced to make the following changes:

```
public class EmailerFactory {
    public Emailer newJapaneseEmailer() { ...
        service.setAddressBook(new PhoneAndEmailBook());
        ...
    public Emailer newFrenchEmailer() {    ...
        service.setAddressBook(new PhoneAndEmailBook());
        ...
    public Emailer newEnglishEmailer() { ...
        service.setAddressBook(new PhoneAndEmailBook());
        ...
}
```

All three of the changes are identical! It is clearly not a desirable scenario. Furthermore, any client code is at the mercy of available factories: You must create new factories for each additional object graph variation. All this spells reams of additional code to write, test, and maintain.

In the case of `Emailer`, following the idea to its inevitable extreme yields:

```
Emailer service = new EmailerFactoryFactory()
                .newAdvancedEmailerFactory()
                .newJapaneseEmailerWithPhoneAndEmail();
```

"General" factory produces simple or advanced factories

Factory for advanced Emailers

Factory producing specific Emailer configurations

It is very difficult to test code like this. I have seen it ruin several projects. Clearly, the Factory pattern technique's drawbacks are serious, especially in larger and more complex code. What we need is a broader mitigation of the core problem.

1.2.3 *The Service Locator pattern*

A *Service Locator* pattern is a kind of Factory. It is a third-party object responsible for producing a fully constructed object graph.

In the typical case, Service Locators are used to find services published by external sources; the service may be an API offered by a bank to transfer funds or a search interface from Google.

These external sources may reside in the same application, machine, or local area network, or they may not. Consider an interface to the NASA Mars Rover several millions of miles away, a simple library for text processing, bundled within an application, or a Remote Enterprise Java Bean (EJB).[2] Look at figure 1.8 for a visual.

Let's look at what a service locator does:

```
Emailer emailer = (Emailer) new ServiceLocator().get("Emailer");
```

Notice that we pass the Service Locator a *key*, in this case the word "Emailer." This tells our locator that we want an `Emailer`. This is significantly different from a Factory that produces only one kind of service. A Service Locator is, therefore, a Factory that can produce *any* kind of service.

Right away this helps reduce a huge amount of repetitive Factory code, in favor of the single Service Locator.

> **JNDI: a Service Locator**
>
> The Java Naming and Directory Interface (JNDI) is a good example of a Service Locator pattern. It is often used by application servers to register resources at start time and later by deployed applications to look them up. Web applications typically use JNDI to look up data sources in this manner.

Let's apply the Service Locator pattern to the earlier example:

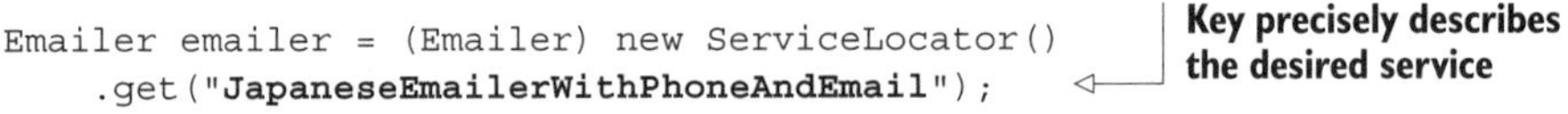

```
Emailer emailer = (Emailer) new ServiceLocator()
    .get("JapaneseEmailerWithPhoneAndEmail");
```


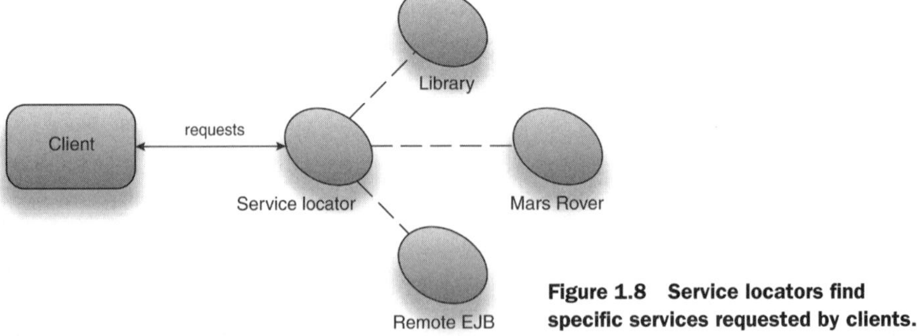

Figure 1.8 Service locators find specific services requested by clients.

[2] A Remote EJB is a type of service exposed by Java EE application servers across a network. For example, a brokerage may expose an order-placing service as a Remote EJB to various client banks.

This code is simple and readable. The identity of a service (its key) is sufficient to obtain exactly the right service and configuration. Now altering the behavior of a service identified by a particular key or fixing bugs within it by changing its object graph will have no effect on dependent code and can be done transparently.

Unfortunately, being a kind of Factory, Service Locators suffer from the same problems of testability and shared state. The keys used to identify a service are opaque and can be confusing to work with, as anyone who has used JNDI can attest. If a key is bound improperly, the wrong type of object may be created, and this error is found out only at runtime. The practice of embedding information about the service within its identifier (namely, `"JapaneseEmailerWithPhoneAndEmail"`) is also verbose and places too much emphasis on arbitrary conventions.

With DI, we take a completely different approach—one that emphasizes testability and concise code that is easy to read and maintain. That's only the beginning; as you will see soon, with DI we can do a great deal more.

1.3 Embracing dependency injection

With dependency injection, we take the best parts of the aforesaid pre-DI solutions and leave behind their drawbacks.

DI enables testability in the same way as construction by hand, via a setter method or constructor injection. DI removes the need for clients to know about their dependencies and how to create them, just as factories do. It leaves behind the problems of shared state and repetitive clutter, by moving construction responsibility to a library.

With DI, clients need know nothing about French or English `Emailers`, let alone French or English `SpellCheckers` and `TextEditors`, in order to use them. This idea of not *explicitly* knowing is central to DI. More accurately, not *asking* for dependencies and instead having them provided to you is an idea called the *Hollywood Principle*.

1.3.1 The Hollywood Principle

The Hollywood Principle is "Don't call us; we'll call you!" Just as Hollywood talent agents use this principle to arrange auditions for actors, so do DI libraries use this principle to provide objects with what they depend on.

This is similar to what we saw in construction by hand (sometimes referred to as *manual* dependency injection). There is one important difference: The task of creating, assembling, and wiring the dependencies into an object graph is performed by an external framework (or library) known as a *dependency injection framework*, or simply a *dependency injector*. Figure 1.9 illustrates this arrangement.

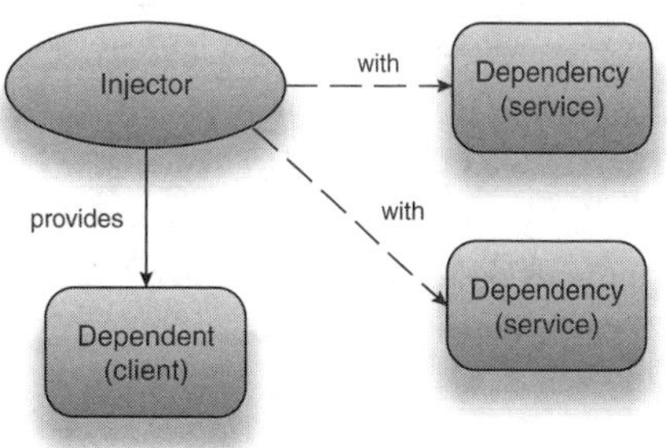

Figure 1.9 The injector provides an object with its dependencies.

Control over the construction, wiring, and assembly of an object graph no longer resides with the clients or services themselves. The Hollywood Principle's reversal of responsibilities is sometimes also known as IoC.

NOTE DI frameworks are sometimes referred to as IoC containers. Examples of such frameworks are PicoContainer (for Java), StructureMap (for C#), and Spring (for Java and C#).

Listing 1.9 shows the Hollywood Principle in action.

Listing 1.9 An `Emailer` and a client

```
public class Emailer {
    ...
    public void send(String text) { .. }
}

public class SimpleEmailClient {                    ❶ SimpleEmailClient depends on Emailer
    private Emailer emailer;
    public SimpleEmailClient(Emailer emailer) {
        this.emailer = emailer;
    }
    public void sendEmail() {                       ❷ Sends an email read from input
        emailer.send(readMessage());
    }
}
```

In this example, our dependent is `SimpleEmailClient` ❶ and the service it uses ❷ is `Emailer`. Notice that neither class is aware of how to construct its graph, nor does either explicitly ask for a service.

In order to send mail, `SimpleEmailClient` does not need to expose anything about `Emailer` or how it works. Put another way, `SimpleEmailClient` encapsulates `Emailer`, and sending email is completely opaque to the user. Constructing and connecting dependencies is now performed by a dependency injector (see figure 1.10).

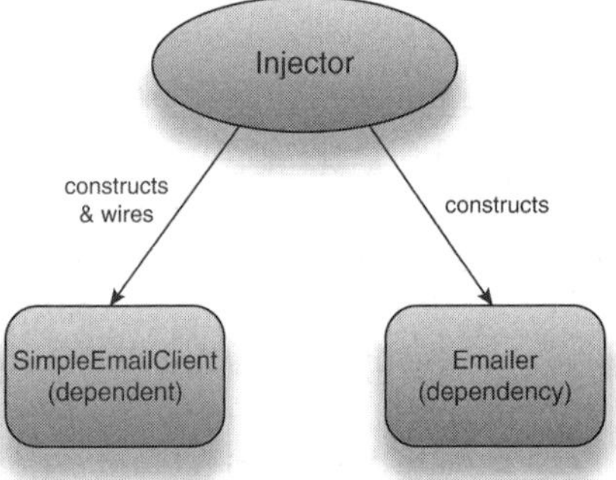

Figure 1.10 The injector constructs and wires `SimpleEmailClient` with a dependency (`Emailer`).

The dependency is shown as a class diagram in figure 1.11.

Notice that `SimpleEmailClient` knows nothing about what kind of `Emailer` it needs or is using to send a message. All it knows is that it accepts *some kind* of `Emailer`, and this dependency is used when needed. Also notice that the client code is now starting to resemble service code; both are free of logic to create or

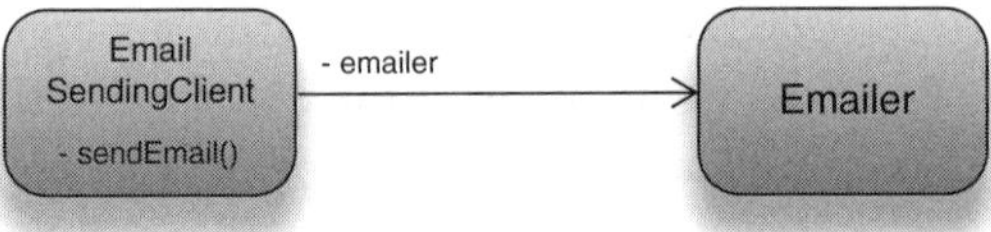

Figure 1.11 Client code that uses an email service provided by dependency injection

locate dependencies. DI facilitates this streamlining, stripping code of distracting clutter and infrastructure logic, leaving purposed, *elementary logic* behind.

We have not yet seen how the wiring is done, as this differs from injector to injector, but what we've seen is still very instructive because it highlights the separation of *infrastructure* code (meant for wiring and construction) from *application* code (the core purpose of a service). The next couple of sections explore this idea, before we jump into the specifics of working with dependency injectors.

1.3.2 Inversion of Control vs. dependency injection

Worthy as they are of a heavyweight bout, these two terms are not really opposed to one another as the heading suggests. You will come across the term IoC quite often, both in the context of dependency injection and outside it. The phrase Inversion of Control is rather vague and connotes a general reversal of responsibilities, which is nonspecific and could equally mean any of the following:

- A module inside a Java EE application server
- An object wired by a dependency injector
- A test method automatically invoked by a framework
- An event handler called on clicking a mouse button

Pedantic users of the term suggest that all of these cases are consistent with its definition and that DI itself is simply one instance of IoC.

In common use, dependency injectors are frequently referred to as *IoC containers.*

In the interest of clarity, for the rest of this book I will abandon the term IoC (and its evil cousin IoC container) in favor of the following, more precise terms:

- *Hollywood Principle*—The idea that a dependent is *contacted* with its dependencies
- *Dependency injector*—A framework or library that embodies the Hollywood Principle
- *Dependency injection*—The range of concerns with designing applications built on these principles

> **Dependency injection**
>
> As near as I can determine, it wasn't until Martin Fowler wrote "Inversion of Control Containers and the Dependency Injection Pattern"[3] that the term dependency injection came into popular use. The term came out of many discussions on the subject among Fowler, the authors of PicoContainer (Paul Hammant and Aslak Hellesøy), Jon Tirsen, and Rod Johnson, among others.

[3] The article has been updated many times over the years. You can read the latest version at http://martinfowler.com/articles/injection.html.

Early frameworks differed by the forms of wiring that they proffered and promoted. Over the years, the efficacy of setter and constructor wiring overtook that of other forms of wiring, and more flexible solutions that emphasized the safety of contracts and the reduction of *repetitive* code emerged. With the rise of related paradigms such as *aspect-oriented programming* (AOP), these features continued to improve. Applications built with DI became streamlined and tolerant to rapid structural and behavioral change.

The modes of configuring a dependency injector also evolved from verbose sets of contracts and configuration files to more concise forms, using new language constructs such as *annotations* and *generics*. Dependency injectors also took better advantage of class manipulation tools like *reflection* and *proxying* and began to exploit design patterns such as *Decorator*[4] and *Builder*,[5] as well as *Domain Specific Languages (DSL)*.

Domain Specific Language (DSL)

Domain Specific Language, or DSL is a language used to solve a specific problem as opposed to a language like C++ that is intended to solve general (or any) problems. DSLs are sometimes used in dependency injection as a precise way of expressing the structural relationship between objects. They are also used to capture other concerns (such as scope) in the *language* of DI. (For more information, see the forthcoming book from Manning Publications, *Building Domain Specific Languages in Boo* by Ayende Rahien.)

A growing emphasis on unit testing continues to be a natural catalyst to the growth of DI popularity. This made for agile programs, which are easily broken down into discrete, modular *units* that are simple to test and swap out with alternative behaviors. Consequently, *loose coupling* is a core driver in the evolution of DI.

Loose coupling

Loose coupling describes an adaptable relationship between a client and a service, where significant changes to the internals of the service have minimal impact on the client. It is generally achieved by placing a rigid contract between client and service so that either may evolve independently, so long as they fulfill the obligations laid down by the contract. Loose coupling is explored in greater detail in chapter 4.

We will explore the best approaches to solving problems with DI and look in detail at bad practices, pitfalls, and corner cases to watch out for, as well as the safety, rigor, and power of DI, properly applied. And most of all we'll see how DI can make your code lean, clean, and something mean.

---

4 Erich Gamma et al, *Design Patterns*: "The Decorator Pattern."

5 Ibid., "The Builder Pattern."

1.4 Dependency injection in the real world

We have now looked at several possible solutions and hinted at a cool alternative called DI. We've also taken an evening stroll down History Lane, turning at the corner of Terminology Boulevard (and somehow visited Hollywood on the way!). Before we proceed to the nuts and bolts of dependency injection, let's survey the landscape to learn what libraries are available, how they work and how they originated.

This is by no means a comparison or evaluation of frameworks; it's a brief introduction. Neither is it meant to be a comprehensive list of options. I will only touch on relatively well-known and widely used DI libraries in Java—and only those that are open source and freely available. Not all of them are purely DI-focused, and very few support the full gamut of DI design patterns described in this book. Nevertheless, each is worth a look.

1.4.1 Java

Java is the birthplace of dependency injection and sports the broadest and most mature set of DI libraries among all platforms. Since many of the problems DI evolved to address are fundamental to Java, DI's effectiveness and prevalence are especially clear in this platform. We'll look at five such libraries ranging from the earliest incarnations of DI in Apache Avalon, through mature, widely adopted libraries like Spring and PicoContainer, to the cutting-edge, modern incarnation in Google, Guice.

Apache Avalon

Apache Avalon is possibly the earliest DI library in the Java world, and it's perhaps the first library that really focused on dependency injection as a core competency. Avalon styled itself as a complete application container, in the days before Java EE and application servers were predominant. Its primary mode of wiring was via custom interfaces, not setter methods or constructors. Avalon also supported myriad lifecycle and event-management interfaces and was popular with many Apache projects. The Apache James mail server (a pure Java SMTP, POP3, and IMAP email server) is built on Avalon.

Avalon is defunct, though Apache James is still going strong. Some of the ideas from Avalon have passed on to another project, Apache Excalibur, whose DI container is named Fortress. Neither Avalon nor Excalibur/Fortress is in common use today.

Spring Framework

Spring Framework is a groundbreaking and cornerstone dependency injection library of the Java world. It is largely responsible for the popularity and evolution of the DI idiom and for a long time was almost synonymous with dependency injection. Spring was created by Rod Johnson and others and was initially meant to solve specific pains in enterprise projects. It was established as an open source project in 2003 and grew rapidly in scope and adoption. Spring provides a vast set of abstractions, modules, and points of integration for enterprise, open source, and commercial libraries. It consists of much more than dependency injection, though DI is its core competency. It primarily supports setter and constructor injection and has a variety of options for managing objects created by its dependency injector. For example, it provides support for both the AspectJ and AopAlliance AOP paradigms.

Spring adds functionality, features, and abstractions for popular third-party libraries at alarming rates. It is extremely well-documented in terms of published reference books as well as online documentation and continues to enjoy widespread growth and adoption.

PicoContainer and NanoContainer

PicoContainer was possibly the first DI library to offer constructor wiring. It was envisioned and built around certain philosophical principles, and many of the discussions found on its website are of a theoretical nature. It was built as a lightweight engine for wiring components together. In this sense it is well-suited to extensions and customization. This makes PicoContainer useful under the covers. PicoContainer supports both setter and constructor injection but clearly demonstrates a bias toward the latter. Due to its nuts-and-bolts nature, many people find PicoContainer difficult to use in applications directly. NanoContainer is a sister project of PicoContainer that attempts to bridge this gap by providing a simple configuration layer, with PicoContainer doing the DI work underneath. NanoContainer also provides other useful extensions.

Apache HiveMind

Apache HiveMind was started by Howard Lewis Ship, the creator of Apache Tapestry, a popular *component-oriented* Java web framework. For a long time Tapestry used HiveMind as its internal dependency injector. Much of the development and popularity of HiveMind has stemmed from this link, though HiveMind and Tapestry have parted company in later releases. HiveMind originally began at a consulting project of Howard's that involved the development and interaction of several hundreds of services. It was primarily used in managing and organizing these services into common, reusable patterns.

HiveMind offers both setter and constructor injection and provides unusual and innovative DI features missing in other popular libraries. For example, HiveMind is able to create and manage *pools* of a service for multiple concurrent clients. Apache HiveMind is not as widely used as some other DI libraries discussed here; however, it has a staunch and loyal following.

Google Guice

Guice (pronounced "Juice") is a hot, new dependency injector created by Bob Lee and others at Google. Guice unabashedly embraces Java 5 language features and strongly emphasizes type and contract safety. It is lightweight and decries verbosity in favor of concise, type-safe, and rigorous configuration. Guice is used heavily at Google, particularly in the vast AdWords application, and a version of it is at the heart of the Struts2 web framework. It supports both setter and constructor injection along with interesting alternatives. Guice's approach to AOP and construction of object graphs is intuitive and simple. Guice is also available inside the Google Web Toolkit (GWT), via its cousin Gin.[6]

---

[6] Google Gin is a port of Guice for the GWT, a JavaScript web framework. Find out more at http://code.google.com/p/google-gin.

It is a new kid on the block, but its popularity is rising and its innovations have already prompted several followers and even some mainstays to emulate its ideas. Guice has a vibrant and thoughtful user community.

1.4.2 DI in other languages and libraries

Several other DI libraries are also available. You could write a whole book on the subject! Some provide extra features, orthogonal to dependency injection, or are simply focused on a different problem space. JBoss Seam is one such framework; it offers complex state management for web applications and integration points for standardized services such as EJBs. It also offers a reasonably sophisticated subset of dependency injection.

As languages, C# and .NET are structurally similar to Java. They are both statically typed, object-oriented languages that need to be compiled. It is no surprise, then, that C# is found in the same problem space as Java and that dependency injectors are applied to equal effect in applications written in C#. However, the prevalence of DI is much lower in the C# world in general. While C# has ports of some Java libraries like Spring and PicoContainer, it also has some innovative DI of its own, particularly in Castle MicroKernel, which does a lot more than just DI. StructureMap, on the other hand, is a mainstay and a more traditional DI library.

Some platforms (or languages) make it harder to design dependency injectors because they lack features such as garbage collection and reflection. C++ is a prime example of such a language. However, it is still possible to write dependency injectors in these languages with other methods that substitute for these tools. For instance, some C++ libraries use *precompilation* and *source code generation* to enable DI.

Still other languages place different (and sometimes fewer) restrictions on types and expressions, allowing objects to take on a more dynamic role in constructing and using services. Python and Ruby are good examples of such *duck-typed* languages. Neither Python nor Ruby programs need to be compiled; their source code is directly *interpreted*, and type checking is done on the fly. Copland is a DI library for Ruby that was inspired by (and is analogous to) Apache HiveMind for Java. Copland uses many of the same terms and principles as HiveMind but is more flexible in certain regards because of the dynamic nature of Ruby.

1.5 Summary

This chapter was an exposition to the subject of building programs in units and has laid the groundwork for DI. Most software is about automating some process in the real world, such as sending a friend a message by email or processing a purchase order. Components in these processes are modeled as a system of objects and methods. When we have vast swaths of components and interactions to manage, constructing and connecting them becomes a tedious and complex task. Development time spent on maintenance, refactoring, and testing can explode without carefully designed architectures. We can reduce all of this to the rather simple-sounding problem of finding and constructing the dependencies, the requisite services of a component (client). However, as you've seen, this is nontrivial when dealing with objects that require different behaviors and does not often scale with typical solutions.

Prior to the use of dependency injectors, there were several solutions of varying effectiveness:

- *Construction by hand*—This involves the client creating and wiring together all of its dependencies. This is a workable solution and certainly conducive to testing, but it scales very poorly as we've merely offloaded the burden of creating and wiring dependencies to clients. It also means clients must know about their dependencies and about *their* implementation details.
- *The Factory pattern*—Clients request a service from an intermediary component known as a Factory. This offloads the burden to Factories and leaves clients relatively lean. Factories have been very successful over the years; however, they pose very real problems for testing and can introduce more with shared state. In very large projects they can cause an explosion of infrastructure code. Code using factories is difficult to test and can be a problem to maintain.
- *The Service Locator pattern*—Essentially a type of Factory, it uses keys to identify services and their specific configurations. The Service Locator solves the explosion-of-factories problem by hiding the details of the service and its configuration from client code. Since it is a Factory, it is also prone to testability and shared state problems. Finally, it requires that a client explicitly request each of its dependencies by an arbitrary key, which can be unclear and abstruse.

Dependency injection offers an innovative alternative via the Hollywood Principle: "Don't call us; we'll call you!" meaning that a component need know nothing about its dependencies nor explicitly ask for them. A third-party library or framework known as the dependency injector is responsible for constructing, assembling, and wiring together clients with services.

DI solves the problem of object graph construction and assembly by applying the Hollywood Principle across components. However, this is just a small window into what is possible when an application is designed and built around DI. We will explore managing state and modifying the behavior and lifecycle of objects in broader contexts. We'll look at the nuances, pitfalls, and corner cases of various configurations and the subtle consequences of particular design choices. This book will equip you with the knowledge and careful understanding you need to design robust, testable, and easily maintainable applications for any purpose or platform. In the next chapter, you'll get a chance to get your hands dirty. We'll dive right in to using some of the DI libraries surveyed in this chapter and contrast their various approaches. Keep a bar of soap handy.

2 Time for injection

This chapter covers:

- Using dependency injection
- Identifying dependencies by keys
- Comparing string, type, and combinatorial keys
- Separating infrastructure from application logic

"We shape our buildings, thereafter they shape us."

—Winston Churchill

In chapter 1, we saw that dependency injection offers a unique and concise solution to the problem of constructing object graphs, with a strong emphasis on unit testing. The crux of this solution is the fact that all your code is freed from constructing dependencies. Code written with DI in mind is behaviorally focused and without distracting clutter. Why is this important?

While the answer may seem self-evident (hard to argue with the less and more precise), it is well worth spelling out:

- *Behaviorally focused*—Presumably, you set out to write code toward a specific purpose, and that purpose is not to construct more objects! Whether writing an email system, a game, or an enterprise messaging system, your primary focus is the behavior of the system. When architectural concerns (such as constructing and locating services) impinge on this logic, it unnecessarily distracts from the original purpose.
- *Modular*—Code designed in discrete, modular units is not only easy to maintain, but it is reusable and easy to package. Individual units are structurally simple to work with. Understanding whether code meets specified requirements is often a difficult proposition for developers. Modular code is focused on small functional subsets (for instance, a spellchecker) and thus is easier to develop.
- *Testable*—Since modules are easy to test for general, purposed behavior without specific awareness of the overall system, it follows that they provide for more robust code. While nominal testability is a benefit in itself, there is much more that concise, loosely coupled code purports. The ability to swap out dependencies with mock counterparts is crucial when testing objects that make use of expensive resources like database connections.

In this chapter, we're going to work with dependency injectors, using various libraries. We'll look at how to identify dependencies, distinguish them from one another, and tell the injector what to do with them. This chapter also examines best practices in configuring dependency injectors and in choosing identifiers (keys) for objects. Let's begin with bootstrapping the injector.

2.1 Bootstrapping the injector

The dependency injector is itself a service like any other. And like any service, it must be constructed and prepared before it can be used. This bootstrap of the injector occurs before any object in the application can benefit from DI. When and how the injector is bootstrapped is often specific to the kind of application in question. It may be done in the following situations:

- In the *init* lifecycle stage of a web application, upon being deployed (figure 2.1)

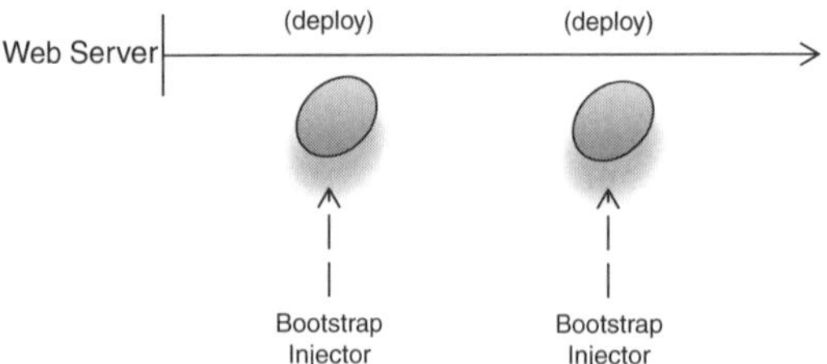

Figure 2.1 Injector is bootstrapped in the init lifecycle stage of a web application, on deployment.

- On *startup* of a desktop program (figure 2.2)

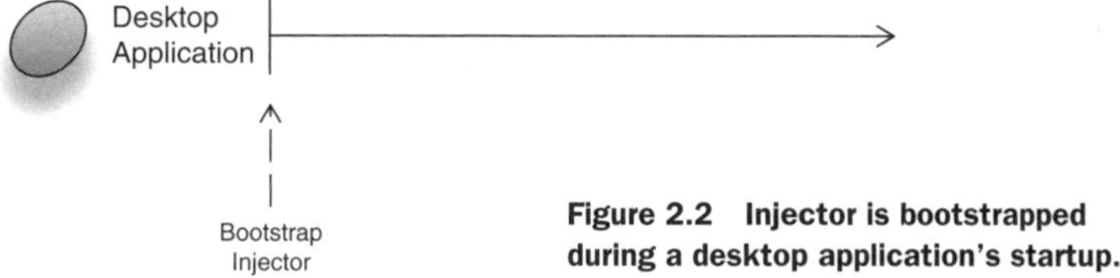

Figure 2.2 Injector is bootstrapped during a desktop application's startup.

- *On demand*, every time it is needed (for instance, on remote invocations [figure 2.3])

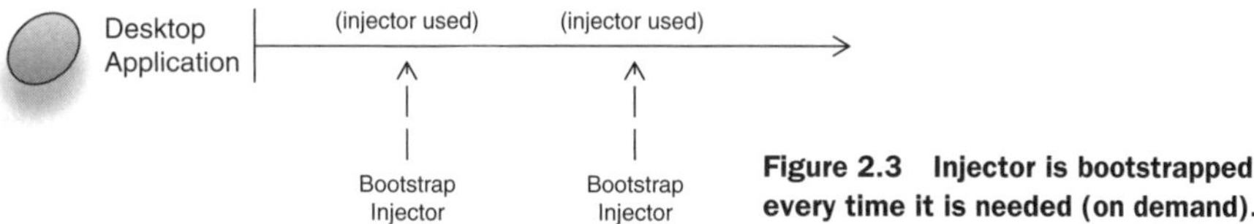

Figure 2.3 Injector is bootstrapped every time it is needed (on demand).

- *Lazily*, when it is *first* needed (figure 2.4)

Figure 2.4 Injector is bootstrapped on first use (lazily).

Each option conforms to a different architectural scenario. None is *the* correct choice for all environments. It is typical to find that injector startup coincides with application startup. Once the injector has been bootstrapped, we can obtain an object from it for use.

2.2 Constructing objects with dependency injection

Let's look at one such scenario with a dependency injector named Guice. In this example, we will let Guice create and assemble an `Emailer` for us and provide it with dependencies (an `English` spellchecker). See figure 2.5.

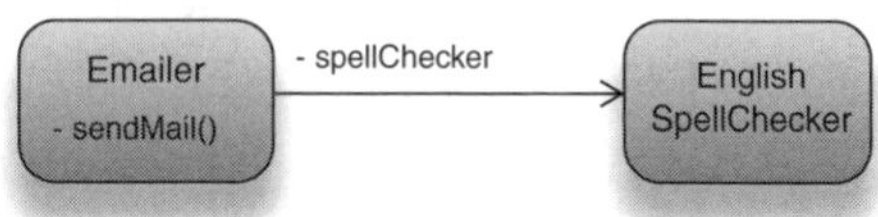

Figure 2.5 A class model of the emailer and English spellchecker

```
Guice.createInjector().getInstance(Emailer.class).send("Hello");
```

Notice that we created the injector and obtained the emailer from it, all in one line—this is an example of the *on-demand* bootstrapping of injectors. In the example, we have done three things worth talking about:

1. Created the injector.
2. Obtained an instance of `Emailer` from the injector.
3. Signaled the `Emailer` to send an email message.

Figure 2.6 illustrates this sequence.

Let's break down this example in code. The first invocation is a simple static method that asks Guice for a new injector:

```
Guice.createInjector()
```

We can think of Guice as a factory class for dependency injectors (recall the Factory pattern from chapter 1). This is fairly straightforward. The second invocation is of greater interest; it asks the injector for an instance of Emailer:

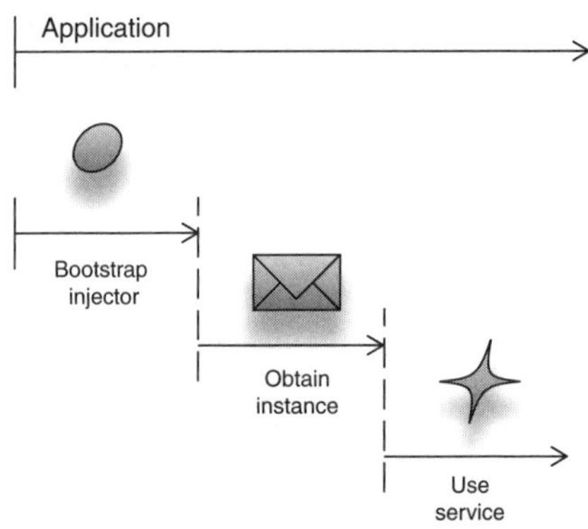

Figure 2.6 Injector obtains emailer for a client, which is then used to send mail.

```
Guice.createInjector().getInstance(Emailer.class)
```

The Emailer obtained from our injector is properly wired with its dependencies, so when it needs to send a message it can call on its SpellChecker to do the spelling verification—all very tidy with a single-use injector:

```
Guice.createInjector().getInstance(Emailer.class).send("Hello!");
```

This, of course, is functionally identical to the more verbose form:

```
Injector injector = Guice.createInjector();
Emailer emailer = injector.getInstance(Emailer.class);
emailer.send("Hello!");
```

This is reasonable at first glance and seems to have brought us some kind of compelling result. However, upon closer inspection it evokes a sense of déjà vu. Remember this?

```
Emailer emailer = (Emailer) new ServiceLocator().get("Emailer");
```

Comparing this to obtaining an emailer from the injector yields more than a suspicious similarity:

```
Emailer emailer = injector.getInstance(Emailer.class);    <-- Ask injector for an Emailer by key
```

It looks as though injector is performing the role of a Service Locator pattern and that I've used Emailer.class as a key that identifies emailers. As we've already noted, keys need not be strings, so it seems I have indeed used a Service Locator. That can't be right, can it? Well, yes, because an injector can itself be used as a Service Locator.

So what is the hype really about? In a sense the injector is an automated, all-purpose service locator prepackaged for convenience. This is a fair characterization, but with *three important differences*, and the hype is really about these three things:

- *Client code (the* Emailer*) is not invoking the injector, unlike with service locators.* Rather, it is the application bootstrapper that invokes the injector. The key difference here is that the latter does not participate in the behavior of the program.

- *Only a root object is obtained from the injector.* This object is generally the *entry point* of an application and is typically requested only once. This means that no matter how many client-service systems exist within the application, their creation, injection, and usage cascades from the root object. For example, an HTTP servlet is a root object, with data-source dependencies injected into it.
- *The injector obtains instances within the current execution context.* In other words, the instance returned may or may not be different depending on the state of the application and the current context. This is known as *scoping* and is a very powerful feature of dependency injection—one that essentially separates it from Service Location. See chapter 5 for more on scopes.

In most real-world applications the act of obtaining and running objects is typically done for you by integration layers, such as the *guice-servlet*[1] extension does with HTTP servlets and Guice. Many DI libraries provide such integration layers out of the box.

This introduces us to the notion that a single unit is an entry point into a program, like a starting line from which other objects (dependencies) stem. The "offspring" of the root object are built and wired as required. In turn, each object may construct and call several of its own dependencies, and so on down the tree of dependencies. This cascading creation of objects is called *viral injection.*

Unlike traditional Service Location patterns this means your code is not *explicitly* dependent on a service (the dependency injector). Of course, apart from this is the not-insignificant fact that you don't have to write, test, or maintain the injector itself.

So what do our `Emailer` (client) and its `SpellChecker` (dependency) look like? Listing 2.1 has one version.

Listing 2.1 An emailer with a spellchecker

```
import com.google.inject.Inject;

public class Emailer {
    private SpellChecker spellChecker;          <-- Dependencies, wired via constructor

    @Inject                                      <-- (1) An annotation tells Guice to use this constructor
    public Emailer(SpellChecker spellChecker) {
        this.spellChecker = spellChecker;
    }

    public void send(String text) {
        spellChecker.check(text);                <-- Dependency used directly when needed
            //send if ok..;
    }
}
```

Notice the `@Inject`[2] annotation (1) placed on `Emailer`'s constructor. This piece of metadata tells Guice to use the annotated constructor. The injector constructs and

1 Guice-servlet allows your HTTP servlets to be created and injected by Guice. A detailed example is provided in chapter 5. For more on guice-servlet, visit http://code.google.com/p/google-guice.

2 The `@Inject` annotation ships with Guice's library distribution.

wires the `Emailer` using it. Guice inspects classes at runtime and determines how to build them. It detects that `SpellChecker` must also be constructed and provided to `Emailer` before it is ready to use.

NOTE Annotations are a feature of Java that allow classes and programs to be enhanced with extra information. Tools, libraries, or even humans can use them to glean additional meaning or intent about the program. Annotations do not manipulate program semantics directly but instead provide a standard way of enhancing them along with appropriate tools.

When `send()` is called, `Emailer` has been wired with a `SpellChecker` and can be called on to `check()` spelling.

In the popular Spring Framework, the same thing is achieved with slightly different annotations:

```
import org.springframework.beans.factory.annotation.Autowired;
import org.springframework.stereotype.Component;

@Component
public class Emailer {
    private SpellChecker spellChecker;

    @Autowired
    public Emailer (SpellChecker spellChecker) {
        this.spellChecker = spellChecker;
    }

    public void send(String text) {
        spellChecker.check(text);
            //send if ok..;
    }
}
```

Instead of @Inject (annotation pointing to `@Autowired`)

What we see here is one way of passing an injector some information via program metadata. In the next section, we'll see how injectors are *configured* in different ways.

2.3 Metadata and injector configuration

Annotations and custom attributes are an elegant and unintrusive form of metadata that helps indicate some information about your code to an injector, namely, which constructor to use (and consequently what its dependencies are).

In essence, what I did was to use the `@Inject` annotation to configure the injector (`@Autowired` and `@Component` for Spring), providing it with the appropriate information it needed to construct the `Emailer`. DI libraries provide a number of mechanisms for configuring the injector (as shown in figure 2.7):

- Using an XML configuration file
- Invoking into a programmatic API
- Using an injection-oriented DSL
- By inference; that is, implicitly from the structure of classes
- By inference from annotated source code

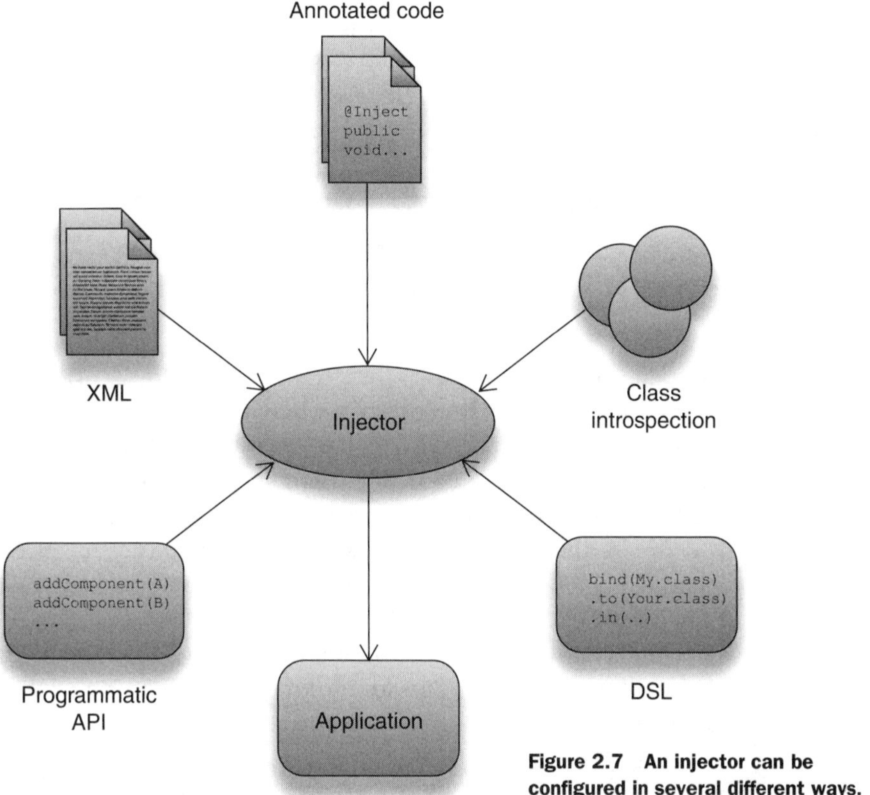

Figure 2.7 An injector can be configured in several different ways.

Or some combination of mechanisms.

That's certainly a lot of options. And choosing among them doesn't always come down to taste. Before judging the effectiveness of each option, let's take our emailer out for a spin with a couple of available options.

2.3.1 *XML injection in Spring*

Spring's primary mode of configuration is an XML file. Though Spring offers many alternatives (we saw one with `@Autowired`), the XML configuration is its most easily identified and common configuration mechanism. Recall our three wonted steps:

- Creating the injector
- Obtaining a component instance from it
- Using the instance to send mail (spamming away!)

In Guice this was written as:

```
Guice.createInjector().getInstance(Emailer.class).send("Hello!");
```

Translating to Spring yields the following:

```
BeanFactory injector = new FileSystemApplicationContext("email.xml");
Emailer emailer = (Emailer) injector.getBean("emailer");
emailer.send("Hello!");
```

Here, `BeanFactory` refers to the Spring dependency injector. The call to `getBean()` is analogous to the original call to `getInstance()`. Both return an instance of `Emailer`. One interesting difference is that we use a string key to identify emailers (and are therefore required to *downcast*[3] it into the variable `emailer`):

```
Emailer emailer = (Emailer) injector.getBean("emailer");
```

Notice that sending an email remains exactly the same in both DI libraries:

```
emailer.send("Hello!");
```

This is an important point, because it means that using code for its original, intended purpose remains exactly the same regardless of what library you choose. And it underlines the fact that dependency injection is not an invasive technique.

Note also how an injector is created. Rather than using a Factory, I've used construction by hand to create a `FileSystemApplicationContext` and assigned it to a variable of type `BeanFactory`. Both `BeanFactory` and `FileSystemApplicationContext` refer to Spring's injector. The latter is a specific kind of `BeanFactory` (just like an `EnglishSpellChecker` is a specific kind of `SpellChecker`).

The file email.xml contains the configuration required for Spring's injector to provide us with an emailer correctly wired with its dependencies. Listing 2.2 shows what email.xml looks like, and figure 2.8 shows how this works.

Listing 2.2 Spring's injector configuration, email.xml

```
<?xml version="1.0" encoding="UTF-8"?>
<beans xmlns="http://www.springframework.org/schema/beans"
    xmlns:xsi="http://www.w3.org/2001/XMLSchema-instance"
    xsi:schemaLocation="http://www.springframework.org/schema/beans

http://www.springframework.org/schema/beans/spring-beans-2.5.xsd"    >

    <bean id="emailer" class="Emailer">
        <constructor-arg ref="spellChecker"/>
    </bean>

    <bean id="spellChecker" class="SpellChecker"/>
</beans>
```

1. Boilerplate to declare this as a Spring configuration file
2. Declare instances of Emailer
3. Inject object bound to "spellChecker"
4. Declare instances of SpellChecker

Let's look at this in some detail. For clarity, we will omit the boilerplate XML schema declaration[4] at the top of the file ❶. First, a <bean> tag ❷ declares a component of

[3] *Downcasting* (or *casting*) is the checked process of converting an instance of a general type into that of a more specific type; this is typically done by assigning the instance to a variable of the target type. In the given case, the general type `Object` is cast into a more specific type `Emailer`.

[4] An XML schema is a formal description of the structure of an XML document toward a particular purpose. In this case, it describes the legal form and structure of a Spring configuration file.

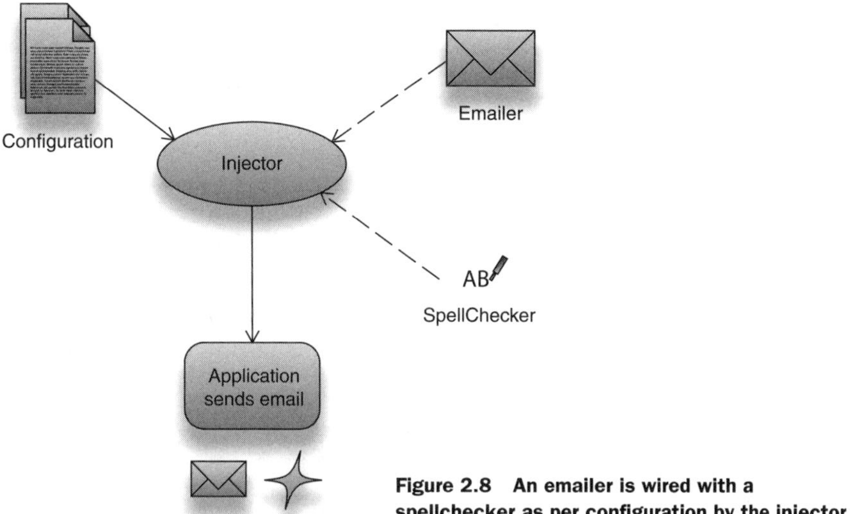

Figure 2.8 An emailer is wired with a spellchecker as per configuration by the injector.

class `Emailer` bound to the string identifier `"emailer."` This identifier is the key used to identify instances of `Emailer` in the vocabulary of the injector.

```
<bean id="emailer" class="Emailer">
```

Recall that in Guice the key served as both identifier as well as the binding to the `Emailer` class and was *implicit*. In Spring's XML, this binding takes the form of an explicit declaration in a `<bean>` element. Dependencies of `Emailer` are similarly declared in their own `<bean>` tags, in this case a `SpellChecker`:

```
<bean id="spellChecker" class="SpellChecker">
```

Now turn your attention back to the first `<bean>` tag ❸, where the interesting part lies:

```
<bean id="emailer" class="Emailer">
    <constructor-arg ref="spellChecker"/>
</bean>
```

The `<constructor-arg>` tag tells Spring to use constructor wiring. It also indicates that `Emailer` instances should be wired with objects identified by a string key, `"spellChecker."` `SpellChecker` itself is declared ❹ in another `<bean>` tag. This method of configuration has the somewhat useful advantage of being explicit about everything, but that is not necessarily a benefit in itself. As you will see later, it can be more flexible under certain circumstances. Also worth mentioning is a more compact rendering that does the same job for us:

```
<beans ...>
     <bean id="emailer" class="Emailer">
        <constructor-arg><bean class="SpellChecker"/></constructor-arg>
    </bean>
</beans>
```

In this case, I've nested the declaration of SpellChecker inside Emailer's constructor-argument tag and omitted its identifier altogether. This is nicer for a couple of reasons:

- The description of SpellChecker is available right inside that of Emailer.
- SpellChecker is not exposed via its own identifier. Therefore it can be obtained only within the context of a Emailer.

Both these ideas provide us with a neat encapsulation of Emailer and its dependencies. Dependency encapsulation means you can't accidentally wire a SpellChecker meant for an Emailer to some other object (a Klingon editor, for example).

This concept of encapsulation is roughly analogous to *class member encapsulation,* which you should be familiar with in Java code. Listing 2.3 revisits our original Emailer's source code for Spring.

Listing 2.3 The emailer, stripped of annotations

```
public class Emailer {
    private SpellChecker spellChecker;

    public Emailer(SpellChecker spellChecker) {
        this.spellChecker = spellChecker;
    }

    public void send(String text) {
        spellChecker.check(text);
        //send if ok...;
    }
}
```

private keyword hides (encapsulates) members

There is no change—except that now I no longer need Guice's annotations and can safely remove them, leaving me with a pristine, shiny Emailer.

2.3.2 From XML to in-code configuration

Both Spring and Guice provide the notion of explicit configuration (in Spring, as you saw, via XML). The advantage to this approach is that you have a central directory of all the services and dependencies used in a particular application. In a large project with many developers working on the same source code, such a directory is especially useful. In Guice this file is called a Module.

Guice modules are regular Java classes that implement the com.google.inject.Module interface (shown in listing 2.4).

Listing 2.4 A typical Guice module

```
import com.google.inject.Binder;
import com.google.inject.Module;

public class MyModule implements Module {
    public void configure(Binder binder) {
        ...
    }
}
```

Services are registered by using the given `binder` and making a sequence of calls that configure Guice accordingly. This is similar to the XML `<bean>` tags you saw in the previous section. Listing 2.5 shows how to declare an emailer's bindings explicitly.

Listing 2.5 Guice module registering emailers

```
import com.google.inject.Binder;
import com.google.inject.Module;

public class EmailModule implements Module {

    public void configure(Binder binder) {
        binder.bind(Emailer.class);           // Register keys/services
        binder.bind(SpellChecker.class);      // explicitly
    }
}
```

This is pretty simple.

TIP To save yourself some typing, extend the `AbstractModule` class, which is a convenience provided by Guice. This marginally neater version with exactly the same semantics is shown in listing 2.6.

Listing 2.6 Slightly neater module registering emailers

```
import com.google.inject.AbstractModule;

public class EmailerModule extends AbstractModule {    // Alternative to implementing Module

    @Override
    protected void configure() {
        bind(Emailer.class);              // Service binding
        bind(SpellChecker.class);         // is more concise
    }
}
```

Listings 2.5 and 2.6 are pretty close to Spring's XML configuration. You should be able to see the similarity quite easily:

```
<beans ...>
    <bean id="emailer" class="Emailer">
        <constructor-arg ref="spellChecker"/>
    </bean>

    <bean id="spellChecker" class="SpellChecker"/>
</beans>
```

Before we look at keys and bindings (tying keys to their services) in greater detail, let's look at a few more cool DI libraries.

2.3.3 *Injection in PicoContainer*

Guice configures the injector with annotations and optionally via inference; similarly Spring provides an XML facility for explicit injector configuration. Yet another alternative is provided by PicoContainer—this is similar to inference but takes the form of a programmatic API.

Figure 2.9 An ironic comic strip about Guice and creator Bob Lee from Eric Burke[5]

First, create the injector. Then grab an emailer from it, and dispatch those endearing greeting emails.

```
MutablePicoContainer injector = new DefaultPicoContainer();
injector.addComponent(Emailer.class);
injector.addComponent(SpellChecker.class);
injector.getComponent(Emailer.class).send("Hello!");
```

This is much closer to the original Guice version with the only real difference being that we use construction by hand to create the injector itself, namely, a `DefaultPicoContainer`. The method `getComponent()` is exactly like `getInstance()` in Guice (and `getBean()` in Spring), taking `Emailer.class` as an identifier.

NOTE Unless you are using PicoContainer 2.0, you will need to *downcast* the returned instance to type `Emailer`. In this example (and for the rest of this book), I've preferred PicoContainer 2.0, as it takes advantage of Java 5 and generics to add a measure of type safety.

What's this line doing here?

```
injector.addComponent(Emailer.class);
```

That appears to be a bit more than the three sweet steps of our wonted familiarity. In fact, what we have done is combine bootstrap and configuration in the same sequence

[5] Read more of Eric's comic strips at http://stuffthathappens.com.

of method calls. The source code for `Emailer` itself does not change. So how does the injector know about `Emailer`'s dependencies? There has been no explicit description of `SpellCheckers` and whether or not to use constructor wiring. Nor have we annotated the class itself with `@Inject` or anything like it.

By default, PicoContainer prefers constructor wiring and greedily looks for available constructors. Greedy, in this sense, refers to the widest set of arguments that it can successfully provide to a class's constructor.

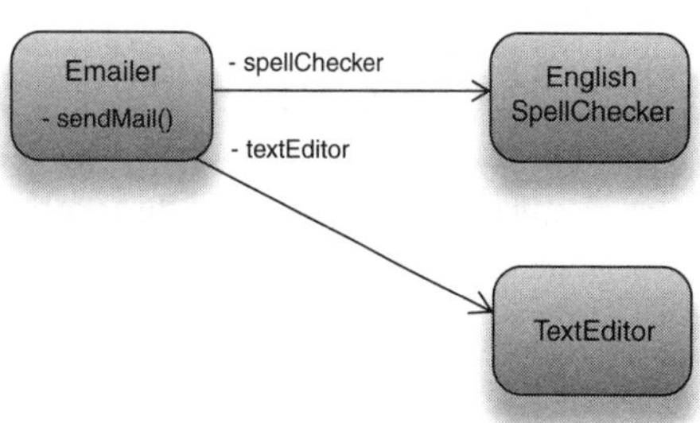

Figure 2.10 Emailer with two dependencies: `SpellChecker` and `TextEditor`

This can seem somewhat counterintuitive, but let's explore an example. For consistency (and because it is cool), I will stick with the emailer. If we imagine that the emailer now requires an editor to write messages in (listing 2.7 and figure 2.10), this can be modeled as a second dependency.

Listing 2.7 The emailer, now with two dependencies

```
public class Emailer {

    private SpellChecker spellChecker;
    private TextEditor editor;

    public Emailer(SpellChecker spellChecker) {
        this.spellChecker = spellChecker;
    }
    public Emailer(SpellChecker spellChecker, TextEditor editor) {
        this.spellChecker = spellChecker;
        this.editor = editor;
    }                                          ❶ Second constructor accepts both dependencies

    public void send() {
        spellChecker.check(editor.getText());
            // send if ok..
    }
}
```

Method `send()` now calls `editor.getText()` ❶ to get the contents of the composed message and send it. Listing 2.8 shows the changes to injector configuration required for this new functionality.

Listing 2.8 Injector bootstrap and using the emailer with its engine

```
MutablePicoContainer injector = new DefaultPicoContainer();
injector.addComponent(Emailer.class);
injector.addComponent(SpellChecker.class);
injector.addComponent(TextEditor.class);
Emailer emailer = injector.getComponent(Emailer.class);    ← Method send() directly retrieves text from the editor
```

This code works because PicoContainer greedily picks the *second* constructor (the one with a greater number of arguments). This default behavior is confusing but fortunately can be changed to suit your preference. We've now seen a couple of forms of configuration that tell a dependency injector how to construct objects. Next we'll use a different idiom: showing the injector how to construct objects.

2.3.4 Revisiting Spring and autowiring

I mentioned in several places that Spring also supports other configuration styles, including the inference style of Guice. One compelling style it offers that you will come across very often is *autowiring*. Autowiring, as the name suggests, is a mode where Spring automatically resolves dependencies by inference on class structure. Back to our email scenario, if this is the structure of the object I want to build with autowiring:

```
public class Emailer {
    private SpellChecker spellChecker;

    public Emailer(SpellChecker spellChecker) {
        this.spellChecker = spellChecker;
    }

    public void send(String text) {
        spellChecker.check(text);
        // send if ok...
    }
}
```

then I can have Spring wire Emailer's SpellChecker dependency without explicitly specifying it:

```
<beans ...>
    <bean id="spellChecker" class="SpellChecker"/>

    <bean id="emailer" class="Emailer" autowire="constructor"/>
</beans>
```

Attribute autowire="constructor" informs the injector to guess dependencies by introspecting on Emailer's constructor. While we still had to register all the available dependency classes in the XML file, there was no need to specify how the graph is wired. Now when an instance of Emailer is constructed, it is automatically wired with a SpellChecker (see figure 2.11):

```
BeanFactory injector = new FileSystemXmlApplicationContext("email.xml");
Emailer emailer = (Emailer) injector.getBean("emailer");
```

And the sending of emails can continue unfettered!

```
emailer.send("Hello!");
```

Constructor autowiring can save you a lot of typing in XML, though it does force you to look in two places to understand your object graph. It is especially useful if most of your dependencies are of unique types, that is, without many variants. And it is particularly useful if you can enforce the convention of only one constructor per class.

From Spring 2.5, you can even resolve the ambiguity between multiple constructors in a class by placing an @Autowired annotation on the particular constructor you

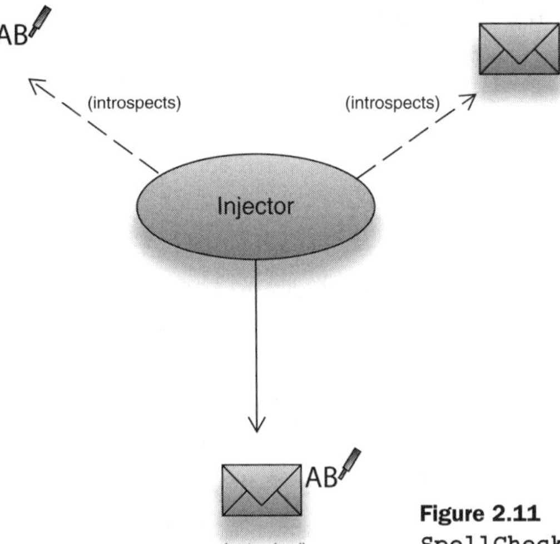

Figure 2.11 Emailer autowired with its `SpellChecker` with no explicit configuration

are interested in. Recall this from earlier in the chapter where we used it in place of `@Inject`. For example:

```
@Component
public class Emailer {
    private SpellChecker spellChecker;

    public Emailer() {
        this.spellChecker = null;
    }

    @Autowired
    public Emailer(SpellChecker spellChecker) {
        this.spellChecker = spellChecker;
    }

    public void send(String text) {
        spellChecker.check(text);
    }
}
```

`@Autowired` performs the same role as Guice's `@Inject` (in addition to `@Component` annotation placed on the class itself). It instructs the injector to choose the annotated constructor when introspecting the class for injection. Remember that you still need to place a <bean> tag in XML to make Spring aware of autowired classes:

```
<beans ...>
    <bean id="spellChecker" class="SpellChecker"/>

    <bean id="emailer" class="Emailer"/>
</beans>
```

Note the absence of any explicit wiring directive (`<constructor-arg>` or `<property>`) that we used in the pure XML configuration system. Note also the more conspicuous absence of the `autowire="..."` attribute, which is unnecessary now that we have `@Autowired`.

Like Guice, this method is both concise and *exemplar.* In other words, what you see in constructor code is what you get in the object graph. The next few sections examine this concept in detail.

2.4 Identifying dependencies for injection

We've already seen that a service generally has some kind of identity, whether an arbitrary string identifier, the class it belongs to, or some other combinatorial key. In this section we will briefly examine a few approaches and the benefits or drawbacks of each.

First, let's formally address what it means to identify components and dependencies. Recall our discussion of the construction and assembly of object graphs from chapter 1. Essentially, a dependency is some implementation of a service. It may only be a flat object with no dependencies of its own. Or it may be an object with a vast graph of interconnected dependencies, which themselves have dependencies, and so on.

To sum up:

- A dependency is any particular permutation of objects in a graph that represents the original service; that is, all permutations obey the same *contract.*
- Permutations of the same service may be thought of as *variants* (or implementations) of that service.

Recall the example of the French and English `Emailers`. They are two variants of the same service (formed by two *different* object graphs). As shown in listing 2.9, dependent `Emailer` is the same for either variant.

Listing 2.9 An email service with French or English spellcheckers

```
public class Emailer {
    private SpellChecker spellChecker;

     public Emailer(SpellChecker spellChecker) {       <-- Injected spellchecker wired via constructor
        this.spellChecker = spellChecker;
    }

    public void send(String text) {                    <-- Provided dependency is used transparently
        spellChecker.check(text);
        // send if ok...
    }
}

interface SpellChecker {                               <-- Interface represents Emailer's dependency
    public boolean check(String text);
}

class FrenchSpellChecker implements SpellChecker {     <-- French implementation of SpellChecker
    public boolean check(String text) {
        //perform some checking...
    }
}
```

```
class EnglishSpellChecker implements SpellChecker {
    public boolean check(String text) {
        //perform some checking...
    }
}
```

English implementation of SpellChecker

Were we to construct them by hand, there would be two possible paths to take. First, for the English email service (the one with the English spellchecker):

```
Emailer emailer = new Emailer(new EnglishSpellChecker());
emailer.send("Hello!");
```

Second, the version with French spelling:

```
Emailer emailer = new Emailer(new FrenchSpellChecker());
emailer.send("Bonjour!");
```

In both these cases, we want an `Emailer` but with different dependencies set. Using a simple string identifier such as `emailer` or a class identifier like `Emailer.class` is clearly insufficient. As an alternative we might try these approaches:

- Use a more specific string identifier, for example `"englishEmailer"` or `"frenchEmailer"`
- Use the class identifier `Emailer.class` together with a discriminator, for example, the ordered pair `[Emailer.class, "english"]`

Existing DI libraries use various methods to solve this problem, usually by falling into one of the two aforementioned paths. Both these options give us an *abstract identity* over a particular service implementation. Once its object graph has been described, a service implementation is easily identified by this abstract identity (which we refer to as its key).

If you wanted to use one particular implementation instead of another, you'd only need to point the dependent to its key. Keys are also essential when we want to leverage other features of dependency injectors, such as:

- *Interception*—Modifying an object's behavior
- *Scope*—Managing an object's state
- *Lifecycle*—Notifying an object of significant events

Keys provide a *binding* between a label and the object graph that implements the service it identifies. The rest of this chapter will focus primarily on the merits and demerits of approaches to keys and bindings.

2.4.1 Identifying by string keys

A key that explicitly spells out the identity of the service implementation should generally have three properties:

- It is *unique* among the set of keys known to an injector; a key must identify only one object graph.

- It is *arbitrary*; it must be able to identify particular, arbitrary service implementations that a user has cooked up. In other words, it has to be more flexible than the service *name* alone.[6]
- It is *explicit*; it must clearly identify the object graph, preferably to the letter of its function.

While these are not hard-and-fast rules, they are good principles to follow. Too often, people dismiss the worth of clear and descriptive keys. Let's look at real-world examples:

A `Set` in Java is a data structure that has many implementations. Among other things, the contract of `Set` disallows duplicate entries. The core Java library ships with the following implementations of `Set`:

- `java.util.TreeSet`—A *binary-tree*[7] implementation of the `Set` service
- `java.util.HashSet`—A *hash-table*[8] implementation of the `Set` service

How should we choose keys for these variants? The names of these implementations give us a good starting point—nominally, `"binaryTreeSet"` and `"hashTableSet."` This certainly isn't rocket science! These keys are explicit, sufficiently different from one another to be unique, and they clearly identify the behavior of the implementation (either binary-tree or hash-table behavior). While this may seem fairly obvious, it is not often the case. You'd be surprised at how many real-world projects are obfuscated with unclear, overlapping keys that say little if anything about an object graph. It is as much for your benefit as the developer and maintainer of an application as it is for the dependency injector itself that you follow these guidelines. Lucid, articulate keys are easily identified and self-documenting, and they go a long way toward preventing accidental misuse, which can be a real nuisance in big projects.

I also strongly encourage use of *namespaces*, for example, `"set.BinaryTree"` and `"set.HashTable,"` which are nicer to read and comprehend than `"binaryTreeSet"` and `"hashTableSet."` Namespaces are a more elegant and natural nomenclature for your *key space* and are eminently more readable than strings of grouped capitalized words. An email service with a French bent might be `"emailer.French,"` and its counterparts might be `"emailer.English,"` `"emailer.Japanese,"` and so forth.

I am especially fond of namespaces in dependency injection. Their value was immediately apparent to me the first time I was on a project with a very large number of XML configuration files. They allowed my team and me to clearly separate services by areas of function and avert the risk of abuse or misapprehension. For instance, data services were prefixed with `dao` (for Data Access Object) and business services with `biz`. Helper objects that sat at the periphery of the core business purpose were confined to a `util`.

---

6 Recall the example of `SpellChecker` (the service) being insufficient to distinguish between its English and French implementations.

7 A binary tree is a data structure in which each stored item may have two successors (or children), starting at a single root item.

8 A hash table is a data structure designed to store and look up entries in a single step using a calculated address known as a hash code.

namespace. I can't emphasize enough how useful this was for us. Consider some of the changes we made in a vast system of objects and dependencies identified solely by string keys (also see figure 2.12):

- `UserDetailsService` became `dao.User`.
- `UserDataUtils` became `util.Users`.
- `DateDataUtils` became `util.Dates`.
- `UserService` became `biz.Users`.

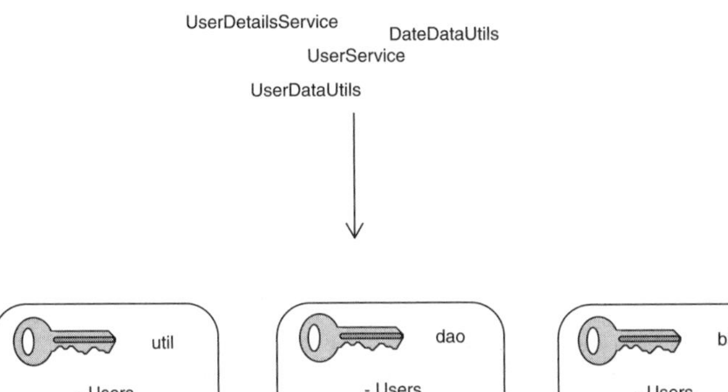

Figure 2.12 Organizing string keys into namespaces

The astute reader will appreciate how much clearer—and more succinct—the latter form is. Of course, there is nothing new or innovative about the concept of namespaces, though one rarely sees it preached in documentation.

Spring and its XML configuration mechanism benefit heavily from this approach. If we were to declare the variant implementations of a `Set`, they may look something like this:

```
<beans ...>
    <bean id="set.HashTable" class="java.util.HashSet"/>

    <bean id="set.BinaryTree" class="java.util.TreeSet"/>
</beans>
```

And obtaining these objects from the injector accords to their keys:

```
BeanFactory injector =
    new FileSystemXmlApplicationContext("treesAndHashes.xml");
Set<?> items = (HashSet<?>) injector.getBean("set.HashTable");
```

For a more complete scenario, consider this pattern for the email service and its two variant spellcheckers (listing 2.10).

Listing 2.10 Variants of an email service using namespaces

```
<beans>
    <bean id="spelling.English" class="EnglishSpellChecker"/>

    <bean id="emailer.English" class="Emailer">
```

```
        <constructor-arg ref="spelling.English"/>
    </bean>

    <bean id="spelling.French" class="FrenchSpellChecker"/>

     <bean id="emailer.French " class="Emailer">
        <constructor-arg ref="spelling.French"/>
    </bean>
</beans>
```

Better yet, listing 2.11 is a more compact, encapsulated version of the same.

Listing 2.11 A compact form of listing 2.10

```
<beans ...>
     <bean id="emailer.English" class="Emailer">
        <constructor-arg><bean class="EnglishSpellChecker"/></constructor-arg>
    </bean>

    <bean id="emailer.French" class="Emailer">
        <constructor-arg><bean class="FrenchSpellChecker"/></constructor-arg>
    </bean>

    <bean id="emailer.Japanese" class="Emailer">
       <constructor-arg><bean class="JapaneseSpellChecker"/></constructor-arg>
    </bean>

</beans>
```

By now, you should be starting to appreciate the value of namespaces, encapsulation, and well-chosen keys. Remember, a well-chosen key is *unique, arbitrary,* and *explicit.* When you must use string keys, choose them wisely. And use namespaces.

To drive the point home, look at the following two setups in pseudocode: one that uses poorly chosen keys and a flat keyspace and a second that conforms to our principles of good key behavior. Listing 2.12 shows an injector configuration with bad keys and no namespaces. Ugly! Wouldn't you agree?

Listing 2.12 Poorly chosen keys for services (in pseudocode configuration)

```
configure() {                                  <-- Start configuration

    personService            { ... }          | Services for personnel
    personDataService        { ... }          | management
    personnelSoapService     { ... }

    userAuth                 { ... }          | Security
    userAuthz                { ... }          | services

    userService              { ... }
    database                 { ... }

    app {
          app = new Application()
          ...                              <-- Wiring logic goes here
    }
}
```

Now compare this with listing 2.13 (and figure 2.13), which presents an improved version of the same configuration. Much better!

Listing 2.13 Good-practice version of listing 2.12

```
configure() {

    define namespace :biz {                          <-- Services organized into biz namespace
        biz.personnel                     { ... }
        biz.user
    }

    define namespace :data {                         <-- Data objects are in data namespace
        data.database                      { ... }
        data.personnel                     { ... }
    }

    define namespace  :soap {
        soap.personnel                     { ... }
    }

    define namespace {
        security.authentication                 { ... }    | Security object keys
        security.authorization                  { ... }    | named lucidly
    }

}
main {
    personnelService = injector.biz.personnel       | Get and use instances
    personnelDao = injector.data.personnel          | from injector

}
```

String keys are flexible, and if chosen well they work well. But well chosen or not, string keys have limitations that can be confounding and rather, well, limiting! Let's talk about some of them.

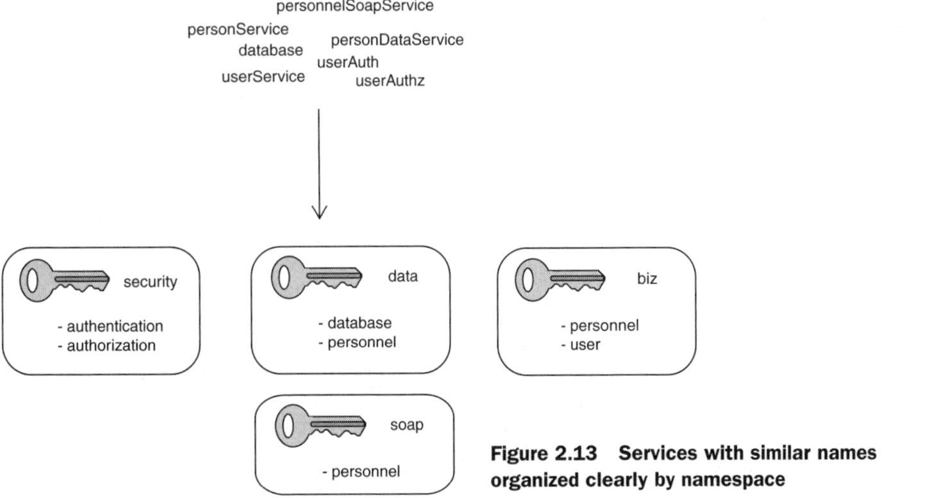

Figure 2.13 Services with similar names organized clearly by namespace

2.4.2 Limitations of string keys

String keys are inherently problematic when one factors human error into the equation. We have all been there. Take the possible ways to spell a common name, for example:

- Alan
- Allan
- Alain
- Allen
- Allun (an Irish variant)

This is a short name (two syllables) and it does not incur the distractions of case and multiple-word capitalization.[9] Yet we can barely agree on a spelling even in the English-speaking world. Mistyping and misreading exacerbates the problem. It is not a stretch to imagine how things can get out of hand very quickly with a large number of services identified by many similar-looking (and sounding) keys. A misspelled key that maps to no valid service can be difficult to detect until well into the runtime of the program.

Furthermore, if you are working with a statically typed language like Java, this is a poor sacrifice to have to make. These languages are supposed to offer guarantees around type validity at compile time. Ideally, one should not have to wait until runtime to detect problems in key bindings.

> **Static and dynamic typing[10]**
>
> Types are specific classes of data in a programming language. For example, the number `32` is of an `Integer` type. Types may also be user defined, such as `Car` or `Song`. Before operations on data can occur, the data's particular type must be determined. This is known as *type resolution*. A *dynamically typed* language resolves types when an operation is *performed*, whereas a *statically typed* language resolves types when an operation is *defined* (typically, but not necessarily, at compile time).

Sometimes tools like IDEs or build agents can help do this extra level of checking for you, during or before compilation. *IntelliJ IDEA*[11] provides plug-ins for Spring for just this purpose. Naturally, it is difficult for any tool to guarantee the correct resolution of dependencies into dependents without bootstrapping the injector and walking across every bound object (or just about every one). As a result, this problem can arise often in injectors that use string keys.

---

9 A phrase or set of words in a key is often delimited by capitalizing each first letter. For example, "Technicolor dream coat" would be written as `TechnicolorDreamCoat` or `technicolorDreamCoat`, which are two forms of the CamelCase convention.

10 Do not confuse static and dynamic typing with *strong* and *weak* typing, or indeed with *duck* typing.

11 IntelliJ IDEA is an advanced Java IDE developed by JetBrains. It is usually at the forefront of innovation in developer productivity. Find out more at http://www.jetbrains.com.

In your injector configuration there is no way to determine the type of a binding if all you have is a string key. Without starting up the injector and inspecting the specific instance for a key, it is hard to determine what type the key is bound to. Take the following example of a game console (the Nintendo Wii) and a game to be played on it:

```
<beans>
     <bean id="nintendo.wii" class="com.nintendo.Wii">
        <constructor-arg ref="game.HalfLife"/>
    </bean>

    <bean id="game.HalfLife" class="com.valve.HalfLifeGame"/>

</beans>
```

Here our keys appear reasonably well chosen: they are unique, arbitrary, and explicit (*and* they use namespaces). I've followed every tenet of good key behavior but something is horribly wrong with this injector configuration. The program crashes when I try to run it. To understand why, delve into the code behind these bindings:

```
package com.nintendo;

public class Wii {
    private WiiGame game;
    public Wii(WiiGame game) {          <-- Game is wired via constructor
        this.game = game;
    }

    public void play() { .. }
}
```

The Nintendo game system takes an argument of type `WiiGame` via its constructor. This dependency represents a game I want to play (I enjoy Half-Life so let's go with that) and is loaded by the game system when `play()` is called. This is the game Half-Life:

```
package com.valve;

public class HalfLife implements PCGame {
    public void load() { .. }
}
```

Oh, no! Half-Life is a game for the PC, *not* the Wii! It is not an instance of `WiiGame` and therefore cannot be wired into `Wii`'s constructor (see figure 2.14).

In Java, executing this program and requesting an instance by key `nintendo.wii` will result in an `UnsatisfiedDependencyException` being thrown. This indicates that the configured binding is of the wrong type for `Wii`'s dependency, and it cannot be converted to the right type.

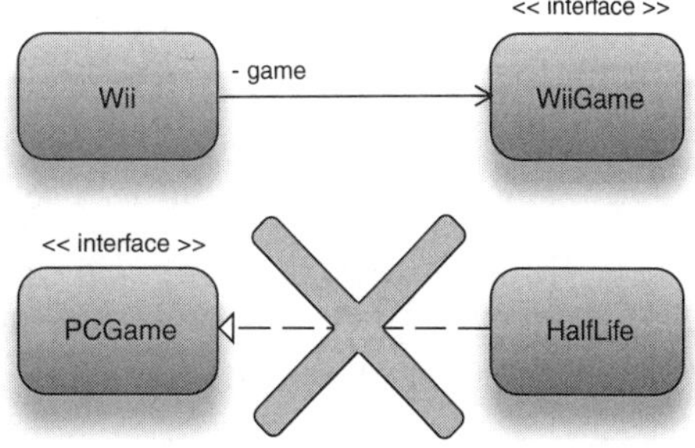

Figure 2.14 Wii and game HalfLife, which implements the wrong interface, `PCGame`

More significant for us, however, is the fact that what appeared to be a perfectly well-written injector configuration turned out to be fatally flawed. Worse, there was no way to detect this until the offending object graph was constructed and used. This highlights a serious limitation of string keys.

Once the problem is identified, we can fix it by selecting the correct implementation of Half-Life. Listing 2.14 shows this fix, illustrated in figure 2.15.

Listing 2.14 The fixed version of games.xml

```
<beans>
     <bean id="nintendo.wii" class="com.nintendo.Wii">
        <constructor-arg ref="game.HalfLife"/>
    </bean>

    <bean id="game.HalfLife" class="com.valve.wii.HalfLife"/>   <-- Changed to a variant of HalfLife

</beans>
```

This time, the game is of the appropriate type and everything works as expected.

```
package com.valve.wii;

public class HalfLife implements WiiGame {    <-- Dependency variant HalfLife is now of the correct type
    public void load() { .. }
}
```

In large applications with many hundreds of object graphs, string identifiers incur many of these problems. No matter what language or injector you decide on, poorly chosen keys are a recipe for disaster. Oh, and use namespaces. Seriously!

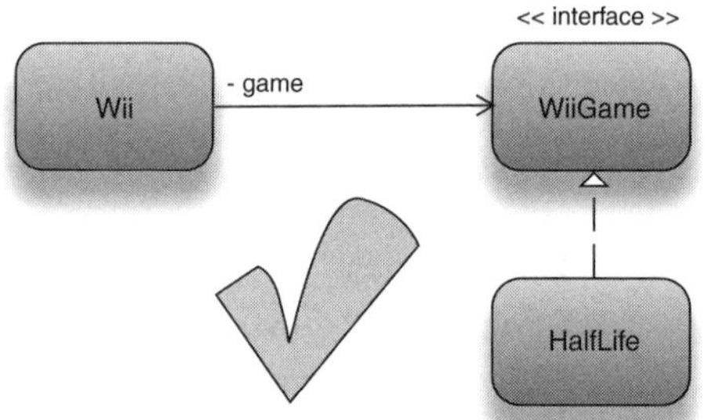

Figure 2.15 `HalfLife` **now correctly implements** `WiiGame`**.**

2.4.3 *Identifying by type*

We have seen how services are identified by a type. Recall some of the examples I've used so far in this book:

- `SpellChecker.class` identifies `EnglishSpellChecker` or `FrenchSpellChecker`.
- `Emailer.class` identifies itself.
- `WiiGame.class` identifies `HalfLife`.
- `Wii.class` identifies itself.

Unlike strings, referring to a type is not quite the same in all languages, but the essential semantic is the same. Java uses *type literals* that are analogous to *string literals* and essentially identify the type directly in code:

- `Set.class`
- `SpellChecker.class`
- `Airplane.class`

Identifying by type is a natural and idiomatic way of referring to a dependency. It is self-descriptive and can be inferred by introspection tools automatically. This has additional advantages in a statically typed language where types are checked at compile time and any errors in types are revealed early.

Look at how identifying by type helps prevent the very error we just saw with string keys and the incorrect wiring of dependencies. Listing 2.15 revisits the broken dependency where the wrong version of the game HalfLife is used in the game console.

Listing 2.15 The class `com.nintendo.Wii` bound to key `nintendo.wii`

```
package com.nintendo;

public class Wii {
    private WiiGame game;
    public Wii(WiiGame game) {          <-- Injected game wired via constructor
        this.game = game;
    }

    public void play() { .. }
}

public class HalfLife implements PCGame {     <-- HalfLife implements the wrong type!
    public void load() { .. }
}
```

This time, instead of XML configuration and Spring, I use Guice and its `Module` binding:

```
public class MyGamesModule extends AbstractModule {     <-- (1) Configured via subclasses of Module or AbstractModule

    @Override
    protected void configure() {
        bind(WiiGame.class).to(HalfLife.class);     <-- (2) This line results in a compiler error
    }
}
```

This injector configuration ❶ will not compile, failing with an error saying there is no such method `to()` ❷ taking an argument of type `HalfLife`. The error is caught nice and early. What the compiler really means is that type key `HalfLife.class` refers to the wrong type. Or, it is *not* an implementation of `WiiGame`. Another nice thing is that bad spelling is also caught early, with a compiler error. IDEs help you catch this kind of error as you are writing code, and let you smart complete the correct values when typing, which is especially nice. We can also achieve a similar end using Spring's JavaConfig configuration mechanism:

```
@Configuration
public class MyGamesConfig {

    @Bean
    public WiiGame game() {          <-- Binding of dependency HalfLife
        return new HalfLife();
    }

    @Bean
    public Wii gameConsole() {
```

```
        return new Wii(game());
    }
}
```

Type checked like normal Java code

Clearly, identifying by type is a winner when compared to plain string keys. PicoContainer also offers identifying by type in a similar fashion to what we've just seen with Guice. However, identifying by type does have serious limitations. In the next sections we'll explore what these are and how they may be overcome.

2.4.4 Limitations of identifying by type

I'll wager you're already familiar with some of the limitations of type (or *class literal* keys). We saw the primary one at the beginning of this section—the inability to distinguish between different implementations of a service. The type key `Car.class` can refer either to `BmwZ4`s or to `ToyotaCamry`s, as shown in figure 2.16.

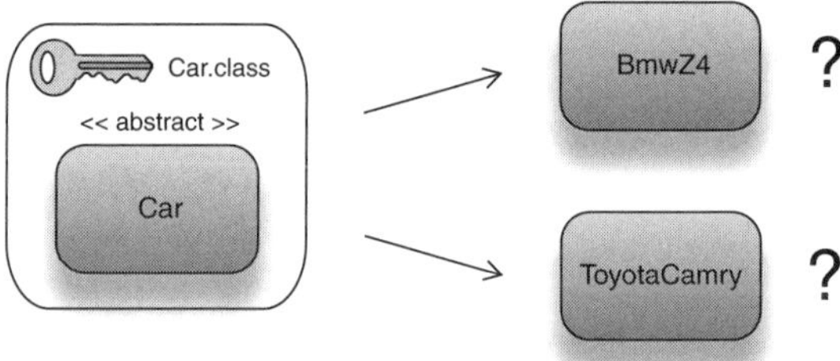

Figure 2.16 Which implementation does type key `Car.class` refer to?

And the injector is none the wiser as to which one to select and wire to clients of `Car`. This is irksome if we wanted to plug in a variety of alternative implementations by just changing keys.

You can refer to a specific implementation *directly* (like `BmwZ4.class` instead of `Car.class`), but this is a poor solution and incurs the same problem of the one default implementation (can't replace it with a `ToyotaCamry`). Worse, it is difficult to test and tightly couples client code to dependencies, which is undesirable.

Identifying by type can be restrictive in other ways. Recall the three holy tenets of well-chosen keys that helped make them lucid and maintainable. Keys must be unique, arbitrary, and explicit. How does identifying by type fare under these tenets?

- *Not unique*—Variant implementations of a service are indistinguishable by type key alone (`BMWZ4`s and `ToyotaCamry`s both have type key `Car.class`).
- *Not arbitrary*—A key bears only the label of the service (that is, the dependency). There is no room to describe arbitrary variants. The game console accepts a `WiiGame`, not `HalfLife` or `SuperMarioBrothers`. Try getting your kid to spend his money on a nondescript, gray disc over a shiny new copy of Half-Life.
- *May or may not be explicit*—One could argue that there is no better explanation of the service's function than its contract. However, were a service contract to leave some details up to its implementations, or likely to other dependencies, we would lose all explicit enunciation, as in an `Emailer` with English spellchecking rather than French (both identified by `Emailer.class`).

It does not fare very well at all: one or possibly none out of three important requisites of good key behavior! Type keys are safer in the context of detecting errors early on, particularly in statically typed languages like Java and C#, but they are rigid and don't offer the breadth of abstraction that string keys do. String keys, on the other hand, are dangerous through misspelling and can be abstruse and opaque if improperly chosen. To summarize: type keys are *safe but inflexible*, and string keys are *flexible but unsafe* and potentially confusing.

It would be ideal if there were a key strategy that was both type and contract safe—and was flexible enough to wire dependents with many implementations that we could identify easily. Fortunately for us, *combinatorial keys* provide the best of both worlds.

2.4.5 Combinatorial keys: a comprehensive solution

Earlier, I described a sample combinatorial key for an English variant of our favorite email service; it looked like this:

```
[Emailer.class, "english"]
```

The ordered pair `[Emailer.class, "english"]` is one case of a combinatorial key consisting of a type key *and* a string key. The type key identifies the service that dependents rely on, in a safe and consistent manner. Its counterpart, the string key, identifies the specific variant that the key is bound to but does so in an abstract manner. Comparing this combinatorial key with a plain string key, the latter clearly has the advantage of type safety. Its second part (the string key) provides a clear advantage over plain type keys because it is able to distinguish between implementations. Let's examine this with a couple of examples:

```
Key 1: [Emailer.class, "english"]
Key 2: [Emailer.class, "french"]
Key X: [Book.class, "dependencyInjection"]
Key Y: [Book.class, "harryPotter"]
```

Keys 1 and 2 identify object graphs of an email service with English and French spellchecking, respectively. Keys X and Y identify two different books.

Another example we've used before is an emailer that depends on a `SpellChecker`:

```
[Emailer.class, "withSpellChecker"]
```

Consider a more complex take on this example, where our emailer depends on a `SpellChecker`, which itself depends on a dictionary to resolve word corrections (as figure 2.17 models).

The combinatorial key identifying this object graph might look something like:

```
[Emailer.class, "withSpellCheckerAndDictionary"]
```

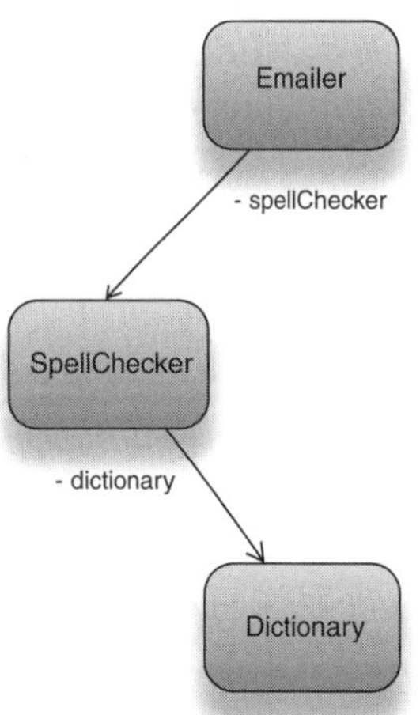

Figure 2.17 A class model of two levels of dependencies below emailer

Even complex object graphs with many permutations are identified easily with combinatorial keys. They also comply with our rules for good key behavior:

- *Keys are unique.* The second part to the ordered pair ensures that two implementations are identified uniquely.
- *Keys are arbitrary.* While the dependency is identified by the first part, any specific behavior exhibited by a custom variant is easily described by the second part of the key.
- *Keys are explicit.* More so than with pure string keys, combinatorial keys are able to identify both the service contract they exhibit and any specific variation to the letter of its function.

So, combinatorial keys are safe, explicit, and able to identify any service variants clearly and precisely. They solve the problems of type-safety that pure string keys can't, and they ease the rigidity of pure type keys. And they do so in an elegant manner. The only drawback is that we have a string part that incurs the problems of misspelling and misuse identified earlier. For example, it is quite easy to see how the following combinatorial keys, relatively safe though they are, can still end up problematic:

```
[Emailer.class, "englihs"]
[Emailer.class, "English"]
[Emailer.class, "francais"]
[Emailer.class, "withFaser"]
[Emailer.class, "with.SpellChecker"]
[Emailer.class, "With.SpellChecker"]
```

Each of these keys will result in an erroneous injector configuration that won't be detected until runtime. While there are certainly far fewer possible *total* errors with this approach, there are nonetheless the same perils and pitfalls so long as we rely on a string key in any consistent and foundational manner. How then can we fix this problem?

It turns out we can still keep all the benefits of combinatorial keys and eliminate the problems that the string part of the key presents. By using an *annotation* in place of the string part of the combinatorial key, we get the benefit of a safe key and the flexibility of an arbitrary and explicit string key.

Consider the following combinatorial keys that are composed of a type and an *annotation* type:

```
[Emailer.class, English.class]
[Emailer.class, WithSpellChecker.class]
[Database.class, FileBased.class]
```

Misspelling the annotation name results in a compiler error, which is an early and clear indication of the problem. This is exactly what we were after. What we have done is effectively replace the string key with a *second* type key. In combination with the service's type key, this retains the qualities of good behavior in well-chosen keys but also eliminates the problems posed by arbitrary, abstract strings. This is quite a comprehensive and elegant solution. The fact that annotations can be reused also makes them good for more than the one service:

```
[Emailer.class, English.class]
[Dictionary.class, English.class]
[SpellChecker.class, English.class]
```

We use the `@English` annotation to distinguish variant implementations of not only the `Emailer` but also the `Dictionary` and `TextEditor` services. These keys are self-documenting and still give us the flexibility of a string key. Since annotations are cheap to create (hardly a couple of lines of code) and reuse, this approach scales nicely too.

Guice embodies the use of type/annotation combinatorial keys and was probably the first library to use this strategy. Listing 2.16 and figure 2.18 show what the injector configuration might look like for the spellchecking service I presented in the previous example.

Listing 2.16 Guice module binding services to combinatorial keys

```
public class SpellingModule extends AbstractModule {

    @Override
    protected void configure() {
        bind(SpellChecker.class)
             .annotatedWith(English.class)
             .to(EnglishSpellChecker.class);

        bind(SpellChecker.class)
             .annotatedWith(French.class)
             .to(FrenchSpellChecker.class);

    }
}
```

Then using either of these services in a client is as simple as using the appropriate annotation:

```
Guice.createInjector(new SpellingModule())
     .getInstance(Key.get(SpellChecker.class, English.class))
     .check("Hello!");
```

When this code is executed, Guice obtains the `SpellChecker` instance bound to the combinatorial key represented by `[SpellChecker.class, English.class]`. Invoking

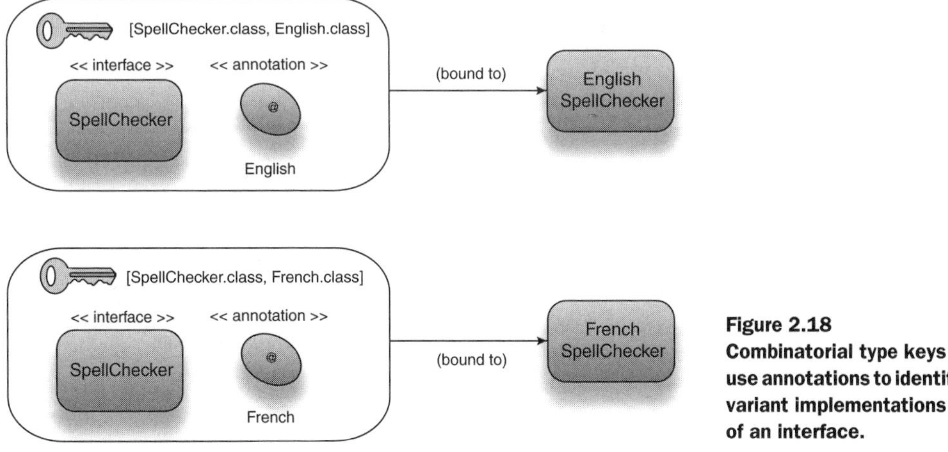

Figure 2.18 Combinatorial type keys use annotations to identify variant implementations of an interface.

the `check()` method on it runs the service method on the correct (that is, English) implementation.

This is also easily done in any *client* of `SpellChecker` via the use of `@English` annotation near the injection point of the dependency. Here's one such example:

```
public class SpellCheckerClient {

    @Inject
    public SpellCheckerClient(@English SpellChecker spellChecker) {
        //use provided spellChecker
    }
}
```

This might strike you as odd—while the client does not depend directly on a specific implementation, it *seems* to couple via the use of `@English` annotation. Doesn't this mean `SpellCheckerClient` is tightly coupled to English spellcheckers? The answer is a surprising no. To understand why, consider the following altered injector configuration:

```
public class SpellingModule extends AbstractModule {

    @Override
    protected void configure() {
        bind(SpellChecker.class)
             .annotatedWith(English.class)
             .to(FrenchSpellChecker.class);
    }
}
```

In this example, I've changed the service implementation bound to the combinatorial key `[SpellChecker.class, English.class]` so that any dependent referring to an `@English` annotated `SpellChecker` will actually receive an implementation of type `FrenchSpellChecker`. There are no errors, and `SpellCheckerClient` is unaware of any change and more importantly *unaffected* by any change. So they aren't really tightly coupled.

No client code needs to change, and we were able to alter configuration transparently.

Similarly, you can build such combinatorial bindings in Spring JavaConfig using types and method names:

```
@Configuration
public class EmailConfig {

    @Bean
    public SpellChecker english() {            <-- Binding of English spellchecker
        return new EnglishSpellChecker();
    }

    @Bean
    public Emailer emailer() {
        return new Emailer(english());          <-- Create an English emailer
    }

}
```

Here, the combinatorial key is [SpellChecker, english()], the latter being the name of the method. It performs a very similar function to the @English annotation we saw just now, though the two approaches differ slightly.

Now let's look at how to take this practice a step further and separate code by area of concern.

2.5 Separating infrastructure and application logic

You have seen how object graphs that represent various services may be created, assembled, and referenced. You have also seen the steps to creating and using dependency injectors and ultimately the objects that they manage for an application. DI libraries differ slightly in the manner in which these steps are achieved and the rigor with which they are performed, but ultimately they all follow the same principles.

Together, these properties make for lean and focused components with code only to deal with their primary business purpose, be it:

- Rendering a web page
- Sending email
- Purchasing stock
- Checking bad spelling

Logic geared toward such purposes is termed *application logic*. Everything else is meant only to support and enhance it. Logic for constructing and assembling object graphs, obtaining connections to databases, setting up network sockets, or crunching text through spellcheckers is all peripheral to the core purpose of the application.

While this *infrastructure logic* is essential to all applications, it is important to distinguish it from the application logic itself. This not only helps keep application logic clear and focused, but it also prevents tests from being polluted with distracting bugs and errors that may have nothing to do with the code's purpose. Dependency injection helps in this regard. Figure 2.19 describes the fundamental injector and object composition that forms the basis of modern architectures.

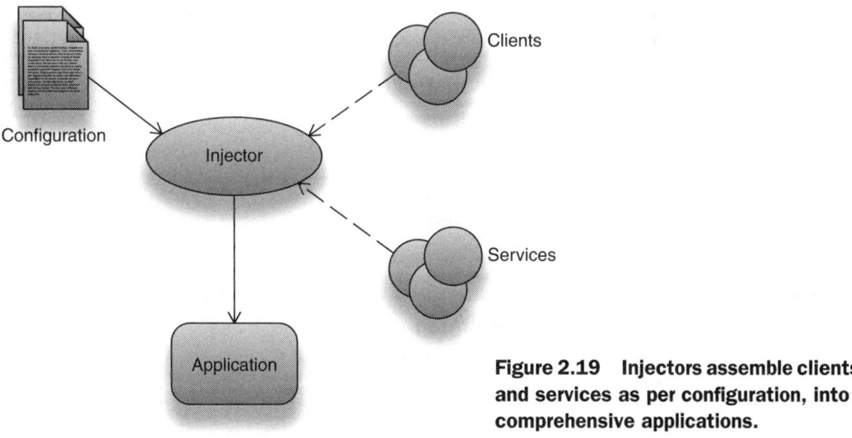

Figure 2.19 Injectors assemble clients and services as per configuration, into comprehensive applications.

Good DI libraries enforce and exemplify this core ideology. They are as much about preventing abuse as they are about proffering best practices or flexibility. As such, a DI library that takes extra steps to prevent you from accidentally shooting yourself in the foot (by checking bindings at compile time, for instance) is preferable. On the other hand, DI libraries that offer a great deal of flexibility (and weak type safety) can draw even experienced developers into traps. This is where careful design is important. Don't be afraid to refactor and redesign your code when you discover violations of good design. A little bit of effort up front to ensure that infrastructure logic remains separate from application logic will go a long way toward keeping your code readable, maintainable, and robust throughout its life.

2.6 Summary

This chapter was a headfirst dive into dependency injectors, their configuration, and their use. You saw how injectors must be bootstrapped with specified configuration and then used to obtain and perform operations on components they build and wire. At first, the injector looks no different to a service locator, and this is roughly correct in the context of obtaining the first, or the root, component from which the rest of an object graph extends.

All services that are used as dependencies are labeled by a key, which the injector uses as a way of referring to them during configuration or service location. The coupling of a key to a particular object graph is called a binding. These bindings determine how components are provided with their dependencies and thus how object graphs are ultimately constructed and wired. There are several kinds of keys, the most common being simply string identifiers, which are common in XML-configured DI libraries such as Spring, StructureMap, and HiveMind. String keys are flexible and provide us with the freedom to describe arbitrary and various assemblies of object graphs that portend a service. Different object graphs that conform to the same set of rules, that are the same service, may be thought of as different *implementations* of that service. String keys allow easy identification of such dependency *variants*.

However, string keys have many limitations, and the fact that they are unrestricted character strings means that they are prone to human error and to misuse and poor design choices. This leads to the necessity of well-chosen string identifiers that portend good key behavior. We defined the characteristics of well-chosen keys as being unique, arbitrary, and explicit. Unique keys ensure that no two object graphs are identified by the same key accidentally and so ensure that there is no ambiguity when a dependency is sought. Arbitrary keys are useful in supporting a variety of custom variants of services, which a creative user may have cooked up. Finally, these keys must also be explicit if they are to exactly describe what a service implementation does as clearly and concisely as is possible. Well-chosen keys combined with the use of namespaces greatly improve readability and also reduce the probability of accidental misuse.

String keys satisfy all of these qualities, but they have serious drawbacks since they lack the knowledge of the type (or class) they represent. This can result in syntactically correct injector configuration that fails at runtime, sometimes even as late as the first use of a faultily configured object graph. In rare cases, it can even result in incorrect dependency wiring without any explicit errors, which is a very scary situation! In a statically typed language like Java, better solutions are imperative to these problems, especially in large projects that make use of *agile* software methods that require rapid, iterative execution of partial units.

An alternative is the use of type keys. These are keys that simply refer to the data type of the service. Type keys solve the misspelling and misuse problem of string keys but sacrifice a lot of flexibility and abstraction in doing so. PicoContainer is one DI library that supports the use of type keys. Their primary limitation is the inability to distinguish between various implementations without directly referring to them in client code. As a result, type keys violate almost all of the requirements of well-chosen keys, though they are safe and help catch errors early, at compile time.

One solution is to combine the two approaches and use type keys to narrow down the service's type and pair it with a string key that distinguishes the specific variant. These are called combinatorial keys, and they provide all of the flexibility of string keys and retain the rigor of type keys. PicoContainer also provides for these hybrid type/string combinatorial keys. However, the use of string identifiers at all still means that there is a risk of misspelling and accidental misuse. Guice provides a comprehensive solution: the use of custom annotation types in place of the string part of a combinatorial key. The combination of the type key referring to a service and an annotation-type key referring to an abstract identifier to distinguish between implementations provides for a compelling mitigation of the problems of even partial string keys.

Finally, whatever DI library you choose, dependency injectors are geared toward the same goals, that is, separate logic meant for constructing and assembling object graphs, managing external resources and connections, and so on from logic that is intended solely for the core purpose of the application. This is called the separation of infrastructure from application logic and is an important part of good design and architecture. The majority of the concepts presented in this book revolve around this core ideology and in many ways serve to emphasize or enhance the importance of this separation. A successful rendition of dependency injection gives you more time to focus effort on application logic and helps make your code testable, maintainable, and concise.

3 Investigating DI

This chapter covers:

- Learning about injection by setter and constructor
- Investigating pros and cons of injection idioms
- Identifying pitfalls in object graph construction
- Learning about reinjecting objects
- Discovering viral injection and cascaded object graphs
- Learning techniques to inject sealed code

"The best way to predict the future is to invent it."

—Alan Kay

Previously we discussed two methods of connecting objects with their dependencies. In the main we have written classes that accept their dependencies via *constructor*. We have also occasionally used a single-argument method called a *setter method* to pass in a dependency. As a recap, here are two such examples from chapter 1:

```
public class Emailer {
    private SpellChecker spellChecker;

    public Emailer(SpellChecker spellChecker) {
        this.spellChecker = spellChecker;
    }
}
```

The same class accepting dependencies by setter:

```
public class Emailer {
    private SpellChecker spellChecker;

    public void setSpellChecker(SpellChecker spellChecker) {
        this.spellChecker = spellChecker;
    }
}
```

These are two common forms of wiring. Many dependency injectors also support other varieties and bias toward or away from these idioms.

The choice between them is not always one of taste alone. There are several consequences to be considered, ranging from scalability to performance, development rigor, type safety, and even software environments. The use of third-party libraries and certain design patterns can also influence the choice of injection idiom.

DI can make your life easier, but like anything else, it requires careful thought and an understanding of pitfalls and traps and the available strategies for dealing with them. The appropriate choice of injection idiom and accompanying design patterns is significant in any architecture. Even if you were to disavow the use of a DI library altogether, you would do well to study the traps, pitfalls, and practices presented in this chapter. They will stand you in good stead for designing and writing healthy code.

In this chapter, we will look at an incarnation of each major idiom and explain when you should choose one over another and why. I provide several strong arguments in favor of constructor injection. However, I will show when setter injection is preferable and how to decide between the two. Understanding injection idioms and the nuances behind them is central to a good grasp of dependency injection and architecture in general. Let's start with the two most common forms.

3.1 Injection idioms

The key to understanding the differences between setter and constructor injection is to understand the differences between methods and constructors. The advantages and limitations arise from these essential language constructs. Constructors have several limitations imposed on them by the language (for example, they can be called only once). On the other hand, they have advantages, such as being able to set final fields. We'll start by examining these limitations and advantages in detail.

3.1.1 Constructor injection

Essentially, a constructor's purpose is to perform initial *setup* work on the instance being constructed, using provided arguments as necessary. This setup work may be wiring of dependencies (what we are typically interested in) or some computation that is necessary prior to the object's use. A constructor has several odd and sometimes confounding restrictions that differentiate it from an ordinary method. A constructor:

- Cannot (does not) return anything.
- Must *complete* before an instance is considered fully constructed.

- Can initialize *final fields*, while a method cannot.
- Can be called only once per instance.
- Cannot be given an arbitrary name—in general, it is named after its class.
- Cannot be *virtual*; you are forced to implement a constructor if you declare it.

A constructor is something of an initialization *hook* and somewhat less than a method, even with a generous definition of methods. Constructors are provided in most object-oriented languages as a means of adequately preparing an object prior to use. The flow chart in figure 3.1 shows the steps taken internally to perform constructor injection.

A more thorough look at the pros and cons of construction injection is available later in this chapter. As we said earlier, setters offer benefits in areas where constructors are limited. They are just like any other method and therefore are more flexible. In the following section, we examine the advantages to this flexibility and where it can sometimes cause problems.

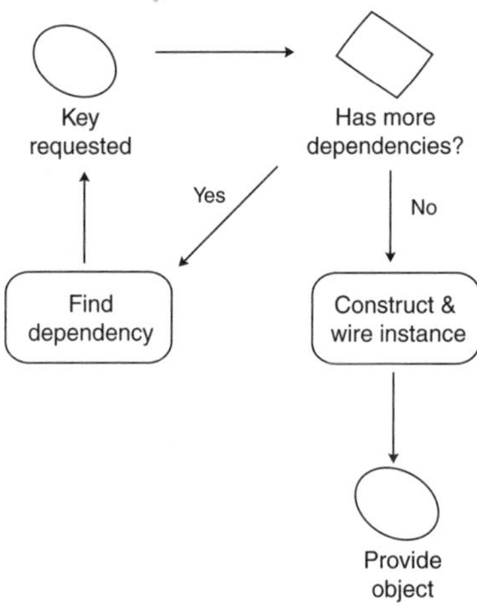

Figure 3.1 Sequence of operations in constructor injection

3.1.2 Setter injection

The other approach we have seen (and the one that is very common) is setter injection. It involves passing an object its dependencies via arguments to a so-called setter method. Let's revisit some of our past uses of setter injection:

```
public class Emailer {
    private SpellChecker spellChecker;

    public void setSpellChecker(SpellChecker spellChecker) {
        this. spellChecker = spellChecker;
    }
}
```

Figure 3.2 depicts the flow of steps in how objects are wired using setter injection. Contrast this with the flow chart presented in figure 3.1.

This sequence is almost identical to that of constructor injection, except that a method named `setSpellChecker()` is used in place of a constructor and the wiring takes place *after* the instance is fully constructed. In common usage, if you want to pass in additional dependencies, you provide additional setters, as shown in listing 3.1 (modeled in figure 3.3).

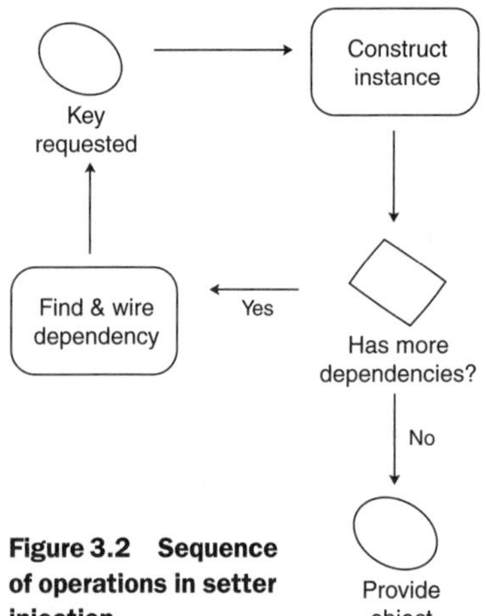

Figure 3.2 Sequence of operations in setter injection

Listing 3.1 A stereo amplifier wired by setter

```
public class Amplifier {
    private Guitar guitar;
    private Speaker speaker;
    private Footpedal footpedal;
    private Synthesizer synthesizer;

    public void setGuitar(Guitar guitar) {
        this.guitar = guitar;
    }

    public void setSpeaker(Speaker speaker) {
        this.speaker = speaker;
    }

    public void setFootpedal(Footpedal footpedal) {
        this.footpedal = footpedal;
    }

    public void setSynthesizer(Synthesizer synthesizer) {
        this.synthesizer = synthesizer;
    }

}
```

Dependencies of a stereo amplifier

Setters for each dependency

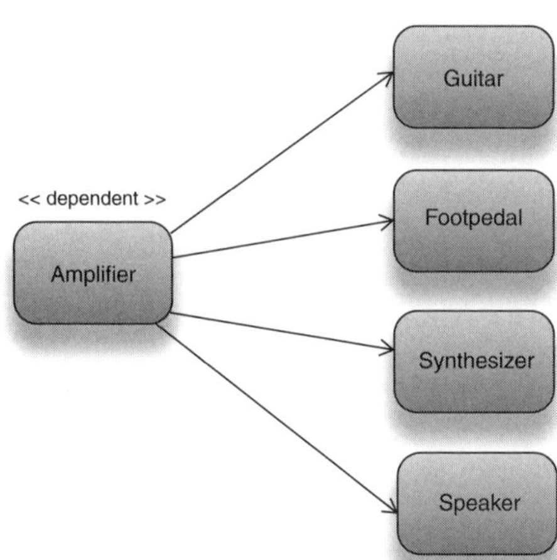

Figure 3.3 Class model of the amplifier and its four dependencies

As with constructor injection, DI libraries diverge slightly in how they are configured to handle setter injection. In Spring parlance, a setter directly refers to a property on the object and is set via the `<property>` XML element, as in listing 3.2.

Listing 3.2 Spring XML configuration for setter injection of `Amplifier`

```
<beans ...>

    <bean id="amplifier" class="stereo.Amplifier">
        <property name="guitar" ref="guitar"/>
        <property name="speaker" ref="speaker"/>
        <property name="footpedal" ref="footpedal"/>
```

```
        <property name="synthesizer" ref="synthesizer"/>
    </bean>

    <bean id="guitar" class="equipment.Guitar"/>

    <bean id="speaker" class="equipment.Speaker"/>

    <bean id="footpedal" class="equipment.Footpedal"/>

    <bean id="synthesizer" class="equipment.Synthesizer"/>

</beans>
```

Here we have declared four <property> tags under bean amplifier that refer (via the ref=".." attribute) to dependencies of Amplifier. Spring knows which setter method we are talking about by matching the name=".." attribute of the <property> tag to the setter method's name (minus the set prefix). So, name="guitar" refers to setGuitar(), name="speaker" to setSpeaker(), and so on. In listing 3.3, we can use encapsulation for a more compact configuration.

Listing 3.3 The same Spring configuration, now with encapsulation

```
<beans ...>

    <bean id="amplifier" class="stereo.Amplifier">
        <property name="guitar">
            <bean class="equipment.Guitar"/>
        </property>

        <property name="speaker">
            <bean class="equipment.Speaker"/>
        </property>

        <property name="footpedal">
            <bean class="equipment.Footpedal"/>
        </property>

        <property name="synthesizer">
            <bean class="equipment.Synthesizer"/>
        </property>
    </bean>

</beans>
```

The elements in bold are encapsulated within <property> declarations. Nothing changes with the code itself. Dependencies are created and wired to the graph when the key amplifier is requested from Spring's injector.

NOTE The order in which these setters are called usually matches the order of the <property> tags. This ordering is unique to the XML configuration mechanism and is not available with autowiring.

As an alternative, listing 3.4 shows what the Guice version of Amplifier would look like.

Listing 3.4 A stereo amplifier wired by setter (using Guice)

```
import com.google.inject.Inject;

public class Amplifier {
    private Guitar guitar;
```

```
    private Speaker speaker;
    private Footpedal footpedal;
    private Synthesizer synthesizer;

    @Inject
    public void setGuitar(Guitar guitar) {
        this.guitar = guitar;
    }

    @Inject
    public void setSpeaker(Speaker speaker) {
        this.speaker = speaker;
    }

    @Inject
    public void setFootpedal(Footpedal footpedal) {
        this.footpedal = footpedal;
    }

    @Inject
    public void setSynthesizer(Synthesizer synthesizer) {
        this.synthesizer = synthesizer;
    }
}
```

The main difference is annotating each setter with `@Inject`.

NOTE The order in which these setters are called is undefined, unlike with Spring's XML configuration.

But one nice thing is that you do not need the setter naming convention in Guice, so you can rewrite this class in a more compact way. Listing 3.5 shows that I have replaced the four separate setters with just one taking four arguments.

Listing 3.5 Compact setter injection (in Java, using Guice)

```
public class Amplifier {
    private Guitar guitar;
    private Speaker speaker;
    private Footpedal footpedal;
    private Synthesizer synthesizer;

    @Inject
    public void set(Guitar guitar, Speaker speaker, Footpedal footpedal,
              Synthesizer synthesizer) {
        this.guitar = guitar;
        this.speaker = speaker;
        this.footpedal = footpedal;
        this.synthesizer = synthesizer;
    }
}
```

Notice that this new setter looks very much like a constructor:

- It returns nothing.
- It accepts a bunch of dependencies.
- It is called only once when the object is created by the injector.

Guice does not place any restrictions on the name or visibility of setters either. So you can hide them from accidental misuse and even give them meaningful names:

```
@Inject
void prepareAmp(Guitar guitar, Speaker speaker, Footpedal footpedal,
           Synthesizer synthesizer) {
    this.guitar = guitar;
    this.speaker = speaker;
    this.footpedal = footpedal;
    this.synthesizer = synthesizer;
}
```

Much nicer, indeed.

Setter injection is easily the most common idiom in use. Many examples and tutorials use setter injection without explaining it or saying why it ought to be used. In fact, setter injection is quite a flexible option and can be very convenient in particular cases. It certainly has a place in the DI spectrum. Yet, it is not an entirely satisfactory situation. A method whose sole purpose is accepting a dependency seems awkward. Worse still, if one is required for each dependency (as in Spring), the number of setters can quickly get out of hand.

This problem is mitigated by the fact that setters are rarely exposed to client code (via interfaces or public classes, for example). Hiding setters makes them less of a danger to abuse. If they are only used by the injector (or by unit tests), there is less risk of objects becoming intertwined.

There are quite a few subtleties (some of the sledgehammer variety!) to deciding when setter injection is appropriate. We will look at them in some detail very shortly. But before that we'll look at some other forms of injection that are less common. Interface injection, in the following section, predates the more-familiar forms. Though it has fallen out of use of late, it's well worth our time to investigate this design idiom.

3.1.3 Interface injection

Interface injection is the idea that an object takes on an *injectable* role itself. In other words, objects receive their dependencies via methods declared in interfaces. In a sense, interface injection is the same as setter injection except that each setter is housed in its own interface. Here's a quick example (listing 3.6).

Listing 3.6 Phaser mounted on a starship via interface wiring

```
public class Starship implements PhaserMountable {
    private Phaser phaser;

    public void mount(Phaser phaser) {        <- This method is called by the injector
        this.phaser = phaser;
    }
}

public interface PhaserMountable {            <- Interface solely for wiring Phasers to dependents
    void mount(Phaser phaser);
}
```

Starship is a kind of PhaserMountable (it *implements* PhaserMountable), which is an interface we've made up solely for the purpose of wiring phasers and starships together. If you wanted to add more dependencies to a starship, you would similarly have to create a *role interface* for each such dependency. Listing 3.7 shows how adding just two more dependencies, a *reactor* and *shuttlecraft*, alters our code.

Listing 3.7 Various dependencies of a starship via interface wiring

```
public class Starship implements PhaserMountable, ReactorMountable,
ShuttleDockable {
    private Phaser phaser;
    private Reactor reactor;
    private Shuttle shuttle;

    public void mount(Phaser phaser) {
        this.phaser = phaser;
    }

    public void mount(Reactor reactor) {
        this.reactor = reactor;
    }

    public void dock(Shuttle shuttle) {
        this.shuttle = shuttle;
    }
}

public interface PhaserMountable {
    void mount(Phaser phaser);
}

public interface ReactorMountable {
    void mount(Reactor reactor);
}

public interface ShuttleDockable {
    void dock(Shuttle shuttle);
}
```

New role interfaces for each additional dependency

The way in which these role interfaces are used by the injector is not a whole lot different from what we saw in some of the other idioms. The now-defunct Apache Avalon framework is the only real exponent of interface injection worth mentioning.

Role interfaces can be used not only to wire dependencies to objects but also to notify them of particular events, such as *initialize, pause, destroy*, and so forth. It is not uncommon for objects managed by interface injection to expose a battery of such interfaces. Listing 3.8 shows a rocket ship that exposes many such roles.

Listing 3.8 A rocket ship with many role interfaces

```
public class Rocket implements EngineMountable, Loadable, Startable,
 Stoppable {
    private Engine engine;
    private Cargo cargo;

    public void mount(Engine engine) {
```

Interface injection methods

```
        this.engine = engine;
    }
                                             Interface injection
    public void load(Cargo cargo) {      <-- methods
        this.cargo = cargo;
    }

    public void start() {                <--
        //start this rocket's engine...     Methods for other
    }                                       infrastructure roles

    public void stop() {                 <--
        //stop this rocket...
    }
}
```

One advantage of interface injection is that you can name the methods-accepting dependencies whatever you want. This gives you the opportunity to use natural, purpose-specific names that are concise and self-explanatory. The method `load(Cargo)` is more intuitive than, say, `setCargo(Cargo)`.

The disadvantages of interface injection are quite obvious. It is extremely verbose. Creating a new interface for each dependency is rather wasteful, and the long string of implemented interfaces following the class definition isn't exactly pretty. These interfaces clutter the class signature and distract attention from other interfaces you may be more interested in. Practically speaking, the fact that the defunct Apache Avalon is the only DI library that offers interface injection also makes it a less-than-attractive option. It is largely an idiom that has gone out of style for these reasons.

As we will see later, some of the ideas behind interface injection form the basis of important design patterns and solutions to several knotty design problems. Another lesser-known injection idiom is *method decoration*, sometimes called *AOP injection*. This form is useful in certain very specific cases and is naturally not very common. However, it may be indispensable for solving particular types of problems, as you will see in the following section.

3.1.4 Method decoration (or AOP injection)

Method decoration is an interesting variation on dependency injection. Method decoration takes the approach that methods rather than objects are the target of injection. This generally means that when they are called, these methods return an injector-provided value instead of their normal value. This requires a fundamental redefinition of a method's behavior and is generally done via some form of *interception*. More often that not, an AOP framework supplies the means of interception. We will look in much greater detail at interception and AOP in chapter 8.

This process is called *decorating* the method and gets its name from the Decorator[1] design pattern.

[1] Decorator design pattern, from *Design Patterns: Elements of Reusable Object-Oriented Software* by Erich Gamma et al. (Addison-Wesley Professional Computing Series, 1994). Sometimes called the "Gang of Four" book.

It is useful if you want to make a Factory out of an *arbitrary method* on your object. The use cases for this are somewhat rare. But it can be a very powerful design pattern if applied correctly. Here's an example:

```
package candy;

public class Dispenser {

    public Pez dispense() {
        return ...;            <-- Dispenses new Pez each time
    }
}

public class Pez { .. }
```

What we're after is for the `dispense()` method to be a Factory for `Pez`. Since we would like `Pez` to be created and wired by the injector, it isn't enough just to manually construct and return an instance:

```
public class Dispenser {

    public Pez dispense() {
        return new Pez(..);        <-- Does not inject Pez correctly
    }
}
```

Clearly we need to bring the injector in, so `Pez`'s dependencies can be correctly wired. One solution is to inject dependencies of `Pez` into `Dispenser` itself, then wire them up manually each time `dispense()` is called:

```
public class Dispenser {
    private Sugar sugar;          <-- Provided by injection

    public Pez dispense() {
        return new Pez(sugar);        <-- Pez is now correctly wired
    }
}
```

This solution looks like it works (at least it compiles and runs), but it doesn't quite give us what we're after:

- The same instance of `Sugar` is wired to every new `Pez`, so we have just moved the problem away one level, not solved it. What we want is *new* `Sugar` for *new* `Pez`.
- `Dispenser` must know how to construct `Pez` and consequently is *tightly coupled* to its internals.
- `Dispenser` is unnecessarily cluttered with `Pez`'s dependencies.

All this looks like we're not putting the injector to full use. So how do we get there? Method decoration provides a compelling solution. To explain how this works, let's rewind to the original example:

```
package candy;

public class Dispenser {

    public Pez dispense() {
```

```
        return ...;      <-- What goes here?
    }
}

public class Pez { .. }
```

Now, in order to make this class legal, we will write a *dummy* implementation of `dispense()`. This implementation does nothing and returns `null` with the understanding that it should never be called or used directly:

```
    public Pez dispense() {
        return null;
    }
```

Now we can proceed to configuring the injector. In listing 3.9 I use Spring to demonstrate.

Listing 3.9 Pez and Dispenser configuration (using Spring), pez.xml

```
<beans ...>
    <bean id="pez" class="candy.Pez">
        <constructor-arg><bean class="candy.Sugar"/></constructor-arg>
    </bean>

    <bean id="dispenser" class="candy.Dispenser"/>
</beans>
```

In listing 3.10, I have configured the injector to construct, assemble, and provide instances of `Pez` and `Dispenser`. However, we're not quite there yet.

Listing 3.10 Pez dispensed with method decoration (using Spring), pez.xml

```
<beans ...>
    <bean id="pez" class="candy.Pez">
        <constructor-arg><bean class="candy.Sugar"/></constructor-arg>
    </bean>

    <bean id="dispenser" class="candy.Dispenser">
        <lookup-method name="dispense" bean="pez"/>
    </bean>
</beans>
```

In listing 3.10, the `<lookup-method>` tag tells Spring to intercept `dispense()` and treat it as a Factory and that it should return object graphs bound to key `pez` when called. Now when we bootstrap and use the injector, we can use `dispense()` to get some candy!

```
BeanFactory injector = new FileSystemXmlApplicationContext("pez.xml");
Dispenser dispenser = (Dispenser) injector.getBean("dispenser");
Pez candy1 = dispenser.dispense();
...
```

For a more detailed look at where method decoration is useful, browse down to the "The Reinjection Problem." Like any powerful DI feature, method decoration is fraught with pitfalls and corner cases. Some of them, particularly regarding method interception, are examined in chapter 8. Carefully consider all of these issues before settling on method decoration as your choice of injection idiom.

Field injection

Guice provides the rather obvious but often-overlooked facility to wire dependencies *directly* into fields of objects (bypassing constructors or setters). This is often useful in writing small test cases or scratch code, and it is particularly so in tutorial and example code where space is limited and meaning must be conveyed in the least-possible number of lines. Consider this rather trivial example:

```
public class BrewingVat {
    @Inject Barley barley;
    @Inject Yeast yeast;

    public Beer brew() {
        //make some beer from ingredients
        ...
    }
}
```

Annotating fields `barley` and `yeast` with `@Inject` tells the injector to wire dependencies directly to them when `BrewingVat` is requested. This happens after the class's constructor has completed and before any annotated setters are called for setter injection. This syntax is compact and easy to read at a glance. However, it is fraught with problems when you consider anything more than the simplest of cases.

Without the ability to set dependencies (whether mocked or real) for testing, unit tests cannot be relied on to indicate the validity of code. It is also not possible to declare field-injected fields immutable, since they are set post construction. So, while field injection is nice and compact (and often good for examples), it has little worth in practice.

With so many options, how do you know what the right choice is?

3.2 Choosing an injection idiom

Well, interface injection is largely unsupported, and we've seen that it is rather verbose and unwieldy, so we can rule it out. Method decoration seems to be something of a corner-case solution, though I maintain that it has its place. That leaves us with constructor and setter injection, which are by far the most dominant forms of the idiom in use today.

The answer to the question of which idiom is the right choice is not simply one of taste, as I have said before. This is a point I can't emphasize too much—there are such important consequences to either choice that potentially lead to difficult, underperformant, and even broken applications. Some of this has to do with objects used in multithreaded environments. Some of it is about testing and maintainability. So you must take special care before choosing an injection idiom. It is well worth the time and effort up front, to avoid intractable problems later. The rest of this chapter is about such problems and how to go about solving them.

3.2.1 Constructor vs. setter injection

The merits and demerits of constructor and setter injection are the same as those for setting *fields* by constructor or setter.

An important practice regards the *state* of fields once set. In most cases we want fields to be set once (at the time the object is created) and never modified again. This means not only that the dependent can rely on its dependencies throughout its life but also that they are ready for use right away. Such fields are said to be *immutable.* If you think of private member variables as a *spatial* form of encapsulation, then immutability is a form of *temporal encapsulation,* that is, unchanging with respect to time. With respect to dependency injection, this can be thought of as *freezing* a completely formed object graph.

Constructor injection affords us the ability to create immutable dependencies by declaring fields as final (modeled in figure 3.4):

```
public class Atlas {
    private final Earth earthOnBack;

    public Atlas(Earth earth) {
         this.earthOnBack = earth;
     }
}
```

Atlas stands today as he did at the time of his (and the earth's) creation, with a fixed, *immutable* earthOnBack. Any attempt, whether accidental or deliberate, to alter field earthOnBack will simply not compile (see listing 3.11). This is a very useful feature because it gives us a strong assurance about the state of an object and means that an object is a *good citizen.*

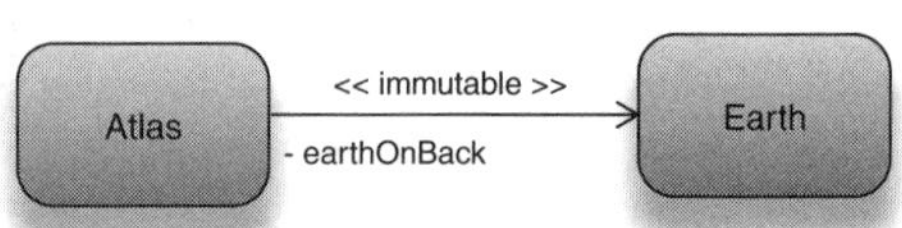

Figure 3.4 Atlas depends on Earth and cannot be changed once wired.

Listing 3.11 An object with immutable fields cannot be modified, once set

```
public class Atlas {
    private final Earth earth;

    public Atlas(Earth earth) {
         this.earth = earth;
        this.earth = null;        <-- Raises a compile error
     }

    public void reset() {
        earth = new Earth();      <-- Raises a compile error
    }
}
```

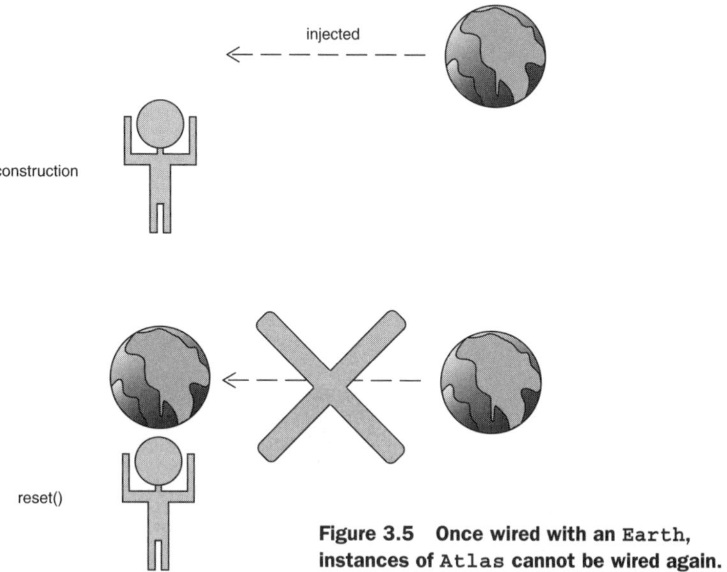

Figure 3.5 Once wired with an `Earth`, instances of `Atlas` cannot be wired again.

Visualize listing 3.11's mutability problem in figure 3.5.

Immutability is essential in application programming. Unfortunately, it is not available using setter injection. Because setter methods are no different from ordinary methods, a compiler can make no guarantees about the *one-call-per-instance* restriction that is needed to ensure field immutability. So score one for constructor injection; it leverages immutability while setter injection can't.

What else can we say about their differences? Plenty: dependencies wired by constructor mean they are wired at the time of the object's creation. The fact that all dependences are wired and that the dependent is ready for use immediately upon construction is a very compelling one. It leads us to the notion of creating *valid* objects that are good citizens. Were a dependency not available (either in a unit test or due to faulty configuration), an early compile error would result. No field can refer to *half-constructed* dependencies. Moreover, a constructor-injected object cannot be created unless *all* dependencies are available. With setter injection such mistakes are easy to make, as shown in listing 3.12 and illustrated in figure 3.6.

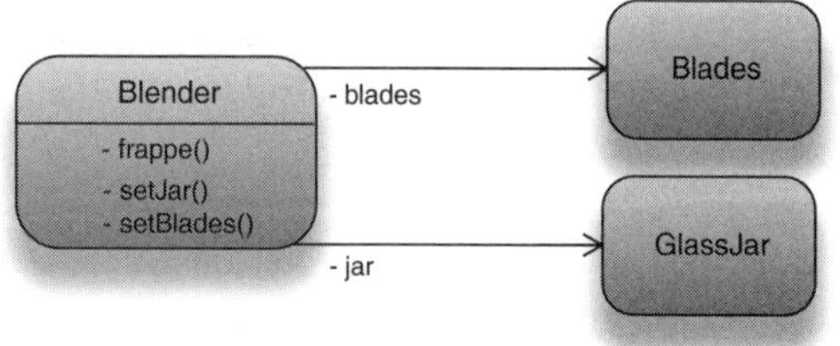

Figure 3.6 `Blender` is setter injected with `Blades` and `GlassJar` (see listing 3.12).

Listing 3.12 Improperly setter-injected object graph (using Guice)

```
public class Blender {
    private GlassJar jar;        <— Wired correctly
    private Blades blades;
```

```
    @Inject
    public void setJar(GlassJar jar) {
        this.jar = jar;
     }

    public void setBlades(Blades blades) {     <-- Oops, missing an @Inject
        this.blades = blades;
    }

    public void frappe() {
        jar.fillWithOranges();
        blades.run();          <-- Exception raised
    }
}
```

A faulty configuration causes much heartache, since it compiles properly and everything *appears* normal. The program in listing 3.12 runs fine until it hits `blades.run()`, which fails by raising a `NullPointerException` since there is no object referenced by field `blades` because it was never set by the injector. Figure 3.7 illustrates the problem.

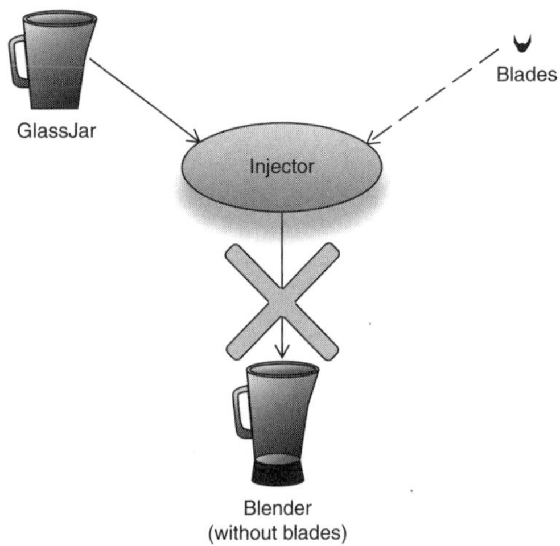

Figure 3.7 `Blender` is incompletely wired, an inadvertent side effect of setter injection.

So let's say you found and fixed the injector configuration (after a bit of pain). Does everything work properly now? No, because you could still encounter this problem in a unit test where dependencies are set manually (without an injector present), as this foolish test of the `Blender` from listing 3.12 does:

```
public class BlenderTest {

    @Test
    public void blendOranges() {
        new Blender().frappe();

        //assert something
     }
}
```

The writer of this test has forgotten to call the appropriate setter methods and prepare the `Blender` correctly before using it. It results in a false negative; that is, an unexpected `NullPointerException` is raised, indicating a test failure when nothing is wrong with `Blender`'s code as such. The reported error is caught only at runtime and isn't particularly intuitive in defining the problem. Worse, you may need to read through a fair thicket of execution traces before discovering the cause of the problem. This exists only with setter injection, since any test with unset dependencies in a constructor won't compile. Score two for constructor injection.

Another problem with setters, as we have already seen, is that their number can very quickly get out of hand. If you have several dependencies, a setter for each dependency can result in a cluttered class with an enormous amount of repetitive code.

On the other hand, the explicitness of setter injection can itself be an advantage. Constructors that take several arguments are difficult to read. Multiple arguments of the same type can also be confusing since the only thing distinguishing them is the order in which they appear, particularly so if you use an IDE like IntelliJ IDEA to generate constructors automatically. For instance, consider the following class wired by constructor:

```
public class Spy {
    private String realName;
    private String britishAlias;
    private String americanAlias;

        public Spy(String name1, String name2, String name3, ...) { .. }
}
```

It is rather difficult to follow how to wire this object. The smallest spelling or ordering mistake could result in an erroneous object graph that goes *completely* undetected (since everything is a `String`). This is a particularly good example because there is no easy way to validate that dependencies have not gotten crossed:

```
new Spy("John Doe", "James Bond", "Don Joe");
```

Everything looks all right, but my `Spy`'s British alias was really `Don Joe` and not the other way around. With setter injection, however, this is clear and explicit (the following example is in Java using setters):

```
Spy spy = new Spy();

spy.setRealName("John Doe");
spy.setBritishAlias("James Bond");
spy.setAmericanAlias("Don Joe");
```

So when you have large numbers of dependencies of the same type, setter injection seems more palatable. This is particularly true for unit tests, which are an important companion to any service and which inject dependencies manually. You'll find more on unit testing and dependency injection in chapter 4. Chalk up a victory for setter injection. One additional problem with constructor injection is that when you have different object graph permutations, the number of constructors can get out of hand very quickly. This is called the *constructor pyramid* problem, and the following section takes an in-depth look at it.

3.2.2 The constructor pyramid problem

Constructor injection also runs into trouble when dealing with objects that are injected differently in different scenarios. Each of these scenarios is like a different *profile* of the object. Listing 3.13 shows the example of an amphibian that has different dependencies when on land than on water.

Listing 3.13 An amphibian can live on land or in water

```
public class Amphibian {
    private Gills gills;
    private Lungs lungs;
    private Heart heart;

    public Amphibian(Heart heart, Gills gills) {      <-- Constructor for life in water
        this.heart = heart;
        this.gills = gills;
    }

    public Amphibian(Heart heart, Lungs lungs) {      <-- Constructor for life on land
        this.heart = heart;
        this.lungs = lungs;
    }

    ...
}
```

When we want a water Amphibian, we construct one with a Heart and Gills. On land, this same Amphibian has a different set of dependencies, mutually exclusive with the water variety (a pair of Lungs). Heart is a common dependency of both Amphibian profiles. The two profiles are modeled in figures 3.8 and 3.9.

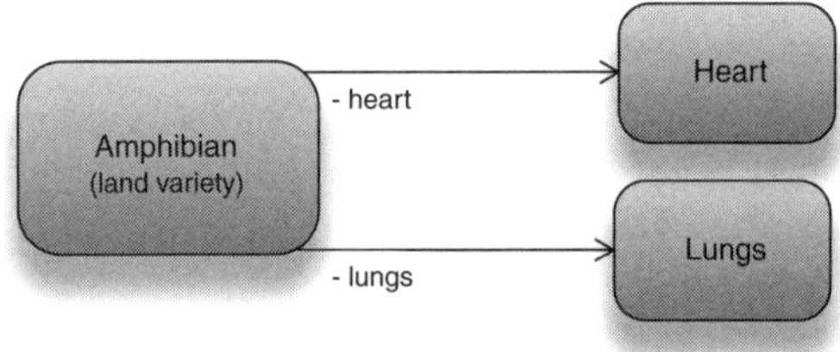

Figure 3.8 The land-dwelling variety of Amphibian depends on a Heart and Lungs.

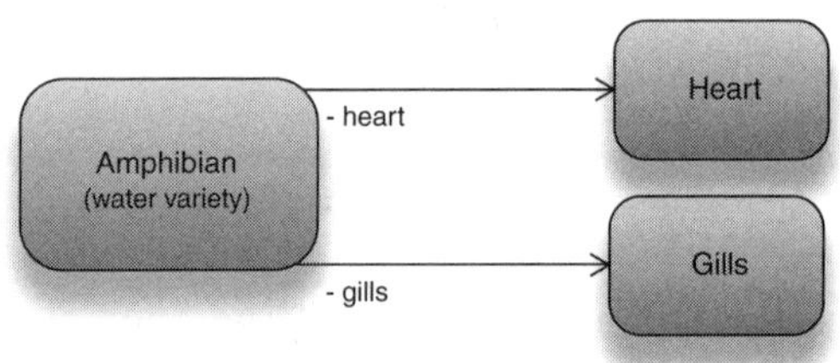

Figure 3.9 The aquatic variety of Amphibian depends on a Heart and Gills.

Ignore for a moment that real amphibians can transition from land to water. Here we require two *mutually exclusive* constructors that match either profile but not both (as listing 3.13 shows). Were you to require more such profiles, there would be more constructors, one for each case. All these constructors differ by is the type of argument they take; unlike setters, they can't have different names. This makes them hard to read and to distinguish from one another. Where an object requires only a partial set of dependencies, additional, smaller constructors need to be written, further adding to the confusion. This issue is called the constructor pyramid problem, because the collection of constructors resembles a rising pyramid. On the other hand, with setters, you can wire any permutation of an object's dependencies without writing any additional code. Score another for setter injection.

Having said all of this, however, the use cases where you require multiple profiles of an object are rare and probably found only in legacy or sealed third-party code. If you find yourself encountering the pyramid problem often, you should ask serious questions about your design before pronouncing setter injection as a mitigant. Another problem when using only constructors is how you connect objects that are dependent on the same instance of each other. This chicken-and-egg problem, though rare, is a serious flaw in constructor injection and is called the *circular reference* problem.

3.2.3 The circular reference problem

Sometimes you run into a case where two objects are dependent on each other. Figure 3.10 shows one such relationship.

Any *symbiotic* relationship between two components embodies this scenario. Parent/child relationships are typical manifestations. One example is shown in listing 3.14.

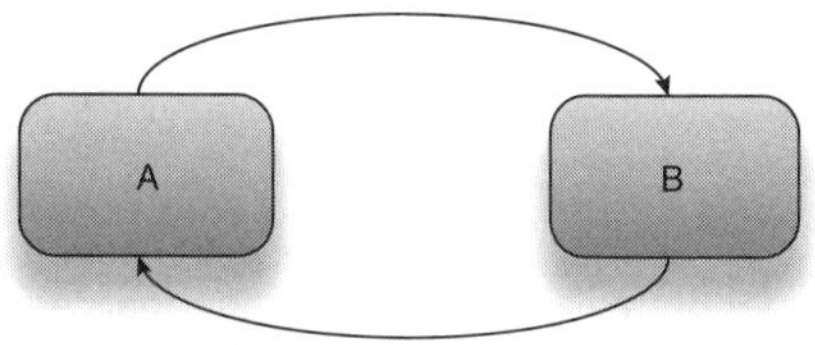

Figure 3.10 A and B are dependent on each other (circular dependency).

Listing 3.14 A host and symbiote interdependency

```
public class Host {
    private final Symbiote symbiote;

    public Host(Symbiote symbiote) {
        this.symbiote = symbiote;
    }
}

public class Symbiote {
    private final Host host;

    public Symbiote(Host host) {
        this.host = host;
    }
}
```

In listing 3.14 both `Host` and `Symbiote` refer to the same instances of each other. `Host` refers to `Symbiote`, which refers back to `Host` in a circle (as described in figure 3.11).

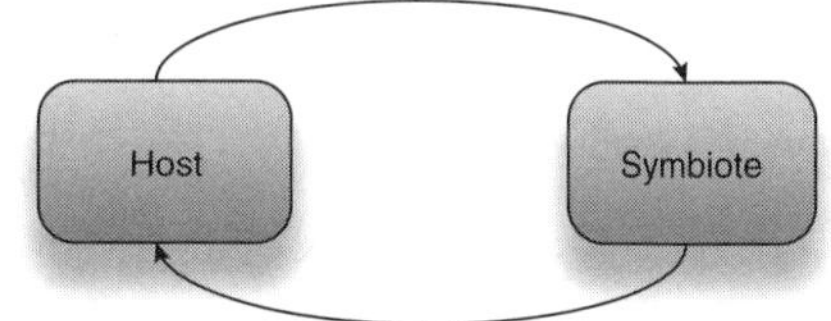

Figure 3.11 `Host` and `Symbiote` are circularly interdependent.

Syntactically, there is no conceivable way to construct these objects so that circularity is satisfied with constructor wiring alone. If you decide to construct `Host` first, it requires a `Symbiote` as dependency to be valid. So you are forced to construct `Symbiote` first; however, the same issue resides with `Symbiote`—#@$! Its only constructor requires a `Host`.

This classic chicken-and-egg scenario is called the circular reference problem.

There is also no easy way to configure an injector to solve the circular reference problem, at least not with the patterns we've examined thus far. You can also imagine indirect circular references where object `A` refers to `B`, which refers to `C`, which itself refers back to `A` (as illustrated in figure 3.12).

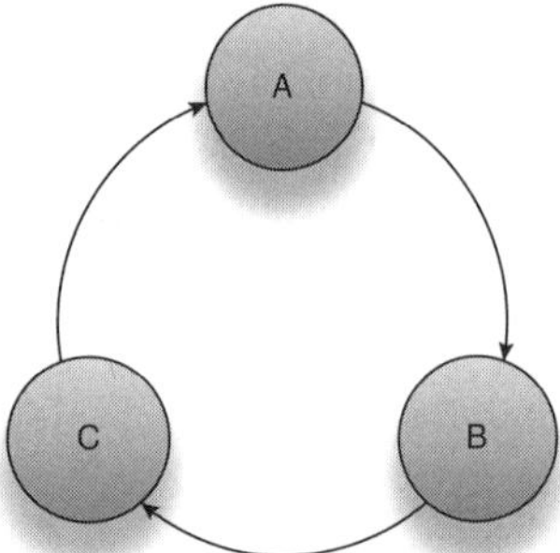

Figure 3.12 Triangular circularity: A depends on B, which depends on C, which depends on A.

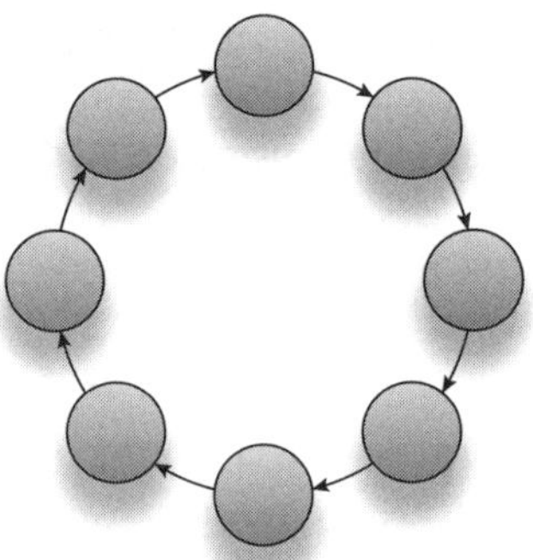

Figure 3.13 Any number of objects may be part of a circular dependency.

In fact, this triangular flavor of circular references is the one more commonly seen. There is no reason why we should stop at three, either. Any number of objects can be added to the circle, and so long as two end points connect, there is no clear strategy for which object to instantiate first. It is the old problem of finding the *beginning* of a cycle (figure 3.13).

The circular reference problem has two compelling solutions that fall, like everything else, between the camps of setter and constructor injection. The first and most obvious solution is simply to switch to setter injection. For our purposes, I'll examine the two-object variety of the circular reference problem (though the same solution is equally applicable to other cases) in listing 3.15.

Listing 3.15 A host and symbiote interdependency with setter injection

```
package example;

public class Host {
    private Symbiote symbiote;

    public void setSymbiote(Symbiote symbiote) {
        this.symbiote = symbiote;
    }
}

public class Symbiote {
    private Host host;

    public void setHost(Host host) {
        this.host = host;
    }
}
```

Then, configuring the injector is straightforward (via setter injection, in Spring):

```
<beans ...>
    <bean id="host" class="example.Host">
        <property name="symbiote" ref="symbiote"/>
    </bean>
```

```
    <bean id="symbiote" class="example.Symbiote">
        <property name="host" ref="host"/>
    </bean>
</beans>
```

Now the circularity is satisfied. When the injector starts up, both `host` and `symbiote` object graphs are constructed via their *nullary* (zero-argument) constructors and then wired by setter to reference each other. Easy enough. Unfortunately there are a couple of serious drawbacks with this choice. The most obvious one is that we can no longer declare either dependency as `final`. So, this solution is less than ideal.

Now let's look at the constructor injection alternative. We already know that we can't directly use constructor wiring to make circular referents point to one another. What alternative is available under these restrictions? One solution that comes to mind is to break the circularity without affecting the *overall* semantic of interdependence. You achieve this by introducing a *proxy*. First let's decouple `Host` and `Symbiote` with interfaces (see listing 3.16).

Listing 3.16 A host and symbiote interdependency, decoupled to use interfaces

```
public interface Host { .. }

public interface Symbiote { .. }

public class HostImpl implements Host {          <-- HostImpl refers to interface Symbiote
    private final Symbiote symbiote;

    public HostImpl(Symbiote symbiote) {
        this.symbiote = symbiote;
    }
}

public class SymbioteImpl implements Symbiote {  <-- SymbioteImpl refers to interface Host
    private final Host host;

    public SymbioteImpl(Host host) {
        this.host = host;
    }
}
```

The class diagram now looks like figure 3.14.

The dependencies of `HostImpl` and `SymbioteImpl` are now on a contract (interface) of each other, rather than a *concrete class*. This is where the proxy comes in:

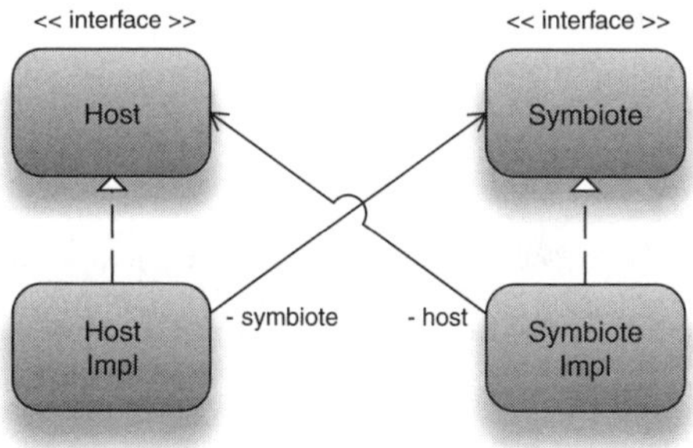

Figure 3.14 A class model for decoupled `Host` and `Symbiote` services (see listing 3.16)

```
public class HostProxy implements Host {
    private Host delegate;

    public void setDelegate(Host delegate) {      <-- HostProxy wired with a Host
        this.delegate = delegate;
    }
}
```

HostProxy, the intermediary, is wired with setter injection allowing HostImpl and SymbioteImpl (the "real" implementations) to declare their fields immutable and use constructor injection. To complete the wiring now, we use the following construction order:

1. Construct HostProxy.
2. Construct SymbioteImpl with the instance of HostProxy (from step 1).
3. Construct HostImpl and wire it with the SymbioteImpl that refers to HostProxy (from step 2).
4. Wire HostProxy to *delegate* HostImpl (from step 3) via setter injection.

Did that do it for us? Indeed—the Host instance now refers to a Symbiote instance that itself holds a reference to the HostProxy. When the SymbioteImpl instance calls any methods on its dependency host, these calls go to HostProxy, which transparently passes them to its delegate, HostImpl. Since HostImpl contains a direct reference to its counterpart SymbioteImpl, the circularity is satisfied, and all is well with the world. Injector configuration for this is shown in listing 3.17.

Listing 3.17 Circular references wired via a proxy (using Spring)

```
<beans>
    <bean id="hostProxy" class="example.HostProxy">
        <property name="delegate" ref="host"/>
    </bean>

    <bean id="host" class="example.HostImpl">
        <constructor-arg ref="symbiote"/>
    </bean>

    <bean id="symbiote" class="example.SymbioteImpl">
        <constructor-arg ref="hostProxy"/>
    </bean>
</beans>
```

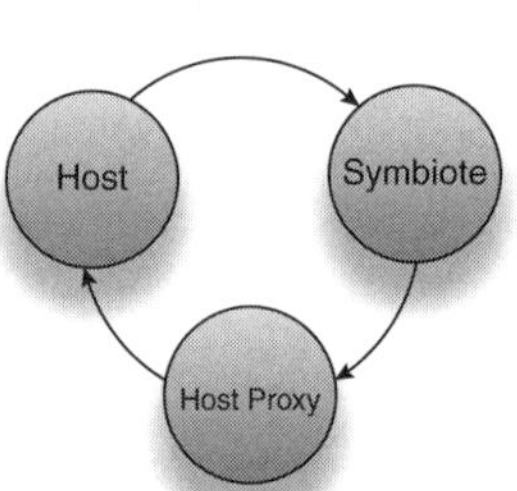

Figure 3.15 Injecting circular referents via a proxy

Figure 3.15 illustrates the solution.

Guice offers a transparent mitigation of this problem (illustrated in figure 3.16). All you need do is configure the injector and bind the relevant keys to one another:

```
public class CircularModule extends AbstractModule {

    @Override
    public void configure() {
        bind(Host.class).to(HostImpl.class).in(Singleton.class);
        bind(Symbiote.class).to(SymbioteImpl.class).in(Singleton.class);

    }
}
```

The Guice injector automatically provides the proxy in the middle. We can also trust the injector to work out the correct order of construction. We don't deal directly with proxies or setter injection or any other infrastructure concern. If you are like me, you find this feature of Guice particularly useful where circular references are warranted. A particular variant of the circular reference problem is the *in-construction* problem. In this scenario, it's impossible to break the cycle even with a proxy. We examine the in-construction problem in the following section.

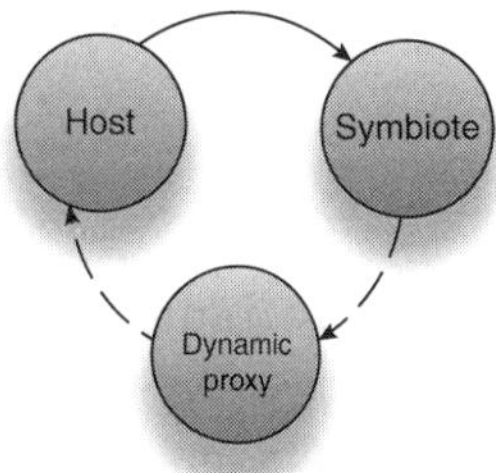

Figure 3.16 Injecting circular referents in Guice with a dynamic proxy

3.2.4 The in-construction problem

Earlier, when describing constructor injection, we said that one of the purposes of a constructor was to "perform some initialization logic" on an object. This may be as simple as setting dependencies on fields or may involve some specific computation needed in order to prepare the object (for example, setting a window's title). The constructor is a good place to put this because you can guarantee that any such logic is run prior to the object being used anywhere. If this computation is expensive, it is worthwhile performing it up front so you don't encumber the object later on.

One close relative of the circular reference problem (section 3.2.3) is where initialization logic requires a dependency that is not yet ready for use. What this typically means is that a circular reference was solved with a proxy, which has not yet been wired with its delegate (recall the four steps to resolving circular references with a proxy, from the previous section). Listing 3.18 illustrates this scenario.

Listing 3.18 Proxy solution inadequate for in-constructor use (using Guice)

```
public interface Host { .. }

public interface Symbiote { .. }

public class HostImpl implements Host {
    private final Symbiote symbiote;

    @Inject
    public HostImpl(Symbiote symbiote) {
        this.symbiote = symbiote;
    }

public int calculateAge() {
// figure out age
}
}

public class SymbioteImpl implements Symbiote {
    private final Host host;
    private final int hostAge;                    <-- Derived property computed on initialization

    @Inject
    public SymbioteImpl(Host host) {
```

```
        this.host = host;
                                                    Computation
        this.hostAge = host.calculateAge();   <-    will fail
    }
}
```

In listing 3.18, both dependents in the circle attempt to use each other within their constructors. One calls a method on the other and is doomed to fail. Since `Host` has been proxied but does not yet hold a valid reference to its delegate, it has no way of passing through calls to the dependency. This is the *in-construction* problem in a nutshell.

Circular references in nature (symbiosis)

Symbiotes in nature are organisms that live in biological dependence on one another. This is a more closely linked relationship than a parent and child. Symbiotes typically cannot survive without their partners. Here are some interesting examples of circular interdependence in nature:

Coral reefs are a symbiosis between coral and various algae that live communally. The algae photosynthesize and excrete food for the coral, which in turn protect and provide a place to live for the algae.

Siboglinid tube worms have no digestive tract. Instead, bacteria that live inside them break down their food into nutrients. In turn, the worms prove the bacteria with a home and a constant supply of food. These fascinating worms were discovered living in hydrothermal vents in the ground.

Several herbivorous animals (plant eaters) have gut fauna living in their stomachs, which help break down plant matter. Plant matter is inherently more difficult to digest because of the thick cell walls plants possess. Like the tube worms, these animals house and provide food for their symbiotes.

The in-construction problem has no obvious solution with constructor injection. The only recourse in such cases is setter injection, as shown in listing 3.19.

Listing 3.19 In-construction problem solved via setter injection (using Guice)

```
public interface Host { .. }

public interface Symbiote { .. }

public class HostImpl implements Host {
    private Symbiote symbiote;

    @Inject
    public void setSymbiote(Symbiote symbiote) {
        this.symbiote = symbiote;
    }

public int calculateAge() {
// figure out age
}
```

```
}

public class SymbioteImpl implements Symbiote {
    private Host host;
    private int hostAge;

    @Inject
    public void setHost(Host host) {
        this.host = host;

        this.hostAge = host.calculateAge();      <-- Initialization logic now works
    }
}
```

Now initialization is guaranteed to succeed because both objects hold references to each other prior to any call to `host.calculateAge()`. This is not the whole story—the in-construction problem can run even deeper. Consider listing 3.20's addendum, which exacerbates the problem.

Listing 3.20 In-construction problem not quite solved

```
public interface Host { .. }

public interface Symbiote { .. }

public class HostImpl implements Host {
    private Symbiote symbiote;
    private int symbioteAge;

    @Inject
    public void setSymbiote(Symbiote symbiote) {
        this.symbiote = symbiote;

        this.symbioteAge = symbiote.calculateAge();      <-- New initialization logic
    }

    ...
}

public class SymbioteImpl implements Symbiote {
    private Host host;
    private int hostAge;

    @Inject
    public void setHost(Host host) {
        this.host = host;

        this.hostAge = host.calculateAge();
    }

    ...
}
```

Now both objects not only *refer* to one another but also *use* each other when dependencies are being wired. Essentially, this is an in-construction *variation* of the circular reference problem. And there is no known solution to this circular initialization mess with constructor injection. In fact, there is no solution to the problem with setter injection either!

More important, this is not really a wiring problem. The issue is with putting objects into a usable *state*. While constructors are the traditional pack mule for this sort of work, they don't quite work in this case. If you find yourself encountering this problem, you are probably better off using lifecycle as a solution. See chapter 7 for an exploration of object lifecycle. Thus far, we've outlined many of the problems with using constructor injection. While many of them are rare, they are nonetheless troubling. Now let's take a look at some of the benefits that really make constructor injection worthwhile.

3.2.5 Constructor injection and object validity

So far, we've talked about several benefits of constructor injection. None are perhaps as significant as *object validity*. Knowing if an object is properly constructed is one of the most overlooked design issues in OOP. Simply having a reference to it is insufficient. Dependencies may not be set, initialization logic may not have run yet, and so on. Even if all this has been achieved in one thread, other participating threads may not agree.

Consider the class in listing 3.21.

Listing 3.21 A class allowing too many unsafe modes of injection

```
public class UnsafeObject {
    private Slippery slippery;        | Dependencies
    private Shady shady;              | wired by setter     | Nullary constructor
                                                           | does nothing
    public UnsafeObject() { }                         <----

    public void setSlippery(Slippery slippery) {
        this.slippery = slippery;
    }

    public void setShady(Shady shady) {
        this.shady = shady;
    }

    public void init() { .. }     <-- Initializer method
}
```

Looking over `UnsafeObject`, it's obvious that dependencies are wired by setter injection. But we're not quite sure why. It has forced both dependencies `slippery` and `shady` to be non-`final`, that is, *mutable*. And it looks like `init()` is expected to be called at some stage before the `UnsafeObject` is ready to perform duties. This object is unsafe, because there are too many ways to construct it incorrectly. Look at the following abusive injector configurations that are permitted by it:

```
<beans ...>
    <bean id="slippery" class="Slippery"/>
    <bean id="shady" class="Shady"/>

    <bean id="unsafe1" class="UnsafeObject"/>
</beans>
```

We have forgotten to set any of its dependencies. No complaints even after the object is constructed and injected. It falls over in a big heap the first time it is used.

```
    <beans ...>
    <bean id="slippery" class="Slippery"/>
    <bean id="shady" class="Shady"/>

    <bean id="unsafe2" class="UnsafeObject">
        <property name="slippery" ref="slippery"/>
    </bean>
</beans>
```

There are still no complaints, and everything will work until dependency `shady` is used. This is potentially riskier (since code using `slippery` will work normally).

```
<beans ...>
    <bean id="slippery" class="Slippery"/>
    <bean id="shady" class="Shady"/>

    <bean id="unsafe4" class="UnsafeObject">
        <property name="slippery" ref="slippery"/>
        <property name="shady" ref="shady"/>
    </bean>
</beans>
```

At first glance, this looks okay. Why is it labeled unsafe? Recall that the `init()` method must be called as part of the object's graduation to readiness. This is among the worst of all cases because no obvious error may come up. Several programmers' days have been wasted over this problem, trivial though it seems at first glance.

```
<beans ...>
    <bean id="slippery" class="Slippery"/>
    <bean id="shady" class="Shady"/>

    <bean id="unsafe5" class="UnsafeObject" init-method="init">
        <property name="slippery" ref="slippery"/>
        <property name="shady" ref="shady"/>
    </bean>
</beans>
```

Finally, a configuration you can rely on! All dependencies are accounted for and the initialization hook is configured correctly. Or is it? Has everything been accounted for? Recall that objects in Spring are singletons by default. This means that other multiple threads are concurrently accessing `unsafe5`. While the injector is itself safe to concurrent accesses of this sort, `UnsafeObject` may not be. The Java Memory Model makes no guarantees about the visibility of non-`final`, non-`volatile` fields across threads. To fix this, you can remove the concept of shared visibility, so an instance is exposed to only a single thread:

```
<beans ...>
    <bean id="slippery" class="Slippery" scope="prototype"/>
    <bean id="shady" class="Shady" scope="prototype"/>

    <bean id="safe" class="UnsafeObject" init-method="init" scope="prototype">
        <property name="slippery" ref="slippery"/>
```

```
        <property name="shady" ref="shady"/>
    </bean>
</beans>
```

The attribute `scope="prototype"` tells the injector to create a new instance of `UnsafeObject` each time it is needed. Now there are no concurrent accesses to `UnsafeObject`. Notice that you are forced to mark both dependencies with `scope="prototype"` as well. Otherwise they may be shared *underneath.*

Well! That was exhaustive. And it involved a lot of configuration just to account for an arbitrary design choice. With constructor injection these problems virtually disappear (as shown in listing 3.22).

Listing 3.22 A safe rewrite of `UnsafeObject` (see listing 3.21)

```
public class SafeObject {
    private final Slippery slippery;          Dependencies wired
    private final Shady shady;                by constructor

    public SafeObject(Slippery slippery, Shady shady) {
        this.slippery = slippery;
        this.shady = shady;                   Initializer runs
                                              inside constructor
        init();
    }

    private void init() { .. }
}
```

`SafeObject` is immune from all of the problems we encountered with its evil cousin. There is only one way to construct it, since it exposes only the one constructor. Both dependencies are declared `final`, making them safely published and thus guaranteed to be visible to all threads. Initialization is done at the end of the constructor. And `init()` is now private, so it can't accidentally be called after construction. Here's the corresponding configuration for `SafeObject` in Guice (it involves placing a single annotation on the class's constructor, as you can see in listing 3.23).

Listing 3.23 Safe object managed by Guice

```
public class SafeObject {
    private final Slippery slippery;
    private final Shady shady;                              Use this
                                                            constructor!
    @Inject
    public SafeObject(Slippery slippery, Shady shady) {
        this.slippery = slippery;
        this.shady = shady;

        init();
    }

    private void init() { .. }
}
```

Constructor injection forces you to create valid, well-behaved objects. Moreover, it prevents you from creating invalid objects by raising errors early. I urge you to consider constructor injection as your first preference, whenever possible. Now, let's look at a problem where some of the more esoteric idioms that we examined earlier in the chapter may prove useful. An example is the partial injection problem, where not all the dependencies are available up front.

3.3 Not all at once: partial injection

Sometimes you don't know about all the dependencies you need right away. Or you are given them later and need to build an object around them. In other cases, you may know about all the dependencies but may need to obtain new ones after each use (as we saw with the Pez dispenser in "Method decoration"). These object graphs can't be described precisely at startup. They need to be built dynamically, at the point of sale.

This introduces to us the idea of a *partial injection*. We'll shortly examine several scenarios where partial (or delayed) injection is useful and see how to go about achieving it. First, we'll look at a scenario where all dependencies are known at construction time but need to be reinjected on each use (because the instance is *used up* and needs to be replenished each time).

3.3.1 The reinjection problem

As the header suggests, this problem is about injecting an object that has already been injected once earlier. Reinjection is typical in cases where you have a *long-lived* dependent with *short-lived* dependencies. More specifically, reinjection is common where a dependency is put into an unusable state after it is used (that is, it has been depleted or used up in some way). You might have a data-holding object, and once it is saved with user input, you may need a new instance for fresh input. Or the dependency may be on a file on disk, which is closed (and disposed) after a single use. There are plenty of incarnations of this problem. Let's look at one purely illustrative case:

```
public class Granny {
    private Apple apple;

    public Granny(Apple apple) {
        this.apple = apple;
    }

    public void eat() {
        apple.consume();
        apple.consume();      <-- Causes an error as apple is already consumed
    }
}
```

Granny is given one apple when she comes into existence. Upon being told to eat(), she consumes that apple but is still hungry. The apple cannot be consumed again since it is already gone. In other words, the *state* of the dependency has changed and it is no longer usable. Apple is short lived, while Granny is long lived, and on each use (every time she eats), she needs a new Apple.

There are a couple of solutions to this problem. You should recall one solution we applied to a similar problem earlier—the Pez dispenser. We could use method decoration to achieve reinjection in this case. But we can't replace `eat()` because it performs a real business task. You could put another method on `Granny`. That would certainly work:

```
public class Granny {

    public Apple getApple() {          <-- Replaced with
        return null;                       method decoration
     }

    public void eat() {
        getApple().consume();
        getApple().consume();
    }
}
```

This is certainly a workable solution. However, it belies our original object graph (of `Granny` depending on an `Apple`) and more importantly is difficult to test. It also relies on a DI library that supports method decoration, and not all of them do. So what are other possible solutions? Common sense says we should be using some kind of Factory, one that can take advantage of DI. The Provider pattern is one such solution.

3.3.2 Reinjection with the Provider pattern

In a nutshell, a Provider pattern is a Factory that the injector creates, wires, and manages. It contains a single method, which *provides* new instances. It is particularly useful for solving the reinjection problem, since a dependent can be wired with a Provider rather than the dependency itself and can obtain instances from it as necessary:

```
public class Granny {

    public Provider<Apple> appleProvider;      <-- Provides apples

    public void eat() {
        appleProvider.get().consume();
        appleProvider.get().consume();
    }
}
```

Notice this line:

```
        appleProvider.get().consume();
```

This effectively says that before we use an apple, we get it from the Provider, meaning that a new `Apple` instance is created each time. This architecture is shown in figure 3.17.

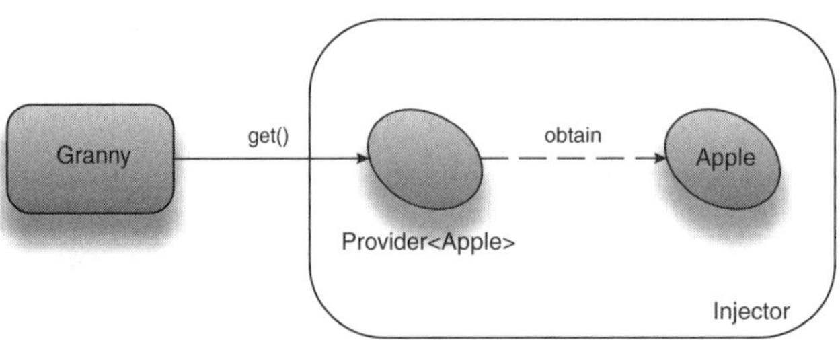

Figure 3.17 `Granny` obtains `Apple` instances from the injector via a provider

There are a couple of things we can say about Providers:

- A Provider is unique (and *specific*) to the type of object it provides. This means you don't do any downcasting on a `get()` as you might do with a Service Locator.
- A Provider's *only* purpose is to provide *scoped* instances of a dependency. Therefore it has just the one method, `get()`.

In Java, which has support for generics, a single provider is all that you need to write. Under this you are free to create as many implementations as needed for each purpose. Guice provides Providers out of the box for all bound types:

```
package com.google.inject;

public interface Provider<T> {
    public T get();
}
```

Method `get()` is fairly straightforward: it says get me an instance of `T`. This may or may not be a new instance depending on the scope of `T`. (For example, if the key is bound as a singleton, the same instance is returned every time.[2]) So, in `Granny`'s case, all that's required is an `@Inject` annotation:

```
public class Granny {

    private Provider<Apple> appleProvider;

    @Inject
    public Granny(Provider<Apple> ap) {          <-- Provider is wired via constructor
        this.appleProvider = ap;
    }

    public void eat() {
        appleProvider.get().consume();
        appleProvider.get().consume();
    }
}
```

You don't need to do anything with the injector configuration because Guice is clever enough to work out how to give you an `Apple` provider. For libraries that don't support this kind of behavior out of the box, you can create a your own `Provider` that does the same trick. Here I've encapsulated a lookup from the injector within a `Provider` for Spring:

```
public class AppleProvider implements Provider<Apple>, BeanFactoryAware {
    private BeanFactory injector;

    public Apple get() {
        return (Apple) injector.getBean("apple");     <-- Apple is looked up from the injector
    }

    public void setBeanFactory(BeanFactory injector) {
        this.injector = injector;
    }
}
```

---

2 See chapter 5 for more on scope.

There are two interesting things about AppleProvider:

- It exposes interface Provider<Apple>, meaning that it's in the business of providing apples.
- It exposes BeanFactoryAware.[3] When it sees this interface, Spring will wire the injector itself to this provider.

The corresponding XML configuration is shown in listing 3.24.

Listing 3.24 Injector configuration for Granny and her Apple provider (in Spring)

```
<beans ...>
    <bean id="appleProvider" class="AppleProvider"/>

    <bean id="granny" class="Granny">
        <constructor-arg ref="appleProvider"/>
    </bean>
</beans>
```

Notice that I didn't have to do anything with AppleProvider. Spring automatically detects that it is an instance of BeanFactoryAware and wires it appropriately. Listing 3.25 shows a slightly more compact, encapsulated version.

Listing 3.25 Encapsulated version of listing 3.24 (in Spring)

```
<beans ...>
    <bean id="granny" class="Granny">
        <constructor-arg><bean class="AppleProvider"/></constructor-arg>
    </bean>
</beans>
```

What if you need to pass in an argument to the dependency? Something that's available only at the time of use, like data from a user, or some resource that acts as a *context* for the dependency. This is a variation on partial injection called the *contextual injection* problem.

3.3.3 The contextual injection problem

You could say that contextual injection and reinjection are related problems. You could even say that contextual injection is a special case of reinjection. These use cases come up quite often, particularly with applications that have some form of external user.

Consider an automated mailing list for a newsletter. Several users sign up with their email addresses, and you periodically send them a copy of your newsletter. The long-lived object in this case is triggered when it's time for an edition of the newsletter to go out, and its context is the newsletter. This is a case of partial injection—where the long-lived object (let's call it NewsletterManager) needs a new instance of a shorter-lived one (let's call this Deliverer) for every newsletter sent out. See figure 3.18 for a visual representation.

---

[3] This is an example of interface injection (which we saw in chapter 2).

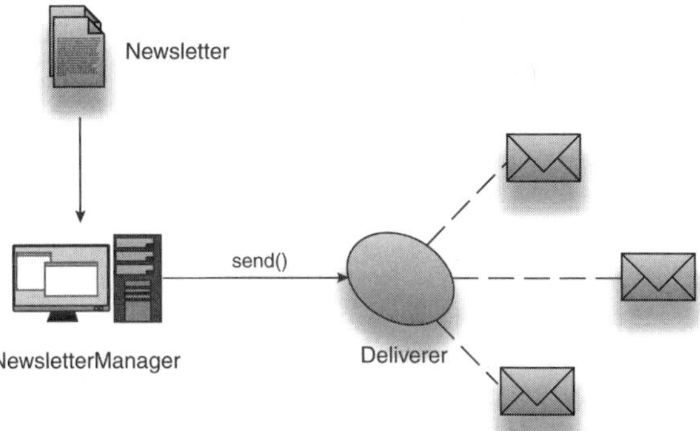

Figure 3.18 A `Deliverer` sends `Newsletters` out to recipients, on prompting by `NewsletterManager`

You could treat this purely as a reinjection problem and pass the newsletter directly to `Deliverer` on every use, say via a setter. Listing 3.26 shows how that might look.

Listing 3.26 A newsletter-sending component and contextual delivery agent

```
public class NewsletterManager {
    private final List<Recipient> recipients;        // Dependencies wired
    private final Provider<Deliverer> deliverer;     // by constructor

    public NewsletterManager(List<Recipient> rs,
                  Provider<Deliverer> dp) {
        this.recipients = rs;
        this.deliverer = dp;
    }

    public void send(Newsletter letter) {
        for (Recipient recipient : recipients) {
            Deliverer d = deliverer.get();
            d.setLetter(letter);                     // Set contextual dependency

            d.deliverTo(recipient);
        }
     }
}

public class Deliverer {
    private Newsletter letter;

    public void setLetter(Newsletter letter) {
        this.letter = letter;
    }

    ...
}
```

In listing 3.26, I've exposed a setter and used a form of manual dependency injection to set the current `Newsletter` (context) on the `Deliverer`. This solution works, but it has the obvious drawbacks that go with using a setter method. What would be really nice is *contextual* constructor injection. And that's brings us to the Assisted Injection pattern.

3.3.4 Contextual injection with the Assisted Injection pattern

Since the contextual injection problem is a relative of reinjection, it follows that their solutions are also related. I used the Provider pattern to solve reinjection. Listing 3.27 reenvisions the newsletter system with a similar pattern: Assisted Injection. Its architecture is described in figure 3.19.

Listing 3.27 A newsletter manager and delivery agent, with Assisted Injection

```
public class NewsletterManager {
    private final List<Recipient> recipients;
    private final AssistedProvider<Deliverer, Newsletter>
            deliverer;                                      // Get dependency for context

    public NewsletterManager(List<Recipient> rs,
                AssistedProvider<Deliverer, Newsletter > dp) {
        this.recipients = rs;
        this.deliverer = dp;
    }

    public void send(Newsletter letter) {
        for (Recipient recipient : recipients) {
            Deliverer d = deliverer.get(letter);            // Alternative to implementing Module

            d.deliverTo(recipient);
        }
    }
}

public interface AssistedProvider<T, C> {
    T get(C context);
}

public class DelivererProvider implements AssistedProvider<Deliverer,
    Newsletter> {

    public Deliverer get(Newsletter letter) {
        return new Deliverer(letter);                       // Construct by hand!
    }
}
```

In listing 3.27, I have two classes of importance:

- `NewsletterManager`—The long-lived, dependent class
- `DelivererProvider`—The Assisted Injection provider, which provides `Deliverer` instances wired with a context (i.e., `Newsletter`)

The other interesting artifact in listing 3.27 is the interface `AssistedProvider`, which takes two type parameters:

- `T` refers to the generic type provided by a call to `get()`.
- `C` refers to the generic type of the context object.

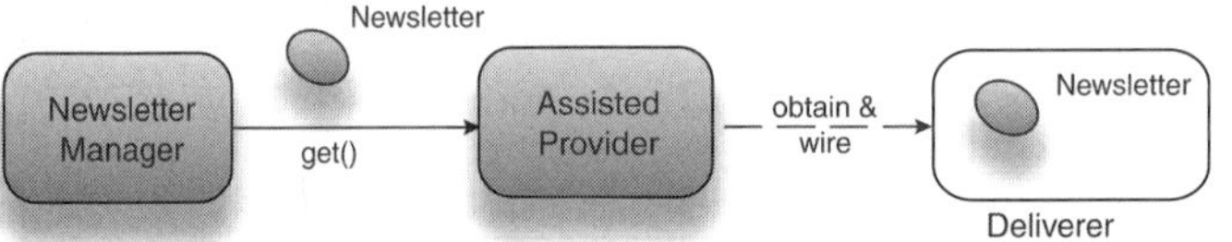

Figure 3.19 `AssistedProvider` **creates a contextualized** `Deliverer` **with the current** `Newsletter`**.**

They let you use `AssistedProvider` in other, similar areas. Like `Provider`, `Assisted-Provider` is a piece of framework code that you can customize to suit your needs.

There's one obvious flaw with this plan. We've used construction by hand in the `AssistedProvider`. That's not ideal because we lose viral dependency injection, interception, scope, and so on. One way to fix it is by using another `Provider` inside the `AssistedProvider`. The trade-off is that we must use setter injection. This is actually a reasonable solution if used sparingly. Listing 3.28 demonstrates it with Guice.

Listing 3.28 A newsletter component, using Assisted Injection

```
public class DelivererProvider implements
    AssistedProvider<Deliverer, Newsletter> {
    private final Provider<Deliverer> deliverer;

    @Inject
    public DelivererProvider(Provider<Deliverer> deliverer) {
        this.deliverer = deliverer;
    }

    public Deliverer get(Newsletter letter) {
        Deliverer d = deliverer.get();
        d.setLetter(letter);

        return d;
    }
}
```

Provider is itself injected

Context set manually

In listing 3.28, we not only get the benefits of dependency injection but also can add the newsletter context to it.

Guice also provides an extension called AssistedInject that can help make this problem easier. AssistedInject lets us declare a Factory-style interface and creates the implementation for us, so we don't have to create the intermediary wiring code by hand. It is also compelling because this means we do not have to use setter injection and can take advantage of all the goodness of constructor injection:

```
import com.google.inject.assistedinject.Assisted;

public class Deliverer {
    private final Newsletter letter;

     @Inject
    public Deliverer(@Assisted Newsletter letter) {
        this.letter = letter;
    }

    ...
}
```

Tells Guice to assist this injection

The `@Assisted` annotation is an indicator to the generated factory that this constructor parameter should be obtained from a factory, rather than use the normal course of injection. The code from listing 3.28 now looks like this:

```
public class NewsletterManager {
    private final List<Recipient> recipients;
    private final DelivererFactory factory;

    public NewsletterManager(List<Recipient> rs,
```

Use an injected factory

```
                     DelivererFactory factory) {
        this.recipients = rs;
        this.factory = factory;
    }

    public void send(Newsletter letter) {
        for (Recipient recipient : recipients) {
            Deliverer d = factory.forLetter(letter);     <-- Get dependency for context

            d.deliverTo(recipient);
        }
     }
}

public interface DelivererFactory {                      <-- Factory backed by Guice
    Deliverer forLetter(Newsletter letter);
}
```

Then in our module, we tell Guice about the `DelivererFactory`:

```
public class NewsletterModule extends AbstractModule {

    @Override
    protected void configure() {
        bind(DelivererFactory.class).toProvider(
             FactoryProvider.newFactory(DelivererFactory.class,
             Newsletter.class));     <-- Context set manually
        ...
    }
}
```

Here, the `FactoryProvider.newFactory()` method is used to create a provider that will create the relevant factory implementation for us. This saves the step of creating a `DelivererFactory` that adds the contextual dependency by hand.

It doesn't take much imagination to see that this too can be insufficient, for instance, if you had two context objects. One mitigant would be to create another kind of `AssistedProvider` with a type signature that supported two contexts:

```
public interface TwoAssistsProvider<T, C1, C2> {
    T get(C1 context1, C2 context2);
}
```

This works, but what about three contexts? Or four? It very quickly gets out of hand. For such cases you will find the Builder pattern much more powerful.

3.3.5 Flexible partial injection with the Builder pattern

If you are familiar with the Gang of Four book on design patterns, you have doubtless heard of the Builder pattern. Builders are often used to assemble object graphs when there are many possible permutations. A Builder is one way to mitigate the constructor pyramid, adding each dependency incrementally. They come in two varieties:

- Using constructor wiring and thus able to produce safe, valid, and immutable objects, but at the sacrifice of injector management
- Using flexible setter wiring (and injector management) but sacrificing the safety of constructor injection

The Builder is a natural solution to all partial-injection problems. Builders can produce objects given only a partial view of their dependencies. In short, that's their job. Listing 3.29 reimagines the reinjection problem with a Builder.

Listing 3.29 Granny gets apples using a Builder

```
public class Granny {

    private AppleBuilder builder;

    @Inject
    public Granny(AppleBuilder b) {          <-- Builder is wired via constructor
        this.builder = b;
    }

    public void eat() {
        builder.build().consume();
        builder.build().consume();
    }
}

public class AppleBuilder {
    public Apple build() {
        return new Apple();                  <-- Construct apples by hand
    }
}
```

In this trivial example, there is no difference between a Builder and provider. Notice that I did not use a generic interface for the Builder. Instead I relied directly on an `AppleBuilder`. Although we had the same level of type-safety with the parameterized `Provider<Apple>`, there's an extra level of flexibility we get with Builders. Let's say that some apples are green and some are red. How would you build them with a provider? You can't directly. One solution might be to create a `Provider<GreenApple>` and `Provider<RedApple>`, but this exposes the underlying implementation (of red or green apples) to a client that shouldn't know these details. Builders give us a much simpler solution:

```
public class Granny {

    private AppleBuilder builder;

    @Inject
    public Granny(AppleBuilder b) {
        this.builder = b;
    }

    public void eat() {
        builder.buildRedApple().consume();
        builder.buildGreenApple().consume();
    }
}
```

While `Granny`'s dependencies don't change, she can still get red or green apples without ever knowing anything about `RedApple` or `GreenApple`. To `Granny`, they are just instances of `Apple`. All this needs is a small addition to `AppleBuilder`:

```
public class AppleBuilder {
    public Apple buildRedApple() {
        return new RedApple();
    }

    public Apple buildGreenApple() {
        return new GreenApple();
    }
}
```

AppleBuilder now encapsulates the construction and any implementation details of Apple (red, green, or otherwise). The dependent, Granny, is kept completely free of implementation details.

Similarly, Builders can be a powerful solution to the contextual injection problem. Listing 3.30 shows this application of the Builder pattern to the newsletter example.

Listing 3.30 A newsletter component, using Builder injection

```
public class NewsletterManager {
    private final List<Recipient> recipients;
    private final DelivererBuilder builder;          <-- Inject a Builder for dependency

    public NewsletterManager(List<Recipient> rs,
                   DelivererBuilder db) {
        this.recipients = rs;
        this.builder = db;
    }

    public void send(Newsletter letter) {
        for (Recipient recipient : recipients) {
            builder.letter(letter);

            Deliverer d = builder.buildDeliverer();       <-- Set context and build dependency

            d.deliverTo(recipient);
        }
     }
}

public class DelivererBuilder {
    private Newsletter letter;

    public void letter(Newsletter letter) {          <-- Setter method accepts context
        this.letter = letter;
    }

    public Deliverer buildDeliverer() {
        return new Deliverer(letter);             <-- Construct with context
    }
}
```

The interesting thing about listing 3.30 is that we have a setter method named letter(), which takes the newsletter (context) object. It temporarily holds the context until it is time to build a Deliverer around it: in the buildDeliverer() method. Using construction by hand, DelivererBuilder ensures that Deliverer instances are wired by constructor (and are thus immutable, valid, and safe). Builders are especially powerful when you have more than one context object to deal with—all you need to do is add setter methods on the Builder. Contrast the following `AssistedProviders` for multiple contexts:

```
public interface TwoAssistsProvider<T, C1, C2> {
    T get(C1 c1, C2 c2);
}

public interface ThreeAssistsProvider<T, C1, C2, C3> {
    T get(C1 c1, C2 c2, C3 c3);
}

...
```

with the builder approach:

```
public class DelivererBuilder {
    private Newsletter letter;
    private String mailServerUrl;
    private int port;

    public void letter(Newsletter letter) {
        this.letter = letter;
    }

    public void mailServerUrl(String url) {
        this.mailServerUrl = url;
    }

    public void port(int port) {
        this.port = port;
    }

    public Deliverer buildDeliverer() {
        return new Deliverer(letter, mailServerUrl, port);
    }
}
```

Now any number of contexts can be set by the `NewsletterManager` (dependent) directly in its `send()` method:

```
    public void send(Newsletter letter) {
        for (Recipient recipient : recipients) {
            builder.letter(letter);
            builder.mailServerUrl("mail.wideplay.com");
            builder.port(21);

            Deliverer d = builder.buildDeliverer();

            d.deliverTo(recipient);
        }
    }
```

These context objects are all set at the time they are needed (on the Builder, rather than the `Deliverer`). This not only allows us to hide actual construction and assembly code but also gives us an abstraction layer between dependent and dependency. If you wanted to ignore the port (defaulting to an SSL port instead), you would change only the appropriate Builder calls. This is useful if you need to make small tweaks in service code without upsetting clients and also for performing some lightweight validation of data (for instance, checking that a port number is within range). Builders also benefit from dependency injection themselves and can do extra setup work if need be. For instance, this Builder transforms email server details into a service for `Deliverer`:

```
public class DelivererBuilder {
    private final MailServerFinder finder;

    private Newsletter newsletter;
    private String mailServerUrl;
    private int port;

    @Inject
    public DelivererBuilder(MailServerFinder finder) {
        this.finder = finder;
    }

    ...

     public Deliverer buildDeliverer() {
        MailServer server = finder.findMailServer(mailServerUrl, port);

        return new Deliverer(letter, server);
    }
```

One important bit of housekeeping: if you are going to reuse a builder, remember to reset it first:

```
     public Deliverer buildDeliverer() {
        try {
            return new Deliverer(letter, mailServerUrl, port);
         } finally {
            letter = null;
            mailServerUrl = null;
            port = -1;
        }
    }
```

Resetting it ensures that a failed Build sequence doesn't contaminate future uses. You could also obtain a new Builder every time (via a provider). This is especially advisable. And it ensures that a Builder is never reused or used concurrently on accident. Thus far, all the code that we've been dealing with has been under our control. Often it may be necessary to work with code that is not under your control and still apply dependency injection to it. This is the problem of injecting objects in sealed code.

3.4 Injecting objects in sealed code

Not all the code you work with is under your control. Many third-party libraries come in binary form and cannot be altered to work with dependency injectors. Adding annotations, refactoring with providers or builders, is out of the question. We'll call this *sealed* code. (Don't confuse this with the C# keyword.)

So if we have no control over sealed code, what can be done to make it work with dependency injection? One answer might be to find a way *not* to use annotations.

3.4.1 Injecting with externalized metadata

Recall some of the early Spring XML configuration. It eliminates the need for annotations, right off the bat, in essence moving configuration metadata from source code to an external location (the XML file). Listing 3.31 shows a sealed class injected purely with externalized metadata.

Listing 3.31 A sealed class injected via external configuration

```
public class Sealed {
    private final Dependency dep;

    public Sealed(Dependency dep) {
        this.dep = dep;
    }
}

<!-- XML injector configuration -->
<beans ...>
    <bean id="sealed" class="Sealed">
        <constructor-arg><bean class="Dependency"/></constructor-arg>
    </bean>
</beans>
```

Here Sealed did not have to change, and the injector configuration is straightforward. This is possible even with Guice, using the module to select the appropriate constructor to inject:

```
public class SealedModule extends AbstractModule {

     @Override
    protected void configure() {
        bind(Sealed.class).toConstructor(sealedConstructor());    <- Bind directly to a constructor of Sealed
    }

     private Constructor<Sealed> sealedConstructor() {
         try {
             return Sealed.class.getConstructor(Dependency.class);    <- Resolve the constructor we want to inject
         } catch(NoSuchMethodException e) {
         addError(e);
             return null;
         }
     }
}
```

This allows us to skip the @Inject annotation and get Guice to directly inject the sealed code.

In Spring, this technique even works with setter injection. See figure 3.20.

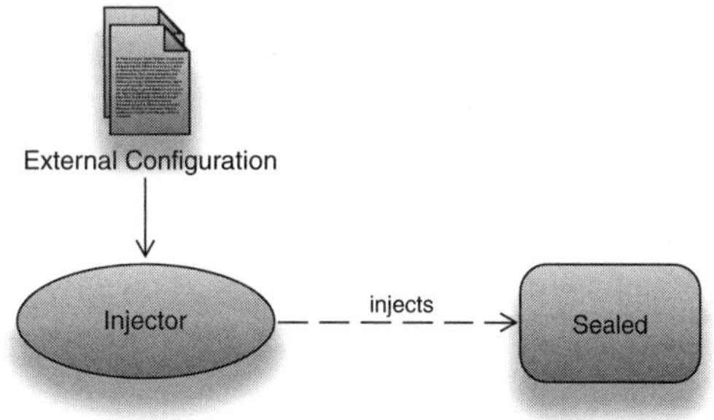

Figure 3.20 External metadata allows you to inject classes in sealed code easily.

But sealed code often throws you more curveballs than this. It may have completely private constructors and expose only a static factory method. This is not uncommon in library code (see listing 3.32).

Listing 3.32 A sealed class injected via external metadata

```
public class Sealed {
    private final Dependency dep;

    private Sealed(Dependency dep) {
        this.dep = dep;
    }

    public static Sealed newInstance(Dependency dep) {
        return new Sealed(dep);
    }
}

<!-- XML injector configuration -->
<beans ...>
    <bean id="sealed" class="Sealed" factory-method="newInstance">
        <constructor-arg><bean class="Dependency"/></constructor-arg>
    </bean>
</beans>
```

Listing 3.32 shows how Spring is able to call on Factory methods just as though they were constructors (the `<constructor-arg>` element now passes arguments to the Factory). If it is an unfriendly factory that completely encapsulates construction, the situation is a bit trickier:

```
public class Sealed {
    private final Dependency dep;

    Sealed(Dependency dep) {
        this.dep = dep;
    }

    public static Sealed newInstance() {
        return new Sealed(new Dependency());
    }
}
```

There is no obvious way to provide the constructor with an instance of `Dependency`. Custom or mock implementations have been removed from the equation, also making testing very difficult. Here's another scenario where the XML falls over:

```
public class Sealed {
    private Dependency dep;

    public Sealed() {
    }

    public void dependOn(Dependency dep) {
        this.dep = dep;
    }
}
```

This class accepts its dependency via setter injection. However, the setter method does not conform to Spring's naming convention. Rather than being named setDependency(), it is called dependOn(). Remember, we can't change any of this code—it is *sealed.*

Even if there were some way around it, misspelling method names can easily cause you much chagrin. The Adapter pattern provides a better solution.

3.4.2 Using the Adapter pattern

The Adapter is yet another design pattern from the Gang of Four book. It allows you to alter the behavior of existing objects by extending them. The following Adapter allows you to inject classes whose constructors are not public (so long as they are not private):

```
public class SealedAdapter extends Sealed {

    @Inject
    public SealedAdapter(Dependency dep) {
        super(dep);
    }
}
```

The call to super(dep) chains to Sealed's hidden constructor. Since SealedAdapter extends Sealed, it can be used by any dependent of Sealed transparently. And it benefits from dependency injection (see figure 3.21).

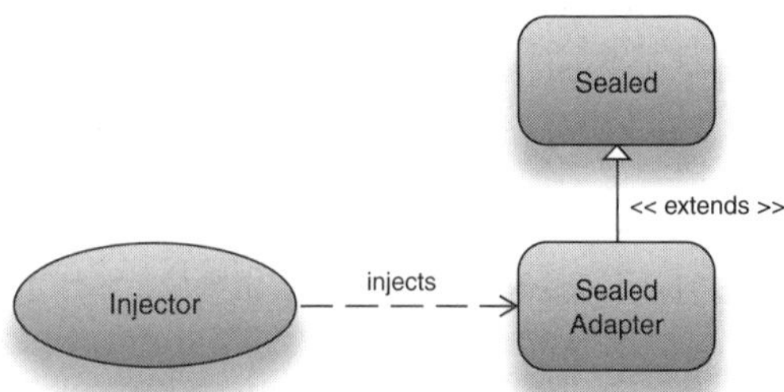

Figure 3.21 SealedAdapter helps Sealed to be injected transparently.

The same solution applies when you have a *package-local* constructor, except you build SealedAdapter into the same package as Sealed.

Similarly, this works with the unconventional setter methods:

```
public class SealedAdapter extends Sealed {

    @Inject
    public SealedAdapter(Dependency dep) {
        dependOn(dep);
    }
}
```

Here's a more convoluted example with both combined:

```
public class SealedAdapter extends Sealed {

    @Inject
    public SealedAdapter(Dependency dep1, Dependency dep2, Dependency dep3) {
        super(dep1);

        dependOn(dep2);
        relyOn(dep3);
    }
}
```

Using an Adapter:

- Any infrastructure logic is cleanly encapsulated within `SealedAdapter`.
- Typing mistakes and misspellings are caught at compile time.
- Dependents of `Sealed` require no code changes (unlike a provider, for example).
- Testing follows the same method as the original sealed class.

Adapters can sometimes be more verbose, but they have no impact on client code. And they can even be passed back to *other* sealed classes transparently, something that's hard to do with providers.

TIP If you're particularly clever, you can bridge the gap between adapter and provider to solve the reinjection problem. Do this by overriding each method of the original component and looking up a new instance as needed with a provider. Then delegate all methods to that instance. It leaves minimal impact on dependent code and is a compelling alternative.

One other interesting option for injecting sealed code is the Builder pattern we saw earlier. You can incrementally add dependencies to a builder and let it decide how to construct the sealed component. Builders are particularly useful with unconventional setters or if there are several constructors or factories to choose from.

3.5 Summary

This chapter was a real workout! First, we explored the injection idioms of setter, constructor, interface, and method decoration. Setter injection has advantages in being flexible, particularly if you don't need every dependency set all of the time. However, it has significant drawbacks since fields can't be made immutable (constant), which is important to preserving object graph integrity. Constructor injection is a compelling alternative, since it does allow you to set immutable fields. It is also useful since you can't accidentally forget to set a dependency (such configuration fails early and fast). Constructor injection is also less verbose and prevents accidental overwriting of previously set dependencies.

However, it too has some drawbacks: If you have several dependencies (or worse, several similar ones), it is difficult to tell them apart. Furthermore, a circular reference (where two components depend on each other) is impossible to resolve with simple constructor wiring. Setter injection helps here, since both objects can be constructed in an incomplete state and later wired to one another. Setter injection also helps avoid the constructor pyramid, which is a design issue when you have multiple profiles of a component, in other words, where a component uses different subsets of its dependencies in different scenarios. Setters are also explicit about the dependencies they wire and thus make for more browsable code.

Constructor injection can be used to solve the circular reference problem, but it requires an intermediary placeholder known as a proxy. Some DI libraries (such as Guice) provide this out of the box, without any additional coding on your part. A related issue, the in-construction problem, where circular interdependents are used before the proxied wiring can complete, can be solved by combining constructor and setter injection or purely with setter injection. Better yet, you can solve this by using a special initializing hook.

However, the drawbacks of field mutability and the vulnerability that setter injection has to accidental invalid construction are too great to ignore. Non-`final` fields are also potentially unsafe to multiple interleaving threads (more on that in chapter 9). So, always try constructor injection first and fall back to setter injection only where you must.

There are also other injection idioms:

- *Interface injection*—This involves exposing role interfaces that are effectively setter methods in their own interface. It has the advantage of being explicit just like setters, and it can be given meaningful names. However, interface injection is extremely verbose and requires several single-use interfaces to be created for the sole purpose of wiring. It is also not supported by many DI libraries.
- *Method decoration*—This involves intercepting a method call and returning an injector-provided value instead. In other words, method decoration turns an ordinary method into a Factory method, but importantly, an injector-backed Factory method. This is useful in some rare cases, but it is difficult to test without an injector and so should be carefully weighed first.
- *Other idioms*—Field injection is a useful utility, where fields are set directly using reflection. This makes for compact classes and is good in tutorial code where space is at a premium. However, it is nearly impossible to test (or replace with mocks) and so should be avoided in production code. Object enhancement is a neat idea that removes the injector from the picture altogether, instead enhancing objects via source code or otherwise leaving them to inject themselves. This is different from Factories or Service Location because it does not pollute source code at development time. There are very few such solutions in practice.

Some components "use up" their dependencies and need them reinjected (within their lifetimes). This introduces a problem, namely reinjection. Reinjection can be solved by the only, which involves the use of a single-method interface that encapsulates the work of constructing a dependency by hand or looks it up from the injector by service location. Providers let you abstract away infrastructure logic from dependent components and are thus a compelling solution to reinjection.

Contextual injection is a related problem. Here, a component may need new dependencies on each use, but more important it needs to provide them with context. This is a form of dependency that is known only at the time of use. Assisted injection can help. A slight variation of the Provider pattern, an Assisted Provider does the same job but passes in the context object to a partially constructed dependency. Since this can quickly get out of hand if you have more than one context object, try looking at the Builder pattern instead. The Builder incrementally absorbs dependencies (context objects or otherwise) and then decides how to construct the original service. It may use constructor wiring or a series of setters or indeed a combination as appropriate. The builder is also an easy solution to the reinjection problem and in such cases is very similar to a provider.

Some code is beyond your control, either third-party libraries, frozen code, or code that can't be changed for some other reasons (such as time constraints). You still need these components, so you need a way to bring them into a modern architecture with dependency injection. DI is really good at this work and at neutralizing such undulations in a large code base. One solution is to use external metadata (if your injector supports it) such as an XML file. This leaves the sealed classes unaffected but still provides them with requisite dependencies. However, if sealed code uses factories or unconventional setter methods, this may be difficult. In this case, the Adapter pattern is a powerful solution. You inject the Adapter as per usual, and then the Adapter decides how to wire the original component. Adapters are a strong solution because they can leave client code unaffected. They are also a transparent alternative to the reinjection problem, though they are sometimes verbose compared to providers.

Dependency injection is about components that are designed, tested, and maintained in discrete modular units that can be assembled, constructed, and deployed in various configurations. It helps separate your code into purposed, uncluttered pieces, which is essential for testing and maintaining code, especially in large projects with many contributors. Chapter 4 examines these ideas in detail, exploring the value of such modular separation and how to achieve it.

4 Building modular applications

This chapter covers:

- Organizing code in modules
- Watching out for tight coupling
- Designing with loose coupling
- Testing code in discrete units
- Working with key rebinding

> *"To define it rudely but not ineptly, engineering is the art of doing that well with one dollar, which any bungler can do with two after a fashion."*
>
> —Arthur Wellesley

So far, we've looked at what it means for objects to be well behaved and classes to be well designed in the small. But in any real-world project, there's also a big picture to be considered. Just as there are principles that help our design of objects in the micro, there are principles for good design in the macro sense. In the coming sections, we'll talk about these design principles and see how to relate them to dependency injection.

Chief among these is testing. DI facilitates *testing* and *testable* code, the latter being an extremely important and often-overlooked condition to successful development. Closely tied to this is the concept of *coupling*, where good classes are linked to the dependencies in ways that facilitate easy replacement and therefore testing—bad ones are not. We'll see how to avoid such cases, and finally we'll look at the advanced case of modifying injector configuration in a running application.

First, let's start at in the micro level and explore the role objects play as the *construction units* of applications.

4.1 Understanding the role of an object

We're all very familiar with objects; you work with them every day and use them to model problems, effortlessly. But let's say for a moment you were asked to define what an object is—what might you say?

You might say an object is:

- A logical grouping of data and related operations
- An instance of a class of things
- A component with specific responsibilities

An object is all these things, but it is also a building block for programs. And as such, the design of objects is paramount to the design of programs themselves. Classes that have a specific, well-defined purpose and stay within clearly defined boundaries are well behaved and reliable. Classes that grow organically, with functionality bolted on when and where required, lead to a world of hurt.

A class can itself be a member of a larger unit of collective responsibilities called a *module*. A module is an independent, contractually sound unit that is focused on a broad part of business responsibility. For example, a *persistence* module may be responsible for storing and retrieving data from a database.

A module may not necessarily be meant for business functionality alone. For example, a *security* module is responsible for guarding unwarranted access to parts of an application. Modules may also be focused on infrastructure or on application logic but typically not both. In other words, a module is:

- *Whole*—A module is a *complete unit* of responsibility. With respect to an application, this means that modules can be picked up and dropped in as needed.
- *Independent*—Unlike an object, a module does not have dependencies on other modules to perform its core function. Apart from some common libraries, a module can be developed and tested independently (that is, in an isolated environment).
- *Contractually sound*—A module conforms to well-defined behavior and can be relied on to behave as expected under all circumstances.
- *Separate*—A module is not invasive of collaborators, and thus it is a discrete unit of functionality.

These qualities of a module are largely important in relation to its collaborators. Many modules interacting with one another through established, patent boundaries form a healthy application. Since modules may be contributed by several different parties (perhaps different teams, sister projects, or even external vendors), it's crucial that they follow these principles. Swapping in replacement modules, for example, replacing persistence in a database with a module that provides persistence in a data cluster or replacing a web presentation module with a desktop GUI, ought to be possible with a minimum of fuss. So long as the overall purpose of the application is maintained, a system of well-designed modules is tolerant to change. Much as different incarnations of an object graph provide variant implementations of a service, different assemblies of modules provide different application semantics. A module is thus an independent, atomic unit of reuse.

Objects and modules that collaborate typically have strong relationships with each other. Often the design of a dependency is influenced by its collaborators. However, each object has its area of responsibility, and well-designed objects stick to their areas without intruding on their collaborators. In other words, each object has its area of concern. Good design keeps those concerns separated.

4.2 Separation of concerns (my pants are too tight!)

Tight pants are very cumbersome! If, like me, you live in a sweltering subtropical environment, they can be especially discomfiting. Similarly, tightly coupled code can cause no end of development pain. It's worth taking the time at the head of a project to prevent such problems from creeping in later.

A big part of modular design is the idea that modules are deployable in different scenarios with little extra effort. The *separation* and *independence* of modules are core to this philosophy, which brings us to the tight-pants problem.

If we take a different perspective on the whole matter, it's not difficult to see that a module is itself a kind of object. The same principles that apply to module design and behavior also apply right down to objects themselves. In the next few sections we'll examine what it means to treat objects with the principle of separation. Earlier we laid down a similar principle: separating infrastructure from application logic so that logic that dealt with construction, organization, and bootstrapping was housed independently from core business logic. If you think of infrastructure as being orthogonal to application logic, then separating the two can be seen as dividing *horizontally* (see figure 4.1).

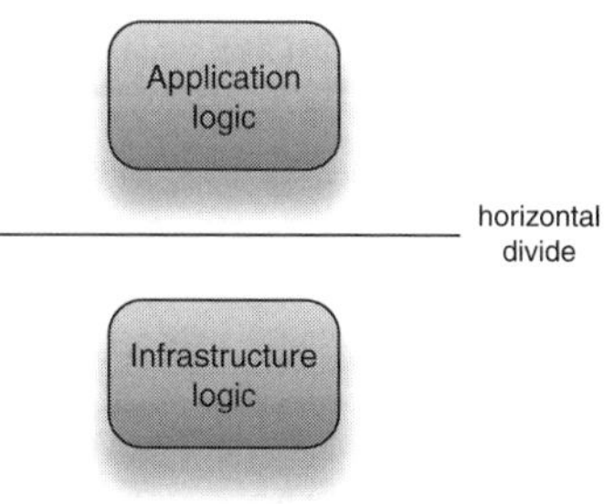

Figure 4.1 Conceptually, application logic sits *on top of* infrastructure logic.

Similarly, logic dealing with different business areas can be separated *vertically* (see figure 4.2).

Checking spelling and editing text are two core parts of any email application. Both deal with application logic and are thus focused on business purpose. However, neither is especially related to the other. It

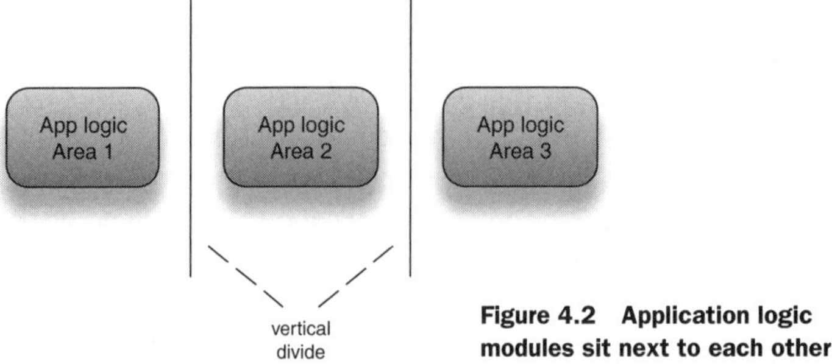

Figure 4.2 Application logic modules sit next to each other.

behooves us to separate them from each other just as we would separate any infrastructure code from the two of them. In other words, separating logic by area of concern is good practice. Figure 4.3 shows a group of modules, separated by area of application as well as infrastructure concern. This kind of modularity is indicative of healthy design.

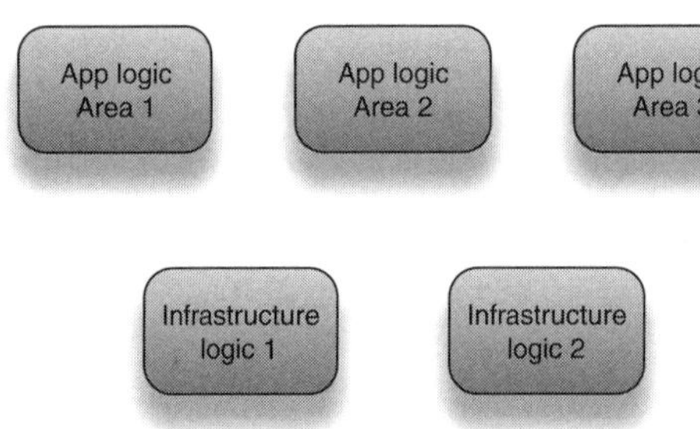

Figure 4.3 An assembly of discrete, separated modules along both infrastructure and core logic lines

When we lose this healthy separation between modules (and indeed objects), things start to get messy. Broadly speaking, this is tight coupling, and it has been a major headache for a very long time in OOP. Many language constructs were developed just to deal with this problem (interfaces and virtual methods, for instance). To know how to write healthy code, one must first be able to recognize tightly coupled code and understand *why* it is a problem.

4.2.1 *Perils of tight coupling*

In chapter 1, we looked at a classic example of tightly coupled code, declared that it was bad, tossed it away, and laid the foundation for DI. Let's resurrect that example and examine it closely (listing 4.1).

Listing 4.1 An email service that checks spelling in English

```
public class Emailer {
    private EnglishSpellChecker spellChecker;

    public Emailer() {
        this.spellChecker = new EnglishSpellChecker();
    }

    ...
}
```

This email service was poorly written because it encapsulated not only its dependencies but also the *creation* of its dependencies. In other words:

- It prevents any external agent (like the injector) from reaching its dependencies.
- It allows for only one *particular* structure of its object graph (created in its constructor).
- It is forced to know how to construct and assemble its dependencies.
- It is forced to know how to construct and assemble dependencies of its dependencies, and so on ad infinitum.

By preventing any external agent from reaching its dependencies, not only does it prevent an injector from creating and wiring them, it prevents a unit test from substituting *mock objects* in their place. This is an important fact because it means the class is *not testable.* Take the test case in listing 4.2 for instance:

Listing 4.2 A test case for `Emailer` using a mocked dependency

```
public class EmailerTest {

    @Test
    public final void ensureSpellingWasChecked() {
        MockSpellChecker mock = new MockSpellChecker();

        new Emailer(mock).send("Hello!");
        assert mock.verifyDidCheckSpelling()      <-- Mock tracks if checkSpelling() was called
            : "failed to check spelling";
    }
}
```

And the mock spellchecker is as follows:

```
public class MockSpellChecker implements SpellChecker {
    private boolean didCheckSpelling = false;

    public boolean check(String text) {        <-- Mocked implementation of interface method
        didCheckSpelling = true;
        return true;
     }

    public boolean verifyDidCheckSpelling() {   <-- Mock-only method reports if spelling was checked
        return didCheckSpelling;
    }
}
```

This test case is impossible to write on `Emailer` as it exists in listing 4.1. That's because there is no constructor or setter available to pass in a mock `SpellChecker`. Mock objects are extremely useful:

- They allow you to test one class and none other. This means that any resultant errors are from that class and none other. In other words, they help you focus on discrete units.
- They allow you to replace computationally expensive dependencies (for instance, those that require hardware resources) with *fake* versions.

- They assert that the class follows the appropriate *contract* when speaking to its dependencies.
- They assert that everything happened as expected and in the expected *order*.

Even if we rewrote the original `Emailer` to take its dependency as an argument, we would still be stuck in this untenable position (see listing 4.3).

Listing 4.3 An email service that checks spelling in English, modified

```
public class Emailer {
    private EnglishSpellChecker spellChecker;

    public Emailer(EnglishSpellChecker spellChecker) {
        this.spellChecker = spellChecker;
    }

    ...
}
```

Now an external agent can set dependencies. However, the problem with testing remains, because `Emailer` is bound inextricably to an `EnglishSpellChecker`. Passing in a mock

```
MockSpellChecker mock = new MockSpellChecker();
new Emailer(mock);
```

results in a compilation error, because `MockSpellChecker` is not an `EnglishSpellChecker`. When a dependent is inextricably bound to its dependencies, code is no longer testable. This, in a nutshell, is tight coupling.

Being tightly coupled to a specific implementation, `Emailer` also prevents you from producing variant implementations. Take the following injector configuration, which tries to assemble an object graph consisting of an `Emailer` with an `EnglishSpellChecker` and a Latin character set in Spring XML (also see figure 4.4):

```
<beans ...>
    <bean id="emailer" class="Emailer">
        <constructor-arg>
            <bean class="EnglishSpellChecker">
                <constructor-arg>
                    <bean class="LatinCharset"/>
                </constructor-arg>
            </bean>
        </constructor-arg>
    </bean>
</beans>
```

Such a configuration is impossible given the tightly coupled object graph. By deciding its own dependencies, `Emailer` prevents any variant of them from being created. This makes for poor reuse and a potential explosion of similar code, since a new kind of `Emailer` would have to be written for each permutation.

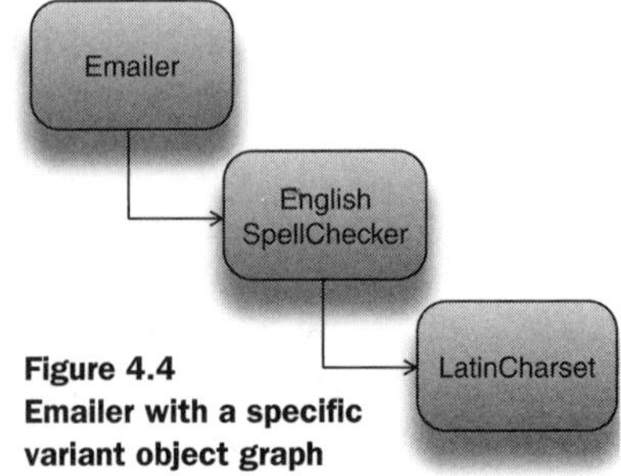

Figure 4.4 Emailer with a specific variant object graph

The example I used in chapter 1 is illustrative of the same problem—we were restricted to English spellcheckers, unable to provide variants in French or Japanese without a parallel deveMlopment effort. Tight coupling also means that we have opened the door in the iron wall separating infrastructure from application logic—something that should raise alarm bells on its own.

4.2.2 Refactoring impacts of tight coupling

We've built up quite a potent argument *against* coupling dependents to their dependencies. There's one major reason we can add that would outweigh all the others: the impact to coupled code when dependencies change. Consider the example in listing 4.4.

Listing 4.4 A utility for searching lists of strings

```
public class StringSearch {
    public String startsWith(ArrayList<String> list, String aString) {
        Iterator<String> iter = list.iterator();     <-- Needs only an iterator
        while(iter.hasNext()) {                           to do its work
            String current = iter.next();

            if (current.startsWith(aString))
                return current;
        }

        return null;
    }

    public boolean contains(ArrayList<String> list, String aString) {
        Iterator<String> iter = list.iterator();     <-- Needs only an iterator
        while(iter.hasNext()) {                           to do its work
            String current = iter.next();

            if (aString.equals(current))
                return true;
        }

        return false;
    }

    ...
}
//elsewhere
String startsWith = new StringSearch().startsWith(myList, "copern");

boolean contains = new StringSearch().contains(myList, "copernicus");
```

`StringSearch` provides a couple of utilities for searching a list of strings. The two methods I have in listing 4.5 test to see if the list contains a particular string and if it contains a partial match. You can imagine many more such utilities that comprehend a list in various ways. Now, what if I wanted to change `StringSearch` so it searched a `HashSet` instead of an `ArrayList`?

Listing 4.5 Impact of refactoring tightly coupled code

```
public class StringSearch {
    public String startsWith(HashSet<String> set, String aString) {
```

```
        Iterator<String> iter = set.iterator();
        while(iter.hasNext()) {
            String current = iter.next();

            if (current.startsWith(aString))
                return current;
        }

        return null;
    }

    public boolean contains(HashSet<String> set, String aString) {
        Iterator<String> iter = set.iterator();
        while(iter.hasNext()) {
            String current = iter.next();

            if (aString.equals(current))
                return true;
        }

        return false;
    }

    ...
}
```

Client code can now search over a `HashSet` instead but only after a significant number of changes to `StringSearch` (one per method):

```
String startsWith = new StringSearch().startsWith(mySet, "copern");
```

```
boolean contains = new StringSearch().contains(mySet, "copernicus");
```

Furthermore, you would have to make a change in every method that the implementation appeared in, and the class is no longer compatible with `ArrayLists`. Any clients already coded to use `ArrayLists` with `StringSearch` must be rewritten to use `HashSets` at a potentially an enormous refactoring cost, which may not even be appropriate in all cases. One way to solve this problem is by making the list a dependency, as shown in listing 4.6.

Listing 4.6 Refactor the list to a dependency

```
public class StringSearch {
    private final HashSet<String> set;

    public StringSearch(HashSet<String> set) {
        this.set = set;
    }

     public String startsWith(String aString) {
        Iterator<String> iter = set.iterator();
        while(iter.hasNext()) {
            String current = iter.next();

            if (current.startsWith(aString))
                return current;
        }
```

```
        return null;
    }

    public boolean contains(String aString) {
        Iterator<String> iter = set.iterator();
        while(iter.hasNext()) {
            String current = iter.next();

            if (aString.equals(current))
                return true;
        }

        return false;
    }

    ...
}
```

Consequently in client code, we can use one instance of the searching class to perform many actions on a set of strings:

```
StringSearch stringSearch = new StringSearch(mySet);

String startsWith = stringSearch.startsWith("copern");

boolean contains = stringSearch.contains("copernicus");
```

One problem is out of the way—we can now search `HashSet`s. And if you had a new requirement in the future to search, say, `TreeSet`s, then the refactoring impact would be much smaller (we'd need to change only the dependency and any clients). But this is still far from ideal. A change every time you choose a different collection data structure is excessive and untenable. We're still feeling the pangs of tight coupling. Listing 4.7 shows how *loose* coupling code cures this ailment.

Listing 4.7 Refactor to a loosely coupled dependency

```
public class StringSearch {
    private final Collection<String> collection;

    public StringSearch(Collection<String> collection) {
        this.collection = collection;
    }

     public String startsWith(String aString) {
        Iterator<String> iter = collection.iterator();
        while(iter.hasNext()) {
            String current = iter.next();

            if (current.startsWith(aString))
                return current;
        }

        return null;
    }

    public boolean contains(String aString) {
        Iterator<String> iter = collection.iterator();
        while(iter.hasNext()) {
```

```
            String current = iter.next();

            if (aString.equals(current))
                return true;
        }

        return false;
    }

    ...
}
```

By placing an abstraction between dependent and dependency (the interface `Collection`), the code loses any awareness of the underlying data structure and interacts with it only through an interface. All of these use cases now work without any coding changes:

```
boolean inList = new StringSearch(myList).contains("copern");

boolean inSet = new StringSearch(mySet).contains("copernicus");

boolean hasKey = new StringSearch(myMap.keySet()).contains("copernicus");

...
```

Now `StringSearch` is completely oblivious to the decisions of clients to use any kind of data structure (so long as they implement the `Collection` interface). You can even add new methods to `StringSearch` without impacting existing clients. This ability of the `Collection` interface to act as a contract for various services is extremely valuable, and you can mimic it in your own services to achieve a similar goal. Services that act according to a contract are well behaved. Going about this can be tricky, and we'll outline some best practices in the next section.

4.2.3 Programming to contract

Loose coupling via interfaces leads nicely to the idea of *programming to contract.* Recall that in chapter 1 we described a service as in part defined by a well-understood set of responsibilities called a contract. Programming to contract means that neither client nor service is aware of the other and communicates only via the contract. The only common ground is the understanding provided by this contract (interface). This means that either can evolve independently so long as both abide by the terms of the contract. A contract is also much more than a means of communication:

- It is a precise specification of behavior.
- It is a metaphor for *real-world* business purpose.
- It is a revelation of intent (of appropriate use).
- It is an inherent mode of documentation.
- It is the keystone for behavior *verification.*

The last point is extremely important because it means that a contract provides the means of testing classes. Verifying that an implementation works as it should is done by testing it against a contract. In a sense, a contract is a *functional requirements specification* for any implementation and one that is native to the programming language itself. Furthermore, a contract represents conceptual purpose and is thus akin to a *business contract.*

When ordering coffee at Starbucks, you follow a well-defined business process:

1 Stand in line.
2 Place your order.
3 Move to the edge of the counter to pick it up.

If Starbucks were to automate this process, the conceptual obligation between you as a client and the attendant would be a *programmatic* contract—probably not too different from listing 4.8.

Listing 4.8 The coffee shop contract!

```
public interface Customer {
    void waitInLine();

    boolean placeOrder(String choice);

    void pickup(Coffee prepared);
}

public interface Attendant {
    boolean takeOrder(String choice);

    Coffee prepareOrder();
}
```

Of course, there are plenty more steps in the real world (exchange of money, for one) but let's set them aside for now. What's important to note is that neither interface says anything about *how* to perform their function, merely *what* that function is. Well-behaved objects adhere strictly to their contracts, and accompanying unit tests help verify that they do. If any class were to violate the terms of its contract, the entire application would be at risk and most probably broken. If Starbucks were out of cappuccino and an order for one were placed, `Attendant.takeOrder()` would be expected to return `false`. If instead it returned `true` but failed to serve the order, this would break `Customers`.

Any class developed to the contract `Customer` or `Attendant` can be a drop-in replacement for either, while leaving the overall Starbucks system behaviorally consistent. Imagine a `BrazilianCustomer` served by a `RoboticAttendant` or perhaps a properly trained `ChimpanzeeCustomer` and `GorillaAttendant`.

Modeling conceptual business purpose goes much further. A carefully developed contract is the cornerstone for communication between business representatives and developers. Developers are clever, mathematical folk who are able to move quickly between abstractions and empiricism. But this is often difficult for representatives of the business who may be unfamiliar with software yet in turn contain all the knowledge about the problem that developers need. A contract can help clarify confusion and provide a bridge for common understanding between abstraction-favoring developers and empirical business folk. While you probably won't be pushing sheets of printed code under their noses, describing the system's interfaces and interoperation forms a reliable basis for communicating ideas around design.

A contract is also a *revelation of intent.* As such, the appropriate manner and context of a service's usage are revealed by its contract definition. This even extends to error handling and recovery. If instead of returning `false`, `Attendant.takeOrder()` threw an `OutOfCoffeeException`, the entire process would fail. Similarly, an `InputStream`'s methods throw `IOException` if there is an error because of hardware failure. `IOException` is explicitly declared on each relevant method and is thus part of the contract. Handling and recovering from such a failure are the responsibility of a client, perhaps by showing a friendly message or by trying the operation again.

Finally, a contract should be simple and readable, clear as to its purpose. Reading through a contract should tell you a lot about the classes that implement it. In this sense, it is an essential form of documentation. Look at this semantic interface from the `StringSearch` example shown earlier:

```
public interface StringSearch {
    boolean contains(String aString);

    String startsWith(String fragment);
}
```

This is a start, but there are several missing pieces. In the simple case of `contains()` we can infer that since it returns a `boolean`, it will return `true` if the string is found. However, what exactly does `startsWith()` return? At a guess, it returns a single successful match. But is this the first match? The last? And what does it return when there are no matches? Clearly, this is an inadequate specification to develop against. One further iteration is shown in listing 4.9.

Listing 4.9 `StringSearch` expressed as a contract

```
public interface StringSearch {

    /**
     * Tests if a string is contained within its list.
     *
     * @param aString Any string to look for.
     * @returns Returns true only if a matching string is found.
     */
    boolean contains(String aString);

    /**
     * Tests if a string in the list begins with a given sequence.
     *
     * @param fragment A partial string to search on.
     * @returns Returns the first match found or null if
     *     none were found.
     */
    String startsWith(String fragment);
}
```

Now StringSearch is clear about its behavior; startsWith() returns the first match or null if no matches are found. The implied benefit of this contractual programming is that code can be discretized into modules and units without their severely affecting one another when they change. DI is a natural fit in providing a framework for programming such loosely coupled code.

4.2.4 Loose coupling with dependency injection

So far, we've seen that loose coupling makes testing, reuse, and evolution of components easy. This makes for modules that are easy to build and maintain. Dependency injection helps by keeping classes relatively free of infrastructure code and by making it easy to assemble objects in various combinations. Because loosely coupled objects rely on contracts to collaborate with dependencies, it is also easy to plug in different implementations, via injection or mocks in a unit test. All it takes is a small change to the binding step. Keeping object graph structure described in one place also makes it easy to find and modify parts of it, with little impact to core application code.

Let's see this in practice. Let's say we have a book catalog, consisting of a library to search and locate books with. By following the principles of loose coupling, we've arrived at the interfaces shown in listing 4.10.

Listing 4.10 A book catalog and its library data service

```
public interface BookCatalog {
    Book search(String criteria);
}

public interface Library {
    Book findByTitle(String title);

    Book findByAuthor(String title);

    Book findByIsbn(String title);
}
```

BookCatalog refers only to the interface Library. Its search() method translates some free-form text search criteria into a search by title, author, or ISBN, subsequently calling the appropriate method on Library. In a simple case, the Library may be implemented as a file-based service, storing and retrieving Book records from disk. In bigger applications it will likely be an external database (like PostgreSQL[1] or Oracle). Altering the catalog system to use a database-backed variant of Library is as simple as changing Library's binding (see listing 4.11) to use the database-driven implementation.

Listing 4.11 A book catalog and a database-backed library service

```
public class BooksModule extends AbstractModule {

    @Override
    protected void configure() {
```

[1] PostgreSQL is an excellent, lightweight, and feature packed open source database. Find out more at http://www.postgresql.org.

```
        bind(Library.class).to(DatabaseLibrary.class);
        bind(BookCatalog.class).to(SimpleBookCatalog.class);
    }
}
```

So long as DatabaseLibrary correctly implements the Library interface, the program continues to work unhindered, and BookCatalog is none the wiser about its underlying storage mechanism. You don't have to compile it again. Listing 4.12 shows another change—this time of the catalog.

Listing 4.12 A desktop-GUI book catalog and a database-backed library service

```
public BooksModule extends AbstractModule {

    @Override
    protected void configure() {
        bind(Library.class).to(DatabaseLibrary.class);
        bind(BookCatalog.class).to(DesktopGUIBookCatalog.class);
    }
}
```

This time it's the Library that's oblivious to the goings on in our application. Loose coupling enables any of our services to evolve down their own paths and yet remain verifiable and behaviorally consistent (figure 4.5 visualizes this evolution), performing the intended service for end users.

Loose assembly of modules is extremely important to testing. It provides a tangible benefit since such code can be constructed easily in tests and given mock dependencies without any additional work. This last part is crucial to writing testable code. In the next section we will see why writing testable code is important and how it helps in developing better application designs in general.

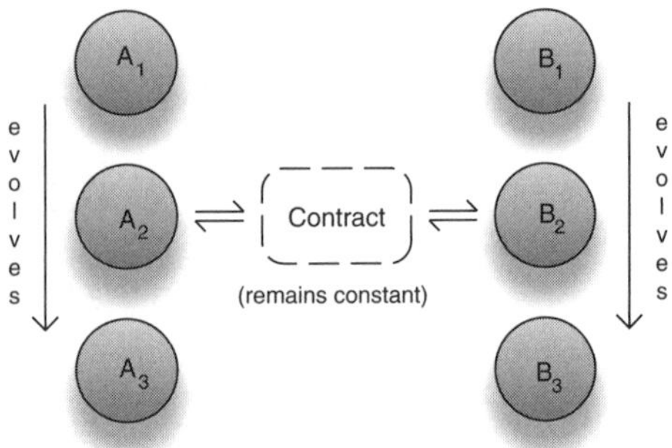

Figure 4.5 Independent evolution of A and B, with no impact to their collaboration

4.3 Testing components

One of the most important parts of software development is testing. Technology pundits argue that there is little value to code that has not been verified by some formal process. Without being able to assert expectations against an object's behavior, there's no way to tell if it fulfills its function. The fact that it compiles correctly, or runs in a deployment environment, is fairly useless in the broad sense. A functional test of an application (say by clicking through menu items in a desktop application) is a mite better than nothing at all, but not significantly so. It ignores several unseen failure points, such as bad data or concurrency bottlenecks.

While functional testing has its place in the quality assurance spectrum, the veracity of code simply can't be met without automated unit and integration tests. These tests provide the following:

- Unit-level assurance of functionality
- Simulation of disaster situations like failing hardware or resource depletion
- Detection of exceptional situations such as bugs in collaborating modules
- Detection of concurrency bottlenecks or thread-unsafe code
- Assurance of regression integrity[2]
- Benchmarking performance under extreme duress

Not only can you test a much broader spectrum of possible scenarios in code, but you can simulate disaster situations and measure performance under various loads. Automated tests are thus a vital part of any application, particularly one that is *programmed to contract.* Testing comes in different flavors, some or all of which can be automated by writing test code. Primary among these is the test accompanying an individual class or unit. This kind of test is independent of the rest of the application and intended to verify just the one unit. These tests are generally called *unit tests* but sometimes are also called *out-of-container* tests. Another form of testing asserts integration behavior between modules in a simulated environment.

4.3.1 Out-of-container (unit) testing

The idea of testing an individual unit of functionality (a class) raises questions about the surrounding environment. What about its dependencies? Its collaborators? Its clients? Testing a unit is *independent* of these surrounds. And this means independent of an injector too. As listing 4.13 shows, unit tests are not concerned with anything but the unit (single class) that they are testing.

Listing 4.13 A unit test of the book catalog, from listing 4.10

```
public class BookCatalogTest {

    @Test
    public final void freeFormSearch() {        <-- Test verifies search
        MockLibrary mock = new MockLibrary();

        new SimpleBookCatalog(mock)
              .search("dependency injection");

        assert mock.foundByKeyword();         <-- Verify mock after search
    }
}
```

We are quite happy to use construction by hand, in particular because there are very few dependencies (all of them mocked) and no dependents besides the test itself. It would be unnecessarily tedious to configure an injector just for a few mocks. If the test passes, there's some assurance that a correctly configured injector will work too, since the test uses normal language constructs. Furthermore, a *mocking framework* can make it a lot easier to create an object with mock dependencies.

2 Regression integrity is the idea that previously verified behavior is maintained on new development iterations, so you don't undo the work that's already been done (and successfully tested).

NOTE EasyMock, Mockito, and JMock are such powerful mock objects frameworks for Java. I would highly recommend Mockito to start with and EasyMock for more sophisticated uses.

This kind of test tests services outside an injector and outside an application—hence the name out-of-container testing. A significant point about this kind of testing is that it forces you to write loosely coupled classes. Classes that rely specifically on injector behavior or on other parts of the application are difficult to test in this fashion because they rely on some dependency that only the final application environment can provide. A database connection is a good example. If it's outside an application, these dependencies are not readily available and must be simulated using mocks.

When you encounter classes whose dependencies cannot be mocked, you should probably rethink design choices. Older versions of EJB encouraged such container-dependent code. Infrastructure concerns like security, transactions, or logging often make things harder since their effects are not directly apparent. Developers tend to want to test everything as a whole and end up hacking together parts of a real application or environment. These don't do justice to testing, because they remove the focus on testing individual units of functionality. Errors raised by such tests may be misleading because of subtle differences in application environments. So when testing, try focusing your attention on a single unit or class, mocking out the rest. If you can do this individually for all units, you will have much more confidence in them and can easily assemble them into working modules.

4.3.2 *I really need my dependencies!*

If the class you're testing does little more than call into its dependencies, you might be tempted to use an injector—at least for the relevant module and mock the rest. It's not unusual to see tests like this:

```
public class BookCatalogTest {
    private Injector injector;

    @BeforeMethod
    public final void setup() {
        injector = Guice.createInjector(new TestBooksModule());
    }

    @Test
    public final void freeFormBookSearch() {
        new SimpleBookCatalog(injector.getInstance(Library.class))
            .search("..");

        ...
    }
}
```

This is a bad idea. Not only will you introduce unnecessary complexity in your tests (they now depend on an injector), but you'll also have to maintain ancillary code in the form of `TestBooksModule`. This is injector configuration that exists purely for the unit test and adds no real value. Furthermore, if there are errors in the injector configuration, the test will fail with a false negative. You may spend hours looking for the bug in the wrong place, wasting time and effort on maintaining code that adds very little value to the test case.

4.3.3 More on mocking dependencies

If your classes do nothing more than call into their dependencies, is it still worth writing unit tests for them? *Absolutely.* In fact, it is imperative if you want to assert your module's integrity in any meaningful way. Verifying the behavior of a service is only half the picture. A class's use of its dependencies is a critical part of its behavior. Mock objects can track and verify that these calls are according to expectation. There are many ways to do this. Let's look at one using EasyMock and writing a behavior script. Listing 4.14 shows such a script for `Library` and verifies its proper use by `BookCatalog`. Remember we're trying to verify that `BookCatalog` depends correctly on `Library`, in other words, that it *uses* `Library` properly.

Listing 4.14 A mock script and assertion of behavior

```
import static org.easymock.EasyMock.*;

public class BookCatalogTest {

    @Test
    public final void freeFormBookSearch() {
        Library mock = createStrictMock(Library.class);

        String criteria = "dependency injection";

        expect(mock.findByAuthor(criteria))          <-- First try author
            .andReturn(null);

        expect(mock.findByKeyword(criteria))         <-- Then try keyword
            .andReturn(null);

        Book di = new Book("dependency injection");
        expect(mock.findByTitle(criteria))           <-- Finally try title
            .andReturn(di);

        replay(mock);                        <-- Signal the mock
                                                 to be ready
        new SimpleBookCatalog(mock)
            .search(criteria);

        verify(mock);    <-- Verify its usage
    }
}
```

In listing 4.14, we script the `Library` mock to expect searches by author and keyword first on each and to return `null`, signaling that no such book exists. Finally, on title search, we return a hand-created instance of book that we're after. This not only asserts the correct use of `Library` by `SimpleBookCatalog` but also asserts correct *order* of use. If `SimpleBookCatalog` were written to prefer searching by title over keyword and author, this test would fail, alerting us to the mistake. To complete the test, we can add yet another assertion that tests the behavior of `SimpleBookCatalog`. Here's the relevant portion from listing 4.14, modified appropriately:

```
Book di = new Book("dependency injection");

 ...
Book result = new SimpleBookCatalog(mock).search(criteria);

assert di.equals(result) : "Unexpected result was returned";
```

Notice that we perform this assertion in addition to the assertions that the mocks provide. Now we have a complete test of `SimpleBookCatalog`. A more elaborate form of testing takes more than one unit into account. This helps detect problems in the coherency between units and determines whether the application behaves well in a broader context. This form of testing is known as integration testing.

4.3.4 Integration testing

So far we've shown how to test individual units and assert their behavior. This ought to be the first step in any development process. We've also lain down reasons for keeping tests independent of an injector or other environment-specific concerns. As your code matures, and the time arrives for a completed module to be integrated into the larger system, new testing concerns arise. These concerns have to do with the interoperation of modules, their dependence on external factors like hardware or database resources, and the overall coherence of the system. Automated tests can help in this regard too, and this flavor of tests is called integration tests.

Integration testing is about testing how various pieces fit together as a whole. Naturally, the dependency injector plays a vital part in this assembly by helping connect modules together in a transparent and cohesive fashion. Figure 4.6 illustrates this architecture.

As figure 4.6 shows, infrastructure concerns like persistence and security are encapsulated in their own modules and interfaced with logic in other modules. The dependency injector is responsible for pulling all of them together to form a coherent whole.

The idea behind integration testing is to simulate user interaction with a system or, if the application is not directly exposed to a human user, to simulate the next most relevant actor. This might be:

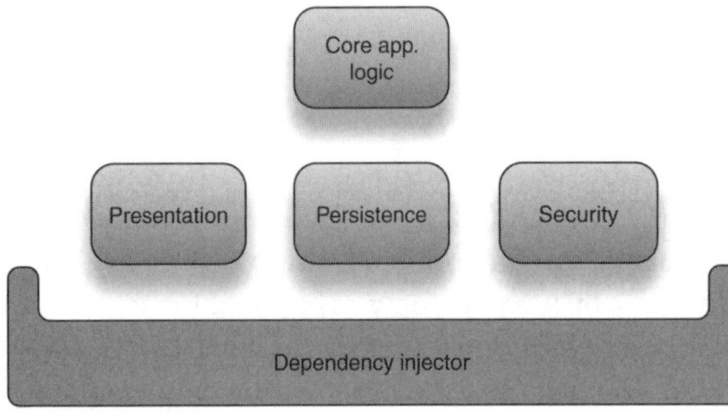

Figure 4.6 Architecture of modules brought together by dependency injection

- A batch of cleared bank checks
- Monitored cooling of a nuclear power plant
- Just about anything else you can imagine

Let's use the example of a web application that serves a page from a database. This will be an automated integration test (listing 4.15).

Listing 4.15 Integration test for a web application

```
public class HomePageIntegrationTest {
    private Injector injector;

    @BeforeTest
    public final void prepareContainer() {
        injector = Guice.createInjector(new WebModule(),
                     new TestPersistenceModule());
    }

    @AfterTest
    public final void cleanup() { .. }

    @Test
    public final void renderHomePage() throws Exception {
        HttpServletRequest request = createMock(..);
        HttpServletResponse response = createMock(..);

        injector.getInstance(HomeServlet.class)
            .service(request, response);

        //assert something about response
    }
}
```

Use a test environment for data resources

Get page servlet from injector and test

There are interesting things about the integration test in listing 4.15. Foremost among them, it looks like we've violated nearly every rule of unit testing. We're using an injector, not mocking anything apart from HTTP request (and response), and using a specialized configuration for tests. Of course, the simple explanation is that this isn't a unit test, so we can ignore these restrictions. But we can do better than that:

- Integration testing is about testing how modules interoperate, so we want to use actual production modules where possible.
- An accurate analog of the production environment is important, so we try to include as many of the variables as we can that go into it: infrastructure modules, the dependency injector, and any external services.
- There will probably be differences between a production and integration environment (such as which database instance to use), and these are captured in a parallel configuration, `TestPersistenceModule`.
- Integration tests are automated, so external interaction must be simulated (for example, this is done by mocking or simulating HTTP requests).

- Integration tests can be expensive, hence the `prepareContainer()` method that runs once before testing begins.
- They also require clean shutdowns of external services (such as database connections and timers), hence the presence of the `cleanup()` method, which runs after testing is complete.

When used properly, integration testing can help reveal errors in configuration and modular assembly. Typically these are environment-specific and often subtle. A healthy codebase will reveal very few coding errors in integration tests, since classes are covered by unit tests. More often than not, one finds that integration tests reveal configuration quirks in libraries or interoperability issues. These tests are an additional safeguard against design flaws in an architecture. However, they are neither the first line of defense (unit tests) nor the final word on application behavior (acceptance tests and QA). But they are a must-have tool to go in the toolbox of any developer.

Next up, we'll take a gander at integration from a number of perspectives. Modular applications can be integrated in various permutations to suit different goals, whether it be testing or deployment on weaker hardware such as a mobile device, where not all of the modules are required.

4.4 Different deployment profiles

We've shown how modules are composite globs of functionality that are like prefab units for big applications. As such, modular applications can be composed in different *profiles*, to different fits. A security module guarding HTTP access can be combined with a presentation module and a file-based persistence module to quickly create a web application. Architectures faithful to modularity principles will be able to evolve better, for instance, by replacing file-based persistence with a module that persists data in an RDBMS database.

While this sounds very simple, it's not always a plug-and-play scenario. Much of it depends on the flexibility of a module and its component classes. The more general and abstract (in other words, loosely coupled) a module's interface, the easier it will be to integrate. This generally comes from experience and natural evolution. Designing a module to be too abstract and all-purposed at the beginning is not a good idea either (and very rarely works).

Once you do have such an architecture, however, there are powerful uses to which it can be put. Chief among those is altering the deployment profile *dynamically*, for instance, by changing injector configuration at runtime. And this is what we call *rebinding*.

4.4.1 Rebinding dependencies

First of all, I must say that altering an injector configuration and the model of objects at runtime is potentially dangerous. Without careful library support, this can mean a loss of some validation and safety features that you would normally get at startup time. It can lead to unpredictable, erratic, and even undetectable bugs. However, if used with care, it can give your application very powerful dynamic features (such as *hot deployment* of changes). This is a fairly advanced use case, so convince yourself first that it is needed and that you can handle the requisite amount of testing and design.

Altering dependency bindings at runtime has several impacts. Injectors are there to give you a leg up, but they can't do everything, and putting them to unusual uses (like rebinding) is fraught with pitfalls:

- Once bound, a key provides instances of its related object until rebound.
- When you rebind a key, all objects already referencing the old binding retain the old instance(s).
- Rebinding is very closely tied to scope. A longer-lived object holding an instance of a key that has been rebound will need to be reinjected or discarded altogether.
- Rebinding is also tied to lifecycle. When significant dependencies are changed, relevant modules may need to be notified (more on this in chapter 7).
- Not all injectors support rebinding, but there are alternative design patterns in such cases.

Injectors that support rebinding are said to be mutable. This says nothing about field or object mutability (which is a different concept altogether). It refers purely to changing the association of a key to an object graph. PicoContainer is one such mutable injector. In the following section, we'll look at how to achieve mutability without a mutable injector, by using the well-known Adapter design pattern.

4.4.2 Mutability with the Adapter pattern

Here we will consider the case of an injector that does not support dynamic rebinding. The problem we're trying to solve is that there isn't enough knowledge while coding to bind all the dependencies appropriately. In other words, the structure of an object graph may change over the life of the application. One very simple solution is to maintain both object graphs and flip a switch when you need to move from one binding to another—something like this:

```
public class LongLived {
    private final DependencyA a;
    private final DependencyB b;          Start with a
    private boolean useA = true;

    public LongLived(DependencyA a, DependencyB b) {
        this.a = a;
        this.b = b;
    }

    public void rebind() {
        useA = false;
    }

    public void go() {
        if (useA)       <-- Work with a
            ...
```

```
        else
            ...     <— Or work with b
    }
}
```

Here the method `rebind()` controls which dependency `LongLived` uses. At some stage in its life, when the rebinding is called for, you need to make a call to `rebind()`.

This works—and probably quite well—but it seems verbose. What's more, it seems like there's a lot of infrastructure logic mixed in with our application. If we've learned anything so far, it's to avoid any such mixing. What's really needed is an abstraction, an intermediary to which we can move the rebinding logic and still remain totally transparent to clients. Providers and builders don't quite work because they either provide new instances of the *same* binding or provide an instance specific to some *context*. But adapters do. They are transparent to dependents (since an adapter extends its *adaptee*) and wrap any infrastructure, keeping it well hidden. Listing 4.16 demonstrates `LongLived` and its dependencies with the adapter pattern.

Listing 4.16 Dynamic rebinding with an adapter

```
public interface Dependency {
    int calculate();
}

public class DependencyAdapter implements Dependency, Rebindable {
    private final DependencyA a;
    private final DependencyB b;
    private boolean useA = true;

    @Inject
    public DependencyAdapter(DependencyA a, DependencyB b) {
        this.a = a;
        this.b = b;
    }

    public void rebind() {
        useA = false;
    }

    public int calculate() {
        if (useA)
            return a.calculate();

        return b.calculate();
    }
}
```

Now most of the infrastructure code has been moved to `DependencyAdapter`. When the rebinding occurs, flag `useA` is set to `false` and the adapter changes, now delegating calls to `DependencyB` instead. One interesting feature of this is the use of a `Rebindable` *role interface*. The control logic for dynamic rebinding is thus itself decoupled from the "rebinding" adapters. All it needs to do is maintain a list of `Rebindables`, go through them, and signal each one to `rebind()` when appropriate. This is neat because the logic of deciding which binding to use is completely known at coding time.

Some injectors even allow *multicasting* to make this an atomic, global process. Multicasting (and lifecycle in general) is explored in depth in chapter 7. Most of all, the use of an adapter ensures our client code is lean and behaviorally focused. Here's what `LongLived` looks like now, after the changes from listing 4.16.

```
public class LongLived {
    private final Dependency dep;

    @Inject
    public LongLived(Dependency dep) {
        this.dep = dep;
    }

    public void go() {
        int result = dep.calculate();
        ...
    }
}
```

That's certainly more concise. Rebinding of the key associated with `Dependency` is now completely transparent to `LongLived`—and any other client code for that matter. This is especially important because it means that unit tests don't have to be rewritten to account for a change in infrastructure. This is a satisfying saving.

4.5 Summary

Objects are discrete functional units of data mixed with operations on that data. In the same sense, larger collections of objects and their responsibilities are known as *modules*. A module is typically a *separate* and *independent* compilation unit. It can be maintained, tested, and developed in isolation. So long as it fulfills the terms of its contract to collaborators, a module can be dropped into any well-designed architecture almost transparently.

Components that are invasive of other components or rely on specific implementation details are said to be *tightly coupled*. Tight coupling is detrimental to maintenance and readability. Moreover, it prevents reuse of utility-style components because they are tightly bound to concrete classes rather than abstractions such as interfaces. This reduces the overall modular integrity of a program. To avoid tight coupling, choose abstractions between a client and service. So long as each fulfills the terms of the mediary contract, either can evolve or be replaced with no impact to the other or to the system as a whole. This flows down to component granularity from the concept of modules. Contracts reveal many other things about a component and about design. These are:

- A business metaphor
- An essential form of (self-) documentation
- A revelation of intent
- A specification for building implementations
- A means of verifying behavior

Code that is modular is also easy to test. Testing specific modules (or components) is a vital part of their development, as it is the primary way to verify their correctness. Tests that rely on components to have dependencies wired are poor tests because they can easily confuse the issue when an error occurs. You may spend hours tracking down whether the component under test is responsible or if one of its dependencies caused the error. The use of mock objects is a powerful remedy to this predicament, and indeed it's an important way to narrow down and verify the behavioral correctness of a piece of code. Never allow injectors or other environment-specific frameworks to creep into unit tests, even as a crutch. Try to use mocks and test units in isolation as much as possible. Code that conforms to this focus is said to be tested out of container.

Once a module has been developed and tested, it is useful to test whether it properly fits together with the rest of the system. This too can be done by automation via integration testing. Integration tests try to be a close analog of the eventual production environment but with some obvious differences (simulated direct user interaction, lower-grade hardware, or external resources). Integration testing can be very useful in detecting bugs caused by the software or hardware environment and by configuration. These are often subtle and not caught easily in unit tests. In a healthy program, integration tests should rarely fail.

In rare cases, it is useful to alter injector configuration dynamically. This is analogous to reassembling the modular structure of the application, but done so at runtime. Not all DI libraries support this kind of functionality directly. One mitigant is to provide dependents with all possible dependencies, then force them to decide which to use as appropriate. This works, but it isn't a great solution because it pollutes application logic with infrastructure concerns. As an alternative solution, the adapter pattern works nicely. It encapsulates any infrastructure logic and can be used in place of the original dependency with no impact to client code. A change in the binding is signaled to the adapter(s) via a rebinding notification, and the adapter shifts to the new binding. While this is a robust and workable solution, it is fraught with potential pitfalls and should be weighed carefully before being embarked upon.

Modular code is wonderful for many reasons. As I've already mentioned, these include testing, reuse, and independent development in isolation. It allows many streams of development (and indeed teams of developers) to work on pieces of a very large composite application and keeps complexity to a minimum. Modularity fits very nicely into dependency injection. DI is not only able to wire and assemble modular code quickly, but it is also able to cast it in different profiles (structures) with minimal impact on collaborators. Thus, dependency injection empowers modular programming.

5 Scope: a fresh breath of state

This chapter covers:

- Understanding what scope means
- Understanding singleton and no scope
- Applying practical scopes for the web

"Still this planet's soil for noble deeds grants scope abounding."

—Johann Goethe

In one sentence, *scope* is a fixed duration of time or method calls in which an object exists. In other words, a scope is a context under which a given key refers to the same instance. Another way to look at this is to think of scope as the amount of time an object's state persists. When the scope context ends, any objects bound under that scope are said to be *out of scope* and cannot be injected again in other instances.

State is important in any application. It is used to incrementally build up data or responsibility. State is also often used to track the context of certain processes, for instance, to track objects in the same database *transaction*.

In this chapter we'll talk about some of the general-purpose scopes: *singleton* and *no scope*. These are scopes that are universally applicable in managing state.

We'll also look at managing state in specific kinds of applications, particularly the web. Managing user-specific state is a major part of scoping for the web, and this is what the *request, session, flash,* and *conversation* scopes provide. We'll look at a couple of implementations of these with regard to Guice and Spring and how they may be applied in building practical web applications. First, we'll take a primer on scopes.

5.1 What is scope?

The real power of scope is that it lets you model the state of your objects declaratively. By telling the injector that a particular key is bound under a scope, you can move the construction and wiring of objects to the injector's purview. This has some important benefits:

- It lets the injector manage the *latent state* of your objects.
- It ensures that your services get new instances of dependencies as needed.
- It implicitly separates state by context (for example, two HTTP requests imply different contexts).
- It reduces the necessity for *state-aware* application logic (which makes code much easier to test and reason about).

Scope properly applied means that code working in a particular context is oblivious to that context. It is the injector's responsibility to manage these contexts. This means not only that you have an added separation between infrastructure and application logic, but also that the same services can be used for many purposes simply by altering their scopes. Take this example of a family bathroom and its toothpaste:

```
family.give("Joanie", injector.getInstance(Toothpaste.class));
family.give("Jackie", injector.getInstance(Toothpaste.class));
family.give("Sachin", injector.getInstance(Toothpaste.class));
```

Looking at this code we can say that the `Toothpaste` is used by Joanie first, then by Jackie, and finally by Sachin. We might also guess that each family member receives the same tube of toothpaste. If the tube were especially small, Sachin might be left with no toothpaste at all (as per figure 5.1).

This is an example of context: All three family members use the same bathroom and therefore have access to the same instance of `Toothpaste`. It is exactly the same as the following program, using construction by hand:

```
Toothpaste toothpaste = new FluorideToothpaste();

family.give("Joanie", toothpaste);
family.give("Jackie", toothpaste);
family.give("Sachin", toothpaste);
```

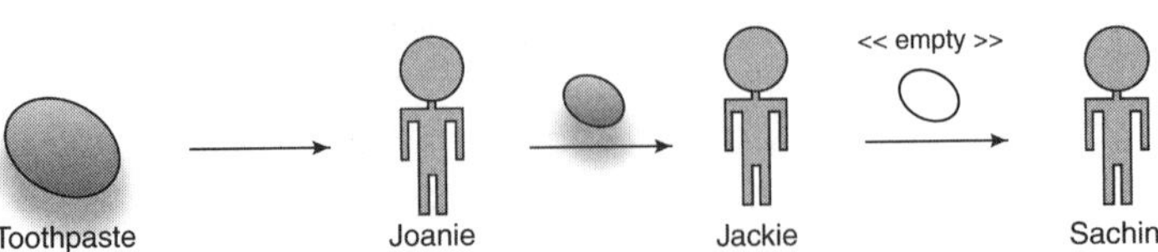

Figure 5.1 The injector distributes the same instance of `Toothpaste` to all family members.

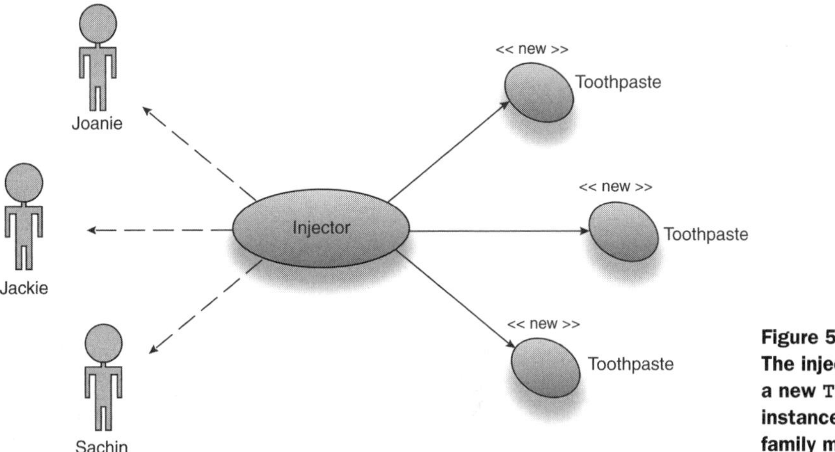

Figure 5.2 The injector creates a new `Toothpaste` instance for each family member.

If this were the whole life of the injector, only one instance of `Toothpaste` would ever be created and used. In other words, `Toothpaste` is bound under *singleton* scope. If each family member had his *own* bathroom (each with its own tube of toothpaste), the semantics would change considerably (figure 5.2).

```
family.give("Joanie", injector.getInstance(Toothpaste.class));
family.give("Jackie", injector.getInstance(Toothpaste.class));
family.give("Sachin", injector.getInstance(Toothpaste.class));
```

Nothing has changed in the code, but now a *new* instance of `Toothpaste` is available to each family member. And now there is no danger of Sachin being deprived of toothpaste by Joanie or Jackie. In this case, the context under which each object operates is unique (that is, its own bathroom). You can think of this as the opposite of singleton scoping. Technically this is like having no scope at all.

5.2 The no scope (or default scope)

In a sense, no scope fulfills the functions of scope, as it

- Provides new instances transparently
- Is managed by the injector
- Associates a service (key) with some context

Or does it? The first two points are indisputable. However, there arises some difficulty in determining exactly what context it represents. To get a better idea of no scope's semantics, let's dissect the example of the toothpaste from earlier. We saw that it took no change in the use of objects to alter their scope. The `family.give()` sequence looks exactly the same for both singleton and no scope:

```
family.give("Joanie", injector.getInstance(Toothpaste.class));
family.give("Jackie", injector.getInstance(Toothpaste.class));
family.give("Sachin", injector.getInstance(Toothpaste.class));
```

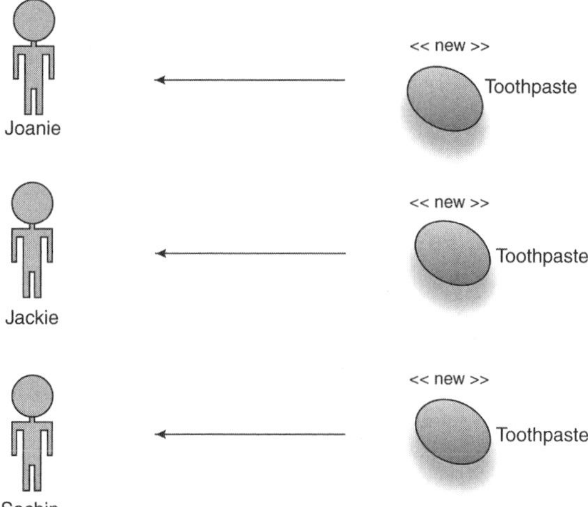

Figure 5.3 Each member of the family receives her own instance of `Toothpaste`.

Or, expanded using construction by hand (modeled in figure 5.3), the same code can be expressed as follows:

```
Toothpaste toothpaste = new FluorideToothpaste();
family.give("Joanie", toothpaste);

toothpaste = new FluorideToothpaste();
family.give("Jackie", toothpaste);

toothpaste = new FluorideToothpaste();
family.give("Sachin", toothpaste);
```

In no scope, every reference to `Toothpaste` implies a new `Toothpaste` instance. We likened this to the family having three bathrooms, one for each member. However, this is not exactly accurate. For instance, if Sachin brushed his teeth twice,

```
family.give("Joanie", injector.getInstance(Toothpaste.class));
family.give("Jackie", injector.getInstance(Toothpaste.class));
family.give("Sachin", injector.getInstance(Toothpaste.class));
family.give("Sachin", injector.getInstance(Toothpaste.class));
```

we would end up with a total of four `Toothpaste` instances (see figure 5.4).

In our conceptual model, there were only three bathrooms. But in practice there were four tubes of toothpaste. This means that no scope cannot be relied on to adhere to any conceptual context. No scope means that every time an injector looks

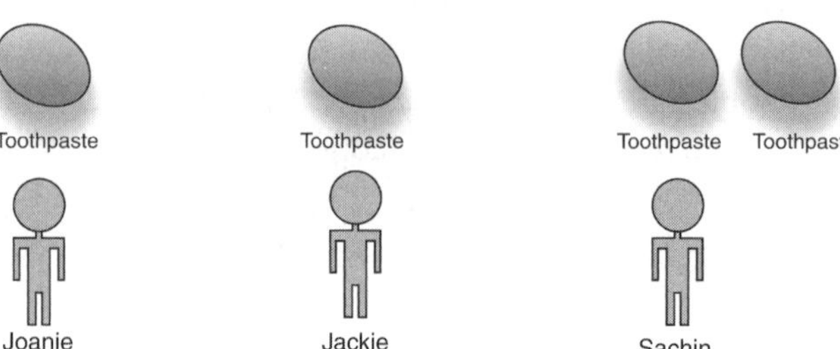

Figure 5.4 There are now four instances of `Toothpaste`, one for each use.

for a given key (one bound under no scope), *it will construct and wire a new instance.* Furthermore, let's say Sachin took Joanie on vacation and only Jackie was left at home. She would brush her teeth once, as follows:

```
family.give("Jackie", injector.getInstance(Toothpaste.class));
```

This would mean only one instance of `Toothpaste` was ever created for the life of the application. This was exactly what happened with singleton scoping, but this time it was purely accidental that it did. Given these two extremes, it is difficult to lay down any kind of strict rules for context with no scope. You could say, perhaps, that no scope is a split-second scope where the context is entirely tied to referents of a key. This would be a reasonable supposition. Contrast singleton and no scope in figure 5.5.

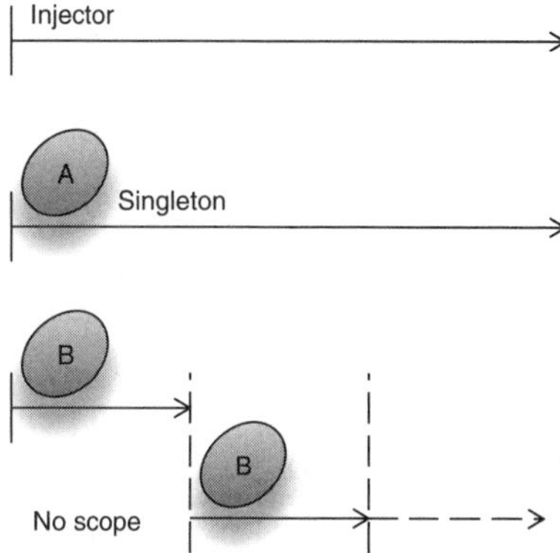

Figure 5.5 Timeline of contexts, contrasting singleton and no scope

No scope is a very powerful tool for working with injector-managed components. This is partly because it allows a certain amount of flexibility in scaling upward. Dependents that exist for longer times (or in *wider* scopes) may safely obtain no-scoped objects as they are required. If you recall the Provider pattern from chapter 4, there is a close similarity. `Granny` obtained new instances of an `Apple` on each use (see listing 5.1, modeled in figure 5.6).

Listing 5.1 An example of no scope using the Provider pattern

```
public class Granny {

    private Provider<Apple> appleProvider;

    public void eat() {
        appleProvider.get().consume();     // Two new Apples
        appleProvider.get().consume();     // created
    }
}
```

In listing 5.1, the `eat()` method uses a provider to retrieve new instances, just as we did for `Toothpaste`, earlier. Here `Apple` is no scoped.

Guice and Spring differ in nomenclature with regard to the no scope. Spring calls it as the *prototype* scope, the idea being that a key (and binding) is a kind of template

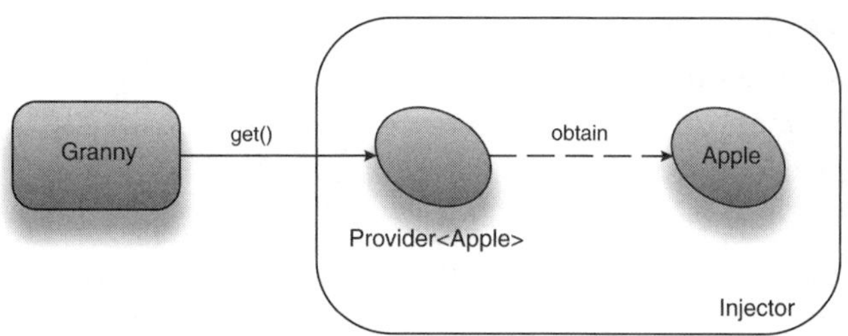

Figure 5.6 `Granny` obtains instances of `Apple` (bound to no scope) from a provider.

(or prototype) for creating new objects. Recall chapter 3, in the section on constructor injection and object validity, where no scoping enabled multiple threads to see independent instances of an object (modeled in figure 5.7):

```
<beans ...>
    <bean id="slippery" class="Slippery" scope="prototype"/>
    <bean id="shady" class="Shady" scope="prototype"/>

    <bean id="safe" class="UnsafeObject" init-method="init" scope="prototype">
        <property name="slippery" ref="slippery">
        <property name="shady" ref="shady">
    </bean>
</beans>
```

This object was actually safe, because any dependents of key *safe* were guaranteed to see new, independent instances of `UnsafeObject`. Like singleton, the name prototype comes from the Gang of Four book, *Design Patterns*. For the rest of this book I will continue to refer to it as, largely because it is a more descriptive name.

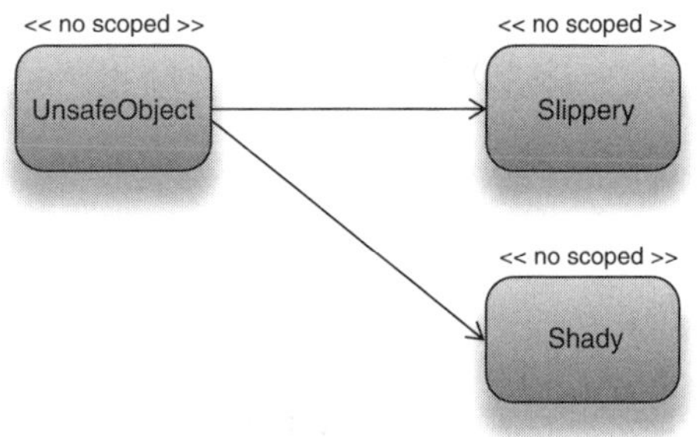

Figure 5.7 `UnsafeObject` and both its dependencies were no scoped.

Like Guice, PicoContainer also assumes the no scope if a key is not explicitly bound to some scope:

```
MutablePicoContainer injector = new DefaultPicoContainer();
injector.addComponent(Toothpaste.class);

family.give("Joanie", injector.getComponent(Toothpaste.class));
family.give("Jackie", injector.getComponent (Toothpaste.class));
...
```

There's almost no difference.

NOTE You will sometimes also hear no scope referred to as the *default* scope. This is a less descriptive name and typically connotes either Guice or PicoContainer (since they *default* to no scope).

While no scope doesn't really lend itself to a context, singleton scope does so quite naturally. Although the design pattern is itself applied in many different ways, we can establish a context quite easily for a singleton.

5.3 The singleton scope

Very simply, a singleton's context is the injector itself. The life of a singleton is tied to the life of the injector (as in figure 5.8).

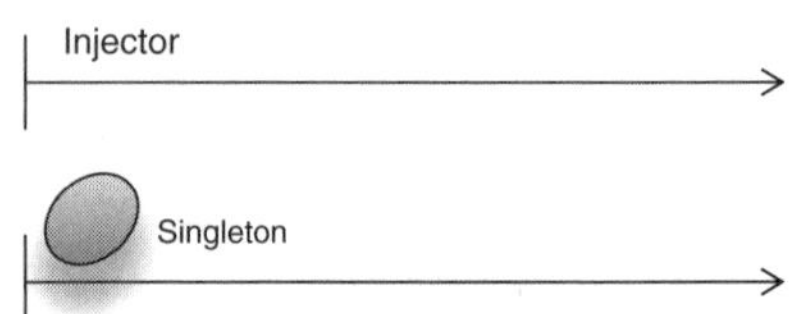

Figure 5.8 Timeline view of an injector and singleton-scoped object `A`

Therefore, only one instance of a singleton is ever created per injector. It is important to emphasize this last point, since it is possible for multiple injectors to exist in the same application. In such a scenario, each injector will hold a different instance of the singleton-scoped object. This is important to understand because many people mistakenly believe that a singleton means one instance for the entire life of an application. In dependency injection, this is not the case. The distinction is subtle and often confusing. In fact, PicoContainer has dropped the term *singleton* and instead refers to it as *cache* scoping.

I persist with *singleton scope*, however, for a few reasons:

- A *singleton-scoped* object is different from a *singleton-patterned* object (more on this shortly).
- The term *singleton* is well known and reasonably well understood, even if its particular semantics are not.
- *Cache scoping* is a different concept altogether (which you will see in the next chapter).

Identifying which service should be a singleton is quite a divisive issue. It is a design decision that should impinge on the nature of a service. If a service represents a conceptual nexus for clients, then it is a likely candidate. For instance, a database *connection pool* is a central port of call for any service that wants to connect to a database (see figure 5.9). Thus, connection pools are good candidates for singleton scoping.

Similarly, services that are stateless (in other words, objects that have no dependencies or whose dependencies are immutable) are good candidates. Since there is no state to manage, no scoping and singleton scoping are both equally viable options. In such cases, the singleton scope has advantages over no scope for a number of reasons:

- Objects can be created at startup (sometimes called *eager instantiation*), saving on construction and wiring overhead.
- There is a single point of reference when stepping through a debugger.
- Maintaining the lone instance saves on memory (memory complexity is *constant* as opposed to *linear* in the case of no scoping; see figure 5.10).

Business objects are perfect candidates for singleton scoping. They hold no state but typically require data-access dependencies. These services are sometimes referred to as

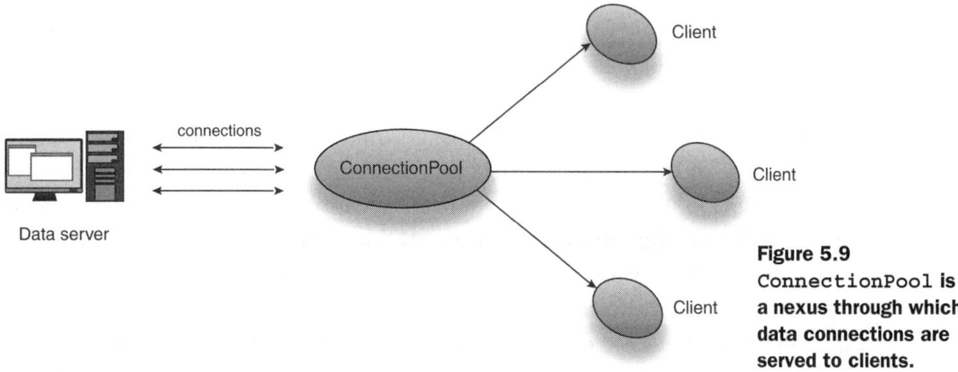

Figure 5.9 **`ConnectionPool` is a nexus through which data connections are served to clients.**

managers or simply business APIs, as in `PersonnelManager`, `SalaryManager`, and `StockOptionsService` in a hypothetical employee payroll system. Any services-oriented APIs are likewise good candidates to be stateless singletons. We'll talk a bit more about *services-oriented architecture* (SOA) in chapter 10.

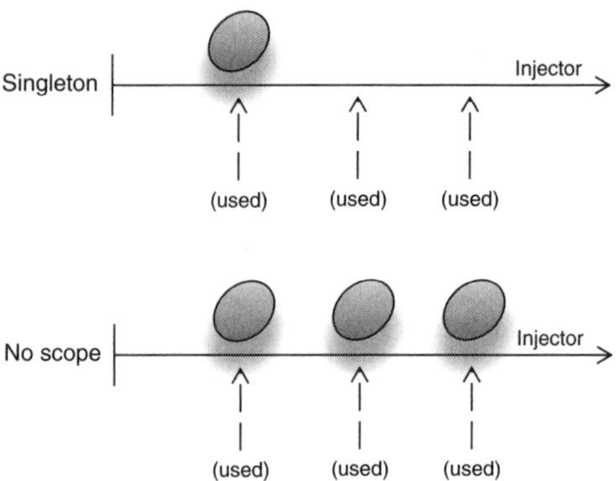

Figure 5.10 Memory usage for a singleton is constant compared to linear for no-scoped instances.

Another oft-stated use case for singletons is when dealing with any object graphs that are expensive to construct and assemble. This may be due to any of the following reasons:

- The object graph itself being very large
- Reliance on slow external resources (like network storage)
- Some difficult computation performed after construction

These aren't good enough reasons in themselves to warrant singleton scoping. Instead you should be asking questions about context. If an external resource is designed to be held open over a long period, then yes, it may warrant singleton scoping, for example, the pool of database connections.

On the other hand, a TCP socket, while potentially expensive to acquire (and cheap to hold onto) may not warrant singleton scoping. If you were writing a game that logs in to a server over a TCP connection when playing against others, you certainly would not want it to be a singleton. If a user happened to log out and back in to a new server in a different network location, a new context for the network service would be established and consequently would need a new instance, not the old singleton instance.

Similarly, the size of the object graph should not play a major role in deciding an object's scope. Object graphs that have several dependencies, which themselves have dependencies, and so on, are not necessarily expensive to construct and assemble. They may have several cheaply buildable parts. So without seeing clear shortcomings in an object's performance, don't be in a rush to optimize it as a singleton. This is a mantra you can repeat to yourself every time you start to speculate and worry about performance in any context.

Computational expense may be a legitimate reason for scoping an object as a singleton, but here too, there are other prevailing concerns. Is the computation a one-time activity? Do its values never change throughout the life of the application? And can you separate the expense of computation from the object itself by, for instance, storing the resultant value in a *memo object*? If you can answer these questions, you may have a singleton on your hands. Remember the singleton litmus test: Should the object exist for the same duration as the injector? In the coming sections, we'll look at how the semantics of the singleton scope affect design in various situations.

Algorithmic (or asymptotic) complexity

Complexity in computing is a measure of the scalability of an algorithm with regard to resources. These resources may be CPU cycles (time complexity), RAM (memory complexity), or any other kind of physical resource that the algorithm may demand (for instance, network bandwidth). Complexity is used to indicate how the algorithm performs with increasing size of input. The input is typically expressed as a number n, indicating the total number of input items. For instance, a text-search algorithm may count the number of characters in a string as its input.

Performance is typically expressed in big Oh notation: $O(n)$ or $O(n^2)$, and so on. Everything is relative to n; the idea is to measure how an algorithm scales for very large values of n. Constant complexity, which is $O(1)$, indicates that the algorithm is independent of n, even for huge values of n. This is considered good because it means the algorithm will only ever consume a fixed amount of resources, regardless of its input.

Going back to the text-search algorithm, it is easy to see that its time complexity is dependent on the size of the input (since every character needs to be searched). This is called *linear complexity* and is usually written as $O(n)$.

In my example of no scoping, the input items are the number of *dependents* of the no-scoped dependency, and the amount of memory allocated scales in proportion to this number. Therefore, its memory complexity is also linear. If I changed to singleton scoping, the memory complexity would be constant, since only the one instance is created and shared by all dependents.

5.3.1 *Singletons in practice*

The important thing to keep in mind about scoping is that a key is bound under a scope, not an object or class. This is true of any scope, not just the singleton. Take the following example of a master terminal that can see several security cameras in a building:

```
<bean id="terminal" class="MasterTerminal" scope="singleton"/>

<bean id="camera.basement" class="SimpleCamera" scope="prototype">
    <constructor-arg ref="terminal"/>
</bean>

<bean id="camera.penthouse" class="SimpleCamera" scope="prototype">
    <constructor-arg ref="terminal"/>
</bean>
```

Notice that I explicitly declare `terminal` as a singleton (by default, Spring beans are all singletons) and both cameras as no scoped (`scope="prototype"`). In this configuration, both `camera.basement` and `camera.penthouse` share the same instance of `MasterTerminal`. Any further keys will also share this instance. Consider this equivalent in Guice, using a module:

```
public class BuildingModule extends AbstractModule {

    @Override
    protected void configure() {
bind(Camera.class).annotatedWith(Basement.class).
➥   to(SimpleCamera.class);
bind(Camera.class).annotatedWith(Penthouse.class).
➥   to(SimpleCamera.class);

        bind(MasterTerminal.class).in(Singleton.class);
    }
}
```

Here we use combinatorial keys (see chapter 2) to identify the basement and penthouse security cameras. Since Guice binds keys under no scope by default, we need only scope `MasterTerminal`:

```
    bind(MasterTerminal.class).in(Singleton.class);
```

This has the same semantics as the Spring configuration. All security camera instances share the same instance of `MasterTerminal`, as shown in figure 5.11.

Another option is to directly annotate `MasterTerminal` as a singleton:

```
@Singleton
public class MasterTerminal { .. }

public class BuildingModule extends AbstractModule {

    @Override
    protected void configure() {
bind(Camera.class).annotatedWith(Basement.class).
➥   to(SimpleCamera.class);
bind(Camera.class).annotatedWith(Penthouse.class).
➥   to(SimpleCamera.class);
                        }
}
```

This lets you skip an explicit binding (see `BuildingModule`). Figure 5.12 shows how a singleton-scoped instance is shared among no-scoped objects.

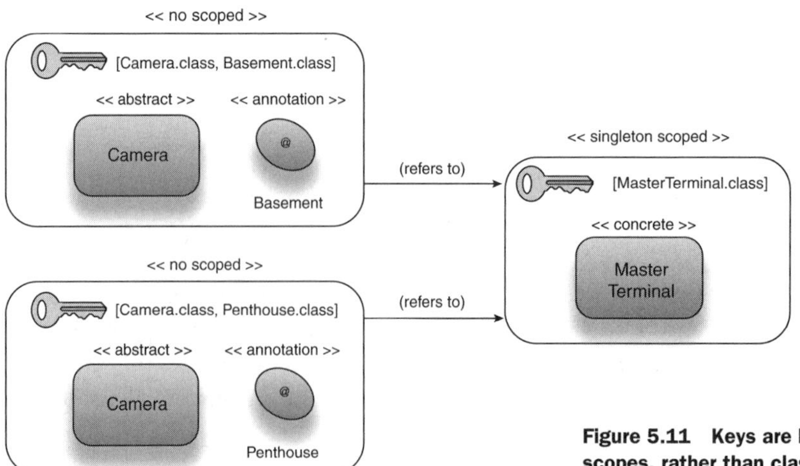

Figure 5.11 Keys are bound under scopes, rather than classes or objects

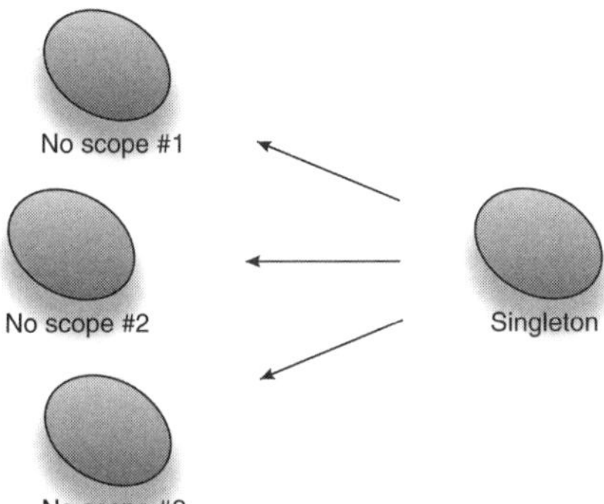

Figure 5.12 A singleton-scoped instance injected into many no-scoped instances

To further illustrate the difference between no scope and singleton scope, let's examine another interesting case. Here is a class `BasementFloor`, which represents a part of the building where security cameras may be installed:

```
public class BasementFloor {
    private final Camera camera1;
    private final Camera camera2;

    @Inject
    public BasementFloor(@Basement Camera camera1,
                         @Basement Camera camera2) {

        this.camera1 = camera1;
        this.camera2 = camera2;
    }
}
```

You might expect that both `camera1` and `camera2` refer to the same instance of security camera, that is, the one identified by key `[Camera, Basement]`. But this is not what happens—`camera1` and `camera2` end up with two different instances of `Camera`. This is because the key `[Camera, Basement]` is bound to no scope (see figure 5.13).

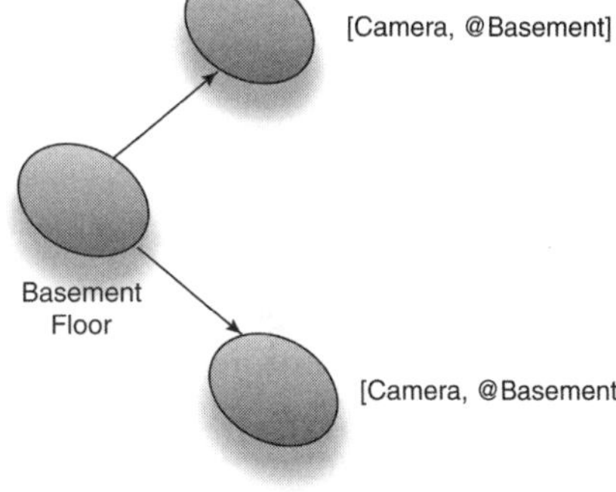

Figure 5.13 `BasementFloor` is wired with two separate instances of no-scoped key `[Camera, @Basement]`.

Similarly, any dependents of `[Camera, Penthouse]` will end up with new, unrelated instances of `Camera`. Consider another class, `Building`, which houses more than one kind of camera:

```
public class Building {
    private final Camera camera1;
    private final Camera camera2;
    private final Camera camera3;
    private final Camera camera4;

    @Inject
    public Building(@Basement Camera camera1,
```

```
                    @Basement Camera camera2,
                    @Penthouse Camera camera3,
                    @Penthouse Camera camera4) {

        this.camera1 = camera1;
        this.camera2 = camera2;
        this.camera3 = camera3;
        this.camera4 = camera4;
    }
}
```

Here, all four fields of `Building` receive different instances of `Camera` even though only two keys are present. This is opposed to the following class, `ControlRoom`, which has four fields that refer to the same instance of `MasterTerminal` but via four references (modeled in figure 5.14):

```
public class ControlRoom {
    private final MasterTerminal terminal1;
    private final MasterTerminal terminal2;
    private final MasterTerminal terminal3;
    private final MasterTerminal terminal4;

    @Inject
    public ControlRoom(MasterTerminal terminal1,
                MasterTerminal terminal2,
                MasterTerminal terminal3,
                MasterTerminal terminal4) {

        this.terminal1 = terminal1;
        this.terminal2 = terminal2;
        this.terminal3 = terminal3;
        this.terminal4 = terminal4;
    }
}
```

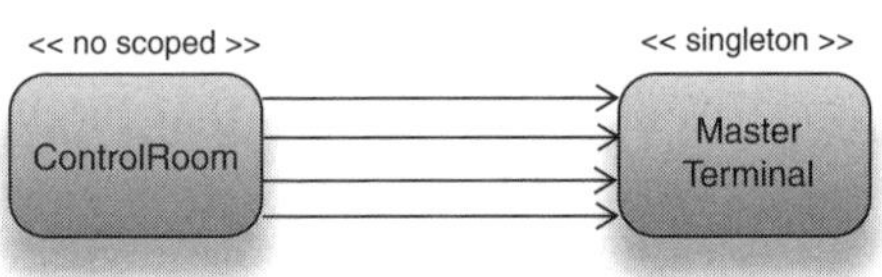

Figure 5.14 All four fields of `ControlRoom` are wired with the same instance of `MasterTerminal`.

If we added a new kind of `MasterTerminal`, bound to a different key, then this would be a different instance. Let's say I add a `MasterTerminal` for the basement only:

```
public class BuildingModule extends AbstractModule {

    @Override
    protected void configure() {
bind(Camera.class).annotatedWith(Basement.class).
➥  to(SimpleCamera.class);
bind(Camera.class).annotatedWith(Penthouse.class).
➥  to(SimpleCamera.class);

bind(MasterTerminal.class).annotatedWith(Master.class).in(Singleton.class);

        bind(MasterTerminal.class).annotatedWith(Basement.class)
            .to(BasementTerminal.class)
            .in(Singleton.class);

    }
}
```

Now any dependents of `[MasterTerminal, Master]` see the same shared instance, but any dependents of key `[MasterTerminal, Basement]` see a different instance. The modified version of `Building` in listing 5.2 illustrates this situation.

Listing 5.2 Object with two different singleton-scoped dependencies

```
public class ControlRoom {
    private final MasterTerminal terminal1;
    private final MasterTerminal terminal2;

    private final MasterTerminal terminal3;
    private final MasterTerminal terminal4;

    @Inject
    public ControlRoom(@Master MasterTerminal terminal1,
                @Master MasterTerminal terminal2,
                @Basement MasterTerminal terminal3,
                @Basement MasterTerminal terminal4) {

        this.terminal1 = terminal1;
        this.terminal2 = terminal2;
        this.terminal3 = terminal3;
        this.terminal4 = terminal4;
    }
}
```

Shared instance of [MasterTerminal, Master]

Shared instance of [MasterTerminal, Basement]

In listing 5.2, `terminal1` and `terminal2` share the same instance of `MasterTerminal`. But `terminal3` and `terminal4` share a different instance. I belabor this point because it is very important to distinguish that a key, rather than an object, is bound under a scope. Singleton scoping allows many instances of the same class to exist and be used by dependents; it allows only one shared instance of a key. This is quite different from the conventional understanding of singletons. This idiom implies a more absolute single instance per application and is definitely problematic. In the following section I'll explain why I go so far as to call it an anti-pattern when compared with the much more erudite singleton scope.

5.3.2 The singleton anti-pattern

You have probably heard a lot of discussion around the web and in technical seminars about the horrors of the singleton as an anti-pattern. Earlier we drew a distinction between *singleton scope*, a feature of DI, and *singleton objects* (or singleton *anti-patterns*), which are the focus of much of this debate. The singleton anti-pattern has several problems. Compounding these problems is the fact that singletons are very useful and therefore employed liberally by developers everywhere.

Its problems however, greatly outweigh its usefulness and should warn you off them for good (especially when dependency injection can save the day with singleton scoping). Let's break this down in code:

```
public class Console {
    private static Console instance = null;

    public static synchronized Console getInstance() {
```

```
        if (null == instance)
            instance = new Console();

        return instance;
    }

    ...
}
```

I'm sure you have seen or written code like this. I certainly have. Its purpose is quite simple; it allows only one instance of `Console` ever to be created for the life of the program (representing the one monitor in a computer, for example). If an instance does not yet exist, it creates one and stores it in a static variable `instance`:

```
if (null == instance)
    instance = new Console();

return instance;
```

The static `getInstance()` method is declared synchronized so that concurrent threads don't accidentally attempt to create instances concurrently. In essence, `getInstance()` is a Factory method—but a special type of Factory that produces only one instance, thereafter returning the stored instance every time. You might say this is the Factory equivalent of singleton scoping.

Apart from all the foibles that Factories bring, note that this immediately causes one major problem. This code is not conducive to testing. If an object relies on `Console.getInstance()` to retrieve a `Console` instance and print something to it, there is no way for us to write a unit test that verifies this behavior. We cannot pass in a substitute `Console` in the following code:

```
public class StockTicker {
    private Console console = Console.getInstance();

    public void tick() {
        //print to console
        ...
    }
}
```

`StockTicker` directly retrieves its dependency from the singleton Factory method. In order to test it with a mock `Console`, you'd have to rewrite `Console` to expose a setter method:

```
public class Console {
    private static Console instance = null;

    public static synchronized Console getInstance() {
        if (null == instance)
            instance = new Console();

        return instance;
    }

    public static synchronized void setInstance(Console console) {
        instance = console;
```

```
    }
    ...
}
```

Patterns that force you to add extra code or infrastructure logic purely for the purposes of testing are poor servants of good design. Nonetheless, now you can test StockTicker:

```
public class StockTickerTest {

    @Test
    public final void printToConsole() {
        Console.setInstance(new MockConsole());
        ...
    }
}
```

But what if there are other tests that need to create their *own* mocked consoles for different purposes (say, a file listing service)? Leaving the mocked instance in place will clobber those tests. To fix that, we have to change the test again:

```
public class StockTickerTest {

    @Test
    public final void printToConsole() {
        Console previous = Console.getInstance();
        try {
            Console.setInstance(new MockConsole());
            ...
        } finally {
            Console.setInstance(previous);
        }
    }
}
```

I wrapped the entire test in a `try/finally` block to ensure that any exceptions thrown by the test do not subvert the `Console` reset.

TIP Depending on your choice of test framework, there may be other methods of doing this. I like to use *TestNG*,[1] which allows the declaration of setup and teardown methods that run before and after each test. See listing 5.3.

Listing 5.3 A test written in TestNG with setup and teardown hooks

```
public class StockTickerTest {
    private Console previous;

    @BeforeMethod
    void setup() {
```

[1] TestNG is a flexible Java testing framework created by Cedric Beust and others. It takes many of the ideas in JUnit and improves on them. Find out more about TestNG at http://www.testng.org and read Cedric's blog at http://beust.com/weblog.

```
        previous = Console.getInstance();
    }

    @Test
    public final void printToConsole() {
        Console.setInstance(new MockConsole());
        ...
    }

    @AfterMethod
    void teardown() {
        Console.setInstance(previous);
    }
}
```

This is a lot of boilerplate to write just to get tests working. It gets worse if you have more than one singleton dependency to mock. Furthermore, if you have many tests running in parallel (in multiple threads), this code doesn't work at all because threads may crisscross and interfere with the singleton. That would make all your tests completely unreliable. This ought to be a showstopper.

If you have more than one injector in an application, the situation grows worse. Singleton objects are shared even *between* injectors and can cause a real headache if you are trying to separate modules by walling them off in their own injectors (see figure 5.15).

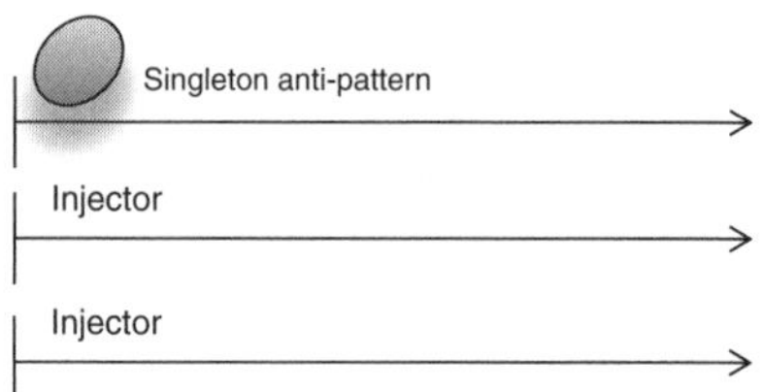

Figure 5.15 Singleton-patterned objects are shared even across injectors.

Moreover, any object created and maintained outside an injector does not benefit from its other powerful features, particularly lifecycle and interception—and the Hollywood Principle. One of the great benefits of DI is that it allows you to quickly bind a key to a different scope simply by changing a line of configuration. That's not possible with the singleton object (figure 5.16).

Its class must be rewritten and retested to introduce scoping semantics. Refactoring between scopes is also a vital part of software development and emerging design. Singleton objects hinder this natural, iterative evolution.

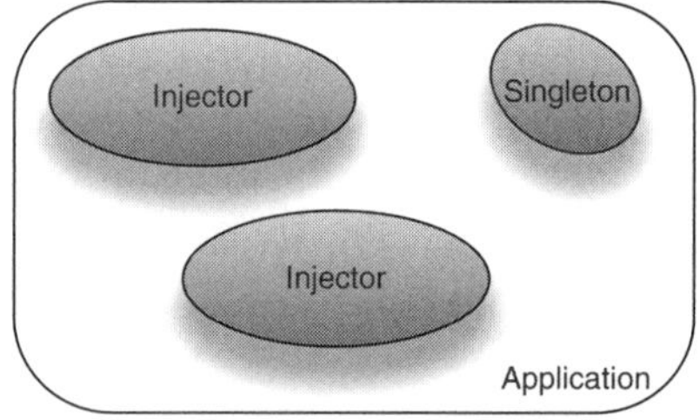

Figure 5.16 Singleton anti-pattern objects sit *outside* dependency injectors.

So to sum up: singleton objects bad, singleton scoping good. Singleton objects make testing difficult if not impossible and are antithetical to good design with dependency injection. Singleton scoping, on the other hand, is a purely injector-driven feature and completely removed from the class in question (figure 5.17).

Singleton scope is thus flexible and grants the usefulness of the Singleton anti-pattern without all of its nasty problems. Scopes have a variety of other uses; they

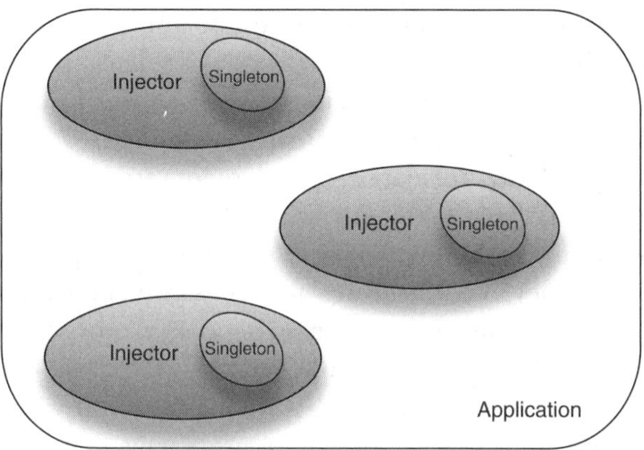

Figure 5.17 Singleton-scoped objects are well-behaved and live inside the injector.

needn't only be applied in the singleton and no scope idioms. In web applications, scopes are extremely useful as unintrusive techniques in maintaining user-specific state. These web-specific scopes are explored in the following section.

5.4 Domain-specific scopes: the web

So far we've seen that scopes are a context in which objects live. When a scope ends, objects bound to it go out of scope. And when it begins again, new objects (of the same keys) come "into scope." Scopes can also be thought of as a period in the objective life of a program where the state of objects is *persistent;* that is, it retains its values for that period. We also examined two of these scopes: the singleton and the no scope. They're rather unique: One sticks around forever, the other a split second. In a sense, these two scopes are universal. Any application has a use for no-scoped objects. And most applications will probably need access to some long-lived service that the singleton context provides.

But there is a whole class of uses that are very specific to a particular problem domain. These are *domain-specific* scopes. They are contexts defined according to the particular behavioral requirements of an application. For example, a movie theater has a specific context for each movie as it is being shown. In a multiplex, several movies may be showing simultaneously, and each of these is a unique context. We can model these contexts as scopes in an injector. A moviegoer watching a showing of the movie *The Princess Bride* is different from one who is watching *Godzilla* in another theater.

An important corollary to this model is that the moviegoer exists for the entire duration of the movie (that is, scope). So if you looked in on the *Godzilla* show, you would expect to see the same members of the audience each time.

The movie scopes are specific to the domain of movie theaters and intimately tied with their semantics. If a moviegoer exits one show just as it is ending and enters another show as it is starting (I used to do this in high school to save money), does it mean the moviegoer is carried across two contexts? Or should its state be lost and a new instance created? We can't answer these questions without getting deeper into the movie theater analogy. More important, the answers to the questions can't be reused in any other problem domain.

One of the most important sets of domain-specific scopes is those around building *web* applications. Web applications have different contexts that emerge from interaction with users. Essentially, web applications are elaborate document retrieval and transmission systems. These are typically HTML documents, which I am sure you are infinitely familiar with. With the evolution of the web, highly interactive web applications have also arisen—to the point where they now closely resemble desktop applications.

However, the basic protocol for transmission of data between a browser and server has remained fairly unchanged. The contexts for a web application have their semantics in this protocol. Unlike a desktop application, a web application will generally have many users simultaneously accessing it. And these users may enter and leave a chain of communications with the web application at will. For example, when checking email via the popular Gmail service from Google, I sign in first (translated as a request for the inbox document), then open a few unread messages (translated as requests for HTML documents), and finally sign out. All this happens with Gmail running constantly on Google's servers. Contrast this with a desktop client like Mozilla Thunderbird, where I perform the same three steps, but they result in the program starting up from scratch and terminating when I've finished (entirely on my desktop). Furthermore, Google's servers host thousands (if not millions) of users doing very similar things simultaneously. Any service that would normally be singleton scoped, for example, my user credentials in Thunderbird, can no longer be a singleton in Gmail.[2] Otherwise, all users would share the same credentials, and we would be able to read each other's mail.

On the other hand, you can't make everything no scoped either. If you do, classes of the Gmail application would be forced to keep passing around user credentials in order to maintain state in a given request, and that would rewind all the benefits originally reaped from scoping. It would also perform rather poorly. Here's where web-specific scopes really help.

All interaction between a user (via a web browser) and a web application occurs inside an *HTTP request* (figure 5.18).

A *request* is—no surprise—a request for a document or, more generally, a resource. To provide this resource, an application might go to a database or a file or perform some *dynamic* computation. All this happens synchronously, that is, while the user is waiting. This entire transaction forms one HTTP request. Objects that live and operate within this context belong to the *request scope*.

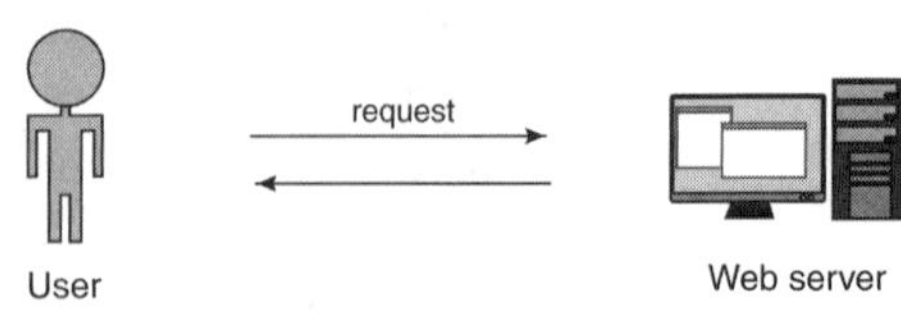

Figure 5.18 Interaction between a web server and a user happens in an HTTP request.

[2] Interesting fact: Gmail's frontend servers use Guice heavily for dependency injection concerns.

5.4.1 HTTP request scope

The request scope is interesting because it isn't strictly a segment in the life of an injector. Since requests can be concurrent, request scopes are also concurrent (but disparate from one another). Let's take the example of an online comic book store. *Sandman* is one of my favorite books, so I do a search for *Sandman* by typing in "sandman" at the appropriate page. To the comics store, this is a request for a document containing a list of *Sandman* titles. Let's call the service that generates this document ComicSearch. ComicSearch must

- Read my search criteria from the incoming request
- Query a database
- Render a list of results

Let's make another service that accesses the database and call this ComicAccess. ComicAccess will in turn depend on database-specific services like connections and statements in order to deliver results. Listing 5.4 describes the code for the comic store so far.

Listing 5.4 Comic store's search and data access components

```
public class ComicSearch {
    private final ComicAccess comicAccess;

    @Inject
    public ComicSearch(ComicAccess comicAccess) {
        this.comicAccess = comicAccess;
    }

    public HTML searchForComics(String criteria) {
        ...
    }
}
```

Now it makes sense for the ComicAccess object to be a singleton—it has no state, connects to a database as needed, and will probably be shared by several clients (other web pages needing to access the comic store). The searchForComics() method takes search criteria (typed in by a user) and returns an HTML object.

NOTE Of course, this is a hypothetical class and the exact form of searchForComics() may be different depending on the web framework you choose. But its semantics remain the same—it takes in search criteria and converts them to an HTML page displaying a list of matches.

ComicSearch is itself stateless (since its only dependency, ComicAccess, is immutable), so we could bind it as a singleton. Given this case, it actually works quite well. Since there is no *request-specific* context, binding ComicSearch either as a singleton or no scope is viable.

Let's expand this example. Let's say we add a requirement that the store shows me items of interest based on my prior purchases. It's not important how it determines my interests, just that it does. Another service, UserContext, will handle this work:

```
public class UserContext {
    private String username;

    private final ComicAccess comicAccess;

    @Inject
    public UserContext(ComicAccess comicAccess) {
        this.comicAccess = comicAccess;
    }

    public List<Comic> getItemsOfInterest() {
        ...
    }

    public void signIn(String username) {
        this.username = username;
    }
}
```

The method `getItemsOfInterest()`scans old purchases using `ComicAccess` and builds a list of suggestions. The interesting part about `UserContext` is its field `username` and method `signIn()`:

```
    public void signIn(String username) {
        this.username = username;
    }
```

When called with an argument, `signIn()` stores the *current* user. You'll notice that `signIn()` is more or less a setter method. But I've deliberately avoided calling it `setUsername()` to distinguish it from a dependency setter. `signIn()` will be called from `ComicSearch`, which itself is triggered by user interaction. Here's the modified code from listing 5.4, reflecting the change:

```
public class ComicSearch {
    private final ComicAccess comicAccess;
    private final UserContext user;

    @Inject
    public ComicSearch(ComicAccess comicAccess, UserContext user) {
        this.comicAccess = comicAccess;
        this.user = user;
    }

    public HTML searchForComics(String criteria, String username) {
        user.signIn(username);

        List<Comic> suggestions = user.getItemsOfInterest();
        ...
    }
}
```

`ComicSearch` is triggered on a request from a user, and method `searchForComics()` is provided with an additional argument, `username`, also extracted from the HTTP request. The `UserContext` object is configured with this username. Now any results it returns will be specific to the current user.

Let's put the `UserContext` to work and expand this another step. We'll add a requirement that the list of results should *not* show any comics that a user has already purchased. One way to do this is with two queries, one with the entire set of results and the second with a history of purchases, displaying only the difference. That sequence would be:

1. Query all matches for criteria from database.
2. Query history of purchases for current user.
3. Iterate every item in step 1, comparing them to every item in step 2, and remove any matches.
4. Display the remainder.

This works, but it seems awfully complex. It is a lot of code to write and a bit superfluous. Furthermore, if these sets are reasonably large and contain a lot of overlap, it could mean doing a large amount of work to bring up results that are simply thrown away. Worse, two queries are two trips to the database, which is expensive and unnecessary in a high-traffic environment.

Another solution is to create a special *finder* method on `ComicAccess` that accepts the username and builds a database query sensitive to this problem. This is much better, because only the relevant results come back and the impact to `ComicSearch` is very small:

```
public HTML searchForComics(String criteria, String username) {
    user.signIn(username);

    List<Comic> suggestions = user.getItemsOfInterest();

    List<Comic> results = comicAccess.searchNoPriorPurchases(criteria,
username);
    ...
}
```

But we can do one better. By moving this work off to `UserContext`, it avoids `ComicSearch` having to know the requisite details for querying comics:

```
public class UserContext {
    private String username;

    private final ComicAccess comicAccess;

    @Inject
    public UserContext(ComicAccess comicAccess) {
        this.comicAccess = comicAccess;
    }

    public List<Comic> getItemsOfInterest() {
        ...
    }

    public List<Comic> searchComics(String criteria) {
        return comicAccess.searchNoPriorPurchases(criteria, username);
    }

    public void signIn(String username) {
        this.username = username;
    }
}
```

Now `ComicSearch` is a lot simpler:

```
public HTML searchForComics(String criteria, String username) {
    user.signIn(username);

    List<Comic> suggestions = user.getItemsOfInterest();

    List<Comic> results = user.searchComics(criteria);
    ...
}
```

The real saving comes with request scoping. We already need to bind `ComicSearch` and `UserContext` in the request scope (because their state is tied to a single user's request). Now let's say that instead of signing in a user in the `searchForComics()` method, we're able to do it at the beginning of a request before the `ComicSearch` page (say, in a servlet *filter*). This is important because it means that authentication logic is separated from business logic. Furthermore, it means code to sign in the user need be written only once and won't have to litter every page:

```
public class ComicSearch {
    private final UserContext user;

    @Inject
    public ComicSearch(UserContext user) {
        this.user = user;
    }

    public HTML searchForComics(String criteria) {
        List<Comic> suggestions = user.getItemsOfInterest();
        List<Comic> results = user.searchComics(criteria);

        ...
    }
}
```

Notice that it is much leaner now and focused on its core purpose. But where has the code for signing in a user gone? Here's one possible way it may have disappeared.

REQUEST SCOPING IN GUICE WITH GUICE-SERVLET

Listing 5.5 shows one implementation using a Java servlet filter and the guice-servlet extension library for Guice.

> **Guice Servlet and Guice**
>
> Guice servlet is an extension to Guice that provides a lot of web-specific functionality, including web-domain scopes (request, session). Guice servlet is registered in web.xml as a filter itself and then later configured using a Guice module. It allows you to manage and intercept servlets or filters via Guice's injector (which is not otherwise possible).
>
> Find out more about guice-servlet at http://code.google.com/p/google-guice.

Listing 5.5 An injector-managed servlet filter using guice-servlet (using Guice)

```
import javax.servlet.Filter;

@Singleton
public class UserFilter implements Filter {
    private final Provider<UserContext> currentUser;

    @Inject
    public UserFilter(Provider<UserContext> currentUser) {
        this.currentUser = currentUser;
    }

    public void doFilter(ServletRequest request, ServletResponse response,
         FilterChain chain) throws IOException, ServletException {

        currentUser.get().signIn(...);          <-- Set up current user

        chain.doFilter(request, response);      <-- Continue processing request
    }

    ...
}
```

There are some interesting things to say about listing 5.5:

- `UserFilter` is a servlet filter applied at the head of every incoming request.
- It is declared under singleton scope (note the `@Singleton` annotation).
- It is injected with a `Provider<UserContext>` so that a *request-scoped* `UserContext` may be obtained each time.
- User credentials are extracted from the request and set on the current `User-Context`.

I use a `Provider<UserContext>` instead of directly injecting a `UserContext` because `UserFilter` is a singleton, and once a singleton is wired with any object, that object gets held onto despite its scope. This is known as *scope-widening injection* and is a problem that I discuss in some detail in the next chapter.

Interestingly enough, in listing 5.4 I was able to use constructor injection to get hold of the `UserContext` provider:

```
@Inject
public UserFilter(Provider<UserContext> currentUser) {
    this.currentUser = currentUser;
}
```

Ordinarily, this wouldn't be possible for a filter registered in web.xml according to the Java Servlet Specification. However, guice-servlet gets around this by sitting between Java servlets and the Guice injector. Listing 5.6 shows how this is done, with a web.xml that is configured to use guice-servlet.

Listing 5.6 web.xml configured with guice-servlet and Guice

```
<?xml version="1.0" encoding="UTF-8"?>       | web.xml namespace
<web-app version="2.4"                       v boilerplate
```

```
        xmlns="http://java.sun.com/xml/ns/j2ee"
        xmlns:xsi="http://www.w3.org/2001/XMLSchema-instance"
        xsi:schemaLocation="http://java.sun.com/xml/ns/j2ee
      http://java.sun.com/xml/ns/j2ee/web-app_2_4.xsd" >

    <listener>
        <listener-class>example.MyGuiceCreator</listener-class
    </listener>

    <filter>
        <filter-name>guiceFilter</filter-name>
        <filter-class>com.google.inject.servlet.GuiceFilter</filter-class>
    </filter>

    <filter-mapping>
        <filter-name>guiceFilter</filter-name>
        <url-pattern>/*</url-pattern>
    </filter-mapping>

</web-app>
```

web.xml namespace boilerplate

Listener creates injector on web app deploy

Filter all URLs through guice-servlet

Guice-servlet's architecture is depicted in figure 5.19.

Notice that in listing 5.6 a servlet context listener named `MyGuiceCreator` is registered. This is a simple class that you create to handle the job of bootstrapping the injector. It is where you tell guice-servlet what filters and servlets you want the Guice injector to manage. Here's what a `MyGuiceCreator` would look like if it were configured to filter all incoming requests with `UserFilter` (to do our authentication work):

```
public class MyGuiceCreator extends GuiceServletContextListener {

    @Override
    protected Injector getInjector() {
        return Guice.createInjector(new ServletModule() {
@Override
            protected void configureServlets() {
                filter("/*").through(UserFilter.class)

            }
        });
    }
}
```

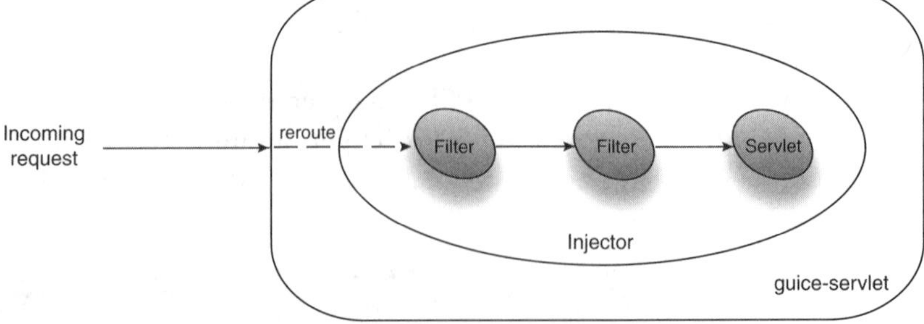

Figure 5.19 Incoming requests are rerouted by guice-servlet to injector-managed filters or servlets.

This code is self-explanatory, but let's go through it anyway. Remember, `MyGuice-Creator` is a class you provide to bootstrap and configure the injector (it must extend `GuiceServletContextListener`). The factory method `Guice.createInjector()` takes instances of Guice's `Module` as argument. You configure filters in guice-servlet via a programmatic API (rather than web.xml):

```
filter("/*").through(UserFilter.class)
```

You could continue adding filters and servlets. Each servlet and filter must be annotated `@Singleton`.

Let's get back to request scoping. By moving code out to the `UserContext` object, every request receives its own instance of `ComicSearch` and `UserContext`. We were able to achieve this transition without any impact to `ComicAccess` and minimal impact to `ComicSearch`. Declarative scoping of objects is thus a very powerful and unintrusive technique.

This is all very well. But how do we actually bind these scopes in Spring, Guice, and others? Let's take a look:

```
import com.google.inject.servlet.RequestScoped;

public class ComicStoreModule extends AbstractModule {

    @Override
    protected void configure() {

    bindComicAccess.class).to(ComicAccessImpl.class).in(Singleton.class);

        bind(UserContext.class).in(RequestScoped.class);
        bind(ComicSearch.class).in(RequestScoped.class);
        ...
    }
}
```

In the example code, I've bound both `UserContext` and `ComicSearch` in `@Request-Scoped`. This is a scope made available by guice-servlet and represents the HTTP request scope in the world of Guice.[3] `ComicAccess` is a simple singleton, and so it is a straightforward binding (to its implementation, `ComicAccessImpl`):

```
bind(ComicAccess.class).to(ComicAccessImpl.class).in(Singleton.class);
```

This same effect can be achieved in Spring with its own set of web-specific scoping utilities. The following section explores the techniques involved there.

REQUEST SCOPING IN SPRING

In Spring's XML configuration mode, these bindings are slightly different (see listing 5.7).

Listing 5.7 Spring XML configuration for the online comic store's components

```
<beans ...>
    <bean id="data.comics" class="ComicAccessImpl" scope="singleton">
```

[3] Don't forget that you need to register guice-servlet's `GuiceFilter` in web.xml, as shown previously.

```
    ...
    </bean>

    <bean id="web.user" class="UserContext" scope="request">
        <constructor-arg ref="data.comics"/>
    </bean>

    <bean id="web.comicSearch" class="ComicSearch" scope="request">
        <constructor-arg ref="data.comics"/>
        <constructor-arg ref="web.user"/>
    </bean>
</beans>
```

The only new thing in listing 5.7 is the attribute `scope="request"` on bindings `web.user` and `web.comicSearch`. Of course, none of the three classes need change at all. Like Guice and guice-servlet, Spring requires additional configuration in web.xml. First off, you need to bootstrap a Spring injector when the web application is deployed. In Guice we used a `ServletContextListener` (recall `MyGuiceCreator`, the subclass of `GuiceServletContextListener`). You do this in Spring too:

```
<web-app ...>
    ...
    <context-param>
        <param-name>contextConfigLocation</param-name>
        <param-value>/WEB-INF/comic-store.xml</param-value>
    </context-param>

    <listener>
        <listener-class>
            org.springframework.web.context.ContextLoaderListener
        </listener-class>
    </listener>
    ...
</web-app>
```

This web.xml is similar to the one we saw earlier with guice-servlet. Notice that we needed to set a context parameter with the name of the XML configuration file. You can think of it as the web equivalent of the following:

```
BeanFactory injector = new FileSystemXmlApplicationContext("WEB-INF/comic-
➥   store.xml");
```

Now we've bootstrapped the injector and told it where to find its configuration. But that's not all; as guice-servlet did for Guice, there's still an integration layer that needs to be configured to get request scopes going:

```
<web-app ...>
    ...
    <listener>
        <listener-class>
            org.springframework.web.context.request.RequestContextListener
        </listener-class>
    </listener>
    ...
</web-app>
```

This listener must appear in addition to the `ContextLoaderListener` shown previously. Now you're set up to shop comics with Spring.

TIP We haven't quite looked at how to configure filters with Spring's injector. Guice-servlet handled this for us via its `GuiceFilter`. Spring does not have this support out of the box. But a sister project, *Spring Security* (formerly *Acegi Security*[4]) does. Spring Security's `FilterToBeanProxy` does a similar job.

Apart from these practical aspects, there are things to keep in mind about request scoping:

- A thread is typically dedicated to a request for the request's entire span. This means that request-scoped objects are not multithreaded.
- It also means that they are generally not thread-safe.
- Integration layers that provide request scoping often cache scoped objects in thread-locals.
- In rare cases, web servers may use multiple threads to service a request (for instance, while processing long-running asynchronous requests). If you are designing a request-scoping library in such a scenario, be aware of thread-local assumptions.

Most of these are pretty low-level and specific to the architecture in question. In the Java servlet world, threads and requests are almost always the same thing (though once completed, a thread may clear its context and proceed to service other requests). So you should be careful to clean up at the end of a request. If you are *designing* request scopes, you should carefully research these potential hazards. Perhaps even more useful than the request scope is the HTTP session scope. This technique allows you to keep objects around between requests in a semantic user session. Using dependency injection, a lot of the glue code to make this happen goes away. Session scoping is thus a powerful tool in the dependency injector's toolbox.

5.4.2 HTTP session scope

An HTTP session scope is the next step up from a request scope. HTTP sessions are an abstraction invented to make up for the fact that the HTTP protocol is stateless. This means that it does not easily allow for long-running interactions with a user to be maintained on the server side. To get around this, developers use clever techniques and string together a series of requests from the same user and call it a session (figure 5.20). An HTTP session has important characteristics:

- A session represents a single, unique user's interaction with a web application.
- A session is composed of one or more requests from the same user.
- Not all requests are necessarily part of a session.
- A session is a kind of store that preserves state between requests.
- The two logical end points of a session are user login and logout.

[4] Find out about Acegi Security at http://www.acegisecurity.org.

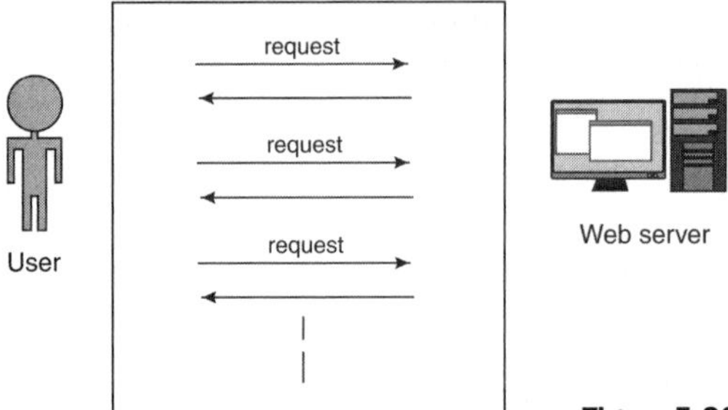

Figure 5.20 A series of related requests from the same user forms an HTTP session.

You can visualize a session as made up of multiple independent requests from the same user (as in figure 5.20). In figure 5.21, each instance of a request-scoped object is unique to that request (R1 to R3). But a *session-scoped* instance is *shared* across all those requests.

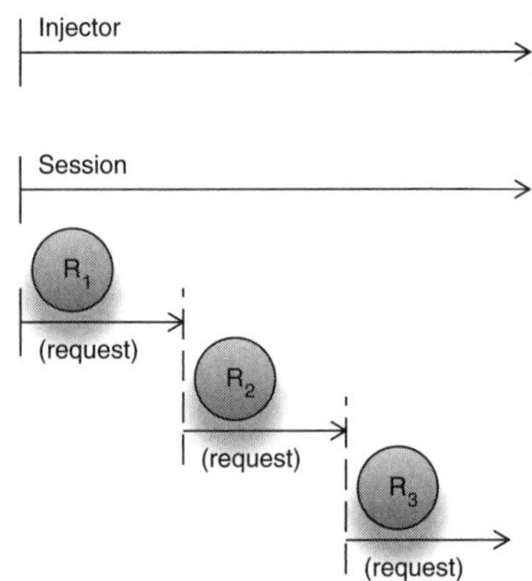

Figure 5.21 A session is composed of independent requests from a user.

Sessions are extremely useful for tracking state relative to a specific user, since a session always exists around one user. These uses include:

- Tracking a user's credentials for security purposes
- Tracking a user's recent activity for quick navigation (for example, breadcrumbs)
- Tracking preferences, to personalize a user's experience
- Caching user-specific information for quick access
- Caching general, constant data for quick access

All these use cases involve storing state temporarily, generally to improve a user's experience through the site. Whether that is about presentation or under the covers, it's about performance. And that's essentially what sessions do. Objects scoped under a session retain their state across requests, essentially continuing from where the last request left off.

Typically, sessions start and end when a user logs in and logs out. This behavior may be customized as necessary. Some requests (for static content, for example) do not participate in a user session and are considered stateless. These requests are independent of sessions, and, generally speaking, services participating in them shouldn't have any user-specific functionality.

Like requests, sessions may also be concurrent. For instance, multiple users who log in at once are said to be in different, unique sessions. While session-scoped instances are shared across requests inside a session, they are independent between sessions. Figure 5.22 shows how this might look in an injector's timeline.

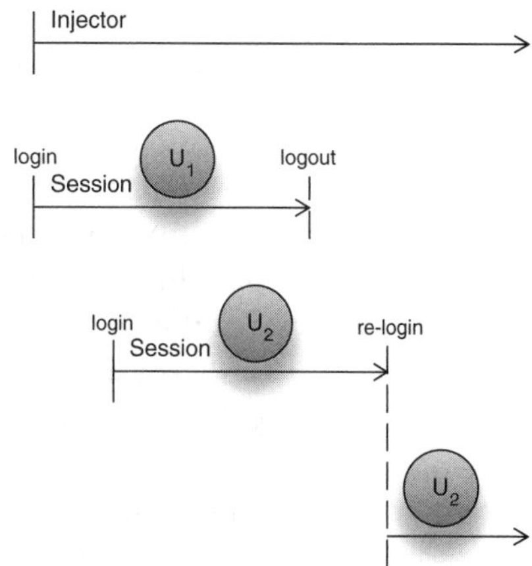

Figure 5.22 Multiple user sessions in the life of an injector

In this figure, U1 is an object that exists in the first user's session, and U2 is a different instance of the same key that exists in the second user's session (it also is an aging Irish rock band). U1 and U2 are completely independent of one another. But within the first user's session, all requests share the same instance (U1)—likewise with the second user and U2. Another interesting point is that the second user's session does not start for a while into the application's life. So there is a time when U2 is out of scope while U1 is in scope, even though both are instances of the same key (let's call it U) bound under session scope.

Another interesting thing about figure 5.22 is that the second user actually logs out and logs back in (at the point marked re-login). This means that there are two instances of U2 for the second user because she started two sessions. The state of U2 prior to the second login is totally independent from the state after the second login. Contrast this with singleton scoping, where instance state would have been shared for the entire life of the injector, regardless of the number of sessions (or users) involved.

Let's go back to the comic store example. We had three important components:

- ComicSearch—A request-scoped service that searched the comic catalog according to given criteria.
- ComicAccess—A singleton-scoped data-access service that acted as a bridge between ComicSearch and a database.
- UserContext—A request-scoped service that was specific to a user; it constructed personalized and filtered search results around a user's behavior.

There was also a filter that set up the UserContext each time, by extracting a username from incoming requests. Can you see any room for improvement? Let's revisit class UserContext to see if it provides any inspiration:

```
public class UserContext {
    private String username;

    private final ComicAccess comicAccess;

    @Inject
    public UserContext(ComicAccess comicAccess) {
        this.comicAccess = comicAccess;
    }

    public List<Comic> getItemsOfInterest() {
        ...
    }

    public List<Comic> searchComics(String criteria) {
        return comicAccess.searchNoPriorPurchases(criteria, username);
```

```
    }

    public void signIn(String username) {
        this.username = username;
    }
}
```

Straight away there is a clear benefit from making this object session scoped. We wouldn't have to sign in the user on every request! It would be enough to do it once, at the start of the session (logical, since this would be where a user logged in) and simply let it be shared across any further requests from the same user. This would be particularly useful if the application loaded user-specific information (such as a user's full name and date of birth) on sign in, since it would save several unnecessary trips to the database on subsequent requests.

Another saving comes from the use case around caching user-specific information for quick access. If we assume that items of interest for a user are unlikely to change within a single session, there is no need to search and collate them on every request. It can be done once and stored in a memo field for further requests. Here's how you might modify `getItemsOfInterest()` to do just that:

```
public class UserContext {
    private List<Comic> itemsOfInterest;        <-- Memo field

    public List<Comic> getItemsOfInterest() {
        if (null == itemsOfInterest) {          <-- Compute once
            ...                                     and memorize
        }

        return itemsOfInterest;
    }

    ...
}
```

By storing computed suggestions in the `itemsOfInterest` memo field, I save a lot of unnecessary computation so long as subsequent requests come from the same user. Each user has her own memo, in their session-scoped `UserContext`.

Binding `UserContext` to session scope is also laughably simple. As far as the injector is concerned, all you need to do is change its binding (we'll do this in Guice and guice-servlet first):

```
import com.google.inject.servlet.RequestScoped;
import com.google.inject.servlet.SessionScoped;

public class ComicStoreModule extends AbstractModule {

    @Override
    protected void configure() {
    bind(ComicAccess.class).to(ComicAccessImpl.class).in(Singleton.class);

        bind(UserContext.class).in(SessionScoped.class);
        bind(ComicSearch.class).in(RequestScoped.class);
        ...
    }
}
```

Earlier we also saw a shortcut notation, where the class was itself annotated. This is possible with session scope too, but first it requires that you to set up a *scoping annotation.* This must be done manually because the web scopes aren't part of the core Guice distribution. It's fairly easy to do:

```
public class ComicStoreModule extends AbstractModule {

    @Override
    protected void configure() {

        install(new ServletModule());

    bind(ComicAccess.class).to(CommicAccessImpl.class).in(Singleton.class);
        bind(ComicSearch.class).in(ServletScopes.REQUEST_SCOPE);
        ...
    }
}
```

Notice that I've removed any explicit binding of `UserContext`. I can now simply annotate the class, and Guice will correctly bind it to the session scope:

```
@SessionScoped
public class UserContext {
...
}
```

You could do the same with request scopes and guice-servlet's `@RequestScoped` annotation.

The Spring equivalent for binding `UserContext` under session scope is also straightforward (once you have the context listeners set up):

```
<beans ...>
    <bean id="data.comics" class="ComicAccessImpl" scope="singleton">
    ...
    </bean>

    <bean id="web.user" class="UserContext" scope="session">
        <constructor-arg ref="data.comics"/>
    </bean>

    <bean id="web.comicSearch" class="ComicSearch" scope="request">
        <constructor-arg ref="data.comics"/>
        <constructor-arg ref="web.user"/>
    </bean>
</beans>
```

No additional configuration of the web server (or servlet container) is required. Cool! Finally, there are a couple of things to keep in mind when working with objects in the session scope:

- Multiple concurrent requests (from the same user) may belong to the same session.
- This means two threads may hit session-scoped objects at once.
- A session-scoped instance, if wired into a singleton, will stick around even when the user has logged out and the session has ended (*scope-widening injection*). Take care that this does not happen. We'll look at remedies in chapter 6.

So how does a session get scoped?

This is a rather tricky question. I said earlier that HTTP sessions are a hack for the fact that the HTTP protocol is *stateless*. This is more or less accurate—the common way of maintaining a user session is to use a browser *cookie*. A cookie is a small file with unique information that a web application can send to a browser as its identity. So, the next time that web browser hits the same URL, it will send back its cookies. When the web application sees this cookie, it "remembers" who is calling and correctly identifies the user—much like an ATM card reminds the bank of who you are. Cookies are specific to a website and URL, so there is no danger of cookies getting crossed between applications.

Not all browsers support cookies, and since some users consider them a risk, even browsers that do may not have them enabled. In these cases we need an alternative way of tracking sessions. One popular alternative is *URL rewriting*. URL rewriting is quite simple. When a browser requests a document, it does so via a URL. Usually this happens when you click a hyperlink on a previous page. Now, instead of the normal URL, the web application rewrites all the hyperlinks sent to a particular user by adding an identifier to it. Then when you (or any user) click the link, your browser requests the rewritten URL. Incoming requests of this nature are filtered and stripped of the extra bit identifying you as a unique user. This information is used to restore your session, and everything continues as normal.

Most web technologies can be configured to use either URL rewriting or cookies as their session continuation strategy. Some, like the *Java Servlet Framework*, automatically detect browser capability and choose the appropriate strategy. The Java Servlet Framework also provides abstractions for HTTP requestsand sessions to make them easy to work with. Guice-servlet and the SpringFramework both provide integration layers that sit over the servlet APIs and enable transparent web scoping with dependency injection.

5.5 Summary

Scope is about managing the state of objects. Service implementations are bound to keys, which are realized as object instances in an application. Without scoping, keys requested from the injector return new instances each time (and each time they are wired as dependencies). This is known as the no scope. Since there is no way of specifying a duration for the time, state may be preserved in these instances. Singleton-scoped keys, on the other hand, are keys that the injector only wires or returns one instance for. In other words, singletons have one instance per key, per injector. This is different from singleton-patterned objects, which enforce one instance per entire application. I decry this flavor of singleton as an anti-pattern because it is nigh on impossible to test with mock substitution and is tricky in concurrently run tests and environments. Such anti-patterned singletons are also shared between multiple injectors in the same application, which may even violate the configuration of the injector. Always choose singleton scoping over singleton patterning.

Thus, scope may be thought of as the choice of instance each time a key is sought from it—whether new, or old, or shared. The singleton and the no scope are universal and have uses in most applications using dependency injection.

However, there is a whole class of scopes that are specific to particular kinds of applications. These scopes are closely tied to contexts specific to a particular problem domain. One such example is the web. Web-specific scopes are popular with many web frameworks and ship out of the box with many DI libraries. The HTTP request scope is the first and simplest of the web scopes. Keys requested from an injector within the same request always return the same instance. When the request completes, these request-scoped objects are discarded, and subsequent requests force the creation of new instances. Request scoping is interesting since the context that a request purports may be concurrent with several other requests. These requests are all walled off in their own unique scopes and keys, and when sought from the injector they are different across these requests.

HTTP session scope is a step up from request scope and is a natural extension of it. An HTTP session is an artificial construct above a string of requests from the same user. Session scope is thus persistent across all these requests (so long as they are from the same user). Sessions are useful for storing user-specific information temporarily, but they are often abused to store data that is relevant only to specific workflows within the user's session. Try to restrict your use of session scope to keeping around user-relevant information only. Good examples are credentials, preferences, and (relatively) constant biographical data.

6 More use cases in scoping

This chapter covers:

- Customizing scope to suit your needs
- Avoiding the perils of improper scoping
- Using advanced scoping: caches and data grids

"A common mistake that people make when trying to design something completely foolproof is to underestimate the ingenuity of complete fools."

—Douglas Adams

As you've just seen in chapter 5, scope is a very powerful tool for managing object state. In particular, it is a tool for making your objects and services *agnostic* of state management. In other words, you allow the injector to worry about the details of state and context, and you keep your objects lean. This has advantages in both productivity and design elegance.

In this chapter we'll look at how to apply these same principles to any *stateful* context and to broaden the applicability of scoping as a tool in dependency injection. Most libraries provide some manner of extending the available scoping functionality. We'll look at how to leverage this in Guice and Spring, in particular.

Closely related are the perils of scoping. While it is extremely powerful as a tool for reversing responsibility, state management can get very tricky to design and build around. We'll look at common pitfalls and some very hairy corner cases, which one would do well to respect. We'll also see how good design can ameliorate or completely avoid these cases and how it can also facilitate good testing.

Finally, I present some ideas for using scope in unusual and potentially interesting ways for very large applications that require enormous scalability. But first, let's lay the groundwork and explore how to customize scope.

6.1 Defining a custom scope

We've had a long look at web scopes. HTTP request and HTTP session scopes provide a useful set of tools for working with context in web applications, particularly for dealing with user interactivity. Most applications (including web apps) are built around some form of data manipulation. In general this data is stored in a relational database like Oracle or PostgreSQL. In object-oriented languages, the same data is modeled as interrelating classes of objects and then mapped to database tables. Objects are marshaled to their counterpart tables, then retrieved as required in future interactions. This is often called *object* (or data) *persistence.*

The process of moving data between application memory (in the form of objects) and database storage (in the form of relational tables) occurs in series of tasks called *transactions.* Let's look at how to treat transactions as a context and define a custom scope around them.

6.1.1 A quick primer on transactions

A transaction is a form of interaction with a data store that is *atomic, consistent, isolated,* and *durable.* Such transactions are sometimes referred to as *ACID transactions.* This is what they imply:

- *Atomicity*—All of the tasks inside a transaction are successful or none are.
- *Consistency*—Data modified by a transaction does not violate prior constraints.
- *Isolation*—Other transactions can never see data in a partial state as it is being transacted.
- *Durability*—This refers to the ability to recover from failures while inside a transaction and leave data consistent.

These transactions extend to your application logic, meaning many different, unrelated components can all participate within a single transaction in order to perform a logical operation on data. Rather than pushing each task through in isolated fashion, it makes sense to combine them as a logical unit under an overall purpose. They are said to be *coarse grained.* When creating an employee record in the database, a transaction may include logic to create annual leave blocks, stock option grants, and other related records. If any one of these tasks fails (for instance, stock could not be assigned because of a shortage), the entire transaction is *rolled back* and no employee is created. This prevents the creation of a partial, *invalid* employee record and keeps the database in a consistent state. A new attempt must be made, once the stock shortage is corrected, in a separate transaction.

Like singletons or HTTP sessions, a transaction is also a specific context within an application. An injector can take advantage of this to reduce the passing around of ancillary data and placeholder objects and generally improve the maintainability of code by moving transactional concerns into *transaction-scoped* dependencies.

6.1.2 Creating a custom transaction scope

Before defining your own scope, it helps to ask a few questions:

- Is the context that this scope represents clearly defined?
- Objects must live for the entire life of this scope; does this work for all scoped instances? You should never have two life spans for a key within a scope.
- Is there going to be more than one thread accessing objects in this scope?

Transaction scope has well-understood start and end points (see figure 6.1). A transaction is also generally confined to one thread of execution. While it's by no means impossible to consider scopes that may be accessed by multiple threads, it is certainly preferable to design scopes that are confined to a single thread. These scopes are inherently simpler and easier to test and reason about. Classes that are bound under thread-confined scopes also don't need to worry about thread-safety, and they are therefore easy to design and test.

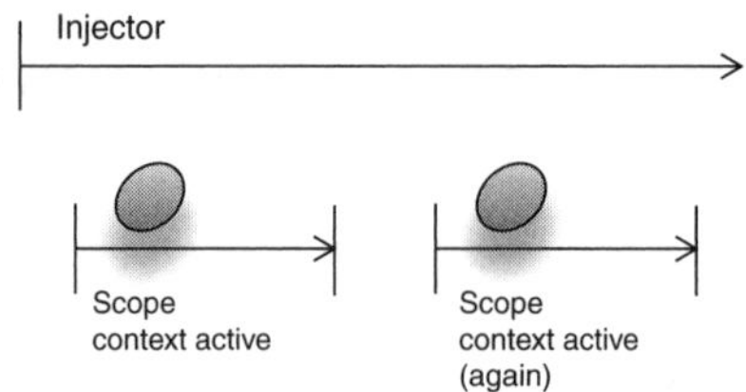

Figure 6.1 A scope generally exists over a repeating context.

So it looks like we're on good ground. Before scoping, let's define a use case. A nuclear power station needs software written to start the reactors and begin the flow of power to an electrical grid. The restriction is that there are three chambers to activate, and they must either all activate or none should. If the chambers are too hot, none must activate. We'll model this as a transaction with a common logical goal, that being the startup of the power station. Listing 6.1 imagines this transactional power station.

Listing 6.1 Three energy chambers activated in concert under a transaction

```
public class PowerStation {
    ...

    public void start() {
        transaction.begin();

        chamber1.fire();
        chamber2.fire();
        chamber3.fire();

        transaction.commit();
    }
}
```

We won't worry too much about the transaction architecture. The important thing is the context that it provides. In `PowerStation`'s case, that context exists for the

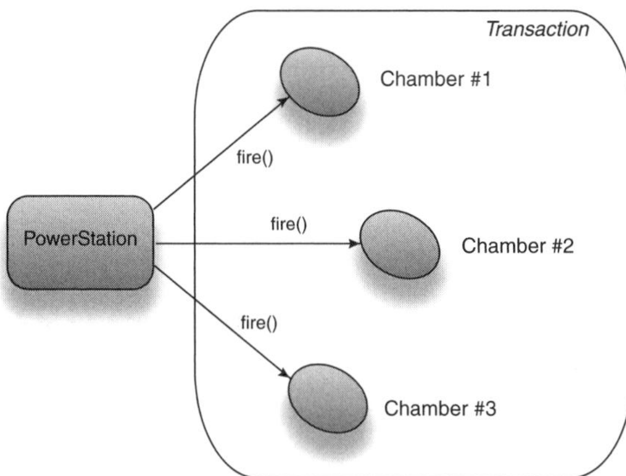

Figure 6.2 `PowerStation` fires all three `Chambers` in a single transaction.

duration of method `start()`, finishing when it returns (figure 6.2 shows a model of this transaction). The call to `transaction.commit()` implies a successful completion of the transaction.

Now let's introduce the failure scenario, where one of the chambers may fail to start by throwing an exception:

```
public void start() {
    transaction.begin();

    boolean failed = false;
    try {
        chamber1.fire();
        chamber2.fire();
        chamber3.fire();

    } catch (StartFailedException e) {
        failed = true;
    } finally {
        if (failed)
            transaction.rollback();
        else
            transaction.commit();
    }
}
```

In this modified version, `start()` expects that one of the chambers may fail, catches the relevant exception (`StartFailedException`), and proceeds to discard the changes to the transaction by rolling it back. The following lines ensure that a failure to start aborts the entire transaction:

```
if (failed)
    transaction.rollback();
else
    transaction.commit();
```

Now let's look at the code in each chamber that may cause the abortive fault:

```
public class Chamber {
    private final Gauge gauge;
```

```
    ...
    public void fire() {
        gauge.measure();

        if (gauge.temperature() > 100)
            throw new StartFailedException();

        ...
    }
}
```

If the chamber's gauge reads above 100, fire() will abort by throwing a StartFailed-Exception, causing the transaction to abort too. This works, but it does not ensure that the cumulative temperature is under control. All three chambers together must have a temperature less than 100, which the code fails to ensure. We need a change to how fire() performs its temperature check. As things stand, Gauge measures the heat level from each chamber independently. In other words, each Chamber has its own Gauge (that is, Gauge is bound under the no scope). To fix the problem, we need to share the gauges among all three chambers. Singleton scoping is not quite right since this would mean *all* dependents of Gauge would share the same instance (perhaps a backup Chamber on the other side of the station or perhaps some component that's not a Chamber at all).

The context for this heat measurement is the starting up of the PowerStation (its start() method). Therefore, the *transaction* scope is an apt fit:

```
@TransactionScoped
public class Gauge { .. }
```

It's shown in figure 6.3 as a class model.

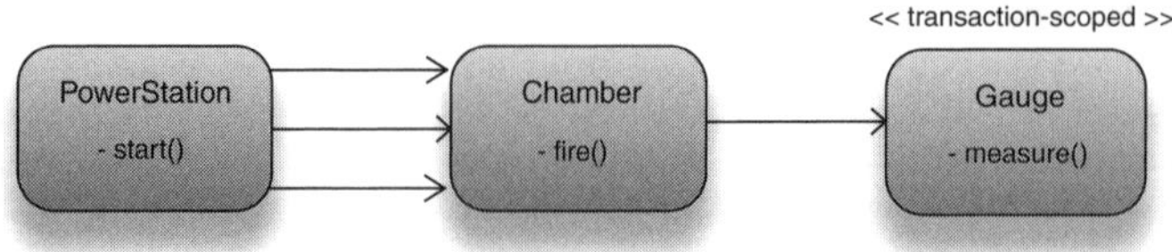

Figure 6.3 A PowerStation's Chamber depends on a transaction-scoped measuring Gauge.

Now when each chamber is fired and consequently measures its heat level, the Gauge correctly reports a cumulative measure of heat from all three chambers. There need be no further changes to PowerStation, Chamber, or any of their methods.

@TransactionScoped is something we just made up (there is certainly no library for it). So how would we go about creating this scope in an injector? The following section answers this question using Guice.

6.1.3 A custom scope in Guice

A scope in Guice is represented by the Scope interface. Scope is as follows:

```
public interface Scope {
    <T> Provider<T> scope(Key<T> key, Provider<T> unscoped);
}
```

A custom scope is required to implement only one method, `scope()`, which returns a scoped instance `Provider`. Recall the Provider pattern from chapter 4. This is the same, except that instead of being used against the reinjection problem, here it's used for providing scoped instances. The two arguments to `scope()` manage the particular object in its context:

- `Key<T> key`—The combinatorial key to be scoped
- `Provider<T> unscoped`—A provider that creates *new* instances of the bound key (in other words, it is a *no-scope* provider)

Use provider `unscoped` when a new context comes to life and new instances need to be provided. When the scope context completes, you simply discard all scoped instances, obtaining new ones from provider `unscoped` instead (see figure 6.4).

Listing 6.2 shows how this is done with the transaction scope.

Listing 6.2 `TransactionScope` implemented in Guice

```
public class TransactionScope implements Scope {
    private final ThreadLocal<Map<Key<?>, Object>> instances
            = new ThreadLocal<Map<Key<?>, Object>>();

    public <T> Provider<T> scope(
final Key<T> key, final Provider<T> unscoped) {

        return new Provider<T>() {      <— Returns a scoped provider

            public T get() {
                Map<Key<?>, Object> map = instances.get();

                if (!map.containsKey(key)) {
                    map.put(key, unscoped.get())        Returns cached or new
                }                                       instance if unavailable

                return (T) map.get(key);
            }
        };
    }

    public void beginScope() {                          <— Sets up a new context
        instances.set(new HashMap<Key<?>, Object>());
    }

    public void endScope() {     <— Closes an existing context
        instances.remove();
    }
}
```

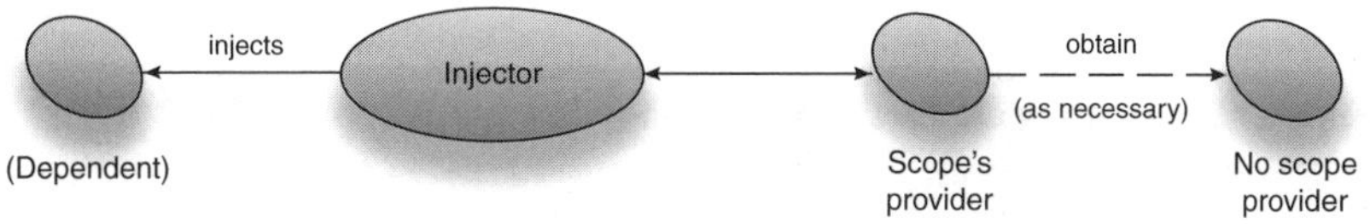

Figure 6.4 The injector obtains instances from a `Scope` provider, which itself may use the no-scope provider.

In listing 6.2, class `TransactionScope` exposes the Guice interface `Scope`. The implemented method `scope()` returns a *scoped* provider that acts as a bridge between the injector and its default no-scope provider. The no-scope provider `unscoped` is used to create new instances as required.

A scoped provider is returned for each key requested in method `scope()`. The provider checks a *thread-local* hash table, returning cached instances for the current thread:

```
 public T get() {
    Map<Key<?>, Object> map = instances.get();

    if (!map.containsKey(key)) {
        map.put(key, unscoped.get());
    }

    return (T) map.get(key);
}
```

If an instance is not already present in the hash table, it is created and cached:

```
if (!map.containsKey(key)) {
    map.put(key, unscoped.get());
}
```

Otherwise, the instance mapped to the given key is returned normally:

```
return (T) map.get(key);
```

This ensures objects that don't yet exist in the current context are created when needed. Method `beginScope()` sets up a context for the current transaction by creating a new hash table to cache objects for the life of the scope (transaction):

```
public void beginScope() {
    instances.set(new HashMap<Key<?>, Object>());
}
```

The hash table maps Guice `Key`s to their scoped instances. Its complement, method `endScope()`, is called by the transaction framework when a transaction completes (either by a successful commit or an abortive rollback), disposing of the cached instances:

```
public void endScope() {
    instances.remove();
}
```

The entire context of the transaction, its scope, and scoped instances are confined to a single thread by using the `ThreadLocal` construct:

```
public class TransactionScope implements Scope {
    private final ThreadLocal<Map<Key<?>, Object>> instances
            = new ThreadLocal<Map<Key<?>, Object>>();
    ...
}
```

`ThreadLocal`s are utilities that allow stored objects to be available only to the storing thread and none other. Because a transaction runs entirely in a single thread, we can be sure that its context will only ever need to be accessed by that thread, and simultaneous transactions are separated from one another by confinement to their respective threads.

Now when a transaction-scoped object (such as `Gauge` from the previous section) is wired to any other object, it is done so inside an active transaction in the *current* thread. When a transaction completes, this instance is lost and any new transactions will see a new instance created. This also applies to concurrent transactions; they are kept walled apart by thread confinement.

Cool! What about when *no* transaction is active and a key is sought? Well, this is a serious problem, and it likely represents an error on the programmer's part. Either she did not start the transaction where it was meant to start or she configured the injector incorrectly. You should add a safety check that reports the error quickly and clearly in such cases:

```
public <T> Provider<T> scope(
final Key<T> key, final Provider<T> unscoped) {

    return new Provider<T>() {

        public T get() {
            Map<Key<?>, Object> map = instances.get();

            if (null == map) {
                throw new
    OutOfScopeException("no transaction was active");
            }

            if (!map.containsKey(key)) {
                map.put(key, unscoped.get());
            }

            return (T) map.get(key);
        }
    };
}
```

This is our sanity check that ensures a proper exception is raised (`OutOfScopeException`) if a transaction-scoped object is sought outside a transaction.

Registering a custom scope in Guice is simple:

```
public class TransactionModule extends AbstractModule {

    @Override
    protected void configure() {
        bindScope(TransactionScoped.class, new TransactionScope());
        ...
    }
}
```

The scoping annotation `@TransactionScoped` is declared as follows:

```
@Retention(RetentionPolicy.RUNTIME)
@ScopeAnnotation
public @interface TransactionScoped { }
```

This is a standard bit of boilerplate that needs to be used when declaring any Guice scope annotation. Notice that `@ScopeAnnotation` is a meta-annotation (an annotation on an annotation), which tells the injector that this is a scoping annotation. Now say that three times fast!

6.1.4 A custom scope in Spring

The same principles of context, instance longevity, and thread-safety apply to all injectors, and Spring is no different. The particular interfaces to expose for scoping, however, are slightly different. Spring also has a `Scope` interface that your scope implementation must expose. But it looks a bit different from Guice's `Scope`. It is shown in listing 6.3.

Listing 6.3 Spring's custom scope interface

```
package org.springframework.beans.factory.config;

public interface Scope {

    Object get(String key, ObjectFactory unscopedProvider);

    Object remove(String key);

    String getConversationId();

    void registerDestructionCallback(String key,
        Runnable destructionCallback);
}
```

Let's take a look at this interface and see how it relates to what we saw in the previous section. First, the scoping provider method:

```
Object get(String key, ObjectFactory unscoped);
```

This is almost identical to Guice's `scope()` method, except that instead of returning a scoped provider, `get()` returns the scoped instance itself. Instead of taking a combinatorial key, it takes a string key. You can think of `get()` as being the provider itself. The second argument, `ObjectFactory`, is an implementation of the Provider pattern (similar to Guice's unscoped `Provider`). It provides no-scoped instances of the given key.

Next, the `remove()` method:

```
Object remove(String key);
```

`remove` evicts any instance stored for the given key in the scope's internal cache (the hash table in `TransactionScope`), and then another method retrieves the scope's identity:

```
String getConversationId();
```

This is an unusually named method. What it essentially points to is the unique identity of the particular scope context. If a transaction were active for the current thread, this method would return a string that uniquely identified this transaction. If we were implementing a session scope, we would return a session ID, unique to a user.

Finally, there's a lifecycle support method:

```
void registerDestructionCallback(String key, Runnable
➥ destructionCallback);
```

registerDestructionCallback() is intended to support lifecycle for specific keys when their instances go out of scope. We won't delve much into this now since lifecycle is coming up in the next chapter.

So what might TransactionScope look like with Spring? Listing 6.4 takes a stab at it.

Listing 6.4 Transaction scope implemented as a custom scope in Spring

```
package my.custom;

public class TransactionScope implements Scope {
    private final ThreadLocal<Map<String, Object>> instances
            = new ThreadLocal<Map<String, Object>>();

    public Object get(String key, ObjectFactory unscoped) {      <-- Scoped instances provider method
        Map<String, Object> map = instances.get();

        if (null == map)
            throw new IllegalStateException("no transaction is active");

        if (!map.containsKey(key)) {
            map.put(key, unscoped.getObject());
        }

        return map.get(key);

    }

    public void beginScope() {          <-- Starts scope context
        instances.set(new HashMap<String, Object>());
    }

    public void endScope() {     <-- Disposes current scope context
        instances.remove();
    }

    public Object remove(String key) {
        if (null == instances.get())
            throw new IllegalStateException("no transaction is active");

        return instances.get().remove(key);     <-- Disposes a specific key from current context
    }

    public String getConversationId() {
        if (null == instances.get())
            throw new IllegalStateException("no transaction is active");

        return instances.get().toString();      <-- A unique string identifying the hash table (context)
    }

    public void registerDestructionCallback(String key,
                Runnable destructionCallback) {
        ...
    }
}
```

Listing 6.4's TransactionScope is very similar to Guice's TransactionScope. The major difference is the three additional methods that Spring requires. For the conversation ID, I return the hash table itself (in String form). This is a simple hack for identifying a context. Depending on the kind of `Map`, this may or may not have good results. You will want to generate a more appropriate identifier in a production version. I also perform a sanity check every time scoping methods are called:

```
if (null == instances.get())
    throw new IllegalStateException("no transaction is active");
```

This is important because it fails fast with a clear and easily identifiable `IllegalStateException`. Countless hours have been wasted because failing code does not indicate exactly what was wrong and where.

Registering this scope with the injector is straightforward, and it involves a bit of simple cut-and-paste code in your injector configuration:

```
<beans ...>
    <bean
➥   class="org.springframework.beans.factory.config.CustomScopeConfigurer">
        <property name="scopes">
            <map>
                <entry key="transaction">
                    <bean class="my.custom.TransactionScope"/>
                </entry>
            </map>
        </property>
    </bean>

    ...
</beans>
```

Then you are free to use it just like any other scope when declaring keys:

```
<bean id="gauge" class="nuclear.Gauge" scope="transaction">
    ...
</bean>
```

Now your new scoped objects can be injected and used as needed. The next section switches around and looks at problems you can encounter when creating your own scopes. It is essential to understand these before you go off and create your own scopes.

6.2 Pitfalls and corner cases in scoping

Letting the injector manage the state of your objects is a wonderful thing when applied properly, but it also attracts danger. Scopes are extremely powerful because they invert the responsibility of managing state, and the injector takes care of passing it around to dependents. It keeps objects free of such concerns and makes them more focused and testable. However, this same power can lead to very grave pitfalls.

Many of these have to do with thread-safety. Some are about construction of object graphs that are striped with objects of different scopes. These pitfalls can lead to a range of unrelated problems that are not immediately apparent, for example, memory leaks, poor performance, or even erratic behavior. The counter to this latent peril is a thorough understanding of problem cases. With that said, let's start with scoping and thread-safety.

6.2.1 Singletons must be thread-safe

Singletons absolutely must be thread-safe—no exceptions. Any serious application has several threads of execution that are continually operating. They may be servicing different users, timers, remote clients, or any of a number of other purposes. A singleton-scoped key directly implies that only one *shared* instance of an object exists in the entire injector (and consequently the application). Multiple threads often end up accessing singleton instances and may even do so concurrently. Chapter 9 discusses the intricacies of threading and objects in detail (with a particular emphasis on Java's thread and memory model).

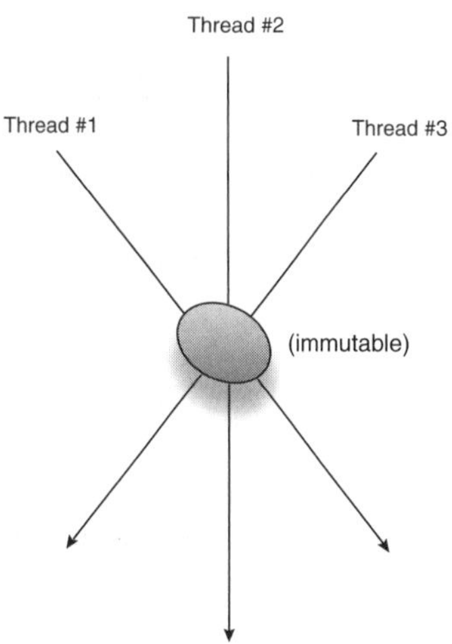

Figure 6.5 Multiple threads may safely use an immutable object.

There are two ways in which you can create thread-safe classes. The simpler and more straightforward is to make them immutable, as shown in figure 6.5.

The fields of the following class are immutable (see how this might look for threads accessing it in figure 6.6):

```
import net.jcip.annotations.Immutable;
...

@Immutable @Singleton
public class MySafeObject{
    private final Dependency dep1;
    private final Dependency dep2;

    @Inject
    public MySafeObject(Dependency dep1, Dependency dep2) {
        this.dep1 = dep1;
        this.dep2 = dep2;
    }

    public Dependency getDep1() { return dep1; }

    public Dependency getDep2() { return dep2; }

    ...
}
```

Notice that `MySafeObject` has no setters and no methods that can alter or affect its dependencies' state. This is good immutable design. The marker annotation `@Immutable` is merely a tag that documents the behavior of `MySafeObject` (it has no effect in practice). Place it on classes that you have designed to be immutable. Don't be confused by its proximity to `@Singleton`; it is there only as documentation. It helps unfamiliar pairs of eyes read, understand, and reason about your classes. It also reduces confusion about intent. This is especially useful when you have bugs, since a colleague can spot the bug and know immediately that it violates design intent.

TIP @Immutable and other thread-safety–related annotations are available from the *Java Concurrency in Practice* website.[1] They are downloadable at the site and provided under a flexible open source license. Neither Guice nor any other injector or production library reacts to the @Immutable annotation.

If their values never change, there is no risk of one thread modifying a value that's out of sync with its rivals. As figure 6.6 shows, mutable singletons, if not properly guarded, can get out of sync between threads.

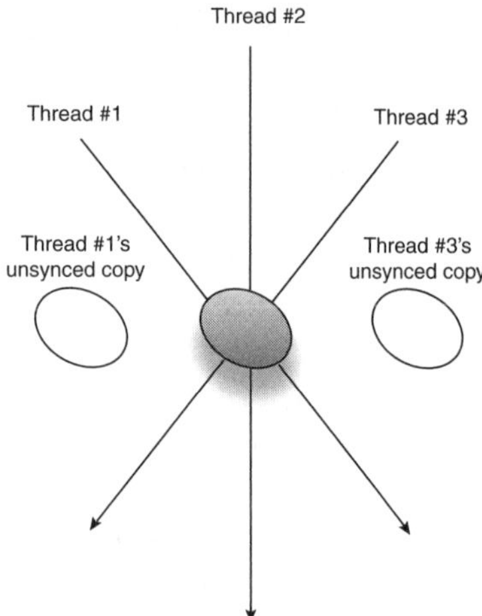

Figure 6.6 All visibility bets are off with multiple threads accessing a mutable object.

With immutable objects, the order of thread execution is irrelevant, so you have fewer problems to design for. Try very hard to make singleton objects immutable. This is by far the simplest and best approach.

Of course, not every singleton can be made immutable. Sometimes you may need to alter the object's state (for example, in a counter or accumulator). If you decide to use setter injection to resolve circular dependencies or the in-construction problem (see chapter 3), you cannot make the class immutable. In these cases, you must carefully design the object and all of its dependencies to be thread-safe. Here I have the same class; it is no longer immutable but thread-safe insofar as it guarantees that all of its dependencies will be visible to all threads:

```
import net.jcip.annotations.ThreadSafe;

@ThreadSafe @Singleton
public class MySafeObject2{
    private volatile Dependency dep1;
    private volatile Dependency dep2;

    @Inject
    public void set(Dependency dep1, Dependency dep2) {
        this.dep1 = dep1;
        this.dep2 = dep2;
    }

    public Dependency getDep1() { return dep1; }

    public Dependency getDep2() { return dep2; }

    ...
}
```

@ThreadSafe, like @Immutable, is intended to convey information about the class's design, nothing more. Java's volatile keyword ensures that the value of a field is kept

1 Find out more at http://jcip.net. Chapter 9 has a lot of detailed information on concurrency and good class and object design. Jump ahead if you are curious.

coherent with all threads. In other words, when MySafeObject2's dependencies are changed using the set() method, they are immediately visible to all threads. This is a very important point, and you will appreciate why when @ThreadSafe is contrasted with the following class:

```
import net.jcip.annotations.NotThreadSafe;

@NotThreadSafe @Singleton
public class MyUnsafeObject {
    private Dependency dep1;
    private Dependency dep2;

    @Inject
    public void set(Dependency dep1, Dependency dep2) {
        this.dep1 = dep1;
        this.dep2 = dep2;
    }

    public Dependency getDep1() { return dep1; }

    public Dependency getDep2() { return dep2; }

    ...
}
```

MyUnsafeObject is critically flawed, because the Java language makes no guarantees that any thread other than the one that set its dependencies will see the dependencies (without additional synchronization). In other words, the memory between threads in non-final, non-volatile fields may be incoherent. The subtle reason has to do with the way Java Virtual Machines (JVM) are designed to manage threads. Threads may keep local, cached copies of non-volatile fields that can quickly get out of sync with one another unless they are synchronized correctly. We'll study this problem and its solutions in greater detail in chapter 9.

Making a class thread-safe is often a difficult and involved process. No simple litmus test exists to say a class is completely thread-safe. Even the best of us can get tripped up when dealing with apparently simple threading and concurrency issues. Your best bet is to reason carefully about a class and its threading environment. Explore plenty of scenarios both common and atypical where a singleton may be used. Try to convince at least one other person of the safety of your code. Actively hunt for flaws; never assume they don't exist. Always validate your assumptions. Test! Test! And test again until you're satisfied.

Thread-safety problems can also present in other ways, particularly when dealing with dependencies that cross scoping boundaries. This is an especially tricky situation called scope widening, which we'll explore in detail in the next section.

6.2.2 Perils of scope-widening injection

I've mentioned a problem called scope-widening injection a few times so far in this book. It came up particularly when wider scoped objects depended on narrower scoped objects, such as a singleton that depends on a no-scoped or request-scoped object. When such a situation is encountered, you end up with a no-scoped (or request-scoped) object that is held by the singleton, and it no longer comes under the purview of its original scope. That means when the context ends, the instance continues to exist as a dependency of the singleton. As you can imagine, this causes a whole swathe of knotty problems that can go undetected. Worse, they won't necessarily cause errors or exceptions to be raised and may appear to be functioning correctly, when really they're opening up a whole bunch of unintended semantics and consequences.

Scope widening also applies to any scopes that are logically of different contexts—even those that may belong to the same scope but refer to separate contexts, such as two separate user sessions. While this kind of scope widening is less likely (due to the walling off between contexts by the injector), it can still occur if a singleton is used to bridge them. I should really say, if a singleton is *abused* as a bridge. Not only does it break the semantics of the scope as understood at the time of its definition, it also can lead to serious performance, maintenance, and correctness problems. Scope widening is tricky, since it cannot easily be addressed by testing either. The simplest kind of peril in scope widening is an object whose scope has ended. This gremlin is called an *out-of-scope object.*

BEWARE THE OUT-OF-SCOPE OBJECT!

Instances that are out of scope present the most serious difficulty of the scope-widening cases. This naïve singleton class depends on a no-scoped component:

```
@Singleton
public class TextReader {
    private final WordCounter counter;

    @Inject
    public TextReader(WordCounter counter) {
        this.counter = counter;
    }

    public void scan(List<String> strings) {

        for(String string : strings)            <-- Count words in all strings
            counter.count(string);

        System.out.println("Total words: " + counter.words());
    }
}
```

TextReader is simple; its method scan() accepts a list of strings and prints the total number of words. Its dependency WordCounter counts the number of words it has received so far:

```
public class WordCounter {
    private int count;

    public void count(String text) {
        count += text.split(" ").length;        <-- Split string around spaces
    }

    public int words() {
        return count;
    }
}
```

So far, so good. Let's try using the `TextReader` to count a few example string sets:

```
Injector injector = Guice.createInjector();
TextReader reader = injector.getInstance(TextReader.class);
reader.scan(Arrays.asList("Dependency injection is good!",
    "Really, it is!"));
```

This code correctly prints a total word count of 7.

```
Total words: 7
```

Now lets extend the example and give it more to do:

```
Injector injector = Guice.createInjector();
     TextReader reader = injector.getInstance(TextReader.class);
reader.scan(Arrays.asList("Dependency injection is good!",
    "Really, it is!"));
reader.scan(Arrays.asList("Dependency injection is terrific!",
    "Use it more!"));
```

What does the program print now?

```
Total words: 7
Total words: 14
```

What went wrong? The second count should have been the same as the first. Double-check the words: There are only seven in both sets. We've been had by scope-widening injection. While you would normally expect the no-scoped `WordCounter` to be disposed of after the first call to `scan()` and a new instance to take its place subsequently, what really happened is that `TextReader` has held onto the original instance. This situation would not improve even if we were to obtain `TextReader` itself twice from the injector:

```
Injector injector = Guice.createInjector();
TextReader reader = injector.getInstance(TextReader.class);
reader.scan(Arrays.asList("Dependency injection is good!",
    "Really, it is!"));

TextReader reader2 = injector.getInstance(TextReader.class);
reader2.scan(Arrays.asList("Dependency injection is terrific!",
    "Use it more!"));
```

This program still prints an incorrect result:

```
Total words: 7
Total words: 14
```

The first run is okay, since at that time all instances (`TextReader` and `WordCounter`) are new ones. But the second run uses the old instance of `WordCounter` as well and so ends up accumulating the word count. If we added a third line this accumulation would continue (visualized in figure 6.7):

```
Injector injector = Guice.createInjector();
     TextReader reader = injector.getInstance(TextReader.class);
reader.scan(Arrays.asList("Dependency injection is good!",
```

```
    "Really, it is!"));

TextReader reader2 = injector.getInstance(TextReader.class);
reader2.scan(Arrays.asList("Dependency injection is terrific!",
    "Use it more!"));

TextReader reader3 = injector.getInstance(TextReader.class);
reader3.scan(Arrays.asList("The quick brown fox", "is really annoying!"));
```

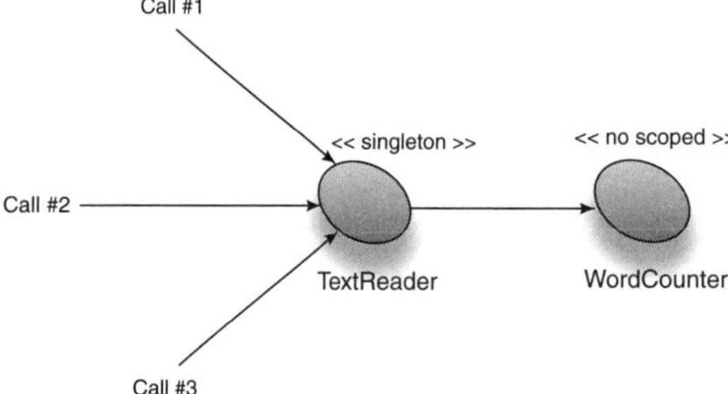

Figure 6.7 `WordCounter`'s scope is widened since it is held by singleton-scoped `TextReader`.

This should print three sets of `7`, but instead it prints

```
Total words: 7
Total words: 14
Total words: 21
```

There are a couple of really easy solutions. The simpler is to remove the discrepancy in scope between `TextReader` and `WordCounter` by choosing the narrowest scope for both, in other words, make `TextReader` no scoped:

```
public class TextReader { .. }
```

Note the missing `@Singleton` annotation, implying no scope. This is shown in figure 6.8.

Now, the program can remain as is:

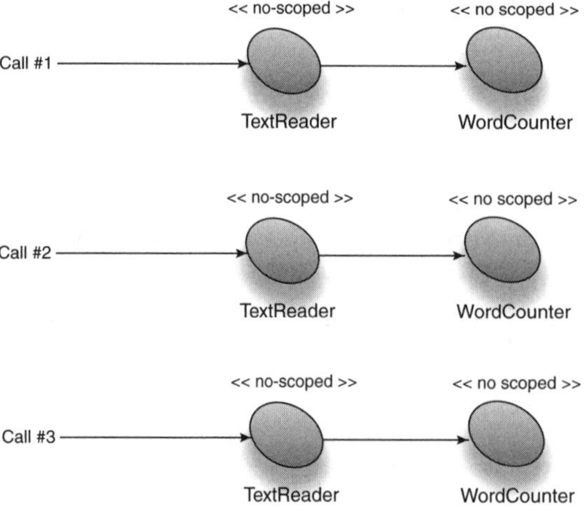

Figure 6.8 Both `TextReader` and its dependent have the same scope and are safe from scope widening.

```
Injector injector = Guice.createInjector();
     TextReader reader = injector.getInstance(TextReader.class);
reader.scan(Arrays.asList("Dependency injection is good!",
    "Really, it is!"));

TextReader reader2 = injector.getInstance(TextReader.class);
reader2.scan(Arrays.asList("Dependency injection is terrific!",
    "Use it more!"));

TextReader reader3 = injector.getInstance(TextReader.class);
reader3.scan(Arrays.asList("The quick brown fox", "is really annoying!"));
```

And it correctly prints the three independent word counts:

```
Total words: 7
Total words: 7
Total words: 7
```

This is an example of scope-widening injection that could not be caught with a unit test. Any test of `WordCounter` would pass, since it does correctly count the number of words in a string. Any test of `TextReader` would also pass, since a mocked `WordCounter` would only assert that correct calls were made to it around its *behavior* rather than around its *state.*

Well, this solution works, but by making `TextReader` no scoped rather than fixing the problem of scope widening, you might say I've sidestepped it. While this is a legitimate solution, there are times when this doesn't work. You need a singleton, and it depends on a no-scoped instance, or, more generally, a wider-scoped object depends on a narrower-scoped object.

Scope widening viewed in this light is a form of the *reinjection problem* (see chapter 3). We can use the same solution to mitigate scope widening. By replacing the narrower-scoped dependency with a provider (and fetching it each time), we allow the injector to intervene when new instances are required:

```
@Singleton
public class TextReader {
    private final Provider<WordCounter> counterProvider;

    @Inject
    public TextReader(Provider<WordCounter> counterProvider) {
        this. counterProvider = counterProvider;
    }

    public void scan(List<String> strings) {
        WordCounter counter = counterProvider.get();

        for(String string : strings)
            counter.count(string);

        System.out.println("Total words: " + counter.words());
    }
}
```

`TextReader` can now go back to being a singleton but continue depending on a no-scoped object without any scope-widening effects. Figure 6.9 imagines how this might work.

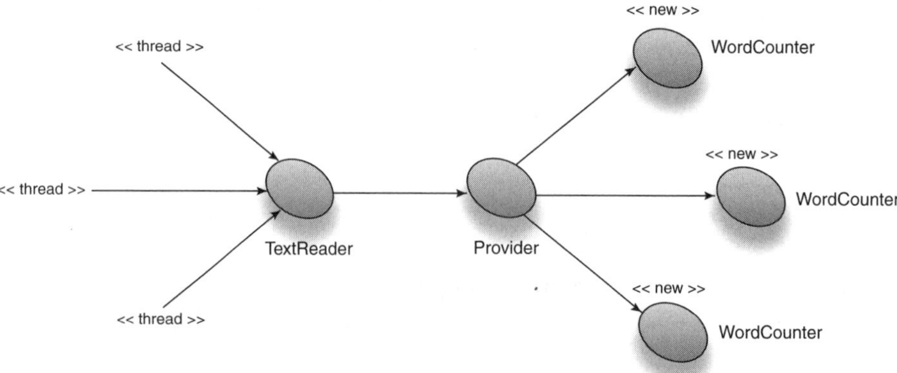

Figure 6.9 A provider acts as an intermediary and prevents widening `WordCounter`'s scope.

Running the program yields the correct word counts:

```
Total words: 7
Total words: 7
Total words: 7
```

One subtle thing to note is that in the new `TextReader`'s `scan()` method we retrieve `WordCounter` once per *method* rather than once per *use*. If we had done this instead:

```
public void scan(List<String> strings) {
    for(String string : strings)
        counterProvider.get().count(string);

    System.out.println("Total words: " +
        counterProvider.get().words());
}
```

we would have ended up with a very different (and rather obnoxious) result:

```
Total words: 0
Total words: 0
Total words: 0
```

There's nothing wrong with the coding of `WordCounter` or its logic, and that's fine. It's just that the statement that prints the count uses a new instance of `WordCounter`, discarding the one that has just run a count. This is one of the perils of stateful behavior. It would probably have had you looking everywhere except where the fault was (that is, in the scoping).

NO, REALLY: BEWARE THE OUT-OF-SCOPE OBJECT!

Out-of-scope objects can also cause bugs in other areas. One common version is the use of an out-of-scope object between (or before) scope contexts (see figure 6.10).

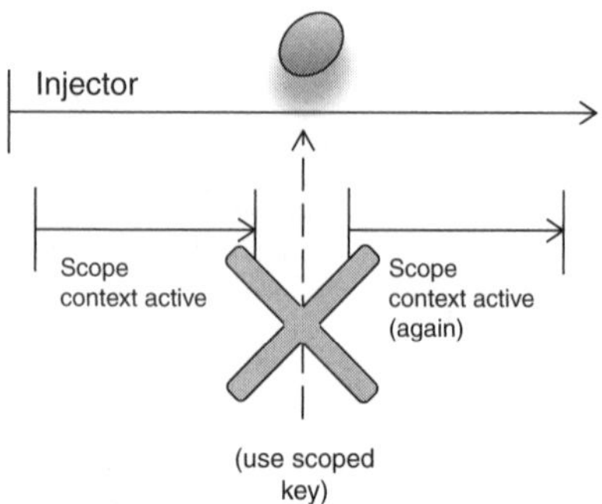

Figure 6.10 Beware of out-of-scope objects used between contexts of a scope.

This is a common problem that users of guice-servlet and Guice post about on the community mailing lists. Consider a servlet managed by guice-servlet:

```
import com.google.inject.servlet.RequestScoped;

@RequestScoped
public class HelloServlet extends HttpServlet {
    public void init(ServletConfig config) { .. }

    ...
}
```

and its injector configuration:

```
Guice.createInjector(new ServletModule() {
        protected void configureServlets() {

            serve("/hello").with(HelloServlet.class);
        }
});
```

Now there is one method of note in HelloServlet: init(), which is called by the guice-servlet on startup of the web application. What's interesting is that HelloServlet is itself request scoped. The servlet lifecycle methods are fired when the web application starts and there are no active requests at the time. The injector (via request scope) immediately detects that there is no active request, so it aborts with an OutOfScopeException (as shown in figure 6.11). This happens at the earliest point of the application's life, so it fails to load the entire web app.

Session scoping a servlet will similarly fail because no user session can be found under which to bring the key into scope. These are all cases of objects being used out of scope and represent serious flaws in the design of a program. In other words, HelloServlet is unavailable for the application to start up. We can use one of the mitigants of the reinjection problem, the Adapter pattern, to solve this problem. Consider this rather plain but functional version of HelloServlet bound with an Adapter:

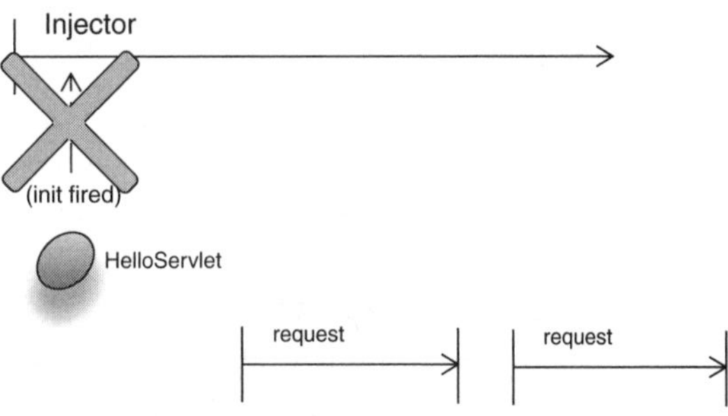

Figure 6.11 Request-scoped HelloServlet is used out of scope, that is, before any requests arrive.

```
@Singleton
public class HelloServletAdapter extends HttpServlet {
    private final Provider<HelloServlet> delegate;

    public void init(ServletConfig config) {
        //do init work
     }

    public void service(HttpServletRequest request,
```

```
        HttpServletResponse response) throws IOException,
➥   ServletException {
        delegate.get().service(request, response);
    }
    ...
}
```

Also the modified injector configuration, using the Adapter instead:

```
Guice.createInjector(new ServletModule() {
        protected void configureServlets() {

            serve("/hello").with(HelloServletAdapter.class);
        }
});
```

HelloServletAdapter is a singleton wrapper around HelloServlet that acts as a go-between. It solves the out-of-scope problem (figure 6.12) by moving the logic for the portions that are outside the scope of HelloServlet into itself. Any calls to its service() method are delegated down to the request-scoped HelloServlet.

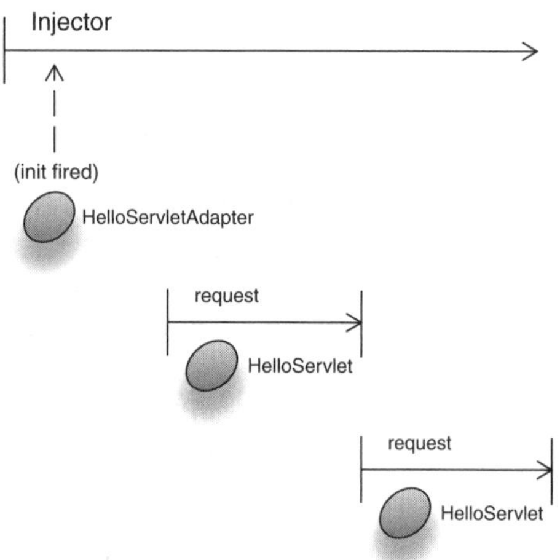

Figure 6.12 A wrapping singleton HelloServletAdapter mitigates the out-of-scope problem.

Since service() is called only during a request, we can rest assured that HelloServlet will always be inside a valid request. Now HelloServlet can keep its scope and still effectively function as expected. Now that we've seen all the domestic problems of scope widening, let's shift gears and look at the truly nasty pitfalls—ones that involve multiple threads and objects in widened scopes.

THREAD-SAFETY REVISITED

Scope widening can also lead to concurrency problems. Wiring any singleton with a narrower-scoped dependency means that it automatically becomes accessible to all the dependents of that singleton. If multiple threads access the singleton object, they are likely to modify its nonsingleton dependencies. If they are not immutable or thread-safe, you may see erratic and unpredictable behavior. Even if they are, they may be underperforming. Thread-safety is a particularly tough subject, since there are so many nuances to the concurrent modification (and access) of state. One of these is the issue of *safe publication,* which is dealt with in chapter 9.

You must take particular care to ensure that singletons never depend on objects that are not thread-safe, or if they do, that these dependencies are guarded properly. Here's an example of a class, scoped as a singleton, that depends on a counting service:

```
@Singleton
public class TextPrinter {
    private final Counter counter;

    public void print(String text) {
        System.out.println(text);

        counter.increment();

        if (counter.getCount() == 100)
            System.out.println("done!");
    }
}
```

`TextPrinter` has a thread *unsafe* dependency, `Counter`, which looks like this:

```
@NotThreadSafe
public class Counter {
    private long count;

    public void increment() {
        count++;
    }

    public long getCount() {
        return count;
    }
}
```

Because many threads hit `TextPrinter`'s methods, `print()` and `printCount()`, they also increment and read `Counter` concurrently. When the number of lines printed hits 100, it prints `"done!"` Unfortunately, the way things stand this may never happen. The counter keeps incrementing, no matter how many threads hit it, so it is logical to assume that `counter` must reach 100 at some point (when a hundred lines are printed):

```
        if (counter.getCount() == 100)
            System.out.println("done!");
```

So what's the problem? Right away there is the problem of memory *coherency*. Class `Counter` is not a singleton and so has been designed without thread-safety in mind. That would be fine were it used at any scope other than singleton (or more strictly, any scope that is confined to single threads). In practice, however, `Counter` has had its scope widened by being wired to `TextPrinter`, which is a singleton. One fix we can try is to make `count` volatile (as we did in a similar example not long ago):

```
//@ThreadSafe?
public class Counter {
    private volatile long count;

    public void increment() {
        count++;
    }

    public long getCount() {
        return count;
    }
}
```

Now, at last, all threads see the same value of count. However, this isn't quite enough. It is conceivable that two threads could run through the print() method at once—the first thread incrementing count to 100 and the second to 101. Then if either the first or second continues down the print() method, it will hit the statement testing whether count is 100. But the count has already hit 101, so the statement evaluates to false and keeps on going. Our base case is never reached, and the program never prints "done!"

Clearly, concurrent access to the counter is not desirable—at least not willy-nilly. To fix this problem, we need to ensure that each thread sees not only the latest value of count but also the value that it has set. In other words, each thread must have access to the counter exclusively. This is known as *mutual exclusion* and is achieved as follows (also illustrated in figure 6.13):

```
@ThreadSafe @Singleton
public class TextPrinter {
    private final Counter counter;

    public synchronized void print(String text) {
        System.out.println(text);

        counter.increment();

        if (counter.getCount() == 100)
            System.out.println("done!");
    }
}
```

The synchronized keyword ensures that no two threads execute method print() concurrently.

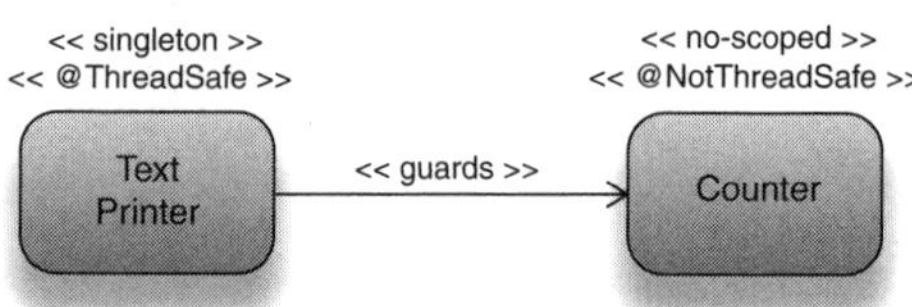

Figure 6.13 Singleton TextPrinter must guard access to its *unsafe* dependencies.

Threads queue up behind one another and execute print() one by one, ensuring that calls to getCount() always return the value set by the same thread in counter.increment() just above. Can we now call Counter thread-safe? It has proper visibility across threads, and it works in singletons that guarded it appropriately. But we can't quite go that far. As a dependency, it can still be used in a *thread-unsafe* manner. So we must leave it thus:

```
@NotThreadSafe
public class Counter {
    private long count;

    public void increment() {
        count++;
    }

    public long getCount() {
        return count;
    }
}
```

Thread-safety is an eternally difficult problem, and it's especially subtle in the case of scope widening since it is hard to detect. Good documentation and modular design will help you go a long way to avert its issues. Scope widening can also create nasty problems that don't involve threads, particularly with memory usage. In the next section we'll look at how this edge case can rear its ugly head and how to solve it.

SCOPE WIDENING AND MEMORY LEAKS

Scope-widening injection certainly has a lot of pitfalls! In Java, a garbage collector runs behind your programs, periodically checking for objects that are no longer in use, *reclaiming* the memory they occupy. Garbage collection is a wonderful feature of modern languages that frees you from having to worry about a large number of memory issues. Memory is automatically allocated to objects when they come into instance. When they're no longer in use, that memory is claimed for reuse.

Memory reclamation is a vital process that helps ensure programs run smoothly and that they can stay up for indefinite periods. Next to hardware failure, memory leaks are the greatest threat to this ability. Memory is said to leak when a programmer expects an object to be reclaimed but the garbage collector can't do so. Usually this is because of programmer oversights (like scope-widening injection). These unreclaimable zombie objects no longer serve any purpose, yet they cannot be claimed by the garbage collector because it cannot verify that they are not in use. Over time these objects can accumulate and consume all of a machine's memory, causing loss of performance and even program crashes.

So how does scope widening feed this problem? Take the case of a singleton. A singleton is held by an injector forever, that is, for the injector's (and usually the application's) entire life span. Therefore, a singleton is never reclaimed during the life of an application. Singletons are generally reclaimed only on shutdown. If any nonsingletons are accidentally wired to a singleton through scope-widening injection, it follows that these objects are also (indirectly) held forever. Here's a naïve example of a servlet that holds onto no-scoped instances on every request:

```
@Singleton
public class BadServlet extends HttpServlet {
    public final Provider<WebPage> page;
    public final List<WebPage> pages = new ArrayList<WebPage>();

    public void service(HttpServletRequest request,
        HttpServletResponse response) {
        pages.add(page.get());

        pages.get(0).handle(request, response);
    }
}
```

`BadServlet` is a frivolous example, but it serves to illustrate how a no-scoped dependency (`WebPage`) can be scope widened and held by a singleton, as shown in figure 6.14.

If you continually refresh the URL served by this servlet, your web server will eventually run out of memory and die with an `OutOfMemoryError`.

A simple solution is to discard instances as soon as they are used:

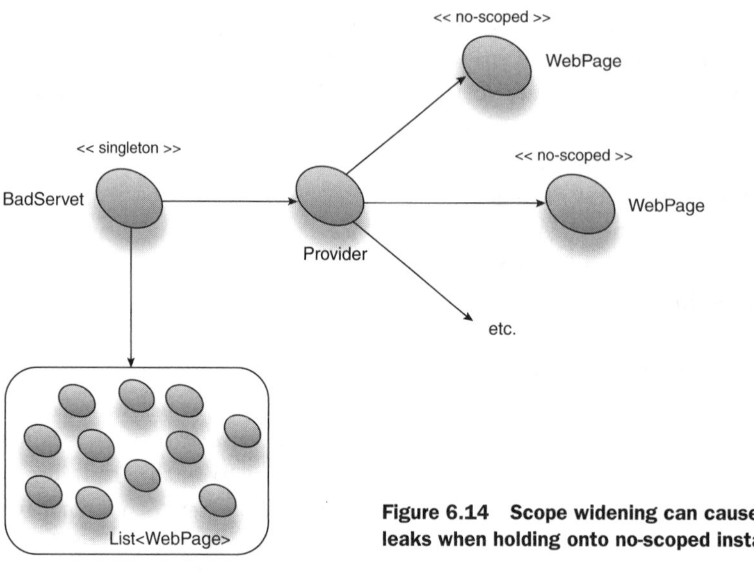

Figure 6.14 Scope widening can cause memory leaks when holding onto no-scoped instances.

```
@Singleton
public class GoodServlet extends HttpServlet {
    public final Provider<WebPage> page;

    public void service(HttpServletRequest request,
        HttpServletResponse response) {
        page.get().handle(request, response);
     }
}
```

The following method uses a no-scoped dependency but discards it immediately:

```
public void service(HttpServletRequest request, HttpServletResponse
➥    response) .. {
    page.get().handle(request, response);
}
```

`GoodServlet` servlet is properly behaved and allows instances of `WebPage` to be reclaimed by the garbage collector, and all is well with the universe. Scope-widening injection contains many such dangers. Avoid it where possible and try to use simpler designs, either by using the narrowest scope available or by choosing the Provider and Adapter design patterns as we've seen.

6.3 Leveraging the power of scopes

If there's one feature of dependency injection that you can't do without (besides wiring), it would be scope. Scopes apply the Hollywood Principle to the state of objects. They are a powerful way of removing boilerplate and infrastructure logic from your code. The importance of this cannot be understated, since it means your code is easier to read and test. Scopes also reduce objects' dependence on one another and therefore simplify your object graphs.

While many DI libraries provide scopes out of the box, and some web frameworks round out the complement with advanced scopes (like *flash* and *conversation*), there's still plenty of room for innovation. We saw just how a custom *transaction* scope can help make components easier to code and test. By pulling the menial labor into behind-the-scenes code, you save yourself a tremendous amount of repetition, coupling, and extra testing. That being said, here are some ideas for leveraging the power of scope.

6.3.1 Cache scope

Objects that are expensive to create (or data that is expensive to retrieve from a store) are especially conducive to in-memory *caching*. Caching is the idea that an object is kept around after its initial fetch, so that additional requests for it can use the cached copy rather than go through the (potentially expensive) process of obtaining it again.

A cache, specifically a disk cache, is powerful in that it can maintain the state of certain important objects across multiple lives of an injector (and, indeed, an application). A particular state can be restored this way for continuing work. In a computer game you play through several difficult levels, then are called away to more mundane pursuits, and so have to close down the game. But you don't want to play through all those levels again. A disk cache can let the application save game state for later resumption. Figure 6.15 imagines how this might look.

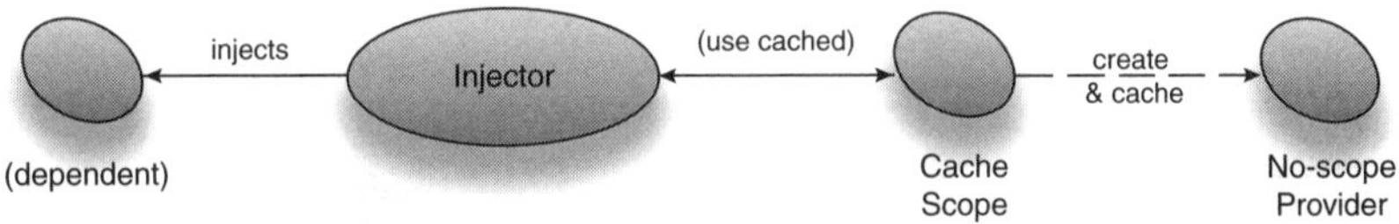

Figure 6.15 The injector obtains instances transparently from the cache scope.

This works in any scenario where long-lived data needs to be saved across injectors. A cache is also powerful for keeping a handle on data constants (such as a list of countries) that rarely change. As the application requests cached items by wiring them in as dependencies, the injector goes to an external store (or creates an instance) for the object. Any subsequent wiring is much faster using the cached copy.

6.3.2 Grid scope

A data grid is very much like a cache in that it is an in-memory store of frequently used data. However, it is a cache that is common across a large number of physical (or logical) machines. These individual machines share objects and act in concert as a *grid*. Grids are sometimes referred to as cluster *caches*. Some sophisticated grids (like Oracle Coherence) do much more than spread objects across a cluster, however. Coherence features querying and updating operations, very much like a database. Grids can also hold objects for very long periods of time, since they are able to distribute the storage load across many more machines than single-disk caches. As a result, they are also often faster and more flexible in clustered applications.

A grid scope that takes advantage of persisting instances in a data grid has no end of useful applications. Grid scoping allows you to transparently cluster a massive number of stateful services and data. This is done transparently so that the load is efficiently balanced across machines without tedious clustering logic and extra service programming. Figures 6.16 and 6.17 show how an instance can be injected in one node and transparently distributed across the grid, to be used by dependents anywhere.

The simplest use case is replication of user credentials across a cluster. A user logged into a single machine may have some relevant data stored in an HTTP session, but if the application is backed by several machines in a cluster, you need to ensure the credentials are also clustered correctly. Grid scoping is a compelling way of creating *single-sign-on* semantics across even different kinds of applications. Single sign-on is the idea that you log in once, on any application in a domain, and you are logged in to all applications on that domain. Here's how you might share a user's relevant information across a data grid:

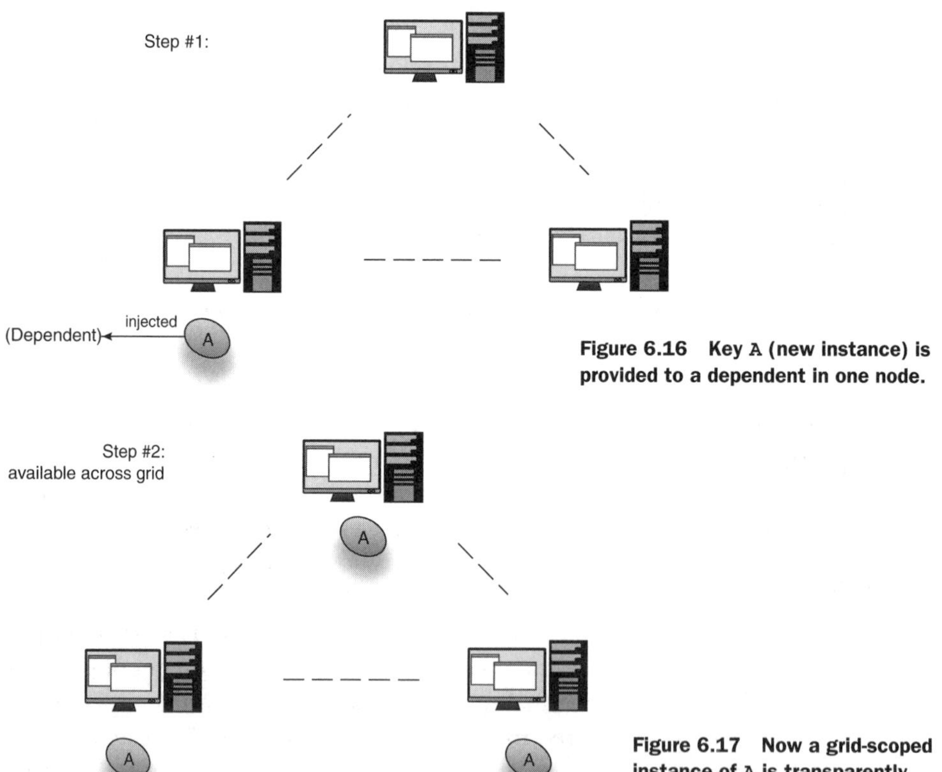

Figure 6.16 Key A (new instance) is provided to a dependent in one node.

Figure 6.17 Now a grid-scoped instance of A is transparently available to the entire grid.

```
@GridScoped @ThreadSafe
public class Users {
    private final Map<String, UserContext> users;

    ...
}

@NotThreadSafe
public class UserContext {
    private String username;
    private boolean isActive;
    private Preferences prefs;

    ...
}
```

Thereafter, servlets, EJBs, service objects, mail components, and many others can all share a user's information by simply injecting the `Users` object. Of all the powerful applications of scope, grid scope is perhaps the most interesting since it offers so much potential for horizontally scaling applications.

6.3.3 Transparent grid computing with DI

The possibilities for client applications to scale and grow are endless, with SOA and enterprise systems cleverly using dependency injection's wonderful design patterns. We've seen the modularity and separation of responsibilities that this can bring. We've also seen how this can help us scale by moving applications off to dedicated hardware. And we've seen the flexibility it can bring in terms of accommodating new business processes and even interbusiness collaboration.

There are a few more exciting possibilities. The kind of scaling we've seen thus far, adding stronger hardware to individual layers of an application, is known as vertical scaling or tiering. You will often hear architectures referred to as an n-tiered or vertically tiered system. This kind of scaling has its advantages, but it can get expensive very quickly. And for very large amounts of traffic, it can even become untenable. An increasingly popular alternative system is known as horizontal scaling.

Horizontal scaling refers to an architecture that increases its processing capacity by the addition of any number of homogenous nodes, each capable of performing the same function as any other. Incoming traffic is evenly distributed across several of these worker machines from a few strong-load distributors. This kind of hardware is both cheap and easily replaceable. And as it turns out, it is extremely powerful when scaling to very large loads.

Apache's Hadoop project is an example of one such homogenous cluster-computing system. It consists of a master machine that distributes a single, computationally expensive task across a number of worker slaves. Then it gathers results from each one and recombines (or reduces) them into an expected total order. This is incredibly useful for searching across large datasets and performing expensive computations that can be broken down into simpler ones.

One possible use of DI would be to apply a similar abstraction over the grid computing network, where one interface and one method call are orchestrated across several machines using a grid service proxy, in much the same way as we used a remote proxy in the SOA case. There are early attempts at performing this sort of orchestration, but most of the effort has been focused on transparent slicing and distribution of tasks around the cluster rather than architectural design patterns for clients of such services. A library like that combined with a thin integration layer for clients could really make dependency injection shine.

6.4 Summary

Injectors are extensible via the definition of custom scopes. These are scopes that match some particular context of a problem domain that would benefit from the application of the Hollywood Principle. Database transaction scope is one such example. Keys bound within this scope return the same instance while a transaction is active in the current thread but return new instances in other transactions (either subsequent or concurrent). Be careful when crafting your own scopes, and adhere to the following principles:

- Define the context of a scope clearly and succinctly.
- Try to keep contexts confined to a single thread.
- Assess whether your scope improves testability of components. If not, stay away! There is no end to the pain that can be caused by a presumed performance or development improvement that ends up not being easy to test.

Custom scopes really require a lot of thought and planning. Objects wired across scoping boundaries can cause serious problems that can go undetected even with comprehensive unit testing.

The problem of "crossing" a scoping boundary is very serious indeed—wiring a narrow-scoped object (that is, a no-scoped one) to a wider-scoped object (a singleton) entirely changes the assumptions about that narrower scope. The instance becomes held by the singleton and effectively lives for the same amount of time. You should try to design an architecture so this scope-widening injection is rare. Binding all keys in the object graph under the narrowest scope is one simple mitigation. However, this doesn't work for all cases; sometimes you need a singleton that depends on a no-scoped (or narrower-scoped) object. You can solve problems in this case by applying the Provider design pattern from chapter 3.

Another issue with scope widening is objects that are out of scope. An out-of-scope object is one for which a key is requested when its bound scope is not active, for example, a request-scoped key wired outside an HTTP request (say, during application startup). Such problems represent design flaws. Rethink the architecture of your long-lived components and their collaborators. If you must, solve the problem with the Adapter pattern, as shown in chapter 3.

A third issue that arises from scope-widening injection is thread-safety. Keys of narrower scope, when wired to a singleton, are susceptible to the action of multiple concurrent threads. It is not enough to secure the singleton component alone; you must guard access to its narrower-scoped dependencies or ensure that they are immutable. This problem often goes undetected and can lead to erratic, unpredictable behavior (without any specific errors being raised), which can be a nightmare to debug. There is no easy way to detect thread-safety issues in scope-widened cases, since unit tests (and even integration tests) are not reliable in this regard. Think about your object graphs and convince yourself (and preferably an educated colleague) that they are thread-safe. Better yet, avoid scope-widening injection altogether.

Finally, scope-widening injection can cause memory leaks if the wider-scoped object holds onto its narrower-scoped dependencies. Memory leaking is impossibly hard to detect and results in arbitrary application crashes, which can be disastrous in production environments.

Although scopes have many pitfalls that may scare you off writing your own, you shouldn't be afraid. These are some positive features of scope:

- Reduction of boilerplate
- Reduction of interdependent code
- Reduction (or removal) of dependence on infrastructure
- Logical use of the Hollywood Principle to create focused, concise code
- Improved testability

The benefits vastly outweigh any perils. Consider the careful use of scopes, and design them according to your problem domain. Scopes can make the use of caches, clusters, and data grids transparent to vastly increase an application's scalability and give it powerful features such as stateful replication.

We've spent two chapters studying the problems and benefits of scope. In the next chapter let's change the theme slightly and look at a broader topic, applicable to all kinds of applications, object lifecycle.

7 From birth to death: object lifecycle

This chapter covers:

- Notifying objects of significant events
- Understanding domain-specific lifecycle
- Initializing lazy and eager singletons
- Customizing lifecycle with multicasting

"I agree with everything you say, but I would attack to the death your right to say it."
—Tom Stoppard

Whether or not lifecycle is a part of dependency injection is a divisive issue. However, like scoping, it can be a powerful tool when used correctly, and it fits closely with dependency injection. In this chapter we'll look at the basic form of lifecycle offered by the language runtime—constructors. We'll also look at managed lifecycle as offered by more elaborate frameworks like servlets and EJBs, to illustrate how lifecycle is domain specific. On the way we'll examine the pitfalls of relying on one-size-fits-all lifecycle models.

Finally, we'll look at how to design and implement a custom lifecycle strategy and design classes that are simple and easy to test. First, let's start by looking at what lifecycle is: events in the life of an application that an object is notified about.

7.1 Significant events in the life of objects

Lifecycle and scope are closely related concepts, so much so that they are occasionally confused with each other. An object's longevity can be seen in these two dimensions. Object longevity with regard to some context (duration, users, threads, and so on) is its scope. Periods in this context indicate various things about an object, for instance, whether it is ready to begin serving clients, or if the object represents a network resource, whether that resource has been closed or abnormally interrupted.

Clearly many of these *states* are specific to the nature of the object. A movie may have a *paused* state in its life; a web application has a *deployed* state, a game has a *game-over* state, and so on. The various states an object goes through in its life are collectively known as its lifecycle. When an object transitions between such states, it is said to undergo lifecycle changes. These are often modeled as events that an object responds to (see figure 7.1).

The most basic lifecycle events are *create* and *destroy*.

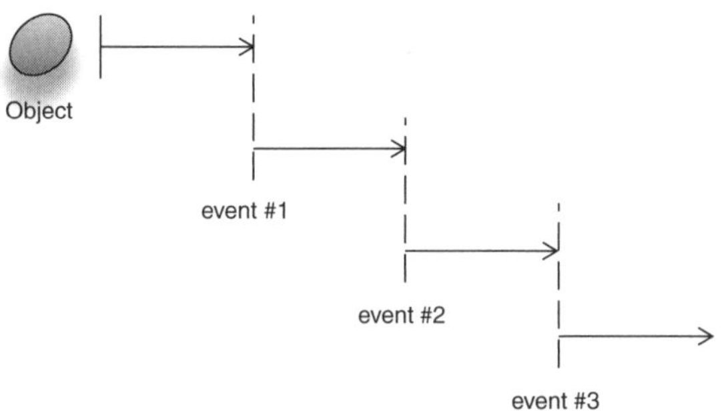

Figure 7.1 An object is notified of events as parts of its lifecycle.

7.1.1 Object creation

Objects come into instance when they are created and are notified about this event by a constructor. Language runtimes support this construct naturally, so this isn't really rocket science. After memory is allocated to an object, its constructor is called, which can perform some initialization logic. Ideally, one would do everything that's necessary on construction (any computation, dependency wiring, and the like) to put an object into a usable state. However, this isn't always possible for reasons that we'll discuss shortly.

In chapter 3 we saw how the constructor is used to wire an object with its dependencies. We saw that it is a powerful technique for creating objects that are good citizens. Good citizenry naturally extends to the lifecycle of an object. Constructing an object (with its dependencies) puts it in a usable state, and thus begins its lifecycle.

Listing 7.1's `Transporter` is notified via its constructor, so that it can prepare itself for use.

Listing 7.1 `Transporter`'s lifecycle is begun with a call to its constructor

```
public class Transporter {
    private final ControlPanel control;
    private final PowerCell cell;
```

```
    public Transporter(ControlPanel control, PowerCell cell) {    <- Constructor
        this.control = control;                                       is notified,
        this.cell = cell;                                             begins
                                                                      lifecycle
        cell.charge();
        control.activate();
}

    public void energize() { .. }    <- Ready to be used

}
```

Figure 7.2 models these classes. In `Transporter`'s case, it calls into its dependencies first (as per figure 7.3).

Following this, `Transporter` is in the ready stage of its life. Method `energize()` can be called safely, to send crew members off on wild planetary adventures (see figure 7.4).

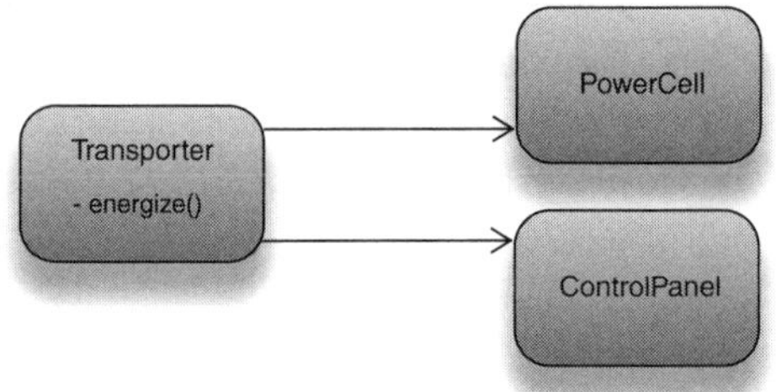

Figure 7.2 A `Transporter` depends on a `PowerCell` and `ControlPanel`.

Furthermore, any preparatory computations are also a natural fit to the constructor:

```
    public Transporter(ControlPanel control, PowerCell cell) {
        this.control = control;
        this.cell = cell;

        cell.charge();
        control.activate();
    }
```

There's nothing spectacular about this example or about using constructors to prepare objects, but the example serves to illustrate the idea behind lifecycle with states

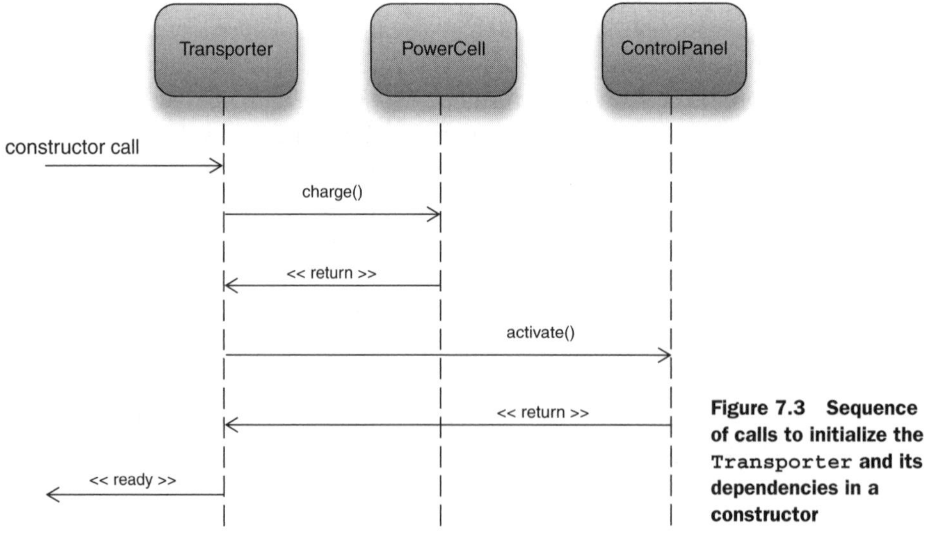

Figure 7.3 Sequence of calls to initialize the `Transporter` and its dependencies in a constructor

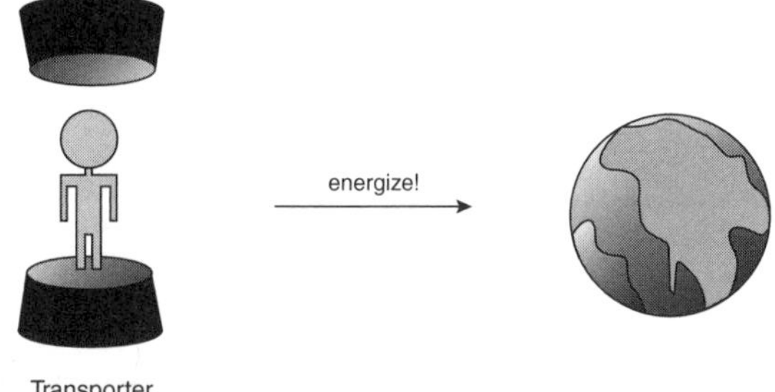

Figure 7.4 Once the constructor lifecycle method runs, we are ready for adventuring!

and about certain tasks that need to be performed to put an object into such states. Similarly, when a service is shut down, resources often need to be relinquished (memory reclaimed, sockets closed, and so on). This occurs when a service is destroyed.

7.1.2 *Object destruction (or finalization)*

In Java, the explicit task of allocating and reclaiming memory is taken care of by the runtime environment. This frees you from having to worry about when to reclaim allocated objects. Premanaged languages like C++ support an explicit *destructor*, which acts as a counterpart to constructors. The destructor is a lifecycle event method, which runs once, just prior to memory being freed. Java has something analogous: *finalizers*. A finalizer is a method that runs just prior to an object being reclaimed by the runtime garbage collector.

Unlike in C++, in Java we cannot guarantee when an object will be reclaimed and therefore when its finalizer runs. The only certainty is that a finalizer *will* be run before the object is reclaimed. This may be often and early (in the case of aggressive garbage collection), or rare and late, or even right at the shutdown of the application itself, or never if the application exits abnormally. For these reasons, disposal of finite resources (such as network sockets or database connections) inside a finalizer is not a good idea.

To illustrate why, let's take the example of a file service that displays the contents of various images in a directory (like a filmstrip preview). This service is described in listing 7.2.

Listing 7.2 This application displays impressions of images on a disk

```
public class Thumbnail {
    private final FileSystem fileSystem;
    private InputStream data;

    public Thumbnail(FileSystem fileSystem) {
        this.fileSystem = fileSystem;
    }

    public Image display(String path) throws IOException {
         data = fileSystem.getPath(path).newInputStream();     <-- InputStream opened on display
         ...
```

```
    }

    @Override
    protected void finalize() throws Throwable {
        data.close();                      <-- InputStream closed
                                               in finalizer (bad!)
        data = null;
        super.finalize();
    }
}
```

Each time the user flips to a new image, the `Thumbnail` object opens a new file and displays it. However, the input stream is closed only inside its `finalize()` method. Since there is no guarantee of when an object may be reclaimed, it's a real possibility that the program will open too many files from the operating system and thus run out of resources (see figure 7.5). This is obviously a poor use of the finalizer lifecycle.

Most times, you will find a better lifecycle method to release finite resources than a finalizer. So, should you never use finalizers? Not quite—there are some rare cases when they come in handy. While you can't rely on a finalizer to release finite resources, you can use a finalizer to *ensure* that a resource has been released previously:

```
@Override
protected void finalize() throws Throwable {
    if (null != data) {
    logger.warning("unclosed thumbnail: " + this);
        data.close();
    }

    data = null;
    super.finalize();
}
```

This is a sanity check that can help in cases where you mistrust clients of your code. Strictly speaking, this isn't common, but it's occasionally useful. Alternatively, you might use logging or profiling APIs inside a finalizer to test predictions about your program's performance.

One other use case for finalizers is releasing memory in collaborating libraries that are not managed. For example, memory resources of a native C library running inside a Java program can be released inside a finalizer by calling a native method (see figure 7.6).

These are corner cases that you are unlikely to encounter in everyday programming. However, it's important to understand the role of finalizers and more important to avoid *abusing* them. More on the pitfalls of finalization is presented in chapter 9.

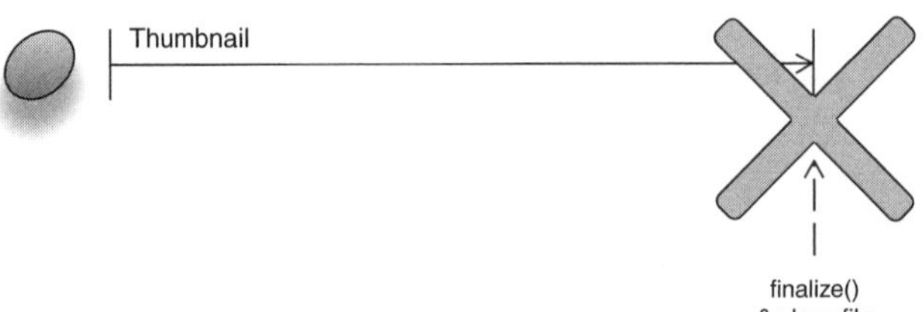

Figure 7.5 Method `finalize()` may run very late, so it's unsuitable for closing finite resources.

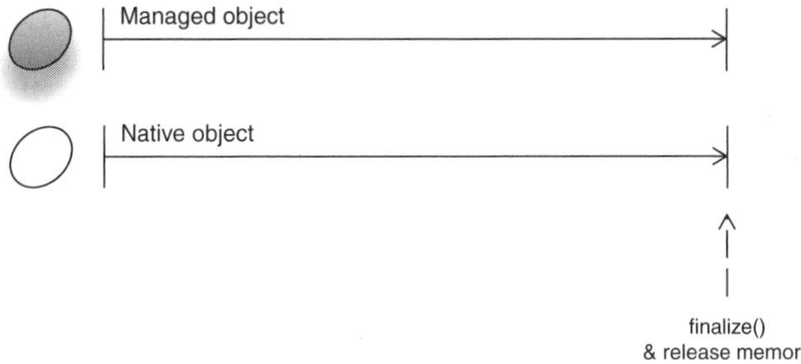

Figure 7.6 It's sometimes useful to release memory in collaborating native libraries with `finalize()`.

Construction and finalization are universal events that apply to any kind of object. But most types of lifecycle apply only to specific classes of objects—and then only in certain application domains. Remember that not all lifecycle is universal and that events are typically specific to particular problem domains.

7.2 One size doesn't fit all (domain-specific lifecycle)

We've seen that constructors are a lifecycle hook on creating objects and that finalizers are their complement prior to destruction. We've also seen that finalizers don't fit all clean-up use cases. Constructors are a bit better, but they too don't fit all initialization use cases. For example, a web application is deployed, and all its objects are constructed quite early. But it may only begin servicing requests at a much later time.

The application doesn't require many of its (finite) resources until that point. In the Java Servlet Framework, this directly translates to a servlet's `init()` method, where resources such as database connections can be acquired and held. Similarly, a network service may be created and configured but is not fully ready until a socket is opened.

This leads to the conclusion that lifecycle events are *not* universal and that the stages in an object's life are *specific* to a problem domain. For instance, the lifecycle of a servlet is very different from the lifecycle of a database connection or that of a movie player. Consequently, the times and frequency of initialization and destruction are dependent on the nature of the service. Web pages are created and destroyed frequently (on each request), while database connection pools are created once and held open almost indefinitely.

In this chapter, we'll look at some of these domains, how they differ, and how to design with them in mind. Let's start by contrasting two very common problem domains that have very different lifecycles: web servlets and database connections.

7.2.1 Contrasting lifecycle scenarios: servlets vs. database connections

A *servlet* is a web component used to render web pages that has three major stages in its lifecycle: *constructed, ready to service,* and *destroyed.* These are demarcated by two lifecycle events: *init* and *destroy.* A servlet's `init()` method is the lifecycle *hook* that's called to notify it of initialization. In other words, when the `init()` method returns, the servlet is expected to be ready for service. Similarly, method `destroy()` is called to notify a servlet that its life has ended. Any cleanup of the servlet's dependencies should be performed here. Once destroyed, a servlet object is never called on to service requests again. Listing 7.3 shows a servlet object that initializes itself in its constructor and opens a connection to the database when notified of the init event. It releases this connection on servlet destruction. This sequence is illustrated in figure 7.7.

Listing 7.3 A Java servlet that starts and cleans up its resources inside lifecycle hooks

```
public class NewsServlet extends HttpServlet {
    private Connection con;
    private final NewsService newsService;

    public NewsServlet() {
        newsService = new NewsService();          <- Create nonfinite dependencies
    }

    @Override
    public void init() throws ServletException {
        try {
            con = DriverManager.getConnection(..);   <- Open database connection
        } catch (SQLException e) {
            ...
        }
    }

    @Override
    public void service(ServletRequest req, ServletResponse res) { .. }

    @Override
    public void destroy() {
        try {
            con.close();                          | Close and release connection
            con = null;                           |
        } catch (SQLException e) {
            ...
        }
    }
}
```

There are some oddities about NewsServlet: Because it is managed directly by the servlet framework, it cannot benefit from dependency injection. Its lifecycle (that is, init() and destroy()) is managed entirely by the servlet container. It introduces the need to create dependencies by hand (or use a factory) and tightly couples the servlet to the underlying data layer. By inserting an integration layer like guice-servlet, we can change all that and have NewsServlet benefit from dependency injection as well as receive the servlet lifecycle events. Listing 7.4 reimagines NewsServlet in this light.

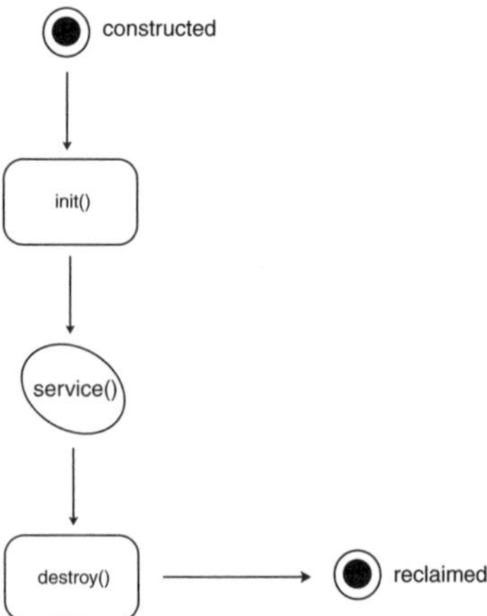

Figure 7.7 Stages in a servlet's lifecycle

Listing 7.4 A version of `NewsServlet` managed by Guice and guice-servlet

```
@Singleton
public class NewsServlet extends HttpServlet {
    private final PersistenceService persistence;
    private final NewsService newsService;

    @Inject
    public NewsServlet(PersistenceService persistence,
       NewsService newsService) {
        this.persistence = persistence;
        this.newsService = newsService;
    }

    @Override
    public void init() {
        persistence.start();
    }

    @Override
    public void service(ServletRequest req, ServletResponse res) { .. }

    @Override
    public void destroy() {
        persistence.shutdown();
    }
}
```

Abstract, nonfinite dependencies are injected

Start persistence service

Shut down persistence service

This version of `NewsServlet` is much neater, not simply because it is injected, but also because its lifecycle can naturally cascade to abstractions underneath. For example, `PersistenceService` may represent a database connection, flat disk file, or even in-memory network storage. Dependency injection in conjunction with the servlet lifecycle makes for simpler, more testable code.

Spring's `DispatcherServlet` provides a similar facility for routing requests from the servlet container to its own custom MVC framework. First you set up the `DispatcherServlet` in web.xml. Then you hook it up to a custom Spring MVC controller that does what you want (and is dependency injected by Spring):

```
<?xml version="1.0" encoding="UTF-8"?>
<beans xmlns="http://www.springframework.org/schema/beans"
       xmlns:xsi="http://www.w3.org/2001/XMLSchema-instance"
       xsi:schemaLocation="http://www.springframework.org/schema/beans
       http://www.springframework.org/schema/beans/spring-beans-2.5.xsd">

    <bean name="/news.html" init-method="init" destroy-method="destroy"
➥  class="c7.NewsController">
      <constructor-arg ref="persistence"/>
      <constructor-arg ref="newsService"/>
    </bean>
    ...
</beans>
```

Here instead of implementing `HttpServlet` directly, we implement Spring's `Controller` interface:

```
import org.springframework.web.servlet.mvc.Controller;
...
public class NewsController implements Controller {
     private final PersistenceService persistence;
     private final NewsService newsService;

     public NewsController(PersistenceService persistence,
        NewsService newsService) {
         this.newsService = newsService; this.persistence = persistence;
     }

     public void init() {
         persistence.start();              <-- Start persistence service
     }

     public ModelAndView handleRequest(HttpServletRequest request,
        HttpServletResponse response) { .. }
     public void destroy() {
         persistence.shutdown();           <-- Shut down persistence service
     }
}
```

Except for the variant `handleRequest()` method, this is very similar to the previous example.

NOTE Notice that we had to specify `init-method` and `destroy-method` in the XML configuration; this is necessary since we're moving from the servlet container to Spring's injector. While these do not exactly coincide (as in the case of Guice Servlet), they perform the same function.

Contrast this with the lifecycle of a different service, such as a database connection. Both can be managed by DI, and both have a role to play in web applications, but they lead very different lives. Listing 7.5 describes a fictional, pooled database connection class.

Listing 7.5 `Connection` wraps a raw database-driver connection for pooling purposes

```
public class PooledConnection {
    private Connection conn;
    private ConnectionState state;

    public synchronized void open() throws SQLException {      <-- Connection is established
        conn = DriverManager.getConnection(..);
    }

    public synchronized void onCheckout() {      <-- Connection is checked out for use
        this.state = IN_USE;
    }

    public synchronized void onReturn() {      <-- Connection is checked back in
        this.state = IDLE;
    }

public synchronized void close() throws SQLException {      <-- Connection is disposed, if not in use
        if (IN_USE == state)
```

```
            throw new IllegalStateException();

        conn.close();
    }
}
```

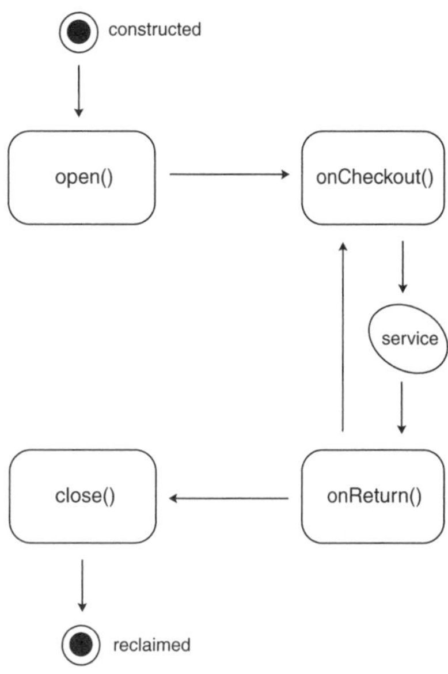

Figure 7.8 Flow of stages in an example database connection's lifecycle

In listing 7.5, there are four lifecycle hooks: `open()`, `close()`, `onCheckout()`, and `onReturn()`. These refer to events in the life of the database connection. `open` and `close` are self-explanatory; `onCheckout()` refers to the connection being taken out of its pool for use. Think of this as checking out a book from your local public library. When notified, the pool-aware connection puts itself in an `IN_USE` state, which is used to ensure that it isn't accidentally closed while serving data. Similarly, `onReturn()` is called when the connection is checked back into its pool, setting it into an `IDLE` state. Figure 7.8 is a flow chart describing the sequence of events in `Connection`'s lifecycle.

Idle connections are safe to close or to perform other background activity on (for example, connection *validation*).

The connection's lifecycle hooks are called from an owning connection pool. As previously said, its usage profile is significantly different from a servlet's—and indeed any other object managed by dependency injectors. The pool itself may be managed by a servlet and cohere with its lifecycle; however, this is not particularly relevant to the connection's lifecycle.

Connection pooling and validation

Connections to RDBMS databases often have timeout values. After a certain period of inactivity, a driver automatically releases a held connection in order to prevent zombie connections from dragging down database performance. Since establishing new connections is potentially expensive, applications create and hold them in pools (at startup), taking the cost up front. Connections are then distributed from the pools to clients and returned after use, avoiding the need to dispose and reestablish connections during the life of busy applications. This is known as *connection pooling*.

If a connection remains idle in a pool for any length of time, it's in danger of being timed out. To prevent this, connection pools execute dummy SQL statements at periodic delays to reset the timer and keep the connection alive. Often these are as simple as `"SELECT 1 FROM DUAL"`, which returns the number `1` from a numerical sequence. This process is known as *connection validation*.

Just as it is difficult to fit connections and servlet into the same lifecycle, it is also difficult for any one lifecycle model to fit all use cases. Many programmers lead themselves into trouble by trying to do just that. One such anti-pattern is trying to apply a converse of the initialization lifecycle event to all services. I call this the destructor anti-pattern.

7.2.2 The Destructor anti-pattern

As we said earlier, finalizers are not well suited to freeing up finite resources in languages with managed memory models. To solve this, many developers use an all-purpose *destroy* lifecycle hook, which is called when the injector (or application itself) is shut down. Spring and PicoContainer provide these all-purpose destroy methods, which are called at some point in the application's lifecycle but not necessarily just when an object is being reclaimed. Here is the file service from earlier in the chapter, modeled using Spring's built-in destroy event:

```
<bean id="thumbnail" class="files.Thumbnail" destroy-method="close">
        <constructor-arg ref="fileSystem"/>
</bean>
```

The attribute `destroy-method=".."` refers to the name of a no-argument method to be called when the injector is shut down. While these are often useful in particular problem domains (such as the servlet lifecycle we saw previously), generalizing this event is not always appropriate. Take the `Thumbnail` example at the head of the chapter; the same problem occurs here as we saw with finalizers. Method `close()` is called when the application exits (Spring's injector calls destroy hooks when the JVM exits). This means that file handles will be held open while images are being viewed. Once again, you can very easily run out of finite OS resources without really using them.

A more sensible solution would be to close each file handle after the image preview has been extracted from it. There isn't a clear way to do that using only the `destroy-method` mechanism or, more generally, using the Destructor pattern.

Thus, indiscriminate use of this all-purpose lifecycle hook can lead to unintuitive designs. It's not uncommon to see Java Swing windows being provided a destructor. Often these are used to dispose of graphical widgets no longer needed within the window. The irony is that Swing widgets don't need to be disposed explicitly. Like any other Java object, Swing widgets are managed and reclaimed by the language runtime and require no explicit memory management.

Without a well-understood destruction hierarchy, it becomes difficult to predict the order in which objects are destroyed. For example:

```
<bean id="thumbnail" class="files.Thumbnail" destroy-method="close">
    <constructor-arg ref="fileSystem"/>
</bean>

<bean id="fileSystem" class="files.ZipFileSystem" destroy-method="close"/>
```

It's difficult to predict the order in which `ZipFileSystem.close()` and `Thumbnail.close()` will be called. If one depends on the other while shutting down, this may lead to accidental illegal states where a dependency has already been closed but a dependent still needs it to shut itself down. It's not unusual to find conditions like the following, to account for just such a scenario:

```
public void close() {
    if (null != reader) {
        if (reader.isOpen())
            reader.someLastMinuteLogic();

        reader = null;
    }

    shutdownMyself();
}
```

Such contortions are abstruse and unnecessary, especially when we have managed memory models and patterns like DI to fall back on. In this light, I strongly discourage using the jack-of-all-trades destroy method or the Destructor anti-pattern. A good alternative is to pick domain-specific finalization patterns. For I/O, Java's `Closeable` interface functions nicely.

7.2.3 Using Java's Closeable interface

Not all objects can be left to garbage collection to be disposed of. Often, an external resource needs to be closed explicitly, at a time other than the application's exit, as we saw in the case of the thumbnail image viewer. Global, one-time destructors are ill-suited for the reasons we've just seen.

An object that acts as a data endpoint can be designed with *closeability* in mind if it exposes the `java.io.Closeable` interface. Here's a definition from the API documentation:

> "*A* `Closeable` *is a source or destination of data that can be closed. The close method is invoked to release resources that the object is holding (such as open files).*"

Modeling finite resources (files, network sockets, and so on) as `Closeables` allows you to redact them into lifecycle stages. For example, a look-ahead caching service could open and read image data in the background. When they are finished being read, these files would be placed into a queue to be closed periodically by a lower-priority thread:

```
@ThreadSafe
public class ResourceCloser implements Runnable {
    @GuardedBy ("lock")
    public final List<Closeable> toClose = new ArrayList<Closeable>();

    private final Object lock = new Object();

    public void run() {
        synchronized(lock) {
            for (Closeable resource : toClose) {
                try {
                    resource.close();
                } catch (IOException e) {
                    ...
                }
```

```
            }
        }
    }

    public void schedule(Closeable resource) {
        synchronized(lock) {
            toClose.add(resource);
        }
    }
}
```

NOTE The annotation @GuardedBy indicates that access to mutable list toClose is guarded by a field named lock. Like @ThreadSafe, @GuardedBy is simply a documenting annotation and has no effect on program semantics.

Resources to be closed are enqueued via the schedule() method and closed periodically by the run() method. We won't worry too much about how this method is scheduled to run or how often. Let it suffice to say that it happens periodically and at a lower priority than other threads in the application. This satisfies the close lifecycle of a file handle and doesn't suffer the problems of destructors. So far, we've looked at how lifecycle is domain-specific and that while objects share common events like construction and finalization, they cannot be shoehorned into initialization and destruction patterns universally. To illustrate, let's examine a scenario that highlights how complex and specific lifecycle can get. Let's look at stateful EJBs, which are common in many real-world business applications.

7.3 A real-world lifecycle scenario: stateful EJBs

So far we've seen fairly simple lifecycle hooks in the form of constructors, some more involved lifecycles with servlets and pooled database connections, and some pitfalls in generalizing these models. Now let's take a look at a more complex case: *stateful EJBs*. EJBs are a programming model for business services. They are managed directly by an application server (commonly, a Java EE application server), and as such their lifecycle is also controlled by it. There are several types of EJBs, suited to various purposes such as persistence, message-passing, and business services. Stateful EJBs at a particular kind of business service are sometimes called *stateful session beans*.

These are basically objects that interact with a client around some specific context. They are called stateful because they can maintain this context across multiple interactions from the same client, in much the same manner as an HTTP session does with a browser client. As of this writing, the EJB specification is in version 3.0, which has some dependency injection features, where EJBs can be provided to one another via annotated fields. Similarly, they also have a controlled lifecycle, where the bean is notified of major events by the application server.

Listing 7.6 is an example of a stateful EJB representing a shopping cart. Its clients may be a website front end (like Amazon.com), a desktop application at a checkout counter, or even another EJB.

Listing 7.6 A stateful EJB representing a returning customer's shopping cart

```
@Remote
public interface ShoppingCart {
    void add(Item item);
    List<Item> list();
}

@Stateful
public class ShoppingCartEjb implements ShoppingCart {
    private List<Item> items = new ArrayList<Item>();
    private double discount;

    @EJB
    private InventoryEjb inventory;        <-- Injected by EJB container

    @PostConstruct
    public void prepareCart() {
        discount = inventory.todaysDiscount() * items.size();   <-- Compute initial discount
    }

    @Remove
    public Status purchase() {
        return inventory.process(items, discount);   <-- Process purchase and dispose EJB
    }

    public void add(Item item) { items.add(item); }      Shopping cart
    public List<Item> list() { return items; }           public methods
}
```

In listing 7.6's `ShoppingCartEjb`, all methods except `add()` and `list()` are EJB lifecycle hooks. Method `prepareCart()` is marked with `@PostConstruct`, indicating to the EJB container that it should be called on initialization. `purchase()` performs a dual role: It processes the order in the shopping cart, returning a status code, and also tells the EJB container to end the stateful bean's lifecycle. Another lifecycle hook, `@PreDestroy`, is available for any explicit cleanup actions that need to occur on a *remove* event.

NOTE The annotation `@EJB` is used in much the same manner as Guice's `@Inject` or Spring's `@Autowired` but only on a field. This tells the EJB container to look up the appropriate EJB and inject an instance. EJB provides basic dependency injection in this fashion. This is undesirable because of the inability to replace with mock objects and for several other reasons outlined in chapters 3 and 4 (EJB does not support constructor injection as of version 3.0).

This is certainly quite a complex set of semantics for a simple shopping cart service. But it gets better—because a stateful EJB is meant to keep a running conversation with its client (until `@Remove` is reached), two more lifecycle hooks are available. These are used to transition a stateful EJB from its active servicing state to a passive state (while the client is off doing other things) and then back again to an active state when the client has returned.

During this passive time, it may be useful to have the shopping cart data stored in a more permanent storage medium like a database or disk cache. EJB provides a `@PrePassivate` lifecycle hook for this purpose:

```
@PrePassivate
public void passivate() {
    cache.store(items);
}
```

This is useful if there is some kind of failure in the application server. On reactivation, you may want to refresh the items in the shopping cart or recompute discounts to ensure that associated data have not become stale. An administrator may have modified the item's price while the stateful EJB was passive. The `@PostActivate` lifecycle hook is called by an EJB container every time a stateful EJB is reactivated:

```
@PostActivate
public void activate() {
    items = inventory.refresh(items);
}
```

While the EJB programming model is not a direct analog of dependency injectors, it nonetheless serves to illustrate how complex, managed lifecycle can work. This entire flow is illustrated in figure 7.9.

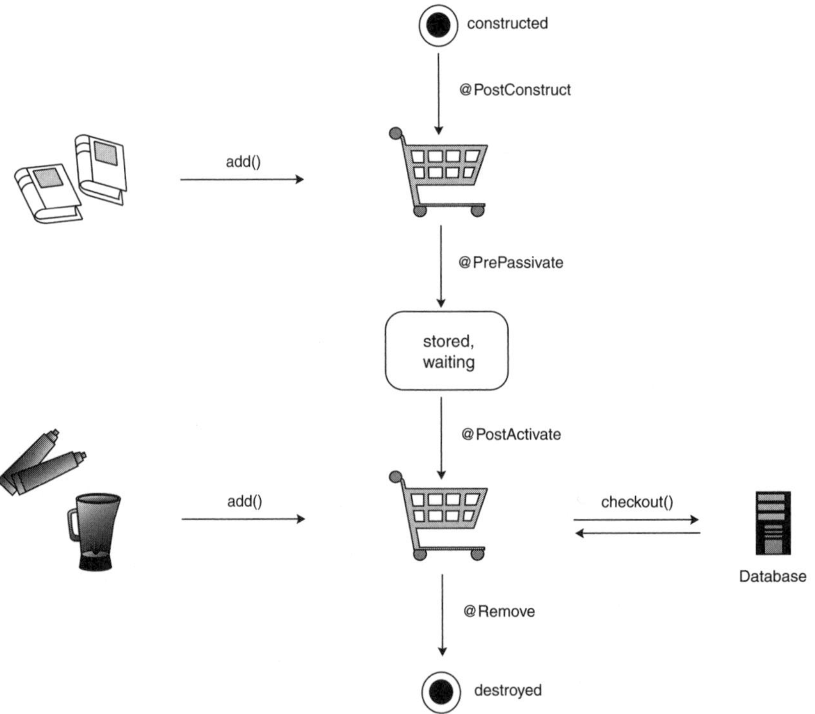

Figure 7.9 The lifecycle of a stateful EJB that models a shopping cart for *returning* clients

You will frequently find the need to apply similar patterns to your own environment, where objects are notified of significant events in their lifespan by an external actor or framework. Keep these examples in mind when designing lifecycle models for your own applications. Another important consideration when designing lifecycle is the timing of events. Not all objects are constructed at the same time. It is often desirable to delay construction until an object is needed. Among other things, this allows for better startup performance and lower memory usage. This type of delayed construction is called *lazy instantiation.*

7.4 Lifecycle and lazy instantiation

Another concept closely related to lifecycle is *on-demand* object construction. We saw this earlier with bootstrapping injectors on demand, per use. It's more common to find dependencies being constructed this way, particularly singleton-scoped objects. Rather than construct a dependency on injector startup, it's created when first needed for injection. In other words, it's created lazily (see figure 7.10).

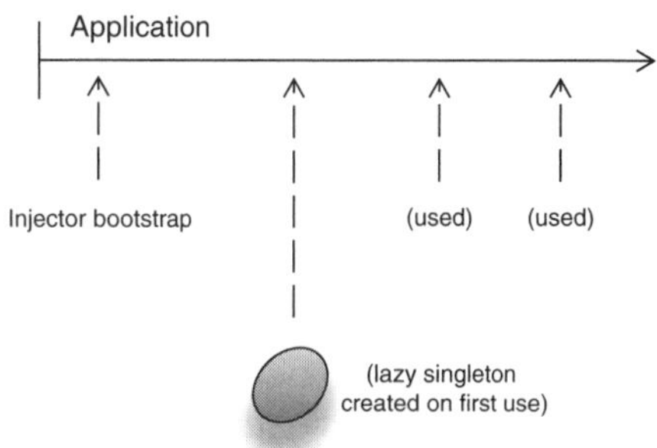

Figure 7.10 Lazily bound objects are created when first used.

Lazy creation of instances is useful when one is unsure whether all injector-managed services will be used early or used at all. If only a few objects are likely to be used early on and the remainder may be used infrequently or at a much later time, it makes sense to delay the work of creating them. This not only saves the injector from a lot of up-front cost but potentially also saves on the amount of memory used. It is especially useful during testing or debugging, where several configured services will probably never be used, or in a desktop or embedded application where fast startup is important.

The converse of lazy instantiation is *eager* instantiation. This is where singleton-scoped objects (in particular) are created along with the injector's bootstrap and cached for later use. Eager instantiation is very useful in large production systems where the performance hit can be taken up front, to make dependencies quickly available subsequently, as illustrated in figure 7.11.

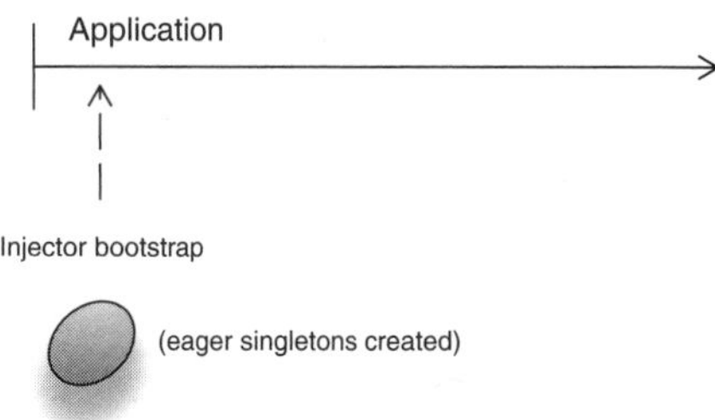

Figure 7.11 Eagerly bound singletons are created along with the injector itself.

The Guice injector can be built with a `Stage` directive, which tells it whether or not to eagerly instantiate singletons:

```
Guice.createInjector(Stage.PRODUCTION, new MyModule());
```

Singletons eagerly created

Or the alternative:

```
Guice.createInjector(Stage.DEVELOPMENT, new MyModule());
```

Singletons lazily created

You can also force certain keys to bind eagerly:

```
bind(MyServiceImpl.class).asEagerSingleton();
```

Or they can bind implicitly, by binding to a preexisting instance:

```
bind(MyService.class).toInstance(new MyServiceImpl());
```

Note that in the latter case, `MyServiceImpl` does not benefit from dependency injection itself, so this method should be avoided as much as possible. In Spring, this is achieved using the `lazy-init=".."` attribute:

```
<bean id="slothful" class="sins.seven.Sloth" lazy-init="true">
...
</bean>
```

Singleton instance `slothful` is created only when it is first needed by the application. By default, all singleton-scoped objects are created eagerly in Spring. Lazy instantiation as a design idiom is quite common. Before you decide to use it, you should consider issues of timing and performance, particularly during startup.

This chapter has thus far dealt with lifecycle events provided by frameworks like Spring and EJB. Now let's explore how we can create our own kinds of lifecycle. The simplest way to do this using a dependency injector is with post-processing.

7.5 Customizing lifecycle with postprocessing

As you've seen, lifecycle is specific to particular use cases and applications. In this case, the injector cannot help you directly, since libraries cannot ship with all possible lifecycle models (obviously). They can help, however, by providing a means for extending the lifecycle model to suit your own requirements.

Libraries like Spring and Guice allow an instance, once created, to be further processed by some general logic. This may include additional wiring, computation, or registering the instance for later retrieval. And it happens before the instance is injected on dependents. This is called *postprocessing* and is perfect for creating a custom lifecycle model (see figure 7.12).

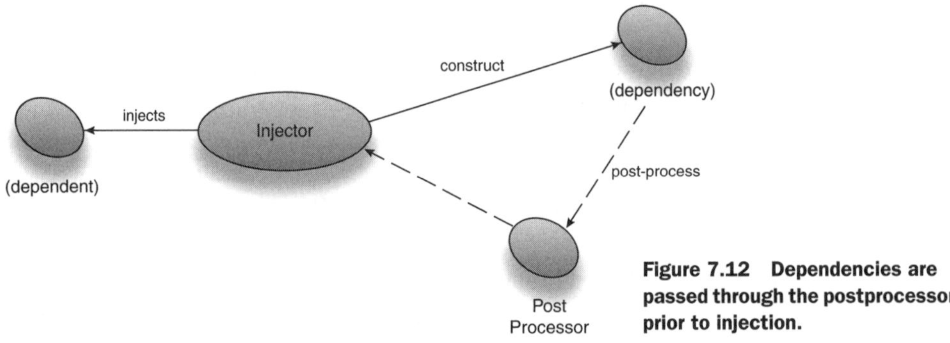

Figure 7.12 Dependencies are passed through the postprocessor prior to injection.

Let's take the example of a shopping arcade where there are several screens showing advertisements and shopping-related information. At midnight, when the arcade closes, these screens need to stop showing ads and display a notice saying that the mall is closed. Each screen's display is controlled from a separate set of feeds, based on their location. Modeling this as lifecycle of a feed (or screen) gives us a flexible and simple solution to the problem.

At midnight a notification is sent to all screens, putting them into a suspended state. Another notification is sent out the next morning when the mall reopens, so that normal programming can resume. Listing 7.7 shows how this `Screen` class would look in Java.

Listing 7.7 A screen with a timed lifecycle, driven by video feeds

```
package arcade;

public class Screen {
    private final Feed daytimeFeed;
    private final Feed overnightFeed;

    public Screen(Feed daytime, Feed overnight) { .. }

    public void suspend() {
        show(overnightFeed);
    }

    public void resume() {
        show(daytimeFeed);
    }

    ...
}
```

Class `Screen` has two interesting methods that embody its lifecycle:

- `suspend()`—Switches the screen to its overnight "mall closed" display
- `resume()`—Restores normal commercial programming

Both methods are specific to the shopping arcade problem domain. We need them to be called at specific times (midnight and early morning) to manage the activity of screens around the mall. The lifecycle sequence for this class is illustrated in figure 7.13.

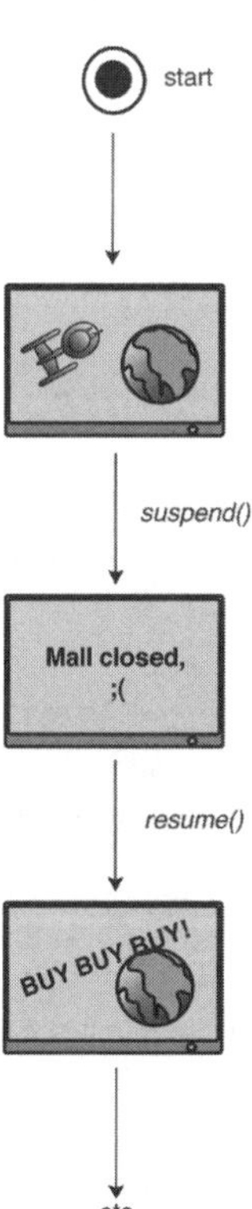

Figure 7.13 Screens around the mall move to a different feed when suspended and resume the next morning.

If all instances of `Screen` are created by a dependency injector, it's possible to postprocess each instance and *register* it for subsequent lifecycle notification. Here's how a postprocessor might look in Spring, along with three independent `Screens` around the arcade:

```
<beans ...>
    ...
    <bean class="arcade.LifecyclePostProcessor"/>

    <bean id="screen.corridor" class="arcade.Screen">
        <constructor-arg ref="daytimeFeed"/>
        <constructor-arg ref="overnightFeed"/>
    </bean>

    <bean id="screen.foodcourt" class="arcade.Screen">
        <constructor-arg ref="daytimeFeed"/>
        <constructor-arg ref="overnightFeed"/>
    </bean>

    <bean id="screen.entrance" class="arcade.Screen">
        <constructor-arg ref="daytimeFeed"/>
        <constructor-arg ref="overnightFeed"/>
    </bean>

</beans>
```

And the postprocessor implementation, which registers available screens for lifecycle management, is as follows:

```
package arcade;

import org.springframework.beans.factory.config.BeanPostProcessor;
import org.springframework.beans.BeansException;

public class LifecyclePostProcessor implements BeanPostProcessor {
    private final List<Screen> screens = new ArrayList<Screen>();

    public Object postProcessAfterInitialization(
        Object object, String key) throws BeansException {

          if (object instanceof Screen)
              screens.add((Screen)object);

          return object;
    }

    public Object postProcessBeforeInitialization(
        Object object, String key) throws BeansException { .. }
}
```

To understand this, let's dissect the `BeanPostProcessor` interface:

```
package org.springframework.beans.factory.config;

import org.springframework.beans.BeansException;

public interface BeanPostProcessor {
    Object postProcessAfterInitialization(
        Object object, String key) throws BeansException;

    Object postProcessBeforeInitialization(
        Object object, String key) throws BeansException;

}
```

Classes exposing this interface must implement the postprocess methods. Their signatures are identical: Both take an instance to postprocess and the string key it is bound to. They also return an `Object`, which is expected to be the *postprocessed* instance. To return the instance unaffected (that is, as per normal), you simply return the object that was passed in. For our purpose, this is exactly what we want. But first we register the instance in a collection of Screens to be used later by the lifecycle system:

```
public Object postProcessAfterInitialization(
    Object object, String key) throws BeansException {

        if (object instanceof Screen)
            screens.add((Screen)object);

        return object;
    }
```

Notice that we're only interested in instances of the Screen class. Subsequently, lifecycle events can be fired on a timer trigger to all screens as necessary:

```
public class LifecyclePostProcessor implements BeanPostProcessor {
    private final List<Screen> screens = new ArrayList<Screen>();

    public void suspendAllScreens() {        <— Called at midnight, by timer
        for (Screen screen : screens)
            screen.suspend();                <— Suspend each screen, in turn
    }

    public Object postProcessAfterInitialization(
        Object object, String key) throws BeansException { .. }

    public Object postProcessBeforeInitialization(
        Object object, String key) throws BeansException { .. }
}
```

Consider its complement, which is called by another timer, when the arcade reopens next morning:

```
    public void resumeAllScreens() {
        for (Screen screen : screens)
            screen.resume();
    }
```

This process can go on continuously every day, so long as the timer thread is in good health, and the screens will correctly switch feeds at the appropriate times. We didn't have to write a timer for each screen, nor did Screens have to keep track of the time themselves. Our single lifecycle manager was sufficient to push events out at the correct time to all Screens. This means not only less code to write but also far less code to *test* and fewer possible points of failure.

Custom post-processing is thus a powerful and flexible technique for creating lifecycle models suited to your application and its particular requirements. Another variant to building custom lifecycle is by multicasting a single method call to many recipients. This system has the advantage of being able to pass arbitrary arguments and even process returned values.

7.6 Customizing lifecycle with multicasting

Multicasting is very similar to what you just saw in section 7.5. Specifically, *multicasting* is the process of dispatching a single method call to multiple recipients. As such, it is perfectly suited to sending lifecycle event notifications to objects managed by an injector. The primary difference between multicasting and the method we used with post-processors is that the framework takes care of broadcasting the event across instances in the injector. This is illustrated in figure 7.14.

This means that you can design your classes to be slightly more decoupled, with less effort. And you can model them according to the traits they embody in a lifecycle model. Listing 7.8 shows how the `Screen` would look if it were designed with multicasting in mind.

Listing 7.8 A screen with a timed lifecycle, designed with lifecycle traits

```
package arcade;

public class Screen implements Suspendable, Resumable {
    private final Feed daytimeFeed;
    private final Feed overnightFeed;

    public Screen(Feed daytime, Feed overnight) { .. }

    public void suspend() {
        show(overnightFeed);
    }

    public void resume() {
        show(daytimeFeed);
    }

    ...
}

public interface Suspendable {
    void suspend();
}

public interface Resumable {
    void resume();
}
```

Here `Suspendable` and `Resumable` are two *traits* that a `Screen` possesses. In other words, they are roles that the `Screen` can embody. This is very similar to the role interfaces that you saw with interface injection in chapter 3. Multicasting is supported in PicoContainer's Gems extension.[1] Listing 7.9 describes a lifecycle manager that uses multicasting to notify `Screen`s.

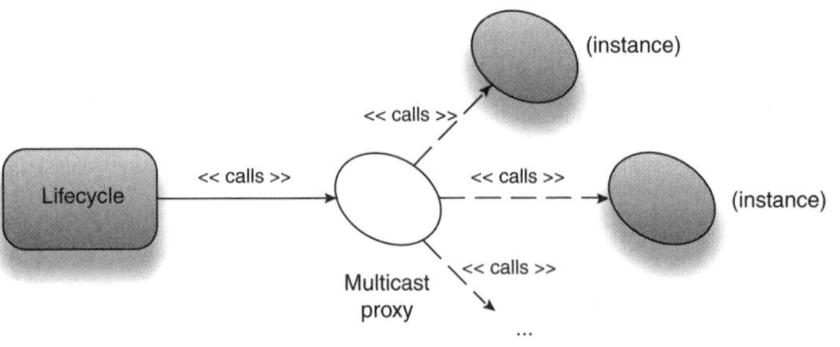

Figure 7.14 A multicast proxy promulgates a single lifecycle call across all managed instances.

[1] Gems are simple, intuitive extensions to the PicoContainer core framework. Find out more at: http://www.picocontainer.org.

Listing 7.9 Lifecycle manager that suspends and resumes services via multicasting

```
package arcade;

import com.thoughtworks.proxy.factory.StandardProxyFactory;
import org.picocontainer.gems.util.Multicaster;
import org.picocontainer.PicoContainer;

public class LifecycleManager {
    private final PicoContainer injector = ..;

    public void suspendAll() {
        Suspendable target = (Suspendable)
                    Multicaster.object(injector, true,
                    new StandardProxyFactory());

        target.suspend();
    }
}
```

First, we create a *multicasting proxy*. This is a dynamically generated implementation of `Suspendable` that transparently delegates its method calls across every instance of `Suspendable` available to the injector:

```
Suspendable target = (Suspendable)
            Multicaster.object(injector, true, new
            StandardProxyFactory());
```

The first argument is the injector to inspect for `Suspendables`. The second tells the multicaster to proceed in the order in which `Suspendables` were originally created by the injector. The last argument is a factory utility, which is used to dynamically create the proxy implementation of `Suspendable`:

```
Suspendable target = (Suspendable)
            Multicaster.object(injector, true, new
            StandardProxyFactory());
```

`StandardProxyFactory` simply uses the JDK tool `java.lang.reflect.Proxy` to create dynamic classes of type `Suspendable`.

This is cool because now the same lifecycle manager can suspend and resume *any* services that expose `Suspendable` and `Resumable`, not just `Screens`. And if the implementation logic of a screen changes (say you move the feed control out into a `Hub`), you don't have to worry about breaking the lifecycle model. Multicasting is thus an evolved form of customizing lifecycle and probably the best choice in most cases.

7.7 Summary

While lifecycle isn't an immediate part of dependency injection, the two are nonetheless closely related. Every object goes through a series of states from construction to destruction that are demarcated by lifecycle *events*. In certain applications objects can be notified of these events by a framework or assisting library.

A class's constructor is the most straightforward and ready form of lifecycle. It is called after memory has been allocated for the object and used to perform some initialization logic, to put the object into a usable state. Dependency injectors often use constructors to provide objects with their dependencies. This is detailed further in chapter 3.

In Java, when an object is about to be reclaimed by the garbage collector, its *finalizer* is called. A finalizer is called at an arbitrary, uncontrollable time, in a separate thread. Finalizers may not run until an application shuts down, or not even then! As a result, finalizers are unreliable for performing cleanup of finite system resources such as file handles or network sockets. Finalizers may be useful in rare cases for sanity checks or for reclaiming memory used in native libraries.

Lifecycle is not a universal concept. Different applications have different requirements for the transitions in state of their services. Lifecycle is thus specific to particular *problem domains*. For example, servlets undergo a separate initialization step well after deployment, to put them into a service-ready state. When a web application is stopped, an explicit destroy event is sent to a servlet. This is very different from a database connection's lifecycle, which may include notifications to set it "idle" or "in use," so validations or disconnects can be performed safely.

Some DI libraries provide a *destroy-method* hook, which is called by the injector on application shutdown. This is unsuitable for most cases for the same reasons that finalizers are. And more specific lifecycle models should be sought, rather than attempt to use this "destructor" anti-pattern. Java's `Closeable` interface is a suitable alternative for releasing finite resources that are data sources or producers. This also indicates that a service is designed with *closeability* in mind, as opposed to being an afterthought as with destructors.

Stateful EJBs are a programming model that supports a very complex lifecycle model, where EJBs are notified by an application server (or EJB container) periodically. Stateful EJBs are akin to HTTP sessions or "conversations" (see chapter 5), where clients may resume a previous interaction with the EJB. These points of resumption and suspension are modeled as lifecycle events to the EJB: postactivate and prepassivate.

An object's lifecycle is also related to timing—singleton-scoped objects can be created immediately, upon injector bootstrap, or lazily, when first needed. Lazy instantiation is useful when startup time is important, such as in a desktop application or when debugging. Eager instantiation is the opposite form, where all singletons are created when the injector starts up. This is useful in production servers where a performance hit can be taken up front, if it means that services can be obtained faster during an application's active life.

Customizing lifecycle is important, and it is useful in many applications. Post-processing is an idiom where an object is passed to a post-processor, prior to being made available for injection. These instances can be inspected and held in a registry for later reference. When a notification needs to be sent, you simply iterate the registry and notify each instance in turn. Spring offers postprocessing via an interface `BeanPostProcessor`.

Lifecycle can also be customized using multicasting. This is very similar to the post-processing technique, except that the framework is responsible for promulgating events to instances managed by the injector. A single method call on an interface is transparently multicast to eligible instances. This is useful in designing more decoupled services that are easier to test and more amenable to refactoring.

Custom lifecycle is a powerful and flexible idiom for reducing boilerplate code and making your code tighter. It allows you to design classes that are more focused and easier to test and maintain. Almost all problem domains have some kind of use for framework lifecycle management. In the next chapter, we'll look at modifying object behavior by intercepting method calls. This can be thought of as the converse of lifecycle, since it involves changing how objects react to their callers rather than propagating events down to them as this chapter showed. As you will see, method interception can be a powerful technique for achieving focused goals across a broad spectrum of services.

8 Managing an object's behavior

This chapter covers:

- Intercepting methods with AOP
- Using transactions, security, and the like
- Watching for perils of proxying
- Avoiding corner cases

"Perfect behavior is born of complete indifference."

—Cesare Pavese

Often one finds that certain types of logic are repeated throughout a program. Many separate parts of an application share similar concerns such as logging, security, or transactions. These are known as *crosscutting concerns.*

Rather than address these concerns in each individual class (as one would do normally), it's easier to address them all at once from a central location. Not only does this reduce repetitive boilerplate code, but it also makes maintenance of existing code less complicated.

Let's look at an example. `Brokerage` is a class that places an order for stock inside a database transaction. Traditionally, we would write code for starting and ending a transaction around each business method:

```
public class Brokerage {
    private final TransactionManager txn;

    public void placeOrder(Order order) {
        txn.beginTransaction();
        try {
            ...
        } catch(DataException e) {
            txn.rollback();
        } finally {
            if(!txn.rolledBack())
                txn.commit();
        }
    }
}
```

This transaction logic uses a `TransactionManager` to start and end a transaction, rolling back on an exception or committing as appropriate. This would be repeated in every method that needed to be transactional.

Now let's look at this if transactions were described declaratively:

```
public class Brokerage {

    @Transactional
    public void placeOrder(Order order) {
        ...
    }
}
```

This is much simpler. By declaring method `placeOrder()` as `@Transactional`, we're able to strip out most of the boilerplate code to wrap an order inside a transaction. Moreover, it removes `Brokerage`'s dependency on a `TransactionManager`, making it simpler to code and test. Also, now all transaction-specific logic is centralized in one place.

`@Transactional` is a piece of metadata that allowed us to declare a transaction around `placeOrder()`. What really happened underneath was that `placeOrder()` was intercepted and wrapped inside a transaction before proceeding normally. This is done via a technique known as aspect-oriented programming (AOP) and is the focus of this chapter. In this chapter we'll look at how to apply this technique to intercept methods on objects that are created by dependency injection and how to insert new behavior around each method. We'll start by examining how method interception is achieved.

8.1 Intercepting methods and AOP

Methods can be intercepted in a number of different ways, depending on the AOP library:

- At compile time, via a specialized compiler
- At load time, by altering class definitions directly
- At runtime, via dynamic proxying

This process is known as *weaving*, as in weaving in the new behavior. The introduced behavior is called *advice*.

Since we are concerned with dependency injection, we'll focus on the runtime flavor of weaving, which is done by the use of dynamic *proxies*.[1] Since DI libraries are responsible for creating objects, they are also able to intercede with proxies for intercepting behavior. This is transparent to any client, since the proxies are merely subclasses of the original types.

> **Dynamic proxies**
>
> A proxy is generated at runtime by a bytecode-generation library. The dynamic class-loading system in Java allows new classes to be defined even at runtime. The JDK core library also provides a utility for generating proxies. Several bytecode-manipulation libraries also exist that are able to do more sophisticated forms of code generation and proxying.

Proxying is a powerful technique. We can use it to replace almost any object created by an injector. Since a proxy possesses all the methods of the original type, it can alter the behavior of any of them.

Let's look at one such scenario where we intercept methods to add logging functionality using Guice.

8.1.1 *A tracing interceptor with Guice*

What we want to do here is trace the execution of every method on a certain class, by printing something to the console. We want to do this using interception rather than adding print statements to each method. Guice lets us do this by binding an interceptor (a utility class containing the advice):

```
import org.aopalliance.intercept.MethodInterceptor;
import org.aopalliance.intercept.MethodInvocation;

public class TracingInterceptor implements MethodInterceptor {
    public Object invoke(MethodInvocation mi) throws Throwable {
        System.out.println("enter " + mi.getMethod().getName());
        try {
            return mi.proceed();
        } finally {
             System.out.println("exit " + mi.getMethod().getName());
        }
    }
}
```

This class is pretty simple; it contains one method—`invoke()`—which is called every time an interception occurs. This method then does the following:

---

[1] We encountered proxies in chapter 3 when dealing with the circular reference problem.

- Prints an alert before proceeding to the intercepted method
- Proceeds and returns the result from the intercepted method
- Prints another alert before returning control to the caller

The last bit is done inside a `finally` block so that any exception thrown by the intercepted method does not subvert the exit trace.

Applying this interceptor is done via Guice's binding API inside any `Module` class, as shown in listing 8.1:

Listing 8.1 A module that applies `TracingInterceptor` to all methods

```
import static com.google.inject.matcher.Matchers.*;

public class MyModule extends AbstractModule {

    @Override
    protected void configure() {
        ...
        bindInterceptor(any(), any(), new TracingInterceptor());
    }
}
```

TIP The `import static` statement at the top of this class makes it possible to omit the class name, `Matchers`, where the `any()` method is defined for convenience. It's a more readable shorthand for writing `Matchers.any()`.

The interesting part about this listing is how the interceptor is bound:

```
bindInterceptor(any(), any(), new TracingInterceptor());
```

The first two parameters are passed `any()`, which represents *any class* and *any method*, respectively. Guice uses these matchers to test for classes and methods to intercept. It comes with several such matchers out of the box, or you can write your own.

Now when we call any methods from objects wired by our injector, the methods will be traced on the console. Let's say `Chef` is one such class:

```
public class Chef {
    public void cook() {
        ...
    }

    public void clean() {
        ...
    }
}
```

Now calling `Chef`'s methods

```
Chef chef = Guice.createInjector(new MyModule())
                .getInstance(Chef.class);

chef.cook();
chef.clean();
```

produces the following output:

```
enter cook
exit cook
enter clean
exit clean
```

`Chef` still has no knowledge of how to print to console. Furthermore, inside a unit test, methods are *not* intercepted, and your test code can focus purely on asserting the relevant business logic.

> **AopAlliance and Guice**
>
> You'll notice that we used an AopAlliance API in this example. The AopAlliance is a public standard defined by many of the early AOP advocates and open source contributors. It's a simple standard that focuses on strong use cases rather than giving you the kitchen sink.
>
> As such, it's not as full featured as some of the other AOP libraries, but on the other hand it's more lightweight and streamlined.

In the next section, we'll look at how to write the same tracing interceptor using a different framework. This will help you see the differences between the two major popular techniques.

8.1.2 A tracing interceptor with Spring

Spring uses a different AOP library (although it also supports the AopAlliance) but works under similar principles. Spring's library is *AspectJ*, which can itself be used independently to provide a whole host of AOP features beyond method interception. For our purposes we'll focus on its Spring incarnation. We'll use the same class `Chef`, but this time we'll intercept it with Spring and AspectJ, as shown in listing 8.2.

Listing 8.2 A tracing interceptor created as an aspect with Spring and AspectJ

```
import org.aspectj.lang.ProceedingJoinPoint;
public class TracingInterceptor {
    public Object trace(ProceedingJoinPoint call) throws Throwable {
        System.out.println("enter " + call.toShortString());
        try {
            return call.proceed();
        } finally {
            System.out.println("exit " + call.toShortString());
        }
    }
}
```

It looks almost the same as our `TracingInterceptor` from Guice. The primary difference is that we do not implement any interface; rather we will tell the injector directly about method `trace()`. This is achieved as shown in listing 8.3.

Listing 8.3 A tracing interceptor configuration with myAspect.xml

```
<?xml version="1.0" encoding="UTF-8"?>
<beans xmlns="http://www.springframework.org/schema/beans"
      xmlns:xsi="http://www.w3.org/2001/XMLSchema-instance"
      xmlns:aop="http://www.springframework.org/schema/aop"
      xsi:schemaLocation="http://www.springframework.org/schema/beans
       http://www.springframework.org/schema/beans/spring-beans-2.5.xsd
       http://www.springframework.org/schema/aop
       http://www.springframework.org/schema/aop/spring-aop-2.5.xsd">

  <bean id="chef" class="example.Chef"/>

  <bean id="tracer" class="example.TracingInterceptor"/>

  <aop:config>
      <aop:aspect ref="tracer">
         <aop:pointcut id="pointcuts.anyMethod"
                     expression="execution(* example.*.*(..))" />
         <aop:around pointcut-ref="pointcuts.anyMethod" method="trace"/>
      </aop:aspect>
  </aop:config>
</beans>
```

This looks like a complex bit of mumbo-jumbo, but it's quite simple. First we declare our `TracingInterceptor` in a <bean> tag, naming it `"tracer"`:

```
<bean id="tracer" class="example.TracingInterceptor"/>
```

Then we declare a *pointcut* using the `<aop:pointcut>` tag provided by Spring:

```
<aop:pointcut id="pointcuts.anyMethod"
              expression="execution(* example.*.*(..))" />
```

The expression "`execution(* example.*.*(..))`" is written in the AspectJ *pointcut language* and tells Spring to intercept the execution of any method with any visibility, name, or arguments from the `example` package. This pointcut expression is the equivalent in AspectJ of a matcher in Guice. Recall the binding expression for matching any method from listing 8.1:

```
bindInterceptor(any(), any(), new TracingInterceptor());
```

AspectJ's pointcut language also allows you to declare matchers of your choosing. Since it is a dedicated language, it doesn't come with any matchers out of the box.

The other tag worth mentioning in listing 8.3 is `<aop:aspect ref="tracer">`. This is the declaration of an *aspect*, which is essentially a binding between a matcher (or pointcut) and an interceptor (advice). It is the semantic equivalent of method `bindInterceptor()` shown earlier. Now running the example

```
BeanFactory injector = new FileSystemXmlApplicationContext("myAspect.xml");
Chef chef = (Chef) injector.getBean("chef");

chef.cook();
chef.clean();
```

produces the expected trace:

```
enter execution(cook)
exit execution(cook)
enter execution(clean)
exit execution(clean)
```

Now that you've seen how to apply method interception at a high level, let's examine how its internals work, by looking at how to work with dynamic proxies and their semantics.

8.1.3 How proxying works

We said earlier that a dynamic proxy is a subclass that is generated at runtime. The fact that it is of the same type means we can transparently replace the original implementation with a proxy and decorate its behavior as we please. Proxying is a tricky subject. The best way to think of it is to imagine a handwritten subclass where all the methods invoke an interceptor instead of doing any real work. The interceptor then decides whether to proceed with the real invocation or effect some alternate behavior instead.

Listing 8.4 shows how such a proxy might look for `Chef`.

Listing 8.4 A static (handwritten) proxy for `Chef`

```
public class ChefProxy extends Chef {
    private final MethodInterceptor interceptor;
    private final Chef chef;

    public ChefProxy(MethodInterceptor interceptor, Chef chef) {
        this.interceptor = interceptor;
        this.chef = chef;
    }

    public void cook() {
        interceptor.invoke(new MethodInvocation() { ... });
    }

    public void clean() {
        interceptor.invoke(new MethodInvocation() { ... });
    }
}
```

Rather than delegate calls directly to the intercepted instance `chef`, this proxy calls the interceptor with a control object, `MethodInvocation`. This control object can be used by `MethodInterceptor` to decide when and how to pass through calls to the original `chef`. These libraries are also able to generate the bytecode for `ChefProxy` on the fly. Let's look one such proxying mechanism.

PROXYING INTERFACES WITH JAVA PROXIES

The Java core library provides tools for dynamically generating proxies. It implements the same design pattern we just saw with a proxy and interceptor pair and is provided as part of the reflection toolset in `java.lang.reflect`. It's limited to proxying interfaces, but this turns out to be sufficient for the majority of use cases. If we imagined that `Chef` was an interface rather than a class,

```
public interface Chef {
    public void cook();

    public void clean();
}
```

we could create a dynamic subclass of `Chef` the following way:

```
import java.lang.reflect.Proxy;
...
Chef proxy = (Chef) Proxy.newProxyInstance(Chef.class.getClassLoader(),
                                           new Class[] { Chef.class },
                                           invocationHandler);
```

The first argument to `Proxy.newProxyInstance()` is the *classloader* in which to define the new proxy:

```
Proxy.newProxyInstance(Chef.class.getClassLoader(), ...)
```

Remember that this is not just a new object we're creating but an entirely new *class*. This can generally be the same as the default (context) classloader or, as in our example, the classloader to which the original interface belongs. It is sometimes useful to customize this, but for most cases you won't need to. You'll see more on this later in the chapter.

The second argument is an array of `Class` objects representing all the interfaces you want this proxy to intercept. In our example, this is just the one interface, `Chef`:

```
Proxy.newProxyInstance(..., new Class[] { Chef.class }, ...);
```

And finally, the last argument is the invocation handler we want the proxy to use:

```
Proxy.newProxyInstance(..., invocationHandler);
```

It must be an object that implements interface `InvocationHandler` from the `java.lang.reflect` package. As you can see, it is very similar to the AopAlliance's `MethodInterceptor`:

```
public interface InvocationHandler {
    Object invoke(Object proxy, Method method, Object[] args);
}
```

Here's a reimagining of the method-tracing interceptor from earlier in this chapter, using JDK `Proxy` and `InvocationHandler` with `Chef`:

```
public class TracingInterceptor implements InvocationHandler {
    private final Chef chef;

    public TracingInterceptor(Chef originalChef) {
        this.chef = originalChef;
    }

    public Object invoke(Object proxy, Method method, Object[] args)
        throws Throwable {
        System.out.println("enter " + method.getName());
        try {
            return method.invoke(chef, args);
```

```
        } finally {
            System.out.println("exit " + method.getName());
        }
    }
}
```

To run it, we use the proxy obtained from `Proxy.newProxyInstance()`:

```
import java.lang.reflect.Proxy;
...
Chef proxy = (Chef) Proxy.newProxyInstance(Chef.class.getClassLoader(),
                                    new Class[] { Chef.class },
                                    new TracingInterceptor(originalChef));

proxy.cook();
proxy.clean();
```

This produces the expected trace:

```
enter cook
exit cook
enter clean
exit clean
```

By constructing `TracingInterceptor` with a constructor argument, `originalChef`, we make it possible for the interceptor to proceed onto *legitimate* calls against the intercepted instance should it need to. In our `invoke()` interception handler, this is illustrated by the reflective method invocation:

```
    Object invoke(Object proxy, Method method, Object[] args)
        throws Throwable {
        System.out.println("enter " + method.getName());
        try {
            return method.invoke(chef, args);
        } finally {
            System.out.println("exit " + method.getName());
        }
    }
```

This is akin to the AopAlliance's `MethodInvocation.proceed()` and AspectJ's `ProceedingJoinPoint.proceed()`.

Although Java provides a fairly powerful API for proxying *interfaces*, it provides no mechanism for proxying *classes*, abstract or otherwise. This is where third-party *bytecode manipulation tools* come in handy.

PROXYING CLASSES WITH CGLIB

A couple of useful libraries provide tools for proxying. Guice and Spring both use a popular library called CGLib[2] to generate proxies under the hood. CGLib fills in nicely where Java's proxy mechanism falls short. It's able to generate the bytecode that would dynamically extend an existing class and override all of its methods, dispatching them to an interceptor instead.

---

[2] CGLib stands for *Code Generation Library*. Find out more about CGLib at http://cglib.sourceforge.net.

If we had a concrete class `FrenchChef`, we would generate a proxy for it as follows:

```
import net.sf.cglib.proxy.Enhancer;
...
Chef chef = (Chef) Enhancer.create(FrenchChef.class,
    new TracingInterceptor());
```

The corresponding `TracingInterceptor` follows the design pattern we're intimately familiar with by now:

```
public class TracingInterceptor implements MethodInterceptor {
    public Object intercept(Object proxy, Method method, Object[] args,
                       MethodProxy methodProxy) throws Throwable {
        System.out.println("enter " + method.getName());
        try {
            return methodProxy.invokeSuper(proxy, args);
        } finally {
            System.out.println("exit " + method.getName());
        }
    }
}
```

The interesting part is that we no longer have to hold onto the original `chef`; CGLib allows us to invoke the corresponding method directly on its superclass:

```
            return methodProxy.invokeSuper(proxy, args);
```

Class proxying can be very powerful if used correctly. It's best used inside dependency injectors (or similar tools) that need to enhance a class's behavior. The consequences of intercepting class methods can be tricky. We'll look at some later in this chapter. It's always generally advisable to use interface proxying where possible, unless you're convinced of the need and its implications.

Of course, there are other problems with interception. One can be too eager to apply this technique. In the next section we'll look at how this can lead to problems.

8.1.4 Too much advice can be dangerous!

As in real life, you can run into trouble when you listen to too much advice. One of the important things to consider is that for each interception, you will incur the overhead of advising methods running before and after the original method. This is generally not an issue if you apply a few interceptors to a few methods. But when the chain gets longer, and it crosscuts critical paths in the application, it can degrade performance.

More important, the order of interception can play spoiler to program semantics. Here is a simple case:

```
public class Template {
    private final String template = "Hello, :name!";

    public String process(String name) {
        return template.replaceAll(":name", name);
    }
}
```

Class Template converts a dynamically provided name into a string containing a greeting. The following code

```
new Template().process("Josh");
```

returns a greeting to Josh:

```
Hello, Josh!
```

Now, using method interception, we can enhance this greeting by decorating it in bold (let's use HTML <b> tags for familiarity):

```
import org.aopalliance.intercept.MethodInterceptor;

public class BoldDecoratingInterceptor implements MethodInterceptor {

    public Object invoke(MethodInvocation mi) throws Throwable {
        String processed = (String)mi.proceed();
        return "<b>" + processed + "</b>";
    }
}
```

We bind this in using a simple matcher:

```
import static com.google.inject.matcher.Matchers.*;
...
   bindInterceptor(subclassesOf(Template.class), any(), new
     BoldDecoratingInterceptor());
```

Now when a client processes anything from a template, it will be decorated in bold:

```
Guice.createInjector(...)
     .getInstance(Template.class)
     .process("Bob");
```

This prints the following:

```
<b>Hello, Bob!</b>
```

So far, so good. Now let's say we want to wrap this whole thing in HTML so it can be rendered in a website. If we had several such templates, another interceptor would save a lot of time and boilerplate code:

```
import org.aopalliance.intercept.MethodInterceptor;

public class HtmlDecoratingInterceptor implements MethodInterceptor {

    public Object invoke(MethodInvocation mi) throws Throwable {
        String processed = (String) mi.proceed();
        return "<html><body>" + processed + "</body></html>";
    }
}
```

Now we have two bits of advice. If you were to naïvely bind in this interceptor at any arbitrary point, it could lead to very unexpected behavior:

```
import static com.google.inject.matcher.Matchers.*;
...
```

```
   bindInterceptor(subclassesOf(Template.class), any(), new
        BoldDecoratingInterceptor());
   bindInterceptor(subclassesOf(Template.class), any(),
        new HtmlDecoratingInterceptor());
```

This would print the following:

```
<b><html><body>Hello, Bob!</body></html></b>
```

Obviously, the order of interception matters. In this trivial example, it's easy for us to see where the problem is and correct it:

```
import static com.google.inject.matcherMatchers.*;
...
   bindInterceptor(subclassesOf(Template.class), any(), new
        HtmlDecoratingInterceptor());
   bindInterceptor(subclassesOf(Template.class), any(), new
        BoldDecoratingInterceptor());
```

Now processing the interceptor chain renders our desired HTML correctly:

```
<html><body><b>Hello, Bob!</b></body></html>
```

This highlights a serious problem that would have gone undetected if we had assumed unit tests were sufficient verification of application behavior. In our example, all interceptors were in the same spot, and it was easy to identify and fix the problem. In more complex codebases, it may not be so straightforward. You should exercise caution when using AOP. In our example, the bold decorator could probably have been written without an interceptor. It probably would have worked better if we had folded it into the template itself.

Later in this chapter we'll show how to protect against the "too much advice" problem with integration tests. For now, let it suffice to say that you should apply interception only in valid use cases. In the next section we'll look at these use cases as applicable to enterprise applications.

8.2 Enterprise use cases for interception

The tracing example was fun, but it's quite a trivial use case. The real advantage of interception comes to light in enterprise use cases, particularly with transactions and security. These may be database transactions or logical groupings of any kind of task. And likewise with security—it may be about authorization to perform a particular action or simply about barring users who aren't logged in.

By far, the most prolific and useful case of interception is to wrap database transactions and reduce the overall level of boilerplate code in business logic methods. There are several ways to go about this; both Guice and Spring provide modules that allow you to use declarative transactions. It's even possible to roll your own, but there are a few edge cases that should lead you to use the library-provided ones, which are thoroughly tested. So let's look at how to achieve transactions with the warp-persist module for Guice.

8.2.1 Transactional methods with warp-persist

Like guice-servlet, which we encountered in chapter 5, warp-persist is a thin module library for Guice that provides support for persistence and transactions. Warp-persist provides integration with the following popular persistence engines:

- Hibernate (a popular object/relational mapping tool)
- Java Persistence API or JPA (a Java standard for object/relational mapping)
- Db4objects (an object database)

Hibernate and JPA both provide a mapping layer between Java objects and relational database tables (stored in an RDBMS like PostgreSQL). And Db4objects is a lightweight object database, which can store and retrieve native objects directly.

Warp-persist sits between the Guice injector and these frameworks, and it reduces the burden on you to wrap and integrate them. It also provides an abstraction over their particular transaction architectures and lets you use matchers to model transactional methods declaratively. Let's take the simple example of storing a new car in a database inventory:

```
import javax.persistence.EntityManager;
import com.wideplay.warp.persist.Transactional;

public class CarInventory {
    private final EntityManager em;
    public CarInventory(EntityManager em) {
        this.em = em;
    }

    @Transactional
    public void newCar(Car car) {
        em.persist(car);
    }
}
```

When a new car arrives, its details are entered into a `Car` object, and it's passed to method `newCar()`, which stores it using the `EntityManager`. The `EntityManager` is an interface provided by JPA that represents a session to the database. Entities (data) may be stored, retrieved, or removed via the `EntityManager` from within transactional methods.

The other important part of `CarInventory` is method `newCar()`, which is annotated `@Transactional`. This is an annotation provided by warp-persist that is used to demarcate a method as being transactional. If we didn't have the declarative approach with `@Transactional`, we would have to write the transaction behavior by hand:

```
    public void newCar(Car car) {
        EntityTransaction txn = em.getTransaction();
        txn.begin();
        boolean succeed = true;
        try {
            em.persist(car);
        } catch (RuntimeException e) {
            txn.rollback();
```

```
            succeed = false;
        } finally {
            if (succeed)
                txn.commit();
        }
    }
```

All of this code is required to correctly determine whether to roll back a transaction and close it properly when finished. This is only a trivial case, since we aren't considering the beginning and closing of the `EntityManager` itself. A session to the database may also need to be opened and closed around transactions.

In listing 8.5, the caught exception is being swallowed after a transaction rollback without any significant action being taken. So, apart from saving yourself a world of repetitive boilerplate, declarative transactions also give you semantic control over the transactional state.

Let's look at how to tell the Guice injector that we're going to use warp-persist (see listing 8.5).

Listing 8.5 A module that configures warp-persist and `@Transactional`

```
import com.wideplay.warp.persist.PersistenceService;
import com.wideplay.warp.persist.jpa.JpaUnit;

public class CarModule extends AbstractModule {

    @Override
    protected void configure() {
        ...
        install(PersistenceService.usingJpa()
                                  .buildModule());

        bindConstant().annotatedWith(JpaUnit.class).to("carDB");
    }
}
```

The method `install()` is a way of telling Guice to add another module to the current one. It is exactly equivalent to passing in each module to the `createInjector()` method individually:

```
Guice.createInjector(new CarModule(), PersistenceService.usingJpa()
                                                        .buildModule());
```

The other important piece of configuration is the constant bound to `"carDB"`:

```
        bindConstant().annotatedWith(JpaUnit.class).to("carDB");
```

This constant is used by warp-persist to determine which persistence unit to connect against. Persistence units are specified in the accompanying persistence.xml configuration file for JPA, which is typically placed in the META-INF/ directory. Here's what it might look like in our imaginary car inventory:

```
<?xml version="1.0" encoding="UTF-8" ?>
<persistence xmlns="http://java.sun.com/xml/ns/persistence"
    xmlns:xsi="http://www.w3.org/2001/XMLSchema-instance"
```

```
    xsi:schemaLocation="http://java.sun.com/xml/ns/persistence
    http://java.sun.com/xml/ns/persistence/persistence_1_0.xsd"
        version="1.0">

    <!-- A JPA Persistence Unit -->
    <persistence-unit name="carDB" transaction-type="RESOURCE_LOCAL">
        <provider>org.hibernate.ejb.HibernatePersistence</provider>

        <!-- JPA entities must be registered here -->
        <class>example.Car</class>

        <properties>
            <!-- vendor-specific properties go here -->
        </properties>
    </persistence-unit>

</persistence>
```

Note that along with the name of the persistence unit, all the persistent classes are listed here. These are classes mapped with JPA annotations, which tell the persistence engine how to map an object to a row in the database. `example.Car` might look something like this:

```
@Entity
public class Car {
    @Id @GeneratedValue
    private Integer id;
    private String name;
    private String model;

    //get + set methods
}
```

When you run this application and call the `newCar()` method with a populated `Car` object,

```
@Inject CarInventory inventory;
...

Car car = new Car("BMW", "325Ci");
inventory.newCar(car);
```

a transaction is automatically started and committed around the call to `newCar()`. This ensures that the `EntityManager` enters the provided `Car` object into its corresponding database table.

Another interesting enterprise use case is that of security. Since interception can be applied from one spot, many parts of an application can be secured with a single, central step. In the following section, we'll explore how to secure groups of methods using Spring AOP and the Spring Security Framework.

8.2.2 Securing methods with Spring Security

Authorization is another common use case for intercepted methods. The pattern is sometimes even applied to web applications where HTTP requests are intercepted by servlet `Filters` and processed against security restrictions.

JPA and object/relational mapping (ORM)

The Java Persistence API is a specification for mapping simple Java objects to relational database tables. It provides a set of standard annotations (`@Entity`, `@Id`, and so on) that are used to map classes and fields to tables and columns. JPA has many vendor implementations, including Hibernate, Oracle TopLink, and Apache OpenJpa. All of these are available under open source licenses, free of charge.

JPA also includes tools for managing database transactions around local resources using a programmatic API. Both Spring and Guice (via warp-persist) provide integration modules for JPA programming models and for declarative transactions; among other niceties.

Find out more about the JPA standard at http://java.sun.com/developer/technicalArticles/J2EE/jpa.

And check out the warp-persist JPA tutorial at http://www.wideplay.com/guicewebextensions2.

Certain methods that provide privileged business functionality can come under the crosscutting banner of security. Like transactions, these methods must first verify that the user driving them has sufficient privileges to execute their functionality. This is a repetitive task that can be moved to the domain of interceptors, which have the rather elegant advantage of being able to suppress secured methods completely. They also allow for declarative management of security across a set of business objects, which is a useful model when applied in very large applications with similar, recurring security concerns.

Let's look at how this is done using Spring Security, an extension to Spring that provides many security features. First, Spring Security is meant primarily for web applications, so enabling it requires a HTTP filter to be present. This gives us a hook into Spring's security stack. Draw up a web.xml like the following:

```
<filter>
    <filter-name>springSecurity</filter-name>
    <filter-class>org.springframework.web.filter.DelegatingFilterProxy</
     filter-class>
</filter>

<filter-mapping>
    <filter-name>springSecurity</filter-name>
    <url-pattern>/*</url-pattern>
</filter-mapping>
```

Much like guice-servlet's `GuiceFilter` (from chapter 5), this filter mapping tells the servlet container to route all requests through Spring Security's `DelegatingFilterProxy`. This Spring-provided filter is able to call into Spring's injector and determine the correct set of security constraints to apply.

Here's a corresponding XML configuration for securing objects of an imaginary class `PhoneService`, managed by the Spring injector:

```
<?xml version="1.0" encoding="UTF-8"?>
<beans xmlns="http://www.springframework.org/schema/beans"
     xmlns:security="http://www.springframework.org/schema/security"
     xmlns:xsi="http://www.w3.org/2001/XMLSchema-instance"
     xsi:schemaLocation="http://www.springframework.org/schema/beans
          http://www.springframework.org/schema/beans/spring-beans-2.5.xsd
          http://www.springframework.org/schema/security

          http://www.springframework.org/schema/security/spring-security-
➥        2.0.xsd">

    <security:http auto-config="true">
        <security:intercept-url pattern="/**" access="ROLE_USER" />
    </security:http>

    <security:authentication-provider>
        <security:user-service>
            <security:user name="josh" password="supersecret"
                authorities="ROLE_USER, ROLE_ADMIN" />
            <security:user name="bob" password="bobby"
                authorities="ROLE_USER" />
        </security:user-service>
    </security:authentication-provider>

    <security:global-method-security>
        <security:protect-pointcut
            expression="execution(* example.PhoneService.*(..))"
                              access="ROLE_ADMIN" />
    </security:global-method-security>
</beans>
```

Wow, that's quite a lot of configuration! Let's look at what it all means. First, we set up automatic configuration to use a whole bunch of defaults for customizable services that Spring Security provides:

```
<security:http auto-config="true">
    <security:intercept-url pattern="/**" access="ROLE_USER" />
</security:http>
```

These are good for our purpose, where we only want to demonstrate security around methods via interception as it applies to dependency injection.

Here we've also asked Spring to intercept all requests coming in and allow access only to users with the privilege ROLE_USER:

```
<security:http auto-config="true">
    <security:intercept-url pattern="/**" access="ROLE_USER" />
</security:http>
```

The path matcher pattern="/**" used by Spring Security[3] is slightly different from the conventional servlet pattern and is equivalent to a URL mapping of "/*" in servlet parlance.

Next, we set up two users, josh and bob, and gave them both ROLE_USER access:

[3] If you're familiar with Ant, note that Spring Security uses Ant-style paths to match against URIs. Ant is a popular build-scripting tool for Java from Apache: http://ant.apache.org/.

```
<security:authentication-provider>
    <security:user-service>
        <security:user name="josh" password="supersecret"
            authorities="ROLE_USER, ROLE_ADMIN" />
        <security:user name="bob" password="bobby"
            authorities="ROLE_USER" />
    </security:user-service>
</security:authentication-provider>
```

This means they will be able to access any page in the web application by default.

Finally, we applied a method security constraint via a *pointcut.* Recall pointcuts from the section early in this chapter on Spring AOP with AspectJ. This pointcut expression matches any method in an imaginary class PhoneService:

```
<security:global-method-security>
    <security:protect-pointcut
       expression="execution(* example.PhoneService.*(..))"
       access="ROLE_ADMIN" />
</security:global-method-security>
```

This security pointcut prevents access to methods in PhoneService from anyone but ROLE_ADMIN users. In our case only josh had this role:

```
<security:user name="josh" password="supersecret"
    authorities="ROLE_USER, ROLE_ADMIN" />
<security:user name="bob" password="bobby" authorities="ROLE_USER" />
```

Let's imagine PhoneService to look something like this:

```
public class PhoneService {
    public Response call(String number) {
        ...
    }

    public void hangUp() {
        ...
    }
}
```

Now if any client code tries to access methods from this class via the Spring injector

```
<bean class="example.PhoneCaller">
    <constructor-arg><bean class="example.PhoneService"/></constructor-arg>
</bean>
```

and the corresponding class,

```
public class PhoneCaller {
    private final PhoneService phone;

    public PhoneCaller(PhoneService phone) {
        this.phone = phone;
    }

    public void doAction() {
        Response response = phone.call("555-1212");
        if (response.notBusy())
```

```
            phone.hangUp();
        }
    }
```

when a user triggers this action (by, for example, clicking a button to call a recipient), Spring Security intercepts calls to `PhoneService.call()` and `PhoneService.hangUp()` and ensures that the user has the appropriate role. If not, an exception is raised and the user is shown an authorization failure message. In this scenario, the target methods are never executed.

This example requires a lot of delving into ancillary topics, such as Spring's web integration layer and related concerns. We've taken only the most cursory glance at this security system, focusing instead on the method interception use case. For a more thorough examination, consult the source code accompanying this chapter and visit http://www.springsource.org for the Spring Security documentation.

In the rest of this chapter, we'll change gears and look at the flip side of all this interception and how basic assumptions in design may need to change depending on how you use AOP.

8.3 Pitfalls and assumptions about interception and proxying

As you saw earlier, proxying is an advanced topic and can involve some pretty low-level semantics dealing with the internals of Java. Thus there are several pitfalls and mistaken assumptions that can lead you astray when working with proxied classes or interfaces. Ideally, a proxy should behave identically to its replaced counterpart. However, this is not always the case.

You can understand and avoid many of the pitfalls if you keep in mind that a proxy is simply a subclass of the original type. Let's look at some of these cases.

8.3.1 Sameness tests are unreliable

If you have a reference to an object, never rely on the sameness (==) test to assert that it's the object you're expecting. An object created by the injector may have been proxied, and though it appears to be the same as the original object, it isn't. This is true even in the case of singletons. Here's such a scenario:

```
final Painting picasso = new Painting("Picasso");

Injector injector = Guice.createInjector(new AbstractModule() {
    protected void configure() {
        bind(Painting.class).toInstance(picasso);
        bindInterceptor(any(), any(), new TracingInterceptor());
    }
});

assert picasso == injector.getInstance(Painting.class);   //will fail
```

In this case, we create an instance outside the injector and bind it via the `bind().toInstance()` directive:

```
final Painting picasso = new Painting("Picasso");

Injector injector = Guice.createInjector(
```

```
...
bind(Painting.class).toInstance(picasso);
...
```

This is an implicit singleton-scoped binding (since we've hand-created the only instance).

Next, we bound in a `TracingInterceptor` like the ones we've seen throughout this chapter. This runs on all classes and all methods:

```
bindInterceptor(any(), any(), new TracingInterceptor());
```

Now, we obtain the bound instance of `Painting` (`picasso`) from the injector and compare it using a sameness assertion to the instance we already know about:

```
assert picasso == injector.getInstance(Painting.class);  //will fail
```

This assertion fails because even though we're semantically talking about the same instance, the physical instances are different. One has been proxied by the injector and the other is a direct reference to the original instance.

A related but much more common anti-pattern is to assume that the class of an available object is the same as the one it is bound to. For example, many logging frameworks publish log messages under the class of an object. Many people naively make the following mistake:

```
import java.util.logging.*;

public class ANoisyService {
    public final Logger log = Logger.getLogger(getClass().getName());

    ...
}
```

This is a dangerous assumption because while it appears as though method `getClass()` will return `Class<ANoisyService>`, in reality it may return the class of the dynamically generated proxy! So instead of logging under `ANoisyLogger`, your log statements may be printing under some unintelligible, generated class name.

Worse than this, if you use `getClass()` to make decisions on application logic, you can find some very erratic and unexpected behavior. Here's an example of a naïve `equals()` method implementation that mistakenly precludes a proxied object from an equality test:

```
public class EqualToNone {
    @Override
    public boolean equals(Object object) {
        if (object == null || object.getClass() != EqualsToNone.class)
            return false;

        ...
    }
}
```

This `equals()` method makes the assumption that subclass instances cannot be semantically equivalent to superclass instances. This is a wrong assumption when any proxied objects are involved. It's not only dependency injectors that need to proxy objects for dynamic behavior modification. Many web frameworks and persistence libraries also employ this design pattern to provide dynamic behavior.

To fix this problem, you should always assume that an object can be proxied and program accordingly:

```
public class EqualToNone {
    @Override
    public boolean equals(Object object) {
        if (!(object instanceof EqualToNone))
            return false;

        ...
    }
}
```

This is a much better implementation that's safe to proxying behavior. Similarly, you should always be explicit about your sameness semantic:

```
import java.util.logging.*;

public class ANoisyService {
    public final Logger log = Logger.getLogger(ANoisySer-
     vice.class.getName());

    ...
}
```

Now, ANoisyService will always publish under the correct logging category regardless of whether or not it has been proxied. Another problem that arises from this situation is the inability to intercept static methods.

8.3.2 Static methods cannot be intercepted

Since proxies are merely subclasses and Java doesn't support overriding static methods, it follows that proxies cannot intercept static methods. However, something more subtle is at work. If you try the following example,

```
public class Super {
    public static void babble() {
        System.out.println("yakity yak");
    }
}

public class Sub extends Super {
    public static void babble() {
        System.out.println("eternal quiet");
    }

    public static void main(String...args) {
        babble();
    }
}
```

and run class Sub from the command line, what do you think it will print? Will the program even compile?

Yes, it will compile! And it prints

```
eternal quiet
```

which appears to all eyes like an overridden static method. We declared a static method `babble()` in `Super` and another static method `babble()` in `Sub`. When we ran `babble()` from `Sub`, it used the subclass's version. This looks very much like overriding instance methods in subclasses. Fortunately there's an explanation: What's really happening is that there are two static methods named `babble()` and the one in `Sub` is hiding the one in `Super` via its lexical context. In other words, if you were to run this from anywhere outside `Sub` or `Super`, you'd have to specify which method you were talking about:

```
import static Super.*;
...
babble();
```

This version correctly prints `"yakity yak"` as expected. So any code that *statically* depends on `Sub` or `Super` must always be explicit about which one it is talking about, meaning that there is no way to substitute a proxied subtype (even were it possible) without the client itself doing so. When you want dynamic behavior, don't place logic in static methods.

Private methods also face the same problem because they cannot be overridden. Although they have access to dynamic state, they cannot be proxied.

8.3.3 Neither can private methods

In Java, methods can have private visibility. A method that is private can't be called from anywhere outside its owning class. This applies to subclasses too, which means that dynamic proxies (which are just subclasses) cannot intercept private methods. If we go back to our `FrenchChef` and alter the visibility of method `clean()` as follows,

```
public class FrenchChef {
    public void cook() {
        ...
    }

    private void clean() {
        ...
    }
}
```

and then run it by adding a `main()` method to its body,

```
    public static void main(String...args) {
        FrenchChef chef = Guice.createInjector(new AbstractModule() {

            @Override
            protected void configure() {
                bind(FrenchChef.class);
                bindInterceptor(any(), any(),
                    new TracingInterceptor());      <-- Trace all methods
            }

        }).getInstance(FrenchChef.class);     <-- Obtain a proxied FrenchChef
```

```
        chef.cook();
        chef.clean();
    }
```

it will produce the following output

```
enter cook
exit cook
```

with no mention of `clean()`. This was not because `clean` did not run; we called it from `main()`, after all. Rather it was because proxying doesn't permit private methods to be intercepted before they're dispatched. A good solution to this problem is to elevate the class's visibility slightly:

```
public class FrenchChef {
    public void cook() {
        ...
    }
    protected void clean() {
        ...
    }
}
```

Protected methods are good candidates for proxying, since they're hidden from all external users except subclasses of the original type. Running the program again produces a more satisfying result:

```
enter cook
exit cook
enter clean
exit clean
```

This is probably the best solution for the majority of cases although it may not always be ideal. While protected methods are hidden from classes outside the current hierarchy, they are still visible to nonproxy subclasses that may exist in different modules. If this is undesirable, Java has yet another visibility level: *package-local* visibility. This makes methods invisible to any code that's outside the owning class's package. Package-local[4] visibility is perfect for hiding methods from subclasses that may extend your class but for which you don't want certain methods shown. These methods can still be intercepted by proxies, because proxies are typically generated within the same package as the original class. Denote package-local visibility by omitting an access keyword:

```
public class FrenchChef {
    public void cook() {
        ...
    }
    void clean() {
        ...
    }
}
```

[4] Package-local visibility is sometimes also called package-private or default visibility.

NOTE I say that proxies are typically generated within the same package, but there are some cases where this may not be true. This behavior is dependent on specific decisions made by the library you're using. Keep an eye out for such decisions. Most dependency injectors can be relied on to place proxies within the same package as their parent classes.

Another variant of this problem (the inability to override certain methods) presents itself when a method has specifically declared itself to be final.

8.3.4 And certainly not final methods!

Methods can be declared as *final* to prevent subclasses from overriding them. The `final` keyword is not a visibility modifier, since it can be applied on public, protected, or package-local methods:

```
public class FrenchChef {
    public final void cook() {
        ...
    }

    void clean() {
        ...
    }
}
```

However, it does prevent a subclass from redefining the method by overriding it. The following code results in a compiler error:

```
public class FrenchSousChef extends FrenchChef {

    @Override
    public void cook() {     <-- Cannot override final method
        ...
    }
}
```

Naturally, this means a proxy can't override it either, and therefore a final method can't be intercepted for behavior modification. The solution in such cases is obviously to remove the final modifier. But if this can't be done for some reason (perhaps you don't have access to the source code), you can wrap the method in a pass-through *delegator*:

```
public class FrenchChefDelegator implements Chef {
    private final FrenchChef delegate;

    public void cook() {
        delegate.cook();     <-- Delegate to original class
    }

    ...
}
```

This class can now be proxied for interception. Method `cook()` is not final so it can be intercepted safely with a proxy. And the class `FrenchChefDelegator` implements `Chef`, so clients of `Chef` are not impacted by the change.

TIP An even better solution would be to proxy the Chef interface directly and pass calls through to the specific implementation. For example, Spring's AOP mechanism allows you to choose interface proxying as the default method. This is also easily accomplished by hand.

The same principle applies to final classes. These are classes that cannot be extended. Not only can their methods not be intercepted, but you can't generate subclasses of them at all:

```
public final class FrenchChef implements Chef {
    public void cook() {
        ...
    }

    public void clean() {
        ...
    }
}
```

The Delegator pattern also works well for this situation:

```
class FrenchChefDelegator implements Chef {
    private final FrenchChef delegate;

    ...

    public void cook() {
        delegate.cook();          <-- Delegate to
    }                                 original class

    public void clean() {
        delegate.clean();         <--
    }

}
```

When in doubt always choose this method over inheritance—even simpler would be proxying the interface directly. Just as final classes and methods cannot be intercepted at runtime, neither can class member fields.

8.3.5 Fields are off limits

Certain flavors of AOP allow you to make deferred modifications to any parts of a codebase. The build-time weaving from AspectJ allows you to alter fields, interfaces implemented, and even static methods. However, neither Spring nor Guice provides this kind of weaving. Almost all use cases for interception can be fulfilled with the runtime weaving flavor that they do provide. However, it does mean that fields, any kind of fields, are off limits with regard to interception.

Let's say FrenchChefs have a dependency on a RecipeBook:

```
public class FrenchChef implements Chef {
    private final RecipeBook recipes;

    public void cook() {
        ...
    }
```

```
    public void clean() {
        ...
    }
}
```

An interceptor can only advise behavior on methods `cook()` and `clean()` but cannot advise anything on recipes. Even if methods on `recipes` were called from `cook()` or `clean()`, an interceptor declared on `FrenchChef` would not be able to trap specific behavior:

```
    private final RecipeBook recipes;

    public void cook() {
        recipes.read("ratatouille");
        ...
    }
```

And a tracing interceptor declared with the specific matcher

```
    bindInterceptor(subclassesOf(Chef.class), any(),
         new TracingInterceptor());
```

will ignore method calls on `RecipeBook` and trace only methods `cook()` and `clean()`. Of course, expanding the matching strategy will allow you to intercept `RecipeBook`'s methods. The following matcher is much better suited:

```
    bindInterceptor(subclassesOf(Chef.class)
➥  .or(subclassesOf(RecipeBook.class)), any(), new TracingInterceptor());
```

The general one we have used earlier in the chapter

```
    bindInterceptor(any(), any(), new TracingInterceptor());
```

will also work nicely:

```
enter cook
enter read
exit read
exit cook
enter clean
exit clean
```

The limitation here is that any intercepted dependency must also have been provided by dependency injection. No dependency injector can intercept methods on objects it doesn't create. For example, the following class

```
public class FrenchChef implements Chef {
    private final RecipeBook recipes = new RecipeBook();

    public void cook() {
        ...
    }

    public void clean() {
        ...
    }
}
```

creates its own dependency (see construction by hand from chapter 1) and therefore subverts the interception mechanism. No matcher will be able to intercept method calls on `RecipeBook` now:

```
enter cook
exit cook
enter clean
exit clean
```

Furthermore, any accesses to scalar fields like primitives or `Strings` are not open to interception whether or not they are injected by the dependency injector:

```
public class FrenchChef implements Chef {
    private int dishesCooked;
    private BigInteger potsWashed;
    private String currently;

    public void cook() {
        dishesCooked++;
        currently = "cooking";
    }

    public void clean() {
        potsWashed = potsWashed.add(BigInteger.ONE);
        currently = "cleaning";
    }
}
```

None of these accesses—whether via method calls or directly by assignment—are visible to interceptors. Typically this is not a problem, but it's something to keep in mind when you're designing services with scalar fields. Of course, not all dependencies will necessarily need interception.

8.3.6 *Unit tests and interception*

One of the nice things about DI is that it doesn't affect the way you write tests. If we were to test a class with many complex dependencies, all we'd need to do would be replace them with mock or stub equivalents. This principle can become somewhat muddied when interception comes into play.

While the imperative behavior of a class is the same in both test and application, its semantic behavior can change advice introduced by AOP. For example, a theme park's ticket-purchase system collects money and dispenses a ticket:

```
public class TicketBooth {
    public Ticket purchase(Money money) {
        if (money.equals(Money.inDollars("200")))
            return new Ticket();

        return Ticket.INSUFFICIENT_FUNDS;
    }
}
```

We can write a unit test for this class quite easily:

```
public class TicketBoothTest {
    @Test
    public void purchaseATicketSuccessfully() {
        Ticket ticket = new TicketBooth().purchase(Money.inDollars("200"));

        assert Ticket.INSUFFICIENT_FUNDS != ticket;    <-- Ensure this is
    }                                                      a valid ticket
}
```

If you decided to modify this behavior by printing a discount coupon for every 100th customer (via an interceptor), the original class's semantic has changed:

```
public class DiscountingInterceptor implements MethodInterceptor {
    private int count;

    public Object invoke(MethodInvocation mi) throws Throwable {
        Ticket ticket = (Ticket)mi.proceed();

        if (Ticket.INSUFFICIENT_FUNDS != ticket         If the customer count
            && (++count % 100) == 0) {             <--  is a multiple of 100

            return new DiscountedTicket(ticket);   <--  Return a
        }                                               discounted ticket

        return ticket;    <-- Return a normal ticket
    }
}
```

The immediate solution that comes to mind is simply to write another unit test, this time around the interceptor:

```
public class DiscountingInterceptorTest {
    @Test
    public void decorateEveryHundredthCall() throws Throwable {
        DiscountingInterceptor discounter = new DiscountingInterceptor();
        MockInvocation mi = new MockInvocation();

        for(int i = 1; i < 101; i++) {                   Call interceptor with
            Object result = discounter.invoke(mi);   <-- a mock invocation

            if (i == 100)
                assert result instanceof DiscountedTicket;   <--
        }
    }                                          On the 100th run, we
}                                              should see a discount
```

But this is not where the difficulty lies. As you saw in "Too much advice can be dangerous!" the combination of two behavioral units can affect total semantic behavior and belie the assertions of individual unit tests. One effective solution is to write an integration test that brings the relevant units together and tests them as they might behave in the eventual application environment.

This is different from a full acceptance test or QA pass, since we're interested in only a particular combination of behaviors and can restrict our attention to the classes we expect to be intercepted:

```
public class DiscountingInterceptorIntegrationTest {
    @Test
```

```
    public void discountEveryHundredthTicket() {
        Injector injector = Guice.createInjector(new AbstractModule() {
            @Override
            protected void configure() {
                bind(TicketBooth.class);
                bindInterceptor(any(), any(),
                    new DiscountingInterceptor());      <-- Apply discount interceptor
            }
        });

        TicketBooth booth = injector.getInstance(TicketBooth.class);

        for(int i = 1; i < 101; i++) {
            Ticket ticket =
                booth.purchase(Money.inDollars("200"));    <-- Call original object 100 times

            if (i == 100)
                assert ticket instanceof DiscountedTicket;
        }

    }
}
```

This test looks very similar to the unit test on the interceptor, but it gives us more confidence about how these units come together. Notice that we call the `TicketBooth.purchase()` method just as clients would in the real application. And its behavior is decorated with interceptors that would also be present in the real app. Where this gets really useful is if we add a second or a third interceptor (as we did in "Too much advice can be dangerous!"); then the confidence that the integration test provides is far greater than the sum of individual unit tests.

When you have any sort of services in your program that rely on side effects like these, it's important to write vertical integration tests to give yourself some assurance on their combined behavior. This will generally be in addition to any unit tests that exist on individual classes. Neither is enough alone, but together they give us sufficient breadth for verifying correct behavior.

8.4 Summary

In this chapter we encountered certain concerns that are global to a program. In traditional approaches, these are addressed individually with repetitive and boilerplate code. A technique known as AOP allows us to centralize this code in one location and apply it many times using a matcher (or pointcut). Matchers allow us to introduce additional behavior before and after business methods execute in a dynamic and declarative fashion. This introduced behavior is known as advice and is typically applied in the form of interceptors.

Interceptors trap the normal behavior of a method and decorate it with the provided advice. They are applied via the use of dynamic proxies, which are generated subclasses of the original class that reroute method calls through an interceptor. The Java core library provides a simple proxying mechanism for generating subclasses of interfaces on the fly. More sophisticated proxy libraries are available for proxying concrete classes too (CGLib is one example).

Because dependency injectors create the services used by an application, they are able to intercede with a proxy that intercepts behavior when applicable. These interceptors can be turned on or off with simple configuration options in both Spring and Guice.

Intercepting methods is a powerful technique for adding dynamic behavior that crosscuts a problem domain. Concerns like security, logging, and transactions are typical use cases for interception. However, it's fraught with pitfalls and requires a thorough understanding if it's to be applied properly, and it has unintended consequences. One pitfall is the order of interception: An interceptor that replaces the returned value of methods (or their arguments) can unintentionally disrupt the behavior of other interceptors yet to run. An integration test that puts together the expected set of interceptors can be a good confidence booster in such cases.

Warp-persist is an integration layer for Guice that allows you to apply transactions declaratively to Hibernate-, JPA-, and Db4objects-driven applications. It provides an `@Transactional` annotation that can be applied to introduce transactionality around any method in an application. Of course, it supports interception without annotations too.

Similarly Spring Security is an AOP-based security framework for Spring applications. Spring Security allows you to declare users and roles and attach them to methods via the use of a pointcut (a matching expression). When a user who is logged into the system executes these methods, an interceptor verifies that he has sufficient privileges, blowing up with an exception if not.

Other things to watch out for with proxies are sameness tests. The == operator tests whether references are equal; it can lead you astray if you test a reference against its intercepted equivalent, since the latter is a dynamically generated proxy. Semantically they refer to the same instance underneath. Equality testing should be applied in such cases. The same also applies to comparing classes of objects directly with the `getClass()` reflective method.

There are several parts of a class and its behaviors that simply cannot be intercepted with runtime proxies. For example, static methods are not attached to any instance, so they cannot be intercepted. Similarly, fields and methods on objects belonging to these fields are off-limits (unless they too have been injected). Methods having `private` visibility or a `final` modifier are also ineligible for proxying and thus behavior modification through interception.

With all these corner cases and pitfalls in mind, you can still apply this technique to great effect in your code. Reducing boilerplate and introducing behavior modification to services late in the game can be a powerful tool. Use interception wisely.

In the next chapter we'll look at some more general design issues specific to very large sets of applications that interact with one another, and we'll show how to use dependency injection in these environments.

9 Best practices in code design

This chapter covers:

- Understanding publication and wiring
- Designing objects to be thread-safe
- Optimizing for concurrency
- Dealing with type-safety
- Using objects in collections

> *"The effort to understand the universe is one of the very few things that lifts human life a little above the level of farce and gives it some of the grace of tragedy."*
>
> —Steven Weinberg

It's often a puzzle to programmers who are new to dependency injection about when to apply it. When it wasn't widely understood, even experienced practitioners applied it too much or too sparingly. The immature state of libraries contributed to this fuzzy application too, giving one the tools but not the discretion of its applicability.

A more fundamental set of confusion arises from the best practices of the language itself. Are these distinct from the patterns relevant to DI? Are they superseded? Or can they coexist (figure 9.1)?

It turns out that such questions are based on the wrong premise entirely. The best practices portended by a language and its engineering fundamentals are the same as those proffered by dependency injection (figure 9.2).

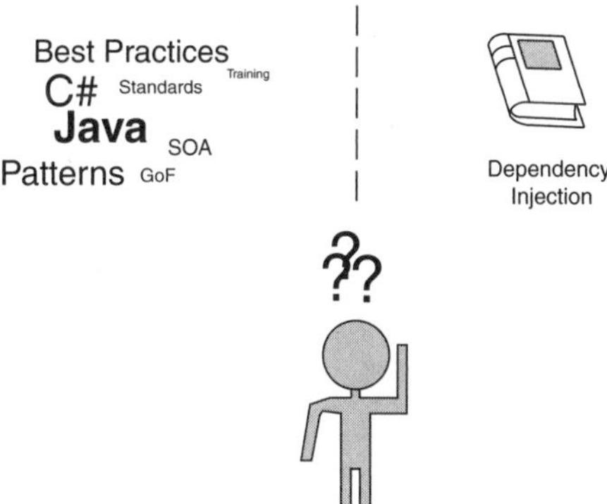

Figure 9.1 Best practices for the language, or architecture with DI?

In other words, design well for the language and problem domain, and you will have designed well for the principles of testing, succinctness, and flexibility.

One of the core problems in multithreaded object-oriented languages is that of visibility. We showed in earlier chapters that altering the state of an object in one thread did not necessarily mean altering its state for all threads. This was particularly relevant with the problem of scope widening discussed in chapters 5 and 6. A more subtle incarnation of this problem occurs during (and immediately after) the construction of an object. Unless carefully designed, its fields may not be properly visible to all threads using it. This is a problem sometimes known as *unsafe publication*, and it's discussed in the following section on object visibility.

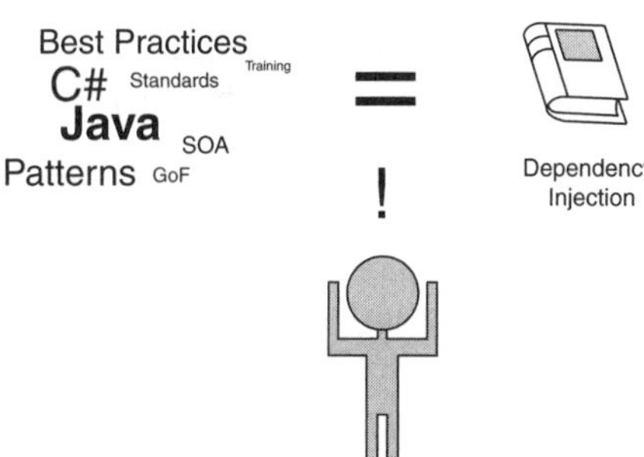

Figure 9.2 Best practices for the language and dependency injection *are the same.*

9.1 Objects and visibility

In chapter 3 we said that a constructor is a special method that runs once immediately after memory allocation of an object, in order to perform initialization work. As such, the object allocated is generally not visible to any other threads of execution than the one creating it. I say "generally," as there are some special circumstances under which objects can be visible.

One of the best ways to understand visibility is to investigate a *hashtable*. A hashtable is a flexible data structure, sometimes called an associative array, that's used to store key-value pairs. Hashtables are ideal for us because they give us a scenario where one thread may come in and change values that are being read by other threads simultaneously, introducing problems of ordering and visibility. Consider a hashtable that stores email addresses by name (we'll use Java's `java.util.HashMap`):

```
Map<String, Email> emails = new HashMap<String, Email>();

emails.put("Dhanji", new Email("dhanji@gmail.com"));     //yes, this is my
                                                         //real email =)
emails.put("Josh", new Email("josh@noemail.com"));
```

```
System.out.println("Dhanji's email address really is "
                   + emails.get("Dhanji"));
```

Reading from this map is fairly straightforward, since there's only one thread of execution through this program (the main thread). We can confidently say that email address values are placed in the map before they're read. This is satisfied by simple lexical ordering. In other words, the put() method is called before the get(). The values are said to be safely published to the reader.

We can elaborate on this example by introducing a second thread:

```
public class UnsafePublication {

    private Map<String, Email> emails = new HashMap<String, Email>();

    public void putEmails() {
        emails.put("Dhanji", new Email("dhanji@gmail.com"));
             emails.put("Josh", new Email("josh@noemail.com"));
    }

    public void read() {
        System.out.println("Dhanji's email address really is "
                           + emails.get("Dhanji"));
    }
}
```

If method putEmails() is called by Thread A and method read() is called by Thread B, there's a danger that the values read() is looking for may not yet be available. This problem cannot be solved by lexical ordering either (see listing 9.1).

Listing 9.1 Unsafe publication of hashtable values

```
public class Main {

    public static void main(String...args) {
        final UnsafePublication pub = new UnsafePublication();

        new Thread(new Runnable() {     <— Thread A
            public void run() {
                pub.putEmails();
            }
        }).start();

        new Thread(new Runnable() {     <— Thread B
            public void run() {
                pub.read();
            }
        }).start();
    }
}
```

In listing 9.1, two threads are started up in order. Thread A has the task of writing emails into the hashtable, while Thread B calls read(), which prints them. Now, even though it appears there is a lexical ordering, there's no guarantee that Thread A will run before Thread B. Several factors are at play. It may be that CPU scheduling preempts the start of Thread A. Or it may be that the compiler believes reordering instructions will lead to better throughput. The point is, once you introduce multiple threads accessing a shared resource, lexical guarantees are no longer valid.

There's a further subtlety with regard to unsafe publication. Even if Thread A did execute on the CPU before Thread B, which we could presumably tell by adding the following print statement,

```
public class UnsafePublication {
    private Map<String, Email> emails = new HashMap<String, Email>();

    public void putEmails() {
        emails.put("Dhanji", new Email("dhanji@gmail.com"));
        emails.put("Josh", new Email("josh@noemail.com"));

        System.out.println("Map updated.");      <-- Trace map update
    }

    public void read() {
        System.out.println("Dhanji's email address really is "
                             + emails.get("Dhanji"));
    }
}
```

there's no guarantee that the program will behave properly. The following program's output is equally likely to happen:

```
Map updated.
Dhanji's email address really is null
```

What's going on? The `"Map updated."` signal was printed in Thread A *before* the read. We should quite certainly have my email address in the hashtable! We can further confound the issue as shown in listing 9.2.

Listing 9.2 Unsafe publication of hashtable values even with apparent verification

```
public class UnsafePublication {
    private Map<String, Email> emails = new HashMap<String, Email>();

    public void putEmails() {
        emails.put("Dhanji", new Email("dhanji@gmail.com"));
        emails.put("Josh", new Email("josh@noemail.com"));

        System.out.println("Map updated.");
        read();                       <-- Ensure map has
    }                                     expected value

    public void read() {
        System.out.println("Dhanji's email address really is "
                             + emails.get("Dhanji"));
    }
}
```

What will this program print? Can it possibly print something as absurd as this?

```
Map updated.
Dhanji's email address really is dhanji@gmail.com
Dhanji's email address really is null
```

Surely, not! In fact, it turns out this is quite possible because a guarantee of order alone is insufficient for safe publication. This is another manifestation of the visibility problems. There are several reasons why Thread B may see a `null` value, even though as far as Thread A is concerned, the map has been updated. We encountered one of these in an earlier chapter when looking at memory coherency. Without sufficient synchronization, the JVM makes no guarantees about visibility of fields between threads. This is a deliberate choice made by the language designers to allow for maximum flexibility in optimizations on various platforms. Thread A's updates to the hashtable may not yet be synchronized with main memory. Thus, they're not published to other threads. So while a thread can see its own updates, there's no assurance that others will. Now let's look at how to correctly publish to all threads.

9.1.1 Safe publication

It's easy to see how this problem can creep into DI as well. Unless properly published, objects may appear incompletely constructed to participating threads, with unavailable or partially constructed dependencies. Consider the equivalent of the hashtable we just saw:

```
public class MoreUnsafePublication {

    private EmailDatabase service;

    public MoreUnsafePublication(EmailDatabase service) {
        this.service = service;     <-- Potentially unsafe publication
    }

    public void read() {
        System.out.println("Dhanji's email address really is "
                              + service.get("Dhanji"));
    }
}
```

`MoreUnsafePublication` is a simple variant of the hashtable that reads an email address using its dependency `EmailDatabase`. This time the issue of publication is not with the hashtable values but with the `EmailDatabase` dependency itself. Threads that call method `read()` cannot rely on the fact that the dependency is available. Without sufficient synchronization, the thread creating the object does not safely publish its fields to other threads. The following could easily result in a `NullPointerException`:

```
    public void read() {
        System.out.println("Dhanji's email address really is "
                              + service.get("Dhanji"));
    }
```

Or worse, it could result in further corruption of the object graph. A very simple solution to this problem is to declare the field as `final`.[1] Final fields are given the guarantee of safe visibility to all threads concerned. Because these fields are generally always set in the constructor, they'll be visible to all threads once the constructor completes.

---

[1] See this article on developerWorks for more information: http://www.ibm.com/developerworks/library/j-jtp03304/

```
public class SafePublication {

    private final EmailDatabase service;

    public SafePublication(EmailDatabase service) {
        this.service = service;
    }

    public void read() {
        System.out.println("Dhanji's email address really is "
                           + service.get("Dhanji"));
    }
}
```

In `SafePublication`, threads may call `read()` and expect dependency `EmailDatabase` to be set correctly. This holds for any thread, even those that did not construct the instance. This is a very simple but powerful solution that's an ideal choice for the vast majority of multithreading problems. It's good practice to declare fields final even if you believe the instance will only ever participate in one thread, as this gives a clear indication of intent.

As we've stated in earlier chapters, thread-safety is a concept very relevant to dependency injection. In the following section, we'll look at exactly what these semantics imply for wiring objects with dependencies.

9.1.2 Safe wiring

We've just seen how we can run into visibility problems between threads. One typically encounters these problems only with singletons. This is because, in general, only singletons are shared by two (or more) threads. Final fields are a safe solution to this problem if you can guarantee that a reference to the object does not escape during construction (we'll look at what escaping means shortly). Many dependency injectors can also help by providing extra synchronization during the construction of singletons. For instance, PicoContainer can be put into a locking mode, which ensures object creation happens in a synchronized state:

```
MutablePicoContainer injector = new DefaultPicoContainer();
injector.as(LOCK, CACHE).addComponent(MyObject.class);
MyObject obj1 = injector.getComponent(MyObject.class);
MyObject obj2 = injector.getComponent(MyObject.class);
```

Instances `obj1` and `obj2` are created in a synchronized fashion, so the dangers of visibility are safely mitigated. The characteristics `LOCK` and `CACHE` instruct PicoContainer to use locking and to create singletons. This would be equivalent to the following:

```
public class SynchronizedPublication {

    private Lock lock = new ReentrantLock();
         private MyObject obj;

    public void constructObj() {

        lock.lock();                          <-- Only one thread may
        try {                                     execute at a time
            obj = new MyObject();
        } finally {
```

```
            lock.unlock();
        }
        //other threads can safely access obj's fields now
    }
}
```

Now, fields of `MyObject` are correctly set and visible to all threads regardless of whether or not they are declared final:

```
public class MyObject {
    private Dependency dep;          <-- Safely published to all threads

    public MyObject(Dependency dep) {
        this.dep = dep;
    }

    ...
}
```

Guice also provides a similar guarantee for all of its singletons. However, despite these niceties, one should *not* rely on the injector to do the work of safe wiring. If you design your classes to be well behaved in threaded environments, they will be safe regardless of whether or not you receive help from libraries. This is especially significant if you want to reuse code in different environments. It's also important when designing objects for concurrency. Furthermore, it's an implicit declaration of intent. When someone comes across your code and the final class members, it's very clear that they weren't meant to be changed. Even if you accidentally try to reassign field values after construction, you can't run afoul of mutability since the compiler alerts you to the problem. Recall that any attempt to modify a final field after construction,

```
public class EarlyWarning {
    private final ImmutableDependency dep;

    public EarlyWarning(ImmutableDependency dep) {
        this.dep = dep;
    }

    public void setImmutableDependency(ImmutableDependency newDep) {
        this.dep = newDep;          <-- Illegal assignment
    }
}
```

results in a clear, fast failure of compilation:

```
Information:Compilation completed with 1 error and 0 warnings
Information:1 error
Information:0 warnings
EarlyWarning.java
    Error:Error:line (9)cannot assign a value to final variable dep
```

The documenting thread-safety annotations, `@Immutable`, `@ThreadSafe`, `@NotThreadSafe`, and `@GuardedBy` that we've used in earlier chapters are an additional clarification of behavioral intent. While the injector can help in minor ways, it's ultimately up to you to create code that's both safe and efficient.

In fact, it's a good principle to design without the injector in mind for all threading cases. DI is meant to help your code become more flexible and testable in design, but it doesn't relieve you of the burden of engineering good code. Or should I say joy?

Another interesting but higher-level consideration is deciding when to use a dependency injector and when not to. This can often be quite tricky, as simplistic as it sounds. Ahead, we'll look at rules of thumb that help in making this decision.

9.2 Objects and design

The question of which classes of objects to manage using dependency injection is often a tricky one. Especially for programmers new to the technique, it can be quite a double-edged sword. Some are overeager to apply it, creating everything with the injector. Some are too careful and use DI sparingly, almost like a Factory or Service Locator. Neither of these extremes is particularly prudent. And both are especially counterproductive in large and complex codebases.

Most of the time, it's quite easy to determine what objects ought to be created and managed by dependency injection. A rule of thumb is to leave anything that's a service or action component to the purview of the injector and any class that models data to traditional, by-hand usage. Now let's see that principle in practice, in dealing with a specific example that uses data and service objects.

9.2.1 On data and services

Let's take the case of an imaginary online auction house. Here you have several objects for managing users, bids, list items, reconciliation, and so forth. These are couched as three primary services, as shown in figure 9.3:

- `AuctionManager`—Manages bids and auction status
- `ItemManager`—Manages list items and descriptions
- `UserManager`—Manages user accounts and history

These three services are classes with several dependencies of their own. For example, `UserManager` needs a DAO to read and write user details to a data store:

```
public class UserManager {
    private final UserDao userDao;

    public UserManager(UserDao userDao) {
        this.userDao = userDao;
    }

    //operations on user...
}
```

Figure 9.3 Three foundational services of the auction house application

`UserDao`, in the example, is our interface to the data store. `UserManager` uses it to create new users, update details such as name and password, and in rare cases mark the account as inactive. Listing 9.3 shows the same class in some detail (also see figure 9.4).

Listing 9.3 `UserManager` performs many operations on user data

```
public class UserManager {
    private final UserDao userDao;

    public UserManager(UserDao userDao) {
        this.userDao = userDao;
    }

    public void createNewUser(User user) {          <-- Registers a new user
        validate(user);
        userDao.save(user);
    }

    public void updatePassword(long userId,         <-- Updates an existing
        String password) {                              user's password
        User user = userDao.read(userId);
        user.setPassword(password);

        validate(user);
        userDao.save(user);
    }
                                                    <-- Sets an account
    public void deactivate(long userId) {               as inactive
        User user = userDao.read(userId);
        user.deactivate();

        userDao.save(user);
    }

    ...
}
```

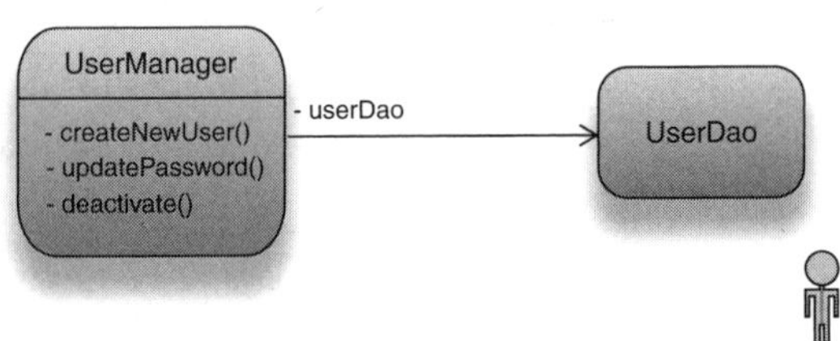

Figure 9.4 A class model of `UserManager` and its dependency, `UserDao`

In listing 9.3, we have three methods that perform some kind of manipulation of the `User` data object. `createNewUser()` registers a new user (represented by an instance of the `User` object) by saving it to a data store:

```
public void createNewUser(User user) {
    validate(user);
    userDao.save(user);
}
```

This method also validates the instance of `user`, ensuring that all the data going in is correct. We don't deal with reporting validation errors at this juncture, since it is already assumed this has been done at the presentation layer (that is, the website). This validation step is purely a safeguard against programmer error. Once we're sure the data is valid, it's passed to `UserDao` to be saved.

Similarly, method `updatePassword()` performs data manipulation on `User`, but this time it's of an instance that already exists. The specific user is identified by a numeric `userId`, and it's the job of `UserDao` to locate and retrieve the relevant instance from the data store:

```
public void updatePassword(long userId, String password) {
    User user = userDao.read(userId);
    user.setPassword(password);

    validate(user);
    userDao.save(user);
}
```

We then set the new password on this instance, signaling a change of password, and resave the details in the same fashion.

The third method in our set of operations deactivates a user account (presumably due to inactivity or violation of terms of use). Aptly named, method `deactivate()` takes in the numeric `userId`, deactivates it, and saves the relevant instance:

```
public void deactivate(long userId) {
    User user = userDao.read(userId);
    user.deactivate();

    userDao.save(user);
}
```

We don't need to validate the `User` this time since we aren't modifying any data in it with untrusted data received from actual user input.

One thing that's clear to us from these three operations is that `UserDao` and `UserManager` are services. The common thread that runs through them is that they perform operations on instances of the `User` class, which is data. Clearly, `UserDao` and `UserManager` are appropriate to be constructed and tested with DI. Class `User`, on the other hand, is constructed often at the presentation layer and has no dependencies. Listing 9.4 describes this data model class (also shown in figure 9.5).

Figure 9.5 Class model of `User` and its properties

Listing 9.4 The `User` data model class

```
public class User {
    private long userId;
    private String name;
    private String password;
    private boolean active = true;

    public User(long userId, String name) {
        this.userId = userId;
        this.name = name;
    }

    public long getUserId() {
```

```
        return userId;
    }

    public String getName() {
        return name;
    }

    public void setName(String name) {
        this.name = name;
    }

    public String getPassword() {
        return password;
    }

    public void setPassword(String password) {
        this.password = password;
    }

    public boolean isActive() {
        return active;
    }

    public void deactivate() {
        this.active = false;
    }
}
```

In listing 9.4, all four fields are *scalar* data types. In other words, they are fields of type `String`, `boolean`, or `long`. And each datum has no real domain semantics. There's nothing special about `Strings`, `booleans`, or `longs` insofar as an auction house is concerned. Consider this in contrast to `User`, which is itself a data type, but one that's specific to the problem domain we're concerned with. It also captures specific operations around that domain (for example, *deactivating* user accounts).

Apart from having no real dependency structure, another interesting point about the `User` class is that almost all of its fields are mutable. Setter methods exist for `name`, `password`, and the `active` flag. This is because `User` models the real-world state of a user's account. Several instances of this class exist, and the specific values of each instance may change gradually over time, that is, when someone changes his password or has his account deactivated.

Clearly, `User` objects are not ideal to be instantiated by DI. There's no gain to be had from interception or lifecycle for `Users`. Scope also doesn't quite fit in this scenario, since all `Users` are no scoped, but at the same time it can persist forever in a data store. Furthermore, there isn't anything significant to test in `User` code. Most methods are dumb setters or accessors, so it's appropriate to create and manage them by hand, like any other scalar object. Listing 9.5 is an example of doing just that from a new-user registration page.

```
@RequestScoped
public class NewUserPage {
    private final UserManager userManager;

    @Inject
```

```
    public NewUserPage(UserManager userManager) {
        this.userManager = userManager;
    }

    public HTML registerNewUser(String name) {
        userManager.createNewUser(new User(nextUserId(), name));

        ...
    }
}
```

NewUserPage represents a web page on the auction website where new users sign up to list and bid on items (see figure 9.6).

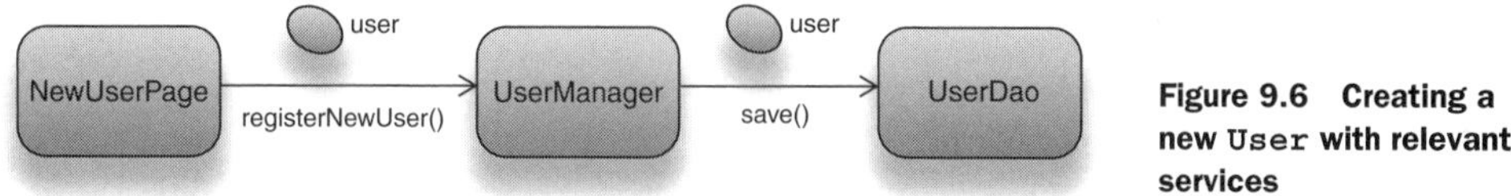

Figure 9.6 Creating a new User with relevant services

It is *HTTP request scoped* as is marked by the @RequestScoped annotation (recall guice-servlet and web scopes from chapter 5):

```
@RequestScoped
public class NewUserPage {
    private final UserManager userManager;

    ...
}
```

NewUserPage also takes data coming in from browser data entry and converts it into a created user by passing it on to the UserManager:

```
    public HTML registerNewUser(String name) {
        userManager.createNewUser(new User(nextUserId(), name));

        ...
    }
```

UserManager is a singleton service that's shared by all instances of the NewUserPage and is called at various data points for purposes like creating users, deactivating their accounts, or changing their details.

The other services, AuctionManager and ItemManager, also model actions on data model objects relating to auctions, list items, and so forth. Here too, the data model objects can be separated from their operations along simple lines (see figure 9.7).

Auctions, Items, ShoppingCarts, Money, and Users are all data classes that are operated on by the aforementioned singleton services and web pages. We can thus make an easy distinction between these classes and those that can benefit from dependency injection.

Another important design principle is *encapsulation*, sometimes called information hiding. In the following section, we'll look at how this applies to DI and techniques for taking advantage of it.

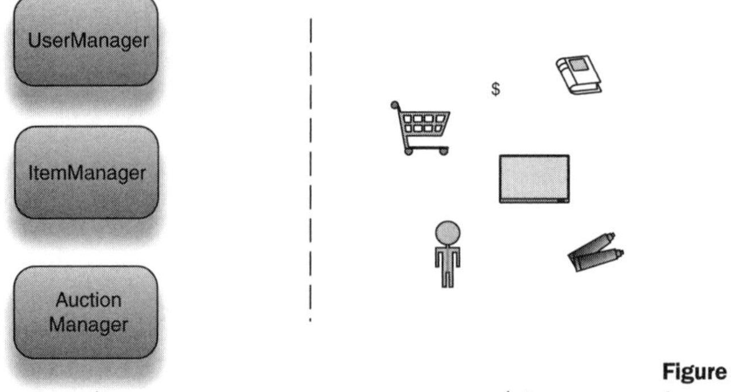

Figure 9.7 Separate data from operations on data.

9.2.2 On better encapsulation

One of the core principles of OOP is encapsulation, that is, the hiding of any information within a component that is relevant *only* to that component. In classes, this takes the form of marking members as `private`. Not only does this make sense in terms of hiding information that's irrelevant to anyone else, it also ensures against accidental *leaking* of semantics.

Leaking of private member fields can be very dangerous since it can lead to tight coupling between components. A class making use of a specific kind of messaging service (say, email messaging) should not expose its implementation details to the outside world. If other classes mistakenly begin using its dependencies, this can lead to tight coupling. Let's take the case of a `Messager` service represented by the following interface

```
public interface Messager {
    void send(Message msg);
}
```

and its email-backed implementation:

```
public class Emailer implements Messager {

    public void send(Message msg) {
        //send message via email...
    }
}
```

`Emailer` converts the incoming generic message into an email and sends it away to recipients. So far so good. Now let's see what happens if we accidentally leak this abstraction:

```
public interface Messager {
    void send(EmailMessage msg);
}
public class Emailer implements Messager {

    public void send(EmailMessage msg) {
```

```
        //send message via email...
    }
}
```

Now, both Messaging and Emailer send EmailMessages in method sendMessage(). While this may seem okay at first glance, a closer examination reveals otherwise. Say you wrote a new kind of messaging service that used the popular *Jabber* instant messaging protocol to send messages:

```
public class JabberMessager implements Messager {

    public void send(JabberMessage msg) {      <-- Does not implement interface method
        //send message via jabber...
    }

    ...
}
```

Because of the leaked abstraction, method send() in JabberMessager does not actually implement send() from the Messager interface. Fortunately, this code will fail on compilation, complaining that the Messager interface is not fully implemented. But we're still stuck with the problem of not being able to change the messaging service's transport—stuck with email, that is. This highlights what is an extremely poor abstraction that has pretty much destroyed our encapsulation. We have effectively exposed the internals of the Emailer class directly and rendered the Messager interface irrelevant.

Of course, this is easily fixed in our case by reverting to the original implementation:

```
public interface Messager {
    void send(Message msg);
}

public class Emailer implements Messager {

    public void send(Message msg) {
        EmailMessage email = convert(msg);      <-- Converts to email-specific message

        //send message via email...
    }
}
```

This version of Emailer correctly converts the incoming implementation-neutral Message object into an EmailMessage, which can be sent over email. Now it's easy for us to create and swap in a JabberMessager system with little difficulty and no impact to client code:

```
public class JabberMessager implements Messager {

    public void send(Message msg) {
        JabberMessage jab = convert(msg);      <-- Converts to Jabber-specific message

        //send message via jabber...
    }

    ...
}
```

JabberMessager now successfully compiles, and the system behaves as expected.

We can take the idea of encapsulation a step further. It isn't always possible to make implementation details private—sometimes implementation classes need to share functionality among themselves. For example, a JabberMessager interface may depend on a JabberMessageConverter and a JabberTransport in order to convert and send the message:

```
public class JabberMessager implements Messager {
    private final JabberTransport transport;              Jabber-specific
    private final JabberMessageConverter converter;       dependencies

    public void send(Message msg) {
        ...
    }
}
```

These are dependencies that exist as public classes. And therefore they can be accessed, subclassed, and used by anyone, leading to a potential horde of tight coupling. In Java, there's an extra layer of visibility that we can take advantage of to prevent anyone outside a package (namespace) from knowing or using classes. This is sometimes called *package-privacy* or *package-local* access. Package-local access has no special keyword and is denoted by the lack of an access specifier. Dependency injectors allow us to take advantage of this special visibility by exposing only service interfaces and configuration from each package, hiding any implementation details within. Let's apply this to the Jabber example with Guice; see listing 9.5.

Listing 9.5 Package encapsulation of the Jabber services

```
package example.messaging;

public interface Messager {
    void send(Message msg);
}

class JabberMessager implements Messager {
    private final JabberTransport transport;
    private final JabberMessageConverter converter;

    public void send(Message msg) {
        ...
    }
}

class JabberTransport {
    ...
}

class JabberMessageConverter {
    ...
}
```

In listing 9.5, all of the implementation classes are declared package-local. They can't be seen from outside the example.messaging package by any classes. Moreover, all communication and use of Jabber services must occur through the Messager interface. This allows us a degree of control over the contract and behavior of our messaging module. It's also easy to specify API behavior to clients, and the documentation for this module is ridiculously simple (nothing more than the single-method Messager interface).

All we need to do to expose Jabber messaging to clients is place a single Guice module in the package, which contains all the nitty-gritty binding details:

```
public class MessagingModule extends AbstractModule {

    @Override
    protected void configure() {
        bind(Messager.class).to(JabberMessager.class);
    }
}
```

The messaging module does nothing more than instruct the injector to use JabberMessager wherever Messaging services are needed. Here's such a user of Jabber messaging:

```
public class MessageClient {
    private final Messager messager;

    public MessageClient(Messager messager) {
        this.messager = messager;
    }

    public void go() {
        messager.send(new Message("Dhanji", "Hi there!"));
    }
}
```

This ensures loose coupling between client code and the messaging module, since clients need only attach to the Messaging interface. We can even use multiple implementations this way and distinguish between them using binding annotations:

```
public class MessagingModule extends AbstractModule {

    @Override
    protected void configure() {
        bind(Messager.class).annotated-
     With(Im.class).to(JabberMessager.class);
        bind(Messager.class).annotatedWith(Mail.class).to(Emailer.class);
    }
}
```

Now clients can choose which implementation to use without coupling to any internals:

```
public class MessageClient {
    private final Messager mailMessager;
    private final Messager imMessager;

    public MessageClient(@Im Messager imMessager, @Mail Messager
        mailMessager) {
        this.imMessager = imMessager;
        this.mailMessager = mailMessager;
    }

    public void go() {
```

```
        Message msg = new Message("Dhanji", "Hi there!");

        imMessager.send(msg);
        mailMessager.send(msg);
    }
}
```

And all is well with the world.

A good example of this kind of encapsulation can be found in the warp-persist integration library we explored in chapter 8. Figure 9.8 is a screenshot of warp-persist's package tree. Notice the classes with a hollow bullet point to the left of them—these are package-local. Public components are restricted to hardly any public classes at all, thus vastly reducing the potential for tight coupling and abstraction leaking.

This is directly reflected in the API documentation for warp-persist. Look at the resulting streamlined and simple Javadoc frame in figure 9.9.

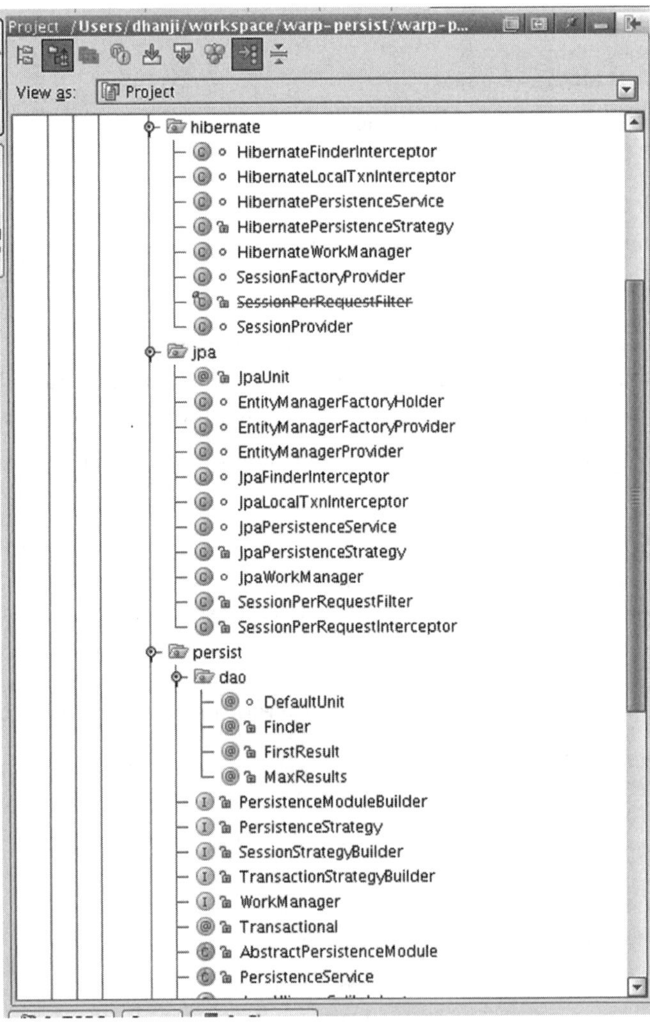

Figure 9.8 Screenshot of warp-persist's package tree (hollow bullets are package-private classes)

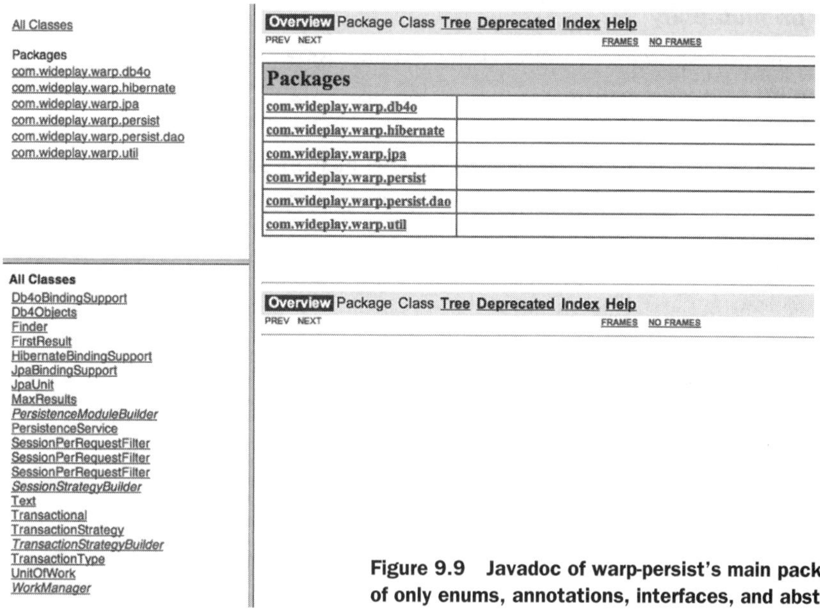

Figure 9.9 Javadoc of warp-persist's main package consisting of only enums, annotations, interfaces, and abstract classes

Neat! A good rule of thumb is to apply package privacy to anything that's not an interface, enum, annotation, or abstract class because these types have very low potential for leaking abstraction logic. You can apply these principles and take advantage of dependency injection to get better encapsulation at the package and module levels.

In previous chapters, we looked at safe design with respect to multiple threads. This often meant correct synchronization. Earlier in this chapter we also looked at visibility. In the following section, we'll take a more performance-focused approach and look at the action of multiple threads concurrently.

9.3 Objects and concurrency

Concurrency is increasingly a very important aspect of modern applications. As we scale to higher levels of traffic and demand, there's a greater need for multiple concurrent threads of execution. Thus, the role of objects managed by the dependency injector is extremely important. Singletons are a particularly significant example of this need.

In a large web application handling several hundreds of requests per minute, a poorly designed singleton can be a serious bottleneck. It introduces ceilings on concurrent performance and can even render the application unscalable under certain conditions.

Poor concurrent behavior is also more common than you might think. And since its effects are highlighted only during performance testing, it can be difficult to identify and mitigate, so it's quite relevant for us to study the effects of concurrency on singletons.

Mutability is an essential variable in this problem, so let's start with that.

9.3.1 More on mutability

Earlier in this chapter we explored the dangers of mutable objects as they manifested in visibility and publication problems. We also established that declaring fields final and making objects immutable was an efficient and robust solution to the thread-safety question. Now we'll explore exactly what it means to be immutable. Some pitfalls are contained within the idea of immutability too. To change things up, let's explore this as a series of puzzles.

IMMUTABLITY PUZZLE 1

Is the following class, `Book`, immutable?

```
public class Book {
    private String title;

    public String getTitle() {
        return title;
    }

    public void setTitle(String title) {
        this.title = title;
    }
}
```

ANSWER 1

This one's easy: no. The value of its `title` field can be changed arbitrarily by calling `setTitle()`, so it is clearly *not* immutable. We can make `Book` immutable by declaring `title` final:

```
public class ImmutableBook {
    private final String title;

    public ImmutableBook(String title) {
        this.title = title;
    }

    public String getTitle() {
        return title;
    }
}
```

Once set in the constructor, the value of `title` cannot change.

IMMUTABLITY PUZZLE 2

Is the following class, `AddressBook`, immutable?

```
public class AddressBook {
    private final String[] names;

    public AddressBook(String[] names) {
        this.names = names;
    }

    public String[] getNames() {
        return names;
    }
}
```

ANSWER 2

The value of the names field is set once in the constructor and is declared final. So AddressBook should be immutable, right? No! In fact, the subtle point is that since names is an array, only the *reference* to it is immutable by declaring it final. The following code is perfectly legal and can potentially lead to a world of hurt where multiple threads are concerned:

```
public class AddressBookMutator {
    private final AddressBook book;

    @Inject
    public AddressBookMutator(AddressBook book) {
        this.book = book;
    }

    public void mutate() {
        String[] names = book.getNames();

        for (int i = 0; i < names.length; i++)
            names[i] = "Censored!";

        for (int i = 0; i < names.length; i++)
            System.out.println(book.getNames()[i]);
    }
}
```

Method mutate() destructively updates the array, even though field names is unchangeable. If you run the program, it prints "Censored!" for every name in the book. The only real solution to this problem is not to use arrays—or to use them very sparingly behind well-understood safeguards and documentation. Choose library collections (such as those found in java.util) classes where possible as these can be guarded by unmodifiable wrappers. See puzzle 3 for an illustration of using java.util.List instead of an array.

IMMUTABLITY PUZZLE 3

Is the following class, BetterAddressBook, immutable?

```
public class BetterAddressBook {
    private final List<String> names;

    public BetterAddressBook(List<String> names) {
        this.names = Collections.unmodifiableList(names);
    }

    public List<String> getNames() {
        return names;
    }
}
```

ANSWER 3

Thankfully, yes; BetterAddressBook is immutable. The wrapper provided by the Collections library ensures that no updates can be made to the list once it has been set. The following code, though it compiles, results in an exception at runtime:

```
BetterAddressBook book = new BetterAddressBook(Arrays.asList(
     "Landau", "Weinberg", "Hawking"));
book.getNames().add(0, "Montana");
```

IMMUTABLITY PUZZLE 4

This is a variant on puzzle 3. Take the same `BetterAddressBook` class we saw earlier. Is it at all possible to construct it in such a way that I can mutate it? You're not allowed to change the code of `BetterAddressBook`.

ANSWER 4

The answer is simple, if a bit confounding:

```
List<String> physicists = new ArrayList<String>();
physicists.addAll(Arrays.asList("Landau", "Weinberg", "Hawking"));

BetterAddressBook book = new BetterAddressBook(physicists);

physicists.add("Einstein");
```

Now an iteration through `BetterAddressBook`'s list of names

```
for (String name : book.getNames())
    System.out.println(name);
```

actually produces the mutated list:

```
Landau
Weinberg
Hawking
Einstein
```

So, really, we must revise what we said in the answer to puzzle 3. `BetterAddressBook` is immutable only if its dependency list is not leaked anywhere else. Better yet, you can rewrite a completely safe version of it by copying the list at the time of its construction:

```
@Immutable
public class BestAddressBook {
    private final List<String> names;

    public BestAddressBook(List<String> names) {
        this.names = Collections.unmodifiableList(
            new ArrayList<String>(names));
    }

    public List<String> getNames() {
        return names;
    }
}
```

Now you're free to leak and mutate the original list,

```
List<String> physicists = new ArrayList<String>();
physicists.addAll(Arrays.asList("Landau", "Weinberg", "Hawking"));

BetterAddressBook book = new BetterAddressBook(physicists);

physicists.clear();
physicists.add("Darwin");
physicists.add("Wallace");
physicists.add("Dawkins");

for (String name : book.getNames())
    System.out.println(name);
```

and BestAddressBook remains unaffected:

```
Landau
Weinberg
Hawking
```

While it may not always be necessary to take such a cautious approach, it's advisable to copy argument lists if you're at all unsure about them escaping into other uses subsequent to construction of the immutable object.

IMMUTABLITY PUZZLE 5

Is the following class, Library, immutable? (Recall Book from puzzle 1.)

```
public class Library {
    private final List<Book> books;

    public Library(List<Book> books) {
        this.books = Collections.unmodifiableList(
            new ArrayList<Book>(books));
    }

    public List<Book> getBooks() {
        return books;
    }
}
```

ANSWER 5

Library depends on a list of Books, but it takes care to wrap the incoming list in an unmodifiable wrapper and copies it prior to doing so. Of course, its only field is final too. Everything looks right—or does it? It turns out that Library is mutable! While the collection of books is unchangeable, there's still the Book object itself, which, as you may recall from the first puzzle, allows its title to be set:

```
Book book = new Book();
book.setTitle("Dependency Injection");

Library library = new Library(Arrays.asList(book));

library.getBooks().get(0).setTitle("The Tempest");     //mutates Library
```

The golden rule with immutability and object graphs is that every dependency of an object must also be immutable. In the case of BestAddressBook, we got lucky, since Strings in Java are already immutable. Take care to ensure that every dependency you have is safely immutable before declaring an object as such. The @Immutable annotations mentioned in chapter 6 help a great deal in conveying and documenting this intent.

While immutability is a desirable goal, often you need to change state in order to do useful work. In the next section we'll look at how to do this and also keep our code performant.

9.3.2 Synchronization vs. concurrency

Sometimes it just happens that you really need mutable objects. It isn't always possible to make everything immutable (though it would be nice!). This need usually arises when you have to maintain some kind of central state in a system that's shared between many or all threads. This is fairly common in large applications. You may need a counter to keep track of the number of requests to a particular resource, or you may be caching heavyweight data in application memory to avoid expensive trips to a database.

Generally, you want to isolate any such use cases and design them very carefully, giving yourself ample slack to test and reason about these multithreaded services. Essentially, such services need to synchronize the data between threads in such a way that the data remains coherent and that threads are not paused for long periods awaiting data. These are two very different problems, with quite different solutions. And they are classed under the headings of *synchronization* and *concurrency*, respectively.

THREAD-SAFE COUNTING

Consider a simple counter. Every time a message is received, it increments the count by one. There are several message handler threads, and they must all update the same counter. If they updated separate counters, there would be no thread-safety problem, but we'd be unable to tell what the total count was. So here's what such a counter might look like:

```
public class MessageCounter {
    private int count;

    public void messageReceived() {
        count++;
    }
}
```

Method `messageReceived()` is called by each message-handling thread upon receiving a message to increment the count. Now, variable `count` is not final and is updated concurrently by more than one thread. So it is very possible that it will get out of sync and read an invalid or corrupt count. A simple solution is to synchronize the counter so that only one thread may increment the count at any given time:

```
public class MessageCounter {
    private int count = 0;

    public synchronized void messageReceived() {
        count++;
    }
}
```

In this version, the singleton-scoped instance of `MessageCounter` itself acts as the lock. Each message-receiving thread must wait its turn in order to acquire the lock, increment the count, and release it. This solution works, and we are assured that the `count` never goes out of sync and that each increment is published safely to all threads.

For this very simple case, the synchronization solution is probably good enough. But think about what happens when there is an enormous number of threads going through the counter. Every one of them must wait to acquire and release the lock before it can proceed with handling the message. This can lead to a serious bottleneck. The problem gets even worse if additional work needs to be done before the counter can be incremented (say, looking up who sent the message from a hashtable). All threads must wait inexorably, until the one holding the lock can finish. This can lead to very poor throughput.

CONCURRENT COUNTING

Concurrent algorithms and data structures are designed with speed and scalability in mind. Multiple threads may liberally hit the critical code without suffering the single-file throughput problems of synchronization. This is accomplished in many ways, primarily by taking advantage of some special *atomic* operations provided by modern CPUs. Atomic operations execute in one go on the CPU and cannot be interrupted by another thread being prioritized while they're executing. Atomic operations are thus somewhat like a very small block of synchronized code that performs just one instruction.

In Java, these are modeled by the `java.util.concurrent.atomic` library and associated data structures found in the `java.util.concurrent` package. Using these we can rewrite the counter to be concurrent rather than sequential:

```
public class MessageCounter {
    private final AtomicInteger count = new AtomicInteger(0);

    public void messageReceived() {
        count.incrementAndGet();
    }
}
```

The method `incrementAndGet()` executes atomically. This is opposed to `count++`, which is actually three operations masquerading as one:

1. Read value from `count`.
2. Increment value by one.
3. Write new value back to `count`.

In the *non-atomic* situation, intervening threads can easily alter `count` concurrently and corrupt its value. With the atomic `incrementAndGet()` this cannot happen.

Furthermore, if a thread is slow in incrementing its count (due to additional work that it's doing, perhaps), this doesn't block other threads from making progress in the meantime as synchronization would. This leads to real concurrency of threads and a substantial increase in throughput.

The value of concurrent data structures becomes more readily apparent when dealing with more complex forms of data, such as those stored in hashtables. Consider the second use case we mentioned, where data is placed into a cache and then looked up by multiple threads to prevent expensive trips to a database. Using a traditional synchronized hashtable this would look as follows:

```
public class SimpleCache {
    private final Map<String, Data> map =
            Collections.synchronizedMap(new HashMap<String, Data>());

    public void set(String key, Data val) {
        map.put(key, val);
    }
```

```
    public Data get(String key) {
        return map.get(key);
    }
}
```

SimpleCache uses a synchronized wrapper around a simple hashtable. This wrapper has a single lock that is acquired on every get() and every put() operation. This is done to safely publish values (as we discussed early in this chapter) to all threads. However, SimpleCache is extremely slow since every thread must wait for the hashmap to perform a lookup operation and release the lock held by the current thread. put() operations can be even worse since they can involve resizing the underlying array when it becomes full. In any high-traffic environment, this is unacceptably underperformant. What we need is for threads to be able to look up values concurrently and perhaps wait only when there are many insertions going on. What we need is a concurrent hashtable:

```
import java.util.concurrent.ConcurrentHashMap;

public class ConcurrentCache {
    private final Map<String, Data> map
        = new ConcurrentHashMap<String, Data>();

    public void set(String key, Data val) {
        map.put(key, val);
    }

    public Data get(String key) {
        return map.get(key);
    }
}
```

This is a special hashtable implementation because it doesn't use locking to read from the map at all! It allows multiple threads to make progress to the same values without requiring a coarse-grained lock as synchronized hashtables do. Instead it locks only on insertion operations but using more fine-grained locks distributed across the hashtable. The keys are partitioned along a configurable number of *stripes*. Each stripe is assigned a lock, and any concurrent insertions to keys in the same stripe must wait for sequential access (just like synchronization). Dividing the table into even a small number of stripes is several times more efficient than locking the entire table every time.

Opt for concurrent data structures wherever you can. And reason carefully about the semantics of making any object a singleton, because you will have to worry about thread safety and concurrency. Finally, conquer your problem by assessing it through the three cordons of immutability, safe publication, and concurrency.

9.4 Summary

This chapter was a thorough workout in best practices and concurrency. Architecturally, the best practices portended by a language and its design patterns are the same as those required by dependency injection. Where possible you should design with testability in mind but *not* rely on the behavior of an injector.

One of the primary problems to face with singletons and objects shared between threads is that of visibility. Dependencies set on an object need to be visible to all threads that use the object. This is known as safe publication. One way to guarantee proper visibility is to make objects immutable. This involves plenty more than merely declaring fields final, as you saw with a series of five puzzles on the topic. Immutability requires that every object in a graph be immutable and that no dependencies "escape" after construction.

Designing objects for better encapsulation is also very important. Dependency injectors like Guice allow you to hide implementation classes in package privacy and expose only interfaces to clients. This helps prevent tight coupling and the accidental leakage of internals. Another important design question is which objects to create and manage via the injector. A rule of thumb is to ask whether an object is a service component or whether it models data. If the latter, there's no benefit to be gained from dependency injection, lifecycle, scope, and so on, and you're better served working with them by hand.

Finally, we explored what it means to be thread-safe in mutable cases. This was especially tricky, since synchronization through locks is insufficient in all cases. In high-traffic environments, you cannot afford to let threads queue up, waiting to acquire a single global lock to a shared resource. The answer is to use concurrent data structures such as those provided by the `java.util.concurrent` library. These data structures purport atomic operations and more fine-grained locking, which allows for better throughput in systems that require a high level of concurrency.

This chapter gave you a solid, low-level grounding in designing code for safe, highly performant Java applications using dependency injection. Next we'll take a broader view and look at how to integrate an application with other libraries and utility frameworks.

10 Integrating with third-party frameworks

This chapter covers:

- Exploring lessons for framework designers
- Exploring framework anti-patterns
- Dealing with type-safety
- Dealing with framework interoperability

"No, no, you're not thinking! You're just being logical."

—Niels Bohr

Our investigation of application design has led us to dependency injection in various forms and working with environments such as web applications, data persistence, filesystems, and GUIs. The techniques we've examined help us tie together the otherwise disparate parts into cohesive modules that are easy to test and maintain.

Such scenarios typically call for the use of utility libraries that facilitate better application design. When you work with persistence, you use an ORM tool like Hibernate. When you work with service clusters, it may be Oracle Coherence.

One of the major impediments to smooth integration between a dependency injector and a given library is that many of these libraries already provide a minimal form of IoC. In other words, they provide some means, usually half baked, to construct and wire objects with dependencies. Generally, these are specific to their areas of need, such as a pluggable connection manager in the case of a persistence engine or a strategy for listening to certain events in the case of a graphical user interface GUI.

Most of the time these solutions focus on only a very specific area and ignore broader requirements for testing and component encapsulation. These typically come with restrictions that make testing and integration difficult—and downright impossible in certain cases. In this chapter, we'll show how this lack of architectural foresight can lead to very poor extensibility solutions and how, with a little bit of thought, a library can be very flexible and easy to integrate with. We'll study popular frameworks that have made the wrong choice by either hiding too much of the component model or by creating their own.

We'll now do a short analysis of how frameworks create fragmentation by each creating its own partial dependency injection idiom.

10.1 Fragmentation of DI solutions

Nearly every application these days does some form of DI. That is, it moves part of its object construction and wiring responsibilities off to configured library code. This can take many forms. In the Java Servlet framework, a very primitive form of this is evident with the registration of servlets and filters in web.xml, as shown in listing 10.1.

Listing 10.1 web.xml is a precursor to solutions using DI

```
<?xml version="1.0" encoding="UTF-8"?>
<web-app version="2.4"
         xmlns="http://java.sun.com/xml/ns/j2ee"
         xmlns:xsi="http://www.w3.org/2001/XMLSchema-instance"
         xsi:schemaLocation="http://java.sun.com/xml/ns/j2ee
         http://java.sun.com/xml/ns/j2ee/web-app_2_4.xsd" >

    <filter>
        <filter-name>webFilter</filter-name>
        <filter-class>
            com.wideplay.example.RequestPrintingFilter
        </filter-class>
    </filter>

    <filter-mapping>
        <filter-name>webFilter</filter-name>
        <url-pattern>/*</url-pattern>
    </filter-mapping>

    <servlet>
        <servlet-name>helloServlet</servlet-name>
        <servlet-class>
            com.wideplay.example.servlets.HelloServlet
        </servlet-class>
    </servlet>
```

```
    <servlet-mapping>
        <servlet-name>helloServlet</servlet-name>
        <url-pattern>/hi/*</url-pattern>
    </servlet-mapping>
</web-app>
```

In listing 10.1, we have a web.xml configuration file for the servlet container that configures a single web application with

- A filter—`com.wideplay.example.RequestPrintingFilter`
- An HTTP servlet—`com.wideplay.example.servlets.HelloServlet`

The filter is a subclass of `javax.servlet.Filter` and performs the simple task of tracing each request by printing its contents. It's configured with the `<filter>` tag as follows:

```
<filter>
    <filter-name>webFilter</filter-name>
    <filter-class>com.wideplay.example.RequestPrintingFilter</filter-class>
</filter>
```

This is reminiscent of Spring's `<bean>` tag, where a similar kind of configuration occurs. By analogy that might be:

```
<bean id="webFilter" class="com.wideplay.example.RequestPrintingFilter"/>
```

Similarly, there's a `<servlet>` tag that allows you to map a `javax.servlet.http.HttpServlet` to a string identifier and URL pattern. The essential difference between this solution and that offered by Spring, Guice, or any other dependency injector is that the servlet framework does not allow you to configure any dependencies for servlets or filters. This is a rather poor state of affairs, since we can virtually guarantee that any serious web application will have many dependencies.

This configuration is fairly restrictive on the structure of servlets (and filters):

- A servlet must have a public, nullary (zero-argument) constructor.
- A servlet class must itself be public and be a concrete type (rather than an interface or abstract class).
- A servlet's methods cannot be intercepted for behavior modification (see chapter 8).
- A servlet must effectively have singleton scope.

We can already see that this is getting to be an inexorable set of restrictions on the design of our application. If all servlets are singletons with nullary constructors, then testing them is very painful.[1] As a result of this and other deficiencies in the programming model, many alternative web frameworks have arisen on top of the servlet framework. These aim to simplify and alleviate the problems portended by the restrictiveness of the servlet programming model, not the least of which has to do with DI (see table 10.1 for a comparison of these solutions).

---

[1] See the problems with testing singletons described in chapter 1 and more comprehensively in chapter 5.

Table 10.1 Java web frameworks (based on servlet) and their solutions for DI

Library	Out-of-box solution	Integrates Spring/Guice/others?	Website
Apache Wicket	Custom factory, no DI	Partially through plug-in.[a]	http://wicket.apache.org
Apache Struts2 (formerly WebWork)	Custom factory, no DI	Fully, depending on plug-in.	http://struts.apache.org
Apache Tapestry 4	Apache HiveMind	Extension integrates Spring through HiveMind lookups.	http://tapestry.apache.org/tapestry4.1
Apache Tapestry 5	TapestryIoC injector	Partially via extension.[b]	http://tapestry.apache.org
JavaServer Faces 1.2	Built-in, very limited DI[c]	Extension integrates variable lookups in Spring.	http://java.sun.com/javaee/javaserverfaces
Spring MVC	Spring IoC	Pretty much tied to Spring.	http://www.springframework.org
Google Sitebricks	Google Guice	Integrates Spring fully via Guice's Spring module.	http://code.google.com/p/google-sitebricks

a. I say partially because Wicket's page objects cannot be constructed by DI libraries (and are therefore constructor injected), even with plug-ins.

b. Tapestry's Spring integration requires special annotations when looking up Spring beans. There is no official support for Guice.

c. JSF's built-in injector lacks support for constructor injection and interception, and it has limitations object identifiers that prevent the use of namespaces (see chapter 2 for an examination of namespaces in dependency identifiers).

As you can see from table 10.1, there isn't a standard programming model for integrating dependency injectors with libraries based around servlets. Only Apache Struts2 and Google Sitebricks fully integrate Guice and Spring.

The situation doesn't get much better with other types of libraries either. The standard EJBs programming model provides its own form of dependency injection that supports direct field injection and basic interception via the `javax.interceptor` library. Direct field injection, as we discussed in chapter 3, is very difficult to test and mandates the presence of nullary constructors, which also means that controlling scope is not an option—all stateless session EJBs (service objects) exist for the duration of a method call. Stateful session EJB*s* are somewhat longer lived, as you saw in chapter 7. But these too are scoped outside your direct control and only marginally longer lived.

Why are we at such a sorry circumstance? Frameworks ought to simplify our lives, not complicate them. The reasons are numerous, but essentially it boils down to the fact that we are only recently learning the value of testability, loose-coupling, scope, and the other benefits ascribed to DI. Moreover, the awareness of how to go about designing with these principles in mind is still maturing. Guice is only a little over two years old itself. PicoContainer's and Spring's modern incarnations are even more recent than that.

That having been said, let's look at what future frameworks and libraries can do to avoid these traps and prevent this sort of unnecessary fragmentation.

10.2 Lessons for framework designers

Most of the critical problems with integration can be avoided if framework designers keep one fundamental principle in mind: *testability*. This means that every bit of client and service code that a framework interacts with ought to be easy to test. This naturally leads to broader concepts like loose coupling, scoping, and modular design. Library components should be easily replaced with mock counterparts. And pluggable functionality should not mandate unnecessary restrictions on user code (servlets requiring a public, nullary constructor, for example).

Replacement with mocks is at once the most essential and most overlooked feature in framework designs. While most frameworks are themselves rigorously tested, they often fail to consider that it is equally important that client code be conducive to testing. This means considering the design of client code as much as the design of APIs and of implementation logic. Frameworks designed with such a leaning often turn out to be easier to use and understand, since there are fewer points of integration, and these are naturally more succinct. Another significant problem is encapsulation—you saw this in the previous chapter when considering the design of your classes. The more public classes you expose, the more danger there is that clients will begin to extend and use them. If you want to make major changes to your framework's architecture or internal design, this process is difficult if your users are heavily tied to several parts of your framework. The Spring Framework's SpringMVC suffers from this. Every single class is public and nonfinal. This means users can bind to any of this code, and it can never change without breaking a lot of client applications.

Even many of Spring's modules extend and use other parts of the framework. This is why people find it very difficult to use Spring modules outside the Spring injector. Spring Security is a classic example of this—many of its components rely strongly on Spring's lifecycle system and on JavaBeans property editors, which make it difficult to port for use with any other dependency injection system or even to use by hand.

Forcing users to extend framework base classes for functionality is also problematic because it blurs the lines between a dependency and a parent class. Composition is a preferable option, because a delegate is easily replaced with a mock or stub for unit and integration testing. Parent class methods are harder to mock and therefore less conducive to testing.

These problems can be classified broadly into three categories:

- Those that prevent testing or make it very difficult
- Those that restrict functionality by subverting interception and scope
- Those that make integration difficult or impossible (the most egregious)

None of these is particularly unavoidable or even necessary, especially if you carefully consider them early in the life of your framework.

Let's start by looking at an egregious instance, the rigid configuration anti-pattern, which makes both testing and integration difficult.

10.2.1 Rigid configuration anti-patterns

Most frameworks provide some form of customization of behavior. This is really a major part of their appeal—for example, Hibernate allows you to use a variety of databases, connection pools, transaction strategies, and so on, taking the basic behavior of the library to the breadth of various use cases. Often this is done via the use of external *resource bundles* such as `.properties` or XML files. Most of this configuration is generally about specifying a certain amount or type of something (`max_connections=..`; or, `timeout=..`; or, `enable_logging=true`; and so on). So this kind of configuration is appropriate.

But sometimes libraries also provide *pluggable* services. They allow you to customize behavior by writing small components, usually adhering to a library interface, and plugging them in. Sometimes they are called plug-ins, other times extensions. But essentially the idea is the same—they are a user-provided dependency of the framework. It is when these plug-ins are configured that things often go wrong in framework integration. Many frameworks will use the same configuration mechanism (XML file or resource bundle) to specify the plug-in. Generally this, too, takes the form of a string name/value pair such as

```
extensibility.plugin=com.example.MyPlugin
```

The property `extensibility.plugin` identifies which plug-in component is being set. On the right side is the name of the user-provided class. On the surface this looks like a clean approach. It is concise, easy to understand, and specifies the needed extension nicely. On closer inspection it reveals several problems that make it both difficult and unwieldy to test and integrate.

TYPE UNSAFE CONFIGURATION ANTI-PATTERN

The gravest of these is probably the disregard for type-safety. Since resource bundles are stored as raw strings, there's no way to verify that the information is present in its appropriate form. You could easily misspell or mistype the configuration parameter or even leave it out completely.

OSCache is a framework that provides real-time caching services for applications. OSCache stores its configuration in a resource bundle named `oscache.properties`. This is loaded by the cache controller when it is started up and then configured. A sample configuration file for OSCache is shown in listing 10.2.

Listing 10.2 A sample `oscache.properties` configuration file

```
cache.memory=false
cache.use.host.domain.in.key=true
cache.path=/tmp

cache.persistence.class=com.opensymphony.oscache.plugins.diskpersistence.
➥  DiskPersistenceListener
```

```
cache.algorithm=com.opensymphony.oscache.base.algorithm.LRUCache
cache.blocking=false
cache.capacity=100
cache.unlimited.disk=false
```

In listing 10.2, we are shown a cache configuration that sets several routine options, such as whether or not to use a disk cache

```
cache.path=/tmp
```

and where to store the files for this disk cache, its capacity, interaction model, and so on:

```
cache.path=/tmp
...
cache.blocking=false
cache.capacity=100
cache.unlimited.disk=false
```

And then, there's one interesting line right in the middle that specifies the kind of caching service to use. In this case it's OSCache's own `DiskPersistenceListener`:

```
cache.persistence.class=com.opensymphony.oscache.plugins.diskpersistence.
➥ DiskPersistenceListener
```

The problem with this is immediately obvious—we have no knowledge when coding this property of whether OSCache supports a `DiskPersistenceListener`. It isn't checked by the compiler. A simple but all-too-common misspelling goes undetected and leaves you with a runtime failure:

```
cache.persistence.class=com.opensymphony.oscache.plugins.diskpersistence.
➥ DiscPersistenceListener
```

This is very similar to the issues with string identifiers (keys) we encountered in chapter 2. Furthermore, even if it is spelled correctly, things may not work as expected unless it implements the correct interface:

```
package com.example.oscache.plugins;

public class MyPersistenceListener {
    ...
}
```

`MyPersistenceListener` is a custom plug-in I've written to persist cache entries in a storage medium of my choice. We can configure OSCache by specifying the property thusly:

```
cache.persistence.class=com.example.oscache.plugins.MyPersistenceListener
```

This is incorrect because `MyPersistenceListener` doesn't implement `PersistenceListener` from OSCache. This error goes undetected until runtime, when the OSCache engine attempts to instantiate `MyPersistenceListener` and use it. The correct code would be

```
package com.example.oscache.plugins;

import com.opensymphony.oscache.base.persistence.PersistenceListener;
```

```
public class MyPersistenceListener implements PersistenceListener {
    ...
}
```

Now, you may be saying, this is only one location where things can go wrong and a bit of extra vigilance is all right. You could write an integration test that will detect the problem—a somewhat verbose but passable solution if used sparingly. But now consider what happens if you misspell the *left-hand* side of the same configuration property:

```
cache.persistance.class=com.example.oscache.plugins.MyPersistenceListener
```

(*Persistence* is spelled with an *e*.)

In this case, not only is there no compile-time check, but any sanity check will completely miss the error! This is because property `cache.persistence.class`, if not explicitly set, will automatically use a default value. Everything appears to be fine, and the configuration throws no errors even in an integration test because you're freely allowed to set as many unknown properties as you like, with no regard to their relevance. Adding values for `cache.persistence.class`, `jokers.friend.is.batman`, and `my.neck.hurts` are all valid properties that a resource bundle won't complain about.

This is a bad state of affairs, since even extra vigilance can let you down. It also leads programmers to resort to things like copying and pasting known working configurations from previous projects or from tutorials.

UNWARRANTED CONSTRAINTS ANTI-PATTERN

This kind of name/value property mapping leads to strange restrictions on user code, particularly, the plug-in code we have been studying—our plug-in is specified using a fully qualified class name:

```
cache.persistence.class=com.example.oscache.plugins.MyPersistenceListener
```

The implication here is that `MyPersistenceListener` must implement interface `PersistenceListener` (as we saw just earlier) but also that `MyPersistenceListener` must have a public nullary constructor that throws no *checked* exceptions:

```
package com.example.oscache.plugins;

import com.opensymphony.oscache.base.persistence;

public class MyPersistenceListener implements PersistenceListener {

    public MyPersistenceListener() {
    }

    ...
}
```

This necessity arises from the fact that OSCache uses *reflection* to instantiate the `MyPersistenceListener` class. Reflective code is used to read and manipulate objects whose types are not immediately known. In our case, there's no source code in OSCache that's aware of `MyPersistenceListener`, yet it must be usable by the original OSCache code in order for plug-ins to work. Using reflection, OSCache is able to construct instances of `MyPersistenceListener` (or any class named in the property) and use them for persistence. Listing 10.3 shows an example of reflective code to create an instance of an unknown class.

Listing 10.3 Creating an object of an unknown class via reflection

```
String className = config.getProperty("cache.persistence.class");

Class<?> listener;
try {
    listener = Class.forName(className);

} catch (ClassNotFoundException e) {
    throw new RuntimeException("failed to find specified class",
        e);
}

Object instance;
try {
    instance = listener.getConstructor().newInstance();
} catch (InstantiationException e) {
    throw new RuntimeException("failed to instantiate listener",
        e);

} catch (IllegalAccessException e) {
    throw new RuntimeException("failed to instantiate listener",
        e);

} catch (InvocationTargetException e) {
    throw new RuntimeException("failed to instantiate listener",
        e);

} catch (NoSuchMethodException e) {
    throw new RuntimeException("failed to instantiate listener",
        e);

}
```

Let's break down this example. First, we need to obtain the name of the class from our configuration property:

```
String className = config.getProperty("cache.persistence.class");
```

This is done using a hypothetical `config` object, which returns values by name from a resource bundle. The string value of our plug-in class is then converted to a `java.lang.Class`, which gives us reflective access to the underlying type:

```
Class<?> listener;
try {
    listener = Class.forName(className);

} catch (ClassNotFoundException e) {
    throw new RuntimeException("failed to find specified class",
        e);
}
```

`Class.forName()` is a method that tries to locate and load the class by its fully qualified name. If it is not found in the classpath of the application, an exception is thrown and we terminate abnormally:

```
try {
    listener = Class.forName(className);

} catch (ClassNotFoundException e) {
    throw new RuntimeException("failed to find specified class",
        e);
}
```

Once the class is successfully loaded, we can try to create an instance of it by obtaining its nullary constructor and calling the method `newInstance()`:

```
Object instance;
try {
    instance = listener.getConstructor().newInstance();
} catch (InstantiationException e) {
    throw new RuntimeException("failed to instantiate listener ",
        e);

} catch (IllegalAccessException e) {
    throw new RuntimeException("failed to instantiate listener",
        e);

} catch (InvocationTargetException e) {
    throw new RuntimeException("failed to instantiate listener",
        e);

} catch (NoSuchMethodException e) {
    throw new RuntimeException("failed to instantiate listener",
        e);

}
```

There are four reasons why creating the instance may fail. And this is captured by the four `catch` clauses in the previous example:

- `InstantiationException`—The specified class was really an interface or abstract class.
- `IllegalAccessException`—Access visibility from the current method is insufficient to call the relevant constructor.
- `InvocationTargetException`—The constructor threw an exception before it completed.
- `NoSuchMethodException`—There is no nullary constructor on the given class.

If none of these four cases occurs, the plug-in can be created and used properly by the framework. Looked at from another point of view, these four exceptions are four restrictions on the design of plug-ins for extending the framework. In other words, these are four restrictions placed on your code if you want to integrate or extend OSCache (or any other library that uses this extensibility idiom):

- You must create and expose a concrete class with `public` visibility.
- This class must also have a `public` constructor.
- This class should not throw checked exceptions.
- It must have a nullary (zero-argument) constructor, which is `public`.

Apart from the restriction of not throwing checked exceptions, these seem to be fairly restrictive. As you saw in the chapter 9, in the section "Objects and design," it's quite desirable to hide implementation details in package-local or private access and expose only interfaces and abstract classes. As you've seen throughout this book, both immutability and testing suffer[2] when you're unable to set dependencies via constructor, since you can't declare them final and they're hard to swap out with mocks.

Without serious contortions like the use of statics and/or the singleton anti-pattern, we are left with a plug-in that can't benefit from DI. Not only does this spell bad weather for testing, but it also means we lose many other benefits such as scoping and interception.

CONSTRAINED LIFECYCLE ANTI-PATTERN

Without scoping or interception, your plug-in code loses much of the handy extra functionality provided by integration libraries like warp-persist and Spring. A persistence listener for cache entries can no longer take advantage of warp-persist's `@Transactional` interceptor, which intercedes in storage code and wraps tasks inside a database transaction. You're forced to write extra code to create and wrap data actions inside a managed database transaction. This similarly applies to other AOP concerns that we encountered in chapter 8, such as security and execution tracing.

Security, transaction, and logging code can no longer be controlled from one location (the interceptor) with configurable matchers and pointcuts. This leads to a fragmentation of crosscutting code, which adds to the maintenance overhead of your architecture.

Scoping is similarly plagued since the one created instance of your plug-in is automatically a singleton. Services that provide contextual database interactivity can no longer be used, since they are dependencies created and managed by an injector that's unavailable to plug-in code. Data actions we perform routinely, like opening a session to the database and storing or retrieving data around that session, cannot be performed directly. This also means that sessions cannot be scoped around individual HTTP requests.

These are all unwarranted constraints placed on user code by a rigid configuration system.

Similarly, a class of anti-patterns that I classify as black box design makes integration and testing extremely difficult. I examine some of these in the following section.

10.2.2 Black box anti-patterns

Another commonly seen symptom of poor design in integration or framework interoperability is the tendency toward *black box* systems. A black box system is something that *completely* hides how it works to the detriment of collaborators. This is not to be confused with the beneficial practice of encapsulation, which involves hiding implementation details to prevent accidental coupling.

[2] For a thorough examination of this, see chapter 4's investigation of testability and chapter 5's section "The singleton anti-pattern."

Black box systems don't so much hide the specific logic of their behaviors as they hide the mechanism by which they operate. Think of this as a runtime analog rigid configuration anti-pattern. Black box anti-patterns allow you to test in very limited ways, and they prevent the use of certain design patterns and practices we've examined by the excessive use of static fields, or abstract base-class functionality.

FRAGILE BASE CLASS ANTI-PATTERN

Many programmers are taught to use inheritance as a means of reusing code. Why rewrite all this great code you've done before? This is a noble enough idea in principle. When applied using class inheritance, it can lead to odd and often confounding problems. The first of these problems is the fragile base class. When you create a subclass to share functionality, you're creating a tight coupling between the new functionality and the base class. The more times you do this, the more tight couplings there are to the base class.

If you're the world's first perfect programmer, this isn't an issue. You would write the perfect base class that never needed to change, even if requirements did, and it would contain all the possible code necessary for its subclasses' evolution. Never mind that it would be enormous and look horrible.

But if you're like everyone else, changes are coming. And they are likely to hurt a lot. Changing functionality in the base class necessitates changing the behavior of all classes that extend it. Furthermore, it's very difficult to always design a correctly extensible base class. Consider the simple case of a queue based on a array-backed list:

```
public class Queue<I> extends ArrayList<I> {
    private int end = -1;                          <-- Start with an empty queue

    public void enqueue(I item) {
        super.add(0, item);
        end++;
    }

    public I dequeue() {
        if (end == -1) return null;            <-- Return null if queue is empty

        end--;
        return super.get(end + 1);
    }
}
```

This is a pretty simple class. `Queue` uses `ArrayList` to represent items it stores. When an item is enqueued (added to the back of the list), it is inserted at index 0 in the `ArrayList`:

```
    public void enqueue(I item) {
        super.add(0, item);
        end++;
    }
```

We increment the `end` index, so we know what the length of the queue is currently. Then when an item is removed from the queue, we decrement the `end` index and return it:

```
    public I dequeue() {
        if (end == -1) return null;

        end--;
        return super.get(end + 1);
    }
```

We need to return the item at `(end + 1)` because this is the last item in the list (pointed at by `end`, before we decremented it). So far, so good; we saved ourselves a lot of array insertion and retrieval code, but now look at what happens when we start using this class in unintended ways:

```
Queue<String> q = new Queue<String>();
q.enqueue("Muse");
q.enqueue("Pearl Jam");
q.clear();
q.enqueue("Nirvana");

System.out.println(q.dequeue());
```

We expect this program to print out `"Nirvana"` and leave the queue in an empty state. But really it throws an `IndexOutOfBoundsException`. Why? It's the fragile base class problem—we've used a method directly from the base class, `ArrayList`, which clears every element in the queue. This seemed natural enough at the time. However, since `Queue` doesn't know about method `clear()`, except via its base class, it doesn't update index `end` when the list is emptied. When `dequeue()` is called, `end` points at index `2` since `enqueue()` has been called three times. In reality, `end` should be pointing at index `0` since there's only one item in the queue.

This has left the queue in a corrupt state, even though the underlying `ArrayList` is functioning as expected. How do we fix this? We could override method `clear()` and have it reset the `end` index:

```
public class Queue<I> extends ArrayList<I> {
    private int end = -1;

    public void enqueue(I item) {
        super.add(0, item);
        end++;
    }

    public I dequeue() {
        if (end == -1) return null;

        end--;
        return super.get(end + 1);
    }

    @Override
    public void clear() {
        end = -1;

        super.clear();
    }
}
```

That's certainly an option, but what about other methods that `ArrayList` provides? Should we override everything? If we do, we're certainly assured that the behavior will be correct, but then we've gained nothing from the inheritance. In fact, we've probably overridden a few methods that have no place in a `Queue` data structure anyway (such as `get(int index)`, which fetches entries by index). We'd have been much better off making the `ArrayList` a dependency of `Queue` and using only those parts of it that we require, as shown in listing 10.4.

Listing 10.4 Replacing inheritance with delegation in class `Queue`

```
public class Queue<I> {
    private int end = -1;
    private final ArrayList<I> list = new ArrayList<I>();

    public void enqueue(I item) {
        list.add(0, item);
        end++;
    }

    public I dequeue() {
        if (end == -1) return null;

        end--;
        return list.get(end + 1);
    }
}
```

Listing 10.4 shows how replacing inheritance with delegation helps solve the fragile base class problem with a much more resilient design pattern. Now we can easily add functionality to the `Queue` with no danger of unintentionally leaking `ArrayList` functionality:

```
public class Queue<I> {
    private int end = -1;
    private final ArrayList<I> list;

    public Queue(ArrayList<I> list) {
        this.list = list;
    }

    public void enqueue(I item) {
        list.add(0, item);
        end++;
    }

    public I dequeue() {
        if (end == -1) return null;

        end--;
        return list.get(end + 1);
    }

    public void clear() {
        end = -1;

        list.clear();
    }
}
```

And now we can use it safely:

```
Queue<String> q = new Queue<String>(new ArrayList<String>());
q.enqueue("Muse");
q.enqueue("Pearl Jam");
q.clear();
q.enqueue("Nirvana");

System.out.println(q.dequeue());
assert null == q.dequeue();
```

This code correctly prints out `"Nirvana"` and leaves the queue empty, and it's a more satisfying solution.

Several open source frameworks make liberal use of abstract base classes to share functionality with little or no regard for the abstract base class problem. Another problem with base classes for sharing code is that they cannot be replaced with a mock object. This makes testing them tricky, especially when you have more than one level of inheritance. The Apache CXF framework has some classes that sport four and five levels of inheritance. Isolating problems can be very difficult in such cases.

While these problems are pretty rough, they're not all insurmountable. Good design can overcome them and lead to the same amount of flexibility with no loss of testing or integration capability. In the following section we'll look at how programmatic configuration can make life easier.

10.3 Programmatic configuration to the rescue

The solution to rigid configuration and black box anti-patterns is surprisingly simple: programmatic configuration. Rather than shoehorn plug-in configuration via the rather lean path of resource bundles (`.properties`, XML, or flat text files), programmatic configuration takes the attitude that configuring plug-ins is the same as DI.

If you start to look at the plug-in as a dependency of the framework, then it becomes simple and natural to write integration between frameworks and injectors, between frameworks and tests, and indeed between various frameworks.

10.3.1 Case study: JSR-303

Bean Validation is the common name for an implementation of the JSR-303[3] specification. Bean Validation is an initiative of the Java Community Process to create a flexible standard for validating data model objects via declarative constraints.

Listing 10.5 shows a typical data model object with annotations representing the declarative constraints acted on by the JSR-303 runtime.

Listing 10.5 A data model object representing a person

```
public class Person {
    @Length(max=150)
    private String name;
```

[3] Find out more about JSR-303 at http://jcp.org/en/jsr/detail?id=303.

```
    @After("1900-01-01")
    private Date bornOn;

    @Email
    private String email;

    @Valid
    private Address home;

    public void setName(String name) {
        this.name = name;
    }

    public Date getBornOn() {
        return bornOn;
    }

    public void setBornOn(Date bornOn) {
        this.bornOn = bornOn;
    }

    public String getEmail() {
        return email;
    }

    public void setEmail(String email) {
        this.email = email;
    }

    public Address getHome() {
        return home;
    }

    public void setHome(Address home) {
        this.home = home;
    }
}

public class Address {
    @NotNull
    @Length(max=200)
    private String line1;

    @Length(max=200)
    private String line2;

    @Zip(message="Zipcode must be five digits exactly")
    private String zipCode;

    @NotNull
    private String city;

    @NotNull
    private String country;

    public String getLine1() {
        return line1;
    }

    public void setLine1(String line1) {
        this.line1 = line1;
```

```
    }

    public String getLine2() {
        return line2;
    }

    public void setLine2(String line2) {
        this.line2 = line2;
    }

    public String getZipCode() {
        return zipCode;
    }

    public void setZipCode(String zipCode) {
        this.zipCode = zipCode;
    }

    public String getCity() {
        return city;
    }

    public void setCity(String city) {
        this.city = city;
    }

    public String getCountry() {
        return country;
    }

    public void setCountry(String country) {
        this.country = country;
    }
}
```

Listing 10.5 is of class `Person`, which represents a person in a hypothetical roster. Each of `Person`'s fields is tagged with an annotation representing a constraint to be applied on instances of the object. Some have an optional `message` attribute, which can be used to customize the error message reported on validation failure:

```
    @Zip(message="Zipcode must be five digits exactly")
    private String zipCode;
```

If all the constraints pass, then the instance is considered valid:

```
Person lincoln = new Person();
lincoln.setName("Abraham Lincoln");
lincoln.setBornOn(new Date());
lincoln.setEmail("abe@lincoln.nowhere");

Address address = new Address();
address.setLine1("1600 Pennsylvania Ave");
address.setZipCode("51245");
address.setCity("Washington, D.C.");
address.setCountry("USA");

lincoln.setHome(address);

List<InvalidValue> errors = validator.validate(lincoln);
System.out.println(String.format("There were %d error(s)", errors.size()));
```

On running this code, you'll see an output of how many errors there were (there were none). Each of the constraints on the code is a custom annotation that we've made up for the purposes of this demonstration. The constraints to which these annotations are attached are determined by the annotation declaration itself. Listing 10.6 illustrates some of the annotations we've used in listing 10.5's example of `Person` and `Address` data classes.

Listing 10.6 Custom annotations that act as constraint-plug-in "configurators"

```
import java.lang.reflect.ElementType
import java.lang.reflect.RetentionPolicy

@Target(ElementType.FIELD)
@Retention(RetentionPolicy.RUNTIME)
@ConstraintValidator(ZipConstraint.class)
public @interface Zip {
    String message() default "Zip invalid";
}

@Target(ElementType.FIELD)
@Retention(RetentionPolicy.RUNTIME)
@ConstraintValidator(LengthConstraint.class)
public @interface Length {
    int min();
    int max();
}

@Target(ElementType.FIELD)
@Retention(RetentionPolicy.RUNTIME)
@ConstraintValidator(NotNullConstraint.class)
public @interface NotNull {
    String message() default "Cannot be null";
}
```

The immediate thing that is apparent from listing 10.6 is that each of these annotations refers to a real validator. In the case of `@Zip`, it refers to class `ZipConstraint`:

```
@Target(ElementType.FIELD)
@Retention(RetentionPolicy.RUNTIME)
@ConstraintValidator(ZipConstraint.class)
public @interface Zip {
    String message() default "Zip invalid";
}
```

Similarly, `@Length`, which validates that fields have a minimum and maximum length, is bound to the `LengthConstraint` class:

```
@Target(ElementType.FIELD)
@Retention(RetentionPolicy.RUNTIME)
@ConstraintValidator(LengthConstraint.class)
public @interface Length {
    int min();
    int max();
}
```

Essentially, this is JSR-303's plug-in configuration mechanism. You use the class name in a *meta-annotation*, to specify which validator plug-in it should use. This is a type-safe meta-annotation that prevents you from registering anything but a subtype of `java.beans.validation.Constraint`, which the validation framework expects.

This is simple and yet quite powerful. We mitigate the problems of misspelling the class name and property name and of specifying the wrong plug-in type all in one stroke. Furthermore, JSR-303 doesn't mandate the use of reflection to create instances of user plug-ins. Unlike the recalcitrants we encountered earlier in this chapter, JSR-303 doesn't have a rigid configuration mechanism and so places no restrictions on your plug-in code.

This is achieved by providing the runtime with a user-written `ConstraintFactory`. This is a simple interface that JSR-303 runtimes use to obtain plug-in instances from your code:

```
/**
* This class manages the creation of constraint validators.
*/
public interface ConstraintFactory {
    /**
    * Instantiate a Constraint.
    *
    * @return Returns a new Constraint instance
    * The ConstraintFactory is <b>not</b> responsible for calling
     Constraint#initialize
    */
    <T extends Constraint> T getInstance(Class<T> constraintClass);
}
```

To take advantage of a dependency injector, you simply register an instance of `ConstraintFactory` that obtains `Constraints` from the injector. Here's a very simple Guice-based implementation that creates an injector and uses it to produce constraints when called on by the JSR-303 runtime:

```
public class GuiceConstraintFactory implements ConstraintFactory {
    private final Injector injector = Guice.createInjector(new MyModule());

    public <T extends Constraint> T getInstance(Class<T> constraintKey) {
        return injector.getInstance(constraintKey);
    }
}
```

This allows you to create constraint plug-ins with their own dependencies and lifecycle, and they can be capable of interception if needed. Let's take a look at an example of the `LengthConstraint`, which was tied to the `@Length` annotation, ensuring a maximum length for strings in listing 10.7.

Listing 10.7 A sample `LengthConstraint` plug-in for checking a string's length

```
/**
 * Check that a string length is between min and max
 *
```

```
 */
public class LengthConstraint implements Constraint<Length> {
    private int min;
    private int max;

    private final StringTools tools;

    @Inject
    public LengthConstraint(StringTools tools) {
        this.tools = tools;
    }

    /**
     * Configure the constraint validator based on the elements
     * specified at the time it was defined.
     *
     * @param constraint the constraint definition
     */
    public void initialize(Length constraint) {
        min = constraint.min();
        max = constraint.max();
    }

    /**
    * Validate a specified value.
    * returns false if the specified value does not conform to the
➥  definition
    * @exception IllegalArgumentException if the object is not of type
➥  String
    */
    public boolean isValid(Object value) {
        if (value == null) return true;

        if ( !(value instanceof String) )
            throw new IllegalArgumentException("Expected String type");

        String string = (String) value;
        return tools.isLengthBetween(min, max, string);
    }
}
```

Inject a string checking utility (annotation on the `@Inject` constructor)

Use dependency to check length (annotation on `return tools.isLengthBetween(min, max, string);`)

In listing 10.7, `LengthConstraint` is dependency injected with `StringTools`, a reusable utility that does the dirty work of checking string length for us. We're able to take advantage of Guice's constructor injection because of the flexibility that JSR-303's `ConstraintFactory` affords us:

```
public class LengthConstraint implements Constraint<Length> {
    private int min;
    private int max;

    private final StringTools tools;

    @Inject
    public LengthConstraint(StringTools tools) {
        this.tools = tools;
    }

    ...
}
```

LengthConstraint dutifully ensures that it's working with a String before passing this on to its dependency to do the hard yards. LengthConstraint is itself configured using an interface method initialize() that provides it with the relevant annotation instance:

```
/**
 * Configure the constraint validator based on the elements
 * specified at the time it was defined.
 *
 * @param constraint the constraint definition
 */
public void initialize(Length constraint) {
    min = constraint.min();
    max = constraint.max();
}
```

Recall that we set this value in the Person class for field name to be between 0 and 150 (see listing 10.5 for the complete Person class):

```
public class Person {
    @Length(max=150)
    private String name;

    ...
}
```

Now, every time the validator runs over an instance of Person,

```
Person lincoln = new Person();
lincoln.setName("Abraham Lincoln");
...
Address address = new Address();
...
lincoln.setHome(address);

List<InvalidValue> errors = validator.validate(lincoln);
```

the LengthConstraint plug-in we wrote will be run. Being flexible in providing us an extension point with the ConstraintFactory and the @ConstraintValidator meta-annotation, JSR-303 rids itself of all the nasty perils of rigid configuration internals. It encourages user code that's easy to test, read, and maintain. And it allows for maximum reuse of service dependencies without any of the encumbering ill effects of static singletons or black box systems.

JSR-303 is an excellent lesson for framework designers who are looking to make their libraries easy to integrate and elegant to work with.

10.4 Summary

In this chapter we looked at the burgeoning problem of integration with third-party frameworks and libraries. Most of the work in software engineering today is done via the use of powerful third-party frameworks, many of which are designed and provided by open source communities such as the Apache Software Foundation or OpenSymphony.

> **Other random indispensable pieces of advice**
>
> *"When wrestling for possession of a sword, the man with the handle always wins."*
>
> —Neal Stephenson (in *Snow Crash*)
>
> *"Technical people are better off not looking at patents. If somebody sues you, you change the algorithm or you just hire a hit-man to whack the stupid git. "*
>
> —Linus Torvalds
>
> *"One should always play fairly when one has the winning cards."*
>
> —Oscar Wilde

Many companies (like Google and ThoughtWorks) are releasing commercially developed libraries as open source for the good of the community at large.

Leveraging these frameworks within an application is an often tedious and difficult task. They're generally designed with a specific type of usage in mind, and integrating them is often a matter of some complexity. The better-designed frameworks provide simple, flexible, and type-safe configuration options that allow you to interact with the framework as you would with any one of your services. Extending such frameworks is typically done via the use of pluggable user code that conforms to a standard interface shipped along with the library. Frameworks that sport rigid configuration such as via the use of resource bundles (`.properties`, XML, or flat text files) cause problems because they place undue restrictions on the classes written for plug-in extensions. Because they are simple strings in a text file, these class names are also prone to misspelling and improper typing and are forced to be publicly accessible.

Moreover, since they're instantiated using reflection, these plug-in classes must have at least one public constructor that accepts no arguments (a *nullary* constructor). This immediately places unwarranted constraints on your code—you cannot declare fields `final` in your plug-in class. Not only does this have grave consequences for visibility, but it also makes your classes hard to test and swap out with mocked dependencies. The restriction on who creates your plug-in class also means that your code cannot take advantage of any of the other benefits of dependency injection. Lifecycle, scoping, and AOP interception must all be given up. This is particularly egregious in a scenario where your plug-in uses the same kind of services that your application does, for instance, a database-backed persistence system. Transactions, database connectivity, and security must all be managed independently from the application by your plug-in code.

The alternative is to share services via the use of static state and the singleton antipattern. This has negative consequences for testing, as you saw in chapter 5.

A well-designed framework, on the other hand, is cognizant of the testability mantra and allows you to configure plug-ins programmatically; that is, within the application itself. JSR-303 is a validation framework that allows you to create constraint plug-ins that are tied to declarative constraints placed on data model objects. These plug-ins are applied universally based on annotation metadata and help specify the validity of a data object. JSR-303's constraint plug-ins are created and configured via the use of a custom `ConstraintFactory` interface. `ConstraintFactory` is a plug-in factory that you provide, which creates instances of the actual constraint plug-ins for JSR-303's runtime.

Programmatic configuration means that your plug-in configuration code is type-safe, contract-safe, and well-defined within the bounds of the framework's usage parameters. It also means that you can control the creation and wiring of your own code, giving it dependencies, scoping, and rigorous testability. This makes it open to all the great benefits of dependency injection that you've so come to love!

In the next chapter you'll apply many of the patterns you've learned up to this point and create a fully functional, running demo application.

11 Dependency injection in action!

This chapter covers:

- Building a complete web application from scratch
- Seeing DI principles in a working application
- Applying useful design patterns
- Solving many common problems

"A computer lets you make more mistakes faster than any invention in human history—with the possible exceptions of handguns and tequila."

—Mitch Radcliffe

In this chapter we'll put all of the things you've learned so far in this book into practice in a real, working application. While there probably aren't enough pages to demonstrate a large enterprise application, we'll look at a succinct application that gives us all the salient features of a broader program.

This program will start from bootstrapping the injector in a web application and walk through designing services for persistence, transactions, and user interactivity. We'll also show how to apply some useful design patterns (such as the

Provider pattern from chapter 5) and ways to properly leverage scope, lifecycle, and interception (AOP).

Let's start by defining what this program will be.

11.1 Crosstalk: a Twitter clone!

I've chosen to do a simple, trivial clone of the popular microblogging service Twitter. (This isn't in the least bit because I spend large chunks of my day on Twitter!) While I was writing this chapter, I thought *crosstalk* was cool code name.

Crosstalk serves as a good illustration of a straightforward yet vastly scalable website that has plenty of user interactivity and data processing needs. These make it an ideal problem domain to showcase the wonderful patterns of dependency injection.

Its requirements are diverse—ranging from persistence and presentation to security and user management. This gives us a good basis for drawing an illustrative architecture from start to finish, in a few pages. First, let's look at these requirements.

11.1.1 Crosstalk's requirements

Our thesis is fairly straightforward: crosstalk allows users to write short text messages (called tweets) on their home page. This engenders some broad requirements. We need to

- Authenticate users when they log on
- Secure their home pages
- Persist tweets in a database

We also need to ensure that the site is scalable and concurrent. In other words, it must be easily tolerant to many users accessing their home pages at once. Given all these requirements, it follows that crosstalk has several layers:

- The presentation layer (website)
- The persistence layer (database mechanism)
- The security layer (authentication and securing pages)

We'll build this application using Google Guice as the injector and Google Sitebricks as the web application framework. Google Sitebricks is a simple, statically typed development system for rendering web pages. It follows the REST idiom, which makes it ideal for building HTML websites.

For persistence, we'll use Hibernate and warp-persist (seen in chapter 8) as the integration bridge with Guice. Let's get started.

11.2 Setting up the application

First, we'll need a layout and structure for the crosstalk application. This needs to follow the Java Servlet standard so that it can be deployed in a servlet container like Apache Tomcat or Mort Bay Jetty. We'll use Jetty for this illustration, since it's very simple to get up and running with. And as the database, we'll go with Hypersonic (sometimes called HSQL), which is an in-memory SQL database that's easy to set up and configure.

Here's the structure we'll start out with for the project (see figure 11.1):

- src—The main source directory, with all our classes
- test—A test sources directory, for our Jetty launcher
- web—The directory for all the web resources (HTML templates, CSS stylesheets)
- web/WEB-INF—A directory required by the servlet container to look for deployment descriptors

The file web.xml is a deployment descriptor that instructs the servlet container about how to configure this web application. We'll use a web.xml file very similar to the one used in chapter 5, when we were dealing with web scopes.

Once you have that layout set up (see figure 11.1), open a project in your favorite IDE and add the libraries shown in table 11.1 to the classpath:

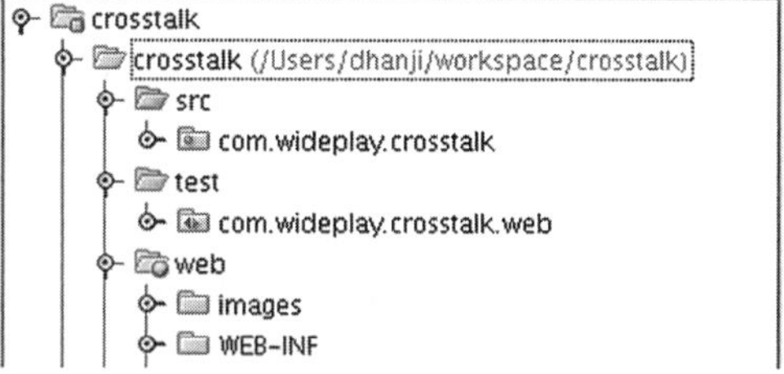

Figure 11.1 The layout of directories for the crosstalk application

Table 11.1 Libraries

Library	Description
guice-2.0.jar	Google Guice core http://code.google.com/p/google-guice/
aopalliance.jar	Guice AOP interface (included with Guice)
google-sitebricks.jar	Google's Sitebricks web framework http://code.google.com/p/google-sitebricks/
guice-servlet-2.0.jar	Servlet integration for Guice (included with Guice
hibernate3.jar	Hibernate core persistence framework https://www.hibernate.org/
hibernate-annotations.jar	Annotations for Hibernate https://www.hibernate.org/
ejb3-persistence.jar	Annotations for Hibernate (included with Hibernate Annotations)
dom4j-1.6.1.jar	Dom4j XML parser (included with Hibernate)
jta.jar	Java Transaction API (included with Hibernate)
cglib-nodep-2.1_3.jar	CGLib used by Hibernate to proxy objects
antlr-2.7.5h3.jar	Antlr compiler library (included with Hibernate)
commons-collections.jar	Apache Collections library (included with Hibernate)
commons-logging.jar	Apache Commons-Logging (required by Hibernate for log output)
warp-persist-2.0-20090214.jar	Warp-persist integrates Hibernate with Guice http://www.wideplay.com/guicewebextensions2

Table 11.1 Libraries *(continued)*

Library	Description
hsqldb.jar	Hypersonic In-Memory SQL database http://hsqldb.org/
servlet-api-2.5-6.1.9.jar	Java Servlet API (included with Jetty)
jetty-6.1.9.jar	Mort Bay Jetty http://www.mortbay.org/jetty
jetty-util-6.1.9.jar	Utilities for working with Jetty
jcip-annotations.jar	The set of annotations used in chapter 10 for thread-safety documentation http://www.javaconcurrencyinpractice.com/

TIP To add these libraries to the classpath in IntelliJ IDEA, open Settings > Project Settings and select the main (crosstalk) module. Then open the Dependencies tab and click Add. Now select Project Library and Add Jar Directory, choosing the directory where all these jars reside (or add them individually using the single-entry module library option).

Once you have all of those lined up, you should be good to go. If you aren't using an IDE, you can place all the jars in a lib directory and specify them individually on the command line.

Now the central configuration for our application will reside in `CrosstalkBootstrap`. This is a simple Java class, a subclass of `GuiceServletContextListener`, from which we'll tell Guice how to wire our services together, as shown in listing 11.1.

Listing 11.1 The Guice configuration for crosstalk (also creates the injector)

```
public final class CrosstalkBootstrap extends GuiceServletContextListener {

    @Override
    protected Injector getInjector() {

        //bind in all of our service dependencies
        final Module services = new ServicesModule();

        //tell Sitebricks to scan this package
        final Module sitebricks = new SitebricksModule() {
            protected void configureSitebricks() {
                scan(CrosstalkBootstrap.class.getPackage());
            }
        };

        //map all incoming requests through the PersistenceFilter
        final Module servlets = new ServletModule() {
                protected void configureServlets() {
                    filter("/*").through(PersistenceFilter.class);

                     install(sitebricks);
                }
        };
```

```
        //finally, create the injector with all our configuration
        return Guice.createInjector(services, servlets);
    }
}
```

It looks pretty simple, but let's examine what this does. By subclassing `GuiceServlet-ContextListener`, we're able to create and register our own injector with guice-servlet and the servlet container itself. This listener must also be registered in web.xml so that it can be called when the application is deployed and made ready to run, as shown in listing 11.2.

Listing 11.2 Web.xml config for guice-servlet and a crosstalk-specific listener

```
<?xml version="1.0" encoding="UTF-8"?>
<web-app xmlns="http://java.sun.com/xml/ns/javaee"
          xmlns:xsi="http://www.w3.org/2001/XMLSchema-instance"
          xsi:schemaLocation="http://java.sun.com/xml/ns/javaee
             http://java.sun.com/xml/ns/javaee/web-app_2_5.xsd"
          version="2.5">

    <filter>
        <filter-name>guiceFilter</filter-name>
        <filter-class>com.google.inject.servlet.GuiceFilter</filter-class>
    </filter>

    <filter-mapping>
        <filter-name>guiceFilter</filter-name>
        <url-pattern>/*</url-pattern>
    </filter-mapping>

    <listener>
        <listener-class>com.wideplay.crosstalk.CrosstalkBootstrap</listener-
     class>
    </listener>

</web-app>
```

Web.xml also creates a filter mapping so that all incoming requests are passed through the guice-servlet `GuiceFilter`. This allows guice-servlet to reroute requests through the filters and servlets configured in Guice's servlet pipeline, allowing us to take advantage of dependency injection idioms, lifecycle, scope and interception. We saw a setup very similar to this in chapter 5. `GuiceFilter` is provided by guice-servlet and requires no special treatment. We map it to `/*` to indicate that all URLs are to be filtered through it:

```
<?xml version="1.0" encoding="UTF-8"?>
<web-app xmlns="http://java.sun.com/xml/ns/javaee"
          xmlns:xsi="http://www.w3.org/2001/XMLSchema-instance"
          xsi:schemaLocation="http://java.sun.com/xml/ns/javaee
             http://java.sun.com/xml/ns/javaee/web-app_2_5.xsd"
          version="2.5">

    <filter>
        <filter-name>guiceFilter</filter-name>
        <filter-class>com.google.inject.servlet.GuiceFilter</filter-class>
```

```
    </filter>

    <filter-mapping>
        <filter-name>guiceFilter</filter-name>
        <url-pattern>/*</url-pattern>
    </filter-mapping>
...
</web-app>
```

This way, all incoming requests are rerouted through guice-servlet's `GuiceFilter`, allowing it to process requests that are specific to crosstalk and pass through requests for static resources like CSS stylesheets and images. Application-specific requests are handled by Google Sitebricks pages, which we'll now go about setting up.

11.3 Configuring Google Sitebricks

Since we'll be using the Google Sitebricks web framework, we'll need to do extra configuration to tell it how to behave. Google Sitebricks has a simple philosophy where individual HTML pages are modeled as Java classes with a backing HTML template. Each such page class is registered against URL patterns in much the same manner as a servlet (or filter). We'll see how this works in a second. But first, let's tell guice-servlet to route all requests through Google Sitebricks, as shown in listing 11.3.

Listing 11.3 `CrosstalkBootstrap` from listing 11.1

```
public final class CrosstalkBootstrap extends
➥   GuiceServletContextListener {

    @Override
    protected Injector getInjector() {
...
        //map all incoming requests through PersistenceFilter
        final Module servlets = new ServletModule() {
                protected void configureServlets() {
                    filter("/*").through(PersistenceFilter.class);

                     install(sitebricks);
                }
        };

        //finally, create the injector with all our configuration
        return Guice.createInjector(services, servlets);
    }
}
```

The line in bold directs Guice to install our web framework, meaning that Google Sitebricks gets a crack at all user requests and can decide which ones to process and which ones it can safely pass on to the servlet container (such as static resources).

Now, we can proceed to look at the Google Sitebricks configuration:

```
public final class CrosstalkBootstrap extends
➥   GuiceServletContextListener {
```

```
    @Override
    protected Injector getInjector() {
...
        //tell sitebricks to scan this package
        final Module sitebricks = new SitebricksModule() {
            @Override
            protected void configureSitebricks() {
                scan(CrosstalkBootstrap.class.getPackage());
            }
        };
    ...
    }
}
```

The method scan(...) tells Google Sitebricks which packages to work with. You may specify as many packages as needed this way.

By providing it with CrosstalkBootstrap's package, we tell Google Sitebricks to scan the entire package tree beginning with com.wideplay.crosstalk and to look for page classes and templates to serve.

Finally, we install one more module in our injector, which will handle all application services. This is, appropriately, the ServicesModule:

```
public final class CrosstalkBootstrap extends
➥ GuiceServletContextListener {

    @Override
    protected Injector getInjector() {

        //bind in all of our service dependencies
        final Module services = new ServicesModule();
...
        //finally, create the injector with all our configuration
        return Guice.createInjector(services, servlets);
    }
}
```

The Guice.createInjector() method is a *varargs* method, meaning that it takes any number of arguments. This is convenient for us as we can pass in our two modules, services and servlets, that configure our persistence and security, respectively. Note that Google Sitebricks web pages are processed by the SitebricksModule. We'll look at the services module in some more detail shortly, but first, let's examine the application's package structure.

11.4 Crosstalk's modularity and service coupling

In this section, we'll look at how crosstalk is broken down into modules by package, service type, and contract. We'll see some of the concepts presented in chapter 4 on modularizing code and in the chapter 10 on packaging clean designs that separate areas of concern.

Crosstalk's packages also expose no implementation details, so that accidental coupling of services does not occur. All collaboration between modules happens through publicly exposed interfaces, with well-defined contracts. Let's see how this structure is achieved.

Crosstalk's packages are organized very simply (shown in figure 11.2).

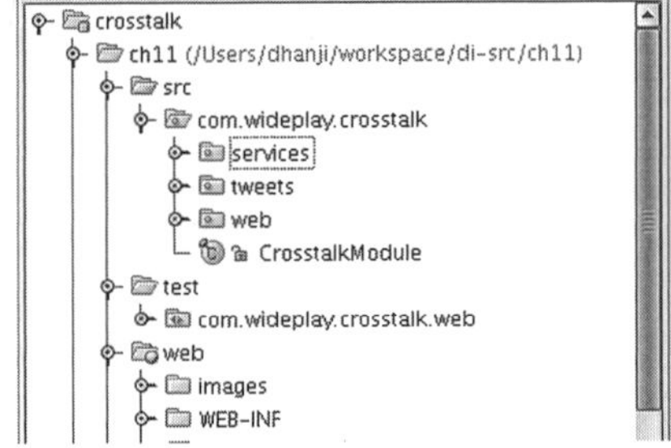

Figure 11.2 The layout of packages in the crosstalk application's src directory

They are divided among the core application services, Google Sitebricks web pages, and any data model classes:

- `com.wideplay.crosstalk.web`—The presentation layer (all page classes go here)
- `com.wideplay.crosstalk.services`—Persistence and security layer
- `com.wideplay.crosstalk.tweets`—The domain model package

Notice that the `services` package exposes only interfaces (apart from the Guice `ServicesModule` configuration class). In chapter 4 we discussed the concept of loose coupling. This allows us to modify specific implementation details without affecting the presentation layer in any way. For example, we may choose to persist the data in a cluster data store rather than Hibernate and HSQL. By changing the implementation of classes in the `services` package, we can do this with no impact to the rest of the application. All implementation classes are hidden away as package-local. Figure 11.3 provides a complete picture of this approach.

You may also notice that the web pages and the data model classes are public. This is because they are used directly by the framework (Google Sitebricks in the web pages' case and Hibernate in the data model's) and configured using flexible annotations, which already alleviate any coupling perils.

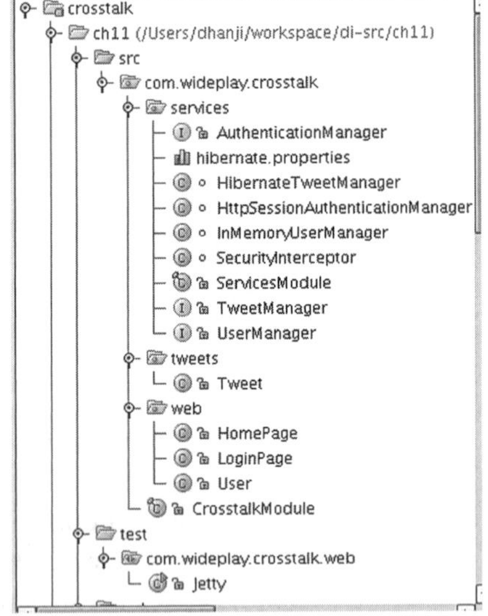

Figure 11.3 All the classes and packages in the eventual crosstalk application

Now that we've taken a bird's-eye tour of the structure, let's get down to it. First, the business end of crosstalk, its user-facing presentation layer.

11.5 The presentation layer

Let's look at some of crosstalk's functionality. Crosstalk's core requirement is the ability to post tweets on a user's home page. For this, we create a class `HomePage`, with a corresponding template in the `web/` resources directory. `HomePage` looks like figure 11.4.

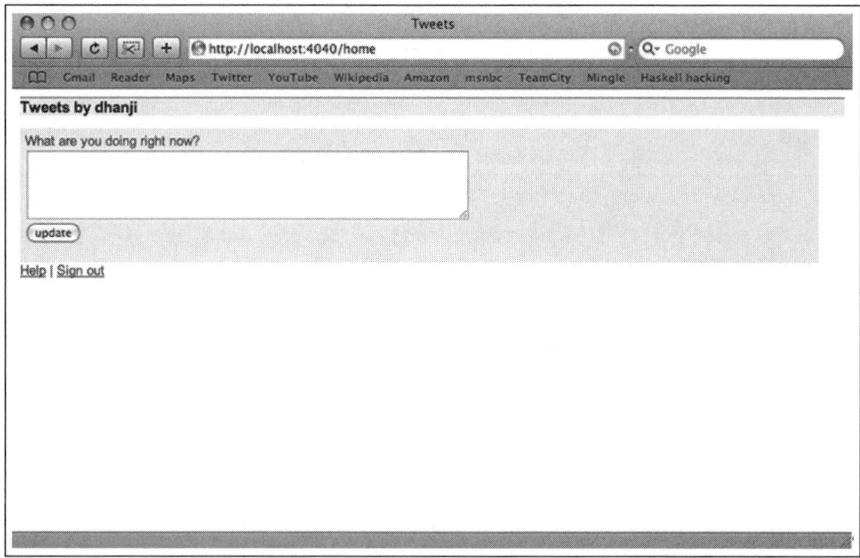

Figure 11.4 A user's home page with no content–it allows users to blog new tweets in a text box.

The Java source code behind `HomePage` is shown in listing 11.4.

Listing 11.4 `HomePage` Sitebricks page class models a crosstalk user's home page

```
package com.wideplay.crosstalk.web;

@At("/home") @Select("action") @RequestScoped
public class HomePage {
    //user context, tracks current user
    private User user;

    //page state variables
    private List<Tweet> tweets;
    private Tweet newTweet = new Tweet();

    //service dependencies
    private final TweetManager tweetManager;

    @Inject
    public HomePage(TweetManager tweetManager, User user) {
        this.tweetManager = tweetManager;
        this.user = user;
    }

    @Get("logout")
    public String logout() {
        user.logout();

        return "/login?message=Bye.";
    }

    @Get
    public String get() {

        //load tweets for current user
```

```
        this.tweets = tweetManager.tweetsFor(user.getUsername());

        //stay on current page
        return null;
    }

    @Post
    public String post() {
        newTweet.setAuthor(user.getUsername());

        //contents are in newTweet, add it to the data store
        tweetManager.addTweet(newTweet);

        //redirect back to this page using a GET
        return "/home";
    }

    //getters/setters...

    public String getUser() {
        return user.getUsername();
    }

    public List<Tweet> getTweets() {
        return tweets;
    }

    public Tweet getNewTweet() {
        return newTweet;
    }
}
```

This looks pretty involved. Let's see what each bit actually means. First, we annotate the class with the `@At` annotation, which tells Google Sitebricks to serve this page at the given URI:

```
@At("/home") @On("action") @RequestScoped
public class HomePage { .. }
```

Now, whenever a user types in URL `http://localhost:8080/home` (assuming the application is deployed at `localhost:8080`), the `HomePage` will be served up by Google Sitebricks. We also see the familiar `@RequestScoped` annotation, which tells Guice to create a new instance of `HomePage` for every incoming request. This is important because it allows us to work with state that's specific to a user without stepping on other users' data, accidentally.

Finally, the `@On` annotation is used to resolve events to fire against. For now, let it suffice to say that `@On` controls which method annotated with `@Get` is called based on an incoming request parameter named `action`.

The visual companion to this page class is its HTML template. This template contains what a user will see. Let's see how it's built.

11.5.1 The HomePage template

`HomePage`'s template is a very simple HTML file. It contains dynamic text, which is provided by binding its data to the request-scoped instance of class `HomePage`, as shown in listing 11.5. It also contains a link to a stylesheet.

Listing 11.5 An HTML template that displays tweets, backed by HomePage

```
<html>
<head>
    <title>Tweets</title>

    <link rel="stylesheet" href="/crosstalk.css"/>
</head>
<body>
    <h2>Tweets by ${user}</h2>

    <div class="box">                          <-- The input box for new tweets
        <div class="box-content">
            <div>What are you doing right now?</div>

            <form action="/home" method="post">
                <textarea name="newTweet.text" rows="5" cols="60" />
                <input type="submit" value="update"/>
            </form>
        </div>
    </div>

    @Repeat(items=tweets, var="tweet")          <-- This div is repeated for every tweet
    <div class="box">
        <div class="box-content">
            ${tweet.text} (${tweet.createdOn})
        </div>
    </div>

    <a href="http://manning.com/prasanna">Help</a> |
    <a href="?action=logout">Sign out</a>
</body>
</html>
```

This line in particular is interesting because it resolves to a property of the HomePage class (that is, one that is accessed via a getter method):

```
<h2>Tweets by ${user}</h2>
```

This heading is dynamically evaluated at runtime by calling HomePage.getUser(). HomePage.getUser() returns the username of the current user logged in to crosstalk:

```
public String getUser() {
    return user.getUsername();
}
```

One other interesting part of the template is the @Repeat annotation:

```
@Repeat(items=tweets, var="tweet")
<div class="box">
    <div class="box-content">
        ${tweet.text} (${tweet.createdOn})
    </div>
</div>
```

This tells Google Sitebricks to repeat the annotated tag (in this case, <div class="box"> over all the items in HomePage's property tweets. For each element in tweets, Google Sitebricks will render out the div tags expanding tweet.text and

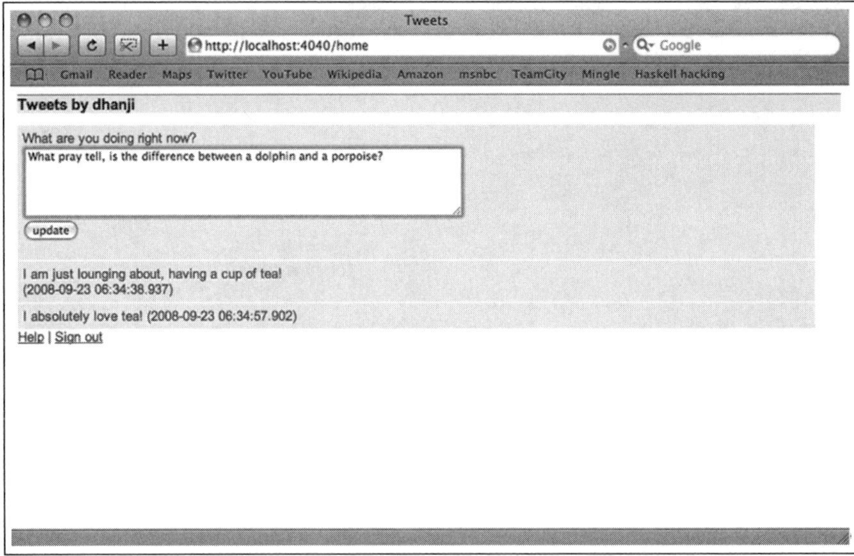

Figure 11.5 A user's home page with blogged content

`tweet.createdOn` properties. In other words, this renders out the list of tweets posted by a user on their home page (see figure 11.5).

The other significant part of this template is the form. Users type their new tweets into a text field and post them by submitting the form:

```
<div>What are you doing right now?</div>

<form action="/home" method="post">
    <textarea name="newTweet.text" rows="5" cols="60" />
    <input type="submit" value="update"/>
</form>
```

Since the form's `textarea` is bound to `newTweet.text`, Google Sitebricks will attempt to write the incoming form post to `HomePage`'s property `newTweet`:

```
@At("/home") @On("action") @RequestScoped
public class HomePage {

    ...

    //page state variables
    private List<Tweet> tweets;
    private Tweet newTweet = new Tweet();

   ...
}
```

This is accomplished by navigating the `getNewTweet()` method to the appropriate setter methods on class `Tweet`, in this case, `setText()`. We take care to create a new instance of `Tweet` every time `HomePage` is created, thus every time it is requested, ensuring that tweets are never overwritten by accident.

Each new tweet entry by a user is recorded and modeled as an instance of class Tweet.

11.5.2 The Tweet domain object

Tweet is the sole class in our domain model, and it consists of simple data fields describing a message, its creation date, and its author, as shown in listing 11.6.

Listing 11.6 Tweet models a tweet message for capturing data and storing it

```
package com.wideplay.crosstalk.tweets;

@Entity
public class Tweet {
    @Id @GeneratedValue
    private Long id;

    private String author;
    private String text;
    private Date createdOn;

    public Tweet () {
        this.createdOn = new Date();          <-- Timestamp new tweets with "now"
    }

    public String getAuthor() {           <--
        return author;
    }

    public String getText() {             <-- Getters/setters for each property
        return text;
    }

    public Date getCreatedOn() {          <--
        return createdOn;
    }

    public void setAuthor(String author) {
        this.author = author;
    }

    public void setText(String text) {
        this.text = text;
    }

    ...
}
```

This class also contains a private field id, which is used by Hibernate to track tweets in the database. This field is annotated with some boilerplate, identifying it as a primary key that's generated automatically:

```
@Id @GeneratedValue
 private Long id;
```

The class itself is annotated with @Entity to indicate to Hibernate that this class is to be treated as a data entity.

NOTE Internally, `@Entity` helps Hibernate separate classes that are mapped to tables from those that may be embedded as additional columns in a larger database table.

All of `Tweet`'s properties have JavaBeans getter and setter methods as per the convention with Hibernate. So far we've seen how this models all of our data and keeps it organized. We need to go a step further and provide `equals()` and `hashCode()` methods to ensure that instances of `Tweet` behave properly in collections. This is also important for any class that Hibernate uses, since it will attempt to compare copies when optimizing for cached access.

`equals()` and `hashCode()` are quite straightforward, as shown in listing 11.7; they take all three data fields into account since together they form the identity of the `Tweet`.

Listing 11.7 `equals()` and `hashCode()` for class `Tweet`, to compare instances

```
@Override
public boolean equals(Object o) {
    if (this == o) return true;
    if (!(o instanceof Tweet)) return false;

    Tweet that = (Tweet) o;

    return this.author.equals(that.author)
            && this.createdOn.equals(that.createdOn)
            && this.text.equals(that.text);
}

@Override
public int hashCode() {
    int result;

    result = (author != null ?
    ➥ author.hashCode() : 0);
    result = 31 * result + (text != null ? text.hashCode() : 0);
    result = 31 * result + (createdOn != null ?
    ➥ createdOn.hashCode() : 0);

    return result;
}
```

If all properties are equal, return true

Hash code is computed from properties and a large prime

The idea is that objects are considered equal if they have the same values for `author`, `text`, and `createdOn`. Put another way, it's impossible to have all three match for two independent tweets. If two are posted at the same time, they will be from different authors. And if they are from the same author, they will necessarily have different creation times.

11.5.3 Users and sessions

In order to track users across independent requests, we must use an HTTP session. However, rather than interact with it directly, crosstalk takes advantage of scoping. The class `User` serves as a context for the current user of the system. Wherever it's referenced from, User points to the user whose HTTP session is currently active. In listing 11.8 we mark User as scoped to the HTTP session by using the @SessionScoped annotation.

Listing 11.8 Session-scoped User tracks information about the current user

```
@SessionScoped @NotThreadSafe
public class User {
    private String username;

    public String getUsername() {
        return username;
    }

    //logs in a user, by setting username to the current session
    public void login(String username) {
        this.username = username;
    }

    //logs out a user, by clearing username from session
    public void logout() {
        this.username = null;
    }
}
```

User does nothing more than store a username for the user who logs in and clears that name when the user logs out. Web page classes and services alike can check to find out whether someone is logged in and, if so, who is logged in by querying this service.

In HomePage, User is directly injected directly as a dependency:

```
@At("/home") @Select("action") @RequestScoped
public class HomePage {
    //user context, tracks current user
    private final User user;

    //page state variables
    private List<Tweet> tweets;
    private Tweet newTweet = new Tweet();

    //service dependencies
    private final TweetManager tweetManager;

    @Inject
    public HomePage(TweetManager tweetManager, User user) {
        this.tweetManager = tweetManager;
        this.user = user;
    }

    ...
}
```

This is safe because the session scope is wider than the request scope. This means that HomePage instances are shorter lived than User instances and therefore run no risk of scope-widening injection. HomePage retrieves a user's tweets by querying the Tweet-Manager for tweets by username:

```
    @Get
    public String get() {
```

```
        //load tweets for current user
        this.tweets = tweetManager.tweetsFor(user.getUsername());

        //stay on current page
        return null;
    }
```

This method is called in normal operation when an HTTP GET request is received by the web server. The annotation `@Get` indicates to Google Sitebricks to use this method as an event handler prior to rendering the page. Once tweets are loaded (and stored in the `tweets` field), the template is rendered displaying all of a user's tweets. You may also have noticed a "Sign out" link on the `HomePage`, which a user clicks to leave the session:

```
<a href="http://manning.com/prasanna">Help</a> |
<a href="?action=logout">Sign out</a>
```

`HomePage` reacts to the sign-out action by logging the user out from the `User` service:

```
    @Get("logout")
    public String logout() {
        user.logout();

        return "/login?message=Bye.";
    }
```

Because of the `@On("action")` annotation at the top of the class, Google Sitebricks knows to call a different event handler. This time, method `logout()` is called since it's annotated with the value-matching action (`@Get("logout")`). The `logout()` method then redirects the user to a login page, where they must log in again to continue using the site:

```
    @Get("logout")
    public String logout() {
        user.logout();

        return "/login?message=Bye.";
    }
```

The login page is both the exit and entry point for the crosstalk website and is also modeled as a Google Sitebricks page.

11.5.4 Logging in and out

`LoginPage`, like `HomePage`, has a Java class and companion template, as shown in figure 11.6.

The template is fairly straightforward. It accepts a `username` and `password`, as shown in listing 11.9 (see figure 11.6 for the web version).

Listing 11.9 An HTML template for `LoginPage` displays login input fields

```
<html>
<head>
    <title>Login</title>
```

```
    <link rel="stylesheet" href="/crosstalk.css"/>
</head>
<body>
    <h2>Please log in to crosstalk.</h2>

    <div class="box">
        <div class="box-content">

            <h3>${message}</h3>          <—— A dynamic success or fail message

            <form action="/login" method="post">      <—— The login form
                <input name="username" type="text" />
                <input name="password" type="password" />

                <input type="submit" value="login"/>
            </form>
        </div>
    </div>

</body>
</html>
```

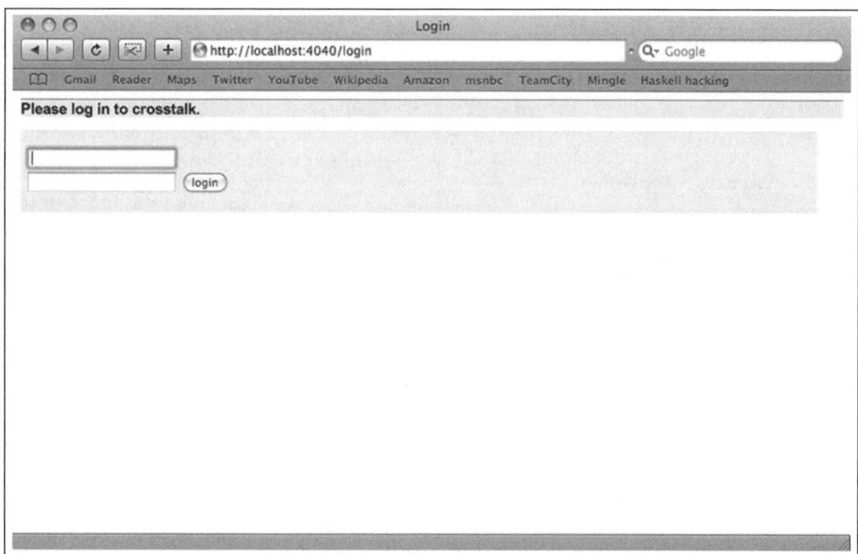

Figure 11.6 All users must log in to use their home page on crosstalk.

This form posts back to `LoginPage` with the entered credentials. `LoginPage` then uses this information to authenticate the user against a `UserManager`, as shown in listing 11.10.

Listing 11.10 Page class `LoginPage` authenticates users logging into crosstalk

```
@At("/login") @RequestScoped
public class LoginPage {
    private String username;
```

```
    private String password;

    private String message = "";

    //service dependencies
    private final UserManager userManager;
    private final User user;

    @Inject
    public LoginPage(UserManager userManager, User user) {
        this.userManager = userManager;
        this.user = user;
    }

    @Post
    public String login() {

        //attempt to authenticate the user
        if (userManager.authenticate(username, password))
            user.login(username);
        else {
            //clear user context from session
            user.logout();

            //stay on this page with error
            return "/login?message=Bad+credentials.";
        }

        //redirect to home page if successfully logged in
        return "/home";
    }

    //getters/setters...
    public void setUsername(String username) {
        this.username = username;
    }

    public void setPassword(String password) {
        this.password = password;
    }

    public String getMessage() {
        return message;
    }

    public void setMessage(String message) {
        this.message = message;
    }
}
```

LoginPage has the standard getters and setters to expose its properties to the template and form input. Method `login()` asks `UserManager` (a data service) whether the username and password are valid:

```
@Post
public String login() {

    //attempt to authenticate the user
    if (userManager.authenticate(username, password))
        user.login(username);
```

```
        else {
            //clear user context from session
            user.logout();

            //stay on this page with error
            return "/login?message=Bad+credentials.";
        }

        //redirect to home page if successfully logged in
        return "/home";
    }
```

If they are valid, `login()` logs the user in via the session-scoped `User` service shown earlier. If not, a redirect is sent back to the login screen with an error message:

```
    @Post
    public String login() {

        //attempt to authenticate the user
        if (userManager.authenticate(username, password))
            user.login(username);
        else {
            //clear user context from session
            user.logout();
            return "/login?message=Bad+credentials.";
        }

        //redirect to home page if successfully logged in
        return "/home";
    }
```

This results in the "Bad credentials" error message as shown in figure 11.7.

Once successfully logged in, the user is sent to their home page to tweet away.

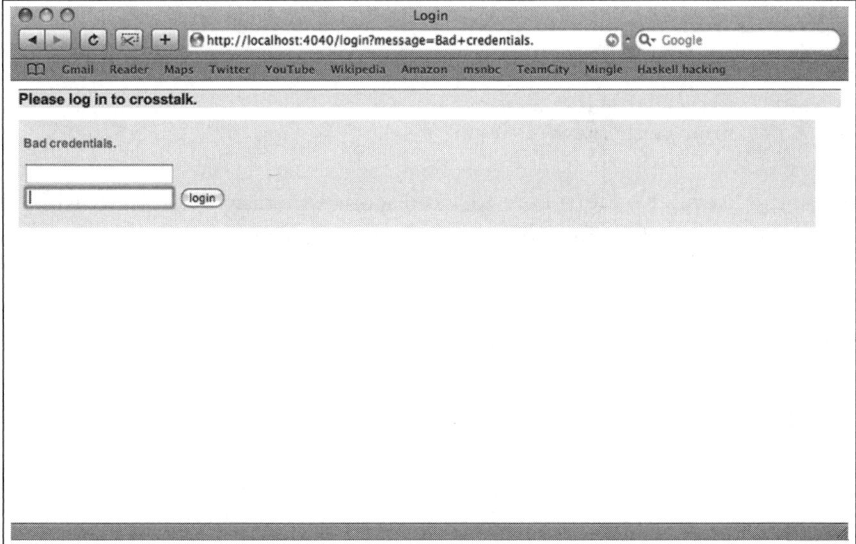

Figure 11.7 Bad usernames or passwords are rejected, appropriately.

11.6 The persistence layer

Data services that crosstalk uses are fairly simple. There's one for managing users (UserManager) and one for managing tweets (TweetManager)—not rocket science. Their implementations are subtly different. Let's look at the TweetManager implementation first, as shown in listing 11.11.

Listing 11.11 Implementation for the TweetManager interface using Hibernate

```
@Immutable @Singleton
class HibernateTweetManager implements TweetManager {

    //the provider pattern helps us prevent scope-widening of sessions
    private final Provider<Session> session;

    @Inject
    public HibernateTweetManager(Provider<Session> session) {
        this.session = session;
    }

    @Finder(query = "from Tweet where author = :author")
    public List<Tweet> tweetsFor(@Named("author") String author) {

        //this method is intercepted by warp-persist DynamicFinders
        // and converted into a query. So you should not see an empty
        // list unless the database contains no Tweets for 'author'.
        return Collections.emptyList();
    }

    public void addTweet(Tweet tweet) {
        session.get().save(tweet);
    }
}
```

HibernateTweetManager implements the TweetManager interface by storing and querying tweets from the database using Hibernate's services. To add a new tweet, we use a session to the database and save a new instance of the Tweet data object:

```
public void addTweet(Tweet tweet) {
    session.get().save(tweet);
}
```

We use the Provider pattern here to avoid scope-widening the session, which is implicitly request scoped. I say implicitly, because its behavior is managed by warp-persist, as you'll see. HibernateTweetManager, like all other classes in the services package, is a thread-safe, immutable singleton. Querying objects is taken care of us by warp-persist's *Dynamic Finders* utility. Annotating the method tweetsFor() with @Finder tells warp-persist to intercept and replace the method with logic that runs the bound query:

```
@Finder(query = "from Tweet where author = :author")
public List<Tweet> tweetsFor(@Named("author") String author) {

    // this method is intercepted by warp-persist DynamicFinders
    // and converted into a query. So you should not see an empty
    // list unless the database contains no Tweets for 'author'.
    return Collections.emptyList();
}
```

The string `"from Tweet where author = :author"` is an HQL (Hibernate Query Language) query, which tells Hibernate to load all tweets with the matching author. The method parameter `author` is annotated with an `@Named("author")` annotation, which binds the parameter into the query at the label `:author`.

TIP For more information on warp-persist and dynamic finders, including tutorials, visit http://www.wideplay.com.

The `UserManager` service by contrast, does not use Hibernate to store users in the database. This is done as a matter of convenience to get us up and running quickly, as shown in listing 11.12.

Listing 11.12 A `UserManager` that uses hard-coded user credentials

```
@Immutable @Singleton
class InMemoryUserManager implements UserManager {
    private final Map<String, String> users;

    public InMemoryUserManager() {
        final Map<String, String> users = new HashMap<String, String>();
        users.put("dhanji", "dirocks");

        //freeze the current hardcoded map so that it is thread-safe
        this.users = Collections.unmodifiableMap(users);
    }

//returns true if a username and password combination is valid
public boolean authenticate(String username, String password) {
        return users.containsKey(username)
            && users.get(username).equals(password);
    }
}
```

A simple hash table is stored in memory in this implementation, and the `authenticate()` method checks values in this hash table. We ensure that this hash table is immutable by wrapping it in an unmodifiable map. You should recall this best practice from chapter 10.

```
    public InMemoryUserManager() {
        final Map<String, String> users = new HashMap<String, String>();
        users.put("dhanji", "dirocks");

        //freeze the current hardcoded map so that it is thread-safe
        this.users = Collections.unmodifiableMap(users);
    }
```

This ensures that `InMemoryUserManager` is both highly concurrent and thread-safe (since it is immutable after construction). In a broader implementation, we'd use a Hibernate version of `UserManager` and have a separate set of pages for users to register and manage their accounts.

Now, let's look at interacting with a data store and retrieving and storing tweet data.

11.6.1 Configuring the persistence layer

As you saw in section 11.2, all the components in the `services` package are separately configured. The `ServicesModule` takes care of this for us and is shown in listing 11.13.

Listing 11.13 Security and persistence configuration (see also listing 11.1)

```
package com.wideplay.crosstalk.services;

public final class ServicesModule extends AbstractModule {
    private static final String HIBERNATE_CONFIG = "hibernate.properties";

    @Override
    protected void configure() {

        //configure persistence services, using hibernate
        install(PersistenceService
                .usingHibernate()
                .across(UnitOfWork.REQUEST)
                .buildModule()
        );

        //configure hibernate with our tweet data model class
        bind(Configuration.class).toInstance(new AnnotationConfiguration()
                .addAnnotatedClass(Tweet.class)
                .setProperties(loadProperties(HIBERNATE_CONFIG))
        );

        //configure crosstalk data services
        bind(TweetManager.class).to(HibernateTweetManager.class);
        bind(UserManager.class).to(InMemoryUserManager.class);

        //configure the in-memory authenticator (with hard-coded users)
        final HttpSessionAuthenticationManager manager =
            new HttpSessionAuthenticationManager();
        bind(AuthenticationManager.class).toInstance(manager);

        //intercept any @Get or @Post method on any page except LoginPage
        bindInterceptor(
                not(subclassesOf(LoginPage.class)),
                annotatedWith(Get.class).or(annotatedWith(Post.class)),

                new SecurityInterceptor(manager)
        );
    }

    private static Properties loadProperties(String props) {
        ...
    }
}
```

First up, we configure warp-persist to use Hibernate and provide us with a Hibernate unit of work (session to the database) every time an HTTP request arrives:

```
install(PersistenceService
        .usingHibernate()
        .across(UnitOfWork.REQUEST)
        .buildModule()
);
```

Then we configure Hibernate itself by binding the `Configuration` class to an annotation-based implementation that contains our `Tweet` domain model class:

```
bind(Configuration.class).toInstance(new AnnotationConfiguration()
        .addAnnotatedClass(Tweet.class)
        .setProperties(loadProperties(HIBERNATE_CONFIG))
);
```

To this configuration, we also add Hibernate configuration properties that tell it which database to use and so on (see the source code accompanying the book for details). The two data services, for users and tweets, are bound directly to their interfaces:

```
bind(TweetManager.class).to(HibernateTweetManager.class);
bind(UserManager.class).to(InMemoryUserManager.class);
```

All this is straightforward. Then we bind another service whose purpose we'll see very shortly:

```
//configure the in-memory authenticator (with hard-coded users)
final HttpSessionAuthenticationManager manager =
    new HttpSessionAuthenticationManager();
bind(AuthenticationManager.class).toInstance(manager);
```

The `AuthenticationManager` is used by crosstalk's security layer to detect whether a user has been authenticated correctly. This level of indirection is required because we can't always directly inject `User` into our services. You'll see why in a second. But first, a `SecurityInterceptor` is bound to all methods annotated with `@Get` and `@Post` except the `LoginPage`:

```
//intercept any @Get or @Post method on any page except LoginPage
bindInterceptor(
        not(subclassesOf(LoginPage.class)),
        annotatedWith(Get.class).or(annotatedWith(Post.class)),

        new SecurityInterceptor(manager)
);
```

This interceptor is used to secure parts of the website by intercepting requests for web pages, allowing us to ensure that only public parts of the site (that is, the login page) are seen by users who are not authenticated and also that only authenticated users may post tweets to their home pages. Let's see how this security interceptor works.

11.7 The security layer

`SecurityInterceptor` is an AOP interceptor that runs on every event method, as shown in listing 11.14. It's intended to guard web pages and prevent them from being displayed to users who aren't properly authenticated.

Listing 11.14 AopAlliance method interceptor applied across the app for security

```
class SecurityInterceptor implements MethodInterceptor {
    private final AuthenticationManager authenticationManager;

    public SecurityInterceptor(
```

```
        AuthenticationManager authenticationManager) {
        this.authenticationManager = authenticationManager;
    }

    public Object invoke(MethodInvocation methodInvocation)
        throws Throwable {

        //proceed with normal execution if a user is logged in
        if (authenticationManager.isLoggedIn()) {
            return methodInvocation.proceed();
        }

        //redirect to login page if the user is not properly logged in!
        return "/login";
    }
}
```

`SecurityInterceptor` is an AopAlliance `MethodInterceptor`,[1] which is triggered every time an HTTP GET or POST handler method is fired by Google Sitebricks (except on `LoginPage`). If a user is logged in, then the method proceeds as normal. If not, a redirect is sent to the login page:

```
    public Object invoke(MethodInvocation methodInvocation)
        throws Throwable {
        ...

        //redirect to the login page if user is not properly logged in!
        return "/login";
    }
```

Method interceptors and their configuration are covered in chapter 8. If you're unsure of how the interception works, consult the section on proxying.

In the next section you'll see how the application's lifespan can be tied to a servlet engine so that it receives notifications about important events in its lifecycle.

11.8 Tying up to the web lifecycle

Our database persistence framework has several expensive operations it must perform when starting up and several cleanup operations when shutting down. These are independent of a unit of work and must occur outside the regular operational life of the web application.

Ideally, this coincides with the web application's own lifecycle and the servlet's `init()` and `destroy()` events. Fortunately for us, warp-persist's `PersistenceFilter` handles all this hard work. On an `init()`, it triggers the creation of connection pools, the creation of tables and resources, and so on. In our case, this also kick-starts the Hypersonic HQSL database in memory. On shutdown of the filter (when `destroy()` is called), it closes down the Hibernate `SessionFactory`.

In addition, the `PersistenceFilter` is necessary to open and close Hibernate units of work on every request. This filter must be registered before installing the `SitebricksModule` so that pages can benefit from the session to the database being open.

---

1 Refer to chapter 8 for details on AOP and interceptors.

So far, we've looked at presentation, persistence and modularity. We've also used interception to provide security and tied everything up with the web lifecycle. Let's now get crosstalk running and give it the real litmus test.

11.9 Finally: up and running!

To run crosstalk, we'll create a simple class with a main method that fires up *Jetty*. We'll put this class in the test/ directory to distinguish it from the application proper. It looks like this:

```
public class Crosstalk {
    public static void main(String... args) throws Exception {
        Server jetty = new Server(8080);      //start at port 8080
        server.addHandler(new WebAppContext("web", "/"));

        jetty.start();
        jetty.join();
    }
}
```

Class `Crosstalk` creates an instance of `Server`, which represents the Jetty web server. We configure it to listen at port `8080` and use the `web/` directory as its resource root. Finally, we also ask it to listen at the root URL context: `"/"`.

Once Jetty is started, it's ready to begin servicing requests. We must use the `join()` method subsequently to prevent the application from exiting too early:

```
        jetty.start();
        jetty.join();
```

Now you're free to run the application (see figure 11.8). Point your browser to `http://localhost:8080/login` to see the login page and start using crosstalk!

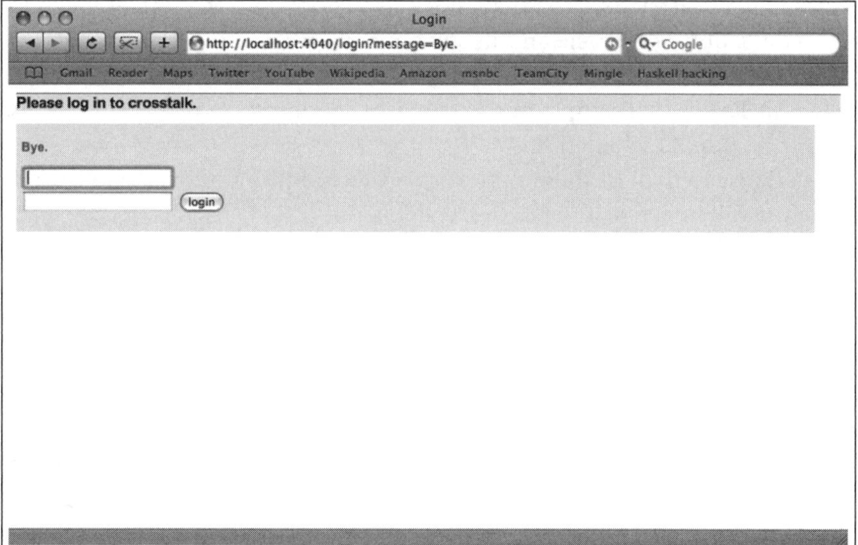

Figure 11.8 See ya!

11.10 Summary

This chapter was an example walkthrough of a real, working web application that embodies many of the concepts you've studied thus far in this book. I chose crosstalk as the problem domain, which is a simple clone of the popular microblogging service Twitter.

Crosstalk starts life as a Guice-based application that uses Hibernate for persistence and Google Sitebricks as the web framework to display web pages and react to user input. We also use Mort Bay Jetty as the servlet container. The injector is bootstrapped (as described in chapter 2) by using the guice-servlet integration layer that allows us to create and configure the injector when the web application is deployed to the servlet container.

Crosstalk consists of three main packages:

- `web`—Contains the web page classes and components
- `services`—Contains the data and security services
- `tweets`—Contains the domain model classes for data persistence

All the components of package `services` are exposed via interfaces, and their implementation details are hidden away as package-local. This is an example of good modularity and loose coupling as shown in chapters 4 and 10.

Web pages are all request-scoped and utilize class `User`, which is a session-scoped service that tracks the current user who is logged in. `LoginPage` ensures that a username is attached to the `User` service upon login, and `HomePage` signs a user out as appropriate. These web components exemplify the ideas presented in chapters 5 and 6 on scoping.

Since starting and stopping the persistence engine is an expensive operation and ideally coincides with the start and close of the web application itself, we register a wrapping `PersistenceFilter` that allows us to hook into the servlet lifecycle. Refer to our investigation of lifecycle and its semantics in greater detail in chapter 7.

The `SecurityInterceptor` was added to secure home pages from users who aren't logged in. This is an example of the behavior modification or AOP interception techniques presented in chapter 8.

Finally, we tied all of these patterns and techniques with the whole application to realize the full benefits of dependency injection!

appendix A: The Butterfly Container

Contributed by Jakob Jenkov

This appendix is about the Butterfly DI DSL called *Butterfly Container Script (BCS)*. We include this appendix to illustrate the last of the four configuration mechanisms mentioned in chapter 2.

A.1 A DSL for dependency injection

What we show here is far from a complete listing of the capabilities of Butterfly Container. Rather we show a few of Butterfly Container's solutions; these problems are also mentioned elsewhere in this book:

- Contextual injection via input parameters
- Reinjection via factory injection

This appendix also looks at a few features made possible by a DSL.

A.2 Application configuration

Butterfly Container is an open source project and is part of a growing collection of components called *Butterfly Components*. Should you be interested in learning more, you can find additional information at http://butterfly.jenkov.com.

A.2.1 The DSL basics

For reasons too involved to discuss here, Butterfly Container was designed to use a DSL tailored to dependency injection for its configuration. This mechanism is somewhat similar to the XML files of Spring, except BCS is not an XML format.

Butterfly Container Script was designed to look like a cross between a standard property file (name = value) and Java code. This was done to make it easier to read, write, and learn since most Java developers are familiar with both Java and property files. This language design also makes it feasible to use BCS files for application configuration (explained later).

A script file consists of one or more bean factories. It's easiest to explain the basics of BCS by using an example:

```
myBean1 = * com.myapp.MyBean();
```

This configuration consists of five parts:

- A factory ID (`myBean1`)
- An equals sign (`=`)
- An instantiation mode (`*`)
- A Factory chain (`com.myapp.MyBean()`)
- A semicolon (`;`)

The Factory ID identifies this Factory. This ID must be unique throughout the container instance. You supply this ID to the container when obtaining an instance or when referencing that factory from other factories.

The equals sign indicates the beginning of the product part of the factory definition.

The instantiation mode is also sometimes referred to as scope. However, not all bean scopes in Butterfly Container are achieved using the instantiation mode. Sometimes a scope is achieved by combining the instantiation mode with a special bean factory, for instance your own bean factory.

BCS currently includes the following instantiation modes:

- `*`—A new instance is created on every call to a Factory.
- `1`—A singleton is created once and returned on every call to a Factory.
- `1T`—One singleton per thread-calling factory is created once and returned on every call to a Factory.
- `1F`—Flyweight; one instance per provided input parameter is created once and returned on every call to a Factory with same input parameter.

The Factory chain defines what object is to be returned by the Factory. In our example that's an instance of the class `com.myapp.Bean`. A Factory can create more than one object when it executes but return only one of them. We'll explain more about the Factory chain later.

The semicolon signals that the Factory chain is finished.

A.2.2 The Factory chain

In the Factory chain of a Factory definition you can call constructors, call methods, and even define local bean factories not visible outside this factory definition. Here's a somewhat more complex example:

```
myBean1 = * com.myapp.MyBean1();
myBean2 = * com.myapp.MyBean2("A Text", myBean1)
                .setMoreText("more text");
```

This configuration consists of two Factories: `myBean1` and `myBean2`. The definition of `myBean1` is pretty much the same as the first example. `myBean2` shows a few new things. First, it contains two constructor parameters to the constructor of the class com.myapp.MyBean2. The second constructor parameter references the myBean1 factory, meaning an instance obtained from this factory should be obtained and injected into the constructor.

The Factory chain contains the method call setMoreText("more text"). This call further configures the MyBean2 instance before returning it. In fact, if the setMoreText() method had returned an object, it would be this object that was returned by the myBean2 Factory and not the MyBean2 instance. Since the setMoreText() method returns void, it's interpreted as returning the instance the method was called on—the MyBean2 instance, in other words. That also means that you can chain method calls on methods returning void, like this:

```
myBean2 = * com.myapp.MyBean2("A Text", myBean1)
            .setMoreText("more text")
            .setAValue(1)
            .setMoreOfSomething("more...");
```

As you can see, the factory now consists of a chain of constructor/method calls, hence the name Factory chain. The Factory chain can be as long as you need it to be.

This is one of the advantages of having a tailored DSL: the freedom to add features like method chaining on methods returning void.

A.2.3 Contextual injection via input parameters

BCS allows contextual injection by enabling factories to receive input parameters. Here's how that looks:

```
myBean1 = * com.myapp.MyBean($0).setValue($1);
myBean2 = * myBean1(com.myapp.SomeBean(), "Value Text");
```

The dollar sign ($) signals that an input parameter is to be injected. The number (0, 1, and so on) specifies which input parameter to inject. As you can see, input parameters are not named or typed. This can lead to type errors in your Factory definitions if you aren't careful. This is one of the limitations of a custom DSL. It's only as advanced as you make it; you don't get Java's full type checking. In reality this is a big problem, as you might think. You can set up unit tests to check the validity of the factories, if you want to.

The myBean2 Factory calls the myBean1 Factory and provides two input parameters to it: a com.myapp.SomeBean instance and the string "Value Text". Notice that each input parameter is itself a Factory chain, so you could also have provided input parameters to the SomeBean instance and called methods on it, like this:

```
myBean1 = * com.myapp.MyBean($0).setValue($1);
myBean2 = * myBean1(com.myapp.SomeBean("config", $0)
                        .setTitle("The Title"),
                    "Value Text");
```

The SomeBean constructor is now given two parameters: the string "config" and the input parameter $0. This input parameter is not the same as the $0 of the myBean1 Factory. The $0 input parameter of the myBean1 Factory is the SomeBean instance. The $0 input parameter of the myBean2 Factory is whatever you provide as first parameter to the myBean2 Factory.

You can also provide input parameters to a Factory when obtaining beans from the container from Java code, like this:

```
MyBean myBean = (MyBean)
    container.instance("myBean1", new SomeBean(), "Value Text");
```

If the method you're trying to inject parameters into is overloaded, it can be hard or even impossible for the container to tell which of the overloaded methods to call. It's therefore possible to specify the type of the injected parameter, like this:

```
    myBean1 = * com.myapp.MyBean((long) $0).setValue((String) $1);
```

A.2.4 Reinjection via factory injection

BCS makes it possible to inject the Factory of a product rather than the product itself. This is done by putting a # in front of the Factory name when referencing it, like this:

```
firstBean  = * com.myapp.FirstBean($0).setValue($1);
secondBean = * com.myapp.SecondBean().setFirstBeanFactory(#firstBean);
```

In the `secondBean` Factory, the `firstBean` Factory is injected into the method `setFirstBeanFactory()`, by referencing the injected Factory as `#firstBean`.

While you could declare the type of the Factory inside the `SecondBean` instance of type `com.jenkov.container.itf.factory.IGlobalFactory`, this would result in a hard reference in your code to a Butterfly Container class. You don't want that. Instead, Butterfly Container is capable of adapting the Factory to your own custom interface as long as the interface has an `instance()` method. Here's an example of such an interface:

```
public interface FirstBeanFactory {
    public FirstBean instance();
}
```

In the `SecondBean` class you can now create a field of the type `FirstBeanFactory`, like this:

```
public class SecondBean {
    protected FirstBeanFactory firstBeanFactory = null;

    public void setFirstBeanFactory(FirstBeanFactory factory){
        this.firstBeanFactory = factory;
    }

    public void doSomething(){
        FirstBean firstBean = this.firstBeanFactory.instance();
    }
}
```

Notice how the use of the `FirstBeanFactory` interface inside the `SecondBean` is perfectly type-safe: no casts and no references to any Butterfly Container–specific classes. You can even specify typed parameters to the `instance()` method. If you look at the Factory definition of `firstBean`, you can see that it actually takes two parameters. You can add them to the `instance()` method like this:

```
public interface FirstBeanFactory {

    public FirstBean instance(long constructorParam, String value);
}
```

These parameters are typed as well, making it easy for maintenance developers to see what types are required by the `firstBean` factory.

You could even call the `instance()` method by the name of the Factory in the container to call, like so:

```
public interface FirstBeanFactory {

    public FirstBean firstBean(long constructorParam,
        String value);
}
```

This can be used to add several Factory methods to the same interface, referencing different Factories in the container, for instance:

```
public interface BeanFactories {

   public long   numberOfConnectionsInPool();
   public String dbUrl();
   public FirstBean firstBean(long constructorParam, String value);
   // etc...
}
```

The container would determine at runtime which Factory to obtain the object from by matching the method name with a factory in the container. It doesn't matter which factory you inject. If your method is called `instance()`, the injected factory is called. If your method is called something else, the Factory having the same name as the method is called.

While this is a powerful feature, you should use it with care. By using named Factory methods in your interface, you create a hard link between the method names and the Factory names. If the Factory names are later changed, the interface methods will stop working and you won't know why, unless you have a unit test determining that it works. You also have the slight disadvantage in that Java doesn't allow the same characters in method names as Butterfly Container allows in Factory names. For instance, if your Factory is named `dao/projectDao`, you cannot name a method in Java `dao/projectDao()`. You can still inject and call the Factory, however, using the method name `instance()`. But then you can have only one method per interface. In most cases, this is sufficient, so it's not a big limitation.

appendix B: SmartyPants for Adobe Flex

Contributed by Josh McDonald

SmartyPants-IOC is a dependency injection framework for use in building Adobe Flex and Flash applications inspired by Google Guice for Java. It's based on key concepts:

- The class+name key
- Injector requests, usually specified via metadata
- Injector rules, specified using an ActionScript-based DSL

B.1 The class+name key

Whether you're telling SmartyPants-IOC what to provide or sitting around with your hand out asking for a dependency, the key is the same: a combination of a class and a name. You must specify the class, but the name is optional.

B.1.1 Injection annotations

How do you actually request that a field be injected? In most circumstances you need to annotate your fields with ActionScript metadata. If you want to request an instance of `IServiceInterface`, the syntax is simple:

```
[Inject]
public var myService:IServiceInterface;
```

Let's say you want to look up a particular string, rather than just anything. For a Web Services Description Language (WSDL) URL, or something along those lines, use this syntax:

```
[Inject(name="mainWSDL")]
public var myServiceWSDL:String;
```

These fields will be injected into your object when it's constructed for you by SmartyPants-IOC or when you call `injector.injectInto(myInstance)`.

SmartyPants-IOC also supports live injections, which when coupled with live rules behave like the Flex SDK's data-binding functionality:

```
//This will be set whenever the source changes
[Inject(name="userName",live)]
public var currentUsername:String;
```

B.2 Injector rules

The injector rules are akin to Guice's bindings, but we use another term to avoid confusion with the Flex SDK's data-binding mechanism. You tell the injector what you'd like it to do, using the DSL. Here are a couple of examples:

```
//Simple singleton rules:
injector.newRule().whenAskedFor(String).named("wsdl")
                  .useInstance("http://www.server.com/soap/service.wsdl");
injector.newRule().whenAskedFor(IServiceInterface)
                  .useSingletonOf(MyServiceImpl);
injector.newRule().whenAskedFor(MyConcreteClass).useSingleton();

//"Live" rules act just like <mx:Binding>
injector.newRule().whenAskedFor(String)
                  .named("userId")
                  .useBindableProperty(this, "userId");
```

B.2.1 But how do I kickstart the whole thing?

Good question! Two ways. First, in an MXML component, this code will inject into your component on the `CreationComplete` event:

```
<?xml version="1.0" encoding="utf-8"?>
<mx:Canvas xmlns:mx="http://www.adobe.com/2006/mxml"
     xmlns:smartypants="http://smartypants.expantra.net/2008">

    <smartypants:RequestInjection/>

    <!-- ...Regular code and MXML... -->

</mx:Canvas>
```

And in ActionScript it's even simpler:

```
SmartyPants.injectInto(this);
```

Hopefully this gives a little more insight into the style and ideas behind SmartyPants-IOC. Be sure to check it out on the Google Code site!

SmartyPants-IOC is hosted on Google Code: http://code.google.com/p/smartypants-ioc/.

index

Symbols

A

B

P

R

S

T